A BREAKTHROUGH IN THE CONCEPT OF A THESAURUS

Now, for the first time, there is a thesaurus which provides a concise definition at every main entry and a brief verbal illustration of the word used in context to help take the guesswork and error out of word selection. Words are clearly distinguished, and the relationship between the main entry and its synonyms is clarified to facilitate proper word choice. Furthermore, because exact synonyms are not always desirable, listings include related words, idiomatic phrases, and antonyms.

THE MERRIAM-WEBSTER THESAURUS represents a whole new concept, one which will delight the general user with its simplicity and the scholar with its completeness. As a guide to more precise and effective use of the language, it is unmatched.

"It is so ample and easy to use that for many it will largely supersede Roget."
—*The Wall Street Journal*

(More....)

RESOUNDING PRAISE
FOR A MAJOR
PUBLISHING EVENT

"This new Merriam-Webster volume represents a genuinely fresh approach to the thesaurus concept evolved by Peter Mark Roget more than a century ago. Because the language itself has vastly grown since Roget's time, this new thesaurus is based on contemporary American-English. Secondly, every entry is not only provided with its synonyms and antonyms but also with idiomatic equivalents, related words and contrasting words, a structure which offers the reader an infinitely broader choice than the original based on a 19th-century English vocabulary....A distinct advance in analysis of language, in accessibility, in contemporaneity, and in convenience."

—*John Barkham Reviews*

"Every home, office, school or library should own a copy....It's so good, it should have been thought of before."

—*The Hartford Courant*

The
Merriam-Webster
Thesaurus

A Merriam-Webster®

PUBLISHED BY POCKET BOOKS NEW YORK

POCKET BOOKS, a Simon & Schuster division of
GULF & WESTERN CORPORATION
1230 Avenue of the Americas, New York, N.Y. 10020

This is the POCKET BOOKS concise edition of
WEBSTER'S COLLEGIATE THESAURUS

Copyright © 1978 by G. & C. Merriam Co.
Philippines copyright © 1978 by G. & C. Merriam Co.

Published by arrangement with G. & C. Merriam Co.
Library of Congress Catalog Card Number: 75-45167

ISBN: 0-671-47621-1

First Pocket Books printing August, 1978

15 14 13 12 11

POCKET and colophon are registered trademarks
of Simon & Schuster.

Printed in the U.S.A.

Preface

WEBSTER'S POCKET THESAURUS is based on the recently published Webster's Collegiate Thesaurus and is designed especially to meet the day-to-day needs of those who want a compact and handy thesaurus. In this book we have been able to eliminate much of the bulk and weight of the larger volume while retaining the basic features that have caused Webster's Collegiate Thesaurus to be so well received.

The basic premise behind both books is that the user of a thesaurus is seeking a more appropriate term than the one he has in mind. This very broad concept is scarcely consonant with the typical thesaurus presentation of "synonyms" and sometimes "antonyms". In point of fact, the user may be seeking a synonym, a word stronger or weaker in force, one of slightly different meaning, a more starchy or more folksy word, an idiomatic phrase that conveys the same idea, or a word that to a greater or less degree contrasts with his starting point. Patently, all these possible uses cannot be subsumed reasonably under the rather unitary notions of "synonym" and "antonym". Perhaps the longevity of Roget's *Thesaurus* rests on the simple fact that in spite of its complexity and lack of guidance, it does spread before the user a greater body of material to browse through than any comparable book heretofore available. Webster's Pocket Thesaurus is designed to present a similar range of material but in a readily available and highly structured form that minimizes the consultant's need to grope and guess.

In earlier Merriam-Webster publications the pattern of supplementing synonym lists with lists of related and contrasted words, words that were relevant to the group under study yet not quite synonyms or antonyms respectively, was extensively tested. This favorably received feature not only allowed more precise delineation of synonyms and antonyms but provided the user with much additional significant and pertinent assistance. The same plan of supplementing synonyms and antonyms with genuinely germane collateral material has been made a feature of this new thesaurus.

Additional features of Webster's Pocket Thesaurus designed to facilitate its use are the provision at each main entry of a concise statement of the segment of denotation in which a group of words can be construed as synonyms, a strictly alphabetical organization, and the entry at its own alphabetical place of each word that appears as a synonym at a main entry. The absence or inadequate handling of the first of these features is a major flaw in most existent thesauruses. Though many justifications have been offered for avoiding the second, they all boil down to the implausible notion that the members of a group of words are synonymous but some are more synonymous than others! Perhaps unfairly, one can't help feeling that the only valid explanation for non-alphabetical listing of properly chosen synonyms appears in one specialized dictionary of synonyms whose author comments. "Apologies are in order, however, for my inability to maintain alphabetical order within the categories, the plea being of course lack of time." Finally, since no one can anticipate where the user's search may start, it seems only logical to enter each synonym in such a way that it can serve as a convenient starting point in his searching.

Though Webster's Pocket Thesaurus is based on Webster's Collegiate Thesaurus, its ultimate authority lies in Webster's Third New International Dictionary and the Merriam-Webster research file of nearly 13,000,000 instances of words in actual use by a wide range of writers and speakers. In preparing the Pocket Thesaurus the chief organizational change was the replacement of the synonym list at each secondary entry with a cross-reference to the appropriate main entry. In addition a few specialized or abstruse entries were eliminated and a few synonyms not likely to be of general interest were dropped.

Webster's Pocket Thesaurus was prepared by Kathleen M. Doherty, assistant editor, under the immediate supervision of E. Ward Gilman, senior editor.

Explanatory Notes

How to Use Webster's Pocket Thesaurus

Every thesaurus user should read these Explanatory Notes because a thorough understanding of the scope, content, and structure of the book is essential to its effective employment. The key lines at the bottom of the text pages direct the user to these Explanatory Notes.

Since the English lexicon contains an incalculable number of fixed combinations, senses, subsenses, and nuances of meaning (for example, Webster's Third New International Dictionary records some 251 distinguishable meanings for the verb *set* and its fixed combinations), *it is essential that the thesaurus be used in conjunction with an adequate dictionary.*

Scope of Webster's Pocket Thesaurus

This book is concerned with the general vocabulary of the English language. Since the user may actually be hindered rather than helped by a vocabulary diluted with obsolete, archaic, or extremely rare terms or with specialized or technical jargon, such words have been omitted.

Structure and Content

Entry Order The body of the book consists of main and secondary entries introduced by alphabetically ordered boldface headwords, as

> **raid** *vb* **1** to make a raid on <Indians *raided* the
> settlers frequently>
> *syn* foray, harass, harry, maraud
> *rel* despoil, devastate, ravage, sack, spoliate,
> waste; loot, plunder, rifle, rob
> **2** *syn* see INVADE 1

> **raider** *n* *syn* see MARAUDER

> **rail** *n* *syn* see RAILING

where *raid, raider,* and *rail* are the headwords introducing either a main entry (as raid *vb* 1), or a secondary entry (as raid *vb* 2, raider *n*, or rail *n*).

Homograph headwords are entered in historical order: the one first used in English is entered first, as

till *prep*
till *conj*
till *vb*

Verbs used predominantly with one or two prepositions or adverbs may be headwords introducing main or secondary entries; in this case, they are entered with the verb segment in boldface type followed by the parenthetical element or elements in lightface type. Such verb + particle combinations immediately follow their base verb in alphabetical order:

put *vb* ———————————— base-verb homograph
put (back) *vb*
put (on) *vb* ————————— verb + particle combinations
put (on *or* upon) *vb*
put *n* ————————————— noun homograph

Fixed verb + adverb collocations commonly entered in dictionaries as two-word verbs have boldface entry at their appropriate alphabetical positions in this book. However, they follow any verb + particle combinations occurring in the same alphabetical sequence:

take *vb* ———————————— base verb
take (from) *vb* ————————— verb + particle combinations
take (to) *vb*
take away *vb* ——————————
take back *vb*
take down *vb* ———————— two-word verb collocations
take in *vb*
take off *vb*

Headwords ordinarily conform to normal dictionary practices: for instance, they are styled as singular nouns or infinitive verbs. Special situations (as plural usage or variant spellings) are signaled by the use of boldface subheads, as

crossroad *n, usu* crossroads *pl but sing or pl in*
constr syn see JUNCTURE 2

woe *n* ...3 *usu* woes *pl* syn see DISASTER

catercorner (*or* catty-corner *or* kitty-corner) *adv*
syn see DIAGONALLY

where crossroads and woes are subheads indicating plural usage, and cattycorner and kitty-corner are subheads showing variant spellings of the headwords.

The Main Entry and Its Basic Elements Each main entry consists of a headword followed by a part-of-speech label, a sense number when needed, a meaning core with a brief verbal illustration, and a list of synonyms. Lists of related words, idiomatic equivalents, contrasted words, and antonyms follow the synonym list if they are called for.

A typical main entry is

calm *adj* **1** free from storm or rough activity < the
wind died and the sea became *calm*>
syn halcyon, hushed, placid, quiet, still, stilly,
untroubled
rel inactive, quiescent, reposing, resting; pacific,
smooth, tranquil, unruffled
idiom calm as a millpond, still as death
con agitated, disturbed, perturbed, restless,
turbulent, uneasy
ant stormy

where the italic part-of-speech label *adj* indicates that the headword is an
adjective. Other such labels used in the book are: *adv* (adverb), *conj* (conjunction), *interj* (interjection), *n* (noun), *prep* (preposition), *pron* (pronoun),
and *vb* (verb).

Individual senses of multisense entries (as **calm** *adj*) are introduced by a
boldface sense number (as **1**).

The meaning core, as at **calm 1**

free from storm or rough activity

indicates the area of meaning in which a group of words (in this case *calm,
halcyon, hushed, placid, quiet, still, stilly,* and *untroubled*) are considered to
be synonymous.

In other words, the meaning core pinpoints the exact relationship between the main-entry headword and its synonyms.

A meaning core may be supplemented by a usage note introduced by a
lightface dash when additional information or comments on syntax or usage are required:

yet *adv* **1** beyond this — used as an intensive to
stress the comparative degree

Some interjections express feelings but otherwise are untranslatable into
substitutable meaning; in such cases, the meaning core itself may be replaced by a usage note:

good-bye *interj* — used as a conventional expression
of good wishes at parting

Each meaning core is followed by a verbal illustration enclosed by angle
brackets, as

< the wind died and the sea became *calm*>

that exemplifies a typical use of the headword (here, **calm**) in its pertinent
sense (1). The verbal illustration also offers the thesaurus user a frame for
testing the suitability of the synonyms and/or related words with regard to
his particular needs. Two verbal illustrations may appear after a meaning
core that is broad enough to subsume alternatives (as both a literal and an
extended use):

see *vb* **1** to take cognizance of by physical
or mental vision < *saw* that the boat was being
driven ashore > < the only one who *saw* the truth >

Such double illustrations have been chosen with discretion and are used sparingly in this book.

The boldface italic abbreviation *syn* introduces a synonym list that appears at each main entry on a line below the meaning core and the verbal illustration. This list may consist of only one synonym (as *here* at **hitherto** *adv* 2) or of many (as *halcyon, hushed, placid, quiet, still, stilly,* and *untroubled* at **calm** *adj* 1). Each synonym in a main-entry list has a boldface entry at its own alphabetical place.

A compare cross-reference may appear at the end of a main-entry *syn* list. This cross-reference introduced by the italic word *compare* is used (1) when two or more groups of synonyms are very closely related and it is felt that the user examining one list should be aware of the existence of the other list or lists:

assassin *n* a person hired or hirable to
commit murder < found out who paid the *assassin* >
syn bravo, cutthroat, gun, gunman, ‖gunsel, gunslinger,
hatchet man, hit man, torpedo, triggerman; *compare* MURDERER

murderer *n* one who kills a human being
< a *murderer* who wouldn't hesitate to kill in cold blood >
syn homicide, killer, manslayer, slayer; *compare* ASSASSIN

and (2) when the user should be warned that certain words have evolved derivative senses that tend to blur precise sense boundaries and consequently cause an overlapping of senses or of meaning, thus making those words somewhat less desirable choices for the user in terms of preciseness than other words in their lists. A comparison of the main entries

ration *n* an amount allotted or made available
especially from a limited supply < saved up their gasoline
ration for a vacation trip >
syn allotment, allowance, apportionment, measure,
meed, part, portion, quantum, quota, share; *compare* SHARE 1

share *n* 1 something belonging to, assumed by, or falling to
one (as in division or apportionment) < wanted his *share* of
the prize money >
syn allotment, allowance, bite, cut, lot,
part, partage, portion, quota, slice; *compare* RATION

reveals the usage overlap of the synonyms *allotment, allowance, part, portion, quota,* and *share* which are indeed valid synonyms at both entries.
The Secondary Entry and Its Basic Elements A secondary entry consists of a boldface headword followed by a part-of-speech label, a boldface sense number when needed, and a *syn* see cross-reference in small capitals directing the user to the appropriate main entry in whose *syn* list the secondary entry appears (followed when needed by a lightface sense number of the main entry). Lists of related words, idiomatic equivalents, contrasted words, or antonyms that are specifically applicable to the secondary-entry headword in the relationship indicated by the *syn* see cross-reference may be included as well. A typical secondary entry is

placid *adj* 1 *syn* see CALM 1
rel irenic, peaceful, serene, unagitated, unstirring
ant roiled

where **placid** is the headword, *adj* is the part-of-speech label, 1 is the sense number of the secondary entry, and *syn* see CALM 1 is the *syn* cross-reference directing the user to the main entry **calm 1** where *placid* is a synonym.

Main and Secondary Entries: Elements Common to Both All, some, or none of the following lists may appear at both main and secondary entries in this order: related words, idiomatic equivalents, contrasted words, and antonyms.

The boldface abbreviation *rel* introduces a list of related words. The related words — words that are almost but not quite synonymous with the headword — are included at an entry next after the synonym list. For example, at the main entry

> **splendid** *adj*...
> 2 extraordinarily or transcendently impressive...
> *syn* glorious, gorgeous, magnificent, proud,
> resplendent, splendiferous, splendorous, sublime,
> superb
> *rel* eminent, illustrious; grand, impressive, lavish,
> luxurious, royal, sumptuous; divine, exquisite,
> lovely; incomparable, matchless, peerless,
> superlative, supreme, unparalleled, unsurpassed;
> surpassing, transcendent

the *rel* list is composed of twenty terms separated into five subgroups that each share a common likeness or relation with the headword and its synonyms. On the other hand, at the secondary entry

> **splendiferous** *adj syn* see SPLENDID 2
> *rel* dazzling, marvelous; smashing, walloping;
> rattling, ripping, screaming, terrific

three subgroups of eight terms were selected as being distinctively related to *splendiferous* rather than to the whole synonym group in the context indicated by the *syn* see cross-reference to **splendid 2**. Related words appearing at a main entry are not ordinarily repeated at the secondary entries. The user should therefore check the main entry when seeking the most complete groupings of related words. Related words as such are not entered in boldface at their own alphabetical places. They may, of course, be synonyms in other lists or head their own main entries.

The boldface italic abbreviation *idiom* introduces a list of idiomatic equivalents that are essentially the same in meaning as the members of a synonym group. An *idiom* list at a main entry includes phrases that are generally pertinent to the entire *syn* list and the headword, as the ones at

> **speak** *vb* 1 to articulate words in order to express
> thoughts...
> *syn* talk, utter, verbalize, vocalize, voice
> *rel*...
> *idiom* break silence, give voice (*or* tongue *or* utterance) to,
> let fall, make public (*or* known), open
> one's mouth (*or* lips), put in (*or* into) words, say one's say,
> speak one's piece

while a secondary-entry list, as the one at

> **retaliate** *vb syn* see RECIPROCATE
> *rel*...
> *idiom* even the score, get back at, get

even with, give in kind, give one a
dose of his own medicine, give one tit for
tat, pay one in his own coin, settle (*or*
square) accounts, turn the tables on

features idioms that are particularly appropriate equivalents of its headword in the context indicated by the *syn* see cross-reference. Idiomatic
equivalents, including those fixed verb + preposition combinations that
function as idioms rather than as literal meanings of the verb are not entered in boldface at their own alphabetical places in this book.

The boldface italic abbreviation *con* introduces a list of contrasted words
— words that are strongly contrastable but not quite antonymous with the
headword — that may appear at an entry:

> **watchful** *adj* paying close attention usually
> with a view to anticipating approaching
> danger or opportunity...
> *syn*...
> *rel*...
> *idiom*...
> *con* careless, heedless, thoughtless; in-
> advertent; absentminded, abstracted,
> faraway

> **alert** *adj* 1 *syn* see WATCHFUL
> *rel*...
> *idiom*...
> *con* inattentive, unmindful; aloof,
> detached, indifferent, unconcerned

At the main entry **watchful** *adj* the *con* list is composed of seven words
separated into three subgroups that each share at least one aspect of contrast to the headword and its *syn* list, while the *con* list at the secondary
entry **alert** 1 comprises six words separated into two such subgroups. Contrasted words appearing at a main entry are not ordinarily repeated at the
secondary entries. The thesaurus user should therefore check the main entry when seeking the most complete groupings of contrasted words. Contrasted words as such are not entered in boldface at their own alphabetical
places. They may, of course, be synonyms in other lists or head their own
main entries.

The boldface italic abbreviation *ant* introduces the last possible element
of a main or secondary entry: an antonym or list of antonyms, as at the
entry

> **perfect** *adj*... 2 ...
> *ant* imperfect

or at the entry

> **quiet** *adj*... 4 not showy or obtrusive...
> *ant* gaudy, loud

When antonyms are drawn from different classes of opposites, members of
the two groups are separated by a semicolon, as at the entry

> **assistance** *n* *syn* see HELP 1   antonyms that are opposites
> *rel*...   with intermediates
> *con*...
> *ant* impediment, impeding;   antonyms that are reverse
> obstructing, obstruction   opposites

Like related and contrasted words, antonyms as such are not entered in boldface at their own alphabetical places. They may, of course, be synonyms in other lists or head their own main entries.

Main and Secondary Entries: The One Arbitrary Rule Ideally, a book such as this should be free of all arbitrary restraints and curtailments. In practice, however, its editors found that one rule was essential: *No word may appear in more than one list at a main or secondary entry.* For example, *nice* is a synonym at **pleasant** *adj* 1. The applicable sense of *nice* is found in Webster's Third New International Dictionary at the entry ¹*nice . . . adj . . .* 7 (binding substitute) +7b, where the definitions are

> : pleasant and satisfying: as . . . b : ENJOYABLE,
> PLEASING, DELIGHTFUL < a *nice* time at
> the party > < *nice* and warm by the fire > < we have
> four *nice* bedrooms upstairs to make them
> comfortable —Willa Cather >

However, one might reasonably construe senses 7e (: MILD, CLEMENT, PLEASING < the *nice* weather of late spring > < the *nice* old days of the past >) and 7g (: FITTING, APPROPRIATE, SUITABLE < the *nice* clothes she wears > < not a *nice* word for use in church >) as a basis for entering *nice* as a related word as well as a synonym at **pleasant** 1, while sense 8 in Webster's Third New International Dictionary

> : most inappropriate : UNPLEASANT, UNATTRACTIVE,
> TREACHEROUS — used ironically < a chronic alcoholic
> is certainly a *nice* one to talk about
> temperance > < a *nice* friend, who would have
> me . . . cover myself with eternal infamy —J.A.
> Froude > < got himself in a *nice* fix >

could be construed as evidence for entering *nice* as both a contrasted word and an antonym at **pleasant** 1. Obviously, the thesaurus user would not be helped by an entry showing any word in such an involved relationship with itself.

Labels, Punctuation, and Symbols

Labels Words that are labeled *cap* or *usu* [ally] *cap* in Webster's Third New International Dictionary are capitalized in this book. Thus, the synonyms *Gehenna, Pandemonium, Sheol,* and *Tophet* are so styled at the main entry **hell** *n* as are the related words *Styx* and *Tartarus.* A term that is capitalized in a main-entry *syn* list is also capitalized when it appears as a boldface secondary entry at its own alphabetical position:

> **Gehenna** *n syn* see HELL

If only one entered sense of a word is capitalized, an italic *cap* label followed by a boldface capitalized subhead is attached to the affected sense:

> **pandemonium** *n* 1 *cap* **Pandemonium** *syn* see HELL
> 2 *syn* see SINK 1
> 3 *syn* see DIN

In addition to the part-of-speech label, an italic plural label may be added when a word or a sense of a word is sometimes, often, usually, or always used in the plural. Typical examples of these labels are found at

years *n pl syn* see OLD AGE

where *pl* indicates that the headword years is always plural in form and construction in this particular application, and at

road *n* 1 *often* roads *pl syn* see HARBOR 3
2 *syn* see WAY 1
3 *syn* see WAY 2

where sense 1 (and only that sense) of the headword road is often but not always used in the plural, and at

minutia *n, usu* minutiae *pl* 1 *syn* see
INS AND OUTS
2 *syn* see TRIVIA

where the label preceding both senses indicates that the headword minutia is usually used in the plural in both of these applications, and at the main entry

trivia *n pl but sometimes sing in constr*

where the label is qualified to show that this plural noun may sometimes be used with a singular verb, and at

common *n* 1 commons *pl but sing or pl in
constr syn* see COMMONALTY

which indicates that common occurs as a plural noun in sense 1 but may occur with either singular or plural verbs, and at

outdoors *n pl but sing in constr* the space where
air is unconfined <every night he let the dog
run in the *outdoors*>

whose label indicates that while the word *outdoors* is a plural noun, it consistently takes a singular verb. Use of these labels conforms to the treatment of plurals in Webster's Third New International Dictionary.

An italic subject guide phrase pointing to something with which the headword is associated may precede a meaning core in a very few instances, as at

set *vb* . . . 11 *of a fowl* to incubate eggs
by crouching upon them . . .

Punctuation A comma links items (as synonyms, idiomatic equivalents, members of a single group or subgroup of related or contrasted words or of antonyms) that are alike in their relation to the headword, as at

conservative *adj* . . . 2 . . .
syn controlled, discreet, moderate, reasonable,
restrained, temperate, unexcessive, unextreme
rel cautious, chary, wary; circumspect, politic, proper,
prudent
con expansive, unconstrained; excessive, freewheeling,
uncontrolled, unrestrained

A semicolon signals a break in continuity and is used in *rel* and *con* lists (as between the two subgroups in the *rel* and *con* lists at **conservative 2** above) to separate subgroups of words which differ in their relation to the headword. A semicolon is also used to separate antonyms that belong to different classes of opposites, as

> **arise** *vb* 1 *syn* see RISE 4
> *ant* recline; slump

where the two antonyms are so separated. A semicolon may also appear at the end of a main-entry *syn* list to introduce a compare cross-reference, as shown at **honorable** *adj* 1:

> *syn* estimable, high-principled, noble,
> sterling, worthy; *compare* VENERABLE 1

Parentheses enclose variant spellings, as at the main entry **cake** *vb* 1 where

> encrust (*or* incrust)

is a synonym, and at the secondary entries, where that particular synonym is styled

> **encrust** (*or* **incrust**) *vb syn* see CAKE 1

Parentheses also enclose a particle or particles usually associated with a base word, as

> **adore** *vb*... 3 to love, admire, or enjoy
> excessively ...
> *syn* dote (on *or* upon), idolize, worship
>
> **dote** (on *or* upon) *vb syn* see ADORE 3

Similarly, parentheses may indicate usage alternatives in idiomatic expressions, as at **slavery** *n* 2 where

> *idiom* the yoke (*or* chains) of slavery

alerts the user that he may choose one of two noun elements when employing this particular idiom. Parentheses are also used in main-entry *syn* lists to enclose plural suffixes of words that are sometimes, often, or usually but not always used in the plural:

> **scad** *n, usu* **scads** *pl* a great number or abundance ...
> *syn* gob(s), heap, jillion, load(s), million,
> oodles, quantities, ...

Parentheses enclose material indicating a typical, or occasionally, a sole object of reference, as in the meaning core of **express** *vb* 2

> to give expression to (*as a thought, an opinion,
> or an emotion*)

where they enclose an adjunct, or at entries such as **abrogate** *vb* 2

> *ant* establish, fix (*as a right, a quality, or
> a custom*)

where an antonym or a group of antonyms are associated with a particular object or objects of reference — a restriction or limitation to which the thesaurus user should be alerted.

Symbols A warning symbol is used in this book in the form of the double bars ‖.

The double bars prefixing some terms warn the user that the employment of such a term may involve a problem of diction too complex for presentation in a thesaurus, or a restriction in usage. Consequently, the thesaurus user should consult a dictionary if he is in doubt about the stylistic level or appropriateness of the word or if he is unfamiliar with its meaning. For example, ‖**fat cat** (a synonym of **notable** *n* 1), ‖**chuff** (a synonym of **sullen** *adj*), and ‖**puxy** (a synonym of **swamp** *n*) are all double-barred in this book because they carry stigmatizing or regional labels in Webster's Third New International Dictionary.

The
Merriam-Webster
Thesaurus

aback *adv syn* see UNAWARES

abaft *adv* toward or at the stern (of a vessel) < headed *abaft* for a smoke >
  syn aft, astern
  rel after, back, behind
  ant forward

abaft *prep* to the rear of < huddled in a nook *abaft* the chimney >
  syn back of, behind

abalienate *vb syn* see TRANSFER 4

abandon *vb* 1 to give up without intent to return or re-claim < *abandoned* his family >
  syn chuck, desert, forsake, quit, renounce, throw over
  rel cast (off), discard, disuse, drop, junk, scrap; reject, repudiate
  idiom have done with, leave flat, quit cold, run out on, turn one's back on (*or* upon), walk out on
  con hold, keep, possess, retain; redeem, rescue, save; acquire, gain, get, procure, win; cherish, foster
  ant re-claim

  2 *syn* see RELINQUISH
  ant retain

abandon *n* 1 *syn* see UNCONSTRAINT

  2 carefree disregard for consequences < behave with *abandon* >
  syn impulsiveness, uninhibitedness, unrestraint; compare UNCONSTRAINT
  rel freedom, liberty, license; exuberance, heedlessness, laxity, laxness, looseness, unruliness, wildness; incontinence, licentiousness, wantonness; fun, games, play, sport
  con constraint, inhibitedness, inhibition, restraint; repression, suppression
  ant self-restraint

abandoned *adj* 1 *syn* see DERELICT 1

  2 free from moral restraint < led a thoroughly *abandoned* life >
  syn dissolute, licentious, profligate, reprobate, self-abandoned, unprincipled
  rel debased, debauched, depraved, perverted, riotous; incorrigible; lascivious, lecherous, lewd, wanton; corrupt, degenerate
  idiom dead to honor, gone to the bad, lost to shame, rotten (to *or* at) the core

  con ethical, high-principled, moral, reputable, virtuous; correct, decent, decorous, proper, seemly
  ant scrupulous, upright

abase *vb syn* see HUMBLE
  rel demote, diminish, downgrade, reduce; fawn, grovel, toady; cower, cringe, truckle
  con elevate, lift, raise
  ant exalt; extol

abash *vb syn* see EMBARRASS 1
  rel abase, demean, humble, humiliate
  idiom make one eat humble pie
  ant embolden, reassure

abashment *n syn* see EMBARRASSMENT

abate *vb* 1 *syn* see ABOLISH 1

  2 *syn* see ANNIHILATE 2

  3 *syn* see DECREASE

  4 to lessen in force or intensity < the storm *abated* slowly >
  syn ‖bate, die (down *or* away), ease off, ebb, fall, let up, lull, moderate, relent, slacken, subside, wane
  rel decrease, diminish, dwindle, lessen, weaken
  idiom run its course
  con augment, expand, extend, increase; mount, rage, soar, surge
  ant revive; rise

abatement *n syn* see DEDUCTION 1
  con enlargement, increase
  ant addition

abbreviate *vb syn* see SHORTEN
  rel attenuate, extenuate
  con enlarge, increase; amplify, dilate, expand
  ant lengthen; extend

ABC *n* 1 *usu* ABC's *pl syn* see ALPHABET 1

  2 *often* ABC's *pl syn* see ALPHABET 2

abdicate *vb* 1 to part formally or definitely with a position of honor or power < the king *abdicated* the throne in order to marry a commoner >
  syn demit, renounce, resign; compare RELINQUISH
  rel abandon, leave, relinquish, surrender; drop; withdraw
  con appropriate, arrogate, confiscate; grab, seize, take over, wrest

ant assume, usurp

2 *syn* see DISCARD

con keep, retain, treasure

abdomen *n* the part of the body between the chest and the pelvis <intense pain in the lower *abdomen*>

syn belly, ‖gut, paunch, stomach, tummy, venter

rel bay window, ‖breadbasket, corporation, pod, pot, potbelly; middle, midriff, midsection

abduct *vb syn* see KIDNAP

rel grab, seize

abecedarian *n syn* see AMATEUR 2

aberrant *adj* 1 *syn* see ABNORMAL 1

rel different, disparate, divergent; eccentric, odd, peculiar, strange; exceptional, unusual

con natural, normal, regular, typical; customary, usual, wonted

ant true (to a type)

2 *syn* see ERRANT 2

aberration *n* 1 *syn* see DEVIATION 1

rel abnormality; mistake, slip; curiosity, oddity, prodigy, rarity

con average, mean, norm; normality

ant conformity; regularity

2 *syn* see INSANITY 1

ant soundness (of mind)

abet *vb* 1 *syn* see INCITE

rel egg, exhort, goad, prod, spur, urge; advocate, countenance, encourage, endorse

con forbid, prevent, prohibit; debar, deter, discourage

2 *syn* see HELP 1

abettor *n syn* see CONFEDERATE

abeyance *n* a state of temporary inactivity <the warm dry weather kept his asthma in *abeyance*>

syn abeyancy, cold storage, doldrums, dormancy, intermission, interruption, latency, quiescence, quiescency, suspension

rel break, interval, pause, respite

con activeness, activity, stir

ant continuance

abeyancy *n syn* see ABEYANCE

ant continuancy

abeyant *adj syn* see LATENT

rel deferred, intermitted, postponed, stayed, suppressed; repressed

con refreshed, renewed, restored

ant active, operative; revived

abhor *vb* 1 *syn* see HATE

2 *syn* see DESPISE

con dote (on or upon), like, love

ant admire

abhorrence *n syn* see ABOMINATION 2

rel distaste, repellency; dismay, horror

con affection, attachment, love

ant admiration; enjoyment

abhorrent *adj* 1 *syn* see HATEFUL 2

ant admirable

2 *syn* see REPUGNANT 1

rel antipathetic; uncongenial, unsympathetic

con alluring, attractive, captivating; enticing, seductive, tempting

ant congenial

abide *vb* 1 *syn* see STAY 2

rel adhere, cleave, cling, stick; dwell, live, reside

con go, leave, quit; move, remove, shift

ant depart

2 *syn* see CONTINUE 1

rel linger; exist, subsist

con avoid, elude, escape, evade

ant pass

3 *syn* see BEAR 10

rel accept, receive; accede, consent

idiom put up with

4 *syn* see RESIDE 1

abiding *adj syn* see SURE 2

rel durable, lasting, perdurable, persistent

con ephemeral, impermanent, short-lived, transient, transitory

ability *n* 1 physical, mental, or legal power to perform <he has the *ability* to accomplish whatever he sets his mind to>

syn adequacy, capability, capacity, competence, might, qualification, qualifiedness

rel address, adroitness, cleverness, dexterity; aptitude, aptness, facility, knack

idiom what it takes

con impotence, inadequacy, incapability, incompetence

ant inability

2 natural or acquired proficiency especially in a particular activity <he has unusual *ability* in planning and designing>

syn command, expertise, expertism, expertness, knack, know-how, mastership, mastery, skill

rel adroitness, deftness, efficiency, handiness, proficiency; ingenuity, resourcefulness; talent

con inadequacy, incompetence, ineffectualness, unfitness; fatuity, futility, inanity

abject *adj syn* see DOWNTRODDEN

abjure *vb* to give up (something formerly adhered to) irrevocably and usually solemnly or formally <an immigrant solemnly *abjuring* allegiance to his former country>

syn forswear, palinode, recall, recant, retract, take back, unsay, withdraw

rel disavow, disown, renounce, repudiate; abandon, desert, forsake; cede, relinquish, surrender

idiom eat one's words

ablaze *adj* 1 *syn* see BURNING 1

2 *syn* see ALIGHT 2

able *adj* possessed of or marked by a high level of efficiency and ability <an *able* student always near the head of his class>

syn au fait, capable, competent, good, proper, qualified, wicked

rel effective, effectual, efficient; expert, proficient, skilled, skillful; alert, clever, keen, sharp; brainy, brilliant, intelligent, smart; enterprising, go-ahead, up-and-coming

con ineffective, ineffectual, inefficient; incapable, incompetent, unqualified; fair, indifferent, mediocre; lackluster, maladroit

ant inept; unable

abnegation *n syn* see RENUNCIATION

abnormal *adj* 1 departing significantly from the normal or a norm <the *abnormal* rains caused flooding>

---

syn synonym(s)   *rel* related word(s)

ant antonym(s)   *con* contrasted word(s)

idiom idiomatic equivalent(s)

‖ use limited; if in doubt, see a dictionary

syn aberrant, anomalous, atypical, deviant, deviative, heteroclite, preternatural, unrepresentative, untypical

rel divergent, offtype; irregular, unnatural; uncustomary, unusual, unwonted; heteromorphic; paratypic

con common, familiar, natural, ordinary, regular, typical; customary, usual, wonted

ant normal

2 *syn* see IRREGULAR 1

abode *n syn* see HABITATION 2

abolish *vb* 1 to bring to an end often by formal or concerted action < *abolish* a tax >

syn abate, abrogate, annihilate, annul, circumduct, invalidate, negate, nullify, quash, undo, vitiate

rel cancel, disallow, disannul, repeal, rescind, revoke, vacate

idiom bring to naught, make void, set aside

con conserve, preserve, save; keep, retain

2 *syn* see ANNIHILATE 2

con found, institute

ant establish

abominable *adj syn* see HATEFUL 2

rel accursed, cursed; loathsome, offensive, repugnant, revolting

con applaudable, commendable

ant laudable (*as practices, customs*); delightful, enjoyable

abominate *vb syn* see HATE

rel curse, damn, objurgate

idiom hold in abomination, take an aversion to

con admire, regard

ant enjoy; esteem

abomination *n* 1 one that is a source of utter disgust or intense dislike < found the new tax form an *abomination* of confused complexity >

syn anathema, bête noire, black beast, bugbear, detestation, hate

rel annoyance, pest, plague, trial; bogey, bugaboo, incubus

con delectation, delight, joy, pleasure; treasure

2 a feeling of extreme disgust and dislike < they hold every indulgence in *abomination* >

syn abhorrence, aversion, detestation, hate, hatred, horror, loathing, repugnance, repugnancy, repulsion, revulsion

rel contempt, despite, disdain, scorn; disfavor, dislike, disrelish, distaste

con admiration, regard, respect; fondness, liking, relish, taste; approbation, approval, countenance, favor; acceptance, tolerance

ant esteem; enjoyment

aboriginal *adj syn* see NATIVE 2

rel primeval, primitive, primordial, pristine; barbarian, barbaric, barbarous, savage

con advanced, progressive; civilized, cultured; sequent, successive

abortion *n syn* see FREAK 2

abortive *adj syn* see FUTILE

rel unformed; immature, unmatured, unripe

con accomplished, completed, concluded, finished

ant consummated

abound *vb syn* see TEEM

abounding *adj syn* see ALIVE 5

rel full, jammed, packed, stuffed

about *adv* 1 in every direction < looked carefully *about* >

syn around, round, round about

2 in a circuitous way or course < took the long way *about* >

syn circuitously, round about

3 *syn* see NEARLY

4 here or there without plan or order < left his tools lying *about* >

syn anyhow, any which way, anywise, around, at random, haphazard, haphazardly, helter-skelter, random, randomly

rel back and forth, hither and thither, to and fro; aimlessly, carelessly, casually

5 in the vicinity < talked to the people standing *about* >

syn near, near-at-hand, nearby

idiom close by

6 in the opposite direction < he turned *about* and saw her >

syn again, around, back, backward, in reverse, round, round about

idiom in one's course

about *prep* 1 in the vicinity of < *about* five miles to go >

syn around, circa, close on, near, nearby, nigh

idiom hard by, not far from

2 *syn* see APROPOS

idiom in point of, with regard to

3 *syn* see OVER 3

4 here and there upon or within < traveled *about* the country >

syn round, through, throughout

idiom all over

about-face *n syn* see REVERSAL 1

above *adv* 1 *syn* see OVER 4

ant below

2 higher on the same page or on a preceding page < earlier examples appear *above*>

syn supra

ant below, infra

above *prep* 1 *syn* see OVER 1

ant below

2 *syn* see BEYOND 2

aboveboard *adj syn* see STRAIGHTFORWARD 2

rel open, scrupulous; artless, ingenuous, unsophisticated

con clandestine, covert, furtive, secret, surreptitious; deceitful; crooked, devious, oblique

ant underhand, underhanded

abracadabra *n syn* see GIBBERISH 3

rel mystification; argot, cant, jargon

abrade *vb* 1 to injure or flaw by frictional action < wind-driven sand *abraded* the glass >

syn chafe, corrade, erode, gall, graze, rub, ruffle, wear

rel corrode, eat away, fret; grate, rasp, scrape

2 *syn* see CHAFE 3

rel burn

3 *syn* see ANNOY 1

rel disorganize, disturb, flurry, rattle; confuse, distract, perturb

con calm, relieve, soothe

Abraham's bosom *n syn* see HEAVEN 2

abreast *adj* 1 *syn* see UP-TO-DATE

2 *syn* see FAMILIAR 3

abridge *vb* 1 to make less by in some manner restricting < laws that *abridge* freedom of speech >
  syn curtail, diminish, lessen, minify
  rel limit, narrow, reduce, restrict; minimize
  con augment, broaden, enlarge, extend
  ant amplify
2 *syn* see SHORTEN
  con amplify, augment, enlarge, increase
  ant expand, extend

abridgment *n* a shortened version of a larger work or treatment produced by condensing and omitting without basic alteration of intent and language < an *abridgment* of a dictionary >
  syn abstract, boildown, breviary, breviate, brief, condensation, conspectus, epitome, synopsis
  rel aperçu, compendium, digest, outline, précis, sketch, syllabus; capsule, summary; sum, summation, summing-up
  con elaboration; paraphrase
  ant expansion

abroad *adv syn* see OVERSEAS

abrogate *vb* 1 *syn* see ANNUL 4
  rel abate, extinguish
  con establish, found; confirm, ratify
  ant institute (*as by enacting or decreeing*)
2 *syn* see ABOLISH 1
  rel extinguish; blot out, cancel, obliterate; ruin, wreck
  con support, uphold
  ant establish, fix (*as a right, a quality, or a custom*)

abrupt *adj* 1 *syn* see PRECIPITATE 2
  rel hastened; casual, informal, unceremonious; quick, speedy
  con dilatory, laggard; easy, relaxed
  ant deliberate, leisurely
2 *syn* see BLUFF
  rel brisk, crisp, sharp; impetuous, quick, ready
  con calm, easy, relaxed
3 *syn* see STEEP 1
  rel perpendicular, plumb, vertical
  con inclined, slanting; flat, level, plane, smooth
  ant sloping

abruptly *adv syn* see SHORT 1

abscess *n* a localized swollen area of infection containing pus < had an *abscess* on his leg >
  syn boil, carbuncle, furuncle, pimple, pustule
  rel lesion, sore, trauma; botch, ulcer

abscond *vb syn* see ESCAPE 1
  rel go, leave, quit, withdraw
  idiom do the disappearing act, skip out, take French leave
  con render, surrender, yield
  ant give (oneself) up

absence *n* the state of being absent or missing < the *absence* of news was disturbing >
  syn dearth, default, defect, lack, ‖miss, privation, want; *compare* FAILURE 3

---

syn synonym(s)   *rel* related word(s)
ant antonym(s)   *con* contrasted word(s)
idiom idiomatic equivalent(s)
‖ use limited; if in doubt, see a dictionary

---

  rel deficiency, drought, inadequacy, insufficiency; exigency, necessity, need; vacuum, void; nonappearance, nonattendance
  con abundance, copiousness, plenty
  ant presence

absent *adj* 1 not now present < all missed their *absent* friend >
  syn away, gone, lacking, missing, omitted, wanting
  ant present
2 *syn* see ABSTRACTED
  rel absorbed; forgetful, heedless
  con attending, hearkening, listening; considerate, thoughtful
  ant attentive

absentminded *adj syn* see ABSTRACTED
  rel unnoticing, unobserving, unperceiving, unseeing; heedless, inattentive
  idiom lost in thought
  con alert; aware
  ant wide-awake

absolute *adj* 1 *syn* see PERFECT 2
  rel pure, sheer, simple
  con circumscribed, limited, partial, restricted
2 *syn* see PURE 2
  rel abstract, ideal; real, true
  con imperfect, incomplete
  ant mixed, qualified
3 *syn* see UTTER
4 exercising power or authority without external restraint < an *absolute* monarch >
  syn arbitrary, autarchic, autocratic, despotic, monocratic, tyrannical, tyrannous; *compare* TOTALITARIAN 1
  rel dictatorial, magisterial; authoritarian, totalitarian; domineering, imperious, masterful; plenipotential, plenipotentiary, unlimited
  con circumscribed, limited, restrained, restricted; constitutional, lawful
5 *syn* see ACTUAL 2
6 *syn* see ULTIMATE 3
  rel ideal, transcendent, transcendental; autonomous, free, independent, sovereign; boundless, eternal, infinite
  con circumscribed, limited, restricted; conditional, contingent, dependent

absolutely *adv syn* see EASILY 2

absolution *n syn* see PARDON
  rel condonation
  con censure, reprehension, reprobation
  ant condemnation

absolve *vb* 1 *syn* see EXEMPT
2 *syn* see EXCULPATE
  rel discharge, free, release
  con condemn, doom, sentence; chasten, discipline, punish
  ant charge (with), hold (to)

absorb *vb* 1 to take in and make a part of one's being < *absorb* knowledge from reading >
  syn assimilate, imbibe, incorporate, inhaust, insorb
  rel embody, imbue, impregnate, infuse, permeate
  con disgorge, eject, expel, vomit; discharge, eliminate, emit, give off, pass
  ant exude, give out
2 *syn* see MONOPOLIZE
  rel concern, engage, immerse, involve, preoccupy
  con diffuse, disperse, scatter

ant dissipate (*as time, attention*)

absorbed *adj syn see* INTENT
 rel involved
 idiom caught up in, up to the elbows (*or* ears) in
 con apathetic, disinterested, indifferent, unconcerned; uninterested; absent, abstracted
 ant distracted

absorbing *adj syn see* ENGROSSING
 ant irksome

abstain *vb* 1 *syn see* DENY 3
 rel abnegate, eschew, forgo; decline, refuse, reject, spurn
 idiom dispense with, do without, let alone
 con pamper; gratify, regale; sate, satiate, surfeit
 ant indulge
2 *syn see* REFRAIN 1

abstemious *adj* marked by restraint in satisfying desires (as for food, drink, or pleasure) < an *abstemious* man, little given to self-indulgence>
 syn abstentious, abstinent, continent, self-restraining, sober, temperate; *compare* SOBER 3
 rel self-abnegating, self-denying; ascetic, austere; sparing
 con greedy, rapacious, voracious; epicurean, sybaritic, voluptuous
 ant gluttonous

abstentious *adj syn see* ABSTEMIOUS
 ant gluttonous

abstinence *n syn see* TEMPERANCE 2
 rel renunciation
 con gorging, sating, surfeiting; immoderateness, overdoing, unrestraint; crapulence, excess, extravagance
 ant self-indulgence

abstinent *adj syn see* ABSTEMIOUS
 ant gluttonous

abstract *adj* 1 having conceptual rather than concrete existence < the *abstract* perfect society>
 syn hypothetical, ideal, theoretical, transcendent, transcendental
 rel academic, impractical, utopian, visionary; speculative, undemonstrable; conceptual, notional; inconcrete
 con corporeal, material, objective, phenomenal, physical; actual, factual, real
 ant concrete
2 *syn see* NEUTRAL

abstract *n syn see* ABRIDGMENT
 con enlargement, expansion
 ant amplification

abstract *vb* 1 *syn see* DETACH
 rel divide, part, separate
 con insinuate, interpolate, interpose
 ant insert, introduce
2 *syn see* STEAL 1

abstracted *adj* withdrawn in mind and inattentive to external matters < seemed *abstracted* and remote>
 syn absent, absentminded, bemused, distrait, faraway, inconscient, lost, preoccupied
 rel engrossed, intent, rapt; oblivious, unmindful, unminding; heedless, inattentive
 idiom in a brown study, lost in thought, lost to the world
 con attentive, vigilant, watchful, wide-awake; noticing, noting, observant, seeing

ant alert

abstruse *adj syn see* RECONDITE
 rel complex, complicated, intricate, knotty; abstract, hypothetical, ideal
 con clear, evident, manifest, palpable; clear, lucid, perspicuous; easy, facile, simple
 ant obvious, plain

absurd *adj syn see* FOOLISH 2
 rel comic, droll, funny; asinine, fatuous, simple; irrational, unreasonable
 con logical, ratiocinative, subtle
 ant rational, sensible

absurdity *n syn see* FOOLISHNESS

abundance *n syn see* PROSPERITY 2
 rel adequacy, competence, enough, plenty, sufficiency; lavishness, prodigality
 idiom enough and to spare
 con deficiency, inadequacy, insufficiency, lack, paucity

abundant *adj syn see* PLENTIFUL
 rel lavish, lush, luxuriant, profuse; crammed, crowded, thick; common
 idiom in good supply
 con infrequent, rare, uncommon; inadequate, scanty
 ant scarce

abuse *vb* 1 *syn see* DECRY 2
 ant praise
2 to put to a bad or improper use < *abuse* the prerogatives of office>
 syn misapply, misemploy, mishandle, misimprove, misuse, pervert, prostitute
 rel mar, spoil; corrupt, debase, desecrate, profane
 idiom make ill use of
 con esteem, honor, respect
3 *syn see* EXPLOIT 2
4 to treat without compassion and usually in a hurtful manner < parents who *abuse* children>
 syn ill-treat, ill-use, maltreat, mistreat, misuse, outrage
 rel damage, harm, hurt, impair, injure; oppress, persecute, wrong; manhandle, mess (up)
 idiom do one dirt, do violence to
 con cherish, prize, treasure; esteem, revere, reverence, venerate
 ant honor, respect

abuse *n* vehemently and usually coarsely expressed condemnation or disapproval < had an unequaled vocabulary of *abuse*>
 syn billingsgate, contumely, invective, obloquy, scurrility, vituperation
 rel calumny, defamation, malignment, mud, vilification; cursing, profanity, swearing; berating, railing, rating, reviling
 con acclaim, laudation, praise; applause, commendation, compliment
 ant adulation

abusive *adj* coarse, insulting, and contemptuous in character or utterance < an *abusive* denunciation>
 syn contumelious, invective, opprobrious, scurrile, scurrilous, truculent, vituperative, vituperatory, vituperous
 rel affronting, insulting, offending, outraging; dirty, odious, offensive; aspersing, maligning, vilifying
 con acclaiming, extolling, lauding, praising; eulogistic, panegyrical; flattering

ant complimentary; respectful

abut *vb syn* see ADJOIN

abutting *adj syn* see ADJACENT 3
rel connecting, joining; impinging
con detached, disengaged; disassociated, disconnected, disjoined, parted, separated

abysm *n syn* see GULF 2

abysmal *adj* 1 *syn* see BOTTOMLESS 2
2 *syn* see DEEP 1
rel illimitable, infinite

abyss *n* 1 *syn* see HELL
2 *syn* see GULF 2
3 *syn* see DEPTH 2

academic *adj* 1 *syn* see PEDANTIC
con ignorant, illiterate, unlettered; down-to-earth, everyday, practical, realistic, straightforward
2 *syn* see THEORETICAL 1
rel impractical, utopian, visionary; chimerical, imaginary

accede *vb syn* see ASSENT
rel concur, cooperate; allow, let, permit
con decline; balk, shy, stick; expostulate, kick, object, protest; fight, oppose, resist, withstand
ant demur

accelerate *vb syn* see SPEED 3
rel drive, impel
idiom get going, make up for lost time
con clog, hamper; delay, detain, slow
ant decelerate; retard

accent *n* 1 *syn* see INFLECTION
2 *syn* see EMPHASIS
rel cadence, meter, rhythm; beat, pulsation, pulse, throb

accentuation *n syn* see EMPHASIS
con evenness, sameness, steadiness, uniformity
ant inaccentuation

accept *vb* 1 *syn* see APPROVE 1
rel fancy, like, relish; admire, esteem
con discountenance, disesteem, dislike, disrelish
ant reject
2 to take or sustain without protest *or* repining <a losing candidate must *accept* the decision of the electorate>
syn bear (with), endure, pocket, swallow, tolerate, tough (out); *compare* BEAR 10
rel acquiesce (in), agree (to *or* with), assent (to), subscribe (to); respect; bow, capitulate, yield
idiom put up with
con disavow, disown; brush (aside), deny, reject, repudiate
3 *syn* see BELIEVE 1
4 *syn* see APPREHEND 1

acceptable *adj* 1 *syn* see DECENT 4
rel average, commonplace, ordinary; bearable, endurable, supportable
con insupportable, intolerable, unbearable, unendurable
ant unacceptable

acceptably *adv syn* see WELL 4

acceptant *adj syn* see RECEPTIVE 1

acceptation *n syn* see MEANING 1

accepted *adj* 1 *syn* see USUAL 1
rel conventional, established, recognized; correct, orthodox, proper, right

---

syn synonym(s)   *rel* related word(s)
ant antonym(s)   *con* contrasted word(s)
idiom idiomatic equivalent(s)
‖ use limited; if in doubt, see a dictionary

---

idiom according to custom (*or* use)
con irregular, questionable, unacceptable, unconventional; incongruent, unconformable, unorthodox
2 *syn* see ORTHODOX 1

acceptive *adj syn* see RECEPTIVE 1

access *n* 1 *syn* see ATTACK 3
rel onset; taking; pang, stitch, twinge
2 *syn* see OUTBURST 1
3 *syn* see DOOR 2
rel passage, route
con departure, retreat, withdrawal
ant egress; outlet

accessible *adj* 1 *syn* see OPEN 4
rel approachable
con limited, restricted; remote
2 *syn* see OPEN 5
ant inaccessible

accession *n syn* see ADDITION
ant discard

accessory *n* 1 *syn* see APPENDAGE
rel accompaniment, concomitant; accretion, addition, increment
2 *syn* see CONFEDERATE
ant principal

accessory *adj syn* see AUXILIARY
rel secondary, subordinate, tributary; coincident, concomitant, concurrent; adventitious, incidental
con constitutional, ingrained, inherent, intrinsic; cardinal, fundamental, vital; essential, indispensable, necessary
ant constituent, integral

accident *n* 1 absence of positive plan or intent <we stopped there by *accident*>
syn chance, fortuity, hap, luck
rel fluke, fortune, hazard
con design, premeditation
ant intent
2 a chance event bringing injury, loss, or distress <the school was closed by an *accident* to the heating system>
syn casualty, misadventure, mischance, mishap
rel calamity, catastrophe, disaster, tragedy; misfortune; chance, destiny, fate, kismet
con foreordination, predestination

accidental *adj* resulting from chance <an *accidental* meeting>
syn casual, chance, contingent, fluky, fortuitous, incidental, odd; *compare* RANDOM, UNINTENTIONAL
rel conditional, dependent; coincident, coincidental; inadvertent, undesigned, unintended, unintentional, unmeant, unplanned, unpurposed, unwitting
con designed, intended, purposed; constitutional, inherent, intrinsic; innate
ant planned; essential

accidentally *adv syn* see INCIDENTALLY 1

acclaim *vb syn* see COMMEND 2
rel cheer, root (for); exalt, magnify; glorify, honor
con berate, revile; damn, execrate, objurgate; censure, denounce
ant vituperate

acclaim *n syn* see APPLAUSE
rel homage, honor, reverence; éclat, glory
con abuse, invective, obloquy; censure, condemnation, denunciation, reprobation
ant vituperation

acclamation *n syn see* APPLAUSE

acclimate *vb syn see* HARDEN 2

acclimatize *vb syn see* HARDEN 2

accolade *n syn see* HONOR 2

accommodate *vb* 1 *syn see* ADAPT
rel bow, defer, submit, yield; alter, change, modify, vary
con alienate, estrange
ant constrain
2 *syn see* HARMONIZE 3
3 *syn see* OBLIGE 2
rel cater (to), humor, indulge
con annoy, harass, harry; irk, vex, worry
ant incommode
4 *syn see* CONTAIN 2
rel encase, enclose
5 *syn see* HARBOR 2

accommodations *n pl* shelter, food, and services (as at a hotel) <searched for *accommodations* as night drew near>
syn lodging, lodgment, room and board
rel bed, room; keep; housing, shelter
idiom bed and breakfast

accompaniment *n* 1 something added to a principal thing usually to increase its impact or effectiveness <her song had a soft orchestral *accompaniment*>
syn augmentation, complement, enhancement, enrichment
rel accessory, addition, supplement; aid, assistance, help
2 an accompanying individual, situation, or occurrence <smog is an inevitable *accompaniment* of excessive numbers of automobiles>
syn associate, companion, concomitant, consort, fellow, mate
rel attendant, colleague, comrade, partner; corollary, equivalent

accompany *vb* to go or be together with <*accompanied* his wife to the theater>
syn attend, bear, ||bring, ||carry, chaperon, companion, company, conduct, consort (with), convoy, escort
rel associate, combine, join, link; defend, guard, protect, safeguard, shield; guide, lead, pilot, steer
idiom bear one company, go along with, go hand in hand with
con leave, quit, withdraw; abandon, forsake

accompanying *adj syn see* CONCOMITANT

accomplice *n syn see* CONFEDERATE
rel aider, assistant, helper; flunky, stooge

accomplish *vb syn see* GAIN 1

accomplished *adj syn see* CONSUMMATE 1
rel adept, expert, masterly, proficient; all-around, many-sided, versatile

accomplishment *n* 1 *syn see* ACQUIREMENT
rel art, craft, skill; adeptness, expertise, expertness, proficiency
2 *syn see* ACTION 1

accord *vb* 1 *syn see* AGREE 4
rel coincide, concur; blend, coalesce, fuse, merge
con differ, disagree; compare, contrast
ant conflict
2 *syn see* GRANT 1
rel allot
con deny, gainsay; refuse; detain, hold, reserve

ant withhold
3 *syn see* GIVE 2

accord *n* 1 *syn see* HARMONY 2
rel affinity, attraction, empathy, sympathy; solidarity, union
idiom community of interest(s)
con conflict, contention, difference; animosity, antipathy, hostility
ant dissension, strife; antagonism
2 *syn see* AGREEMENT 2
3 *syn see* HARMONY 1

accordant *adj syn see* HARMONIOUS 2

accordingly *adv syn see* THEREFORE
idiom by reason of that (*or* this), for that (*or* this) reason

according to *prep syn see* BY 5

accost *vb* 1 *syn see* ADDRESS 7
rel buttonhole
con ignore, overlook, slight; avoid, elude, evade, shun
2 to approach boldly or in a challenging or sometimes a defensive manner <*accosted* by a beggar who demanded money>
syn confront, face, front
rel affront, insult, offend, outrage; annoy, bother; challenge, dare, outface
idiom come face to face with, meet face to face
3 *syn see* ADDRESS 4
rel call (to), hail, halloo; buttonhole; dog, hound, pester, worry

accouchement *n syn see* CONFINEMENT 2

account *n* 1 *syn see* BILL 1
2 *syn see* USE 3
con immateriality, inconsequence, insignificance, unimportance; bootlessness, fruitlessness, futility
3 *syn see* WORTH 1
4 *syn see* REGARD 4
rel consequence, dignity, distinction, note; reputation, repute
5 *syn see* EXPLANATION 2
6 *syn see* SCORE 4
7 a statement of real or purported events, occurrences, or conditions <wrote an *account* of his travels>
syn chronicle, history, narrative, report, story, version; *compare* STORY 2

account *vb* 1 *syn see* CONSIDER 3
rel appraise, assess, estimate, evaluate, rate; esteem
con underestimate, underrate, undervalue
2 *syn see* EXPLAIN 3
rel answer, elucidate, expound, interpret

accountable *adj syn see* RESPONSIBLE
con absolute, arbitrary, autocratic; imperious, magisterial, masterful
ant unaccountable

accouter *vb syn see* FURNISH 1
rel attire, dress; adorn, deck, decorate, embellish; fix (up), prepare, ready

accouterment *n, usu* accouterments *pl syn see* EQUIPMENT
rel appointment(s); furnishing(s); bravery, regalia, trappings

accredit *vb* 1 *syn see* APPROVE 1
rel commend, recommend; attest, certify, vouch (for)
con belittle, deprecate, depreciate, disapprove; reject, repudiate
2 *syn see* ASCRIBE

3 *syn* see AUTHORIZE 1
rel introduce, present

accretion *n syn* see ADDITION
rel enlargement; attachment, joining,
uniting; adjunct, appendage

accroach *vb* 1 *syn* see ARROGATE 1
2 *syn* see APPROPRIATE 1

accumulate *vb* to bring together and form
a store of < *accumulate* knowledge >
syn amass, cumulate, garner, hive, lay up,
roll up, stockpile, store (up), uplay; *compare* HOARD
rel assemble, collect, gather, lay by, lay
down, lay in; heap, mass, pile, stock;
fund, hoard, treasure
idiom squirrel away
con decrease, diminish, lessen; deal, dispense, distribute, dole (out); dispel, disperse, scatter; consume, expend, spend,
use, use up
ant dissipate

accumulation *n* a mass, quantity, or number that has accumulated < an *accumulation* of rubbish >
syn agglomeration, aggregation, amassment, collection, colluvies, conglomeration, cumulation, hoard, trove
rel bank, heap, mass, pile; cumulus, reserve, stock, store
con dispersal, dispersion, scattering

accumulative *adj syn* see CUMULATIVE
rel aggregative, conglomerative; augmen-
tative, multiplicative
con contractile, contractive, reducing,
reductive; dispelling, dispersing, dispersive,
dissipative, scattering

accuracy *n syn* see PRECISION

accurate *adj* 1 *syn* see CORRECT 2
con slipshod, slovenly; careless, heedless,
lax
ant inaccurate
2 *syn* see CERTAIN 3

accurately *adv syn* see JUST 1

accursed *adj syn* see EXECRABLE 1
rel abhorrent, abominable, detestable,
hateful, odious; offensive, repugnant, revolting
con admirable, estimable; honorable;
divine, holy, sacred
ant blessed

accuse *vb* to declare one guilty of a fault
or offense < *accused* her daughter of neglecting her children >
syn arraign, charge, criminate, impeach,
incriminate, inculpate, indict, tax
rel blame, censure, criticize, denounce,
reprobate; complain
idiom bring charges (against), point the
finger at, prefer charges (against)
con absolve, acquit, exonerate, vindicate;
accept, approve, endorse, sanction
ant exculpate

accustom *vb* to make something familiar
or acceptable through use or experience
< *accustom* oneself to city life >
syn familiarize, habituate, inure, use,
wont
rel accommodate, adapt, adjust; acclimatize, harden, season

---

syn synonym(s)   *rel* related word(s)
ant antonym(s)   *con* contrasted word(s)
idiom idiomatic equivalent(s)
‖ use limited; if in doubt, see a dictionary

---

con alienate, estrange, wean; abjure, reject, repudiate; rebuff, repel, repulse, scorn
ant disaccustom

accustomed *adj* 1 *syn* see HABITUAL 2
2 *syn* see USUAL 1
rel commonplace, everyday; conventional,
regulation, standard
con infrequent, occasional, uncommon;
erratic, odd, peculiar, queer, singular
ant unaccustomed

ace *n* 1 *syn* see HAIR
2 *syn* see PARTICLE

acedia *n syn* see SLOTH 2

acerb *adj* 1 *syn* see SOUR 1
2 *syn* see SARCASTIC

acerbate *vb syn* see EXACERBATE

acerbic *adj* 1 *syn* see SOUR 1
2 *syn* see SARCASTIC

acerbity *n* 1 *syn* see ACRIMONY
rel acidity, sourness, tartness; crabbed-
ness, dourness, saturninity, surliness;
acridity, bitterness; harshness, roughness
con blandness, gentleness, mildness,
smoothness; amiability, complaisance,
good nature
ant mellowness
2 *syn* see SARCASM

acetose *adj syn* see SOUR 1

ache *vb* 1 *syn* see HURT 4
2 *syn* see COMPASSIONATE
rel deplore; sorrow (over); comfort, console, solace
3 *syn* see LONG

ache *n syn* see PAIN 1
rel injury; rack
con alleviation, assuagement, mitigation,
relief; comfort, ease

acheronian *adj syn* see GLOOMY 3

acherontic *adj syn* see GLOOMY 3

achieve *vb* 1 *syn* see PERFORM 2
rel complete, conclude, finish; conquer,
overcome, surmount
idiom bring to a happy issue, bring to
pass
con begin, commence, start
ant fail (in or to do)
2 *syn* see GAIN 1
rel acquire, get, obtain, secure; actualize;
arrive, come
idiom gain one's end
con depart, deviate, swerve; avoid, elude,
escape, shun
ant miss

achievement *n* 1 *syn* see FEAT 2
con omission, slighting
ant failure
2 *syn* see ACQUIREMENT

Achilles' heel *n syn* see SOFT SPOT 2

aching *adj syn* see PAINFUL 1
rel achy

acicular *adj syn* see POINTED 1

aciculate *adj syn* see POINTED 1

acid *adj syn* see SOUR 1
con bland, mild, neutral
ant sweet; alkaline, basic

acidulous *adj syn* see SOUR 1
rel biting, cutting, sharp; piquant, pungent
con bland, mild, neutral; mellow, smooth,
suave
ant saccharine

acknowledge *vb* 1 to show often grudgingly by word or deed that one knows of

and agrees to or with something < *acknowledge* the justice of a complaint >
syn admit, allow, avow, concede, confess, fess (up), grant, let on, own, own up
rel disclose, divulge, reveal, tell; announce, declare, proclaim, publish
con disallow, disavow, disown, ||nix, reject; contradict, gainsay, impugn, negate, negative
ant deny

2 to take notice of and accept as being as stated < he is generally *acknowledged* to be the leader in his profession >
syn admit, agree, recognize
rel accept, receive; concede, consider, deem, hold, view
con disregard, neglect, slight; reject, repudiate, spurn
ant ignore

acknowledgment *n syn see* CREDIT 4

acme *n syn see* APEX 2

acoustic *adj syn see* AUDITORY

acquaint *vb* **1** *syn see* INTRODUCE 4
idiom make acquainted
2 *syn see* INFORM 2
rel disclose, divulge, reveal; accustom, habituate
con hold, hold back, reserve, withhold; conceal, hide

acquaintance *n* **1** knowledge of something based on personal exposure < had a considerable *acquaintance* with modern poetry >
syn experience, familiarity, intimacy, inwardness
rel apprehension, grasp, ken; appreciation, awareness, consciousness
con inexperience, unfamiliarity; greenness, verdancy
2 *syn see* FRIEND
rel associate, companion, comrade, crony
con outsider, stranger

acquainted *adj syn see* FAMILIAR 3

acquiesce *vb syn see* ASSENT
rel accommodate, adapt, adjust, reconcile; bow, coincide, concur
con balk, demur, shy (away); kick, protest, remonstrate; differ, dissent
ant object

acquiescence *n* weak or passive agreement to what is asked or demanded < his childish *acquiescence* to all claims on his time >
syn compliance, conformity, resignation
rel complaisance; submissiveness; deference
con contumaciousness, insubordination; independence, self-assurance
ant rebellion, rebelliousness

acquiescent *adj syn see* PASSIVE 2

acquire *vb* **1** *syn see* GET 1
rel achieve, reach; add
con alienate, convey, transfer; abandon, relinquish, surrender, yield
ant forfeit
2 *syn see* EARN 1
rel accumulate, amass, collect, cumulate, garner
3 *syn see* DEVELOP 4

acquirement *n* a power or skill that results from persistent endeavor and cultivation < proud of his scholastic *acquirements* >

syn accomplishment, achievement, acquisition, attainment, finish
rel accretion, addition; advance, advancement; education, erudition, knowledge
con dearth, defect, lack, privation, want

acquisition *n syn see* ACQUIREMENT
rel accession, increment; assets, belongings, means, possessions

acquisitive *adj syn see* COVETOUS
rel demanding, exacting, exigent
con eschewing, forbearing, forgoing; sacrificing
ant abnegating, self-denying

acquit *vb* **1** *syn see* EXCULPATE
rel discharge, free, liberate, release; justify
con condemn, damn, doom, proscribe, sentence
ant convict
2 *syn see* BEHAVE 1

acres *n pl syn see* ESTATE 3

acrid *adj* having or being a noticeable, persistent, and usually unpleasant flavor or sometimes odor < the tonic had an *acrid* aftertaste >
syn amaroidal, astringent, austere, bitter, harsh, sharp
rel biting, caustic, cutting; piquant, pungent; cloying, oversweet, saccharine
con palatable, sapid, tasty, toothsome; delectable, delicious, luscious
ant savory

acrimonious *adj syn see* ANGRY
rel cranky, cross, irascible, splenetic, testy; belligerent, contentious, quarrelsome
con benign, benignant, kind, kindly
ant irenic, peaceable

acrimony *n* sharpness or rancor manifested in words, manner, or disposition < the dispute was renewed with increasing *acrimony* >
syn acerbity, asperity, mordancy
rel bitterness, ill will, malevolence, malice, malignity, spite, spleen; animosity, animus, antipathy, rancor
con civility, courtesy, graciousness, politeness; diplomacy, urbanity
ant suavity

acroamatic *adj syn see* RECONDITE

across *adv* **1** so as to intersect the length of something < cut the board *across* >
syn athwart, crossways, crosswise
2 *syn see* OVER 1

across *prep* from one side to the other < drew the curtain *across* the window >
syn athwart, cross, over

act *vb* **1** to present a role or performance on or as if on the stage < *acted* the part of Hamlet's father >
syn discourse, do, enact, impersonate, perform, personate, play, playact
rel characterize, portray, represent; masquerade; counterfeit, feign, sham, simulate
2 *syn see* ASSUME 4
idiom act a part, put on an act (of)
3 *syn see* BEHAVE 1
rel perform
4 to perform the duties or function of < he *acted* as president for over a year >
syn function, officiate, serve
idiom do duty (as), discharge the office (of), serve in the office (or capacity) of
5 to perform especially in an indicated way < the laxative *acted* quickly >

syn behave, function, operate, perform, react, take, work
idiom take effect
6 *syn* see FUNCTION 3

act *n syn* see ACTION 1
rel exploit, feat

actify *vb syn* see VITALIZE

acting *adj syn* see TEMPORARY

action *n* 1 something done or effected < a kindly *action* >
syn accomplishment, act, deed, doing, thing
rel discharge, effectuation, execution, fulfillment, performance; activity, behavior, operation, reaction, work; procedure, proceeding, process
2 *syn* see BATTLE
rel affray, combat, conflict, fray
3 *syn* see SERVICE 1
4 *syn* see SUIT 1

activate *vb syn* see VITALIZE
rel arouse, awaken, rally, rouse, stir, wake, waken
ant arrest

active *adj* 1 being at work or in effective operation < marginal mines that are *active* only when prices are high >
syn alive, dynamic, functioning, live, operative, running, working
rel assiduous, busy, diligent, industrious; energetic, strenuous, vigorous; alert, wideawake; rushing
con dormant, latent, quiescent; idle, inert, passive, supine; dead, dull, slow
ant inactive; abeyant
2 *syn* see AGILE
rel animated, spirited, vivacious; flexible, graceful, supple
con inert, lumpish, torpid
ant inactive
3 *syn* see ENERGETIC 2
rel expeditious, prompt, ready
con disinterested, indifferent, unconcerned

actively *adv syn* see SERIOUSLY 1

activity *n syn* see EXERCISE 2

activize *vb syn* see VITALIZE

actor *n* 1 one who takes part in an exhibition simulating happenings in real life < had been an *actor* on the stage and in television >
syn impersonator, mime, mimic, mummer, performer, playactor, player, thespian, trouper
2 *syn* see PARTICIPANT
rel mainstay, supporter, sustainer, upholder
con abettor, backer, patron; promoter

actual *adj* 1 existing in act < our *actual* intentions >
syn existent, extant
ant possible, potential
2 existing in or based on fact < problems of *actual* life >
syn absolute, factual, genuine, hard, positive, sure-enough
rel commonplace, everyday, ordinary, routine, usual; concrete, real, tangible
con conjectural, hypothetical, theoretical; putative, reputed, supposititious

ant apparent, nominal
3 *syn* see REAL 3
rel material, objective, phenomenal, physical; authentic, bona fide, legitimate
con abstract, transcendent, transcendental; academic, speculative, theoretical; fabulous, fictitious, mythical
ant ideal; imaginary

actuality *n* 1 *syn* see EXISTENCE 1
rel actualization, externalization, incarnation, materialization; achievement, attainment
con abstraction, ideality, transcendence
ant possibility, potentiality
2 something that has existence < the *actualities* of daily life >
syn materiality, reality
rel basis, essence, substance; embodiment, incarnation
3 *syn* see FACT 1

actually *n syn* see VERY 1

actuate *vb* 1 *syn* see MOVE 5
2 *syn* see MOBILIZE 1
rel excite, galvanize, provoke; arouse, rouse, stir; vitalize

act up *vb syn* see CUT UP 2

acumen *n syn* see WIT 3
rel acuteness, sharpness
con denseness, density, slowness
ant obtuseness, obtusity

acuminate *adj syn* see POINTED 1

acuminous *adj syn* see POINTED 1

acute *adj* 1 *syn* see POINTED 1
rel barbed, prickly, spiky, spined, spiny
ant blunt
2 *syn* see SHARP 4
rel cutting, incisive, trenchant; piercing
con crass, dense, dull, slow, stupid
ant obtuse
3 perceiving clearly and sensitively < an *acute* ear >
syn keen, perceptive, sensitive, sharp
rel observant, penetrating, probing; accurate, meticulous, precise
con imperceptive, insensitive; imprecise, inaccurate; inexact, uncritical
ant dull
4 elevated in pitch < an *acute* note >
syn argute, high, piercing, piping, sharp, shrill, thin, treble
rel penetrating; reedy, screechy, shrieky, shrilly, squeaky; tinny
con bass, deep, low
ant grave
5 *syn* see SHARP 8
6 serious to the point of approaching a crisis < an *acute* housing shortage >
syn climacteric, critical, crucial, desperate, dire
rel afflictive, grave, serious; aggravated, intensified; dangerous, hazardous, menacing, perilous, precarious, threatening; exigent, urgent

adage *n syn* see SAYING

adamant *adj syn* see INFLEXIBLE 2
rel immobile, immovable; unsubmitting
con placable, relenting, submitting; complaisant, obliging; subdued, submissive
ant yielding

adamantine *adj syn* see INFLEXIBLE 2
rel immobile, immovable; unsubmitting
con placable, relenting, submitting; complaisant, obliging; subdued, submissive

---

syn synonym(s)   *rel* related word(s)
ant antonym(s)   *con* contrasted word(s)
idiom idiomatic equivalent(s)
‖ use limited; if in doubt, see a dictionary

ant yielding

adapt *vb* to bring into correspondence or make suitable < *adapted* himself easily to the company he found himself with >
syn accommodate, adjust, conform, fit, quadrate, reconcile, square, suit, tailor, tailor-make
rel qualify, temper; acclimate, acclimatize
ant unfit

adaptable *adj* 1 *syn* see VERSATILE
2 *syn* see PLASTIC
con intractable, irreconcilable, nonconforming, refractory, unaccommodating
ant inadaptable, unadaptable

adapted *adj syn* see ASSORTED 2

add *vb* 1 to bring in or join on something more so as to form a larger or more inclusive whole < *added* music to his accomplishments >
syn annex, append, subjoin, superadd, take on
rel affix, attach, fasten, superimpose, tack (on); augment, enlarge, increase; burden, clutter, cumber, encumber, saddle
con abstract, detach; curtail, decrease, diminish, lessen, reduce
ant deduct, subtract
2 to combine numbers or quantities into one sum < *add* up a column of figures >
syn cast, figure, foot, sum, summate, tot, total, totalize, tote
rel calculate, compute, estimate, reckon; score, tally

added *adj syn* see ADDITIONAL

addendum *n*, sometimes **addenda** *pl* but *sing* or *pl* in *constr syn* see APPENDIX 1

addict *vb syn* see HABITUATE 2
rel bias, dispose, incline, predispose; address, apply, direct
con alienate, estrange; detach, disengage, disincline, indispose
ant wean

addict *n* a person who by habit or strong inclination indulges in something < a science fiction *addict* >
syn aficionado, buff, devotee, fan, habitué, hound, lover, votary
rel enthusiast, fanatic, zealot; hobbyist, putterer, tinkerer

addition *n* something that tends to increase something else (as in size, number, or content) < there are several new *additions* to our staff >
syn accession, accretion, augmentation, increase, increment, raise, rise
rel accessory, adjunct, appanage, appurtenance, supplement; continuation, extension, rider; accrual, accruement, accumulation
con deduction, lessening, reduction

additional *adj* being or coming by way of addition < gave *additional* reasons to justify his position >
syn added, another, else, farther, fresh, further, more, new, other
rel accessory, adscititious, collateral, extra, supplemental, supplementary

additionally *adv* 1 *syn* see ALSO 2
2 *syn* see AGAIN 4

additive *adj syn* see CUMULATIVE
rel component, constituent, elemental

additory *adj syn* see CUMULATIVE

addle *vb syn* see CONFUSE 2

rel confound, dumbfound, nonplus; amaze, astound, flabbergast
idiom addle one's wits
con animate, enliven, quicken, vivify
ant refresh (*mentally*)

address *vb* 1 *syn* see DIRECT 2
2 *syn* see SEND 1
3 to occupy (oneself or one's attention or efforts) with something < *addressed* himself to the job and soon finished it >
syn apply, bend, buckle (down), devote, direct, give, throw, turn
rel associate, connect, couple, link, relate; aim, level, point
idiom bring (oneself) into relation with something, tax (one's energies) with something
con disregard, ignore, overlook
4 to communicate directly to or with < *addressed* the governor with his petition >
syn accost, apply (to), approach, bespeak, memorialize
rel speak (to), talk (with); appeal (to); apostrophize; petition
con ignore, overlook, pass up, slight; avoid, cut, disregard
5 *syn* see TALK 7
6 to affix directions for delivery < *address* a letter >
syn direct, superscribe
7 to seek the attention of usually orally and in order to gain recognition < *address* a stranger to ask directions >
syn accost, call (to), greet, hail, salute
rel converse, speak, talk
idiom attract one's attention
8 to direct one's attention to in the role of a suitor < ready to marry the first man that *addressed* her >
syn court, make up (to), pursue, spark, sue, sweetheart, woo
rel attend, escort, squire; neck, pet, romance, rush, smooch, spoon
idiom make a play for, pay (one's) addresses to, run after

address *n* 1 the quality or state of being ready or skillful < to bring off such a coup requires *address* >
syn adroitness, deftness, dexterity, dexterousness, prowess, readiness, skill, sleight; *compare* TACT
rel competence, efficiency, expertise, know-how, proficiency; craft, finesse; ingeniousness, ingenuity, resourcefulness
con inadequacy, ineptitude, ineptness, unskillfulness; awkwardness, clumsiness, gawkiness, lubberliness, stupidity
2 *syn* see TACT
rel dexterity, ease, facility; cleverness, readiness; affability, graciousness
con awkwardness, clumsiness, gaucheness; boorishness, churlishness
ant maladroitness
3 *syn* see BEARING 1
4 *syn* see SPEECH 2

adduce *vb* to bring forward for consideration < *adduce* evidence in support of a hypothesis >
syn advance, allege, cite, lay, offer, present
rel animadvert, comment, commentate, remark; document, exemplify, illustrate;

prefer, proffer, propose, submit, suggest, tender

add up *vb syn* see AMOUNT 1

add up (to) *vb syn* see MEAN 2

adept *n syn* see EXPERT
ant bungler, incompetent

adept *adj syn* see PROFICIENT
rel clever; adroit, deft, dexterous
con amateurish, dabbling, dilettantish; awkward, clumsy, maladroit
ant bungling, inapt, inept

adequacy *n* 1 *syn* see ABILITY 1
rel equality, satisfactoriness, sufficiency
idiom enough on the ball
ant inadequacy, inadequateness
2 *syn* see ENOUGH

adequate *adj* 1 *syn* see SUFFICIENT 1
con meager, scanty, sparse
ant inadequate, unadequate
2 *syn* see DECENT 4

adequately *adv* 1 *syn* see ENOUGH 1
2 *syn* see WELL 4

adequation *n syn* see EQUIVALENCE

adhere *vb syn* see STICK 2
rel combine, join, link, unite
con disjoin, disunite

adherence *n* 1 a physical adhering < the close *adherence* of scales to a plant bud >
syn adhesion, bond, cling, clinging, coherence, cohesion, stickage, sticking
rel agglutination, cementation, concretion, conglutination; congelation, set, setting, solidification
con detachment, disjunction, parting, separation
2 *syn* see ATTACHMENT 1
con fickleness, inconstancy

adherent *n syn* see FOLLOWER
rel backer, champion, upholder
con apostate, recreant; deserter, forsaker; adversary, antagonist, opponent
ant renegade

adhesion *n* 1 *syn* see ADHERENCE 1
ant nonadhesion
2 *syn* see ATTACHMENT 1
con fickleness, inconstancy

adhesive *adj syn* see STICKY 1

adieu *interj syn* see GOOD-BYE

adieu *n syn* see PARTING

ad interim *adj syn* see TEMPORARY
ant permanent

adipose *adj syn* see FATTY 1

adiposity *n syn* see OBESITY

adit *n syn* see DOOR 2

adjacent *adj* 1 *syn* see NEIGHBORING
ant remote
2 *syn* see CONVENIENT 2
3 having a common border < the brothers built on *adjacent* lots >
syn abutting, adjoining, approximal, bordering, conterminous, contiguous, juxtaposed, touching
rel closest, nearest, next; consecutive, successive; attached, connected, joined, linked
con distant, far, remote, removed; parted, separated
ant nonadjacent

adjoin *vb* to be contiguous or adjacent to < the new suburb *adjoins* farmland >
syn abut, border, butt (on *or* against), communicate, join, line, march, neighbor, touch, verge
rel meet, run (into); end

adjoining *adj syn* see ADJACENT 3
ant detached

adjourn *vb* 1 *syn* see DEFER
rel curb, hold back, restrain
con advance, expedite, further, promote
2 to bring to a formal close < *adjourn* the legislature >
syn dissolve, prorogate, prorogue, recess, rise, terminate
rel break up, close, disband, discontinue, disperse; stay, suspend
con open; mobilize, muster, rally
ant convene, convoke

adjudge *vb syn* see JUDGE 1
rel accord, allot, assign, award, grant

adjudicate *vb syn* see JUDGE 1

adjunct *n syn* see APPENDAGE
rel accretion, addition; appanage; affix, attachment, fixture

adjust *vb* 1 *syn* see ADAPT
rel accord, correspond; attune, harmonize
2 to alter so as to make efficient or more efficient < *adjust* a carburetor >
syn fix, regulate, tune (up)
rel correct, rectify, right; balance, stabilize, steady, trim, true; arrange, order, rig
idiom make right, put (*or* set) in order, put right (*or* to rights), set right (*or* to rights)
con disarrange, disorder, disturb, upset
ant derange
3 *syn* see HABITUATE 2

adjuvant *adj syn* see AUXILIARY
rel synergistic
con antagonistic, negating, negativing, neutralizing; hindering, impeding, obstructing
ant counteractive

ad-lib *vb syn* see IMPROVISE

admeasure *vb syn* see ALLOT

admeasurement *n syn* see SIZE 1

adminicular *adj syn* see CORROBORATIVE

administer *vb* 1 to supervise the affairs or the provision, use, or conduct of especially in the capacity of an agent or steward < *administer* justice >
syn administrate, carry out, execute, govern, render
rel conduct, direct, manage, run, supervise
2 to provide in appropriate amount < *administer* a laxative >
syn apportion, deal (out), dispense, dole (out), mete (out), portion (out), share out
rel distribute, give, give out, issue; allot, assign, consign; allocate, ration
3 *syn* see GIVE 10

administrate *vb syn* see ADMINISTER 1

administrator *n syn* see EXECUTIVE

admirable *adj syn* see WORTHY 1

admiration *n* 1 *syn* see WONDER 1
rel surprise; ecstasy, rapture, transport
con aloofness, indifference, unconcern
2 *syn* see REGARD 4
rel appreciation; adoration, reverence, veneration, worship
con detestation, hate, hatred, loathing; dislike, disrelish, distaste

---

syn synonym(s)   *rel* related word(s)
ant antonym(s)   *con* contrasted word(s)
idiom idiomatic equivalent(s)
‖ use limited; if in doubt, see a dictionary

ant abhorrence

admire *vb* **1** to view with an elevated feeling of pleasure < *admired* the scene that spread out before them >
syn appreciate, cherish, delight (in), relish; *compare* APPRECIATE 1
rel adore, revere, reverence, venerate, worship
idiom go into raptures over, take delight in
con disesteem, disfavor, dislike, disrelish, mislike
ant disdain
2 to hold in high esteem < *admired* his ability to get things done >
syn consider, esteem, regard, respect
rel appreciate, cherish, prize, treasure, value
idiom have (*or* hold) a high opinion of, rate highly, set (great) store by, think much (*or* highly) of
con abominate, detest, hate, loathe; contemn, despise, disdain, scorn
ant abhor

admirer *n syn see* AMATEUR 1

admissible *adj syn see* PERMISSIBLE

admission *n syn see* DOOR 2

admit *vb* **1** *syn see* TAKE 10
rel allow, permit, suffer; entertain, harbor, house, lodge, shelter
con debar, exclude, shut out; bar, block, hinder, obstruct
ant eject, expel
2 *syn see* ACKNOWLEDGE 1
rel acquiesce, agree, assent, subscribe
ant gainsay
3 *syn see* ENTER 2
rel induct, initiate, install; insert, interject, interpose
con debar, shut out; eject, expel, oust
ant exclude
4 *syn see* ACKNOWLEDGE 2

admittance *n syn see* DOOR 2

admix *vb syn see* MIX 1

admixture *n* **1** an added ingredient that alters the character of something < her love had a marring *admixture* of selfishness >
syn adulterant, alloy, denaturant
rel doctor, fortification, taint; accretion, addition; bit, dash, shade, smack, spice, tinge
2 *syn see* MIXTURE

admonish *vb syn see* REPROVE
rel caution, forewarn, warn
idiom have a word with
con applaud, approve, compliment
ant commend

admonishing *adj syn see* MONITORY

admonishment *n syn see* REBUKE

admonition *n* **1** *syn see* REBUKE
2 *syn see* WARNING

admonitory *adj syn see* MONITORY

ado *n syn see* STIR 1
rel effort, exertion, pains, trouble; confusion, hurly-burly, turmoil, uproar
con calm, peace, serenity, tranquillity; quiet, silence, stillness

adolescence *n syn see* YOUTH 1
ant senescence

adopt *vb* to make one's own what in some fashion one owes to another < *adopt* a new style >
syn embrace, espouse, take on, take up
rel affect, assume; appropriate, arrogate, take, usurp; domesticate, naturalize
idiom adapt to one's own ends, go in for
con reject, spurn; abjure, forswear, renounce
ant discard; repudiate

adoption *n syn see* ESPOUSAL 4

adorable *adj* **1** *syn see* LOVABLE
2 *syn see* DELIGHTFUL

adoration *n* deep, ardent, and often excessive attachment or love < the *adoration* given popular heroes >
syn idolatry, idolization, worship
rel affection, attachment, devotion, love; crush, infatuation, passion, weakness
con antipathy, aversion; disfavor, dislike, distaste
ant detestation

adore *vb* **1** *syn see* REVERE
rel extol, laud, praise
con curse, execrate
2 *syn see* LOVE 2
3 to love, admire, or enjoy excessively < she *adores* and spoils her grandchildren >
syn dote (on *or* upon), idolize, worship
rel admire, esteem, love; coddle, indulge, pamper, spoil
idiom be silly over
con abhor, abominate, hate, loathe; contemn, despise, disdain, scorn
ant detest
4 *syn see* LOVE 1

adorn *vb* to add something nonessential to enhance the appearance or beauty of < a hat *adorned* with feathers >
syn beautify, bedeck, deck, decorate, dress (up), embellish, garnish, ornament, prank, trim
rel enrich, furbish, smarten, spruce (up); bedizen, dandify, fancy up; enhance, heighten, intensify
con clear, divest, expose, strip, uncover; deface, mar, scar, spoil
ant disfigure

ad rem *adj syn see* RELEVANT

adroit *adj* **1** *syn see* DEXTEROUS 1
ant maladroit
2 *syn see* SKILLFUL 2
3 *syn see* CLEVER 4
rel astute, perspicacious, shrewd; intelligent, quick-witted, smart; artful, subtle
con dense, dull, stupid; apathetic, heavy, impassive, phlegmatic, stodgy
ant stolid

adroitness *n* **1** *syn see* ADDRESS 1
2 *syn see* ART 1

adscititious *adj syn see* ADVENTITIOUS

adulation *n syn see* FLATTERY
rel acclaim, applause
ant abuse

adult *adj syn see* MATURE 1
rel aged
con adolescent, pubescent
ant juvenile, puerile

adulterant *n syn see* ADMIXTURE 1

adulterate *vb* to alter fraudulently usually for profit < sausage *adulterated* with cereal products >
syn debase, doctor, dope (up), load, sophisticate, weight

rel cut, dilute; denaturalize, denature, manipulate, tamper (with); defile, impurify, pollute, taint; deacon

con better, improve; augment, fortify, supplement

ant refine

adumbrate *vb* **1** to give a hint or indication of something to come < social unrest that *adumbrated* the revolt >

syn foreshadow, hint, prefigurate, prefigure, shadow (forth); *compare* SUGGEST 5

rel augur, bode, forebode, foretell, portend, presage; lower, menace, threaten; symbolize, typify

idiom cast its shadow before

2 *syn* see FORETELL

rel argue, bespeak, betoken, indicate

3 *syn* see SKETCH

4 *syn* see SUGGEST 5

rel denote, mean, signify

5 *syn* see OBSCURE

adumbration *n syn* see SHADE 1

rel hint, intimation, suggestion; sign, symptom, token; emblem, symbol, type

con disclosure, discovery, divulgence

ant revelation

advance *vb* **1** to cause to proceed or progress toward a goal < warm rains *advanced* the crops >

syn encourage, forward, foster, further, promote, serve

rel aid, assist, help; accelerate, quicken, speed

con hinder, impede; delay, slow; curb, restrain

ant retard; check

2 to raise in rank or position < was *advanced* to the presidency >

syn elevate, prefer, promote, upgrade

rel aggrandize, exalt, raise, uplift; glorify, immortalize, magnify

ant hold back; reduce (*in rank*)

3 *syn* see LEND

4 *syn* see ADDUCE

rel air, broach, expose

5 to go forward in space or time or toward an objective < prices *advanced* sharply >

syn get along, get on, march, move, proceed, progress

rel heighten, increase, intensify; develop, mature

idiom forge ahead, gain ground, get ahead, make headway (*or* progress), make one's way, make rapid strides

con retire, retreat, retrograde, withdraw

ant recede

advance *n* **1** *syn* see PROGRESS 2

2 forward movement especially on a course of action or development < the recent *advance* of technology >

syn advancement, anabasis, headway, march, ongoing, proficiency, progress

rel betterment, furtherance, improvement; development, evolution; breakthrough

con retreat, retrogression; ebbing, retiring, withdrawal

ant recession

3 *syn* see OVERTURE 1

rel offer, proffer

advanced *adj* **1** *syn* see PRECOCIOUS

con retrograde, retrogressive

ant backward

2 *syn* see LIBERAL 3

rel adventurous, daring, venturesome

ant conservative

advancement *n* **1** the act of raising or the status of being raised in grade, rank, or dignity < his *advancement* in his profession was rapid >

syn elevation, preference, preferment, prelation, promotion, upgrading

rel aggrandizement, dignification, magnification, raising, uplifting

con demotion, downgrading, reduction

ant degradation

2 *syn* see ADVANCE 2

advantage *n* **1** *syn* see BETTER 2

2 *syn* see WELFARE

3 something giving one person or side a position of superiority (as in a contest) < he had the *advantage* of greater height >

syn allowance, bulge, ‖deadwood, draw, edge, handicap, head start, odds, ‖overhand, start, vantage; *compare* BETTER 2

rel drop, jump, lead, running start; ascendancy, domination, leadership; mastery, superiority, upper hand, whip hand

idiom ace in the hole, inside track

con embarrassment, hamper, hindrance, impediment, inconvenience

ant disadvantage

4 *syn* see USE 3

rel betterment, improvement; enhancement; heightening

con damage, harm, hurt; injury

ant detriment

5 *syn* see GOOD 1

advantage *vb* *syn* see BENEFIT

advantageous *adj* **1** yielding a profit < sold on very *advantageous* terms >

syn gainful, good, lucrative, moneymaking, paying, profitable, remunerative, wellpaying, worthwhile

rel acceptable, agreeable, desirable, pleasing, satisfactory, satisfying

idiom in the black, paying its (own) way

con disadvantageous, unfavorable, unprofitable; damaging, hurtful

2 *syn* see GOOD 1

rel remedial, salutary; conducive, contributory, implemental, instrumental; advisable, expedient

con unfavorable; inconvenient; deleterious, detrimental

ant disadvantageous

advenient *adj syn* see ADVENTITIOUS

advent *n* *syn* see ARRIVAL 1

rel approach, nearing

ant exit

advential *adj syn* see ADVENTITIOUS

adventitious *adj* coming from without and not participating in the fundamental nature of something < *adventitious* notions that have corrupted the primitive doctrine >

syn adscititious, advenient, advential, supervenient

rel accidental, casual, contingent, fortuitous, incidental

---

syn synonym(s)   *rel* related word(s)
ant antonym(s)   *con* contrasted word(s)
idiom idiomatic equivalent(s)
‖ use limited: if in doubt, see a dictionary

con constitutional, essential, intrinsic; inborn, inbred, innate
ant inherent

adventure *n* an undertaking or experience that involves hazard and requires boldness < recounted the *adventures* of his solitary voyage >
syn emprise, enterprise, exploit, feat, gest, venture
rel hazard, peril, risk; quest; achievement

adventure *vb syn see* VENTURE 1

adventuresome *adj syn see* ADVENTUROUS
ant unadventurous; cautious

adventurous *adj* courting danger or exposing oneself to danger beyond the call of duty or courage < *adventurous* boys scrambled over the cliff face >
syn adventuresome, audacious, daredevil, daring, foolhardy, rash, reckless, temerarious, venturesome, venturous
rel bold, doughty, intrepid; brash, harebrained, hotheaded, impetuous, imprudent, madcap, overconfident
con shrinking, timid, timorous; afraid, alarmed, fearful, scared; apprehensive, uneasy
ant unadventurous; cautious

adversary *n syn see* OPPONENT
rel assaulter, attacker
con backer, supporter, upholder
ant ally

adverse *adj* 1 acting against or in a contrary direction < hindered by *adverse* forces >
syn antagonistic, anti, antipathetic, opposed, opposing, oppugnant
rel contrary, counter, counteractive; hindering, impeding, obstructive; hostile, unfriendly
con coactive, collaborative, cooperative; adjuvant, synergistic; favorable, propitious
2 being opposed to one's interests < an *adverse* balance of trade >
syn detrimental, negative, unfavorable
rel deleterious, harmful, hurtful, injurious; disadvantageous, prejudicial, unpropitious, unsatisfactory
con advantageous, favorable, positive, propitious, satisfactory

adversity *n syn see* MISFORTUNE
rel distress, misery, suffering; deprivation, destitution, indigence, poverty
con bliss, felicity, happiness; comfort, ease
ant prosperity

advert *vb syn see* REFER 3
rel animadvert, note, notice, observe, remark
con disregard, ignore, neglect, overlook

advertent *adj syn see* ATTENTIVE 1

advertise *vb* 1 *syn see* DECLARE 1
rel recount, relate, report; communicate, impart; ballyhoo, promote, propagandize, publicize
con conceal, repress, suppress; bury, hide, obscure
2 *syn see* PUBLICIZE
3 *syn see* PROMOTE 3

advertisement *n syn see* DECLARATION
rel ballyhoo, promotion, propaganda, publicity

advertising *n syn see* PUBLICITY

advice *n* 1 recommendation regarding a decision or course of conduct < benefited from his *advice* on study habits >
syn advisement, counsel
rel direction, guidance, instruction, teaching; admonition; caution, cautioning, forewarning, warning
2 *syn see* NEWS

advisable *adj syn see* EXPEDIENT
rel commendable, desirable; becoming, seemly, suitable; sensible
ant inadvisable

advise *vb* 1 *syn see* COUNSEL
rel caution, forewarn, warn; coax, induce, persuade, win (over)
con bedazzle, misadvise, mislead
2 *syn see* CONFER 2
rel deliberate
3 *syn see* INFORM 2
rel disclose, let out, reveal; communicate, impart

advised *adj syn see* DELIBERATE 1
rel intended, intentional, meant; knowing, purposeful, willful

advisement *n syn see* ADVICE 1

advocate *n syn see* EXPONENT

advocate *vb* 1 *syn see* ENCOURAGE 2
2 *syn see* SUPPORT 2
rel justify, vindicate; advance, forward, promote
idiom hold a brief for
con assail, attack; combat, fight, oppose
ant impugn

aegis *n* 1 *syn see* DEFENSE 1
2 *syn see* BACKING

aeneous *adj syn see* BRAZEN 4

aeon *n syn see* AGE 2

aerial *adj* 1 *syn see* AIRY 1
2 *syn see* LOFTY 6
3 *syn see* AIRY 3
rel immaterial, incorporeal; impalpable, imperceptible, imponderable

aesthete *n syn see* CONNOISSEUR
rel perfectionist, stickler; fussbudget, old maid
con barbarian; clod, lout, oaf

affable *adj* 1 *syn see* GRACIOUS 1
rel courteous, polite; suave, urbane; loquacious, talkative
con crabbed, glum, surly; reticent, withdrawn; silent, taciturn, uncommunicative
ant reserved
2 *syn see* GENTLE 2

affair *n* 1 something done or dealt with < trying to get at the truth of the *affair* >
syn business, concern, matter, shooting match, thing
rel care, lookout, responsibility; pie, proceeding
idiom cup of tea
2 *syn see* BUSINESS 8
3 *syn see* LOVE AFFAIR
4 *syn see* AMOUR 2

affect *vb* 1 *syn see* ASSUME 4
2 *syn see* FREQUENT

affect *vb* to produce a usually mental or emotional effect on one capable of reaction < much *affected* by the touching scene >
syn carry, get, impress, influence, inspire, move, strike, sway, touch
rel actuate, draw, drive, impel; penetrate, pierce

idiom work on

affectation *n syn see* POSE 2
  rel ostentation, pretentiousness
  con ingenuousness, naiveté, naturalness, simplicity, unsophistication
  ant artlessness

affected *adj* 1 *syn see* INTERESTED
  2 *syn see* SELF-CONSCIOUS
  3 *syn see* GENTEEL 3
  4 *syn see* PRECIOUS 4
  5 *syn see* ARTIFICIAL 3

affecting *adj syn see* MOVING 2
  rel piteous, pitiable, pitiful; distressful, distressing, disturbing, troubling

affection *n* 1 *syn see* FEELING 3
  rel leaning, penchant, propensity; bias, predilection; bent, faculty, turn
  con aversion, hate, hatred; dislike, distaste
  ant antipathy
  2 *syn see* LOVE 1
  rel sympathy, tenderness, warmth; attention, concern, interest; doting, enjoying
  con coolness, frigidity
  ant coldness

affection *vb syn see* LOVE 2

affection *n* 1 *syn see* DISEASE 1
  rel access, attack, paroxysm, spell; derangement, disordering, disturbance
  2 *syn see* QUALITY 1

affectionate *adj syn see* LOVING
  rel sympathetic, tender, warm
  con apathetic, impassive, stolid; remote, uninterested, withdrawn
  ant cold; undemonstrative

affective *adj syn see* EMOTIONAL 2

affectivity *n syn see* FEELING 3

affianced *adj syn see* ENGAGED 2

affianced *n syn see* BETROTHED

affiche *n syn see* POSTER

affiliated *adj syn see* RELATED
  con autonomous, free, independent
  ant unaffiliated

affiliation *n syn see* ASSOCIATION 1

affinity *n* 1 *syn see* ATTRACTION 2
  con antipathy, aversion; dislike, distaste; repugnance, repellency, repulsion
  2 *syn see* LIKENESS
  rel accord

affirm *vb syn see* ASSERT 1
  rel attest, certify, guarantee, vouch, witness; say, state
  con debate

affirmative *adj syn see* POSITIVE 6

affix *vb syn see* FASTEN 1
  rel add, annex, append, subjoin
  con disengage, disjoin
  ant detach

afflation *n syn see* INSPIRATION

afflatus *n syn see* INSPIRATION

afflict *vb* to inflict upon one something hard to endure <he was *afflicted* with boils>
  syn agonize, crucify, excruciate, harrow, martyr, martyrize, rack, smite, strike, torment, torture, try, wring
  rel annoy, harass, harry, pester, plague, press, worry; bother, irk, vex; lacerate, wound

---

con console, delight, gladden, please, rejoice; ease, relieve, solace
  ant comfort

afflicted *adj syn see* WOEFUL 1

affliction *n* 1 *syn see* TRIAL 1
  rel mischance, mishap
  con alleviation, assuagement, easement, relief
  ant consolation, solace
  2 *syn see* SORROW
  3 *syn see* SICKNESS 1

afflictive *adj* 1 *syn see* PAINFUL 1
  2 *syn see* DEPLORABLE
  3 *syn see* BITTER 2

affluent *adj syn see* RICH 1
  rel acquisitive, grasping
  con poor; bankrupt, impoverished
  ant impecunious; straitened

affranchise *vb syn see* ENFRANCHISE

affray *n* 1 *syn see* BRAWL 2
  2 *syn see* CLASH 2

affright *vb syn see* FRIGHTEN
  rel bewilder, confound
  con animate, fire, inspire
  ant embolden, nerve

affront *vb* 1 *syn see* OFFEND 3
  rel criticize, dispraise
  con compliment; laud, praise; dignify, honor
  2 *syn see* CONFRONT 1

affront *n* a speech or an action designed to impugn the honor or worth of someone or something <her costume was an *affront* to the solemnity of the occasion>
  syn contumely, despite, indignity, insult, slap
  rel dishonor, flouting, offense, outrage, slight; aspersion, barb, defamation, dig
  idiom slap in the face
  con deference, homage, honor; adulation, compliment, flattery

aficionado *n syn see* ADDICT

afield *adj syn see* AMISS 2

afire *adj* 1 *syn see* BURNING 1
  2 *syn see* ALIGHT 2

aflame *adj* 1 *syn see* BURNING 1
  2 *syn see* ALIGHT 2

aflicker *adj syn see* ALIGHT 2, ablaze, afire, aflame, aglow

à fond *adv syn see* WELL 3

aforementioned *adj syn see* SUCH 1

aforesaid *adj syn see* SUCH 1

aforethought *adj syn see* DELIBERATE 1

afraid *adj* 1 suffering the effects of apprehension, fear, or terror <too *afraid* to even cry for help>
  syn aghast, anxious, ‖ascared, fearful, frightened, scared, scary, terrified; *compare* FEARFUL 2
  rel shrinking, shy, timid, timorous; cautious, chary, wary; jumpy, skittish
  idiom frightened out of one's wits, in a (blue) funk, scared to death, terror stricken
  con confident, dauntless, fearless; assured, collected, poised, self-possessed
  ant unafraid
  2 *syn see* FEARFUL 2
  idiom all of a twitter (*or* flutter)
  ant unafraid; sanguine
  3 *syn see* DISINCLINED

afresh *adv* 1 *syn see* OVER 7
  2 *syn see* NEW

‖**African dominoes** *n pl syn* see DICE

aft *adv syn* see ABAFT
  rel hind, posterior
  con ahead, before, forward
  ant fore

after *adv* so as to follow in time or space
  < *after*, we turned toward home >
  syn afterward, afterwhile, behind, by and
  by, infra, later, latterly, next, subsequently
  rel abaft, aft, astern
  idiom after a time (*or* while), in the wake
  of
  con ahead, forward
  ant before

after *prep* **1** so as to resemble or follow in
  some respect < named *after* his father >
  syn for, from
  2 later in time or lower in place or rank
  < *after* our discussion >
  syn behind, below, following, next, since,
  subsequent to
  con ante, ere, in advance of, preceding,
  prior to
  ant before
  3 *syn* see BEYOND 1

after *adj* **1** *syn* see SUBSEQUENT 1
  2 *syn* see POSTERIOR 2
  con antecedent, preceding, prior

after all *adv syn* see HOWEVER

aftereffect *n syn* see EFFECT 1
  rel remainder, residual, residuum

afterlife *n* **1** *syn* see ETERNITY 2
  2 *syn* see HEREAFTER 2

afterlight *n syn* see REVIEW 5

aftermath *n syn* see EFFECT 1
  rel remainder, residual, residuum

aftertime *n syn* see FUTURE

afterward *adv syn* see AFTER

afterward *n syn* see FUTURE

afterwhile *adv syn* see AFTER

afterword *n syn* see EPILOGUE 1

afterworld *n syn* see HEREAFTER 2

again *adv* **1** *syn* see ABOUT 6
  2 *syn* see OVER 7
  3 *syn* see THEN 1
  4 as another point, fact, or instance
  < *again*, consider taxes >
  syn additionally, also, besides, further, in
  addition, then; *compare* ALSO 2
  idiom by the same token, into the bargain, on top of that
  5 as an alternative and especially a converse < he may win and *again* he may
  not >
  syn contra, contrariwise, contrary, contrawise, conversely, oppositely, vice versa;
  compare HOWEVER
  idiom at the same time, be that as it may,
  just the same, on the other hand

again and again *adv syn* see OFTEN

against *prep* **1** directly opposite < stood
  against the crowd and shouted for order >
  syn contra, facing, fronting, over against,
  toward, vis-à-vis
  idiom counter to, face to face with
  2 so as to touch < vines trained *against*
  the wall >
  syn to, touching
  idiom in contact with, next to
  3 *syn* see VERSUS 1
  4 without being prevented or obstructed
  by < succeeded *against* grave handicaps >
  syn despite, in spite of, notwithstanding,
  regardless of

  idiom in the face of
  5 *syn* see FROM 2
  6 *syn* see APROPOS

agape *adj syn* see AGHAST 2

age *n* **1** *syn* see OLD AGE
  ant youth
  2 *often* **ages** *pl* a long or seemingly long
  period of time < haven't seen her for
  ages >
  syn aeon, blue moon, coon's age, dog's
  age, donkey's years, eternity, long
  idiom month of Sundays, ‖right smart
  spell
  con flash, instant, minute, moment, second, split second, trice
  3 *syn* see PERIOD 2

age *vb syn* see MATURE

aged *adj* **1** being in the declining phase of
  life < *aged* pensioners >
  syn ancient, elderly, old, olden
  rel pensioned (off), retired, superannuated; senior; hoary, patriarchal, venerable;
  doddering, senescent, senile, tottery
  idiom along in years, getting on, getting
  on (*or* along) in years, gray with age, on
  one's last legs, stricken with years
  con juvenile, puerile
  ant youthful
  2 *syn* see ANCIENT 1
  3 *syn* see RIPE 3

ageless *adj syn* see ETERNAL 4

agency *n syn* see MEAN 2
  rel antecedent, cause, determinant; gear

agenda *n syn* see PROGRAM 1

agent *n* **1** *syn* see MEAN 2
  rel doer, executive, executor, performer;
  actor, worker; activator, energizer
  2 one who acts for another < diplomatic
  agents serving abroad >
  syn assignee, attorney, deputy, factor,
  proxy; *compare* DELEGATE
  rel go-between, middleman; instrument,
  minister, tool; commissioner, institor,
  proctor, procurator, representative, steward; buyer, commissionaire
  ant principal
  3 *syn* see SPY

age-old *adj syn* see ANCIENT 1

agglomerate *n syn* see AGGREGATE 1
  rel heap, mass, pile

agglomeration *n* **1** *syn* see ACCUMULA-
  TION
  rel association, combination
  2 *syn* see AGGREGATE 1

aggrandize *vb* **1** *syn* see INCREASE 1
  rel amplify, build up
  2 *syn* see EXALT 1
  ant belittle

aggrandizement *n syn* see APOTHEOSIS 2

aggravate *vb* **1** *syn* see INTENSIFY
  rel augment, enlarge, increase, multiply;
  aggrandize
  con extenuate, palliate
  ant alleviate
  2 *syn* see IRRITATE
  rel disturb, perturb, upset; annoy, bedevil
  con calm, tranquilize
  ant appease

aggravation *n syn* see ANNOYANCE 1

aggregate *vb syn* see AMOUNT 1

aggregate *n* **1** a mass or body formed of
  particles or parts that retain their individuality < an *aggregate* of ill-planned arguments >

syn agglomerate, agglomeration, aggregation, conglomerate, conglomeration; *compare* ACCUMULATION
ant constituent, element
2 *syn* see BODY 5
ant individual, unit; particular
3 *syn* see WHOLE 1

aggregation *n* **1** *syn* see AGGREGATE 1
ant constituent, element
2 *syn* see ACCUMULATION
rel backlog, reserve, stockpile
3 *syn* see GATHERING 2

aggress *vb syn* see ATTACK 1

aggression *n* **1** *syn* see ATTACK 1
2 *syn* see ATTACK 2
rel incursion, inroad, invasion, raid; irruption
ant resistance

aggressive *adj* marked by bold determination and readiness for conflict <an *aggressive* fighter >
syn assertive, assertory, militant, pushful, pushing, pushy, self-assertive
rel belligerent, combative, contentious, scrappy; domineering, imperious, masterful, tough; energetic, hard-hitting, strenuous, vigorous
con passive, unassertive; meek, submissive, yielding

aggressiveness *n syn* see ATTACK 2

aggrieve *vb* **1** *syn* see DISTRESS 2
rel abuse, misuse, outrage; pain
con delight, gladden, please
2 *syn* see WRONG
rel afflict, torment, try; annoy, harass, harry, plague, worry
con benefit, profit

aghast *adj* **1** *syn* see AFRAID 1
rel appalled, horrified, horror-struck; undone, unmanned
idiom scared stiff (*or* white)
2 struck by an intense emotional reaction (as surprise, disgust, or bewilderment) < *aghast* at the lack of discipline >
syn agape, confounded, dismayed, dumbfounded, overwhelmed, shocked, thunderstruck
rel agog, amazed, startled; awed, awestricken; astonished, flabbergasted, surprised
idiom struck all of a heap, taken aback, unable to believe one's eyes (*or* senses)
con acceptant, acquiescent, tolerant

agile *adj* acting or moving with easy alacrity <an *agile* mind >
syn active, brisk, brisky, catty, lively, nimble, sprightly, spry, volant, yare, zippy
rel adroit, deft, dexterous; fleet, quick, speedy; limber, lissome, lithe, supple; light-footed, tripping
con inactive, inert, passive; heavy, lethargic, logy; dull, slow, sluggish
ant torpid

agitable *adj syn* see EXCITABLE

agitate *vb* **1** *syn* see SHAKE 4
rel bounce, joggle, jounce; actuate, drive, impel, move
con lull, quiet, still

2 *syn* see DISCOMPOSE 1
rel exasperate, irritate, peeve, provoke, rile, ruffle
ant calm, tranquilize
3 *syn* see DISCUSS 1
rel air, broach, ventilate; consider; assail, attack

agitation *n syn* see COMMOTION 2
rel ado, bustle, disturbance, stir
ant tranquillity

agitator *n syn* see INSTIGATOR

aglow *adj syn* see ALIGHT 2
rel gleaming, glowing, shining; lucent, luminous, radiant

agnate *adj* **1** *syn* see RELATED
2 *syn* see LIKE

agog *adj syn* see EAGER
rel aroused, roused, stirred; excited, galvanized, stimulated; restive; zestful
ant aloof

agonize *vb* **1** *syn* see AFFLICT
rel distress, trouble; chafe, fret, gall
2 *syn* see WRITHE 1
rel bear, endure, suffer

agonizing *adj syn* see EXCRUCIATING
rel exquisite, fierce, intense, vehement, violent

agony *n syn* see DISTRESS
con repose, rest

agrarian *adj syn* see WILD 1

agree *vb* **1** *syn* see ACKNOWLEDGE 2
rel allow, concede, grant, own
con except, exclude
ant deny
2 *syn* see ASSENT
rel allow, concede, grant; receive; acknowledge, admit
con expostulate, kick, object, remonstrate; balk, demur, jib; oppose, resist, withstand
ant protest (against); differ (with)
3 to achieve harmony (as of opinion, feeling, or purpose) <they *agreed* finally on all major issues>
syn coincide, concert, concord, concur, harmonize
rel coact, cooperate, unite
idiom fall in with, hit it off with
con bicker, quarrel, squabble, wrangle; argue, debate, dispute, hassle
ant differ; disagree
4 to exist or go together without conflict or incongruity <his conclusion *agrees* with the evidence>
syn accord, check, check out, cohere, comport, conform, consist, consort, correspond, dovetail, fit (in), ǁgee, go, harmonize, jibe, march, quadrate, rhyme, square, suit, tally
rel approach, equal, match, rival, touch; complete, fulfill, round out, supplement
idiom go hand in hand
con negate, negative, nullify; clash, conflict, jar
ant differ (from)

agree (with) *vb syn* see SUIT 4

agreeability *n syn* see AMENITY 1

agreeable *adj* **1** *syn* see PLEASANT 1
rel delectable, delightful
ant disagreeable
2 *syn* see CONSONANT 1
con conflicting, inharmonious, jarring, uncongenial

agreeableness *n syn* see AMENITY 1

---

syn synonym(s)   *rel* related word(s)
ant antonym(s)   *con* contrasted word(s)
idiom idiomatic equivalent(s)
ǁ use limited: if in doubt, see a dictionary

agreed *adv syn* see YES 1

agreement *n* 1 *syn* see HARMONY 2

ant disagreement

2 a settlement reached by parties to a dispute or negotiation <the company has reached an *agreement* with the striking workers>

syn accord, deal, understanding; *compare* CONTRACT

rel cartel, concordat, convention, entente, pact; compact, contract, covenant, treaty; engagement

3 *syn* see TREATY

4 *syn* see CONTRACT

agrestal *adj syn* see WILD 1

agrestic *adj syn* see RURAL

agriculture *n* the science or business of raising useful plants and animals <opening the country for *agriculture*>

syn farming, husbandry

aground *adj* being or becoming forced onto the ground or shore <the boat is *aground* and breaking up>

syn beached, grounded, stranded

idiom high and dry, on the rocks

ant afloat

ahead *adv* 1 *syn* see BEFORE 1

con after

ant behind

2 further on in the direction in question <the road stretched *ahead* toward the west>

syn alee, forth, forward, onward

ahead of *prep syn* see BEFORE 1

aid *vb syn* see HELP 1

rel alleviate, lighten, mitigate, relieve

ant impede

aid *n* 1 *syn* see HELP 1

2 *syn* see HELP 2

rel alleviation, assuagement, mitigation; backing, support

idiom a leg up

con check, curb, restraint; bar, obstacle, obstruction

ant impediment

3 *syn* see HELPER

4 *syn* see ASSISTANT 2

rel aider, befriender, benefactor, ministrant, succorer; striker

aidant *adj syn* see HELPFUL 1

aide *n syn* see ASSISTANT 2

aide-de-camp *n syn* see ASSISTANT 2

aiding *adj syn* see HELPFUL 1

ail *vb syn* see TROUBLE 1

rel afflict, try

idiom be the matter (with), give one trouble

con alleviate, ease, relieve; comfort, console, solace

ailing *adj syn* see UNWELL

rel debilitated, enfeebled, gone, strengthless, weak; droopy, limp, sapless, spiritless

con hale, lusty, robust, rugged, vigorous

ailment *n* 1 *syn* see DISEASE

2 *syn* see UNREST

aim *vb* 1 *syn* see DIRECT 2

rel concentrate, fix, focus

idiom draw a bead on, take aim

2 to have as a controlling desire something that transcends one's present capacity for attainment <from a boy he had *aimed* at high office>

syn aspire, pant

rel attempt, endeavor, essay, strive, try; design, intend, propose, purpose; covet, crave, yearn (for)

idiom have an eye to, reach for the stars, set one's eyes upon

3 *syn* see INTEND 2

rel choose, desire, want, wish; expect

idiom have (*or* keep) in view, promise oneself (to)

4 *syn* see SLANT 2

aim *n syn* see AMBITION 2

rel desideratum, desire, idol, urge

idiom end in view

aimless *adj syn* see RANDOM

air *n* 1 *syn* see BEARING 1

rel manner, style

2 *usu* **airs** *pl syn* see POSE 2

rel loftiness, ostentation, pretentiousness, show; complacency, self-importance, vainglory, vanity

3 a pervading influence that colors outward appearance or apparent character <the village had an *air* of decay>

syn atmosphere, aura, feel, feeling, mood, semblance

rel character, property, quality

con basis, essence, reality

4 *syn* see MELODY

air *vb syn* see EXPRESS 2

rel discover, divulge, reveal; broadcast, declare, proclaim, publish

idiom make public, noise (*or* sound) abroad, spread far and wide

airless *adj syn* see STUFFY 1

airman *n syn* see PILOT 2

airy *adj* 1 of or relating to air <clouds drifting on *airy* currents>

syn aerial, atmospheric, pneumatic

rel gaseous, vaporous

2 *syn* see LOFTY 6

rel exposed, windswept; supernal

3 resembling or suggesting air especially in lightness or lack of substance <*airy* persiflage>

syn aerial, ethereal, vaporous, vapory

rel frivolous, light, volatile; rare, rarefied, tenuous, thin; dainty, delicate, diaphanous, exquisite, spiritual

con corporeal, material, physical; bulky, massive, massy

ant substantial

4 *syn* see ELASTIC 2

rel animated, high-spirited, spirited

5 *syn* see WINDY 1

akin *adj* 1 *syn* see RELATED

2 *syn* see LIKE

rel kindred; according, agreeing, conforming, harmonizing

con extraneous, foreign

ant alien

alacrity *n* promptness in responding or acting <accepted the invitation with *alacrity*>

syn dispatch, expedition, goodwill, promptitude, readiness

rel briskness, eagerness; enthusiasm, fervor, heartiness, zeal; promptness, quickness

con hesitation, procrastination, temporization, vacillation; apathy, indifference, lethargy, phlegm, sluggishness

ant dilatoriness

a la mode *adj syn* see STYLISH

alarm *n* 1 a signal that warns or calls to action <the door's squeak gave the *alarm*>
syn alert, SOS, tocsin
rel caution, forewarning, prenotice, warning
2 *syn see* FEAR 1
rel upset; strain, stress, tension
con calmness, serenity, tranquillity; equanimity, sangfroid
ant assurance; composure

alarm *vb syn see* FRIGHTEN
rel amaze, astonish, surprise
idiom give one a turn
con comfort, console, solace
ant assure, relieve

alarmable *adj syn see* EXCITABLE
albeit *conj syn see* THOUGH
album *n syn see* ANTHOLOGY
alcohol *n syn see* LIQUOR 2
alcoholic *adj syn see* SPIRITUOUS
alcoholized *adj syn see* INTOXICATED 1
alcove *n syn see* SUMMERHOUSE
alee *adv syn see* AHEAD 2
alehouse *n* an establishment serving primarily beer and ale <warm country *alehouses*>
syn beer garden, beer hall, ‖beerhouse, bierstube, mughouse, stube; *compare* BAR 4
rel barrelhouse, bistro, bottle club, brasserie, cabaret, café, honky-tonk, nightclub, rathskeller, roadhouse, wineshop
alembicated *adj syn see* PRECIOUS 4
alert *adj* 1 *syn see* WATCHFUL
rel attentive, heedful, mindful; careful
idiom all eyes and ears, on (one's) guard, on the alert
con inattentive, unmindful; aloof, detached, indifferent, unconcerned
2 *syn see* INTELLIGENT 2
rel apt, prompt, quick, ready
con lackadaisical, languid, listless
3 *syn see* LIVELY 1
rel frisky; mercurial
idiom full of ''·
con inactive, ·lolent
ant inert

alert *n syn see* ALARM 1
alfresco *adj syn see* OUTDOOR
algetic *adj syn see* PAINFUL 1
alias *n syn see* PSEUDONYM
alibi *n syn see* EXCUSE 1
alien *adj syn see* EXTRINSIC
rel exotic, outlandish, strange; incompatible, incongruous, inconsonant
con cognate, kindred, related; compatible, congenial, congruous, consonant; germane, material, pertinent, relevant
ant akin; assimilable
alien *n syn see* STRANGER
con national, subject
ant citizen
alien *vb* 1 *syn see* ESTRANGE
rel alter, change, convert
con accommodate, adjust, conform, reconcile
ant unite; reunite

2 *syn see* TRANSFER 4
rel give up, hand over, relinquish
alienate *vb* 1 *syn see* TRANSFER 4
rel give up, hand over, relinquish
2 *syn see* ESTRANGE
rel alter, change, convert
con accommodate, adjust, conform, reconcile
ant unite; reunite
alienation *n* 1 *syn see* ESTRANGEMENT
2 *syn see* INSANITY 1
alight *vb* to come to rest after or as if after a flight, a descent, or a fall <snowflakes *alighting* on the bare trees>
syn land, light, perch, roost, set down, settle, sit down, touch down
rel drop, fall, tumble
con arise, ascend, rise, soar
alight *adj* 1 *syn see* BURNING 1
2 made bright by or as if by fire <her face *alight* with joy>
syn ablaze, afire, aflame, aflicker, aglow
rel bright, effulgent, fulgent, refulgent; blazing, flaming, flaring, glowing
con dark, dusky, gloomy, heavy, lowery, shadowed, shadowy
align *vb syn see* LINE 1
rel adjust, fix, regulate
con unsettle
alike *adj syn see* LIKE
con separate
ant unlike; different
alikeness *n syn see* LIKENESS
aliment *n syn see* FOOD 2
alimentary *adj syn see* NUTRITIVE 1
alimentation *n syn see* LIVING
alimentative *adj syn see* NUTRITIVE 1
alimony *n syn see* LIVING
alive *adj* 1 *syn see* LIVING 1
con inactive, inert
ant dead, defunct
2 *syn see* EXTANT 1
3 *syn see* ACTIVE 1
rel fresh, green, verdant
con dormant, inactive, quiescent
ant dead, extinct
4 *syn see* AWARE
rel vigilant, watchful, wide-awake; intelligent, quick-witted
con heedless, inattentive, oblivious, unmindful; careless, neglectful, negligent
ant blind (to)
5 full of vigorous life, animation, or activity <the streets were *alive* with shoppers>
syn abounding, overflowing, replete, rife, swarming, teeming, thronged
rel crowded, populous, thick; filled, flush, full
con barren, empty, vacant, void; unoccupied, unpopulated, untenanted
all *adj* 1 *syn see* WHOLE 4
rel full, plenary
2 each member or individual of <*all* my friends came with me>
syn each, every
ant no
all *adv* 1 without exception <the money was *all* spent>
syn all in all, altogether, exactly, in toto, just, purely, quite, stick, totally, utterly, wholly
idiom in its entirety

---

2 *syn* see APIECE

all *pron* 1 *syn* see EVERYTHING
2 *syn* see EVERYBODY

all *n syn* see WHOLE 1

all—around *adj* 1 *syn* see VERSATILE
rel complete, consummate
2 not narrowly particularized < taking an *all-around* view of the problem >
syn comprehensive, general, global, inclusive, overall, sweeping
rel broad, extensive, panoramic, wide; all-inclusive, unexcluding, unexclusive, wide-ranging; synoptic
con express, particular, specific; narrow, precise, restricted; individual, singular

allay *vb* 1 *syn* see RELIEVE 1
con arouse, rouse, stir; excite, provoke, stimulate; aggravate, enhance
ant intensify
2 *syn* see CALM
rel ease, soften, subdue; deaden, dull, temper; disburden, disembarrass, disencumber; deliver, free, release
con aggravate, enhance, heighten, magnify, worsen
ant intensify

all but *adv* 1 *syn* see NEARLY
2 *syn* see ALMOST 2

allege *vb syn* see ADDUCE
rel affirm, assert, avouch, avow, declare, profess; recite, recount, rehearse, state
con contradict, deny, gainsay, impugn, negate, negative; controvert, disprove, rebut, refute
ant contravene

alleged *adj* of questionable truth or genuineness < had doubts of the *alleged* miracle >
syn ostensible, pretended, professed, purported, so-called, supposed; *compare* SUPPOSED 1
rel credible, plausible, specious; doubtful, dubious, questionable; self-styled, soi-disant, would-be
idiom in name only
con authentic, bona fide, genuine, veritable; actual, real, true; delusory, erroneous, fallacious, false, illusory, imaginary, unreal

allegiance *n syn* see FIDELITY 1
rel firmness; consecration, dedication, deference, homage, honor
con alienation, disaffection; disloyalty, treason

allegiant *adj syn* see FAITHFUL 1

allegory *n* 1 a method of indirect representation (as in literature or art) of ideas or truths < by *allegory* such abstractions as love and fear can be depicted >
syn figuration, symbolism, symbolization, typification
2 a literary form that tells a story to present a truth or enforce a moral < Orwell's *Animal Farm* is a well-known English *allegory* >
syn apologue, fable, myth, parable; *compare* MYTH 1

allergy *n syn* see ANTIPATHY 2
rel rejection, repulsion, revulsion
con affinity, attraction, sympathy

alleviate *vb syn* see RELIEVE 1
rel cure, remedy
idiom temper the wind to the shorn lamb
con augment, heighten, intensify

ant aggravate

alleviation *n syn* see EASE 3

all—fired *adj syn* see UTTER

alliance *n* 1 *syn* see ASSOCIATION 1
2 an association (as of nations) for a common object < a world *alliance* in support of peace >
syn anschluss, coalition, confederacy, confederation, federation, league, union; *compare* UNIFICATION
rel association, club, order, society

allied *adj syn* see RELATED
rel linked, united; parallel, similar
con alien, extraneous, foreign; discrete, separate, several
ant unallied

all in *adj syn* see EFFETE 2
idiom at last gasp

all in all *adv* 1 *syn* see ALL 1
2 *syn* see ALTOGETHER 3

allineate *vb syn* see LINE 1

allness *n syn* see ENTIRETY 1

allocate *vb* 1 *syn* see ALLOT
con reserve, sequester, stockpile
2 *syn* see DESIGNATE 3

allocution *n syn* see SPEECH 2

allot *vb* to give as one's share, portion, role, or place < *allotted* himself a daily hour for exercise >
syn admeasure, allocate, allow, apportion, assign, give, lot, mete (out)
rel deal (out), dispense, distribute, dole (out); equip, fit out, furnish; accord, grant, vouchsafe; appoint, ordain, prescribe
con detain, hold, hold back, keep, retain, withhold; appropriate, arrogate, confiscate

allotment *n* 1 *syn* see SHARE 1
2 *syn* see RATION

all—out *adj syn* see TOTAL 5

all over *adv syn* see EVERYWHERE 1

allover *adj syn* see OMNIPRESENT

‖**all—overs** *n pl syn* see JITTERS

allow *vb* 1 *syn* see ALLOT
rel bestow, confer
con refuse
2 *syn* see ACKNOWLEDGE 1
rel accede, acquiesce, assent
con confute, refute; reject
ant disallow
3 *syn* see LET 2
rel brook, endure, stand, tolerate; defer, submit, yield
con avert, prevent, ward (off)
ant inhibit

allowable *adj syn* see PERMISSIBLE

allowance *n* 1 *syn* see RATION
rel assignment; appropriation, grant, subsidy
2 *syn* see SHARE 1
3 *syn* see ADVANTAGE 3
rel aid, assistance, help; bounty, grant, subsidy
4 *syn* see PERMISSION
rel countenance, favor; indulgence, toleration
con refusal, rejection; contradiction, contravention, negation
5 a taking into account of extenuating circumstances or of contingencies < we must make *allowance* for the inexperience of youth >
syn concession
rel accommodation, adaptation, adjustment; extenuation, mitigation, palliation

alloy *n* **1** *syn* see ADMIXTURE 1
2 *syn* see MIXTURE
all-powerful *adj* *syn* see OMNIPOTENT
all right *adv* *syn* see YES 1
all right *adj* *syn* see DECENT 4
all round (*or* **all around**) *adv* *syn* see EVERYWHERE 1
all there *adj* *syn* see SANE 2
all told *adv* *syn* see ALTOGETHER 3
allude *vb* *syn* see REFER 3
    rel hint, imply, intimate, suggest
allure *vb* **1** *syn* see ATTRACT 1
    rel delude; woo
    con avoid, elude, eschew, shun; alienate, disaffect, estrange, wean
    2 *syn* see LURE
allure *n* *syn* see CHARM 3
allurement *n* **1** *syn* see ATTRACTION 1
    2 *syn* see LURE 2
alluring *adj* *syn* see ATTRACTIVE 1
    rel appetizing; beguiling; delusive
    con repellent; disagreeable, displeasing, uninviting, unlikable, unpleasant
    ant repulsive
almighty *adj* *syn* see OMNIPOTENT
almost *adv* **1** *syn* see NEARLY
    2 not actually but in effect < he paid *almost* nothing for it >
    syn all but, as good as, much as, essentially, practically, well-nigh; *compare* VIRTUALLY
    idiom for all practical purposes, in effect, just about, to all intents and purposes
alms *n pl* *syn* see DONATION
aloft *adv* *syn* see OVER 4
    rel high; skyward, upward
    idiom in the clouds
alone *adj* **1** separated from others < the house was *alone* on a windy ridge >
    syn apart, detached, isolate, isolated, removed, unaccompanied
    rel out-of-the-way, private, remote, retired, secluded, withdrawn
    idiom off the beaten track
    con adjacent, close-by, near-at-hand, nearly, neighboring, nigh
    2 *syn* see LONE 1
    3 having no equal or rival and being single in kind or excellence < a drug *alone* in its curative powers >
    syn matchless, only, peerless, unequaled, unique, unmatched, unparalleled, unrivaled; *compare* SUPREME
    rel inimitable; incomparable, unexcelled, unsurpassed; excellent, good, superior
    idiom second to none
    con common, commonplace, everyday, ordinary, usual; accustomed, conventional, customary, regular
    4 *syn* see ONLY 2
alone *adv* *syn* see ONLY 1
aloneness *n* *syn* see SOLITUDE
along *adv* **1** so as to make forward progress < hurrying *along* toward town >
    syn forth, forward, on, onward; *compare* AHEAD 2
    2 *syn* see ALSO 2
alongside *prep* *syn* see BESIDE 1

aloof *adj* **1** *syn* see INDIFFERENT 2
    rel arrogant, disdainful, haughty, proud; chilly, cold, cool, frigid; constrained, reserved, restrained, reticent, standoffish
    con affable, companionable, gregarious, sociable, social; friendly, neighborly
    ant familiar; outgoing
    2 *syn* see UNSOCIABLE
alp *n* *syn* see MOUNTAIN 1
alpha *n* *syn* see BEGINNING
    ant omega
alphabet *n* **1** a set of characters in which a language can be written < the Greek *alphabet* >
    syn ABC(s), christcross-row, letters
    2 the simplest fundamental part or level < learning the *alphabet* of science >
    syn ABC's, elements, fundamentals, grammar, principles, rudiments
    rel beginning, commencement, start; outset
    idiom first steps
    con entirety, total, whole; details, minutiae, trivia
already *adv* **1** *syn* see BEFORE 2
    2 *syn* see EVEN 2
also *adv* **1** in the same manner < those *also* serve who support the workers >
    syn correspondingly, likewise, similarly, so
    idiom in like manner
    2 in addition to that < he was stern but *also* just >
    syn additionally, along, as well, besides, futhermore, item, likewise, more, moreover, still, too, withal, yea, yet
    idiom into the bargain, on top of that, to boot
    3 *syn* see AGAIN 4
alter *vb* **1** *syn* see CHANGE 1
    rel accommodate, adapt, adjust, moderate, modulate, temper; doctor
    idiom work a change (in)
    con conserve, keep, preserve, retain
    ant fix
    2 *syn* see STERILIZE
alteration *n* **1** *syn* see CHANGE 1
    rel accommodation, adaptation, adjustment; conversion, metamorphosis, transformation; fluctuation, shilly-shally, vacillation, wavering
    con perdurability, permanence, stability; continuance, endurance, persistence
    ant fixation, fixity
    2 *syn* see TRANSITION
    3 *syn* see CONVERSION 2
altercate *vb* *syn* see QUARREL
    rel agitate, argue, debate, dispute
    con accord, get along; accommodate, adapt, adjust, conform
    ant concur
altercation *n* *syn* see QUARREL
    rel argument; combat, contest
    con agreement, concord, consonance, harmony, empathy, like-mindedness, sympathy, understanding
    ant accord; concurrence
alterity *n* *syn* see DISSIMILARITY
alternate *adj* **1** *syn* see INTERMITTENT
    rel alternant, alternating, rotating; complementary, corresponding, reciprocal
    con sequent, successive
    ant consecutive

---

syn synonym(s)   *rel* related word(s)
ant antonym(s)   *con* contrasted word(s)
idiom idiomatic equivalent(s)
‖ use limited; if in doubt, see a dictionary

2 *syn* see SUBSTITUTE 1
rel equivalent, proxy, replacing; exchangeable, interchangeable; makeshift, provisional, tentative

alternate *vb syn* see ROTATE 2
rel fluctuate, oscillate, sway, waver; recur, return, revert
con follow, succeed

alternate *n syn* see SUBSTITUTE

alternately *adv syn* see INSTEAD

alternation *n syn* see SUCCESSION 2
rel recurrence, return, reversion; reappearance, repetition

alternative *adj syn* see SUBSTITUTE 1
rel equivalent, proxy, replacing; exchangeable, interchangeable; makeshift, provisional, tentative

alternative *n syn* see CHOICE 1
rel attainable, contingency, possibility

alternatively *adv syn* see INSTEAD

although *conj syn* see THOUGH

altitude *n syn* see HEIGHT
rel apex, eminence, peak, summit
con depth

altitudinous *adj syn* see HIGH 1

altogether *adv* 1 *syn* see WELL 3
2 *syn* see ALL 1
3 as a total < *altogether* it cost over a thousand dollars>
syn all told, in all, quite
idiom taken together
4 with minor exceptions or flaws < *altogether* the party was a success>
syn all in all, by and large, en masse, generally, on the whole
idiom all things considered, as a whole, for the most part, generally speaking, in the main

altruistic *adj syn* see CHARITABLE 1
rel considerate, kind, unselfish; bounteous, bountiful, generous, liberal, openhanded; bighearted, magnanimous, nobleminded
con egotistic, self-centered, selfish, self-seeking; illiberal, mean, niggardly, stingy, ungenerous
ant egoistic

always *adv* 1 on every relevant occasion < *always* made the same mistake>
syn constantly, continuously, ever, invariably, perpetually
rel frequently, often, regularly, usually
idiom in every case (*or* instance), without exception
con rarely, seldom
ant never
2 *syn* see EVER 2

||**amah** *n syn* see NURSEMAID

amalgam *n syn* see MIXTURE

amalgamate *vb syn* see MIX 1
rel compact, consolidate, unify
con crumble, decompose, disintegrate; disperse, dissipate, scatter

amalgamation *n* 1 *syn* see MIXTURE
2 *syn* see CONSOLIDATION 2

amaranthine *adj syn* see EVERLASTING 1

amaroidal *adj syn* see ACRID

amass *vb syn* see ACCUMULATE
ant distribute

amassment *n syn* see ACCUMULATION

amateur *n* 1 one having a marked and usually informed taste or liking for something < an *amateur* of fine fabrics>

syn admirer, devotee, fan, fancier, votary
rel crank, enthusiast, faddist, infatuate,
||nut, zealot; aesthete, cognoscente, connoisseur, dilettante; illuminato, illuminist
con abecedarian, dabbler, tyro; adept, expert
2 one who follows a pursuit without attaining mastery or professional status < a nation handicapped by *amateurs* in high office>
syn abecedarian, dabbler, dilettante, nonprofessional, smatterer, tyro, uninitiate
rel beginner, greenhorn, neophyte; apprentice, novice, probationer; potterer, putterer, tinker
con adept, virtuoso, wizard
ant expert, master; professional

amateurish *adj* lacking or marked by lack of expert skill or finish < an *amateurish* actor>
syn dabbling, dilettante, dilettantish, dilettantist, jackleg, unaccomplished, unfinished, ungifted, unskilled
rel clumsy, crude, green, raw, untutored; defective, deficient, faulty, flawed
con accomplished, expert, gifted, skilled
ant professional

amative *adj syn* see EROTIC

amatory *adj syn* see EROTIC
rel admiring, attracted, yearning

amaze *vb syn* see SURPRISE 2
rel affect, impress, move, strike, touch

amaze *n syn* see WONDER 2
rel confoundment; surprise

amazement *n syn* see WONDER 2
rel confoundment; surprise

amazing *adj syn* see MARVELOUS 1

amazon *n syn* see VIRAGO

ambidextrous *adj* 1 *syn* see TWO-HANDED 2
2 *syn* see VERSATILE
3 *syn* see INSINCERE

ambience *n syn* see ENVIRONMENT

ambient *n syn* see ENVIRONMENT

ambiguity *n* expression or an expression obscure because subject to more than one interpretation < a speech full of *ambiguities*>
syn amphibology, double entendre, double meaning, equivocality, equivocation, equivoque, tergiversation
rel dodge, evasion, hedge, quibble, shift, subterfuge; cavil, haggling, hair-splitting, quibbling; obscurity, uncertainty, vagueness
con definiteness, expressness, specificity; clearness, exactness, precision
ant explicitness; lucidity

ambiguous *adj* 1 *syn* see OBSCURE 3
rel doubtful, dubious, questionable
con clear, lucid, perspicuous; categorical, express, specific
ant explicit
2 *syn* see DOUBTFUL 1

ambit *n* 1 *syn* see CIRCUMFERENCE
2 *syn* see RANGE 2

ambition *n* 1 strong desire for advancement < a life ruled by *ambition*>
syn ambitiousness, aspiration, pretension
rel drive, go-ahead, push; anxiety, avidity, eagerness, keenness; energy, enterprise, spirit; goad, incentive, motive, spur
con contentment, satisfaction; faineance, indolence, lethargy, sloth

2 an object of desire or intent < his *ambition* was to have enough to live on without working >
syn aim, goal, mark, objective, quaesitum, target; *compare* INTENTION
rel design, intent, purpose; desire, fancy, hope, wish; dream, ideal, nirvana
3 *syn see* ENTERPRISE 4

ambitious *adj* 1 marked by intense desire for advancement (as in power, fame, or wealth) < a ruthlessly *ambitious* politician >
syn aspiring, emulous, vaulting
rel aggressive, enterprising, go-ahead, pushing, up-and-doing; energetic, hard-working, indefatigable; anxious, avid, eager, keen
con apathetic, phlegmatic, stolid; faineant, indolent, lazy, slothful
2 of a kind to try or exceed one's powers of performance < an *ambitious* scheme to recover gold from seawater >
syn grandiose, lofty, pretentious, utopian, visionary
rel audacious, bold, daring; chimerical, extravagant, high-flown, impractical, unrealistic
con easy, plain, straightforward; feasible, practicable, realistic; unpretentious
ant modest

ambitiousness *n syn see* AMBITION 1
ambivalent *adj syn see* EQUIVOCAL 2
amble *vb syn see* SAUNTER
rel dally, dawdle, dillydally, loiter
ambrosial *adj* 1 *syn see* DELIGHTFUL
2 *syn see* SWEET 2
ambulant *adj syn see* ITINERANT
ant bedfast, bedridden
ambulate *vb syn see* WALK 1
ambulatory *adj syn see* ITINERANT
ambuscade *n syn see* AMBUSH
ambush *vb syn see* SURPRISE 1
rel assail, assault, attack; ensnare, entrap, snare, trap
ambush *n* a device to entrap an enemy by lying in hiding until a surprise attack is feasible < planned an *ambush* on the cliff above the trail >
syn ambuscade, ambushment
rel lure, snare, trap; blind, cover, hideout, retreat
ambushment *n syn see* AMBUSH
ameliorate *vb* 1 *syn see* IMPROVE 1
rel alleviate, lighten, mitigate, relieve
con damage, harm, hurt, impair, injure, mar, spoil; aggravate, intensify
ant worsen; deteriorate
2 *syn see* IMPROVE 3
amenable *adj* 1 *syn see* RESPONSIBLE
rel open, subject; dependent, subordinate
con autarchic, free
ant independent (of); autonomous
2 *syn see* OBEDIENT
rel subdued, tame; receptive, responsive, willing; adaptable, impressionable, malleable, plastic, pliable, pliant
con fierce, mulish, obstinate, stubborn, truculent

ant recalcitrant, refractory
amend *vb* 1 *syn see* CORRECT 1
rel repair; elevate, lift, raise
con corrupt, debauch, deprave, pervert, vitiate
ant debase
2 *syn see* IMPROVE 1
rel advance, forward, promote
ant worsen; impair
amends *n pl syn see* REPARATION
amenity *n* 1 the quality of being pleasant or agreeable < a discussion conducted in perfect *amenity* > < the *amenity* of the climate >
syn agreeability, agreeableness, amiability, cordiality, enjoyableness, geniality, gratefulness, pleasance, pleasantness, sweetness and light
rel attractiveness, charm, delightfulness; fascination, pleasingness
con disagreeableness, distastefulness, unattractiveness, unpleasantness
2 a feature that makes for pleasantness or ease < among the *amenities* of the house is central air-conditioning >
syn comfort, convenience, facility
rel betterment, enhancement, enrichment, improvement; excellence, merit, quality, virtue
con difficulty, hardship, trial, vicissitude
3 *pl amenities syn see* MANNER 5
4 *syn see* LUXURY
5 *syn see* COURTESY 1
rel civility, courteousness, politeness; affability, cordiality, geniality, graciousness, sociability
con discourtesy, impoliteness, incivility; affront, indignity, insult; acrimony
ant rudeness
ament *n syn see* FOOL 4
amerce *vb syn see* PENALIZE
amercement *n syn see* FINE
amiability *n syn see* AMENITY 1
amiable *adj* 1 of a generally agreeable nature especially in social interaction < the meeting ended on an *amiable* note >
syn complaisant, easy, good-humored, good-natured, good-tempered, lenient, mild, obliging
rel affable, cordial, genial, gracious; courteous, mannerly; benign, benignant, kind, kindly; responsive, warm, warmhearted
idiom easy to get along with
con discourteous, ill-mannered, ill-natured, impolite, rude; crabbed, dour, unsociable
ant unamiable; surly
2 *syn see* GENTLE 2
amicable *adj* 1 characterized by peaceableness and goodwill < the negotiators joined in *amicable* discussion >
syn friendly, neighborly
rel empathic, like-minded, sympathetic, understanding; accordant, agreeing, concordant, frictionless, harmonious; pacific, peaceable, peaceful
con bellicose, belligerent, combative, contentious, pugnacious, quarrelsome; antipathetic, hostile, suspicious, uncooperative
2 *syn see* HARMONIOUS 3
amical *adj syn see* HARMONIOUS 3
amid *prep* 1 in or into the central part of < the bomb burst *amid* the crowd >

---

syn synonym(s)   *rel* related word(s)
ant antonym(s)   *con* contrasted word(s)
idiom idiomatic equivalent(s)
‖ use limited; if in doubt, see a dictionary

syn among, mid, midst

idiom in (*or* into) the middle of, in (*or* into) the midst of, in (*or* into) the thick of

2 *syn* see AMONG 1

3 *syn* see DURING

amigo *n syn* see FRIEND

amiss *adv* 1 in a mistaken, inappropriate, or reprehensible way <I feel you judge him *amiss* >

syn faultily, incorrectly, wrongly

rel inaccurately; indiscreetly, unwisely

con accurately, correctly, properly, rightly; cleverly, wisely

ant right

2 out of the proper course <our planning had gone *amiss* >

syn afield, astray, awry, badly, unfavorably, wrong; *compare* HARD 5

idiom beside (*or* off) the mark

con auspiciously, famously, favorably, promisingly, propitiously, well

ant aright

amiss *adj* 1 *syn* see BAD 1

2 *syn* see FAULTY

3 *syn* see BLAMEWORTHY

amity *n syn* see GOODWILL 1

rel accord, agreement, concord, harmony; amicableness, neighborliness

con animosity, antagonism, antipathy, hostility; conflict, contention, discord, dissension, strife

ant enmity

amnesty *n syn* see PARDON

among *prep* 1 surrounded by <the valley nestled *among* high mountains>

syn amid, mid, midst

2 *syn* see AMID 1

3 *syn* see BETWEEN

amorist *n syn* see GALLANT 2

amorous *adj syn* see EROTIC

rel enamored, infatuated; lustful

con aloof, detached, indifferent; cold, cool; apathetic, impassive, unconcerned

ant frigid

amorousness *n syn* see LOVE 2

amorphous *adj syn* see FORMLESS

amount *vb* 1 to make up as a total <their expenses *amounted* to just a hundred dollars>

syn add up, aggregate, come, number, run (to *or* into), sum (to *or* into), total

rel comprehend, comprise, embody, include, incorporate, reach, subsume

2 to be essentially equivalent <that utter terror that *amounts* to madness>

syn approach, correspond (to), equal, match, partake (of), rival, touch

rel hint, imply, intimate, smack (of), suggest

idiom be near to, come to the same thing as, have all the earmarks (*or* features) of

amount *n* 1 *syn* see BODY 5

2 *syn* see SUBSTANCE 2

amour *n* 1 *syn* see LOVE AFFAIR

2 an illicit or informal sexual relation <memoirs devoted to accounts of his *amours* >

syn affair, intrigue, liaison

rel entanglement, intimacy, relationship; love affair, romance

3 *syn* see LOVE 2

amour propre *n* 1 *syn* see PRIDE 2

2 *syn* see CONCEIT 2

rel complacency, self-complacency, self-satisfaction, smugness; pride

amphibological *adj syn* see OBSCURE 3

amphibology *n syn* see AMBIGUITY

ample *adj* 1 *syn* see SPACIOUS

rel distended, expanded, inflated, swollen

con scant, skimpy, spare; cramped, exiguous, narrow, strait

ant meager; circumscribed

2 *syn* see PLENTIFUL

rel lavish, prodigal, profuse; handsome

idiom enough and to spare

con scrimpy, spare, sparse; beggarly, miserable, niggardly

ant meager, scant

amplify *vb* 1 *syn* see EXPAND 4

rel augment, extend, increase; unfold

con abbreviate, shorten

ant abridge, condense

2 *syn* see EXPAND 3

amplitude *n* 1 *syn* see SIZE 2

2 *syn* see BREADTH 2

con closeness, limitation, restriction, straitness

ant narrowness

3 *syn* see EXPANSE

rel bigness, greatness, largeness; capaciousness, commodiousness, roominess, spaciousness

con circumscription, restriction

ant straitness; limitation

amply *adv syn* see WELL 4

amulet *n syn* see CHARM 2

rel lucky piece, rabbit-foot

amuse *vb* to pass or cause to pass time in pleasant or agreeable activity <simple toys to *amuse* children on long trips>

syn divert, entertain, recreate

rel absorb, distract, engross; animate, enliven, fleet, quicken; beguile, charm, delight, enchant, fascinate, wile; while

con fatigue, irk, jade, pall (on), tire, wear (on), weary; bore, ennui

amusement *n syn* see ENTERTAINMENT

ana *n syn* see ANTHOLOGY

anabasis *n syn* see ADVANCE 2

anachronism *n* 1 a chronological error <*anachronisms* of several centuries mar some earlier chronicles>

syn misdate, misdating, mistiming, parachronism

rel antedate, anticipation, prochronism, prolepsis; metachronism, postdate

2 one that is inappropriately situated especially in time <born centuries too late, he was an *anachronism* in modern urban society>

syn solecism

rel bevue, faux pas, gaffe; defect, flaw, mistake, slip

anadem *n syn* see WREATH

anagogic *adj syn* see MYSTICAL 1

rel esoteric, occult, recondite; allegorical, symbolical

analects *n pl syn* see ANTHOLOGY

analgesic *n syn* see ANODYNE 1

ant irritant

analogous *adj syn* see LIKE

rel convertible, corresponding, interchangeable; kindred

analogue *n syn* see PARALLEL

rel cognate, congener

analogy *n* 1 *syn* see LIKENESS

2 expression or an expression involving explicit or implied comparison of things basically unlike but with some striking similarities <God can be described only by *analogy*>
syn metaphor, simile, similitude
rel ambiguity, equivocation, equivoque, tergiversation
con demonstration, description, formulation

analphabet *n syn* see ILLITERATE

analysis *n* 1 separation of a whole into its fundamental elements or constituent parts <*analysis* of a problem>
syn breakdown, breakup, dissection, resolution
rel division, separation; decomposition, disintegration
con combination, union; concatenation, integration, unification
ant synthesis
2 *syn* see EXAMINATION

analytic *adj syn* see LOGICAL 2
rel deep, profound; acute, keen, sharp; penetrating, piercing
con constructive, creative, inventive

analytical *adj syn* see LOGICAL 2

analyze *vb* to divide a complex whole into its constituent parts or elements <*analyze* the plot of a novel>
syn anatomize, break down, decompose, decompound, dissect, resolve
rel divide, part, separate; assort, classify, pigeonhole; examine, inspect, investigate, scrutinize
con articulate, concatenate, integrate
ant compose, compound; construct

anamnesis *n syn* see MEMORY 2

Ananias *n syn* see LIAR

anarch *n syn* see REBEL

anarchism *n* 1 a political theory opposed to all forms of government and advocating voluntary cooperation and interaction of individuals and groups in satisfying their common needs <the doubtful premises of *anarchism* about human nature>
syn anarchy
rel utopianism; communism, Marxism, syndicalism
con absolutism, authoritarianism, dictatorship; elitism
2 *syn* see DISORDER 2

anarchist *n syn* see REBEL

anarchy *n* 1 absence of effective government or the resulting social disorder <complete *anarchy* followed the breakdown of communications>
syn chaos, lawlessness, mobocracy, ochlocracy
rel confusion, disorder, disorganization
idiom mob rule (*or* law), reign of terror
2 *syn* see ANARCHISM
3 *syn* see DISORDER 2

anastomose *vb syn* see INTERJOIN

anathema *n* 1 *syn* see CURSE 1
rel censure, condemnation, denunciation, reprehension, reprobation, reproof
con eulogy, laudation, praise

2 *syn* see ABOMINATION 1
rel leper, pariah, outcast, untouchable

anathematize *vb syn* see EXECRATE 1
rel impugn, reproach
con approbate, approve, countenance, endorse, favor

anatomize *vb syn* see ANALYZE

ancestor *n* 1 a person from whom one is descended <proud of his pioneer *ancestors*>
syn antecedent (used in pl.), ascendant, forebear, forefather, primogenitor, progenitor
ant descendant
2 *syn* see FORERUNNER 2

ancestry *n* one's progenitors or their character or quality as a whole <a man of noble *ancestry*>
syn blood, descent, extraction, lineage, origin, pedigree
rel family, kindred, line, race, stock; derivation, source; breed, breeding
ant descendants; posterity

anchor *vb syn* see FASTEN 2
rel imbed, plant
idiom make fast (*or* secure)

anchorage *n syn* see HARBOR 3

ancient *adj* 1 persisting from the distant past <an *ancient* monument>
syn aged, age-old, antediluvian, antique, hoary, Noachian, old, timeworn, venerable; compare OBSOLETE
rel primal, primeval, primordial, pristine; forgotten, immemorial, remote, traditional; ageless, dateless
idiom old as time, older than God (*or* the hills), out of the dim past
con current, fresh, new, novel, prevailing, up-to-date
ant modern
2 *syn* see AGED 1
rel doddering, doting, fading, sinking, waning, wasting
idiom old as Methuselah (*or* the hills)

ancient *n syn* see OLDSTER

ancilla *n syn* see HELPER

ancillary *adj* 1 *syn* see AUXILIARY
2 *syn* see CONCOMITANT

androgynous *adj syn* see BISEXUAL

android *n syn* see ROBOT 1

anecdote *n syn* see STORY 2
rel recital, relation; episode, event, incident

anemic *adj syn* see PALE 2

anent *prep syn* see APROPOS

anesthetic *adj syn* see INSENSIBLE 5
rel impenetrable, impermeable, impervious; obtuse
con responsive, sensitive

anesthetic *n syn* see ANODYNE 1
ant stimulant

anesthetized *adj syn* see NUMB 1

anew *adv* 1 *syn* see OVER 7
2 *syn* see NEW

anfractuous *adj syn* see WINDING

angel *n syn* see SPONSOR
rel ‖butter-and-egg man

angelic *adj syn* see SAINTLY

anger *n* emotional excitement induced by intense displeasure <a man easily aroused to *anger*>
syn fury, indignation, ire, mad, rage, wrath

---

syn synonym(s)   *rel* related word(s)
ant antonym(s)   *con* contrasted word(s)
idiom idiomatic equivalent(s)
‖ use limited; if in doubt, see a dictionary

rel ‖dander, dudgeon, ‖Dutch, huff, ‖monkey, pet, pique, temper: annoyance, exasperation, infuriation, irritation
ant forbearance

anger *vb* 1 to make angry < their constant heedless interruptions *angered* her >
syn enrage, incense, infuriate, ire, mad, madden, steam up, umbrage
rel annoy, irk, vex; aggravate, exasperate, irritate, nettle, provoke, rile; affront, offend, outrage
idiom burn one up, make one hot under the collar, put (*or* get) one's dander up, set one by the ears
con appease, conciliate, mollify, placate, propitiate, soothe
ant gratify; pacify
2 to be or become angry < he *angers* easily >
syn blow up, boil, boil over, bristle, burn, flare (up), fume, rage, seethe
rel chafe, fret, stew; rant, rave, storm
idiom breathe fire, fly into a rage, get hot under the collar, get one's blood (*or* dander) up, hit the ceiling, lose one's temper, see red
ant calm (down)

angle *vb syn* see HINT 4

angle *n* 1 *syn* see VIEWPOINT 2
2 *syn* see PHASE
rel detail, item, particular
3 *syn* see TURN 4

angle *vb* 1 *syn* see SLANT 2
2 *syn* see SLANT 3

angry *adj* feeling or showing strong displeasure or bad temper < *angry* at the children's lack of consideration >
syn acrimonious, choleric, heated, indignant, irate, ireful, mad, ‖pissed, ‖pissed off, shirty, waxy, wrathful, wrathy, wroth, wrothful, wrothy
rel aggravated, exasperated, perturbed, put out, riley, upset, uptight, worked up, wrought (up); angered, enraged, incensed, infuriate, infuriated, maddened, sore, vexed; orey-eyed, red-faced, wild-eyed
idiom foaming at the mouth, hot under the collar, in a taking, in a temper (*or* rage), mad as a hornet (*or* wet hen)
con calm, placid, tolerant; content, pleased, satisfied

anguish *n syn* see SORROW
rel anxiety, worry; ache, pain, pang, throe; torment, torture
con comfort, consolation, solace; alleviation, assuagement, mitigation
ant relief

angular *adj* 1 *syn* see RUDE 1
2 *syn* see LEAN
rel lathy, ribby, weedy
con chubby, chuffy
ant rotund

anima *n syn* see SOUL 1

animadversion *n* a remark or statement that constitutes an adverse and usually uncharitable criticism < her spiteful *animadversions* on her neighbors' children >
syn aspersion, obloquy, reflection, slam, slur, stricture
rel censure, criticism, reprehension; accusation, imputation, insinuation; captiousness, carping, caviling, faultfinding
con acclaim, extolling, laudation, praise; approbation, approval

ant commendation

animadvert *vb syn* see REMARK 2
rel declare, say, state, tell, utter; descant, dilate, expatiate, perorate; adduce, offer, present
con disregard, ignore, overlook

animal *n syn* see BEAST

animal *adj* 1 *syn* see BRUTISH
2 *syn* see CARNAL 2
rel bestial, brutal, brutish
con intellectual, mental, psychic; reasoning, thinking; nonphysical, spiritual
ant rational

animalism *n syn* see ANIMALITY
rel lasciviousness, lecherousness, lechery, licentiousness, lustfulness, unchastity; sensualism, sensuality, voluptuousness

animality *n* the animal aspect or quality of human beings or human nature < his violent reaction was sheer *animality* >
syn animalism, carnality, fleshliness
rel maleness, masculinity, virility; sensuality; brutishness, coarseness, grossness
ant spirituality

animalize *vb syn* see DEBASE 1

animate *adj* 1 *syn* see LIVING 1
rel breathing, viable
ant inanimate
2 *syn* see LIVELY 1
rel active, dynamic, live; activated, energized, vitalized
con dead, inanimate, lifeless; passive
ant inert

animate *vb* 1 *syn* see ENCOURAGE 1
rel invigorate, refresh, renew; fortify, reinforce, strengthen
idiom give a lift (to), put on (*or* upon) one's mettle, raise the spirits of
2 *syn* see QUICKEN 1
3 *syn* see FIRE 2
rel activate, actuate, motivate; drive, impel, move
con check, curb, restrain; frustrate, thwart
ant inhibit

animated *adj* 1 *syn* see LIVING 1
rel activated, energized, vitalized
con passive
ant inert
2 *syn* see LIVELY 1
rel exuberant, high-spirited, zestful
con enervated, spiritless; comatose
ant dejected, depressed

animating *adj syn* see INVIGORATING

animation *n syn* see SPIRIT 5

animosity *n syn* see ENMITY
con amity; esteem
ant goodwill

animus *n* 1 *syn* see INTENTION
2 *syn* see SOUL 1
3 *syn* see ENMITY
rel grudge; bias, discrimination, prejudice
con partiality, predilection; sympathy
ant favor

annals *n pl syn* see HISTORY 2

annex *vb* 1 *syn* see ADD 1
rel associate, connect, join, link, unite
con disengage; divorce, part, separate
2 *syn* see GET 1
3 *syn* see APPROPRIATE 1
4 *syn* see STEAL 1

annex *n* a subsidiary structure associated with a main building < built an *annex* to the museum to hold a new collection >

syn arm, block, ell, extension, wing
rel addition, continuation

annihilate *vb* 1 *syn* see ABOLISH 1
2 to destroy utterly < matter cannot be *annihilated* >
syn abate, abolish, blot out, eradicate, exterminate, extinguish, extirpate, murder, root out, uncreate, uproot, wipe (out)
rel cancel, efface, erase, expunge, obliterate
con renew, restore; create, discover, invent; fashion, forge, form, make, shape
3 *syn* see DESTROY 1
4 *syn* see SLAUGHTER 3
rel rout
5 *syn* see CRUSH 5

annihilative *adj syn* see DESTRUCTIVE

annotate *vb* to add or append comment < *annotate* a volume of poems >
syn gloss
rel construe, elucidate, explain, expound; comment, commentate, remark

announce *vb* 1 *syn* see DECLARE 1
rel communicate, impart
con hush (up), smother, stifle, suppress
2 to point to as a future occurrence or development < the shortening days *announce* the coming of winter >
syn forerun, foreshow, harbinger, herald, preindicate, presage
rel augur, forebode, forecast, foretell, predict
3 *syn* see INDICATE 2
rel present, set forth, show (forth)

announcement *n syn* see DECLARATION
rel affirmation, assertion, averment, statement

annoy *vb* 1 to disturb and upset nervously < her persistent prying soon *annoyed* her hostess >
syn abrade, bother, ‖bug, chafe, exercise, fret, gall, irk, provoke, ruffle, vex; *compare* IRRITATE
rel agitate, disturb, perturb, upset
idiom get in one's hair
con comfort, console, solace; content, gratify, please, satisfy
ant soothe
2 *syn* see WORRY 1
rel badger, bait, chivy, heckle, hector; chafe, distress, gall, rub
idiom get (*or* grate) on one's nerves, rub one the wrong way
con disregard, ignore, overlook; appease, calm, dulcify, mollify; cool, lull, subdue

annoyance *n* 1 the act of annoying < devoted himself to the *annoyance* of his patient wife >
syn bothering, harassment, irking, provocation, provoking, vexation, vexing
rel pestering, teasing
2 the state or feeling of being annoyed < her *annoyance* increased as he continued to pester her >
syn aggravation, bother, botheration, exasperation, pother
rel anger, indignation, ire, wrath; aversion, repugnance, repulsion, revulsion; disgust, dislike, distaste

con appreciation, enjoyment, liking, pleasure
3 something that causes an annoyed state or feeling < his constant baiting was an *annoyance* to her >
syn besetment, bother, botheration, botherment, exasperation, irritant, nuisance, pest, pester, ‖pesterment, plague
rel affliction, aggravation, distress, provocation, trial; riding

annual *n syn* see YEARBOOK

annuary *n syn* see YEARBOOK

annul *vb* 1 *syn* see ERASE
rel abstract, dispose (of), eliminate, remove
2 *syn* see NEUTRALIZE
rel outweigh, overbalance
3 *syn* see ABOLISH 1
rel counteract, negative, neutralize; blot out, cancel, efface, obliterate; extinguish
idiom make void, set aside
con enact, ordain, pass
4 to deprive of legal validity, force, or authority < *annul* a marriage >
syn abrogate, discharge, dissolve, quash, vacate, void
rel abolish, cancel, countermand, invalidate, nullify, undo
idiom make void

annunciate *vb syn* see DECLARE 1
rel affirm, assert, asseverate, aver; profess, protest; pronounce, state

anodyne *n* 1 something used to relieve or prevent pain < opium and its derivatives are still our most potent *anodynes* >
syn analgesic, anesthetic, pain-killer
rel calmative, depressant, sedative, tranquilizer; hypnotic, somnifacient, soporific, stupefacient
2 something that soothes or, often, dulls or deadens the senses or sensibilities < the kind of religion that is no more than an *anodyne* >
syn narcotic, nepenthe, opiate
ant energizer, stimulant; irritant

anomalous *adj* 1 *syn* see IRREGULAR 1
rel monstrous, prodigious
2 *syn* see ABNORMAL 1
rel foreign, peculiar, singular, strange; monstrous, prodigious
con accustomed, customary, usual, wonted

anon *adv* 1 *syn* see PRESENTLY 1
2 *syn* see THEN 1

anonym *n syn* see PSEUDONYM

anonymous *adj* not identified by name < saved by an *anonymous* hero >
syn innominate, nameless, undesignated, unnamed
rel incognito, unidentified, unknown, unrecognized, unspecified
ant named, onymous

another *adj* 1 *syn* see THAT 1
2 *syn* see ADDITIONAL
rel second

anschauung *n syn* see INTUITION

anschluss *n syn* see ALLIANCE 2

answer *n* 1 something spoken or written by way of return to a question or demand < a sullen *answer* >
syn antiphon, rejoinder, reply, respond, response, retort, return

---

syn synonym(s)   *rel* related word(s)
ant antonym(s)   *con* contrasted word(s)
idiom idiomatic equivalent(s)
‖ use limited; if in doubt, see a dictionary

rel comment, observation, remark; defense, justification; rebuttal, refutation; replication

con inquiry, interrogation, query, question, quiz

2 something attained by mental effort and especially by computation < got the *answer* by trial-and-error methods>

syn result, solution

answer *vb* 1 to say, write, or do something in response (as to a question) < *answered* his critics with documented facts>

syn come in, rejoin, reply, respond, retort, return

rel acknowledge, recognize; disprove, rebut, refute; countercharge, recriminate

idiom come back (at), make reply (to)

con ask, inquire, interrogate, query, question, quiz

2 *syn* see SATISFY 5

answerable *adj syn* see RESPONSIBLE

rel bound, compelled, constrained, duty-bound, obligated, obliged

Antaean *adj syn* see HUGE

antagonism *n* 1 *syn* see ENMITY

rel opposition, oppugnancy, resistance, withstanding; clashing, conflict, difference, disagreement, discord, friction

con concord, consonance, harmony; agreement, understanding

ant accord; comity

2 an opposing state, action, or position < the natural *antagonism* of predators and prey>

syn antithesis, con, contradistinction, contraposition, contrariety, opposition, oppose

rel disagreement, discrepancy, disparity, incongruity; annulling, negation, nullification; counteraction

con agreement, congruity; alliance, association, rapport; empathy, sympathy

antagonist *n syn* see OPPONENT

con adherent, henchman, partisan

ant supporter

antagonistic *adj* 1 *syn* see BITTER 1

2 *syn* see ADVERSE 1

rel discordant, incompatible, inconsonant; averse, disinclined, indisposed, unwilling; conflicting, hostile

con advantageous, beneficial; auspicious, benign, propitious

ant favorable

3 *syn* see ANTIPATHETIC 1

rel adverse, counter, counteractive, reactive; discordant; antonymous, opposing, oppugnant

ante *adv syn* see BEFORE 1

ante *prep syn* see BEFORE 1

ante *n syn* see BET

antecede *vb syn* see PRECEDE 2

antecedence *n syn* see PRIORITY

antecedent *n* 1 *syn* see CAUSE 1

rel forebear, forerunner, precursor; agency, instrumentality, means

con sequel; upshot

ant consequence

2 *syn* see FORERUNNER 2

3 — used in pl. *syn* see ANCESTOR 1

antecedent *adj syn* see PRECEDING

ant consequent; subsequent

antecedently *adv syn* see BEFORE 1

antecessor *n syn* see FORERUNNER 2

antedate *vb syn* see PRECEDE 2

antediluvian *adj syn* see ANCIENT 1

antediluvian *n syn* see FOGY

anterior *adj syn* see PRECEDING

con after, back, hind, hinder, rear

ant posterior

anthology *n* a collection of selected artistic and especially literary pieces or passages < an *anthology* of sacred music>

syn album, ana, analects, florilegium, garland, miscellany, omnibus, posy

rel collection, compilation; delectus, treasure-house, treasury

anthropoid *adj* resembling man < *anthropoid* apes>

syn anthropomorphic, anthropomorphous, humanoid, manlike

anthropomorphic *adj syn* see ANTHROPOID

anthropomorphous *adj syn* see ANTHROPOID

anti *n syn* see OPPONENT

anti *adj syn* see ADVERSE 1

ant pro

antic *n syn* see PRANK

rel artifice, wile; romp

antic *adj* 1 *syn* see FANTASTIC 2

rel foolish; comic, comical, farcical, laughable, ludicrous

con prudent, sensible, wise; conventional, formal; grave, sedate, serious, solemn, somber

2 characterized by a light gay quality < a briskly *antic* and delightful tale>

syn frolicsome, playful, rollicking, sprightly

rel gay, lively, spirited; light, whimsical; casual, easy, suave

con constrained, controlled, curbed, guarded, inhibited, restrained

3 *syn* see PLAYFUL 1

anticipant *adj syn* see EXPECTANT 1

anticipate *vb* 1 *syn* see PREVENT 1

rel forecast, foretell, presage

idiom be one step ahead of

con disregard, ignore, neglect, overlook, slight

2 *syn* see FORESEE

rel await, contemplate, expect; foretaste

idiom be on the lookout (or watch) for, look forward to, look (or watch) out for

anticipation *n syn* see EXPECTANCY 1

anticipative *adj syn* see EXPECTANT 1

anticipatory *adj syn* see EXPECTANT 1

antidote *n syn* see REMEDY 2

rel negator, neutralizer, nullifier; offset; backfire

antipasto *n syn* see APPETIZER

antipathetic *adj* 1 having a natural or inherent opposition < national needs *antipathetic* to peace>

syn antagonistic, clashing, conflicting, contrariant, contrary, discordant

rel antipodal, antithetical, antonymous, contradictory, opposite

idiom at cross purposes, at daggers drawn, at war with one another

con agreeing, consonant, correspondent, harmonious; coactive, collaborative, cooperative

ant concordant

2 arousing marked aversion or dislike < found his sister's husband in every way *antipathetic*>

syn aversive, kindless, repellent, repugnant, uncongenial, ungenial, unsympathetic

rel abhorrent, obnoxious; disgustful, disgusting, distasteful, loathsome, repulsive

con compatible, consonant, sympathetic; alluring, attractive, charming; agreeable, pleasant, pleasing, satisfying, soothing

ant congenial

3 *syn* see ADVERSE 1

antipathy *n* 1 *syn* see ENMITY

rel disrelish, distaste, repellency, repugnance; avoidance, escape, eschewal, evasion

con liking, partiality, predilection, prepossession; attachment, love; attraction, taste (for)

ant affection (for)

2 the state of mind induced by what is antipathetic <a strong *antipathy* to modern art>

syn allergy, aversion, dyspathy

rel abhorrence, dislike, disrelish, distaste, repellency, repugnance; avoidance, escape, eschewal, evasion

con liking, partiality, predilection, prepossession; affection, attachment, love; attraction

ant taste (for)

antiphon *n syn* see ANSWER 1

antipodal *adj syn* see OPPOSITE

antipode *n syn* see OPPOSITE

antipodean *adj syn* see OPPOSITE

antipole *n syn* see OPPOSITE

antiquate *vb syn* see OUTDATE

antiquated *adj syn* see OLD-FASHIONED

con modern, new, novel

ant modernistic

antique *adj* 1 *syn* see ANCIENT 1

rel ancestral, dateless, immemorial, legendary, time-honored, traditional

con advanced, current, recent

2 *syn* see OLD-FASHIONED

antisocial *adj* averse to the society of others <a pure scholar, remote and *antisocial*>

syn eremitic, misanthropic, reclusive, reserved, solitary, standoffish

rel ascetic, austere, cold, remote; cynical, introverted, withdrawn

con affable, friendly, gregarious; communicative, outgoing, sociable

ant social

antithesis *n* 1 *syn* see ANTAGONISM 2

2 *syn* see OPPOSITE

antithetical *adj syn* see OPPOSITE

anxiety *n syn* see CARE 2

rel doubt, mistrust, uncertainty; distress, misery, suffering; dread; panic

con composure, equanimity, sangfroid; aplomb, confidence, self-possession; certainty, certitude, faith, trust

ant security

anxious *adj* 1 *syn* see AFRAID 1

rel agitated, apprehensive, jittery, perturbed, upset, worried; alarmed, bothered, disquieted, troubled, uneasy

idiom ill at ease

con calm, collected, cool, easy, imperturbable, unruffled; assured, confident, sanguine, sure

2 *syn* see EAGER

rel importunate, pressing, urgent

idiom all agog, bursting to

con averse, disinclined, hesitant, indisposed, reluctant

ant loath

anyhow *adv syn* see ABOUT 4

anytime *adv syn* see EVER 4

anyway *adv syn* see EVER 5

any which way *adv syn* see ABOUT 4

anywise *adv* 1 *syn* see ABOUT 4

2 *syn* see EVER 5

A1 *adj syn* see EXCELLENT

space *adv syn* see FAST 2

apart *adv* 1 as a discrete item <taken *apart*, his view seemed sound enough>

syn independently, individually, one by one, separately, severally, singly

idiom one at a time

2 excluded from consideration <these slips *apart*, he had done very well>

syn aside

idiom to one side

3 in or into parts <tore the sheets *apart*>

syn asunder, sky-high

idiom all to pieces, to bits (*or* flinders)

apart *adj syn* see ALONE 1

apart *from prep syn* see EXCEPT

apartheid *n syn* see SEGREGATION

apartment *n* 1 a set of rooms (as in a private house or a block) rented or leased for use as a dwelling place <had a tiny top-floor *apartment*>

syn ‖chambers, flat, lodging(s), rental, rooms, suite, tenement

2 *syn* see ROOM 1

apathetic *adj syn* see IMPASSIVE 1

rel dull, inert, languid, sluggish, torpid; anesthetic, impassible, insensible, insensitive; callous, unmoved, untouched; limp, spiritless

con aroused, awake, aware, conscious, impressionable, perceptive, receptive; vigilant, watchful, wide-awake

ant alert

apathy *n* 1 lack of emotional responsiveness <hid her sorrow behind a dull brooding *apathy*>

syn impassivity, insensibility, phlegm, stoicism, stolidity, unresponsiveness

rel inertness, passivity, supineness; aloofness, detachment, indifference, unconcern; lethargy, torpidity, torpor; listlessness, numbness, stupefaction, stupor

con ardor, fervor, passion, responsiveness, warmth; alertness, awareness, concern, solicitude

ant zeal; enthusiasm

2 lack of interest or concern <public *apathy* toward the school crisis>

syn disinterest, disregard, heedlessness, indifference, insouciance, lassitude, lethargy, listlessness, unconcern, unmindfulness

rel callousness, hardness, insensitivity, obduracy, unawareness; coldness, halfheartedness, lukewarmness; calmness, dispassion, dispassionateness

con attentiveness, concern, heedfulness, interest; awareness, mindfulness, sensitiv-

---

syn synonym(s)   *rel* related word(s)
ant antonym(s)   *con* contrasted word(s)
idiom idiomatic equivalent(s)
‖ use limited; if in doubt, see a dictionary

ity, solicitude; ardency, fervency, passion, warmth, zeal

ape *vb syn* see MIMIC
rel caricature; emulate, rival
idiom make like

aperçu *n syn* see COMPENDIUM 1

aperitive *adj syn* see PALATABLE

aperture *n* a discontinuity allowing passage <the mouse squeezed through a narrow *aperture* in the wall>
syn hole, opening, orifice, outlet, vent
rel discontinuity, gap, hiatus, interstice; bore, perforation, pinhole, prick, puncture; chasm, cleft, cut, gash, slash, slit; breach, break, rupture

apery *n syn* see MIMICRY

apex *n* 1 *syn* see TOP 1
rel extremity, limit, spire
ant nadir
2 the culminating point <the *apex* of his career>
syn acme, apogee, capsheaf, capstone, climax, comble, crescendo, crest, crown, culmen, culmination, meridian, ne plus ultra, noon, noontide, peak, pinnacle, sublimity, summit, zenith
rel last word, prime, quintessence, ultimate; achievement, attainment, consummation, realization
ant nadir
3 *syn* see POINT 9
rel cap, crest, peak, prominence, spire

aphorism *n syn* see MAXIM

aphrodisia *n syn* see LUST 2

aphrodisiac *adj syn* see EROTIC
ant anaphrodisiac

apiarist *n syn* see BEEKEEPER

apical *adj syn* see TOP 1

apiculturist *n syn* see BEEKEEPER

apiece *adv* by, for, or to each one <gave the boys a dollar *apiece*>
syn all, aside, each, ‖per, per capita, per caput
rel individually, one by one, respectively, severally, singly, successively

apish *adj syn* see SLAVISH 3

aplomb *n syn* see CONFIDENCE 2
rel poise, savoir faire; coolness, imperturbability, levelheadedness, nonchalance; composure, ease, easiness, equanimity, sangfroid
idiom presence of mind
con bewilderment, distraction, perplexity; befuddlement, confusion, fluster, fuddlement; discomfiture, embarrassment, perturbation
ant shyness

apocalypse *n syn* see REVELATION
rel envisioning, foresight, precognition, prevision

apocalyptic *adj* 1 *syn* see PROPHETIC
2 *syn* see OMINOUS

apocryphal *adj syn* see SPURIOUS 3
rel false, erroneous, inaccurate, incorrect, untrue, wrong; doubtful, dubious, questionable
idiom open to question
con accurate, correct, established, factual, true, truthful, veracious; authentic

apogee *n syn* see APEX 2

Apollyon *n syn* see DEVIL 1

apologetic *adj syn* see REMORSEFUL

apologetical *adj syn* see APOLOGY 1

apologia *n syn* see APOLOGY 1
rel clarification, elucidation, explanation, interpretation

apologue *n syn* see ALLEGORY 2

apology *n* 1 a presentation intended to justify or defend something <the white paper is essentially an *apology* for recent foreign policy>
syn apologetic, apologia, defense, justification; *compare* EXCUSE 1
rel excuse, extenuation, mitigation, palliation; advocating, advocation, championing, espousal, espousing, support
idiom pleading one's cause, putting in a good word for, speaking up for
con blame, censure, condemnation, decrial, reprehension, reprobation
2 an acknowledgment expressing regret for a wrong, improper, or discommoding act <murmured a brief *apology* for her lateness>
syn excuse, regrets; *compare* EXCUSE 1
rel amends, atonement; acknowledgment, admission, concession, confession, mea culpa; reparation, redress, satisfaction
3 *syn* see EXCUSE 3

aporetic *adj syn* see INCREDULOUS

apostasy *n syn* see DEFECTION
rel perfidy, treacherousness

apostate *n syn* see RENEGADE
rel bolter; dissenter, nonconformist, recusant
con adherent, follower, partisan; convert, proselyte

apostatize *vb syn* see DEFECT

a posteriori *adj syn* see INDUCTIVE

apostle *n syn* see MISSIONARY

apothecary *n syn* see DRUGGIST

apothegm *n syn* see MAXIM

apotheosis *n* 1 the consummate form, example, or instance (as of a quality) <the *apotheosis* of vulgarity>
syn epitome, last word, quintessence, ultimate; *compare* EMBODIMENT
rel acme, culmination, height, peak, summit
idiom ‖the living end
2 a raising to a state of eminent triumph or glory <the *apotheosis* of a folk hero>
syn aggrandizement, deification, dignification, exaltation, glorification
rel elevation, ennoblement, enshrinement, idolization, immortalization, lionization
con debasement, defamation, degradation, denigration, sullying

appall *vb syn* see DISMAY 1
rel awe, faze, overawe
con brace (up), buck up, cheer (up); assure, hearten, inspire, inspirit
ant embolden, nerve

appalling *adj syn* see FEARFUL 3
rel daunting, dismaying, horrifying; bewildering, confounding, dumbfounding
con assuring, heartening, inspiriting
ant reassuring

appanage *n syn* see RIGHT 2

apparatus *n syn* see EQUIPMENT
rel implement, instrument, tool, utensil; furnishings, provisions, supplies

apparel *vb syn* see CLOTHE
rel appoint
con bare, denude
ant divest

apparel n syn see CLOTHES

apparent adj 1 syn see CLEAR 5
  rel ponderable; noticeable, prominent;
  discernible, observable, perceivable
  idiom plain as day, plain to be seen
  con ambiguous, hidden, obscure
  ant inapparent
  2 being other than seems to be the case
  < her apparent goodwill masked an inner
  loathing >
  syn Barmecidal, illusive, illusory, ostensible, seeming, semblant
  rel deceptive, delusive, delusory, misleading; credible, plausible, specious; factitious, fake, false, pseudo, sham, supposititious, suppositious
  con genuine, true, valid; basic, essential,
  fundamental, inherent, intrinsic
  ant actual, real

apparently adv syn see OSTENSIBLY

apparition n a visible appearance of something not present and especially of a dead
  person < illusions that the superstitious
  see as apparitions >
  syn bogey, eidolon, ghost, ‖haunt, phantasm, phantom, revenant, shade, shadow,
  specter, spectrum, spirit, ‖spook, umbra,
  wraith
  rel delusion, hallucination, illusion; corposant, foxfire, ignis fatuus, jack-o'-lantern, marshfire, Saint Elmo's fire, will-o'-the-wisp

appeal n 1 syn see PRAYER
  rel asking, requesting, solicitation
  con claim, demand, exaction; kick, objection, protest
  2 syn see ATTRACTION 1
  3 syn see CHARM 3
  rel draw; pleasantness
  con disagreeableness, unpleasantness

appeal vb 1 syn see BEG
  2 syn see PETITION
  3 syn see INTEREST

appealing adj syn see ATTRACTIVE 1

appear vb 1 to become visible < the sun
  appeared from behind a cloud >
  syn emerge, loom, show
  rel arrive, come; arise, emanate, issue,
  materialize, outcrop, rise, spring
  idiom come in sight, come into view,
  meet (or strike) the eye, show one's face
  con go, leave; depart, retire, withdraw
  ant disappear, vanish
  2 syn see SEEM
  idiom give an appearance of, strike one as

appearance n 1 the state or form in which
  one appears < his disheveled appearance
  surprised his guests >
  syn aspect, look, mien, seeming
  rel air, bearing, countenance, demeanor,
  manner
  2 usu appearances pl outward and often
  deceptive indication or look < to all appearances he was guilty >
  syn face, guise, seeming, semblance,
  show, showing, simulacrum; compare
  MASK

rel fiction, make-believe, pretense, pretension; disguise, facade, front, masquerade,
  outside, pose
  idiom outward show
  con fact, reality, truth

appease vb 1 syn see PACIFY
  rel calm (down), ease, soothe; extenuate,
  gloss (over), palliate, whitewash
  con annoy, bother, irk, vex; anger, enrage, incense, infuriate; discompose, disturb, perturb, upset
  ant exasperate
  2 syn see SATISFY 3
  rel ease, relieve; cater (to), coddle, pamper, spoil
  ant aggravate

appellation n syn see NAME 1

appellative n syn see NAME 1

append vb syn see ADD 1

appendage n something accompanying or
  attached to another thing to which it is
  usually subordinate or nonessential < people to whom culture is a mere appendage
  to life >
  syn accessory, adjunct, appendix, appurtenance
  rel auxiliary, incidental, subsidiary, supplement; collateral, extra, nonessential

appendix n 1 additional material subjoined
  to a writing and especially a book < a
  dictionary with an appendix of new
  words >
  syn addendum, codicil, rider, supplement
  2 rel APPENDAGE, accessory, adjunct,
  appurtenance

apperception n syn see RECOGNITION 1
  rel apprehension, grasp, perception; comprehension, understanding

appertain vb 1 syn see BELONG 2
  2 syn see BEAR (on or upon)

appetence n syn see APPETITE 1

appetent adj syn see EAGER
  rel craving, desirous, lusting, yearning
  idiom consumed with desire

appetite n 1 a natural enjoyment of food
  < all fell to with a hearty appetite >
  syn appetence, stomach, taste
  rel gluttony, greed, hunger, voracity;
  epicurism, gourmandise
  2 syn see DESIRE 1
  rel cupidity, greed, urgency
  con abnegation, asceticism, renunciation,
  self-denial; distaste, revulsion
  3 an attraction toward something < had a
  great appetite for gossip >
  syn fondness, inclination, liking, soft
  spot, taste, weakness
  rel bent, bias, flair, leaning, penchant,
  proclivity, propensity
  con disinclination, dislike, distaste; disinterest, unconcern

appetition n syn see DESIRE 1

appetizer n food or drink served before a
  meal to stimulate appetite < appetizers
  such as cocktails, and canapés >
  syn antipasto, hors d'oeuvre, whet,
  zakuska
  rel dainty, delicacy, goody, tidbit; savory

appetizing adj syn see PALATABLE
  ant disgusting, nauseating

applaud vb 1 syn see COMMEND 2
  rel boost, plug
  ant censure; admonish

---

2 to express enthusiastic approval < *applauded* wildly when his team won a point>
syn cheer, rise (to), root
rel acclaim, extol, laud, praise; eulogize, glorify, magnify, panegyrize
con deride, mock, ridicule, taunt; contemn, disdain, scorn, scout
ant boo; hiss

applause *n* public expression of approbation < her appearance was greeted with *applause*>
syn acclaim, acclamation, plaudit(s)
rel cheers, hand, ovation, round; cheering, clapping, rooting
con derision, mockery, ridicule, taunting; Bronx cheer, raspberry
ant booing, hissing

‖**apple knocker** *n syn see* RUSTIC

apple-polish *vb syn see* FAWN

apple-polisher *n syn see* SYCOPHANT

‖**applesauce** *n syn see* NONSENSE 2

appliance *n syn see* USE 1

applicability *n syn see* USE 3
con irrelevance, unsuitability
ant inapplicability

applicable *adj* **1** *syn see* RELEVANT
rel alliable, associable, compatible, congenial, connective
con incompatible, uncongenial; inappropriate, unfit, unsuitable
ant inapplicable
2 *syn see* FIT 1
rel correct, good, seemly
idiom as it ought to be, as it should be
con improper, incorrect

applicant *n syn see* CANDIDATE

application *n* **1** *syn see* ATTENTION 1
rel busyness, zeal; energy, indefatigability
con bemusement, wool-gathering; faineance, laziness, sloth
ant indolence
2 *syn see* USE 1
3 *syn see* EXERCISE 1
4 *syn see* PRAYER

applicative *adj syn see* RELEVANT

applicatory *adj syn see* RELEVANT

apply *vb* **1** *syn see* ADDRESS 3
rel set about, take on, undertake; drudge, grind, toil
idiom burn the midnight oil, keep one's nose to the grindstone, work like a horse (*or* dog *or* ‖nigger); concern (oneself) with something, set (one's hand) to something
con let slide, neglect, pass over, slight
2 *syn see* BEAR (on *or* upon)
idiom come into relation with
3 *syn see* RESORT 2
rel appeal, petition; beg, beseech, entreat, implore, supplicate; importune, press, urge
idiom make application to
4 *syn see* USE 2

apply (to) *vb syn see* ADDRESS 4

appoint *vb* **1** *syn see* DESIGNATE 2
rel accredit, authorize, commission
con cashier, discharge, dismiss; debar, exclude, reject
2 *syn see* FURNISH 1
rel embellish, enrich, furbish, garnish; dress up, set off, spruce (up)
con denude, dismantle, divest, strip

appointment *n* **1** *syn see* JOB 2
2 *syn see* ENGAGEMENT 3

apportion *vb* **1** *syn see* ALLOT
rel divide, partition, share
con assemble, collect, gather
2 to separate something into shares with care and accuracy and distribute it among a number < Christ *apportioned* the loaves and fishes>
syn divide, ‖divvy, parcel, portion, prorate, quota, ration, share, ‖shift
rel accord, award, bestow, distribute; give, grant, present; part, separate, split
3 *syn see* ADMINISTER 2
rel dish out, serve

apportionment *n syn see* RATION

apposite *adj syn see* RELEVANT
rel felicitous, happy; opportune, pat, seasonable, timely
idiom to the point (*or* purpose)
con awkward, inept; casual, haphazard, hit-or-miss, random
ant inapposite, inapt

appositeness *n syn see* ORDER 11

appraisal *n* **1** *syn see* ESTIMATE 1
2 *syn see* ESTIMATION 1

appraise *vb syn see* ESTIMATE 1
rel adjudge, deem, esteem, judge; audit, examine, inspect, scrutinize
idiom set (*or* place) a value on, take the measure of

appraisement *n syn see* ESTIMATE 1
2 *syn see* ESTIMATION 1

appreciable *adj syn see* PERCEPTIBLE
rel noticeable; apparent, clear, evident, manifest, obvious, plain; concrete, material, real, substantial
con impalpable, imperceptible, imponderable, insensible, intangible
ant inappreciable

appreciate *vb* **1** to hold in high estimation < *appreciate* the kindness of a friend>
syn apprize, cherish, esteem, prize, treasure, value; *compare* ADMIRE 1
rel admire, regard, respect; adore, ‖eat up, enjoy, like, love, relish
idiom rate highly, set great store by, think much (*or* well) of
con contemn, disapprove, disdain, scorn; decry, depreciate, disparage
ant despise
2 *syn see* ADMIRE 1
rel enjoy, like, savor
con contemn, disdain, scorn
3 *syn see* KNOW 1
rel catch, seize, take in

appreciation *n syn see* TESTIMONIAL 3

apprehend *vb* **1** to recognize the existence or meaning of < as a child learns to *apprehend* the relation between naughtiness and punishment>
syn accept, catch, compass, comprehend, conceive, cotton (to *or* on to), ‖dig, follow, grasp, make out, see, take, take in, tumble (to), twig, understand
rel realize, recognize, sense; absorb, digest, seize; catch on, wise (up); penetrate
idiom catch (*or* get) the drift of, get the idea, get through one's head, make head or tail of
ant misapprehend
2 *syn see* ARREST 2
3 *syn see* FORESEE
rel dread, fear

idiom be on pins and needles, have one's heart in one's mouth, wait with bated breath
4 *syn* see KNOW 1
idiom be acquainted with, be cognizant of

apprehensible *adj syn* see UNDERSTAND-ABLE

apprehension *n* **1** *syn* see IDEA
2 *syn* see ARREST
3 fear that something is going or will go wrong <had the strongest *apprehension* about her sister's health>
syn apprehensiveness, foreboding, misgiving, premonition, prenotion, presage, presentiment
rel agitation, angst, anxiety, care, concern, disquiet, disquietude, solicitude, unease, uneasiness, worry; alarm, dread, fear, panic
idiom the anxious seat
con assurance, composure, equanimity, sangfroid, self-possession; faith, reliance, trust
ant confidence

apprehensive *adj* **1** *syn* see AWARE
2 *syn* see FEARFUL 2
ant confident

apprehensiveness *n* *syn* see APPREHENSION 3

apprentice *n* *syn* see NOVICE
rel starter; amateur
con adept, expert, specialist

apprenticed *adj syn* see BOUND 2

apprise *vb syn* see INFORM 2
rel announce, communicate, declare, proclaim, publish; disclose, discover, divulge, reveal, tell
idiom make known to, serve (one) notice

apprize *vb syn* see APPRECIATE 1

approach *vb* **1** to come or go near or nearer <as a boy *approaches* manhood>
syn approximate, near, nigh
rel achieve, arrive (at), attain, gain, hit, make, reach; draw on
idiom come to close quarters with
con recede, retire, retreat, withdraw; depart, go, leave
2 *syn* see ADDRESS 4
rel advise, confer, consult, counsel, negotiate, parley; beg, beseech, entreat, implore, plead, supplicate
3 *syn* see REACH 3
4 *syn* see AMOUNT 2
con depart, deviate, digress; differ, disaccord, disharmonize, vary
5 *syn* see BORDER 3

approach *n syn* see OVERTURE 1
rel attempt, endeavor, essay, try; call, invitation
ant withdrawal

approaching *adj syn* see FORTHCOMING

approbate *vb syn* see APPROVE 1

approbation *n* warmly commending acceptance or agreement <expressed *approbation* of their progress>
syn approval, benediction, blessing, favor, OK (*or* okay)

---

syn synonym(s)   *rel* related word(s)
ant antonym(s)   *con* contrasted word(s)
idiom idiomatic equivalent(s)
‖ use limited; if in doubt, see a dictionary

rel commendation, countenance, goodwill, sanction; admiration, esteem, liking, regard, respect; pleasure, satisfaction
con censure, condemnation, criticism, disapproval, disfavor, reprehension; annoyance, disgust, irritation; distress, regret, sorrow
ant disapprobation

approbative *adj syn* see FAVORABLE 1

approbatory *adj syn* see FAVORABLE 1

appropinquity *n syn* see PROXIMITY

appropriate *vb* **1** to take over as if by preeminent right <limitations on the right of the state to *appropriate* private property>
syn accroach, annex, arrogate, commandeer, confiscate, expropriate, preempt, seize, sequester, take; compare ARROGATE 1
rel grab, grasp, snatch; claim, exact, extort, wrench; conscript, draft, press
idiom help oneself to, lay hold of, make free with, take possession of
2 *syn* see STEAL 1
rel despoil, spoil; forage, raid
3 *syn* see ARROGATE 1

appropriate *adj* **1** *syn* see FIT 1
rel apposite, germane, pertinent, relevant; opportune, pat, seasonable, timely
con incompatible, incongruous, inconsonant
ant inappropriate
2 *syn* see GOOD 2
rel agreeable, desirable, enjoyable, pleasant; acceptable, admissible, eligible, entitled, right, worthy
con disagreeable undesirable, unpleasant; inadmissible, ineligible, unworthy, wrong
ant inappropriate
3 *syn* see JUST 3
con unfair, unjustified, unmerited, unreasonable; unsuitable
ant inappropriate
4 *syn* see TRUE 7
ant inappropriate

appropriately *adv syn* see WELL 4

appropriateness *n* **1** *syn* see USE 3
2 *syn* see ORDER 11

appropriation *n* property (as money) set apart or given by official or formal action for a predetermined use by others <an increased *appropriation* for public housing>
syn grant, subsidy, subvention
rel allotment, allowance, stipend; aid, assistance, grant-in-aid, help

approval *n syn* see APPROBATION
rel applause, commendation, compliment; acceptance, endorsement, sanction, suffrage
con depreciation, derogation, disparagement
ant disapproval

approve *vb* **1** to find acceptable <they were unable to *approve* his behavior>
syn accept, approbate, countenance, favor, go (for), hold (with)
rel back (up), stand by, support, sustain, uphold; bear, endure, put up (with), tolerate
idiom be in favor of, pat on the back, take kindly to, think well (*or* highly) of, view with approval (*or* favor)

con deprecate, disfavor, dislike, frown (on *or* upon); object (to), oppose

ant disapprove

2 to give an often formal expression of approval and support <the committee *approved* the plans for the new clubhouse>

syn accredit, certify, endorse, OK (*or* okay), sanction

rel applaud, compliment, commend; confirm, initial, ratify; clear

con refuse, reject, repudiate, spurn; censure, condemn, criticize, reprehend, reprobate

ant disapprove

approving *adj syn* see FAVORABLE 1

approximal *adj syn* see ADJACENT 3

approximate *adj* 1 *syn* see COMPARATIVE

2 *syn* see RUDE 3

approximate *vb* 1 *syn* see APPROACH 1

idiom be in the neighborhood of

2 *syn* see ESTIMATE 3

approximately *adv syn* see NEARLY

idiom in round numbers, right about

ant exactly, precisely

appulse *n syn* see IMPACT

appurtenance *n syn* see APPENDAGE

rel appointment (*usu* appointments *pl*), equipment, furnishings, furniture

appurtenant *adj syn* see AUXILIARY

a priori *adj syn* see DEDUCTIVE

apriorism *n syn* see ASSUMPTION 2

apropos *adj syn* see RELEVANT

rel meet, proper

con clumsy, gauche, inappropriate, inept

ant malapropos

apropos *prep* in reference to <it is impossible to reach a decision *apropos* this matter at present>

syn about, against, anent, as for, as regards, as respects, as to, concerning, in re, in respect to, re, regarding, respecting, touching, toward, with respect to

apt *adj* 1 having a tendency or inclination <it is *apt* to be cool late in the evening>

syn given, inclined, liable, likely, prone

rel disposed, minded, predisposed

con averse, disinclined, indisposed, loath; doubtful, improbable, unlikely

2 *syn* see FIT 1

rel apposite, apropos, pertinent, relevant; compelling, convincing, telling; exact, nice, precise

con awkward, clumsy, maladroit

ant inapt, inept

3 *syn* see QUICK 2

rel alert, brainy, bright; gifted, talented

con laggard

aptness *n* 1 *syn* see ORDER 11

rel helpfulness, propitiousness

2 *syn* see GIFT 2

‖**apurpose** *adv syn* see INTENTIONALLY

apyrous *adj syn* see NONCOMBUSTIBLE

aquake *adj syn* see TREMULOUS

aqua vitae *n syn* see LIQUOR 2

aqueduct *n syn* see CHANNEL 1

aquiculture *n syn* see HYDROPONICS

aquiver *adj syn* see TREMULOUS

arab *n* 1 *syn* see VAGABOND

‖2 *syn* see PEDDLER

arable *adj* suitable for tilling and for growing crops <used their *arable* land intensively>

syn cultivable, cultivatable, tillable

rel fat, fertile, fruitful, productive

con barren, sterile, unfertile, unfruitful, unproductive

arbiter *n syn* see JUDGE 1

rel moderator

arbitrary *adj* 1 characterized by or given to willful and often unwise or irrational choices and demands <a proud fitful *arbitrary* nature>

syn capricious, erratic, freakish, vagarious, wayward, whimsical, whimsied

rel undisciplined, unruly, wild, willful; arrogant, unconstrained, unreasonable; careless, heedless, impetuous, indiscreet, precipitate, rash; kooky, screwball, zany

con circumspect, discreet, heedful, judicious, politic, reflective; calculating, discriminative, judicial, prudent, well-advised

2 *syn* see ABSOLUTE 4

rel authoritarian, dictatorial, magisterial, oracular

con lawful, legal, licit, rightful

ant legitimate

arbitrate *vb syn* see JUDGE 1

rel intermediate, intervene, mediate; appease, placate, soothe

arbitrator *n* 1 *syn* see MODERATOR

2 *syn* see JUDGE 1

arbor *n* a shelter (as in a garden) formed of vines or branches or of latticework covered with climbing shrubs or vines <the children picnicked under the *arbor*>

syn bower, pergola

rel belvedere, casino, gazebo, summerhouse

arc *n syn* see CURVE

arcadia *n syn* see UTOPIA

arcane *adj syn* see MYSTERIOUS

rel eerie, uncanny, weird; anagogic, mystical

arced *adj syn* see CURVED

arch *n syn* see CURVE

arch *adj* 1 *syn* see FIRST 3

rel conspicuous, notable, noteworthy; extraordinary, extreme

2 *syn* see SAUCY 1

rel impish, mischievous, playful, roguish, waggish; bold, cheeky, cocky, flippant, fresh; derisive, mocking, twitting

con modest, quiet, respectful, submissive

3 *syn* see COY 2

archaic *adj* 1 *syn* see OLD-FASHIONED

idiom behind the times, of the old school

con fresh, modern, new, novel; fashionable

ant up-to-date

2 *syn* see PRIMITIVE 3

arched *adj syn* see CURVED

archetypal *adj syn* see TYPICAL 1

archetype *n* 1 *syn* see ORIGINAL 1

2 *syn* see MODEL 2

archfiend *n syn* see DEVIL 2

archilochian *adj syn* see SARCASTIC

archimage *n syn* see MAGICIAN 1

architect *n syn* see FATHER 2

architecture *n syn* see MAKEUP 1

archive *n, usu* **archives** *pl* 1 *syn* see LIBRARY

2 *syn* see DOCUMENT

rel papers, parchments, scrolls, writings; clippings, cuttings, excerpts, extracts, fragments, gleanings, remains

arciform *adj syn* see CURVED

arctic *adj syn* see COLD 1
rel bitter, boreal, hyperborean; numbing, rigorous; hibernal, hiemal
idiom cold as charity, cold enough to freeze a brass monkey
ant torrid

ardent *adj* 1 *syn* see IMPASSIONED
rel enthusiastic, urgent; avid, desirous, eager, keen
con calm, composed, imperturbable, nonchalant; apathetic, impassive, phlegmatic; disinterested, dispassionate, impartial, uninterested
ant cool
2 very deep or moving < had an *ardent* longing for knowledge >
syn extreme, intense
rel crying, importunate, insistent, urgent; great, mighty, powerful, strong
con feeble, minimal, slight, trivial
3 *syn* see EAGER
rel hasty, impetuous, impulsive, precipitate; fervid, fiery, hectic, hot; uncontrolled, ungoverned; earnest, intent, urgent, vehement
con dull, heavy, inert, leaden, lumpish; languid, lethargic, listless; apathetic, impassive, phlegmatic
ant easygoing
4 *syn* see FAITHFUL 1
5 *syn* see HOT 1
6 *syn* see SPIRITUOUS

ardor *n* 1 *syn* see PASSION 6
rel avidity; gusto, spirit, verve, zest; excitement, galvanization, quickening, stimulation
con aloofness, detachment, disinterest, unconcern; apathy, lackadaisy, languor, listlessness
ant coolness; indifference
2 *syn* see EAGERNESS
rel ardency, fervor, warmth
3 *syn* see FIDELITY 1
rel adoration, love, worship

arduous *adj* 1 *syn* see HARD 6
2 *syn* see STEEP 1
3 *syn* see TIGHT 4

arduously *adv syn* see HARD 8
con easily, facilely
ant effortlessly

area *n* 1 a distinguishable extent of surface and especially of the earth's surface < a large wooded *area* >
syn belt, region, territory, tract, zone
rel expanse, stretch; district, locality, place; lot, plot, section; terrain; circuit
2 *syn* see LOCALITY 1

arena *n syn* see SCENE 4

arete *n syn* see EXCELLENCE

argent *adj syn* see SILVERY

argentate *adj syn* see SILVERY

argenteous *adj syn* see SILVERY

argentine *adj syn* see SILVERY

argot *n syn* see DIALECT 2

arguable *adj syn* see MOOT

argue *vb* 1 *syn* see DISCUSS 1

rel analyze, investigate, review, sift, study, ventilate; expostulate, object, protest, remonstrate
2 to contend in words < *arguing* about who should answer the phone >
syn argufy, bicker, dispute, hassle, quibble, squabble, wrangle; *compare* QUARREL
rel differ, disaccord, disagree, dissent; balk, demur, jib; clash, conflict
idiom bandy words, have it out, join (*or* take) issue
con accord, agree, concur
3 *syn* see INDICATE 2
4 *syn* see MAINTAIN 2

argue (into) *vb syn* see INDUCE 1

argufy *vb syn* see ARGUE 2

argument *n* 1 *syn* see REASON 3
rel basis, foundation; position, posture, stance, standpoint
2 a vigorous often heated discussion of a moot question < their continuing *argument* over household expenses >
syn contention, controversy, dispute, hurrah, rumpus
rel argumentation, debate, disputation, polemic; disagreement, dissension, squabbling; embroilment, fuss, hassle, wrangle
3 *syn* see SUBJECT 2
rel position, proposition, statement, thesis

argumentation *n* the act or art or an exercise of one's powers of argument < noted for his skill in *argumentation* >
syn debate, dialectic, disputation, forensic, mooting
rel argument, controversy, dispute; declamation, elocution, eloquence, oratory, rhetoric

argumentative *adj syn* see CONTENTIOUS 2

argute *adj* 1 *syn* see SHREWD
2 *syn* see ACUTE 4

aria *n syn* see SONG 2

arid *adj* 1 *syn* see DRY 1
rel barren, infertile, sterile, unfruitful
con fecund, fertile, fruitful
2 lacking in interest or liveliness < some of the most *arid* prose ever written >
syn bromidic, dry, dryasdust, dull, dusty, insipid, tedious, uninteresting, weariful, wearisome; *compare* TEPID 2, UNORIGINAL
rel drab, dreary, flat, heavy, lackluster, leaden, unanimated, unlively; academic, bookish, pedantic; boring, humdrum, monotonous, unimaginative, uninspired
con appealing, bright, lively, sparkling, stimulating, vigorous, vivid

aright *adv syn* see WELL 1

arise *vb* 1 *syn* see RISE 4
ant recline; slump
2 *syn* see ROLL OUT
3 *syn* see SPRING 1
rel ensue, follow, succeed
4 *syn* see BEGIN 2

aristarch *n syn* see CRITIC

aristo *n syn* see GENTLEMAN

aristocracy *n* the highest stratum of a society < the self-centered attitude of some *aristocracies* >
syn aristoi, blue blood, carriage trade, crème de la crème, elite, flower, gentility, gentry, haut monde, optimacy, patriciate, quality, society, upper class, upper crust, who's who

---

syn synonym(s)   *rel* related word(s)
ant antonym(s)   *con* contrasted word(s)
idiom idiomatic equivalent(s)
|| use limited; if in doubt, see a dictionary

rel nobility, noblesse, patricians; county; beau monde, bon ton, jet set, smart set
con canaille, mob, rabble, riffraff; commoners, commons, masses, people, plebeians

aristocrat *n syn* see GENTLEMAN
ant commoner

aristoi *n syn* see ARISTOCRACY

arithmetic *n syn* see COMPUTATION

arm *n* 1 *syn* see INLET
2 *syn* see ANNEX
3 *syn* see POWER 4

arm *vb syn* see FURNISH 1
rel prepare, ready
idiom put in (or into) shape
ant disarm

armament *n syn* see DEFENSE 1

armamentarium *n syn* see SUPPLY

armed forces *n pl syn* see TROOP 2

armistice *n syn* see TRUCE

armor *n syn* see DEFENSE 1
rel cloak, mantle, shroud, veil; buckler, cover, screen, shelter

armory *n* a place where military arms and supplies are stored < the problem of weapon theft from *armories* >
syn arsenal, depot, dump, magazine

army *n syn* see MULTITUDE 1
rel crush, horde, mob, press, throng

aroma *n* 1 *syn* see FRAGRANCE
2 *syn* see SMELL 1
rel fetor, mephitis, reek, stench, stink

aromal *adj syn* see SWEET 2
rel penetrating, piquant, pungent
ant acrid

aromatic *adj syn* see SWEET 2
ant acrid

aromatize *vb syn* see SCENT 2

around *adv* 1 *syn* see ABOUT 1
2 *syn* see THROUGH 1
3 *syn* see ABOUT 4
4 *syn* see ABOUT 6

around *prep syn* see ABOUT 1

around *adj syn* see EXTANT 1

around-the-clock *adj syn* see CONTINUAL

arouse *vb syn* see STIR 1
rel alert, excite, work up; electrify, thrill; fire, inflame
idiom fan the fire (or flame), raise to fever heat, set on fire, stir one's blood (or feelings)
con allay, alleviate, assuage, ease, mitigate, relieve; mollify, pacify, placate
ant calm, quiet

arraign *vb syn* see ACCUSE
rel cite, summon; test, try
idiom bring to book, call to account
con absolve, acquit, exculpate, exonerate, vindicate; defend, justify

arrange *vb* 1 *syn* see ORDER 1
rel assort, categorize, pigeonhole, sort
con disorder, disorganize, disturb, unsettle; confuse, jumble, muddle, tumble; disperse, scatter
ant derange, disarrange
2 *syn* see DESIGN 3
3 *syn* see PLAN 2
4 *syn* see NEGOTIATE 1
rel design, plan, project, scheme
5 *syn* see HARMONIZE 4

arrangement *n syn* see ORDER 3
rel layout, lineup, setup; method, system

arrant *adj* 1 *syn* see UTTER
rel plain, pure, regular, sheer
2 *syn* see SHAMELESS

array *vb* 1 *syn* see ORDER 1
ant disarray
2 *syn* see CLOTHE

array *n* 1 *syn* see GROUP 3
2 *syn* see DISPLAY 2
rel exhibition, exposing, showing; arranging, marshaling, ordering

arrear *n*, *usu* arrears *pl syn* see DEBT 3

arrearage *n* 1 *syn* see DEBT 3
2 *syn* see INDEBTEDNESS 1

arrect *adj* 1 *syn* see ERECT
2 *syn* see ATTENTIVE 1

arrest *vb* 1 to bring to a halt < science cannot yet *arrest* the process of aging>
syn check, halt, interrupt, stall, stay; *compare* STOP 3
rel balk, frustrate, thwart; choke, obstruct, stop (up); delay, detain, hamper, hinder, restrain, retard; interfere, interpose, intervene; contain, stem, withstand
idiom bring to a halt (or stand or standstill), bring up short, check in full career, cut short
con advance, forward, further, promote; expedite, hasten, quicken, speed
2 to take and hold in custody under authority of the law < *arrested* for murder>
syn apprehend, ‖bust, detain, nab, pick up, pinch, pull in, run in; *compare* CATCH 1
rel immure, imprison, incarcerate, jail, lock (up), ‖slough; attach
idiom lay by the heels, lay hands on
con discharge, free, liberate, release

arrest *n* the taking and holding of a person in custody under authority of the law < unwilling to submit to *arrest*>
syn apprehension, arrestation, arrestment, detention, ‖nab, pickup, pinch
rel capture, catch, collar, seizure, taking
con discharge, freeing, liberation, release

arrestation *n syn* see ARREST

arresting *adj syn* see NOTICEABLE
rel attractive, enchanting, fascinating; affective, appealing, impressive, moving, touching
idiom enough to make one stop and take notice
con common, familiar, ordinary, run-of-the-mill; hackneyed, stereotyped, trite

arrestive *adj syn* see NOTICEABLE

arrestment *n syn* see ARREST

arride *vb syn* see PLEASE 2
rel beguile, divert, entertain, recreate
idiom tickle one's fancy
con bore, ennui, jade, weary

arrival *n* 1 the reaching of a destination < the train was late in its *arrival* >
syn advent, coming
rel appearance, emergence, entrance, issuance, manifestation
con disappearance, going, leaving, withdrawal; recession, retirement, retreat
ant departure
2 *syn* see SUCCESS

arrive *vb* 1 *syn* see COME 1
con get away, go, retire
ant depart
2 *syn* see SUCCEED 3

arriviste *n syn* see UPSTART

arrogance *n syn* see PRIDE 3
ant humility

arrogant *adj* 1 *syn* see PROUD 1
rel domineering, imperative, peremptory;
affected, artificial, highfalutin, mannered,
showy
idiom too big for one's britches
con humble; deferential, submissive; abject, obsequious, subservient, truckling
ant meek
2 *syn* see POMPOUS 1

arrogate *vb* 1 to claim or take over in a
high-handed manner < *arrogated* to himself the right to make all decisions >
syn accroach, appropriate, assume, commandeer, preempt, usurp; *compare* APPRO-
PRIATE 1
rel annex, preempt, preoccupy, sequester;
grab, seize, take, take over
idiom help oneself to, make free with,
take into one's own hands
con cede, relinquish, resign, surrender,
yield
ant renounce
2 *syn* see APPROPRIATE 1

arrondi *adj syn* see CURVED

arroyo *n syn* see RAVINE

*****arse** *n syn* see BUTTOCKS

arsenal *n* 1 *syn* see ARMORY
2 *syn* see DEPOT 2

arsonist *n syn* see INCENDIARY

arsy-varsy *adj syn* see UPSIDE-DOWN 2

art *n* 1 a usually acquired proficiency in
doing or performing < there's an *art* to
competent public speaking >
syn adroitness, craft, cunning, dexterity,
expertise, know-how, skill
rel capability, competence, handiness,
proficiency; address, finesse, ||savvy
con clumsiness, maladroitness
2 *syn* see CUNNING 2
rel acuteness, astuteness
con candor, frankness, sincerity; direct-
ness, straightforewardness, bluffness,
bluntness
3 *syn* see TRADE 1

artery *n syn* see WAY 1

artful *adj syn* see SLY 2
rel diplomatic, oily, politic, smooth,
suave; facile, specious, superficial; adroit,
dexterous
ant artless

artfulness *n syn* see CUNNING 2

article *n* 1 *syn* see POINT 1
rel division, section, segment
2 *syn* see ESSAY 2
rel critique, manifesto, report, statement,
study, survey
3 *syn* see THING 3
rel detail, particular

articled *adj syn* see BOUND 2

articulate *adj* 1 *syn* see VOCAL 1
rel clear, distinct, intelligible
ant inarticulate; dumb
2 *syn* see VOCAL 3
rel meaningful, significant; garrulous,
prolix, talkative; uttering, venting

ant inarticulate

articulate *vb* 1 *syn* see INTEGRATE 3
rel connect, join, relate; methodize, order,
organize, systematize; adjust, coordinate,
harmonize, regulate; assemble, collect,
gather; unify
con dissect, resolve; divide, part, separate
2 to form speech sounds < regional differences in *articulating* the letter *r* >
syn enunciate, phonate, pronounce, say
rel sound, utter

articulation *n syn* see VOCALIZATION

artifice *n* 1 *syn* see CUNNING 2
rel ingenuity, inventiveness, originality;
adroitness, cleverness, keenness, quickness,
shrewdness; adeptness, proficiency
2 *syn* see TRICK 1
rel chicane, chicanery, trickery; knavery,
rascality, skulduggery; deceit, dissimulation, duplicity, guile

artificial *adj* 1 *syn* see SYNTHETIC
rel fabricated, fashioned, made
con native
ant natural
2 taking the place of something else and
especially of something finer or more
costly < *artificial* diamonds >
syn dummy, ersatz, false, imitation,
mock, sham, simulated, spurious, substitute; *compare* FICTITIOUS 2, SPURIOUS 3
rel fake, papier-mâché, ||pretend, unreal;
hollow, painted
con authentic, bona fide, genuine, real,
sure-enough, true, veritable
3 lacking in spontaneity and genuineness
< exchanged *artificial* smiles >
syn affected, assumed, feigned, put-on,
spurious
rel histrionic, insincere, overdone, quaint,
stagy, theatrical, unnatural; cute, cutesy,
goody-goody, mincing, overrefined, sim-
pering; contrived, forced, labored
con genuine, sincere, spontaneous, unaffected

artist *n syn* see EXPERT
rel ace, crackerjack, first-rater, shark,
topnotcher; genius, prodigy, wonder

artiste *n syn* see EXPERT

artless *adj syn* see NATURAL 5
rel free, relaxed; aboveboard, forthright,
straightforward; childlike, trusting, unsuspicious; untouched, virginal
con cunning, insidious, sly, wily; calculating, designing, intriguing, scheming; artificial, insincere
ant artful; affected

arty *adj syn* see PRETENTIOUS 3

arty-crafty *adj syn* see PRETENTIOUS 3

as *conj syn* see BECAUSE

as a rule *adv syn* see USUALLY 2

||**ascared** *adj syn* see AFRAID 1

ascend *vb* 1 to move upward to or toward
a summit < *ascend* a mountain >
syn climb, escalade, escalate, mount,
scale, upclimb, upgo
rel clamber, get up, scramble, shin; crest,
surmount, top
idiom scale the heights, work one's way
up
ant descend
2 *syn* see RISE 4

ascendancy *n syn* see SUPREMACY

ascendant *n* 1 *syn* see SUPREMACY

---

syn synonym(s)   *rel* related word(s)
ant antonym(s)   *con* contrasted word(s)
idiom idiomatic equivalent(s)
|| use limited; if in doubt, see a dictionary

2 *syn* see ANCESTOR 1
rel forerunner, precursor, predecessor
ant descendant

ascendant *adj syn* see DOMINANT 1

ascension *n syn* see ASCENT

ascent *n* a moving upward or an upward movement <the slow *ascent* of the creaky old elevator>
syn ascension, rise, rising
rel elevation, raising, uplifting
ant descent

ascertain *vb syn* see DISCOVER 3
rel ask, inquire, interrogate, query, question; appraise, inspect, observe, survey, view; consider, contemplate, study, weigh
con assume, presume; conjecture, guess, surmise

ascetic *adj syn* see SEVERE 1
rel abstemious, abstinent, forbearing; self-abasing, self-abnegating, self-denying, self-forgetful, selfless; disciplined, restrained, schooled, trained
con epicurean, sensual, sensuous, sybaritic; abandoned, dissolute, licentious, self-indulgent
ant luxurious, voluptuous

ascribe *vb* to refer especially to a supposed cause, source, or author <a manuscript commonly *ascribed* to Saint Augustine>
syn accredit, assign, attribute, charge, credit, impute, lay, refer
rel attach (to), connect (with), fix (on or upon), pin (on), saddle (on or upon or with); affix, fasten; conjecture, guess, surmise; adduce, advance, allege, cite

aseptic *adj syn* see UNDEMONSTRATIVE

as for *prep syn* see APROPOS

as good as *adv* 1 *syn* see NEARLY
2 *syn* see ALMOST 2

ash *n* the residue left when material is consumed by fire <cold whitened *ash* on the hearth>
syn ashes, cinders, clinkers
rel dross, scoria, slag; charcoal, coal(s), coke, ember(s); fumes, smoke, soot

ashake *adj syn* see TREMULOUS

ashamed *adj* humiliated or disconcerted usually by feelings of guilt, disgrace, or impropriety <*ashamed* of her brother's noisy boasting>
syn chagrined, mortified, shamed
rel abashed, discomfited, embarrassed; abased, humbled, humiliated; abject, hangdog, mean; contrite, penitent, repentant
idiom unable to show one's face
con arrogant, assured, overbearing, self-assured; vain, vainglorious
ant proud

ashen *adj syn* see PALE 1
rel corpselike, ghostly, macabre; blanched, bleached, decolorized, faded

ashes *n pl syn* see ASH

ashiver *adj syn* see TREMULOUS

ashy *adj syn* see PALE 1

aside *adv* 1 in a slanting or sloping direction <his head hung *aside* as if he lacked the strength to hold it up>
syn aslant, aslope, obliquely, sideways, sidewise, slant, slantingly, slantingways, slantly, slantways, slantwise, ||slaunchways, slopeways; compare SIDEWAYS 1
rel askance, askant, askew, awry; downgrade, downhill

con erectly, uprightly, vertically
2 *syn* see APART 2
3 *syn* see APIECE

||**aside** *prep syn* see NEAR 2

aside *n syn* see DIGRESSION

aside from *prep syn* see EXCEPT

asinine *adj syn* see SIMPLE 3
rel puerile; absurd, irrational, unreasonable
con prudent, sage, sane, sapient, wise; clever, intelligent, knowing, smart; rational, reasonable
ant judicious, sensible

ask *vb* 1 to call upon for an answer or information <*asked* him to explain his behavior>
syn catechize, examine, inquire, interrogate, query, question, quiz
rel argue, canvass, debate, deliberate, discuss, review, talk (over)
con answer, rejoin, reply, respond, retort
2 to seek to obtain by making one's needs or desires known <*asked* for time to consider the problem>
syn bespeak, desire, request, solicit
rel claim, demand, exact, require; beg, beseech, entreat, implore, importune
idiom put in for
3 *syn* see DEMAND 2
4 *syn* see INVITE
rel canvass, request, seek

askance *adv* 1 *syn* see AWRY 1
ant directly
2 with absence of approval or trust <a proceeding one must view more than a little *askance*>
syn distrustfully, doubtfully, mistrustfully, skeptically, suspiciously
rel captiously, critically, cynically, doubtingly; deprecatingly, depreciatively, disparagingly
con approvingly, favorably

askant *adv syn* see AWRY 1
ant directly

asker *n syn* see SUPPLIANT

askew *adv syn* see AWRY 1
ant straight

aslant *adv syn* see ASIDE 1

asleep *adj* 1 *syn* see DEAD 1
2 *syn* see NUMB 1
3 *syn* see INACTIVE

as long as *conj syn* see BECAUSE

aslope *adv syn* see ASIDE 1

as much as *adv syn* see ALMOST 2

asomatous *adj syn* see IMMATERIAL 1

aspect *n* 1 *syn* see APPEARANCE 1
rel countenance, face, visage; air, bearing, port, presence
2 *syn* see PHASE
rel point of view, slant, standpoint

asperity *n* 1 *syn* see DIFFICULTY 1
rel austerity, bitterness, grimness, harshness, inclemency, severity, stringency
con blandness, gentleness, mildness, softness
2 *syn* see INEQUALITY 1
3 *syn* see ACRIMONY
rel harshness, keenness, roughness, sharpness; irritability, snappishness, tartness, waspishness
con blandness, smoothness, suavity, urbanity; courtesy, gallantry
ant amenity

asperous *adj syn* see ROUGH 1
asperse *vb* 1 *syn* see MALIGN
  rel deride, mock, taunt; affront, insult, offend
  con applaud, commend, compliment
  2 *syn* see BAPTIZE
aspersion *n syn* see ANIMADVERSION
  rel abuse, invective, muck, vituperation; backbiting, calumny, detraction, scandal, slander; lampoon, libel, pasquinade, skit, squib
  con eulogy, extolling, laudation, praise; acclaim, acclamation, applause, plaudits; commendation, compliment
asphyxiate *vb syn* see SUFFOCATE
aspirant *n syn* see CANDIDATE
aspiration *n syn* see AMBITION 1
  rel aim, direction, goal, objective; desire, lust, passion, urge
aspire *vb* 1 *syn* see AIM 2
  rel hunger, long, pine, thirst; bid (for), strain (for *or* after), struggle (for), try (for)
  idiom cry for the moon, have at heart, have one's heart set on, reach for (*or* keep one's eyes on) the stars
  con condescend, deign, look down (on); grovel, stoop, wallow
  2 *syn* see RISE 4
aspiring *adj syn* see AMBITIOUS 1
  rel desirous, impassioned, urgent; wanting, wishful, yearning
as regards *prep syn* see APROPOS
as respects *prep syn* see APROPOS
ass *n* 1 *syn* see DONKEY 1
  2 *syn* see FOOL 1
*****ass** *n syn* see BUTTOCKS
assail *vb syn* see ATTACK 1
  rel beat, belabor, buffet, pound, pummel
  idiom round on
assailment *n syn* see ATTACK 1
assassin *n* a person hired or hirable to commit murder <found out who paid the *assassin* >
  syn bravo, cutthroat, gun, gunman, ‖gunsel, gunslinger, hatchet man, hit man, torpedo, triggerman; *compare* MURDERER
  rel apache, desperado, goon, ‖gorilla, highbinder, strong arm, thug
assassinate *vb syn* see MURDER 1
assault *n syn* see ATTACK 1
  rel brush, clash, invasion, melee, skirmish; brawl, contest, fracas, set-to
assault *vb syn* see ATTACK 1
  rel battle, fight, war; clash, collide, encounter, engage; skirmish
assay *vb* 1 *syn* see TRY 5
  rel venture
  idiom make an effort to
  2 *syn* see ESTIMATE 1
  rel demonstrate, prove, test, try; analyze, resolve; calculate, compute, reckon
assemblage *n syn* see GATHERING 1
assemble *vb* 1 *syn* see CONVOKE
  2 *syn* see GATHER 6
  rel associate, combine, unite; convene, convoke
  con dispel, dissipate, scatter; leave, part, quit, separate

---

  ant disperse
  3 *syn* see GROUP 1
  rel accumulate, aggregate, amass, garner; bunch, clump; bank, heap, mound, pile, stack
  con dispel, dissipate, scatter; leave, part, quit, separate; break up, disband
  ant disperse
  4 *syn* see MAKE 3
assembly *n* 1 *syn* see GATHERING 2
  rel association, band, conclave, party, troupe
  2 *syn* see GROUP 1
  rel crowd, push; faction, interest, sect, wing; brotherhood, fellowship, fraternity
  con masses, multitude; canaille, rabble, riffraff, ruck, trash
assent *vb* to give or express one's consent or concurrence <*assented* grudgingly to her plans for the evening>
  syn accede, acquiesce, agree, consent, subscribe, yes
  rel adopt, embrace, espouse; accept; abide, bear (with), endure, stand, suffer, tolerate; down, stomach, swallow, take; defer, relent, submit, yield
  idiom be at one with, cast one's vote for, give the nod of approval, go along with, see eye to eye with
  con rebuff, refuse, reject, scorn, scout, spurn; deny, gainsay
  ant dissent
assert *vb* 1 to state firmly, positively, or assuredly <he continued to *assert* his innocence>
  syn affirm, aver, avouch, avow, constate, declare, depose, predicate, profess, protest
  rel adduce, advance, allege, cite, claim, pretend; announce, broadcast, disseminate, proclaim, promulgate, publish, spread
  idiom have it
  con contradict, contravene, dispute, gainsay, negate, negative, traverse; confute, disprove, rebut, refute
  ant deny; controvert
  2 *syn* see MAINTAIN 2
  rel declare, express, utter, voice; advance, state, stipulate, submit
assertive *adj* 1 *syn* see EMPHATIC
  2 *syn* see AGGRESSIVE
  rel affirmative; arbitrary, dogmatic, peremptory, positive; assured, certain, cocksure, opinionated, opinionative, self-assured, sure; confident, presumptuous, sanguine, self-confident
  con bashful, diffident, modest, shy; amenable, biddable, docile, submissive
  ant retiring; acquiescent
assertory *adj syn* see AGGRESSIVE
assess *vb* 1 *syn* see LEVY
  2 *syn* see ESTIMATE 1
  rel calculate, compute; account, consider, deem, reckon, weigh
assessment *n* 1 *syn* see ESTIMATION 1
  2 *syn* see ESTIMATE 1
  3 *syn* see TAX 1
asset *n* 1 assets *pl syn* see MEAN 3
  rel bankroll, money; equity; principal
  ant liabilities
  2 *syn* see CREDIT 3
  rel distinction, glory, honor, ornament
  con detriment, disadvantage, discredit, liability

---

syn synonym(s)   *rel* related word(s)
ant antonym(s)   *con* contrasted word(s)
idiom idiomatic equivalent(s)
‖ use limited; if in doubt, see a dictionary

ant handicap

asshead *n syn* see FOOL 1

assiduous *adj* marked by careful attention or persistent application <learned to speak French fluently by *assiduous* practice>
syn diligent, industrious, operose, sedulous; *compare* BUSY 1
rel hardworking, laborious, moiling; indefatigable, tireless, untiring, unwearied, zealous
idiom hard at it
con casual, haphazard, happy-go-lucky, hit-or-miss, intermittent, random; careless, lax, remiss, slack, sloppy, slovenly; indolent, lazy, slothful
ant desultory

assiduously *adv syn* see HARD 3

assign *vb 1 syn* see TRANSFER 4
2 *syn* see ALLOT
rel establish, fix, set, settle
3 *syn* see ASCRIBE
rel associate, link, relate; classify, pigeonhole
4 *syn* see PRESCRIBE 2
rel decide, determine; commit, consign, entrust, relegate

assignation *n syn* see ENGAGEMENT 3
rel agreement, arrangement, understanding; get-together

assignee *n syn* see AGENT 2

assignment *n syn* see TASK 1
rel incumbency, liability, obligation, responsibility

assimilate *vb 1 syn* see ABSORB 1
rel imbue, infuse, ingrain, inoculate, leaven, suffuse; adopt, embrace, espouse; corner, engross, monopolize
2 *syn* see EQUATE 2

assimilation *n syn* see RECOGNITION 1
rel awareness, consciousness, mindfulness

assist *vb syn* see HELP 1
rel accompany, attend, escort; concur, cooperate
con clog, fetter, trammel; forestall, prevent; burden, encumber, handicap, tax, weigh down
ant hamper; impede

assist *n syn* see HELP 1

assistance *n syn* see HELP 1
rel backing, supporting, upholding; advantage, avail, profit, use; appropriation, grant, subsidy, subvention
con checking, hampering, hindering, hindrance; balking, foiling, frustration, thwarting
ant impediment, impeding; obstructing, obstruction

assistant *n 1 syn* see HELPER
2 a person who takes over part of the duties of a superior <started as *assistant* to the secretary>
syn aid, aide, aide-de-camp, coadjutant, coadjutor, lieutenant
rel acolyte, attendant, second; flunky, henchman, minion, stooge; girl Friday, right-hand man; agent, attorney, deputy, factor, proxy; fall guy, patsy; co-worker, workfellow, yokemate

assistive *adj syn* see HELPFUL 1

assize *n 1 syn* see LAW 1
2 *syn* see STANDARD 4

associate *vb syn* see JOIN 1

rel amalgamate, blend, coalesce, merge, mingle, mix; ally, confederate, federate, league
con alienate, estrange; divide, divorce, part

associate *n 1 syn* see PARTNER
rel affiliate, ally, confederate, leaguer; abettor, accomplice, collaborator
2 *syn* see COLLEAGUE
3 a person regularly frequenting the company of another <a man is judged by the *associates* he keeps>
syn buddy, chum, comate, companion, comrade, crony, ‖cully, pal, running mate; *compare* FRIEND
rel acquaintance, friend, sympathizer; confidant, familiar, intimate; brother-in-arms, comrade-in-arms
4 *syn* see ACCOMPANIMENT 2
rel complement, correlate, correlative, counterpart, match; correspondent
con competitor, rival; adversary, antagonist, opponent

association *n 1* the quality or state of being associated <worked in close *association* with the courts>
syn affiliation, alliance, cahoots, combination, conjointment, conjunction, connection, hookup, partnership, tie-up, togetherness
rel coaction, collaboration, concert, cooperation, teamwork; conviviality, gaiety, joviality, sociability
con aloofness, apartness, disjunction, disunion, isolation, separation
ant disassociation, dissociation
2 an organization of persons sharing a common interest or purpose <a buyers' *association*>
syn brotherhood, club, congress, fellowship, fraternity, guild, league, order, society, sodality, union
rel alliance, axis, bloc, coalition, federation, organization; faction, interest, sect, wing; combine, gang, machine, ring
3 *syn* see LEAGUE 4
4 something (as a feeling or recollection) associated in the mind with a particular person or thing <the thought of her childhood home always carried an *association* of loving warmth>
syn connotation, hint, implication, overtone, suggestion, undertone
rel image, picture, vision; appearance, fantasy, illusion, mirage

assort *vb* to arrange systematically <*assort* yarn by color>
syn categorize, class, classify, group, pigeonhole
rel arrange, methodize, order, systematize; distribute, divide, separate; screen, sift; stratify
con derange, disarrange, disorder, disorganize; commingle, jumble, mingle, mix, scramble

assorted *adj 1 syn* see MISCELLANEOUS
con chosen, picked, preferred, selected
2 corresponding in such manner or degree as to be appropriately associated <they made a well-*assorted* pair>
syn adapted, conformable, fitted, matched, suited
rel chosen, picked, preferred, selected; associated, bracketed, coupled, linked

con confused, disordered, fouled-up, hay-wire, jumbled, muddled, scrambled

assortment *n* 1 *syn* see VARIETY 2

2 *syn* see MISCELLANY 1

assuage *vb* 1 *syn* see RELIEVE 1

rel placate

con augment, increase, recruit, reinforce; enhance, exaggerate, heighten, intensify, magnify, strengthen

ant exacerbate

2 *syn* see PACIFY

rel calm, ease, relax, slack, slacken, soothe

con annoy, inflame, nettle, provoke, ruffle, vex

as such *adv* *syn* see PER SE

assumably *adv* *syn* see PRESUMABLY

assume *vb* 1 *syn* see DON 2

2 *syn* see DON 1

3 *syn* see ARROGATE 1

rel grab, seize, snatch, take

idiom take over the helm, take possession (*or* command)

4 to take on or present a false or deceptive appearance < their gaiety was *assumed* >

syn act, affect, bluff, counterfeit, fake, feign, pretend, put on, sham, simulate

rel camouflage, cloak, conceal, disguise, dissemble, hide, mask

idiom make believe

5 *syn* see PRESUPPOSE

rel affirm, assert, aver, predicate, profess; allow, concede, grant

6 *syn* see UNDERSTAND 3

assumed *adj* *syn* see ARTIFICIAL 3

rel factitious, synthetic; deceptive, delusory, illusory, insubstantial, unreal

con authentic, bona fide, genuine, veritable; real, true

assumption *n* 1 *syn* see PRESUPPOSITION

2 something that is taken for granted or advanced as fact < decisions based on *assumptions* about the nature of society >

syn apriorism, posit, postulate, postulation, premise, presumption, presupposition, supposition, thesis

rel conjecture, guess, surmise; hypothesis, theory; axiom, fundamental, law, principle, theorem

assurance *n* 1 *syn* see WORD 8

rel parole, promise, troth; plight; agreement, compact, covenant, pact, understanding

2 *syn* see CERTAINTY

rel credit; dependence, reliance, trust

con suspicion, uncertainty; disbelief, incredulity, unbelief

ant mistrust; dubiousness

3 *syn* see SAFETY

4 *syn* see CONFIDENCE 2

rel composure, equanimity, sangfroid

con agitation, disquiet, jumpiness, nervousness, shakiness, skittishness; anxiety, doubt, foreboding, funk, perturbation, trepidation

ant alarm

5 *syn* see TEMERITY

rel brazenness, cockiness, presumption; conceit, self-conceit, self-importance, vanity

con diffidence, modesty, shyness, timidity; self-deprecation, self-effacement, unassumingness, unpretentiousness

assure *vb* 1 *syn* see ENSURE

con abash, discomfit, embarrass; buffalo, bulldoze, cow, daunt, intimidate, shake; demoralize, disquiet, unman, unnerve

ant alarm

2 to make one sure or certain of something < pinched his arm to *assure* himself he was awake >

syn convince, persuade, satisfy

idiom bring (*or* drive) home to, lead one to believe, sell one on something

assured *adj* 1 *syn* see CONFIDENT 1

rel collected, composed, cool, imperturbable, unflappable, unruffled; game, plucky, resolute, spunky

con abashed, discomfited, disconcerted, embarrassed, rattled; hesitant, insecure, reluctant, uncertain; apprehensive, timorous

2 *syn* see DECIDED 1

rel certain, fixed, set

con ambiguous, uncertain; enigmatic, mysterious, obscure

assuredness *n* *syn* see CERTAINTY

astern *adv* *syn* see ABAFT

rel rear

con ahead, before, forward

as to *prep* 1 *syn* see APROPOS

2 *syn* see BY 5

astonish *vb* *syn* see SURPRISE 2

rel overwhelm; affright, alarm, terrify

astonishing *adj* *syn* see MARVELOUS 1

astound *vb* *syn* see SURPRISE 2

astounding *adj* *syn* see MARVELOUS 1

astral *adj* 1 *syn* see STELLAR 1

2 *syn* see DREAMY 1

3 *syn* see EXALTED 1

astray *adv* *syn* see AMISS 2

astricted *adj* *syn* see CONSTIPATED

astringent *adj* 1 *syn* see ACRID

rel puckery

con bland, mellow, mild

2 *syn* see SEVERE 1

rel biting, cutting, incisive, penetrating, piercing, stabbing; brisk, caustic, keen, sharp

con lax, loose, relaxed, slack, weak; unexacting

3 *syn* see TONIC 1

astucious *adj* *syn* see SHREWD

rel discreet, foresighted, prudent; cunning, sly, wily

con ingenuous, naive, simple, unsophisticated; dull, heavy, obtuse, slow; arid, barren, staid, stuffy, uninspired

ant gullible

astucity *n* *syn* see WIT 3

astute *adj* 1 *syn* see SHREWD

rel discreet, foresighted, prudent; cunning, sly, wily

con ingenuous, naive, simple, unsophisticated; dull, heavy, obtuse, slow; arid, barren, staid, stuffy, uninspired

ant gullible

2 *syn* see SLY 2

rel subtile, subtle; keen, knowing, sharp

idiom slippery as an eel, too clever by half

---

syn synonym(s)   *rel* related word(s)

ant antonym(s)   *con* contrasted word(s)

idiom idiomatic equivalent(s)

‖ use limited; if in doubt, see a dictionary

con aboveboard, forthright, straightforward; ingenuous, naive, simple, unsophisticated

astuteness *n syn* see WIT 3

asudden *adv syn* see SHORT 1

asunder *adv syn* see APART 3
idiom all to pieces, one part from the other, to shreds

as usual *adv syn* see USUALLY 1

asweat *adj syn* see SWEATY

as well *adv* 1 *syn* see ALSO 2
idiom over and above
2 *syn* see EVEN 1

as well as *prep syn* see BESIDES 1

as yet *adv syn* see HITHERTO 1

asylum *n* 1 *syn* see SHELTER 1
2 *syn* see REFUGE 1
rel inviolability; security
3 an institution for the care of the insane <demand for improved *asylums*>
syn booby hatch, ∥bughouse, crazy house, loony bin, madhouse, ∥nuthouse
rel farm, home, institution, sanatorium
idiom ∥funny farm, insane (*or* lunatic) asylum, mental hospital (*or* institution), state hospital

asymmetric *adj syn* see LOPSIDED

at all *adv* 1 *syn* see EVER 5
2 *syn* see EVER 4

ataraxy *n syn* see EQUANIMITY

atavism *n syn* see REVERSION 1

ataxia *n syn* see CONFUSION 3

at close hand *adv syn* see CLOSE

atelier *n syn* see STUDIO

athenaeum *n syn* see LIBRARY

athirst *adj* 1 *syn* see THIRSTY 1
rel dehydrated, desiccated, dried up
2 *syn* see EAGER
con lackadaisical, languid, listless; autistic, withdrawn

athletic *adj syn* see MUSCULAR 2
rel active, energetic, strenuous, vigorous
con delicate; decadent, effete, flabby, soft

athletics *n pl* physical activities engaged in for exercise or pleasure <went in heavily for *athletics*>
syn games, sports
rel calisthenics, exercise, gymnastics; drill, practice, workout; amusement, diversion, entertainment, pastime, recreation

athwart *adv* 1 *syn* see ACROSS 1
2 *syn* see OVER 1

athwart *prep syn* see ACROSS

atiptoe *adj syn* see EXPECTANT 1

atmosphere *n* 1 *syn* see AIR 3
rel character, flavor, property, quality; characteristic, individuality, peculiarity; impression, suggestion
2 *syn* see ENVIRONMENT

atmospheric *adj syn* see AIRY 1

atom *n syn* see PARTICLE
rel dash, touch, trace; shade, smack, spice, soupçon, suggestion, suspicion, tincture, tinge

atomize *vb syn* see DESTROY 1

at once *adv* 1 *syn* see TOGETHER 1
2 *syn* see AWAY 3

atone *vb syn* see EXPIATE
rel compensate, pay, recompense, satisfy; appease, conciliate, propitiate
idiom set one's house in order

stone (for) *vb syn* see COMPENSATE 1

atramentous *adj syn* see BLACK 1

at random *adv syn* see ABOUT 4

atrocious *adj* 1 *syn* see OUTRAGEOUS 2
rel flagitious, infamous, iniquitous, vicious; barbarous, savage; glaring, rank; abominable, contemptible, despicable, execrable, odious, vile
con fine, righteous, upright, virtuous; benign, gentle, kindly
ant humane
2 *syn* see OFFENSIVE
rel displeasing, distasteful
con alluring, magnetic

atrociousness *n syn* see ENORMITY 1

atrocity *n syn* see ENORMITY 1

atrophy *n syn* see DETERIORATION 1

attach *vb syn* see FASTEN 1
rel associate; add, annex, append; bind, tie
con disassociate, dissociate; disembarrass, disencumber, disengage, disentangle
ant detach

attachment *n* 1 the state of being firmly attached to someone or something (as by affection, sympathy, or self-interest) <his *attachment* to an outworn code>
syn adherence, adhesion, constancy, faithfulness, fidelity, loyalty
rel firmness, staunchness, steadfastness; allegiance, devotion, fealty
con disloyalty, faithlessness, infidelity, unfaithfulness; aloofness, distance, remoteness; disinterest, disregard, unconcern, unmindfulness
ant detachment
2 *syn* see LOVE 1
rel piety; devotedness
con antipathy, disinclination, dislike; alienation, disaffection, estrangement
ant aversion

attack *vb* 1 to act in violent opposition <cavalry *attacked* the Indian camp>
syn aggress, assail, assault, beset, fall (on *or* upon), storm, strike
rel invade, irrupt; charge, raid, rush; besiege, blockade, encompass, invest; beleaguer, beset, harass, harry, press; turn (on)
idiom gang up on, light into, sail into, set upon, take the offensive
con defend, guard, protect, shield; combat, oppose, resist, withstand
2 to begin to work vigorously (as at a task) <*attack* a problem>
syn bang away (at), tackle
rel buckle (to *or* down *or* down to), fall to, pitch in, wade (in *or* into)
idiom address (*or* apply *or* devote) oneself to, give oneself up to
con dawdle, lag, poke, putter

attack *n* 1 an act of attacking especially in the form of an attempt to injure, destroy, or defame <insecticides that are essential for successful *attack* on insect pests>
syn aggression, assailment, assault, offense, offensive, onfall, onset, onslaught
rel charge, descent, drive, foray, push, raid, sally, sortie; blitz, incursion, inroad, surprise; action, battle
con championing, justification, protection, support, vindication; opposition, resistance; defending, guarding, protecting, sheltering
ant defense

2 action or an attitude in a struggle that calls for or is opposed by defense < his policy had always been one of *attack* >
syn aggression, aggressiveness, belligerence, combativeness, fight, pugnacity
rel bellicosity, chauvinism, jingoism, warmongering; activation, militarization, mobilization, muster
con submissiveness, yielding
3 an episode of bodily or mental disorder < a sudden *attack* of dizziness >
syn access, fit, seizure, spell, throe, turn; *compare* SIEGE
rel outbreak, paroxysm, spasm; affection, ailment, complaint, disease, disorder

attain *vb syn* see GAIN 1
idiom gain one's end, make good

attainable *adj syn* see AVAILABLE 1

attainment *n syn* see ACQUIREMENT

attempt *vb syn* see TRY 5
rel begin, commence, inaugurate, initiate, start; venture
idiom give (something) a try, take a crack (or whack) at
con accomplish, achieve, effect, execute, fulfill, perform; attain, compass, gain, reach
ant succeed

attempt *n* an effort made to do or accomplish something, < made a determined *attempt* to improve her writing >
syn endeavor, essay, hassle, striving, struggle, trial, try, undertaking
rel care, effort, pains, trouble; beginning, commencement, initiation, offer, shy, start
con accomplishment, achievement, attainment, finish, fulfillment

attend *vb* 1 *syn* see LISTEN
idiom be attentive (to), give heed (to)
2 *syn* see TEND 2
rel govern, oversee, supervise; direct, handle, manage, regulate, run; aid, assist, help
3 *syn* see ACCOMPANY
rel associate, fraternize, join, mingle, mix

attendant *adj syn* see CONCOMITANT

attendant *n syn* see HELPER

attending *adj syn* see CONCOMITANT

attention *n* 1 a focusing of the mind on something < gave the problem careful *attention* >
syn application, concentration, consideration, debate, deliberation, heed, study
rel assiduity, diligence, industry, sedulity, sedulousness; notice, observation, regard, remark; absorption, engrossment, immersion, intentness
con absence, absentmindedness, abstraction, detachment, remoteness, withdrawal; disinterest, indifference, unconcern, unmindfulness
ant inattention
2 *syn* see NOTICE 1
rel awareness, consciousness, mindfulness, sensibility
con disregard, heedlessness, insensibility, unawareness, unconsciousness
3 *syn* see COURTESY 1

rel deference, homage, honor, reverence; benignity; considerateness, consideration, kindliness, solicitude
con neglect, negligence; aloofness, indifference, unconcern; discourtesy

attentive *adj* 1 concentrating one's attention on something < listeners *attentive* to the speaker's appeal >
syn advertent, arrect, heedful, intentive, observant, regardful
rel alert, aware, mindful; agog, eager, interested, keen; concentrating, earnest, intent; open-eared, open-eyed
idiom all ears (or eyes), on the ball, paying attention
con absorbed, abstracted, bemused, preoccupied; absentminded, daydreaming, faraway, oblivious, wandering, woolgathering
ant absent; inattentive
2 *syn* see THOUGHTFUL 3
con aloof, indifferent
ant inattentive; neglectful

attenuate *vb* 1 *syn* see THIN 1
rel lessen; sap; dissipate; constrict, contract, deflate, shrink
con amplify, dilate, distend, expand, inflate, swell; augment, enlarge, increase; enrich
2 *syn* see WEAKEN 1
3 *syn* see THIN 2

attenuate *adj* 1 *syn* see THIN 1
2 *syn* see THIN 2

attenuated *adj syn* see THIN 2

attest *vb* 1 *syn* see CERTIFY 1
rel confirm, corroborate, substantiate, verify; support, sustain, uphold, warrant; affirm, asseverate, depone, swear, testify
con confute, controvert, disprove, refute; contradict, deny, gainsay
2 *syn* see INDICATE 2
rel authenticate, confirm, substantiate
con falsify, misrepresent; distort, garble, pervert, twist, warp
ant belie
3 *syn* see TESTIFY 1

attestation *n syn* see TESTIMONY

at times *adv syn* see SOMETIMES

attire *vb syn* see CLOTHE
rel accouter, appoint, arm, equip, outfit
con bare, denude, dismantle, strip
ant divest

attire *n syn* see CLOTHES

attirement *n syn* see CLOTHES

attitude *n* 1 *syn* see POSTURE 1
rel air, demeanor, port, presence
2 *syn* see POSITION 1
rel point of view; bias, predilection, prejudice, prepossession

attitudinize *vb syn* see POSE 4

attorney *n* 1 *syn* see AGENT 2
rel alternate, locum tenens, stand-in, substitute, supply
2 *syn* see LAWYER

attorney-at-law *n syn* see LAWYER

attract *vb* 1 to exert an irresistible or compelling influence on < her beauty *attracted* all eyes >
syn allure, bewitch, captivate, charm, draw, enchant, fascinate, magnetize, wile
rel entice, lure, seduce, tempt; beguile, draw (in), intrigue, inveigle, suck (in); enrapture, entrance; court, invite, solicit

---

syn synonym(s)   *rel* related word(s)
ant antonym(s)   *con* contrasted word(s)
idiom idiomatic equivalent(s)
‖ use limited; if in doubt, see a dictionary

con fend (off), hold (off *or* away), rebuff, repulse; disgust, offend, revolt

ant repel

2 *syn* see INTEREST

attracting *adj syn* see ATTRACTIVE 1

attraction *n* 1 a quality that elicits admiration or pleased responsiveness <yielding to the *attraction* of the balmy afternoon>

syn allurement, appeal, attractiveness, call, draw, drawing power, lure, pull, seduction

rel charm, glamour, interest; delight, pleasure; bait, hook, snare

con offensiveness, repulsiveness, ugliness

2 a relationship characteristic of individuals that are drawn together naturally or involuntarily and exert a degree of influence on one another <the *attraction* between iron and the magnet>

syn affinity, sympathy

rel accord, concord, harmony

idiom drawing together

con conflict, discord, friction, tension

attractive *adj* 1 having the power to attract <an area *attractive* to wildlife>

syn alluring, appealing, attracting, bewitching, captivating, charming, drawing, enchanting, engaging, fascinating, glamorous, magnetic, mesmeric, prepossessing, seductive, siren

rel beautiful, bonny, comely, fair, lovely, pretty; Circean, enticing, fetching, luring, tempting; interesting, taking, winning; beckoning, come-hither, inviting, provocative, tantalizing, teasing; likable, simpatico

con abhorrent, distasteful, obnoxious, repugnant; loathsome, offensive, repulsive, revolting; antipathetic, unsympathetic

ant repellent, repelling; forbidding

2 *syn* see BEAUTIFUL

rel agreeable, goodly, ||likely, pleasing, sightly

con homely, ill-favored, plain, uncomely, unprepossessing

ant unattractive

attractiveness *n syn* see ATTRACTION 1

attribute *n* 1 *syn* see QUALITY 1

rel particularity, singularity, specialty; brand, earmark, impress, stamp

2 *syn* see SYMBOL 1

attribute *vb syn* see ASCRIBE

rel calendar, chronologize, date, place

attrition *n syn* see PENITENCE

attritional *adj syn* see REMORSEFUL

attune *vb syn* see HARMONIZE 3

rel balance, compensate, counterbalance; accord, agree; fix, rectify, regulate

idiom put in tune, set to rights (*or* in order)

con divide, separate, wean

||**atween** *prep syn* see BETWEEN 2

||**atwixt** *prep syn* see BETWEEN 2

atypical *adj syn* see ABNORMAL 1

rel irregular, unnatural; different, divergent; exceptional, odd, peculiar, queer, strange

con customary, usual

ant typical; representative

auberge *n syn* see HOTEL

au courant *adj* 1 *syn* see AWARE

2 *syn* see UP-TO-DATE

3 *syn* see FAMILIAR 3

audacious *adj* 1 *syn* see BRAVE 1

rel adventurous, daredevil, daring, foolhardy, rash, reckless, venturesome; brash, brazen, shameless

con calculating, cautious, chary, wary; judicious, prudent, sane, wise; careful, circumspect, discreet

2 *syn* see ADVENTUROUS

rel fearless, valiant, valorous

con careful, circumspect, discreet; calculating, cautious, chary, wary

3 *syn* see INSOLENT 2

4 free from constraint and formality <found life an *audacious* ever-changing adventure>

syn uncurbed, ungoverned, unhampered, uninhibited, unrestrained, untrammeled

rel emancipated, free, independent; easy, relaxed; careless, heedless, thoughtless; self-absorbed, self-centered, selfish

con checked, curbed, governed, hampered, inhibited, restrained, trammeled; careful, cautious, heedful, mindful, thoughtful; considerate, generous, self-abnegating, self-effacing; drab, dull, pedestrian

audacity *n syn* see TEMERITY

rel cheek, effrontery, face, gall; brass, brazenness, cockiness; forwardness, impudence, resolution; courage, mettle, spirit

con calculation, caution, wariness; shyness, timidity, timorousness; agitation, disquiet, nervousness, perturbation, trepidation

ant circumspection

audible *adj syn* see AURAL 1

ant inaudible

audience *n* 1 *syn* see HEARING 2

rel attention, consideration, ear

2 *syn* see FOLLOWING 2

rel admirers, devotees, fanciers, fans, votaries

audile *adj syn* see AUDITORY

audit *n syn* see EXAMINATION

rel investigation, probe; check, control, corrective

audition *n syn* see HEARING 2

auditory *adj* of, relating to, or experienced through the sense of hearing <*auditory* disorders>

syn acoustic, audile, aural; *compare* AURAL 1

au fait *adj* 1 *syn* see ABLE

2 *syn* see FAMILIAR 3

3 *syn* see DECOROUS 1

au fond *adv syn* see ESSENTIALLY 1

Augean stable *n syn* see SINK 1

aught (*or* ought) *n syn* see ZERO 1

augment *vb* 1 *syn* see INCREASE 1

2 *syn* see INCREASE 2

augment *vb syn* see INCREASE 1

rel exalt, hike, raise

con attenuate, decrease, dwindle; abridge; alleviate, assuage, relieve

ant abate

augmentation *n* 1 *syn* see ACCOMPANIMENT 1

rel adjunct, annex, attachment, fixture, reinforcement; bonus, boot, extra, plus

2 *syn* see ADDITION

con subtraction

augur *n syn* see PROPHET

augur *vb* 1 *syn* see FORETELL

rel argue, bespeak, indicate

2 to indicate or suggest a future probability < their enthusiasm *augurs* well for the success of the enterprise >
syn betoken, bode, forebode, foreshadow, foreshow, foretoken, omen, portend, presage, promise
rel hint, imply, intimate, suggest; prefigure, shadow (forth)
idiom bid fair to, give promise (*or* fair promise) of, hold out hope of, lead one to believe (*or* expect)

augury *n syn* see FORETOKEN
rel anticipation, premonition, presentiment
con accomplishment, effecting, effectuation, fulfillment, actualization, materialization, realization; appearance, emergence, forthcoming, issuance

august *adj syn* see GRAND 1
rel splendid, sublime, superb; impressive, moving, striking; awe-inspiring, awful, fearful, overwhelming

au naturel *adj syn* see NUDE 2

aura *n syn* see AIR 3
rel appearance, aspect, suggestion; aureole, radiance

aural *adj* **1** heard or perceived with the ear < responded to *aural* stimuli >
syn audible, auricular; *compare* AUDITORY
2 *syn* see AUDITORY

aureate *adj syn* see RHETORICAL
rel baroque, rococo
con moderate, quiet, restrained, sober, temperate
ant austere

auricular *n syn* see AURAL 1

aurora *n syn* see DAWN 1

auslander *n syn* see STRANGER

auspex *n syn* see PROPHET

auspices *n pl syn* see BACKING

auspicious *adj* **1** *syn* see FAVORABLE 5
rel hopeful; golden, halcyon, roseate, rosy
con ominous, portentous, unpropitious; adverse, antagonistic
ant inauspicious; ill-omened
2 *syn* see TIMELY 1

austere *adj* **1** *syn* see SEVERE 1
rel bald, bare, simple, unadorned, undecorated, unembellished, unornamented; earnest, grave, serious, sober, somber
con complicated, elaborate, fancy, flamboyant, fussy, ornate; frivolous, light, light-minded, shallow, superficial
2 *syn* see ACRID
rel biting, keen, rough
con bland, mellow, smooth, soft
3 *syn* see GRIM 2

autarchic *adj* **1** *syn* see ABSOLUTE 4
rel commanding, dogmatic, imperious; nonconstitutional, undemocratic
2 *syn* see FREE 1
rel self-dependent, self-reliant, self-sufficient

autarkic *adj syn* see FREE 1
rel self-dependent, self-reliant, self-sufficient

---

authentic *adj* **1** worthy of acceptance because of accuracy < an *authentic* portrayal of ancient customs >
syn convincing, credible, faithful, trustworthy, trusty
rel accurate, dependable, factual, reliable, sure; solid, sound, straight, valid; authoritative, cathedral, official, standard
idiom all wool and a yard wide; to be depended (*or* relied) on
con incredible, unconvincing, untrustworthy; equivocal, obscure, uncertain, vague; hypothetical, purported, putative, supposed, supposititious; debatable, doubtful, questionable; nonstandard
ant inauthentic
2 being exactly as appears or is claimed < an *authentic* masterpiece >
syn blown-in-the-bottle, bona fide, genuine, indubitable, pukka, questionless, real, right, simon-pure, sure-enough, true, undoubted, undubitable, unquestionable, veritable, very
rel cognizable, identifiable, knowable, recognizable; honest, pure, unadulterated, unalloyed
con deceptive, delusive, delusory, false, misleading, wrong; unidentifiable, unrecognizable
ant spurious
3 *syn* see CERTAIN 3

authenticate *vb* **1** *syn* see CONFIRM 2
rel accredit, approve, endorse; demonstrate, prove, test, try; avouch, vouch (for)
con reject, repudiate, spurn; contradict, deny, negate
ant impugn

author *n syn* see FATHER 2
rel origin, source; ancestor, parent, procreator

authoritarian *adj* **1** *syn* see DICTATORIAL
rel heavy-handed, high-handed, oppressive, strict, stringent
ant libertarian; anarchistic
2 *syn* see TOTALITARIAN 1
rel fascistic, nazi, patriarchal
ant democratic

authoritative *adj* **1** *syn* see OFFICIAL
2 *syn* see TRUE 9
rel attested, authenticated, circumstantiated, confirmed, proven, validated, verified; convincing, indisputable, irrefutable, sure, unrefutable; cathedral, cathedratic
con contestable, controversial, debatable, disputable, refutable; dubious, questionable, suspect, unreliable
3 *syn* see DICTATORIAL
4 *syn* see ORTHODOX 1

authority *n* **1** *syn* see EXPERT
2 *syn* see POWER 1
rel governance, government, rule
3 *syn* see INFLUENCE 1
rel example, exemplar, ideal, model, pattern, standard; force, power, pressure

authorization *n syn* see PERMISSION

authorize *vb* **1** to invest with power or the right to act < I did not *authorize* him to speak for me >
syn accredit, commission, empower, enable, license
rel approve, countenance, endorse; aid, assist, help, support, subserve; advance, facilitate, forward, further, promote

con bar, disallow, enjoin, forbid, interdict, prohibit
2 *syn* see ENTITLE 2
rel allow, let, permit; approve, countenance, endorse
idiom give one the right to
3 *syn* see INVEST 2
auto *n syn* see CAR
auto *vb* 1 *syn* see DRIVE 5
2 *syn* see RIDE 1
autobiographer *n syn* see BIOGRAPHER
autobiographist *n syn* see BIOGRAPHER
autobiography *n syn* see BIOGRAPHY
rel diary, journal, letters
autocar *n syn* see CAR
autochthonous *adj syn* see NATIVE 2
con alien, extraneous, extrinsic, foreign; imported, introduced
ant naturalized
autocracy *n syn* see TYRANNY
autocratic *adj syn* see ABSOLUTE 4
rel arrogant, haughty, overbearing, overweening
con deferential, submissive, yielding; forbearing, indulgent, lenient, tolerant
autodidactic *adj syn* see SELF-TAUGHT
autograph *vb syn* see SIGN 1
autognosis *n syn* see SELF-KNOWLEDGE
autoist *n syn* see MOTORIST
automatic *adj* 1 *syn* see SPONTANEOUS
rel prompt, quick, ready; accustomed, confirmed, habitual, habituated
2 *syn* see PERFUNCTORY
automaton *n* 1 *syn* see ROBOT 1
2 *syn* see ROBOT 2
automobile *n syn* see CAR
automobilist *n syn* see MOTORIST
autonomous *adj syn* see FREE 1
rel self-governed; unconstrained, uncontrolled, unsubordinated
con controlled, subordinated; governed, ruled; affiliated, allied
autopsy *n* examination of the body after death usually to determine the cause of death < the *autopsy* of a murder victim >
syn necropsy, ‖post, postmortem, postmortem examination
autoschediasm *n syn* see IMPROVISATION
autoschediastic *adj syn* see EXTEMPORANEOUS
auxiliary *adj* capable of supplying or intended to supply aid or support < an *auxiliary* police unit >
syn accessory, adjuvant, ancillary, appurtenant, collateral, contributory, subservient, subsidiary
rel complementary, supplementary; peripheral, secondary, subordinate, tributary; backing, supporting, upholding; aiding, assisting, helping
con chief, leading, main, principal; sole, solitary, unique
avail *vb syn* see BENEFIT
rel answer, fill, fulfill, meet, satisfy
con damage, harm, hurt, injure
avail *n syn* see USE 3
rel interest; appositeness, suitability
con inappropriateness, unsuitableness
available *adj* 1 that is accessible or may be obtained < the best pen *available* at the present time >
syn attainable, disponible, gettable, obtainable, procurable, securable

rel accessible, convenient, handy
idiom to be had
con unattainable, unobtainable; absent, deficient, lacking, missing
ant unavailable
2 *syn* see PURCHASABLE 1
avarice *n syn* see CUPIDITY
rel frugality, parsimony, thrift; miserliness, niggardliness, parsimoniousness, stinginess; acquisitiveness, covetousness, graspingness, piggishness
con extravagance; bountifulness, bounty, generosity, liberality, munificence, openhandedness
ant prodigality
avariciousness *n syn* see CUPIDITY
avenge *vb* to inflict punishment by way of repayment for < *avenge* an insult >
syn redress, revenge, venge, vindicate
rel compensate, pay (back), pay out, recompense, repay, requite, retaliate, retribute; chasten, chastise, punish; correct, right
idiom get an eye for an eye, get even with, settle accounts, wreak one's vengeance
con condone, disregard, ignore, overlook; absolve, amnesty, forgive, pardon, remit; bear, endure, stand, suffer, tolerate
avengement *n syn* see RETALIATION
avenging *n syn* see RETALIATION
avenue *n* 1 *syn* see WAY 1
‖**2** *syn* see DRIVEWAY
aver *vb syn* see ASSERT 1
rel defend, hold, justify, maintain
con deny
average *n* something (as a number, quantity, or condition) that represents a middle point between extremes < somewhat sweeter than *average* >
syn mean, median, norm, par
ant maximum; minimum
average *adj syn* see MEDIUM
rel common, familiar, ordinary; customary, usual
idiom common or garden variety
con choice, excellent, exceptional, prime, superior; conspicuous, noticeable, outstanding, prominent; bad, inferior, lowgrade, poor, punk
averagely *adv syn* see ENOUGH 2
avernal *adj syn* see INFERNAL 2
averse *adj syn* see DISINCLINED
rel balky, contrary, perverse; flinching, quailing, recoiling, resistant, shrinking; uncongenial, unsympathetic
ant avid (of *or* for)
aversion *n* 1 *syn* see DISLIKE
rel antagonism, antipathy, hostility; dread, fear, horror
con bias, partiality; leaning, propensity, taste
ant predilection
2 *syn* see ANTIPATHY 2
rel abhorrence, distaste, repellency, repugnance, repulsion, revulsion; disgust, dread, loathing
con bias, partiality, penchant; flair, inclination, leaning, taste
ant attachment; predilection
3 *syn* see ABOMINATION 2
ant delight
aversive *adj syn* see ANTIPATHETIC 2

avert *vb* **1** *syn* see TURN 6
  rel remove, transfer
  2 *syn* see PREVENT 2
  rel anticipate; balk, foil, frustrate, thwart; check, halt, stay, stop
  con advance, further, promote

aviary *n* a house, enclosure, or large cage for confining live birds < the zoo's *aviary* >
  syn birdhouse
  rel dovecote, dovehouse; columbary, pigeon house

aviator *n* *syn* see PILOT 2

avid *adj* *syn* see EAGER
  rel covetous, craving, desirous, wanting, wishful; importunate, insistent, pressing, urgent; gluttonous, omnivorous
  con aloof, disinterested, uninterested; disinclined, indisposed, loath
  ant indifferent; averse

avidity *n* *syn* see CUPIDITY

avoid *vb* *syn* see ESCAPE 2
  rel avert, deflect, divert, obviate, prevent, ward (off), debar, exclude, preclude, forbid, prohibit
  idiom give a miss (*or* a wide berth), have no truck with, set one's face against, steer clear of, turn one's back on
  con court, invite, solicit
  ant face; meet

avoidance *n* *syn* see ESCAPE 2

avouch *vb* *syn* see ASSERT 1
  rel confirm, corroborate; acknowledge, admit, confess, own
  con deny, impugn

avow *vb* **1** *syn* see ASSERT 1
  rel defend, maintain, vindicate; asseverate, swear, testify
  2 *syn* see ACKNOWLEDGE 1
  con repudiate, withdraw

avowry *n* *syn* see PATRON SAINT

await *vb* *syn* see EXPECT 1
  rel abide, stay, wait
  idiom bide one's time, sweat (*or* tough) it out

awake *vb* *syn* see WAKE 1

awake *adj* *syn* see AWARE
  rel vigilant, watchful; aroused, awakened, roused, stirred up; excited
  con drowsy, sleepy, slumberous, somnolent; inactive, inert, supine

awaken *vb* **1** *syn* see WAKE 1
  2 *syn* see STIR 1
  rel fire, inflame; alert
  idiom stir the feelings (*or* blood) of
  con arrest, check, retard, subdue; calm, compose, restrain

awanting *prep* *syn* see WITHOUT 2

award *vb* **1** *syn* see GRANT 1
  rel allocate, allot, apportion, assign; dower, endow, endue
  2 *syn* see GIVE 2

award *n* *syn* see HONOR 2

aware *adj* marked by realization, perception, or knowledge often of something not generally realized, perceived, or known < *aware* of her own inner weakness >
  syn alive, apprehensive, au courant, awake, cognizant, conscious, conversant,

knowing, mindful, sensible, sentient, ware, witting
  rel acquainted, apprised, informed; alert, heedful; impressionable, perceptive, receptive
  con anesthetic, impassible, insensible, insensitive; ignorant, unknowing
  ant unaware

awash *adj* *syn* see FULL 1

away *adv* **1** from this or that place < come *away* at once >
  syn hence, thence
  rel forth, out, therefrom
  2 at some distance from a place expressed or implied < he lived several blocks *away* >
  syn off, over
  rel afar, far; apart, aside
  3 without hesitation or delay < fire *away* when you see the target >
  syn at once, directly, first off, forthwith, immediately, instanter, instantly, now, PDQ, right, right away, right off, straight, straight away, straight off, straightway
  rel momentarily, promptly, ‖pronto, punctually; expeditiously, quickly, speedily, swiftly

away *adj* *syn* see ABSENT 1

awe *n* *syn* see REVERENCE 2
  rel esteem, regard, respect, veneration, worship; admiration, amazement, wonder, wonderment
  con despite, scorn; arrogance, insolence, superciliousness

awe *vb* *syn* see FRIGHTEN

aweless *adj* *syn* see BRAVE 1

awful *adj* *syn* see FEARFUL 3
  rel impressive, moving; august, imposing, majestic; splendid, superb; grave, serious, solemn; ominous, portentous

‖**awful** *adv* *syn* see VERY 1

awfully *adv* *syn* see VERY 1

awkward *adj* **1** *syn* see CLUMSY 1
  rel blundering, bumbling; bungling; clownish, lubberly, oafish; cumbrous, hulking, ponderous
  idiom all thumbs
  2 marked by a lack of grace, ease, skill, or fitness (as in action or speech) < his *awkward* approach to the problem >
  syn bumbling, clumsy, gauche, halting, ham-handed, heavy-handed, inept, lumbering, maladroit, unhandy, unhappy, wooden; *compare* CLUMSY 1
  rel rigid, stiff; discomfited, disconcerted, embarrassed; bunglesome, bungling, inefficient, inexpert, unskillful
  con adept, adroit, dexterous, expert, finished, polished, proficient, skilled, skillful, smooth; easy, effortless, facile, simple
  ant deft; graceful
  3 *syn* see INCONVENIENT
  4 *syn* see INFELICITOUS

awry *adv* (*or adj*) **1** deviating from a straight line or direction < the coverlet was pulled *awry* >
  syn askance, askant, askew, ‖cam, cocks-a-hoop, cockeyed, crookedly
  rel aside, aslant, obliquely, slantways
  con even, straight, true; directly, undeviatingly
  2 *syn* see AMISS 2
  rel erroneously, faultily, untruly; aside

---

syn synonym(s)   *rel* related word(s)
ant antonym(s)   *con* contrasted word(s)
idiom idiomatic equivalent(s)
‖ use limited; if in doubt, see a dictionary

ax *vb syn* see DISMISS 3
axiom *n* 1 *syn* see PRINCIPLE 1
  2 *syn* see MAXIM

‖ayah *n syn* see NURSEMAID
aye *adv syn* see YES 1

B

Babbitt *n syn* see PHILISTINE
babblative *adj syn* see TALKATIVE
babble *vb* 1 *syn* see GIBBER
  2 to talk nonsensically < silly people *babbling* on about trivia >
    syn blabber, blather, drivel, drool, gabble, prate, prattle, twaddle, ‖waffle
    rel clack, jaw, rattle, run on, yak, yammer, yap
    idiom run off at the mouth
  3 *syn* see CHAT 1
babble *n* 1 *syn* see CHATTER
  2 *syn* see GIBBERISH 1
babe *n syn* see BABY 1
babel *n syn* see DIN
    con bush, noiselessness; peace, quiet, silence
babushka *n syn* see KERCHIEF 1
baby *n* 1 a very young child esp. in the first year of life < the love of a mother for her *baby* >
    syn babe, bantling, infant, neonate, newborn
    rel bambino, little one, toddler, tot; nursling, suckling, weanling; bratling
    idiom babe in arms
  2 *syn* see WEAKLING
  ‖3 *syn* see GIRL FRIEND 2
baby *vb* to treat with special, excessive, or fond care < *baby* a sick husband >
    syn cater (to), cocker, coddle, cosset, cotton, humor, indulge, mollycoddle, pamper, spoil
    rel dry-nurse, wet-nurse; dote (on *or* upon), favor; gratify, please, satisfy
    con control, discipline, restrain; abuse, illtreat, ill-use, mistreat, oppress; neglect, overlook, slight
baby buggy *n syn* see BABY CARRIAGE
baby carriage *n* a four-wheeled push carriage with a folding top for a baby < used the *baby carriage* to wheel home firewood >
    syn baby buggy, bassinet, ‖perambulator, ‖pram
babyhood *n syn* see INFANCY 1
babyish *adj syn* see CHILDISH
bacchanal *n syn* see ORGY 2
bacchanalia *n syn* see ORGY 2
back *n* 1 the surface or part most remote from the front < the *back* of his neck >
    syn posterior, rear, rearward
    rel extremity, tail; reverse
    con anterior
    ant front
  2 *syn* see SPINE
back *adv syn* see ABOUT 6
back *adj* 1 distant from settled areas < *back* regions in the hill country >
    syn frontier, outlandish, remote, unsettled
    rel uncultivated, uninhabited, unoccupied, unpopulated, wild

    con built-up, settled, urban
  2 *syn* see POSTERIOR 2
    ant front
back *vb* 1 *syn* see SUPPORT 2
    rel aid, assist, help; abet
  2 *syn* see CAPITALIZE
  3 *syn* see MOUNT 5
  4 *syn* see RECEDE 1
    con advance, progress
back answer *n syn* see RETORT 2
backbiting *n syn* see DETRACTION
    rel animadversion, reflection, stricture; abuse, invective, obloquy, vituperation
    con accolade, commendation, encomium, eulogy, laudation, paean, panegyric, praise, tribute; adulation, blarney, compliment, flattery, soft soap
backbiting *adj syn* see LIBELOUS
backbone *n* 1 *syn* see SPINE
  2 *syn* see FORTITUDE
    rel hardihood; heart
    con irresoluteness, irresolution
    ant backbonelessness, spinelessness
  3 *syn* see MAINSTAY
backchat *n syn* see BANTER
backcountry *n syn* see FRONTIER 2
‖backdoor trots *n pl but sing or pl in constr syn* see DIARRHEA
back down *vb* to withdraw from a previous agreement or stand < a politician *backing down* on an earlier promise >
    syn back off, back out, backpedal, backwater, crawfish (out), cry off, declare off, renege, resile, welsh
    rel disavow, recall, recant, retract, take back, withdraw; backtrack; beg off, weasel (out); balk, demur, hold back, stickle
    idiom get out of, go back on
backer *n syn* see SPONSOR
    rel ally, protagonist; bankroller, ‖grubstaker, ‖meal ticket, promoter
backer-up *n syn* see SPONSOR
backfire *vb* to have the reverse of the desired effect < the new policy *backfired* disastrously >
    syn backlash, boomerang, bounce (back), kick back
    rel fall (through), fizzle, miscarry, miss, ricochet
    idiom come to grief, go on the rocks, ‖lay an egg
    con come off, succeed, work out
backhouse *n syn* see PRIVY 1
backing *n* aid or support given to an undertaking < the project had the *backing* of the city fathers >
    syn aegis, auspices, patronage, sponsorship
    rel championship, cooperation, fosterage; guidance, tutelage; encouragement; assistance, help, support
backland *n syn* see FRONTIER 2

backlash *vb syn* see BACKFIRE

backlog *n syn* see RESERVE

back of *prep syn* see ABAFT

back off *vb syn* see BACK DOWN

back out *vb syn* see BACK DOWN

backpack *n* a carrying case (as of canvas or nylon) held on the back by shoulder straps < carried his supplies in a *backpack* >
syn haversack, knapsack, pack, packsack, rucksack

backpedal *vb syn* see BACK DOWN
rel dodge, duck, elude, evade, get around, shirk, sidestep

backset *n syn* see SETBACK

backside *n syn* see BUTTOCKS

backslide *vb syn* see LAPSE
rel regress, retrovert, return, revert; defect, desert, tergiversate, turn
idiom fall away, fall (*or* sink *or* slide *or* slip) back into, give in to

backsliding *n syn* see LAPSE 2

backstabbing *n syn* see DETRACTION

backstage *adj or adv* off or away from the part of the stage visible to the audience < *backstage* sounds that gave the impression of a storm >
syn offstage
idiom behind the scenes
ant onstage

backstop *vb syn* see SUPPORT 2

back talk *n* impudent and insolent talk < do as you're told and no *back talk* >
syn guff, ||jaw, ||lip, mouth, sass, sauce
rel cheek, impudence, insolence

||backveld *n syn* see FRONTIER 2

backward *adv syn* see ABOUT 6

backward *adj* 1 directed, turned, or executed backward < the *backward* swimming of the crayfish >
syn retral, retrograde
rel inverted, reversed
ant advance, forward
2 *syn* see DISINCLINED
rel bashful, diffident
3 *syn* see SHY 1
4 *syn* see RETARDED
5 holding to outworn or traditional views, ideas, or principles < had a *backward* attitude toward social inferiors >
syn benighted, ignorant, unenlightened, unprogressive
rel conservative, reactionary; obtuse, stupid, thickheaded; bigoted, hidebound, narrow; blind; unenlightened, uninformed
con advanced, aware, enlightened, forward-looking, progressive, unbenighted
6 not developing or progressing especially in economic and social areas < *backward* nations using primitive farming methods >
syn behindhand, underdeveloped, undeveloped, unprogressive
rel poor, struggling; medieval; benighted, retarded, uncultivated, uncultured
idiom behind the times
con forward-looking, progressive; civilized, cultivated, cultured; modern
ant advanced

---

syn synonym(s)   *rel* related word(s)
ant antonym(s)   *con* contrasted word(s)
idiom idiomatic equivalent(s)
|| use limited; if in doubt, see a dictionary

backwash *n syn* see FRONTIER 2

backwater *n syn* see FRONTIER 2

backwater *vb syn* see BACK DOWN
rel dodge, duck, elude, evade, get around, shirk, sidestep

backwoods *n pl but sing or pl in constr syn* see FRONTIER 2

||backwoodser *n syn* see RUSTIC

backwoodsman *n syn* see RUSTIC

bad *adj* 1 falling short of a standard of what is satisfactory < a *bad* repair job >
syn amiss, ||bum, ||crappy, dissatisfactory, poor, ||punk, rotten, unsatisfactory, up, wrong
rel deficient, inadequate, inferior; careless, slipshod; defective, disordered, off, unsound; execrable, ||lousy, miserable, ||pisspoor, wretched; inadmissible, objectionable, unacceptable; insufferable, intolerable
idiom below par, not up to snuff (*or* scratch)
con excellent, fine, meritorious; acceptable, adequate, sound
2 *syn* see WRONG 1
rel arrant, peccant; graceless, improper, indecorous, untoward; disorderly, misbehaving, naughty, rowdy ruffianly, unruly; froward, perverse
ant good
3 *syn* see EVIL 5
4 *syn* see EVIL 6
5 having undergone decay < one *bad* apple can spoil the barrel >
syn decayed, putrid, rotten, spoiled
rel fusty, stale; mildewed, moldered, moldy, moth-eaten, musty, rancid, worm-eaten, decomposed, putrefied, putrefacted; tainted, turned
con crisp, dewy, fresh, sweet, unspoiled; choice, picked, prime
ant good
6 *syn* see NAUGHTY 1
7 *syn* see TOUGH 8
8 arousing discomfort or distaste < a *bad* smell >
syn ||chiselly, disagreeable, displeasing, rotten, sour, unhappy, unpleasant
rel disgusting, foul, nauseating, noisome, noxious, offensive, repulsive, sickening; abhorrent, hateful, loathsome, obnoxious; uneasy; thankless, ungrateful; distasteful, distressing, sticky; ungracious, unhandsome
con agreeable, pleasant, pleasing, refreshing, soothing; unoffensive
9 *syn* see HARMFUL
10 *syn* see DOWNCAST
11 *syn* see NULL

bad actor *n syn* see TROUBLEMAKER

bad books *n pl syn* see DISLIKE

badge *n* 1 *syn* see INSIGNIA
2 *syn* see HONOR 2

badger *vb syn* see BAIT 2
rel plague, tease, worry

badinage *n syn* see BANTER
rel chaffing, guying, japery, joshing, kidding, sport

badland *n syn* see WASTE 1

||bad lot *n syn* see WASTREL 1

badly *adv* 1 *syn* see HARD 5
2 *syn* see AMISS 2
ant well

badman *n syn* see OUTLAW
rel criminal, villain; hood, hoodlum, hooligan, thug; blackguard, devil, knave, rascal, rapscallion, rascallion, rogue, scoundrel

bad-tempered *adj syn* see ILL-TEMPERED
rel cantankerous, cranky, crusty, temperamental, touchy
con forbearing, long-suffering, patient
ant good-tempered

Baedeker *n syn* see HANDBOOK

baffle *vb syn* see FRUSTRATE 1
rel confound, dumbfound, flummox, mystify, nonplus; puzzle; addle, ball up, befuddle, confuse, fog, mix up, muddle; discomfit, disconcert, embarrass, faze, rattle
con enlighten, illuminate

bag *n* 1 a container made of a flexible material and open or opening at the top <a grocery *bag* >
syn ||poke, pouch, sack
||2 *syn* see HAG 2

bag *vb syn* see CATCH 1
rel clench, ||cop, ||glom, hook, land, nab, net, sack, scoop
idiom lay by the heels

baggage *n syn* see WANTON

||**bagged** *adj syn* see INTOXICATED 1

||**bagnio** *n syn* see BROTHEL

bail *n syn* see GUARANTEE 1

bail *vb syn* see DIP 2

bailiwick *n syn* see FIELD
rel district, jurisdiction, neighborhood, place, quarter, realm; beat, circuit, round, walk

bait *vb* 1 *syn* see MOLEST
2 to persist in tormenting or harassing another < *baiting* him with gibes about his humble origin>
syn badger, bullyrag, chivy, heckle, hector, hound, ride
rel annoy, bother, bedevil, devil, rag, worry; harass, harry, haze, vex; ||bug, nag, pester, push around
3 *syn* see LURE

bait *n* 1 *syn* see LURE 2
||2 *syn* see SNACK

bake *vb* 1 *syn* see BURN 3
2 *syn* see FIRE 6

baking *adj syn* see HOT 1

balance *n* 1 the stability resulting from the equalization of opposing forces <keeping his emotional *balance* when under stress>
syn counterpoise, equilibrium, equipoise, equiponderation, poise, stasis
rel collectedness, composure, cool, coolness, coolth, equanimity, repose, sangfroid; aplomb, assurance, self-assurance, self-possession; control, self-control, stability, steadiness; stagnancy, stagnation
con imbalance, unbalance; instability, nervousness, shakiness, uncontrol, unsteadiness
2 *syn* see SYMMETRY
rel congruity, consistency, correspondence, sameness
con disbalance, disharmony, disproportion, incongruity, inconsistency, irregularity, overbalance, unbalance
ant imbalance
3 *syn* see REMAINDER

balance *vb syn* see COMPENSATE 1

rel adjust, attune, harmonize, tune; accord, agree, correspond; even, level, square
idiom strike a balance

bald *adj* 1 *syn* see HAIRLESS
rel bobbed, clipped, cropped, polled, shaven, sheared
con bushy, hairy, hirsute, shaggy; unshaven, unshorn; fleecy, furry, woolly; downy, fuzzy, pilose, pubescent
2 *syn* see BARE 1
rel austere, severe; plain, unadorned, undecorated, unembellished, ungarnished, unornamented; colorless, lackluster, lifeless, lusterless, uncolored

balderdash *n syn* see NONSENSE 2

baldhead *n* one who has a bald head
syn baldpate, ||baldy, ||skinhead

baldpate *n syn* see BALDHEAD

||**baldy** *n syn* see BALDHEAD

balefire *n syn* see BEACON 1

baleful *adj syn* see SINISTER
rel deadly, evil, harmful, pernicious; bodeful, foreboding; unfavorable, unpromising
con auspicious, benign, favorable, promising, propitious; advantageous, beneficial
ant beneficent
2 *syn* see OMINOUS

balk *n syn* see TIMBER 2

balk *vb* 1 *syn* see FRUSTRATE 1
idiom stand in the way of
con back, support, uphold; aid, assist, help
ant forward
2 *syn* see DEMUR
rel decline, refuse, turn down; flinch, hang back, quail, recoil, shrink
con capitulate, give in

balky *adj syn* see CONTRARY 3
rel immovable, inflexible, unbending, unmanageable; averse, disinclined, hesitant, indisposed, loath, reluctant
con subdued, submissive, tame

ball *n* a more or less spherical body or mass <a *ball* of string>
syn globe, orb, rondure, round, sphere
rel egg, oval, ovoid

ball *vb* to form into a more or less spherical body or mass < *balled* the cookie dough with her hands>
syn conglobate, conglobe, ensphere, round, sphere
rel bead, pill; clot, wad

balladmonger *n syn* see POETASTER

ball and chain *n* 1 *syn* see RESTRICTION 1
||2 *syn* see WIFE

ballast *vb syn* see STABILIZE

ballerina *n syn* see DANCER

ballet girl *n syn* see DANCER

ballot *n* 1 a piece of paper used to cast a vote in an election <deliberately spoiled his *ballot* >
syn ticket, vote
rel Australian ballot, Indiana ballot, Massachusetts ballot, office-block ballot, office-group ballot, party-column ballot, secret ballot
2 *syn* see SUFFRAGE

ballot *vb syn* see ELECT 2

||**ballup** *n syn* see CONFUSION 3

ball up *vb syn* see CONFUSE 2

ballyhoo *vb syn* see TOUT

balm *n* 1 *syn* see OINTMENT

  2 *syn* see FRAGRANCE

balm *vb syn* see CALM

balmy *adj* 1 *syn* see SWEET 2

  rel musky; refreshing, rejuvenating, restorative; pleasant, pleasing

  2 *syn* see GENTLE 1

  rel agreeable, delightful, gratifying, pleasant, pleasing; allaying, assuaging, balsamic, easing, lightening, relieving, soothing

  con annoying, bothering, bothersome, irking, irksome, vexing

  ‖3 *syn* see FOOLISH 2

‖**baloney** *n syn* see NONSENSE 2

balustrade *n syn* see RAILING

bamboozle *vb syn* see DUPE

  rel bilk, diddle, swindle

ban *vb syn* see FORBID

  rel illegalize, outlaw

  con approve, authorize; suffer, tolerate

ban *n syn* see TABOO

banal *adj syn* see INSIPID 3

  rel hackneyed, pedestrian, trite, warmed-over; bromidic, commonplace, corny, platitudinous, stock; bewhiskered, hoary, old; asinine, fatuous, silly, simple

  con fresh, new, novel; different, uncommon, unusual; stimulating, zesty; choice, rare, recherché

  ant original

banality *n syn* see COMMONPLACE

banausic *adj* 1 *syn* see DULL 9

  2 *syn* see MATERIALISTIC

band *n syn* see STRIP 1

  rel belt, border, edge, line; tape; fascia, taenia; streak, vein

band *vb* 1 *syn* see BELT 1

  2 *syn* see UNITE 2

  rel amalgamate, unionize; consociate; club, team (up)

  con disintegrate, disperse, dissolve, separate

  ant break up, disband

band *n* 1 *syn* see COMPANY 4

  rel assembly, bevy, body, bunch, covey, group; detachment, detail

  2 *syn* see GROUP 1

  3 *syn* see ORCHESTRA

bandage *vb* to cover with a bandage < *bandage* wounds >

  syn bind, dress

bandanna *n syn* see KERCHIEF 1

bandar–log *n syn* see CHATTERBOX

bandbox *adj syn* see DAPPER

bandeau *n syn* see STRIP 1

banderole *n syn* see FLAG

‖**bandido** *n syn* see OUTLAW

  rel brigand, footpad, highwayman, holdup man; bravo, cutthroat, gunman, villain; gangster, mobster, racketeer

banding *n syn* see STRIP 1

bandit *n* 1 *syn* see OUTLAW

  rel brigand, footpad, highwayman, holdup man; bravo, cutthroat, villain; gangster, mobster, racketeer; jayhawker

  2 *syn* see MARAUDER

bandwagon *n syn* see FASHION 3

bandy *vb syn* see EXCHANGE 3

  rel chuck, flip, pitch, throw, toss; banter; answer, repay, retort

  idiom bat (*or* beat) back and forth

bandy *adj syn* see BOWLEGGED

bandy–legged *adj syn* see BOWLEGGED

bane *n* 1 *syn* see POISON

  2 *syn* see DOWNFALL 2

baneful *adj* 1 *syn* see PERNICIOUS

  rel injurious; insalubrious, noisome, unhealthy, unwholesome

  con benign, favorable, propitious; advantageous, helpful, profitable; healthful, salubrious, salutary, wholesome

  ant beneficial

  2 *syn* see OMINOUS

‖**bang** *vb syn* see SURPASS 1

bang *n* 1 *syn* see BLOW 1

  2 a loud percussive or explosive noise < slammed the book shut with a *bang* >

  syn blast, boom, burst, clap, crack, crash, slam, smash, wham

  rel noise, report, sound; discharge, explosion, pop, shot; howl, roar, roll, rumble, thunder

  3 *syn* see THRILL

  4 *syn* see SMASH 6

  5 *syn* see VIGOR 2

bang *adv syn* see JUST 1

bang away (at) *vb syn* see ATTACK 2

bang–up *adj syn* see EXCELLENT

banish *vb* to eject by force or authority from a country, state, or sovereignty < *banish* an enemy of the king >

  syn cast out, deport, displace, exile, expatriate, expel, expulse, ‖fag, ostracize, oust, relegate, run out, transport; *compare* EJECT 1

  rel disfellowship, excommunicate, rusticate; debar, exclude, shut out; drive out, eject, evict, turn out; bump, can, cashier, discharge, dismiss, fire, put out, sack; blackball, blacklist, boycott

banishment *n syn* see EXILE 1

banister *n syn* see RAILING

bank *n* 1 *syn* see PILE 1

  rel snowbank, snowdrift; cloudage, fogbank

  2 *syn* see SHORE

  rel bankside, levee, riverfront, streamside; lakefront, lakeside, lakeside, margin; oceanfront, seabank, seabeach, seaboard, seafront, sea frontage, sea line, sea sands, shingle

  idiom water's edge

bank *vb syn* see HEAP 1

  rel compact, concentrate

bank *vb* to place money in a bank < *banks* half his paycheck every week >

  syn deposit

  rel invest, lay aside, lay away, salt away, salt down, save, set aside, sock away; cache, coffer, hoard, squirrel (away), stash

  con draw out, take out, withdraw; disburse, expend, fork (over *or* out), lay out, pay (out), spend

bank (on *or* upon) *vb syn* see RELY (on *or* upon)

  rel intend, plan; bet (on), gamble (on), stake, venture, wager

  idiom bank the rent on, bet one's bottom dollar on, go bail on, lay money on

---

syn synonym(s)   *rel* related word(s)
ant antonym(s)   *con* contrasted word(s)
idiom idiomatic equivalent(s)
‖ use limited; if in doubt, see a dictionary

bankroll *vb syn* see CAPITALIZE

bankrupt *vb* 1 *syn* see DEPLETE
rel break, impair, incapacitate
con rebuild, repair, restore, revive; augment, bolster, fortify, strengthen
2 *syn* see STRIP 2
3 *syn* see RUIN 3
4 *syn* see RUIN 2

banned *adj* 1 *syn* see FORBIDDEN
2 *syn* see CONTRABAND

banner *n syn* see FLAG
rel banneret

banner *adj syn* see EXCELLENT

bannerol *n syn* see FLAG

banquet *n syn* see DINNER
rel bridale, feed, ǁgaudy, harvest home, repast, ǁtuck, ǁtuck-in, ǁtuck-out

bantam *adj* 1 *syn* see SMALL 1
2 *syn* see SAUCY 1

banter *vb* 1 to make fun of good-naturedly
< the students resented their teacher's *bantering* them about mistakes >
syn chaff, fool, fun, jest, ǁjive, joke, jolly, josh, kid, rag, razz, rib
rel deride, guy, mock, quiz, rally, ridicule, satirize, taunt, tease, twit
idiom make fun of, make merry with, poke fun at
ǁ2 *syn* see FACE 3
ǁ3 *syn* see COAX

banter *n* animated back-and-forth exchange of remarks < entertained the group with their jolly *banter* >
syn backchat, badinage, ǁcross talk, persiflage, repartee, snip-snap
rel chitchat, gossip, gossipry, small talk; rallying, teasing; exchange, give-and-take
con debate, deliberation, discussion

bantling *n syn* see BABY 1

baptismal name *n syn* see GIVEN NAME

baptize *vb* 1 to administer the rite of baptism < a child *baptized* in the Catholic Church >
syn asperse, christen, immerse, sprinkle
rel cleanse, purify, regenerate
2 *syn* see NAME 1

bar *n* 1 a solid piece of material usually rectangular and considerably longer than it is wide < a *bar* of gold >
syn billet, ingot, rod, slab, stick, strip
2 something that stands in the way of some objective < his religion was a *bar* to membership in that exclusive club >
syn barricade, barrier, blank wall, block, blockade, fence, roadblock, stop, wall
rel clog, encumbrance, hamper, hindrance, impediment; hurdle, obstacle, obstruction, stumbling block; check, checkrein, control, curb; bamboo curtain, iron curtain; difficulty, hardship, vicissitude
3 *syn* see OBSTACLE
rel check, checkrein, control, curb
con accommodation, convenience, facility, service
ant advantage
4 *syn* see COURT 2
5 a room or public establishment where alcoholic beverages are served < nightly discussions in the *bar* >
syn barroom, ǁboozer, ǁbucket shop, buvette, cantina, cocktail lounge, drinkery, drunkery, ǁgin mill, ǁgroggery, ǁgrogshop, lounge, pothouse, pub, ǁpublic house,

ǁrum-hole, rummery, ǁrum-mill, rumshop, saloon, tap, taproom, tavern, watering hole, watering place; *compare* ALEHOUSE
rel barrelhouse, bistro, bottle club, cabaret, café, dive, honky-tonk, nightclub, rathskeller, roadhouse, wineshop

bar *vb* 1 *syn* see LIMIT 2
2 *syn* see EXCLUDE
rel block, hinder; leave out, omit, pass over; banish, deport, exile, ostracize
con accept, receive, welcome; allow, let, permit
ant admit, include
3 *syn* see HINDER
rel halt, stop
con back, support, uphold

bar *prep syn* see EXCEPT

barathrum *n syn* see HELL

barb *n syn* see SHAFT 2

barbarian *adj* 1 of, relating to, or characteristic of people that are not fully civilized < the *barbarian* tribes that sacked Rome >
syn barbaric, barbarous, Gothic, Hunnic, Hunnish, rude, savage, uncivil, uncivilized, uncultivated, wild
rel heathenish, vandal, vandalic; backward, coarse, crude, ill-mannered, primitive, rough; untamed; uncouth, uncultured; beastish, bloodthirsty, brutal, cruel, ferocious, inhuman
con gentle, peaceful, subdued, submissive, tame; cultured, enlightened, humane, sophisticated; genteel, refined, well-bred, well-mannered
ant civilized
2 *syn* see BARBARIC 1

barbaric *adj* 1 marked by a lack of restraint, cultivated taste, and refinement < the *barbaric* use of color and ornament >
syn barbarian, barbarous, graceless, outlandish, tasteless, vulgar, wild
rel coarse, crude, rough, rude, uncouth; flamboyant, florid, ornate, ostentatious, showy; blatant, flashy, garish, gaudy, loud, tawdry; cacophonous, ʰarsh, raucous; aggressive
con quiet, restrained, soft, subdued; concinnous, cultivated, elegant, polished, refined; smooth, sophisticated, urbane
2 *syn* see BARBARIAN 1

barbarism *n* a word or expression which in form or use offends against contemporary standards of correctness or purity in a language < many writers consider *irregardless* a *barbarism* >
syn corruption, impropriety, slangism, solecism, vernacularism, vernacularity, vulgarism
rel neologism; colloquialism, foreignism; shibboleth; Goldwynism, Irish bull, malaprop, malapropism, spoonerism; caconym; error, lapse, misuse, slip

barbarous *adj* 1 *syn* see BARBARIAN 1
2 *syn* see OUTRAGEOUS 1
3 *syn* see BARBARIC 1
rel backward, benighted, cretinous, ignorant, illiterate, lowbrow, philistine, uneducated, unlettered, unread, unschooled, untaught, untutored
con aware, informed, sophisticated, with-it; finished, polished, rounded; well-bred,

well-mannered; educated, intelligent, learned, schooled; erudite, well-read
4 *syn* see FIERCE 1
rel heartless, uncompassionate, unmerciful; atrocious, monstrous, outrageous; bloody, butcherly, sanguinary; fiendish, sadistic
con forbearing, lenient, merciful, tolerant; compassionate, sympathetic, tender; benevolent, humane, humanitarian
ant clement

barbate *adj syn* see BEARDED

barber *n* one whose occupation is primarily cutting hair
syn haircutter
rel coiffeur, coiffeuse, friseur, hairdresser, hair stylist; beautician, cosmetologist; clipper, cropper, shaver

bard *n* 1 a poet-singer who sang or recited verse to the accompaniment of a stringed instrument (as a harp) < *bards* were the theater of olden times >
syn jongleur, minstrel, troubadour
rel meistersinger, minnesinger, rhapsodist; gleeman; skald; conteur
2 *syn* see POET

bardlet *n syn* see POETASTER

bardling *n syn* see POETASTER

bare *adj* 1 lacking a natural or usual cover or finish < the room looked *bare* without curtains and pictures >
syn bald, naked, nude
rel denuded, dismantled, divested, peeled, stripped, uncovered; baldish, depilated, hairless; unattired, unclad, unclothed, undressed, unrobed; arid, bleak, desert, desolate
con attired, clad, clothed, dressed, garbed; furry, hairy; green, leafy, luxuriant, verdant; complete, consummate, finished, perfect
ant covered
2 *syn* see OPEN 2
3 *syn* see EMPTY 1
rel barren, depleted, destitute, dried-up, emptied, exhausted; unfilled, unstocked, unsupplied
con bountiful, bursting, chock-full, complete, crammed, laden, overflowing, overfull, replete, stuffed; full, stocked, supplied
4 *syn* see VERY 4

bare *vb syn* see STRIP 2
rel disclose, exhibit, expose, reveal, show, unveil
con camouflage, cloak, disguise, dissemble, mask; apparel, attire, dress, garb, invest, robe
ant cover

barefaced *adj syn* see SHAMELESS
rel blunt, candid, frank, open, plain, temerarious; indecent, indecorous, unseemly
con covert, secret, secretive, stealthy; cautious, circumspect, discreet, tactful
ant furtive

barefisted *adj or adv syn* see BARE-HANDED

barefoot *adj* 1 wearing no shoes or stockings < always went *barefoot* in the summer >
syn shoeless, unsandaled, unshod
con socked, stockinged; sockless; booted, sandaled, shod
2 *syn* see DISCALCED

bare-handed *adj or adv* without covering on the hands < box *bare-handed* >
syn barefisted, bareknuckle
ant gloved

bareknuckle *adj or adv syn* see BARE-HANDED

barely *adv syn* see JUST 2
con amply; adequately, enough, sufficiently

barf *vb syn* see VOMIT

bargain *n* 1 an advantageous purchase < at that price the car is a *bargain* >
syn buy, closeout, pennyworth, steal
rel deal; giveaway
con cheat, flimflam, gouge, sticking, sting
2 *syn* see CONTRACT

bargain *vb* 1 *syn* see HAGGLE 2
rel arrange, confer, negotiate; compromise
2 *syn* see TRADE 1

barge *vb syn* see LUMBER

bark *vb syn* see SNAP 1

barkeeper *n* 1 *syn* see SALOONKEEPER
2 *syn* see BARTENDER

||**barmaid** *n syn* see BARTENDER

barman *n syn* see BARTENDER

Barmecidal *adj syn* see APPARENT 2

barnacle *n syn* see PARASITE

||**barney** *n syn* see QUARREL

barnyard *adj syn* see OBSCENE 2

baron *n syn* see MAGNATE

baronial *adj syn* see GRAND 1

baroque *adj syn* see ORNATE
rel embellished, gilt, ornamented, scrolled
con austere, gray

barrage *n* a vigorous expulsion or projection of many things at once < the announcement was met with a *barrage* of protests >
syn bombardment, broadside, burst, cannonade, drumfire, fusillade, hail, salvo, shower, storm, volley
rel burst, eruption, flare, outburst, stream, surge, tornado

barrel *n* 1 *syn* see CASK
2 *syn* see MUCH

barrel *vb syn* see HURRY 2

barrelhouse *n syn* see DIVE

barrelhouse *vb syn* see HURRY 2

barren *adj* 1 *syn* see STERILE 1
rel childless, fallow, heirless, issueless
con pregnant; fertile
ant fecund
2 deficient in production of vegetation and especially crops < *barren* deserts and wastelands >
syn hardscrabble, infertile, unbearing, unfertile, unproductive
rel fallow; irreclaimable, uncultivable, unhusbanded, untillable, wild; bleak, depleted, improverished, poor, worn-out; vegetationless, verdureless; arid, desert, dry, parched
con arable, fruitful, productive; fat, rich; lush, luxuriant; green, verdant, verdurous
ant fertile

barren *n syn* see WASTE 1

barricade *n syn* see BAR 2
barrier *n syn* see BAR 2
barring *prep syn* see EXCEPT
barroom *n syn* see BAR 5
bar sinister *n syn* see STIGMA
bartender *n* one who serves alcoholic beverages at a bar <worked for some years as a *bartender* >
syn barkeeper, ||barmaid, barman, mixologist, tapster; *compare* SALOONKEEPER
barter *vb syn* see TRADE 1
basal *adj* 1 *syn* see FUNDAMENTAL 1
rel pedimental; bottommost, lowermost, lowest, nethermost, undermost
con highest, uppermost
2 *syn* see ELEMENTARY 1
base *n* 1 something on which another thing is reared or built or by which it is supported or fixed in place <the *base* of a lamp>
syn basement, basis, bed, bedrock, bottom, footing, foundation, ground, groundwork, hardpan, infrastructure, rest, seat, seating, substratum, substruction, substructure, underpinning, understructure; *compare* BASIS 1
rel bolster, buttress, framework, prop, stand, stay, support; foot
2 *syn* see BASIS 1
3 *syn* see BOTTOM 3
base *vb* to supply or to serve as a basis <*based* his accusation on sound evidence>
syn bottom, establish, found, ground, predicate, rest, stay
rel build, construct, fix, plant, seat, set up
base *adj* 1 *syn* see IGNOBLE 1
2 *syn* see CHEAP 2
3 contemptible because beneath minimal standards of human decency <a *base* lying cheat>
syn despicable, ignoble, low, low-down, servile, sordid, squalid, ugly, vile, wretched; *compare* CONTEMPTIBLE
rel beggarly, lousy, sorry; abominable, disgraceful, loathsome; bad, evil, wicked; base-minded, low-minded, meanspirited; caitiff, cowardly, dastardly, recreant; unworthy; dirty, filthy; degrading, humiliating, ignominious
con honest, honorable, upright; virtuous; ethical, moral, righteous; fair, forbearing, open-minded, patient, reasonable, tolerant, understanding
ant noble
baseborn *adj* 1 *syn* see IGNOBLE 1
2 *syn* see ILLEGITIMATE 1
baseless *adj* being without cause or occasion <anxious old ladies with their *baseless* fears>
syn bottomless, foundationless, gratuitous, groundless, uncalled-for, unfounded, ungrounded, unwarranted
rel false, wrong; indefensible, reasonless, unjustifiable, unsolid, unsupported, unsustained, untenable; empty, idle, vain; needless, pointless, senseless, unnecessary, unneeded
con actual, real, reasonable, true; authentic, bona fide, genuine, valid
basement *n syn* see BASE 1
bash *n* 1 *syn* see BLOW 1

2 *syn* see SHINDIG 1
bashful *adj syn* see SHY 1
rel timorous; recoiling, shrinking, mousy; abashed, embarrassed; blushful
con assured, bold, intrepid; arrogant, barefaced, brazen, impudent, shameless; loquacious, talkative
ant brash, forward
basic *adj* 1 *syn* see FUNDAMENTAL 1
rel capital, chief, main, principal
2 *syn* see ELEMENTAL 1
basic *n syn* see ESSENTIAL 1
basically *adv syn* see ESSENTIALLY 1
basin *n syn* see DEPRESSION 2
basis *n* 1 something that supports or sustains anything immaterial <his argument rested on a *basis* of conjecture>
syn base, bedrock, footing, foundation, ground, groundwork, infrastructure, root, substratum, underpinning; *compare* BASE 1
rel axiom, fundamental, law, principle, theorem; assumption, postulate, premise, presumption, presupposition; essence, heart
2 *syn* see BASE 1
3 something serving as a reason or justification for an action or opinion <resented such a challenge without *basis* or reason>
syn foundation, warrant
rel call, justification, right; ground(s), reason
bask *vb* 1 *syn* see SUN
2 *syn* see WALLOW 3
bassinet *n syn* see BABY CARRIAGE
bastard *n* 1 one born out of wedlock <bore a *bastard* before she was fifteen>
syn by-blow, catch colt, chance child, come-by-chance, filius nullius, filius populi, illegitimate, love child, natural child, whoreson, woods colt
2 *syn* see HYBRID
bastard *adj* 1 *syn* see ILLEGITIMATE 1
2 *syn* see SPURIOUS 3
bastardize *vb syn* see DEBASE 1
bastardy *n syn* see ILLEGITIMACY 1
baste *vb* 1 *syn* see BEAT 1
rel clobber, ||larrup, mill, whip
2 *syn* see SCOLD 1
bastille *n syn* see JAIL
bastille *vb syn* see IMPRISON
bastinado *n syn* see BLOW 1
bastion *n syn* see BULWARK
bat *n* 1 *syn* see BLOW 1
2 *syn* see CUDGEL
||3 *syn* see SPEED 2
4 *syn* see BINGE 1
||bat *n syn* see HAG 2
bat *vb syn* see WANDER 1
bat *vb syn* see WINK
batch *n syn* see GROUP 3
bate *vb* ||1 *syn* see ABATE 4
||2 *syn* see DECREASE
3 *syn* see EXCLUDE
bath *n, usu* **baths** *pl syn* see SPA 1
||bath *vb syn* see BATHE 1
bathe *vb* 1 to clean oneself with a bath <*bathed* only on Saturday nights>
syn ||bath, shower, tub, wash
rel soap; douse, soak
2 to flow or splash against <waves *bathed* the rocky shore>
syn lap, lave, lip, wash
rel drench, soak, sop, souse; flush

bathetic *adj* **1** *syn* see TRITE

2 *syn* see SENTIMENTAL

bathtub gin *n* *syn* see MOONSHINE 2

bating *prep* *syn* see EXCEPT

baton *n* *syn* see CUDGEL

batter *vb* **1** to affect (as by repeated blows) so severely as to disfigure or damage < so *battered* in the fight he couldn't even crawl away > < a boat *battered* to pieces by stormy seas >
syn ||bung up, mangle, maul
rel disable, disfigure; maim, mutilate; cripple, lame; bruise, contuse, lacerate; baste, clobber, pummel; shatter, wreck
idiom beat black and blue, beat to pieces (*or* shreds), beat within an inch of one's life

2 *syn* see BEAT 1

battery *n* *syn* see GROUP 3

battle *n* a hostile meeting between opposing military forces < the *battle* continued until nightfall >
syn action, engagement
rel brush, clash, encounter, pitched battle, scrimmage, skirmish; assault, attack, onset, onslaught, sortie; combat, conflict, contest, fight; hostilities

battle *vb* *syn* see CONTEND 1
rel clash, scrimmage; assail, assault, attack, bombard

battle cry *n* a word or phrase used as a slogan by a faction < "death to the invader" was the *battle cry* >
syn cry, motto, rallying cry, war cry; *compare* CATCHWORD

battlesome *adj* *syn* see QUARRELSOME 2

||**batty** *adj* *syn* see INSANE 1

bauble *n* *syn* see KNICKKNACK

bavardage *n* *syn* see SMALL TALK

bawd *n* *syn* see PROSTITUTE

bawdy house *n* *syn* see BROTHEL

bawl *vb* **1** *syn* see ROAR
rel holler, scream, screech, shout, shriek, squall, yammer, yell

2 to cry and weep loudly or lustily especially from distress < the baby *bawled* and kicked when its bottle was taken away >
syn howl, squall, wail, yowl; *compare* CRY 2, ROAR
rel blubber, boohoo, cry, sob, weep

bawl out *vb* *syn* see SCOLD 1
rel condemn, denounce
idiom read a lecture (*or* lesson)

bay *n*, *usu* **bays** *pl* *syn* see HONOR 2

bay *vb* *syn* see HOWL 1

bay *n* *syn* see INLET

baygall *n* *syn* see SWAMP

bayou *n* *syn* see INLET

bay window *n* *syn* see POTBELLY

bazoo *n* ||**1** *syn* see MOUTH 1

2 *syn* see RASPBERRY

be *vb* to have actuality or reality < I think, therefore I *am* >
syn breathe, exist, live, move, subsist
rel hold, obtain, stand; abide, continue, endure, go on, persist, prevail, remain; come

beach *n* *syn* see SHORE

rel oceanfront; lakeshore, lakeside

beach *vb* *syn* see SHIPWRECK 1

beached *adj* *syn* see AGROUND

beacon *n* **1** a signal fire usually on an elevated place < a *beacon* on the hill to warn of danger >
syn balefire, watchfire
rel flare; bonfire

2 *syn* see LIGHTHOUSE

beak *n* **1** *syn* see BILL 1

2 *syn* see NOSE 1

3 *syn* see PROMONTORY

||**4** *syn* see JUDGE 2

beak *vb* *syn* see PECK 1

be-all and end-all *n* **1** *syn* see ESSENCE 2

2 *syn* see WHOLE 1

beam *n* **1** *syn* see TIMBER 2

2 *syn* see RAY 1

3 *syn* see BUTTOCKS

beam *vb* **1** *syn* see SHINE 1

2 *syn* see SMILE

beaming *adj* *syn* see BRIGHT 1

||**bean** *n* *syn* see HEAD 1

beanery *n* *syn* see EATING HOUSE

beany *adj* *syn* see SPIRITED 2

bear *vb* **1** *syn* see CARRY 1
rel shoulder

2 *syn* see BEHAVE 1

3 to have attached to one < the bottle *bears* the label "poisonous" >
syn carry, have, possess
rel display, exhibit, show
con lack, need, want

4 *syn* see ACCOMPANY

5 to give birth to offspring < she has *borne* several children >
syn ||birth, ||born, bring forth, deliver
idiom bring abed, bring to bed, bring to birth, give birth to, have a baby
con abort, miscarry

6 *syn* see PRESS 8

7 *syn* see PRESS 1

8 *syn* see PROCREATE 1

9 to bring forth a product < the apple trees *bear* every year >
syn produce, turn out, yield
rel breed, engender, generate, propagate, reproduce; fructify, fruit; fabricate, fashion, form, make, shape; create, invent

10 to put up with something trying or difficult < can't *bear* the tension of the work >
syn abide, brook, digest, endure, go, lump, stand, ||stick, stick out, stomach, suffer, support, sustain, swallow, sweat out, take, tolerate; *compare* ACCEPT 2
rel afflict, torment, torture, try; allow, condone, countenance, permit; acquiesce, bow, defer, submit, yield
idiom make do, put up with, take lying down
con decline, refuse, reject, spurn; avoid, bypass, elude, evade, shun

11 *syn* see HEAD 3

bear (on *or* upon) *vb* to have a connection especially logically < this situation *bears* directly upon the question under discussion >
syn appertain, apply, pertain, relate
rel refer; affect, concern, involve, touch; correspond, parallel
idiom have to do with, tie in with

---

syn synonym(s)   *rel* related word(s)
ant antonym(s)   *con* contrasted word(s)
idiom idiomatic equivalent(s)
|| use limited; if in doubt, see a dictionary

bear (with) *vb syn* see ACCEPT 2

bearable *adj* capable of being borne < his outrageous behavior is hardly *bearable* >
syn endurable, livable, sufferable, supportable, sustainable, tolerable
rel acceptable, admissible, allowable, satisfactory
con insufferable, insupportable, intolerable, unendurable, unsupportable
ant unbearable

beard *n* the natural growth of hair on a man's face < some men look better with *beards* >
syn beaver, whiskers; *compare* SIDE-WHISKERS
rel charley, galways, goatee, imperial, spade beard, Vandyke; fuzz

beard *vb syn* see FACE 3
idiom beard the lion in his den

bearded *adj* having a beard < an old *bearded* philosopher >
syn barbate, bewhiskered, whiskered
rel beardy; goateed; hairy; stubbed, stubbly, unshaven
con barefaced, clean-faced, clean-shaven, shaven, smooth-faced, whiskerless
ant beardless

bear down *vb syn* see CONQUER 1

bearer *n* 1 *syn* see MESSENGER
2 a man who carries baggage and supplies for travelers < native *bearers* serving the safari >
syn carrier, drogher, porter
rel boy, cargador, coolie; redcap, skycap

bearing *n* 1 the way in which or the quality by which a person outwardly manifests his personality < a dowager with a regal *bearing* >
syn address, air, comportment, demeanor, deportment, mien, port, presence, set
rel aspect, brow, look; attitude, carriage, pose, posture, stand; poise; display, front; behavior, conduct
2 *syn* see BIRTH 1

bearish *adj syn* see CANTANKEROUS

bear out *vb syn* see CONFIRM 2

bear up *vb syn* see SUPPORT 4

beast *n* a lower animal as distinguished from man < *beasts* of the field >
syn animal, brute, creature, ||critter
rel beastie, varmint; quadruped

beastly *adj syn* see BRUTISH

beat *vb* 1 to strike repeatedly < robbed and *beaten* by thugs >
syn baste, batter, belabor, buffet, drub, ||dump, hammer, lam, lambaste, paste, pelt, pound, pummel, thrash, tromp, wallop, whop
rel bastinado, baton, bludgeon, cudgel, fustigate, pistol-whip; flog, lace, lash, tan, whip; lay on, maul, muss up, rough (up)
idiom give one beans, rain blows on
2 *syn* see WHIP 2
3 *syn* see SCOUR 2
4 *syn* see WHIP 3
5 *syn* see WAG
6 *syn* see HAMMER 1
7 *syn* see SURPASS 1
idiom beat (all) hollow
8 *syn* see NONPLUS 1
9 *syn* see CHEAT
10 *syn* see FRUSTRATE 1
11 *syn* see SCOOP 3

12 *syn* see PULSATE
13 *syn* see WIN 1

beat *n* 1 *syn* see RHYTHM
2 *syn* see SCOOP

beat down *vb syn* see CONQUER 1

beating *n syn* see DEFEAT 1
rel lump(s)

beatitude *n syn* see HAPPINESS
rel ecstasy, rapture, transport
con affliction, trial, tribulation; anguish, grief, sorrow, woe; agony, suffering
ant despair, dolor

beau *n* 1 *syn* see BOYFRIEND 1
2 *syn* see BOYFRIEND 2

Beau Brummel *n syn* see FOP

beau ideal *n syn* see MODEL 2
idiom shining example

||**beaut** *n syn* see BEAUTY

beauteous *adj syn* see BEAUTIFUL

beautiful *adj* very pleasing or delightful to look at < the most *beautiful* woman in the world >
syn attractive, beauteous, ||bonny, comely, fair, good-looking, handsome, lovely, pretty, pulchritudinous, stunning, well-favored
rel choice, elegant, exquisite; glorious, resplendent, splendid, sublime, superb; eye-appealing, eye-filling, ||proper; personable, pleasing
con offensive, repugnant, repulsive, revolting; homely, plain, ordinary, unattractive, unbeauteous, uncomely, unhandsome, unlovely, unpretty
ant ugly, unbeautiful

beautiful people *n pl syn* see SMART SET

beautify *vb syn* see ADORN
rel glamorize, prettify
con deface, disfigure; damage, mar, spoil
ant uglify

beauty *n* a physically attractive woman < a charming woman and a *beauty* to boot >
syn ||beaut, eyeful, knockout, looker, lovely, stunner
rel charmer, dazzler, dream, eye-opener, good-looker, peach; belle, toast
idiom raving beauty
con dog, gorgon, hag, slattern, witch

beaver *n syn* see BEARD

becalm *vb syn* see CALM

because *conj* for the reason that < I left *because* I was bored >
syn as, as long as, ||being, 'cause, considering, for, inasmuch as, now, seeing, since, whereas
idiom in view of the fact

because of *prep syn* see OVER 6

becloud *vb* 1 *syn* see OBSCURE
rel befuddle, confuse, perplex, puzzle
con illuminate
2 *syn* see CONFUSE 4

become *vb* 1 to commence to be < *became* sick yesterday >
syn come, ||come over, get, go, grow, run, turn, wax
rel arise, mount, rise, soar
idiom get to be, turn out to be
2 *syn* see SUIT 4
3 *syn* see FLATTER

becoming *adj syn* see DECOROUS 1
rel attractive, flattering; tasteful

con unattractive, unflattering; distasteful; inappropriate, unfitting, unrespectable, unsuitable
ant unbecoming

becomingly *adv syn* see WELL 4

becrush *vb syn* see CRUSH 2

bed *n syn* see BASE 1

bed *vb* 1 to put to bed <getting the children *bedded* >
  syn tuck (in)
  rel cradle
2 *syn* see RETIRE 4

bedamn *vb syn* see SWEAR 3

bedaub *vb syn* see SMEAR 1

bedaze *vb syn* see DAZE 2

bedazzle *vb syn* see DAZE 1

bedcover *n syn* see BEDSPREAD

bedeck *vb syn* see ADORN
  rel bedaub, bedizen

bedevil *vb syn* see WORRY 1

bedfast *adj syn* see BEDRIDDEN

bedim *vb syn* see OBSCURE
  con highlight, illuminate

bedlamite *n syn* see LUNATIC 1

bedlamite *adj syn* see INSANE 1

bedog *vb syn* see TAIL

bedraggled *adj syn* see SHABBY 1

bedridden *adj* confined to one's bed by illness or injury <a *bedridden* invalid >
  syn bedfast
  rel confined, incapacitated, laid up; feeble, infirm, sickly, weak
  idiom flat on one's back
  con healed, mended; hale, healthy, whole
  ant ambulant; ambulatory

bedrock *n syn* see BASE 1
2 *syn* see BASIS 1

bedspread *n* an often ornamental outer covering for a bed <an appliquéd *bedspread* >
  syn bedcover, counterpane, coverlet, ‖coverlid, spread

bee *n syn* see CAPRICE
  rel idea; impulse

beef *n* 1 *syn* see MUSCLE 1
2 *syn* see POWER 4
3 *syn* see QUARREL

‖**beef** *vb syn* see GRIPE

beef (up) *vb syn* see INCREASE 1

beefheaded *adj syn* see STUPID 1

beef-witted *adj syn* see STUPID 1

beefy *adj syn* see HUSKY 1

beekeeper *n* one who engages in the production of and caring for bees and honey <special masks and gloves for *beekeepers* >
  syn apiarist, apiculturist, beeman, beemaster

beeline *vb syn* see HURRY 2

Beelzebub *n syn* see DEVIL 1

beeman *n syn* see BEEKEEPER

beemaster *n syn* see BEEKEEPER

beer garden *n syn* see ALEHOUSE

beer hall *n syn* see ALEHOUSE

‖**beerhouse** *n syn* see ALEHOUSE

beetle *vb* 1 *syn* see HANG 4
2 *syn* see BULGE

beetlehead *n syn* see DUNCE

---

beetleheaded *adj syn* see STUPID 1

‖**beezer** *n syn* see NOSE 1

befall *vb syn* see HAPPEN 1

befit *vb syn* see SUIT 4

befitting *adj* 1 *syn* see FIT 1
  ant unbefitting
2 *syn* see DECOROUS 1

befittingly *adv syn* see WELL 1

befog *vb* 1 *syn* see OBSCURE
2 *syn* see CONFUSE 4
3 *syn* see PUZZLE

befool *vb syn* see DUPE

before *adv* 1 so as to precede something in order or time <racing on *before* to give warning >
  syn ahead, ante, antecedently, beforehand, fore, forward, in advance, precedently, previous
  con behind; abaft, aft, astern
  ant after
2 in time past <had heard that joke *before* >
  syn already, earlier, erstwhile, formerly, heretofore, once, previously; *compare* THEN 1
  ant after
3 until now or then <you'll get it tomorrow and not *before* >
  syn beforehand, earlier, sooner

before *prep* 1 coming before in space or time <be home *before* dark >
  syn ahead of, ante, ere, in advance of, preceding, prior to, to; *compare* UNTIL
  con since, subsequent to
  ant after
2 in the presence of <stood *before* the court >
  syn confronting, facing
  idiom face to face with
3 *syn* see UNTIL

beforehand *adv* 1 *syn* see BEFORE 1
2 *syn* see BEFORE 3

befoul *vb* 1 *syn* see CONTAMINATE 2
2 *syn* see MALIGN

befuddle *vb syn* see CONFUSE 2
  rel daze

befuddlement *n syn* see HAZE 2
  rel confusion, mix-up
  con clearheadedness, lucidness

beg *vb* to ask for or ask one for something urgently <beg one's life from an attacker> < *beg* a stranger for help>
  syn appeal, beseech, brace, conjure, crave, entreat, implore, importune, invoke, plead, pray, supplicate
  rel ask, call (on), request, solicit; petition, sue; besiege, demand, press; nag, worry
  idiom throw oneself at the feet of (*or* on the mercy of)
  con hint, intimate, suggest

‖**begats** *n pl* 1 *syn* see GENEALOGY
2 *syn* see OFFSPRING

begem *vb syn* see BEJEWEL

beget *vb* 1 *syn* see FATHER 1
2 *syn* see PROCREATE 1

beggar *n* 1 one who begs especially habitually or as a livelihood < *beggars* crying out to tourists>
  syn bummer, cadger, moocher, panhandler, ‖schnorrer
  rel deadbeat, freeloader, sponge, sponger; ‖bindle stiff, hobo, tramp
2 *syn* see SUPPLIANT

---

syn synonym(s)   *rel* related word(s)
ant antonym(s)   *con* contrasted word(s)
idiom idiomatic equivalent(s)
‖ use limited; if in doubt, see a dictionary

3 *syn* see PAUPER

beggared *adj syn* see POOR 1

beggarly *adj syn* see CONTEMPTIBLE

rel wretched; ‖cheesy, trashy; measly, paltry

beggary *n* 1 *syn* see POVERTY 1

2 *syn* see MENDICANCY

begin *vb* 1 to carry out the first act or step of an action or operation < *began* his lecture with a joke >

syn commence, embark (on *or* upon), enter, get off, inaugurate, initiate, jump (off), kick off, launch, lead off, open, set to, start, take up, tee off

rel establish, found, institute; introduce, usher in; broach; attack, tackle; prepare; break in; dig in

idiom get the show on the road, get to work, get underway

con cease, desist, discontinue, quit, stop; close, complete, conclude, finish, terminate; abandon, forsake, leave, quit; back out, renege, withdraw

ant end

2 to come into existence < not since civilization *began* has there been such distress >

syn arise, commence, originate, start; *compare* SPRING 1

rel spring; open

idiom raise its head

con end, finish, terminate

beginner *n syn* see NOVICE

beginning *n* the first part or stage of a process or development < the first few chapters at the *beginning* of the novel >

syn alpha, birth, commencement, dawn, dawning, day spring, genesis, onset, opening, opening gun, outset, outstart, setout, start

rel creation, inception, origin, origination, root, source, spring; anlage, rudiment, sprout; prologue; appearance, emergence, rise; incipiency, infancy

idiom the word go

con consummation, termination; closing, completion, conclusion; omega

ant end, ending

beginning *adj* 1 *syn* see INITIAL 1

2 *syn* see ELEMENTARY

begird *vb* 1 *syn* see BELT 1

2 *syn* see SURROUND 1

begirdle *vb* 1 *syn* see BELT 1

begone *vb syn* see GET OUT 1

begrime *vb syn* see SOIL 2

begrudge *vb syn* see ENVY

beguile *vb* 1 *syn* see MANIPULATE 2

2 *syn* see DECEIVE

rel entice, lure, seduce

3 *syn* see WHILE

beguiling *adj syn* see MISLEADING

béguin *n syn* see INFATUATION

behave *vb* 1 to act in a specified way < *behave* as people of good breeding should >

syn acquit, act, bear, carry, comport, conduct, demean, deport, disport, do, go on, move, quit

rel control, direct, manage

idiom make as if (*or* as though); be on one's best behavior, mind one's p's and q's

ant misbehave, misconduct

2 *syn* see ACT 5

behavior *n* one's actions in general or on a particular occasion < his flustered *behavior* before women >

syn comportment, conduct, deportment, tenue

rel bearing, demeanor, mien; action, manner, way

con misbehavior, misconduct

behead *vb* to sever the head < nobles *beheaded* for treason >

syn decapitate, decollate, guillotine, head, neck

idiom bring to the block

behemoth *n syn* see GIANT

behemothic *adj syn* see HUGE

behest *n syn* see COMMAND 1

rel demand; prompting, request, solicitation

behind *adv syn* see AFTER

behind *prep* 1 *syn* see ABAFT

2 *syn* see AFTER 2

behind *n syn* see BUTTOCKS

behindhand *adj* 1 *syn* see NEGLIGENT

2 *syn* see BACKWARD 6

3 *syn* see TARDY

ant beforehand

behold *vb syn* see SEE 1

beholden *adj syn* see INDEBTED

beholder *n syn* see SPECTATOR

being *n* 1 *syn* see EXISTENCE 1

rel character, individuality, personality

ant nonbeing

2 *syn* see THING 4

3 *syn* see ENTITY 1

4 *syn* see ESSENCE 1

5 *syn* see HUMAN

‖**being** *conj syn* see BECAUSE

bejewel *vb* to ornament with or as if with jewels < a *bejeweled* headdress > < cobwebs all *bejeweled* with glittering morning dew >

syn begem, beset, enjewel, gem, jewel

rel bespangle, spangle; diamond; encrust

belabor *vb syn* see BEAT 1

belated *adj* 1 *syn* see TARDY

2 *syn* see OLD-FASHIONED

belch *vb* 1 to expel gas suddenly from the stomach through the mouth < ate and ate until he *belched* >

syn burp, eruct, eructate

2 *syn* see ERUPT 1

beldam *n* 1 a woman of advanced years < a crotchety *beldam* hunched over the fire >

syn dame, gammer, grandam; *compare* GAFFER, OLDSTER

rel grandmother, granny; grand dame; matron; matriarch

idiom old girl

con damsel, lass, maid, miss

2 *syn* see HAG 2

beleaguer *vb* 1 *syn* see BESIEGE

rel siege, storm

idiom set upon from all sides

2 *syn* see WORRY 1

belfry *n* 1 *syn* see BELL TOWER

‖2 *syn* see HEAD 1

belie *vb syn* see MISREPRESENT

rel contradict, contravene, negative; controvert, disprove; conceal, disguise, hide

con bespeak, betoken, indicate; disclose, discover, reveal

ant attest

belief *n* 1 the act of assenting intellectually to something proposed as true or the state of mind of one who so assents < offered ready *belief* to anyone he trusted >
syn credence, credit, faith
rel assurance, certainty, certitude, conviction, sureness; acquiescence, assent; trust; credibility, trustworthiness
con distrust, doubt, mistrust, uncertainty; incredulity; question
ant disbelief, unbelief
2 *syn* see OPINION
rel doctrine, dogma, fundamental, law, precept, principle; concept, idea

believable *adj* worthy of belief < the author's bizarre characterizations are hardly *believable* >
syn colorable, credible, creditable, plausible
rel likely, possible, probable, tenable; conceivable, rational, reasonable; presumable, supposable; unquestionable; convincing, impressive, persuasive, satisfying; meaningful, solid, substantial
con improbable, unlikely; doubtable, doubtful, dubious, fishy, questionable; specious; implausible, incredible; inconceivable, untenable; fabulous, mythological
ant unbelievable

believe *vb* 1 to have a firm conviction in the reality of something < *believes* in ghosts >
syn accept, ‖buy, swallow
rel accredit, credit, trust; admit
idiom have no doubts about, hold the belief that, take (*or* accept) as gospel, take at one's word, take one's word for
con discredit, distrust, doubt, mistrust, question, suspect; challenge, dispute, reject, turn down
ant disbelieve, misbelieve
2 *syn* see FEEL 3
3 *syn* see UNDERSTAND 3

belittle *vb* *syn* see DECRY 2
rel criticize, discredit; underestimate, underrate, undervalue
con intensify; boast, crow
ant aggrandize; magnify

belittlement *n* *syn* see DETRACTION

bell *vb* *syn* see RING

‖**bell cow** *n* *syn* see LEADER 1

bellicose *adj* *syn* see BELLIGERENT
rel aggressive, assertive; factious, fighting, rebellious
idiom full of fight
con gentle, moderate, temperate
ant amicable; pacific

belligerence *n* *syn* see ATTACK 2

belligerent *adj* having or taking an aggressive or fighting attitude < a *belligerent* reply to a diplomatic note >
syn bellicose, combative, contentious, gladiatorial, militant, pugnacious, quarrelsome, ‖ructious, scrappy, truculent, warlike; *compare* QUARRELSOME 2
rel battling, fighting, warring; attacking, invading; aggressive, antagonistic, fierce, hostile; ardent, hot, hot-tempered

---

syn synonym(s)   *rel* related word(s)
ant antonym(s)   *con* contrasted word(s)
idiom idiomatic equivalent(s)
‖ use limited; if in doubt, see a dictionary

---

con neutral; pacific, pacifist, peaceable, peaceful; conciliatory; amicable
ant friendly

‖**belling** *n* *syn* see SHIVAREE

bellow *vb* *syn* see ROAR
rel bark, bay, yelp; cry, wail; low, moo

bell ringer *n* *syn* see SMASH 6

bell tower *n* a tower that supports or shelters a bell or group of bells < a *bell tower* stood free from the church >
syn belfry, campanile, carillon

bellwether *n* *syn* see LEADER 1

belly *n* *syn* see ABDOMEN

bellyache *n* *syn* see STOMACHACHE

‖**bellyache** *vb* *syn* see GRIPE

‖**bellyacher** *n* *syn* see GROUCH

belong *vb* 1 to be suitable, appropriate, or advantageous or to be in a proper or fitting place or situation < the boxes *belong* in the attic >
syn fit, go, set
rel become, befit, suit; accord, agree, chime, harmonize; correspond, match, tally
idiom have one's place
2 to be the property of (a person or thing) < the books *belong* to the library >
syn appertain, pertain, vest
3 to be an attribute, part, adjunct, or function (of a person or thing) < good humor and wit *belong* to his personality >
syn indwell, inhere
idiom run in one's blood (*or* family)

belongings *n pl* *syn* see POSSESSION 2

beloved *adj* *syn* see FAVORITE 1

beloved *n* 1 *syn* see SWEETHEART 1
2 *syn* see GIRL FRIEND 2
3 *syn* see BOYFRIEND 2

below *adv* 1 in or at a lower position than something expressed or implied < several business establishments were situated *below* >
syn beneath, under, underneath
ant above
2 lower on the same page or on a following page < for additional examples see *below* >
syn infra
ant above, supra

below *prep* 1 in a lower position relative to some other object or place < lives just *below* me >
syn beneath, under, underneath
con over
ant above
2 *syn* see AFTER 2

belt *n* 1 a strip of flexible material worn around the waist < a leather *belt* >
syn ceinture, cincture, girdle, sash, waistband
rel baldric, cummerbund; band
2 *syn* see AREA 1
rel stretch, strip

belt *vb* 1 to bind about or around with or as if with a belt < gold lamé *belting* the gown >
syn band, begird, begirdle, cincture, encincture, engird, engirdle, gird, girdle
rel tie (up); loop; sash; circle, encircle, ring
2 *syn* see SLAM 1

belt *n* *syn* see BLOW 1

belvedere *n* *syn* see SUMMERHOUSE

bemean *vb syn* see HUMBLE

bemedaled *adj* having or wearing decorations especially as awarded by the military <the general's *bemedaled* uniform>
syn beribboned, decorated

bemired *adj syn* see MUDDY 1

bemoan *vb syn* see DEPLORE 1
rel regret; complain
con applaud, cheer, huzzah; delight, jubilate, rejoice
ant exult

bemuse *vb syn* see DAZE 2
rel addle; perplex, puzzle
con enlighten, illuminate

bemused *adj syn* see ABSTRACTED

benchmark *n syn* see STANDARD 3

bend *vb* 1 *syn* see CURVE
rel arch, curl, double, hook
ant straighten
2 *syn* see GIVE 12
3 *syn* see INCLINE 3
4 *syn* see ADDRESS 3

bend (over) *vb syn* see HANG 4

bend *n* 1 *syn* see TURN 2
2 *syn* see TURN 4
3 *syn* see CURVE

bender *n syn* see BINGE 1

bending *adj syn* see CROOKED 1

beneath *adv syn* see BELOW 1

beneath *prep syn* see BELOW 1
ant above, over

benediction *n* 1 *syn* see BLESSING 1
2 *syn* see GRACE 1
3 *syn* see APPROBATION
4 *syn* see GOOD 1

benefact *vb syn* see HELP 1

benefaction *n syn* see DONATION

benefic *adj syn* see GOOD 1
rel desirable, pleasing, satisfying
con damaging, harmful, injurious
ant malefic

beneficence *n syn* see DONATION

beneficial *adj syn* see GOOD 1
rel salutary, wholesome
con baneful, deleterious, noxious, pernicious
ant detrimental, harmful

benefit *n* 1 *syn* see GOOD 1
2 *syn* see WELFARE
rel account, behalf, sake; gain, profit
con catastrophe, disaster, misfortune; detriment
ant harm, ill

benefit *vb* to be useful or profitable to <medicines that *benefit* mankind>
syn advantage, avail, profit, serve, work (for)
rel advance, ameliorate, better, contribute (to), favor, improve; relieve, succor; build, further, promote; aid, assist, help
idiom do a world of good
con hinder, impede; damage, impair, injure; distress, upset; afflict, anguish; oppose
ant harm, hurt

benet *vb syn* see CATCH 1

benevolence *n* 1 *syn* see GOODWILL 1
con animosity, bitterness, ill will; antagonism, hostility; inimicality, unkindliness; stinginess
2 *syn* see GIFT 1

benevolent *adj* 1 *syn* see GENEROUS 1
rel beneficent; charitable; humane; compassionate, tenderhearted

con cruel, inhuman, malicious, spiteful
ant malevolent
2 *syn* see CHARITABLE 1
rel bighearted, freehearted, generous, greathearted, largehearted, liberal, openhanded; public-spirited; do-good
con niggardly, stingy; callous, indifferent, insensitive, unconcerned, unfeeling

benighted *adj* 1 *syn* see IGNORANT 1
rel backward, unenlightened; uninformed
idiom in the dark
con informed, intelligent
2 *syn* see BACKWARD 5

benightedness *n syn* see IGNORANCE 1

benign *adj* 1 *syn* see KIND
rel gracious
con malevolent, malicious, malignant, spiteful; acrid, caustic, mordant
ant malign
2 *syn* see FAVORABLE 5
rel gentle, mild; benevolent, charitable, humane; clement, forbearing, merciful
con menacing, threatening
ant malign

benignant *adj syn* see KIND
rel mild; gracious
con malevolent, malicious, spiteful; relentless
ant malignant

benison *n syn* see BLESSING 1

bent *n* 1 *syn* see LEANING 2
2 *syn* see GIFT 2
con antipathy, aversion; inability, incapacity

bent *adj* 1 *syn* see CURVED
2 *syn* see DECIDED 2

benumb *vb* 1 *syn* see DEADEN 1
2 *syn* see DAZE 2

benumbed *adj syn* see NUMB 1

bequeath *vb* 1 *syn* see WILL
con disinherit, exheridate
2 *syn* see HAND DOWN

bequest *n syn* see LEGACY 1

berate *vb syn* see SCOLD 1
con acclaim, praise; applaud; commend, compliment

berceuse *n syn* see LULLABY

bereave *vb syn* see DEPRIVE 2

bereaved *adj* suffering the death of a loved one <the *bereaved* family>
syn bereft
rel distressed, sorrowing

bereft *adj syn* see BEREAVED

beribboned *adj syn* see BEMEDALED

berth *n* 1 *syn* see WHARF
2 *syn* see JOB 2

beseech *vb syn* see BEG

beset *vb* 1 *syn* see BEJEWEL
2 *syn* see ATTACK 1
3 *syn* see BESIEGE
4 *syn* see INFEST 1
5 *syn* see SURROUND 1
idiom come at from all directions (or sides)

besetment *n syn* see ANNOYANCE 3

beside *prep* 1 at or by the side of <left the car *beside* the road>
syn alongside, by, ‖forenet, next to
rel near, opposite
2 *syn* see NEAR 2
3 *syn* see BESIDES 1
4 *syn* see EXCEPT

besides *adv* 1 *syn* see ALSO 2

idiom at that
2 *syn* see AGAIN 4
besides *prep* 1 in addition to < *besides*
being tall, he's thin >
syn as well as, beside, beyond, over and
above
idiom along with, together with
2 *syn* see EXCEPT 1
besides *adj syn* see ADDITIONAL
besiege *vb* to surround an enemy in a
fortified or strong position so as to prevent ingress and egress < Troy was *be-
sieged* by Greeks for ten years >
syn beleaguer, beset, blockade, invest
rel encircle, encompass, hem (in), surround; trap; assail, assault, attack
besmear *vb* 1 *syn* see SMEAR 1
2 *syn* see TAINT 1
besmirch *vb syn* see TAINT 1
besoil *vb syn* see SOIL 2
besotted *adj syn* see INFATUATED
bespangle *vb syn* see SPANGLE 1
bespatter *vb* 1 *syn* see SPOT 1
2 *syn* see MALIGN
bespeak *vb* 1 *syn* see RESERVE 2
2 *syn* see ADDRESS 4
3 *syn* see ASK 2
idiom put in for
4 *syn* see INDICATE 2
bespeckle *vb syn* see SPECKLE 1
bespectacled *adj* having or wearing
glasses < *bespectacled* thesaurists >
syn spectacled
bespot *vb syn* see SPOT 1
besprinkle *vb syn* see SPRINKLE 1
best *adj* much more than half < passed the
best part of a month at the shore >
syn better, ‖bettermost, greater, largest,
most
best *vb* 1 *syn* see CONQUER 2
2 *syn* see SURPASS 1
3 *syn* see DEFEAT 2
best *n* the choicest one or part < always
gave the *best* that she had >
syn choice, cream, elite, fat, flower, pick,
pride, prime, primrose, prize, top
rel gem; nonesuch, nonpareil; exemplar,
model, paragon, pattern
idiom cock of the walk, flower of the
flock, one in a thousand (*or* million)
ant worst
bestain *vb syn* see STAIN 1
‖**best bib and tucker** *n syn* see FINERY
best girl *n syn* see GIRL FRIEND 1
bestial *adj syn* see BRUTISH
bestialize *vb syn* see DEBASE 1
bestir *vb syn* see STIR 1
bestow *vb* 1 *syn* see USE 2
2 *syn* see STOW
3 *syn* see HARBOR 2
4 *syn* see GIVE 1
bestower *n syn* see DONOR
bestrew *vb syn* see STREW 1
bestride *vb syn* see MOUNT 5
2 to sit with one leg on each side < boys
bestriding a fallen log >
syn straddle, ‖striddle, stride
bet *n* something of value (as money) staked
on a winner-take-all basis on the outcome

of an uncertainty < laid a *bet* at three to
one on the champion >
syn ante, pot, stake, wager
bet *vb syn* see GAMBLE 1
bête noire *n syn* see ABOMINATION 1
bethink *vb syn* see REMEMBER
betide *vb syn* see HAPPEN 1
betimes *adv* 1 *syn* see EARLY 1
2 *syn* see EARLY 2
‖3 *syn* see SOMETIMES
betoken *vb* 1 *syn* see INDICATE 2
2 *syn* see AUGUR 2
betray *vb* 1 *syn* see DECEIVE
rel ensnare, entrap, snare, trap
2 to prove faithless or treacherous < *betrayed* his own people by going over to
the enemy >
syn cross, double-cross, sell, sell out,
‖split
rel desert, renegade; give away, inform,
turn in; collaborate; apostatize
idiom act (*or* play) the traitor, break
faith, round on, sell down the river
3 *syn* see REVEAL 1
rel demonstrate, evidence, evince, manifest, show; betoken, indicate
con defend, guard, protect, safeguard,
shield
betrayer *n syn* see INFORMER
betrothal *n syn* see ENGAGEMENT 2
betrothed *n* either member of a couple
engaged to be married
syn affianced, intended
rel fiancé, husband-to-be; bride-to-be,
fiancée, wife-to-be
betrothed *adj syn* see ENGAGED 2
betrothing *n syn* see ENGAGEMENT 2
betrothment *n syn* see ENGAGEMENT 2
better *adj* 1 *syn* see BEST
2 more worthy or pleasing than an alternative < it is *better* to lose gracefully than
to win arrogantly >
syn ‖bettermost, preferable, superior;
compare GOOD
rel exceeding, exceptional, surpassing;
choice, desirable, excellent
idiom more than a match for
ant worse
better *adv syn* see MORE 2
ant worse
better *n* 1 *syn* see SUPERIOR
2 a superior or winning position < had
the *better* of the argument >
syn advantage, superiority, upper hand,
victory, whip hand; *compare* ADVANTAGE
3
rel success, triumph, win
con collapse, defeat, disadvantage, loss;
beating, drubbing, licking
ant worse
better *vb* 1 *syn* see IMPROVE 1
ant worsen
2 *syn* see SURPASS 1
‖**bettermost** *adj* 1 *syn* see BETTER 2
2 *syn* see BEST
between *prep* 1 *syn* in common to (as in position, in a distribution, or in participation)
 < a treaty *between* three powers >
syn among
2 in the time, space, or interval that sepa-
rates < *between* the ages 12 and 20 >
syn ‖atween, ‖atwixt, ‖betwixt, in between, tween, twixt

---

syn synonym(s)   *rel* related word(s)
ant antonym(s)   *con* contrasted word(s)
idiom idiomatic equivalent(s)
‖ use limited; if in doubt, see a dictionary

‖**betwixt** *prep syn* see BETWEEN 2
bevel *n syn* see DIAGONAL
beveled *adj syn* see DIAGONAL
‖**bever** *n syn* see SNACK
beverage *n syn* see DRINK 1
bevy *n syn* see GROUP 1
bewail *vb syn* see DEPLORE 1
ant rejoice
beware *vb* to be cautious < *beware* of the dog >
syn look out, mind, watch out
rel attend, heed, notice, watch
idiom be on one's guard, be on the lookout (*or* watch), keep at a safe distance, take care (*or* heed)
con disregard, ignore, neglect
bewhiskered *adj syn* see BEARDED
bewilder *vb* 1 *syn* see PUZZLE
rel baffle, fuddle, muddle
2 *syn* see CONFUSE 2
bewitch *vb* 1 to practice witchcraft on < medicine men who *bewitch* ignorant tribesmen >
syn charm, enchant, ensorcell, hex, spell, voodoo, witch
rel bedevil, demonize, overlook, possess, sorcerize; beglamour, dazzle, trick
idiom cast a spell on (*or* over), give (*or* cast) the evil eye, put a curse on
2 *syn* see ATTRACT 1
rel beglamour, ‖snow
bewitched *adj syn* see ENAMORED 3
bewitching *adj syn* see ATTRACTIVE 1
con forbidding, grim
bewitchment *n syn* see MAGIC 1
beyond *adv* 1 on or to the farther side < a house with mountains *beyond* >
syn farther, further, ‖yon, yonder
2 *syn* see OVER 1
beyond *prep* 1 on or to the farther side of < the store is just *beyond* the next house >
syn after, outside, past, without
2 out of the reach, sphere, or comprehension of < it's *beyond* me how he did it >
syn above, past
idiom beyond one's depth (*or* power), over (*or* above) one's head, too deep (*or* much) for
3 *syn* see BESIDES 1
beyond *adj syn* see ADDITIONAL
beyond *n syn* see HEREAFTER 2
‖**b'hoy** *n syn* see TOUGH
bias *n* 1 *syn* see LEANING 2
2 *syn* see PREJUDICE
rel inclination, predisposition; slant, standpoint, viewpoint
con dispassionateness; fairness, justness
bias *adj syn* see DIAGONAL
bias *vb* 1 *syn* see SLANT 3
2 *syn* see INCLINE 3
3 *syn* see PREJUDICE 2
biased *adj* 1 *syn* see DIAGONAL
2 exhibiting or characterized by a highly personal and unreasoned distortion of judgment < a *biased* estimate of the book's worth >
syn colored, jaundiced, one-sided, partial, partisan, prejudiced, prepossessed, tendentious, unindifferent, unneutral, warped
rel bent, disposed, inclined, predisposed; influenced, interested, swayed; opinionated
con detached, dispassionate, impartial, neutral, open-minded; fair, honest, just
ant unbiased
bibber *n syn* see DRUNKARD
bibble-babble *n syn* see CHATTER
bibelot *n syn* see KNICKKNACK
Bible *n* the sacred volume of Christians < students of the *Bible* >
syn Book, Holy Writ, Sacred Writ, Scripture
idiom Book of Books, Good Book, Word of God
bibliopole *n syn* see BOOKDEALER
bicker *vb* 1 *syn* see ARGUE 2
rel battle, contend, fight, war
2 *syn* see QUARREL
3 *syn* see RATTLE 1
bickering *n syn* see QUARREL
bicycle *n* a pedal-propelled vehicle with two wheels tandem, a steering handle, and a saddle seat < ten-speed *bicycles* >
syn bike, cycle, two-wheeler, velocipede
bid *vb* 1 *syn* see COMMAND
rel summon
con interdict, prohibit
ant forbid
2 *syn* see INVITE
rel request
biddable *adj syn* see OBEDIENT
rel amiable, good-natured, obliging
con mulish, obstinate, stiff-necked, stubborn
ant recalcitrant
bidding *n syn* see COMMAND
rel call, summoning
biddy *n* 1 *syn* see MAID 2
2 *syn* see HAG 2
bide *vb* 1 *syn* see STAY 2
rel continue
2 *syn* see RESIDE 1
bierstube *n syn* see ALEHOUSE
biff *n syn* see BLOW 1
‖**biff** *vb syn* see STRIKE 2
‖**biffy** *n syn* see PRIVY 1
bifold *adj syn* see TWOFOLD 1
big *adj* 1 of significant size or scope < a *big* expanse of mud > < *big* plans >
syn considerable, extensive, hefty, large, large-scale, major, sizable
rel bumper, hulking, whacking, whopping; clumsy, unwieldy; ample, biggish, capacious, commodious, comprehensive, copious, roomy, spacious, voluminous; distended, inflated, swollen
con paltry, piddling, trivial; slight, small; insignificant; minute, tiny, wee
ant little
2 *syn* see LARGE 1
3 *syn* see PREGNANT 1
4 *syn* see FULL 1
rel flushed, overflowing; cloyed, glutted, sated, satiated, satisfied
idiom full to bursting (*or* overflowing), full to the ears, stuffed to the gills
con empty
5 *syn* see IMPORTANT 1
6 *syn* see PRETENTIOUS 3
7 *syn* see GENEROUS 1
big *adv syn* see VERY 1
big *n syn* see NOTABLE 1
big boy *n syn* see NOTABLE 1
‖**big bug** *n syn* see NOTABLE 1
‖**big cheese** *n syn* see NOTABLE 1
‖**big chief** *n syn* see NOTABLE 1
biggety *adj syn* see WISE 5

||biggie *n syn* see NOTABLE 1

big gun *n syn* see NOTABLE 1

||big house *n syn* see JAIL

bight *n syn* see INLET

big name *n syn* see CELEBRITY 2

bigness *n syn* see SIZE 2

||big noise *n syn* see NOTABLE 1

bigot *n syn* see ENTHUSIAST

  rel approver, liker, relisher; mumpsimus, racist, segregationist

  con depreciator, disparager, knocker; disliker, disrelisher, hater, loather, misliker

bigoted *adj syn* see ILLIBERAL

  rel lily-white; conservative

big shot *n syn* see NOTABLE 1

big-timer *n syn* see NOTABLE 1

||big wheel *n syn* see NOTABLE 1

bigwig *n syn* see NOTABLE 1

bike *n syn* see BICYCLE

bilge *n syn* see NONSENSE 2

bilk *vb* 1 *syn* see FRUSTRATE 1

  con fulfill

  2 *syn* see CHEAT

  3 *syn* see ESCAPE 2

  rel dodge, shake

bill *n* 1 the jaws of a bird with their projecting horny covering < the huge *bill* of the toucan >

  syn beak, neb, nib, pecker

  2 *syn* see PROMONTORY

  3 *syn* see VISOR 1

bill *n* 1 a statement of the amount due a creditor < *bills* from the grocer and doctor >

  syn account, invoice, reckoning, score, statement, tab

  rel charges, damage

  idiom statement of account

  2 *syn* see CHECK 1

  3 *syn* see POSTER

  4 *syn* see DOLLAR

billet *n syn* see JOB 2

billet *vb* 1 to assign quarters to soldiers < the troops were *billeted* in private homes >

  syn canton, quarter

  rel bed, house, lodge, put up; bestow

  2 *syn* see HARBOR 2

billet *n syn* see BAR 1

billet–doux *n syn* see LOVE LETTER

billingsgate *n syn* see ABUSE

billy *n syn* see CUDGEL

billy club *n syn* see CUDGEL

||bim *n syn* see WANTON

bimanal *adj syn* see TWO-HANDED 2

bimanual *adj syn* see TWO-HANDED 1

||bimbo *n syn* see WANTON

binary *adj syn* see TWOFOLD 1

bind *vb* 1 *syn* see TIE 1

  con release

  ant unloose

  2 *syn* see BANDAGE

||bindle stiff *n syn* see VAGABOND

||bing *n syn* see PILE 1

binge *n* 1 a drunken revel < hung over after a weekend *binge* >

  syn bat, bender, blowoff, booze, brannigan, bum; bust, carousal, carouse, compotation, drunk, jag, orgy, ran-tan, rowdy-

dow, soak, souse, spree, tear, ||time, toot, wassail

  rel bacchanal, bacchanalia, debauch; blast, ||blowout; ||bun

  2 *syn* see SPREE 1

bio *n syn* see BIOGRAPHY

biocide *n syn* see PESTICIDE

biographer *n* one who writes a biography < irresponsible *biographers* whose work is more fiction than fact >

  syn autobiographer, autobiographist, Boswell, memoirist

biography *n* a more or less detailed account of the events and circumstances of a person's life < wrote a *biography* of his grandfather >

  syn autobiography, bio, confessions, life, memoir

  rel diary, journal, letters; adventures, history, story; profile; obit, obituary

biologic *n syn* see DRUG 1

bird *n syn* see RASPBERRY

birdbrain *n syn* see SCATTERBRAIN

birdhouse *n syn* see AVIARY

birdman *n syn* see PILOT 2

bird–witted *adj syn* see GIDDY 1

birr *n syn* see ENERGY 2

birth *n* 1 the act or process of bringing forth young from the womb < had a very hard *birth* after a prolonged labor >

  syn bearing, ||birthing, childbearing, childbirth, delivery, parturition

  rel abortion, miscarriage, slip

  2 *syn* see BEGINNING

birth *vb* ||1 *syn* see BEAR 5

  2 *syn* see SPRING 1

birth control *n* control of the number of children born especially by preventing or lessening the frequency of conception < cultural and religious aspects of *birth control* >

  syn contraception

  rel rhythm method; planned parenthood; vasectomy; (the) pill

||birthing *n syn* see BIRTH 1

birthmark *n* 1 a congenital pigmented area on the skin < *birthmarks* often appear on the neck >

  syn mole, nevus

  2 *syn* see CHARACTERISTIC 1

birth pang *n, usu* birth pangs *pl syn* see LABOR 2

birthright *n* 1 *syn* see RIGHT 2

  2 *syn* see HERITAGE 1

bisexual *adj* being structurally and functionally both male and female < many lower animals are *bisexual* >

  syn androgynous, hermaphrodite, hermaphroditic

bistered *adj syn* see DARK 3

bistro *n syn* see NIGHTCLUB

bit *n* 1 *syn* see MORSEL 1

  2 *syn* see PARTICLE

  3 *syn* see END 4

  4 *syn* see WHILE 1

bit *vb syn* see RESTRAIN 1

bit by bit *adv syn* see GRADUALLY

||bitch *vb* 1 *syn* see GRIPE

  2 *syn* see DECEIVE

bitch (up) *vb syn* see BOTCH

bitchy *adj syn* see MALICIOUS

bite *vb* 1 to seize with the teeth so that they enter < *bite* into a pear >

---

syn synonym(s) *rel* related word(s)

ant antonym(s) *con* contrasted word(s)

idiom idiomatic equivalent(s)

|| use limited; if in doubt, see a dictionary

syn champ, chomp
rel gnaw, nibble, tooth; ||chaw, chew, crunch, masticate, munch, scrunch; eat
idiom sink one's teeth into
2 *syn* see EAT 3
3 *syn* see SMART
bite *n* 1 *syn* see MORSEL 1
2 *syn* see SNACK
3 *syn* see SHARE 1
biting *adj syn* see INCISIVE
||**bitsy** *adj syn* see TINY
bitter *adj* 1 *syn* see ACRID
rel acerb, acid, bitterish
con delicious; bland, flat, insipid
2 difficult to accept mentally < the *bitter* truth >
syn afflictive, distasteful, galling, grievous, painful, unpalatable
rel annoying, distressing, disturbing, woeful; bad, disagreeable, displeasing, offensive, unpleasant; galling, provoking, vexatious
con agreeable, gratifying, satisfying
3 marked by intense animosity < *bitter* contempt >
syn antagonistic, hostile, rancorous, virulent, vitriolic
rel alienated, divided, estranged; irreconcilable
4 *syn* see SEVERE 3
con mild, springlike, summery
bitter-ender *n syn* see DIEHARD 1
bitterly *adv syn* see HARD 6
bivouac *vb syn* see CAMP
||**bivvy** *vb syn* see CAMP
bizarre *adj* 1 *syn* see STRANGE 4
2 *syn* see FANTASTIC 2
con normal, ordinary, regular
blab *n syn* see CHATTER
blab *n syn* see GOSSIP
blab (out) *vb syn* see REVEAL 1
blabber *vb syn* see BABBLE 2
blabber *n syn* see CHATTER
blabber *n syn* see CHATTERBOX
blabbermouth *n syn* see CHATTERBOX
blabmouth *n syn* see CHATTERBOX
black *adj* 1 having the color of soot or coal < a *black* hearse >
syn atramentous, ebon, ebony, inky, jet, jetty, onyx, pitch-black, pitch-dark, pitchy, raven, sable
rel blackish; charcoal, slate; piceous; dusky, swart, swarthy; brunet
idiom black as a crow (*or* a shoe *or* the ace of spades), black as hell (*or* night)
ant white
2 *syn* see DIRTY 1
3 *syn* see GLOOMY 3
4 *syn* see UTTER
black *vb syn* see BRUISE 1
black (out) *vb syn* see ERASE
black and white *n syn* see PRINT 2
black-a-vised *adj syn* see DARK 3
black beast *n syn* see ABOMINATION 1
||**blackcoat** *n syn* see CLERGYMAN
black dog *n syn* see SADNESS
blacken *vb syn* see MALIGN
idiom blacken one's good name, give one a black eye, throw mud at
black eye *n* 1 a bruise about the eye < got a *black eye* in a fight >
syn mouse, shiner
rel contusion

2 *syn* see STIGMA
blackguard *n syn* see VILLAIN 1
black out *vb syn* see FAINT
blackout *n syn* see FAINT
blague *n syn* see NONSENSE 2
blah *n syn* see NONSENSE 2
blah *adj syn* see DULL 9
blamable *adj syn* see BLAMEWORTHY
blame *vb syn* see CRITICIZE
rel accuse, charge; impute
idiom lay at one's door (*or* doorstep), lay (*or* put) the blame on
con exculpate, vindicate; praise
blame *n* responsibility for misdeed or delinquency < accepted the *blame* for his foolish act >
syn culpability, fault, guilt, onus
rel accountability, answerability, liability; accusation, charge, imputation; censure, condemnation, denunciation, reprehension
idiom burden of guilt
con commendation, compliment; acclaim, applause, praise
blamed *adj* 1 *syn* see DAMNED 2
2 *syn* see UTTER
blameful *adj syn* see BLAMEWORTHY
blameless *adj* 1 *syn* see INNOCENT 2
2 *syn* see GOOD 11
rel unimpeachable
ant blameworthy
blameworthy *adj* deserving reproach and punishment < though not criminal, his behavior was certainly *blameworthy* >
syn amiss, blamable, blameful, censurable, culpable, demeritorious, guilty, reprehensible, sinful, unholy
rel illaudable, uncommendable, unpraiseworthy, unpretty; delinquent, faultful; punishable; foolish, irresponsible, reckless
idiom at fault, to blame
con faultless, flawless, impeccable, irreproachable, unimpeachable; guiltless, innocent, sinless; creditable, high-principled, upright
ant blameless; unblamable
blanch *vb syn* see WHITEN 1
blanch (over) *vb syn* see PALLIATE
blanch *vb syn* see RECOIL
blanched *adj syn* see PALE 1
bland *adj* 1 *syn* see SUAVE
rel good-natured, ingratiating
con bluff, crusty, gruff
ant brusque
2 *syn* see GENTLE 1
3 *syn* see INSIPID 3
con pungent, savory, spicy, zestful
blandish *vb syn* see COAX
rel flatter; beguile, charm
con threaten
blandishment *n syn* see FLATTERY
blank *adj* 1 *syn* see EXPRESSIONLESS
2 *syn* see UTTER
blank *n syn* see OMISSION
blank check *n syn* see CARTE BLANCHE
blanket *vb syn* see COVER 3
blankety-blank *adj* 1 *syn* see DAMNED 2
2 *syn* see UTTER
blankness *n syn* see VACUITY 2
blank wall *n syn* see BAR 2
blare *vb* 1 *syn* see BLAZE
2 *syn* see SCREAM 4
blaring *adj syn* see LOUD 1

blarney *vb syn* see COAX
blarney *n syn* see FLATTERY
blasé *adj syn* see SOPHISTICATED 2
 con awed, wide-eyed; artless, naive, natural, unsophisticated
blasphemous *adj syn* see SACRILEGIOUS
blasphemy *n* 1 impious or irreverent language <cursing God is *blasphemy*>
 syn cursing, cussing, execration, imprecation, profanity, swearing
 rel affront, indignity, insult; abuse, billingsgate, scurrility, vituperation
 con reverence, veneration, worship
 ant adoration
 2 *syn* see PROFANATION
 rel abuse, befouling, shaming
blast *n syn* see BANG 1
blast *vb* 1 to ruin or to injure severely, suddenly, or surprisingly <we'll have no peaches; frost *blasted* the blossoms this year>
 syn blight, dash, nip
 rel destroy, ruin, wreck; damage, injure, spoil; shrivel, stunt, wither
 2 *syn* see SLAM 1
 3 *syn* see WHIP 2
blasted *adj* 1 *syn* see DAMNED 2
 2 *syn* see UTTER
blat *vb syn* see EXCLAIM
blatant *adj* 1 *syn* see VOCIFEROUS
 rel screaming; obtrusive
 con modest, soft-spoken
 2 *syn* see GAUDY
 3 *syn* see SHAMELESS
blather *vb syn* see BABBLE 2
blather *n syn* see NONSENSE 2
blatherskite *n syn* see NONSENSE 2
‖**blatter** *n syn* see CHATTER
blaze *vb* to burn or appear to burn brightly <the hot sun *blazed* down>
 syn blare, flame, flare, glare, glow
 rel illuminate, illumine, light; radiate, shine; coruscate, fulgurate, scintillate, sparkle; incandesce
blaze (abroad) *vb syn* see DECLARE 1
blazes *n pl syn* see HELL
blazing *adj* 1 *syn* see BURNING 1
 2 *syn* see IMPASSIONED
blazon *vb syn* see DECLARE 1
bleach *vb syn* see WHITEN 1
bleak *adj* 1 *syn* see GRIM 2
 2 *syn* see GLOOMY 3
blear *vb syn* see DULL 4
blear *adj syn* see FAINT 2
blear-eyed *adj syn* see STUPID 1
blear-witted *adj syn* see STUPID 1
bleary *adj* 1 *syn* see FAINT 2
 2 *syn* see EFFETE 2
bleat *vb syn* see GRIPE
bleed *vb* 1 *syn* see EXUDE
 2 *syn* see FLEECE 1
bleeding *adj* 1 *syn* see DAMNED 2
 2 *syn* see UTTER
blemish *vb syn* see INJURE 1
blemish *n* an imperfection (as a spot or crack) <a *blemish* on the face>
 syn defect, flaw, vice
 rel fault, scar; blister, blotch, disfigurement, pockmark, wart; catch, snag, tear

---

syn synonym(s)   *rel* related word(s)
ant antonym(s)   *con* contrasted word(s)
idiom idiomatic equivalent(s)
‖ use limited; if in doubt, see a dictionary

---

blench *vb syn* see RECOIL
blench *vb syn* see WHITEN 1
blend *vb* 1 *syn* see MIX 1
 rel combine, integrate
 con resolve, separate
 2 *syn* see HARMONIZE 4
blend *n syn* see MIXTURE
blending *adj syn* see HARMONIOUS 1
bless *vb* 1 to make holy by religious rite or word <the priest *blessed* the water and wine>
 syn consecrate, hallow, sanctify
 rel dedicate
 con defile, desecrate, profane
 2 *syn* see PRAISE 2
blessed *adj* 1 *syn* see HOLY 1
 2 *syn* see DAMNED 2
 3 *syn* see UTTER
blessedness *n syn* see HAPPINESS
 con agony, suffering
 ant misery
blessing *n* 1 an expression or utterance of good wishes <on departing, he received his father's *blessing*>
 syn benediction, benison
 rel Godspeed, valediction
 2 *syn* see APPROBATION
 3 *syn* see GOOD 1
 4 *syn* see GRACE 1
‖**bless out** *vb syn* see SCOLD 1
blight *vb syn* see BLAST 1
blighted *adj* 1 *syn* see DAMNED 2
 2 *syn* see UTTER
‖**blighter** *n syn* see WRETCH 1
blimp *n* 1 *syn* see FATTY
 2 *syn* see REACTIONARY
 3 *cap syn* see STUFFED SHIRT
blind *adj* 1 lacking the power to see <kittens are *blind* at birth>
 syn ‖dark, eyeless, sightless, stone-blind, visionless
 rel dim-sighted, purblind, short-sighted; blindish; blindfolded; unseeing
 idiom blind as a bat
 con seeing, sighted; keen, sharp
 2 *syn* see INTOXICATED 1
 3 *syn* see DULL 7
blind *vb syn* see DAZE 1
blind *n* 1 *syn* see FRONT 3
 2 *syn* see DECOY 2
blind alley *n syn* see DEAD END
blinding *adj* 1 *syn* see DAMNED 2
 2 *syn* see UTTER
blink *vb* 1 *syn* see WINK
 2 to shine intermittently <we'll signal by *blinking* the headlights>
 syn flash, flicker, twinkle
 rel glimmer, scintillate, shimmer
blink (at) *vb syn* see CONNIVE 1
blink (at *or* away) *vb syn* see NEGLECT 1
‖**blinking** *adj* 1 *syn* see DAMNED 2
 2 *syn* see UTTER
blip *vb* 1 *syn* see SLAP 1
 2 *syn* see CENSOR
bliss *n* 1 *syn* see HAPPINESS
 con dolor, misery, woe
 ant anguish
 2 *syn* see HEAVEN 2
blissful *adj* 1 *syn* see HAPPINESS
 rel ecstasy, euphoria, exaltation; heaven, paradise
blister *vb syn* see LAMBASTE 3
blistering *adj* 1 *syn* see HOT 1

‖2 *syn* see DAMNED 2
blithe *adj* 1 *syn* see CHEERFUL 1
　2 *syn* see MERRY
　ant atrabilious, morose
blithering *adj syn* see UTTER
blithesome *adj syn* see MERRY
blitz *vb syn* see BOMBARD
‖**bloat** *n syn* see DRUNKARD
bloated *adj syn* see POMPOUS 1
bloc *n syn* see COMBINATION 2
block *n syn* 1 see BAR 2
　2 *syn* see ANNEX
block *vb syn* 1 see HINDER
　2 *syn* see INTERCEPT
　3 *syn* see FILL 1
block (out) *vb syn* see SKETCH
blockade *n syn* 1 see BAR 2
　‖2 *syn* see MOONSHINE 2
blockade *vb syn* see BESIEGE
block and block *adj syn* see FULL 1
blockhead *n syn* see DUNCE
blockheaded *adj syn* see STUPID 1
blockish *adj syn* see STUPID 1
block out *vb syn* see SCREEN 3
‖**bloke** *n syn* see MAN 3
blond *adj* 1 of a pale soft yellow color
　< *blond* hair >
　syn flaxen, golden, straw
　rel blondish; platinum; champagne, tow-
　headed
　con dark; brunet
　2 *syn* see FAIR 3
blood *n* 1 the fluid that circulates in the
　heart, arteries, capillaries, and veins of a
　vertebrate animal < *blood* covered the
　battlefield >
　syn ‖claret, gore
　rel ichor; humor
　2 *syn* see ANCESTRY
　3 *syn* see MURDER
　4 *syn* see FOP
blood-and-guts *adj syn* see INTENSIVE 2
bloodbath *n syn* see MASSACRE
bloodless *adj* 1 *syn* see PALE 2
　rel colorless; lifeless
　con alive; vigorous; florid
　ant plethoric; sanguine
　2 *syn* see INSENSIBLE 5
bloodshed *n syn* see MASSACRE
bloodstained *adj syn* see BLOODY 1
bloodsucker *n syn* see PARASITE
bloodthirsty *adj syn* see MURDEROUS
bloody *adj* 1 affected by or involving the
　shedding of blood < a *bloody* knife >
　< when will this long and *bloody* conflict
　cease? >
　syn bloodstained, ensanguined, gory,
　imbrued, sanguinary, sanguine, sanguine-
　ous
　rel bloodthirsty, grim, murderous, slaugh-
　terous; cutthroat, red-handed
　2 *syn* see MURDEROUS
bloom *n* 1 *syn* see FLOWER 1
　2 a state or time of beauty, freshness, and
　vigor < the *bloom* of youth >
　syn blossom, flush
　rel glow
　3 a rosy appearance of the cheeks < re-
　covered all her health and *bloom* >
　syn blossom, blush, flush, glow
bloom *vb syn* see BLOSSOM
‖**blooming** *adj* 1 *syn* see DAMNED 2
　2 *syn* see UTTER

blooper *n* 1 *syn* see ERROR 2
　2 *syn* see FAUX PAS
blossom *n* 1 *syn* see FLOWER 1
　rel capitulum, corymb, cyme, infloves-
　cence, panicle, raceme, spike, umbel
　2 *syn* see BLOOM 2
　3 *syn* see BLOOM 3
blossom *vb* to produce flowers or be in
　flower < lilacs *blossom* in the spring >
　syn bloom, blow, burgeon, effloresce,
　flower, outbloom
　rel bud; leaf; shoot; open, unfold
　idiom burst into bloom, come into flower,
　put forth blossoms (or flowers or bloom)
　con fade, fall, wither
blot *n syn* see STIGMA
　rel blemish, flaw, defect
blot *vb syn* see STAIN 1
blotch *vb syn* see SPLOTCH
blot out *vb* 1 *syn* see ERASE
　2 *syn* see ANNIHILATE 2
‖**blotter** *n syn* see DRUNKARD
‖**blotto** *adj syn* see INTOXICATED 1
bloviate *vb syn* see ORATE
blow *vb* 1 to produce a current of air on
　< let the wind *blow* your hair dry >
　syn fan, ruffle, wind, winnow
　2 *syn* see BOAST
　3 *syn* see PANT
　4 *syn* see WASTE 2
　5 *syn* see TREAT 1
　‖6 *syn* see BOTCH
　7 *syn* see GO 2
blow *n syn* see BREAK 4
blow *vb syn* see BLOSSOM
blow *n* 1 a forceful sharp stroke (as with
　the fist or an instrument) < struck him a
　sudden *blow* >
　syn bang, bash, bastinado, bat, belt, biff,
　bop, crack, ‖ding, ‖douse, pound, slam,
　slosh, smack, smash, sock, ‖swap, thwack,
　wallop, ‖welt, whack, whop; *compare*
　CUFF, HIT 1
　rel recumbentibus, slug, ‖souse; clip, pelt,
　plug, punch, swat
　2 *syn* see IMPACT
blow-by-blow *adj syn* see CIRCUMSTAN-
　TIAL
blowen *n syn* see HARLOT 1
blower *n syn* see BRAGGART
blowhard *n syn* see BRAGGART
‖**blow in** *vb syn* see COME 1
blown-in-the-bottle *adj syn* see AU-
　THENTIC 2
‖**blow off** *vb syn* see GRIPE
blowoff *n syn* see BINGE 1
‖**blowout** *n syn* see SHINDIG 1
blowsy *adj syn* see SLATTERNLY
　ant spruce
blow up *vb* 1 *syn* see EXPLODE 1
　2 *syn* see DISCREDIT 2
　3 *syn* see ANGER 2
blowy *adj syn* see WINDY 1
blub *vb syn* see CRY 2
blubber *vb syn* see CRY 2
bludgeon *n syn* see CUDGEL
bludgeon *vb syn* see INTIMIDATE
blue *adj* 1 *syn* see DOWNCAST
　2 *syn* see RISQUÉ
　3 *syn* see UTTER
blue *n syn* see OCEAN
blue blood *n* 1 *syn* see GENTLEMAN
　2 *syn* see ARISTOCRACY

‖**bluebottle** n syn see POLICEMAN

bluecoat n syn see POLICEMAN

blue-eyed adj syn see FAVORITE 1

blue moon n syn see AGE 2

bluenose n syn see PRUDE

bluenosed adj syn see PRIM 1

blueprint n syn see PLAN 1
  rel outline, sketch

blueprint vb syn see PLAN 2

blue-ribbon adj syn see EXCELLENT

blues n pl but sometimes sing in constr syn
  see SADNESS

bluff adj direct and unceremonious in
  speech or manner < bluff aggressive questions >
  syn abrupt, blunt, breviloquent, brief,
  brusque, crusty, curt, gruff, rough, short,
  short-spoken, snippety, snippy
  rel hearty, honest, sincere; barefaced,
  candid, direct, forthright, frank, no-nonsense, outspoken, plainspoken, straightforward; bearish, rude, tactless; sharp, tart;
  laconic, terse
  idiom to the point
  con civil, courteous, courtly, gallant,
  polite; diplomatic, urbane
  ant smooth, suave

bluff vb 1 syn see DECEIVE
  rel fool, joke, trick
  2 syn see ASSUME 4

blunder vb 1 syn see STUMBLE 3
  2 syn see WALLOW 2
  3 syn see BOTCH

blunder (away) vb syn see WASTE 2

blunder n syn see ERROR 2

blunderbuss n syn see STUMBLEBUM

blunderer n syn see STUMBLEBUM

blunt adj 1 syn see DULL 6
  rel unpointed, unsharp; insensitive
  con acuminate, acute
  ant keen, sharp
  2 syn see BLUFF
  con politic, smooth, suave
  ant subtle; tactful

blunt vb 1 syn see DULL 3
  2 syn see DEADEN 1
  3 syn see DULL 5
  4 syn see WEAKEN 1

‖**blunt** n syn see MONEY

blur n syn see STIGMA

blur vb 1 syn see TAINT 1
  2 syn see CONFUSE 4
  3 syn see DULL 4

blurb n syn see PUFF 3

blurt (out) vb syn see EXCLAIM

blush vb to turn or glow red in the face
  < blushed from embarrassment >
  syn color, crimson, flush, glow, mantle,
  pink, pinken, redden, rose, rouge

blush n syn see BLOOM 3

bluster vb 1 syn see ROAR
  rel blast, storm, rage
  2 syn see INTIMIDATE

blustering adj syn see WILD 6

blustery adj syn see WILD 6

board vb 1 to get aboard of < boarded the
  wrong bus >
  syn embark

---

  rel embus, emplane, entrain
  idiom get on
  con debus, deplane, detrain; land
  ant debark, disembark, get off
  2 syn see HARBOR 2
  rel care (for), cherish, nurture, tend

board n 1 **boards** pl syn see DRAMA
  2 syn see TABLE 1

boast vb to express pride in oneself or
  one's accomplishments < boasting about
  all the girl friends he had >
  syn blow, brag, cock-a-doodle-doo, crow,
  gasconade, mouth, prate, puff, rodomontade, vaunt
  rel pique, plume, preen, pride, quack;
  gush, vapor; aggrandize, exalt, glory, triumph; bluster; ‖bounce, bully, ruffle,
  swash, swashbuckle, swagger; flaunt, parade, show off
  idiom blow one's horn, congratulate oneself, hug oneself, pat oneself on the back
  con belittle, decry, degrade, disparage,
  knock, minimize, run down
  ant depreciate

boaster n syn see BRAGGART

boastful adj given to or characterized by
  boasting < a boastful old windbag >
  syn braggadocian, braggart, braggy, rodomontade, self-glorifying, vaunting
  rel arrogant, pretentious; cock-a-hoop,
  exultant; big-headed, conceited, swelled-
  headed; self-aggrandizing, self-applauding,
  self-flattering, vainglorious
  idiom having a high opinion of oneself,
  seeing oneself larger than life
  con self-depreciating, self-effacing, unassuming; bashful, demure, sheepish, shy,
  timid; quiet, reserved, restrained, retiring
  ant modest

bob vb syn see TAP 1

bobbery n syn see BRAWL 2

bobble vb syn see BOTCH

‖**bobby** n syn see POLICEMAN

‖**bodacious** adj syn see NOTEWORTHY

bode vb syn see AUGUR 2

bodement n syn see FORETOKEN

bodiless adj syn see IMMATERIAL 1

bodily adj of or relating to the human
  body < bodily pain >
  syn carnal, corporal, corporeal, fleshly,
  physical, somatic
  rel animal, sensual
  con intellectual, mental, psychic, psychological; spiritual, unworldly

boding n syn see FORETOKEN

body n 1 syn see HUMAN
  2 syn see CORPSE
  3 the main, central, or essential part < the
  body of the discussion dealt with ways to
  ensure equal opportunities for all >
  syn bulk, core, corpus, mass, staple, substance; compare ESSENCE 2, SUBSTANCE 2,
  TENOR 1
  rel majority; sum, total, whole; basis,
  crux, fundamental, gravamen; gist, pith
  con angle, aspect, facet, feature, side;
  accessory, extension, offshoot, side issue
  4 a discrete portion of matter < unknown bodies in space >
  syn bulk, mass, object, volume
  5 a determinable or measurable whole
  < collected a large body of evidence >
  syn aggregate, amount, budget, bulk,
  quantity, quantum, total

---

  syn synonym(s)   rel related word(s)
  ant antonym(s)   con contrasted word(s)
  idiom idiomatic equivalent(s)
  ‖ use limited; if in doubt, see a dictionary

rel extent, range; number, stock, sum, whole
6 *syn* see GROUP 3
7 *syn* see SUBSTANCE 2
body (forth) *vb syn* see REPRESENT 2
boeotian *n syn* see PHILISTINE
bog *n syn* see SWAMP
bog (down) *vb syn* see DELAY 1
bogey *n syn* see APPARITION
boggle *vb* 1 *syn* see DEMUR
2 *syn* see BOTCH
3 *syn* see STAGGER 5
bogus *adj syn* see COUNTERFEIT
rel forged; imitation
con bona fide, good
ant authentic, genuine, real
Bohemian *n* a person (as an artist) who has an unconventional life-style that often reflects protest against or indifference to convention < a gathering place for radicals and *Bohemians* >
syn maverick, nonconformist
rel beat, beatnik, dropout, hippie; iconoclast; eccentric, original; recusant
con conformer, conventionalist, formalist, pedant
bohunk *n syn* see OAF 1
boil *n syn* see ABSCESS
boil *vb* 1 *syn* see SEETHE 4
2 to prepare (as food) in a liquid heated to the point that it begins to give off steam < *boil* eggs >
syn parboil, seethe, simmer, stew
rel coddle, poach; decoct; steam
3 *syn* see ANGER 2
4 *syn* see RUSH 1
boil down *vb syn* see SIMPLIFY
boildown *n syn* see ABRIDGMENT
‖**boiled** *adj syn* see INTOXICATED 1
boiling *adj syn* see HOT 1
boil over *vb syn* see ANGER 2
boisterous *adj* 1 *syn* see TURBULENT 1
2 *syn* see VOCIFEROUS
rel brawling, noisy, riotous, rollicking, rowdy
con sedate, sober, staid; noiseless
‖**boko** *n syn* see NOSE 1
bold *adj* 1 *syn* see BRAVE 1
con pusillanimous, shrinking, timid, timorous
ant cowardly
2 *syn* see WISE 5
rel audacious; bluff
con mousy, quiet, shy
3 *syn* see INSOLENT 2
‖**boldacious** *adj syn* see INSOLENT 2
bold-faced *adj syn* see WISE 5
boldhearted *adj syn* see BRAVE 1
boldness *n syn* see INSOLENCE
bollix *vb syn* see BOTCH
Bolshevik *n syn* see COMMUNIST
‖**Bolshie** *n syn* see COMMUNIST
bolster *vb* 1 *syn* see SUPPORT 4
rel reinforce, strengthen
2 *syn* see SUPPORT 5
bolt *n syn* see THUNDERBOLT
bolt *vb* 1 *syn* see START 1
2 *syn* see RUSH 1
3 *syn* see RUN 2
4 *syn* see EXCLAIM
5 *syn* see GULP
bomb *n* 1 *syn* see FAILURE 5
‖2 *syn* see FORTUNE 4

bomb *vb syn* see BOMBARD
bombard *vb* to assault with bombs or shells < cities *bombarded* by planes and artillery >
syn blitz, bomb, cannonade, shell
rel barrage, strafe, strike
idiom open up on, pour a broadside into
bombardment *n syn* see BARRAGE
bombast *n* pretentious inflated speech or writing < adolescent *bombast* about Youth and Destiny >
syn fustian, highfalutin, lexiphanicism, rant, rhapsody, rhetoric, rodomontade
rel grandiloquence, magniloquence; flatulence, orotundity, tumidity, turgidity; heroics, pyrotechnics, sesquipedality; Johnsonese; spread-eagleism; nonsense
idiom purple prose
bombastic *adj syn* see RHETORICAL
rel flatulent
con unimpassioned; unaffected
‖**bombed** *adj syn* see INTOXICATED 1
bombinate *vb syn* see HUM
bona fide *adj syn* see AUTHENTIC 2
bona fides *n syn* see GOOD FAITH
bonanza *n* a place of great abundance or a source of great wealth or opportunity < the town proved to be a *bonanza* for entrepreneurs >
syn eldorado, Golconda, gold mine, mine, treasure-house, treasure trove, treasury
bond *n* 1 *usu* **bonds** *pl syn* see SHACKLE
2 *syn* see CONTRACT
3 a uniting or binding element or force < the *bonds* of friendship >
syn knot, ligament, ligature, link, nexus, tie, vinculum, yoke
rel bridge, connection, connective, liaison; interrelationship, relationship
4 *syn* see ADHERENCE 1
5 *syn* see GUARANTEE 1
bondage *n* the state of subjection to an owner or master < prisoners sold into *bondage* >
syn enslavement, helotry, peonage, serfage, serfdom, servility, servitude, slavery, thrall, thralldom, villenage, yoke
rel subjection, subjugation
con freedom, independence, liberty
bondman *n syn* see SLAVE 1
bondslave *n syn* see SLAVE 1
bondsman *n syn* see SLAVE 1
bone *n* 1 **bones** *pl syn* see DICE
‖2 *syn* see DOLLAR
bone (up) *vb syn* see CRAM 2
bone-dry *adj* 1 *syn* see DRY 1
2 *syn* see DRY 3
bonehead *n syn* see DUNCE
boneless *adj syn* see WEAK 4
boner *n* 1 *syn* see ERROR 2
2 *syn* see FAUX PAS
boneyard *n syn* see CEMETERY
bong *vb syn* see RING
boniface *n syn* see SALOONKEEPER
‖**bonkers** *adj syn* see INSANE 1
bonne bouche *n syn* see DELICACY
‖**bonnet** *n syn* see DECOY 2
‖**bonny** *adj syn* see BEAUTIFUL
bon vivant *n syn* see EPICURE
rel bon viveur, boulevardier, high liver, man-about-town, sport
bony *adj syn* see LEAN
boo *n syn* see RASPBERRY

boo *n syn see* MARIJUANA

boob *n* **1** *syn see* DUNCE

  2 *syn see* PHILISTINE

‖**boo–boo** *n syn see* FAUX PAS

booby *n syn see* DUNCE

booby hatch *n syn see* ASYLUM 3

booby trap *n syn see* PITFALL

boodle *n* **1** *syn see* FORTUNE 4

  2 *syn see* SPOIL

boodle *vb syn see* CHEAT

boohoo *vb syn see* CRY 2

book *n* **1** a collection of folded, cut, bound, and usually printed sheets < a *book* of poems >

  syn tome, volume

  rel publication, work, writing; scroll; booklet, brochure, folder, leaflet, magazine, pamphlet; compendium, handbook, manual, monograph, textbook, tract, treatise; codex; novel

  2 *cap* Book *syn see* BIBLE

book *vb* **1** *syn see* LIST 3

  2 *syn see* TIME 1

  3 *syn see* RESERVE 2

bookdealer *n* one who deals in books < sold his library to a *bookdealer* >

  syn bibliopole, bookman, bookseller

  rel bouquiniste

bookie *n syn see* BOOKMAKER

bookish *adj syn see* PEDANTIC

  rel booksy, highbrow

book–learned *adj syn see* PEDANTIC

bookmaker *n* one who determines odds and receives and pays off bets < *bookmakers* who welsh on paying off winners >

  syn bookie, layer

  rel pricemaker; runner

bookman *n syn see* BOOKDEALER

bookseller *n syn see* BOOKDEALER

booky *adj syn see* BOOKDEALER

boom *n* **1** *syn see* BANG 2

  2 *syn see* PROSPERITY 4

boomerang *vb syn see* BACKFIRE

booming *adj syn see* FLOURISHING

boon *n* **1** *syn see* GIFT 1

  2 *syn see* GOOD 1

boon *adj syn see* MERRY

‖**boondocks** *n pl syn see* FRONTIER 2

‖**boonies** *n pl syn see* FRONTIER 2

boor *n* an uncouth ungainly fellow < an ill-mannered *boor* >

  syn ‖bosthoon, chuff, churl, clodhopper, clown, grobian, mucker

  rel barbarian, vulgarian; looby, lubber; farmer, loon, rustic, swain; ‖carl; bohunk; boob, buffoon, oaf

  con slicker, smoothy; gentleman; cosmopolitan, cosmopolite, sophisticate

boorish *adj* uncouth in manner or appearance < a *boorish* fellow lacking all grace >

  syn churlish, cloddish, clodhopping, clownish, ill-bred, loutish, lowbred, lubberly, lumpish, robustious, rugged, swainish, uncivilized, uncultured, unpolished, unrefined; *compare* COARSE 3

  rel barbarian, barbaric, outlandish, tasteless, vulgar; bucolic, countrified, inurbane, provincial, rustic, yokelish; ill-mannered,

impolite, rude, uncivil, ungracious; graceless, unpoised

  con cultivated, cultured, refined; suave, urbane; courteous, courtly, genteel, polite, well-bred; graceful, gracious, poised

boost *vb* **1** *syn see* RAISE 9

  2 *syn see* INCREASE 1

  3 *syn see* PROMOTE 3

  ‖**4** *syn see* SHOPLIFT

boost *n syn see* RISE 3

‖**booster** *n syn see* DECOY 1

boot *n* **1** *syn see* THRILL

  2 *syn see* NOVICE

boot (out) *vb* **1** *syn see* EJECT 1

  2 *syn see* DISMISS 3

‖**boot hill** *n syn see* CEMETERY

bootleg *n syn see* MOONSHINE 2

bootleg *vb syn see* SMUGGLE

bootless *adj syn see* FUTILE

  rel frustrating; profitless, worthless

bootlick *vb syn see* FAWN

bootlick *n syn see* SYCOPHANT

bootlicker *n syn see* SYCOPHANT

bootlicking *adj syn see* FAWNING

booty *n syn see* SPOIL

booze *vb syn see* DRINK 3

booze *n* **1** *syn see* LIQUOR 2

  2 *syn see* BINGE 1

‖**boozed** *adj syn see* INTOXICATED 1

boozehound *n syn see* DRUNKARD

boozer *n* **1** *syn see* DRUNKARD

  ‖**2** *syn see* BAR 5

‖**boozy** *adj syn see* INTOXICATED 1

bop *n syn see* BLOW 1

borasca *n syn see* POVERTY 1

bordello *n syn see* BROTHEL

border *n* **1** a line or relatively narrow space that marks the outermost bound of something < the *border* of the rug >

  syn brim, brink, edge, fringe, hem, margin, perimeter, periphery, rim, selvage, skirt, verge; *compare* CIRCUMFERENCE

  rel butts and bounds, lines, metes and bounds; bound, circumference, confine, end, extremity, limit, termination; boundary, frontier, march, pale; beginning, door, entrance, threshold; sideline; lip

  con inside, interior; recesses; center; body, bulk, mass, whole

  2 *syn see* FRONTIER 1

border *vb* **1** to form a border to < hedges *border* the park >

  syn bound, define, edge, fringe, hem, margin, outline, rim, skirt, surround, verge

  rel circumscribe, encircle, enclose, frame; contour, delineate, mark (off), outline, set off; flank, line, side; trim

  2 *syn see* ADJOIN

  3 to come to be closely similiar to a specified thing < ideas that *border* on the absurd >

  syn approach, trench, verge

  rel approximate, compare, near

  idiom come close (*or* near) to

bordering *adj syn see* ADJACENT 3

borderland *n syn see* FRONTIER 1

borderline *adj syn see* DOUBTFUL 1

bore *vb* **1** *syn see* PERFORATE

  2 *syn see* GAZE 1

bore *vb* to induce a state of boredom in < *bored* to death by his endless sermon >

  syn ennui, pall, tire, weary

  rel jade; fatigue, wear; annoy, irk, irritate; afflict, bother, discomfort

---

syn synonym(s)   *rel* related word(s)
ant antonym(s)   *con* contrasted word(s)
idiom idiomatic equivalent(s)
‖ use limited; if in doubt, see a dictionary

idiom put one to sleep
  con amuse, entertain; excite, fascinate,
  intrigue; absorb, beguile, engross, enthrall,
  grip; enliven, freshen, invigorate, quicken,
  stimulate
  ant interest
boreal *adj syn see* COLD 1
boredom *n syn see* TEDIUM
  rel fatigue, weariness; disgust, distaste
  con amusement, diversion, entertainment;
  excitement, fascination; engrossment, enthrallment
boresome *adj syn see* IRKSOME
  rel deadly, dreary, dull, humdrum, monotonous
  con amusing, entertaining; exciting, fascinating, intriguing; absorbing, engrossing,
  enthralling, gripping, stimulating
  ant interesting
boring *adj syn see* IRKSOME
born *adj syn see* INHERENT
‖**born** *vb syn see* BEAR 5
borné *adj syn see* LITTLE 2
bosh *n syn see* NONSENSE 2
bosom *n syn see* HEART 1
bosomy *adj syn see* BUXOM
boss *n syn see* LEADER 2
‖**boss** *adj syn see* EXCELLENT
boss *vb syn see* SUPERVISE
bossy *adj syn see* MASTERFUL 1
‖**bosthoon** *n syn see* BOOR
Boswell *n syn see* BIOGRAPHER
botch *vb* to do or proceed ineffectively or
  badly through clumsiness, stupidity, or
  lack of ability <a complete incompetent
  —*botches* everything he puts his hand
  to>
  syn bitch (up), ‖blow, blunder, bobble,
  boggle, bollix, ‖bugger up, bumble, bungle,
  cobble, dub, flub, fluff, foozle, fumble,
  goof (up), gum (up), louse up, mess,
  ‖muck, mucker, muff, ‖screw (up)
  rel butcher, mangle, murder, mutilate;
  mar, ruin, spoil; destroy, wreck; hash;
  tinker;   misconduct,   mishandle,
  mismanage; confuse, disorder
  idiom play (*or* wreak) havoc with, play
  hell with
botch *n syn see* MESS 3
botchery *n syn see* MESS 3
botchy *adj syn see* SLIPSHOD 3
bother *vb* 1 *syn see* DISCOMPOSE 1
  2 *syn see* ANNOY 1
bother *n* 1 *syn see* ANNOYANCE 2
  2 *syn see* ANNOYANCE 3
  3 *syn see* INCONVENIENCE
botheration *n* 1 *syn see* ANNOYANCE 2
  2 *syn see* ANNOYANCE 3
bothering *n syn see* ANNOYANCE 1
botherment *n syn see* ANNOYANCE 3
bothersomeness *n   syn   see* INCON-
  VENIENCE
bottega *n syn see* STUDIO
bottle (up) *vb* 1 *syn see* RESTRAIN
  2 *syn see* CORNER
bottom *n* 1 the under surface as opposed
  to the top surface <gum was stuck to the
  bottom of her shoe>
  syn sole, underneath, underside, undersurface
  rel belly, underbelly, underbody; base,
  floor, foot, ground
  con acme, apex, cap, crest, crown, tip,
  upper

ant top
  2 *syn see* BUTTOCKS
  3 the lower or lowest point <the *bottom*
  of the page>
  syn base, foot, nadir
  rel basement, floor, ground; end; low
  con acme, apex, pinnacle, zenith
  ant top
  4 *syn see* BASE 1
  5 *syn see* ESSENCE 2
bottom *vb syn see* BASE
bottom *adj* 1 *syn see* BOTTOMMOST
  2 *syn see* FUNDAMENTAL 1
bottom dog *n syn see* VICTIM 2
bottomless *adj* 1 *syn see* BASELESS
  rel reasonless, unjustifiable, unsupportable
  2 extremely deep <the *bottomless* sea>
  syn abysmal, fathomless, plumbless,
  plummetless, soundless, unfathomable;
  compare DEEP 1
  rel endless, infinite
bottommost *adj* that is at the very bottom
  <the ladder's *bottommost* rung>
  syn bottom, lowermost, lowest, nethermost, rock-bottom, undermost
  con top, upper, uppermost
  ant topmost
bough *n syn see* LIMB
bought *adj syn see* READY-MADE
‖**boughten** *adj syn see* READY-MADE
boulevard *n syn see* WAY 1
bounce *vb* 1 *syn see* JUMP 1
  2 *syn see* DISMISS 3
  ‖3 *syn see* INTIMIDATE
bounce (back) *vb* 1 *syn see* RECOVER 3
  2 *syn see* BACKFIRE
bouncer *n* ‖1 *syn see* LIE
  rel exaggeration, hyperbole, overstatement
  idiom tall tale
  2 a person employed to restrain or eject
  disorderly persons (as at a bar) <tossed
  out by the *bouncer*>
  syn chucker, ‖chucker-out, houseman
  rel goon, muscleman, strong arm
bouncy *adj syn see* ELASTIC 2
bound *n* 1 *usu* bounds *pl syn see* ENVI-
  RONS 1
  2 *syn see* LIMIT 1
bound *vb* 1 *syn see* DEMARCATE 1
  2 *syn see* BORDER 1
bound *adj* 1 *syn see* FINITE
  2 obliged to serve a master or in a clearly
  defined capacity for a certain length of
  time by the terms of a contract or mutual
  agreement <brought to the American
  colonies as a *bound* servant>
  syn apprenticed, articled, indentured
  rel contracted; enslaved
  con free, freed
  3 *syn see* CONSTIPATED
bound *vb syn see* JUMP 1
boundary *n syn see* ENVIRONS 1
bounded *adj syn see* FINITE
  ant unbounded
bounder *n syn see* CAD
boundless *adj syn see* LIMITLESS
bounteous *adj* 1 *syn see* LIBERAL 1
  con cheap, illiberal, scant
  ant niggardly
  2 *syn see* PLENTIFUL
  con insufficient, scant, sparse
bountiful *adj* 1 *syn see* LIBERAL 1

2 *syn* see PLENTIFUL

bouquet *n* 1 cut flowers arranged for wear or display <a *bouquet* of spring flowers>
syn nosegay, posy
rel arrangement; boutonniere, corsage; spray; wreath; garland, festoon; lei
2 *syn* see COMPLIMENT 1
3 *syn* see FRAGRANCE

Bourbon *n* *syn* see REACTIONARY

bout *n* 1 *syn* see SPELL 1
2 *syn* see SIEGE

boutade *n* *syn* see CAPRICE

bow *vb* *syn* see YIELD 2

bow *n* 1 *syn* see CURVE
2 *syn* see TURN 4

bow *vb* *syn* see CURVE

bowdlerize *vb* *syn* see CENSOR

bowed *adj* 1 *syn* see CURVED
2 *syn* see BOWLEGGED

bowel *vb* *syn* see EVISCERATE

bower *n* *syn* see ARBOR

bowery *n* *syn* see SKID ROW

bowl *n* *syn* see STADIUM

||**bowl** (down *or* out) *vb* *syn* see WHIP 2

bowl (down *or* over) *vb* *syn* see FELL 1

bowlegged *adj* having legs bent outward <a *bowlegged* cowboy>
syn bandy, bandy-legged, bowed
rel bent, crooked, curved, misshapen

bowwow *n* *syn* see DOG 1

||**box** *n* 1 *syn* see HUT
2 *syn* see PREDICAMENT

box *n* *syn* see CUFF

box *vb* *syn* see SLAP 1

boxing *n* the art of attack and defense with the fists practiced as a sport <he liked *boxing*—at least as a spectator sport>
syn fisticuffs, prizefighting, pugilism, ring

boy *n* 1 a male person not fully matured <a *boy* of nine>
syn lad, laddie, shaveling, son, stripling, tad
rel gamin, ragamuffin, street arab, urchin; hobbledehoy, whippersnapper; schoolboy
idiom little shaver, small fry
2 *syn* see MAN 3

boyfriend *n* 1 a man who is a woman's usual or preferred escort or companion <went to the movies with her *boyfriend*>
syn beau, gentleman friend, swain, young man
rel admirer
2 a man who shares with a woman a strong and usually sexually oriented mutual attraction <moved in with her *boyfriend*>
syn beau, beloved, flame, inamorato, lover, steady, sweetheart, truelove
rel crush, heartthrob; fiancé
3 *syn* see LOVER 1

brabble *vb* *syn* see QUARREL

brabble *n* 1 *syn* see QUARREL
2 *syn* see CHATTER

brace *n* 1 *syn* see COUPLE
2 *syn* see SUPPORT 3
3 braces *pl* *syn* see SUSPENDERS

brace *vb* 1 *syn* see GIRD 3

2 *syn* see SUPPORT 4
3 *syn* see BEG

bracing *adj* *syn* see INVIGORATING

bracket *vb* 1 *syn* see JOIN 1
2 *syn* see COMPARE 2

brag *vb* *syn* see BOAST
con apologize, deprecate

braggadocian *adj* *syn* see BOASTFUL

braggadocio *n* *syn* see BRAGGART

braggart *n* one who boasts <too much of a *braggart* about his strength>
syn blower, blowhard, boaster, braggadocio, bragger, ||gasbag, puckfist, rodomont, rodomontade, vaunter
rel bluffer, blusterer, loudmouth, miles gloriosus, ranter, raver, windbag
con Milquetoast

braggart *adj* *syn* see BOASTFUL

bragger *n* *syn* see BRAGGART

braggy *adj* *syn* see BOASTFUL

Brahmin *n* *syn* see INTELLECTUAL 2

brain *n* 1 *syn* see MIND 1
2 *syn* see INTELLECT 2
3 often brains *pl* *syn* see INTELLIGENCE 1

brainchild *n* *syn* see INVENTION

brainless *adj* *syn* see SIMPLE 3

brainpower *n* *syn* see INTELLIGENCE 1

brainsick *adj* *syn* see INSANE 1

brainwork *n* *syn* see THOUGHT 1

brainy *adj* *syn* see INTELLIGENT 2

brake *vb* *syn* see HINDER
rel slow, stop

branch *n* 1 *syn* see LIMB
rel branchlet
2 *syn* see CREEK 2

brand *n* 1 *syn* see MARK 7
2 *syn* see STIGMA

brandish *vb* *syn* see SHOW 4

brand-new *adj* conspicuously new and unused <a *brand-new* car right out of the showroom>
syn fire-new, mint, spang-new, spanking-new, span-new, spick-and-span
rel untouched, unused; clean, fresh, pristine
con hand-me-down, secondhand, used; outworn, shabby, worn, worn-out
ant old

brannigan *n* 1 *syn* see BINGE 1
2 *syn* see QUARREL

brash *adj* 1 *syn* see RASH 1
2 *syn* see EXUBERANT 1
3 *syn* see TACTLESS
4 *syn* see PRESUMPTUOUS
rel bold, brazen; rash, reckless; headlong, impetuous; cocksure

brashness *n* 1 *syn* see TEMERITY
2 *syn* see EFFRONTERY

brass *n* ||1 *syn* see MONEY
2 *syn* see EFFRONTERY

brassbound *adj* 1 *syn* see ILLIBERAL
2 *syn* see INFLEXIBLE 2
3 *syn* see PRESUMPTUOUS

brass hat *n* *syn* see SUPERIOR

brassy *adj* 1 *syn* see SHAMELESS
2 *syn* see BRAZEN 4

brave *adj* 1 having or showing no fear when faced with something dangerous, difficult, or unknown <made a *brave* attempt to save the burning house>
syn audacious, aweless, bold, boldhearted, bravehearted, chin-up, courageous, dauntless, doughty, fearless, gallant, game, greathearted, ||gutsy, heroic, intrepid, lion-

---

syn synonym(s)   *rel* related word(s)
ant antonym(s)   *con* contrasted word(s)
idiom idiomatic equivalent(s)
|| use limited; if in doubt, see a dictionary

hearted, manful, manly, ‖plucked, plucky, soldierly, spunky, stalwart, stout, stout-hearted, unafraid, unblenched, unblench-ing, undauntable, undaunted, unfearful, unfearing, valiant, valorous

rel daring, defiant, gritty, hardy, mettle-some, resolute, spirited, steadfast, unap-prehensive, undismayed, unflinching, un-frightened, unquailing, unshrinking, un-swerving, unwincing, unyielding, venture-some; chivalrous, noble, preux; confident

con cringing, flinching, frightened, pusil-lanimous, scared, shrinking, timid; chick-enhearted, fainthearted, lily-livered, nerve-less, soft, spineless, unmanly, weakhearted, weak-kneed, yellow

ant cowardly, craven

2 *syn* see COLORFUL

3 *syn* see GOOD 1

brave *vb syn* see FACE 3

con avoid

bravehearted *adj syn* see BRAVE 1

bravery *n syn* see FINERY

bravo *n syn* see ASSASSIN

brawl *vb syn* see QUARREL

brawl *n* 1 *syn* see QUARREL

2 a rough, noisy, and often prolonged hand-to-hand fight usually involving sev-eral people < windows and furniture were broken in the barroom *brawl* >

syn affray, bobbery, broil, dogfight, don-nybrook, fight, fracas, fray, free-for-all, knock-down-and-drag-out, maul, melee, mellay, ‖muss, rough-and-tumble, row, rowdydow, ruction, scrap, scrimmage, scuffle, set-to; *compare* QUARREL

rel fistfight, fisticuffs, slugfest; struggle, tussle; conflict, contention, contest, riot; altercation, embroilment, imbroglio, quar-rel, wrangle; commotion, disturbance, eruption, hubbub, pandemonium, ruckus, rumpus, turn-to, ‖turnup, upheaval, up-roar; incident, ‖rumble

idiom a coming to blows, exchange of blows

brawling *adj syn* see QUARRELSOME 2

brawlsome *adj syn* see QUARRELSOME 2

brawly *adj syn* see QUARRELSOME 2

brawn *n syn* see MUSCLE 1

brawny *adj syn* see MUSCULAR 2

rel lusty, red-blooded, vigorous, vital; tough

con lanky, lean, rawboned, skinny, thin

ant scrawny

bray *vb syn* see PULVERIZE 1

brazen *adj* 1 *syn* see INSOLENT 2

2 *syn* see SHAMELESS

3 *syn* see GAUDY

4 of the color of polished brass < a *brazen* sky at sunset >

syn aeneous, brassy

rel bronze

brazenfaced *adj syn* see SHAMELESS

breach *n* 1 the act or offense of failing to keep the law or to do what law, duty, or obligation requires < sued for *breach* of contract > < his behavior was a gross *breach* of good manners >

syn contravention, infraction, infringe-ment, transgression, trespass, violation

rel disregard, nonobservance; delin-quency, dereliction, neglect

con conformance, conformity, observance

ant observance

2 *syn* see GAP 1

3 an interruption of accustomed friendly relations < a trivial misunderstanding caused a *breach* between the brothers >

syn break, fissure, fracture, rent, rift, rupture, schism, split; *compare* SCHISM 3

rel division, separation, severance; alien-ation, estrangement; difference, discord, disharmony, dissension, disunity, strife, variance; secession, withdrawal; falling-out, quarrel

idiom parting of ways

con integrity, solidarity, union, unity; communion, community; accord, concord, harmony

4 *syn* see GAP 2

breach *vb* 1 *syn* see OPEN 3

rel bore, penetrate

2 *syn* see VIOLATE 1

bread *n* 1 *syn* see FOOD 1

2 *syn* see LIVING

‖3 *syn* see MONEY

bread and butter *n syn* see LIVING

breadth *n* 1 *syn* see EXPANSE

2 spaciousness of extent < the *breadth* of his knowledge on the subject is awe-some >

syn amplitude, comprehensiveness, full-ness, scope, wideness

rel compass, gamut, orbit, range, reach, sweep; expanse, spread, stretch

con limitation, restriction

ant narrowness

breadthen *vb syn* see BROADEN

break *vb* 1 *syn* see GIVE 12

2 *syn* see PLOW

3 *syn* see VIOLATE 1

ant observe

4 *syn* see ESCAPE 1

5 *syn* see FAIL 5

idiom go broke

6 *syn* see RUIN 3

7 *syn* see DEGRADE 1

8 *syn* see DISPROVE 1

9 *syn* see COMMUNICATE 1

10 *syn* see SOLVE 2

11 *syn* see DECODE

12 *syn* see HAPPEN 1

13 *syn* see GET OUT 2

‖14 *syn* see CLEAR 9

break *n* 1 *syn* see GAP 1

2 *syn* see GAP 3

3 *syn* see INTERLUDE

4 a usually short rest period < took a *break* for coffee >

syn blow, breath, breather, breathing space (*or* spell), respite, ten; *compare* PAUSE

5 *syn* see BREACH 3

6 *syn* see FAUX PAS

7 *syn* see OPPORTUNITY

breakable *adj syn* see FRAGILE 1

break down *vb* 1 *syn* see ANALYZE

2 *syn* see DECAY

3 *syn* see COLLAPSE 2

breakdown *n* 1 *syn* see NERVOUS BREAK-DOWN

2 *syn* see COLLAPSE 2

3 *syn* see ANALYSIS 1

break in *vb* 1 *syn* see HOUSEBREAK

idiom break and enter

2 *syn* see INTERRUPT 2

breakneck *adj syn* see FAST 3
break out *vb syn* see ERUPT 2
breakout *n syn* see ESCAPE 1
breakthrough *n syn* see RISE 3
break up *vb* 1 *syn* see SEPARATE 1
  2 *syn* see DISBAND
breakup *n syn* see ANALYSIS 1
breast *n syn* see HEART 1
breast-feed *vb syn* see NURSE 1
breastwork *n syn* see BULWARK
breath *n* 1 *syn* see HINT 2
  2 *syn* see BREAK 4
breathe *vb* 1 *syn* see BE
  2 *syn* see REST 3
  3 to draw (as air) into and expel from the
  lungs < *breathe* clean air >
    syn respire
    rel exhale, inhale
  4 *syn* see CONFIDE 1
breathe (in) *vb syn* see INHALE
breathe (out) *vb syn* see EXHALE
breather *n syn* see BREAK 4
breathing *n syn* see INSTANT 1
breathing space (or spell) *n syn* see
  BREAK 4
breathless *adj* 1 *syn* see EAGER
  2 *syn* see STUFFY 1
bred-in-the-bone *adj syn* see INVETER-
  ATE 1
breech *n syn* see BUTTOCKS
breed *vb* 1 *syn* see PROCREATE 1
  2 *syn* see FATHER 1
  3 *syn* see GENERATE 3
  4 *syn* see GROW 1
breed *n syn* see TYPE
breeding *n syn* see CULTURE
    rel civility, courtesy, gentility, grace
    con barbarism, boorishness; coarseness,
    grossness; discourtesy, rudeness
    ant vulgarity
breeding ground *n* a place or environment which favors growth < the slum was
  a *breeding ground* for crime >
    syn forcing bed, forcing house, hotbed,
    hothouse
breeze *n syn* see SNAP 1
breeze *vb* to proceed quickly and easily
  < *breezed* through customs >
    syn waltz, zip
    rel skim, slide, slip
    con drag, falter, flag, lag, trail
breezy *adj* 1 *syn* see WINDY 1
  2 *syn* see EASYGOING 3
breviary *n syn* see ABRIDGMENT
breviate *n syn* see ABRIDGMENT
breviloquent *adj* 1 *syn* see CONCISE
  2 *syn* see BLUFF
brew *vb syn* see LOOM 1
brew *n syn* see MISCELLANY 1
bribable *adj syn* see VENAL 1
bribe *vb* to give or promise money or favor
  to a person in a position of trust to influence his judgment or conduct < *bribed* a
  building inspector >
    syn buy, buy off, fix, have, ‖lubricate,
    sop, square, tamper (with)
    rel approach; corrupt, instigate, suborn;
    soften (up), sweeten

    idiom grease the palm (*or* hand), oil the
    palm (*or* hand), tickle the palm
bridal *n syn* see WEDDING
bridewell *n syn* see JAIL
bridle *vb syn* see RESTRAIN 1
    rel repress, suppress; control, manage;
    govern, rule
    con air, express, utter, ventilate, voice
    ant vent
brief *adj* 1 *syn* see SHORT 1
    rel fleeting, momentary, passing, transient
    ant long
  2 *syn* see CONCISE
  3 *syn* see BLUFF
brief *n syn* see ABRIDGMENT
briefly *adv* in a few words < be answered
  briefly and to the point >
    syn concisely, in brief, in short, laconi-
    cally, shortly, succinctly, tersely
    rel accurately, crisply, exactly, precisely
    idiom in a capsule, in a nutshell, in a
    word, to make a long story short
    con diffusely, long-windedly, profusely,
    prolixly, protractedly, verbosely, wordily;
    at length, comprehensively, fully
brig *n syn* see JAIL
brigand *n syn* see MARAUDER
bright *adj* 1 shining or glowing with light
  < the *bright* sun >
    syn beaming, brilliant, effulgent, fulgent,
    incandescent, lambent, ‖ucent, lucid, lumi-
    nous, lustrous, radiant, refulgent
    rel clear, light, undimmed; illuminated,
    lighted; coruscating, flashing, gleaming,
    glistening, glittering, scintillating, shim-
    mering, sparkling; blazing, flaming, glow-
    ing; burnished, polished, shiny; sunshiny
    con dark, dusky, gloomy, murky, tene-
    brous; colorless, drab, dreary, lackluster,
    leaden; somber; cloudy, gray, overcast,
    shadowy; moonless, starless, sunless; faint,
    pale, weak
    ant dim; dull
  2 *syn* see COLORFUL
  3 *syn* see GLAD 2
  4 *syn* see FAVORABLE 5
  5 *syn* see INTELLIGENT 2
    rel advanced, precocious
    con retarded
    ant dense, dull
  6 *syn* see LIVELY 1
brilliant *adj* 1 *syn* see BRIGHT 1
    ant subdued
  2 *syn* see INTELLIGENT 2
    rel erudite, learned; sage, wise
brim *n syn* see BORDER 1
brimful *adj* 1 *syn* see FULL 1
  2 *syn* see BIG 3
brimming *adj* 1 *syn* see FULL 1
  2 *syn* see BIG 3
brine *n syn* see OCEAN
bring *vb* 1 *syn* see CONVERT 1
  ‖2 *syn* see ACCOMPANY
  3 *syn* see SELL 4
bring about *vb syn* see EFFECT 1
bring around *vb syn* see INDUCE 1
bring down *vb syn* see FELL 1
bring forth *vb syn* see BEAR 5
bring in *vb* 1 *syn* see YIELD 5
  2 *syn* see SELL 4
  3 *syn* see BIG 3
bring off *vb syn* see EFFECT 2
bring out *vb syn* see SAY 1

---

syn synonym(s)   *rel* related word(s)
ant antonym(s)   *con* contrasted word(s)
idiom idiomatic equivalent(s)
‖ use limited; if in doubt, see a dictionary

bring up vb **1** to give a child a parent's fostering care <the orphan was *brought up* by his aunt >
syn ‖fetch up, raise, rear
rel breed, cultivate, foster, nurture; feed, nourish, provide (for); discipline, educate, train
con abuse, ill-use, maltreat; neglect
2 *syn* see STOP 4
3 *syn* see REFER 3
4 *syn* see BROACH
5 *syn* see VOMIT

brink n **1** *syn* see BORDER 1
2 *syn* see VERGE 2

‖**briny** n *syn* see OCEAN

brio n *syn* see SPIRIT 5

brisk adj *syn* see AGILE
rel adroit; quick
con inactive, torpid
ant sluggish

brisky adj *syn* see AGILE

bristle vb *syn* see ANGER 2

brittle adj *syn* see SHORT 6

broach n *syn* see BROOCH

broach vb to open up (a subject) for discussion <would be awkward to *broach* the matter now>
syn bring up, introduce, moot, ventilate
rel interject, interpose; mention, speak (about); propose, suggest
con hush (up), quash, stifle, suppress; black out, censor

broad adj **1** *syn* see LIBERAL 3
2 *syn* see EXTENSIVE 1
3 *syn* see RISQUÉ

broadcast n *syn* see DECLARATION

broadcast vb **1** *syn* see STREW 1
2 *syn* see DECLARE 1
rel communicate, radio, televise, transmit
idiom spread a report, spread far and wide

broaden vb to grow or become broad or broader <the street *broadens* into an avenue>
syn breadthen, widen
rel expand; spread (out); open
con contract, shrink; slim, thin
ant narrow

broad-minded adj *syn* see LIBERAL 3

broadside n *syn* see BARRAGE

Brobdingnagian adj *syn* see HUGE

brocard n *syn* see MAXIM

‖**brogue** vb *syn* see IDLE

broil vb *syn* see BURN 3

broil n *syn* see BRAWL 2

broiling adj *syn* see HOT 1

broke adj *syn* see POOR 1

broken-down adj *syn* see SHABBY 1

broker n *syn* see GO-BETWEEN 2

bromide n *syn* see COMMONPLACE

bromidic adj *syn* see ARID 2

‖**Bronx cheer** n *syn* see RASPBERRY

brooch n an ornament with a pin or clasp now worn usually by women <a diamond *brooch*>
syn broach, clip, pin

brood n *syn* see OFFSPRING

brood vb **1** *syn* see SET 11
2 *syn* see MOPE 1

brook vb *syn* see BEAR 10

brook n *syn* see CREEK 2

brothel n an establishment where prostitutes ply their trade <madam of the local *brothel*>
syn bagnio, bawdy house, bordello, call house, cathouse, crib, disorderly house, fancy house, ‖hookshop, ‖joyhouse, lupanar, parlor house, seraglio, sporting house, stew, whorehouse
idiom house of ill fame (*or* repute), house of prostitution

brotherhood n *syn* see ASSOCIATION 2

brouhaha n **1** *syn* see DIN
2 *syn* see COMMOTION 3

brow n *syn* see FOREHEAD

browbeat vb *syn* see INTIMIDATE

browbeater n *syn* see BULLY 1

brownie n *syn* see FAIRY

‖**brownnose** vb *syn* see FAWN

‖**brownnose** n *syn* see SYCOPHANT

‖**brownnoser** n *syn* see SYCOPHANT

brown study n *syn* see REVERIE

browse vb to read through, study, or examine cursorily <*browsed* through the book looking for illustrations>
syn dip (into), flip (through), glance (at *or* over), leaf (through), riff (through), riffle (through), run (through *or* over), scan, skim (through), thumb (through)
rel go (through *or* over), look (over), peruse, skip (through)
idiom give the once over, run the eye over
con examine, study; delve (into), dig (into)
ant pore (over)

bruise n an injury involving rupture of small blood vessels and discoloration without break in the overlying skin <got an ugly *bruise* when he fell>
syn contusion; *compare* BLACK EYE
rel ‖boo-boo; abrasion, scrape, scratch
idiom black-and-blue spot (*or* mark)

bruise vb **1** to inflict a bruise on <fell down and *bruised* his hip>
syn black, contuse
rel batter, ‖bung up
2 *syn* see CRUSH 2

bruit (about) vb *syn* see DECLARE 1
rel hint, intimate, rumor, suggest

bruja n *syn* see WITCH 1

brume n *syn* see HAZE 1

brummagem adj *syn* see COUNTERFEIT

brunet adj *syn* see DARK 3

brush vb to touch or strike lightly (as in passing) <they *brushed* fenders but no real damage was done>
syn glance, graze, kiss, shave, skim
rel bump, clash, collide, sideswipe; clip, contact, scrape, touch

brush n **1** *syn* see ENCOUNTER
rel clash, engagement
2 *syn* see CLASH 2

brush up vb *syn* see TOUCH UP

brusque adj *syn* see BLUFF

brutal adj **1** *syn* see BRUTISH
2 *syn* see SEVERE 3

brutalize vb *syn* see DEBASE 1

brute adj *syn* see BRUTISH

brute n *syn* see BEAST

brutish adj marked by animal traits and by a lack of man's dignity or refinement <a graceless *brutish* hulk of a man>
syn animal, beastly, bestial, brutal, brute, feral, ferine, swinish
rel animalistic; coarse, crude; base, low, mean, scurvy, vile

bubble *vb* **1** *syn* see SLOSH 1
  2 *syn* see SEETHE 4
bubble *n syn* see PIPE DREAM
buccaneer *n syn* see PIRATE
buck *n* **1** *syn* see MAN 3
  2 *syn* see POP
  || **3** *syn* see DOLLAR
  4 *syn* see SAWHORSE
buck *vb* **1** *syn* see RESIST
  2 *syn* see CARRY 1
  3 *syn* see PASS 9
buck (off) *vb syn* see THROW 2
buck *vb syn* see PULVERIZE 1
|| **bucket** *n syn* see JAIL
bucket *vb syn* see HURRY 2
|| **bucket shop** *n syn* see BAR 3
buckle (down) *vb* **1** *syn* see ADDRESS 3
  2 *syn* see PITCH IN 1
buckle (under) *vb syn* see YIELD 2
buckram *adj syn* see STIFF 4
buck up *vb syn* see COMFORT
bucolic *adj syn* see RURAL
  ant urbane
bucolic *n syn* see RUSTIC
bud *n* **1** *syn* see CHILD 1
  2 *syn* see SEED 2
buddy *n syn* see ASSOCIATE 3
|| **buddy–buddy** *adj syn* see INTIMATE 4
|| **budge** *n syn* see LIQUOR 2
|| **budget** *n syn* see BODY 5
budtime *n syn* see SPRING 5
buff *n syn* see ADDICT
buff *vb syn* see POLISH 1
buffalo *vb* **1** *syn* see FRUSTRATE 1
  2 *syn* see NONPLUS 1
buff–bare *adj syn* see NUDE 2
buffet *n syn* see CUFF
buffet *vb* **1** *syn* see SLAP 1
  2 *syn* see BEAT 1
|| **buffet** *n syn* see EATING HOUSE
|| **bufflehead** *n syn* see DUNCE
|| **buffle–headed** *adj syn* see SIMPLE 3
buffoon *n syn* see CLOWN 1
|| **buffy** *adj syn* see INTOXICATED 1
bug *n syn* see ENTHUSIAST
bug *vb syn* see ANNOY 1
bugbear *n syn* see ABOMINATION 1
|| **bugger** *n syn* see SNOT 1
|| **bugger** *n syn* see EXHAUST 4
bugger up *vb syn* see BOTCH
|| **buggy** *adj* **1** *syn* see ENTHUSIASTIC
  2 *syn* see INSANE 1
|| **buggy** *n syn* see CAR
|| **bughouse** *n syn* see ASYLUM 3
|| **bughouse** *adj syn* see INSANE 1
|| **bugs** *adj* **1** *syn* see INSANE 1
  2 *syn* see ENTHUSIASTIC
build *vb* **1** to form or fashion a structure
< will *build* either a garage or carport >
  syn construct, erect, put up, raise, rear,
uprear; *compare* ERECT 3, MAKE 3
  rel fabricate, fashion, frame, manufacture;
run up, throw up; prefabricate
  con demolish, destroy, dismantle, level,
pull down, raze, take down, tear down,
wreck
  2 *syn* see MAKE 3
  3 *syn* see INCREASE 1

  4 *syn* see INCREASE 2
build (on) *vb syn* see RELY (on *or* upon)
build *n syn* see PHYSIQUE
  rel conformation
building *n* a usually roofed and walled
structure built for permanent use < a
building with four apartments >
  syn fabric, structure; *compare* EDIFICE,
HUT
build up *vb* **1** *syn* see ERECT 5
  2 *syn* see PUBLICIZE
buildup *n syn* see PUBLICITY
|| **built** *adj syn* see CURVACEOUS
built–in *adj syn* see INHERENT
bulge *vb* to extend outward beyond the
usual or normal line < the box was so full
that the sides *bulged* >
  syn beetle, jut, overhang, poke, pouch,
pout, project, protrude, protuberate, stand
out, stick out
  rel bag, belly, dilate, distend, expand,
swell
bulge *n* **1** *syn* see PROJECTION 1
  rel bump, lump, swelling
  con depression, hollow, pit
  2 *syn* see ADVANTAGE 3
bulk *vb syn* see LOOM 3
bulk *n* **1** a body of usually material substance that constitutes a thing or unit
< his industry was proven by the *bulk* of
his accomplishment > < a great dark *bulk*
blocked the alley >
  syn mass, volume
  rel bigness, greatness, largeness, magnitude, quantity, totality
  2 *syn* see BODY 4
  3 *syn* see BODY 5
  4 *syn* see BODY 3
bulk *vb syn* see LARGE 1
bull *n* **1** *syn* see ERROR 2
  || **2** *syn* see NONSENSE 2
  || **3** *syn* see POLICEMAN
bull *adj syn* see LARGE 1
|| **bull band** *n syn* see SHIVAREE
bulldoze *vb* **1** *syn* see INTIMIDATE
  rel menace, threaten; harass, harry
  2 *syn* see PUSH 1
bulldozer *n syn* see BULLY 1
bullet *vb syn* see HURRY 2
bullfighter *n* one who fights bulls
< moved with the grace of an experienced
bullfighter >
  syn matador, toreador, torero
  rel banderillero; cuadrillero; picador;
cuadrilla
bullheaded *adj syn* see OBSTINATE
bullwork *n syn* see WORK 2
bully *n* **1** an insolent, overbearing person
who persists in tormenting another < a
big *bully* who picked on little kids >
  syn browbeater, bulldozer, harasser, harrier, hector, intimidator; *compare* TOUGH
  rel annoyer, antagonizer, heckler, persecu-
tor, pest, tease, tormenter
  2 *syn* see PIMP 1
bully *adj syn* see EXCELLENT
bully *vb syn* see INTIMIDATE
  rel torment, torture; menace, threaten
  ant coax
bullyboy *n syn* see TOUGH
bullyrag *vb* **1** *syn* see INTIMIDATE
  2 *syn* see BAIT 2
bulwark *n* an aboveground defensive structure that forms part of a fortification

---

syn synonym(s)   *rel* related word(s)
ant antonym(s)   *con* contrasted word(s)
idiom idiomatic equivalent(s)
|| use limited; if in doubt, see a dictionary

< the *bulwarks* were woefully under-
manned >
syn bastion, breastwork, parapet, rampart
rel citadel, fort, fortress, stronghold
con bunker, dugout
bulwark *vb syn* see DEFEND 1
‖**bum** *vb syn* see HUM
bum *vb syn* see IDLE
bum *n* 1 *syn* see VAGABOND
 2 *syn* see SLUGGARD
‖**bum** *adj syn* see BAD 1
bum *n syn* see BINGE 1
bumble *vb syn* see HUM
bumble *vb* 1 *syn* see BOTCH
 2 *syn* see STUMBLE 3
bumbling *adj syn* see AWKWARD 2
‖**bumfuzzle** *vb syn* see CONFUSE 2
bummel *vb syn* see SAUNTER
bummer *n* 1 *syn* see BEGGAR 1
 2 *syn* see MARAUDER
bumming *n syn* see MENDICANCY
bump *vb* 1 to meet with or come up
against forcibly < the two cars *bumped*
with a great crumpling of fenders >
syn clash, collide, ‖prang
rel bang, carom, crash, hit, knock, slam,
strike; impinge; jar, jolt
idiom whang together
 2 *syn* see HAPPEN 1
 3 *syn* see DEGRADE 1
bump *n* 1 *syn* see IMPACT
 2 a swelling of tissue usually resulting
from a blow < fell and got a *bump* on his
head >
syn bunch, knot, lump, ‖pumpknot
rel protuberance, swelling
 3 a marked unevenness in a road surface
likely to jolt a passing vehicle
syn ‖cahot, thank-you-ma'am
rel chuckhole, mudhole, pothole, rut
 4 *syn* see GIFT 2
bumpkin *n syn* see RUSTIC
bump off *vb syn* see MURDER 1
‖**bump-off** *n syn* see MURDER
bunch *n* 1 *syn* see BUMP 2
 2 *syn* see GROUP 3
 3 *syn* see SET 2
 4 *syn* see GROUP 1
bunco steerer *n syn* see SWINDLER
bundle *n* 1 *syn* see GROUP 3
 2 *syn* see FORTUNE 4
bundle up *vb* to dress warmly < *bundle
up*, it's cold outside >
syn ‖hap, muffle, wrap (up)
rel envelop, mummify, swaddle, swathe
‖**bung** *vb syn* see THROW 1
bung-full *adj syn* see FULL 1
bungle *vb syn* see BOTCH
bungle *n syn* see ERROR 2
bungler *n syn* see STUMBLEBUM
‖**bung up** *vb syn* see BATTER 1
bunk *vb syn* see HARBOR 2
‖**bunk** *vb syn* see ESCAPE 1
bunk *n syn* see NONSENSE 2
‖**bunk** *vb syn* see DECEIVE
bunkum *n syn* see NONSENSE 2
‖**bunkum** *adj* 1 *syn* see EXCELLENT
 2 *syn* see HEALTHY 1
Bunyanesque *adj syn* see HUGE
buoy (up) *vb syn* see SUPPORT 5
buoyancy *n syn* see EBULLIENCE
buoyant *adj syn* see ELASTIC 2
burble *vb* 1 *syn* see SLOSH 1

 2 *syn* see CHAT 1
burden *n* 1 *syn* see LOAD 1
 2 *syn* see LOAD 3
burden *vb* to lay a heavy load on or to lie
like a heavy load on a person or thing
< *burdened* his men with needless heavy
work > < I won't *burden* you with this
lengthy story >
syn charge, clog, cumber, encumber, lade,
load, lumber, saddle, task, tax, weigh,
weight
rel overburden, overload, overweigh;
handicap; afflict, oppress
idiom bear down on (*or* upon)
con alleviate, ease, lighten, relieve, unload; disburden, disencumber
ant unburden
burden *n syn* see SUBSTANCE 2
burdensome *adj syn* see ONEROUS
burdensomely *adv syn* see HARD 8
bureaucrat *n* a member of a bureaucracy
< *bureaucrats* were blamed for the error >
syn mandarin
rel civil servant, functionary, official
burg *n* a small, insignificant, remote town
< the *burg* had only two stores and one
gas station >
syn hick town, jerkwater town, mudhole,
one-horse town, Podunk, tank town, whis-
tle-stop
rel cowtown; crossroads; jumping-off
place; hamlet, village
con city, metropolis
burgee *n syn* see FLAG
burgeon *vb* 1 *syn* see INCREASE 2
 2 *syn* see BLOSSOM
burghal *adj syn* see URBAN
burgher *n syn* see TOWNSMAN
burglarize *vb* to commit an act of breaking open and entering with a felonious
purpose the dwelling house of another by
night < that night several homes were
burglarized >
syn burgle; compare HOUSEBREAK, ROB
1
rel knock over, rob; ransack, rifle; screw
burgle *vb syn* see BURGLARIZE
burial *n* 1 *syn* see GRAVE
 2 the act or ceremony of burying < his
burial took place yesterday >
syn entombment, inhumation, interment,
sepulture
rel burying, exequies, funeral, obsequies;
deposition; deep six
con disinterment, exhumation
burial ground *n syn* see CEMETERY
buried *adj syn* see ULTERIOR
burke *vb* 1 *syn* see SUPPRESS 3
 2 *syn* see SKIRT 3
burlesque *n* 1 *syn* see MOCKERY 2
 2 *syn* see CARICATURE 2
burlesque *vb syn* see MIMIC
burly *adj syn* see HUSKY 1
‖**burn** *n syn* see CREEK 1
burn *vb* 1 *syn* see SHINE 1
 2 to undergo combustion < the wood is
too green to *burn* >
syn combust
rel fire, flame, ignite, kindle, light; consume, use; smolder, sputter
 3 to be hot as if on fire < sand *burning* in
the blazing sun >
syn bake, broil, cook, melt, roast, scorch,
swelter

rel parch, toast, warm; char
con chill, cool, freeze
4 *syn* see ANGER 2
5 *syn* see SMART
6 *syn* see FIRE 6
‖**7** *syn* see CHEAT
burn (up) *vb syn* see IRRITATE
burnable *adj syn* see COMBUSTIBLE 1
burning *adj* **1** on fire <the *burning* house>
syn ablaze, afire, aflame, alight, blazing, conflagrant, fiery, flaming, flaring, ignited, lighted
rel aglow, glowing, incandescent
idiom in flames
con burned-out, cold
2 *syn* see HOT 1
ant icy
3 *syn* see FEVERISH 2
4 *syn* see IMPASSIONED
5 *syn* see PRESSING
burnish *vb syn* see POLISH 1
burnished *adj syn* see LUSTROUS 1
burn off *vb syn* see CLEAR 9
burnsides *n pl syn* see SIDE-WHISKERS
burp *vb syn* see BELCH 1
burro *n syn* see DONKEY 1
burrow *n* **1** *syn* see LAIR 1
2 *syn* see HOVEL
burrow *vb syn* see SNUGGLE
burst *vb* **1** *syn* see EXPLODE 1
2 *syn* see SHATTER 1
3 *syn* see PLUNGE 2
burst (forth) *vb syn* see ERUPT 2
burst *n* **1** *syn* see OUTBREAK 1
2 *syn* see OUTBURST 1
3 *syn* see BANG 2
4 *syn* see BARRAGE
bury *vb* **1** to deposit (a corpse) in or as if in the earth <the pharaohs were *buried* in pyramids> < *buried* at sea>
syn entomb, inhume, inter, lay away, plant, put away, sepulcher, sepulture, tomb; *compare* ENTOMB 1
rel inurn; coffin
idiom consign to the grave, lay to rest, put six feet under
con dig (up), disentomb, disinter, exhume, untomb; burn, cremate
2 *syn* see HIDE
burying ground *n syn* see CEMETERY
‖**bus** *n syn* see CAR
bush *n syn* see FRONTIER 2
‖**bush up** *vb syn* see HIDE
bushwa *n syn* see NONSENSE 2
business *n* **1** *syn* see FUNCTION 1
2 *syn* see PATRONAGE 2
3 *syn* see WORK 1
4 activity concerned with the supplying and distribution of commodities <the lumber *business* depends heavily on the housing *business*>
syn commerce, industry, trade, traffic
5 *syn* see ENTERPRISE 3
6 *syn* see AFFAIR 1
7 *syn* see DOODAD
8 something personal to oneself <that is none of your *business*>

---

syn synonym(s) *rel* related word(s)
ant antonym(s) *con* contrasted word(s)
idiom idiomatic equivalent(s)
‖ use limited; if in doubt, see a dictionary

---

syn affair, concern, lookout, occasions, palaver
businessman *n syn* see MERCHANT
buss *vb syn* see KISS 1
bust *vb* **1** *syn* see RUIN 3
2 *syn* see DEGRADE 1
ant promote
3 *syn* see FAIL 5
‖**4** *syn* see ARREST 2
bust *n* ‖**1** *syn* see CUFF
2 *syn* see FAILURE 5
3 *syn* see BINGE 1
4 *syn* see RAID 2
‖**busthead** *n syn* see MOONSHINE 2
bustle *vb syn* see HURRY 2
bustle *n* **1** *syn* see STIR 1
2 *syn* see COMMOTION 4
bustling *adj* full of activity <a *bustling* frontier town>
syn busy, fussy, hopping, humming, hustling, lively, popping
rel active, brisk, energetic
idiom on its way, on the go (or move), up and doing
busty *adj syn* see BUXOM
busy *adj* **1** engaged in activity <I can't stop to talk. I'm *busy*>
syn employed, engaged, occupied, working; *compare* ASSIDUOUS
idiom at work, on the fly
con idle, inactive
ant free
2 *syn* see BUSTLING
3 *syn* see IMPERTINENT 2
busy *vb syn* see ENGAGE 4
busybody *n* one who concerns himself with affairs not his own <a meddlesome *busybody* who saw all and tattled all she saw>
syn butt-in, ‖buttinsky, intermeddler, kibitzer, meddler, Meddlesome Mattie, nose, nosey Parker, Paul Pry, polypragmatist, pragmatic, pragmatist, prier (or pryer), quidnunc, rubber, rubberneck, snoop, ‖sticky-beak; *compare* GOSSIP 1, INFORMER
rel gossip, gossipmonger, newsmonger, rumormonger, scandalmonger, tabby, talebearer, telltale
idiom curiosity shop, question box
busybody *vb* **1** *syn* see SNOOP
2 *syn* see MEDDLE
but *conj* **1** *syn* see ONLY
2 *syn* see EXCEPT 1
but *prep syn* see EXCEPT
but *adv* **1** *syn* see ONLY 1
2 *syn* see JUST 3
butcher *vb* **1** *syn* see SLAUGHTER 1
2 *syn* see SLAUGHTER 2
butchery *n syn* see MASSACRE
butt *n* **1** *syn* see TARGET 1
2 *syn* see LAUGHINGSTOCK
3 *syn* see FOOL 3
butt (on *or* against) *vb syn* see ADJOIN
‖**butt** *n* **1** *syn* see BUTTOCKS
2 *syn* see CIGARETTE
butt *n syn* see CASK
butterball *n syn* see FATTY
butt in *vb* **1** *syn* see INTRUDE 1
con abstain, forbear, restrain
2 *syn* see MEDDLE
butt-in *n syn* see BUSYBODY
‖**buttinsky** *n syn* see BUSYBODY

buttocks *n pl* the part of the back on which a person sits <gave the boy a whack across the *buttocks*>
syn backside, beam, behind, bottom, breech, ‖butt, ‖can, cheeks, derriere, ‖duff, fanny, fundament, hams, haunches, heinie (or hiney), hind end, ‖hinder, hunkers, ‖keister, nates, podex, posterior, rear, rear end, rump, seat, ‖stern, tail, tail end, ‖tokus, ‖twat
idiom seat of one's pants

button-down *adj syn see* CONVENTIONAL 1

buttress *n syn see* SUPPORT 3

buttress *vb syn see* SUPPORT 4

buvette *n syn see* BAR 4

buxom *adj* having an amply developed bosom <a *buxom* young woman>
syn bosomy, busty, chesty, full-bosomed; *compare* CURVACEOUS
rel ‖stacked; full-figured, Junoesque, shapely, well-developed, well-proportioned

buy *vb* 1 to acquire something for money or the equivalent <*bought* a new car>
syn purchase, take
rel acquire, get, obtain, procure
ant sell
2 *syn see* RANSOM
3 *syn see* BRIBE
‖4 *syn see* BELIEVE 1

buy *n syn see* BARGAIN 1

buyable *adj syn see* VENAL 1

buyer *n syn see* PURCHASER

buy off *vb syn see* BRIBE

buzz *vb* 1 *syn see* HUM
2 *syn see* HISS
‖3 *syn see* TELEPHONE

buzz *n syn see* REPORT 1

‖**buzzed** *adj syn see* INTOXICATED 1

by *prep* 1 *syn see* BESIDE 1
2 *syn see* NEAR 2
3 *syn see* VIA 1
4 *syn see* VIA 2

5 with reference to <sorted *by* color>
syn according to, as to

by *adv syn see* OVER 5

by *interj syn see* GOOD-BYE

by all odds *adv syn see* FAR AND AWAY

by a long shot *adv syn see* FAR AND AWAY

by and by *adv* 1 *syn see* AFTER
2 *syn see* PRESENTLY 1

by-and-by *n syn see* FUTURE

by and large *adv syn see* ALTOGETHER 3

by-blow *n syn see* BASTARD 1

by dint of *prep syn see* VIA 2

bye-bye *interj syn see* GOOD-BYE

by far *adv syn see* FAR AND AWAY

bygone *adj* 1 *syn see* FORMER 2
2 *syn see* OLD-FASHIONED
3 *syn see* EXTINCT 2

by long odds *adv syn see* FAR AND AWAY

by means of *prep syn see* VIA 2

byname *n syn see* NICKNAME

by odds *adv syn see* FAR AND AWAY

by ordinary *adv syn see* USUALLY 2

bypass *vb* 1 *syn see* SKIRT 2
2 *syn see* SKIRT 3

byplace *n syn see* NOOK

by-product *n syn see* OUTGROWTH 2

by-sitter *n syn see* SPECTATOR

bystander *n syn see* SPECTATOR

by stealth *adv syn see* SECRETLY

by-talk *n syn see* SMALL TALK

by the bye *adv syn see* INCIDENTALLY 2

by the way *adv syn see* INCIDENTALLY 2

by-the-way *adj syn see* INDIFFERENT 2

by virtue of *prep syn see* VIA 2

by way of *prep* 1 *syn see* VIA 1
2 *syn see* VIA 2

byword *n* 1 *syn see* SAYING
2 *syn see* CATCHWORD
3 *syn see* NICKNAME

Byzantine *adj syn see* COMPLEX 2

C

cab *n syn see* TAXICAB

‖**cab** *n syn see* CRUD

cabal *n* 1 *syn see* CLIQUE
2 *syn see* PLOT 2

cabalistic *adj syn see* MYSTERIOUS

cabaret *n syn see* NIGHTCLUB

‖**cabbage** *n syn see* MONEY

cabbage *vb syn see* STEAL 1

cabbagehead *n syn see* DUNCE

cabin *n syn see* HUT

‖**caboose** *n syn see* HUT

‖**caboose** *n syn see* JAIL

ca' canny *n syn see* SLOWDOWN 2

cache *vb syn see* HIDE
con discover, unearth

cachet *n syn see* STATUS 2

‖**cack** *vb syn see* VOMIT

cackle *vb syn see* CHAT 1

cackle *n syn see* CHATTER

cacophonic *adj syn see* DISSONANT 1

cacophonous *adj syn see* DISSONANT 1

cad *n* a person without gentlemanly instincts <gloated over his rival's distress like the *cad* that he was>
syn bounder, cur, rotter, yellow dog
rel boor, churl, clown, lout; guttersnipe, mucker, vulgarian; ‖creep; bastard, heel, louse, rat, stinker
idiom Jack Nasty
ant gentleman

cadaver *n syn see* CORPSE

cadaverous *adj* 1 *syn see* GHASTLY 2
2 *syn see* EMACIATED
rel careworn, haggard, pinched, worn

cadence *n syn see* RHYTHM
rel accent, accentuation, emphasis, stress; pulsation, pulse, throb

cadency *n syn see* RHYTHM

cadet *n syn see* PIMP 1

cadger *n syn see* BEGGAR 1

cadging *n syn see* MENDICANCY

caducity *n syn see* OLD AGE
rel childishness, dotardy, dotingness

café n 1 syn see EATING HOUSE

   2 syn see NIGHTCLUB

cage vb syn see ENCLOSE 1

   rel imprison, incarcerate, jail

cagey adj syn see SHREWD

cageyness n syn see CUNNING 2

cahoots n pl syn see ASSOCIATION 1

‖**cahot** n syn see BUMP 3

cajole vb syn see COAX

   rel beguile, deceive, delude; tantalize; crowd, push

cake vb 1 to cover with a surface layer < the floor was *caked* with filth >

   syn crust, encrust (*or* incrust), incrustate, rime

   rel besmear, coat, smear, spread; cover, daub

   2 syn see HARDEN 1

   rel compress, condense, contract, shrink

cakewalk n syn see RUNAWAY

calaboose n syn see JAIL

calamitous adj 1 syn see FATAL 2

   2 syn see DEPLORABLE

calamity n syn see DISASTER

   rel collapse, ruin, wreck; affliction, cross, trial, tribulation, visitation

   con fortune, luck; benefaction; favor, gift

   ant boon

calamity howler n syn see PESSIMIST

calculate vb to determine or approximate a mathematical value (as speed, cost, or quantity) < *calculate* the cost of a new car >

   syn cipher, compute, estimate, figure, reckon

   rel consider, study, weigh; ascertain, determine, discover; appraise, evaluate, price, value; assess, prize, rate

   con conjecture, guess, surmise

calculate (on *or* upon) vb syn see RELY (on *or* upon)

calculating adj syn see CAUTIOUS

   rel artful, crafty, cunning, guileful, sly, wily

   con improvident, imprudent, indiscreet

   ant rash, reckless

calculation n syn see COMPUTATION

calembour n syn see PUN

calendar n syn see PROGRAM 1

calenture n syn see PASSION 6

caliber n 1 syn see QUALITY 2

   rel ability, capability, capacity; force, power

   2 syn see QUALITY 3

caliginous adj syn see DARK 1

call vb 1 to speak or utter in a loud distinct carrying voice < *call* for help >

   syn cry, hallo, holler, hollo, shout, vociferate, yell; *compare* SHOUT 1

   rel bawl, bellow, hoot, howl, roar, scream, screech, shriek, shrill, whoop, yowl

   con murmur, whisper

   2 syn see DEMAND 1

   3 syn see SUMMON 2

   rel assemble, collect, gather, round up; bid, invite

   4 syn see CONVOKE

   5 syn see TELEPHONE

   6 syn see NAME 1

   7 syn see PREDICT 2

   8 syn see ESTIMATE 3

   9 syn see PORETELL

   10 syn see VISIT 2

call (for) vb syn see DEMAND 2

call (to) vb syn see ADDRESS 7

call n 1 the natural vocal sound of an animal and especially a bird < the clear *call* of a bellbird >

   syn cry, note, song

   rel cheep, chirp, peep, twitter, warble

   2 syn see ATTRACTION 1

   3 syn see OCCASION 3

   4 syn see VISIT 1

call down vb syn see REPROVE

caller n syn see VISITOR 1

‖**callet** n syn see PROSTITUTE

call girl n syn see PROSTITUTE

call house n syn see BROTHEL

calligraphy n syn see HANDWRITING

call in vb syn see SUMMON 2

calling n 1 syn see MISSION

   2 syn see TRADE 1

   3 syn see WORK 1

‖**callithump** n syn see SHIVAREE

call off vb syn see CANCEL 1

callous adj syn see UNFEELING 2

   rel indurated, set

callow adj 1 syn see YOUNG 1

   2 syn see INEXPERIENCED

callowness n syn see INEXPERIENCE

call up vb to summon for active military duty < *called up* the army reserves >

   syn order up; *compare* DRAFT 1

   rel mobilize

   idiom call to the colors

   ant discharge, muster out

calm n syn see QUIET 1

calm adj 1 free from storm or rough activity < the wind died and the sea became *calm* >

   syn halcyon, hushed, placid, quiet, still, stilly, untroubled

   rel inactive, quiescent, reposing, resting; pacific, smooth, tranquil, unruffled

   idiom calm as a millpond, still as death

   con agitated, disturbed, perturbed, restless, turbulent, uneasy

   ant stormy

   2 free from mental or emotional distress or agitation < a man who remained *calm* under stress >

   syn collected, composed, easy, easygoing, placid, poised, possessed, self-composed, self-possessed, serene, tranquil

   rel cool, imperturbable, nonchalant, unflappable, unruffled; even-tempered, impassive, phlegmatic, steady; firm, stable, staunch

   con discomposed, disturbed, perturbed, upset; anxious, bothered, confused, nervous; fidgety, jittery, jumpy, shaky, tense

   ant agitated

calm vb to relieve from or bring to an end whatever distresses, agitates, or disturbs < that inner faith that *calms* the troubled spirit >

   syn allay, balm, becalm, compose, lull, quiet, ‖quieten, settle, soothe, ‖soother, still, tranquilize

---

syn synonym(s)   rel related word(s)
ant antonym(s)   con contrasted word(s)
idiom idiomatic equivalent(s)
‖ use limited; if in doubt, see a dictionary

rel alleviate, assuage, mitigate, relieve; appease, mollify, pacify, placate; relax, steady

con bother, discompose, disquiet, disturb, flurry, perturb, stir up, upset

ant agitate; arouse

calmant *n syn see* SEDATIVE

calmative *n syn see* SEDATIVE

calmness *n syn see* EQUANIMITY

calumniate *vb syn see* MALIGN

ant eulogize; vindicate

calumnious *adj syn see* LIBELOUS

calumny *n syn see* DETRACTION

rel animadversion, reflection, stricture

con encomium, panegyric, tribute; adulation, compliment, flattery

ant eulogy; vindication

calvary *n syn see* TRIAL 1

‖**cam** *adv syn see* AWRY 1

camaraderie *n* a spirit of friendly goodwill typical of comrades < the easy *camaraderie* of a cozy neighborhood bar >

syn comradery, good-fellowship

rel affability, friendliness, gregariousness, sociability; cheer, conviviality, jollity

con aloofness, coldness, frigidity, inaccessibility, reclusiveness, remoteness, self-containment; exclusiveness, self-sufficiency, unsociability

camarilla *n syn see* CLIQUE

cameraman *n syn see* PHOTOGRAPHER

camerist *n syn see* PHOTOGRAPHER

camouflage *vb syn see* DISGUISE

rel becloud, befog, dim

camp *n* 1 a place where a number of people (as vacationers or soldiers) live temporarily together in usually more or less casual housing < planned to summer at a fishing *camp* in Maine >

syn campground, encampment

2 *syn see* CLIQUE

3 *syn see* HUT

camp *vb* to live temporarily in a camp or the outdoors < *camped* under the trees for the night >

syn bivouac, ‖bivvy, encamp, ‖laager, ‖maroon, tent

idiom rough it

con decamp

campanile *n syn see* BELL TOWER

campestral *adj syn see* RURAL

camp follower *n syn see* PROSTITUTE

campground *n syn see* CAMP 1

‖**cample** *vb syn see* SCOLD 1

‖**can** *n* 1 *syn see* JAIL

2 *syn see* TOILET

3 *syn see* BUTTOCKS

‖**can** *vb syn see* DISMISS 3

Canaan *n syn see* HEAVEN 2

canaille *n syn see* RABBLE 2

canal *n syn see* CHANNEL 1

canard *n syn see* LIE

rel hoax, humbug, mare's-nest, sell, spoof; artifice, dodge, trick

‖**canary** *n syn see* INFORMER

cancel *vb* 1 *syn see* ERASE

2 to give up something previously arranged or agreed on < decided to *cancel* his appointment with the dentist >

syn call off, drop, scrub

rel end, terminate; annul, invalidate, rescind, revoke; give up, relinquish, surrender

cancel (out) *vb syn see* NEUTRALIZE

candid *adj* 1 *syn see* FAIR 4

rel aboveboard, forthright, straightforward; honest, scrupulous, upright

2 *syn see* FRANK

ant evasive

candidate *n* one who seeks an office, honor, position, or award < examining *candidates* for editorial positions >

syn applicant, aspirant, hopeful, seeker

rel nominee; dark horse; also-ran, has-been; campaigner, electioneerer, stumper, whistle-stopper

candy *vb syn see* SUGARCOAT 1

canine *n syn see* DOG 1

canker *vb syn see* DEBASE 1

cankered *adj syn see* CANTANKEROUS

cannabis *n syn see* MARIJUANA

canned *adj* 1 *syn see* CONDENSED

‖2 *syn see* INTOXICATED 1

cannibalic *adj syn see* FIERCE 1

canniness *n* 1 *syn see* PRUDENCE 1

2 *syn see* CUNNING 2

‖**cannon** *n syn see* PICKPOCKET

cannonade *n syn see* BARRAGE

cannonade *vb syn see* BOMBARD

canny *adj* 1 *syn see* CLEVER 4

2 *syn see* SPARING

3 *syn see* WISE 4

canon *n* 1 *syn see* LAW 1

2 *syn see* DOCTRINE

canonical *adj syn see* ORTHODOX 1

‖**cant** *adj syn see* LIVELY 1

cant *vb syn see* SLANT 1

cant *n* 1 *syn see* DIALECT 2

rel diction, language, phraseology, vocabulary; idiom, speech

2 *syn see* TERMINOLOGY

3 *syn see* HYPOCRISY

cantankerous *adj* habitually ill-humored, irritable, and disagreeable < one of our more *cantankerous* fellow workers >

syn bearish, cankered, cranky, cross-grained, crotchety, ornery, rantankerous, vinegarish, vinegary, waspish, waspy; *compare* IRASCIBLE, IRRITABLE

rel dour, morose, sour; crabbed, cross, crusty, huffy, petulant, prickly, snappish; dyspeptic, ill-conditioned, ill-natured; liverish

idiom like a bear with a sore paw

con benign, kindly, mellow, mild; amiable, congenial, friendly, pleasant, well-disposed; benevolent, gracious, kind

canter *n syn see* VAGABOND

cantina *n syn see* BAR 5

canting *adj syn see* HYPOCRITICAL

canton *vb syn see* BILLET 1

‖**canty** *adj syn see* LIVELY 1

canvass *vb* 1 *syn see* SCRUTINIZE 1

2 *syn see* DISCUSS 1

3 *syn see* SOLICIT 1

cap *vb* 1 *syn see* SURMOUNT 3

‖2 *syn see* PUZZLE

3 *syn see* COVER 3

4 *syn see* SURPASS 1

5 *syn see* CLIMAX

capability *n* 1 *syn see* ABILITY 1

rel art, craft, cunning, skill

con inability, disability

ant incapability, incompetence

2 *syn see* EFFICACY 1

capable *adj syn see* ABLE

ant incapable

capacious *adj syn* see SPACIOUS
rel dilatable, distensible, expandable,
expansive, extensile; abundant, copious,
plentiful
ant exiguous

capacity *n* 1 *syn* see ABILITY 1
rel bent, faculty, gift, knack, talent, twin;
caliber, stature
con impotence, ineffectiveness, powerlessness
ant incapacity
2 *syn* see STATUS 1

cape *n syn* see PROMONTORY

caper *vb syn* see GAMBOL
idiom cut capers

caper *n* 1 *syn* see ESCAPADE
2 *syn* see PRANK
rel devilment, impishness, mischief, roguery, waggishness

‖**capernoited** *adj syn* see INTOXICATED 1

capital *adj* 1 *syn* see EGREGIOUS
2 *syn* see CHIEF 2
rel cardinal, essential, vital; basic, fundamental, underlying
3 *syn* see EXCELLENT

capital *n syn* see MEAN 3

capitalize *vb* to supply capital for or to
< agreed to *capitalize* the venture >
syn back, bankroll, finance, grubstake,
stake
rel aid, assist, help, subsidize, support;
fund; promote, sponsor

capitulate *vb syn* see YIELD 2

capitulation *n syn* see SURRENDER

capper *n syn* see DECOY 2

caprice *n* an arbitrary, impulsive, and
often illogical notion or change of mind
< given to sudden *caprices* and random
fancies >
syn bee, boutade, conceit, crank, crotchet,
fancy, freak, humor, maggot, megrim,
notion, vagary, whigmaleerie, whim,
whimsy
rel mood, temper, vein; contrariety, inconsistency, perversity; characteristic,
foible, habit, mannerism, peculiarity, trait,
trick

capricious *adj* 1 *syn* see ARBITRARY 1
2 *syn* see INCONSTANT 1
rel humorsome, moody; effervescent
con constant, steady
ant steadfast
3 *syn* see UNCERTAIN 1

capsheaf *n syn* see APEX 2

capstone *n syn* see APEX 2

capsule *adj syn* see CONDENSED

caption *n* an explanatory or identifying
comment accompanying a pictorial illustration < the *captions* were under the
wrong figures >
syn legend, underline

captious *adj syn* see CRITICAL 1
rel demanding, exacting, finicky; contrary, perverse; irritable, peevish, petulant,
snappish, snappy, testy
con judicious, sensible, wise; rational,
reasonable; knowing, knowledgeable

---

syn synonym(s)   *rel* related word(s)
ant antonym(s)   *con* contrasted word(s)
idiom idiomatic equivalent(s)
‖ use limited; if in doubt, see a dictionary

captivate *vb syn* see ATTRACT 1
rel delight, gratify, please; enterall, grip,
hold, mesmerize, spellbind
ant repulse

captivated *adj syn* see ENAMORED 3

captivating *adj syn* see ATTRACTIVE 1

capture *vb syn* see CATCH 1

Capuan *adj syn* see LUXURIOUS 3

car *n* a usually private passenger-carrying
automotive vehicle < drove a shabby old
car >
syn auto, autocar, automobile, buggy,
‖bus, machine, motor, motorcar
rel coach, convertible, coupe, hardtop,
limousine, phaeton, roadster, runabout,
sedan, station wagon, touring car; ‖crate,
‖clunker, ‖heap, ‖jalopy, junker, ‖wreck

caravansary *n syn* see HOTEL

carbon *n syn* see REPRODUCTION

carbon copy *n syn* see REPRODUCTION

carbuncle *n syn* see ABSCESS

carcass *n syn* see CORPSE

‖**carcel** *n syn* see JAIL

card *n* 1 *syn* see WAG 1
2 *syn* see PROGRAM 1
3 *syn* see MENU

card *vb syn* see SCHEDULE 1

cardboard *adj syn* see STIFF 4
rel unlifelike, unreal, unrealistic

cardinal *adj* 1 *syn* see ESSENTIAL 2
2 *syn* see CENTRAL 1

care *n* 1 *syn* see SORROW
rel strain, stress, tension
2 a burdened or disquieted state of mind
< a mind full of *care* and sadness >
syn anxiety, concern, concernment, disquiet, disquietude, solicitude, unease, uneasiness, worry
rel apprehension, foreboding, misgiving,
suspense; agitation, disturbance, perturbation; alarm, consternation, dismay, fear
con calm, ease, peace, quietude; assurance, comfort, easiness
3 *syn* see TRIAL 2
4 serious and heedful attentiveness < attended his words with *care* >
syn carefulness, concern, consciousness,
heed, heedfulness, regard; *compare* ATTEN-
TION 1
rel curiosity; enthusiasm, interest; consideration, solicitude, thoughtfulness; effort,
exertion, pains, trouble; alertness, vigilance, watchfulness
con carelessness, disregard, heedlessness,
unconcern; boredom, disinterest, ennui
5 *syn* see OVERSIGHT 1
6 *syn* see CUSTODY

care (for) *vb* 1 *syn* see TEND 2
2 *syn* see MINISTER (to)
idiom take care of

careen *vb syn* see LURCH 2

career *vb syn* see COURSE

carefree *adj* 1 *syn* see HAPPY-GO-LUCKY
2 *syn* see IRRESPONSIBLE

careful *adj* 1 *syn* see CAUTIOUS
rel attentive, heedful, observant
2 closely attentive to details or showing
such attention < *careful* workmanship >
syn conscientious, conscionable, exact,
fussy, heedful, meticulous, painstaking,
punctilious, punctual, scrupulous
rel accurate, nice, precise; deliberate,
studied; foresighted, provident, prudent;

critical, discriminating, finical, finicky; observant, particular, religious; duteous, dutiful, intent
con disorderly, lax, negligent, slack, slipshod, slovenly; heedless, neglectful, remiss
ant careless

carefulness *n syn see* CARE 4

careless *adj* 1 lacking in or showing lack of care and attention < *careless* of the harm his neglect might do to others> <unwilling to accept such *careless* shoddy work>
syn feckless, heedless, inadvertent, irreflective, thoughtless, uncaring, unheeding, unrecking, unreflective, unthinking; *compare* INCAUTIOUS, RASH 1
rel forgetful, inattentive, oblivious, unmindful; lax, neglectful, negligent, slack, unconcerned, uninterested; inadequate, incapable, unfit, unqualified
con careful, heedful, thoughtful; concerned, considerate, punctilious, scrupulous
ant careful
2 *syn see* IRRESPONSIBLE
3 *syn see* NEGLIGENT
4 *syn see* SLIPSHOD 3
5 *syn see* SLOVENLY 1

caress *vb* to express interest, affection, or love by touching or handling < *caress* a frightened child>
syn cosset, cuddle, dandle, fondle, love, pet
rel cocker, coddle, indulge, pamper; coquet, dally, flirt, toy, trifle; nuzzle, pat, stroke

careworn *adj syn see* HAGGARD
rel distressed, troubled; exhausted, fagged, jaded, tuckered
ant carefree

cargo *n syn see* LOAD 1

caricature *n* 1 *syn see* MOCKERY 2
2 a grotesque or bizarre imitation <a doting attentiveness that was a sickly *caricature* of motherhood>
syn burlesque, parody, takeoff, travesty
rel lampoon, libel, pasquinade; laughingstock, mockery; cheat, fake, imitation, phony, sham; bosh, bunk, gammon, hokum, moonshine; clinquant, pinchbeck, shoddy, tinsel

carillon *n syn see* BELL TOWER

caritas *n syn see* MERCY

cark *vb* 1 *syn see* TROUBLE 1
2 *syn see* WORRY 3

carnage *n syn see* MASSACRE

carnal *adj* 1 *syn see* BODILY
rel material, substantial; earthly, earthy
2 characterized by physical rather than intellectual or spiritual orientation <giving too much heed to the *carnal* aspects of day-to-day life>
syn animal, fleshly, sensual; *compare* SENSUOUS
rel bodily, corporal, corporeal, physical; coarse, gross, obscene, vulgar; earthly, earthy, mundane, temporal, worldly; lascivious, lewd, lustful, wanton; Pandemic, sensuous
con ethical, moral, noble, righteous, virtuous; aerial, ethereal, otherworldly, supernal; chaste, decent, modest, pure
ant spiritual; intellectual

carnality *n syn see* ANIMALITY

carom *vb syn see* GLANCE 1

carousal *n syn see* BINGE 1

carouse *n syn see* BINGE 1

carouse *vb syn see* REVEL 1

carp (at) *vb syn see* NAG

carper *n syn see* CRITIC

‖**carpet** *vb syn see* SCOLD 1
idiom call on the carpet, take to task

carpet knight *n syn see* HEDONIST

carping *adj syn see* CRITICAL 1
rel blaming, criticizing, reprehending, reprobating; jawing, railing, upbraiding; blameful, condemnatory, damnatory, objurgatory, reproachful, reprobatory
con applauding, commendatory, complimentary; approving, endorsing; extolling, laudatory, praiseful
ant fulsome

carriage *n* 1 *syn see* TRANSPORTATION 1
2 *syn see* POSTURE 1

carriageable *adj syn see* PORTABLE

carriage trade *n syn see* ARISTOCRACY

carrier *n* 1 *syn see* BEARER 2
2 *syn see* MESSENGER
3 *syn see* VECTOR

carrot *n syn see* REWARD

carry *vb* 1 to be the agent or means by which someone or something is shifted from one place to another < *carried* the child on his shoulder>
syn bear, buck, convey, ferry, ‖hump, ‖jag, lug, pack, tote, transport
rel bring, fetch, take; move, remove, shift, transfer; send, transmit
‖2 *syn see* ACCOMPANY
3 *syn see* AFFECT
4 *syn see* BEAR 3
5 *syn see* CONDUCT 4
6 *syn see* BEHAVE 1
7 *syn see* SUPPORT 4
8 *syn see* STOCK

carrying *n syn see* TRANSPORTATION 1

carry off *vb syn see* KILL 1

carry on *vb* 1 *syn see* CONDUCT 3
2 *syn see* CUT UP 2
3 *syn see* PERSEVERE

carry out *vb* 1 *syn see* ADMINISTER 1
rel complete, finalize; discharge, effect, effectuate, fulfill; prosecute, transact
idiom put in force (*or* into effect); sign, seal, and deliver
2 *syn see* EFFECT 2

carrytale *n syn see* GOSSIP 1

carry through *vb* 1 *syn see* EFFECT 2
2 *syn see* CONTINUE 1

carte blanche *n* full discretionary power <was given *carte blanche* to build, landscape, and furnish the house>
syn blank check, free hand
rel license, prerogative, right; authority, power; say, say-so
idiom power of attorney

carte d'entrée *n syn see* TICKET 2

carte du jour *n syn see* MENU

cartel *n* 1 *syn see* DEFIANCE 1
rel gage, gauntlet, glove; blow, slap
2 *syn see* SYNDICATE
rel corporation; multinational; consortium, merger

carve *vb* 1 *syn see* CUT 5
2 *syn see* SCULPTURE

Casanova *n* 1 *syn see* GALLANT 2

2 *syn* see WOLF

cascade *n syn* see WATERFALL

||**cascade** *vb syn* see VOMIT

case *n* 1 *syn* see EVENT 4
  2 *syn* see ORDER 9
  3 *syn* see SUIT 1
  4 *syn* see INSTANCE
  rel circumstance, episode, event, incident, occurrence; condition, situation, state
  5 *syn* see ECCENTRIC

case *n syn* see HULL

||**case** *vb syn* see SCRUTINIZE 1

case history *n syn* see INSTANCE

cash *n syn* see MONEY

cashier *vb* 1 *syn* see DISMISS 3
  rel eject, expel, oust; bar, eliminate, exclude; pass over, shelve
  con appoint, designate, elect, name; employ, engage, hire
  2 *syn* see DISCARD

cash in *vb syn* see DIE 1

cask *n* a vessel made of staves, headings, and hoops <a *cask* of cider>
  syn barrel, butt, hogshead, keg, pipe, tun

Cassandra *n syn* see PESSIMIST

cassock *n syn* see CLERGYMAN

cast *vb* 1 *syn* see THROW 1
  rel broadcast, disperse, distribute, scatter
  2 *syn* see DIRECT 2
  3 *syn* see DISCARD
  rel abandon, leave, relinquish, surrender, yield; dismiss, drop
  |4 *syn* see VOMIT
  5 *syn* see ADD 2
  6 *syn* see PLAN 2

cast *n* 1 *syn* see LOOK 2
  2 *syn* see PREDICTION
  3 *syn* see COLOR 1
  4 *syn* see HINT 2
  5 *syn* see TYPE
  6 *syn* see FORM 1

cast about *vb syn* see SEEK 1

cast away *vb* 1 *syn* see WASTE 2
  2 *syn* see SHIPWRECK 1

castaway *n syn* see OUTCAST

cast down *vb syn* see HUMBLE

cast down *adj syn* see DOWNCAST

castigate *vb* 1 *syn* see PUNISH 1
  rel baste, beat, belabor, drub, pummel, thrash; berate, rail, rate, tongue-lash, upbraid, wig; penalize
  2 *syn* see LAMBASTE 3

castigation *n syn* see PUNISHMENT

castigatory *adj syn* see PUNITIVE

castle *n syn* see MANSION

castle-builder *n syn* see DREAMER

cast out *vb* 1 *syn* see BANISH
  ||2 *syn* see QUARREL

castrate *vb* 1 *syn* see STERILIZE
  2 *syn* see UNNERVE
  rel bleed, drain, empty, exhaust

casual *adj* 1 *syn* see ACCIDENTAL
  rel unplanned, unpremeditated; extemporaneous, extempore, impromptu, improvised, offhand; impulsive, spontaneous
  con advised, considered, deliberate, intentional, planned, premeditated, studied
  ant deliberate

2 *syn* see INDIFFERENT 2
  3 *syn* see EASYGOING 3
  con ceremonial, conventional, formal
  4 *syn* see LITTLE 3

casually *adv syn* see INCIDENTALLY 1

casualty *n* 1 *syn* see ACCIDENT 2
  2 *syn* see FATALITY 2
  3 *syn* see VICTIM 2

casuistry *n syn* see FALLACY 2

|**cat** *n syn* see MAN 3

|**cat** *vb syn* see VOMIT

cataclysm *n* 1 *syn* see FLOOD 2
  2 *syn* see DISASTER

cataclysmic *adj syn* see FATAL 2

catacomb *n syn* see CRYPT

catalog *n syn* see LIST
  rel program, prospectus, syllabus

catalog *vb* 1 *syn* see INVENTORY
  2 *syn* see LIST 3
  rel admit, enter, introduce; count, enumerate, number

catalyst *n syn* see STIMULUS

cataplasm *n syn* see POULTICE

cataract *n* 1 *syn* see WATERFALL
  2 *syn* see FLOOD 2

catastrophe *n syn* see DISASTER

catastrophic *adj syn* see FATAL 2

catcall *n syn* see RASPBERRY

catch *vb* 1 to obtain physical mastery and possession of <the cat *caught* a mouse>
  syn bag, capture, collar, ||cotch, get, nail, prehend, secure, take; *compare* ARREST 2, SEIZE 2
  rel clutch, grab, snatch; clasp, grasp, grip; ensnare, entangle, entrap, snare, tangle, trap
  con free, release
  ant miss
  2 *syn* see SEIZE 2
  3 to put at a disadvantage or bring under control by or as if by enmeshing in a net <*caught* in the fallacy of his own argument>
  syn benet, catch up, ensnare, entangle, entrap, snare, tangle, trap; *compare* ENTANGLE 3
  rel baffle, confound, nonplus, perplex, stick, stump; abash, disturb, embarrass, put out; confuse, flurry, fluster, rattle
  4 *syn* see DUPE
  5 *syn* see FIND 1
  6 *syn* see MARRY 1
  7 to come up with often unexpectedly <the storm *caught* them unawares>
  syn ||cotch, overhaul, overtake, take
  rel reach
  idiom come upon
  8 *syn* see SEIZE 3
  9 *syn* see INTERCEPT
  10 *syn* see CONTRACT 1
  idiom fall ill (of *or* with), fall victim to
  11 *syn* see FASTEN 2
  12 *syn* see STRIKE 2
  13 *syn* see APPREHEND 1

catch colt *n syn* see BASTARD

catching *adj* 1 *syn* see INFECTIOUS 2
  2 *syn* see INFECTIOUS 3

catch on *vb syn* see DISCOVER 3

catchphrase *n syn* see CATCHWORD

catchpole *n syn* see DELEGATE

catch up *vb* 1 *syn* see CATCH 3
  2 *syn* see ENTHRALL 2

catchword *n* a word or phrase that catches the eye or ear and is repeated so

---

syn synonym(s)   *rel* related word(s)
ant antonym(s)   *con* contrasted word(s)
idiom idiomatic equivalent(s)
|| use limited; if in doubt, see a dictionary

often that it becomes representative of a political party, school of thought, or point of view <"new deal" became the *catchword* of supporters and critics of Franklin Roosevelt>
  syn byword, catchphrase, phrase, shibboleth, slogan, watchword; compare BATTLE CRY
  rel household word; maxim, motto
catchy *adj syn see* FITFUL
catechize *vb syn see* ASK 1
categorical *adj* 1 *syn see* ULTIMATE 3
  con conjectural, hypothetical, suppositious; conditional, contingent, dependent, relative
 2 *syn see* EXPLICIT
  rel certain, positive, sure; direct, downright, forthright
  con ambiguous; doubtful, dubious, problematic, questionable
 3 *syn see* POSITIVE 1
categorically *adv syn see* EXPRESSLY 1
categorize *vb syn see* ASSORT
  rel identify, nail down, peg, put down
category *n syn see* CLASS 1
cater (to) *vb* 1 *syn see* BABY
  idiom make much of
 2 *syn see* INDULGE 1
cateran *n syn see* MARAUDER
catercorner (*or* **catty-corner** *or* **kittys corner**) *adv syn see* DIAGONALLY
cater–cousin *n syn see* FRIEND
caterwaul *vb syn see* QUARREL
catharsis *n syn see* PURIFICATION
catholic *adj* 1 *syn see* UNIVERSAL 2
  rel comprehensive, inclusive; general, generic, indeterminate; extensive, large-scale
  ant parochial; provincial
 2 *syn see* ECLECTIC 2
catholicon *n syn see* PANACEA
cathouse *n syn see* BROTHEL
catlike *adj syn see* STEALTHY 2
catnap *n syn see* NAP
catnap *vb syn see* NAP
‖catouse *n syn see* COMMOTION 3
cat's-paw *n syn see* TOOL 2
catty *adj* 1 *syn see* STEALTHY 2
 2 *syn see* AGILE
 3 *syn see* MALICIOUS
‖caulk (off) *vb syn see* NAP
‖caulker *n syn see* DRAM
causatum *n syn see* EFFECT 1
cause *n* 1 that (as a person, fact, or condition) which is responsible for an effect <the storm was the *cause* of all our difficulties>
  syn antecedent, determinant, occasion, reason
  rel goad, impulse, incentive, inducement, motive, spring; origin, prime mover, root, source; author, creator, generator, originator
  con consequence, effect, issue, outcome, result
 2 *syn see* MOTIVE 1
 3 *syn see* OCCASION 3
 4 *syn see* SUIT 1
cause *vb* 1 *syn see* GENERATE 3
 2 *syn see* EFFECT 2
  rel elicit, evoke, provoke
  idiom be at the root of, give origin to, set on foot

'cause *conj syn see* BECAUSE
causerie *n syn see* CHAT 2
caustic *adj* 1 marked by sharp and often witty incisiveness <a *caustic* critic>
  syn mordacious, mordant, salty, scathing, trenchant; compare SARCASTIC
  rel biting, cutting, incisive; acrid, bitter, pungent, tart; acute, keen, sharp; ironic, sarcastic, satiric, stinging; harsh, rough, severe, stringent; crisp, pithy, succinct, terse
  con gentle, mild; cordial, gracious; bland, diplomatic, suave, urbane
  ant genial
 2 *syn see* SARCASTIC
causticity *n syn see* SARCASM
caution *n* 1 *syn see* WARNING
 2 *syn see* PRUDENCE 1
caution *vb syn see* WARN 1
cautionary *adj syn see* MONITORY
cautioning *adj syn see* MONITORY
cautious *adj* marked by careful prudence especially in reducing or avoiding risk or danger <a *cautious* approach to marriage>
  syn calculating, careful, chary, circumspect, considerate, discreet, gingerly, guarded, safe, wary
  rel alert, vigilant, watchful; cagey, canny, cozy, foresighted, precautious, shrewd; forethoughtful, prethoughtful, provident, prudent; calculating, scheming, shrewd; expedient, judicious, politic
  idiom on one's guard, on the safe side, playing it safe
  con daring, rash, reckless, venturesome; headlong, impetuous, precipitate
  ant adventurous, temerarious
cavalier *adj syn see* PROUD 1
cave *n* a usually natural underground chamber <the limestone *caves* of Kentucky>
  syn cavern, grotto, subterrane, subterranean
cave *vb* 1 *syn see* GIVE 12
 2 *syn see* YIELD 2
cave (in) *vb syn see* COLLAPSE 2
caveat *n syn see* WARNING
cavern *n syn see* CAVE
cavernous *adj* 1 suggestive of a cave <a *cavernous* fireplace that gulped in wood>
  syn chasmal, gaping, yawning
  rel commodious, vast
 2 *syn see* HOLLOW 1
cavil *vb syn see* QUIBBLE 1
caviler *n syn see* CRITIC
caviling *adj syn see* CRITICAL 1
  rel contrary, perverse; demanding, exacting; finicky, fussy, picky; mean, petty, small; hairsplitting, niggling, nitpicking
  con amiable, complaisant, good-natured, tolerant; accommodating, easy, obliging
cavillous *adj syn see* CRITICAL 1
cavity *n syn see* HOLE 3
cavort *vb syn see* GAMBOL
  rel carry on, cut up, horse (around), horseplay, roughhouse
caw *vb syn see* SQUALL 1
cease *vb syn see* STOP 3
  rel close, conclude, end, finish, terminate; intermit
  con continue, persist; extend, prolong, protract; arise, originate, rise, spring

cease *n syn* see END 2

cease-fire *n syn* see TRUCE

ceaseless *adj syn* 1 *syn* see CONTINUAL
2 *syn* see EVERLASTING 1

cede *vb* 1 *syn* see RELINQUISH
rel accord, concede, grant, vouchsafe
con hold, hold back, keep back, retain, withhold
2 *syn* see TRANSFER 4

ceinture *n syn* see BELT 1

‖**celeb** *n syn* see CELEBRITY 2

celebrate *vb* 1 *syn* see KEEP 2
2 *syn* see PRAISE 2

celebrated *adj syn* see FAMOUS 2

celebrious *adj syn* see FAMOUS 2

celebrity *n* 1 *syn* see FAME 2
ant obscurity
2 a widely known and popularly esteemed person < youngsters making a great to-do over sports *celebrities* >
syn big name, ‖celeb, luminary, name, notability, notable, somebody
rel hero, immortal, mahatma, star, superstar; lion; personage, worthy; cynosure
idiom center of attraction, person of note (or mark)
con back number; nobody

celerity *n* 1 *syn* see HASTE 1
rel alacrity, briskness, legerity
2 *syn* see SPEED 2

celestial *adj* of, relating to, or befitting heaven or the heavens < *celestial* music from an angelic choir >
syn empyreal, empyrean, heavenly
rel ethereal, supernal, transcendental; otherworldly, unearthly, transmundane; beatific, blessed, elysian, Olympian
con earthly, earthy, mundane, sublunary, worldly; chthonian, hellish, infernal
ant terrestrial, uncelestial

cemetery *n* a piece of land used for burying the dead < the quiet peace of a country *cemetery* >
syn ‖boneyard, ‖boot hill, burial ground, burying ground, God's acre, graveyard, memorial park, necropolis, polyandrium, potter's field
rel churchyard; catacomb
idiom city of the dead

censor *vb* to remove matter considered objectionable by expurgation or alteration < *censor* a movie >
syn blip, bowdlerize, expurgate, screen
rel cut out, excise, exscind; blue-pencil, delete, edit, red-pencil; bleach, clean (up), purge, purify; narrow, restrain, restrict

censorious *adj syn* see CRITICAL 1
rel chiding, reproachful, reproaching; condemnatory, condemning, denouncing, denunciatory, reprehending; accusatory, culpatory
con acclaiming, acclamatory, extolling, laudatory, lauding, praising; adulatory, complimentary, flattering
ant eulogistic

censurable *adj syn* see BLAMEWORTHY
rel improper, incorrect, objectionable, wrong, wrongful; discreditable, doubtful, questionable; inadmissible, unacceptable

con correct, proper, right; acceptable, admissible; creditable
ant uncensurable

censure *vb syn* see CRITICIZE
rel rebuke, reprimand, reproach, reprove; contemn, disdain, scorn, scout, strafe; disallow, disapprove, oppose, reject, stigmatize
con applaud, compliment, recommend; allow, approve, support
ant commend

center *n* 1 a point or part in a surface or solid more or less equidistant from the periphery < the *center* of the earth >
syn core, middle, midpoint, midst
rel inside, interior
con circumference, compass, perimeter, periphery; bounds, confines, limits
2 one eminent in or central to a particular activity, condition, or interest < a *center* of international trade >
syn focal point, focus, heart, hub, nerve center, polestar, seat; *compare* ESSENCE 2
3 a source or point of origin (as of an influence, pressure, or effect) < the group proved a *center* of discontent >
syn core, heart, pith, quick, root
rel activator, dynamo, energizer, stimulant

center *adj* 1 *syn* see MIDDLE 1
2 *syn* see MIDDLE 2

centermost *adj syn* see MIDDLE 1

central *adj* 1 occupying a dominant or supremely important position < the *central* theme of American foreign policy >
syn cardinal, overriding, overruling, pivotal, ruling
rel dominant, paramount, predominant, preponderant; important, significant; outstanding, salient, signal; chief, essential, foremost, leading, main; all-absorbing, controlling, master; focal, key; basic, fundamental, primary, radical
con insignificant, minor, trivial, unimportant; borderline, marginal
ant peripheral
2 *syn* see MIDDLE 2

centralizing *adj syn* see INTEGRATIVE

‖**centripetal** *adj syn* see INTEGRATIVE

‖**cep** *prep syn* see EXCEPT

cerate *n syn* see OINTMENT

cerberus *n syn* see CUSTODIAN

cerebral *adj* 1 *syn* see MENTAL 1
2 *syn* see INTELLECTUAL 2

cerebrate *vb syn* see THINK 5

cerebration *n syn* see THOUGHT 1

ceremonial *adj* stressing or concerned with careful attention to form and detail < his *ceremonial* approach to everyday life >
syn ceremonious, conventional, formal, solemn, stately
rel mannered, studied, stylized; liturgical, ritual, ritualistic; august, courtly, imposing, lofty; fixed, rigid, set, starchy, stiff
con casual, easy, informal, relaxed; artless, ingenuous, open, sincere

ceremonial *n* 1 *syn* see FORM 2
2 *syn* see RITE 2

ceremonious *adj syn* see CEREMONIAL
rel decorous, proper, seemly; impressive, moving, striking; grandiose, imposing, majestic
ant unceremonious

---

syn synonym(s)   *rel* related word(s)
ant antonym(s)   *con* contrasted word(s)
idiom idiomatic equivalent(s)
‖ use limited; if in doubt, see a dictionary

ceremony n 1 *syn* see FORM 2
2 *syn* see RITE 2

certain adj 1 *syn* see FIRM 4
rel assured, certified, guaranteed, warranted; ensured, insured, sure
2 constituting an indeterminate and otherwise unidentified part of a group or whole < *certain* students dispute this finding >
syn some, various
rel a, an, one; many, numerous; divers, several, sundry
con no; all
3 being such beyond a doubt < no *certain* likeness of this saint survives >
syn accurate, authentic, dependable, reliable
rel credible, plausible, well-grounded
con counterfeit, false, spurious; controversial, doubtful, dubious, questionable
ant uncertain
4 *syn* see INFALLIBLE 2
5 *syn* see POSITIVE 3
rel confirmable, demonstrable, establishable, provable, verifiable; doubtless, trustworthy, unerring
con controversial, iffy
ant uncertain
6 *syn* see INEVITABLE
rel indefeasible, irrevocable, unalterable, written; fated, predestinated, predetermined
ant uncertain
7 *syn* see SURE 5
rel assured, confident, sanguine
con hesitant, indecisive, vague, wavering; doubtful, dubious, questionable
ant uncertain

certainty n a state of mind in which one is free from doubt < answered with complete *certainty* >
syn assurance, assuredness, certitude, confidence, conviction, sureness, surety
rel belief, credence, faith; absoluteness, definiteness, dogmatism, positiveness, positivism; firmness, staunchness, steadiness
con doubt, mistrust, skepticism, unsureness; fluctuation, irresolution, shifting, trimming, vacillation, wavering; obscurity, vagueness
ant uncertainty

certify vb 1 to testify usually formally and in writing to the truth or genuineness of something < *certify* a student's college transcript >
syn attest, vouch, witness
rel assert, aver, avouch, avow, profess
2 *syn* see WARRANT 2
3 *syn* see APPROVE 2
rel authorize, commission, license
con antagonize, counter, oppose

certitude n *syn* see CERTAINTY
rel cocksureness
con uncertainty
ant doubt

‖**cess** n *syn* see TAX 1
cessation n *syn* see END 2
cesspit n *syn* see SINK 1
cesspool n *syn* see SINK 1
‖**chack** n *syn* see SNACK
chafe vb 1 *syn* see ANNOY 1
2 *syn* see ABRADE 1
3 to make sore or raw through friction < the high stiff collar *chafed* his neck >

syn abrade, excoriate, fret, gall, rub
rel damage, hurt, impair, injure; flay, peel, skin; inflame, irritate; graze, scrape, scratch
con ease, relieve, soothe

chaff vb *syn* see BANTER 1
idiom make merry over

chaffer vb *syn* see HAGGLE 2
rel beg, coax, plead

chafing adj *syn* see IMPATIENT 1

chagrined adj *syn* see ASHAMED
rel crushed, disconcerted; discomposed, perturbed, upset
idiom put out of countenance

chain n 1 **chains** pl *syn* see SHACKLE
2 *syn* see SUCCESSION 2
3 *syn* see SYNDICATE

chain adj 1 *syn* see CUMULATIVE
2 *syn* see TRITE

chair vb *syn* see PRESIDE

chair car n *syn* see PARLOR CAR

chalk (out) vb *syn* see SKETCH

chalk up vb *syn* see GET 1

challenge vb 1 *syn* see DEMAND 1
2 *syn* see QUESTION 2
3 *syn* see FACE 3
rel question; dispute; strive, struggle, try
idiom throw down the (or one's) gage
con by-pass, evade
4 *syn* see STIR 1

challenge n 1 *syn* see DEMUR 2
2 *syn* see DEFIANCE 1
rel calling, claiming, demanding, exacting; importuning, insistence

chamber n 1 *syn* see ROOM 1
‖2 **chambers** pl *syn* see APARTMENT 1
chamber vb *syn* see HARBOR 1

champ vb 1 *syn* see CHEW 1
rel crush, macerate, mash, smash
2 *syn* see BITE 1
rel nibble, nip; gum, mouth, mumble; peck, pick

champaign n *syn* see FIELD

champion n *syn* see EXPONENT

champion vb *syn* see SUPPORT 2
rel battle, contend, fight (for)
idiom put in a good word for, stand behind (or back of), stand up for
con resist, withstand; denounce, condemn
ant combat

champion adj *syn* see EXCELLENT
rel distinguished, illustrious, outstanding, splendid
2 *syn* see FIRST 3

chance n 1 *syn* see ACCIDENT 1
con certainty, inevitability, necessity; destiny, fate, foreordination, predestination
ant law
2 an unpurposed, unpredictable, and uncontrollable master force < the folly of depending on *chance* for success in life >
syn fortune, hazard, luck
rel advantage, break, fluke; fate, lot; contingency
3 *syn* see OPPORTUNITY
rel likelihood, possibility, probability; outlook, prospect

chance vb 1 *syn* see HAPPEN 1
2 *syn* see HAPPEN 2
3 *syn* see GAMBLE 2
4 *syn* see VENTURE 1
idiom put at (or in) hazard

con cherish, protect, safeguard, secure

chance *adj syn see* ACCIDENTAL
rel careless, heedless, offhand

chance child *n syn see* BASTARD 1

chancy *adj* 1 *syn see* UNCERTAIN 1
rel hazardous, risky, speculative, unsound; precarious, ticklish, touchy, tricky
idiom hanging by a thread, on thin ice (*or* slippery ground)
con safe, secure, sound, stable
2 *syn see* DANGEROUS 1

change *vb* 1 to make or become different
< *changed* her will again and again >
< our needs *change* as we grow older >
syn alter, modify, mutate, refashion, turn, vary; *compare* TRANSFORM
rel convert, metamorphose, transform, transmute; diversify, variegate; exchange, interchange
idiom go (*or* pass through) a change
con establish, fix, set
2 *syn see* TRANSFORM
3 *syn see* REVERSE 1
4 *syn see* STERILIZE
5 to make substitution for or among < it's time to *change* the subject >
syn replace, shift
rel exchange, swap, trade; substitute
6 *syn see* EXCHANGE 2

change *n* 1 a making different < saw a gradual *change* of attitude in the community >
syn alteration, modification, mutation, turn, variation
rel aberration, deviation, divergence; diversification; shift; innovation
ant uniformity
2 a result of such change < amazed at the *changes* in the town >
syn innovation, mutation, novelty, permutation, sport, vicissitude
rel conversion, metamorphosis, transformation, transmutation; shift, substitute, surrogate; avatar

changeable *adj* 1 alterable or changing under slight provocation < *changeable* April weather >
syn changeful, fluid, mobile, mutable, protean, unsettled, unstable, unsteady, variable, weathery; *compare* INCONSTANT 1, MUTABLE 2
rel adaptable, impressionable, plastic, pliant; ever-changing, kaleidoscopic; restless, unfixed; inconstant, uncertain, vicissitudinous
con constant, invariable, permanent; certain, fixed, immutable, unalterable, unmodifiable; abiding, enduring, persistent
ant unchangeable; unchanging
2 *syn see* MUTABLE 2
3 *syn see* INCONSTANT 1

changeabout *n syn see* REVERSAL 1

changeful *adj syn see* CHANGEABLE 1
rel active, dynamic, live; lively, vigorous
con durable, lasting, perdurable, stable; steady, uniform
ant changeless, unchanging

changeover *n syn see* CONVERSION 2

channel *n* 1 passage through which a fluid (as water) flows or is led < the river cut a new *channel* to the sea >
syn aqueduct, canal, conduit, course, duct, watercourse
rel pass, passage, way
2 *syn see* MEAN 2
3 *syn see* PIPELINE

channel *vb syn see* CONDUCT 4

chant *vb syn see* SING 1

chaos *n* 1 *syn see* CONFUSION 3
2 *syn see* ANARCHY 1
rel misrule, unruliness

chap *n syn see* MAN 3

chaperon *vb* 1 *syn see* ACCOMPANY
rel guide, overlook, oversee, supervise
2 *syn see* SUPERVISE

chapfallen *adj syn see* DOWNCAST

chaplet *n syn see* WREATH

character *n* 1 an arbitrary or conventional device used in writing or printing < an inscription in runic *characters* >
syn mark, sign, symbol
rel cipher, device, monogram; letter
2 *syn see* CHARACTERISTIC 1
3 *syn see* QUALITY 1
rel distinction, uniqueness, uniquity
4 *syn see* TYPE
5 *syn see* DISPOSITION 3
rel soul, spirit; courage, mettle, resolution; intellect, intelligence, mind
6 *syn see* ROLE 1
7 *syn see* STATUS 1
8 *syn see* CREDENTIALS
9 *syn see* NOTABLE 1
10 *syn see* ECCENTRIC
||11 *syn see* HUMAN
12 *syn see* REPUTATION 2

character assassination *n syn see* DETRACTION

characteristic *adj* being or revealing a quality specific or identifying to an individual or group < her *characteristic* down-to-earth approach to a problem >
syn diacritic, diagnostic, distinctive, idiosyncratic, individual, peculiar, proper
rel especial, particular, special, specific; natural, normal, regular, typical
con general, generic, universal
ant uncharacteristic

characteristic *n* 1 something that marks or sets apart < *characteristics* that distinguish man from lower primates >
syn birthmark, character, feature, point, trait; *compare* QUALITY 1
rel badge, mark, sign, token; flavor, odor, savor, smack, tang; differentia; singularity
2 *syn see* QUALITY 1

characterize *vb* 1 *syn see* SKETCH
2 to be a peculiar or significant quality or feature of something < a man *characterized* by quiet dignity >
syn distinguish, individualize, individuate, mark, qualify, signalize, singularize
rel define, describe, differentiate, identify; peculiarize, personalize
idiom be a feature of

characterless *adj* lacking in character or solid qualities < a drab *characterless* little man that no one ever seemed to notice >
syn namby-pamby, pantywaist, wishy-washy
rel childish, infantile; sissified, sissy, unmanly; futile, weak; impotent, powerless

---

syn synonym(s)   *rel* related word(s)
ant antonym(s)   *con* contrasted word(s)
idiom idiomatic equivalent(s)
|| use limited; if in doubt, see a dictionary

con manly, strong, vigorous, virile

charade *n syn* see PRETENSE 2

chare *n syn* see TASK 1

charge *vb 1 syn* see BURDEN
2 *syn* see LOAD 3
3 *syn* see PERMEATE
4 *syn* see ENTRUST 1
5 *syn* see COMMAND
rel ask, request, solicit; adjure
6 *syn* see ACCUSE
rel impugn, reprehend, reproach
idiom bring (*or* prefer) charges
con excuse, forgive, pardon, remit; acquit
ant absolve
7 *syn* see ASCRIBE
8 *syn* see RUSH 1

charge *n 1 syn* see LOAD 3
rel business, devoir, place
2 *syn* see OBLIGATION 2
3 *syn* see OVERSIGHT 1
4 *syn* see COMMAND 1
5 *syn* see PRICE 1

chargeless *adj syn* see FREE 5

charger *n syn* see COURSER

charioteer *vb syn* see DRIVE 5

charisma *n syn* see CHARM 3

charitable *adj* 1 having or showing interest in or concern for the welfare of others
<spent generously for *charitable* aid to
the needy>
syn altruistic, benevolent, eleemosynary,
good, humane, humanitarian, philanthropic
rel accommodating, helpful, obliging;
benign, kindhearted, kindly, sympathetic
2 *syn* see FORBEARING
rel benevolent, considerate, kindly,
thoughtful
con cold, harsh, heartless, unfeeling
ant uncharitable

charity *n 1 syn* see MERCY
rel affection, attachment, love; altruism,
benevolence, humaneness; kindliness; amity, friendliness, goodwill
con malevolence, malignancy, malignity,
spite, spleen
ant ill will, malice
2 *syn* see DONATION

charivari *n syn* see SHIVAREE

charlatan *n* one who pretends unscrupu-
lously to knowledge or skill <the professions overrun with *charlatans* and ro-
gues>
syn mountebank, quack, quacksalver,
quackster, saltimbanque; *compare* IMPOS-
TER
rel bluff, four-flusher, sham

Charlie McCarthy *n syn* see STOOGE 1

charm *n 1 syn* see SPELL
2 an object worn or cherished to ward off
evil or attract good fortune <the Indian
medicine bag is essentially a *charm*>
syn amulet, fetish, juju, luck, mascot,
periapt, phylactery, talisman, zemi
3 a quality or combination of qualities
that is wholly attractive and irresistible
<the *charm* of her smile>
syn allure, appeal, charisma, fascination,
glamour, magnetism, witchcraft, witchery
rel allurement, attraction, attractiveness,
lure; agreeableness, delightfulness, gratefulness

con hatefulness, obnoxiousness, odiousness, repulsiveness; distastefulness, unpleasantness

charm *vb 1 syn* see ATTRACT 1
2 *syn* see BEWITCH 1

charmed *adj syn* see ENAMORED 3

charmer *n syn* see MAGICIAN 1

charming *adj syn* see ATTRACTIVE 1
ant charmless

chart *n* 1 a stylized or symbolic depiction
of something incapable of direct verbal or
pictorial representation (as because of
complexity or abstractness) <a *chart* of
anticipated economic progress>
syn graph, map
rel plan, plat, plot, scheme
2 *syn* see TABLE 2

chart *vb syn* see PLAN 2

charter *n syn* see DEED 1

charter *vb syn* see HIRE 1

chary *adj* 1 *syn* see CAUTIOUS
rel disinclined, hesitant, loath, reluctant;
economical, frugal, sparing, thrifty; constrained, inhibited, restrained
2 *syn* see SPARING

chase *vb* 1 *syn* see FOLLOW 2
con flee, fly
2 *syn* see HUNT 1
3 *syn* see EJECT 1
4 *syn* see RUSH 1
5 *syn* see COURSE

chase *n syn* see HUNTING
2 *syn* see GAME 3

chaser *n syn* see WOLF

chasm *n* 1 *syn* see GULF 2
2 *syn* see RAVINE
3 *syn* see OMISSION
4 *syn* see SCHISM 3

chasmal *adj syn* see CAVERNOUS 1

chaste *adj* free from every trace of the
lewd or salacious <was as *chaste* in language as in conduct>
syn clean, decent, immaculate, modest,
pure, spotless, stainless, unblemished,
undefiled, unsullied
rel ethical, moral, righteous, virtuous;
maidenly, virgin, virginal; becoming, decorous, proper, seemly; abstinent, continent
con coarse, gross, obscene, ribald, vulgar;
lascivious, lecherous, licentious, lustful;
gluttonous, incontinent, self-indulgent
ant unchaste

chasten *vb syn* see PUNISH 1
rel abase, humble, humiliate; afflict, try
con baby, humor, indulge, spoil
ant pamper

chastise *vb syn* see PUNISH 1
rel baste, beat, belabor, pummel, thrash

chastisement *n syn* see PUNISHMENT

chat *vb* 1 to emit a ready flow of inconsequential talk <*chats* on the phone for
hours>
syn babble, burble, cackle, chatter, chin-
chin, clack, clatter, ||dish, dither, gab,
gabble, ||gas, jaw, ||natter, patter, prate,
prattle, rattle, run on, smatter, talk, tinkle, twaddle, twiddle, twitter, yak, yakety-
yak, yammer, yatter; *compare* CONVERSE
rel yap; blab, gossip; gush, lallygag; confabulate
idiom beat one's gums, ||chew the fat (*or*
rag), ||shoot (*or* bat) the breeze, ||shoot (*or*
sling) the bull

con discourse, expound; declaim, harangue, hold forth, orate, preach
2 *syn* see CONVERSE

chat *n* 1 *syn* see CHATTER
2 an informal conversation < had a satisfactory little *chat* with the new assistant >
syn causerie, chin, prose, rap, talk, yarn; *compare* CONVERSATION 2
rel gossip, tête-à-tête
idiom bull session, rap session
con debate, deliberation, discussion
3 *syn* see CONVERSATION 1

chateau *n syn* see MANSION

chattel *n* 1 **chattels** *pl syn* see POSSESSION 2
2 *syn* see SLAVE 1

chatter *vb* 1 *syn* see GIBBER
2 *syn* see CHAT 1

chatter *n* idle and often loud and incessant talk < schoolgirl *chatter* >
syn babble, bibble-babble, blab, blabber, ||blatter, brabble, cackle, chat, chin-chin, ||chin music, chitchat, chitter-chatter, clack, gab, gabble, gibble-gabble, jabber, palaver, prate, prattle, stultiloquence, talkee-talkee, tittle-tattle, yak, yakety-yak, yak-yak, yatter
rel ||bull, gossip, small talk
idiom tongue wagging

chatterbox *n* one who engages in chatter < that old *chatterbox* will talk your arm off >
syn bandar-log, blabber, blabbermouth, blabmouth, chatterer, chewet, gabber, jabberer, magpie, prater, prattler
rel busybody, gossip, newsmonger, quidnunc, scandalmonger, tabby, tattletale

chatterer *n syn* see CHATTERBOX

chatty *adj syn* see TALKATIVE

||**chaw** *vb* 1 *syn* see CHEW 1
2 *syn* see PONDER 2

chawbacon *n syn* see RUSTIC

cheap *adj* 1 costing little < produce is usually *cheaper* in summer >
syn inexpensive, low, low-cost, low-priced, popular, reasonable, uncostly, undear
rel bargain-basement, bargain-counter, cut-rate, reduced; dirt-cheap
con dear, high, high-priced
ant costly, expensive
2 of inferior quality < *cheap* furniture is never a bargain >
syn base, cheesy, common, mean, ||ornery, paltry, poor, rubbishing, rubbishly, rubbishy, shoddy, sleazy, tatty, trashy, trumpery; *compare* INFERIOR 2
rel cheap-jack, valueless, worthless; flashy, garish, meretricious, tawdry; brummagem, fake, phony, sham; bad, rotten, terrible
con capital, excellent, fine, good; first-class, first-rate, high-class, high-grade, superior, tip-top, top-notch
ant precious
3 *syn* see CONTEMPTIBLE
rel wrong; base, low, vile; measly, paltry, petty, trifling

ant noble

cheapen *vb syn* see DEPRECIATE 1

cheap-jack (*or* **cheap-john**) *n syn* see PEDDLER

cheapskate *n syn* see MISER

cheat *n* 1 *syn* see DECEPTION 1
2 *syn* see IMPOSTURE
rel bamboozlement, cozening, hoaxing; chicane, chicanery, trickery
3 *syn* see SWINDLER

cheat *vb* to obtain something (as money) from or an advantage over by dishonesty and trickery < *cheated* out of his inheritance by a grasping lawyer >
syn beat, bilk, boodle, ||burn, chisel, chouse, cozen, ||crook, defraud, diddle, do, ||doodle, ||dry-shave, ||duff, flimflam, gyp, ||mace, ||mump, overreach, ream, ||screw, sucker, swindle, take; *compare* EXTORT 1, FLEECE 1
rel befool, dupe, fool, gull, slick; bunco, con, fudge, short; beguile, deceive, delude, double-cross, mislead

cheater *n syn* see SWINDLER

check *vb* 1 *syn* see ARREST 1
rel cease, desist, discontinue, stop; repress, suppress; circumvent, foil, frustrate, thwart
ant expedite
2 *syn* see RESTRAIN 1
rel baffle, balk; obviate, preclude, prevent
ant accelerate (*of speed*); advance (*as of hopes, plans*); release (*of feelings, energies*)
3 *syn* see TRY 1
4 *syn* see AGREE 4

check *n* 1 *syn* see SETBACK
2 a statement of charges for food and drink consumed (as at a restaurant) < shocked at the size of the *check* >
syn bill, tab
rel damage, score

check out *vb* ||1 *syn* see DIE 1
2 *syn* see AGREE 4

check over *vb syn* see SCRUTINIZE 1

check-over *n syn* see EXAMINATION

check up *vb syn* see SCRUTINIZE 1

checkup *n syn* see EXAMINATION

cheek *n* 1 **cheeks** *pl syn* see BUTTOCKS
2 *syn* see EFFRONTERY

cheeky *adj syn* see WISE 5

cheep *vb syn* see CHIRP

cheer *vb* 1 *syn* see COMFORT 1
2 *syn* see ENCOURAGE 1
3 *syn* see APPLAUD 2

cheerful *adj* 1 marked by or suggestive of lighthearted ease of mind and spirit < a *cheerful* smile >
syn blithe, cheery, ||chirk, chirpy, chirrupy, lightsome, sunbeamy, sunny; *compare* LIVELY 1
rel airy, carefree, debonair, jaunty; animated, gay, lighthearted, lively, vivacious; buoyant, corky
idiom in good (*or* high) spirits, of good cheer
con blue, dejected, depressed, melancholy; dispirited, heavyhearted, joyless, mournful, sorrowful, woeful; dour, morose, saturnine, sullen; doleful, lugubrious; austere, forbidding, grim, stern
ant gloomy, glum
2 *syn* see GLAD 2
ant cheerless

syn synonym(s)   *rel* related word(s)
ant antonym(s)   *con* contrasted word(s)
idiom idiomatic equivalent(s)
|| use limited; if in doubt, see a dictionary

‖**cheerio** *interj syn* see GOOD-BYE
cheerless *adj syn* see GLOOMY 3
  rel dejecting
  ant cheerful
cheery *adj* 1 *syn* see GLAD 2
  2 *syn* see CHEERFUL 1
cheeseparer *n syn* see MISER
cheeseparing *adj syn* see STINGY
  rel cheap, grudging, mean, shabby; illiberal
cheesy *adj syn* see CHEAP 2
chef d'oeuvre *n* 1 *syn* see MASTERPIECE 1
  2 *syn* see SHOWPIECE
‖**chemist** *n syn* see DRUGGIST
cherish *vb* 1 *syn* see NURSE 2
  rel conserve, preserve, save; entertain, harbor, keep, shelter; defend, guard, safeguard, shield
  con reject, repudiate, scorn
  ant abandon
  2 *syn* see APPRECIATE 1
  rel revere, reverence, venerate
  idiom hold in high esteem
  con disregard, forget, ignore, overlook, slight
  ant neglect
  3 *syn* see ADMIRE 1
‖**cherry** *n syn* see VIRGINITY
chest *n syn* see TREASURY 2
chesty *adj syn* see BUXOM
chew *vb* 1 to crush or grind with the teeth < *chew* your food well >
  syn champ, ‖chaw, chomp, ‖chonk, chumble, chump, crunch, masticate, munch, ruminate, scrunch
  rel bite; gnaw, nibble; consume, devour, eat; gum, mumble
  ‖2 *syn* see SCOLD 1
chewet *n syn* see CHATTERBOX
‖**chew out** *vb syn* see SCOLD 1
chiaus *n syn* see SWINDLER
chic *n syn* see FASHION 3
chic *adj syn* see STYLISH
chicane *vb* 1 *syn* see QUIBBLE 1
  2 *syn* see DUPE
chicane *n syn* see DECEPTION 1
  rel artifice, feint, gambit, maneuver, ploy, ruse, stratagem, trick, wile; furtiveness, surreptitiousness, underhandedness
  con forthrightness, straightforwardness
chicanery *n syn* see DECEPTION 1
  rel intrigue, machination, plot; furtiveness, surreptitiousness, underhandedness
  con forthrightness, straightforwardness; honesty, honor, integrity, probity
chichi *adj* 1 *syn* see SHOWY
  2 *syn* see PRECIOUS 4
chick *n* 1 *syn* see CHILD 1
  ‖2 *syn* see GIRL FRIEND 1
chickabiddy *n syn* see CHILD 1
chicken *n syn* see COWARD
‖**chicken** *adj syn* see COWARDLY
chide *vb syn* see REPROVE
  rel berate, rate, scold, upbraid
  con applaud, compliment; approve, endorse, sanction
  ant commend
chiding *n syn* see REBUKE
chief *n* 1 *syn* see LEADER 2
  rel dictator, duce, führer
  2 *syn* see NOTABLE 1
chief *adj* 1 *syn* see FIRST 3

2 standing apart by reason of superior importance, significance, or influence < his *chief* claim to consideration is his unquestionable uprightness >
  syn capital, ‖cock, dominant, main, major, number one, outstanding, predominant, preeminent, principal, star, stellar
  rel primal, primary, prime; important, prominent, significant; consequential, momentous, weighty; effective, potent, telling; controlling, master, ruling
  con inconsequential, minor, trivial, unimportant; collateral, contingent, secondary
chiefly *adv syn* see GENERALLY 1
chieftain *n syn* see LEADER 2
chiffer *n syn* see NUMBER
child *n* 1 a young person < a movie for both *children* and adults >
  syn bud, chick, chickabiddy, chit, juvenile, kid, moppet, ‖nipper, puss, youngling, young one, youngster, youth
  rel minor; adolescent, teenager, teener, teenybopper; brat, bratling, dickens, runabout; cherub, innocent, lamb, sweetling
  idiom a slip of a boy (*or* girl), small fry, young hopeful
  ant adult, grown-up
  2 **children** *pl syn* see OFFSPRING
childbearing *n* 1 *syn* see BIRTH 1
  2 *syn* see LABOR 2
childbed *n syn* see CONFINEMENT 2
childbirth *n* 1 *syn* see BIRTH 1
  2 *syn* see LABOR 2
childing *adj* 1 *syn* see PREGNANT 1
  2 *syn* see FERTILE
childish *adj* significantly deficient in maturity < a *childish* and spiteful attitude >
  syn babyish, immature, infantile, infantine, prekindergarten, puerile
  rel asinine, fatuous, foolish, silly, simple; naive, unsophisticated; arrested, backward, moronic, retarded, slow, ‖wanting
  ant adult
child's play *n syn* see SNAP 1
chill *vb syn* see DISCOURAGE 1
chill *adj* 1 *syn* see COLD 1
  2 *syn* see COLD 2
  rel distant, formal, reserved, solitary, standoffish, uncompanionable, withdrawn; abstracted, disinterested, uninterested
  con easy, gregarious, informal; sociable
chiller *n syn* see THRILLER
chillsome *adj syn* see COLD 1
chilly *adj syn* see COLD 1
chime *n syn* see HARMONY 2
chime *vb syn* see RING
chime in *vb* 1 *syn* see INTERRUPT 2
  2 *syn* see SAY 1
chimera *n syn* see PIPE DREAM
chimerical *adj syn* see FICTITIOUS 1
  rel ambitious, pretentious, utopian; deceptive, delusive, delusory; fabulous, mythical; absurd, preposterous
  con believable, plausible, rational, reasonable; possible, practicable
  ant feasible
chiming *adj syn* see HARMONIOUS 1
chin *n syn* see CHAT 2
chin *vb syn* see CONVERSE
chin–chin *vb syn* see CHAT 1
chin–chin *n syn* see CHATTER
‖**chinchy** *adj syn* see STINGY
chine *n syn* see RIDGE 1

Chinese puzzle *n syn* see MYSTERY
Chinese wall *n syn* see OBSTACLE
chink *n syn* see CRACK 3
  rel interruption
chink *vb syn* see JINGLE
||**chink** *n syn* see MONEY
||**chinkle** *vb syn* see JINGLE
||**chin music** *n syn* see CHATTER
chintzy *adj syn* see GAUDY
chin–up *adj syn* see BRAVE 1
chip *vb syn* see CHIRP
chip in *vb* 1 *syn* see CONTRIBUTE 1
  2 *syn* see INTERRUPT 2
chipper *vb syn* see CHIRP
chipper *adj* 1 *syn* see LIVELY 1
  2 *syn* see NEAT 2
||**chippy** *n syn* see DOXY 1
||**chips** *n pl syn* see MONEY
chirk *adj* 1 *syn* see LIVELY 1
  2 *syn* see CHEERFUL 1
chirk (up) *vb syn* see ENCOURAGE 1
||**chirm** *n syn* see DIN
||**chirm** *vb syn* see CHIRP
chirography *n syn* see HANDWRITING
chirp *vb* to make a short, sharp, and usually repetitive sound < sparrows *chirping*
  on the lawn >
  syn cheep, chip, chipper, ||chirm, chirrup,
  clutter, peep, twoodle, tweet, twitter
chirpy *adj syn* see CHEERFUL
chirrup *vb syn* see CHIRP
chirrupy *adj syn* see CHEERFUL 1
chisel *vb* 1 *syn* see SCULPTURE
  2 *syn* see CHEAT
chisel (in) *vb syn* see INTRUDE 1
||**chiselly** *adj syn* see BAD 8
chit *n syn* see CHILD 1
chit *n syn* see NOTE 2
chitchat *n* 1 *syn* see CHATTER
  2 *syn* see SMALL TALK
chitter *vb syn* see CHIRP
chitter–chatter *n* 1 *syn* see CHATTER
  2 *syn* see SMALL TALK
chivalrous *adj syn* see GENEROUS 1
  rel knightly, manly, noble
  con churlish common, low
chivy *vb* 1 *syn* see FOLLOW 2
  2 *syn* see BAIT 2
  rel afflict, torment, try; chase, pursue,
  trail
choate *adj syn* see WHOLE 3
chockablock *adj syn* see FULL 1
chock–full *adj syn* see FULL 1
choice *n* 1 the act, right, opportunity, or
  faculty of choosing or deciding < the
  choice lies with the electorate >
  syn alternative, ||druthers, election, op-
  tion, preference, selection
  rel decision, determination, finding, judgment, verdict; appraisal, evaluation, rating
  2 *syn* see BEST
choice *adj* having qualities that appeal to a
  fine or highly refined taste < a few *choice*
  spirits gathered nightly to discuss the
  day's events >
  syn dainty, delicate, elegant, exquisite,
  rare, recherché, select, superior
  rel incomparable, peerless, preeminent,
  prime, superlative, supreme, surpassing,

transcendent, unsurpassed; chosen, culled,
picked, selected
  con common, ordinary; average, fair,
  mediocre, medium, middling, run-of-the-
  mill, second-rate; drab, dull, lackluster,
  lusterless
  ant indifferent
||**choicy** *adj syn* see NICE 1
choke *vb* 1 to check normal breathing
  especially by compressing or obstructing
  the windpipe < *choked* by a bone in the
  throat >
  syn strangle, throttle; *compare* SUFFO-
  CATE
  2 *syn* see SUFFOCATE
  3 *syn* see FILL 1
  4 *syn* see LOAD 3
choke (off) *vb syn* see SILENCE
||**chokey** *n syn* see JAIL
choking *n syn* see REPRESSION 1
choleric *adj* 1 *syn* see IRASCIBLE
  rel acrimonious, angry, fiery, indignant,
  irate, mad, spunky, wrathful, wroth; captious, carping, faultfinding
  con calm, serene, tranquil; composed,
  cool, nonchalant
  ant placid
  2 *syn* see ANGRY
chomp *vb* 1 *syn* see CHEW 1
  2 *syn* see BITE 1
||**chonk** *vb syn* see CHEW 1
choose *vb* 1 to fix upon one among alternatives as the one to be taken, accepted,
  or adopted < *chose* the largest apple but
  found it sour >
  syn cull, elect, mark, opt (for), optate,
  pick, pick out, prefer, select, single (out),
  take
  rel adopt, embrace, espouse; crave, desire,
  love, want, wish
  con decline, refuse, repudiate, spurn;
  abnegate, forbear, forgo
  ant reject; eschew
  2 *syn* see WILL 1
  rel favor, prefer
  ||3 *syn* see DESIRE 1
choosy *adj syn* see NICE 1
chop *vb* 1 *syn* see FELL 2
  2 to cut into fragments by repeated
  strokes < *chop* meat and onions for
  hash >
  syn hash, mince
  rel cut up, dice, fragment
  idiom cut to bits, make mincemeat of
chop *n syn* see CUFF
chop–chop *adv syn* see FAST 2
chore *n* 1 *syn* see TASK 1
  2 *syn* see TASK 2
  rel trial, tribulation
chortle *vb syn* see LAUGH
chorus *n syn* see HARMONY 1
chosen *adj syn* see SELECT 1
chouse *n syn* see TRICK 1
chouse *vb syn* see CHEAT
||**chow** *n* 1 *syn* see FOOD 1
  2 *syn* see MEAL
chowchow *adj syn* see MISCELLANEOUS
chowchow *n syn* see MISCELLANY 1
chowderhead *n syn* see DUNCE
chrism *n syn* see OINTMENT
christcross–row *n syn* see ALPHABET 1
christen *vb* 1 *syn* see BAPTIZE
  2 *syn* see NAME 1

---

syn synonym(s)   *rel* related word(s)
ant antonym(s)   *con* contrasted word(s)
idiom idiomatic equivalent(s)
|| use limited; if in doubt, see a dictionary

Christian *adj syn* see DECOROUS 1

Christian name *n syn* see GIVEN NAME

Christmas *n* a festival or holiday commemorating the birth of Christ < gave presents on *Christmas*>
syn Nativity, noel, Xmas, yule, yuletide

chronic *adj* 1 *syn* see HABITUAL 2
2 *syn* see USUAL 1

chronicle *n* 1 *syn* see HISTORY 2
2 *syn* see ACCOUNT 7
rel narration, recital, recountal

chthonian *adj syn* see INFERNAL 1

chthonic *adj syn* see INFERNAL 1

chubby *adj syn* see ROTUND 2
ant slim

chuck *vb* 1 *syn* see DISCARD
2 *syn* see EJECT 1
3 *syn* see ABANDON 1
||**chuck** *syn* see HARBOR 3

chucker *n syn* see BOUNCER 2

||**chucker-out** *n syn* see BOUNCER 2

chuckhole *n syn* see POTHOLE

chuckle *vb syn* see LAUGH

chucklehead *n syn* see DUNCE

chuckleheaded *adj syn* see STUPID 1

chuff *n* 1 *syn* see BOOR
2 *syn* see MISER

||**chuff** *adj syn* see SULLEN

chuffy *adj syn* see STOCKY

||**chuffy** *adj syn* see SULLEN

chum *n syn* see ASSOCIATE 3

chumble *vb syn* see CHEW 1

chummy *adj* 1 *syn* see FAMILIAR 1
2 *syn* see INTIMATE 4

chump *n* ||1 *syn* see HEAD 1
2 *syn* see DUNCE
3 *syn* see FOOL 3

chump *vb syn* see CHEW 1

||**chumpy** *adj syn* see STOCKY

chunk *n syn* see LUMP 1

chunky *adj syn* see STOCKY
rel chubby, rotund

||**chunter** *vb syn* see MUMBLE

church *n* 1 *syn* see HOUSE OF WORSHIP
2 *syn* see RELIGION 2

church *adj syn* see ECCLESIASTICAL

churchly *adj syn* see ECCLESIASTICAL

churchman *n syn* see CLERGYMAN

churchmanly *adj syn* see ECCLESIASTICAL

churl *n syn* see BOOR
ant aristocrat, gentleman

churlish *adj syn* see BOORISH
rel crude, discourteous; blunt, brusque, crusty, curt, gruff; dour, surly; naive, unschooled
con bland, politic, smooth; polished, sophisticated
ant courtly

churn *vb syn* see SEETHE 4

chute *n syn* see WATERFALL

cicatrix *n syn* see SCAR

cicatrize *vb syn* see SCAR

||**cig** *n syn* see CIGARETTE

cigarette *n* a paper-wrapped tube of finely cut smoking tobacco < dependence on *cigarettes*>
syn ||butt, ||cig, ||coffin nail, fag, ||gasper, ||pill, ||skag, smoke

cimmerian *adj syn* see INFERNAL 2

cinch *n syn* see SNAP 1

cinch *vb syn* see ENSURE

cincture *n syn* see BELT 1

cincture *vb syn* see BELT 1

cinders *n pl syn* see ASH

cine *n syn* see MOVIE

||**cinema** *n syn* see MOVIE

cipher *n* 1 *syn* see ZERO 1
2 *syn* see NUMBER
3 *syn* see MONOGRAM
4 *syn* see NONENTITY

cipher *vb* 1 *syn* see CALCULATE
||2 *syn* see SOLVE 2

ciphering *n syn* see COMPUTATION

circa *prep syn* see ABOUT 1

Circean *adj syn* see ENTICING

circle *n* 1 *syn* see RANGE 2
2 *syn* see CYCLE 1
3 *syn* see SET 5
rel acquaintance; cronies, friends, intimates; associates, companions, comrades
4 *syn* see CLIQUE

circle *vb* 1 *syn* see SURROUND 1
2 *syn* see TURN 1

circuit *n* 1 *syn* see CIRCUMFERENCE
rel course, route, way; journey, tour, travels, trip
2 *syn* see REVOLUTION 1
3 *syn* see TOUR 2
4 *syn* see LEAGUE 4

circuitous *adj syn* see INDIRECT 1
ant straight

circuitously *adv syn* see ABOUT 2

circular *adj* 1 *syn* see ROUND 1
2 *syn* see INDIRECT 1

circulate *vb* 1 *syn* see SPREAD 1
rel exchange, interchange; flow; revolve, rotate
2 *syn* see MOBILIZE 1

circulation *n syn* see REVOLUTION 1

circulator *n syn* see GOSSIP 1

circumambages *n pl syn* see VERBIAGE 1

circumambulate *vb syn* see WANDER 1

circumbendibus *n syn* see VERBIAGE 1

circumduct *vb* 1 *syn* see TURN 1
2 *syn* see ABOLISH

circumference *n* a continuous line or course about an area < strolled along the *circumference* of the reservoir >
syn ambit, circuit, compass, perimeter, periphery; *compare* BORDER 1
rel boundary, bounds, confines, limits; border, margin, rim

circumlocution *n syn* see VERBIAGE 1
con conciseness, concision, pithiness, succinctness, terseness; compactness

circumnavigate *vb syn* see SKIRT 2

circumscribe *vb syn* see LIMIT 2
rel fetter, hamper, trammel
con amplify, distend, inflate, swell; enlarge
ant dilate, expand

circumscribed *adj syn* see DEFINITE 1
rel bound, bounded, finite; confined, cramped, strait

circumscription *n* 1 *syn* see RESTRICTION 1
2 *syn* see RESTRICTION 2

circumspect *adj syn* see CAUTIOUS
rel meticulous, punctilious, scrupulous
con adventurous, daredevil, foolhardy; careless, heedless; bold
ant audacious

circumstance *n syn* see OCCURRENCE
rel detail, item, particular; component, constituent, element, factor

2 *syn* see FATE

circumstantial *adj* marked by careful attention to relevant details < gave a *circumstantial* account of his adventure >
syn blow-by-blow, clocklike, detailed, full, itemized, minute, particular, particularized, thorough
rel accurate, exact, nice, precise; complete, replete; close, strict
con compendious, concise, laconic, pithy, short, succinct, terse; abbreviated, curtailed, cut, pruned, shortened, trimmed
ant abridged; summary

circumvent *vb* 1 *syn* see FRUSTRATE 1
rel befool, dupe, hoodwink, trick; avoid, elude, escape, evade
ant conform (*to laws, orders*); cooperate (*with persons*)
2 *syn* see SKIRT 2
3 *syn* see SKIRT 3

circumvolution *n* *syn* see REVOLUTION 1

cit *n* *syn* see TOWNSMAN

citadel *n* *syn* see FORT

citation *n* *syn* see ENCOMIUM
rel award, guerdon, reward

cite *vb* 1 *syn* see REMEMBER
2 *syn* see MENTION
3 *syn* see ADDUCE
rel count, enumerate, number, tell

citizen *n* *syn* see TOWNSMAN
2 a person regarded as a member of a sovereign state, entitled to its protection, and subject to its laws < the subtle bond between the *citizen* and the nation >
syn national, subject
con foreigner, stranger
ant alien

city *adj* *syn* see URBAN

civic *adj* *syn* see PUBLIC 1

civil *adj* *syn* see PUBLIC 1
2 adequate in courtesy < made a *civil* inquiry about their health >
syn courteous, genteel, mannerly, polite, well-mannered; *compare* COURTLY
rel cultivated, refined, well-bred; accommodating, affable, cordial, obliging; bland, diplomatic, gracious, politic, suave, urbane
con boorish, churlish, loutish, uncouth; discourteous, ill-mannered, impolite, ungracious
ant uncivil; rude

civilities *n pl* *syn* see MANNER 5

civilized *adj* 1 *syn* see DECOROUS 1
2 *syn* see SUAVE

Civitas Dei *n* *syn* see HEAVEN 2

||**clabber** *vb* *syn* see CURDLE

clack *vb* 1 *syn* see CHAT 1
2 *syn* see RATTLE 1

clack *n* 1 *syn* see CHATTER
2 *syn* see GOSSIP 1

clad *vb* 1 *syn* see CLOTHE
2 *syn* see SHEATHE

||**claggy** *adj* 1 *syn* see STICKY 1
2 *syn* see MUDDY 1

claim *vb* 1 *syn* see DEMAND 1
rel adduce, advance, allege; assert, defend, justify, maintain, vindicate
con abnegate, forgo; refuse, reject, repudiate; disavow, disown

ant disclaim; renounce
2 *syn* see MAINTAIN 2

claim *n* 1 a real or assumed right to demand something as one's own or one's due < his genial wit was his greatest *claim* to fame >
syn ||dibs, pretense, pretension, title
rel birthright, prerogative, privilege, right; affirmation, assertion, declaration, protestation
2 *syn* see INTEREST 1

clamant *adj* *syn* see PRESSING

clamber *vb* *syn* see SCRAMBLE 1

clamor *n* 1 *syn* see COMMOTION 4
2 *syn* see DIN
3 *syn* see COMMOTION 1

clamor *vb* *syn* see ROAR
rel claim, demand; agitate, debate, dispute
idiom make the welkin ring, raise the roof

clamorous *adj* 1 *syn* see VOCIFEROUS
rel articulate, eloquent, vocal, voluble; adjuring, begging, imploring, importunate
ant taciturn
2 *syn* see PRESSING

clamp *n* *syn* see HOLD

clampdown *n* *syn* see REPRESSION 2

clan *n* 1 *syn* see FAMILY 1
2 *syn* see CLIQUE

clandestine *adj* *syn* see SECRET 1
rel illegitimate, illicit; artful, foxy, sly
con aboveboard, forthright, straightforward
ant open

clandestinely *adv* *syn* see SECRETLY

clangorous *adj* *syn* see NOISY

clap *n* *syn* see BANG 1

claptrap *n* *syn* see NONSENSE 2

||**claret** *n* *syn* see BLOOD 1

clarify *vb* 1 *syn* see PURIFY 1
2 to make clear and understandable < felt a need to *clarify* his position on the question >
syn clear, clear up, elucidate, explain, illuminate, illustrate; *compare* EXPLAIN 1
rel settle, straighten out; define, delineate, formulate; analyze, break down, simplify
idiom make plain
con befog, cloud, obfuscate, obscure; confuse, foul up, muddle, ||snafu

clarion *adj* *syn* see FAIR 2

clarity *n* notable precision of thought or expression < *clarity* of expression depends on use of exactly the right words in precisely the right way >
syn clearness, limpidity, lucidity, perspicuity, plainness
rel articulateness, articulation; care, exactitude, fussiness, meticulousness, nicety, precision; accuracy, correctitude, propriety
con haziness, imprecision, indefiniteness, unclearness, vagueness; inexactness, laxity, looseness, sloppiness, slovenliness
ant obscurity

||**clarty** *adj* 1 *syn* see MUDDY 1
2 *syn* see STICKY 1

clash *vb* 1 *syn* see BUMP 1
2 to be markedly out of harmony < garish colors that *clashed* almost painfully >
syn conflict, disaccord, discord, disharmonize, jangle, jar, mismatch
rel fret, gall, grate, try
idiom swear at one another

---

syn synonym(s)   *rel* related word(s)
ant antonym(s)   *con* contrasted word(s)
idiom idiomatic equivalent(s)
|| use limited; if in doubt, see a dictionary

con accord, blend, conform, correspond; fit, meet, suit

ant harmonize

clash *n* 1 *syn* see IMPACT

2 a sharp and usually brief conflict especially between military units < recurrent border *clashes* >

syn affray, brush, fray, melee, mellay, scrimmage, skirmish

rel brawl, broil, fracas, riot, row, rumpus, scrap, set-to; action, battle, conflict, engagement; embroilment, encounter

idiom clash of arms, passage at (*or* of) arms

clashing *adj syn* see ANTIPATHETIC 1

clasp *n syn* see HOLD

clasp *vb* 1 *syn* see EMBRACE 1

2 *syn* see TAKE 4

class *n* 1 a unit or a subunit of a larger whole made up of members sharing one or more characteristics < miniaturization of circuitry made possible a whole new *class* of small computers and calculators >

syn category, grade, group, grouping, league, pigeonhole, tier

rel brand, color, description, feather, genre, grain, ilk, kidney, kind, nature, order, sort, stamp, style, type: bracket, branch, denomination, division, head, section; genus, species

2 *syn* see QUALITY 2

3 *syn* see TYPE

class *vb* 1 *syn* see ASSORT

2 to put into an appropriate class < he is generally *classed* among our leading theoretical physicists >

syn classify, evaluate, grade, rank, rate

rel appraise, gauge, judge; divide, part, separate; allot, assign; account, assess, consider, hold, reckon, regard; mark, score

classic *adj* 1 *syn* see EXCELLENT

2 *syn* see VINTAGE 1

3 *syn* see TYPICAL 1

classic *n syn* see MASTERPIECE 1

classical *adj* 1 *syn* see EXCELLENT

2 *syn* see VINTAGE 1

3 *syn* see TYPICAL 1

classify *vb* 1 *syn* see ASSORT

2 *syn* see CLASS 2

classy *adj syn* see STYLISH

clatter *vb* 1 *syn* see RATTLE 1

2 *syn* see CHAT 1

clatter *n syn* see COMMOTION 4

clattery *adj syn* see NOISY

claviger *n syn* see CUSTODIAN

clawback *n syn* see SYCOPHANT

clean *adj* 1 free from dirt < kept a *clean* house in a dirty neighborhood >

syn cleanly, immaculate, spotless, taintless, unsoiled, unsullied

rel bright, shining, sparkling; fresh, pure, untainted; wholesome

idiom clean as a whistle (*or* new penny)

con dingy, grimy, grubby, messy, mussy, slovenly; filthy, foul, noisome

ant dirty, unclean

2 *syn* see INNOCENT 2

3 *syn* see CHASTE

ant unclean

4 *syn* see FAIR 5

clean *vb* 1 *syn* see PURIFY 1

2 to make clean < *cleaned* his car every week >

syn cleanse, clean up

rel do, neaten, order, police, spruce, straighten (up), tidy, trim; brighten, freshen, furbish, recondition; renew, renovate

idiom make spick-and-span

con begrime, daub, dirty, sully; besmirch, defile, foul, pollute

ant soil

3 *syn* see DRESS 3

clean-cut *adj syn* see EXPLICIT

clean-limbed *adj syn* see SHAPELY

cleanly *adj syn* see CLEAN 1

rel neat, orderly, spick-and-span, tidy, trim; dainty, fastidious, fussy, nice

con disheveled, disorderly, slipshod, sloppy, slovenly, unkempt

ant uncleanly

cleanse *vb* 1 *syn* see CLEAN 2

rel disinfect, sanitize, sterilize

2 *syn* see PURIFY 1

3 *syn* see PURIFY 2

cleansing *n syn* see PURIFICATION

clean up *vb* 1 *syn* see CLEAR 6

2 *syn* see CLEAN 2

3 *syn* see SETTLE 7

clean up (on) *vb syn* see WHIP 2

clear *adj* 1 *syn* see FAIR 2

2 *syn* see TRANSPARENT 1

3 *syn* see TRANSLUCENT 3

rel milky, opalescent

4 free from obscurity or ambiguity < his account of the accident was perfectly *clear* >

syn clear-cut, crystal, lucent, lucid, luculent, luminous, pellucid, perspicuous, translucent, transparent, transpicuous, unambiguous, unblurred; *compare* UNDERSTANDABLE

rel apprehensible, comprehensible, graspable, knowable, understandable; plain, simple, straightforward, uncomplicated, unperplexed; defined, definite

idiom clear as day (*or* crystal), plain as the nose on one's face

con clouded, dark, mysterious, unclear; hazy, ill-defined, vague

ant obscure

5 readily perceived or apprehended < a *clear* case of embezzlement >

syn apparent, conspicuous, distinct, evident, manifest, obvious, open-and-shut, openhanded, palpable, patent, plain, straightforward, unambiguous, unequivocal, univocal, unmistakable; *compare* SELF-EXPLANATORY, UNDERSTANDABLE

rel appreciable, perceptible, recognizable, sensible, tangible; overt, public, published, unhidden, unobscured; exact, precise

con dim, dusky, gloomy, murky; cryptic, dark, enigmatic, equivocal, indistinct, vague; arcane, esoteric, mysterious, occult

ant obscure

6 *syn* see EMPTY 1

clear *adv syn* see WELL 3

clear *vb* 1 *syn* see EXCULPATE

2 *syn* see CLARIFY 2

3 *syn* see VACATE 2

4 *syn* see RID

rel eliminate, rule out; clean, cleanse

5 to make right by presenting what is due < *clear* one's accounts >

syn clear off, discharge, liquidate, pay, pay up, quit, satisfy, settle, square

rel close, pay off, repay, sink, solve
6 to obtain as a profit or return <he *cleared* several thousand on the deal>
syn clean up, gain, make, net
rel acquire, get, obtain, secure; earn, win; accumulate, gather, glean, pick up
7 *syn* see EXTRICATE 2
8 to pass over or by <*cleared* the hurdle with perfect form>
syn hurdle, leap, negotiate, over, over-leap, surmount, vault
9 to become fair <the weather *cleared* later in the day>
syn ||break, burn off
rel ameliorate, better, improve, meliorate; settle, stabilize
10 *syn* see VANISH

clear away *vb* 1 *syn* see REMOVE 4
2 *syn* see EXTRICATE 2
clear-cut *adj* 1 *syn* see CLEAR 4
2 *syn* see EXPLICIT
3 *syn* see INCISIVE
rel clear, distinct, manifest, plain; definite, explicit, express; exact, nice, precise
con fogged, hazy, misty; confused, mud-dled; obscured, overcast
4 *syn* see DECIDED 1
rel indubitable, undisputed, undoubted, unquestioned
idiom beyond a shade (*or* shadow) of doubt, past dispute
clearness *n* *syn* see CLARITY
clear off *vb* *syn* see CLEAR 5
clear out *vb* *syn* see GET OUT 1
clear-sightedness *n* *syn* see WIT 3
clear up *vb* 1 *syn* see CLARIFY 2
2 *syn* see SOLVE 2
cleavage *n* *syn* see SCHISM 3
cleave *vb* *syn* see STICK 2
rel associate, combine, conjoin, join, link, unite
con alienate, disaffect, disunite, estrange, separate
cleave *vb* 1 *syn* see CUT 5
2 *syn* see TEAR 1
rel divide, divorce, separate; chop, hew
con join, link, unite; attach, fasten
cleft *n* 1 *syn* see CRACK 3
2 *syn* see RAVINE
3 *syn* see SCHISM 3
clemency *n* 1 *syn* see MERCY
rel gentleness, mildness; equitableness, fairness, justness
con austerity, severity, sternness; rigidity, rigorousness, strictness; inexorableness, inflexibility, obduracy
ant harshness
2 *syn* see FORBEARANCE 2
rel endurance, sufferance
con firmness, hardness, inflexibility, obdu-rateness, relentlessness, rigidity
ant harshness
clement *adj* *syn* see FORBEARING
rel compassionate, sympathetic, tender; benign, benignant, kind, kindly; benevo-lent, charitable, humane
con austere, severe, stern; rigid, rigorous, strict, stringent

ant harsh; barbarous
clench *n* *syn* see HOLD
clergyman *n* one duly ordained to the service of God in the Christian church <the responsibility of the *clergyman* to the whole community>
syn ||blackcoat, cassock, churchman, cleric, clerical, clerk, ||devil-dodger, divine, ||dominie, ecclesiast, ecclesiastic, ||Holy Joe, minister, parson, preacher, pul-pitarian, pulpiteer, pulpiter, reverend, sermonizer, sky pilot
rel evangelist, missionary; chaplain, cu-rate, pastor, vicar; father, priest, shepherd; predicant
idiom man of God, man of the cloth
cleric *n* *syn* see CLERGYMAN
clerical *n* *syn* see CLERGYMAN
clerisy *n* *syn* see INTELLIGENTSIA
clerk *n* *syn* see CLERGYMAN
clerkish *adj* *syn* see NICE 1
clever *adj* 1 *syn* see SKILLFUL 2
2 *syn* see DEXTEROUS 1
3 *syn* see INTELLIGENT 2
rel apt, prompt, quick, ready; able, capa-ble, competent; all-around, many-sided, versatile
idiom quick as a flash, sharp (*or* smart) as a whip
con asinine, fatuous, foolish, simple
ant dull
4 highly skilled in devising or contriving <very *clever* about getting her own way>
syn adroit, canny, ||coony, cunning, dex-terous, ingenious, ||sleighty, slim, sly; com-pare SKILLFUL 2
rel able, adept, expert, handy, masterly, proficient, skilled, skillful; capable, compe-tent, qualified; crafty, deceitful, slick, tricky
con awkward, clumsy, gauche, inept, maladroit; dilatory, laggard, slow, slug-gish; incapable, incompetent, inept, un-qualified
5 pleasing because of aptness, sparkle, and usually wit <delighted her audience with a series of *clever* comparisons>
syn good, scintillating, smart, sprightly
rel bright, brilliant, coruscating, dazzling, sparkling; piquant, racy, salty; fanciful, whimsical; amusing, entertaining, pleasing; facetious, funny, humorous, witty; laugh-able, risible
con drab, dull, humdrum, monotonous, stodgy; barren, empty, inane; fatuous, pointless; absurd, foolish, nonsensical, ridiculous
ant stupid
||**cleverly** *adv* *syn* see WELL 3
cliché *n* *syn* see COMMONPLACE
cliché *adj* *syn* see TRITE
clichéd *adj* *syn* see TRITE
click *vb* *syn* see SUCCEED 2
client *n* *syn* see CUSTOMER
clientage *n* *syn* see FOLLOWING 2
clientele *n* *syn* see FOLLOWING 2
climacteric *adj* *syn* see ACUTE 6
climate *n* *syn* see ENVIRONMENT
climatize *vb* *syn* see HARDEN 2
climax *n* *syn* see APEX 2
climax *vb* to bring to or come to a satisfy-ing termination <the feast was *climaxed* by a glorious plum pudding>

---

syn synonym(s)   *rel* related word(s)
ant antonym(s)   *con* contrasted word(s)
idiom idiomatic equivalent(s)
|| use limited; if in doubt, see a dictionary

syn cap, crown, culminate, finish off, round off, top off

rel content, please, satisfy; conclude, end, finish, terminate

climb vb syn see ASCEND 1

‖**clinch** vb syn see EMBRACE 1

clinch n syn see HOLD

clincher n syn see TRUMP CARD

cling vb syn see STICK 2

cling n syn see ADHERENCE 1

clinging n syn see ADHERENCE 1

clink vb syn see JINGLE

‖**clink** n syn see JAIL

clinkers n pl syn see ASH

‖**clip** vb syn see EMBRACE 1

clip n syn see BROOCH

clip vb 1 syn see CUT 6

2 syn see MOW

3 syn see REDUCE 2

4 syn see OVERCHARGE 1

clique n a narrowly exclusive group of people usually held together by a common often selfish interest or purpose <there was a politically minded *clique* on the campus>

syn cabal, camarilla, camp, circle, clan, coterie, in-group, mob, ring; compare SET 5

clitter vb syn see RATTLE 1

cloak n syn see MASK 2

cloak vb syn see DISGUISE

rel blanket, curtain, screen, shroud, veil

ant uncloak

clobber vb‖1 syn see WHIP 2

2 syn see SLAM 1

clochard n syn see VAGABOND

clock vb syn see TIME 2

‖**clock** vb syn see SET 11

clocklike adj syn see CIRCUMSTANTIAL

clockwise adj syn see RIGHT-HANDED

clod n 1 syn see LUMP 1

2 syn see DUNCE

cloddish adj syn see BOORISH

clodhopper n 1 syn see RUSTIC

2 syn see BOOR

clodhopping adj syn see BOORISH

clodpate n syn see DUNCE

clodpoll n syn see DUNCE

clog n syn see ENCUMBRANCE

clog vb 1 syn see BURDEN

2 syn see HAMPER

3 syn see FILL 1

cloggy adj syn see STICKY 1

cloister vb syn see SECLUDE

cloistered adj syn see SECLUDED

clonk vb syn see THUD

‖**Cloot** n, usu **Cloots** pl syn see DEVIL 1

‖**Clootie** n syn see DEVIL 1

close vb 1 to fill an opening with an appropriate closure <be sure to *close* the gate>

syn ‖put to, shut

rel bang, clap, slam; block, choke, clog, obstruct, occlude, stop; debar, exclude

ant open

2 syn see SCREEN 3

3 to bring or come to a limit or to a natural or appropriate stopping point <*closed* the meeting as soon as the discussion was over>

syn complete, conclude, consummate, determine, do, end, finish, halt, terminate, ultimate, wind up, wrap up

rel cease, desist, quit, stop; finalize, write off

idiom call it a day, set a period to

con begin, commence, enter (on or upon), inaugurate, initiate, start

4 syn see FILL 1

5 syn see DECREASE

6 syn see MEET 6

close n 1 syn see END 2

2 syn see FINALE

ant opening

‖**close** n syn see COURT 1

close adj 1 syn see SILENT 3

idiom close as a clam

con candid, frank, plain

ant open

2 syn see STUFFY 1

rel humid, muggy, sticky

3 syn see STINGY

ant liberal

4 having the constituent parts massed closely together <a paper of fine *close* texture>

syn compact, crowded, dense, thick, tight

rel compacted, compressed, condensed, consolidated, constricted, contracted; firm, solid, substantial; impenetrable, impermeable; close-grained

con lax, loose, slack; unconsolidated

5 syn see TIGHT 3

6 not far removed (as in space, time, or relationship) from something stipulated or understood <true and veritable are *close* synonyms> <the park is very *close* to the river> <it is *close* to closing time>

syn immediate, near, near-at-hand, nearly, nigh, proximate; compare NEIGHBORING

rel abutting, adjacent, adjoining, contiguous; convenient, handy; nearest, nearmost, next

idiom at hand, at one's fingers' ends (or fingertips), under one's nose

con distant, far, faraway, far-off, removed

ant remote

7 syn see FAMILIAR 1

con cool, remote, withdrawn

ant aloof

close adv into proximity with respect to space, time, or approach <hoping to come *closer* to the truth of the matter>

syn at close hand, hard, near, nearby, nigh

rel almost, nearabout, nearly

idiom as near as no matter (or never mind), in hailing (or spitting) distance, within an inch (or an ace) of, within a stone's throw

con afar, distantly, far

ant remotely

close-at-hand adj 1 syn see NEIGHBORING

2 syn see CONVENIENT 2

close-by adj 1 syn see NEIGHBORING

2 syn see CONVENIENT 2

closed adj syn see SELF-SUFFICIENT

closed book n syn see MYSTERY

closed-minded adj syn see OBSTINATE

closefisted adj syn see STINGY

rel clinging, clutching, grasping, keeping, tenacious

close in vb syn see ENCLOSE 1

close-lipped adj syn see SILENT 3

closely adv syn see HARD 4

rel carefully, heedfully, mindfully, thoughtfully; meticulously, minutely, punctiliously, scrupulously *con* carelessly, heedlessly, thoughtlessly

closemouthed *adj syn* see SILENT 3

close off *vb syn* see ISOLATE

close on *prep syn* see ABOUT 1

close out *vb syn* see SELL OUT 1

closeout *n syn* see BARGAIN 1

‖**closet** *n syn* see PRIVY 1

closet *adj* 1 *syn* see PRIVATE 1
   2 *syn* see THEORETICAL 1

close–tongued *adj syn* see SILENT 3

closing *n syn* see END 2

closing *adj syn* see LAST

closure *n syn* see END 2

clot *n syn* see GROUP 3

clot *vb syn* see COAGULATE

clothe *vb* to cover with or as if with garments <forests *clothe* the rocky slopes>
   syn apparel, array, attire, clad, dress,
enclothe, garb, garment, raiment
   rel costume, do up, dress up, tog (up *or*
out); cloak, mantle, robe; accouter, equip,
outfit, rig (out); bedrape, drape, swathe;
endue, invest
   con dismantle, divest, strip
   ant unclothe

clothes *n pl* a person's garments as a
whole <dressed in new *clothes* from the
skin out>
   syn apparel, attire, attirement, clothing,
dress, duds, habiliment(s), rags, raiment,
rigging, things, togs
   rel array, garb, toggery, vestments, ves-
ture; costume, getup, outfit, rig

clothing *n* 1 *syn* see CLOTHES
   2 *syn* see ROLE 1

cloud *n syn* see MULTITUDE 1

cloud *vb* 1 *syn* see OBSCURE
   rel addle, befuddle, confuse, muddle;
distract, perplex, puzzle
   2 *syn* see CONFUSE 4
   3 *syn* see TAINT 1

clouded *adj syn* see DOUBTFUL 1

cloudless *adj syn* see FAIR 2

cloudy *adj* 1 *syn* see OVERCAST
   2 *syn* see HAZY
   3 *syn* see MURKY 3

clough *n syn* see RAVINE

clout *n* 1 *syn* see CUFF
   2 *syn* see PULL 2

clout *vb* 1 *syn* see STRIKE 2
   ‖2 *syn* see STEAL 1

clove *n syn* see RAVINE

clown *n* 1 *syn* see RUSTIC
   2 *syn* see BOOR
   3 a performer (as in a circus) who enter-
tains by grotesque appearance and actions
<children delighted by the antics of the
clowns>
   syn buffoon, harlequin, merry-andrew,
zany
   rel comedian; fool, jester, mountebank;
mime, mummer
   4 *syn* see ZANY 2

clownish *adj syn* see BOORISH
   rel awkward, clumsy, gauche; green, raw,
rough, rude, uncouth
   ant urbane

cloy *vb syn* see SATIATE

---

con excite, pique, provoke, stimulate
   ant whet

club *n* 1 *syn* see CUDGEL
   2 *syn* see ASSOCIATION 2

club car *n syn* see PARLOR CAR

‖**cluck** *n syn* see DUNCE

clue *n syn* see HINT 1

clue (*or* **clew**) *vb syn* see INFORM 2

clump *n* 1 *syn* see GROUP 3
   rel clutter, hodgepodge, jumble, omnium-
gatherum
   2 *syn* see LUMP 1

clump *vb syn* see LUMBER

clumsy *adj* 1 lacking in physical ease and
grace usually because of coarse cumbersome build or poor coordination <a
clumsy boy constantly stumbling over his
own feet> <the *clumsy* gait of a young
puppy>
   syn awkward, gawky, lumbering, lumpish, splathering, splay, ungainly; *compare*
AWKWARD 2
   rel butterfingered, heavy-handed, left-
handed, unhandy; graceless, inelegant,
uncouth; bulky, hulking, unwieldy
   idiom all thumbs, fingers all thumbs
   con comely, shapely, well-formed, well-
proportioned; apt, deft, handy, quick,
ready
   2 *syn* see AWKWARD 2

clunk *n syn* see THUD

clunker *n syn* see JALOPY

cluster *n* 1 *syn* see GROUP 3
   2 *syn* see GROUP 1

cluster *vb syn* see GROUP 1
   rel accumulate, aggregate, associate, cumulate; bundle, package, parcel

clutch *vb syn* see SEIZE 2
   rel clench, clinch, gripe; cherish, harbor,
hold, keep

clutch *n syn* see HOLD

clutch *n syn* see GROUP 3

clutter *n* 1 *syn* see CONFUSION 3
   2 a disordered nondescript mass or group
<a *clutter* of ornaments on the mantel>
   syn hash, hugger-mugger, jumble, jungle,
litter, mash, mishmash, muddle, rummage,
scramble, shuffle, tumble
   rel hodgepodge, macédoine, medley, mélange; disarray, mess, muss, ruck
   con arrangement, array, order; grouping,
ordering, pigeonholing, ranking, sorting

‖**cly** *vb syn* see STEAL 1

coact *vb syn* see INTERACT

coacting *adj syn* see COOPERATIVE

coactive *adj syn* see COOPERATIVE

coadjutant *n syn* see ASSISTANT 2

coadjute *vb syn* see UNITE 2

coadjutor *n syn* see ASSISTANT 2

coadunate *vb syn* see JOIN 1

coadunation *n syn* see UNIFICATION

coagment *vb syn* see JOIN 1

coagulate *vb* to alter by chemical reaction
from a liquid to a more or less firm jelly
<the blood *coagulated* and closed the
wound>
   syn clot, congeal, gel, gelate, gelatinize,
jell, jellify, jelly, set
   rel concrete, harden, solidify; curdle,
inspissate; compact, concentrate, consolidate; coalesce; freeze; dehydrate, dry;
condense, thicken
   con deliquesce, fluidify, liquefy, liquesce;
flux, fuse, melt, run

---

syn synonym(s)   *rel* related word(s)
ant antonym(s)   *con* contrasted word(s)
idiom idiomatic equivalent(s)
‖ use limited; if in doubt, see a dictionary

coalesce *vb syn* see JOIN 1
 rel adhere, cleave, cling, stick; blend, fuse, merge, mingle, mix
coalition *n* 1 *syn* see UNIFICATION
 2 *syn* see COMBINATION 2
 3 *syn* see ALLIANCE 2
coarct *vb syn* see RESTRAIN 1
coarse *adj* 1 made up of relatively large particles < *coarse* sand >
 syn grainy, granular
 rel caked, cakey, lumpy, particulate
 2 *syn* see CRUDE 5
 3 deficient in refinement of manner and delicacy of feeling < a *coarse* practical man lacking all social graces >
 syn crass, crude, gross, incult, inelegant, low, raw, rough, rude, uncouth, uncultivated, uncultured, unrefined, vulgar; *compare* BOORISH
 rel raffish, roughneck, rowdy, vulgarian; common, tacky
 con considerate, courtly, gracious; cultivated, polished, refined
 4 *syn* see OBSCENE 2
 ‖5 *syn* see WILD 6
coast *n syn* see SHORE
coast *vb syn* see SLIDE 6
coax *vb* to influence or persuade by artful ingratiation < *coaxed* her friend to help her with her work >
 syn ‖barter, blandish, blarney, cajole, con, soft-soap, sweet-talk, wheedle
 rel pester, plague, tease; importune, press, urge; get, induce, persuade, prevail; entice, inveigle, lure, tempt; butter (up)
 con coerce, compel, constrain, force, oblige; browbeat, bulldoze, cow, intimidate
 ant bully
cob *vb syn* see SURPASS 1
cobble *vb syn* see BOTCH
 rel confuse, foul up, snafu, snarl (up)
cobweb *n syn* see WEB 2
cock *n* 1 *syn* see FAUCET
 2 *syn* see LEADER 2
 ‖3 *syn* see NONSENSE 2
‖**cock** *adj syn* see CHIEF 2
‖**cock** *vb syn* see LORD
cock *n syn* see PILE 1
cock *n syn* see HEAP 1
cock-a-doodle-doo *vb syn* see BOAST
cock-a-hoop *adj* 1 *syn* see EXULTANT
 2 *syn* see AWRY 1
Cockaigne *n syn* see UTOPIA
cock-and-bull story *n syn* see LIE
cock-a-whoop *adj syn* see EXULTANT
cockcrow *n syn* see DAWN 1
cockcrowing *n syn* see DAWN 1
cocker *vb syn* see BABY
‖**cocket** *adj syn* see SAUCY 1
cockeyed *adj* 1 *syn* see AWRY 1
 2 *syn* see INTOXICATED 1
cockle *vb syn* see RIPPLE
cocksure *adj syn* see SURE 5
cocktail lounge *n syn* see BAR 5
‖**coco** *n syn* see HEAD 1
coconspirator *n syn* see CONFEDERATE
‖**coconut** *n syn* see HEAD 1
cocotte *n syn* see PROSTITUTE
coddle *vb syn* see BABY
codicil *n syn* see APPENDIX 1
coefficient *adj syn* see COOPERATIVE
coerce *vb syn* see FORCE 2

rel beset, push, urge; browbeat, bulldoze, bully, cow, intimidate; menace, terrorize, threaten
coercion *n syn* see FORCE 4
 rel menace, menacing, threat, threatening
coetaneous *adj syn* see CONTEMPORARY 1
coeval *adj syn* see CONTEMPORARY 1
coexistent *adj syn* see CONTEMPORARY 1
coexisting *adj syn* see CONTEMPORARY 1
coffee shop *n syn* see EATING HOUSE
coffer *n syn* see TREASURY 2
‖**coffin nail** *n syn* see CIGARETTE
cogency *n syn* see POINT 3
 rel pertinence, relevance; bearing, concern, connection
cogent *adj* 1 *syn* see VALID
 rel compelling, constraining, forceful, forcible, potent, powerful, puissant; inducing, persuasive, justified, well-founded, well-grounded
 con ineffective, ineffectual, inefficacious; feeble, forceless, impotent, powerless, weak
 2 *syn* see WELL-FOUNDED
 rel consequential, influential, momentous, weighty; meaningful, significant
cogitable *adj syn* see THINKABLE 1
cogitate *vb* 1 *syn* see THINK 5
 rel conceive, envisage, envision, imagine
 2 *syn* see PLOT
cogitation *n syn* see THOUGHT 1
cogitative *adj syn* see THOUGHTFUL 1
cognate *adj syn* see RELATED
 rel common, general, generic, universal
 con different, disparate, divergent, diverse, various
cognizance *n syn* see NOTICE 1
cognizant *adj syn* see AWARE
 con forgetful, oblivious, unmindful; heedless, ignoring, neglectful, slighting, unmindful
 ant ignorant
cognize *vb syn* see KNOW 1
cognomen *n syn* see NAME 1
cognoscente *n syn* see CONNOISSEUR
 rel ‖dab, proficient, specialist; authority, critic, judge
cohere *vb* 1 *syn* see STICK 2
 rel blend, coalesce, fuse, merge; associate, combine, connect, join, unite
 con disembarrass, disentangle, untangle
 2 *syn* see AGREE 4
coherence *n* 1 *syn* see ADHERENCE 1
 rel integrity, solidarity, union, unity
 ant incoherence
 2 *syn* see CONSISTENCY
cohesion *n* 1 *syn* see ADHERENCE 1
 ant incohesion
 2 *syn* see SOLIDARITY
cohort *n* 1 *syn* see PARTNER
 2 *syn* see FOLLOWER
coil *n syn* see COMMOTION 3
coil *vb syn* see WIND 2
 rel revolve, rotate, turn
‖**coin** *n syn* see MONEY
 idiom coin of the realm
coinage *n syn* see INVENTION
coincide *vb syn* see AGREE 3
 rel accord, correspond, jibe, tally; equal, match
 con deviate, divagate, divaricate, diverge; bias, skew, twist, warp

ant differ

coincident *adj syn* see CONCOMITANT

coincidentally *adv syn* see TOGETHER 1

coincidently *adv syn* see TOGETHER 1

coinstantaneously *adv* *syn* see TO-
GETHER 1

cojones *n pl syn* see COURAGE

cold *adj* 1 marked by a deficiency of
warmth <a *cold* day>
syn arctic, chill, chillsome, chilly, cool,
freezing, frigid, frore, frosty, gelid, glacial,
icy, nippy, shivery
rel biting, bleak, chilling, cutting, nipping, polar, raw, sharp; frozen, iced, wintry; bracing, brisk, crisp, snappy
con calid, genial, mild
ant warm

2 lacking cordiality or emotional warmth
<a *cold* greeting>
syn chill, emotionless, frigid, glacial, icy,
indifferent, unemotional
rel unenthusiastic, unresponsive, unsympathetic
con cordial, friendly, genial, hearty,
warm; empathic, sympathetic

3 *syn* see MATTER-OF-FACT 3

4 *syn* see FRIGID 3
ant hot

5 *syn* see GLOOMY 3

6 *syn* see DEAD 1

7 *syn* see INSENSIBLE 1

cold-blooded *adj* 1 *syn* see UNFEELING 2

2 *syn* see MATTER-OF-FACT 3

cold feet *n syn* see FEAR 1

coldhearted *adj syn* see UNFEELING 2
ant warmhearted

‖**cold meat** *n syn* see CORPSE

cold-shoulder *vb syn* see CUT 7

cold storage *n syn* see ABEYANCE

colic *n syn* see STOMACHACHE

coliseum *n syn* see STADIUM

‖**coll** *vb syn* see EMBRACE 1

collapse *vb* 1 *syn* see GIVE 12
rel break up, disintegrate, shatter
idiom fall to pieces

2 to lose energy, stamina, or control under stress <exhausted to the point of
collapsing helplessly on the bed>
syn break down, cave (in), drop, ‖flake
out, give out, peg out, succumb, wilt
rel droop, fail, languish, weaken; exhaust,
fag, flag, play out, tire, weary
con enliven, invigorate, stimulate

collapse *n* 1 *syn* see NERVOUS BREAK-
DOWN

2 a sudden and grave failure <the *collapse* of an overextended market>
syn breakdown, crack-up, crash, debacle,
smash, smashup, wreck
rel breakup, disorganization, disruption,
undoing; cataclysm, catastrophe; destruction, ruination, ruining; failure

collar *vb* 1 *syn* see CORNER

2 *syn* see CATCH 1

3 *syn* see STEAL 1

collate *vb syn* see COMPARE 2

collateral *adj* 1 *syn* see CONCOMITANT

2 *syn* see INDIRECT 1

---

syn synonym(s)   *rel* related word(s)
ant antonym(s)   *con* contrasted word(s)
idiom idiomatic equivalent(s)
‖ use limited; if in doubt, see a dictionary

3 *syn* see CORROBORATIVE

4 *syn* see SUBORDINATE
rel allied, cognate, kindred, related; complementary, corresponding, reciprocal
con major, prominent

5 *syn* see AUXILIARY

‖**collateral** *n syn* see REFUSE

colleague *n* one affiliated with another
usually through a common office or profession <he claims to speak for his *colleagues* in the Senate>
syn associate, compatriot, compeer, confrere
rel consociate, copartner, fellow, partner;
co-worker, workfellow; buddy, chum,
companion, crony, pal; aide, assistant,
helper

collect *vb* 1 *syn* see GATHER 6
con assort, sort; sever, sunder; deal, dispense, divide, dole
ant disperse; distribute

2 *syn* see INFER

3 *syn* see COMPOSE 4

4 *syn* see GROUP 1
rel align, array, dispose, marshal, order,
rank
con broadcast, disperse, distribute, scatter

collected *adj* 1 *syn* see CALM 2
rel peaceful, quiet, still
ant distraught

2 *syn* see COOL 2
rel assured, confident, sanguine, sure;
complacent, self-satisfied, smug
con disordered, troubled

collection *n* 1 *syn* see GATHERING 2
rel band, crew, outfit, party

2 *syn* see ACCUMULATION
rel assortment, medley, miscellany, variety; bunch, clump, cluster, group; armamentarium; boiling, caboodle, kit, lot

‖**college** *n syn* see JAIL

collide *vb syn* see BUMP 1
rel atomize, fragment, pulverize, shatter,
smash, splinter; break up, crunch, scrap

collimate *vb syn* see PARALLEL 2

collision *n syn* see IMPACT
rel dilapidation, ruin, wreck; demolish-
ment, destruction

collocate *vb syn* see PARALLEL 2

collogue *vb* ‖1 *syn* see PLOT

2 *syn* see CONFER 2

colloque *vb syn* see CONVERSE

colloquial *adj syn* see VERNACULAR

colloquial *n syn* see VERNACULAR 3

colloquium *n syn* see CONFERENCE 2

colloquy *n* 1 *syn* see CONVERSATION 1

2 *syn* see CONVERSATION 2

3 *syn* see CONFERENCE 2

collude *vb syn* see PLOT

collusion *n syn* see COMPLICITY

colluvies *n syn* see ACCUMULATION

2 *syn* see MISCELLANY 1

collywobbles *n pl but sing or pl in constr*
syn see STOMACHACHE

Colonel Blimp *n syn* see STUFFED SHIRT

color *n* 1 a property of a visible thing
recognizable only when rays of light fall
upon it and serving to distinguish things
otherwise visually identical (as in size,
shape, or texture) <the green *color* of
foliage turns rainbow-hued in autumn>
syn cast, hue, shade, tinge, tint, tone

2 *syn* see MASK 2

3 *syn* see VERISIMILITUDE

4 *syn* see POSITION 1

5 *syn* see FLAG

6 something used to impart visible color to something <dyed her curtains with one of the new easy-to-use *colors*>
syn colorant, dye, dyestuff, pigment, stain, tincture

color *vb* 1 *syn* see EMBROIDER
rel disguise, distort, fake, misrepresent
con constrain, minimize, reduce, soften, temper; blue-pencil, censor, edit

2 *syn* see MISREPRESENT

3 *syn* see BLUSH

colorable *adj syn* see BELIEVABLE
rel cogent, compelling, convincing, sound, telling, valid

colorant *n syn* see COLOR 6

colored *adj syn* see BIASED 2

colorful *adj* making a fine display of usually showy color <a *colorful* bed of asters>
syn brave, bright, colory, gay, vivid
rel blatant, florid, garish, gaudy, loud; flashy, showy, splashy
con blanched, bleached, pallid, wan; dim, dull, faint, pale, weak
ant colorless

coloring *n* 1 *syn* see MASK 2

2 *syn* see EXAGGERATION

colorless *adj* 1 *syn* see PALE 1

2 lacking in sparkle and vitality <an accurate but *colorless* recital of facts>
syn drab, dull, flat, lackluster, lifeless, lusterless, prosaic, prosy
rel blurry, hazy, obscure, vague; feeble, insipid, milk-and-water, namby-pamby, weak, wishy-washy; unimaginative, uninspired
con clear, concise, exact, precise; exciting, provocative, rousing, stimulating, stirring
ant colorful

3 *syn* see NEUTRAL
rel aloof, remote, withdrawn

colory *adj syn* see COLORFUL

colossal *adj syn* see HUGE

colporteur *n syn* see MISSIONARY

colt *n syn* see NOVICE

coltish *adj syn* see PLAYFUL 1

columbary *n syn* see DOVECOTE

column *n* 1 *syn* see PILLAR 1

2 *syn* see SUPPORT 3

coma *n* 1 *syn* see FAINT

2 *syn* see LETHARGY 1

comate *n syn* see ASSOCIATE 3

comatose *adj* 1 *syn* see INSENSIBLE 2

2 *syn* see LETHARGIC
rel anesthetic, impassible, insensitive
ant awake

comb *vb* 1 *syn* see SORT 2

2 *syn* see SCOUR 2
rel examine, inspect, scrutinize; investigate, probe, sift

combat *vb syn* see RESIST
rel battle, contend, war

combat *n syn* see SERVICE 1

combative *adj syn* see BELLIGERENT
rel energetic, strenuous, vigorous; manful, manly, virile
ant pacifistic

combativeness *n syn* see ATTACK 2

‖**combe** *n syn* see VALLEY

combination *n* 1 *syn* see UNIFICATION

2 individuals or organized interests banded together to further a common end <a *combination* of citizens devoted to holding down taxes>
syn bloc, coalition, combine, faction, party, ring
rel cartel, pool, syndicate, trust; cabal, circle, clique, coterie, set

3 *syn* see ASSOCIATION 5

combine *vb* 1 *syn* see JOIN 1
rel amalgamate, blend, commingle, fuse, mingle, mix; consolidate, unify
con divide, divorce, part
ant separate

2 *syn* see EMBODY 2

3 *syn* see UNITE 2
rel agree, coincide; merge, pool

combine *n* 1 *syn* see COMBINATION 2

2 *syn* see SYNDICATE

comble *n syn* see APEX 2

combust *vb syn* see BURN 2

combustible *adj* 1 capable of catching or being set on fire <*combustible* materials should be stored away from open fire>
syn burnable, flammable, ignitable, inflammable
rel comburent, combustive; burning, firing, igniting, kindling
con fireproof; flameproof, nonflammable; fire-resistant, fire-resistive, fire-retardant
ant incombustible, noncombustible

2 *syn* see EXCITABLE

come *vb* 1 to attain to a destination <when will they *come*>
syn arrive, ‖blow in, get, get in, reach, show, show up, turn up
rel approach, near, nigh
con depart, leave, quit, retreat, withdraw
ant go

2 *syn* see AMOUNT 1

3 *syn* see HAPPEN 1

4 *syn* see BECOME 1

come (from) *vb* 1 *syn* see SPRING

2 *syn* see ORIGINATE 5

come (in) *vb syn* see ENTER 1

comeback *n syn* see RETORT 2

come by *vb syn* see VISIT 2

come-by-chance *n syn* see BASTARD 1

comedian *n* 1 *syn* see HUMORIST 2

2 *syn* see WAG 1

come down (with) *vb syn* see CONTRACT 1

comedown *n* a loss of status <bitter over their *comedown* in the world>
syn descent, discomfiture, down; *compare* SETBACK
rel collapse, crash, downfall, fall, ruin, smash, undoing, wreck
con advance, headway, progress
ant rise

comedy *n syn* see HUMOR 4

come in *vb syn* see ANSWER 1

comely *adj* 1 *syn* see BEAUTIFUL
ant homely

2 *syn* see DECOROUS 1

come off *vb* 1 *syn* see SUCCEED 2

2 *syn* see HAPPEN 1

come-off *n syn* see ESCAPE 2

come-on *n* 1 *syn* see LURE 2

‖2 *syn* see FOOL 3

3 *syn* see SWINDLER

come out *vb* 1 *syn* see GET OUT 2

2 *syn* see DEBUT

come out (with) *vb syn* see SAY 1

come over *vb* 1 *syn* see VISIT 2
  2 *syn* see BECOME 1

come round *vb syn* see RECOVER 2

comestible *adj syn* see EDIBLE

comestibles *n pl syn* see FOOD 1

come through *vb* 1 *syn* see SURVIVE 2
  2 *syn* see CONTRIBUTE 1

comeuppance *n syn* see DUE 1

comfort *n* 1 *syn* see HELP 1
  2 *syn* see AMENITY 2

comfort *vb* to make or try to make
brighter a person overcome by grief or
misery < *comforting* her widowed sister
with words of hope>
  syn buck up, cheer, console, solace, upraise
  rel brighten, gladden, lighten; allay, alleviate, assuage, mitigate, relieve; refresh,
renew, restore; reassure, commiserate,
condole, sympathize
  idiom give a lift to
  con torment, torture, try; distress, trouble, worry; annoy, irk, vex
  ant afflict; bother

comfortable *adj* 1 *syn* see SUFFICIENT 1
  2 enjoying or providing conditions that
make for comfort and security < lived in
a *comfortable* home on a quiet street>
  syn comfy, cozy, cushy, easeful, easy,
snug, soft
  rel agreeable, grateful, gratifying, welcome; pleasant, pleasing, restful; comforting, consoling, solacing; content, pleased,
satisfied
  con distressing, perturbing, troubling;
annoying, bothering, irking, vexing; inferior, miserable, poor, substandard,
wretched
  ant uncomfortable
  3 *syn* see PROSPEROUS 3
  idiom in comfortable circumstances

||**comforter** *n syn* see QUILT

comforter *n syn* see QUILT

comfortless *adj syn* see UNCOMFORT-
ABLE

comfy *adj syn* see COMFORTABLE 2

comic *adj syn* see LAUGHABLE
  rel antic, fantastic, grotesque; mocking,
ridiculing
  ant tragic

comic *n syn* see HUMORIST 2

comical *adj syn* see LAUGHABLE
  rel absurd, foolish, silly; impish, roguish,
sportive, waggish
  con doleful, dolorous, lugubrious, melancholy
  ant pathetic

comicality *n syn* see HUMOR 4

comicalness *n syn* see HUMOR 4

coming *n syn* see ARRIVAL 2

coming *adj* 1 *syn* see FORTHCOMING
  2 *syn* see NEXT

coming in *n*, *usu* comings in *pl syn* see
REVENUE

comingle *vb syn* see MIX 1

comity *n syn* see GOODWILL 1

rel accord, concord, harmony; camaraderie, companionship, comradeship, good-
fellowship

comma *n syn* see PAUSE

command *vb* to issue orders or an order to
< the general *commanded* the troops to
advance>
  syn bid, charge, direct, enjoin, instruct,
order, tell, warn
  rel demand, exact, require; coerce, compel, constrain, force, oblige; conduct, control, manage; ask, call (on), request, say
  ant comply, obey

command *n* 1 a direction that must or
should be obeyed < failure to obey a direct *command* subjects the soldier to
grave penalties>
  syn behest, bidding, charge, dictate, injunction, mandate, order, word
  rel direction, directive, instruction; canon,
law, ordinance, precept, rule, statute;
devoir, duty, obligation, responsibility
  2 *syn* see POWER 1
  rel rule
  3 *syn* see ABILITY 2
  rel aplomb, assurance, confidence, poise
  con incertitude, insecurity, uncertainty,
unsureness; indecisiveness, vagueness

commandeer *vb* 1 *syn* see APPROPRIATE
1
  2 *syn* see ARROGATE 1

comme il faut *adj syn* see DECOROUS 1

commemorate *vb* 1 *syn* see KEEP 2
  2 *syn* see MEMORIALIZE 2

commemorative *adj syn* see MEMORIAL

commemoratory *adj syn* see MEMORIAL

commence *vb* 1 *syn* see BEGIN 1
  2 *syn* see BEGIN 2
  idiom come into being (*or* existence)

commencement *n syn* see BEGINNING

commend *vb* 1 *syn* see COMMIT 1
  rel resign, yield; proffer, tender
  2 to indicate one's warm approval < the
teacher *commended* her pupils' studious
attitude>
  syn acclaim, applaud, compliment, hail,
kudize, praise, recommend, ||roose
  rel eulogize, extol; approve, countenance,
endorse, support
  con blame, criticize, reprehend, reprobate;
chide, rebuke, reprimand, reproach, reprove
  ant censure; admonish

commendable *adj syn* see WORTHY 1

commensurable *adj syn* see PROPOR-
TIONAL

commensurate *adj syn* see PROPOR-
TIONAL

comment *n* 1 *syn* see REMARK 2
  2 *syn* see CRITICISM

comment *vb syn* see REMARK 2
  rel construe, elucidate, explain, explicate;
expound; annotate, gloss

commentary *n syn* see REMARK 2

commentate *vb syn* see REMARK 2

commerce *n* 1 *syn* see CONTACT 2
  2 a situation characterized by mutual
exchange (as of ideas) < those who feel
that art should have no *commerce* with
morality>
  syn communion, dealings, intercourse,
traffic, truck

---

syn synonym(s)   *rel* related word(s)
ant antonym(s)   *con* contrasted word(s)
idiom idiomatic equivalent(s)
|| use limited; if in doubt, see a dictionary

rel communication, congress, contact, exchange, interchange, intercommunication; basis, common ground, takeoff

3 *syn* see BUSINESS 4

commie *n syn* see COMMUNIST

commination *n syn* see CURSE 1

commingle *vb syn* see MIX 1
rel integrate, unify

comminute *vb syn* see PULVERIZE 1

commiserable *adj syn* see PITIFUL 1

commiserate *vb syn* see COMPASSIONATE

commiseration *n syn* see PITY

commission *vb* 1 *syn* see AUTHORIZE 1
rel appoint, designate, name, nominate; bid, charge, command, enjoin, instruct, order

2 *syn* see DELEGATE

commit *vb* 1 to assign (as to a person) especially for use or safekeeping <it is unwise to *commit* all power and authority to one man> <sainted beings who *commit* their spirits to God>
syn commend, confide, consign, entrust, hand over, relegate, turn over
rel allocate, allot, assign, destine, ordain; move, remove, shift, transfer; deliver, give, offer, submit; delegate, deputize
idiom give into the charge (or hands) of
2 to be responsible for or guilty of (an offense or wrongdoing) <*commit* a crime>
syn perpetuate, pull
rel accomplish, achieve, do, effectuate, execute, perform, pull off; contravene, transgress, trespass, violate; offend, scandalize, sin

commitment *n syn* see OBLIGATION 2

committal *n syn* see OBLIGATION 2

commix *vb syn* see MIX 1

commixture *n syn* see MIXTURE

commodious *adj syn* see SPACIOUS
con cramped, narrow, strait
ant incommodious

commodities *n pl syn* see MERCHANDISE
rel articles, items, things

common *adj* 1 generally shared in or participated in by members of a community <our *common* civic responsibilities>
syn communal, conjoint, conjunct, intermutual, joint, mutual, public, shared
rel general, generic, universal; like, reciprocal, similar; corporate
con personal, private, restricted
ant individual

2 *syn* see GENERAL 2
rel popular, public

3 *syn* see IMPURE 3

4 taking place often <a *common* occurrence>
syn customary, everyday, familiar, frequent
rel repetitious, routine, usual
con infrequent, occasional, unfrequent; casual, chance, incidental
ant rare, uncommon

5 *syn* see GENERAL

6 conforming to a type without noteworthy excellences or faults <just a *common* everyday sort trying to get by in life>
syn commonplace, ordinary, prosaic, uneventful, unexceptional, unnoteworthy

rel down-to-earth, matter-of-fact, prosy, unexciting; dull, flat, trite, stale, uninteresting
con exceptional, noteworthy, remarkable; excellent, marvelous, prodigious, wonderful; aberrant, divergent, eccentric
ant extraordinary

7 *syn* see DECENT 4

8 *syn* see CHEAP 2

9 *syn* see INFERIOR 2

‖10 *syn* see EASYGOING 3

common *n* 1 commons *pl but sing or pl in constr syn* see COMMONALTY
2 an often improved and ornamentally planted open space for public use in a built-up area <in summer a band played on the village *common*>
syn green, plaza, square
rel garden, park, pleasance, pleasure ground

commonage *n syn* see COMMONALTY

commonalty *n* persons without rank or authority or the political estate made up of these <laws that both the gentles and the *commonalty* recognized as just>
syn commonage, commoners, common men, commune, people, plebeians, plebes, plebs, populace, rank and file, third estate
rel masses, mob, multitude, proletariat, public
con aristocracy, elite, gentility, nobility; classes, gentry, nobs

commoners *n pl syn* see COMMONALTY

commonition *n syn* see WARNING

commonly *adv syn* see USUALLY 2
idiom more often than not

common men *n pl syn* see COMMONALTY

commonplace *n* an idea or expression deficient in originality or freshness <lazily exchanging *commonplaces* over their beer>
syn banality, bromide, cliché, platitude, prosaicism, prosaism, rubber stamp, shibboleth, tag, truism
rel chestnut, corn, prose, stereotype; inanity, shallowness, wishy-washiness; threadbareness, triteness
ant profundity

commonplace *adj* 1 *syn* see COMMON 6

2 *syn* see GENERAL 1

3 *syn* see PROSAIC 3

4 *syn* see TRITE
idiom a dime a dozen, as everyday as breakfast

common sense *n syn* see SENSE 6

commorancy *n syn* see HABITATION 2

commotion *n* 1 a state of often disorderly civic unrest <the whole city was in *commotion* over the new restrictions>
syn clamor, convulsion, ferment, outcry, tumult, upheaval, upturn
rel insurgence, insurrection, mutiny, rebellion, revolt, riot, uprising
2 a state of usually mental or emotional excitement <this challenge threw him into great *commotion* of mind>
syn agitation, confusion, dither, flap, lather, pother, stew, tumult, turbulence, turmoil
rel discomposure, disquiet, flurry, fluster, perturbation, upset; annoyance, bother, irritation, vexation; strain, tension
con calm, placidity, quietude, relaxation, serenity

3 a noisy and often unruly disturbance
< the children created a *commotion* over
missing the circus >

syn brouhaha, ‖catouse, coil, foofaraw,
furore, fuss, hurrah, ruckus, rumpus, shindig, shindy, to-do, uproar

rel din, hubbub, bullabaloo, pandemonium, racket; fracas, ruction, row

4 a state of noisy confusion < never saw
such *commotion* as the time the old sow
got out and knocked the preacher into the
midden >

syn bustle, clamor, clatter, hassle, hubbub, hurly-burly, lather, moil, pother,
rowdydow, ruction, storm, to-do, tows
row, tumult, turmoil, uproar, whirl,
whoopla; *compare* DIN, STIR 1

con calmness, order, peace, quiet

commove *vb syn* see ELATE

communal *adj syn* see COMMON 1

commune *n syn* see COMMONALTY

communicable *adj* 1 *syn* see INFECTIOUS
2

2 *syn* see COMMUNICATIVE

communicate *vb* 1 to make known < *communicated* the whole story under a pledge
of secrecy >

syn break, convey, impart, pass on, transmit

rel betray, disclose, discover, divulge, ‖let
out, reveal, tell; hint, imply, let on, suggest; broadcast, disseminate, publicize

con conceal, hide, obscure, screen, veil;
dissemble, distort, garble, twist, warp;
camouflage, disguise

2 *syn* see ADJOIN

communication *n* 1 *syn* see MESSAGE 1

2 *syn* see CONTACT 2

3 interchange of thoughts or opinions
through shared symbols < the difficulties
of *communication* between people of different cultural backgrounds >

syn communion, converse, intercommunication, intercourse

rel exchange, interchange; conversing,
discussing, talking; conversation, discussion, talk; advice, intelligence, news, tidings

communicative *adj* inclined to talk freely
and sometimes indiscreetly < too *communicative* to be trusted with a secret >

syn communicable, expansive; *compare*
FRANK

rel garrulous, loquacious, talkative, voluble; conversational; demonstrative, effusive, gushing

con constrained, guarded, inhibited, restrained; bridled, controlled, curbed

communion *n* 1 *syn* see COMMERCE 2

2 *syn* see COMMUNICATION 3

3 *syn* see CONTACT 2

4 *syn* see RELIGION 2

Communist *n* a member of the Russian
Communist party < restructuring of Rus-
sia by the *Communists* >

syn Bolshevik, ‖Bolshie, commie, comrade, Red

rel fellow traveler, pink, pinko; Leninist,
Marxist, Stalinist, Trotskyist; apparatchik

community *n syn* see SOCIETY 3

commutable *adj syn* see INTERCHANGE-
ABLE

commute *vb syn* see TRANSFORM

compact *adj* 1 *syn* see PITHY

2 *syn* see CLOSE 4

rel hard; appressed, bunched, packed

con loose, slack, unconstrained; rare,
tenuous, thin

compact *vb* 1 *syn* see UNIFY 1

rel compress, condense, contract; combine, unite; set, solidify

con disperse, dissipate; fluff, loosen

compact *n syn* see CONTRACT

compacting *adj syn* see INTEGRATIVE

companion *n* 1 *syn* see ASSOCIATE 3

rel colleague, fellow, partner; chaperon,
escort

2 *syn* see MATE 5

3 *syn* see ACCOMPANIMENT 2

companion *vb syn* see ACCOMPANY

companionable *adj syn* see SOCIAL 1

rel amiable, complacent, good-natured

con uncongenial, unsympathetic; reserved,
taciturn, uncommunicative

companionship *n syn* see COMPANY 1

company *n* 1 association between individuals especially on pleasant or intimate
terms < we always enjoyed his *company* >

syn companionship, fellowship, society

rel camaraderie, comradeship, consociation

2 persons visiting especially in one's house
< invited *company* for dinner >

syn guests, visitors; *compare* VISITOR 1

3 *syn* see GATHERING 2

4 a group of persons associated in a joint
effort or for a common purpose < a *company* of thieves lay in wait by the highway >

syn band, corps, outfit, party, troop,
troupe

rel crew, gang, pack, team; circle, clique,
coterie, set; association, club, order, society; crowd, horde, mob, throng; group

5 *syn* see ENTERPRISE 3

company *vb syn* see ACCOMPANY

comparable *adj syn* see LIKE

ant disparate

comparative *adj* being such in comparison
with an expressed or implied standard or
absolute < living in *comparative* poverty >

syn approximate, near, relative

rel equivalent, like, similar

con genuine, real, true

ant absolute

compare *vb* 1 *syn* see EQUATE 2

2 to examine side by side or point by
point in order to establish likenesses and
differences < *compare* the effects of two
diets on weight loss >

syn bracket, collate, contrast

rel approach, equal, match, rival, touch;
examine, inspect, observe, scan, scrutinize,
size (up); consider, contemplate, ponder,
study, weigh

comparison *n syn* see LIKENESS

compass *vb* 1 *syn* see SURROUND 1

2 *syn* see GET 1

3 *syn* see APPREHEND 1

compass *n* 1 *syn* see CIRCUMFERENCE

rel domain, field, sphere; enclosure

---

2 syn see ENVIRONS 1

3 syn see RANGE 2

rel bounds, limits; circumscription, limitation, restriction

compassion *n* **1** syn see SYMPATHY 2

rel charity, clemency, grace, lenity, mercy; benevolence, humaneness, humanity

con aloofness, indifference, unconcern; cruelty, harshness, mercilessness; implacability, relentlessness

2 syn see PITY

compassionate *adj* syn see TENDER

rel clement, forbearing; piteous, pitiful

con grim, implacable, merciless, relentless, unrelenting; adamant, inexorable, inflexible, obdurate

compassionate *vb* to feel or express compassion for < a kindly man who *compassionated* all human misery >

syn ache, commiserate, feel (for), pity, sympathize (with)

rel grieve (over), regret, repine; lament, mourn, sorrow (for *or* over); deplore

con accept, endure, tolerate; disregard, ignore, overlook, pass over

compassionless *adj* syn see UNFEELING 2

compatible syn see CONSONANT 1

rel comparable, fit, fitting, meet, proper, suitable

ant incompatible

compatriot *n* syn see COLLEAGUE

compeer *n* syn see COLLEAGUE

compel *vb* syn see FORCE 2

compellation *n* syn see NAME 1

compendiary *adj* syn see CONCISE

compendious *adj* syn see CONCISE

rel close, compact

con amplified, elaborated, expanded, inflated; complete, full

compendium *n* **1** a condensed treatment of a subject < prepared a *compendium* of the state laws dealing with education >

syn aperçu, digest, pandect, précis, sketch, survey, syllabus, sylloge

rel abridgment, abstract, brief, conspectus, epitome; overview

con elaboration, expansion

2 syn see HANDBOOK

compenetrate *vb* syn see PERMEATE

compensate *vb* **1** to make good the defects of < her kind heart *compensated* for her nosy ways >

syn atone (for), balance, counterbalance, counterpoise, countervail, make up, offset, outweigh, redeem, set off

rel abrogate, annul, invalidate, negate, nullify; counteract, negative, neutralize; better, fix (up), improve, repair; redress

idiom make amends (*or* reparations), make matters right

2 syn see PAY 1

3 to make proper payment to (as for injury, loss, or damage) < *compensated* a worker injured on the job >

syn indemnify, pay, recompense, reimburse, remunerate, repay, requite

rel recoup, refund

idiom make restitution (*or* reparation)

compensation *n* syn see REPARATION

compete *vb* **1** to strive to gain mastery or obtain a prize < students *competing* for a scholarship >

syn contend, contest, rival, vie

rel dispute; battle, fight, strive, struggle; attempt, essay, try

2 syn see RIVAL 2

rel approach, equal, match, touch

competence *n* **1** syn see ENOUGH

2 syn see ABILITY 1

rel appropriateness, fitness, suitability

ant incompetence

competent *adj* **1** syn see ABLE

rel adept, finished, masterly, polished

ant incompetent

2 syn see SUFFICIENT 1

competition *n* **1** syn see CONTEST 1

2 syn see CONTEST 2

3 syn see RIVAL

competitor *n* syn see RIVAL

complacence *n* syn see CONCEIT 2

complacency *n* syn see CONCEIT 2

complacent *adj* feeling or showing an often excessive or unjustified satisfaction and pleasure in one's status, possessions, or attainments < had the *complacent* air of superiority that often mars an ignorant self-made man >

syn priggish, self-complacent, self-contented, self-pleased, self-satisfied, smug

rel assured, confident, self-assured, self-confident, self-possessed; conceited, egoistic, egotistic

con humble, modest; diffident, shy

complain *vb* to express discontent, resentment, or regret usually peaceably and as if seeking sympathy < a nice girl but given to *complaining* over trifles >

syn fuss, kick, murmur, repine, wail, whine; *compare* GRIPE 2, GRUMBLE 1

rel fret, worry; nag, pester

idiom air a grievance, find fault, register a complaint, sing (*or* cry) the blues

con accept, condone, countenance, tolerate

complainer *n* syn see GROUCH

complaint *n* syn see DISEASE 1

complaisant *adj* syn see AMIABLE 1

rel accommodating, agreeable, generous, indulgent; submissive

con harsh, rigorous, stern; determined, firm, masterful

complement *n* **1** something that makes up a deficiency in another thing < bought the farm with its *complement* of equipment and livestock >

syn supplement

rel correlate, counterpart; makeweight

2 syn see ACCOMPANIMENT 1

3 syn see COUNTERPART 1

complete *adj* **1** syn see WHOLE 3

2 syn see UNABRIDGED

3 syn see WHOLE 4

4 brought to completion < each *complete* revolution of the earth >

syn completed, concluded, done, down, ended, finished, terminated, through

rel accomplished, achieved, effected, executed, realized; attained, compassed

idiom all over, done with, set at rest

ant incomplete

5 syn see EXHAUSTIVE

ant incomplete

6 syn see UTTER

complete *vb* **1** syn see CLOSE 3

rel accomplish, achieve, discharge, effect, execute, fulfill, perform

idiom carry through, go through with
2 *syn* see FULFILL 1

completed *adj syn* see COMPLETE 4

completely *adv* 1 *syn* see DOWN 2
idiom down to the ground
2 *syn* see THOROUGHLY 2
3 *syn* see WELL 3

completeness *n* 1 *syn* see ENTIRETY 1
2 *syn* see INTEGRITY 2

complex *adj* 1 made up of two or more separable or identifiable elements < the *complex* vascular system of higher plants >
syn composite, compound
rel blended, compounded, mingled, mixed; heterogeneous, varied; elaborate, intricate, involved; complicated, confused, mixed-up
con homogeneous, uniform
ant simple
2 difficult to comprehend because of a multiplicity of interrelated elements < a *complex* plot to undermine the government by discrediting its leaders >
syn Byzantine, complicated, daedal, elaborate, gordian, intricate, involved, knotty, labyrinthine, sophisticated
rel bewildering, confusing, distracting, disturbing; baffling, confounding, mysterious, mystifying, perplexing, puzzling, equivocal, obscure, vague; involute, involuted, reticular
con clear, defined, definite, distinct, plain, recognizable, uncomplicated, uninvolved; comprehensible, explicable, intelligible, knowable
ant simple

complex *n syn* see SYSTEM 1
con constituent, element, factor; member, part, piece, portion; detail, item, particular
ant component

complexion *n syn* see DISPOSITION 3
rel kind, sort, style, type

complexion *vb syn* see TINT

complexionless *adj syn* see PALE 1

compliance *n syn* see ACQUIESCENCE
rel amenability, docility, obedience, tractability; deference, submission, submissiveness
con contumacy, obstinacy, stubbornness
ant frowardness

complicate *vb* to make complex, involved, or difficult < a disagreement *complicated* by intense personal animosities >
syn entangle, ǁmuck, muddle, perplex, ravel, snarl, tangle
rel jumble, ǁsnafu; derange, disarrange, disorder, mix up, upset
con arrange, order; disentangle, straighten (out), untangle
ant simplify

complicated *adj* 1 *syn* see ELABORATE 2
2 *syn* see COMPLEX 2
rel arduous, difficult, hard; abstruse, recondite
con easy, facile, light; clear-cut, precise, straightforward
ant simple

---

complicity *n* association with an improper or unlawful activity < failed to prove his *complicity* in the cover-up >
syn collusion, connivance
rel implication, involvement; engineering, machination, manipulation, wire-pulling

compliment *n* 1 an expression of regard or praise < a man meriting the *compliments* and homage of his fellows >
syn bouquet, kudo, orchid(s)
rel trade-last; laud, laudation, praise; accolade, commendation, honor; blessing(s), congratulation(s), felicitation(s); encomium, eulogy, tribute
con dig, gibe, jeer, slam
ant taunt
ǁ2 *syn* see GIFT 1

compliment *vb syn* see COMMEND 2
idiom take off one's hat to
con belittle, decry, denigrate, depreciate, disparage, run down

complimentary *adj syn* see FREE 5

comply *vb syn* see OBEY

component *n syn* see ELEMENT 2
con admixture, amalgam, blend, compound, mixture
ant composite; complex

comport *vb* 1 *syn* see AGREE 4
2 *syn* see BEHAVE 1

comportment *n* 1 *syn* see BEARING 1
2 *syn* see BEHAVIOR

compose *vb* 1 *syn* see CONSTITUTE 1
rel consist (of)
2 to bring into being by mental and especially artistic effort < *compose* a ballad or a history of England >
syn create
rel devise, invent, make up, originate; dream up
3 *syn* see CALM
rel ease, lessen, soften; comfort, console, solace
con agitate, embroil, trouble, unsettle
ant discompose
4 to bring oneself or one's emotions under control < *composed* himself and turned to face the new attack >
syn collect, contain, control, cool, recollect, rein, repress, restrain, simmer down, smother, suppress
rel down, mitigate, moderate, modulate, pocket, temper, tune down; bottle (up), check, hold in; ease (off *or* up), let up, relax, slacken
idiom calm down, control one's feelings (or emotions), get hold of oneself, master one's feelings, pull oneself together

composed *adj* 1 *syn* see CALM 2
2 *syn* see COOL 2
rel quiet, still; sedate, serious, staid; repressed, suppressed
con concerned, worried
ant discomposed, ruffled

composite *adj syn* see COMPLEX 1

composite *n syn* see MIXTURE
rel combination, union

composition *n* 1 *syn* see MAKEUP 1
2 *syn* see COMPROMISE
3 *syn* see ESSAY 2

compos mentis *adj syn* see SANE 2

compost *n syn* see MIXTURE

composure *n syn* see EQUANIMITY
ant discomposure, perturbation

compotation *n syn* see BINGE 1

compound *vb* 1 *syn* see JOIN 1
2 *syn* see MIX 1
3 *syn* see INCREASE 1

compound *adj syn* see COMPLEX 1

compound *n syn* see MIXTURE

comprehend *vb* 1 *syn* see APPREHEND 1
2 *syn* see KNOW 1
rel envisage, envision, see
3 *syn* see INCLUDE

comprehendible *adj syn* see UNDER-
STANDABLE
ant incomprehendible

comprehensible *adj syn* see UNDER-
STANDABLE
ant incomprehensible

comprehensive *adj* 1 *syn* see ENCYCLO-
PEDIC
2 *syn* see ALL-AROUND 2
idiom in depth

comprehensiveness *n syn* see BREADTH
2

compress *vb* 1 *syn* see CONTRACT 3
rel compact, consolidate; cram, crowd,
press, squeeze
con disperse, dissipate, scatter
ant stretch; spread
2 *syn* see PRESS 1

comprise *vb syn* see CONSTITUTE 1

compromise *n* a settlement reached by
mutual concession <the company and the
union agreed to a *compromise* on fringe
benefits>
syn composition
rel golden mean, mean, middle ground,
middle way; agreement, compact, contract, pact; arrangement, bargain, understanding
idiom happy medium

compromise *vb syn* see ENDANGER
rel blast, blight, mar, queer, ruin, spoil
idiom cook one's goose; play havoc (*or*
hob) with, settle one's hash

compulsatory *adj syn* see MANDATORY

compulsion *n syn* see FORCE 4
rel driving, impelling, pressing; exigency,
necessity, need; pressure, stress
con coaxing, inducing, persuasion; choice,
election, option, preference

compulsory *adj syn* see MANDATORY

compunction *n* 1 *syn* see PENITENCE
rel conscience, conscientiousness, punctili-
ousness, scrupulosity, scrupulousness
con brazenness, callousness, hardness,
insensitivity; disinterest, indifference, unconcern; obduracy, recalcitrance
2 *syn* see QUALM
rel disinclination; hesitancy, hesitation

compunctious *adj syn* see REMORSEFUL

computation *n* the act or action of calculating mathematically <by his *computation* they could not possibly afford a new
car>
syn arithmetic, calculation, ciphering,
estimation, figuring, reckoning

compute *vb syn* see CALCULATE

comrade *n* 1 *syn* see ASSOCIATE 3
rel consort, fellow, mate; adjunct, ally,
auxiliary
2 *syn* see COMMUNIST

comradery *n syn* see CAMARADERIE

comstock *n syn* see PRUDE

con *vb* 1 *syn* see SCRUTINIZE 1
2 *syn* see MEMORIZE

con *n* 1 *syn* see OPPONENT
ant pro
2 *syn* see ANTAGONISM 2

con *vb* 1 *syn* see DUPE
2 *syn* see COAX

||con *n syn* see CONVICT

concatenate *vb syn* see INTEGRATE 3

concavity *n syn* see DEPRESSION 2

conceal *vb syn* see HIDE
rel camouflage, disguise, dissemble
idiom keep (something) dark
con betray, divulge; evidence, evince,
manifest
ant reveal

concealed *adj syn* see ULTERIOR

concede *vb* 1 *syn* see ACKNOWLEDGE 1
rel cede, relinquish, waive
con agitate, argue, debate, discuss; answer, confute, refute; controvert
ant dispute
2 *syn* see GRANT 1
con refuse, reject
ant deny

conceit *n* 1 *syn* see IDEA
2 an attitude of regarding oneself with
favor <his constant boasting was an
indication of *conceit*>
syn amour propre, complacence, complacency, conceitedness, consequence, egoism,
egotism, narcissism, outrecuidance, pride,
self-admiration, self-complacency, self=
conceit, self-consequence, self-esteem, self=
exaltation, self-glory, self-importance, self=
love, self-opinion, self-pride, swelled head,
swellheadedness, vainglory, vainness, vanity
rel assurance, pomposity, self-partiality,
smugness, stuffiness
con humbleness, humility, self-depreciation, unpretentiousness
ant modesty
3 *syn* see CAPRICE

||conceit *vb syn* see UNDERSTAND 3

conceited *adj syn* see VAIN 3

conceitedness *n syn* see CONCEIT 2

||conceity *adj syn* see VAIN 3

conceivable *adj* 1 *syn* see THINKABLE 2
2 *syn* see PROBABLE

conceive *vb* 1 *syn* see THINK 1
rel excogitate, cogitate, speculate; meditate, ponder, ruminate
2 *syn* see APPREHEND 1
rel heed, mark, note, notice, observe,
remark
3 *syn* see UNDERSTAND 3
rel judge; deem, feel

concenter *vb* 1 *syn* see FASTEN 3
2 *syn* see CONVERGE

concentrate *vb* 1 *syn* see FASTEN 3
rel establish, set, settle
2 *syn* see UNIFY 1
rel assemble, collect, gather; heap, mass,
pile
con dispel, disperse; attenuate, dilute,
extenuate, rarefy, thin; dispense, distribute
ant dissipate
3 *syn* see CONTRACT 3
4 *syn* see CONVERGE

concentrated *adj* 1 *syn* see STRONG 3
2 *syn* see WHOLE 5
rel complete, entire, total
3 *syn* see INTENSE 1

concentrating *adj syn* see INTEGRATIVE

concentration *n syn* see ATTENTION 1
  rel enthrallment, raptness
  ant distraction

concept *n syn* see IDEA
  con percept, sensation, sense-datum, sensum

conception *n syn* see IDEA

conceptual *adj* existing or dealing with what exists only in the mind < *conceptual* analysis of a problem >
  syn ideal, ideational, notional
  rel abstract, transcendent, transcendental; absolute, categorical, ultimate; obscure, remote; fanciful, imaginary, visionary
  con practical, pragmatic, realistic; concrete, material, substantial, tangible

concern *n* 1 *syn* see INTEREST 3
  2 *syn* see AFFAIR 1
  3 *syn* see BUSINESS 8
  4 *syn* see CARE 4
  5 *syn* see CONSIDERATION 3
  6 *syn* see UNCERTAINTY
  rel faltering, irresolution; apprehension, misgiving; inquietude, suspense
  7 *syn* see CARE 2
  rel attention, consideration, thoughtfulness
  con aloofness, incuriousness, indifference
  ant unconcern
  8 *syn* see ENTERPRISE 3
  9 *syn* see GADGET 1

concerned *adj syn* see INTERESTED

concerning *prep syn* see APROPOS

concernment *n syn* see CARE 2

concert *vb* 1 *syn* see NEGOTIATE 1
  rel argue, debate, discuss; concur, cooperate, unite
  2 *syn* see AGREE 3

concert *n syn* see HARMONY 1

concession *n syn* see ALLOWANCE 5

conciliate *vb syn* see PACIFY
  rel intervene, mediate; persuade, prevail; calm, quiet, soothe, tranquilize
  con alienate, disaffect, estrange; foment, incite; excite, pique, provoke, stimulate
  ant antagonize

concise *adj* presented with or given to brevity of expression < a *concise* statement of the problem > < a very *concise* thinker >
  syn breviloquent, brief, compendiary, compendious, curt, laconic, short, short and sweet, succinct, summary, terse; *compare* PITHY
  rel abridged, compressed, condensed; marrowy, meaty, pithy; lean
  con diffuse, long-winded, prolix, rambling, voluble, wordy
  ant redundant; verbose

concisely *adv syn* see BRIEFLY

conclude *vb* 1 *syn* see DECIDE
  2 *syn* see CLOSE 3
  idiom ring down the curtain
  ant open
  3 *syn* see INFER

concluded *adj syn* see COMPLETE 4

concluding *adj syn* see LAST

ant opening

conclusion *n* 1 *syn* see INFERENCE 2
  2 *syn* see FINALE
  3 *syn* see END 2
  4 *syn* see DECISION 1

conclusive *adj* putting an end to debate or question usually by reason of irrefutability < the evidence was *conclusive* and no defense was possible >
  syn definitive
  rel cogent, compelling, convincing, telling; incontrovertible, irrefragable, irrefrangible, irrefutable, unanswerable; deciding, decisive, determinant, determinate, determinative; clear, precise, unambiguous
  con doubtful, dubious, problematic, questionable; credible, plausible, specious; ambiguous, cryptic, enigmatic, obscure
  ant inconclusive

concoct *vb syn* see CONTRIVE 2
  rel conceive, envisage, envision; create, discover, originate

concomitant *adj* occurring in company with < good manners are likely to be *concomitant* with good behavior >
  syn accompanying, ancillary, attendant, attending, coincident, collateral, incident, satellite
  rel accessory, adjuvant, supplementary; correlative, corresponding

concomitant *n syn* see ACCOMPANIMENT 2

concord *n* 1 *syn* see HARMONY 2
  rel amity, comity, friendship, goodwill; calmness, peace, placidity, serenity, tranquillity
  con conflict, contention, difference, dissension, strife, variance
  ant discord
  2 *syn* see HARMONY 3
  3 *syn* see HARMONY 1
  4 *syn* see TREATY

concord *vb syn* see AGREE 3

concordance *n syn* see HARMONY 2

concordant *adj syn* see HARMONIOUS 2

concours *n syn* see CONTEST 2

concourse *n* a coming, flocking, or flowing together < they doubt the universe originated in a chance *concourse* of atoms >
  syn concursion, confluence, gathering, junction, meeting
  rel association, joining, linkage
  con disassociation, parting, separation

concrete *vb* 1 *syn* see HARDEN 1
  2 *syn* see JOIN 1

concupiscence *n syn* see LUST 2

concupiscent *adj syn* see LUSTFUL 2

concur *vb* 1 *syn* see UNITE 2
  rel accord, agree, harmonize, jibe
  2 *syn* see AGREE 3
  rel accede, acquiesce, assent, consent
  ant contend; altercate

concurrent *adj syn* see CONTEMPORARY 1

concurrently *adv syn* see TOGETHER 1

concursion *n syn* see CONCOURSE

concuss *vb* 1 *syn* see SHAKE 4
  2 *syn* see FORCE 2

concussion *n syn* see IMPACT
  rel beating, buffeting, jarring, jolting, pounding, shaking; blow, clip, clout

condemn *vb syn* see CRITICIZE
  rel belittle, decry, depreciate, disparage; deprecate, disapprove

---

syn synonym(s)   *rel* related word(s)
ant antonym(s)   *con* contrasted word(s)
idiom idiomatic equivalent(s)
‖ use limited; if in doubt, see a dictionary

idiom damn with faint praise, find fault with

con applaud, commend, compliment; acclaim, eulogize, extol, laud, praise; condone, excuse, forgive, pardon

2 *syn* see SENTENCE

con deliver, redeem, rescue, save

condemned *adj syn* see DAMNED 1

rel fallen, fated

condensation *n syn* see ABRIDGMENT

condense *vb* 1 *syn* see CONTRACT 3

rel compact, consolidate; curtail, minimize

con amplify

2 *syn* see EPITOMIZE 1

con broaden, expand, extend, widen

ant amplify

condensed *adj* made shorter and typically simpler <a *condensed* biography>

syn canned, capsule, epitomized, pocket, potted

rel abbreviated, abridged, bobbed, bobtail, bobtailed, curtailed, shortened

con elaborated, polished, refined; amplified, enlarged, expanded

condescend *vb syn* see STOOP 1

condign *adj syn* see JUST 3

rel grim, rigorous, stern, strict, stringent; atrocious, awful, dreadful, horrible

condition *n* 1 something that limits or qualifies an agreement or offer <included the *condition* that any heir contesting the will would be automatically disinherited>

syn provision, proviso, reservation, stipulation, strings, terms

rel prerequisite, requirement, requisite; exception, exemption, limitation, modification, qualification, restriction, saving clause

2 *syn* see ESSENTIAL 2

3 *syn* see STATE 1

4 *syn* see ORDER 9

5 *syn* see ORDER 10

6 *syn* see DISEASE 1

conditional *adj* 1 containing or dependent on a condition <our agreement is *conditional* on your raising the needed funds>

syn provisional, provisionary, provisory, tentative

rel iffy, obscure, uncertain; limited, modified, qualified, restricted

con fixed, set, sure

ant unconditional

2 *syn* see DEPENDENT 1

rel provisional, tentative; problematic, questionable; fortuitous, incidental

ant unconditional

condonable *adj syn* see JUSTIFIABLE

rel acceptable, tolerable

condone *vb syn* see EXCUSE 1

rel disregard, forget, ignore, overlook

con deplore, deprecate, disapprove; impugn, reproach

conduce *vb syn* see CONTRIBUTE 2

conduct *n* 1 *syn* see OVERSIGHT 1

2 *syn* see BEHAVIOR

rel bearing, demeanor, mien, posture, stance

conduct *vb* 1 *syn* see GUIDE

2 *syn* see ACCOMPANY

rel convey, transmit

3 to have the direction of and responsibility for <he had *conducted* a small market for many years>

syn carry on, direct, keep, manage, operate, ordain, run

rel administer, handle, head, oversee, supervise; arrange, control, keep up, order, regulate, rule; engineer, lead, pilot, steer

4 to act as a conduit for <shady transactions that *conducted* profits away from the stockholders>

syn carry, channel, convey, funnel, pipe, siphon, traject, transmit

rel remove, separate, take away, withdraw

5 *syn* see BEHAVE 1

conduit *n* 1 *syn* see CHANNEL 1

2 *syn* see PIPELINE

confab *vb syn* see CONFER 2

confabulate *vb syn* see CONFER 2

confabulation *n* 1 *syn* see CONVERSATION 1

2 *syn* see CONVERSATION 2

3 *syn* see CONFERENCE 1

confederacy *n syn* see ALLIANCE 2

confederate *n* one associated with another or others in a wrong or unlawful act <conspiring with his *confederates* to overthrow the government>

syn abettor, accessory, accomplice, coconspirator, conspirator

rel collaborator, fellow traveler; associate, colleague, fellow, partner

confederation *n syn* see ALLIANCE 2

confer *vb* 1 *syn* see GIVE 2

rel allot, provide; vouchsafe

2 to carry on a conversation or discussion usually directed toward reaching a decision or settlement <the President *conferred* with his cabinet about the scandal>

syn advise, collogue, confab, confabulate, consult, huddle, parley, powwow, treat

rel bargain, chaffer, deal, negotiate; argue, debate, discuss; converse, speak, talk

idiom put one's head together with

conference *n* 1 an interchanging of views <took several hours of *conference* to find a solution to the problem>

syn confabulation, deliberation, discussion, rap, ventilation

2 a meeting for the purpose of serious discussion and interchange of views <the association held a *conference* on the problems of aging>

syn colloquium, colloquy, palaver, rap session, seminar

rel round robin, round table

3 *syn* see TALK 4

4 *syn* see LEAGUE 4

conferrer *n syn* see DONOR

confess *vb syn* see ACKNOWLEDGE 1

idiom make a clean breast, open one's heart

confessions *n pl syn* see BIOGRAPHY

confidant *n syn* see FRIEND

confide *vb* 1 to tell confidentially <shyly *confided* her secret>

syn breathe, whisper

rel hint, insinuate, intimate, suggest

con advertise, broadcast, proclaim, publish

2 *syn* see COMMIT 1

rel bestow, present

confidence *n* 1 *syn* see TRUST 1

con distrust, mistrust; despair, hopelessness

ant doubt; apprehension

2 a feeling or showing of adequacy and reliance on oneself and one's powers < had serene *confidence* in his own ability to win through >

syn aplomb, assurance, self-assurance, self-assuredness, self-confidence, self-trust; *compare* EQUANIMITY

rel courage, mettle, resolution, spirit, tenacity; brashness, impudence, presumption

con apprehension, incertitude, misgiving, self-depreciation, self-doubt, uncertitude

ant diffidence

3 *syn* see CERTAINTY

4 *syn* see EFFRONTERY

confidence man *n syn* see SWINDLER

confident *adj* 1 marked by a strong, fearless, and bold belief in oneself and one's capacities < faced his accusers with a *confident* air >

syn assured, sanguine, secure, self-assured, self-confident, undoubtful

rel certain, cocksure, cocky, perky, positive, sure; self-possessed, self-reliant; bold, brave, courageous, dauntless, fearless, intrepid, unafraid, undaunted, valiant

con jittery, nervous, uneasy; afraid, daunted, fearful; doubtful, dubious

ant apprehensive

2 *syn* see SURE 5

3 *syn* see PRESUMPTUOUS

confidential *adj* 1 *syn* see PRIVATE 1

2 *syn* see FAMILIAR 1

rel secret; tried, trustworthy, trusty

configuration *n syn* see FORM 1

confine *vb* 1 *syn* see LIMIT 2

2 *syn* see IMPRISON

confine *n, usu* confines *pl* 1 *syn* see ENVIRONS 1

2 *syn* see LIMIT 1

rel circumference, compass, periphery

3 *syn* see RANGE 2

confined *adj syn* see CRAMPED

confinement *n* 1 *syn* see RESTRICTION 2

2 the state attending and consequent to childbirth < had a long difficult *confinement* >

syn accouchement, childbed, lying-in

rel parturition; labor, travail

confirm *vb* 1 *syn* see RATIFY

rel accede, acquiesce, assent, consent, subscribe; validate

idiom make good

con decline, refuse, reject

2 to attest to the truth, genuineness, accuracy, or validity of something < a surprise witness *confirmed* his account of the incident >

syn authenticate, bear out, corroborate, justify, substantiate, validate, verify

rel attest, certify, vouch, witness; back, support, underpin, uphold, warrant; check, check out

con confute, controvert, disprove, refute; contravene, gainsay, impugn, negative, traverse

ant deny; contradict

---

syn synonym(s)   *rel* related word(s)
ant antonym(s)   *con* contrasted word(s)
idiom idiomatic equivalent(s)
‖ use limited; if in doubt, see a dictionary

confirm (in) *vb syn* see HABITUATE 2

confirmation *n syn* see TESTIMONY

confirmative *adj   syn   see   COR-ROBORATIVE**

confirmatory *adj   syn   see   COR-ROBORATIVE**

confirmed *adj* 1 *syn* see HABITUAL 2

2 *syn* see INVETERATE 1

confiscate *vb syn* see APPROPRIATE 1

confiture *n syn* see JAM

conflagrant *adj syn* see BURNING 1

conflagration *n syn* see FIRE 1

conflict *n* 1 *syn* see CONTEST 1

rel argument, controversy, dispute

2 *syn* see CONTEST 2

3 *syn* see DISCORD

conflict *vb syn* see CLASH 2

rel differ, disagree, vary; disturb, interfere

idiom run against the tide

conflicting *adj* 1 *syn* see ANTIPATHETIC 1

2 *syn* see INCONSONANT 1

confluence *n syn* see CONCOURSE

conform *vb* 1 *syn* see ADAPT

rel attune, harmonize, tune

2 *syn* see AGREE 4

con conflict, differ, disagree

ant diverge

3 *syn* see HARMONIZE 3

4 *syn* see OBEY

idiom toe the line

conformable *adj syn* see ASSORTED 2

rel appropriate, fitting, suitable; applicable, usable

conformation *n syn* see FORM 1

conforming *adj syn* see DECOROUS 1

conformity *n* 1 *syn* see CONSISTENCY

2 *syn* see ACQUIESCENCE

confound *vb* 1 *syn* see PUZZLE

idiom take aback

2 *syn* see MISTAKE 1

ant discriminate, distinguish

3 *syn* see EMBARRASS

4 *syn* see DISPROVE 1

confounded *adj* 1 *syn* see AGHAST 2

2 *syn* see DAMNED 2

3 *syn* see UTTER

confoundedly *adv syn* see EVER 6

confrere *n* 1 *syn* see COLLEAGUE

2 *syn* see PARTNER

confront *vb* 1 to stand over against in the role of an adversary or enemy < he *confronted* his accusers with perfect aplomb >

syn affront, encounter, face, meet; *compare* MEET 6

rel beard, brave, challenge, defy; flout, scorn, scout; oppose, resist, withstand

idiom come to close quarters with, come up against

con avoid, elude, evade

2 *syn* see ACCOST 2

confronting *prep syn* see BEFORE 2

confuse *vb* 1 *syn* see EMBARRASS

2 to make unclear in mind or purpose < found the city hustle and noise very *confusing* >

syn addle, ball up, befuddle, bewilder, ‖bumfuzzle, discombobulate, distract, dizzy, fluster, fuddle, mix up, ‖mizzle, ‖momble, muddle, mull, throw off, throw out

rel misguide, mislead; agitate, bother, discompose, disquiet, flurry, perturb, upset

3 *syn* see PUZZLE

4 to make indistinct the elements or true character of (as a discussion) < *confuse* an issue in a debate>

syn becloud, befog, blur, cloud, fog, muddy

rel complicate, confound, involve, mix up

idiom lose in a fog

con clarify, elucidate; simplify

5 to throw into disorder < surging waves *confused* the waters> <her accounts were totally *confused*>

syn foul up, jumble, mix up, muddle, ||snafu, snarl up, tumble; *compare* DISORDER 1

rel derange, disarrange, disorder, disorganize, disturb, mess (up), unsettle

idiom put in a flutter, throw into confusion

6 *syn* see MISREPRESENT

7 *syn* see MISTAKE 1

ant differentiate

confusion *n* 1 *syn* see RUIN 3

2 *syn* see EMBARRASSMENT

3 a condition in which things are out of their normal or proper places or relationships <the room was in complete *confusion*>

syn ataxia, ||ballup, chaos, clutter, disarray, disorder, huddle, misorder, muddle, ||mullock, pell-mell, snarl, topsy-turviness

rel derangement, disarrangement, disturbance; foul-up, mess, mix-up, muck, ||mux, ||snafu; babel, din, hullabaloo, pandemonium

con methodization, ordering, organization, systematization; method, order, system

4 *syn* see COMMOTION 1

rel disorder, disorganization, disturbance; discomfiture, embarrassment

confute *vb* *syn* see DISPROVE 1

congé *n* *syn* see PARTING

congeal *vb* 1 *syn* see HARDEN 1

rel chill, cool, freeze

2 *syn* see COAGULATE

congenial *adj* 1 *syn* see HARMONIOUS 3

ant uncongenial

2 *syn* see CONSONANT 1

rel companionable, cooperative, social; affable, cordial, genial, gracious, sociable; pleasant, pleasing

ant uncongenial; antipathetic (*of persons*); abhorrent (*of tasks, responsibilities*)

3 *syn* see PLEASANT 1

4 *syn* see GRACIOUS 1

congenital *adj* 1 *syn* see INNATE 1

2 *syn* see INHERENT

congeries *n* *syn* see GATHERING 2

congest *vb* *syn* see FILL 1

conglobate *vb* *syn* see BALL

conglobe *vb* *syn* see BALL

conglomerate *adj* *syn* see MISCELLANEOUS

conglomerate *n* 1 *syn* see AGGREGATE 1

2 *syn* see SYNDICATE

conglomeration *n* 1 *syn* see ACCUMULATION

2 *syn* see AGGREGATE 1

congratulate *vb* to express to another one's pleasure in his good fortune or success < *congratulate* a friend when he wins a race>

syn felicitate

rel applaud, laud, praise; bless, compliment

idiom pat one on the back, tender (*or* offer) congratulation, wish one joy, wish one well

con belittle, depreciate, disparage, knock, run down, slur

congregate *vb* *syn* see GATHER 6

rel swarm, teem

ant disperse

congregation *n* *syn* see GATHERING 2

rel audience, disciples, following, public

congress *n* *syn* see ASSOCIATION 2

congress *vb* *syn* see GATHER 6

congruity *n* *syn* see CONSISTENCY

congruous *adj* 1 *syn* see CONSONANT 1

rel appropriate, fit, fitting, meet; proper, seemly

ant incongruous

2 *syn* see HARMONIOUS 2

conjectural *adj* *syn* see SUPPOSED 1

con demonstrated; unquestionable

conjecture *n* *syn* see THEORY 2

ant fact

conjecture *vb* to draw an inference from slight or inadequate evidence <when he failed to arrive on time she *conjectured* that he was drinking again>

syn guess, presume, pretend, suppose, surmise, think; *compare* INFER, UNDERSTAND 3

rel assume, expect, suspect; believe, deem, feel; conceive, fancy, imagine; conclude, estimate, gather, glean, infer, judge

idiom hazard a conjecture, take for granted

con demonstrate, prove, test, try; ascertain, determine, discover, learn

conjoin *vb* 1 *syn* see JOIN 1

2 *syn* see UNITE 2

conjoint *adj* 1 *syn* see COMMON 1

2 *syn* see COOPERATIVE

conjointly *adv* *syn* see TOGETHER 3

conjointment *n* *syn* see ASSOCIATION 1

conjugal *adj* *syn* see MATRIMONIAL

conjugality *n* *syn* see MARRIAGE 2

conjugate *vb* *syn* see JOIN 1

conjunct *adj* *syn* see COMMON 1

conjunction *n* *syn* see ASSOCIATION 1

conjuration *n* *syn* see SPELL

conjure *vb* *syn* see BEG

conjurer *n* 1 *syn* see MAGICIAN 1

2 *syn* see MAGICIAN 2

conjuring *n* 1 *syn* see MAGIC 1

2 *syn* see MAGIC 2

conjury *n* *syn* see MAGIC 1

||**conk** *n* 1 *syn* see NOSE 1

2 *syn* see HEAD 1

||**conk** *n* *syn* see HIT 1

conk *vb* *syn* see DIE 1

con man *n* *syn* see SWINDLER

rel shill

con mark, sucker, victim; greenhorn

connate *adj* 1 *syn* see INNATE 1

2 *syn* see INHERENT

3 *syn* see RELATED

connatural *adj* 1 *syn* see INNATE 1

2 *syn* see RELATED

connect *vb* *syn* see JOIN 1

ant disconnect

connection *n* 1 *syn* see ASSOCIATION 1

2 *syn* see JOINT 1

3 *syn* see JOB 2

4 *syn* see RELIGION 2

connivance *n syn* see COMPLICITY

connive *vb* 1 to secretly favor or sympathize with something improper or illicit < *connive* at treason >

syn blink (at), wink (at)

rel condone, disregard, ignore, overlook, tolerate

idiom close (*or* shut) one's eyes to, let go by (*or* get by) one's eye, regard with indulgence

con disapprove, disfavor, frown (at *or* upon); disallow, reject, repudiate; disdain, scorn, scout, spurn

2 *syn* see PLOT

connoisseur *n* a person who enjoys with discrimination and appreciation of subtleties and details especially in matters of culture or art < a *connoisseur* of fine wines >

syn aesthete, cognoscente, dilettante

rel bon vivant, epicure, gourmet; adept, authority, critic, expert

con abecedarian, amateur, dabbler, tyro

connotation *n syn* see ASSOCIATION 4

connote *vb syn* see MEAN 2

2 *syn* see SUGGEST 1

connubial *adj syn* see MATRIMONIAL

connubiality *n syn* see MARRIAGE 1

conquer *vb* 1 to overcome or gain dominion over by force of arms < leaders who have tried and failed to *conquer* the world >

syn bear down, beat down, crush, defeat, overpower, reduce, subdue, subjugate, vanquish; *compare* DEFEAT 2, OVERTHROW 2, WHIP 2, WIN 1

rel baffle, balk, circumvent, foil, frustrate, outwit, override, thwart; bend, control, master, overmaster, subject, worst

idiom bring one to one's knees, trample in the dust, trample underfoot

con bow, cave, give up, succumb, yield; capitulate, submit, surrender

2 to gain mastery over something by getting the better of obstacles and difficulties < trials faced by the men who *conquered* Mount Everest >

syn best, master, overcome, prevail, triumph; *compare* OVERCOME 1

3 *syn* see OVERCOME 1

conqueror *n syn* see VICTOR 1

conquest *n syn* see VICTORY 1

rel defeating, overthrow, rout, routing, subdual

consanguine *adj syn* see RELATED

‖**consarned** *adj* 1 *syn* see DAMNED 2

2 *syn* see UTTER

conscience *n syn* see QUALM

conscienceless *adj syn* see UNSCRUPULOUS

rel devious, shifty, tricky, unfair

ant conscientious

conscientious *adj* 1 *syn* see UPRIGHT 2

ant conscienceless

2 *syn* see CAREFUL 2

conscionable *adj syn* see CAREFUL 2

conscious *adj* 1 *syn* see AWARE

rel noticing, noting, perceiving, remarking; vigilant, watchful

con forgetful, oblivious, unmindful; disregarding, ignoring, overlooking

ant unconscious

2 *syn* see SELF-CONSCIOUS

consciousness *n syn* see CARE 4

conscribe *vb syn* see DRAFT 1

conscript *vb syn* see DRAFT 1

consecrate *vb* 1 *syn* see DEVOTE 1

con desecrate, profane; defile, pollute

2 *syn* see BLESS 1

consecrated *adj syn* see HOLY 1

consecution *n* 1 *syn* see ORDER 5

2 *syn* see SUCCESSION 2

consecutive *adj* following one after another in orderly fashion < it rained for five *consecutive* days >

syn sequent, sequential, serial, subsequent, subsequential, succedent, succeeding, successional, successive; *compare* NEXT

rel after, ensuing, following, later; enlarging, increasing, progressive

con antecedent, preceding, prior

consecutively *adv syn* see TOGETHER 2

consent *vb syn* see ASSENT

rel allow, let, permit; approve, sanction; concur

con decline; balk, demur, stick, stickle

consent *n* 1 *syn* see PERMISSION

2 *syn* see AGREEMENT 2

consentaneous *adj syn* see UNANIMOUS

consentient *adj syn* see UNANIMOUS

consequence *n* 1 *syn* see EFFECT 1

con origin, root, source

ant antecedent

2 *syn* see IMPORTANCE

rel exigency, need; fame, honor, renown, reputation, repute

3 *syn* see STATUS 2

4 *syn* see CONCEIT 2

consequent *adj syn* see RATIONAL

consequential *adj syn* see IMPORTANT 1

consequently *adv syn* see THEREFORE

conservancy *n syn* see CONSERVATION 1

conservation *n* 1 a deliberate planned guarding and protecting of something felt as precious < *conservation* of our natural resources >

syn conservancy, husbanding, preserval, preservation, salvation, saving

rel attention, care, cherishing, protection; control, directing, governing, management, managing, supervising, supervision

con neglect, squandering, waste

2 *syn* see PRESERVATION 1

conservative *adj* 1 tending to resist or oppose change < took a very *conservative* stance politically >

syn die-hard, fogyish, old-line, orthodox, reactionary, right, tory, traditionalistic

con modern, progressive, radical

ant advanced

2 kept or keeping within bounds < equally *conservative* in speech and action >

syn controlled, discreet, moderate, reasonable, restrained, temperate, unexcessive, unextreme

rel cautious, chary, wary; circumspect, politic, proper, prudent

---

syn synonym(s)   *rel* related word(s)

ant antonym(s)   *con* contrasted word(s)

idiom idiomatic equivalent(s)

‖ use limited; if in doubt, see a dictionary

con expansive, unconstrained; excessive, freewheeling, uncontrolled, unrestrained

conservative *n syn* see DIEHARD 1

conservatory *n syn* see GREENHOUSE

conserve *vb syn* see SAVE 3
rel keep up, maintain, support, sustain
con dissipate, fritter, squander, waste

conserve *n syn* see JAM

consider *vb* 1 to give serious thought to < *consider* the risk you would be taking >
syn contemplate, excogitate, mind, perpend, ponder, study, think (out *or* over), weigh
rel meditate, muse, ruminate; cogitate, reason, reflect, speculate, think; examine, inspect, look (at), scan, scrutinize, see
idiom bestow thought to, chew the cud over, revolve (*or* turn over) in one's mind
con disregard, ignore, neglect, overlook, slight
2 *syn* see EYE 1
rel envisage, envision
3 to come to view, judge, or classify < be *considered* thrift essential to success >
syn account, deem, reckon, regard, view; *compare* FEEL 3
rel conceive, fancy, imagine, think; conclude, gather, infer, judge, rule
4 *syn* see ADMIRE 2
5 *syn* see FEEL 3

considerable *adj* 1 *syn* see IMPORTANT 1
2 tending more to the large than the small < buckled down with his ax and made a *considerable* impression on the woodpile >
syn good, respectable, ||right smart, sensible, sizable, ||smart
rel able, capable, competent; active, effective, efficacious; important, notable, significant; goodly, pretty, substantial, tidy
con insignificant, meager, slight, trivial; big, grand, great, huge
3 *syn* see BIG 1

considerably *adv syn* see WELL 8

considerate *adj* 1 *syn* see CAUTIOUS
2 *syn* see THOUGHTFUL 3
rel kind, kindly; compassionate, sympathetic, tender, warmhearted; amiable, complaisant, obliging
ant inconsiderate
3 *syn* see GENEROUS 1

considerately *adv syn* see WELL 2
rel solicitously, tenderly; altruistically, benevolently, charitably
con austerely, harshly, severely, strictly

considerateness *n syn* see CONSIDERATION 3

consideration *n* 1 *syn* see ATTENTION 1
2 *syn* see MOTIVE 1
3 thoughtful and sympathetic attention < showed great *consideration* to the needs of others >
syn concern, considerateness, regard, solicitude
rel awareness, heed, heedfulness, mindfulness; forbearance, mercy, quarter
con disregard, heedlessness, unconcern, unmindfulness; inconsiderateness; contempt, despite, disdain, disinterest, scorn
4 *syn* see REGARD 4

considered *adj syn* see DELIBERATE 1
rel intentional, voluntary, willful
con impulsive, instinctive, spontaneous; headlong, impetuous, precipitate

ant unconsidered

considering *conj syn* see BECAUSE

consign *vb* 1 *syn* see COMMIT 1
rel resign, surrender, yield
2 *syn* see SEND 1

consist *vb* 1 to have existence or a place < our national strength *consists* not solely in military readiness >
syn dwell, exist, inhere, lie, reside
rel be, subsist; abide, repose, rest
idiom have one's (*or* a) place
2 *syn* see AGREE 4

consistency *n* agreement or harmony of parts, traits, or features < his adversary had to admit the *consistency* of his position >
syn coherence, conformity, congruity, correspondence; *compare* HARMONY 2
rel agreement, concord, consonance; likeness, similarity; apposition, aptness, felicity, fitness, suitability
con incoherence, incongruity; impropriety, inappropriateness, unsuitability
ant inconsistency

consistent *adj* 1 *syn* see SAME 3
2 *syn* see CONSONANT 1

consistently *adv syn* see USUALLY 1

consociate *n syn* see PARTNER

console *vb syn* see COMFORT
rel calm, relieve, tranquilize; animate, hearten, inspirit
idiom lift the spirits of
con agitate, discompose, disquiet, disturb, perturb, upset

consolidate *vb syn* see UNIFY 1
rel amalgamate, blend, fuse, merge; set, solidify
con part, sever, sunder; liquefy, melt

consolidating *adj syn* see INTEGRATIVE

consolidation *n* 1 *syn* see UNIFICATION
2 a union of two or more businesses < *consolidation* is often accompanied by a new corporate name >
syn amalgamation, merger
ant dissolution

consonance *n* 1 *syn* see HARMONY 2
con discrepancy, incompatibility, incongruousness
ant discord
2 *syn* see HARMONY 1
ant dissonance

consonant *adj* 1 conforming (as to a pattern, a standard, or a relationship) without discord or difficulty < his performance was seldom *consonant* with his very real abilities >
syn agreeable, compatible, congenial, congruous, consistent, sympathetic; *compare* HARMONIOUS 2
rel accordant, conformable, harmonious; coincident, concurrent; en rapport
con discordant, discrepant; incompatible, incongruous, inconsistent
ant inconsonant
2 *syn* see HARMONIOUS 1
ant dissonant
3 *syn* see LIKE
4 *syn* see RESONANT

consort *n* 1 *syn* see ACCOMPANIMENT 2
2 *syn* see SPOUSE

consort *vb syn* see AGREE 4

consort (with) *vb syn* see ACCOMPANY

consortium *n syn* see ASSOCIATION 2

conspectus *n syn* see ABRIDGMENT
conspicuous *adj* **1** *syn* see CLEAR 5
2 *syn* see NOTICEABLE
rel celebrated, eminent, illustrious; showy
con common, everyday, ordinary; covert,
secret; concealed, hidden
ant inconspicuous
conspiracy *n syn* see PLOT 2
rel sedition, treason; disloyalty, faithlessness, falsity, perfidiousness, perfidy,
treacherousness, treachery
con faith, faithfulness, fealty, loyalty
conspirator *n syn* see CONFEDERATE
conspire *vb syn* see PLOT
||**constable** *n syn* see POLICEMAN
constancy *n syn* see ATTACHMENT 1
constant *adj* **1** *syn* see FAITHFUL 1
rel abiding, clinging, enduring, lasting,
persistent, persisting
con capricious, mercurial
ant fickle, inconstant
2 *syn* see INFLEXIBLE 3
con fluctuant, fluctuating, fluctuational,
unstable
ant inconstant, variable
3 *syn* see SAME 3
4 *syn* see STEADY 2
5 *syn* see CONTINUAL
rel chronic, confirmed, inveterate; dogged,
obstinate, pertinacious; persevering
con alternate, intermittent, recurrent;
infrequent, occasional, sporadic
ant fitful
constantly *adv syn* see ALWAYS 1
idiom day after day, day in, day out
ant occasionally
constate *vb syn* see ASSERT 1
consternate *vb syn* see DISMAY 1
consternation *n syn* see FEAR 1
rel confusion, muddle, muddlement; bewilderment, distraction, perplexity
con composure, equanimity, phlegm,
sangfroid; aplomb, poise, self-command,
self-possession
constipate *vb syn* see STULTIFY
constipated *adj* being unable to defecate
regularly and without difficulty < com-
plained that she was constantly *constipated* >
syn astricted, bound, costive, obstipated
constituent *n syn* see ELEMENT 2
rel division, fraction, part, portion
con complex, economy, organism, system;
amalgam, blend, composite, compound
ant aggregate, whole
constitute *vb* **1** to be all or a fundamental
part of the substance of < water *constitutes* the greater part of the human
body >
syn compose, comprise, form, make,
make up
rel embody, incorporate, integrate; complement, complete, fill out, flesh (out)
2 *syn* see ENACT 1
3 *syn* see FOUND 2
constitution *n* **1** *syn* see PHYSIQUE
2 *syn* see MAKEUP 1
constitutional *adj syn* see INHERENT

con anomalous, irregular, unnatural
ant advenient
constitutional *n syn* see WALK 1
rel ambulation, footwork, legwork, per-
ambulation
constitutive *adj syn* see ESSENTIAL 2
constrain *vb* **1** *syn* see FORCE 2
2 *syn* see RESTRAIN 1
3 *syn* see DENY 3
rel abridge, curtail, deprive; ban, bar,
disallow, enjoin
4 *syn* see IMPRISON
5 *syn* see PRESS 1
6 *syn* see DISTRESS 2
constrained *adj syn* see RESERVED 1
constrainment *n syn* see RESTRICTION 2
constraint *n* **1** *syn* see FORCE 4
rel repression, suppression; driving, impelling, impulsion; goad, motive, spring,
spur
2 *syn* see RESTRICTION 2
constrict *vb* **1** *syn* see CONTRACT 3
rel curb, restrain; circumscribe, confine,
limit, restrict
con enlarge, expand, increase, maximize
2 to make narrow or narrower < the muscles that *constrict* the sphincter >
syn constringe, narrow
rel gather, plait, pucker; compress, constrain, squeeze; astringe
con broaden, dilate, distend, widen
ant expand
constringe *vb syn* see CONSTRICT 2
construal *n syn* see EXPLANATION 1
construct *vb* **1** *syn* see MAKE 3
2 *syn* see BUILD 1
3 *syn* see ERECT 5
construction *n* **1** *syn* see MAKEUP 1
2 *syn* see EXPLANATION 1
constructive *adj syn* see IMPLICIT 2
rel inferential, ratiocinative; construable,
interpretable, renderable
con clear, evident, obvious, patent
ant manifest
construe *vb syn* see EXPLAIN 1
consuetude *n syn* see HABIT 1
consult *vb syn* see CONFER 2
rel cogitate, counsel, deliberate, consider,
examine, review
consume *vb* **1** to bring to an end by or as
if by the action of a destroying force
< the village was *consumed* by fire >
syn devour, eat, eat up, exhaust, use up
rel destroy, raze, ruin, wreck; annihilate,
extinguish; crush, overwhelm, suppress
con bolster, brace, buttress, hold up,
prop, stay, support, sustain; build, construct, create, make, produce; renew, restore
2 *syn* see WASTE 2
3 *syn* see GO 4
4 *syn* see EAT 1
5 to eat or drink usually gluttonously or
without measure < *consumed* dozens of
burgers and a case of beer >
syn polish off, punish, put away, put
down, shift, swill; *compare* EAT 1
rel absorb, ingest; devour, gobble (up),
gorge, wolf; down, gulp, guzzle, inhale,
swallow
idiom dispose of
6 *syn* see MONOPOLIZE
consumedly *adv syn* see EVER 6

---

syn synonym(s)   *rel* related word(s)
ant antonym(s)   *con* contrasted word(s)
idiom idiomatic equivalent(s)
|| use limited; if in doubt, see a dictionary

consuming *adj syn* see ENGROSSING

consummate *adj* 1 brought to the highest possible point of perfection < the difficult allegro passages displayed her *consummate* skill >
syn accomplished, finished, perfected, ripe, virtuosic; *compare* PERFECT 2
rel faultless, flawless, impeccable, perfect; practiced, skilled, trained; able, gifted, talented; inimitable, peerless, superb, superlative, supreme, transcendent, unsurpassable
con callow, crude, green, raw, rough, uncouth; defective, deficient, inadequate
2 *syn* see UTTER

consummate *vb syn* see CLOSE 3

consumption *n syn* see TUBERCULOSIS

contact *n* 1 the state of being in or coming into close association or connection < shuddered at the *contact* of his icy hand >
syn contingence, touch
rel closeness, contiguity, nearness, propinquity, proximity; impingement, taction, touching; association, connection, relation; oneness, union, unity
con breach, break, rift, rupture, split; insularity, isolation, seclusion, segregation, separation; distance, farness, remoteness
2 a situation permitting exchange of ideas and opinions < tried for several days to get in *contact* with her brother >
syn commerce, communication, communion, intercommunication, intercourse
rel association, companionship, fellowship; oneness, union, unity; accord, concord, harmony, rapport; empathy, sympathy, understanding

contact *vb syn* see REACH 4

contagion *n syn* see POISON
rel contamination, corruption, pollution, taint; miasma

contagious *adj* 1 *syn* see INFECTIOUS 2
2 *syn* see INFECTIOUS 3

contain *vb* 1 *syn* see COMPOSE 4
2 to have or be capable of having within < the box *contained* family papers > < a mug that will *contain* a quart of ale >
syn accommodate, hold
rel harbor, house, lodge, shelter; admit, receive, take, take in
3 *syn* see INCLUDE

contaminate *vb* 1 to debase by making impure or unclean < feared her child's morals would be *contaminated* by others >
syn defile, pollute, soil, taint; *compare* TAINT 1
rel corrupt, debase, debauch, deprave, pervert, vitiate; harm, injure, spoil
con better, elevate, improve
ant purify
2 to render unfit for use by the introduction of unwholesome or undesirable elements < water *contaminated* by sewage >
syn befoul, foul, pollute
rel infect; poison; dirty, soil
ant purify

contemn *vb syn* see DESPISE

contemplate *vb* 1 *syn* see EYE 1
rel ponder, reflect, study; examine, inspect, scan, scrutinize
2 *syn* see CONSIDER 1

rel drift, roam
3 *syn* see INTEND 2
idiom have in view

contemplative *adj syn* see THOUGHTFUL 1
rel musing, weighing; reasoning
idiom in a brown study

contemporaneous *adj syn* see CONTEMPORARY 1

contemporary *adj* 1 existing or occurring at the same time < the story has come down from several *contemporary* sources >
syn coetaneous, coeval, coexistent, coexisting, concurrent, contemporaneous, simultaneous, synchronal, synchronic, synchronous
rel accompanying, attendant, attending, coincident, concomitant; current, existing, present; associated, connected, linked, related
con antecedent, foregoing, preceding, previous, prior; ensuing, following, succeeding
2 *syn* see PRESENT 3
3 *syn* see UP-TO-DATE

contempt *n* 1 *syn* see DESPITE 1
rel antipathy, aversion; distaste, repugnance
con awe, fear, reverence
ant regard
2 *syn* see DISGRACE
3 *syn* see DEFIANCE 2

contemptible *adj* arousing or meriting scorn or disdain < a *contemptible* attempt to blame his wife for his failure >
syn beggarly, cheap, despicable, despisable, mean, pitiable, pitiful, scummy, scurvy, shabby, sorry; *compare* BASE 3
rel abhorrent, abominable, detestable, hateful, odious; abject, ignoble, sordid; bad, inferior, poor, sad; disgusting, scrimy, shameful; outcast
con creditable, estimable, honorable, noble; high-minded, high-principled, principled, true, upright; honest, square, straight
ant admirable

contend *vb* 1 to strive in opposition to someone or something < *contending* against the temptation to look behind him >
syn battle, fight, oppugn, tug, war
rel combat, oppose, resist, withstand; contest, cope (with), vie
2 *syn* see MAINTAIN 2
rel report, say, tell; charge, enjoin, urge; dictate, prescribe
3 *syn* see COMPETE 1
rel combat, oppose, resist, withstand; confront, encounter, face, meet, stand

content *vb syn* see SATISFY 3
rel delight, thrill, tickle; bewitch, captivate, charm, enrapture
con disappoint, dishearten, displease
ant discontent

contention *n* 1 *syn* see DISCORD
rel altercation, quarrel, squabble, wrangle; argument, controversy, dispute
con agreement, coincidence, concurrence
2 *syn* see ARGUMENT 2
3 *syn* see THESIS 1

contentious *adj* 1 *syn* see BELLIGERENT
rel contrary, froward, perverse; captious, carping, caviling, faultfinding

con calm, serene, tranquil; amiable, complaisant, good-natured, obliging
ant peaceable

2 prone to wordy contention <a *contentious* old chap, always ready for an argument>
syn argumentative, controversial, disputatious, litigious, polemical
rel fiery, hasty, hotheaded, impetuous, peppery; belligerent, bellicose, scrappy
con amiable, complaisant, good-natured, obliging; agreeable, cooperative, understanding

conterminous *adj syn* see ADJACENT 3

contest *vb* 1 *syn* see COMPETE 1
rel endeavor
2 *syn* see RESIST

contest *n* 1 earnest struggle for superiority or victory <the rival factions continued in *contest* for several years>
syn competition, conflict, emulation, rivalry, strife, striving, tug-of-war, warfare
rel brush, encounter, skirmish; action, battle, engagement

2 a competitive encounter between groups or individuals <there were *contests* of skill and of wit>
syn competition, concours, conflict, meet, meeting, rencontre
rel proving, testing, trial, trying

contestation *n syn* see THESIS 1

contiguity *n syn* see PROXIMITY

contiguous *adj* 1 *syn* see ADJACENT 3
rel close, near, nearby, nigh
con apart, separate; distant, remote
2 *syn* see NEIGHBORING

contiguously *adv syn* see IMMEDIATELY 1

contiguousness *n syn* see PROXIMITY

continence *n syn* see TEMPERANCE 2
rel self-restraint; moderation, temperateness; chasteness, chastity, purity
con self-indulgence; excessiveness, inordinateness; lasciviousness, lecherousness, lewdness, licentiousness, wantonness
ant incontinence

continent *adj syn* see ABSTEMIOUS
rel bridled, curbed, inhibited, restrained; chaste, pure
con self-indulgent, spoiled
ant incontinent

contingence *n syn* see CONTACT 1

contingency *n syn* see JUNCTURE 2
rel break, chance, occasion, opportunity

contingent *adj* 1 *syn* see ACCIDENTAL
rel unanticipated, unforeseeable, unforeseen; likely, possible, probable
con certain, inevitable, necessary
2 *syn* see DEPENDENT 1

continual *adj* continuing without intermission and seemingly without end <they were tired of her *continual* nagging>
syn around-the-clock, ceaseless, constant, continuous, endless, everlasting, incessant, interminable, minutely, perpetual, timeless, unceasing, unending, unintermitted, unintermittent, uninterrupted, unremitting
rel abiding, enduring, persistent, persisting, staying; unvarying; unchanging, un-

failing, unflagging, unwaning; relentless, running, steady
con ephemeral, evanescent, impermanent, short-lived, temporary, transient, transitory

continually *adv syn* see TOGETHER 2

continuance *n syn* see RUN 2
rel constancy, longevity, permanence; survival

continuation *n* 1 uninterrupted existence or succession <the *continuation* of political disorder in Northern Ireland>
syn continuity, duration, endurance, persistence
rel extension, prolongation, protraction
ant termination
2 *syn* see RUN 2
ant cessation

continue *vb* 1 to remain indefinitely in existence or in a particular state or course <many traditional beliefs still *continue*> <do you expect to *continue* in school for the rest of your life?>
syn abide, carry through, endure, last, perdure, persist
rel carry on, carry over, ride, run on; outlast, outlive, survive; remain, stay
con cease, desist, discontinue, quit; arrest, check, interrupt; defer, intermit, postpone, stay, suspend
ant discontinue
2 *syn* see RESUME 2

continuing *adj syn* see OLD 2

continuity *n syn* see CONTINUATION 1

continuous *adj syn* see CONTINUAL
ant discontinuous

continuously *adv* 1 *syn* see TOGETHER 2
2 *syn* see ALWAYS 1

contort *vb syn* see DEFORM
rel bend, curve, twist

contour *n syn* see OUTLINE

contra *prep syn* see AGAINST 1

contra *adv syn* see AGAIN 5

contra *n syn* see OPPOSITE

contraband *adj* prohibited or excluded by law or treaty <fur or feathers from endangered species are *contraband* in advanced nations>
syn banned, hot
rel disapproved, proscribed, taboo; forbidden, prohibited; excluded, shut out

contraband *vb syn* see SMUGGLE

contraception *n syn* see BIRTH CONTROL

contract *n* a usually legally enforceable arrangement between two or more parties <a *contract* for a new roof>
syn agreement, bargain, bond, compact, convention, covenant, pact, transaction; *compare* AGREEMENT 2, TREATY

contract *vb* 1 to become affected by a disease or disorder <*contracted* a severe cold that later turned into pneumonia>
syn catch, come down (with), get, sicken (with *or* of), take
rel acquire, obtain; decline, fail, sink, weaken; afflict, derange, disorder, indispose, upset; bring on, cause, induce; succumb (to)
idiom be laid by the heels by, fall (a) victim to
2 *syn* see INCUR
3 to make or become smaller in bulk or volume <*contract* a muscle>

syn synonym(s)   *rel* related word(s)
ant antonym(s)   *con* contrasted word(s)
idiom idiomatic equivalent(s)
|| use limited; if in doubt, see a dictionary

syn compress, concentrate, condense, constrict, shrink

rel decrease, diminish, dwindle, lessen, reduce

con dilate, distend, inflate, swell

ant expand

contracted *adj syn* see ENGAGED 2

contradict *vb syn* see DENY 4

rel dispute; belie, falsify, garble

con authenticate, substantiate, verify

ant corroborate; confirm

contradiction *n syn* see DENIAL 2

contradictory *n syn* see OPPOSITE

contradictory *adj syn* see OPPOSITE

rel negating, nullifying; adverse, antagonistic, counteractive

con agreeing, jibing, squaring, tallying

ant corroboratory; confirmatory

contradistinction *n syn* see ANTAGONISM 2

contraposition *n syn* see ANTAGONISM 2

contraption *n syn* see DEVICE 2

contrariant *n syn* see ANTIPATHETIC 1

contrariety *n syn* see ANTAGONISM 2

contrariwise *adv syn* see AGAIN 5

idiom on (*or* to) the contrary

contrary *n syn* see OPPOSITE

contrary *adj* 1 *syn* see OPPOSITE

2 *syn* see ANTIPATHETIC 1

3 obstinately self-willed in refusing to concur, conform, or submit <why be *contrary* about something that you cannot change>

syn balky, cross-grained, froward, ornery, perverse, restive, wayward, wrongheaded

rel headstrong, intractable, recalcitrant, refractory, unruly; contumacious, insubordinate, rebellious; dissentient, dissident, nonconforming, nonconformist, recusant; obstinate, stubborn

con amenable, biddable, docile, obedient, tractable; amiable, obliging; acquiescent, compliant; forbearing, long-suffering, tolerant

ant complaisant

contrary *adv syn* see AGAIN 5

contrast *vb syn* see COMPARE 2

contravene *vb* 1 *syn* see VIOLATE 1

rel encroach, intrude, overstep, trespass

2 *syn* see DENY 4

rel combat, fight, oppose, resist; abjure, disclaim, disown, exclude, reject, repudiate, spurn

con accept, agree, subscribe (to); admit, allow, own

ant uphold (*as a principle*); allege (*as a right or claim*)

contravention *n syn* see BREACH 1

rel crime, offense, sin, vice

contrawise *adv syn* see AGAIN 5

contretemps *n syn* see MISFORTUNE

contribute *vb* 1 to give in common with others < *contribute* to a fund for handicapped children>

syn chip in, come through, kick in, pitch in, subscribe; *compare* GIVE 1

idiom put something in the pot, sweeten the kitty

2 to have a share in something (as an act or effect) <careful planning *contributed* greatly to the success of the project>

syn conduce, redound, tend

rel aid, help, assist; add (to), augment, supplement; fortify, recruit, reinforce, strengthen

idiom do one's bit, have a hand in

con detract, minus, subtract, take away

contribution *n syn* see DONATION

contributory *adj syn* see AUXILIARY

contrite *adj syn* see REMORSEFUL

contriteness *n syn* see PENITENCE

contrition *n syn* see PENITENCE

contriturate *vb syn* see PULVERIZE 1

contrivance *n* 1 *syn* see DEVICE 2

2 *syn* see INVENTION

contrive *vb* 1 *syn* see PLOT

rel develop, elaborate, work out

2 to use ingenuity in making or doing or achieving an end < *contrived* a useful camp stove from a few bricks and a piece of screen>

syn concoct, cook (up), devise, dream up, formulate, frame, hatch (up), invent, make up, vamp (up)

rel plan, plot, project, scheme; fabricate, fashion, make, manufacture; handle, manipulate, move; rig

control *vb* 1 *syn* see COMPOSE 4

rel adjust, regulate; curb, master, quell, subdue

2 *syn* see GOVERN 3

rel regulate, supervise; discipline

idiom put through the mill (*or* a course of sprouts), take in hand

control *n syn* see POWER 1

controlled *adj syn* see CONSERVATIVE 2

controversial *adj syn* see CONTENTIOUS 2

controversy *n* 1 *syn* see ARGUMENT 2

2 *syn* see QUARREL

controvert *vb syn* see DISPROVE 1

rel challenge, oppugn, question

contumacious *adj syn* see INSUBORDINATE

rel contrary, froward, perverse; alienated, disaffected, estranged, irreconcilable

con acquiescent, compliant, resigned

ant obedient

contumacy *n syn* see DEFIANCE 2

contumelious *adj* 1 *syn* see ABUSIVE

2 *syn* see INSOLENT 2

ant obsequious

contumely *n* 1 *syn* see ABUSE

rel animadversion, aspersion, reflection, stricture

idiom hard (*or* bitter) words

2 *syn* see AFFRONT

confuse *vb syn* see BRUISE 1

contusion *n syn* see BRUISE

conundrum *n syn* see MYSTERY

convalesce *vb syn* see IMPROVE 3

convenance *n syn* see FORM 3

convene *vb* 1 to begin a session (as of a legislature or conference) <the council *convened* at 10 o'clock>

syn meet, open, sit

idiom hold a meeting (*or* session)

2 *syn* see SUMMON 2

rel convoke, muster

3 *syn* see CONVOKE

convenience *n* 1 *syn* see AMENITY 2

2 *syn* see TOILET

convenience *vb syn* see OBLIGE 2

convenient *adj* 1 *syn* see GOOD 2

2 situated within easy reach <left his glasses *convenient* to his book>

syn adjacent, close-at-hand, close-by, handy, near-at-hand, nearby
rel close, near, nigh; immediate, next
idiom at one's beck and call, at one's fingertips, in one's immediate neighborhood, under one's nose
ant inconvenient

convention *n* 1 *syn* see TREATY
2 *syn* see CONTRACT
rel accord, understanding
3 *syn* see FORM 3
rel canon, law, precept, rule; custom, practice

conventional *adj* 1 according with or based on generally accepted and well-established usage < took a very *conventional* view of his duty >
syn button-down, orthodox, square, straight; *compare* TRADITIONAL 1
rel moderate, sober, temperate; constrained, restrained; dependable, reliable, responsible; conscientious, fastidious, nice, punctilious, scrupulous; conservative, traditionalistic
ant unconventional
2 *syn* see TRADITIONAL 1
3 *syn* see CEREMONIAL
rel decent, decorous, proper, seemly; correct, precise, right
con lax, negligent, remiss, slack; artless, ingenuous, naive, natural, simple, unsophisticated
ant unconventional

converge *vb* to come to or trend toward a common point < the main streets *converge* on a central square >
syn concenter, concentrate, focus, meet
idiom come to a center, come (*or* run) together

conversant *adj* 1 *syn* see AWARE
ant ignorant
2 *syn* see FAMILIAR 3
rel sensible; up-to-date; apprehending, comprehending, perceptive, percipient
con unfamiliar; nescient
ant unconversant

conversation *n* 1 oral exchange of information or ideas < leaned against the fence in casual *conversation* >
syn chat, colloquy, confabulation, converse, dialogue, parley
rel discussion; discourse, speech, talk
2 an instance of conversational exchange < had a long *conversation* about family problems >
syn colloquy, confabulation, dialogue, talk; *compare* CHAT 2
rel debate, deliberation, discussion, ventilation; comment, observation, remark; cross talk, repartee

conversation piece *n* *syn* see CURIOSITY 2

converse *vb* to engage in conversation < they *conversed* quietly while waiting for their friend >
syn chat, chin, colloque, talk, visit, yarn; *compare* CHAT 1

converse (in) *vb* *syn* see SPEAK 3

converse *n* 1 *syn* see CONVERSATION 1
2 *syn* see COMMUNICATION 3

converse *adj* *syn* see OPPOSITE

converse *n* *syn* see OPPOSITE

conversely *adv* *syn* see AGAIN 5

conversion *n* 1 fundamental alteration in one's system of beliefs < Judaism does not encourage *conversion* of gentiles >
syn metanoia, rebirth
rel about-face, reversal, turning; reclamation, regeneration
idiom change of heart
2 change of one thing to another usually by substitution < *conversion* of locomotives from steam to diesel power >
syn alteration, changeover, shift, transformation
rel change, modification, qualification; metamorphosis, mutation, permutation, transmutation; innovation, novelty

convert *vb* 1 to induce (another or others) to accept the validity of something (as a belief, course of action, or point of view) < Chinese missionaries *converted* many Japanese to Buddhism >
syn bring, lead, move, persuade
rel redeem, reform, save; bend, bias, incline, sway; actuate, budge, impel; proselyte, proselytize
2 *syn* see TRANSFORM
rel fabricate, forge, make, manufacture; apply, employ, use, utilize

convey *vb* 1 *syn* see CARRY 1
2 *syn* see COMMUNICATE 1
rel project, put across
3 *syn* see TRANSFER 4
rel commit, consign, relegate
4 *syn* see CONDUCT 4

conveyance *n* 1 *syn* see TRANSPORTATION 1
2 *syn* see DEED 3
3 *syn* see VEHICLE 3

convict *n* a person serving time in prison after conviction as a criminal < mixing hardened *convicts* with juvenile offenders >
syn ‖con, jailbird, ‖lag, loser, prison bird
rel long-termer, longtimer; ‖stir bug; recidivist, repeater

conviction *n* 1 *syn* see CERTAINTY
con dubiety, dubiosity, uncertainty; disbelief, incredulity, unbelief
2 *syn* see OPINION
rel doctrine, dogma, tenet

convince *vb* 1 *syn* see ASSURE 2
2 *syn* see INDUCE 1

convincing *adj* 1 *syn* see AUTHENTIC 1
2 *syn* see VALID

convivial *adj* *syn* see SOCIAL 1
rel lively, vivacious; jocund, jolly, merry
con grave, sedate, serious, sober, solemn, somber; reserved, reticent, silent
ant taciturn; stolid

convoke *vb* to bring together by or as if by summons < the ruler *convoked* his council >
syn assemble, call, convene, summon; *compare* SUMMON 2
rel collect, congregate, gather; ask, bid, invite, request; meet, sit
con adjourn, close, dissolve, prorogue, recess, suspend; disperse, scatter

convoluted *adj* *syn* see WINDING

---

syn synonym(s)   *rel* related word(s)
ant antonym(s)   *con* contrasted word(s)
idiom idiomatic equivalent(s)
‖ use limited; if in doubt, see a dictionary

convoy *vb syn* see ACCOMPANY
  rel defend, guard, protect, safeguard, shield

convulse *vb syn* see SHAKE 4

convulsion *n syn* see COMMOTION 1
  rel cataclysm, disaster; quaking, rocking, shaking, tottering, trembling

cook *vb* 1 to make ready or fit for eating by the use of heat <liked everything well=cooked >
  syn do
  2 *syn* see BURN 3

cook (up) *vb syn* see CONTRIVE 2

cookshop *n syn* see EATING HOUSE

cool *adj* 1 *syn* see COLD 1
  ant warm
  2 freed or giving the impression of freedom from all agitation or excitement <they looked *cool* and very formidable>
  syn collected, composed, disimpassioned, imperturbable, nonchalant, unflappable, unruffled; compare HAPPY-GO-LUCKY
  rel calm, placid, serene, tranquil; aloof, detached, indifferent; impassive, phlegmatic, stolid; assured, confident, self-possessed
  con fervent, fervid, impassioned, passionate, perfervid; discomposed, disturbed, flurried, flustered, perturbed, upset
  ant ardent; agitated
  3 *syn* see UNSOCIABLE
  ‖4 *syn* see MARVELOUS 2

cool *vb* 1 *syn* see COMPOSE 4
  2 *syn* see MURDER 1

cooler *n syn* see JAIL

coolness *n syn* see EQUANIMITY

‖**coon** *vb syn* see STEAL 1

coon's age *n syn* see AGE 2

‖**coony** *adj syn* see CLEVER 4

coop *n syn* see JAIL

coop *vb syn* see ENCLOSE 1
  rel bar, block, hinder, impede, obstruct

cooperate *vb syn* see UNITE 2
  rel agree, coincide
  con annul, negate, nullify; negative, neutralize
  ant counteract

cooperative *adj* involving joint action in producing a result <the need of *cooperative* efforts to effect lasting social change>
  syn coacting, coactive, coefficient, conjoint, synergetic, synergic
  rel collaborative, concerted; noncompetitive, uncompetitive
  con competitive, emulous, rivaling, vying; antagonistic, conflicting, oppugnant
  ant counteractive

coordinate *vb syn* see HARMONIZE 3

coordinate *n* 1 *syn* see OPPOSITE NUMBER
  2 *syn* see MATE 5

‖**cop** *vb syn* see STEAL 1

cop *n syn* see POLICEMAN

copartner *n syn* see PARTNER

copious *adj syn* see PLENTIFUL
  rel exuberant, lush, luxuriant
  con exiguous, scant, scanty, scrimpy, spare, sparse; slender, slight, slim, tenuous, thin
  ant meager

‖**cop out** *vb syn* see DIE 1

‖**copper** *n syn* see POLICEMAN

copy *n* 1 *syn* see IMITATION

2 *syn* see REPRODUCTION
  rel counterpart, parallel; impress, impression, imprint, print; effigy, image, likeness
  ant original

copy *vb* to make a copy of <had her more valuable jewelry *copied* >
  syn duplicate, imitate, reduplicate, replicate, reproduce
  rel ditto, repeat; counterfeit, fake, sham, simulate; ape, burlesque, mock, parody, take off, travesty
  ant originate

coquet *vb syn* see TRIFLE 1

coquette *n syn* see FLIRT

coquettish *adj syn* see COY 2

cordial *adj syn* see GRACIOUS 1
  rel responsive, sympathetic, tender, warm, warmhearted; heartfelt, hearty, sincere, wholehearted
  con cold, cool, frigid, frosty; aloof, detached, disinterested, indifferent; reserved, silent, taciturn

cordiality *n syn* see AMENITY 1
  rel responsiveness, sympathy, understanding, warmth; mutuality, reciprocity; approbation, approval, favor
  con cross-purposes, difference, disagreement, misunderstanding, odds, variance; disapprobation, disapproval, disfavor

core *n* 1 *syn* see CENTER 1
  2 *syn* see BODY 3
  3 *syn* see SUBSTANCE 2
  rel consequence, import, importance, significance
  4 *syn* see CENTER 3
  rel base, basis, foundation; beginning, commencement, origin, start

‖**corker** *n syn* ‖DILLY, crackerjack, ‖daisy, dandy, humdinger, jim-dandy, knockout, ‖lalapalooza, ‖lulu, nifty

corkscrew *vb syn* see WIND 2

corner *n* 1 *syn* see PREDICAMENT
  2 *syn* see MONOPOLY

corner *vb* to get into one's control or a position from which escape is difficult <*cornered* him at a party and tried to borrow a hundred dollars>
  syn bottle (up), collar, tree
  rel bother, disturb, put out, trouble; capture, catch, nab, seize, trap
  idiom chase up a tree, drive (or run) into a corner, get (or have) on the ropes

cornerwise *adv syn* see DIAGONALLY

corny *adj syn* see TRITE

corollary *n syn* see EFFECT 1

coronal *n syn* see WREATH

coronet *n syn* see WREATH

corporal *adj syn* see BODILY

corporation *n syn* see POTBELLY

corporeal *adj* 1 *syn* see BODILY
  2 *syn* see MATERIAL 1

corps *n syn* see COMPANY 4

corpse *n* a dead body especially of a human being <concealed the *corpse* under some rubbish>
  syn body, cadaver, carcass, ‖cold meat, ‖deader, mort, remains, stiff
  rel carrion; bones

corpselike *adj* 1 *syn* see DEATHLY 1
  2 *syn* see GHASTLY 2

corpsy *adj syn* see DEATHLY 1

corpulence *n syn* see OBESITY

corpulent *adj syn* see FAT 2

corpus *n* 1 *syn* see BODY 3

2 *syn* see OEUVRE

corrade *vb syn* see ABRADE 1

corral *vb syn* see ENCLOSE 1

correct *vb* 1 to set right something that is wrong < *correct* a misstatement >

syn amend, emend, mend, rectify, right

rel ameliorate, better, improve; redress, remedy, revise; make over, reform; adjust, fix, regulate

con damage, harm, hurt, impair, injure, mar, spoil

2 *syn* see PUNISH 1

con baby, coddle, cosset, humor, indulge, pamper, spoil

correct *adj* 1 *syn* see DECOROUS 1

rel careful, meticulous, punctilious, scrupulous

2 conforming to or agreeing with fact < the *correct* solution to the problem >

syn accurate, exact, nice, precise, proper, right, rigorous

rel faithful, true, undistorted, veracious, veridical; faultless, flawless, impeccable, perfect

con fallacious, false, wrong; defective, faulty, flawed, imperfect

ant incorrect

correction *n syn* see PUNISHMENT

correctitude *n syn* see ORDER 7

corrective *n syn* see REMEDY 2

correctly *adv syn* see WELL 1

correctness *n* 1 *syn* see ORDER 7

2 *syn* see PRECISION

correlate *n* 1 *syn* see COUNTERPART 1

2 *syn* see PARALLEL

correspond *vb syn* see AGREE 4

correspond (to) *vb syn* see AMOUNT 2

correspondence *n syn* see CONSISTENCY

ant divergence

correspondent *n syn* see PARALLEL

corresponding *adj syn* see LIKE

correspondingly *adv syn* see ALSO 1

corridor *n syn* see PASSAGE 4

corrival *n syn* see RIVAL

corroborate *vb syn* see CONFIRM 2

con invalidate, negate, nullify

ant contradict

corroborative *adj* serving or tending to corroborate < *corroborative* evidence >

syn adminicular, collateral, confirmational, confirmatory, corroboratory, verificatory

rel ancillary, auxiliary, supplementary, supportive; assisting, helping

con confutative, refutative, refutatory; contradictory, negatory

corroboratory *adj syn* see CORROBORATIVE

corrode *vb syn* see EAT 3

corrosive *adj syn* see SARCASTIC

corrosiveness *n syn* see SARCASM

corrugation *n syn* see WRINKLE

corrupt *vb* 1 *syn* see DEBASE 1

rel abase, degrade; ruin, wreck

con amend, correct, reform

2 *syn* see DECAY

rel befoul, defile, foul; smirch, tarnish

corrupt *adj* 1 *syn* see VICIOUS 2

rel crooked, devious, oblique; baneful, deleterious, detrimental, noxious, pernicious; abased, degraded, low

2 seeking sordid advantage with little regard to moral or legal bars < a *corrupt* politician >

syn mercenary, praetorian, unethical, unprincipled, unscrupulous, venal; *compare* CROOKED 2, VENAL 1

rel undependable, unreliable, untrustworthy; faithless, inconstant, unfaithful; double-dealing, perfidious, treacherous, two-faced; bribable, corruptible; blackguardly, knavish, reprobate

con ethical, principled, scrupulous, upright; dependable, reliable, trustworthy, trusty

3 *syn* see CROOKED 2

corrupted *adj syn* see DEBASED

corruptible *adj syn* see VENAL 1

corruption *n* 1 *syn* see VICE 1

2 *syn* see BARBARISM

corsair *n syn* see PIRATE

coruscate *vb syn* see FLASH 1

coruscation *n syn* see FLASH 1

corybantic *adj syn* see FURIOUS 2

coryphée *n syn* see DANCER

cosmic *adj syn* see UNIVERSAL 2

cosmopolitan *adj* 1 exhibiting or characterized by a sophistication and savoir faire arising from cultured urban life and wide travel < had a thoroughly *cosmopolitan* outlook on life >

syn metropolitan, urbane; *compare* SOPHISTICATED 2

rel civilized, polished, smooth; sophisticated, worldly-wise; cultivated, cultured

con boorish, cloddish, rude, rustic; insular, parochial, provincial

2 *syn* see UNIVERSAL 2

cosmos (*or* **kosmos**) *n syn* see UNIVERSE

cosset *vb* 1 *syn* see CARESS

2 *syn* see BABY

cost *n* 1 *syn* see PRICE 1

2 *syn* see EXPENSE 1

3 *syn* see EXPENSE 2

costive *adj* 1 *syn* see CONSTIPATED

2 *syn* see STINGY

costless *adj syn* see FREE 5

costly *adj* 1 commanding or being a large price < the scarcer an item becomes the more *costly* it is >

syn dear, expensive, high; *compare* PRECIOUS 1

rel excessive, exorbitant, extravagant, inordinate, steep, stiff; fancy, premium, top

con inexpensive, low, low-priced, reasonable

ant cheap

2 *syn* see PRECIOUS 1

costume *n* style of clothing and adornment < her *costume* was always suitable to the occasion >

syn dress, getup, guise, outfit, rig, setout, turnout

rel fashion, mode, style

cot *n syn* see HUT

‖**cotch** *vb* 1 *syn* see SEIZE 2

2 *syn* see CATCH 1

3 *syn* see CATCH 7

coterie *n syn* see CLIQUE

cottage *n syn* see HUT

---

syn synonym(s)   *rel* related word(s)

ant antonym(s)   *con* contrasted word(s)

idiom idiomatic equivalent(s)

‖ use limited; if in doubt, see a dictionary

cotton vb 1 syn see BABY
  2 syn see FAWN
cotton (to or on to) vb syn see APPREHEND 1
cottony adj syn see SOFT 3
couch vb 1 syn see WORD
  2 syn see LOWER 3
couch n syn see LAIR 1
couleur de rose adj syn see HOPEFUL 2
couloir n syn see PASSAGE 4
counsel n syn see ADVICE 1
counsel vb to give advice to or about
  < counseled him to wait for a more propitious occasion >
  syn advise, recommend
  rel admonish, reprehend, warn; direct, order, prescribe; charge, enjoin, prompt, urge; advocate, suggest
count vb 1 to ascertain the total of units in a collection by noting one after another
  < counted the sheep in the pasture >
  syn enumerate, number, numerate, tale, tally, tell
  rel add, cast, figure, foot, sum, tot, total; calculate, compute, estimate, reckon; tell off
  2 syn see MATTER
  3 syn see WEIGH 3
count (on) vb syn see RELY (on or upon)
count (on or upon) vb syn see EXPECT 1
countenance n 1 syn see LOOK 2
  idiom (the) cut of one's jib
  2 syn see FACE 1
countenance vb 1 syn see ENCOURAGE 2
  rel applaud, commend; back, champion, support, uphold
  con deride, ridicule; criticize, reprehend, reprobate; reproach, reprove
  2 syn see APPROVE 1
counter vb syn see OPPOSE 1
counter n syn see OPPOSITE
counter adj syn see OPPOSITE
  rel hostile, inimical; adverse, antagonistic, anti, oppugnant; hindering, impeding, obstructive
counteract vb syn see NEUTRALIZE
  rel correct, fix, rectify, right
  con cooperate, coordinate, synergize; back, reinforce, support
counteractant n syn see REMEDY 2
counteractive n syn see REMEDY 2
counteragent n syn see REMEDY 2
counterbalance vb syn see COMPENSATE 1
  rel amend, correct, rectify
  con overbalance, unbalance
counterblow n syn see RETALIATION
countercheck vb syn see NEUTRALIZE
counterfactual adj syn see FALSE 1
counterfeit vb syn see ASSUME 4
  rel ape, copy, imitate, mimic
counterfeit adj being an imitation intended to mislead or deceive < counterfeit money > < counterfeit sympathy >
  syn bogus, brummagem, fake, false, phony, pinchbeck, pseudo, sham, snide, spurious; compare SPURIOUS 3
  rel feigned, pretended, simulated; deceptive, delusive, delusory, misleading; fraudulent
  con authentic, veritable; actual, real, true; unquestionable, valid

  ant bona fide, genuine
counterfeit n syn see IMPOSTURE
  rel copy, facsimile, reproduction; dummy, simulacrum
countermeasure n syn see REMEDY 2
counterpane n syn see BEDSPREAD
counterpart n 1 something that completes or complements < export controls as a counterpart of domestic distribution controls >
  syn complement, correlate, pendant; compare PARALLEL
  rel analogue, correlate, correspondent; equal, equivalent, like, match
  con counterpoint, opposite
  2 syn see PARALLEL
  3 syn see EQUAL
  4 syn see OPPOSITE NUMBER
counterpoise n syn see BALANCE 1
counterpoise vb syn see COMPENSATE 1
  rel ballast, poise, stabilize, steady, trim
  con capsize, overturn, upset
counterpole n syn see OPPOSITE
countersign n syn see PASSWORD 1
counterstep n syn see REMEDY 2
countertype n syn see PARALLEL
countervail vb syn see COMPENSATE 1
  rel amend, correct, rectify; foil, frustrate, thwart; overcome, surmount
countless adj syn see INNUMERABLE
count out vb syn see EXCLUDE
countrified adj syn see RURAL
country n the nation-state to which one belongs or from which one originated
  < returned to his own country after years of exile >
  syn fatherland, home, homeland, land, mother country, motherland, soil
country adj syn see RURAL
country jake n syn see RUSTIC
countryman n syn see RUSTIC
couple vb 1 syn see JOIN 1
  2 syn see HITCH 2
  rel hook up, ||inspan
couple n two individuals of the same or a similar kind that occur, function, or are considered together < a couple of ideas for improving the book > < the happiest couple I know >
  syn brace, doublet, duo, dyad, pair, twosome
  rel span, team, yoke
coupling n syn see JOINT 1
courage n a quality of mind or temperament that enables one to stand fast in the face of opposition, hardship, or danger < had the kind of courage that could appreciate a danger yet steadfastly face it >
  syn cojones, dauntlessness, guts, heart, mettle, ||moxie, pluck, resolution, spirit, spunk; compare FORTITUDE
  rel audacity, boldness, bravery, doughtiness, fearlessness, intrepidity; gallantry, heroism, valor; backbone, fortitude, grit, sand; assurance, determination, firmness, persistence, tenacity
  con chickenheartedness, faintheartedness, unmanliness, yellowness; baseness, cravenness, poltroonery, pusillanimity; timidity, timorousness
  ant cowardice
courageous adj syn see BRAVE 1

rel fiery, high-spirited; strong, tenacious

con afraid, apprehensive, fearful

ant pusillanimous

courier *n syn* see MESSENGER

course *n* 1 *syn* see WAY 2

rel circuit, orbit, range, scope

2 *syn* see CHANNEL 2

3 way of acting or proceeding < hard to decide on the best *course* to follow >

syn line, policy, polity, procedure, program

rel design, pattern, plan, platform, scheme; manner, system, way

idiom course of action

4 *syn* see PROGRESS 2

5 *syn* see SUCCESSION 2

course *vb* to proceed with great celerity (as in pursuing or competing) < the fox *coursed* after the hare >

syn career, chase, race, rush, speed, tear; compare RUSH 1

rel hasten, hurry, bustle; dart, dash, scamper, scoot, scurry; run, sprint

idiom step on the gas, stir one's stumps

courser *n* a strong vigorous horse formerly used in mounted combat < heroes mounted on great fiery *coursers* >

syn charger, war-horse

court *n* 1 an open space wholly or partly enclosed (as by buildings or walls) < the window looked on the *court* >

syn ||close, courtyard, curtilage, enclosure, quad, quadrangle, yard

2 a place or the persons assembled for the administration of justice < the *court* was called to order >

syn bar, lawcourt, tribunal

3 *syn* see JUDGE 2

court *vb syn* see ADDRESS 8

rel allure, attract, captivate, charm

courteous *adj syn* see CIVIL 2

rel attentive, considerate, thoughtful

con blunt, brusque, curt, gruff; insolent, overbearing, supercilious

ant discourteous

courtesan *n syn* see HARLOT 1

courtesy *n* 1 courteous behavior or a courteous act < noted for her *courtesy* and graciousness > < such little *courtesies* take little time but often brighten lonely lives >

syn amenity, attention, gallantry

rel affability, cordiality, geniality, graciousness; comity, complaisance; chivalry, civility, courteousness, courtliness; attentiveness, considerateness, consideration, thoughtfulness

con boorishness, churlishness; impoliteness, incivility, rudeness, ungraciousness

ant discourtesy

2 *syn* see FAVOR 4

courtly *adj* marked by elaborate and often ceremonious courtesy < this was indeed a *courtly* gentleman of the old school >

syn gallant, gracious, preux, stately; compare CIVIL 2

rel august, dignified, imposing, lofty; prim, starchy, stiff, stilted, studied; ceremonious, conventional, formal; civilized

con discourteous, ill-mannered, impolite, rude, uncivil, ungracious; boorish, coarse, gross, loutish, uncouth, vulgar

ant churlish

courtyard *n syn* see COURT 1

cousinage *n syn* see KIN 2

cousinhood *n syn* see KIN 2

cove *n syn* see INLET

covenant *n syn* see CONTRACT

covenant *vb syn* see VOW

rel agree, concur

cover *vb* 1 *syn* see DEFEND 1

2 *syn* see HIDE

3 to spread over or put something over < a smile *covered* her face > < *cover* the garden with manure >

syn blanket, cap, crown, overcast, overlay, overspread

rel conceal, hide, screen; defend, protect, shield; enclose, enfold, envelop, shroud, wrap; overspread, superimpose, superpose

con display, exhibit, expose

ant bare, uncover

4 *syn* see TRAVEL 2

5 *syn* see SET 11

cover *n* 1 *syn* see SHELTER 1

rel concealment, hiding, screen; safety, security

ant exposure

2 *syn* see MASK 2

coverlet *n syn* see BEDSPREAD

||**coverlid** *n syn* see BEDSPREAD

covert *adj* 1 *syn* see SECRET 1

rel camouflaged, cloaked, disguised, dissembled, masked

con candid, frank, open

ant overt

2 *syn* see ULTERIOR

con direct, forthright; honest, square, straight

covert *n syn* see SHELTER 1

covertly *adv syn* see SECRETLY

covet *vb syn* see DESIRE 1

con abjure, forswear

ant renounce

covetous *adj* having or marked by an urgent and often unscrupulous desire for possessions < the *covetous* eye of an avid collector >

syn acquisitive, desirous, grabby, grasping, greedy, itchy, prehensile

rel esurient, gluttonous, rapacious, ravenous, voracious; hoggish, lickerish, piggish, swinish; avid, eager, keen; envious, jealous; grudging, selfish

con generous, liberal, munificent; ungrudging, unselfish; abstemious, abstinent, ascetic, austere; moderate, restrained, temperate

covey *n syn* see GROUP 1

covin *n syn* see PLOT 2

cow *vb syn* see INTIMIDATE

rel appall, daunt, dismay; abash, discomfit, disconcert, embarrass, faze, rattle

con cower, cringe, fawn, toady, truckle

coward *n* one who shows or yields to ignoble fear < a treacherous *coward* who betrayed his friends to save his own skin >

syn chicken, craven, dastard, funk, funker, poltroon, quitter, yellowbelly

rel baby, fraidycat, invertebrate, jellyfish, milksop, scaredy-cat; caitiff, recreant

con gallant, hero, palladin, stalwart; ideal, model, pattern, standard

---

coward *adj syn* see COWARDLY

cowardly *adj* marked by or arising from a base lack of courage <a *cowardly* desertion>
syn ||chicken, coward, cowhearted, craven, gutless, lily-livered, milk-livered, poltroon, poltroonish, poor-spirited, pusillanimous, spunkless, unmanly, white-livered, yellow
rel afraid, chickenhearted, fainthearted, fearful, timid, timorous; funky, panicky; caitiff, dastardly, recreant, vile, worthless
con courageous, fearless, intrepid, valiant; daring, reckless, temerarious
ant brave

cower *vb syn* see FAWN
rel blench, flinch, quail, recoil, shrink, wince
con browbeat, bulldoze, bully, cow, intimidate; bristle, strut, swagger

cowering *adj syn* see FAWNING

cowhearted *adj syn* see COWARDLY

coxcomb *n syn* see FOP

coy *adj* 1 *syn* see SHY 1
rel decent, decorous, nice, proper, seemly
con brash, brazen, impudent
2 marked by a light playful artlessness <glanced up with a *coy* twinkle in her eye>
syn arch, coquettish, roguish
rel capricious, kittenish, lively, mischievous, playful, skittish
con serious, sober, thoughtful

cozen *vb* 1 *syn* see CHEAT
2 *syn* see DECEIVE

cozy *adj* 1 *syn* see COMFORTABLE 2
rel safe, secure
2 *syn* see INTIMATE 4

crab *vb syn* see GRIPE
idiom fret and fume

crab *n syn* see GROUCH

crabbed *adj syn* see SULLEN
rel blunt, brusque, crusty, gruff; choleric, cranky, splenetic, testy; huffy, irascible, irritable, snappish
con amiable, complaisant, good-natured, obliging; benign, benignant, kind, kindly; agreeable, pleasing; affable, genial, gracious

crabber *n syn* see GROUCH

crabby *adj syn* see SULLEN

crabwise *adv syn* see SIDEWAYS 1

crack *vb syn* see DECODE
rel puzzle out

crack *n* 1 *syn* see BANG 2
rel splintering, splitting; percussion
2 *syn* see JOKE 1
rel dig, fling, potshot
idiom flash of wit
3 a usually narrow opening, break, or discontinuity made by splitting and rupture <a *crack* in the ice>
syn chink, cleft, fissure, rift, rima, rimation, rime, split
rel rent; discontinuity, interstice, interval; cranny, niche; crevasse, crevice
4 *syn* see INSTANT 1
idiom flash of lightning
5 *syn* see BLOW 1
6 *syn* see FLING 1

crack *adj syn* see PROFICIENT
rel excellent, superior

crackbrain *n syn* see CRACKPOT
idiom cracked wit

crackbrained *adj syn* see INSANE 1

crackdown *n syn* see REPRESSION 2
rel quashing
idiom lowering the boom

cracked *adj syn* see INSANE 1
idiom ||off in the upper story

crackerjack *n syn* ||DILLY, ||corker, ||daisy, dandy, humdinger, jim-dandy, knockout, ||lalapalooza, ||lulu, nifty

crackerjack *adj syn* see PROFICIENT

||**crackers** *adj syn* see INSANE 1

cracking *adj syn* see MONSTROUS 1

crackpot *n* one given to extremely eccentric or lunatic ideas or actions <a *crackpot* who wrote threatening letters to public figures>
syn crackbrain, crank, cuckoo, ||ding-a=ling, harebrain, kook, lunatic, nut, screwball
rel case, character, ||dingbat, eccentric, oddball, oddity, ||wack; loon, loony, madman, maniac

crack-up *n* 1 *syn* see NERVOUS BREAKDOWN
2 *syn* see CRASH 3
3 *syn* see COLLAPSE 2
rel decline, deterioration

||**cracky** *adj syn* see INSANE 1

cradlesong *n syn* see LULLABY

craft *n* 1 *syn* see ART 1
2 *syn* see TRADE 1
rel job
3 *syn* see CUNNING 2

craftiness *n syn* see CUNNING 2

crafty *adj syn* see SLY 2
rel adroit, clever, tidy; acute, keen, sharp; deceitful, fawning, ||sleekit, ||sleeky

cragged *adj syn* see ROUGH 1

craggy *adj syn* see ROUGH 1

cram *vb* 1 to fill (a limited space) forcibly with more than is practicable or fitting <*crammed* the suitcase chock-full and had to sit on it to close it>
syn jam, jam-pack, ||pang, ram, stuff, tamp; *compare* LOAD 3, PRESS 7
rel pack, stive; fill, heap; chock, choke; press, shove, thrust; drive, force; squeeze, wedge
2 *syn* see PRESS 7
3 *syn* see GULP
rel overeat
idiom pack it in
4 to study intensively or under pressure <had to *cram* all night before the exam>
syn bone (up), ||mug (up)
rel study; review
idiom burn the midnight oil

cram-full *adj syn* see FULL 1

crammed *adj syn* see FULL 1
idiom crammed full, crammed to the bursting point, fit (or ready) to burst
ant emptied

cramp *n* 1 *syn* see RESTRICTION 1
rel shackle
2 *syn* see RESTRICTION 2
rel constipation, stultification

cramp *adj syn* see CRAMPED

cramped *adj* having insufficient size or capacity <a *cramped* cubbyhole of an office>
syn confined, cramp, incommodious, squeezy, ||tucked up
rel close, narrow, tight, two-by-four; little, minute, small, tiny

con commodious, unconfined
ant spacious

crank *n* 1 *syn* see CAPRICE
2 *syn* see CRACKPOT
rel freak
3 *syn* see GROUCH

cranky *adj* 1 *syn* see INSANE 1
2 *syn* see CANTANKEROUS
rel contrary, difficult, froward, perverse
3 *syn* see IRASCIBLE
rel bad-humored, ill-humored; disagreeable; ugly
idiom out of sorts

cranny *n* *syn* see NOOK

‖**crap** *n* *syn* see NONSENSE 2

‖**crap out** *vb* *syn* see FAINT

‖**crappy** *adj* *syn* see BAD 1

crash *vb* *syn* see FAIL 5
ant skyrocket

crash *n* 1 *syn* see BANG 2
2 *syn* see IMPACT
3 a wrecking or smashing especially of a vehicle < an air *crash* >
syn crack-up, pileup, ‖prang, smash, smashup, ‖stramash, wreck
rel accident; collision
4 *syn* see COLLAPSE 1

crashing *adj* *syn* see UTTER

crass *adj* *syn* see COARSE 3
rel churlish, loutish
ant refined

crate *n* *syn* see JALOPY

crave *vb* 1 *syn* see BEG
2 *syn* see DESIRE 1
con contemn, despise, disdain, scorn
ant spurn
3 *syn* see LONG
idiom have a craving for
4 *syn* see DEMAND 2

craven *adj* *syn* see COWARDLY

craven *n* *syn* see COWARD

craving *n* *syn* see DESIRE 1

crawfish (out) *vb* *syn* see BACK DOWN

crawl *vb* 1 *syn* see CREEP 1
rel grovel; worm
2 *syn* see TEEM
‖3 *syn* see LAMBASTE 3

craze *vb* *syn* see MADDEN 1

craze *n* *syn* see FASHION 3
rel enthusiasm, fever

crazed *adj* *syn* see INSANE 1

craziness *n* *syn* see FOOLISHNESS

crazy *adj* 1 *syn* see INSANE 1
rel doting, gaga, moonstruck; beheaded, silly; erratic, possessed
idiom as crazy as a loon, having a screw loose, having bats in one's belfry, not having all one's marbles (*or* buttons)
ant sane
2 *syn* see FOOLISH 2
rel goofy, senseless
idiom beyond the realm of reason, out of all reason
con practical, reasonable, reasoned, sensible
ant sane

‖**crazy** *adv* *syn* see VERY 1

crazy house *n* *syn* see ASYLUM 3

---

syn synonym(s)   *rel* related word(s)
ant antonym(s)   *con* contrasted word(s)
idiom idiomatic equivalent(s)
‖ use limited; if in doubt, see a dictionary

cream *n* 1 *syn* see OINTMENT
2 *syn* see BEST
idiom (the) top cream

‖**cream** *vb* *syn* see WHIP 2

crease *n* *syn* see WRINKLE

create *vb* 1 *syn* see GENERATE 1
idiom call into being
2 *syn* see FOUND 2
3 *syn* see COMPOSE 2
rel conceive, formulate; imagine

creation *n* *syn* see UNIVERSE

creative *adj* *syn* see INVENTIVE
rel causal, institutive, occasional; Promethean
ant uncreative

creator *n* *syn* see FATHER 2
rel brain(s), brainpower, mastermind

creature *n* 1 *syn* see BEAST
2 *syn* see HUMAN
3 *syn* see SYCOPHANT

credence *n* *syn* see BELIEF 1
rel acceptance, accepting, admission, admitting; confidence, reliance, trust
con skepticism; distrust, mistrust; disbelief, incredulity, unbelief

credentials *n pl* something presented or held by one as proof that he is what or who he claims to be < her academic *credentials* were excellent >
syn character, recommendation, reference, testimonial
rel document(s), documentation, paper(s), voucher; accreditation, certification, endorsement, sanction

credible *adj* 1 *syn* see BELIEVABLE
rel satisfying, satisfactory; solid, sound, straight, valid
idiom to be believed
con unsatisfactory; preposterous, ridiculous
ant incredible
2 *syn* see AUTHENTIC 1
rel likely, probable; rational, reasonable; conclusive, determinative
ant incredible

credit *n* 1 *syn* see BELIEF 1
rel confidence, reliance, trust
2 *syn* see INFLUENCE 1
rel fame, renown, reputation, repute
con disrepute, ignominy, obloquy, opprobrium
ant discredit
3 one that enhances another < he is a *credit* to his family >
syn asset
rel honor
4 favorable notice or attention resulting from an action or achievement < took all the *credit* for the idea >
syn acknowledgment, recognition
rel attention, notice; distinction, fame, honor; glory, kudos

credit *vb* 1 *syn* see FEEL 3
con disbelieve, pooh-pooh
ant discredit
2 *syn* see ASCRIBE

creditable *adj* 1 *syn* see BELIEVABLE
ant discreditable
2 *syn* see RESPECTABLE 1
rel satisfactory; suitable
ant discreditable

credo *n* *syn* see IDEOLOGY

credulous *adj* ready or inclined to believe especially on slight or insufficient evidence < deceiving the *credulous* young girls >
syn unsuspecting, unsuspicious, unwary
rel believing; accepting, unquestioning; trustful, trusting; green, inexperienced; naive, simple, unsophisticated; dupable, gullible
con mistrustful, suspecting, suspicious; careful, wary; doubtful, doubting, questioning
ant incredulous, skeptical

creed *n* 1 *syn* see RELIGION 1
2 *syn* see RELIGION 2
3 *syn* see IDEOLOGY

creek *n* ‖1 *syn* see INLET
rel ria
2 a natural stream of water normally smaller than and often tributary to a river < went wading in the *creek* >
syn ‖branch, brook, ‖burn, ‖crick, gill, race, ‖rindle, ‖rithe, rivulet, ‖run, runnel, stream
rel ‖beck, brooklet, ‖rigolet, rill, rillet, runlet, streamlet; freshet; ditch, watercourse; wadi

creep *vb* 1 to move along a surface in a prone or crouching position < a cat *creeping* through the grass >
syn crawl, slide, snake
rel glide, slither; sneak, steal, tiptoe; edge, inch; sniggle, wriggle
2 *syn* see STEAL 3
3 *syn* see SNEAK

crème de la crème *n* *syn* see ARISTOCRACY

crepehanger *n* *syn* see PESSIMIST

crescendo *n* *syn* see APEX 2

crest *n* 1 *syn* see TOP 1
rel cap
2 *syn* see RIDGE 1
3 *syn* see APEX 2

crest *vb* *syn* see SURMOUNT 3

crestfallen *adj* *syn* see DOWNCAST
idiom ‖in a funk
ant elated

cretin *n* *syn* see FOOL 4
rel zombie

crew *n* *syn* see GROUP 1
rel aggregation, collection, congregation; gang, retinue, set

crib *n* 1 *syn* see BROTHEL
2 *syn* see PONY
rel plagiarism

‖**crib** *vb* *syn* see GRIPE

‖**crick** *n* *syn* see CREEK 2

crime *n* 1 a serious breach of the public law < armed robbery is a *crime* >
syn misdeed, offense
rel criminality, illegality, lawlessness; delict, delictum; breach, break, infringement, transgression, violation; wrong, wrongdoing; felony
2 *syn* see EVIL 3

crimeless *adj* *syn* see INNOCENT 2

criminal *adj* *syn* see UNLAWFUL

criminal *n* one who has committed a usually serious offense < car thieves and other *criminals* >
syn felon, lawbreaker, malefactor, offender
rel scofflaw; transgressor, trespasser, wrongdoer; crook, ‖twicer; gangster, hood,

mobster, racketeer, thug; fugitive, outlaw; convict, jailbird

criminate *vb* *syn* see ACCUSE
ant exonerate

crimp *vb* 1 *syn* see CRUMPLE 1
2 *syn* see RESTRAIN 1

crimp *n* *syn* see OBSTACLE

crimple *vb* *syn* see CRUMPLE 1

crimson *vb* *syn* see BLUSH
ant blanch

cringe *vb* *syn* see FAWN
rel blench, flinch, quail, recoil, wince; ‖croodle, crouch, shrink
idiom bow and scrape, eat dirt

cringing *adj* *syn* see FAWNING
rel obeisant, prostrate
idiom bowing and scraping, eating dirt, eating humble pie, on one's hands and knees

crinkle *vb* *syn* see CRUMPLE 1

crinkle *n* *syn* see WRINKLE
rel crimp

cripple *vb* 1 *syn* see MAIM
rel lame
2 *syn* see PARALYZE 1
3 *syn* see WEAKEN 1

crisis *n* *syn* see JUNCTURE 2

crisp *adj* 1 *syn* see SHORT 6
con flabby, flaccid, limp
2 *syn* see INCISIVE
rel piquing, provoking, stimulating

crisscross *vb* *syn* see INTERSECT

criterion *n* *syn* see STANDARD 3
rel adjudgment, judgment

critic *n* one given to harsh or captious judgment < chronic *critics* of the administration >
syn aristarch, carper, caviler, criticizer, faultfinder, knocker, momus, smellfungus, Zoilus
rel Monday morning quarterback; nitpicker, quibbler; belittler, disparager; complainer; censurer; muckraker, mudslinger
con backer, supporter; partisan; advocate, champion, protagonist

critic *adj* *syn* see CRITICAL 1

critical *adj* 1 exhibiting the spirit of one who looks for and points out faults and defects < constant *critical* comments about her attire >
syn captious, carping, caviling, cavillous, censorious, critic, fau̱ltfinding, hypercritical, overcritical
rel discerning, discriminating, penetrating; finicky, fussy, particular; belittling, demeaning, disparaging, humbling, lowering
con cursory, shallow, superficial; encouraging, flattering, praising
ant uncritical
2 *syn* see ACUTE 6
rel conclusive, decisive, determinative; consequential, important, momentous, significant, weighty

criticism *n* a discourse that evaluates or analyzes something (as a work of art or literature) < read every *criticism* of the new play >
syn comment, critique, notice, review, reviewal
rel analysis, examination, study; commentary, observation; opinion; appraisal, assessment, estimate, rating

criticize *vb* to make adverse comments about (someone or something) openly,

often publicly, and with varying severity < *criticized* his opponent's liberal views >
syn blame, censure, condemn, cut up, denounce, denunciate, knock, pan, rap, reprehend, reprobate, skin; *compare* LAMBASTE 3, REPROVE, SCOLD 1
rel blast, castigate, fulminate (against), fustigate, roast, scathe
idiom find fault with, pull (*or* pick *or* tear) to pieces, take to task
con approve, countenance, endorse, OK (*or* okay)
ant praise

criticizer *n syn* CRITIC, aristarch, carper, caviler, faultfinder, knocker, momus, smellfungus, Zoilus

critique *n syn* see CRITICISM

||**critter** *n syn* see BEAST

croak *vb* 1 *syn* see GRUMBLE 1
rel complain, quarrel
||2 *syn* see DIE 1

||**croaker** *n syn* see PHYSICIAN

croaking *adj syn* see HOARSE 1

croaky *adj syn* see HOARSE 1

||**crocked** *adj syn* see INTOXICATED 1

crone *n syn* see HAG 2
rel frump, slattern, sloven

crony *n syn* see ASSOCIATE 3
idiom bosom buddy

||**crooch** *vb syn* see CROUCH

||**croodle** *vb syn* see SNUGGLE

crook *vb* 1 *syn* see CURVE
||2 *syn* see STEAL 1
||3 *syn* see CHEAT

crooked *adj* 1 departing from a straight line or course < a *crooked* road >
syn bending, curving, devious, twisting; *compare* CURVED, WINDING
rel oblique; circuitous, indirect, roundabout; errant, meandering, rambling, serpentine, snaky, tortuous, winding; zigzag
con direct, undeviating
ant straight
2 deviating from rectitude < *crooked* police officers on the take >
syn corrupt, dishonest, snide; *compare* CORRUPT 2, VENAL 1
rel devious, indirect, shifty, underhand; double-dealing, fraudulent; deceitful, lying, untruthful; ruthless, unscrupulous
con aboveboard, forthright, straightforward; conscientious, honorable, just, proper, righteous, scrupulous, upright
ant honest, straight

crookedly *adv syn* see AWRY 1
ant straight

crop *n syn* see HARVEST 2

crop *vb* 1 *syn* see TOP 1
rel chop, hew, slash; detach, disengage
2 *syn* see MOW
3 *syn* see CUT 6
rel snip

cropping *n syn* see HARVEST 1

cross *n* 1 *syn* see TRIAL 1
idiom a cross to bear
2 *syn* see HYBRID

cross *vb* 1 *syn* see DENY 4
2 *syn* see BETRAY 2

idiom bite the hand that feeds one, stab in the back
3 *syn* see TRAVERSE 4
4 to cause (an animal or plant) to breed with one of a different kind < *crossing* a horse with an ass results in a mule >
syn crossbreed, cross-mate, hybridize, interbreed, intercross
rel mongrelize
5 *syn* see INTERSECT
idiom lie (*or* be) athwart

cross *adj syn* see IRASCIBLE
rel captious, carping, caviling, faultfinding
idiom cross as a bear

cross *prep syn* see ACROSS

crossbred *n syn* see HYBRID

crossbreed *vb syn* see CROSS 4

crossbreed *n syn* see HYBRID

crosscut *vb syn* see INTERSECT

cross-examination *n* a thorough, typically formal questioning for full information < *cross-examination* of a hostile witness >
syn grill, grilling, interrogation, third degree
rel debriefing; questioning

cross-grained *adj* 1 *syn* see CANTANKEROUS
2 *syn* see CONTRARY 3
rel difficult

crossing *adj syn* see TRANSVERSE

cross-mate *vb syn* see CROSS 4

crosspatch *n syn* see GROUCH

crossroad *n*, *usu* crossroads *pl but sing or pl in constr syn* see JUNCTURE 2

||**cross talk** *n syn* see BANTER

crossways *adv syn* see ACROSS 1
rel transversely; askew, awry, crisscross
con lengthwise
ant longways

crosswise *adv syn* see ACROSS 1
con longways
ant lengthwise

crosswise *adj syn* see TRANSVERSE
ant lengthwise

crotchet *n syn* see CAPRICE
rel eccentricity, kink, kinkiness, quirk, twist
idiom bee in one's bonnet (*or* brain), flea in one's nose, kink in one's horn, maggot in one's brain

crotchety *adj syn* see CANTANKEROUS

crouch *vb* to stoop low with the limbs close to the body < *crouched* behind a rock and watched >
syn ||crooch, huddle, hunch, scrooch (down); *compare* SQUAT
rel bend, bow, dip, duck; hunker (down), ||quat, squat, stoop, ||swat; cower, cringe, flinch, quail, wince; grovel

crow *vb syn* see BOAST
rel cry, exult, jubilate

crowd *vb* 1 *syn* see PRESS 1
rel ram, shove
2 *syn* see PRESS 7
rel bunch, cluster

crowd *n* 1 a usually large group of people < a *crowd* gathered before the palace >
syn crush, drove, horde, multitude, press, push, squash, throng; *compare* MULTITUDE 1
rel army, host, legion; flock, gaggle, herd, swarm; mob, rabble, rout

---

syn synonym(s)   *rel* related word(s)
ant antonym(s)   *con* contrasted word(s)
idiom idiomatic equivalent(s)
|| use limited; if in doubt, see a dictionary

2 *syn* see GATHERING 2

rel huddle, parley; troop; herd; rally

3 *syn* see MULTITUDE 1

4 *syn* see SET 5

crowded *adj* 1 *syn* see FULL 1

rel overcharged, overloaded

ant uncrowded

2 *syn* see CLOSE 4

ant uncrowded

crown *n* 1 *syn* see TOP 1

2 *syn* see WREATH

rel diadem, tiara

3 *syn* see APEX 2

crown *vb* 1 *syn* see SURMOUNT 3

2 *syn* see COVER 3

3 *syn* see CLIMAX

crown (with) *vb syn* see ENDOW 1

crucial *adj syn* see ACUTE 6

rel deciding, decisive, important; necessary, vital; clamorous, compelling, crying, imperative, insistent, pressing

crucible *n syn* see TRIAL 1

crucify *vb syn* see AFFLICT

rel bedevil, bother, browbeat

idiom kill by inches, nail to the cross, put on the rack

crud *n* a deposit or incrustation of something filthy, greasy, or sticky < machinery all covered with *crud* >

syn ||cab, goo, gook, gunk; compare GOO 1

rel filth, muck, slime, sludge; debris, junk, rubbish, trash

||cruddle *vb syn* see CURDLE

crude *adj* 1 *syn* see UNREFINED 3

2 *syn* see COARSE 3

rel backward, ignorant, unenlightened; boorish, cloddish, clodhopping, ill-bred, loutish, lowbred; savage; insensible

3 *syn* see RUDE 1

rel immature, unmatured; coarse, graceless

con cultivated, cultured, refined; developed, matured, ripened

ant consummate, finished

4 *syn* see OBSCENE 2

rel blue, risqué

idiom rated X

5 rough in plan or execution < *crude* imitations, completely lacking in the original artistry >

syn coarse, inexpert, prentice; compare RUDE 1

rel amateurish, unproficient, unskilled, untaught, untrained; raw, rough, rude, unfinished, unpolished; inadequate, ineffective, inferior, poor

con finished, perfected, polished

ant expert

cruel *adj syn* see FIERCE 1

rel atrocious, heinous, monstrous, outrageous; bestial, bloodthirsty, brutish; heartless, implacable, relentless; impiteous, unpitying

con compassionate, sympathetic, tender; clement, forbearing, lenient, merciful; humane, kindly

||cruise *vb syn* see GO 1

cruise *n syn* see VOYAGE

rel sail

||cruiser *n syn* see PROSTITUTE

crumb *n syn* see PARTICLE

crumble *vb syn* see DECAY

rel mush, squash

crumbly *adj syn* see SHORT 6

rel rubbery

||crump *adj syn* see SHORT 6

crumple *vb* 1 to press or twist into folds or wrinkles < *crumple* a piece of paper >

syn crimp, crimple, crinkle, ||crunkle, rimple, ruck (up), ||ruckle, rumple, screw, scrunch, wrinkle

rel crease, fold; buckle, cockle; wad

ant smooth

2 *syn* see GIVE 12

crunch *vb syn* see CHEW 1

crunchy *adj syn* see SHORT 6

||crunkle *vb syn* see CRUMPLE 1

crusading *adj syn* see EVANGELICAL

crush *vb* 1 *syn* see PRESS 3

rel ||scruze, squeeze

2 to reduce or be reduced to a pulpy or broken mass < *crushed* rose petals >

syn becrush, bruise, mash, ||mush (up), pulp, squash

rel press, squeeze; contuse, ||batter, maim; beat, pound; dash, quash, ||quat, smash; comminute, powder, pulverize, triturate

3 *syn* see PULVERIZE 1

4 *syn* see PRESS 1

5 to bring to an end by destroying or defeating < the police *crushed* the rebellion >

syn annihilate, extinguish, put down, quash, quell, quench, squash, suppress; compare SUPPRESS 2

rel ||quelch, repress, squelch, strangle; beat down, conquer, defeat, subdue, subjugate; ruin, wreck; abolish, demolish, destroy; blot out, obliterate

idiom crush (or grind) under one's heel, ride down into the dust, roll (or trample) in the dust

6 *syn* see CONQUER 1

idiom bring one to his knees

7 *syn* see PRESS 7

crush *n* 1 *syn* see CROWD 1

2 *syn* see INFATUATION

rel calf love, puppy love

||crust *n syn* see EFFRONTERY

crust *vb syn* see CAKE 1

crusty *adj* 1 *syn* see BLUFF

rel irritable, snappish, waspish; choleric, cranky, irascible, splenetic, testy; crabbed, dour, saturnine, surly

2 *syn* see OBSCENE 2

crux *n syn* see SUBSTANCE 2

cry *vb* 1 *syn* see CALL 1

rel bleat

2 to show distress, grief, or pain by tears and usually incoherent utterances < the little girl *cried* when she fell down >

syn blub, blubber, boohoo, ||pipe, sob, wail, weep; compare BAWL 2, WHIMPER

rel sniff, snivel, whimper, whine; break down, choke up; groan, moan, sigh; bemoan, bewail, keen, lament, mourn, sorrow; bawl, howl, squall, yowl

idiom cry one's eyes (or heart) out, ||pipe one's eye, shed tears

3 *syn* see SHOUT 1

4 *syn* see PUBLICIZE

cry *n* 1 *syn* see BATTLE CRY

rel slogan

2 *syn* see REPORT 1

3 *syn* see FASHION 3

4 *syn* see CALL 1
  rel screech, squawk; squeak; caw
cry down *vb syn* see DECRY 2
  ant cry up
crying *adj* 1 *syn* see PRESSING
  rel necessary, needed
  2 *syn* see OUTRAGEOUS 2
cry off *vb syn* see BACK DOWN
cry out *vb syn* see EXCLAIM
crypt *n* a subterranean chamber < a burial
  crypt >
  syn catacomb, undercroft, vault
  rel cell; chamber, compartment, room;
  cave, cavern, grotto
cryptanalyze *vb syn* see DECODE
cryptic *adj* being intentionally obscure and
  mysterious < the senator made some *cryp-*
  tic statements about intelligence operations >
  syn dark, Delphian, enigmatic, mystifying; *compare* OBSCURE 3
  rel equivocal, murky, obscure, opaque,
  tenebrous, unclear, uninformative, vague;
  incomprehensible, inexplicable, strange,
  unfathomable; abstruse, mysterious; evasive, secretive
crystal *adj syn* see CLEAR 4
  idiom clear as crystal, crystal clear
cry up *vb syn* see PRAISE 2
  idiom beat the drum for, praise to the
  skies
  ant cry down
cubby *n syn* see CUBBYHOLE
cubbyhole *n* an excessively small room or
  place < a cramped *cubbyhole* of an office >
  syn cubby, mousehole, pigeonhole
  rel recess; niche; cubicle
  idiom hole in the wall
‖**cubes** *n pl syn* see DICE
cuckoo *n syn* see CRACKPOT
cuckoo *adj syn* see INSANE 1
cuddle *vb* 1 *syn* see CARESS
  rel embrace, enfold, hold
  2 *syn* see SNUGGLE
cudgel *n* a short solid stick used as a
  weapon or an instrument of punishment
  < beat the prisoner with a *cudgel* >
  syn bat, baton, billy, billy club, bludgeon,
  club, knobkerrie, mace, nightstick, ‖shille-
  lagh, spontoon, truncheon, war club
  rel birch, cane, ferule, hickory, paddle,
  rattan, rod, switch; blackjack; quarterstaff;
  bastinado
cue *n syn* see HINT 1
cuff *vb syn* see SLAP 1
cuff *n* a sharp blow typically delivered with
  the hand < gave him a good *cuff* in the
  face >
  syn box, buffet, ‖bust, chop, clout, haymaker, ‖paste, poke, punch, slap, smack,
  sock, spank, ‖spat, ‖swack; *compare* BLOW
  1, HIT 1
  rel bat, blow, clip, wallop
cul–de–sac *n syn* see DEAD END
  rel stalemate
cull *vb* 1 *syn* see GLEAN
  rel accumulate, amass, collect, round up

2 *syn* see CHOOSE 1
  rel discriminate
  idiom separate the sheep from the goats,
  separate the wheat from the chaff
‖**cull** *n syn* see FOOL 3
‖**cully** *n syn* see ASSOCIATE 3
culmen *n syn* see APEX 2
culminate *vb syn* see CLIMAX
culmination *n syn* see APEX 2
  rel extremity, limit, maximum
culpability *n syn* see BLAME
  con blamelessness, innocence
  ant inculpability
culpable *adj syn* see BLAMEWORTHY
  rel impeachable, indictable
  ant inculpable
cult *n* 1 *syn* see RELIGION 1
  2 *syn* see RELIGION 2
cultivable *adj syn* see ARABLE
  ant uncultivable
cultivatable *adj syn* see ARABLE
  ant uncultivatable
cultivate *vb* 1 *syn* see TILL
  rel crop, farm, manage
  2 *syn* see NURSE 2
  rel raise, rear; educate, instruct, teach,
  train; ameliorate, better, improve
  con disregard, ignore, neglect, slight
  3 *syn* see GROW 1
  rel develop, mature, ripen
cultivated *adj syn* see GENTEEL 1
  rel courteous, polite
  ant uncultivated
cultivation *n syn* see CULTURE
culture *n* enlightenment and excellence of
  taste acquired by intellectual and aesthetic
  training < a man of *culture* is known by
  his reading >
  syn breeding, cultivation, polish, refinement
  rel education, enlightenment, erudition,
  learning; gentility, manners; discrimination, taste; savoir-faire, sophistication,
  urbanity; class, elegance
  con greenness, ignorance, inexperience,
  verdancy; crudeness, vulgarity
cultured *adj syn* see GENTEEL 1
  rel educated, enlightened, erudite,
  learned, literate; civilized
  ant uncultured
culverhouse *n syn* see DOVECOTE
cumber *vb syn* see BURDEN
cumbersome *adj syn* see UNWIELDY
  rel irksome, tiresome, wearisome
cumbrance *n syn* see ENCUMBRANCE
  rel burden, charge, pressure
cumbrous *adj syn* see UNWIELDY
  rel clogging, hampering, hindering, impeding
cumshaw *n syn* see GRATUITY
cumulate *vb syn* see ACCUMULATE
  rel obtain, secure
  ant dissipate
cumulation *n syn* see ACCUMULATION
  rel stockpile; snowball
cumulative *adj* increasing or produced by
  addition of like or similar things < the
  cumulative effect of several drugs >
  syn accumulative, additive, additory,
  chain, summative
  rel accumulated, amassed; augmenting,
  increasing, multiplying; advancing, heightening, intensifying, magnifying, snowball-
  ing

---

syn synonym(s)   *rel* related word(s)
ant antonym(s)   *con* contrasted word(s)
idiom idiomatic equivalent(s)
‖ use limited; if in doubt, see a dictionary

con dispersed, dissipated, scattered

cunning *adj* 1 *syn see* CLEVER 4
rel well-devised, well-laid, well-planned; crackerjack, masterful
idiom too clever by half
2 *syn see* SLY 2
rel acute, keen, sharp; knowing, smart; wary
idiom not to be caught with chaff
con artless, naive, unsophisticated

cunning *n* 1 *syn see* ART 1
rel deftness, dexterousness; adeptness, expertness; cleverness, ingeniousness, ingenuity
2 skill in devising or using indirect or subtle methods <a woman able to maneuver people with great *cunning* >
syn art, artfulness, artifice, cageyness, canniness, craft, craftiness, foxiness, slyness, wiliness
rel savvy, sharpness, shrewdness; cleverness, ingeniousness, ingenuity; agility, facility, finesse, slickness; subtlety; insidiousness, shiftiness, trickiness
3 *syn see* DECEIT 1
idiom satanic cunning, the cunning of the serpent

cupidity *n* intense desire for possessions and wealth <the sight of so much money aroused his *cupidity* >
syn avarice, avariciousness, avidity, greed, rapacity
rel acquisitiveness, greediness, possessiveness, rapaciousness; eagerness, voracity; craving, desire; lust; infatuation, passion

cur *n* 1 *syn see* SNOT 1
rel riffraff
2 *syn see* CAD

curative *adj* restoring or tending to restore to a state of normalcy or health <a *curative* drug>
syn curing, healing, remedial, remedying, restorative, sanative, sanatory, vulnerary, wholesome
rel medicable, medicative, medicinal; corrective, therapeutic, invigorating, tonic; beneficial, helpful, salutary, wholesome

curb *vb* 1 *syn see* HAMPER
2 *syn see* DENY 3
rel repress, suppress
ant goad
3 *syn see* RESTRAIN 1
rel fetter, hamper, hog-tie, manacle, shackle
idiom hold in leash, keep a tight rein on
con unbridle, unleash
ant spur

curd *vb syn see* CURDLE

curdle *vb* to cause to become coagulated or thickened and often sour <hot weather will *curdle* milk>
syn ‖clabber, ‖cruddle, curd, ‖lopper, turn
rel clot, coagulate, condense, thicken; ferment; go off, sour, spoil

cure *n* 1 *syn see* REMEDY 1
2 *syn see* REMEDY 2

cure *vb* to rectify an unhealthy or undesirable condition <aspirin *cured* his headache>
syn heal, remedy
rel doctor, medicate; restore; ameliorate, better, improve

cure-all *n syn see* PANACEA

cureless *adj syn see* HOPELESS 2

curing *adj syn see* CURATIVE

curio *n syn see* KNICKKNACK

curiosity *n* 1 *syn see* INTEREST 3
rel inquisitiveness, questioning
ant disinterest
2 something that arouses interest especially because of uncommon or exotic characteristics <an architectural *curiosity* >
syn conversation piece, oddity
rel exception, nonesuch, rarity; marvel, prodigy, wonder; anomaly; freak, monstrosity
idiom something to write home about

curious *adj* 1 *syn see* INQUISITIVE 1
rel searching; analytical; prurient
ant incurious
2 interested in what is not one's personal or proper concern <a *curious* old woman prying into her neighbors' affairs>
syn inquisitive, inquisitorial, inquisitory, ‖nibby, nosy, peery, prying, snoopy
rel interfering, intermeddling, meddling, tampering; examining, inspecting, scrutinizing; impertinent, intrusive, meddlesome
idiom consumed (*or* burning *or* eaten up) with curiosity, curious as a cat (*or* monkey)
con aloof, detached, disinterested, indifferent, unconcerned, uninterested; apathetic, impassive, phlegmatic, stolid
ant incurious
3 *syn see* STRANGE 4

curl *vb syn see* WIND 2
rel crook; roll; ringlet; kink
con straighten, unkink, unwind
ant uncurl

currency *n syn see* MONEY

current *adj* 1 *syn see* PRESENT
rel topical, up-to-date
con antiquated, antique, obsolete
2 *syn see* PREVAILING
rel accustomed, customary; a la mode, fashionable, modern, popular
ant antique

current *n* 1 *syn see* FLOW
2 *syn see* TENDENCY 1

curry *vb syn see* WHIP 2

curse *n* 1 a denunciation that conveys a wish or threat of evil <the dying man's *curse* against his family>
syn anathema, commination, imprecation, malediction, malison
rel execration, objurgation; damning, denunciation; blasphemy, profanation, profanity, sacrilege
ant blessing
2 *syn see* SWEARWORD
3 *syn see* PLAGUE 1

curse *vb* 1 *syn see* EXECRATE 1
rel blaspheme; blight; doom
idiom call down curses on the head of, call down evil on
ant bless
2 *syn see* SWEAR 3
idiom ‖curse up a storm

cursed *adj* 1 *syn see* DAMNED 2
rel hateful
2 *syn see* EXECRABLE 1
rel disgusting; odious
ant blessed

cursing *n syn see* BLASPHEMY 1

cursive *adj syn* see EASY 9

cursory *adj syn* see SUPERFICIAL 2
rel fast, hasty, hurried, quick, rapid, speedy, swift; brief, short; casual, desultory, haphazard, random
con careful, meticulous, scrupulous
ant painstaking

curt *adj* 1 *syn* see CONCISE
2 *syn* see BLUFF
rel imperious, peremptory
ant voluble

curtail *vb* 1 *syn* see SHORTEN
ant prolong, protract
2 *syn* see ABRIDGE 1
ant extend

curtains *n pl but sing in constr syn* see DEATH 1

curtilage *n syn* see COURT 1

curvaceous *adj* having a shapely figure marked by pronounced curves <*curvaceous* bikini-clad girls swarmed over the beach>
syn ||built, curvesome, curvilinear, curvy, Junoesque, rounded, ||stacked, well-developed; *compare* BUXOM, SHAPELY
rel shapeful, shapely, statuesque, well-proportioned; attractive, charming, pleasing
idiom ||built (*or* stacked) like a brick outhouse

curvation *n syn* see CURVE

curvature *n syn* see CURVE

curve *vb* to swerve or cause to swerve from a straight line or course <the road *curves* to the right>
syn bend, bow, crook, round; *compare* WIND 2
rel deflect, divert, turn; deviate, swerve, veer; coil, curl, spiral, twist, wind; incurve
ant straighten

curve *n* something (as a line or surface) that curves or is curved <a slight *curve* to her eyebrows>
syn arc, arch, bend, bow, curvation, curvature, round
rel incurvation, incurvature; inflection; rondure; circuit, circumference, compass

curved *adj* having or characterized by a curve or curves <a *curved* vault>
syn arced, arched, arciform, arrondi, bent, bowed, curvilinear, round, rounded; *compare* CROOKED 1
rel declinate; embowed, incurvate, incurved; excurved; bending, twisted, twisting
ant straight

curvesome *adj syn* see CURVACEOUS

curvilinear *adj* 1 *syn* see CURVED
2 *syn* see CURVACEOUS

curving *adj syn* see CROOKED 1

curvy *adj syn* see CURVACEOUS

cushy *adj syn* see COMFORTABLE 2

cusp *n syn* see POINT 9

cuspidate *adj syn* see POINTED 1

cuss *n* 1 *syn* see SWEARWORD
2 *syn* see MAN 3

cuss *vb syn* see SWEAR 3
idiom ||cuss up a blue streak

---

syn synonym(s)   *rel* related word(s)
ant antonym(s)   *con* contrasted word(s)
idiom idiomatic equivalent(s)
|| use limited; if in doubt, see a dictionary

cussed *adj syn* see DAMNED 2

cussing *adj syn* see BLASPHEMY 1

cussword *n syn* see SWEARWORD

custodian *n* one that guards, protects, or maintains (as property or records) <was the *custodian* of the manor for many years>
syn cerberus, claviger, ||custodier, custos, guardian, keeper, warden, watchdog
rel curator, steward; castellan, governor; overseer, supervisor

||**custodier** *n syn* see CUSTODIAN

custody *n* the act or duty of guarding and preserving <the government has *custody* of all state gifts>
syn care, guardianship, keeping, safekeeping, trust, ward
rel caretaking; charge, management, supervision
con departure, deviation, shift; exception; irregularity

custom *n* 1 *syn* see HABIT 1
rel precedent; ritual; mold; fixture, institution; prescription, rubric; canon, law, precept, rule
idiom matter of course
con departure, deviation, shift; exception; irregularity
2 *syn* see PATRONAGE 2

custom *adj syn* see CUSTOM-MADE

customarily *adv syn* see USUALLY 1
rel conventionally, traditionally; normally, ordinarily; routinely
idiom as a matter of course
con rarely; never
ant occasionally

customary *adj* 1 *syn* see USUAL 1
rel acknowledged, recognized, understood; standard; conventional, orthodox, traditional; prescriptive, regulation, stipulated
idiom being the customary (*or* usual) thing
con occasional; infrequent, inhabitual, sporadic, uncommon; irregular
ant uncustomary
2 *syn* see COMMON 4
rel household, popular; general, universal
ant uncustomary

custom-built *adj syn* see CUSTOM-MADE

customer *n* one that patronizes or uses the services of something (as a store or restaurant) <many *customers* in the shop>
syn client, patron
rel buyer, consumer, purchaser, shopper

customized *adj syn* see CUSTOM-MADE

custom-made *adj* made according to personal order and individual specifications <he always wore a *custom-made* suit>
syn custom, custom-built, customized, custom-tailored, made-to-order, tailor-made
ant mass-produced

custom-tailored *adj syn* see CUSTOM-MADE

custos *n syn* see CUSTODIAN

cut *vb* 1 to penetrate with or as if with a sharp edge <*cut* his hand on a broken bottle>
syn gash, incise, pierce, slash, slice, slit
rel cleave, dissever, sever, sunder; rend, rip, tear; lacerate, wound
2 *syn* see SHORTEN
3 *syn* see REDUCE 2

4 *syn* see MOW

5 to penetrate and divide with an edged tool or instrument < *cut* the melon into slices >

syn carve, cleave, dissect, dissever, sever, slice, split, sunder

rel divide, part, separate; chop, dice, hash, mince, mow

idiom lay open

6 to reduce by severing parts < the barber *cut* his hair too short >

syn clip, crop, pare, prune, shave, shear, skive, trim

rel cut back, dock, lop, poll, pollard, shrub; amputate; curtail

7 to refuse social recognition especially by way of rebuke < his friends *cut* him after the scandal broke >

syn cold-shoulder, ostracize, snob, snub

rel disdain, ignore, rebuff, reject, slight, turn away; affront, insult, offend

idiom give the cold shoulder (to), show one his place, slam the door in one's face, slam the door on, slap one in the face, turn aside (*or* away) from, turn one's back (on *or* upon)

8 *syn* see DILUTE

9 *syn* see FELL 2

10 *syn* see OPERATE 2

cut *n* 1 *syn* see PART 1

2 *syn* see SHARE 1

3 *syn* see TRENCH

4 *syn* see TYPE

cut *adj syn* see INTOXICATED 1

cut back *vb* 1 *syn* see SHORTEN

2 *syn* see REDUCE 2

cut down *vb syn* see REDUCE 2

cut in *vb syn* see INTRUDE 1

cut off *vb* 1 *syn* see KILL 1

2 *syn* see INTERCEPT

3 *syn* see ISOLATE

4 *syn* see DISINHERIT 1

cutoff *n syn* see SHORTCUT

cut out *vb* 1 *syn* see EXCISE

2 *syn* see SUPPLANT 1

cutpurse *n syn* see PICKPOCKET

cutthroat *n syn* see ASSASSIN

cutting *adj syn* see INCISIVE

rel piercing, probing

cut up *vb* 1 *syn* see CRITICIZE

2 to behave in a boisterously comic or unruly manner < children *cutting up* in front of company >

syn act up, carry on, horse, horseplay

rel caper, cavort, romp; clown; show off; roughhouse; misbehave

idiom cut a dido (*or* shine), cut up rough, ||kick up a shindy, raise Cain (*or* Ned), whoop it up

cutup *n syn* see ZANY 2

cycle *n* 1 a complete course of recurrent operations or events < a 24-hour *cycle* of medication >

syn circle, round, wheel; *compare* SUCCESSION 2

rel chain, sequel, sequence, series; course, run; circuit, loop, ring

2 *syn* see BICYCLE

cyclone *n syn* see TORNADO

cyclopean *adj syn* see HUGE

ant lilliputian

cynical *adj syn* see SARDONIC

cyprian *n syn* see WANTON

czar *n syn* see MAGNATE

D

dab *vb syn* see SMEAR 1

||**dab** *n syn* see EXPERT

dabbler *n syn* see AMATEUR 2

con adept, artist, connoisseur; expert, master, professional

dabbling *adj syn* see AMATEURISH

rel sciolistic, shallow, sophomoric, superficial

con adept, capable, competent

||**dabster** *n syn* see EXPERT

dad *n syn* see FATHER 1

dada *n syn* see FATHER 1

dad-blamed *adj* 1 *syn* see DAMNED 2

2 *syn* see UTTER

dad-blasted *adj* 1 *syn* see DAMNED 2

2 *syn* see UTTER

dad-burned *adj* 1 *syn* see DAMNED 2

2 *syn* see UTTER

daddy *n syn* see FATHER 1

daedal *adj syn* see COMPLEX 2

daffy *adj syn* see INSANE 1

daft *adj syn* see INSANE 1

daily *adj* of each or every day < *daily* prayers for the dead >

syn diurnal, quotidian

con nocturnal; alternate, intermittent, periodic, recurrent, spasmodic; erratic, fitful, fluctuating, infrequent, irregular; occasional, sporadic

ant nightly

dainty *n syn* see DELICACY

dainty *adj* 1 *syn* see CHOICE

rel beautiful, bonay, fair, lovely, pretty; delectable, delicious, delightful; airy, diaphanous, ethereal, light

con coarse, vulgar

ant gross

2 *syn* see NICE 1

rel acute, penetrative, perceptive

con careless, neglectful, negligent, thoughtless

||**daisy** *n syn* ||DILLY, ||corker, crackerjack, dandy, humdinger, jim-dandy, knockout, ||lalapalooza, ||lulu, nifty

dale *n syn* see VALLEY

dally *vb* 1 *syn* see TRIFLE 1

rel frolic, gambol, play, rollick, romp, sport; caress, cosset, cuddle, dandle, fondle, pet

2 *syn* see DELAY 2

con fleet, rush, scurry, skedaddle

ant hasten

dam *vb syn* see HINDER

rel repress, suppress

con air, express, utter, vent

damage *n syn* see INJURY 1
   rel impairment, marring; deterioration, dilapidation, disrepair, ruining, wrecking; deleteriousness, disadvantage, drawback
   con amelioration, betterment, improvement; benefit, profit; advantage, service, use
   ant repair

damage *vb syn* see INJURE 1
   rel demolish, destroy, raze, ruin, wreck; deteriorate, dilapidate; abuse, ill-treat, maltreat, mistreat, misuse, outrage
   con ameliorate, amend, better, improve; mend
   ant repair

damaged *adj* having been injured < *damaged* merchandise >
   syn flawed, impaired, marred, spoiled
   rel blemished, broken, imperfect, injured, unsound
   con flawless, good, intact, unbroken, unhurt, unimpaired, uninjured, unmarred, whole; corrected, improved, rectified, repaired
   ant undamaged

damaging *adj syn* see HARMFUL

dame *n* 1 *syn* see MATRIARCH
   2 *syn* see BELDAM 1

damn *vb* 1 *syn* see SENTENCE
   rel castigate, discipline, penalize, punish; banish, cast out, expel
   con deliver, ransom, redeem, rescue; reward
   ant save
   2 *syn* see EXECRATE 1
   rel abominate; vituperate
   3 *syn* see SWEAR 3

damn *n syn* see PARTICLE

damnable *adj* 1 *syn* see EXECRABLE 1
   rel abhorrent, abominable, detestable, hateful, odious; damned
   con admirable, commendable, estimable; laudable, praiseworthy
   2 *syn* see DAMNED 2
   3 *syn* see UTTER

damned *adj* 1 being doomed to eternal punishment < a *damned* soul >
   syn condemned, doomed, lost
   rel anathematized, cursed, reprobate; done for
   idiom gone to blazes, hell bound
   con delivered, ransomed, redeemed
   ant saved
   2 deserving censure or strong disapproval —often used as a generalized expression of annoyance < this *damned* door won't open >
   syn blamed, blankety-blank, blasted, bleeding, blessed, blighted, blinding, ‖blinking, ‖blistering, ‖blooming, confounded, ‖consarned, cursed, cussed, dad-blamed, dad-blasted, dad-burned, damnable, dang, darn (*or* durn), dashed, dog-gone, dratted, execrable, goldarn, infernal, perishing, so-and-so
   3 *syn* see UTTER

damned *adv syn* see VERY 1

---

syn synonym(s)   *rel* related word(s)
ant antonym(s)   *con* contrasted word(s)
idiom idiomatic equivalent(s)
‖ use limited; if in doubt, see a dictionary

damp *adj* slightly or relatively wet < her dress was still *damp* >
   syn dampish, dank, moist, moisty, wettish
   rel drenched, saturated, soaked, soaking; soggy, water-logged
   con arid, dry

dampen *vb syn* see MUFFLE 2

dampish *adj syn* see DAMP

damsel *n syn* see GIRL 1

dance *vb* 1 to perform a rhythmic and patterned succession of steps usually to music < the band was good enough to *dance* to >
   syn foot (it), hoof (it), prance, step, tread
   rel shuffle, trip, truck
   idiom ‖cut a rug, trip the light fantastic
   2 *syn* see FLIT 2
   rel quaver, quiver, shake, tremble, wobble

dancer *n* a professional performer of dances < *dancers* performing a ballet >
   syn ballerina, ballet girl, coryphée, dancing girl, danseur, danseuse, figurant, figurante, hoofer
   rel chorine, chorus boy, chorus girl, chorus man; danseur noble, premier danseur, premiere danseuse, prima ballerina

dancing girl *n syn* see DANCER

dandle *vb syn* see CARESS
   rel disport, play, sport

dandy *n* 1 *syn* see FOP
   con clod, lout, lump, oaf, slob, slouch
   ant sloven
   2 *syn* ‖DILLY, ‖corker, crackerjack, ‖daisy, humdinger, jim-dandy, ‖lalapalozza, ‖lulu, nifty, peach

‖dandy *adj* 1 *syn* see MARVELOUS 2
   2 *syn* see EXCELLENT
   rel grand, hunky-dory, keen, nifty, swell
   idiom fine and dandy
   con ‖bum, ‖crummy, grim, ‖lousy, ‖putrid, rotten
   ant blah

dang *adj* 1 *syn* see DAMNED 2
   2 *syn* see UTTER

danger *n* the state of being exposed to injury, pain, or loss < they are seeking a place where children can play without *danger* >
   syn hazard, jeopardy, peril, risk
   rel menace, precariousness, threat; emergency, exigency, pass; precipice
   idiom dangerous ground, thin ice
   con safety; exemption, immunity; defense, guard, protection, safeguard, shield
   ant security

dangerous *adj* 1 attended by or involving the possibility of injury, pain, or loss < a *dangerous* crossing >
   syn chancy, ‖dangersome, hairy, hazardous, jeopardous, parlous, perilous, risky, treacherous, unhealthy, unsound, wicked; *compare* GRAVE 3
   rel insecure, precarious, uncertain, unsafe; chance, haphazard, hit-or-miss, random; critical, menacing, serious, threatening
   idiom beset (*or* fraught) with danger, on a collision course
   con certain, reliable; harmless, innocent
   ant safe, secure
   2 *syn* see GRAVE 3

‖dangersome *adj syn* see DANGEROUS 1

dangle *vb syn* see HANG 1

dank *adj syn* see DAMP

danseur *n syn* see DANCER

danseuse *n syn* see DANCER

dap *vb syn* see GLANCE 1

dapper *adj* trimly neat and tidy < a *dapper* dresser, always neat as a pin >
syn bandbox, doggish, doggy, natty, sassy, sparkish, spiffy, spruce, sprucy, well-groomed; *compare* NEAT 2, STYLISH
rel chichi; jaunty, rakish; showy
con dowdy, drab, unstylish; disheveled, disordered, slipshod, sloppy, slovenly, unkempt, untidy; blowsy, dowdy, frowsy, shabby, slatternly

dappled *adj syn* see VARIEGATED
con pure, smooth, spotless, unbroken, uniform

dare *vb syn* see FACE 3
rel change, hazard, risk
idiom take the bull by the horns
con avoid, evade; flee, run

dare *n syn* see DEFIANCE 1

daredevil *adj syn* see ADVENTUROUS
con timid, timorous; cautious, chary, circumspect, wary; discreet, judicious, prudent, sane, sensible

daring *adj syn* see ADVENTUROUS

dark *adj* 1 deficient in light < a *dark* room >
syn caliginous, dim, dun, dusk, dusky, gloomy, lightless, murky, obscure, somber, tenebrous, unilluminated
rel cloudy, dull, shadowy, shady; pitch-black, pitch-dark
con bright, brilliant, luminous, radiant; enlightened, illuminated, illumined, lighted
ant light
2 *syn* see CRYPTIC
rel abstruse, esoteric, hidden, occult, recondite; anagogic, cabalistic, darkling, mystic, mystical; complicated, intricate, knotty
con clear, perspicuous; easy, facile, light, simple
ant lucid
3 of dark complexion < her *dark* good looks >
syn bistered, black-a-vised, brunet, dark-skinned, dusky, swart, swarth, swarthy
con blond, fair, light; ruddy, tawny
‖4 *syn* see BLIND 1

darken *vb syn* see OBSCURE
ant illuminate

dark-skinned *adj syn* see DARK 3

darling *n syn* see SWEETHEART 1

darling *adj* 1 *syn* see FAVORITE 1
2 *syn* see DELIGHTFUL

darn (*or* durn) *adj* 1 *syn* see DAMNED 2
2 *syn* see UTTER

dart *n syn* see SHAFT 2

dart *vb syn* see FLY 1
rel hasten, hurry, precipitate, speed; run, scamper, scoot, scurry, sprint, spurt
con dally, dawdle, delay, linger, tarry; lumber, plod, slog, trudge

dash *vb* 1 *syn* see RUSH 1
rel run, scamper, scoot, scurry, sprint
con dally, dawdle, delay, linger, tarry; lumber, plod, slog, trudge
2 *syn* see RUN 1
3 *syn* see BLAST 1
4 *syn* see FRUSTRATE 1

dash *n* 1 *syn* see SPIRIT 5
rel energy, force, might, power, strength; intensity, vehemence; impressiveness

con apathy, dullness, languor, lethargy, listlessness, sluggishness, stagnation, torpor
2 *syn* see HINT 2
rel impress, impression, stamp

dashed *adj* 1 *syn* see DAMNED 2
2 *syn* see UTTER

dashing *adj* 1 *syn* see LIVELY 1
2 *syn* see STYLISH
rel flashy, flaunting; dapper, jaunty, spiffy, spruce
idiom cutting a fine figure
con unfashionable, unstylish; modest, unostentatious, unpretentious
ant drab

dastard *n syn* see COWARD

date *vb* to go or take on a date < he *dated* her several times that winter >
syn see, take out
rel accompany, escort; court, woo
idiom go out with

date *n* 1 *syn* see ENGAGEMENT 3
2 *syn* see ESCORT 1

dated *adj syn* see OLD-FASHIONED
ant up-to-the-minute

dateless *adj syn* see ETERNAL 4
ant ephemeral

daub *vb syn* see SMEAR 1
rel spatter, speckle, spot; dapple, fleck, variegate

daunt *vb syn* see DISMAY 1
rel browbeat, bully, cow, intimidate; baffle, foil, frustrate, thwart
con arouse, awaken, rally, rouse, stir, waken; actuate, drive, impel, move; activate, energize, vitalize
ant enhearten

dauntless *adj syn* see BRAVE 1
rel indomitable, invincible, unconquerable
con hesitant, reluctant
ant poltroon

dauntlessness *n syn* see COURAGE
ant poltroonery

dawdle *vb* 1 *syn* see IDLE
2 *syn* see DELAY 2
rel amble, saunter, stroll; stay, wait; toy, trifle; fritter, waste
idiom fritter away time
con arouse, rally, rouse, stir; hasten, hurry, speed

dawdler *n syn* see LAGGARD

dawn *n* 1 the first appearance of light in the morning < birds which sing at *dawn* >
syn aurora, cockcrow, cockcrowing, dawning, daybreak, daylight, light, morn, morning, sunrise, sunup
rel prime
idiom break of day, crack of dawn, first blush (*or* flush) of day, first light, peep of day, the wee small hours
2 *syn* see BEGINNING
ant sunset

dawning *n* 1 *syn* see DAWN 1
2 *syn* see BEGINNING
ant sunset

day *n* 1 the time of light between one night and the next < waiting for *day* to dawn >
syn daylight, daytime
rel light, sunlight, sunshine
con dark, nighttime
ant night
2 *usu* days *pl syn* see PERIOD 2

daybreak n syn see DAWN 1

daydream n syn see FANCY 4
rel conceiving, fancying, imagination, imagining
con substantiality, tangibility; authenticity, truth, verity

daydreaming adj syn see DREAMY 1

daydreamy adj syn see DREAMY 1

daylight n 1 syn see DAWN 1
syn see DAY 1

dayspring n syn see BEGINNING

daystar n syn see SUN 1

daytime n syn see DAY 1

daze vb 1 to confuse with light <the bright sunlight *dazed* him>
syn bedazzle, blind, dazzle
rel overcome, overpower, overwhelm; dizzy
2 to dull or deaden the powers of the mind through some disturbing experience or influence <*dazed* by the news of the accident>
syn bedaze, bemuse, benumb, paralyze, petrify, stun, stupefy
rel bewilder, confound, disorder, distract, dumbfound, mystify; befuddle, confuse, fuddle, muddle; dazzle, dizzy; rock
con enhance, expand, heighten, sharpen; alert, arouse, waken

daze n syn see HAZE 2

dazzle vb syn see DAZE 1

dead adj 1 devoid of life <a *dead* person>
syn asleep, cold, deceased, defunct, departed, exanimate, extinct, inanimate, late, lifeless, spiritless, unanimated
rel bloodless, breathless; gone, reposing; inactive, inert; belowground, buried
idiom dead as a doornail, gone the way of all flesh, out of one's misery, pushing up daisies
con animate, animated, living, vital; being, existing; active, live
ant alive
2 syn see DEATHLY 1
rel insensible, insentient, numb, unfeeling, unresponsive; inanimate, unconscious
con feeling, responsive, sensitive, sentient; animate, animated, living, spirited, vivacious
ant alive
3 syn see NUMB 1
4 syn see OBSOLETE
ant living; viable
5 syn see EXTINCT 2
6 syn see DULL 7
rel bleak, dismal
con glorious, resplendent
7 syn see UTTER

dead adv syn see DIRECTLY 1

deaden vb 1 to impair in vigor, force, activity, or sensation <the news *deadened* his distress>
syn benumb, blunt, desensitize, dull, mull, numb
rel anesthetize, paralyze, unnerve; stun, stupefy
con animate, vivify, energize, invigorate; activate, vitalize

---

---

ant enliven
2 syn see MUFFLE 2

dead end n a course which leads to nothing further <had reached a *dead end* in negotiations>
syn blind alley, cul-de-sac, impasse, pocket
rel corner, hole; deadlock, halt, standstill; bottleneck

deadened adj 1 syn see DEATHLY 1
2 syn see NUMB 1

‖**deader** n syn see CORPSE

deadfall n syn see PITFALL

deadliness n syn see FATALITY 1

deadlock n syn see DRAW 4
rel condition, posture, situation, state; dilemma, plight, predicament, quandary
con decision, determination, resolution, solution

deadly adj 1 causing or causative of death <a *deadly* disease>
syn deathly, fatal, lethal, mortal, mortiferous, pestilent, pestilential; compare PERNICIOUS
rel destroying, destructive; killing, slaying; internecine; baneful, noxious, pernicious; poisonous, toxic, virulent
con healthful, healthy, wholesome; advantageous, beneficial, restorative, sanative
2 syn see PERNICIOUS
con harmless, innocuous, inoffensive, unoffending
3 syn see DEATHLY 1

deadpan adj syn see EXPRESSIONLESS

dead to rights adv syn see RED-HANDED

deadweight n syn see LOAD 3

‖**deadwood** n syn see ADVANTAGE 3

deaf adj syn see OBSTINATE

deal vb 1 syn see DISTRIBUTE 1
rel partake, participate, share
con receive, take; detain, hold, hold back, keep, retain, withhold; appropriate, arrogate, confiscate
2 syn see GIVE 10
rel impart, mete, render
con annul, cancel, remove, rescind, revoke

deal (out) vb syn see ADMINISTER 2
rel dish, dish out, help, serve; offer, present, proffer, tender
con hold, hold back, keep, retain, withhold

deal (with) vb syn see TREAT 2
rel control, direct; clear, rid, unburden
con misconduct, misdirect, mishandle, mismanage; disregard, ignore, neglect; burden, cumber, encumber

deal n 1 syn see AGREEMENT 2
2 treatment received in a transaction from another <a fair *deal*>
syn shake

dealer n syn see MERCHANT

dealings n pl syn see COMMERCE 1
rel affairs, business, concerns, doings, matters, things; proceedings

deambulatory adj syn see ITINERANT

dean n syn see LEADER 1

dear adj 1 syn see FAVORITE 1
2 syn see LOVING
3 syn see COSTLY 1
con inexpensive, low, moderate, modest, nominal
ant cheap

dear n syn see SWEETHEART 1

dearth *n syn* see ABSENCE
rel infrequency, rareness, scarcity, uncommonness; exiguousness, meagerness, scantiness, scantness; paucity, insufficiency
con superfluity, surplus; lavishness, prodigality, profusion
ant excess

death *n* 1 the end or the ending of life < *death* of a man > < *death* of an enterprise >
syn curtains, decease, defunction, demise, dissolution, grim reaper, (the) Pale Horse, passing, quietus, silence, sleep
rel annihilation, ending, expiration, extinction, grave, termination
idiom crossing the bar
ant life
2 *syn* see FATALITY 2

deathful *adj syn* see DEATHLY 1

deathless *adj syn* see IMMORTAL 1
rel eternal; abiding, lasting, persisting

deathlike *adj* 1 *syn* see DEATHLY 1
2 *syn* see GHASTLY 2

deathly *adj* 1 suggesting death (as in inertness or appearance) < fell in a *deathly* faint >
syn corpselike, corpsy, dead, deadened, deadly, deathful, deathlike
rel cadaverous, haggard, wasted; ghastly, grisly, gruesome, macabre; appalling, dreadful, horrible
con healthy, hearty, robust; stout, sturdy; energetic, strenuous, vigorous
2 *syn* see DEADLY 1

debacle *n* 1 *syn* see DEFEAT 1
2 *syn* see COLLAPSE 2

debar *vb syn* see EXCLUDE
rel forbid, interdict; block, hinder, impede, obstruct
con accept, receive; allow, let, permit
ant admit

debark *vb syn* see DISEMBARK

debase *vb* 1 to cause to become impaired in quality or character < vulgarly outrageous movies that *debase* the taste of the people >
syn animalize, bastardize, bestialize, brutalize, canker, corrupt, debauch, demoralize, deprave, pervert, poison, rot, stain, vitiate, warp; compare ADULTERATE
rel damage, harm, impair, injure, mar, spoil; contaminate, defile, dishonor, pollute, taint; commercialize
con enhance, heighten; lift, raise; ameliorate, better, improve
ant elevate; amend
2 *syn* see HUMBLE
rel cripple, debilitate, disable, enfeeble, sap, undermine, weaken
con acclaim, laud, praise; refresh, rejuvenate, renew, restore
3 *syn* see ADULTERATE
rel damage, impair, worsen; corrupt, defile, spoil
idiom play the devil (*or* the mischief) with
con amend, upgrade

debased *adj* being lowered in quality or character < became *debased* in his greed for money >
syn corrupted, debauched, depraved, perverted, vitiate, vitiated
rel decadent, degenerate, degenerated, deteriorated; abandoned, dissolute, profligate, reprobate

con ameliorated, bettered, improved; elevated, lifted, raised
ant elevated

debatable *adj syn* see MOOT
ant undebatable

debate *n* 1 *syn* see ARGUMENTATION
rel controverting, rebutting, refuting
2 *syn* see ATTENTION 1

debate *vb syn* see DISCUSS 1
rel altercate, quarrel, wrangle; confute, controvert, disprove, rebut, refute; demonstrate, prove; contend, contest
con agree, coincide, concur; affirm, aver, maintain, profess

debauch *vb* 1 *syn* see DEBASE 1
rel decoy, inveigle, lure, seduce, tempt
con amend, remedy; clean, cleanse, purge, purify; preserve, reclaim, save
2 *syn* see SEDUCE 2

debauch *n syn* see ORGY 2

debauched *adj syn* see DEBASED
rel lascivious, lecherous, lewd, libertine, libidinous, licentious, wanton
con delivered, reclaimed, redeemed, rescued, saved; chaste, decent, pure; moral, virtuous; continent, temperate

debilitate *vb syn* see WEAKEN 1
rel devitalize; attenuate, extenuate; harm, hurt, mar, spoil
con energize, vitalize; fortify, reinforce, strengthen; refresh, rejuvenate, renew, restore; rally, rouse, stir
ant invigorate

debility *n syn* see INFIRMITY 1

debris *n syn* see REFUSE
rel dregs, dross, rubble

debt *n* 1 *syn* see EVIL 2
2 *syn* see INDEBTEDNESS 1
3 something (as money) that is owed < struggling to get ahead of his *debts* >
syn arrear(s), arrearage, due, indebtedness, liability; compare INDEBTEDNESS 1
rel default, deficit, delinquency, nonpayment, outstandings; debit, demurrage
con asset, credit; compensation, refund, reimbursement, remuneration

debunk *vb syn* see EXPOSE 4

debut *vb* to make one's formal entrance into society < she *debuted* on her 20th birthday >
syn come out
idiom make one's bow

decadence *n syn* see DETERIORATION 1
rel regress, regression, regressiveness, retrogradation, retrograding, retrogression, retrogressiveness; debasement, degradation
con advance, progress, progression; amelioration, bettering, betterment, improvement
ant rise; flourishing

decadent *adj syn* see EFFETE 3

decamp *vb* 1 *syn* see GET OUT 1
2 *syn* see ESCAPE 1
rel exit, go, leave, quit, retire, withdraw; avoid, elude, evade, shun
con arrive, come

decapitate *vb* 1 *syn* see BEHEAD
2 *syn* see DESTROY 1

decay *vb* to undergo or to cause to undergo destructive changes < apples *decaying* in the basket >
syn break down, corrupt, crumble, decompose, disintegrate, molder, ‖perish, putrefy, putresce, rot, spoil, taint, turn

rel deteriorate; debilitate, enfeeble, sap, undermine, weaken; contaminate, defile, pollute; dilapidate, ruin, wreck; curdle, ferment, sour, work; dry-rot

idiom go bad, go to pot, go to seed, go to wrack and ruin

con mature, ripen; refresh, renew, restore; activate, energize, vitalize; cleanse, purify; galvanize, quicken, stimulate, strengthen

decayed *adj* 1 *syn* see EFFETE 3

2 *syn* see BAD 5

decease *n* *syn* see DEATH 1

decease *vb* *syn* see DIE 1

deceased *adj* *syn* see DEAD 1

deceit *n* 1 the act or practice of imposing upon the credulity of others by dishonesty, fraud, or trickery <he was full of *deceit* in his business dealings>

syn cunning, dissemblance, dissimulation, duplicity, guile

rel chicane, chicanery, deception, double-dealing, fraud, trickery; artifice, craft; cheating, cozening, defrauding, entrapping, overreaching, trapping

con honesty, scrupulosity, scrupulousness, uprightness; candidness, candor, frankness, openness; forthrightness, straightforwardness

2 *syn* see IMPOSTURE

deceitful *adj* *syn* see DISHONEST 1

rel artful, crafty, cunning, foxy, guileful, insidious, sly, tricky, wily; clandestine, furtive, stealthy, underhand, underhanded; deceptive, delusive, delusory, misleading

con assuring, convincing, reassuring

ant trustworthy

deceive *vb* to lead astray or frustrate by underhandedness <advertising that *deceives* the public>

syn beguile, betray, ‖bitch, bluff, ‖bunk, cozen, delude, double-cross, four-flush, humbug, illude, juggle, mislead, mock, sell out, suck in, take in, two-time

rel cheat, defraud, do, overreach; circumvent, outwit; bamboozle, befool, dupe, gull, hoax, hoodwink, spoof, trick, victimize; throw off

idiom pull one's leg, pull the wool over one's eyes, put something over (*or* across), take for a ride, take into camp, throw off the scent (*or* track)

con correct, disabuse, rectify, unblind; acquaint, advise, apprise, inform

ant undeceive; enlighten

deceiving *adj* *syn* see MISLEADING

ant undeceiving; enlightening

decelerate *vb* *syn* see DELAY 1

ant accelerate

decency *n* *rel* appropriateness, fittingness, fitness, suitability; ceremoniousness, conventionality, formality

con impropriety, indecorousness, unseemliness; inappropriateness, unfitness, unsuitability; discourteousness, impoliteness, rudeness

ant indecency

decent *adj* 1 *syn* see DECOROUS 1

---

con awkward, clumsy, gauche, inept, maladroit; discomfiting, disconcerting, embarrassing; crude, rough, rude, uncouth

2 *syn* see CHASTE

rel noble; good, right; rigid, strict; ascetic, austere, severe

con lewd; libertine, wanton; abandoned, dissolute, profligate, reprobate

ant indecent; obscene

3 *syn* see RESPECTABLE 5

4 better than mediocre but less than excellent <the accommodations were *decent*>

syn acceptable, adequate, all right, common, good, respectable, right, satisfactory, sufficient, tolerable, unexceptional, unexceptionable, unimpeachable, unobjectionable; *compare* RESPECTABLE 5, SUFFICIENT 1

rel average, fair, mediocre, middling

con imperfect, inadequate, unacceptable, unsatisfactory; excellent, fine, superior

5 *syn* see SUFFICIENT 1

decently *adv* *syn* see WELL 1

deception *n* 1 the act of deliberately deceiving <resort to falsehood and *deception* in avoiding the tax>

syn cheat, chicane, chicanery, dipsy-doodle, dirt, dishonesty, double-dealing, dupery, fourberie, fraud, hanky-panky, high-binding, indirection, sharp practice, subterfuge, ‖suck-in, trickery

rel cunning, deceit, dissimulation, duplicity, guile; cheating, cozening, defrauding, overreaching; bamboozling, befooling, duping, gulling, hoaxing, hoodwinking; manipulation; ride, ‖snow job

con candidness, frankness, openness; honesty, integrity, probity; artlessness, ingenuousness, naiveté

2 *syn* see IMPOSTURE

rel delusion, hallucination, illusion, mirage

3 *syn* see FALLACY 2

deceptive *adj* *syn* see MISLEADING

rel colorable, plausible, specious; apparent, illusory, ostensible, seeming

con authentic, bona fide, genuine, veritable; actual, real, true; dependable, reliable, trustworthy

deceptiveness *n* *syn* see FALLACY 2

decide *vb* to come or to cause to come to a conclusion <he *decided* how to solve the problem>

syn conclude, determine, figure, resolve, rule, settle

rel gather; adjudge, adjudicate, judge; conjecture, guess, surmise; establish, fix, set

idiom cast the die, make up one's mind, settle in one's mind

con falter, hesitate, vacillate, waver; fluctuate, oscillate; balk, demur, scruple, shy

decided *adj* 1 beyond any doubt or ambiguity <a *decided* advantage over her opponent>

syn assured, clear-cut, definite, pronounced

rel determined, resolved; certain, positive, sure; categorical, explicit, express, unequivocal; clear, obvious, unmistakable, runaway

con doubtful, dubious, problematic, uncertain; equivocal, obscure, vague

---

syn synonym(s)   *rel* related word(s)
ant antonym(s)   *con* contrasted word(s)
idiom idiomatic equivalent(s)
‖ use limited; if in doubt, see a dictionary

ant questionable

2 free from doubt or wavering < he had a *decided* manner >
syn bent, decisive, determined, intent, resolute, resolved, set, settled
rel certain, cocksure, positive, sure; iron-jawed; established, fixed; earnest, purposeful, serious; unfaltering, unhesitating, unwavering
con doubtful, dubious, irresolute, uncertain; faltering, hesitant, vacillating, wavering; undetermined, unresolved, unsettled, unsure
ant undecided
3 *syn* see POSITIVE 1

decidedness *n syn* see DECISION 2

decimate *vb* **1** *syn* see DESTROY 1
2 *syn* see SLAUGHTER 3

decipher *vb* **1** *syn* see DECODE
ant cipher, encipher
2 *syn* see SOLVE 2
rel paraphrase, translate; analyze, break down
idiom find the key of
con misconstrue, misinterpret, misunderstand; confuse, muddle; bewilder, confound, mystify, puzzle; jumble, mix, scramble

decision *n* **1** a position arrived at after consideration < the *decision* of the committee remains firm >
syn conclusion, determination, resolution, settlement
rel accord, agreement, understanding; accommodation, adjustment, arrangement; compromise, reconciliation; choice, preference, selection
con deadlock, draw, stalemate, standoff, tie
2 freedom from doubt or wavering < a man of unusual *decision* >
syn decidedness, determination, firmness, purposefulness, purposiveness, resoluteness, resolution, resolve
rel doggedness, obstinacy, obstinance, perseverance, persistence, stubbornness; earnestness, seriousness; backbone, fortitude, grit, pluck
con changeableness, indetermination, irresolution; uncertainty, unsureness; faltering, fluctuation, hesitation, vacillation, wavering
ant indecision

decisive *adj syn* see DECIDED 2
rel imperative, imperious, masterful, peremptory; assured, self-assured, self-confident; steadfast, unswerving, unwavering
con fluctuating, oscillating; hesitant, reluctant; doubtful, dubious, irresolute, uncertain, undecided
ant indecisive

deck *vb syn* see ADORN
rel apparel, array, attire, clothe, dress; accouter, appoint, furnish
con deface, disfigure; impair, mar, spoil; contort, deform, distort; dismantle, divest, strip

deck (out) *vb syn* see DRESS UP 1

declaim *vb syn* see ORATE

declamatory *adj syn* see RHETORICAL

declaration *n* the act of declaring, proclaiming, or publicly announcing < a *declaration* of war >
syn advertisement, announcement, broadcast, proclamation, promulgation, pronouncement, pronunciamento, publication
rel information, notice, notification; communication; disclosure, revelation; report, statement; acknowledgment, avowal
con concealment, hiding; denial, disaffirmation; recall, recantation, retraction, revocation

declare *vb* **1** to make known openly or publicly < *declared* his intention to run for the senate >
syn advertise, announce, annunciate, blaze (abroad), blazon, broadcast, bruit (about), disseminate, proclaim, promulgate, publish, sound, toot, vend
rel acquaint, advise, apprise, inform, notify; communicate, impart; pronounce; disclose, discover, divulge, reveal; report
idiom declare oneself, make public (*or* known)
con hold, hold back, keep back, reserve, withhold; recall, recant, retract, revoke
2 *syn* see ASSERT 1
rel air, broach, express, utter, vent, ventilate, voice; acknowledge, admit, own
idiom have one's say
con controvert; deny; repress, suppress; conceal, hide
3 *syn* see SAY 1
rel broach, express, voice
idiom speak one's piece

declare off *vb syn* see BACK DOWN

declass *vb syn* see DEGRADE 1
rel disbar, exclude, rule out; abash, discomfit, disconcert
con aggrandize, exalt, magnify

déclassé *adj syn* see INFERIOR 2

declension *n syn* see DETERIORATION 1
rel regression, regressiveness, retrogression, retrogressiveness; dilapidation, ruination
con ascension, ascent; rise, rising; advance, progress, progression; development, maturation

declination *n* **1** *syn* see DETERIORATION 1
2 *syn* see FAILURE 4

decline *vb* **1** *syn* see SET 12
ant ascend
2 *syn* see FAIL 1
rel backslide, lapse, relapse; slide; return, revert; recede, retrograde; abate, ebb, subside, wane
idiom go downhill, take a turn for the worse
con advance, progress; develop, mature; gain, recover
3 *syn* see DETERIORATE 1
4 to turn away by not accepting, receiving, or considering < he *declined* the invitation >
syn disapprove, dismiss, refuse, reject, reprobate, repudiate, spurn, turn down
rel balk, boggle, demur, jib, scruple, shy, stick, stickle; abstain, forbear, refrain; deny, gainsay; abjure, renounce; bypass
idiom send regrets
con receive, take; accede, acquiesce, assent, consent; choose, select; adopt, embrace, espouse
ant accept

decline *n* **1** *syn* see FAILURE 4

rel devitalization, weakening

con advancement, progress; recovery; development, maturation

2 *syn* see DETERIORATION 1

rel comedown, descent, drop, fall, falling off, slump; ebb, wane; backsliding, lapse, relapse

con development, evolution

3 a downward movement (as in price or value) <stocks suffered a *decline* in the market>

syn dip, downslide, downswing, downtrend, downturn, drop, falloff, sag, slide, slip, slump

rel lapse, loss, lowering; depression; decrease, drop-off, sell-off

con upswing, uptrend, upturn

4 *syn* see DESCENT 4

declivate *adj syn* see INCLINED 3

declivitous *adj syn* see INCLINED 3

declivity *n syn* see DESCENT 4

ant acclivity

decode *vb* to convert code into ordinary language <*decode* a message>

syn break, crack, cryptanalyze, decipher, decrypt

rel anagram; render, translate; ‖dope out, figure out, make out; resolve, solve, unfold, unravel, unriddle, work, work out; elucidate, explain, interpret

con cipher, codify, encipher; anagrammatize

ant code, encode, encrypt

decollate *vb syn* see BEHEAD

decolor *vb syn* see WHITEN 1

rel wash out; achromatize, fume, peroxide

con blacken; dye, imbue, stain, tinge, tint; paint, shade

ant color

decolorize *vb syn* see WHITEN 1

ant color

decompose *vb* **1** *syn* see ANALYZE

con combine, join, link, write; synthesize, unify; amalgamate, merge, mix

ant compound

2 *syn* see DECAY

rel deliquesce, liquefy, melt; break up, dissolve

decompound *vb syn* see ANALYZE

ant compound

decorate *vb syn* see ADORN

rel accouter, appoint, equip, furnish, outfit

con impair, injure, mar, spoil; blot, blotch, foul, mutilate, scar, uglify; dismantle, divest, strip

decorated *adj syn* see BEMEDALED

decoration *n syn* see HONOR 2

decorous *adj* **1** conforming to an accepted standard of propriety or good form <*decorous* behavior seems regrettably out of fashion>

syn au fait, becoming, befitting, Christian, civilized, comely, conforming, correct, decent, de rigueur, done, nice, proper, respectable, right, seemly

rel ceremonial, ceremonious, conventional, formal; dignified, elegant; appropri-

ate, fit, fitting, meet, seasonable, suitable; prim, punctilious, rigid, stiff, stuffy

con blatant, clamorous, obstreperous, strident; aggressive, assertive, pushing, pushy; coarse, gross, vulgar; easy, fast, loose; improper, incorrect, unbecoming

ant indecorous

2 *syn* see GOOD 13

decorously *adv syn* see WELL 1

decorousness *n syn* see ORDER 7

rel ceremoniousness, conventionality, formality, solemnity; convenance, convention, form, usage

con inappropriateness, incorrectness; unfitness, unsuitability, unsuitableness; disorder, misbehavior, misconduct, misdeed, misdemeanor

ant indecorousness

decorticate *vb syn* see SKIN 2

rel bark; scalp; denude, divest

decorum *n* **1** socially acceptable behavior or accepted standards of this <they found his conduct quite lacking in *decorum*>

syn decency, dignity, etiquette, propriety, seemliness

rel convenance, convention, form, usage

con laxity, laxness, license, slackness; carelessness, heedlessness, inconsiderateness, mannerlessness; inappropriateness, incorrectness

ant indecorum

2 *syn* see ORDER 7

rel ceremoniousness, conventionality, formality, solemnity; convenance, convention, form, usage

con inappropriateness, incorrectness; unfitness, unsuitability, unsuitableness; disorder, misbehavior, misconduct, misdeed, misdemeanor

ant indecorum; license

3 *usu* decorums *syn* see MANNER 3

decoy *n* **1** *syn* see LURE 2

rel chicane, chicanery, deception, trickery; drawing card

con rebuff, repellence, repellency, repellent, repugnance, repulse, repulsion

2 a person used as a lure <used the detective as a *decoy* to catch the pushers>

syn blind, ‖bonnet, ‖booster, capper, shill, shillaber, stick

rel lugger, roper, steerer; come-on, front, plant, stall

decoy *vb syn* see LURE

rel deceive, delude, mislead; ensorcell, wile

con disgust, repel, sicken; offend, repulse, revolt

decrease *vb* to grow less especially gradually <his influence *decreased* as a new generation grew up>

syn abate, bate, close, diminish, drain (away), dwindle, lessen, peak (out), peter (out), rebate, recede, reduce, taper, taper off

rel abbreviate, abridge, clip, curtail, retrench, shorten, trim; contract, shrink; allay, alleviate, ease, lighten, mitigate; ebb, subside; cut, cut back, cut down, lower; deduct, subtract

con augment, enlarge, multiply; elongate, extend, lengthen, prolong, protract; amplify, dilate, distend, expand, swell; accumulate, amass

---

syn synonym(s)   *rel* related word(s)

ant antonym(s)   *con* contrasted word(s)

idiom idiomatic equivalent(s)

‖ use limited; if in doubt, see a dictionary

ant increase

decree *n* 1 *syn* see EDICT 1

2 *syn* see LAW 1

rel behest, bidding, injunction, order; charge, charging, direction, instruction; announcement, declaration, proclamation, promulgation, pronouncement

decree *vb syn* see DICTATE

rel compel, constrain, force, oblige; demand, require

decrepit *adj* 1 *syn* see WEAK 1

rel haggard, wasted, worn; aged, old, superannuated; creaky, quavering, shaking, tottering

con strong; lusty, hale, healthy, hearty, robust, sound, well

ant sturdy

2 *syn* see SHABBY 1

rel damaged, impaired, injured, marred, spoiled; cast-off, ragged, used; slipshod, sloppy, unkempt

decrepitude *n syn* see INFIRMITY 1

ant vigor

decretum *n syn* see LAW 1

decry *vb* 1 *syn* see DEPRECIATE 1

2 to indicate one's low opinion of something < *decrying* his opponent's character >

syn abuse, belittle, cry down, depreciate, derogate, detract (from), diminish, discount, disparage, disprize, downcry, ‖low-rate, minimize, opprobriate, run down, take (from), take away, write off

rel deprecate, disapprove; censure, condemn, criticize; denounce, reprehend, reprobate; asperse, calumniate, defame, malign, traduce, vilify; discredit, disgrace

idiom bring into discredit, cast a slur upon, cast blame upon, throw stones at

con acclaim, eulogize, laud, praise; aggrandize, exalt, magnify; applaud, commend, compliment, recommend; endorse, sanction; approve, countenance, favor

ant extol, puff

decrypt *vb syn* see DECODE

decumbent *adj syn* see PRONE 4

decussate *vb syn* see INTERSECT

dedicate *vb syn* see DEVOTE 1

rel address, apply, direct, give, surrender; commit, confide, consign, entrust; allot, appropriate, assign, set (aside)

idiom give over to

dedition *n syn* see SURRENDER

deduce *vb syn* see INFER

rel cogitate; consider, deem, regard; conceive, fancy, imagine; assume, presume, presuppose; read (into)

idiom take to mean

deducible *adj syn* see DEDUCTIVE

deduct *vb* 1 to take away one quantity from another < *deduct* the cost from his bill >

syn discount, draw back, knock off, substract, subtract, take, take away, take off, take out

rel decrease, diminish, lessen, reduce; roll back

con cast, figure, sum, tot, total

ant add

2 *syn* see INFER

deduction *n* 1 an amount subtracted from a sum < *deductions* from gross income >

syn abatement, discount, rebate, reduction, subtraction

rel allowance, credit, cut; decrease, decrement, depreciation, diminution; charge-off, offtake, takeoff, write-off; dockage

con accession, accretion, augmentation, increase, increment, raise, rise; appreciation

ant addition

2 *syn* see INFERENCE 1

3 *syn* see INFERENCE 2

rel cogitation, deliberation, reasoning, reflection, speculation, thinking; consideration, contemplation; meditation, mulling, musing, pondering, rumination

deductive *adj* that can be deduced or developed from premises < *deductive* laws >

syn a priori, deducible, derivable, dogmatic, reasoned

rel illative, inferential, ratiocinative; conjectural, hypothetical, purported, putative, supposed, suppositious; academic, speculative, theoretical

con categorical, definite, explicit, express; instinctive, intuitive

deed *n* 1 *syn* see ACTION 1

2 *syn* see FEAT 2

rel gaining, securing, winning; adventure, enterprise, quest; cause, crusade

idiom bold stroke

3 a written, signed, and usually sealed instrument that spells out some bargain, transfer, or contract < the *deed* to the property >

syn charter, conveyance

rel bargain, compact, contract, covenant, pact

deed *vb syn* see TRANSFER 4

deem *vb* 1 *syn* see CONSIDER 3

rel conjecture, guess, surmise, suspect, ‖suspicion, understand; ‖allow, assume, believe, ‖calculate, daresay, divine, expect, presume, suppose

idiom hold to be true

2 *syn* see FEEL 3

idiom take for granted

de-emphasize *vb syn* see SOFT-PEDAL

deep *adj* 1 having great extension downward or inward < a *deep* well > < a *deep* closet >

syn abysmal, profound; *compare* BOTTOMLESS 2

con depthless, shallow, superficial, unprofound; flat, level, plain, plane

ant shallow

2 *syn* see INTENSIVE

3 *syn* see RECONDITE

rel complex, complicated, intricate; arcane, mysterious; concealed, hidden

con easy, facile, simple; apparent, clear, distinct, evident, manifest, obvious; lucid, perspicuous; depthless, shallow, superficial, unprofound

4 *syn* see SLY 2

rel shrewd; acute, keen, knowing, sharp; contriving, intriguing, plotting

con ingenuous, naive, simple, unsophisticated; aboveboard, forthright, straightforward

5 *syn* see INTENT

rel abstracted, concentrated; centered, fixed, focused, set

con distracted, diverted; detached, disinterested, indifferent, unconcerned, uninterested

deep *n syn* see OCEAN

deep-dyed *adj syn* see INVETERATE 1

deepen *vb syn* see INTENSIFY

deepness *n* 1 *syn* see DEPTH 1
ant shallowness
2 *syn* see DEPTH 2

deep-rooted *adj syn* see INVETERATE 1

deep-seated *adj* 1 *syn* see INHERENT
2 *syn* see INVETERATE 1
rel constitutional, immanent, indwelling, ingrained, inherent, intrinsic; deep, profound; inner, internal, inward; implanted; infixed
con peripheral, shallow, superficial, surface; adventitious, casual, chance, incidental
ant skin-deep

||**deep-six** *vb syn* see DISCARD

deep water *n syn* see PREDICAMENT

deface *vb* to mar the appearance of < *deface* the wall with graffiti >
syn disfashion, disfeature, disfigure
rel blemish, damage, harm, impair, injure, mar, spoil; contort, deform, distort, misshape; batter, mangle, mutilate; demolish, destroy; dilapidate, ruin, wreck
con mend, patch, repair; freshen, improve, refurbish, renew, restore; adorn, beautify, deck, decorate, embellish, ornament

defacer *n syn* see VANDAL

de facto *adv syn* see VERY 2

defalcation *n syn* see FAILURE 3
rel laxness, negligence, remissness, slackness; failing, fault
con discharge, effectuation, execution, fulfillment; completion, conclusion

defamation *n syn* see DETRACTION
ant puffery

defamatory *adj syn* see LIBELOUS

defame *vb syn* see MALIGN
rel belie, misrepresent
idiom cast a slur on, throw mud at
con applaud, commend, compliment; exalt, magnify; back, champion, support, uphold
ant laud; puff

default *n* 1 *syn* see FAILURE 1
rel deficiency, fault, imperfection, shortcoming; lapse, weakness; disregard, omission, overlooking, slight
2 *syn* see ABSENCE

defeasance *n syn* see DEFEAT 1

defeat *vb* 1 *syn* see CONQUER 1
rel bar, block, hinder, impede, obstruct; repress, suppress
idiom beat all hollow, get the better of, grind into the dust, ||have by the short hairs
con capitulate, defer, give in, submit; back down, withdraw
2 to win a victory over < *defeated* his opponent in the race >
syn beat, down, outdo, ||pip, worst; *compare* CONQUER 1, WHIP 2
rel outfight, outgame; nose out
idiom get the better of

defeat *n* 1 an overthrow especially of an army in battle < the brigade suffered a *defeat* >

---

syn beating, debacle, defeasance, discomfiture, downcast, downthrow, drubbing, ||dusting, licking, overthrow, rout, shellacking, thrashing, trouncing, vanquishment, warming
rel bafflement, check, foil, frustration; rebuff, repulse, reversal, reverse, setback; ||cleaning, ||cleanup, clobbering, lambasting
con conquest, triumph; gaining, securing, winning; ascendancy, supremacy
ant victory
2 *syn* see FAILURE 2

defeater *n syn* see VICTOR 1
ant defeated

defect *n* 1 *syn* see BLEMISH
rel failing, fault, foible, frailty; infirmity, weakness; deficiency, imperfection, shortcoming
con excellence, faultlessness, impeccability; merit, perfection, virtue
2 *syn* see ABSENCE
rel scantiness, scarceness, scarcity, shortage
con overage, overplus, superfluity, surplus, surplusage
ant excess

defect *vb* to desert a cause or party often in order to espouse another < he *defected* from the Communist party >
syn apostatize, desert, rat, renounce, repudiate, tergiversate, tergiverse, turn
rel abandon, forsake; back out, renege, withdraw; depart, go, leave, quit; reject, spurn
idiom change sides, go back on, go over, turn one's coat, walk (*or* run) out on
con adhere (to), cling (to), hang on, stick (to *or* with); cherish, cultivate, foster

defection *n* conscious abandonment of allegiance or duty < *defection* from family responsibilities in times of trouble >
syn apostasy, desertion, falseness, recreancy, tergiversation
rel alienation, disaffection, estrangement; disloyalty, faithlessness; abandonment, forsaking; divorce, parting, runout, separation, sundering; disownment, rejection, repudiation
idiom running out on, ||taking a runout powder
con constancy, faithfulness, loyalty, resoluteness, staunchness, steadfastness; allegiance, fealty, fidelity; dependability, reliability, trustworthiness

defective *adj* 1 *syn* see FAULTY
rel broken, damaged, impaired, injured
con faultless, flawless, impeccable, unblemished, undamaged
ant defectless
2 *syn* see DEFICIENT 1
rel corrupted, debased, vitiated; deranged, disordered, disturbed, unsettled; unhealthy, unsound
con entire, perfect, whole; complete, full, plenary; healthy, sound
ant intact; defectless

defector *n syn* see RENEGADE

defend *vb* 1 to keep safe (as from danger or against attack) < *defend* the country from aggression >
syn bulwark, cover, fend, guard, protect, safeguard, screen, secure, shield

---

syn synonym(s)   *rel* related word(s)
ant antonym(s)   *con* contrasted word(s)
idiom idiomatic equivalent(s)
|| use limited; if in doubt, see a dictionary

rel avert, prevent, ward; oppose, resist, withstand; battle, contend, fight, war; conserve, preserve, save
idiom stand on the defensive, stave off from
con aggress, assail, assault, fall (on *or* upon); bombard, storm; beset, besiege, overrun; capitulate, cave, submit, yield
ant attack
2 *syn* see MAINTAIN 2
rel air, express, utter, vent, voice; account, explain, justify, rationalize; back, champion, support, uphold
idiom speak (*or* stand *or* stick) up for
con contradict, deny, gainsay, traverse; confute, controvert, disprove, rebut, refute

defendable *adj syn* see TENABLE 1
ant undefendable

defense *n* 1 means or method of defending <the skunk's powerful *defense* against attackers>
syn aegis, armament, armor, guard, protection, safeguard, security, shield, ward
rel arms, munitions, weaponry, weapons; fastness, fort, fortress, stronghold
con aggression, offense, offensive
ant attack
2 *syn* see APOLOGY 1
rel answer, rejoinder, reply, response, retort, return; exculpation, excuse, explanation, rationalization
con censure, condemnation, criticism, decrial, reprehension, reprobation, reproof; assault, attack, onset, onslaught

defenseless *adj syn* see HELPLESS 1

defensible *adj* 1 *syn* see TENABLE 1
ant indefensible
2 *syn* see JUSTIFIABLE
ant indefensible

defer *vb* to delay an action or proceeding <decided to *defer* voting until the next meeting>
syn adjourn, delay, hold off, hold over, hold up, intermit, lay over, postpone, prorogue, put off, put over, remit, shelve, stand over, stay, suspend, waive
rel detain, retard, slow; block, hinder, impede, obstruct; stall; extend, lengthen, prolong, protract
idiom hold up on, lay to one side, put on ice, set aside
con accelerate, hasten, hurry, speed; expedite, further, promote
ant advance

defer *vb syn* see YIELD 2
rel accede, acquiesce, agree, assent; accommodate, adapt, adjust, conform; cringe, fawn, truckle
con combat, fight, oppose, resist; object, remonstrate; balk, demur, stickle, strain
ant withstand

deference *n syn* see HONOR 1
rel acquiescence, compliance; submission, submissiveness
con insolence, irreverence; disesteem, disfavor; discourtesy, incivility, rudeness
ant disrespect

deferential *adj* 1 *syn* see RESPECTFUL
2 *syn* see INGRATIATING

defi *n syn* see DEFIANCE 1

defiance *n* 1 the act or an instance of defying <presented a *defiance* to his rival>
syn cartel, challenge, dare, defi, defy, stump
rel call, muster, summons; command, enjoinder, order
con capitulation, submission, surrender
2 disposition to resist or unwillingness to brook opposition <exhibited *defiance* toward his teacher>
syn contempt, contumacy, despite, recalcitrance, stubbornness
rel factiousness, insubordination, insurgency, rebelliousness; headstrongness, intractableness, unruliness; boldness, bravado, brazenness, impudence, insolence; audacity, effrontery, hardihood, temerity; contrariness, perversity
con acquiescence, compliance; amenableness, docility, obedience, tractableness; submissiveness

deficiency *n* 1 *syn* see FAILURE 3
rel absence, default, defect, want
con copiousness, plenty; great deal, heap, lot, much
2 *syn* see IMPERFECTION
rel dearth, defect, lack, privation, want; default, dereliction, miscarriage, neglect
ant excess

deficient *adj* 1 showing lack of something necessary <*deficient* in judgment>
syn defective, ‖half-assed, inadequate, incomplete, insufficient, lacking, uncomplete, wanting
rel faulty, flawed, imperfect, unsound; damaged, impaired, injured, marred; amiss, bad, unsatisfactory
idiom in want of
con complete, entire, intact, whole; acceptable, adequate, sufficient
2 *syn* see SHORT 3
rel infrequent, rare, uncommon
idiom found wanting
con excessive, extravagant, immoderate, inordinate; enough, satisfactory, sufficing
ant adequate, sufficient

deficit *n syn* see FAILURE 3
con copiousness, plenty; excess, surplus, surplusage

defile *vb* 1 *syn* see CONTAMINATE 1
rel desecrate, profane; befoul, dirty, foul, sully, tarnish
con consecrate, hallow
ant cleanse; purify
2 *syn* see RAPE
rel dishonor, shame, soil, sully
3 *syn* see TAINT 1

defiled *adj syn* see IMPURE

define *vb* 1 *syn* see PRESCRIBE 2
rel circumscribe, limit, mark (off), mark (out); designate, delineate, describe
con confound, confuse, mistake
2 *syn* see BORDER 1
3 *syn* see ETCH 2
rel explain, expound, interpret

definite *adj* 1 having distinct or certain limits <*definite* dimensions>
syn circumscribed, determinate, fixed, limited, narrow, precise, restricted
rel assigned, defined, prescribed; established, set; decided, determined, settled
con ambiguous, obscure, vague; unconditional, unlimited, unqualified, unrestricted; indeterminate, uncircumscribed; imprecise, loose, undefined

ant indefinite
2 *syn* see EXPLICIT
rel complete, full; downright, forthright;
incisive
con doubtful, dubious, questionable; ambiguous
ant indefinite; equivocal
3 *syn* see POSITIVE 1
4 *syn* see DECIDED 1
ant uncertain
definitely *adv* 1 *syn* see EXPRESSLY 1
2 *syn* see EASILY 2
definiteness *n syn* see PRECISION
ant indefiniteness
definitive *adj* 1 *syn* see CONCLUSIVE
rel determining, settling; concluding,
final, last, terminal, ultimate; closing,
completing, ending, finishing, terminating;
absolute, categorical
con inconclusive, indecisive; temporary,
transitory
ant provisional, tentative
2 *syn* see EXPLICIT
rel actual, real
con doubtful, dubious, questionable; ambiguous
ant indefinitive
definitiveness *n syn* see PRECISION
ant indefinitiveness, indefinitude
definitude *n syn* see PRECISION
ant indefinitiveness, indefinitude
deflect *vb* 1 *syn* see TURN 6
rel disperse, swerve; hook, skew
2 *syn* see WARD 1
rel hold off, keep off
deflection *n* 1 *syn* see DEVIATION 1
rel bending, curving, twisting; departing,
swerve, swerving, veer, veering
2 *syn* see TURN 2
deflorate *vb syn* see RAPE
deflower *vb* 1 *syn* see RAPE
2 *syn* see RAVAGE
deform *vb* to mar or spoil by or as if by
twisting <a face *deformed* by bitterness>
syn contort, distort, misshape, torture,
warp, wind
rel batter, cripple, maim, mangle, mutilate; deface, disfigure; damage, impair,
injure, mar, spoil; blemish, flaw; screw
(up), squinch
deformity *n* a physical blemish or disfigurement <the dwarf's humpback *deformity*>
syn distortion, malconformation, malformation, misshape
rel defacement, deformation, disfigurement; damage, impairment, injury; aberration, abnormality; irregularity, unnaturalness
defraud *vb syn* see CHEAT
rel bamboozle, hoax, trick; circumvent,
foil, outwit; fleece, milk, stick; take in
idiom do out of, put over a fast one, take
to the cleaner's
defrauder *n syn* see SWINDLER
deft *adj syn* see DEXTEROUS 1
rel agile, brisk, fleet; apt, prompt, quick,
ready; adept, crack, crackerjack; ingenious, neat

con heavy-handed, unskillful; blundering,
bungling, butterfingered; rigid, stiff,
wooden
ant awkward, unhandy
deftness *n syn* see ADDRESS 1
rel agility, fleetness, nimbleness; assuredness, confidence
con incompetence, inefficiency; clumsiness, heavy-handedness, maladroitness
ant awkwardness
defunct *adj* 1 *syn* see DEAD 1
rel inactive, inert
ant alive; live
2 *syn* see EXTINCT 2
ant surviving
defunction *n syn* see DEATH 1
defy *vb syn* see FACE 3
rel deride, mock, ridicule; gibe, flout;
scorn, scout, spurn; disregard, ignore
idiom fling (or throw) down the gauntlet,
hurl defiance at
con blench, flinch, quail, shrink
ant recoil
defy *n syn* see DEFIANCE 1
dégagé *adj syn* see EASYGOING 3
ant mannered
degeneracy *n syn* see DETERIORATION 1
degenerate *adj* 1 *syn* see EFFETE 3
rel deteriorating, retrograde, retrogressive,
worsening; failing, sinking
2 *syn* see VICIOUS 2
rel degraded, demeaned
con ethical, moral, virtuous; honorable,
just, upright
ant regenerate
degenerate *vb syn* see DETERIORATE 1
rel corrupt, deprave, vitiate; backslide,
lapse; return, revert
con improve, upgrade; lift, uplift
degeneration *n syn* see DETERIORATION
1
rel regression, regressiveness, retrogression, retrogressiveness; depreciation; corruption, depravation, depravedness, depravity, perversion
con regeneracy, regenerateness; progress,
progression
ant regeneration
degradation *n syn* see DEMOTION
ant advancement; elevation
degrade *vb* 1 to lower in station, rank, or
grade <*degraded* in rank for miscon-
duct>
syn break, bump, bust, declass, demerit,
demote, disgrade, disrate, downgrade, put
down, reduce
rel abase, debase, humble, humiliate,
lower; disbar, rule out
con advance, further; boost, lift, raise;
enhance, heighten
ant elevate
2 *syn* see HUMBLE
rel belittle, decry, derogate, detract, disparage; diminish, lessen, reduce
con elevate, raise; acclaim, extol, laud,
praise
ant uplift
degree *n* 1 a unitary component of a process, course, or order of classification
<advanced by *degrees*>
syn grade, notch, rung, stage, step
2 relative size or character of the parts or
components in a complex whole compared
with other like things <the *degree* of

---

syn synonym(s)　　*rel* related word(s)
ant antonym(s)　*con* contrasted word(s)
idiom idiomatic equivalent(s)
‖ use limited; if in doubt, see a dictionary

difference between the two jobs> <his
work demands a high *degree* of intelli-
gence>
syn proportion, rate, ratio, scale
rel dimension; extent, magnitude, measure, size

dégringolade n **syn** see DETERIORATION
1

dehydrate vb **syn** see DRY 1
ant hydrate; rehydrate

deific adj **syn** see DIVINE 1
2 **syn** see DIVINE 2

deification n **syn** see APOTHEOSIS 2

deign vb **syn** see STOOP 1

deject vb **syn** see DISCOURAGE 1
ant exhilarate; cheer

dejected adj **syn** see DOWNCAST
idiom down in the dumps (*or* mouth), in
the dumps
ant animated

dejection n **syn** see SADNESS
rel despair, desperation
ant exhilaration

dekko vb **syn** see SEE 2

delay vb 1 to cause to be late or behind in
movement or progress <was *delayed* by
traffic>
syn bog (down), decelerate, detain, embog, hang up, mire, retard, set back,
slacken, slow (up *or* down)
rel block, hinder, impede, obstruct; defer,
hold over, hold up, intermit, postpone,
put off, stay, suspend; arrest, check, interrupt
idiom hang fire
con accelerate, hasten, hurry, precipitate,
quicken, speed; advance, forward, further,
promote
ant expedite
2 to move or act slowly so that progress
or work is retarded <their landlord kept
delaying in making repairs>
syn dally, dawdle, dilly, dillydally, drag,
lag, linger, loiter, mull, poke, procrastinate, put off, tarry, trail
rel hang back, idle, wait; drone; falter,
hesitate, vacillate, waver
idiom take one's own sweet (*or* good)
time
ant hasten, hurry
3 **syn** see DEFER

delectable adj **syn** see DELIGHTFUL
rel choice, dainty, delicate, exquisite, rare;
palatable, sapid, savory, tasty, toothsome
con loathsome, offensive, repulsive, revolting
ant distasteful

delectate vb **syn** see PLEASE 2

delectation n 1 **syn** see PLEASURE 2
rel gratification, gratifying, regalement,
regaling; enjoyment, relish
ant distaste
2 **syn** see ENJOYMENT 1

deleerit adj **syn** see INTOXICATED 1

delegate n a person standing in the place
of another or others <was a *delegate* to
the convention>
syn catchpole, deputy, representant, representative; compare AGENT 1
rel agent, factor, proxy; alternate, replacement, stand-in, substitute, surrogate;
mouthpiece, spokesman; emissary, envoy

delegate vb to appoint as one's representative <*delegated* her to watch the chil-
dren>
syn commission, depute, deputize
rel ascribe, assign, charge; appoint, designate, name; choose, pick, select

delete vb **syn** see ERASE
rel eliminate, exclude, rule out; omit

deleterious adj **syn** see HARMFUL
rel destroying, destructive; ruining, ruinous
con advantageous, profitable; healthful,
healthy, salubrious, wholesome
ant salutary

deliberate adj 1 arrived at after due
thought <a *deliberate* judgment>
syn advised, aforethought, considered,
designed, premeditated, prepense, studied,
studious, thought-out
rel planned, projected, schemed; calcu-
lated; careful, meticulous, scrupulous;
foresighted, forethoughtful, provident,
prudent
con chance, chancy, desultory, haphazard,
happy-go-lucky, hit-or-miss, random; aimless, designless, purposeless; hasty, hurried; abrupt, impetuous, sudden; automatic, instinctive, spontaneous
ant casual
2 **syn** see VOLUNTARY
rel intended, meant, meditated, purposed;
determined, purposeful; aware, cognizant,
conscious
con careless, heedless, inadvertent,
thoughtless; unintended, unpurposed
ant impulsive
3 **syn** see SLOW 2
rel calculating, cautious, chary, circumspect, wary; careful, heedful; collected,
composed, cool, imperturbable
con hasty, headlong, impetuous, sudden
ant abrupt, precipitate

deliberate vb 1 **syn** see PONDER 2
2 **syn** see THINK 5
rel excogitate, study, weigh; argue, debate, discuss, talk over

deliberately adv **syn** see INTENTIONALLY

deliberation n 1 **syn** see ATTENTION 1
2 **syn** see THOUGHT 1
3 **syn** see CONFERENCE 1

delicacy n something special and delicious
to eat <fresh fruit in the winter was once
an uncommon *delicacy*>
syn bonne bouche, dainty, goody, kickshaw, morsel, tidbit (*or* titbit), treat
rel banquet, feast, regale; eosseting, indulgence, luxury
idiom choice bit, dish fit for a king

delicate adj 1 **syn** see CHOICE
rel delectable, delicious, delightful; balmy,
gentle, lenient, mild, soft; aerial, airy,
ethereal
con coarse, crude, vulgar
ant gross
2 **syn** see FINE 1
3 **syn** see NICE 1
rel perceptive, sensitive
con insensitive, undiscriminating, unperceptive
4 **syn** see FRAGILE 1
5 lacking in strength or substance <a
delicate constitution>
syn flimsy, slight

rel feeble, fragile, frail, weak; sickly, unhealthy; decrepit, infirm

con stalwart, stout, strong, sturdy, tenacious, tough; hale, healthy, robust, sound, well, wholesome

6 *syn* see TACTFUL

rel adept, expert, masterly, proficient; discreet, foresighted, prudent; careful, heedful; cautious, wary

con impolitic; imprudent, indiscreet; awkward, clumsy, gauche, inept, maladroit; unskillful

7 marked by or requiring tact <a *delicate* situation>

syn precarious, sensitive, ticklish, touchy, tricky

rel uncertain, unpredictable; hair-trigger, volatile; sticky

delicatesse *n syn* see TACT

ant indelicacy

delicious *adj syn* see DELIGHTFUL

rel appetizing, palatable, sapid, savory, toothsome; choice, dainty, delicate, exquisite, rare

con banal, flat, inane, insipid, jejune, wishy-washy

delight *vb* 1 *syn* see EXULT

2 *syn* see PLEASE 2

rel amuse, divert, entertain; allure, attract, charm, enchant, fascinate; enrapture, entrance, transport

con aggrieve, distress, pain, trouble; afflict, try; grieve; bother, irk; bore

delight (in) *vb* 1 *syn* see ADMIRE 1

rel enjoy, like, savor; eat up, luxuriate (in)

con abhor, abominate, hate, loathe

2 *syn* see LOVE 1

delight *n syn* see PLEASURE 2

rel glee, hilarity, jollity, mirth; ecstasy, rapture, transport; contentment, satisfaction; relish

con abhorrence, detestation, hate, hatred; dislike, distaste; discontent, dissatisfaction

ant aversion; disappointment

delightful *adj* highly pleasing to the senses or to aesthetic taste <a *delightful* view>

syn adorable, ambrosial, darling, delectable, delicious, heavenly, luscious, lush, scrumptious, yummy

rel charming, enchanting, fascinating; alluring, attractive; beautiful, fair, lovely; ineffable; agreeable, gratifying, pleasant, pleasing; satisfying

con miserable, wretched; distasteful, obnoxious, repellent, repugnant; abhorrent, detestable, hateful, odious; boring, irksome, tedious; distressing, troubling

ant abominable, horrid

delimit *vb* 1 *syn* see DEMARCATE 1

rel decide

2 *syn* see LIMIT 2

delimitate *vb* 1 *syn* see DEMARCATE 1

2 *syn* see LIMIT 2

delineate *vb* 1 *syn* see REPRESENT 1

rel design, plan; evoke, paint

2 *syn* see ETCH 2

delineation *n* 1 *syn* see REPRESENTATION

rel design, plan; evocation, painting; account, story, version

2 *syn* see OUTLINE

delinquency *n syn* see FAILURE 1

rel nonobservance; nonfulfillment; lapse, weakness

delinquent *adj syn* see NEGLIGENT

deliquesce *vb syn* see LIQUEFY

rel decay, decompose, disintegrate

con cake, harden, indurate, set, solidify

delirious *adj* 1 disordered in mind especially temporarily <*delirious* from the fever>

syn raving, wandering

rel deranged, disarranged, disordered, disturbed, unsettled; bewildered, confused, distracted; rambling; irrational, unreasonable; crazed, crazy, demented, insane, lunatic, mad, maniac

idiom out of one's head (*or* mind)

con rational, reasonable; sane, sensible; comatose, unconscious

2 *syn* see FURIOUS 2

rel overexcited, overwrought; ecstatic, rapturous, transported; delighted, enthused, thrilled

idiom all agog, beside oneself

con collected, composed, easy, relaxed; unexcited, unmoved, unstimulated

delirium *n* frenzied excitement or wild enthusiasm <in a *delirium* of patriotic feeling>

syn frenzy, furor

rel ardor, enthusiasm, fervor, passion, zeal; ecstasy, rapture, transport

con nonchalance, sangfroid; indifference, unconcern

ant apathy

deliver *vb* 1 *syn* see RESCUE

con immure, imprison, incarcerate, intern, jail; capture, catch, ensnare, entrap, snare, trap; condemn, damn, doom

2 *syn* see GIVE 3

rel relinquish, resign, surrender, yield

con keep, retain

3 *syn* see BEAR 5

4 *syn* see SAY 1

rel broach, express, vent, voice; communicate, impart

5 *syn* see GIVE 10

rel dispatch, send, transmit; fling, hurl, pitch, throw

delivery *n syn* see BIRTH 1

Delphian *adj* 1 *syn* see PROPHETIC

2 *syn* see CRYPTIC

delude *vb syn* see DECEIVE

idiom play tricks (*or* a trick) on

con enlighten, illume, illuminate, illustrate, light, lighten; elucidate, explain

deluding *adj syn* see MISLEADING

deluge *n syn* see FLOOD 1

rel flux; overrunning

deluge *vb* 1 to flow over so as to submerge or enclose <the lowlands were completely *deluged*>

syn drown, engulf, flood, inundate, overflow, overwhelm, submerge, swamp, whelm

rel overrun; flush, gush, pour, sluice, stream

2 *syn* see WET

con dehydrate, desiccate, dry, parch

---

syn synonym(s)   *rel* related word(s)

ant antonym(s)   *con* contrasted word(s)

idiom idiomatic equivalent(s)

‖ use limited; if in doubt, see a dictionary

3 to affect overwhelmingly as if by a deluge of water <he was *deluged* by telephone calls>
syn flood, overwhelm, swamp, whelm
rel overcome; oversupply; abound, teem

delusion *n* **1** something accepted as true that is actually false or unreal <people who suffer from *delusions* of persecution>
syn hallucination, ignis fatuus, illusion, mirage, phantasm
rel chicane, chicanery, deception, trickery; cheat, counterfeit, deceit, fake, fraud, humbug, imposture, sham; daydream, dream, fancy, fantasy, figment, vision; apparition, eidolon, ghost, phantom, shade
ant reality
2 *syn* see FALLACY 2
ant verity

delusive *adj syn* see MISLEADING
rel chimerical, fanciful, fantastic, imaginary, quixotic, visionary; apparent, illusory, ostensible, seeming
con authentic, bona fide, genuine, veritable; actual, real, true

delusory *adj syn* see MISLEADING

deluxe *adj syn* see LUXURIOUS 3
rel choice, dainty, delicate, elegant, exquisite, rare, recherché
con coarse, common, ordinary; inelegant

delve *vb* ‖ **1** *syn* see DIG 1
rel gouge (out), hollow (out), scoop (out), quarry (out); burrow, tunnel; comb, ferret out, search, seek
2 *syn* see MINE

delve (into) *vb syn* see EXPLORE

delve *n syn* see HOLE 1

delving *n syn* see INQUIRY 1

demagogue *n* a leader who makes use of popular prejudices and false claims especially for political advantage <*demagogues* who endanger the orderly processes of democratic government>
syn rabble-rouser
rel fomenter, inciter, instigator; agitator, firebrand, hothead, incendiary, inflamer; troublemaker

demand *n* **1** *syn* see REQUIREMENT 1
2 *syn* see NEED 3

demand *vb* **1** to ask for something as or as if one's right or due <the physician *demanded* payment of his bill>
syn call, challenge, claim, exact, postulate, require, requisition, solicit
rel ask, request; bid, charge, command, direct, enjoin, order; cite, summon, summons; coerce, compel, constrain, force, oblige; necessitate
con cede, relinquish, resign, waive; allow, concede, grant; give, offer, tender
2 to have as a need or requirement <it *demands* considerable practice to master the piano>
syn ask, call (for), crave, necessitate, require, take
rel fail, lack, need, want
idiom need (*or* want), doing, stand in need of

demanding *adj syn* see ONEROUS
rel rigid, rigorous, severe, stern, strict, stringent; crying, imperative, importunate, instant, pressing, urgent
ant undemanding

demarcate *vb* **1** to mark the limits of <*demarcate* the boundary between two countries>
syn bound, delimit, delimitate, determine, limit, mark (out)
rel establish, fix, set; assign, define, prescribe; circumscribe, confine, restrict
2 *syn* see DISTINGUISH
rel insulate, isolate, seclude, segregate, sequester

demean *vb syn* see BEHAVE 1

demean *vb syn* see HUMBLE
rel belittle, decry, derogate, detract, disparage; contemn, despise, scorn
con elevate, enhance, heighten

demeanor *n syn* see BEARING 1
rel behavior, conduct

dement *n syn* see LUNATIC 1

demented *adj syn* see INSANE 1
rel delirious, frenzied, hysterical

demerit *n syn* see IMPERFECTION

demerit *vb syn* see DEGRADE 1

demeritorious *adj syn* see BLAMEWORTHY
ant meritorious

demesne *n syn* see FIELD

demigod *n syn* see SUPERMAN

demimondaine *n syn* see HARLOT 1

demimonde *n syn* see HARLOT 1

demirep *n syn* see HARLOT 1

demise *vb syn* see DIE 1

demise *n syn* see DEATH 1
rel annihilation, ending, expiration, extinction

demit *vb syn* see ABDICATE 1

demit *vb syn* see LOWER 3

demiurgic *adj syn* see INVENTIVE

‖**demob** *vb syn* see DISCHARGE 7
ant mobilize

demobilize *vb syn* see DISCHARGE 7
rel break up, disband, dispel, disperse, scatter; retire, withdraw
ant mobilize

democratic *adj* of or relating to a political system in which the supreme power is held and exercised by the people <a *democratic* government>
syn popular, self-governing, self-ruling
rel representative; libertarian
con totalitarian; absolute, arbitrary, autocratic, despotic; tyrannical, tyrannous; fascistic, nazi, patriarchal
ant authoritarian; undemocratic

démodé *adj syn* see OLD-FASHIONED
ant a la mode

demoded *adj syn* see OLD-FASHIONED
ant a la mode

demolish *vb syn* see DESTROY 1
rel dilapidate; crush, smash; break, burst, crack
con build, erect, frame, raise, rear
ant construct; rebuild
2 *syn* see TOTAL 3

demon *n syn* see DEVIL 2

demoniac *adj syn* see FIENDISH
rel crazed, crazy, insane, maniac; fired, inspired
con celestial, heavenly
ant angelic

demonian *adj syn* see FIENDISH
rel crazed, crazy, insane, maniac; fired, inspired
con celestial, heavenly

ant angelic

demonic *adj syn* see FIENDISH
rel crazed, crazy, insane, maniac; fired, inspired
con celestial, heavenly
ant angelic

demonstrate *vb* 1 *syn* see SHOW 2
rel display, exhibit, expose, flaunt, parade; explain, set forth
idiom go to show
con conceal, hide, secrete; camouflage, cloak, disguise, dissemble, mask
2 *syn* see PROVE 1
rel authenticate, validate
3 *syn* see ESTABLISH 6

demonstration *n syn* see EXHIBITION 1

demonstrative *adj* marked by display of feeling < was *demonstrative* in his welcome >
syn expansive, outgoing, unconstrained, unreserved, unrestrained
rel affectionate, loving; effusive, outpouring, profuse; candid, frank, open, outspoken, plain
con constrained, reserved, restrained, reticent, taciturn; bashful, shy; retiring, shrinking; introverted; aloof, detached, indifferent, unconcerned; chilly, cold, frigid, glacial, icy
ant undemonstrative

demoralize *vb* 1 *syn* see DEBASE 1
rel debilitate, undermine, weaken; damp, dampen
2 *syn* see DISCOURAGE 1
rel agitate, disturb, upset; disarrange, disorder, disorganize, unsettle; confuse, jumble, muddle, snarl; debilitate, undermine, weaken; unman, unnerve
con arrange, order, organize; energize, fortify, invigorate, strengthen

demote *vb syn* see DEGRADE 1
rel demean, lower
ant promote

demotion *n* the action or an instance of demoting < received a *demotion* from sergeant to corporal >
syn degradation, downgrading, reduction
rel debasement, humbling, humiliation; blackballing, disbarment, exclusion, suspension
con advancement, preferment, upgrading; aggrandizement; boost, elevation, lift, raise
ant promotion

demur *vb* to object or have scruples < he *demurred* at any horseplay >
syn balk, boggle, gag, jib, scruple, shy, stick, stickle, strain, stumble
rel falter, hesitate, vacillate, waver; combat, fight, oppose, resist; expostulate, object, protest, remonstrate; deprecate, disapprove
con accept, admit, receive, take; acquiesce, agree, assent, consent, subscribe, yes; concur; defer, relent, succumb, submit, yield
ant accede

demur *n* 1 *syn* see QUALM

rel faltering, hesitancy, hesitation; aversion, disinclination, loathness; expostulation, protest
con promptness, quickness, readiness
2 the act of objecting or taking exception < accepted without *demur* >
syn challenge, demurral, demurrer, difficulty, objection, protest, question, remonstrance, remonstration
rel reluctance, unwillingness; faltering, hesitancy, hesitation; deprecation, disapproval; protestation; difference, disagreement, dissent, variance
con acquiescence, agreement, assent, consent; concurrence; submission

demure *adj syn* see SHY 1
rel decent, decorous, nice, proper, seemly; prim; earnest, serious, solemn; close, reserved, reticent, silent
con impertinent, intrusive, meddlesome, obtrusive, officious; brash, forward, unbashful, unretiring

demurral *n syn* see DEMUR 2
demurrer *n syn* see DEMUR 2
den *n* 1 *syn* see LAIR 1
2 *syn* see HIDEOUT
3 *syn* see SINK 1
denaturant *n syn* see ADMIXTURE 1
denial *n* 1 refusal to satisfy a request or desire < *denial* of his visiting privileges >
syn disallowance, refusal, rejection
rel declination, nonacceptance
con allowing, conceding, grant, letting; leave, permission, sufferance
2 refusal to admit the truth < his *denial* that he took the money >
syn contradiction, gainsaying, negation
rel controversion, disproof, rebuttal, refutal, refutation; refusal, rejection, repudiation
con acknowledgment, avowal, confession; affirmation, assertion, confirmation
ant admission
3 *syn* see RENUNCIATION
rel abstaining, refraining
con indulgence, self-indulgence; overdoing, overindulgence

denigrate *vb syn* see MALIGN
denizen *n* 1 *syn* see INHABITANT
rel citizen, national, subject
2 *syn* see HABITUÉ 1
denominate *vb syn* see NAME 1
denomination *n* 1 *syn* see NAME 1
2 *syn* see RELIGION 2
denotative *adj syn* see INDICATIVE
denote *vb syn* see MEAN 2
rel insinuate; announce, argue, bespeak, prove
denotive *adj syn* see INDICATIVE
denounce *vb syn* see CRITICIZE
rel accuse, arraign, charge, impeach, incriminate, indict, tax; revile, vituperate; delate, inform
idiom cry harrow (*or* haro)
con panegyrize, praise
ant eulogize
de novo *adv syn* see OVER 7
dense *adj* 1 *syn* see CLOSE 4
rel heaped, massed, piled; crammed, crowded, jam-packed
con dispersed, dissipated, scattered; rare, thin; exiguous, meager, scant, scanty, spare

---

syn synonym(s)   *rel* related word(s)
ant antonym(s)   *con* contrasted word(s)
idiom idiomatic equivalent(s)
‖ use limited; if in doubt, see a dictionary

ant sparse; tenuous

2 *syn* see STUPID 1

rel obtuse; impassive, phlegmatic, stolid; lethargic, sluggish, torpid

ant subtle; bright

denticulate *adj syn* see SERRATE

denudate *vb syn* see STRIP 2

denude *vb* 1 *syn* see STRIP 1

2 *syn* see STRIP 2

denuded *adj syn* see OPEN 2

denunciate *vb syn* see CRITICIZE

rel delate, inform; menace, threaten

ant eulogize

deny *vb* 1 *syn* see DISCLAIM

rel abandon, desert, forsake

con adopt, embrace, espouse; recognize

ant acknowledge; admit

2 to refuse to grant < he was unwilling to *deny* the child's request >

syn disallow, keep back, refuse, withhold

idiom say no to, turn thumbs down on

con allow, concede, let, permit; afford, give

ant grant

3 to restrain (as oneself) from or forgo what is pleasant or satisfying < decided to *deny* himself a second piece of pie >

syn abstain, constrain, curb, hold back, refrain

rel eschew, forbear, forgo, sacrifice; inhibit, restrain; avoid, shun

con overdo, overindulge

ant indulge

4 to refuse to accept as true, valid, or worthy of consideration < *denying* the existence of witches >

syn contradict, contravene, cross, disaffirm, gainsay, impugn, negate, negative, traverse

rel decline, refuse, reject, repudiate; confute, controvert, disprove, rebut, refute; downface

con affirm, assert, aver; allow, grant; authenticate, corroborate, substantiate, validate, verify; avow, confess; claim, submit

ant concede; confirm

depart *vb* 1 *syn* see GO 2

rel set out, start, strike out, toddle

con linger, stay, tarry, wait; come; approach, near

ant arrive; abide, remain

2 *syn* see DIE 1

con exist, live, survive

3 *syn* see SWERVE 2

rel abandon, desert, forsake; reject, repudiate; cast, discard; differ, disagree, dissent, vary

4 *syn* see DIGRESS 2

departed *adj* 1 *syn* see DEAD 1

idiom called home, gone to a better land

2 *syn* see EXTINCT 2

departing *adj syn* see PARTING

departure *n* 1 the act of going, coming out, or leaving a place < the hasty *departure* of the refugees >

syn egress, egression, exit, exiting, exodus, offgoing, setting-out, withdrawal

rel going, leaving, quitting, retreat; decampment, flight; farewell, leave-taking

con coming, entering, ingress

ant arrival

2 *syn* see DEVIATION 1

rel rambling, straying, wandering

depend *vb syn* see HANG 1

depend (on *or* upon) *vb* 1 to rest or to be contingent upon something uncertain, variable, or indeterminable < our trip *depends* upon the weather >

syn hang (on *or* upon), hinge (on *or* upon), ||pend, stand (on *or* upon), turn (on *or* upon)

rel base, bottom, found, ground, rest, stay

idiom hang in the balance

2 *syn* see RELY (on *or* upon)

rel incline, lean

dependable *adj* 1 *syn* see RELIABLE 1

rel assured, confident, sure; responsible; constant, faithful, loyal, staunch, steadfast, steady

idiom as good as one's word, to be counted on

con capricious, fickle, inconstant, mercurial, unstable; dishonest, lying, mendacious, untruthful

ant independable, undependable

2 *syn* see TRUE 9

3 *syn* see CERTAIN 3

dependence *n syn* see TRUST 1

dependent *adj* 1 determined or conditioned by another < a conclusion that is *dependent* on a premise >

syn conditional, contingent, relative, reliant

rel exposed, liable, open, subject, susceptible; iffy, provisional, provisory; uncertain; circumscribed, limited, restricted

con categorical, ultimate; boundless, eternal, illimitable, uncircumscribed; basal, basic, fundamental, primary, underived

ant absolute; infinite; original

2 *syn* see SUBORDINATE

rel counting, depending, reckoning, relying, trusting; accessory, ancillary, appurtenant; abased, debased, humbled

con principal; paramount, predominant, preponderant, preponderating, sovereign

ant independent

depict *vb syn* see REPRESENT 1

rel narrate, recite, recount, rehearse, relate, report, state; outline, sketch

depiction *n syn* see REPRESENTATION

deplete *vb* to bring to a low estate by depriving of something essential < an epidemic which *depletes* an army of manpower >

syn bankrupt, drain, draw, draw down, exhaust, impoverish, use up

rel cripple, debilitate, disable, enfeeble, sap, undermine, weaken; decrease, diminish, lessen, reduce; bleed, draw off, dry up, empty, milk; consume, expend, finish, spend, wash up

idiom dig into

con augment, enlarge, increase; bolster, fortify, strengthen; rebuild, repair, restore, revive

ant renew, replace

depleted *adj syn* see EFFETE 2

rel sapped, weakened

con augmented, enlarged, increased

deplorable *adj* of a kind to cause great distress < a *deplorable* loss of life >

syn afflictive, calamitous, dire, distressing, dolorous, grievous, heartbreaking, heartrending, lamentable, mournful, regrettable, unfortunate, woeful

rel awful, dreadful, terrible; horrifying, intolerable, overwhelming, sickening, unbearable; miserable, wretched; disastrous

idiom as bad as bad can be, as bad as can be

con beneficial, helpful, salutary; advantageous, favorable, propitious

deplore *vb* 1 to manifest grief or sorrow for something < *deplore* the death of a close friend>

syn bemoan, bewail, grieve, lament, moan, weep

rel deprecate, disapprove; mourn, sorrow; cry, keen, wail

con boast, brag, crow, vaunt; rejoice

2 *syn* see REGRET

depone *vb syn* see TESTIFY 2

deport *vb* 1 *syn* see BEHAVE 1

2 *syn* see BANISH

deportation *n syn* see EXILE 1

deportment *n* 1 *syn* see BEHAVIOR

2 *syn* see BEARING 1

depose *vb* 1 to remove from a throne or other high position < trying to *depose* the king in favor of his brother> < *deposed* industrial leaders>

syn dethrone, discrown, disenthrone, displace, disthrone, uncrown, unmake

rel overthrow, subvert, upset; chuck, dismiss, eject, oust, throw out

con inaugurate, induct, install, instate, invest; crown, enthrone, throne

2 *syn* see ASSERT 1

3 *syn* see TESTIFY 2

deposit *vb syn* see BANK

rel put by, store, stow

deposit *n syn* see SEDIMENT

depository *n syn* see DEPOT 2

depot *n* 1 *syn* see ARMORY

2 a place where something is deposited or stored < a gasoline *depot* >

syn arsenal, depository, magazine, repository, store, storehouse

rel storeroom, warehouse

3 *syn* see RAILROAD STATION

rel terminal, terminus

deprave *vb syn* see DEBASE 1

con elevate, ennoble, exalt, raise, uplift

depraved *adj* 1 *syn* see DEBASED

rel degenerate, infamous, vicious, villainous; degraded; twisted, warped

con scrupulous, upright

2 *syn* see VICIOUS 1

depravity *n syn* see VICE 1

deprecate *vb syn* see DISAPPROVE 1

rel bemoan, bewail, deplore, lament; derogate, detract

ant endorse

depreciate *vb* 1 to reduce the value of < *depreciate* the dollar>

syn cheapen, decry, devalorize, devaluate, devalue, downgrade, lower, mark down, soften, underprize, underrate, undervalue, write down, write off

rel depress; abate, decrease, diminish, dwindle, lessen, reduce; erode

---

con augment, increase; bloat, blow up, expand, inflate; amplify, magnify

ant appreciate

2 *syn* see DECRY 2

rel underestimate, underrate, undervalue; discountenance, disfavor, disesteem

con cherish, prize, treasure, value; comprehend, understand

ant appreciate

depreciation *n syn* see DETRACTION

depreciative *adj syn* see DEROGATORY

rel underestimating, underrating, undervaluing

ant appreciative

depreciatory *adj syn* see DEROGATORY

rel underestimating, underrating, undervaluing

ant appreciative

depredate *vb syn* see RAVAGE

depredator *n syn* see MARAUDER

depress *vb* 1 *syn* see LOWER 3

2 to lower in spirit or mood < the thought of all his debts *depressed* him>

syn oppress, press, sadden, weigh down

rel ail, distress, trouble; afflict, torment, try; contrist, deject, discourage, dishearten, dispirit; bother, disturb, perturb, upset

con delight, gladden, gratify, please, rejoice; excite, inspire, stimulate; brighten, cheer up, encourage; buoy, elevate

ant elate, exhilarate; cheer

depressant *adj syn* see GLOOMY 3

depressed *adj* 1 *syn* see DOWNCAST

rel lugubrious, melancholy

ant exhilarated; animated

2 *syn* see UNDERPRIVILEGED

depressing *adj* 1 *syn* see GLOOMY 3

con cheering, elevating, uplifting; exciting, inspiring

ant exhilarating

2 *syn* see SAD 2

depression *n* 1 *syn* see SADNESS

rel boredom, doldrums, ennui, tedium

con glee, hilarity, mirth

ant buoyancy; elation

2 a low spot < a *depression* in the land >

syn basin, concavity, dip, hollow, sag, sink, sinkage, sinkhole; *compare* NOTCH 1

rel cavity, hole, pocket, vacuity, vacuum, void; crater, pit; scoop

3 a period of lowered economic activity and extensive unemployment < indicators that warn of a coming *depression* >

syn recession, slump, stagnation

rel crash, decline, dislocation, drop; sag; paralysis; ||stagflation

con expansion; booming, development, growth; advancement, progress

ant boom

depressive *adj syn* see GLOOMY 3

deprivation *n syn* see PRIVATION 2

deprive *vb* 1 *syn* see STRIP 2

2 to prevent one from possessing < to *deprive* a person of his civil rights>

syn bereave, disinherit, dispossess, divest, lose, oust, rob; *compare* STRIP 2

rel dock; bare, denude, dismantle, strip

con furnish, give, supply; clothe, endow, equip, fit (out), invest, outfit

ant provide

deprived *adj syn* see UNDERPRIVILEGED

deprivement *n syn* see PRIVATION 2

---

syn synonym(s)   *rel* related word(s)

ant antonym(s)   *con* contrasted word(s)

idiom idiomatic equivalent(s)

|| use limited; if in doubt, see a dictionary

depth *n* 1 the perpendicular extent or measurement downward from a surface < measured the *depth* of the river >
syn deepness, drop
rel profoundness, profundity; lowness; sounding; draft
con shallowness; altitude, elevation
2 the quality of being profound (as in insight) or full (as of knowledge) < her answer showed she had great *depth* in that subject >
syn abyss, deepness, profoundness, profundity
rel sense, wisdom, wiseness; brain, intellect, intelligence; keenness, sharpness
con shallowness, superficiality, unprofoundness; sciolism, smatter, smattering

depthless *adj syn see* SUPERFICIAL 2
depurate *vb syn see* PURIFY 1
depute *vb syn see* DELEGATE
deputize *vb syn see* DELEGATE
deputy *n* 1 *syn see* AGENT 2
rel substitute, surrogate; replacement
2 *syn see* DELEGATE
derange *vb* 1 *syn see* DISORDER 1
rel perturb; discommode, incommode inconvenience
con compose, settle
ant arrange; adjust
2 *syn see* UPSET 5
3 *syn see* MADDEN 1
deranged *adj syn see* INSANE 1
rel disarranged, disordered, disturbed
derangement *n syn see* INSANITY 1
rel disarrangement, disorder; confusion; disturbance; unsoundness
derelict *adj* 1 given up especially by the owner or occupant < a *derelict* old home>
syn abandoned, deserted, desolate, forsaken, lorn, solitary, uncouth
rel dilapidated, dingy, faded, run-down, seedy, shabby, threadbare
con cherished, prized, treasured; attended, kept up, maintained
2 *syn see* NEGLIGENT
rel irresponsible, undependable, unreliable, untrustworthy
con dependable, reliable, responsible, trustworthy; careful, heedful, thoughtful
ant faithful
derelict *n* 1 *syn see* OUTCAST
2 *syn see* VAGABOND
dereliction *n syn see* FAILURE 1
rel abuse, misuse, outrage
ant faithfulness
deride *vb syn see* RIDICULE
rel banter, chaff, jolly, kid, rag, rib
de rigueur *adj syn see* DECOROUS 1
derision *n syn see* LAUGHINGSTOCK
derivable *adj syn see* DEDUCTIVE
derivate *adj syn see* SECONDARY 2
derivation *n syn see* SOURCE
derivational *adj syn see* SECONDARY 2
derivative *adj syn see* SECONDARY 2
ant underivative
derivative *n syn see* OUTGROWTH 2
derive *vb* 1 to reach (as a conclusion) as an end point of reasoning and observation < evidence from which he *derived* a startling new set of axioms >
syn educe, evolve, excogitate

rel conclude, deduce, gather, infer, judge; arrive (at), elicit, extract, reach; develop, elaborate, formulate, put (together), work out
2 *syn see* INFER
3 *syn see* TAKE 14
derive (from) *vb syn see* SPRING 1
derived *adj syn see* SECONDARY 2
dernier cri *n syn see* FASHION 3
dernier ressort *n syn see* RESOURCE 3
derogate *vb syn see* DECRY 2
rel decrease, lessen, reduce; discredit, disgrace
con enhance, heighten, intensify
derogatory *adj* designed or tending to belittle < *derogatory* comments about the actor's performance >
syn depreciative, depreciatory, detracting, disadvantageous, disparaging, dyslogistic, pejorative, slighting, uncomplimentary
rel belittling, decrying, minimizing; aspersing, calumnious, defamatory, maligning, vilifying; degrading, demeaning, humiliating; despiteful, malevolent, malicious, spiteful; contumelious, disdainful, scornful
con admiring, esteeming; acclaiming, laudatory, praising; appreciative
ant complimentary
derout *vb syn see* ROUT 1
derriere *n syn see* BUTTOCKS
descant *n* 1 *syn see* MELODY
2 *syn see* SONG 2
descant *vb syn see* DISCOURSE 1
descend *vb* 1 *syn see* FALL 1
ant rise
2 *syn see* STOOP 2
3 *syn see* DETERIORATE 1
descendant *n* 1 **descendants** *pl syn see* OFFSPRING
ant ascendants, ancestors
2 *syn see* OUTGROWTH 2
descent *n* 1 the act or process of passing from a higher to a lower level or state < a parachute *descent* > < his slow *descent* to the gutter >
syn drop, fall
rel plummeting, plunging, sinking
con rise, upswing, upturn; advance, headway, progress, progression; betterment, improvement
ant ascent
2 *syn see* COMEDOWN
3 *syn see* ANCESTRY
4 an inclination downward < the steep *descent* of the mountain >
syn decline, declivity, dip, drop, fall
rel downgrade, grade, gradient, incline, slope; drop, drop-off
con acclivity, upgrade, uphill
ant ascent, rise
describe *vb* 1 *syn see* RELATE 1
rel communicate, impart; transmit; construe, elucidate, explain, explicate, expound; exemplify, illustrate; characterize, distinguish
2 *syn see* REPRESENT 1
description *n* 1 *syn see* REPRESENTATION
2 a descriptive statement < a fascinating *description* of his adventures >
syn narration, recital, recountal, recounting

rel anecdote, narrative, story, tale, yarn; account, chronicle, version; report, statement

3 *syn* see TYPE

descry *vb* 1 *syn* see SEE 1

2 *syn* see FIND 1

rel appreciate, comprehend, understand; realize

desecrate *adj syn* see RAVAGE

desecrated *adj syn* see IMPURE 3

desecration *n syn* see PROFANATION

ant consecration

desensitize *vb syn* see DEADEN 1

ant sensitize

desert *n syn* see WASTE 1

desert *n usu* deserts *pl syn* see DUE 1

rel chastening, chastisement, discipline, disciplining, punishment

idiom just deserts

desert *vb* 1 *syn* see ABANDON 1

rel depart, go, leave

con adhere, cohere

ant cleave (to), stick (to)

2 *syn* see DEFECT

rel abscond, decamp, escape, flee, fly

idiom go over the hill

con abide, remain, stay

deserted *adj syn* see DERELICT 1

rel empty, vacant; uninhabited, unoccupied; bare, barren

desertion *n syn* see DEFECTION

rel perfidiousness, perfidy, treacherousness, treachery

deserve *vb syn* see EARN 2

rel gain, get, win; demand

idiom have it coming

deserved *adj syn* see JUST 3

ant undeserved

deserving *n syn* see DUE 1

deserving *adj syn* see WORTHY 1

ant undeserving

desexualize *vb syn* see STERILIZE

desiccate *vb* 1 *syn* see DRY 1

2 to drain or be drained of emotional or intellectual vitality < this book is *desiccated* by undue concentration on statistics >

syn devitalize, dry up

rel deplete, drain, exhaust; divest; decay, fade, shrivel, wither, wizen

con brighten, enliven

desiderate *vb syn* see DESIRE 1

desight *n syn* see EYESORE

design *vb* 1 *syn* see INTEND 2

2 *syn* see PLAN 1

rel delineate, diagram; create, invent; construct, fashion, form, frame, produce; contrive

con accomplish, achieve, effect, execute, fulfill, perform

3 to work out the arrangement of the parts of < *design* an urban center >

syn arrange, lay out, map (out), plan, set out; *compare* PLAN 2

rel delineate, diagram, draft, outline, sketch

design *n* 1 *syn* see PLAN 1

rel delineation, diagram, draft, outline, sketch, tracing; creation, invention

---

con accomplishment, achievement, execution, fulfillment, performance

2 *syn* see INTENTION

rel conation, volition, will; deliberation, reflection, thinking, thought; intrigue, machination, plot

con accident, chance, fortuity, hap; impulse

3 *syn* see FIGURE 3

4 *syn* see MAKEUP 1

designate *vb* 1 *syn* see NAME 1

2 to declare a person one's choice < *designated* him to fill the position >

syn appoint, finger, make, name, nominate, tap

rel choose, elect, opt, pick, select, single; assign, delegate, depute; dictate

con disapprove, disfavor, object (to), oppose; disallow, reject, turn down

3 to set aside (as funds) for a specific use < *designated* the income to be used for charity >

syn allocate, earmark

rel specify; appropriate, reserve; stipulate; allot, apportion, mete (out)

designation *n syn* see NAME 1

rel identification, recognition; classification, pigeonhole, pigeonholing

designative *adj syn* see INDICATIVE

designed *adj syn* see DELIBERATE 1

rel decided, determined, resolved

con casual, chance, contingent, fluky, fortuitous, incidental; impulsive, spontaneous; natural, normal, regular, typical

ant accidental

designedly *adv syn* see INTENTIONALLY

designless *adj syn* see RANDOM

desire *n* 1 a longing for something that promises enjoyment or satisfaction < he had a strong *desire* for fame and fortune >

syn appetite, appetition, craving, itch, lust, passion, urge

rel hankering, hunger, hungering, longing, pining, thirst, thirsting, yearning; desideratum, desiderium; avarice, cupidity, greed, rapacity; concupiscence, eros

con abhorrence, repellency, repugnance, repulsion; aversion, disfavor, dislike

ant distaste

2 *syn* see LUST 2

desire *vb* 1 to have a longing for something < men who *desire* success >

syn ||choose, covet, crave, desiderate, want, wish

rel hanker, hunger, long, pine, thirst, yearn; enjoy, fancy, like; aim, aspire, pant

idiom set one's eyes (*or* heart) upon

con abhor, abominate, detest, hate, loath; decline, refuse, reject, repudiate, spurn

2 *syn* see ASK 2

desired *adj syn* see TRUE 7

desirous *adj syn* see COVETOUS

desist *vb syn* see STOP 3

rel abstain, forbear; abandon, relinquish, resign, yield

idiom have done with

con continue; persevere

ant persist

desistance *n syn* see END 2

desk *n* a table, frame, or case with a sloping or horizontal surface especially for writing < sat meditating at her *desk* >

syn escritoire, secretaire, secretary, writing desk

---

rel lectern, reading desk

desolate *adj* 1 *syn see* DERELICT 1
rel empty, vacant; uninhabited, unoccupied
2 *syn see* INCONSOLABLE
3 *syn see* GLOOMY 3
rel bare, barren; destitute, poor, poverty‑stricken; dark, murky

desolate *vb syn see* RAVAGE

despair *vb* to lose all hope or confidence < *despaired* of winning >
syn despond, give up
rel abandon, drop, relinquish, renounce, resign, surrender, yield
idiom lose heart (*or* courage *or* faith *or* hope)
con await, count (on), depend (on), hope, look (for); trust (in *or* to)
ant expect

despairing *adj syn see* DESPONDENT
rel atrabilious, melancholic, melancholy; cynical, misanthropic, pessimistic; depressed, oppressed, weighed down
con optimistic, roseate, rose‑colored; assured, confident, sanguine, sure
ant hopeful

desperado *n syn see* OUTLAW
rel convict, criminal, lawbreaker

desperate *adj* 1 *syn see* DESPONDENT
rel foolhardy, rash, reckless, venturesome; headlong, precipitate; baffled, balked, circumvented, foiled, frustrated, outwitted, thwarted
con collected, composed, cool, nonchalant; assured, confident, sanguine, sure
2 *syn see* ACUTE 6
3 *syn see* INTENSE 1
4 *syn see* OUTRAGEOUS 2

despicable *adj* 1 *syn see* CONTEMPTIBLE
rel disgraceful, disreputable, ignominious, infamous, loathsome
con applaudable, commendable
ant laudable, praiseworthy
2 *syn see* BASE 3

despisable *adj syn see* CONTEMPTIBLE

despisal *n syn see* DESPITE 1

despise *vb* to regard as beneath one's notice and unworthy of consideration or interest < he had always *despised* the weak >
syn abhor, contemn, disdain, look down, scorn, scout
rel abominate, detest, execrate, hate, loathe; reject, repudiate, spurn; avoid, eschew, renounce, shun; disregard, ignore, overlook, slight, snub
idiom have no use for, look down one's nose at
con apprize, cherish, prize, treasure, value; admire, regard, respect
ant appreciate, esteem

despisement *n syn see* DESPITE 1

despite *n* 1 the feeling or attitude of despising < felt *despite* toward the lowly >
syn contempt, despisal, despisement, disdain, disparagement, scorn
rel disdainfulness, insolence, superciliousness; abhorrence, abomination, detestation, hate, hatred, loathing; rejection, repudiation, spurning; aversion, disfavor, dislike, distaste; cold shoulder, rebuff, slight, snub; disgust, loathing
con admiration, esteem, honor, regard, respect; attraction, liking

2 *syn see* MALICE
rel contempt, disdain, scorn; abhorrence, abomination, detestation, hate, hatred, loathing
con admiration, esteem, respect: awe, fear, reverence
ant appreciation
3 *syn see* DEFIANCE 2
rel harm, hurt, injury
4 *syn see* AFFRONT
rel cut, discourtesy, incivility; rebuff, slight, snub

despite *prep syn see* AGAINST 4

despiteful *adj syn see* MALICIOUS

despitefulness *n syn see* MALICE

despoil *vb syn see* RAVAGE

despoiler *n* 1 *syn see* MARAUDER
2 *syn see* VANDAL

despond *vb* 1 *syn see* DESPAIR
rel droop, sag; languish
idiom reach the depths
con expect, hope, look
2 *syn see* MOPE 1

despondent *adj* having lost all or nearly all hope < *despondent* about his health >
syn despairing, desperate, desponding, forlorn, hopeless
rel grieving, mourning, sorrowful; dejected, depressed, melancholy, sad; disconsolate, dispirited, downcast, woebegone; discouraged, disheartened
con cheerful, glad, happy, joyful, joyous; buoyant, elastic, resilient, volatile; hopeful, optimistic
ant lighthearted

desponding *adj syn see* DESPONDENT

despot *n syn see* TYRANT

despotic *adj syn see* ABSOLUTE 4

despotism *n syn see* TYRANNY

despotize *vb syn see* TYRANNIZE

desquamate *vb syn see* SCALE 2

destine *vb syn see* PREDESTINE 1

destiny *n syn see* FATE
rel design, goal, intent, intention, objective

destitute *adj* 1 *syn see* DEVOID
rel deficient; bankrupt, bankrupted, depleted, drained, exhausted; divested, stripped
con complete, full, replete
2 *syn see* POOR 1
rel depleted, drained, exhausted
idiom on one's uppers, on the rocks
con comfortable, prosperous, well‑fixed, well‑off, well‑to‑do
ant opulent

destituteness *n syn see* POVERTY 1
rel absence, dearth, lack; adversity, misfortune
con competence, sufficiency
ant opulence

destitution *n syn see* POVERTY 1
rel absence, dearth, lack, privation, want; adversity, misfortune
con competence, sufficiency
ant opulence

destroy *vb* 1 to bring to ruin < the army *destroyed* the enemy village > < his health was finally *destroyed* by drink >
syn annihilate, atomize, decapitate, decimate, demolish, destruct, discreate, dismantle, dissolve, dynamite, pull down, pulverize, quench, raze, rub out, ruin, ruinate, shatter, shoot, smash, tear down.

unbuild, undo, unframe, unmake, wrack, wreck; *compare* TOTAL 3

rel abolish, extinguish; devastate, pillage, ravage, sack, waste; eradicate, exterminate, extirpate, wipe; mangle, mutilate; rubble; doom

idiom blow to bits, bring to an end, dispose of, tear to shreds

con establish, found, institute, organize; fabricate, fashion, forge, form, make, manufacture, shape; conserve, preserve, protect, save

2 *syn* see KILL 1

destroyer *n* 1 *syn* see VANDAL
　2 *syn* see DOWNFALL 2

destruct *vb syn* see DESTROY 1

destruction *n* 1 *syn* see DOWNFALL 2
　2 *syn* see RUIN 3

destructive *adj* having the capability, property, or effect of destroying <a *destructive* windstorm> <his brother was a *destructive* influence in his life>

syn annihilative, ruinous, shattering, wrackful, wreckful

rel calamitous, disastrous, deadly, fatal, lethal, mortal; consumptive; internecine; baneful, deleterious, detrimental

con creative, formative; harmless, innocuous, inoffensive; helpful, improving

ant constructive

desuetude *n* 1 *syn* see END 2
　2 *syn* see DISUSE

desultory *adj* 1 *syn* see FITFUL

rel erratic; shifting, vagrant, wavering

con constant, invariable, unchanging, unfailing

ant steady

2 *syn* see RANDOM

rel fitful, spasmodic; disorderly, unmethodical, unsystematic; capricious, fickle, inconstant, mercurial

con orderly, systematic

ant assiduous; methodical

detach *vb* to remove one thing from another with which it is in union or association <*detach* sheets from a loose-leaf book>

syn abstract, disassociate, disconnect, disengage, dissociate, uncouple, unfix

rel cut off; divorce, part, separate, sever, sunder; disjoin, disunite; disassemble, dismantle, dismember, dismount; disaffiliate

idiom take apart

con fasten, fix; bind, tie; combine, conjoin, unite

ant affix, attach

detached *adj* 1 *syn* see ALONE 1

rel separate, unconnected

con abutting, adjacent; connected, joined, linked

ant adjoining; attached

2 *syn* see INDIFFERENT 2

con anxious, concerned, solicitous; self-centered, selfish

ant interested

3 *syn* see NEUTRAL

rel distant, remote, removed

---

syn synonym(s)　　*rel* related word(s)
ant antonym(s)　　*con* contrasted word(s)
idiom idiomatic equivalent(s)
‖ use limited; if in doubt, see a dictionary

---

detachment *n syn* see SEPARATION 1

detail *n syn* see POINT 1

con anatomy, framework, skeleton, structure; bulk, mass; design, plan

detail *vb syn* see SPECIFY 3

detailed *adj syn* see CIRCUMSTANTIAL

rel abundant, copious; exhausting, exhaustive, thoroughgoing

detailedly *adv syn* see THOROUGHLY 2

detain *vb* 1 *syn* see ARREST 2

rel buttonhole, hold, restrain

2 *syn* see KEEP 5

3 *syn* see DELAY 1

rel check, curb, inhibit, restrain

detect *vb syn* see FIND 1

detectable *adj syn* see PERCEPTIBLE

detection *n syn* see DISCOVERY

detective *n* one employed or engaged in detecting lawbreakers or in getting information that is not readily or publicly accessible <used *detectives* to locate the missing witness>

syn dick, ‖eye, gumshoe, hawkshaw, investigator, plainclothesman, Sherlock, Sherlock Holmes, sleuth, ‖tec; *compare* INFORMER, PRIVATE DETECTIVE

rel G-man; roper; shoofly

detention *n syn* see ARREST

rel imprisonment, incarceration, internment

deter *vb* 1 *syn* see DISSUADE

rel prevent; block, hinder, impede, obstruct; debar, shut out; frighten, scare; inhibit, restrain

con abet, incite, instigate; excite, provoke, stimulate; actuate, motivate

2 *syn* see PREVENT 2

deteriorate *vb* 1 to pass from a higher to a lower type or condition <the road quickly *deteriorated* into a bumpy path>

syn decline, degenerate, descend, disimprove, disintegrate, retrograde, rot, sink, worsen

rel crumble, decay, decompose; impair, mar, spoil; debilitate, undermine, weaken; depreciate, lessen

idiom be the worse for wear, go downhill, go to pot (or the dogs)

con better, improve; advance, progress; enhance, heighten

ant ameliorate

2 *syn* see FAIL 1

deterioration *n* 1 a falling from a higher to a lower level (as of quality or character) <the *deterioration* of business during the depression>

syn atrophy, decadence, declension, declination, decline, degeneracy, degeneration, dégringolade, devaluation, devolution, downfall, downgrade, ruin

rel impairment, spoiling; crumbling, decay, decaying, decomposition, disintegration, dissolution, dry rot, rotting; debasement, degradation; depreciation, lessening; dislocation, disruption

con betterment, help; enhancement, heightening, improvement

ant amelioration

2 *syn* see FAILURE 4

con convalescence, recovering, recuperation

ant improvement

determinable *adj syn* see TERMINABLE

determinant *n syn see* CAUSE 1
rel factor; authority, influence, weight

determinate *adj* 1 *syn see* INFLEXIBLE 3
2 *syn see* DEFINITE 1
ant indeterminate

determinate *vb syn see* IDENTIFY

determination *n* 1 *syn see* DECISION 1
2 *syn see* DECISION 2
ant indetermination

determine *vb* 1 *syn see* ESTABLISH 6
rel fix, set; settle
2 *syn see* PREDESTINE 1
3 *syn see* DEMARCATE 1
4 *syn see* DECIDE
rel bias, dispose, incline, predispose; actuate, drive, impel, move; induce, persuade
5 *syn see* CLOSE 3
6 *syn see* DISCOVER 3

determined *adj syn see* DECIDED 2
rel earnest, purposeful, serious; unfaltering, unhesitating, unwavering
con unresolved, unsettled; hesitating, hesitant, wavering
ant undetermined

detest *vb syn see* HATE
rel reject, repudiate, spurn
con love; appreciate, treasure, value
ant adore

detestable *adj syn see* HATEFUL 2
rel sorry; atrocious, heinous, monstrous, outrageous
ant adorable

detestation *n* 1 *syn see* ABOMINATION 2
rel antipathy, disgust
con affection, attachment, love; forbearance, indulgence, tolerance
ant adoration
2 *syn see* ABOMINATION 1
ant adoration

dethrone *vb syn see* DEPOSE 1
ant enthrone, throne

detonate *vb syn see* EXPLODE 1

detour *n* an indirect course often temporarily replacing part of a usual route <a *detour* around road construction> <took a *detour* to show him the lake>
syn roundabout, runaround
rel bypass

detour *vb syn see* SKIRT 2

detract (from) *vb syn see* DECRY 2
rel libel, slander; decrease, lessen, reduce
con enhance, heighten, intensify

detracting *adj* 1 *syn see* DEROGATORY
2 *syn see* LIBELOUS

detraction *n* the expression of damaging or malicious opinions <his persistent *detraction* of his rival's motives was wholly unfair>
syn backbiting, backstabbing, belittlement, calumny, character assassination, defamation, depreciation, disparagement, scandal, slander, sycophancy, tale
rel damage, harm, hurt, injury; injustice, wrong; aspersion, calumniation, libel, libeling, maligning, slandering, traducing, vilification
con enhancement, heightening, laudation, praise; approbation, approval
ant commendation

detractive *adj syn see* LIBELOUS

detractory *adj syn see* LIBELOUS

detriment *n syn see* DISADVANTAGE
rel damage, harm, hurt, injury, mischief; impairment, marring, spoiling

ant advantage, benefit

detrimental *adj syn see* HARMFUL
con aiding, helpful, helping; harmless
ant beneficial
2 *syn see* ADVERSE 2

de trop *adj syn see* SUPERFLUOUS

detruncate *vb syn see* TOP 1

deuced *adj syn see* UTTER

||**deval** *vb syn see* STOP 3

devalorize *vb syn see* DEPRECIATE 1

devaluate *vb syn see* DEPRECIATE 1

devaluation *n syn see* DETERIORATION 1

devalue *vb syn see* DEPRECIATE 1

devast *vb syn see* RAVAGE

devastate *vb syn see* RAVAGE

devastation *n syn see* RUIN 3

||**devel** *vb syn see* STRIKE 2

develop *vb* 1 *syn see* EXPAND 4
2 *syn see* UNFOLD 3
rel actualize, materialize, realize
3 *syn see* MATURE
rel dilate, expand; enroot, establish; flourish, prosper, thrive
con shrivel, wither, wizen
4 to come to have usually gradually <*develop* a taste for dry wine>
syn acquire, form
rel gain, get, obtain; achieve, attain, reach
5 *syn see* HAPPEN 1

development *n* progressive advance from a lower or simpler to a higher or more complex form <*development* of a seed into a plant> <*development* of an industry>
syn evolution, evolvement, flowering, growth, progress, progression, unfolding, upgrowth
rel advance, advancement, ongoing
con decadence, declension, degeneration, deterioration, devolution
ant decline

deviant *adj* 1 *syn see* ABNORMAL 1
con normal; natural
2 *syn see* IRREGULAR 1

deviate *vb* 1 *syn see* SWERVE 2
2 *syn see* ERR
idiom deviate from the path of virtue

deviation *n* 1 departure from a course or procedure or from a norm or standard <no *deviation* from traditional methods was permitted>
syn aberration, deflection, departure, divergence, diversion, turning
rel alteration, change, modification, variation; breach, transgression, violation; anomaly, failing, fault; blunder, error, lapse
con accordance, agreement, conformance, conformity, correspondence
2 *syn see* TURN 2

deviative *adj syn see* ABNORMAL 1

device *n* 1 *syn see* TRICK 1
2 something (as a mechanical device) that performs a function or effects a desired end <invented many handy household *devices*>
syn contraption, contrivance; *compare* GADGET 1
rel appliance, implement, instrument, tool, utensil; apparatus, machine, mechanism; expedient, makeshift, resort, resource, shift; creation, invention; dingus, doohickey, hickey, thingumbob
3 *syn see* FIGURE 3

rel attribute, emblem, symbol, type; insignia, motto

deviceful *adj syn see* INVENTIVE

devil *n* 1 *often cap* the personal supreme spirit of evil and unrighteousness in Jewish and Christian theology
syn Apollyon, Beelzebub, ‖Cloot(s), ‖Clootie, diablo, fiend, Lucifer, Old Gooseberry, Old Nick, Old Scratch, Satan, serpent
rel cacodemon; dybbuk
idiom Prince of Darkness
2 an extremely and malignantly wicked person < he was a *devil* who would stop at nothing to get what he wanted >
syn Archfiend, demon, fiend, Satan, Succubus; *compare* SCAMP, VILLAIN 1
rel blackguard, caitiff, knave; scoundrel, villain; beast, brute
3 *syn see* SCAMP

‖**devil-devil** *n syn see* SPELL

‖**devil-dodger** *n syn see* CLERGYMAN

deviling *n syn see* IMP 1

devilish *adj* 1 *syn see* FIENDISH
rel iniquitous, nefarious, villainous; accursed, cursed, damnable, execrable; bad, evil, wicked
ant angelic
2 *syn see* SATANIC 1

devilkin *n syn see* IMP 1

devil-may-care *adj syn see* WILD 7
rel rash, reckless
con careful, heedful, responsible, thoughtful

devilment *n syn see* MISCHIEVOUSNESS

devilry *n syn see* MISCHIEVOUSNESS

‖**devil's-bones** *n pl syn see* DICE

deviltry *n syn see* MISCHIEVOUSNESS

devious *adj* 1 *syn see* OBSCURE 2
2 *syn see* CROOKED 1
rel deviating, digressing, diverting
ant straightforward
3 *syn see* ERRATIC 1
4 *syn see* ERRANT 2
rel artful, crafty, cunning, foxy, insidious, sly, tricky
5 *syn see* UNDERHAND
ant straightforward

devise *n syn see* LEGACY 1

devise *vb* 1 *syn see* PLAN 2
2 *syn see* CONTRIVE 2
rel create, discover; forge, form, shape; design
3 *syn see* PLOT
4 *syn see* WILL

devitalize *vb syn see* DESICCATE 2
rel deprive; eviscerate, weaken
ant vitalize

devoid *adj* showing a want or lack < a poem *devoid* of worth >
syn destitute, empty, innocent, void
rel bare, barren; lacking, wanting; deficient
con filled, full; furnished, provided, supplied
ant replete

devoir *n* 1 *syn see* OBLIGATION 2
2 *syn see* TASK 1

devolution *n syn see* DETERIORATION 1
rel regression, regressiveness, retrogression, retrogressiveness; receding, recession, retrogradation, retrograding
con development; progress, progression
ant evolution

devote *vb* 1 to set apart for a particular and often a better or higher use or end < a woman who *devotes* her life to helping others >
syn consecrate, dedicate, hallow
rel sanctify, vow; commit, confide, consign, entrust
idiom set apart
2 *syn see* GIVE 1
3 *syn see* ADDRESS 3
rel attempt, endeavor, strive, struggle, try; employ, use, utilize

devote (to) *vb syn see* HABITUATE 2
rel attach, wrap (up)

devoted *adj syn see* LOVING
rel constant, faithful, loyal, true; thoughtful; fervid, zealous

devotee *n* 1 *syn see* ADDICT
2 *syn see* AMATEUR 1

devotion *n* 1 *syn see* FIDELITY 1
rel enthusiasm, fervor, passion, zeal; affection, attachment, love; consecration, dedication, devotement
2 *syn see* LOVE 1

devour *vb* 1 *syn see* EAT 1
2 *syn see* EAT UP 1
idiom eat like a horse, eat one's head off
3 *syn see* CONSUME 1
4 *syn see* RAVAGE
rel demolish, destroy; ruin, wreck; dissipate, squander
5 to exhibit avid interest in or enjoyment of < the crowd *devoured* the lurid scene >
syn ‖eat up
rel delight (in), enjoy, rejoice (in), relish, revel (in); feast (on), gloat (over *or* on)
con avoid, eschew, shun

devout *adj* showing fervor in the practice of religion < a *devout* churchgoer >
syn godly, holy, pietistic, pious, prayerful, religious
rel ardent, fervent, fervid, zealous; adoring, revering, venerating, worshiping
con impious, irreligious, ungodly, unholy; irreverent; apostate, backsliding
ant undevout

dexter *adj syn see* FAVORABLE 5
ant sinister

dexterity *n* 1 *syn see* ADDRESS 1
rel adeptness, skillfulness; effortlessness, smoothness
con awkwardness, maladroitness
ant clumsiness
2 *syn see* ART 1

dexterous *adj* 1 ready and skilled in physical movements < a *dexterous* worker >
syn adroit, clever, deft, handy, neat-handed, nimble
rel agile; adept, expert, masterly, proficient, skilled, skillful; easy, effortless, facile, smooth
con awkward, gauche, inept, maladroit
ant clumsy
2 *syn see* CLEVER 4

dexterousness *n syn see* ADDRESS 1
ant clumsiness

dextrorotatory *adj syn see* RIGHT-HANDED

---

syn synonym(s)   *rel* related word(s)
ant antonym(s)   *con* contrasted word(s)
idiom idiomatic equivalent(s)
‖ use limited; if in doubt, see a dictionary

ant levorotatory

diablerie *n* 1 *syn* see MISCHIEVOUSNESS
  2 *syn* see EVIL 3

diablo *n syn* see DEVIL 1

diabolic *adj* 1 *syn* see SATANIC 1
  2 *syn* see FIENDISH
  rel evil, ill, wicked
  ant angelic

diabolism *n syn* see SATANISM

diabolonian *adj syn* see FIENDISH

diacritic *adj syn* see CHARACTERISTIC

diagnose *vb syn* see IDENTIFY

diagnostic *adj syn* see CHARACTERISTIC

diagnosticate *vb syn* see IDENTIFY

diagonal *adj* between horizontal and vertical in direction < cloth with a *diagonal* stripe >
  syn bevel, beveled, bias, biased, slanted, slanting; *compare* INCLINED 3

diagonally *adv* in a line running across from corner to corner < decided to place the couch *diagonally* at the end of the room >
  syn catercorner (*or* catty-corner *or* kitty-corner), cornerwise, slantingways, slantways, slantwise, ‖slaunchways
  idiom on the bias
  con parallelly, square, straight

‖**dial** *n syn* see FACE 1

dial *vb syn* see TUNE 3

dialect *n* 1 *syn* see LANGUAGE 1
  2 a form of language that is not recognized as standard < the Doric *dialect* of ancient Greece >
  syn argot, cant, jargon, lingo, patois, patter, slang, vernacular; *compare* TERMINOLOGY, VERNACULAR 3
  rel localism, provincialism, regionalism

dialectic *n syn* see ARGUMENTATION

dialogue *n* 1 *syn* see CONVERSATION 1
  2 *syn* see CONVERSATION 2

diametric *adj syn* see OPPOSITE

diapason *n syn* see MELODY

diaphanous *adj syn* see FILMY

diarrhea *n* abnormally frequent intestinal evacuations with more or less fluid stools < they were taken with severe *diarrhea* >
  syn backdoor trots, dysentery, flux, ‖runs, scour(s), ‖squirts
  idiom Montezuma's revenge, summer complaint

diatribe *n syn* see TIRADE

‖**dibs** *n pl* 1 *syn* see MONEY
  2 *syn* see CLAIM 1

dice *n pl, sing* **die** a pair or set of small cubes marked on each face with from one to six spots and used in various games and in gambling by being shaken and thrown to come to rest at random < staked everything on a cast of *dice* >
  syn ‖African dominoes, bones, ‖cubes, ‖devil's-bones, ‖ivory, ‖tats

dice *vb syn* see DISCARD

dichotomize *vb syn* see SEPARATE 1

dick *n* 1 *syn* see DETECTIVE

dicker *vb syn* see HAGGLE 2

dickey *adj syn* see WEAK 2

dictate *vb* to promulgate expressly something to be followed, observed, obeyed, or accepted < the commission *dictated* the policies to be followed >
  syn decree, impose, lay down, ordain, prescribe, set

rel control, direct, manage; guide, lead; govern, rule; say, tell, utter; bid, charge, command, enjoin, instruct, order

dictate *n syn* see COMMAND 1

dictative *adj syn* see DICTATORIAL

dictator *n syn* see TYRANT

dictatorial *adj* imposing one's will or opinions on others < the chief was inclined to be *dictatorial* with his subordinates >
  syn authoritarian, authoritative, dictative, doctrinaire, dogmatic, magisterial; *compare* TOTALITARIAN 1
  rel bossy, domineering, imperative, imperious, masterful, peremptory; absolute, arbitrary, autocratic, despotic, tyrannical; arrogant, haughty, overbearing, proud; firm, stern
  con amenable, biddable, docile, obedient, tractable; menial, obsequious, servile, slavish, subservient

dictatorship *n syn* see TYRANNY

diction *n syn* see WORDING

dictionary *n syn* see TERMINOLOGY

dictum *n syn* see MAXIM

‖**dicty** *adj syn* see SNOBBISH

didactic *adj* overburdened with instruction and the proprieties < his speech to the new freshmen was painfully *didactic* >
  syn moral, moralizing, preachy, schoolmasterish, sermonic, sermonizing, teachy
  rel advisory, exhortative, hortative; preceptive
  ant undidactic

‖**didder** *vb syn* see SHAKE 1

diddle *vb* 1 *syn* see IDLE
  2 *syn* see CHEAT

diddle-daddle *vb syn* see IDLE

diddler *n syn* see SWINDLER

dido *n* 1 *usu* **didoes** *pl syn* see PRANK
  2 *syn* see KNICKKNACK

die *vb* 1 to pass from physical life < he *died* at an advanced age >
  syn cash in, ‖check out, conk, ‖cop out, ‖croak, decease, demise, depart, drop, expire, go, ‖kick in, ‖kick off, pass, pass away, pass out, peg out, perish, pip, pop off, ‖snuff (out), succumb, ‖swelt
  idiom be gathered to one's fathers, bite the dust (*or* ground), breathe one's last, cash in one's checks (*or* chips), give up the ghost, ‖kick the bucket, ‖kick up one's heels, meet one's end, shuffle off this mortal coil, ‖snuff it, turn up one's toes (to the daisies)
  con be, exist, subsist; flourish, thrive
  ant live
  2 *syn* see PERISH 2

die (down *or* away) *vb syn* see ABATE 4
  rel recede; disappear
  con ascend, mount, rise
  ant come up

die *n* 1 see DICE
  ‖2 *syn* see TOY 2

die-away *adj syn* see LANGUID

diehard *n* 1 an irreconcilable opponent of change < party *diehards* who would make no concessions >
  syn bitter-ender, conservative, fundamentalist, old liner, praetorian, pullback, right, rightist, right wing, right-winger, standpat, standpatter, tory; *compare* REACTIONARY

rel mossback, old fogy, stick-in-the-mud; intransigent; true blue; right-center

con liberal, progressive, radical

2 *syn* see REACTIONARY

die-hard *adj syn* see CONSERVATIVE 1

differ *vb* 1 to be unlike or distinct in nature, form, or characteristics < the houses *differ* only in a few minor details >

syn disagree, vary

rel depart, deviate, diverge

con accord, conform, correspond

ant agree

2 to be of unlike or opposite opinion < men who *differ* on religious matters >

syn disaccord, disagree, discord, dissent, divide, vary

rel clash, conflict, jar; bicker, quarrel, squabble; argue, debate, dispute; oppose, protest (against)

idiom differ in opinion, hold opposite views

con coincide, concert, concur, harmonize; accord, conform, correspond

ant agree

difference *n* 1 *syn* see DISSIMILARITY

rel modification, variation

con equivalence, equivalency, sameness

ant resemblance

2 *syn* see DISCORD

rel clash, conflict

3 *syn* see VARIANCE 1

difference *vb syn* see KNOW 4

different *adj* 1 unlike in kind or character < could hardly be more *different* >

syn disparate, dissimilar, distant, divergent, diverse, other, otherwise, unalike, unequal, unlike, unsimilar, various

rel particular, single; distinctive, individual, peculiar; divers, sundry

con akin, analogous, comparable, like, parallel, similar, uniform; equal, equivalent, self-same

ant alike, identical, same

2 *syn* see DISTINCT 1

differential *adj syn* see DISCRIMINATORY

differentiate *vb syn* see KNOW 4

rel comprehend, understand

con confound, mistake

ant confuse

differently *adv syn* see OTHERWISE 1

difficile *adj syn* see HARD 6

difficult *adj syn* see HARD 6

rel problem, problematic

idiom easier said than done, no picnic, tough sledding

ant simple

difficulty *adv syn* see HARD 8

difficulty *n* 1 something obstructing one's course and demanding effort and endurance if one's end is to be attained < he encountered great *difficulties* on his way to success >

syn asperity, hardness, hardship, rigor, vicissitude

rel impediment, obstacle, obstruction, snag; dilemma, fix, jam, pickle, plight, predicament, quandary, scrape; emergency, exigency, pass, pinch, strait; bother, inconvenience, problem, trouble

idiom hard nut to crack, hard row to hoe, heavy sledding

2 *syn* see DEMUR 2

3 *syn* see QUARREL

diffident *adj syn* see SHY 1

rel blenching, flinching, shrinking; hesitant, reluctant

con assured, presumptuous, sanguine, sure; self-assured, self-confident, self-possessed, self-reliant; brazen, impudent, shameless

ant confident

difform *adj syn* see LOPSIDED

diffuse *adj syn* see WORDY

rel exuberant, lavish, profuse; casual, desultory, random; lax, loose, slack; lengthy, long

con concentrated; condensed

ant succinct

diffuse *vb* 1 *syn* see SPREAD 1

rel extend; expand

con compact, consolidate; center, centralize, focus

ant concentrate

2 *syn* see INTERFUSE 2

dig *vb* 1 to loosen and turn over or remove (as soil) with or as if with a spade < *dig* for potatoes > < *dug* through her drawer looking for the scarf >

syn ‖delve, excavate, grub, shovel, spade

rel quarry; enter, penetrate, pierce, probe; dig up, root, rootle, root out

2 to form by digging < *dig* a trench >

syn dig out, excavate, scoop, shovel, spade

3 *syn* see THRUST 2

‖4 *syn* see RESIDE 1

5 *syn* see POKE 1

‖6 *syn* see APPREHEND 1

7 *syn* see ENJOY 1

dig (into) *vb syn* see EXPLORE

dig *n* 1 *syn* see POKE 1

2 *syn* see SITE 3

digest *n* *syn* see COMPENDIUM 1

rel abridgment, synopsis

digest *vb* 1 *syn* see BEAR 10

2 *syn* see EPITOMIZE 1

digit *n* *syn* see NUMBER

dignification *n* *syn* see APOTHEOSIS 2

dignify *vb syn* see EXALT 1

con abase, debase

ant demean

dignitary *n* *syn* see NOTABLE 1

dignity *n* 1 *syn* see STATUS 2

2 *syn* see DECORUM 1

rel excellence, merit, perfection, virtue; ethicalness, ethics, morality, nobleness, nobility

con impropriety, indecency, indecorum, unseemliness

3 *syn* see ELEGANCE

rel augustness, grandeur, grandness, magnificence, majesty, nobleness, nobility; address, poise

dig out *vb* 1 *syn* see DIG 2

2 *syn* see RUMMAGE 3

digress *vb* 1 *syn* see SWERVE 2

2 to turn aside from the main subject of attention or course of argument < he *digressed* into too many side issues >

syn depart, divagate, diverge, excurse, ramble, stray, wander

rel drift, roam

---

syn synonym(s)   *rel* related word(s)
ant antonym(s)   *con* contrasted word(s)
idiom idiomatic equivalent(s)
‖ use limited; if in doubt, see a dictionary

idiom get off the subject, go off on a tangent

con advance, proceed, progress

digression *n* a departure from a subject or theme < a *digression* from the main point of the speech >

syn aside, discursion, divagation, excursion, excursus, parenthesis

rel episode, excurse, incident, underaction; deflection, deviation, divergence; departure; drifting, rambling, straying, wandering

‖**dike** (out *or* up) *vb syn* see DRESS UP 1

dilapidate *vb syn* see RUIN 2

rel crumble, decay, decompose, disintegrate; disregard, forget, ignore, neglect, overlook, slight

con mend, rebuild, repair; rejuvenate, renew, renovate, restore

dilapidated *adj syn* see SHABBY 1

rel damaged, impaired, injured, marred; crumbled, decayed

dilate *vb syn* see EXPAND 3

rel augment, enlarge, increase; extend, lengthen, prolong, protract; broaden, widen

con compress, condense, contract, shrink; attenuate

ant circumscribe; constrict

dilate (on *or* upon) *vb syn* see DISCOURSE 1

rel describe, narrate, recite, recount, rehearse, relate

con abbreviate, abridge, curtail, shorten

dilatory *adj syn* see SLOW 2

rel lax, neglectful, negligent, remiss, slack

con assiduous, busy, industrious, sedulous; prompt, quick, ready; hasty, impetuous, precipitate

ant diligent

dilemma *n syn* see PREDICAMENT

rel bewilderment, mystification, perplexity

idiom horns of a dilemma

dilettante *n* 1 *syn* see CONNOISSEUR

2 *syn* see AMATEUR 2

dilettante *adj syn* see AMATEURISH

dilettantish *adj syn* see AMATEURISH

dilettantist *adj syn* see AMATEURISH

diligent *adj syn* see ASSIDUOUS

rel persevering, persistent, persisting; unflagging

con deliberate, laggard, leisurely, slow; desultory

ant dilatory

‖**dilly** *adj syn* see FOOLISH 2

‖**dilly** *n* one that is remarkable or extraordinary of its kind < came up with a *dilly* of an idea to sell the product >

syn ‖corker, crackerjack, ‖daisy, dandy, ‖dinger, ‖doozer, humdinger, jim-dandy, knockout, ‖lalapalooza, ‖lulu, nifty, peach, ‖pip, pippin, ripper, ripsnorter, rouser

dilly *vb syn* see DELAY 2

dillydally *vb syn* see DELAY 2

dilute *vb* to make less strong or concentrated < *dilute* acid >

syn cut, thin, weaken

rel moderate, qualify, temper; deliquesce, liquefy; alter, modify

con enrich, fortify, richen, upgrade; condense, densify, evaporate, thicken

ant concentrate

dilute *adj* of relatively low strength or concentration < *dilute* acid >

syn diluted, thin, washy, watered-down, waterish, watery, weak

rel reduced; adulterated, sophisticated; impaired, impoverished, weakened

con condensed, densified, thickened

ant concentrated

diluted *adj syn* see DILUTE

ant concentrated

dim *adj* 1 *syn* see DARK 1

ant bright

2 *syn* see DULL 7

‖3 *syn* see DULL 9

4 *syn* see FAINT 2

con manifest, plain

ant distinct

dim *vb* 1 *syn* see OBSCURE

2 *syn* see DULL 1

3 *syn* see DULL 4

dime novel *n* a usually paperback melodramatic novel < read mostly *dime novels* >

syn dreadful, penny dreadful, shilling shocker, shocker, yellowback

rel bloodcurdler, chiller, ‖killer-diller; thriller; pulp

dimension *n* 1 *usu* dimensions *pl syn* see SIZE 1

2 *usu* dimensions *pl syn* see RANGE 2

dimensionality *n syn* see SIZE 1

diminish *vb* 1 *syn* see ABRIDGE 1

2 *syn* see DECREASE

rel ebb, subside, wane; moderate, temper; attenuate, extenuate

con aggravate, enhance, heighten, intensify

3 *syn* see DECRY 2

diminutive *adj syn* see TINY

‖**dimmet** *n syn* see EVENING 1

dimple *vb syn* see RIPPLE

‖**dimps** *n syn* see EVENING 1

dim-sighted *adj syn* see PURBLIND

‖**dimpsy** *n syn* see EVENING 1

dimwit *n syn* see DUNCE

dim-witted *adj syn* see RETARDED

con alert, keen

din *n* a welter of discordant sounds < the *din* of a machine shop >

syn babel, brouhaha, ‖chirm, clamor, hubbub, hullabaloo, jangle, music, pandemonium, racket, racketry, tintamarre, tumult, uproar; *compare* COMMOTION 4

rel blatancy, boisterousness, clamorousness, stridency; bedlam; clangor, clatter, rattle; clash, percussion; ‖row; noise, sound

con calm, lull, quietude, stillness; concord, consonance, harmony; melody, musicality, tunefulness

diner *n syn* see EATING HOUSE

dinero *n syn* see MONEY

ding *vb* 1 *syn* see STRIKE 2

2 *syn* see SURPASS 1

‖**ding** *n syn* see BLOW 1

ding-a-ling *n syn* see CRACKPOT

dingdong *adv syn* see HARD 3

dinge *n syn* see SADNESS

‖**dinger** *n syn* ‖DILLY, ‖corker, crackerjack, ‖daisy, dandy, humdinger, jim-dandy, knockout, ‖lalapalooza, ‖lulu

dingus *n syn* see DOODAD

dingy *adj syn* see SHABBY 1

rel grimed, smirched, soiled, sullied, tarnished; dull; dusky, gloomy, murky *con* bright, brilliant, luminous, shining; clean, cleanly

dining table *n syn see* TABLE 1

dinky *adj syn see* MINOR 2

||**dinky-di** *adj syn see* FAITHFUL 1

dinner *n* a usually elaborate meal served to guests or a group often to mark an occasion or honor an individual < the annual club *dinner* >
syn banquet, feast, regale, spread
rel ||blowout, festival, fete, junket; breakfast, collation, luncheon

dinner table *n syn see* TABLE 1

dinosauric *adj syn see* HUGE

||**dinsome** *adj syn see* VOCIFEROUS

dint *n syn see* POWER 4

dip *vb* 1 to plunge or thrust momentarily or partially under the surface of a liquid < *dip* a dress in cleansing fluid >
syn douse, duck, dunk, immerse, souse, submerge, submerse
rel pitch, plunge
2 to lift a portion of by reaching below the surface with something shaped to hold liquid < *dip* drinking water from a spring >
syn bail, lade, ladle, scoop
rel dish, spoon; bucket (up *or* out), draw
||3 *syn see* PAWN
4 *syn see* DUCK 2
5 *syn see* PLUMMET
6 *syn see* SET 12
7 *syn see* SWERVE 1

dip (into) *vb syn see* BROWSE

dip *n* 1 *syn see* DESCENT 4
2 *syn see* DECLINE 3
3 *syn see* DEPRESSION 2
||4 *syn see* PICKPOCKET

diplomacy *n syn see* TACT

diplomatic *adj syn see* TACTFUL
rel bland, smooth; courteous, polite; astute, shrewd; artful, crafty, guileful, wily
ant undiplomatic

||**dippy** *adj syn see* FOOLISH 2

dipsy-doodle *n syn see* DECEPTION 1

dire *adj* 1 *syn see* FEARFUL 3
2 *syn see* DEPLORABLE
rel depressing, oppressing
3 *syn see* OMINOUS
4 *syn see* PRESSING
5 *syn see* ACUTE 6

direct *vb* 1 *syn see* ADDRESS 6
2 to turn something toward its appointed or intended mark or goal < *directed* his eyes to the door >
syn address, aim, cast, head, incline, lay, level, ||point, present, set, train, turn, zero (in)
rel beam; divert; fasten, focus
3 *syn see* ADDRESS 3
rel fix, set, settle
con deflect, divert; deviate, digress, diverge, swerve
4 *syn see* GUIDE
ant misdirect
5 *syn see* GOVERN 1
6 *syn see* CONDUCT 3
7 *syn see* COMMAND

rel assign, define, prescribe

direct *adj* 1 being or passing in a straight line of descent from parent to offspring < *direct* ancestors >
syn lineal
2 admitting free or continuous passage < a *direct* route to the beach >
syn straight, straightforward, through, uninterrupted
rel linear; continuous, unbroken, undeviating, unswerving
con circuitous, roundabout
ant indirect
3 *syn see* FRANK
ant devious
4 marked by absence of an intervening agency, instrumentality, or influence < he had no *direct* knowledge of the crime >
syn firsthand, immediate, primary
rel contiguous, next, proximate
ant indirect

direct *adv* 1 *syn see* DIRECTLY 1
2 *syn see* VERBATIM

direction *n* 1 *syn see* VIEWPOINT 2

directive *n* 1 *syn see* EDICT 1
2 *syn see* MEMORANDUM 2
3 *syn see* MESSAGE 1

directly *adv* 1 without deviation of course < the turnpike runs *directly* east and west >
syn dead, direct, due, right, straight, straightly, undeviatingly
idiom as the crow flies, in a beeline
con circuitously, deviously, round about; discursively, ramblingly
ant indirectly
2 *syn see* VERBATIM
3 *syn see* IMMEDIATELY 1
4 *syn see* AWAY 3
5 *syn see* PRESENTLY 1

direful *adj* 1 *syn see* FEARFUL 3
2 *syn see* OMINOUS

dirt *n* 1 *syn see* EARTH 2
2 *syn see* DECEPTION 1

dirt poor *adj syn see* POOR 1

dirty *adj* 1 soiled or begrimed with dirt < wash those *dirty* hands >
syn black, dungy, filthy, foul, grubby, impure, mucky, murky, nasty, soily, sordid, squalid, unclean, uncleanly
rel contaminated, defiled, polluted, tainted; dreggy; draggled, draggletailed, draggly
idiom dirty as a pig
con immaculate, spotless; unsoiled, unspotted, unsullied
ant clean
2 *syn see* IMPURE 1
ant clean
3 *syn see* OBSCENE 2
4 *syn see* WILD 6

dirty *vb* 1 *syn see* SOIL 2
ant clean
2 *syn see* TAINT 1
idiom dirty one's hands

disability *n syn see* DISADVANTAGE

disable *vb* 1 *syn see* DISQUALIFY
2 *syn see* PARALYZE 1
3 *syn see* WEAKEN 1
rel harm, hurt, mar, spoil; batter, maim, mangle, mutilate; ruin, wreck
con restore, resuscitate, revive, revivify
ant rehabilitate

---

syn synonym(s)   *rel* related word(s)
ant antonym(s)   *con* contrasted word(s)
idiom idiomatic equivalent(s)
|| use limited; if in doubt, see a dictionary

disabuse vb to set free from mistakes (as in reasoning or judgment) <he was *disabused* of his belief when the facts were presented>
  syn purge, undeceive, undelude
  rel amend, correct, emend, rectify, redress; disillude, disillusion, unblind; enlighten, illuminate; free, liberate, release
  idiom open one's eyes, prick the (or one's) bubble, puncture one's balloon, set (or put) right (or straight)
  con deceive, delude, mislead; dupe, gull

disaccord vb 1 *syn* see CLASH 2
  2 *syn* see DIFFER 2
  ant accord

disaccord n *syn* see DISCORD
  ant accord

disacknowledge vb *syn* see DISCLAIM

disadvantage n an unfavorable or prejudicial quality or circumstance <the machine has two serious *disadvantages*>
  syn detriment, disability, drawback, handicap
  rel bar, impediment, obstacle, obstruction; blocking, hamper, hindrance, imposition
  con aid, assistance, help; service, usefulness, utility, value, worth
  ant advantage

disadvantaged adj *syn* see UNDERPRIVILEGED
  ant advantaged

disadvantageous adj *syn* see DEROGATORY

disadvise vb *syn* see DISSUADE

disaffect vb *syn* see ESTRANGE
  rel agitate, discompose, disquiet, disturb, upset
  ant win (over)

disaffection n *syn* see ESTRANGEMENT

disaffirm vb *syn* see DENY 4

disagree vb 1 *syn* see DIFFER 1
  ant agree
  2 *syn* see DIFFER 2
  ant agree

disagreeable adj 1 *syn* see BAD 8
  rel annoying, distressing, disturbing, woeful
  ant agreeable
  2 *syn* see IRRITABLE
  ant agreeable

disallow vb 1 *syn* see DENY 2
  con accede, acquiesce, assent
  ant allow
  2 *syn* see DISCLAIM
  rel debar, exclude, shut out
  ant allow

disallowance n *syn* see DENIAL 1

disappear vb *syn* see VANISH
  rel go, leave
  ant appear

disappoint vb *syn* see FRUSTRATE 1

disapprove vb 1 to feel or express an objection <*disapprove* of his actions>
  syn deprecate, discommend, discountenance, disesteem, disfavor, frown, object
  rel blame, censure, condemn, criticize, denounce, reprehend, reprobate; decry, depreciate, detract, disparage, dispraise; expostulate, remonstrate
  idiom look askance at, make a wry face at, not go for, take a dim view of, take exception to

con applaud, commend, compliment, recommend; accredit, certify, endorse, sanction; approbate, countenance, favor
  ant approve
  2 *syn* see DECLINE 4

disarm vb 1 *syn* see PARALYZE 1
  2 to influence favorably by persuasive words or acts <*disarmed* by her smile>
  syn unarm, unsteel, win (over)
  rel allure, attract, bewitch, captivate, charm, enchant, fascinate
  con alert, caution, tip (off), warn
  ant arm

disarming adj *syn* ingratiating, deferential, ingratiatory, insinuating, insinuative, saccharine, silken, silky

disarrange vb *syn* see DISORDER 1
  rel mislay, misplace; displace, replace; overturn
  ant arrange

disarray n *syn* see CONFUSION 3
  con arrangement, marshaling

disarray vb *syn* see DISORDER 1
  ant array

disassemble vb *syn* see DISMOUNT

disassociate vb *syn* see DETACH

disaster n a sudden calamitous event bringing great damage, loss, or destruction <a flood *disaster* struck the valley>
  syn calamity, cataclysm, catastrophe, misadventure, tragedy, woe(s)
  rel accident, casualty, fatality, mishap; adversity, distress, misadventure, mischance, misfortune; rock(s)

disastrous adj *syn* see FATAL 2
  rel hapless, luckless, unfortunate; destructive
  con fortunate, happy, lucky, providential

disavow vb *syn* see DISCLAIM
  rel impugn, negate, negative
  con allow, concede, grant; assert, justify, maintain
  ant avow

disband vb to cease to exist as a unit <the dance group *disbanded* after a farewell concert>
  syn break up, disperse, dissolve
  rel dispel, dissipate, scatter; dichotomize, disjoin, disjoint, dissect, dissever, disunite, divide, divorce, part, separate, sever, sunder
  idiom go their several ways, part company
  con combine, concur, conjoin, cooperate, unite; assemble, collect, congregate, gather; call up, summon
  ant band

disbelief n *syn* see UNBELIEF
  rel atheism, deism; rejection, repudiation, spurning
  con credence, credit, faith
  ant belief

disbelieve vb to hold not to be true or real <*disbelieved* his professions of sincerity>
  syn discredit, unbelieve
  rel distrust, doubt, mistrust, question, suspect; eschew, reject, scorn, scout
  con accept, ||buy, swallow
  ant believe

disbelieving adj *syn* see INCREDULOUS

disbodied adj *syn* see IMMATERIAL 1

disburden vb *syn* see UNLOAD

disburse vb 1 *syn* see SPEND 1

2 *syn* see DISTRIBUTE 1

disbursement *n syn* see EXPENSE 1

discalceate *adj syn* see DISCALCED

discalced *adj* wearing only sandals on the feet < *discalced* monks>
syn barefoot, discalceate
con calced, shod

discard *vb* to get rid of < *discard* old clothes > <people who *discard* traditional values>
syn abdicate, cashier, cast, chuck, ‖deep-six, ‖dice, ditch, dump, jettison, junk, lay aside, reject, scrap, shed, ‖shoot, shuck (off), slough, throw away, throw out, wash out
rel abandon, desert, forsake; repudiate, spurn; dismiss, eject, oust
idiom do away with, let go by the board
con adopt, embrace, espouse, take on, take up; employ, use, utilize; hold, hold back, keep, retain; cherish, esteem, nurture

discarding *n syn* see DISPOSAL 2

discarnate *adj syn* see IMMATERIAL 1
ant carnate, incarnate

discept *vb syn* see DISCUSS 1

discern *vb* 1 *syn* see SEE 1
rel ascertain, discover; anticipate, apprehend, divine, foresee
2 *syn* see KNOW 4

discernible *adj syn* see PERCEPTIBLE
ant indiscernible

discerning *adj syn* see WISE 1
ant undiscerning

discernment *n syn* see WIT 3
rel intuition, reason; sagaciousness, sagacity
con crassness, density, slowness; blindness

discharge *vb* 1 *syn* see UNLOAD
2 *syn* see EXEMPT
3 *syn* see SHOOT 1
4 *syn* see FREE
rel dismiss, eject, expel, oust; eliminate, exclude
5 to give outlet to <the river *discharges* its waters into the bay>
syn disembogue, emit, flow, give off, pour, void
rel eject, exude, release
6 *syn* see DISMISS 3
rel displace, replace, supersede, supplant
con hire; contract
ant engage
7 to release from service with the armed forces < *discharged* from the army with the rank of sergeant>
syn ‖demob, demobilize, muster out, separate
rel disenroll; deactivate, inactivate; bounce, cashier, dismiss, drop, fire, sack
8 *syn* see CLEAR 5
9 *syn* see ANNUL 4

discinct *adj syn* see NEGLIGENT

disciple *n syn* see FOLLOWER
rel enthusiast, fanatic, zealot

disciplinary *adj syn* see PUNITIVE

discipline *n* 1 *syn* see PUNISHMENT
2 *syn* see WILL 3

discipline *vb* 1 *syn* see PUNISH 1

---

syn synonym(s)   *rel* related word(s)
ant antonym(s)   *con* contrasted word(s)
idiom idiomatic equivalent(s)
‖ use limited; if in doubt, see a dictionary

rel overcome, reduce, subdue, subjugate; bridle, check, curb, inhibit, restrain
2 *syn* see TEACH
rel guide, lead; conduct, control, direct, manage

disclaim *vb* to refuse to admit, accept, or approve <the senator *disclaimed* the comment attributed to him > < *disclaim* responsibility for a subordinate's mistake>
syn deny, disacknowledge, disallow, disavow, disown, repudiate
rel contradict, contravene, gainsay, traverse; refuse, reject, spurn; deprecate; belittle, disparage, minimize; abjure, forswear, recant, renounce, retract; challenge, criticize
idiom turn one's back on, wash one's hands of
con acknowledge, avow, own; accept, admit, receive, take
ant claim

disclose *vb* 1 *syn* see OPEN 2
2 *syn* see REVEAL 1
rel acknowledge, admit, avow, confess, own
idiom make public
con conceal, hide; camouflage, cloak, disguise, dissemble, mask

discolor *vb* 1 *syn* see TAINT 1
2 *syn* see STAIN 1

discolor *adj syn* see VARIEGATED

discombobulate *vb* 1 *syn* see DISCOMPOSE 1
2 *syn* see CONFUSE 2

discomfit *vb syn* see EMBARRASS
rel annoy, bother, irk, vex; disturb, perturb, upset

discomfiture *n* 1 *syn* see DEFEAT 1
2 *syn* see COMEDOWN
3 *syn* see EMBARRASSMENT
rel agitation, disquiet, perturbation, upset; commotion; prickles

discomforting *adj syn* see UNCOMFORTABLE
ant comforting

discommend *vb syn* see DISAPPROVE 1
rel admonish; criticize, reprehend; censure
con approve, endorse, sanction
ant commend; recommend

discommode *vb syn* see INCONVENIENCE
rel flurry, fluster, perturb, upset; bother, irk, vex

discommoding *adj syn* see INCONVENIENT

discommodious *adj syn* see INCONVENIENT

discompose *vb* 1 to destroy or impair one's capacity for collected thought or decisive action < *discomposed* by the rudeness of his friend>
syn agitate, bother, discombobulate, dismay, disquiet, disturb, flurry, fluster, perturb, unhinge, unsettle, untune, upset; *compare* EMBARRASS
rel disagree; annoy, irk, vex; harass, harry, pester, plague, worry
con calm, quiet, settle, soothe, tranquilize; allay, alleviate, assuage; appease, conciliate, mollify, pacify, placate, propitiate
ant compose
2 *syn* see DISORDER 1
ant compose

discomposure *n syn* see EMBARRASSMENT

ant composure

disconcert *vb syn* see EMBARRASS
rel bewilder, nonplus, perplex, puzzle

disconcertion *n syn* see EMBARRASS-MENT

disconcertment *n syn* see EMBARRASS-MENT

disconfirm *vb syn* see DISPROVE 1

disconnect *vb syn* see DETACH
ant connect

disconnected *adj syn* see INCOHERENT 2
ant connected

disconsolate *adj* 1 *syn* see DOWNCAST
rel comfortless, inconsolable; sorrowful, woeful; doleful, melancholy; unhappy
ant cheerful
2 *syn* see INCONSOLABLE
3 *syn* see GLOOMY 3
ant cheerful, cheery

disconsonant *adj syn* see INCONSONANT 1

discontent *adj syn* see DISCONTENTED
ant content

discontented *adj* showing or expressing a sense of grievance or thwarted aspirations or desires < *discontented* with his position >
syn discontent, disgruntled, dissatisfied, malcontent, malcontented, uncontent, uncontented, ungratified
rel disquieted, disturbed, perturbed, restless, upset; displeased; unhappy
con satisfied; gratified, pleased; happy; elated, exultant, jubilant, triumphant
ant contented

discontinuance *n syn* see END 2
ant continuance, continuation

discontinuation *n syn* see END 2
ant continuance, continuation

discontinue *vb syn* see STOP 3
ant continue

discontinuity *n syn* see GAP 1
ant continuity

discontinuous *adj syn* see INCOHERENT 2
ant continuous

‖**disconvenience** *n syn* see INCONVE-NIENCE
ant convenience

‖**disconvenience** *vb syn* see INCONVE-NIENCE
ant convenience

discord *n* the state of those who disagree and lack harmony < a household full of turmoil and *discord* >
syn conflict, contention, difference, disaccord, disharmony, dispeace, dissension, dissent, dissidence, dissonance, disunion, disunity, division, inharmony, mischief, strife, unpeace, variance
rel discrepancy, incompatibility, incongruity, inconsistency, inconsonance, uncongeniality; animosity, antagonism, antipathy, enmity, hostility, rancor; polarization; collision
con accord, consonance; agreement, concordance, concurrence
ant concord, harmony

discord *vb* 1 *syn* see CLASH 2
ant concord, harmonize
2 *syn* see DIFFER 2
ant accord

discordant *adj* 1 *syn* see INHARMONIOUS 2

2 *syn* see INCONSONANT 1
con according, agreeing, congenial, harmonious, harmonizing
ant concordant
3 *syn* see ANTIPATHETIC 1
ant concordant
4 *syn* see DISSONANT 1

discotheque *n syn* see NIGHTCLUB

discount *n syn* see DEDUCTION 1

discount *vb* 1 *syn* see DEDUCT 1
con boost, hike, increase, mark up, raise
2 *syn* see NEGLECT
3 *syn* see DECRY 2

discountenance *vb* 1 *syn* see EMBARRASS
idiom put out of countenance
2 *syn* see DISAPPROVE 1
rel reproach, reprove
con encourage, favor
ant countenance

discourage *vb* 1 to weaken the stamina, interest, or zeal of < the long winter and lack of fuel *discouraged* the settlers >
syn chill, deject, demoralize, dishearten, disparage, dispirit
rel depress, weigh; afflict, try; damp, dampen, droop; distress, trouble; bother, irk, vex
idiom take the heart out of
con cheer, embolden, hearten, inspirit, nerve, steel
ant encourage
2 *syn* see DISSUADE
rel check, inhibit, restrain; prevent; frighten, scare
idiom lay a wet blanket on, throw cold water on
con advocate, countenance, favor; approve, back, endorse
ant encourage

discouraging *adj syn* see GLOOMY 3
rel deterring; hindering
ant encouraging

discourse *n* 1 *syn* see SPEECH 1
2 a systematic, serious, and often learned exposition of a subject or topic < his *discourses* during the seminar were long remembered >
syn disquisition, dissertation, memoir, monograph, monography, thesis, tractate, treatise
rel article, essay, paper; lecture, sermon; rhetoric, speech, talk

discourse *vb* 1 to express oneself especially formally and at length < *discourses* knowledgeably about the laws of nature >
syn descant, dilate (on or upon), discuss, dissert, dissertate, expatiate, sermonize
rel converse, speak, talk, voice; argue, dispute; harangue, lecture, orate, perorate; amplify, develop, elaborate, enlarge, expand; explain, expound; comment, commentate, remark
2 *syn* see ACT 1

discourteous *adj syn* see RUDE 6
con chivalrous, civil, courtly, gallant
ant courteous

discover *vb* 1 *syn* see EXPOSE 4
2 *syn* see REVEAL 1
rel advertise, proclaim, publish
con repress, suppress
3 to become or be made aware of something not previously known < *discover* a secret >

syn ascertain, catch on, determine, find
out, hear, learn, see, tumble, unearth
rel descry, detect, encounter, espy, hit (on
or upon), meet (with), spot; discern, note,
observe, perceive
idiom get wise to
con miss, overlook; disregard, ignore

discovery n the gaining knowledge of or
ascertaining the existence of something
previously unknown or unrecognized
< the *discovery* of a new chemical ele-
ment >
syn detection, espial, find, strike, unearthing
rel disclosure, exposition, exposure, revelation, uncovering

discreate vb syn see DESTROY 1
discredit vb 1 syn see DISBELIEVE
ant credit
2 to deprive of credibility < he *discredited*
the rumor immediately >
syn blow up, disprove, explode, puncture,
shoot
rel expose, show up; destroy, ruin
idiom bring to naught, knock the bottom
out of, not leave a leg to stand on
con accept, believe, credit
discredit n syn see DISGRACE
ant credit
discreditable adj syn see DISREPUTABLE
1
discreet adj 1 syn see CAUTIOUS
con foolhardy
ant indiscreet
2 syn see PLAIN 1
3 syn see CONSERVATIVE 2
discreetness n syn see PRUDENCE 1
ant indiscreetness
discrepancy n syn see DISSIMILARITY
discrepant adj syn see INCONSONANT 1
rel different, disparate, divergent, diverse;
disagreeing, varying
con agreeing, conforming, corresponding,
jibing, squaring, tallying; alike, identical,
like, parallel, similar, uniform
discrepate vb syn see KNOW 4
discrete adj syn see DISTINCT 1
con blended, fused, merged, mingled
ant indiscrete
discretion n syn see PRUDENCE 1
rel moderation, restraint; gumption, judgment, sense, wisdom
con asininity, fatuousness, foolishness,
simplicity; foolhardiness, rashness, recklessness
ant indiscretion
discretionary adj syn see OPTIONAL
discriminate vb syn see KNOW 4
rel note, perceive, remark; collate, compare, contrast
ant confound
discriminating adj syn see ECLECTIC 1
rel careful; judicious, prudent, wise
ant undiscriminating
discrimination n syn see WIT 3
rel judgment, sense
con crassness, density, slowness
discriminative adj syn see DISCRIMINA-
TORY

ant undiscriminative
discriminatory adj applying or favoring
discrimination in treatment < *discriminatory* employment practices against wom-
en >
syn discriminative
rel biased, inequitable, partial, partisan,
prejudiced, prepossessed, unfair, unjust
con dispassionate, equal, equitable, fair,
impartial, just, objective, unbiased, uncolored, unprejudiced
ant nondiscriminatory
discrown vb syn see DEPOSE 1
disculpate vb syn see EXCULPATE
ant inculpate
discumber vb syn see EXTRICATE 2
discursion n syn see DIGRESSION
discuss vb 1 to exchange views about
something in order to arrive at the truth
or to convince others < met to *discuss*
community needs >
syn agitate, argue, canvass, debate, dis-
cept, dispute, ||kick around, moot, pro and
con, thrash out, toss (around)
rel deliberate, hash over, reason (out),
talk over; consider, weigh
idiom consider pro and con, go into,
reason the point
2 syn see DISCOURSE 1
rel elucidate, explicate, interpret
discussion n syn see CONFERENCE 1
disdain n 1 syn see DESPITE 1
rel antipathy, aversion; arrogance, haughtiness, insolence, superciliousness
con awe, fear, reverence
2 syn see PRIDE 3
disdain vb syn see DESPISE
con accept, receive, take; acknowledge,
admit, own; esteem, respect
ant admire
disdainful adj syn see PROUD 1
rel rejecting, repudiating, spurning; con-
temning, despising, scorning, scouting;
antipathetic, averse, unsympathetic
ant admiring; respectful
disdainfulness n syn see PRIDE 3
disease n 1 a kind or instance of impairment of a living being that interferes with
normal bodily function < tuberculosis has
become a controllable *disease* >
syn affection, ailment, complaint, condition, disorder, ill, infirmity, malady, sickness, syndrome; compare INFIRMITY 1,
SICKNESS 1
rel bug, ||epizootic, ||misery, virus
2 syn see INFIRMITY 1
ant health
diseasedness n syn see SICKNESS 1
disedge vb syn see DULL 3
disembark vb to go ashore out of a ship
< *disembark* at the next port >
syn debark, land
rel put in
con board, get on
ant embark
disembarrass vb syn see EXTRICATE 2
rel clear, rid, unburden
ant embarrass
disembodied adj syn see IMMATERIAL 1
disembogue vb syn see DISCHARGE 5
disembowel vb syn see EVISCERATE
disembroil vb syn see EXTRICATE 2
ant enbroil

---

syn synonym(s)   rel related word(s)
ant antonym(s)   con contrasted word(s)
idiom idiomatic equivalent(s)
|| use limited; if in doubt, see a dictionary

disemploy vb syn see DISMISS 3
disenable vb syn see DISQUALIFY
disenchanted adj syn see SOPHISTICATED 2
disencumber vb syn see EXTRICATE 2
  rel alleviate, lighten, relieve
  con depress, oppress, weigh
  ant encumber
disenfranchise vb syn see DISFRANCHISE
disengage vb 1 syn see DETACH
  rel free, liberate, release
  con associate, connect, join, link, unite
  ant engage
  2 syn see LOOSE 3
disentangle vb syn see EXTRICATE 2
  rel detach, disengage; part, separate, sever, sunder
  con enmesh, involve
  ant entangle, tangle
disenthrall vb syn see FREE
disenthrone vb syn see DEPOSE 1
disentranced adj syn see SOPHISTICATED 2
disentwine vb syn see EXTRICATE 2
disesteem vb 1 syn see DISAPPROVE 1
disesteem n syn see DISGRACE
  ant esteem
disfashion vb syn see DEFACE
disfavor n 1 syn see DISLIKE
  rel distrust, mistrust
  con approbation, approval; admiration, esteem, liking, regard, respect
  ant favor
  2 syn see DISGRACE
disfavor vb syn see DISAPPROVE 1
  con approve, accept, approbate, countenance, go (for), hold (with)
  ant favor
disfeature vb syn see DEFACE
disfigure vb syn see DEFACE
  ant adorn
disfranchise vb to deprive of a legal right and especially of the right to vote < people subtly disfranchised by community apathy>
  syn disenfranchise
  rel deprive, take away
  ant affranchise, enfranchise, franchise
disgorge vb 1 syn see VOMIT
  2 syn see ERUPT 1
disgrace n the state of one who has lost esteem and good repute < retired in disgrace after the scandal became public>
  syn contempt, discredit, disesteem, disfavor, dishonor, disrepute, ignominy, infamy, obloquy, odium, opprobrium, shame
  rel abasement, debasement, debasing, degradation, humbling, humiliation; black eye, blot, brand, spot, stain, stigma
  con admiration, regard; awe, fear, reverence; fame, glory, honor, renown, repute
  ant esteem, respect
disgraceful adj syn see DISREPUTABLE 1
  ant respectable; respectworthy
disgracious adj syn see RUDE 6
  ant gracious
disgrade vb syn see DEGRADE 1
disgruntled adj syn see DISCONTENTED
disguise vb to alter so as to hide the true appearance or character of < disguised herself with a wig > < disguised his anger behind a false geniality>
  syn camouflage, cloak, dissemble, dissimulate, dress up, mask

  rel conceal, hide; obfuscate, obscure; belie, falsify, garble, misrepresent; affect, assume, counterfeit, feign, pretend, sham, simulate
  con display, exhibit, expose, flaunt, parade, show; betray, disclose, discover, reveal
disguise n 1 syn see MASK 2
  rel deception, delusion; speciousness
  2 syn see PRETENSE 2
disguised adj syn see INTOXICATED 1
disguisement n syn see MASK 2
disgust vb to be offensive to the taste or sensibilities of < the sight of filth disgusted him >
  syn nauseate, reluct, repel, repulse, revolt, sicken
  rel offend, outrage
  idiom make one sick, stick in one's craw (or crop or gizzard), turn one's stomach
  con charm, entice, tempt; delight, gratify, please, rejoice, tickle
disgusted adj syn see FED UP
disgusting adj syn see OFFENSIVE
‖**dish** vb syn see CHAT 1
disharmonic adj syn see DISSONANT 1
  ant harmonic, harmonious
disharmonious adj syn see DISSONANT 1
  ant harmonic, harmonious
disharmonize vb syn see CLASH 2
  ant harmonize
disharmony n syn see DISCORD
  ant harmony
dishearten vb syn see DISCOURAGE 1
  ant hearten
disheartening adj syn see GLOOMY 3
  rel despondent, pessimistic
  con encouraging, optimistic
  ant heartening
disheveled adj syn see SLOVENLY 1
dishonest adj 1 unworthy of trust or belief < made a dishonest report on their progress>
  syn deceitful, knavish, lying, mendacious, roguish, shifty, unhonest, untruthful
  rel crooked, devious, furtive, oblique; faithless, false, perfidious, untrustworthy; cheating, cozening, ‖cronk, defrauding, double-dealing, fraudulent, swindling, two-faced; insidious, tricky
  con conscientious, honorable, just, scrupulous, upright; aboveboard, forthright, straightforward; candid, fair, frank, open, plain; dependable, reliable, sure, trustworthy, trusty
  ant honest
  2 syn see CROOKED 2
dishonesty n syn see DECEPTION 1
dishonor n syn see DISGRACE
  con reverence, veneration; authority, credit, influence, prestige, weight
  ant honor
dishonorable adj syn see DISREPUTABLE 1
  ant honorable
dish out vb syn see GIVE 3
disillusioned adj syn see SOPHISTICATED 2
  con beguiled, deceived, deluded, misled
disimpassioned adj syn see COOL 2
  ant heated, impassioned
disimprison vb syn see FREE
  ant imprison

disimprove *vb syn* see DETERIORATE 1
ant improve

disinclination *n syn* see DISLIKE
ant inclination

disinclined *adj* lacking the will or desire to do something < *disinclined* to accept his story>
syn afraid, averse, backward, hesitant, indisposed, loath, reluctant, shy, uneager, unwilling, unwishful
rel antipathetic, unsympathetic; doubtful, dubious; opposing, resisting; balking, boggling, shying, sticking, stickling; objecting, protesting
con anxious, avid, eager, keen; disposed, predisposed, ready, willing
ant inclined

disingenuous *adj* lacking in candor and often giving a false appearance of simple frankness <had a *disingenuous* way of asking for advice when he really wanted help>
syn uncandid, unfrank
rel false, feigned, insincere, left-handed; artful, crafty, cunning, foxy, guileful, insidious, sly, tricky, wily; devious, indirect, oblique
con artless, naive, natural, simple, unsophisticated; candid, frank, open, plain; sincere, unfeigned; aboveboard, direct, straightforward
ant ingenuous

disinherit *vb* 1 to deprive (an heir apparent) of the right to inherit <the father *disinherited* his wayward son in his will>
syn cut off
rel disown, repudiate; dispossess
idiom cut off without a cent
2 *syn* see DEPRIVE 2

disinhume *vb syn* see EXHUME
ant inhume

disintegrate *vb* 1 *syn* see DECAY
rel deliquesce; disperse, dissipate, scatter
con articulate, concatenate; blend, coalesce, fuse, merge; associate, combine, conjoin, connect, join, link, unite
2 *syn* see DETERIORATE 1

disinter *vb syn* see EXHUME
ant inter

disinterest *n syn* see APATHY 2
ant interest

disinterested *adj* 1 *syn* see INDIFFERENT 2
rel negative, neutral
con concerned, curious; fervent, impassioned, passionate
ant interested
2 *syn* see NEUTRAL
rel fair, just, impartial, unbiased
con biased, prejudiced; involved
ant concerned

disject *vb syn* see STREW 1

disjoin *vb syn* see SEPARATE 1

disjoint *vb* 1 *syn* see SEPARATE 1
2 *syn* see DISORDER 1

disjointed *adj syn* see INCOHERENT 2

dislike *n* a state of mind or feeling marked by an inner avoidance of something usu-

ally felt as unpleasant or repugnant <a pronounced *dislike* for mathematics>
syn aversion, bad books, disfavor, disinclination, disliking, displeasure, disrelish, dissatisfaction, distaste, indisposition
rel detestation, hate, hatred; deprecation, disapproval; prejudice, scunner
idiom a derry on
con affection, attachment, love; partiality, predilection, preference
ant liking

disliking *n syn* see DISLIKE
ant liking

dislimb *vb syn* see MAIM

dislimn *vb syn* see OBSCURE

dislocate *vb* 1 *syn* see DISORDER 1
2 *syn* see MOVE 4

disloyal *adj syn* see FAITHLESS
rel alienated, disaffected, estranged
ant loyal

disloyalty *n* 1 *syn* see INFIDELITY
ant loyalty
2 *syn* see TREACHERY
ant loyalty

dismal *adj syn* see GLOOMY 3
con animated, gay, lively; cheerful

dismals *n pl, used with the syn* see SADNESS

dismantle *vb* 1 *syn* see STRIP 2
con appoint, equip, outfit
2 *syn* see DESTROY 1
3 *syn* see REVOKE 2
4 *syn* see DISMOUNT

dismay *n syn* see FEAR 1
con aplomb, assurance, confidence, self-possession; mettle, resolution, spirit

dismay *vb* 1 to unnerve and check by arousing fear, apprehension, or aversion < *dismayed* by the task that lay ahead>
syn appall, consternate, daunt, horrify, shake
rel bewilder, confound, dumbfound, mystify, nonplus, perplex, puzzle; abash, discomfit, disconcert, embarrass, faze, rattle; discourage, dishearten; affright, alarm, frighten, scare, terrify
idiom set one back on one's heels, take aback
con assure, ensure, secure; excite, galvanize, pique, provoke, quicken, stimulate
2 *syn* see DISCOMPOSE 1

dismayed *adj syn* see AGHAST 2
rel discomfited, disconcerted, fazed, rattled
ant undismayed

dismember *vb* 1 *syn* see MAIM
rel part, separate, sever, sunder
2 *syn* see DISMOUNT

dismiss *vb* 1 *syn* see DIVORCE 2
2 *syn* see DECLINE 4
3 to let go from one's employ or service <during the recession thousands of employees were *dismissed*>
syn ax, boot (out), bounce, ‖can, cashier, discharge, disemploy, drop, fire, kick out, let out, sack, terminate, turn off
rel depose, displace, furlough, lay off, remove, retire, suspend, unseat; reject, turn away; riff
idiom give one the gate (*or* one's walking papers), let go; give the ax (*or* the can) to
con hire; contract, engage; get, obtain, procure, secure

---

syn synonym(s)   *rel* related word(s)
ant antonym(s)   *con* contrasted word(s)
idiom idiomatic equivalent(s)
‖ use limited; if in doubt, see a dictionary

ant employ

4 *syn* see EJECT 1

rel cast, discard, shed, slough

idiom send one to Coventry

5 to refuse to consider seriously < *dismisses* the other performers as mere amateurs >

syn kiss off, pooh-pooh

rel deride, mock, rally, ridicule, taunt, twit; flout, gibe, gird, jeer, scoff; contemn, despise, disdain, scorn, scout; reject

dismissive *adj syn* see PROUD 1

dismount *vb* to take down or apart from an assembled position < *dismount* a revolver for cleaning >

syn disassemble, dismantle, dismember, take down

rel detach, disengage; disconnect, disjoin, disunite, separate

idiom take apart, take to pieces

con assemble, construct, put together; combine, unite

disobedient *adj* refusing or neglecting to obey < the *disobedient* child refused to come in >

syn naughty, obstreperous, unruly; *compare* CONTRARY 3, NAUGHTY 1

rel headstrong, recalcitrant, willful; contumacious, insubordinate, rebellious

con amenable, biddable, docile, tractable; decorous, good, well-behaved

ant obedient

disoblige *vb syn* see INCONVENIENCE

con accommodate, convenience, favor

ant oblige

disorder *n* 1 *syn* see CONFUSION 3

con orderliness; pattern, plan

ant order

2 breach of public order < the overthrow of the government caused *disorder* in the country >

syn anarchism, anarchy, distemper, misrule, riot

rel anomie; agitation, commotion, convulsion, tumult, turbulence, turmoil, upheaval

ant order

3 *syn* see DISEASE 1

4 *syn* see SICKNESS 1

disorder *vb* 1 to undo the fixed or proper order of something < *disorder* the carefully arranged contents of a drawer >

syn derange, disarrange, disarray, discompose, disjoint, dislocate, disorganize, disrupt, distemper, disturb, jumble, ‖mammock, mess (up), mix up, muddle, muss (up), ‖mux, rummage, shuffle, tumble, unsettle, upset; *compare* CONFUSE 5

rel ball up, embroil; dishevel, rumple

idiom make hay of

con arrange, marshal, methodize, organize, systematize; align, array, line, line up, range; adjust, fix, regulate

ant order

2 *syn* see UPSET 5

disordered *adj* 1 *syn* see INCOHERENT 2

2 *syn* see INSANE 1

disorderly *adj syn* see TURBULENT 1

disorderly house *n syn* see BROTHEL

disorganize *vb syn* see DISORDER 1

ant organize

disown *vb syn* see DISCLAIM

ant own

disparage *vb* 1 *syn* see DECRY 2

ant applaud

2 *syn* see DISCOURAGE 1

disparagement *n* 1 *syn* see DETRACTION

rel animadversion, aspersion, reflection, stricture

2 *syn* see DESPITE 1

disparaging *adj syn* see DEROGATORY

rel underestimating, underrating, undervaluing

con acclaiming, extolling, praising; exalting, magnifying

disparate *adj syn* see DIFFERENT 1

rel discordant, discrepant, incompatible, inconsistent, inconsonant; distinct, separate

ant analogous, comparable

disparity *n* the state of being different (as in degree, rank, excellence, or number) < the *disparity* between the rich and the poor > < their stories showed significant *disparity* >

syn disproportion, imparity, inequality, unevenness

rel alterity, difference, dissemblance, dissimilarity, dissimilitude, distinction, divergence, divergency, otherness, unlikeness

con adequation, equality, equatability, equivalence, equivalency, sameness; correlation, correspondence, likeness; evenness

ant parity

dispassionate *adj* 1 *syn* see NEUTRAL

rel imperturbable, unflappable, unruffled

con fervent, vehement; intemperate

2 *syn* see FAIR 4

rel aloof, indifferent; frank, open; aboveboard, straightforward

dispatch *vb* 1 *syn* see SEND 1

rel hasten, quicken, speed

2 *syn* see KILL 1

3 *syn* see EAT UP 1

dispatch *n* 1 *syn* see HASTE 1

con dawdling, loitering, procrastination

ant delay

2 *syn* see ALACRITY

rel diligence, industriousness

dispeace *n syn* see DISCORD

dispel *vb syn* see SCATTER 1

rel dismiss, eject, expel, oust; crumble, disintegrate

dispensable *adj* capable of being dispensed with < many household gadgets are readily *dispensable* >

syn nonessential, unessential, unrequired

rel needless, unnecessary, unneeded; minor, trivial, unimportant

con essential, imperative, necessary, necessitous, required; vital

ant indispensable

dispensation *n syn* see FAVOR 4

dispense *vb* 1 *syn* see DISTRIBUTE 1

2 *syn* see GIVE 3

rel portion, prorate

3 *syn* see ADMINISTER 2

4 *syn* see HANDLE 2

5 *syn* see EXEMPT

disperse *vb* 1 *syn* see SCATTER 1

rel discharge, dismiss

con call, cite, convene, convoke, summon

ant assemble, congregate; collect

2 *syn* see DISTRIBUTE 1

3 *syn* see SPREAD 1

4 *syn* see DISBAND

dispirit *vb syn* see DISCOURAGE 1

idiom dampen (*or* lower) one's spirits
ant inspirit

dispirited *adj syn* see DOWNCAST
rel melancholy, sad
ant high-spirited, inspirited

dispiriting *adj syn* see GLOOMY 3
rel dejecting, distressing; oppressing
ant inspiriting

displace *vb* 1 *syn* see BANISH
2 *syn* see DEPOSE 1
3 *syn* see SUPPLANT 1

displaced person *n syn* see REFUGEE

displacement *n syn* see EXILE 1

display *vb* 1 *syn* see OPEN 2
rel demonstrate, evidence, evince, lay out, manifest, show
con camouflage, cloak, disguise, dissemble, mask; conceal, hide, secrete
2 *syn* see SHOW 4
3 *syn* see SHOW 1

display *n* 1 *syn* see EXHIBITION 1
2 a striking or spectacular exhibition <a parvenu's *display* of wealth>
syn array, fanfare, panoply, parade, pomp, shine, show
rel ostentation, ostentatiousness, pretension, pretentiousness, showiness; setout

displeasing *adj syn* see BAD 8
rel annoying, bothersome, irksome, vexing
con agreeable, gratifying, pleasant
ant pleasing

displeasure *n syn* see DISLIKE
rel anger; vexation
con delight, enjoyment
ant pleasure

disponible *adj syn* see AVAILABLE 1

disport *n syn* see PLAY 1
rel jollity, merriment

disport *vb* 1 *syn* see SHOW 4
2 *syn* see BEHAVE 1
3 *syn* see PLAY 1

disposal *n* 1 *syn* see ORDER 3
2 the act of ridding oneself of something <incinerators used for the *disposal* of trash>
syn discarding, disposition, dumping, jettison, junking, relegation, riddance, scrapping, throwing away
rel chucking, clearance; demolishing, demolition, destroying, destruction
con acquirement, acquisition; accumulation, collection, cumulation, deposit, hoard, trove

dispose *vb* 1 *syn* see INCLINE 3
ant indispose
2 *syn* see ORDER 1

disposed *adj syn* see WILLING 1
ant indisposed

disposition *n* 1 *syn* see DISPOSAL 2
rel control, controlling, direction, management
2 *syn* see ORDER 3
3 the complex of especially mental and emotional qualities that distinguish an individual <a man of irritable *disposition*>

syn character, complexion, humor, individualism, individuality, makeup, nature, personality, temper, temperament
rel mood, tone, vein; cast, stamp, tenor, type; being; identity
idiom frame of mind
4 *syn* see LEANING 2

dispossess *vb syn* see DEPRIVE 2
con provide, supply

dispossession *n syn* see PRIVATION 2

dispraise *vb syn* see DECRY 2
ant praise

disproportion *n syn* see DISPARITY

disproportional *adj syn* see LOPSIDED

disproportionate *adj syn* see LOPSIDED
ant proportionate

disprove *vb* 1 to show by presenting evidence that something is not true <the defendant's claims were *disproved* by the testimony>
syn break, confound, confute, controvert, disconfirm, evert, rebut, refute
rel contravene, impugn, negative, traverse; overthrow, overturn
con evidence, show; demonstrate, display, illustrate, manifest; argue, bespeak, tell
ant prove
2 *syn* see DISCREDIT 2

disputable *adj syn* see MOOT 1

disputation *n syn* see ARGUMENTATION

disputatious *adj syn* see CONTENTIOUS 2

dispute *vb* 1 *syn* see ARGUE 2
con give in, surrender
2 *syn* see DISCUSS 1
rel confute, controvert, disprove, rebut, refute
con allow, grant
ant concede
3 *syn* see QUESTION 2
4 *syn* see RESIST

dispute *n* 1 *syn* see ARGUMENT 2
rel conflict, discord, dissension, strife
2 *syn* see QUARREL

disqualified *adj syn* see UNFIT 2
ant qualified

disqualify *vb* to deprive of a power, right, or privilege <a conviction of perjury *disqualified* him from being a witness>
syn disable, disenable, incapacitate
rel bar, bate, debar, eliminate, except, exclude, rule out, suspend
con empower, enable
ant qualify

disquiet *vb syn* see DISCOMPOSE 1
rel distress, trouble
con calm, compose, lull, still
ant quiet, soothe, tranquilize

disquiet *n* 1 *syn* see CARE 2
ant quiet
2 *syn* see UNREST
ant quiet

disquietude *n* 1 *syn* see CARE 2
2 *syn* see UNREST
ant quietness, quietude

disquisition *n syn* see DISCOURSE 2
rel inquiry, investigation; argumentation, debate, disputation

disquisitive *adj syn* see INQUISITIVE 1

disrate *vb syn* see DEGRADE 1

disregard *vb syn* see NEGLECT
con attend, mind, tend, watch; note, notice, observe, remark
ant regard

---

syn synonym(s)   *rel* related word(s)
ant antonym(s)   *con* contrasted word(s)
idiom idiomatic equivalent(s)
‖ use limited; if in doubt, see a dictionary

disregard n syn see APATHY 2
  rel forgetting, ignoring, neglecting, omission, omitting, overlooking, slighting
  con consideration, thoughtfulness
disregardful adj syn see NEGLIGENT
  ant regardful
disrelish n syn see DISLIKE
  ant relish
disremember vb syn see FORGET 1
disreputable adj 1 not reputable or decent < was punished for his *disreputable* conduct >
  syn discreditable, disgraceful, dishonorable, ignominious, inglorious, shabby, shady, shameful, shoddy, unrespectable
  rel abject, mean, sordid; beggarly, cheap, contemptible, despicable, pitiable, scurvy, sorry
  con admirable, creditable, estimable, honorable, respectable
  ant reputable
  2 syn see SHABBY 1
disrepute n syn see DISGRACE
  ant repute
disrespect n syn see INSOLENCE
  ant respect
disrespectful adj syn see RUDE 6
  ant respectful
disrobe vb 1 syn see STRIP 1
  2 syn see STRIP 2
disrupt vb 1 syn see OPEN 3
  2 syn see DISORDER 1
dissatisfaction n syn see DISLIKE
  ant satisfaction
dissatisfactory adj syn see BAD 1
  ant satisfactory
dissatisfied adj syn see DISCONTENTED
  rel annoyed, bothered, irked, vexed
  con content, contented, gratified
  ant satisfied
dissect vb 1 syn see SEPARATE 1
  2 syn see CUT 5
  rel penetrate, pierce, probe
  3 syn see ANALYZE
dissection n syn see ANALYSIS 1
  rel examination, inspection, review, scrutiny; criticism, critique
dissemblance n syn see DISSIMILARITY
  ant resemblance, semblance
dissemblance n syn see DECEIT 1
dissemble vb syn see DISGUISE
  con demonstrate, evidence, evince, manifest, show
dissembler n syn see HYPOCRITE
disseminate vb 1 syn see SPREAD 1
  2 syn see DECLARE 1
  3 syn see STREW 1
dissension n syn see DISCORD
  rel altercation, bickering, quarrel, wrangle; argument, controversy, dispute
  con amity, friendship, goodwill
  ant accord; comity
dissent vb syn see DIFFER 2
  rel balk, boggle, demur, shy, stickle
  con acquiesce, agree, subscribe
  ant assent; concur
dissent n 1 syn see DISCORD
  2 syn see HERESY
  rel disagreement, nonagreement, nonconcurrence
dissenter n syn see HERETIC
dissert vb syn see DISCOURSE 1
dissertate vb syn see DISCOURSE 1

dissertation n syn see DISCOURSE 2
  rel exposition; argumentation, disputation
dissever vb 1 syn see SEPARATE 1
  2 syn see CUT 5
dissidence n 1 syn see DISCORD
  2 syn see HERESY
dissident adj syn see HERETICAL
dissident n syn see HERETIC
dissimilar adj syn see DIFFERENT 1
  rel antithetical, antonymous, contradictory, contrary, opposite
  ant similar
dissimilarity n lack of agreement or correspondence or an instance of this < the *dissimilarities* in the cultures of the two countries >
  syn alterity, difference, discrepancy, dissemblance, dissimilitude, distance, distinction, divarication, divergence, divergency, otherness, unlikeness
  rel disparity, diversity; discordance, incongruity, inconsistency, inconsonance; discord, variance; severance; offset, margin
  con affinity, analogy, likeness, resemblance, similitude; accordance, congruity, consistency, consonance; agreement, conformity, correspondence
  ant similarity
dissimilitude n syn see DISSIMILARITY
  ant similitude
dissimulate vb syn see DISGUISE
dissimulation n syn see DECEIT 1
  rel camouflaging, cloaking, disguising, dissembling, masking; concealing, hiding, secreting; feigning, pretending, pretense, shamming; hypocrisy, pharisaism, sanctimony
dissimulator n syn see HYPOCRITE
dissipate vb 1 syn see SCATTER 1
  rel crumble, disintegrate
  ant accumulate; concentrate (*as efforts, thoughts*)
  2 syn see WASTE 2
  rel disappear, evanesce, evaporate, vanish
  ant absorb (*as time, attention*)
dissipation n syn see ENTERTAINMENT
dissociate vb syn see DETACH
  rel alienate, estrange
  ant associate
dissolute adj syn see ABANDONED 2
  rel lax, light, loose, slack, wanton, wayward; fast, raffish, rakish, wild
dissolution n 1 syn see SEPARATION 1
  2 syn see DEATH 1
dissolve vb 1 syn see DESTROY 1
  2 syn see ADJOURN 2
  3 syn see ANNUL 4
  4 syn see LIQUEFY
  5 syn see SOLVE 2
  6 syn see DISBAND
dissonance n syn see DISCORD
dissonant adj 1 marked by a mingling of discordant sounds < the two bands playing different pieces at the same time sounded *dissonant* >
  syn cacophonic, cacophonous, discordant, disharmonic, disharmonious, immusical, inharmonic, inharmonious, rude, unharmonious, unmusical
  rel grating, harsh, hoarse, jarring, raucous, rugged, strident
  con blending, chiming, concerted, harmonic, symphonious; euphonious, harmo-

nious, mellifluous, mellow, melodious, musical; agreeable, pleasing

ant consonant

2 *syn* see INCONSONANT 1

dissuade *vb* to turn one aside from a purpose, a project, or a plan < they tried to *dissuade* a friend from making a mistake >

syn deter, disadvise, discourage, divert

rel derail, throw off; advise, counsel; exhort, prick, urge

idiom talk out of

con get, induce, prevail; affect, influence, touch

ant persuade

distance *n* 1 an extent of areal or linear measure < he did not know the *distance* he had walked >

syn length, stretch

rel area, extent; ambit, compass, extension, orbit, purview, radius, range, reach, scope, sweep

2 the length of a literal or figurative course traversed or to be traversed < he had come a long *distance* from his pitiful beginnings >

syn way, ways

rel extent, size; piece, spell

3 *syn* see EXPANSE

4 *syn* see DISSIMILARITY

distance *vb syn* see OUTSTRIP 1

distant *adj* 1 not close in space, time, or relationship < traveling to a more *distant* place > < the *distant* days of the Pilgrim fathers > < a *distant* cousin >

syn far, faraway, far-flung, far-off, off-lying, outlying, remote, removed

rel apart, isolated, obscure, out-of-the-way, retired, secret; secluded, sequestered

idiom at a distance

con close, near, nearby, next, nigh; adjacent, adjoining, contiguous

2 *syn* see DIFFERENT 1

3 *syn* see UNSOCIABLE

rel arrogant, haughty, proud; modest, retiring, shy

con forward, presuming, ‖pushy, self-assertive

distaste *n syn* see DISLIKE

rel abhorrence, repugnance, repulsion, revulsion; antipathy, hostility

con relish, zest; appetite, desire; enjoyment

ant taste

distasteful *adj* 1 *syn* see UNPALATABLE 1

ant tasteful, tasty

2 *syn* see BITTER 2

rel obnoxious, repellent, repugnant, repulsive; abominable, detestable, hateful, odious

con agreeable, grateful, gratifying, pleasant, pleasing, welcome

distemper *vb syn* see DISORDER 1

distemper *n syn* see DISORDER 2

distend *vb syn* see EXPAND 3

rel augment, enlarge, increase; extend, lengthen

ant constrict

dismrone *vb syn* see DEPOSE 1

---

syn synonym(s)   *rel* related word(s)

ant antonym(s)   *con* contrasted word(s)

idiom idiomatic equivalent(s)

‖ use limited; if in doubt, see a dictionary

distill *vb syn* see DRIP

distinct *adj* 1 capable of being distinguished as differing < the novel has two related, but nevertheless *distinct*. plots >

syn different, discrete, diverse, separate, several, various

rel distinctive, individual, peculiar; particular, single, sole; especial, individual, special, specific; disparate, dissimilar, divergent

con identical, same, selfsame; corresponding, equivalent, like, similar

ant indistinguishable

2 *syn* see CLEAR 5

rel defined, prescribed; categorical, definite, explicit, express, specific; lucid, perspicuous; clear-cut, incisive, trenchant

con faint, obscure

ant indistinct; nebulous

distinction *n* 1 *syn* see DISSIMILARITY

con affinity, analogy, likeness, similarity, similitude

ant indistinction, resemblance

2 *syn* see EMINENCE 1

3 *syn* see HONOR 2

distinctive *adj syn* see CHARACTERISTIC

rel separate, single, unique; discrete, distinct, several

con common, familiar, ordinary, popular, vulgar; alike, analogous, comparable, identical, like, parallel; equal, equivalent, same

distinctively *adv syn* see ESPECIALLY 1

distinctiveness *n syn* see INDIVIDUALITY 3

distingué *adj syn* see GENTEEL 1

distinguish *vb* 1 *syn* see KNOW 4

rel divide, part; detach, disengage; demarcate, set off

con confuse, mistake

ant confound

2 *syn* see EXALT 1

3 *syn* see CHARACTERIZE 2

idiom set apart

4 *syn* see SEE 1

5 *syn* see IDENTIFY

distinguished *adj syn* see FAMOUS 2

rel courtly, dignified, grand, imposing, stately

ant undistinguished

distort *vb* 1 *syn* see MISREPRESENT

rel misconstrue, misinterpret; alter, change

2 *syn* see DEFORM

rel bend, curve, twist

distortion *n syn* see DEFORMITY

distract *vb* 1 *syn* see CONFUSE 2

2 *syn* see MADDEN 1

distracted *adj syn* see DISTRAUGHT

distraction *n* 1 *syn* see INSANITY 1

2 *syn* see ENTERTAINMENT

distrait *adj* 1 *syn* see ABSTRACTED

2 *syn* see DISTRAUGHT

distraught *adj* 1 agitated with doubt or mental conflict < *distraught* over the health of her child >

syn distracted, distrait, distressed, harassed, tormented, troubled, worried

rel agitated, concerned, discomposed, flustered, perturbed, upset; addled, confused, muddled; bewildered, nonplussed

idiom beside oneself

con composed, cool, imperturbable, nonchalant, unflappable, unruffled; calm, tranquil; unconcerned, undisturbed, unworried

ant collected

2 *syn* see INSANE 1

distress *n* the state of being in serious trouble or in mental or physical anguish <in great *distress* over the decision he had to make>

syn agony, dolor, misery, passion, suffering

rel affliction, cross, trial, tribulation, visitation; anguish, grief, heartbreak, sorrow, woe; exigency, pass, pinch, strait; difficulty, hardship, rigor, vicissitude; ache, pain, pang, throe, twinge

con comfort, comforting, consolation, solace, solacing; allaying, alleviation, assuagement, ease, relief, relieving; ease, peace, security

distress *vb* 1 *syn* see TRY 2

rel afflict, rack, torment, torture

con allay, alleviate, assuage, lighten, mitigate, relieve

2 to cause pain or suffering to <the death of his longtime friend *distressed* him deeply>

syn aggrieve, constrain, grieve, hurt, injure, pain

rel harass, strain, stress, try, trouble; depress, oppress, weigh

con comfort, console, solace; aid, assist, help

3 *syn* see TROUBLE 1

rel annoy, harry, pester, plague

distressed *adj syn* see DISTRAUGHT

distressing *adj syn* see DEPLORABLE

distribute *vb* 1 to give out, usually in shares, to each member of a group <*distributed* his possessions among his heirs>

syn deal, disburse, dispense, disperse, divide, ‖divvy, dole (out), lot (out), measure (out), partition

rel allocate, allot, apportion, assign, mete (out); parcel, portion, prorate, ration; administer; dribble; bestow, donate, give, present

con assemble, gather; accumulate, hoard

ant amass; collect

2 *syn* see SPREAD 1

distribution *n syn* see ORDER 3

district *n* 1 *syn* see QUARTER 2

2 *syn* see LOCALITY 1

rel division, parcel

distrust *vb* to have no trust or confidence in <he *distrusted* most politicians>

syn doubt, misdoubt, mistrust, suspect, ‖suspicion

rel disbelieve, discredit, unbelieve

con bank, count, depend, reckon, rely; commit, confide, consign, entrust

ant trust

distrustful *adj syn* see SUSPICIOUS 2

distrustfully *adv syn* see ASKANCE 2

disturb *vb* 1 *syn* see MOVE 4

2 *syn* see DISCOMPOSE 1

rel alarm, frighten, scare, terrify; bewilder, distract, perplex, puzzle; discommode, incommode, inconvenience, trouble

3 *syn* see DISORDER 1

rel displace, replace; move, remove, shift; interfere, intermeddle, meddle, tamper

con establish, fix, set, settle; adjust, regulate

disunify *vb syn* see ESTRANGE

disunion *n* 1 *syn* see SEPARATION 1

2 *syn* see DISCORD

disunite *vb* 1 *syn* see SEPARATE 1

2 *syn* see ESTRANGE

disunity *n syn* see DISCORD

disusage *n syn* see DISUSE

disuse *n* cessation of use, practice, or exercise <to keep the mind from falling into *disuse*, one must exercise one's reading abilities> <his muscles became atrophied from *disuse*>

syn desuetude, disusage

con appliance, application, employment, operation, play, usance; exercise

ant use

disused *adj syn* see OBSOLETE

ditch *n syn* see TRENCH

ditch *vb* 1 *syn* see DISCARD

‖2 *syn* see HIDE

‖**dite** *n syn* see PARTICLE

dither *vb* 1 *syn* see SHAKE 1

2 *syn* see HESITATE

3 *syn* see CHAT 1

dither *n* 1 *syn* see JITTERS

2 *syn* see COMMOTION 2

dithyrambic *adj syn* see IMPASSIONED

ditto *n syn* see REPRODUCTION

ditty *n syn* see SONG 2

diurnal *adj syn* see DAILY

ant nocturnal

diuturnal *adj syn* see LASTING

divagate *vb syn* see DIGRESS 2

divagation *n syn* see DIGRESSION

divarication *n syn* see DISSIMILARITY

dive *vb syn* see PLUNGE 2

rel bound, jump, leap, spring; impel, move

dive *n* a shabby or disreputable place for drinking or entertainment <got a schooner of beer at the *dive* down the street>

syn barrelhouse, hangout, honky-tonk, joint

rel dump, hole; bar, barroom, lounge, pothouse, pub, saloon, taproom, tavern

‖**diver** *n syn* see PICKPOCKET

diverge *vb* 1 *syn* see SWERVE 2

rel differ, disagree, vary; divide, part, separate

ant converge; conform

2 *syn* see DIGRESS 2

divergence *n* 1 *syn* see DISSIMILARITY

rel diversity, variety

con accord, concord, consonance, harmony

ant conformity, correspondence

2 *syn* see DEVIATION 1

rel division, parting, separation; differing, disagreeing, varying

con agreement, coincidence, concurrence

ant convergence

divergency *n syn* see DISSIMILARITY

divergent *adj* 1 *syn* see DIFFERENT 1

rel antithetical, contradictory, contrary, opposite; aberrant, abnormal, atypical

con alike, identical, parallel, same

ant convergent

2 *syn* see IRREGULAR 1

divers *adj syn* see SEVERAL 3

divers *pron, pl in constr syn* see SUNDRY

diverse *adj* 1 *syn* see DIFFERENT 1

rel contrasted, contrasting, contrastive; contradictory, contrary, opposite

con equal, equivalent, same
ant identical, selfsame
2 *syn* see DISTINCT 1
idiom of every description
3 *syn* see MANIFOLD
diversely *adv syn* see OTHERWISE 1
diverseness *n syn* see VARIETY 1
diversiform *adj syn* see MANIFOLD
diversion *n* 1 *syn* see DEVIATION 1
2 *syn* see PLAY 1
3 *syn* see ENTERTAINMENT
rel frivolity, levity
4 *syn* see ENJOYMENT 1
diversity *n syn* see VARIETY 1
rel difference, dissimilarity, distinction, divergence, divergency, unlikeness
ant uniformity; identity
divert *vb* 1 *syn* see TURN 6
rel swerve; alter, change, modify
con fix, set, settle
2 *syn* see DISSUADE
rel abstract, detach, disengage
3 *syn* see AMUSE
rel delight, gladden, please, regale, tickle
divertissement *n syn* see ENTERTAINMENT
divest *vb* 1 *syn* see STRIP 2
ant invest, vest; apparel, attire, clothe
2 *syn* see DEPRIVE 2
rel despoil, plunder, spoil
ant invest, vest
divestiture *n syn* see PRIVATION 2
divide *vb* 1 *syn* see SEPARATE 1
rel carve, chop, cut
ant unite
2 *syn* see DISTRIBUTE 1
3 *syn* see APPORTION 2
rel allocate, allot, assign
4 *syn* see DIFFER 2
rel part, separate
con combine, concur, conjoin, cooperate
ant unite
dividend *n syn* see REWARD
divine *n syn* see CLERGYMAN
divine *vb syn* see FORESEE
divine *adj* 1 of or relating to God or a god <the *divine* will>
syn deific, godly
rel chthonian
2 like or like that of God or a god <men who aspire to *divine* honors>
syn deific, godlike
rel extramundane, superhuman, superphysical, transmundane
3 *syn* see MARVELOUS 1
division *n* 1 *syn* see PART 1
2 *syn* see SEPARATION 1
3 *syn* see DISCORD
divorce *n syn* see SEPARATION 1
divorce *vb* 1 *syn* see SEPARATE 1
rel disaffect, wean
2 to end a marriage by legal action <unable to agree, they decided to *divorce*> < *divorced* his wife>
syn dismiss, put away, unmarry
rel break up, separate, split; annul, cancel
divorcement *n syn* see SEPARATION 1
divulge *vb syn* see REVEAL 1

rel proclaim; gossip, tattle
‖**divvy** *vb* 1 *syn* see DISTRIBUTE 1
2 *syn* see APPORTION 2
‖**dizzard** *n syn* see DUNCE
dizzy *adj* 1 *syn* see GIDDY 1
rel asinine, fatuous, foolish; inane
2 affected by a sensation of being whirled about or around <the speed with which she dispatched her tasks made the onlookers *dizzy*>
syn giddy, light, light-headed, swimming, swimmy, vertiginous
rel reeling, whirling; bewildered, confounded, distracted, puzzled; addled, befuddled, confused, dazed, dazzled, fuddled, muddled
idiom with spots before one's eyes
3 *syn* see EXCESSIVE 1
dizzy *vb syn* see CONFUSE 2
do *vb* 1 *syn* see PERFORM 2
2 *syn* see CLOSE 3
3 *syn* see ACT 1
4 *syn* see CHEAT
idiom do out of, sell one a bill of goods
5 *syn* see COOK 1
6 *syn* see BEHAVE 1
7 *syn* see SHIFT 5
8 *syn* see HAPPEN 1
9 *syn* see TRAVEL 2
10 *syn* see SERVE 3
11 *syn* see SERVE 5
‖**do** *n syn* see SUCCESS
doable *adj syn* see POSSIBLE 1
doc *n syn* see PHYSICIAN
docile *adj syn* see OBEDIENT
rel adaptable, pliable, pliant
con obstinate, self-willed, stubborn, willful
ant indocile; ungovernable, unruly
‖**docious** *adj syn* see OBEDIENT
dock *n syn* see WHARF
docket *n syn* see PROGRAM 1
doctor *n syn* see PHYSICIAN
doctor *vb* 1 *syn* see TREAT 4
2 *syn* see MEND 2
3 *syn* see ADULTERATE
doctrinaire *adj syn* see DICTATORIAL
rel bullheaded, dogged, mulish, obstinate, pertinacious, pigheaded, stiff-necked, stubborn
ant undoctrinaire
doctrine *n* a principle accepted as valid and authoritative <the *doctrine* of evolution>
syn canon, dogma, tenet
rel instruction, teaching; axiom, basic, fundamental, principle
idiom article of belief (or faith)
document *n* something preserved and serving as evidence (as of an event, a situation, or the culture of a period) <ceramic and flint artifacts provide our only *document* of this ancient people>
syn archive(s), monument, record
rel evidence, testimony
doddering *adj syn* see SENILE
doddery *adj syn* see SENILE
dodge *vb* 1 to avoid or evade by some maneuver or shift <*dodging* in and out among the crowd> < *dodged* his pursuer with ease>
syn duck, fence, parry, shirk, sidestep
rel malinger; avoid, elude, escape, evade, skirt; slide, slip; short-circuit

---

syn synonym(s)   *rel* related word(s)
ant antonym(s)   *con* contrasted word(s)
idiom idiomatic equivalent(s)

‖ use limited; if in doubt, see a dictionary

idiom fight shy of
con ‖banter, beard, brave, challenge, dare, defy, front, venture; confront, encounter, meet
ant face
2 *syn* see EQUIVOCATE 2
dodo *n syn* see DUNCE
‖**dods** *n pl syn* see SULK
‖**dodunk** *n syn* see DUNCE
doff *vb syn* see REMOVE 3
do for *vb syn* see HELP 1
dofunny *n syn* see DOODAD
dog *n* 1 a highly variable carnivorous domesticated mammal <many households have *dogs* as pets>
syn bowwow, canine, hound, ‖pooch, tyke
rel pup, puppy; cur, ‖feist, mongrel, mutt
2 *syn* see SNOT 1
3 *syn* see FRANKFURTER
4 *syn* see JALOPY
dog *vb syn* see TAIL
Dogberry *n syn* see POLICEMAN
dogfall *n syn* see DRAW 4
dogfight *n syn* see BRAWL 2
dogged *adj* 1 *syn* see INFLEXIBLE 2
2 *syn* see PERSISTENT 1
doggery *n syn* see RABBLE 2
doggish *adj syn* see DAPPER
doggone *adj* 1 *syn* see DAMNED 2
2 *syn* see UTTER
doggy *adj syn* see DAPPER
dogma *n syn* see DOCTRINE
rel belief, conviction, persuasion, view
dogmatic *adj* 1 *syn* see DICTATORIAL
2 *syn* see DEDUCTIVE
dog nap *n syn* see NAP
dog's age *n syn* see AGE 2
do in *vb* 1 *syn* see RUIN 2
2 *syn* see MURDER 1
3 *syn* see EXHAUST 4
doing *n syn* see ACTION 1
doit *n syn* see PARTICLE
doldrums *n pl* 1 *syn* see TEDIUM
rel blues, dejection, depression, dumps, gloom; apathy, disinterest, indifference, listlessness
con high spirits, spirits
2 *syn* see ABEYANCE
rel depression, retardation, slump, stagnation; inactivity
dole (out) *vb* 1 *syn* see ADMINISTER 2
2 *syn* see DISTRIBUTE 1
‖**dole** *n* 1 *syn* see SORROW
2 *syn* see MISFORTUNE
doleful *adj* 1 *syn* see DOWNCAST
2 *syn* see WOEFUL 1
3 *syn* see MELANCHOLY 2
rel grieving, mourning, sorrowing; piteous, pitiful
con blithe, blithesome, radiant, sparkling, sunny
ant cheerful, cheery
dolefuls *n pl, used with the syn* see SADNESS
dolent *adj syn* see WOEFUL 1
dolesome *adj syn* see MELANCHOLY 2
dolittle *n syn* see SLUGGARD
dollar *n* a currency bill representing one hundred cents <had a single *dollar* left>
syn bill, ‖bone, ‖buck, ‖fish, frogskin, ‖ironman, oner, rock, ‖skin, ‖smacker, smackeroo
dollop *n syn* see DRAM 1

doll out *vb syn* see DRESS UP 1
doll up *vb syn* see DRESS UP 1
dolor *n syn* see DISTRESS
con blessedness, bliss, felicity, happiness
ant beatitude
dolorous *adj* 1 *syn* see DEPLORABLE
2 *syn* see WOEFUL 1
3 *syn* see MELANCHOLY 2
dolt *n syn* see DUNCE
dolthead *n syn* see DUNCE
doltish *adj syn* see STUPID 1
domain *n syn* see FIELD
‖**dome** *n syn* see HEAD 1
domestic *adj* 1 of or relating to the household or family < *domestic* chores required to maintain a home>
syn family, home, household
con civic, public; personal, private; business, occupational, professional
2 of, relating to, or carried on within an indicated or implied country <charts of *domestic* as well as foreign waters>
syn home, ‖inland, internal, intestine, municipal, national, native
ant foreign
3 *syn* see TAME
domesticate *vb* to adapt (an animal or plant) to life in intimate association with and to the advantage of man <the man who *domesticated* the first dog>
syn domesticize, domiciliate, master, tame
rel gentle, subdue; housebreak; break, bust, train
domesticated *adj syn* see TAME
domesticize *vb syn* see DOMESTICATE
domicile *n syn* see HABITATION 2
domicile *vb syn* see HARBOR 2
domiciliate *vb* 1 *syn* see HARBOR 2
2 *syn* see DOMESTICATE
dominance *n syn* see SUPREMACY
dominant *adj* 1 superior to all others in power, influence, or importance <the Sumerians were a *dominant* race of ancient times>
syn ascendant, master, outweighing, overbalancing, overbearing, overweighing, paramount, predominant, predominate, preponderant, prevalent, regnant, sovereign
rel prevailing; preeminent, supreme, surpassing, transcendent; chief, first, foremost, leading, main, principal; governing, ruling
con collateral, dependent, secondary, subject, tributary; unimportant
ant subordinate
2 *syn* see CHIEF 2
dominate *vb* 1 *syn* see GOVERN 3
2 *syn* see RULE 2
3 *syn* see OVERLOOK 2
domination *n* 1 *syn* see SUPREMACY
2 *syn* see POWER 1
dominator *n syn* see LEADER 2
domineer *n syn* see RULE 2
domineering *adj syn* see MASTERFUL 1
rel arrogant, insolent, lordly
con obsequious, servile, slavish; bootlicking, groveling, sycophantic, toadying
ant subservient; fawning
‖**dominie** *n syn* see CLERGYMAN
dominion *n* 1 *syn* see SUPREMACY
2 *syn* see FIELD
3 *syn* see OWNERSHIP

domino *n syn* see MASK 1

domitae naturae *adj syn* see TAME

don *vb* 1 to place on one's person (an article of clothing) < *donned* a raincoat for his trip>
syn assume, draw on, get on, huddle (on), put on, slip (on), throw
rel apparel, array, attire, clad, clothe, dress, enclothe, garb, garment, raiment
con cast, pull (off), remove, take off, throw (off); unclothe, undress; disrobe
ant doff

2 to clothe or envelop oneself in < able to *don* a new personality at will>
syn assume, pull, put on, strike, take on
rel camouflage, color, disguise; belie, falsify, garble, misrepresent

donate *vb syn* see GIVE 1

donation *n* a gift of money or its equivalent to a charity, humanitarian cause, or public institution < sought *donations* for victims of the flood>
syn alms, benefaction, beneficence, charity, contribution, offering
rel aid, assistance, help, relief; philanthropy; bequest, endowment; appropriation, grant, subsidy, subvention; allowance, dole, pittance, ration

donator *n syn* see DONOR

done *adj* 1 *syn* see DECOROUS 1
2 *syn* see COMPLETE 4
3 *syn* see EFFETE 2
4 *syn* see THROUGH 4

done for *adj syn* see THROUGH 3

done in *adj syn* see EFFETE 2

‖**doney** *n syn* see GIRL FRIEND 1

‖**donicker** *n syn* see TOILET

Don Juan *n* 1 *syn* see GALLANT 2
2 *syn* see WOLF

donk *n syn* see DONKEY 1

donkey *n* 1 the domestic ass < the *donkey*, a typical pack animal>
syn ass, burro, donk, jackass, ‖moke, ‖neddy, ‖Rocky Mountain canary
rel ‖dickey, jack; hinny, mule; jennet, jenny, jenny ass
2 *syn* see FOOL 1

donkeyish *adj syn* see FOOLISH 2

donkey's years *n pl syn* see AGE 2

donkeywork *n syn* see WORK 2

donnybrook *n syn* see BRAWL 2

donor *n* one that gives something to another < a *donor* of funds to research foundations>
syn bestower, conferrer, donator, giver, presenter
rel contributor, subscriber

do-nothing *n syn* see SLUGGARD

‖**donsie** *adj syn* see UNWELL

doodad *n* something trivial which is hard to classify or whose name is unknown < wondered what the little round *doodad* was for>
syn business, dingus, dofunny, doohickey, gadget, gizmo, ‖hootenanny, jigger, rigamajig, thingum, thingumajig, thingumbob, thingummy; *compare* GADGET 1, WHAT-DO-YOU-CALL-IT

doodle *n syn* see FOOL 1

‖**doodle** *n syn* see CHEAT

doodle *vb syn* see FIDDLE 2

doohickey *n syn* see DOODAD

doom *n syn* see FATE
rel calamity, cataclysm, catastrophe, disaster, tragedy

doom *vb syn* see SENTENCE

doom (to) *vb syn* see PREDESTINE 1

doomed *adj syn* see DAMNED 1

doomful *adj syn* see OMINOUS

door *n* 1 an opening by which one can enter or leave a structure and especially a building < looked through the front *door*>
syn doorway, entrance, entranceway, entry, entryway, portal

2 a means or right of entering, approaching, or participating < viewed education as the *door* to success>
syn access, adit, admission, admittance, entrance, entrée, entry, ingress, way

doormat *n syn* see WEAKLING

doorway *n syn* see DOOR 1

‖**doozer** *n syn* ‖DILLY, ‖corker, ‖daisy, dandy, ‖dinger, humdinger, jim-dandy, ‖lalapalooza, ‖lulu, peach

dope *n* 1 *syn* see DRUG 2
2 *syn* see DUNCE

dope (up) *vb syn* see ADULTERATE

doped *adj syn* see DRUGGED

‖**dope out** *vb* 1 *syn* see SOLVE 2
2 *syn* see INFER
3 *syn* see PLAN 2

dopey *adj syn* see LETHARGIC

do-re-mi *n syn* see MONEY

‖**dorm** *vb syn* see DOZE

dormancy *n syn* see ABEYANCE

dormant *adj syn* see LATENT
ant active

‖**dort** *vb syn* see SULK

dorts *n pl syn* see SULK

‖**dorty** *adj syn* see SULLEN

doss *n syn* see SLEEP 1

doss *vb syn* see SLEEP

dot *n syn* see POINT 11

dot *vb* 1 *syn* see SPECKLE 1
2 *syn* see SPOT 2

dot *n syn* see DOWRY

dotage *n* advanced age accompanied by a decline of mental poise and alertness < a doddering eighty-year-old entering his *dotage*>
syn second childhood, senility; *compare* OLD AGE
rel decrepitude, feebleness, infirmity; age, elderliness, senectitude
con adolescence, youth; maturity

dote (on *or* **upon)** *vb syn* see ADORE 3
rel enjoy, fancy, like
idiom be sweet on
ant loathe

‖**doted** *adj syn* see SENILE

doting *adj* 1 *syn* see SENILE
2 *syn* see LOVING
rel asinine, fatuous, foolish, silly, simple

dottiness *n syn* see FOOLISHNESS

dotty *adj* 1 *syn* see INFATUATED
2 *syn* see FOOLISH 2

double *adj* 1 *syn* see TWOFOLD 1
2 *syn* see TWIN
3 *syn* see TWOFOLD 2
4 *syn* see INSINCERE

---

syn synonym(s)   *rel* related word(s)
ant antonym(s)   *con* contrasted word(s)
idiom idiomatic equivalent(s)
‖ use limited; if in doubt, see a dictionary

double n 1 syn see MATE 5

2 syn see IMAGE 1

3 syn see TURN 2

rel departure, digression, divergence, swerving, veering

double vb 1 to make twice as great or as many < doubled the amount of his salary >

syn dualize, dupe, duplicate

rel replicate; amplify, augment, enlarge, increase, magnify; supplement

con decrease, lessen, minimize

ant halve

2 to make of two thicknesses by turning or bending usually in the middle < he doubled the towel for better absorbency >

syn fold

rel pleat, plicate, turn over

3 syn see ESCAPE 2

4 syn see DUB

double-barreled adj 1 syn see TWOFOLD 2

2 syn see TWOFOLD 1

double-cross vb 1 syn see DECEIVE

2 syn see BETRAY 2

double-dealer n syn see SWINDLER

double-dealing n syn see DECEPTION 1

double-dealing adj syn see INSINCERE

double-distilled adj syn see UTTER

||**double-dog dare** vb syn see FACE 3

double-dome n syn see INTELLECTUAL 2

double-dyed adj syn see UTTER

double-edged adj syn see OBSCURE 3

double entendre n syn see AMBIGUITY

double-faced adj 1 syn see OBSCURE 3

2 syn see INSINCERE

doublehearted adj syn see INSINCERE

double meaning n syn see AMBIGUITY

double-minded adj 1 syn see VACILLATING 2

idiom of two minds

2 syn see INSINCERE

doublet n syn see COUPLE

double-talk n 1 syn see NONSENSE 2

2 syn see GOBBLEDYGOOK

double-tongued adj syn see INSINCERE

doubt vb 1 syn see QUESTION 2

2 syn see DISTRUST

con accredit, credit, trust; accept, believe, ||buy, swallow

doubt n syn see UNCERTAINTY

rel dubiousness, questionableness; disbelief, incredulity, unbelief

con dependence, faith, reliance, trust

ant certitude; confidence

doubtable adj syn see DOUBTFUL 1

ant undoubtable

doubter n syn see SKEPTIC

doubtful adj 1 not having or affording assurance of the certainty or soundness of something or someone < their chance of success is doubtful >

syn ambiguous, borderline, clouded, doubtable, dubious, dubitable, equivocal, fishy, impugnable, indecisive, open, precarious, problematic, queasy, shady, shaky, suspect, suspicious, uncertain, unclear, undecided, uneasy, unsettled, unstable, unsure; compare MOOT

rel question-begging; touch-and-go; chancy, insecure, questionable, speculative; hazy, obscure; unlikely; contingent, iffy

idiom at issue, in dispute, in doubt, in question

con decisive, open-and-shut, positive, sure; inarguable, incontestable, unarguable, undeniable, undoubted, unquestionable

ant indubitable

2 syn see MOOT

3 syn see IMPROBABLE 1

doubtfully adv syn see ASKANCE 2

doubtfulness n syn see UNCERTAINTY

doubting Thomas n syn see SKEPTIC

doubtless adv 1 syn see EASILY 2

2 syn see PRESUMABLY

doubtlessly adv 1 syn see WELL 7

ant doubtfully

2 syn see EASILY 2

dough n syn see MONEY

doughface n syn see MASK 1

||**doughhead** n syn see DUNCE

doughty adj syn see BRAVE 1

doughy adj syn see PALE 1

do up vb syn see MEND 2

dour adj 1 syn see GRIM 2

rel rigid, rigorous, strict; implacable

2 syn see SULLEN

||**douse** n syn see BLOW 1

douse vb syn see REMOVE 3

douse vb 1 syn see DIP 1

2 syn see WET

con bake, dehydrate, desiccate, dry, parch

3 syn see SPLASH

4 syn see EXTINGUISH 1

||**dout** vb syn see EXTINGUISH 1

dove n syn see PACIFIST

ant hawk

dovecote n a small compartmented raised house or box for domestic pigeons < old countryseats with elaborate stone dovecotes >

syn columbary, culverhouse, dovehouse, pigeon house, pigeonry

rel aviary, birdhouse; perch, roost

dovehouse n syn see DOVECOTE

||**dover** n syn see NAP

dovetail vb syn see AGREE 4

dowager n syn see MATRIARCH

dowd n syn see SLATTERN 1

dowdy n syn see SLATTERN 1

dowdy adj 1 syn see SLATTERNLY

con chic, fashionable, modish, stylish; flashy, garish, gaudy

ant smart

2 syn see TACKY 2

ant smart

3 syn see OLD-FASHIONED

dower n syn see DOWRY

dower vb syn see ENDOW 1

rel accouter, appoint, equip, furnish, outfit

||**dowly** adj syn see OVERCAST

down adv 1 from a higher to a lower level < the land sloped down toward the sea >

syn downward, downwardly, downwards, netherwards

rel below, earthward, groundward; downgrade, downhill, downslope

con aloft, upward, upwardly, upwards

ant up

2 to completion < wash down the car >

syn completely, fully, through-and-through

idiom from top to bottom

3 syn see SERIOUSLY 1

down adj 1 syn see SLOW 3

2 *syn* see DOWNCAST
ant up
3 *syn* see SICK 1
4 *syn* see LOWER
ant up
5 *syn* see COMPLETE 4
down *n syn* see COMEDOWN
down *vb* 1 *syn* see SWALLOW 1
2 *syn* see DEFEAT 2
3 *syn* see FELL 1
4 *syn* see KILL 1
5 *syn* see OVERCOME 1
down *n* a soft fluffy material or covering
< the *down* on a peach >
syn floss, flue, fluff, fur, fuzz, lint, pile
down-and-out *n syn* see PAUPER
down-at-heel *adj syn* see SHABBY 1
downcast *n syn* see DEFEAT 1
downcast *adj* low in spirits < felt *downcast*
by the rejection >
syn bad, blue, cast down, chapfallen,
crestfallen, dejected, depressed, disconsolate, dispirited, doleful, down, downhearted, down-in-the-mouth, downthrown,
droopy, dull, heartsick, heartsore, hipped,
low, low-spirited, mopey, soul-sick, spiritless, sunk, woebegone; *compare* SAD 1
rel discouraged, disheartened; oppressed,
weighed down; distressed, troubled; despondent, forlorn; listless; broody; moody;
gloomy, glum, morose
idiom in the depths
con cheerful, happy, joyous, lighthearted;
excited, exhilarated, intoxicated; buoyed
up, gladdened; encouraged, heartened;
animated, gay, lively, sprightly, vivacious;
delighted, pleased
ant elated
downcry *vb syn* see DECRY 2
downfall *n* 1 *syn* see DETERIORATION 1
rel comedown, descent, discomfiture,
down
2 something that causes a downfall
< drink was his *downfall* >
syn bane, destroyer, destruction, ruin,
ruination, undoing
rel headache, problem, trouble
idiom road to ruin
con aid, help, support
downgrade *n syn* see DETERIORATION 1
ant upgrade
downgrade *vb* 1 *syn* see DEPRECIATE 1
ant upgrade
2 *syn* see DEGRADE 1
ant upgrade
downgrading *n syn* see DEMOTION
ant upgrading
downhearted *adj syn* see DOWNCAST
down-in-the-mouth *adj syn* see DOWN-
CAST
downright *adj* 1 *syn* see UTTER
2 being what is stated beyond any possibility of doubt < a *downright* lie >
syn flat, indubitable, unquestionable, up-
and-down; *compare* POSITIVE 3
rel out-and-out, sure-enough; absolute,
positive; certain, clear
downside-up *adj syn* see UPSIDE-DOWN 2

---

downslide *n syn* see DECLINE 3
downswing *n syn* see DECLINE 3
downthrow *n syn* see DEFEAT 1
downthrown *adj syn* see DOWNCAST
down-to-date *adj syn* see UP-TO-DATE
down-to-earth *adj syn* see REALISTIC
downtrend *n syn* see DECLINE 3
downtrodden *adj* oppressed by superior
power < the *downtrodden* peasants >
syn abject, underfoot
rel oppressed, persecuted; abused, mal-
treated, mistreated
downturn *n syn* see DECLINE 3
downward *adv syn* see DOWN 1
ant upward
downwardly *adv syn* see DOWN 1
ant upwardly
downwards *adv syn* see DOWN 1
ant upwards
||**downy** *adj syn* see SLY 2
dowry *n* the money, goods, or estate that a
woman brings to her husband in marriage
< from a poor family, she came to her
marriage with no *dowry* >
syn dot, dower, marriage portion
con bride-price, bridewealth; settlement
doxy *n* 1 a usually young woman who
engages in promiscuous sexual intercourse
< a *doxy* who frequented singles bars >
syn ||chippy, floozy, grisette, light-o'-love,
nymphet, party girl, roundheel,
tart, ||tootsie; *compare* HARLOT 1, PROSTI-
TUTE, WANTON
idiom woman of easy virtue
||2 *syn* see MISTRESS
doyen *n* 1 *syn* see LEADER 1
2 *syn* see EXPERT
doze *vb* to sleep lightly < he was inclined
to *doze* at his desk >
syn ||dorm, drowse, ||sloom, slumber,
||snooze, ||sog; *compare* NAP, SLEEP
doze (off) *vb* to fall into a light sleep
< *dozed* off while sitting before the fire >
syn drop off, drowse (off)
idiom drift off
doze *n* a light sleep < was caught in a *doze*
at his desk >
syn drowse, ||sloom, slumber; *compare*
NAP, SLEEP 1
dozy *adj syn* see SLEEPY 1
DP *n syn* see REFUGEE
drab *n* 1 *syn* see HAG 2
2 *syn* see SLATTERN 1
3 *syn* see PROSTITUTE
drab *adj* 1 *syn* see DULL 8
2 *syn* see COLORLESS 2
rel bleak, desolate, dismal, dispiriting,
dreary; dingy, faded
con bright, brilliant, luminous
draconian *adj syn* see RIGID 3
draffy *adj syn* see WORTHLESS 1
draft *n syn* see DRINK 3, drag, drain, drench, ||peg,
swig, swill
draft *vb* 1 to enroll in the armed forces by
compulsion < *drafted* when he was barely
eighteen >
syn conscribe, conscript; *compare* CALL
UP
rel induct; enlist, enroll, muster (in *or*
out); impress, press
2 *syn* see SKETCH
3 to formulate and produce < *drafting*
plans to meet an emergency >

---

syn synonym(s)   *rel* related word(s)
ant antonym(s)   *con* contrasted word(s)
idiom idiomatic equivalent(s)
|| use limited; if in doubt, see a dictionary

syn draw up, formulate, frame, make, prepare

rel concoct, contrive, devise, invent; fabricate, fashion, forge, form, manufacture, shape; plan, project; outline, sketch

4 *syn* see DRAIN 1

drag *n* 1 *syn* see DRAW 1

2 *syn* see DRINK 3

‖3 *syn* see PULL 2

‖4 *syn* see WAY 1

drag *vb* 1 *syn* see PULL 2

con propel, push, shove, thrust; drive, impel, move

2 *syn* see DELAY 2

idiom drag one's feet (*or* heels)

con hasten, hurry

3 to hang down and be drawn behind < her dress *dragged* in the dust >

syn draggle, trail, traipse

rel droop, hang, sag

‖**drag down** *vb syn* see EARN 1

dragging *adj syn* see LONG 2

draggle *vb syn* see DRAG 3

draggle-tail *n syn* see SLATTERN 1

draggletailed *adj syn* see SLATTERNLY

dragoon *vb syn* see INTIMIDATE

drain *vb* 1 to draw off (liquid) by degrees < *drain* the water from the swimming pool >

syn draft, draw, draw off, pump, siphon, tap

rel milk; bleed; suck; empty, exhaust

2 *syn* see TIRE 1

3 *syn* see DEPLETE

idiom bleed white

drain (away) *vb syn* see DECREASE

drain *n syn* see DRINK 3

drained *adj syn* see EFFETE 2

dram *n* 1 a small quantity of something (as alcoholic liquor) to drink < a *dram* of brandy helped to break his chill >

syn ‖caulker, dollop, drop, jolt, nip, shot, slug, snifter, snort, snorter, spot, toothful, tot, ‖wet

rel draft, drink, ‖peg, potation, pull, swig, swill; finger; jigger; dash; ‖splash; snack; quick one

2 *syn* see PARTICLE

drama *n* dramatic art, literature, or affairs < was interested in *drama* during his college years >

syn boards, footlights, (the) stage, theater

rel show business

dramatic *adj* 1 of or relating to drama < made no objections to his son's *dramatic* ambitions >

syn dramaturgic, histrionic, theatral, theatric, theatrical, thespian

2 *syn* see THEATRICAL 2

ant undramatic

dramatist *n syn* see PLAYWRIGHT

dramatizer *n syn* see PLAYWRIGHT

dramaturge *n syn* see PLAYWRIGHT

dramaturgic *adj syn* see DRAMATIC 1

drape *vb* 1 *syn* see SWATHE

2 *syn* see SPRAWL

dratted *adj syn* see DAMNED 2

draw *vb* 1 *syn* see PULL 2

rel bring, fetch; educe, elicit, evoke, extract

con propel, push, shove, thrust; drive, impel, move

2 *syn* see DRAIN 1

3 *syn* see ATTRACT 1

4 *syn* see INDUCE 1

5 *syn* see TAKE 14

6 *syn* see INFER

7 *syn* see EXTEND 3

8 *syn* see DEPLETE

9 *syn* see EVISCERATE

draw *n* 1 a sucking pull on something (as a sipping straw or cigarette) < took a long *draw* on his pipe before answering >

syn drag, puff, pull

rel smoke; inhale

2 *syn* see ADVANTAGE 3

3 *syn* see ATTRACTION 1

4 an indecisive ending to a contest or competition < the prizefight ended in a *draw* >

syn deadlock, dogfall, stalemate, standoff, tie

rel dead heat, photo finish; standstill

con loss; win

draw back *vb syn* see DEDUCT 1

drawback *n syn* see DISADVANTAGE

rel evil, ill; inconvenience, trouble

con advantage, edge

draw down *vb* 1 *syn* see EARN 1

2 *syn* see DEPLETE

draw in *vb syn* see INDUCE 1

drawing *adj syn* see ATTRACTIVE 1

drawing power *n syn* see ATTRACTION 1

drawing room *n syn* see SALON 1

drawn *adj syn* see HAGGARD

con hale, robust

drawn-out *adj syn* see LONG 2

draw off *vb syn* see DRAIN 1

rel abstract; withdraw; move, remove, shift, transfer

draw on *vb* 1 *syn* see EFFECT 2

2 *syn* see INDUCE 1

3 *syn* see DON 1

draw out *vb syn* see EXTEND 3

draw up *vb* 1 *syn* see DRAFT 3

2 *syn* see STOP 4

dray horse *n syn* see SLAVE 2

dread *n syn* see FEAR 1

dreadful *adj syn* see FEARFUL 3

‖**dreadful** *adv syn* see VERY 1

dreadful *n syn* see DIME NOVEL

dreadfully *adv syn* see VERY 1

dream *n* 1 *syn* see FANCY 4

2 *syn* see PIPE DREAM

dream *vb syn* see LONG

dreamer *n* one whose conduct is guided more by ideals than practicalities < a *dreamer* proposing glorious plans impossible to make work >

syn castle-builder, idealist, ideologue, utopian, visionary

rel daydreamer, illusionist, lotus-eater, wishful thinker; Don Quixote: theorist

con pragmatist, realist; Babbitt, Philistine; pedant

dream up *vb syn* see CONTRIVE 2

dreamy *adj* 1 given to dreaming, reverie, or fancy < a *dreamy* and most impractical person >

syn astral, daydreaming, daydreamy, otherworldly, unworldly, visionary

rel fanciful, idealistic, romantic, whimsical

con down-to-earth, practical, pragmatic, realistic; actual, factual

2 *syn* see MARVELOUS 2

drear *adj syn* see GLOOMY 3

dreary *adj* **1** *syn* see GLOOMY 3
2 *syn* see DULL 9
dreck *n syn* see REFUSE
dreg *n, usu* **dregs** *pl* **1** *syn* see SEDIMENT
2 *syn* see RABBLE 2
‖**dreich** *adj syn* see LONG 2
drench *n syn* see DRINK 3
drench *vb* **1** *syn* see WET
rel dip, duck, dunk, immerse, submerge
2 *syn* see SOAK 1
3 *syn* see POUR 3
drenched *adj syn* see WET 1
dress *vb* **1** *syn* see CLOTHE
ant undress
2 *syn* see BANDAGE
3 to remove the entrails from < *dress* fish,
fowl, or game >
syn clean, gut
rel butcher, slaughter
4 *syn* see TILL
rel fertilize, topdress
dress (up) *vb syn* see ADORN
dress *n* **1** *syn* see CLOTHES
2 *syn* see COSTUME
dress down *vb syn* see SCOLD 1
dress up *vb* **1** to attire in best or formal
clothes < *dressed up* to go to the theater >
syn deck (out), ‖dike (out *or* up), doll
out, doll up, ‖dude up, fix up, gussy up,
prank, ‖prick (up), primp, prink (up),
slick, smarten (up), smug, spiff, spruce
(up), tog (out *or* up), ‖toggle, trick (off.
out, *or* up)
rel prettify, pretty (up); apparel, array,
attire, clad, clothe, dress, enclothe, garb,
garment, raiment; overdress; preen; prim
(up)
idiom dress fit to kill, dress to the nines.
put on the dog
2 *syn* see DISGUISE
drib *vb syn* see DRIP
drib *n syn* see DROP 1
dribble *vb* **1** *syn* see DRIP
2 *syn* see DROOL 2
dribble (away) *vb syn* see WASTE 2
dribble *n syn* see PITTANCE
driblet *n* **1** *syn* see PITTANCE
2 *syn* see DROP 1
drift *n* **1** *syn* see FLOW
2 *syn* see PILE 1
rel array, batch, bunch, bundle, clump,
cluster, clutch, group, lot, parcel, set
‖**3** *syn* see DROVE 2
4 *syn* see TENDENCY 1
rel motion, movement, progress, progression; aim, intent, intention, purpose
5 *syn* see LEANING 2
6 *syn* see TENOR 1
rel direction, line, set
drift *vb* **1** to become carried or floated
along < cakes of ice *drifting* along the
stream >
syn float, ride, wash
rel dart, fly, sail, scud, shoot, skim;
dance, flicker, flit, flitter, flutter, hover
2 *syn* see SAUNTER
3 *syn* see WANDER 1
4 *syn* see SLIDE 6

drifter *n* **1** *syn* see ROVER
2 *syn* see VAGABOND
driftwood *n* vagrant impoverished people
< the *driftwood* of skid row >
syn flotsam, jetsam, wreckage
drill *vb* **1** *syn* see PERFORATE
2 *syn* see EXERCISE 3
rel accustom, habituate
drill *n syn* see EXERCISE 3
drilling *n syn* see EXERCISE 3
drink *vb* **1** to take in (potable liquid) < the
boys *drank* all the soda >
syn imbibe, quaff, sip, sup (off *or* up),
swallow, toss
rel drain, gulp, guzzle, slosh, slurp, swig,
swill; wash down
idiom wet one's whistle
2 to salute and wish honor and health to
(a person) by raising and then drinking
from a vessel < *drink* to the bride and
groom >
syn pledge, toast
rel honor, salute; wet
3 to partake of alcoholic liquors especially
habitually or to excess < he *drinks* but
does not smoke >
syn booze, guzzle, imbibe, liquor (up),
‖lush (up), nip, soak, swig, swill, swizzle,
tank up, tipple, tope
idiom bend the elbow, cheer the inner
man, drink like a fish, go on a binge, hit
the bottle, take a nip
drink *n* **1** liquid suitable for swallowing
< able to make palatable *drink* from
seawater >
syn beverage, drinkable, liquor, potable
rel liquid; brew; potion
2 *syn* see LIQUOR 2
3 a portion of potable liquid < took a
drink from the cup >
syn draft, drag, drain, drench, ‖peg, swig,
swill
rel draw, pull; finger, jigger; libation
4 *syn* see OCEAN
drinkable *adj syn* see POTABLE
drinkable *n syn* see DRINK 1
drinkery *n syn* see BAR 5
drip *vb* to let fall drops of moisture or
liquid < trees *dripping* after the rain >
syn distill, drib, dribble, drop, trickle,
trill, weep
rel spatter, sprinkle, spurtle; gush, pour,
sluice, stream
‖**drip** *n* **1** *syn* see NONSENSE 1
2 *syn* see DUNCE
dripping *adj syn* see WET 1
drippy *adj syn* see SENTIMENTAL
drive *vb* **1** *syn* see MOVE 5
rel coerce, compel, force; incite, instigate
con check, curb, inhibit, restrain; guide,
lead, pilot, steer
2 *syn* see PUSH 1
3 to urge along (as cattle) < cowboys
driving the great herds north >
syn ‖drove, herd, run
rel shepherd; wrangle; egg, exhort, goad,
prick, prod, punch, sic, spur, urge
4 *syn* see THRUST 2
5 to operate and steer (a motor vehicle)
< *drive* a car >
syn auto, charioteer, motor, pilot, tool,
wheel

---

syn synonym(s)   *rel* related word(s)
ant antonym(s)   *con* contrasted word(s)
idiom idiomatic equivalent(s)
‖ use limited; if in doubt, see a dictionary

rel operate. run, work; guide, steer; roll; chauffeur

6 *syn* see IMPRESS 3

7 *syn* see PLUNGE 2

8 *syn* see LABOR 1

drive *n* **1** a short trip in a vehicle <took a *drive* around town>

syn ride, spin, turn; *compare* TRIP 1

rel whirl; joyride; excursion, outing

2 *syn* see DRIVEWAY

3 *syn* see ENTERPRISE 4

4 *syn* see VIGOR 2

rel impetus, momentum, speed, velocity

drivel *vb* **1** *syn* see DROOL 2

2 *syn* see BABBLE 2

3 *syn* see WASTE 2

drivel *n* **1** *syn* see NONSENSE 2

2 *syn* see GIBBERISH 1

driveling *adj* *syn* see INSIPID 3

driver *n* *syn* see MOTORIST

driveway *n* a private road giving access from a public way <the *driveway* to a house>

syn ‖avenue, drive

rel court, place, row, street

driving *adj* *syn* see ENERGETIC 2

drizzle *vb* *syn* see SPRINKLE 5

drogher *n* *syn* see BEARER 2

drôlerie *n* *syn* see JOKE 1

droll *adj* *syn* see LAUGHABLE

rel absurd, preposterous

droll *n* *syn* see HUMORIST 2

drollery *n* **1** *syn* see JOKE 1

2 *syn* see HUMOR 4

drollness *n* *syn* see HUMOR 4

drone *vb* **1** *syn* see HUM

2 *syn* see IDLE

drony *adj* *syn* see LAZY

drool *vb* **1** to secrete or become filled with saliva usually in anticipation of food <mouths *drooled* as we waited for dinner>

syn water

idiom water at the mouth

2 to let saliva or some other substance flow from the mouth <babies often *drool* uncontrollably>

syn dribble, drivel, salivate, slabber, slaver, slobber

3 *syn* see ENTHUSE 2

4 *syn* see BABBLE 2

drool *n* *syn* see NONSENSE 2

droop *vb* **1** *syn* see SLOUCH

2 *syn* see LOWER 3

3 to become literally or figuratively limp through loss of vigor or freshness <he walked along, his shoulders *drooping* from exhaustion>

syn flag, sag, swag, wilt

rel drop, fall, sink, slump, subside; dangle, hang, loll, lop, sling, suspend; decline, deteriorate, ‖dwine, fade, fail, languish, weaken

droopy *adj* *syn* see DOWNCAST

drop *n* **1** the quantity of fluid that falls in one spherical mass <a *drop* of rain>

syn drib, driblet, droplet, globule, gobbet

rel dribble, drip, trickle

2 *syn* see PARTICLE

3 *syn* see DRAM

4 *syn* see DESCENT 4

5 *syn* see DESCENT 1

6 *syn* see DECLINE 3

7 *syn* see DEPTH 1

drop *vb* **1** *syn* see FALL 2

2 *syn* see FALL 1

ant mount

3 *syn* see PLUMMET

rel slide, slip

con rally, rebound; ascend, climb; soar

ant mount

4 *syn* see COLLAPSE 2

rel backslide, lapse, relapse

5 *syn* see DIE 1

6 *syn* see DRIP

7 *syn* see FELL 1

8 *syn* see QUIT 6

9 *syn* see CANCEL 2

10 *syn* see DISMISS 3

11 *syn* see LOSE 2

12 *syn* see LOSE 1

drop (in *or* **by)** *vb* *syn* see VISIT 2

drop (off) *vb* *syn* see SLIP 6

droplet *n* *syn* see DROP 1

drop off *vb* *syn* see DOZE (off)

dropsical *adj* *syn* see INFLATED

dropsied *adj* *syn* see INFLATED

drossy *adj* *syn* see WORTHLESS 1

droughty *adj* *syn* see DRY 1

‖drouk *vb* *syn* see SOAK 1

drove *n* **1** *syn* see CROWD 1

2 a group of domestic animals reared or handled as a unit <a *drove* of cattle>

syn ‖drift, flock, herd

rel drive; pack; school

‖drove *vb* *syn* see DRIVE 3

drown *vb* **1** *syn* see OVERWHELM 4

2 *syn* see DELUGE 1

3 *syn* see WET

drowse *vb* *syn* see DOZE

drowse (off) *vb* *syn* see DOZE (off)

drowse *n* *syn* see DOZE

drowsy *adj* *syn* see SLEEPY 1

rel lackadaisical, languid, languorous

con alert, vigilant, watchful; active, dynamic, live; animated, lively, vivacious

drub *vb* **1** *syn* see BEAT 1

2 *syn* see LAMBASTE 3

3 *syn* see WHIP 2

drubbing *n* *syn* see DEFEAT 1

drudge *vb* to perform hard, menial, or monotonous work <*drudged* all day washing floors>

syn grind, grub, ‖muck, plod, slave, slog, toil

rel hammer, peg (away *or* at *or* on), plow, plug, pound (away); perform, work

idiom keep one's nose to the grindstone

con idle, laze, loaf, lounge; dally, dawdle, potter, putter; cheat, chisel

drudge *n* **1** *syn* see SLAVE 2

2 *syn* see WORK 2

3 *syn* see HACK 2

drudgery *n* *syn* see WORK 2

drudging *adj* *syn* see IRKSOME

drug *n* **1** a substance used by itself or in a mixture in the treatment or diagnosis of disease <a life-sustaining *drug*>

syn biologic, medicinal, pharmaceutic, pharmaceutical

rel cure, medicament, medication, medicine, physic, remedy, specific; simple

2 a narcotic substance or preparation <depended on *drugs* to make life bearable>

syn dope, ‖hop, narcotic, opiate

drugged *adj* being under the influence of a drug taken for nonmedical purposes < was *drugged* on LSD >
　syn doped, high, hopped-up, spaced-out, stoned, tripped out, turned on, ‖wiped out, zonked
　idiom on a trip
　ant straight

druggist *n* one who deals in medicinal drugs
　syn apothecary, ‖chemist, pharmacist
　rel pharmacologist

drum *vb syn* see SOLICIT 1

drumfire *n syn* see BARRAGE

drumhead *adj syn* see SUMMARY 2

drum up *vb syn* see SOLICIT 1

drunk *adj syn* see INTOXICATED 1
　rel drinking, drinky
　idiom roaring drunk
　con bone-dry, dry
　ant sober

drunk *n* 1 *syn* see BINGE 1
　2 *syn* see DRUNKARD

drunkard *n* one who drinks alcoholic liquors to excess < *drunkards* lurching homeward when the bar finally closes >
　syn bibber, ‖bloat, ‖blotter, boozehound, boozer, drunk, fuddler, guzzler, inebriate, lush, ‖lusher, rumdum, rummy, ‖rumpot, ‖shicker, soak, soaker, sot, sponge, stiff, swillbowl, swiller, tippler, toper, tosspot
　rel alcoholic, dipsomaniac; wino; drammer
　idiom elbow bender (*or* crooker)
　ant teetotaler

drunken *adj syn* see INTOXICATED 1

drunkery *n syn* see BAR 5

‖**druthers** *n syn* see CHOICE 1

dry *adj* 1 devoid of or deficient in moisture < preferred a *dry* climate >
　syn arid, bone-dry, droughty, moistureless, sere, thirsty, unwatered, waterless
　rel baked, dehydrated, desiccated, parched; bald, bare, barren; depleted, drained, exhausted, impoverished; juiceless, sapless, sapped
　con drenched, dripping, saturated, soaked, soaking, sodden, sopping, soppy, soused, wringing-wet; damp, dank, humid, moist; exuberant, lush, luxuriant, prodigal, profuse
　ant wet
　2 *syn* see THIRSTY 1
　3 marked by the absence of or abstention from alcoholic beverages < a *dry* party >
　syn bone-dry, teetotal
　ant wet
　4 *syn* see IMPASSIVE 1
　5 *syn* see ARID 2
　6 *syn* see PLAIN 1
　7 *syn* see SOUR 1
　ant sweet
　8 *syn* see HARSH 3

dry *vb* 1 to treat or affect so as to deprive of moisture < clothes *dried* in the wind >
　syn dehydrate, desiccate, exsiccate, parch, sear
　rel evaporate; anhydrate; deplete, drain, exhaust; shrivel, wither, wizen

---

syn synonym(s)　　*rel* related word(s)
ant antonym(s)　　*con* contrasted word(s)
idiom idiomatic equivalent(s)
‖ use limited; if in doubt, see a dictionary

　con deluge, douse, drench, soak, sop, souse; damp, dampen, moisten
　ant wet
　2 *syn* see HARDEN 1

dryasdust *adj syn* see ARID 2

dry land *n syn* see EARTH 2

‖**dry-shave** *vb syn* see CHEAT

dry up *vb* 1 *syn* see DESICCATE 2
　2 *syn* see WITHER
　3 *syn* see SHUT UP 2

dual *adj* 1 *syn* see TWOFOLD 1
　2 *syn* see TWIN

dualistic *adj syn* see TWOFOLD 1

dualize *vb syn* see DOUBLE 1

dub *vb* 1 *syn* see NAME 1
　2 *syn* see BOTCH

dub *vb* to provide (a motion-picture film) with a new sound track (as for substituting dialogue in a foreign language) < *dubbed* the Italian movie into English >
　syn double

dubiety *n syn* see UNCERTAINTY
　rel hesitancy; faltering, vacillation, wavering
　con decidedness, decisiveness
　ant decision

dubiosity *n syn* see UNCERTAINTY
　rel addlement, confusion, muddlement; faltering, vacillation, wavering
　con cocksureness, positiveness
　ant decidedness

dubious *adj* 1 *syn* see MOOT
　2 *syn* see DOUBTFUL 1
　rel skeptical; mistrustful; disinclined, hesitant, reluctant
　con dependable, tried, trustworthy, trusty; certain, positive, sure
　ant cocksure; reliable
　3 *syn* see IMPROBABLE 1
　4 *syn* see UNRELIABLE 1
　ant trustworthy

dubitable *adj syn* see DOUBTFUL 1
　ant indubitable

dubitancy *n syn* see UNCERTAINTY

duce *n syn* see TYRANT

‖**duck** *n syn* see ECCENTRIC

duck *vb* 1 *syn* see DIP 1
　2 to lower (as the head or body) quickly < had to *duck* his head to get through the door >
　syn dip, stoop
　rel bend; bow
　3 *syn* see DODGE 1
　rel avert, prevent, ward
　4 *syn* see ESCAPE 2

duck soup *n syn* see SNAP 1

duct *n syn* see CHANNEL 1

ductile *adj syn* see PLASTIC
　rel responsive; submitting; fluid, liquid
　con intractable, refractory; adamant, obdurate

ductus *n syn* see HANDWRITING

dud *n syn* see FAILURE 5

dude *n syn* see FOP

‖**dude up** *vb syn* see DRESS UP 1

dudgeon *n syn* see OFFENSE 2
　rel fury, ire, rage, wrath; humor, mood, temper

duds *n pl* 1 *syn* see CLOTHES
　‖2 *syn* see RAGS 1

due *adj* 1 *syn* see JUST 3
　rel good, right; equitable, fair, just; coming, earned

con excessive, exorbitant, extravagant, immoderate, inordinate; deficient

ant undue

2 having reached the date at which payment is required < a note that would become *due* after eighteen months >

syn mature, payable

3 *syn* see UNPAID 2

due *n* **1** what one fairly has coming < the artist has finally been accorded his *due* >

syn comeuppance, desert(s), deserving, lumps, merit, right(s)

rel deservedness, dueness, entitlement; compensation, payment, recompense, recompensing, repayment, satisfaction; reprisal, retaliation, retribution, revenge, vengeance; guerdon, need, reward

idiom what is coming to one

2 *syn* see DEBT 3

due *adv syn* see DIRECTLY 1

duel *vb syn* see RESIST

due to *prep syn* see OVER 6

‖**duff** *vb syn* see CHEAT

duff *n syn* see BUTTOCKS

duffer *n* ‖1 *syn* see PEDDLER

2 *syn* see DUNCE

dulcet *adj* **1** *syn* see MELODIOUS 1

con grinding, rasping, scraping, scratching

ant grating

2 *syn* see SWEET 1

dull *adj* **1** *syn* see STUPID 1

ant sharp

2 *syn* see RETARDED

con advanced, precocious

3 *syn* see INSENSIBLE 5

4 *syn* see DOWNCAST

5 *syn* see COLORLESS 2

ant bright

6 lacking sharpness of edge or point < a knife with a *dull* blade >

syn blunt, obtuse

rel blunted, dulled, unsharpened

con honed, keen, razor-sharp, unblunted, whetted

ant sharp

7 lacking warmth, luster, or brilliance < a smooth *dull* finish >

syn blind, dead, dim, flat, lackluster, lusterless, mat, muted

rel cold, dingy, drab, dun, leaden, somber; deadened, lifeless

con beaming, bright, brilliant, effulgent, fulgent, incandescent, lambent, lucent, lucid, luminous, lustrous, radiant, refulgent; burnished, polished, shiny

8 cloudy in color < a *dull* brown >

syn drab, muddy, murky, subfusc

rel blurry, cloudy, hazy; flat, lackluster, lifeless, lusterless; mousy

ant clear; rich

9 being so unvaried or uninteresting as to provoke boredom or tedium < any routine constantly repeated can become *dull* >

syn banausic, blah, ‖dim, dreary, humdrum, monotone, monotonous, pedestrian, plodding, poky, stodgy

rel boring, irksome, tedious, tiring, wearisome; brainless; exhausting, fagging, fatiguing

con animating, exciting, stimulating; gay, spritely

ant lively

10 *syn* see OVERCAST

11 *syn* see ARID 2

rel matter-of-fact, prosaic, prosy; bloodless

idiom dull as ditchwater

con exciting, stimulating

ant lively

dull *vb* **1** to make less clear, distinct, or bright < colors *dulled* by the sun >

syn dim, fade, muddy, pale, tarnish

rel discolor, wash out; blur

con brighten, freshen, intensify

2 *syn* see DEADEN 1

ant sharpen

3 to deprive of sharpness (as of edge or point) < *dull* a spade >

syn blunt, disedge, obtund, turn

idiom take the edge off

con edge, hone

ant sharpen

4 to impair one or more of the senses < age had *dulled* his hearing >

syn blear, blur, dim

rel debilitate, enfeeble, weaken; darken; retard, slow

ant sharpen

5 to make slow or obtuse < his mind had been *dulled* by drink >

syn blunt, hebetate, stupefy

rel becloud, befog, cloud, darken, dim; benumb, deaden, numb; retard, slow

con quicken, stimulate, whet

ant sharpen

dullard *n syn* see DUNCE

dullhead *n syn* see DUNCE

dullness *n syn* see LETHARGY 1

rel denseness, stupidity

con edge, incisiveness, keenness

ant sharpness

dumb *adj* **1** lacking the power to speak < deaf and *dumb* from birth >

syn inarticulate, mute, silent, speechless, unarticulate, voiceless; compare SILENT 2

ant articulate

2 *syn* see SILENT 2

rel incoherent, indistinct, maundering, tongue-tied

3 *syn* see SILENT 3

con speaking, talking; talkative, verbose

4 *syn* see STUPID 1

idiom dumb as an ox

dumb (up) *vb syn* see SHUT UP 2

dumbbell *n syn* see DUNCE

‖**dumb bunny** *n syn* see DUNCE

‖**dumb cluck** *n syn* see DUNCE

dumbfound *vb* **1** *syn* see SURPRISE 2

2 *syn* see STAGGER 5

dumbfounded *adj syn* see AGHAST 2

‖**dumbhead** *n syn* see DUNCE

‖**dummkopf** *n syn* see DUNCE

dummy *n* **1** *syn* see DUNCE

2 *syn* see STOOGE 1

dummy *adj syn* see ARTIFICIAL 2

‖**dummy (up)** *vb syn* see SHUT UP 2

dump *vb* **1** *syn* see DISCARD

‖**2** *syn* see BEAT 1

dump *n* **1** *syn* see ARMORY

2 *syn* see STY 1

dumping *n syn* see DISPOSAL 2

dumpling *n syn* see FATTY

dumps *n pl syn* see SADNESS

idiom low spirits

dumpy *adj syn* see STOCKY

rel formless, shapeless, unformed

dun *adj syn see* DARK 1

dun *vb syn see* WORRY 1

dunce *n* a dull-witted person < the traditional *dunce* in pointed cap>
syn beetlehead, blockhead, bonehead, boob, booby, ‖bufflehead, cabbagehead, chowderhead, chucklehead, chump, clod, clodpate, clodpoll, ‖cluck, dimwit, ‖dizzard, dodo, ‖dodunk, dolt, dolthead, dope, ‖doughhead, ‖drip, duffer, dullard, dullhead, dumbbell, ‖dumb bunny, ‖dumb cluck, ‖dumbhead, ‖dummkopf, dummy, dunderhead, dunderpate, fathead, featherweight, goof, ‖goon, hammerhead, idiot, ignoramus, ironhead, knothead, knucklehead, lackwit, lame-brain, lunk, lunkhead, ‖moonraker, moron, muddlehead, mug, muggins, mutt, muttonhead, nitwit, noddy, noodle, numskull, oaf, pinhead, poke, prune, pumpkin head, put, ‖schnook, simp, simpleton, ‖spoon, squarehead, ‖stunpoll, ‖stupe, stupid, thickhead, thickskull, turnip, wantwit, woodenhead, zombie
rel lightweight; ass, donkey, fool, imbecile, jackass, jerk, nincompoop, ninny, ‖schmo, ‖schmuck; birdbrain, featherbrain, scatterbrain
idiom dumb ox, Simple Simon
con brain, highbrow, intellectual, thinker, wit; pundit, sage, savant, scholar, wise man; prodigy, wizard; genius, mastermind

duncical *adj syn see* STUPID 1

dunderhead *n syn see* DUNCE

dunderpate *n syn see* DUNCE

dundrearies *n pl syn see* SIDE-WHISKERS

dungeon *n* a close dark prison or vault commonly underground < the prisoners were kept in lightless *dungeons* >
syn oubliette
rel vault; black hole; cell; jail, prison

dungy *adj syn see* DIRTY 1

dunk *vb syn see* DIP 1
rel saturate, soak, sop

duo *n syn see* COUPLE

dupe *n syn see* FOOL 3

dupe *vb* to delude by underhand methods < the public is easily *duped* by extravagant claims in advertising >
syn bamboozle, befool, catch, chicane, con, dust, flimflam, fool, gull, hoax, hoodwink, hornswoggle, job, kid, pigeon, ‖rig, spoof, trick, victimize
rel beguile, betray, deceive, delude, double-cross, mislead; cheat, cozen, defraud, overreach; baffle, circumvent, outwit
idiom pull one's leg, put something over (or across)
con enlighten, inform, wise (up)

dupe *vb syn see* DOUBLE 1

dupery *n syn see* DECEPTION 1

duple *adj syn see* TWOFOLD 1

duplex *adj syn see* TWOFOLD 1

duplicate *adj syn see* SAME 2

duplicate *n* 1 *syn see* REPRODUCTION
rel analogue, counterpart, parallel
2 *syn see* MATE 5

---

duplicate *vb* 1 *syn see* DOUBLE 1
2 *syn see* COPY

duplicitous *adj syn see* UNDERHAND

duplicity *n* 1 *syn see* DECEIT 1
rel faithlessness, perfidiousness, perfidy, treacherousness, treachery

durable *adj syn see* LASTING
rel stout, strong, tenacious
con feeble, fragile, frail, weak

duration *n* 1 *syn see* CONTINUATION 1
2 *syn see* RUN 2
3 *syn see* TERM 2

duress *n syn see* FORCE 4

during *prep* in the course of < *during* the disorder some men kept their heads>
syn amid, mid, midst, over, throughout

dusk *adj syn see* DARK 1

dusk *n syn see* EVENING 1

‖**dusk dark** *n syn see* EVENING 1

dusky *adj* 1 *syn see* DARK 3
2 *syn see* DARK 1
3 *syn see* GLOOMY 3
4 *syn see* OBSCURE 3

dust *n* 1 *syn see* DUSTING
2 *syn see* QUARREL
‖3 *syn see* REFUSE

dust *vb* 1 *syn see* SPRINKLE 1
2 *syn see* WHIP 2
3 *syn see* DUPE
idiom throw dust in one's eyes
‖4 *syn see* HURRY 2

dusting *n* 1 a small quantity lightly applied to or sprinkled on < a *dusting* of sugar on the cake>
syn dust, powdering, sprinkling
‖2 *syn see* DEFEAT 1

‖**dust off** *vb syn see* MURDER 1

dustup *n syn see* QUARREL

dusty *adj syn see* ARID 2

Dutch *n syn see* TROUBLE 3

duteous *adj syn see* RESPECTFUL

dutiful *adj syn see* RESPECTFUL

duty *n* 1 *syn see* OBLIGATION 2
rel accountability, amenability, answerability, liability
2 *syn see* FUNCTION 1
3 *syn see* LOAD 3
4 *syn see* TAX 1
5 *syn see* TASK 1
6 *syn see* USE 4

dwarf *n* a very small person < she was a tiny little thing, almost a *dwarf* >
syn homunculus, hop-o'-my-thumb, Lilliputian, manikin, midge, midget, peewee, pygmy, runt, Tom Thumb
rel ‖ribe, ‖shrimp, wart; dwarfling; minimus
ant giant

dwarf *vb syn see* STUNT

dwarf *adj syn see* TINY

dwarfish *adj syn see* TINY

dwell *vb* 1 *syn see* RESIDE 1
2 *syn see* CONSIST 1

dweller *n syn see* INHABITANT

dwelling *n syn see* HABITATION 2

dwindle *vb* 1 *syn see* DECREASE
rel ebb, subside, wane; attenuate, extenuate, thin; moderate; disappear
2 *syn see* FAIL 3

‖**dwine** *vb syn see* FAIL 1

dyad *n syn see* COUPLE

dye *n syn see* COLOR 6

dyed-in-the-wool *adj syn see* INVETERATE 1

---

syn synonym(s)   *rel* related word(s)
ant antonym(s)   *con* contrasted word(s)
idiom idiomatic equivalent(s)
‖ use limited; if in doubt, see a dictionary

dyestuff *n syn* see COLOR 6

dying *adj syn* see MORIBUND

dynamic *adj* 1 *syn* see ACTIVE 1
rel activating, energizing, vitalizing
ant static

2 *syn* see VIGOROUS
rel forceful, forcible; intense, vehement, violent
con idle, inactive, passive

ant :nert

dynamite *vb syn* see DESTROY 1

dynamo *n syn* see HUSTLER 1

dysentery *n syn* see DIARRHEA

dyslogistic *adj syn* see DEROGATORY
ant eulogistic

dyspathy *n syn* see ANTIPATHY 2

dyspeptic *adj syn* see ILL-TEMPERED

dysphoria *n syn* see SADNESS

E

each *adj syn* see ALL 2
rel any, several, various; particular, respective, specific

each *adv syn* see APIECE
idiom a shot, a throw, a whack

eager *adj* moved by a strong and urgent desire or interest < young executives *eager* to succeed >
syn agog, anxious, appetent, ardent, athirst, avid, breathless, impatient, keen, raring, solicitous, thirsty
rel enthusiastic, gung ho, heated, hot; ambitious, intent; acquisitive, covetous, craving, desirous, hankering, ‖honing, hungry, longing, pining, wishful, yearning; impatient, restive, restless
idiom champing at the bit, ready and willing
con aloof, disinterested, incurious, indifferent, unconcerned, uninterested; apathetic, detached, impassive, stolid
ant listless

eagerness *n* a strong and urgent desire or interest < an *eagerness* to learn >
syn ardor, enthusiasm, zing
rel alacrity, avidity, keenness, quickness; ambition; gusto, ‖mustard, zest
con lackadaisicality, languor, lethargy; aloofness, disinterest; apathy, deliberation, detachment, impassivity, stolidity
ant listlessness

eagle eye *n syn* see EYE 3

eagle-eyed *adj syn* see SHARP-EYED

ear *n syn* see NOTICE 1

earlier *adv* 1 *syn* see BEFORE 2

2 *syn* see HITHERTO 1

3 *syn* see BEFORE 3

earliest *adj syn* see FIRST 2
con final, terminal, ultimate
ant latest

early *adv* 1 at or nearly at the beginning of a period, course, process, or series < it is much too *early* to guess the outcome >
syn betimes, seasonably, soon, timely
rel first

2 in advance of the expected or usual time < these apples bear *early* and heavy >
syn betimes, oversoon, prematurely
rel beforehand
idiom ahead of time, bright and early

early *adj* 1 of, relating to, or occurring near the beginning of a period of time, a development, or a series < *early* Renaissance > < *early* art forms >
syn primitive, primordial

rel original, pristine; ancient, antediluvian, antiquated, primal, primeval; antecedent, preceding, prevenient, prior
con conclusive, final, last, terminal, ultimate; eventual; intermediate, middle, midmost
ant late

2 occurring before the expected or usual time < an *early* death > < an *early* peach >
syn overearly, oversoon, premature, previous, ‖soon, untimely; *compare* PRECOCIOUS
rel anticipative, anticipatory, precipitant, precocious; unanticipated, unexpected
con slow, tardy; anticipated, expected
ant late

earmark *vb syn* see DESIGNATE 3

earn *vb* 1 to receive as return for effort < *earn* a living wage >
syn acquire, bring in, ‖drag down, draw down, gain, get, knock down, make, win
rel attain, effect, obtain, procure, realize, receive, secure

2 to be or make worthy of < his devotion to duty *earned* him a promotion >
syn deserve, merit, rate
rel bag, come by, harvest, net, reap, score

earnest *n syn* see EARNESTNESS
rel attention, interest; enthusiasm, warmth, zeal
ant jest, play

earnest *adj syn* see SERIOUS 1
rel ardent, enthusiastic, passionate, pressing, warm, zealous; assiduous, busy, diligent, industrious, perseverant, sedulous; sincere, wholehearted, whole-souled
con buoyant, effervescent, elastic, flippant, light
ant frivolous

earnest *n syn* see PLEDGE 1

earnestly *adv* 1 *syn* see HARD 3
rel seriously, soberly, solemnly, thoughtfully; zealously

2 *syn* see SERIOUSLY 1

earnestness *n* a state of freedom from all jesting or trifling < he studied with great *earnestness* >
syn earnest, intentness, serious-mindedness, seriousness
rel doggedness, perseverance, persistence; decision, determination, firmness, purposefulness, resolve; absorption, attentiveness, concentration, engrossment; deliberation; gravity, sobriety

con levity, lightness; shallowness, superficiality; carelessness, slackness
ant frivolity

earnings *n pl syn* see PROFIT

earshot *n* the range within which something (as a voice) may be heard < the gossips were still within *earshot* of her >
syn hearing, sound
idiom carrying (*or* bearing) distance

earsplitting *adj syn* see LOUD 1
rel penetrating, shrill

earth *n* 1 the entire area in which man lives and acts < expect the destruction of the *earth* >
syn globe, (the) planet, world
rel orb, sphere; cosmos, creation, macrocosm, universe, vale
2 areas of land as distinguished from sea and air < clayey *earth*, difficult to drain >
syn dirt, dry land, ground, land, soil, terra firma
rel clay, gravel, humus, loam, mud, sand; fill, subsoil; terrain, turf; clod

earthlike *adj syn* see EARTHY 1

earthly *adj* 1 of, relating to, or characteristic of this earth or man's life on earth < *earthly* pursuits >
syn mundane, sublunary, tellurian, telluric, terrene, terrestrial, uncelestial, worldly
rel carnal, corporeal, earthbound, physical; material, temporal; unspiritual
con celestial, empyreal, empyrean, heavenly; ideal, utopian; divine, spiritual
2 *syn* see PROBABLE
rel imaginable, potential

earthquake *n* a shaking or trembling of the earth that is volcanic or tectonic in origin < homes destroyed by *earthquakes* >
syn quake, ‖quaker, shake, shock, temblor (*or* tremblor), tremor

earthy *adj* 1 consisting of, resembling, or suggesting earth < a stale *earthy* smell >
syn earthlike, terrene, terrestrial
rel clayey, dusty, muddy, sandy
2 *syn* see EARTHLY 1
3 *syn* see MATERIALISTIC
4 *syn* see REALISTIC
ant impractical

ease *n* 1 *syn* see REST 1
rel idleness, inactivity, inertia, inertness, passivity, supinity; calmness, security
con labor, toil, travail; adversity, difficulty; burden, care, worry
2 *syn* see UNCONSTRAINT
3 freedom from or mitigation of pain < medication brought him instant *ease* >
syn alleviation, easement, mitigation, relief
rel decrease, diminishment, moderation, reduction; calming, soothing
con discomfort, unrest; agony, pain
4 *syn* see READINESS 3
rel adroitness, artfulness, cleverness, deftness, effortlessness, expertise, expertness, fluency, knack, poise, skillfulness, smoothness; efficiency, dispatch

con awkwardness, clumsiness, maladroitness, stiffness, woodenness; constraint; inconvenience, pains; exertion
ant effort
5 *syn* see PROSPERITY 2

ease *vb* 1 *syn* see RELIEVE 1
rel deaden, dull; ameliorate, help
con afflict, torment
2 *syn* see LOOSE 5
rel disengage, free, release
con bind, restrain, tighten
3 to make less difficult < new laws that will *ease* voting requirements >
syn facilitate
rel aid, assist, better, help, improve; forward, further, promote, speed
idiom clear (*or* prepare) the way (for), grease the wheels, open the door (to *or* for)
con hinder, impede, retard

easeful *adj syn* see COMFORTABLE 2

easement *n syn* see EASE 3
rel allayment, appeasement, assuagement, mollification

ease off *vb* 1 *syn* see LOOSE 5
2 *syn* see ABATE 4
3 *syn* see RELAX 2

easily *adv* 1 without discomfort, difficulty, or reluctance < *easily* translated the document >
syn effortlessly, facilely, freely, lightly, readily, smoothly, well
rel competently, dexterously, efficiently, fluently, handily, simply
idiom hands down, slick as a whistle
con awkwardly, clumsily, ineptly, stiffly; arduously, wearily
ant laboriously
2 without question < this is *easily* the best course of action >
syn absolutely, definitely, doubtless, doubtlessly, positively, unequivocally, unquestionably
rel actually, assuredly, certainly, clearly, decidedly, indeed, really, truly, undoubtedly
idiom no doubt
con apparently, perhaps, probably, seemingly; doubtfully, equivocally, questionably
3 *syn* see WELL 7

easy *adj* 1 causing or involving little or no difficulty < an *easy* solution >
syn effortless, facile, light, royal, simple, smooth, untroublesome
rel apparent, clear, distinct, evident, manifest, obvious, plain; clear-cut, straightforward, uncomplicated, uncompounded, uninvolved
idiom easy as falling off a log, easy as pie, nothing to it
con arduous, difficult, troublesome; abstruse, complex, complicated, intricate, knotty
ant hard
2 *syn* see FORBEARING
rel compassionate, condoning, excusing, forgiving, pardoning, sympathetic; benign, kindly; lax, moderate, soft; humoring, mollycoddling, pampering, spoiling
con austere, exacting, rigid, severe, stern, strict, stringent
3 easily taken advantage of or imposed upon < he was *easy* prey to her wiles >

---

syn synonym(s) *rel* related word(s)
ant antonym(s) *con* contrasted word(s)
idiom idiomatic equivalent(s)
‖ use limited; if in doubt, see a dictionary

syn fleeceable, gullible, naive, susceptible

rel credulous, trusting, unmistrusting, unsuspicious; deceivable, deludable, dupable, exploitable; artless, dewy-eyed, green, simple, unsophisticated

con critical, cynical, disbelieving, mistrustful, scoffing, skeptical, suspicious, unbelieving

4 *syn* see FAST 7

5 *syn* see COMFORTABLE 2

rel secure

con discontented, dissatisfied; miserable

ant uncomfortable

6 *syn* see AMIABLE 1

rel familiar, gregarious, informal; courtly, diplomatic, pleasant, polite, sociable; smooth, suave, urbane

con brusque, curt, unfriendly, unpleasant; constrained, embarrassed, formal, restrained; discourteous, impolite, undiplomatic, ungracious; stiff, unsocial, withdrawn, wooden

ant ill at ease

7 *syn* see CALM 2

rel relaxed; lethargic, unambitious

con agitated, tense, troubled, uptight

8 *syn* see PROSPEROUS 3

rel successful, thriving

idiom in easy circumstances, on easy street

con straitened

9 marked by ready facility (as of expression) <an *easy* style of writing>

syn cursive, effortless, flowing, fluent, running, smooth

rel facile; graceful

con effortful, labored

ant difficult

easygoing *adj* **1** *syn* see CALM 2

con agitated, flurried, flustered, harassed; anxious, concerned, upset, worried

ant uptight

2 *syn* see LAZY

rel apathetic, careless, indifferent, unconcerned; unambitious

con active, ambitious, diligent, dynamic, energetic, industrious, live, vigorous

3 not constrained or bound by rigid standards <enjoyed the *easygoing* morality of a commune>

syn breezy, casual, ‖common, dégagé, informal, low-pressure, relaxed, ‖sonsy, unconstrained, unfussy, unreserved

rel affable, folksy; flexible, lax, moderate, offhand, off-handed, unaffected; carefree, devil-may-care, happy-go-lucky; outgiving; uninhibited

idiom free and easy

con ceremonious, decorous, formal, proper, stuffy; constrained, inflexible, inhibited, restrained, rigid, starchy, stiff

easy mark *n* **1** *syn* see POOL 3

2 *syn* see SOFT TOUCH 1

‖**easy rider** *n* **1** *syn* see SYCOPHANT

2 *syn* see PIMP 1

easy street *n* *syn* see PROSPERITY 2

eat *vb* **1** to take in as food <they quickly *ate* a hearty breakfast>

syn consume, devour, feed (on), ingest, meal, partake (of), take; *compare* CONSUME 2

rel banquet, feast, gormandize; eat up, gobble (up *or* down), gorge (on), ‖mop (up), polish off, scoff; breakfast, dine,

lunch, snack, sup; mouth, ‖muckamuck, nibble, pick

idiom break bread, get away with, have (*or* take) a bite, take nourishment, ‖put on the feed bag

2 *syn* see CONSUME 1

3 to consume gradually <the acid *ate* the surface of the copper>

syn bite, corrode, eat away, erode, gnaw, scour, wear (away)

rel nibble (away); consume, decompose, disintegrate, dissolve

eatable *adj* *syn* see EDIBLE

eat away *vb* *syn* see EAT 3

eating house *n* a cheap often small restaurant <grabbed a quick sandwich at a local *eating house*>

syn beanery, ‖buffet, café, coffee shop, cookshop, diner, ‖greasy spoon, ‖hashery, ‖hash house, lunch counter (*or* bar), luncheonette, lunchroom, lunch wagon (*or* cart), quick-lunch, sandwich shop, snack bar (*or* counter)

rel cafeteria, eatery, tearoom; trattoria

‖**eats** *n pl* *syn* see FOOD 1

eat up *vb* **1** to eat completely and without delay <*eat up* your dinner before it gets cold>

syn devour, dispatch, polish off

rel down, eat; bolt, gobble (up *or* down), gorge (on), ‖mop (up), wolf

2 *syn* see CONSUME 1

‖**3** *syn* see DEVOUR 5

rel luxuriate (in), riot (in), wallow (in)

idiom be beside oneself over, be thrilled to death by, smack one's lips over, take delight in

‖**4** *syn* see LOVE 1

ebb *vb* *syn* see ABATE 4

rel decline, peter (out); recede, retreat, retrograde

con ascend, increase, mount, rise; advance, progress

ant flow

ebbing *n* *syn* see FAILURE 4

rel declining, sinking

ebon *adj* *syn* see BLACK 1

ebony *adj* *syn* see BLACK 1

ebullience *n* lively or enthusiastic expression of thoughts or feelings <her bubbling *ebullience* was infectious>

syn buoyancy, effervescence, exuberance, exuberancy

rel animation, enthusiasm, gaiety, highspiritedness, liveliness, vitality, vivaciousness, vivacity; agitation, excitement, exhilaration, ferment

con apathy, impassivity, languor, lethargy, listlessness, passivity, sluggishness, stolidity, torpidity, torpor; enervation, inactivity, inertia, lifelessness; disinterest, unconcern, uninterest

ebullient *adj* *syn* see EXUBERANT 1

eccentric *adj* **1** not having the same center <*eccentric* spheres>

syn off-center

rel uncentered; off-balance, unbalanced

con centered; balanced

ant concentric

2 *syn* see STRANGE 4

rel anomalous, irregular, unnatural; exceptionable, exceptional, quirky, quizzical; beheaded, ‖dippy, wacky; fantastic, grotesque *con* customary, habitual; natural, normal, regular, typical

eccentric *n* one who deviates from established patterns especially in odd or whimsical ways <an *eccentric* who filled his house with statues of himself>
syn case, character, ||duck, oddball, oddity, original, quiz, ||spook, ||wack, zombie
rel bohemian, maverick, nonconformist, unconformist; dissenter, heretic; caution, coot, ||geezer; crackpot, crank, freak, kook, screwball
idiom queer duck (*or* potato)
con conformer, conformist, conventionalist, traditionalist; bore, bromide, dullard

ecclesiast *n syn see* CLERGYMAN

ecclesiastic *n syn see* CLERGYMAN

ecclesiastical *adj* of, relating to, or belonging to a church especially as an established institution < *ecclesiastical* law>
syn church, churchly, churchmanly, spiritual
rel apostolic, canonical, episcopal, episcopalian, evangelistic, theological; clerical, ministerial, papal, pastoral, patriarchal, pontifical, prelatial, priestly, rabbinical, sacerdotal; cathedralesque, churchlike, pantheonic, synagogal, synagogical, tabernacular, templelike
con lay, secular

ecdysiast *n syn see* STRIPTEASER

echelon *n syn see* LINE 5

echoic *adj syn see* ONOMATOPOEIC

éclat *n syn see* FAME 2
rel bang, brilliance, brilliancy, display, luster, notice- ableness, prominence, remarkableness; distinction, standing; kudos
con oblivion, obscurity; contempt, derision, scorn

eclectic *adj* 1 selecting what appears to be the best from various doctrines, methods, or styles <an *eclectic* taste in music>
syn discriminating, select, selective
rel elective, selecting; choosing, choosy, discerning, fastidious, finicky, fussy, particular, picky
2 composed of elements drawn from various sources <an *eclectic* art incorporating romanticism and impressionism>
syn catholic
rel broad, comprehensive, inclusive; assorted, mingled, mixed; diverse, diversified, heterogeneous, multifarious, multiform, varied; derived, unoriginal
con distinctive, narrow; new, original

eclipse *vb syn see* OBSCURE

economical *adj syn see* SPARING
rel careful, forehanded, prudent; economizing, penny-wise; cheeseparing, close, mean, miserly, niggardly, penny-pinching, penurious, scrimping, skimping, spare, stingy
con generous, lavish, wasteful
ant extravagant

economic poison *n syn see* PESTICIDE

economize *vb* to avoid unnecessary waste or expense < *economize* on food by using leftovers>

syn save
rel conserve; scrimp, skimp
con dissipate, scatter, waste
ant squander, throw away

economy *n* careful management of material resources <retired people often must learn to practice *economy*>
syn forehandedness, frugality, husbandry, providence, prudence, thrift, thriftiness
rel meanness, miserliness, niggardliness, parcity, parsimony, scrimping, skimping, stinginess; carefulness, discretion
con improvidence, lavishness, prodigality, squandering, thriftlessness, wastefulness
ant extravagance

ecstasy *n* intense exaltation of mind and feelings <was in *ecstasy* over flying>
syn heaven, rapture, rhapsody, seventh heaven, transport; *compare* EXHILARATION
rel beatitude, blessedness, bliss, blissfulness, felicity, gladness, happiness; delectation, delight, elation, joy, joyfulness, overjoyfulness, pleasure; enchantment, euphoria, intoxication, madness; exaltation, inspiration; paradise; afflatus, frenzy, fury
idiom cloud nine
con dejection, downheartedness, lowness, lowspiritedness, oppression; blues, dumps, melancholy
ant depression

ecumenical *adj syn see* UNIVERSAL 2
rel heaven-wide; all-comprehending, all-comprehensive, all-covering, all-including, all-pervading; comprehensive, general, inclusive
con diocesan, local, parochial, provincial; circumscribed, insular, limited, narrow, restricted

edacious *adj syn see* VORACIOUS

eddy *n* a swirling mass especially of water <dark *eddies* in the flooded stream>
syn maelstrom, vortex, whirl, whirlpool
rel gurge, surge, swirl, twirl, whirl; back current, back stream, countercurrent, counterflow, counterflux; backwash, backwater

eddy *vb syn see* SWIRL

edge *n* 1 *syn see* BORDER 1
rel end, extremity; ledge, side
con area, surface
2 a cutting quality <there was an *edge* to his voice as he answered>
syn incisiveness, keenness, sharpness
rel bite, cut, sting; knife-edge, razor-edge; acerbity, acidity, acridity, causticity; astringency, stringency; acuteness, penetration, shrillness, thinness
3 *syn see* VERGE 2
4 *syn see* ADVANTAGE 3
con bar, encumbrance, obstacle; disadvantage

edge *vb* 1 *syn see* SHARPEN
2 *syn see* BORDER 1
3 *syn see* SIDLE

edge in *vb syn see* INSINUATE 3

edgy *adj* 1 *syn see* TENSE 2
rel skittish; excitable, excited, highstrung, overstrung; irritable, touchy; impatient, restless
idiom on edge
con detached; peaceful, placid; patient
2 *syn see* EXCITABLE

---

syn synonym(s)   *rel* related word(s)
ant antonym(s)   *con* contrasted word(s)
idiom idiomatic equivalent(s)
|| use limited; if in doubt, see a dictionary

edible *adj* suitable for use as food < *edible* plant products >
syn comestible, eatable, esculent
rel digestible; nourishing, nutritious, nutritive; palatable, savory, succulent, tasty, toothsome
ant inedible

edibles *n pl syn* see FOOD 1

edict *n* 1 a publicly proclaimed order or rule of conduct by a competent authority < a government *edict* regarding curfew enforcement >
syn decree, directive, ruling, ukase
rel instrument; order; manifesto, proclamation, pronouncement, pronunciamiento; bull
2 *syn* see LAW 1

edifice *n* a large, magnificent, or massive building < a marble *edifice* now used as a museum >
syn erection, pile, structure; *compare* BUILDING, HUT

edify *vb syn* see ILLUMINATE 2
rel better, enhance; elucidate; educate, instruct, teach
con debase, deprave

edition *n* the total number of copies of the same work printed during a stretch of time < the initial *edition* of 50,000 copies was exhausted in a month >
syn impression, printing, reissue, reprinting

educate *vb syn* see TEACH
rel cultivate, nurture; brief, explain, inform

education *n* 1 the act or process of educating < devoted himself to the *education* of illiterate adults >
syn instruction, schooling, teaching, training, tuition, tutelage
rel coaching, pedagogy, tutorage, tutoring, tutorship; direction, guidance
2 the product or result of being educated < obtained his *education* in local schools and in college >
syn erudition, knowledge, learning, scholarship, science
rel culture, edification, enlightenment, learnedness, literacy
con ignorance, illiteracy

educational *adj syn* see INFORMATIVE

educative *adj syn* see INFORMATIVE

educe *vb* 1 to draw out something hidden, latent, or reserved < *educed* important information from the witness >
syn elicit, evince, evoke, extort, extract, milk
rel drag, draw, draw out, pull, wrest, wring; gain, get, obtain, procure, secure; distill
con miss, overlook, pass over
2 *syn* see DERIVE 1
rel reason (out), think (out)

eerie *adj syn* see WEIRD 1
rel bizarre, fantastic, grotesque; arcane; crawly

efface *vb syn* see ERASE
rel eradicate, extirpate; eliminate, exclude, rule out

effect *n* 1 a condition or occurrence traceable to a cause < the *effect* of the medicine was dizziness >
syn aftereffect, aftermath, causatum, consequence, corollary, end product, event,

eventuality, issue, outcome, precipitate, result, sequel, sequence, upshot
rel pursuance; development, fruit, outgrowth, ramification; denouement, repercussion; conclusion, end; side effect
con antecedent, determinant, occasion, reason; base, basis, foundation, ground, groundwork
ant cause
2 effects *pl syn* see POSSESSION 2

effect *vb* 1 to induce to come into being < specific genes *effect* specific bodily characters >
syn bring about, cause, draw on, make, produce, secure
rel conceive, create, generate; bring on, induce; enact, render, turn out, yield
con impede, limit, restrict; repress, suppress
2 to carry to a successful conclusion < found a pass that allowed them to *effect* passage through the mountains >
syn bring off, carry out, carry through, effectuate; *compare* FULFILL 1, PERFORM 2
rel actualize, realize; achieve, procure
con fail, fall down
3 *syn* see ENFORCE

effective *adj* producing or capable of producing a result < an *effective* rebuke >
syn effectual, efficacious, efficient, virtuous
rel adequate, capable, competent; cogent, compelling, convincing, sound, telling, valid; able, active, dynamic; operative, useful; direct
con abortive, bootless, fruitless, futile, vain; empty, hollow, idle, nugatory, otiose, pointless; inoperative, useless, worthless
ant ineffective

effectiveness *n* 1 *syn* see POINT 3
rel forcefulness, potency, power, strength, verve, vigor
con impotence, weakness
ant ineffectiveness
2 *syn* see EFFICIENCY 1
3 *syn* see EFFICACY 1

effectual *adj syn* see EFFECTIVE
rel accomplishing, achieving, effecting, fulfilling; practicable, sound, useful, valid, workable; conclusive, decisive, determinative, influential; authoritative, potent, powerful, strong, toothy
con impotent, weak
ant ineffectual

effectuate *vb syn* see EFFECT 2

effeminate *adj* lacking manly strength and purpose < an *effeminate* preoccupation with trifles >
syn epicene, Miss-Nancyish, pansified, prissy, sissified, sissy, unmanly
rel chichi, old-maidish, overnice, precious; foppish, sappy, silken
ant manly, masculine

effervescence *n syn* see EBULLIENCE
rel bubbling, ebullition, fizzing, foaming
con deadness, flatness, staleness

effervescent *adj* 1 *syn* see EXUBERANT 1
2 *syn* see ELASTIC 2
rel animated, boiling, bubbly, excited, gay, lively, sparkling, sprightly, vivacious; gleeful, hilarious, jolly, mirthful
con lifeless, listless, subdued; earnest, sedate, serious, solemn

effete *adj* **1** *syn* see STERILE 1

2 having lost energy or drive < *effete*, weary, burned out revolutionaries >
syn all in, bleary, depleted, done, done in, drained, exhausted, far-gone, spent, used up, washed-out, worn-out
rel consumed; debilitated, enfeebled, fatigued
idiom on one's last legs, out on one's feet
con alive, lively, vigorous, vital

3 having lost character < a soft, *effete* society >
syn decadent, decayed, degenerate, over-ripe
rel decaying, declining; soft, weak; dissolute, immoral

efficacious *adj* *syn* see EFFECTIVE
rel active, operative, productive; influential, potent, powerful, puissant, strong
con abortive; impotent, powerless, useless, vain, weak
ant inefficacious

efficacy *n* **1** the power to produce an effect < *efficacy* of the drug >
syn capability, effectiveness, efficiency, potency
rel capableness, productiveness, use; adequacy, capacity, sufficiency
con ineffectiveness, inefficiency; uselessness, worthlessness
ant inefficacy

2 *syn* see EFFICIENCY 1

efficiency *n* **1** the capacity to produce desired results with a minimum expenditure of energy, time, or resources < demands a high degree of *efficiency* on the job >
syn effectiveness, efficacy, performance
rel ability, address, adeptness, competence, expertise, know-how, proficiency, prowess, skill; capability, resourcefulness; productivity
con inadequacy, incompetence, ineffectiveness; unproductiveness
ant inefficiency

2 *syn* see EFFICACY 1

efficient *adj* *syn* see EFFECTIVE
rel able, capable, competent, fitted, qualified; adept, expert, masterly, proficient, skilled, skillful
con incapable, incompetent, inexpert, unadept, unproficient, unqualified, unsuitable; unproductive; ineffectual
ant inefficient

effloresce *vb* *syn* see BLOSSOM

effort *n* **1** the active use of energy in producing a result < thought the job wasn't worth the *effort* >
syn elbow grease, exertion, pains, trouble, while
rel labor, toil, travail, work; energy, force, might, power, puissance; attempt, endeavor, essay
idiom sweat of one's brow
con adroitness, facility, smoothness; do-nothingness, inaction, indolence, inertia, lackadaisicalness, languor, laziness
ant ease

2 *syn* see TASK 2

effortful *adj* *syn* see HARD 6

effortless *adj* **1** *syn* see EASY 1
rel adept, expert, masterly, proficient, ready, skilled, skillful
con laborious, toilsome, trying
ant painstaking

2 *syn* see EASY 9

effortlessly *adv* *syn* see EASILY 1
rel adeptly, adroitly, efficiently, expertly, proficiently, skillfully
con painstakingly
ant arduously, laboriously

effrontery *n* flagrant disregard of courtesy or propriety and an arrogant assumption of privilege < had the *effrontery* to insult her father >
syn brashness, brass, cheek, confidence, ||crust, face, gall, nerve, presumption; *compare* INSOLENCE
rel audacity, hardihood, temerity; assurance, self-assurance, self-confidence; brazenness, impudence; impertinence, insolence
con courtesy, grace, propriety

effulgent *adj* *syn* see BRIGHT 1
rel vivid; glorious, resplendent, splendid
con dark, dusky, gloomy, murky

effusive *adj* unduly demonstrative < *effusive* assurances of undying love >
syn gushing, gushy, slobbering, slobbery, sloppy
rel expansive, fulsome, outpouring, profuse; demonstrative, unconstrained, unreserved, unrestrained; cloying, slushy; smarmy
con close, restrained, reticent, taciturn; bashful, modest, shy
ant reserved

egg (on) *vb* *syn* see URGE
rel agitate, excite, pique, stimulate; instigate; arouse, drive, rally, stir up, whip (on or up)
con arrest, bridle

egghead *n* *syn* see INTELLECTUAL 2

egocentric *adj* **1** concerned with the individual person rather than society < an *egocentric* approach to world problems >
syn individualist, individualistic
rel self-centered, selfish

2 concerned only with one's own activities or needs and usually tending to self-assertion or self-satisfaction < an *egocentric* man, lacking feeling for others >
syn egoistic, egomaniacal, egotistic, self-absorbed, self-centered, self-concerned, self-interested, self-involved, selfish, self-seeking, self-serving; *compare* POMPOUS 1
rel conceited, narcissistic, self-affected, self-applauding, self-conceited, self-concentered, self-indulgent, self-loving, stuck-up, vainglorious; megalomaniac
idiom wrapped up in oneself

egoism *n* **1** *syn* see EGOTISM 1
rel self-assurance, self-confidence, self-possession
ant altruism

2 *syn* see CONCEIT 2
rel self-satisfaction
con meekness, modesty
ant humility

egoistic *adj* *syn* see EGOCENTRIC 2
rel individualistic; self-satisfied, swell-headed

---

syn synonym(s)   *rel* related word(s)
ant antonym(s)   *con* contrasted word(s)
idiom idiomatic equivalent(s)

|| use limited; if in doubt, see a dictionary

con humble, modest
ant altruistic

egomaniacal *adj syn* see EGOCENTRIC 2
rel self-exalting, self-glorifying, vainglorious

egotism *n* 1 an exaggerated sense of one's own importance <in believing that he was indispensable, he exhibited consummate *egotism*>
syn egoism, self-importance
rel conceit, conceitedness, narcissism, self-esteem, self-love, vainness; boastfulness, boasting, bragging, gasconade, gasconism, megalomania, vaunting
con humility, lowliness; bashfulness, diffidence, shyness; modesty
ant altruism
2 *syn* see CONCEIT 2
rel arrogance, superiority; contempt
con humbleness, self-effacement
ant humility

egotistic *adj syn* see EGOCENTRIC 2
rel boastful, cocky, inflated, pretentious, proud, puffed up, self-satisfied; conceited, stuck-up
idiom in love with oneself, stuck on oneself
con humble, modest; self-effacing, shy

egregious *adj* conspicuously bad or objectionable <an *egregious* mistake>
syn capital, flagrant, glaring, gross, rank
rel arrant, outright, stark; infamous, nefarious, notorious; atrocious, deplorable, heinous, monstrous, outrageous, preposterous
con measly, minor, petty, piddling, slender, slight, trifling, trivial

egress *n* 1 *syn* see DEPARTURE 1
rel emergence, emerging
con coming, entering; arrival
ant ingress
2 a place or means of going out <a gate providing *egress* from the pasture>
syn exit, outlet
rel opening, passage; escape
idiom way out
con entrance, entry, entryway
ant access, ingress

egression *n syn* see DEPARTURE 1
con entrance, entering
ant ingression

eidolon *n syn* see APPARITION

ejaculate *vb syn* see EXCLAIM
rel call (out), shout, vociferate, yell

eject *vb* 1 to drive or force (somebody) out <*eject* an intruder from one's home>
syn boot (out), chase, chuck, dismiss, evict, extrude, kick out, out, throw out; *compare* BANISH
rel displace, dispossess; drive off, rout, run off; debar, disbar, eliminate, exclude, rule out, shut out; bump, cashier, discharge, fire, sack; discard, shed; reject, repudiate, spurn
idiom give one his walking papers, send packing, show one the door
con accept, admit, install, receive; entertain, harbor, house, lodge, shelter
2 *syn* see ERUPT 1

elaborate *adj* 1 *syn* see COMPLEX 2
2 marked by complexity of detail or ornament <an *elaborate* coiffure>
syn complicated, fancy, intricate

rel detailed, highly-wrought; decorated, dressy, embellished, ornate; elegant; busy, overdone, overworked, overwrought
con common, ordinary, plain, unpolished; inartificial, inornate, natural
ant simple

elaborate *vb* 1 *syn* see EXPAND 4
rel comment, discuss, dwell (upon); clarify, explain, expound, interpret
2 *syn* see UNFOLD 3

élan *n syn* see SPIRIT 5
rel impetus

élan vital *n syn* see SOUL 1

elapse *vb syn* see PASS 3
rel flow, glide, pass (by), slide, slip (by); lapse, run out

elastic *adj* 1 able to withstand strain without being permanently affected or injured <a rubber band is *elastic*>
syn flexible, resilient, springy, stretch, stretchy, supple, whippy
rel ductile, malleable, pliable, pliant, plastic, rubberlike, rubbery; adaptable, moldable, stretchable, yielding; bouncy, limber, lithe
con brittle; inflexible, stiff, tense
ant rigid
2 able to recover quickly from depression and maintain high spirits <had an *elastic* optimistic nature>
syn airy, bouncy, buoyant, effervescent, expansive, resilient, volatile
rel animated, gay, lively, sprightly, vivacious; ebullient, high-spirited, mettlesome, soaring, spirited; adaptable, recuperative
con blue, dejected, depressed, gloomy, melancholy, sad; flaccid, limp

elate *vb* to elevate the spirits of <the phenomenal sales record *elated* him>
syn commove, excite, exhilarate, inspire, set up, spirit (up), stimulate
rel brighten, cheer, cheer up, encourage; delight, gladden, gratify, overjoy; buoy, elevate, exalt, uplift
con distress; oppress, weigh; weary
ant depress

elated *adj syn* see INTOXICATED 2
rel enchanted, enraptured, exalted, transported; delighted, ecstatic, euphoric, exultant, jubilant, overjoyed
idiom in heaven, in seventh heaven, on cloud nine
con blue, deflated, unhappy

elation *n* 1 the quality or state of being elated <felt great *elation* when he won the presidential nomination>
syn euphoria, exaltation, exhilaration
rel buoyancy; happiness, joy; excitement; rapture, transport
idiom stars in one's eyes
con blues, depression; distress, misery, sadness, unhappiness
ant deflation
2 *syn* see EUPHORIA 2
ant depression

elbow *vb syn* see PUSH 2

elbowroom *n syn* see ROOM 3
rel space

elder *n* 1 *syn* see SENIOR 2
2 *syn* see OLDSTER
3 *syn* see SUPERIOR

elderliness *n syn* see OLD AGE

elderly *adj syn* see AGED 1

rel aging, declining
con juvenile, young
ant youthful

eldorado *n syn see* BONANZA

elect *adj syn see* SELECT 1
rel choice, rare; hand-picked, singled out;
designated, destined, ordained; delivered,
redeemed, saved
con refused, rejected, repudiated, spurned;
disdained, scorned; damned, doomed,
reprobate

elect *vb 1 syn see* CHOOSE 1
rel decide, determine, resolve, settle; conclude, judge; accept, admit, receive
con reject; dismiss, eject, expel, oust
ant abjure
2 to select by or as if by ballot < the
board of directors *elected* a new chairman >
syn ballot, vote (in)
rel choose, designate, name, opt, pick,
select, single; nominate; appoint
3 *syn see* WILL

election *n syn see* CHOICE 1

elective *adj syn see* OPTIONAL

electrify *vb syn see* THRILL
rel provoke; jar, stagger, stun

eleemosynary *adj syn see* CHARITABLE 1
rel beneficent, generous, liberal, munificent, openhanded
con close, parsimonious, tight

elegance *n* impressive beauty of form,
appearance, or behavior < the sumptuous
elegance of the furnishings >
syn dignity, grace
rel beauty, charm; cultivation, culture,
polish, refinement, sophistication, style,
taste, tastefulness; lushness, magnificence,
ornateness, poshness, richness, splendor,
sumptuousness
con grotesqueness, ugliness; clumsiness,
crudeness, roughness, rudeness; austerity,
bareness, inornateness, severity

elegant *adj syn see* CHOICE
rel august, grand, majestic, noble, stately;
beautiful, graceful, handsome, lovely;
cultivated, cultured, finished, polished,
refined, tasteful; luxurious, opulent, sumptuous
con crude, rough, rude, uncouth; grotesque

element *n 1 syn see* ESSENTIAL 1
2 one of the parts, substances, or principles that make up a compound or complex whole < analyzed the various *elements* of the problem >
syn component, constituent, factor, ingredient; *compare* POINT 1
rel fundamental, principle; item, member,
part, particle, piece, portion; detail, particular; aspect, facet, feature, view
con bulk, mass, volume; entirety, whole;
sum, total, totality
ant composite, compound
3 elements *pl syn see* ALPHABET 2
rel basics, basis, foundations, groundwork; outlines
4 *syn see* POINT 1

---

rel division, member, section, sector,
segment

elemental *adj 1* of, relating to, or being an
ultimate and irreducible element < such
elemental aspects of life as sex and nutrition >
syn basic, elementary, essential, fundamental, primitive, substratal, underlying
rel primary, prime, primordial; inherent,
intrinsic, radical
con secondary, subordinate; casual, incidental, trivial, unimportant
2 *syn see* ELEMENTARY 1
3 *syn see* INHERENT

elementary *adj 1* of, relating to, or dealing
with the simplest principles of something
< can't handle the most *elementary* deci-
sion-making >
syn basal, beginning, elemental, rudimental, rudimentary, simplest
rel introductory, prefatory, preliminary;
easy, simple; rude, unsubtle
con complex, complicated, elaborate,
intricate, labyrinthine; sophisticated
ant advanced
2 *syn see* ELEMENTAL 1

elephantine *adj 1 syn see* HUGE
con slender, slight, slim, thin; dainty
2 *syn see* PONDEROUS 2
rel awkward, clumsy, graceless, maladroit, ungraceful
con graceful, nimble, quick

elevate *vb 1 syn see* LIFT 1
rel ensky, erect
con cut (down), deflate, depress, scale
(down)
ant lower
2 *syn see* ADVANCE 2
rel boost; enhance, glorify, heighten
con demote, downgrade, lower, reduce;
abase, debase, degrade

elevated *adj 1* being positioned above a
surface < an *elevated* monorail >
syn lifted, raised, upheaved, uplifted,
upraised, uprisen
rel high; aerial
con ground-level, low, lowered, low-lying,
unelevated
ant sunken
2 being on a high moral or intellectual
plane < *elevated* ideas >
syn high-minded, moral, noble
rel ethical, honorable, righteous, upright,
upstanding, virtuous
con base, ignoble, mean; immoral, low,
unethical; intolerable, unacceptable
3 *syn see* GRAND 3
4 being exceedingly dignified in form,
tone, or style < an *elevated* prose style >
syn eloquent, high, lofty
rel dignified, formal; grand, grandiloquent, grandiose, high-flown, majestic,
stately, towering
con informal; lowly, unassuming

elevation *n 1 syn see* HEIGHT
rel acclivity, ascent, rise
con depression, descent; flatness, levelness
2 *syn see* ADVANCEMENT 1
rel advance, boost, raise; ennoblement,
exaltation, glorification, lionization; apotheosis, deification, immortalization, magnification
con downgrading; depreciation, detraction, disparagement

ant degradation

elf *n syn see* FAIRY

elicit *vb syn see* EDUCE 1
rel bring, fetch
con eschew, forego; abandon

elide *vb syn see* NEGLECT

eligible *adj* qualified to be or worthy of being chosen <an *eligible* bachelor>
syn fit, suitable
rel acceptable, desirable, likely, preferable, seemly; capable, fitted, qualified, suited, worthy; marriageable, nubile; visitable
con undesirable; disqualified, unfit, unqualified, unsuitable, unworthy
ant ineligible

eliminate *vb* 1 *syn see* EXCLUDE
rel freeze out, shut out; dismiss, ‖dump, eject, evict, expel, oust; delete, erase, expunge
con accept, receive
2 *syn see* REMOVE 4
3 *syn see* PURGE 3

elite *n* 1 *syn see* BEST
rel elect, pink, select; ‖hoi polloi
idiom cream of the crop, crème de la crème, pick of the bunch
2 *syn see* ARISTOCRACY
rel drawing rooms; Four Hundred; beautiful people, jet set, smart set
idiom high society, horsey set
con hoi polloi, (the) masses, mob, peasantry, people, proletariat, rabble

elixir *n syn see* PANACEA
rel balm, cure, therapy, therapeutic

ell *n syn see* ANNEX

elocution *n syn see* ORATORY

elongate *vb syn see* EXTEND 3
rel drag (out); string
con contract, draw in; compress; curtail, retrench; shrink
ant abbreviate, shorten

elongate *adj syn see* LONG 1
rel lengthened
ant abbreviated, shortened

elongated *adj syn see* LONG 1
rel drawn (out), lengthened, prolonged, prolonged, protracted, stretched
con contracted, drawn (in), shrunken
ant shortened

elongation *n syn see* EXTENSION 1

elope *vb* to go away secretly usually with the intention of marrying <decided to *elope* rather than endure a big wedding>
syn run away
idiom go to Gretna Green

eloquence *n* discourse marked by force and persuasiveness suggesting strong feeling <read the poem with *eloquence*>
syn expression, expressiveness, expressivity, facundity
rel meaningfulness, persuasiveness; fervor, force, forcefulness, passion, power, spirit, vigor

eloquent *adj* 1 *syn see* VOCAL 3
rel forceful, potent, powerful; ardent, fervent, fervid, impassioned, passionate; glib, silver-tongued, voluble
con inarticulate, ineffective, weak
2 *syn see* EXPRESSIVE
rel graphic, indicative, revealing, suggestive, telling; affecting, impressive, moving, poignant, touching

3 *syn see* ELEVATED 4

else *adv syn see* OTHERWISE 2

else *adj syn see* ADDITIONAL

‖**elseways** *adv syn see* OTHERWISE 2

elsewise *adv syn see* OTHERWISE 2

elucidate *vb syn see* CLARIFY 2
rel exemplify; demonstrate, prove; annotate, spell out; enlighten
con confuse; darken

elude *vb syn see* ESCAPE 2
rel baffle, circumvent, foil, frustrate, outwit, thwart; flee, fly
idiom give the slip
con accost, face; chase, follow, pursue, tag, tail, trail

elusion *n syn see* ESCAPE 2

elusive *adj* not easily perceived, grasped, comprehended, pinned down, or isolated <inspiration need not be forever *elusive*> <they finally isolated the *elusive* virus that caused the disease>
syn elusory, evasive, intangible
rel evanescent, fleeting, fugitive; baffling, imponderable, incomprehensible, mysterious; insubstantial, phantom

elusory *adj syn see* ELUSIVE
rel nebulous, vague

elvish *adj syn see* PLAYFUL 2

elysium *n syn see* HEAVEN 2

emaciated *adj* being very lean through loss of flesh (as from hunger or disease) <*emaciated* bony hands clutched at him>
syn cadaverous, gaunt, skeletal, wasted
rel bony, lean, scrawny, skinny, wizened; starved, underfed, undernourished
idiom all skin and bones, thin as a rail
con fit, husky, solid, well-fed, well-nourished; chubby, plump, portly, rotund, stocky, stout; corpulent, obese
ant fleshy

emanate *vb syn see* SPRING 1
rel initiate; emit, exude, radiate

emancipate *vb syn see* FREE
ant enslave

emasculate *vb syn see* UNNERVE
rel debilitate, devitalize
con energize, vitalize

emasculate *adj syn see* WEAK 4

embark *vb syn see* BOARD 1

embark (on *or* upon) *vb syn see* BEGIN 1

embarrass *vb* to throw into a state of self-conscious distress <bawdy stories *embarrassed* her>
syn abash, confound, confuse, discomfit, disconcert, discountenance, faze, rattle; *compare* DISCOMPOSE 1
rel agitate, bother, discompose, flurry, fluster, perturb; nonplus; chagrin, distress, vex; queer
idiom put on the spot, put to the blush
con calm, relieve, soothe

embarrassing *adj syn see* INCONVENIENT

embarrassment *n* the quality, state, or condition of being embarrassed <felt great *embarrassment* when she fell down>
syn abashment, confusion, discomfiture, discomposure, disconcertion, disconcertment, unease, uneasiness
rel constraint, stain; agitation, discombobulation, perturbation; chagrin, distress, vexation; humiliation, mortification; difficulty, Queer Street

con assurance, calm, imperturbability, savoir faire

embed vb syn see ENTRENCH 1

embellish vb 1 syn see ADORN
rel apparel, array, ||doll up, dress up, emblaze, embroider, enrich, furbish
con bare, denude, divest, strip
2 syn see EMBROIDER

embellishment n syn see EXAGGERATION
rel floridity, ostentation

embezzle vb to appropriate dishonestly and fraudulently to one's own use < embezzled a trust fund >
syn misappropriate, peculate
rel loot, pilfer, steal, thieve

embitter vb syn see EXACERBATE
rel bitter, sour

emblem n 1 syn see SYMBOL 1
2 syn see INSIGNIA

emblematize vb syn see REPRESENT 2

embodiment n a concrete or actual entity in which something (as an idea, principle, or type) is embodied < he is the embodiment of all our hopes >
syn incarnation, personification; compare APOTHEOSIS 1
rel manifestation; prosopopoeia; archetype; apotheosis, epitome, quintessence

embody vb 1 to make an abstraction concrete or perceptible often by representation in human or animal form < Dickens embodied hypocrisy in his Uriah Heep >
syn exteriorize, externalize, incarnate, manifest, materialize, objectify, personalize, personify, personize, substantiate; compare REPRESENT 2
rel actualize, hypostatize, realize, reify, symbolize, typify; demonstrate, evince, exemplify, exhibit, illustrate, show (forth)
ant disembody
2 to cause to become a body or part of another body < embodied a revenue provision in the new law >
syn combine, incorporate, integrate
rel absorb, amalgamate, assimilate, blend, consolidate, fuse, merge, unify
3 syn see INCLUDE
rel compose, consist (of), constitute
4 syn see REPRESENT 2

embog vb syn see DELAY 1

embolden vb syn see ENCOURAGE 1
rel impel; inspire; chance, hazard, venture
con deter, discourage
ant abash

embouchement n syn see MOUTH 5

embouchure n syn see MOUTH 5

embowel vb syn see EVISCERATE

embrace vb 1 to gather into one's arms usually as a gesture of affection < embraced his wife >
syn clasp, ||clinch, ||clip, ||coll, enfold, hug, press, squeeze
rel cling, grip, hold; encircle, entwine, envelop, enwind, fold, lock, twine, wrap; cuddle, fondle, nuzzle, snuggle; cradle, hold
idiom ||go into a clinch

2 syn see ADOPT
rel accept, accommodate, admit, incorporate, receive, take (over), take in; seize (upon), welcome
con reject; abjure, deny, forswear, renounce
ant spurn
3 syn see INCLUDE
rel compose, cover, enclose, hold

embracement n syn see ESPOUSAL 4

embracing n syn see ESPOUSAL 4

embrangle vb syn see ENTANGLE 3

embroider vb to give an elaborate account of, often with florid language and fictitious details < embroidered the story of his adventures in the army >
syn color, embellish, exaggerate, fudge, magnify, overcharge, overdraw, overpaint, overstate, pad, stretch
rel aggrandize, amplify, build up, distend, elaborate, enhance, enlarge (upon), expand; dramatize, hyperbolize, overdo, overelaborate, overembellish, overemphasize, overestimate
idiom lay it on thick, stretch (or strain) the truth
con deemphasize, minimize, play (down), underestimate, understate

embroidering n syn see EXAGGERATION

embroil vb syn see INVOLVE 1

embroilment n 1 syn see QUARREL
2 syn see ENTANGLEMENT 1

embryo n syn see SEED 2

emend vb syn see CORRECT 1
rel alter, edit, emendate; polish, retouch

emerge vb syn see APPEAR 1
rel derive, originate, spring, stem; arise, materialize, rise; come (forth), come out, emanate, flow, issue (forth); proceed
idiom appear on the horizon, come on the scene, come out in the open, come to light, make its appearance
con disappear, fade, fade (out); evaporate; dissolve

emergency n syn see JUNCTURE 2
rel difficulty, extremity; clutch, fix, hole, pinch, push, squeeze, vicissitude; climax
idiom turn of events

emigrant n one that leaves one place to settle in another < a city teeming with emigrants from many lands >
syn immigrant, migrant
rel alien, displaced person, DP, émigré, evacuee, exile, expatriate, fugitive, refugee; migrator, migratory
con aborigine, native

emigrate vb syn see MIGRATE

émigré n 1 a person forced to immigrate usually for political reasons < a city filled with White Russian émigrés >
syn exile, expatriate, expellee
rel emigrant, immigrant; alien, displaced person, DP, evacuee, fugitive, refugee
2 syn see REFUGEE

eminence n 1 a condition, position, or state of great importance or superiority < the eminence of the presidency >
syn distinction, illustriousness, kudos, preeminence, prestige, prominence, prominency, renown
rel greatness, loftiness, prepotency, significance, superiority; authority, credit, dignity, importance, influence, power, weight;

---

fame, famousness, glory, honor, reputation, repute
con insignificance, unimportance; obscurity
2 *syn* see NOTABLE 1
3 a natural elevation < the house stood on an *eminence* overlooking the river >
syn projection, prominence
rel peak, raise, rise, uprise; altitude, elevation, height; highness, loftiness
con cavity, depression, dip
eminency *n syn* see FORTE
eminent *adj syn* see FAMOUS 2
rel well-known; august, dominant, exalted, important, lofty, noble, preeminent; big league, big-name, big-time
con uncelebrated, unremarkable, unrenowned; common, lowly
eminently *adv syn* see VERY 1
emissary *n syn* see MESSENGER
emit *vb* 1 *syn* see DISCHARGE 5
2 to discharge something such as moisture, vapor, or fumes < a smokestack *emitting* effluents >
syn give off, give out, issue, release, throw off, vent
rel discharge, evacuate, expel; let out, loose, pass (off); pour (out); reek; drip, emanate, excrete, extrude, exude, ooze, secrete; exhale, expire
emolument *n syn* see WAGE
rel guerdon
emote *vb* to give expression to emotion especially on or as if on the stage < she *emotes*, postures, and harangues at the slightest provocation >
syn emotionalize
rel gush, sentimentalize; carry on, rage, rant, storm, take on
emotion *n syn* see FEELING 3
rel excitability, responsiveness, sensibility, sensitiveness, sensitivity, susceptibilities; sensation
con coldness, detachment, reserve, unfeelingness
emotionable *adj syn* see EMOTIONAL 1
emotional *adj* 1 dominated by, prone to, or moved by emotion < an irritable *emotional* woman who was easily upset by trivialities >
syn emotionable, feeling, sensitive, sentient
rel responsive, susceptible, susceptive; softhearted, sympathetic; ardent, fervent, passionate; rhapsodic, rhapsodical
con cold, detached, insensitive, reserved, taciturn, unfeeling
ant emotionless, unemotional
2 appealing to or arousing emotion < an *emotional* sermon >
syn affective, emotive, moving; compare MOVING 2
rel affecting, stirring, touching
emotionalize *vb syn* see EMOTE
emotionless *adj* 1 *syn* see COLD 2
rel nonemotional, undemonstrative; cool, dispassionate, distant, immovable, impassive, remote, reserved; heartless, unfeeling
con responsive, softhearted, sympathetic; ardent, fervent, passionate
ant emotional
2 *syn* see MATTER-OF-FACT 3
emotive *adj syn* see EMOTIONAL 2

empathy *n syn* see SYMPATHY 2
rel accord, affinity, communion, compatibility, concord, congeniality, fellow feeling, rapport, responsiveness, warmth; appreciation, comprehension, understanding
idiom community of interests
con animosity, animus, antagonism, antipathy, enmity
emphasis *n* force brought to bear on something to bring out what is important < the school's *emphasis* on discipline >
syn accent, accentuation, stress
rel attention; force, insistence; weight
emphasize *vb* to give more emphasis to especially by displaying more or less prominently < the papers *emphasized* crime stories >
syn feature, italicize, play (up), stress, underline, underscore
rel accent, accentuate, charge, highlight, mark, pinpoint, point (up), punctuate, spotlight; assert, press
idiom bear down on (*or* upon)
con depreciate, minimize, play (down), shrug off, underrate, understate
ant de-emphasize
emphatic *adj* marked by, uttered with, or made prominent by stress or emphasis < made his point in an *emphatic* argument >
syn assertive, forceful, insistent, resounding
rel aggressive, energetic, insistive, vigorous; accented, accentuated, assertative, decided, emphasized, marked, pointed, stressed, underlined
con insipid, milk-and-water, unaggressive, unassertive, weak, wishy-washy; de-emphasized, played (down), understated
ant unemphatic
empirical *adj* originating in, relying on, or based on factual information, observation, or direct sense experience < an *empirical* basis for an ethical theory >
syn experient, experiential, experimental
rel observational; factual
con conjectural, speculative, unproved, unsubstantiated; ideal, imagined
ant theoretical
employ *vb* 1 *syn* see USE 2
rel avail, exert, practice, work; devote, engross, monopolize
2 to provide with a job that pays wages < *employed* a new draftsman >
syn engage, hire, put on, take on
rel add, contract (for), obtain, procure, retain, secure, sign (on *or* up)
employable *adj syn* see OPEN 5
employed *adj syn* see BUSY 1
employment *n* 1 *syn* see USE 1
rel purpose; disposition, exercise, exploitation, handling, utilization
2 *syn* see EXERCISE 1
3 *syn* see WORK 1
rel assignment, mission; office, position, post, situation; function
4 the act of employing for wages < handled the *employment* of new workers >
syn engagement, engaging, hiring
rel enlistment, enrollment, recruitment, signing on
empower *vb* 1 *syn* see INVEST 2

2 *syn* see AUTHORIZE 1

3 *syn* see ENABLE 2

rel endow, invest; authorize, charge, commission, entitle, entrust, license, privilege, sanction

con debar, disallow, disbar, exclude, rule out, shut out

emprise *n syn* see ADVENTURE

emptiness *n syn* see VACUITY 2

emptor *n syn* see PURCHASER

empty *adj* 1 lacking contents that could or should be present <an *empty* apartment> <the whole book is *empty* of meaning>

syn bare, clear, stark, vacant, vacuous, void

rel barren, blank; abandoned, deserted, emptied, forsaken, godforsaken, unfilled, unfurnished uninhabited, untenanted, vacated; destitute, devoid; depleted, drained, exhausted

con complete, replete; filled, occupied, packed, teeming

ant full

2 *syn* see VAIN 1

rel paltry, petty, trifling, trivial; banal, flat, inane, ineffectual, insipid, jejune, vapid; dumb, fatuous, foolish, ignorant, silly, simple

con meaningful, pregnant, significant; authentic, bona fide, genuine, veritable

3 *syn* see EXPRESSIONLESS

4 *syn* see DEVOID

empty *vb syn* see VACATE 2

empty-headed *adj* 1 *syn* see GIDDY 1

rel brainless, rattleheaded; ignorant, simple

2 *syn* see VACUOUS 2

3 *syn* see IGNORANT 1

empyreal *adj syn* see CELESTIAL

rel aerial, airy; extraterrestrial; divine, holy, spiritual, sublime

ant terrestrial

empyrean *adj syn* see CELESTIAL

empyrean *n* 1 *syn* see HEAVEN 2

2 *syn* see SKY

emulate *vb syn* see RIVAL 2

rel challenge, outvie

emulation *n syn* see CONTEST 1

emulative *adj syn* see SLAVISH 3

emulous *adj syn* see AMBITIOUS 1

rel aiming, striving; agog, athirst; competitive, vying

con unambitious, unaspiring; detached, disinterested, uninterested

enable *vb* 1 *syn* see AUTHORIZE 1

rel allow, let, permit, sanction

2 to render able often by giving power, strength, or competence to <his education *enabled* him to find an excellent job>

syn empower

rel allow, let, permit; condition, fit, prepare, qualify, ready

con inhibit, preclude, prevent; disallow, enjoin, forbid, prohibit

enact *vb* 1 to cause to be by legal and authoritative act <*enact* a law>

---

syn constitute, establish, make

rel bring about, institute; authorize, decree, proclaim; accomplish, carry (through), effect, effectuate, execute, legislate, pass, put (through), ratify

con abolish, abrogate, annul, cancel, invalidate, nullify, rescind, revoke; overturn

ant repeal

2 *syn* see ACT 1

rel depict, portray, represent

enamored *adj* 1 moved by intense sexual attraction <became more desperately *enamored* of the man every day>

syn mashed, smitten, soft (on), spoony (over *or* on)

rel infatuated; crazy (over *or* about), mad (about), nuts (about), silly (over *or* about), wild (about); amorous, devoted, loving

idiom head over heels in love, stuck on, sweet on

2 *syn* see INFATUATED

3 taking great pleasure in something <found herself *enamored* of those huge English teas>

syn bewitched, captivated, charmed, enchanted, entranced, fascinated

rel fond

encamp *vb syn* see CAMP

encampment *n syn* see CAMP 1

enceinte *adj syn* see PREGNANT 1

enchant *vb* 1 *syn* see BEWITCH 1

2 *syn* see ATTRACT 1

rel delight, enthrall, please, send, thrill; mesmerize

idiom carry away, knock dead

con disillusion, dissatisfy, let down

ant disenchant

enchanted *adj syn* see ENAMORED 3

rel delighted, pleased; pixilated

ant disenchanted

enchanter *n syn* see MAGICIAN 1

enchanting *adj syn* see ATTRACTIVE 1

rel attractive, pleasing; delectable, delightful; beguiling, enthralling, entrancing, intriguing, witching; exciting, sirenic

con repellent

enchantment *n syn* see MAGIC 1

enchantress *n syn* see WITCH 1

enchiridion *n syn* see HANDBOOK

rel book, text

encincture *vb syn* see BELT 1

encircle *vb syn* see SURROUND 1

rel band, cincture, circuit, enring; halo, wreathe

enclose *vb* 1 to shut up or confine by or as if by barriers <a valley *enclosed* by mountains>

syn cage, close in, coop, corral, envelop, fence, hedge, hem, immure, mew, mure, pen, shut in, wall

rel bound, circumscribe, confine, contain, limit, restrict; circle, compass, encircle, encompass, surround; environ; enlock

2 *syn* see ENFOLD 1

enclosure *n syn* see COURT 1

enclothe *vb syn* see CLOTHE

encomiastic *adj syn* see EULOGISTIC

encomium *n* a formal expression of praise <an unstinted *encomium* of a national hero>

syn citation, eulogy, panegyric, salutation, tribute

rel approval, kudos, laud, laudation, magnification, praise; acclaim, acclamation, applause, plaudits; accolade, commendation, compliment

con abuse, invective, obloquy, vituperation; criticism, critique, faultfinding

encompass *vb* 1 *syn* see SURROUND 1

rel bound, delimit

2 *syn* see INCLUDE

encounter *vb* 1 *syn* see CONFRONT 1

rel clash, collide, conflict

2 *syn* see ENGAGE 5

3 *syn* see MEET 6

rel ‖bump (into), come (across), run (across), run (into)

idiom cross the path of, fall in with, meet up with

con miss, pass (by)

4 *syn* see FIND 1

encounter *n* a sudden, hostile, and usually brief confrontation or dispute between factions or persons <a sharp courtroom *encounter* between opposing lawyers>

syn brush, run-in, set-to, skirmish, velitation

rel conflict, contest; scrap; fray, fight; battle; argument, contention, quarrel

encourage *vb* 1 to fill with courage or strength of purpose especially in preparation for a hard task <the teacher's praise *encouraged* the student to try harder>

syn animate, cheer, chirk (up), embolden, enhearten, hearten, inspirit, nerve, ‖pearten (up), steel, strengthen; *compare* SUPPORT 5

rel assure, reassure; boost, excite, galvanize, pique, provoke,· quicken, stimulate; buck up, buoy (up), energize, fortify, invigorate; rally, stir

idiom give a shot in the arm

con deject, depress, discourage, dishearten, dispirit; affright, caution, frighten

ant discourage

2 to give the support of one's approval to <the government openly *encouraged* East‐West détente>

syn advocate, countenance, favor

rel approve, back, endorse, go (for), sanction, subscribe (to); abet, assist, reinforce, support, sustain; incite, instigate; induce, prevail

idiom lend one's countenance to, lend one's favor (or support) to, smile upon

con deter, dissuade, divert, hinder; inhibit, restrain; disapprove

ant discourage

3 *syn* see ADVANCE 1

rel patronize, push, support; develop, improve, subsidize

con weaken; check, retard, slow

ant discourage

encouraging *adj syn* see HOPEFUL 2

encroach *vb syn* see TRESPASS 2

rel barge (in), ‖bust (in), butt (in), chisel (in), horn (in), muscle (in), worm (in); interfere, interpose, intervene, meddle; overstep

idiom foist oneself upon, stick one's nose in (or into)

con ignore, let (alone), pass over; avoid

encrust (or **incrust**) *vb syn* see CAKE 1

encumber *vb syn* see BURDEN

rel freight; discommode, incommode, inconvenience; fetter, hamper, handicap; block, impede, obstruct; oppress, overburden

encumbrance *n* something that impedes and makes action difficult <told his story simply without the *encumbrance* of unnecessary details>

syn clog, cumbrance, hindrance, impedance, impediment

rel disadvantage, handicap, load; difficulty, hardship, inconvenience

con aid; catalyst, impetus, stimulus

ant assist, assistance

encyclopedic *adj* embracing, comprehensively treating, or informed in a wide range of subjects <an *encyclopedic* article on world history>

syn comprehensive, inclusive

rel all-comprehensive, all-embracing, all-inclusive, complete; extensive, general; discursive

end *n* 1 *syn* see LIMIT 1

rel borderline, tip; extreme, extremity

con center, hub, middle

2 ceasing of a course (as of action or activity) or the point at which something ceases <the *end* of the war>

syn cease, cessation, close, closing, closure, conclusion, desistance, desuetude, discontinuance, discontinuation, ending, finish, period, stop, termination, terminus; *compare* FINALE

rel consummation, culmination; expiration; coda, curtains, finale, finality, finis, terminal, windup

idiom cutoff point, end of the line, stopping point

con genesis, inception

ant beginning

3 *syn* see FINALE

4 something residual <melted down candle *ends*>

syn bit, fragment, scrap

rel butt end, fag end, leaving, remainder, remnant, residue; part, particle, piece

end *vb syn* see CLOSE 3

ant begin

endable *adj syn* see TERMINABLE

endanger *vb* to bring into peril (as of harm or disaster) <conspirators who were *endangering* the cause of freedom>

syn compromise, hazard, imperil, jeopard, jeopardize, jeopardy, menace, peril, risk

rel expose, lay (open); chance, venture

con guard, protect, shelter, shield; preserve, save

endeavor *vb syn* see TRY 5

rel determine, intend, purpose; address, apply, bid (for), drive (at), go (for); strain

endeavor *n syn* see ATTEMPT

rel exertion, push; labor, toil, travail, work

ended *adj syn* see COMPLETE 4

endemic *adj syn* see NATIVE 2

rel home-bred, native-born

con pandemic; extraneous, extrinsic

ant exotic

ending *n* 1 *syn* see END 2

ant beginning

2 *syn* see FINALE

endless *adj* 1 *syn* see LIMITLESS

2 *syn* see EVERLASTING 1

rel constant, continuous; deathless, immortal, undying; boundless, limitless unbounded, unlimited; self-perpetuating

3 *syn* see CONTINUAL

rel overlong

endorse *vb syn see* APPROVE 2
rel attest, authenticate, pass (on *or* upon),
vouch, witness; command, recommend;
advocate, back (up), champion, stand by,
support, uphold
con deprecate, disapprove; anathematize,
denounce

endorsement *n syn see* SANCTION

endow *vb* 1 to furnish or provide with a
gift, talent, or good quality <poets *endowed* with genius>
syn crown (with), dower, endue
rel bestow, confer; accord, award, grant;
empower, enable; enhance, enrich,
heighten
con bare, denude, divest, strip; despoil,
ravage, spoliate; deplete, drain, exhaust
2 to furnish, (as an institution) with a
store of capital < *endowed* a hospital >
syn finance, fund, subsidize
rel found, organize; bequeath, contribute,
donate, subscribe, support; award, grant;
back, promote, sponsor; provide, supply
con beggar, impoverish, pauperize; drain,
draw (on)

end product *n syn see* EFFECT 1

endue *vb syn see* ENDOW 1
rel clothe, invest, vest; accouter, equip,
furnish, outfit

endurable *adj syn see* BEARABLE

endurance *n* 1 *syn see* CONTINUATION 1
2 *syn see* TOLERANCE 1

endure *vb* 1 *syn see* CONTINUE 1
rel bide, linger
con crumble, decay, disintegrate; collapse,
fall
ant perish
2 *syn see* ACCEPT 2
rel stand, submit (to), suffer, sustain;
undergo
con break, collapse, give in, resign
3 *syn see* BEAR 10

enduring *adj* 1 *syn see* LASTING
ant fleeting
2 *syn see* OLD 2
3 *syn see* SURE 2
rel durable, resolute, solid, sound, stable,
staunch, sturdy, substantial
con capricious, changeable, fickle, inconstant, mercurial, unstable, variable

endways *adv syn see* LENGTHWISE

endwise *adv syn see* LENGTHWISE

enemy *n* an individual or group that is
hostile toward another <the senator was
blackmailed by a political *enemy* >
syn foe
rel adversary, antagonist, opponent; assailant, attacker, combatant, invader;
competitor, contender, emulator, rival
con benefactor, friend, supporter; ally,
collaborator, colleague, confederate,
friendly; adherent, follower, partisan, upholder

energetic *adj* 1 *syn see* VIGOROUS
rel aggressive, emphatic, vibrant; indefatigable
con easygoing; faineant, idle, languorous,
lethargic

2 disposed to or having a capacity for
action < an *energetic* campaign worker>
syn active, driving, enterprising, lively
rel animated, breezy, brisk, fresh, kinetic,
peppy, spirited, sprightly, spry, vivacious,
zippy
idiom full of go (*or* life *or* pep *or* zip)
con apathetic, inert; lethargic, limp, listless, passive, phlegmatic, spiritless, spunkless
ant inactive

energetically *adv syn see* HARD 1
rel firmly, strenuously; busily, industri-
ously, zealously
idiom at full tilt
con idly, lazily, lethargically, listlessly;
slowly
ant unenergetically

energize *vb* 1 *syn see* VITALIZE
idiom put pep (*or* zip) into
con emasculate, enervate; debilitate, enfeeble
2 *syn see* STRENGTHEN 2
rel arm, empower, enable; build (up),
sustain
con daunt

energy *n* 1 *syn see* POWER 4
rel activity, operativeness; forcefulness,
mightiness, powerfulness
con impotence; decrepitude, feebleness,
weakness; powerlessness
ant inertia
2 vigorous and effectual application and
operation of power <work with *energy* >
syn birr, go, hardihood, ‖moxie, pep,
potency, tuck, vigor; *compare* VIGOR 2
rel application, effectiveness, efficacy;
effort, operativeness; toughness
con kef, languor, lethargy, listlessness,
sluggishness; ergophobia

enervate *vb syn see* UNNERVE
rel debilitate, devitalize, disable; exhaust,
fatigue, jade, tire, weary
con activate, energize, vitalize; galvanize,
quicken, stimulate

enervated *adj syn see* LANGUID
rel debilitated, devitalized, enfeebled,
undermined, weakened; exhausted, fatigued, run-down, tired, weary; decadent,
degenerate, degenerated, deteriorated
con active, animated, energetic, lusty,
strenuous, vigorous, vital; strong, sturdy,
tenacious, tough

enfant terrible *n syn see* SCAMP

enfeeble *vb syn see* WEAKEN 1
rel devitalize, exhaust
con galvanize; harden, strengthen
ant fortify

enfold *vb* 1 to surround or cover closely
< a heavy fog *enfolded* the ships>
syn enclose, enshroud, envelop, enwrap,
invest, shroud, veil, wrap; *compare*
SWATHE
rel cover, drape; encase, ensheathe; encircle, encompass, environ, gird, girdle, surround
2 *syn see* EMBRACE 1

enforce *vb* to put something into effect or
operation < *enforce* a law >
syn effect, implement, invoke
rel accomplish, administer, carry (out *or*
through); discharge, execute, fulfill, perform; compel, force, oblige

---

syn synonym(s)   *rel* related word(s)
ant antonym(s)   *con* contrasted word(s)
idiom idiomatic equivalent(s)
‖ use limited; if in doubt, see a dictionary

con disregard, forget, ignore, neglect; relax

enfranchise *vb* to admit to full political rights as a freeman or citizen < slaves were emancipated in 1863 but were not *enfranchised* until the fifteenth amendment went into effect in 1870 >
syn affranchise, franchise
rel emancipate, free, liberate, release; deliver, extricate, rescue
con enslave, oppress, subject
ant disenfranchise, disfranchise

engage *vb* **1** to come into contact and interlock with < the teeth of one gear wheel *engaging* those of another >
syn intermesh, mesh
rel interact, interlace, interlock, interplay
con free, release
ant disengage
2 *syn* see PROMISE 1
rel commit; bind, tie; affiance, betroth, troth
3 *syn* see EMPLOY 2
con dismiss, eject, fire
ant discharge
4 to hold the attention of < the puzzle *engaged* him all evening >
syn busy, engross, immerse, occupy, soak
rel absorb, imbue, involve; arrest, captivate, enthrall, fascinate, grip; monopolize, preengage, preoccupy
5 to enter into contest or conflict with < ordered to seek out and *engage* the enemy fleet >
syn encounter, face, meet, take on
rel assault, attack, strike; battle, fight
idiom do battle with, join battle with
con elude, escape, evade

engaged *adj* **1** *syn* see BUSY 1
ant unengaged
2 pledged in marriage < the *engaged* couple made a charming pair >
syn affianced, betrothed, contracted, intended, plighted, ‖promised
rel committed, pledged
con free, uncommitted, unpledged
ant unengaged
3 *syn* see INTENT

engagement *n* **1** *syn* see PROMISE
2 the act or state of being engaged to be married < the couple recently announced their *engagement* >
syn betrothal, betrothing, betrothment, espousal, troth
rel pledge, plight, promise
ant disengagement
3 a promise to be in an agreed place at a specified time, usually for a particular purpose < had an *engagement* with him for nine that evening >
syn appointment, assignation, date, rendezvous, tryst
rel arrangement, invitation; interview, get-together, meeting, visit
4 *syn* see EMPLOYMENT 4
5 *syn* see BATTLE

engaging *adj* **1** *syn* see ATTRACTIVE 1
2 *syn* see SWEET 1
rel alluring, appealing, attractive, captivating, charming, enchanting, entrancing, fetching; fascinating, interesting, intriguing
con repellent, repelling, repulsive; unappealing, unattractive, uninteresting

ant loathsome

engaging *n* *syn* see EMPLOYMENT 4

engender *vb* *syn* see GENERATE 3
rel develop; excite, stimulate; arouse, quicken, rouse, stir

engineer *vb* to contrive or plan out usually with subtle skill or craft < *engineered* an agreement between the two rival governments >
syn finagle, machinate, maneuver, wangle; *compare* MANIPULATE 2
rel arrange, contrive, devise, mastermind, plan (out), set up; intrigue, plot, scheme; manage, manipulate, negotiate; put (over), put (through), swing
idiom pull strings (or wires)

engird *vb* *syn* see BELT 1

engirdle *vb* *syn* see BELT 1

englut *vb* *syn* see GULP

engrave *vb* **1** to cut into a surface usually with a graving tool in order to form an inscription or a pictorial illustration < *engraved* a banknote design on the copper plate >
syn etch, grave, incise
rel chase, enchase; carve; inscribe
2 to impress deeply < the incident was *engraved* in his memory >
syn etch, impress, imprint, inscribe
rel carve; fix; instill; print; embed, entrench, infix, ingrain, root

engross *vb* **1** *syn* see WRITE
rel enscroll, scroll; superscribe
2 *syn* see MONOPOLIZE
rel apply, fill, occupy, preoccupy; assimilate, take up; arrest, engage, grip, ‖hog, hold, immerse, involve; attract, captivate, enthrall
con bewilder, distract; disperse, dissipate, scatter
3 *syn* see ENGAGE 4

engrossed *adj* *syn* see INTENT
rel consumed, monopolized, occupied; submerged; assiduous, busy, diligent, industrious, sedulous
idiom caught up in, lost in, taken up with
con detached, disinterested, indifferent, unconcerned, uninterested

engrossing *adj* gripping the attention completely so as to exclude everything else < the *engrossing* nature of his task made the time pass quickly >
syn absorbing, consuming, monopolizing
rel all-consuming, controlling, gripping; interesting, intriguing; exciting, provoking, stimulating; obsessing, preoccupying
con boring, drab, dull, monotonous; unentertaining, unexciting, uninteresting

engulf *vb* *syn* see DELUGE 1

enhance *vb* **1** *syn* see INTENSIFY
rel elevate, lift, raise; enlarge (upon), exaggerate, strengthen; augment, build (up), increase; adorn, beautify, embellish, embroider
con belittle, deprecate, detract, minimize
2 *syn* see FLATTER

enhancement *n* *syn* see ACCOMPANIMENT 1
rel improvement, intensification

enhearten *vb* *syn* see ENCOURAGE 1

enigma *n* *syn* see MYSTERY
rel crux, knot, puzzler, sticker; bewilderment, perplexity, question, question mark

idiom hard nut to crack

enigmatic *adj syn* see CRYPTIC

enisle *vb syn* see ISOLATE

enjewel *vb syn* see BEJEWEL

enjoin *vb* 1 *syn* see COMMAND
  rel decree, dictate, impose, prescribe, rule; adjure, advise, counsel; admonish, caution, forewarn
  con acquiesce, agree, comply, conform, obey, submit, yield
  2 *syn* see FORBID
  rel deny, disallow

enjoy *vb* 1 to take pleasure in or receive satisfaction from < *enjoyed* the meal >
  syn ∥dig, go, like, ∥mind, relish
  rel cotton (to); take (to); appreciate, dote (on *or* upon), fancy, love; delight (in), drink (in), eat up, luxuriate (in), savor
  con abhor, abominate, detest, hate, loathe; condemn, despise, scorn
  2 *syn* see HAVE 1
  rel fill, occupy, maintain; boast, command

enjoyableness *n syn* see AMENITY 1
  rel attractiveness, pleasingness, pleasurableness; niceness

enjoyment *n* 1 an attitude, circumstance, or favorable response to a stimulus that tends to make one gratified or happy < gave himself up to vigorous *enjoyment* of his pipe >
  syn delectation, diversion, pleasure, relish; *compare* PLEASURE 2
  rel delight, joy; amusement, entertainment; indulgence, savor; recreation, relaxation; gratification, satisfaction
  con abhorrence, antipathy, aversion; repugnance, repulsion
  2 *syn* see PLEASURE 2

enkindle *vb syn* see LIGHT 2

enlarge *vb* 1 *syn* see INCREASE 1
  rel add (to), embroider, exaggerate; grow, stretch, widen
  con attenuate; abridge; compress
  2 *syn* see EXPAND 4
  3 *syn* see INCREASE 2

enlargement *n syn* see EXPANSION 2

enlighten *vb syn* see ILLUMINATE 2
  rel direct, educate, guide, inform, instruct, school, teach, train; acquaint, advise, apprise, inform
  con bewilder, confuse, mystify, perplex, puzzle; addle, fuddle, muddle

enlightening *adj* tending to dissipate ignorance or increase knowledge and awareness < an *enlightening* glimpse of government in action >
  syn illuminant, illuminating, illuminative, illumining
  rel broadening, edifying, educational, instructive; clarifying, elucidative, explanatory
  con unedifying, uninstructive; confusing, obfuscatory, obscuring

enlist *vb syn* see ENTER 3

enliven *vb syn* see QUICKEN 1
  rel refresh, rejuvenate, renew, restore; excite, galvanize, invigorate, jazz (up), pep (up), provoke, stimulate; amuse, cheer,

divert, entertain, recreate; exhilarate, fire, inspire
  idiom give (new) life to
  con depress, oppress, weigh
  ant subdue

en masse *adv syn* see ALTOGETHER 3

enmesh *vb syn* see ENTANGLE 3
  rel drag (into), draw (in), hook, tangle; embarrass, implicate
  idiom make party to
  con disembarrass, disentangle
  ant extricate

enmeshment *n syn* see ENTANGLEMENT 1

enmity *n* deep-seated dislike or ill will or a manifestation of such feeling < the country had experienced generations of racial *enmity* >
  syn animosity, animus, antagonism, antipathy, hostility, rancor
  rel uncordiality, unfriendliness; alienation, dead set, disaffection, estrangement; abhorrence, detestation, dislike, hate, hatred, loathing; aversion; bad blood, bitterness, daggers, gall, ill will, malevolence, malice, malignancy, malignity, spite, spleen
  con amicability, cordiality, friendliness, neighborliness; comity, empathy, friendship, goodwill, sympathy, understanding
  ant amity

ennoble *vb syn* see EXALT 1

ennui *n syn* see TEDIUM
  rel blues, dejection, depression, dumps, melancholy, sadness; boredness; fatigue, languidness, languor, listlessness, spiritlessness, tiredness, weariness; satiety, surfeit

ennui *vb syn* see BORE
  con enliven, stimulate, vitalize

enormity *n* 1 the quality or state of being abnormally, monstrously, or outrageously evil < the utter *enormity* of the crime >
  syn atrociousness, atrocity, heinousness, monstrousness
  rel grossness, outrage, outrageousness, rankness; depravity; flagrancy
  con excusableness, remissibility, veniality; bearableness, tolerability
  2 the quality or state of being huge < the *enormity* of the task confounded him >
  syn enormousness, hugeness, immensity, magnitude, tremendousness, vastness
  rel bigness, greatness, massiveness; graveness, seriousness, weightiness
  con diminutiveness, minuteness, smallness, tininess; triviality, unimportance

enormous *adj syn* see HUGE
  rel stupendous
  ant tiny

enormousness *n syn* see ENORMITY 2
  rel monstrousness, prodigiousness, stupendousness

enough *adj syn* see SUFFICIENT 1

enough *adv* 1 in or to a degree or quantity that satisfies some condition < unstable *enough* to react with water >
  syn adequately, sufficiently
  rel abundantly, amply; acceptably, admissibly, satisfactorily; commensurately, proportionately
  2 in a tolerable degree < she sang well *enough* >

---

syn synonym(s) *rel* related word(s)
ant antonym(s) *con* contrasted word(s)
idiom idiomatic equivalent(s)
∥ use limited; if in doubt, see a dictionary

syn averagely, fairly, moderately, passably, rather, so-so, tolerably

rel acceptably, decently, satisfactorily

enough *n* as much as is needed or wanted <we have *enough* for all of our needs>

syn adequacy, competence, sufficiency, sufficient

rel abundance, ampleness, plenty

con inadequateness; deficiency, deficit, lack, shortage, want; outage, ullage, wantage

ant inadequacy, insufficiency

enounce *vb syn* see ENUNCIATE 1

enrage *vb syn* see ANGER 1

idiom make one's blood boil, work up into a passion

ant placate

enrapture *vb syn* see TRANSPORT 2

rel elate, gladden, gratify, please, rejoice; allure, attract, captivate, charm, enchant, enthrall, fascinate

enravish *vb syn* see TRANSPORT 2

enrich *vb* to make financially rich or richer <*enriched* himself through speculation>

syn richen

enrichment *n syn* see ACCOMPANIMENT 1

enroll *vb* 1 to take in (as a person) by entering identification in a list, catalog, or roll <the school *enrolls* about 800 students>

syn list, register

rel enter, insert; catalog, inscribe, record; enlist, line (up), recruit, sign (up); join, matriculate

con discard, omit, reject

2 *syn* see LIST 3

3 *syn* see ENTER 3

ensample *n* 1 *syn* see MODEL 2

2 *syn* see EXAMPLE 3

ensanguined *adj syn* see BLOODY 1

ensconce *vb* 1 *syn* see HIDE

2 to establish or place firmly, comfortably, or snugly <was happily *ensconced* on the sofa before the fire>

syn install, settle

rel establish, fix, locate, place, plant, seat, set, situate, station

ensepulcher *vb syn* see ENTOMB 1

enshroud *vb syn* see ENFOLD 1

rel cloak, conceal, curtain, hide

con disclose, display, illustrate, open (up), reveal, show, uncover, unveil

ensign *n syn* see FLAG

enslave *vb* to reduce to and hold in a state of servitude <free peasants reduced to serfdom or *enslaved*>

syn enthrall, subjugate

rel disenfranchise, disfranchise; subject; oppress, shackle, yoke

con affranchise, enfranchise; free, liberate

ant emancipate

enslavement *n syn* see BONDAGE

ensnare *vb syn* see CATCH 3

rel decoy, entice, inveigle, lure; hook, net, snag; bag, capture

ensnarl *vb* 1 *syn* see ENTANGLE 1

2 *syn* see ENTANGLE 3

ensorcell *vb syn* see BEWITCH 1

ensorcellment *n syn* see MAGIC 1

ensphere *vb syn* see BALL

ensue *vb syn* see FOLLOW 1

rel derive, emanate, issue, proceed, stem; attend, result

idiom be subsequent (to), come next

con antecede, forerun, preface

ensuing *adj* 1 *syn* see SUBSEQUENT 1

2 *syn* see NEXT

ensure *vb* to make something certain or sure <provisions *ensuring* that the rank and file have a voice in union policy-making>

syn assure, cinch, insure, secure

rel certify, guarantee, warrant; arrange, establish, provide, set out

enswathe *vb syn* see SWATHE

entangle *vb* 1 to twist or interweave so as to make separation difficult <*entangled* the yarn>

syn ensnarl, intertangle, perplex, snarl, tangle

rel intertwine, interweave, ‖snirl, twist; ball up

2 *syn* see COMPLICATE

3 to catch or hold as if in a net from which escape is difficult <a firm hopelessly *entangled* in financial difficulties>

syn embrangle, enmesh, ensnarl, trammel; compare CATCH 3, INVOLVE 1

rel burden, clog, fetter, hamper, impede; bag, capture, catch, ensnare, entrap, snare, trap; discomfit, embarrass, embroil

con extricate, untangle; detach, disengage; clear, free; disburden, unfetter

ant disentangle

4 *syn* see CATCH 3

entanglement *n* 1 the condition of being deeply involved or closely linked often in an embarrassing or compromising way <*entanglements* with underworld figures tarnished his reputation>

syn embroilment, enmeshment, involvement; compare WEB 2

rel ensnarement; affair, intrigue, liaison; association, contact

2 *syn* see WEB 2

enter *vb* 1 to come or go into some place or thing <he *entered* the room>

syn come (in), go in, ingress, penetrate

rel pierce, probe

idiom set foot in

con egress, exit, go out, leave; come out, emerge, sally; escape, flee

ant issue

2 to cause or permit to go in or into <*enter* synonyms in a thesaurus>

syn admit, introduce

rel inject, insert, intercalate, interpolate, put (in), set down; docket, inscribe, list, post, record, register; enroll

3 to make or become a member of <decided to *enter* the army>

syn enlist, enroll, join (up), muster, sign on, sign up

rel come (into), go (into)

idiom get oneself into, take up (*or* out) membership (in)

4 *syn* see BEGIN 1

enterprise *n* 1 *syn* see ADVENTURE

rel attempt, effort, endeavor, striving, struggle; campaign, cause, project, pursuit, task, undertaking; deed

2 *syn* see PROJECT 2

rel speculation

3 a unit of economic or business organization or activity <an economy encouraging the expansion of small, privately owned *enterprises*>

syn business, company, concern, establishment, firm, house, outfit

rel interest; organization; corporation; industry

4 readiness to attempt or engage in what requires energy or daring <complained about his brother's lack of *enterprise* >

syn ambition, drive, get-up-and-go, initiative, push; *compare* VIGOR 2

rel ambitiousness, eagerness, energy, enthusiasm, ‖hustle, vigor; boldness, courage, daring, venturesomeness; inventiveness, self-reliance

con languor, lethargy; indolence, laziness, sloth; apathy, inertia

enterprising *adj* **1** *syn* see ENERGETIC 2

rel aggressive, ambitious, busy, eager, hustling, pushing, up-and-coming; adventurous, venturesome

2 showing initiative, resolution, and determined effort (as in pursuing a course or a career) <an *enterprising* young man likely to go far>

syn go-ahead, gumptious, up-and-coming

rel aggressive, pushing; diligent, hardworking, industrious, zealous; ambitious, aspiring, craving, hungry, itching, lusting, yearning; audacious, daring, dashing, venturesome

idiom on one's toes

ant unenterprising

entertain *vb* **1** *syn* see HARBOR 2

rel invite; admit, receive; cherish, cultivate, foster; feed, nourish

con banish, eject, throw out; ignore, neglect

2 *syn* see AMUSE

rel delight, enliven, gladden, gratify, please, regale, rejoice

entertainment *n* something diverting, amusing, or entertaining <staged a floor show as *entertainment* for her guests>

syn amusement, dissipation, distraction, diversion, divertissement, recreation

rel disport, play, sport; enjoyment, gaiety, pleasure; relaxation, relief

enthrall *vb* **1** *syn* see ENSLAVE

rel master, subdue

con emancipate

2 to hold spellbound <told mystery stories that *enthralled* his playmates>

syn catch up, fascinate, grip, hold, mesmerize, spellbind

rel absorb, engage, preoccupy; charm, enchant, engross, intrigue

con bore, ennui, weary

enthuse *vb* **1** *syn* see THRILL

2 to show great enthusiasm <tourists *enthusing* over the medieval towns>

syn drool, rave, rhapsodize, rhapsody

con censure, criticize; belittle, depreciate, disparage, dispraise, knock, undervalue

enthusiasm *n* **1** *syn* see PASSION 6

rel craze, fascination, infatuation, mania

con impassivity, phlegm, stolidity; aloofness, detachment, indifference, unconcern

ant apathy

2 *syn* see EAGERNESS

rel earnest, interest; ebullience, élan

enthusiast *n* a person who manifests extreme and often uncritical ardor, fervor, or devotion in an attachment <an increasing number of ecology *enthusiasts* >

syn bigot, bug, fanatic, fiend, freak, maniac, nut, zealot

rel addict, aficionado, buff, bum, devotee, fan, habitué, lover, votary; partisan, supporter; bear, extremist

con depreciator, detractor, disparager, knocker

enthusiastic *adj* filled with or marked by enthusiasm <was *enthusiastic* about golf>

syn ‖buggy, ‖bugs, gung ho, keen, nutty, warm, zealous

rel ardent, devoted, eager, fervent, hearty, spirited; gaga, ‖gone (on), hopped-up; hipped, obsessed; passionate, vascular; rabid

con apathetic, detached, indifferent, reluctant, uninterested

ant unenthusiastic

entice *vb* *syn* see LURE

con alarm, fright, frighten (off), terrify

ant scare (off)

enticement *n* *syn* see LURE 2

enticing *adj* being extremely and often dangerously attractive <she looked at him with an *enticing* smile>

syn Circean, fetching, luring, tempting

rel attractive, beguiling, bewitching, enchanting, fascinating, intriguing, inviting, siren, witching; captivating; likable, pleasant, pleasing

entify *vb* *syn* see MATERIALIZE 2

entire *adj* **1** *syn* see WHOLE 3

rel all, gross; plenary

con incomplete, unfinished; limited, qualified

ant partial

2 *syn* see WHOLE 1

rel concatenated, integrated; compacted, consolidated, unified

con broken (up); faulty

ant impaired

3 *syn* see WHOLE 4

entirely *adv* **1** *syn* see WELL 3

2 *syn* see ONLY 1

entireness *n* **1** *syn* see ENTIRETY 1

con incompleteness

2 *syn* see INTEGRITY 2

entirety *n* **1** the state of being complete <the striking *entirety* and self-sufficiency of the feudal community>

syn allness, completeness, entireness, oneness, totality, wholeness

rel collectiveness, unity; integrity, plenitude; comprehensiveness, omneity, universality

con disunity, division, separateness; fragmentation, incompleteness

2 *syn* see WHOLE 1

rel collectivity, complex, everything

con component, detail, element, item, part

ant particular

entitle *vb* **1** *syn* see NAME 1

2 to furnish with proper authority or grounds for seeking or claiming something <this ticket *entitles* the bearer to free admission>

---

syn authorize, qualify
rel empower, license; allow, enable, let, permit

entity *n* **1** one that has real and independent existence <each *entity* of the series requires separate study>
syn being, existence, existent, individual, something, thing
rel body, object
2 *syn* see THING 4
3 *syn* see WHOLE 2

entomb *vb* **1** to deposit in or as if in a tomb <relics *entombed* in pyramids>
syn ensepulcher, sepulcher, sepulture, tomb; *compare* BURY 1
rel bury, inhume, inter, ||plant; inurn; enshrine, shrine
con dig (up), disinhume, disinter, exhume, unbury
ant disentomb
2 *syn* see BURY 1

entombment *n* *syn* see BURIAL 2

entourage *n* one's attendants or subordinates <the queen's *entourage*>
syn following, retinue, suite, train
rel associates, attendants, courtiers, followers, retainers; hangers-on, sycophants, toadies

entrails *n pl* the internal organs of the body <some of the *entrails* are valued as food>
syn gut(s), innards, insides, internals, inwards, ||pudding(s), stuffing, tripes, viscera
rel bowels, intestines; vitals; giblets, pluck, purtenance

entrammel *vb* *syn* see HAMPER
con assist, expedite, facilitate; extricate

entrance *n* **1** the act or fact of going in or coming in <awaited the *entrance* of the army into the city>
syn entry, ingress, ingression
rel arrival, coming, incoming; ingoing; penetration
con departure, egress, emergence, emerging, emigration, exit
ant egression, exiting
2 *syn* see DOOR 1
rel access, aperture, opening, threshold
ant exit
3 *syn* see DOOR 2
rel open door

entrance *vb* *syn* see TRANSPORT 2
rel gladden, please, rejoice; attract, bewitch, captivate, charm, enchant, fascinate; enthrall, hypnotize, spellbind
con disappoint, disgust, repel, repulse; bore

entranced *adj* *syn* see ENAMORED 3

entranceway *n* *syn* see DOOR 1

entrap *vb* **1** *syn* see CATCH 3
2 *syn* see LURE

entreat *vb* *syn* see BEG
rel blandish, coax, wheedle; pester, plague, press, urge

entreaty *n* *syn* see PRAYER

entrée *n* *syn* see DOOR 2
rel introduction; open door

entrench *vb* **1** to establish so solidly or strongly as to make dislodgment or change extremely difficult <prejudices *entrenched* for generations>
syn embed, fix, infix, ingrain, lodge, root

rel found, ground; implant; confirm, define, establish, settle, strengthen
con eliminate, eradicate, root out, uproot; banish, cast out, eject, expel; remove
ant dislodge
2 *syn* see TRESPASS 2
rel interfere, intervene
idiom break in upon, stick one's nose into

entrenched *adj* *syn* see INVETERATE 1

entrepreneur *n* **1** one who owns, launches, manages, and assumes the risks of an economic venture <theatrical *entrepreneurs* making fortunes from successful shows>
syn undertaker
rel organizer; backer, impresario; contractor; administrator, manager; producer; promoter
2 *syn* see GO-BETWEEN 2

entrust *vb* **1** to confer a trust upon <*entrusted* him with responsibility for completing the work>
syn charge, trust
rel confer, impose; delegate, relegate; allocate, allot, assign
2 *syn* see COMMIT 1
rel deliver, deposit, leave, trust; bank, count, depend, reckon, rely
idiom give in trust

entry *n* **1** *syn* see ENTRANCE 1
2 *syn* see DOOR 1
rel access, opening, threshold
con egress
ant exit
3 *syn* see DOOR 2

entryway *n* *syn* see DOOR 1
rel threshold
con egress
ant exit

entwine *vb* *syn* see WIND 2
rel entangle, entwist, interlace, interplait, intertwine, interweave; enmesh
con uncoil, undo, unravel, untwine, untwist, unwind, unwrap; straighten (out)

enumerate *vb* **1** *syn* see COUNT 1
2 to specify one after the other <*enumerated* the advantages of his position>
syn list, numerate, tick off
rel run (over), tell off; identify, mention, recite, recount, relate, specify
3 *syn* see ITEMIZE 1

enunciate *vb* **1** to make a definite or systematic statement of <was the first to *enunciate* the modern principle of inertia>
syn enounce, state
rel develop, formulate, outline, postulate; advance, lay down, submit; announce, declare, proclaim; affirm; show
idiom set forth
2 *syn* see ARTICULATE 2
rel express, intone, modulate, vocalize, voice

envelop *vb* **1** *syn* see ENFOLD 1
rel cloak, hide, mask
2 *syn* see SWATHE
3 *syn* see ENCLOSE 1
rel guard, protect, shield

envenom *vb* *syn* see EXACERBATE

envious *adj* maliciously grudging another's advantages <*envious* of her rival's charm>
syn envying, green-eyed, invidious, jealous

rel coveting, covetous, grasping, greedy;
begrudging, grudging; appetent, desirous,
longing, yearning; resentful, umbrageous
idiom green with envy
con benign, benignant; generous, kind;
tolerant; unconcerned, uninterested

enviousness *n syn see* ENVY

environ *vb syn see* SURROUND 1
rel enclose, fence, go (around)

environment *n* surrounding or associated
matters that influence or modify a course
of development < the socioeconomic *environment* in Germany that produced Hitler >
syn ambience, ambient, atmosphere, climate, medium, milieu, mise-en-scène, surroundings
rel habitat; backdrop, background, context, setting; situation, status

environs *n pl* 1 an enclosing line or margin
< several thousand businesses located
within the *environs* of the city >
syn bound(s), boundary, compass, con-
fine(s), limits, precinct(s), purlieus; *compare* LIMIT 1
rel fringes
2 the suburban areas or districts around a
city or heavily populated area < a new
system of parks for the national capital
and its *environs* >
syn outskirt(s), purlieus, suburbs
rel locality, neighborhood, vicinity; surroundings

envisage *vb syn see* THINK 1
rel behold, grasp, look (upon), picture,
regard, survey, view; externalize, materialize, objectify; foresee
idiom form a mental picture of, have a
picture of, picture to oneself, view in the
mind's eye

envision *vb syn see* THINK 1
rel call up, conjure up, summon up; picture, view; foresee
idiom have a mental picture of, picture to
oneself, view in the mind's eye

envoy *n* 1 a representative with a rank
between an ambassador and a minister
resident who is accredited to a foreign
government < the President received the
envoy from Spain >
syn envoy extraordinary, minister plenipotentiary
rel ambassador, attaché, chargé d'affaires,
consul, councillor, internuncio, legate,
minister, nuncio; diplomat
2 *syn see* MESSENGER

envoy extraordinary *n syn see* ENVOY 1

envy *n* spiteful malice and resentment over
another's advantage < his lavish life-style
provoked *envy* among his colleagues >
syn enviousness, invidiousness, jealousy
rel covetousness; grudging; resentment

envy *vb* to experience envy < while she
outwardly criticized her sister's looks, she
secretly *envied* them >
syn begrudge, grudge
rel covet, crave, desire, hanker, long,
want, yearn

idiom be green with envy

envying *adj syn see* ENVIOUS

enwrap *vb* 1 *syn see* SWATHE
2 *syn see* ENFOLD 1
rel enswathe, swaddle, swathe; sheathe

ephemeral *adj syn see* TRANSIENT
rel brief, short, temporary, unenduring;
episodic
idiom here today and gone tomorrow
con endless, enduring, eternal, everlasting,
lasting
ant perpetual

epicene *adj syn see* EFFEMINATE

epicure *n* one who takes great and fastidious pleasure in eating and drinking < was
a real *epicure*, and his dinners were excellent >
syn bon vivant, gastronome, gastronomer,
gastronomist, gourmand, gourmet
rel amateur, connoisseur, epicurean; glutton, ravener; high liver

epicurean *adj syn see* SENSUOUS

epidemic *n* the sudden widespread occurrence of something felt to resemble an
epidemic disease < an *epidemic* of art
forgeries >
syn outbreak, plague, rash; *compare* OUT-
BREAK 1

epigrammatic *adj syn see* PITHY

epilogue *n* 1 the final part that rounds out
or completes the design of a nondramatic
literary work < the author wrote an *epilogue* to his book explaining that some of
his earlier impressions were wrong >
syn afterword
rel postlude; conclusion, ending
con prelude; foreword, introduction, preface
ant prologue
2 something that resembles an epilogue in
rounding out or giving point to something
else < an incident that can be regarded as
an *epilogue* to the history of Roman Britain >
syn sequel
rel follow-up, postscript
ant prologue

episode *n syn see* OCCURRENCE

epistle *n syn see* LETTER 2
rel communication

epitaph *n* an inscription on a tombstone in
memory of the one buried there
syn hic jacet

epitome *n* 1 *syn see* ABRIDGMENT
2 *syn see* SUMMARY
3 *syn see* APOTHEOSIS 1

epitomize *vb* 1 to make or give an epitome
of < a report which *epitomizes* one of the
most complex theories of all time >
syn condense, digest, inventory, nutshell,
sum, summarize, summate, sum up, synopsize
rel boil down, capsulize; outline, tabulate
con elaborate, enlarge (on), expand
2 to serve as the typical representation or
ideal expression of < he *epitomized* safe,
dull conservatism >
syn exemplify, typify
rel embody, incarnate, incorporate, personify, represent, symbolize
3 *syn see* REPRESENT 2

epitomized *adj syn see* CONDENSED

epoch *n syn see* PERIOD 2

---

syn synonym(s)   *rel* related word(s)
ant antonym(s)   *con* contrasted word(s)
idiom idiomatic equivalent(s)
|| use limited; if in doubt, see a dictionary

rel interval, term

epochal *adj* uniquely or highly significant < had to make an *epochal* decision: whether or not to declare war >
syn momentous
rel consequential, far-reaching, important; unmatched, unparalleled
con inconsequential, minor, petty, small-time, trivial, unimportant

equable *adj syn* see STEADY 2
rel methodical, orderly, regular, systematic; immutable, invariable, unchangeable; equal, equivalent, same
con variable; fitful, spasmodic
ant inequable, unequable

equal *adj* 1 *syn* see SAME 2
rel equable, even, uniform; alike; like; commensurate, corresponding, proportionate
idiom one and the same
con different, disparate, divergent, diverse, varied; un- alike, unequable, uneven; irregular
ant unequal
2 *syn* see FAIR 4
idiom without distinction
con discriminating, discriminative, unfair
ant inequitable
3 *syn* see EVEN 3
4 *syn* see EVEN 4
5 *syn* see PROPORTIONAL

equal *n* one that is equal to another in status, achievement, value, meaning, or effect < he has no *equal* in common sense and honesty >
syn counterpart, equivalent, like, match; *compare* OPPOSITE NUMBER, PARALLEL
rel companion, fellow, mate, peer; alter ego, double, twin; competitor, rival; similar

equal *vb* 1 *syn* see AMOUNT 2
rel compare, parallel; accord, agree, square, tally; reach
idiom amount to the same thing
2 *syn* see EVEN 2
3 to make or produce something equal to (as in quality or value) < *equal* that if you can >
syn match, measure up, meet, rival, tie, touch
rel beat, top

equality *n syn* see EQUIVALENCE

equalize *vb* 1 to make equal in amount, degree, or status < *equalize* educational opportunities >
syn equate, even
rel balance, level, square
2 *syn* see EVEN 2

equally *adv* 1 *syn* see EVENLY 1
2 *syn* see EVENLY 2

equanimity *n* the characteristic quality of one who is self-possessed and not easily disturbed or perturbed < faced disaster with bland *equanimity* >
syn ataraxy, calmness, composure, coolness, imperturbability, phlegm, sangfroid, self-possession; *compare* CONFIDENCE 2
rel balance, equilibrium, equipoise, poise; aplomb, assurance, confidence, self-assurance; detachment; placidity, serenity, tranquillity
con alarm, anxiety, apprehension; excitability, nervousness; agitation, discomposure, disquiet, disturbance, perturbation

equatability *n syn* see EQUIVALENCE

equate *vb* 1 *syn* see EQUALIZE 1
2 to treat, represent, or regard as equal, equivalent, or comparable < *equated* retreat with cowardice >
syn assimilate, compare, liken, match, paragon, parallel
rel associate, relate, similize; consider, hold, regard, represent, treat

equidistant *adj syn* see MIDDLE 1

equilibrium *n syn* see BALANCE 1
rel stabilization, steadiness, steadying; counterbalance, counterpoise
con top-heaviness

equip *vb syn* see FURNISH 1
rel provide, supply; fit (out), rig (up or out), turn (out); gear, prepare, qualify

equipment *n* items needed for the performance of a task or useful in effecting an end < the *equipment* for the polar expedition included ships, instruments, sleds, dogs, and supplies >
syn accouterment(s), apparatus, gear, habiliments, machinery, material(s), matériel, outfit, paraphernalia, tackle, tackling
rel accessories, appurtenances, attachments, fittings, trappings; baggage, belonging(s), impedimenta, rig, things, traps; equipage, provisioning, provisions

equipoise *n syn* see BALANCE 1
rel counterbalance, counterpoise, counterweight

equiponderation *n syn* see BALANCE 1

equitable *adj* 1 *syn* see FAIR 4
rel level, stable; equivalent, identical, same
idiom fair and square
con discriminatory
ant inequitable, unfair
2 *syn* see EVEN 3

equity *n syn* see JUSTICE 1
rel equitableness, justness
con bias, discrimination, partiality, unfairness
ant inequity

equivalence *n* the state or property of being equivalent or the result of making equivalent < the *equivalence* of paper money and coins >
syn adequation, equality, equatability, equivalency, par, parity, sameness
rel likeness; compatibility, correlation, correspondence; exchangeability, interchangeability
con discrepancy, disparity, divergence, incompatibility, inequality, unlikeness
ant difference

equivalency *n syn* see EQUIVALENCE

equivalent *adj* 1 *syn* see SAME 2
rel commensurate, proportionate; convertible, correlative, corresponding, parallel, reciprocal, substitute
con disparate, divergent, diverse, various; discordant, discrepant, incompatible, inconsonant
ant unlike
2 *syn* see LIKE

equivalent *n syn* see EQUAL
rel obverse, reciprocal, substitute; parallel

equivocal *adj* 1 *syn* see OBSCURE 3
rel hazy, indistinct; doubtful, dubious, questionable; indeterminate, multivocal
idiom clear as mud

con clear, distinct, understandable; categorical, explicit, unambiguous, univocal; certain, conclusive

ant unequivocal

2 characterized by a mixture of opposing feelings < an *equivocal* attitude toward the expensive proposal >

syn ambivalent

rel uncertain, undecided

idiom having mixed (*or* divided) feelings

con assured, certain, decided, sure

3 *syn* see DOUBTFUL 1

rel disreputable

idiom open to question

con credible

equivocality *n syn* see AMBIGUITY

equivocate *vb* 1 *syn* see LIE

rel elude, escape, evade

2 to avoid committing oneself by speaking evasively < he'd rather be brutally frank with them than *equivocate* on that issue >

syn dodge, evade, hedge, pussyfoot, shuffle, sidestep, tergiversate, tergiverse, weasel; *compare* SKIRT 3

rel cavil, prevaricate, quibble; fence, parry; avoid, elude, eschew

idiom beat around (*or* about) the bush, beg the question, mince words

equivocating *adj syn* see EVASIVE 1

rel deceptive, delusive, misleading

equivocation *n* 1 *syn* see AMBIGUITY

rel hedging; coloring, distortion, misrepresentation; deceit, dissimulation, duplicity

ant explicitness

2 *syn* see FALLACY 2

rel haggling, quibbling; fib, fibbing, lie, lying

equivoque *n syn* see AMBIGUITY

era *n syn* see PERIOD 2

rel term; stage

eradicate *vb syn* see ANNIHILATE 2

rel demolish, destroy, raze; liquidate, purge

con establish, fix, set; implant, inculcate, instill; breed, engender, generate, propagate

erase *vb* to eliminate or neutralize with or as if with a stroke of the pen < time has *erased* their sad memories > < *erase* an error >

syn annul, black (out), blot out, cancel, delete, efface, expunge, obliterate, wipe (out), x (out)

rel disannul, negate, nullify; abolish, blank (out), cross (off *or* out), cut out, dele, eliminate, excise, extirpate, rub out, scrape, sponge (out), strike (out); neutralize; remove, take out, withdraw

con impress, imprint, print, stamp; insert; reinstate, renew, restore

ere *prep syn* see BEFORE 1

erect *adj* standing up straight < the dog's *erect* ears pricked forward >

syn arrect, raised, stand-up, straight-up, upright, upstanding

rel erectile; elevated, lifted, upraised; perpendicular, standing, vertical

con decumbent, flat, prostrate, recumbent; drooping, hanging, pendent

erect *vb* 1 *syn* see BUILD 1

2 *syn* see MAKE 3

rel compose, create; make up, run up

con demolish, destroy, tear up, unbuild, wreck

3 to fix in an upright position < *erected* a flagpole >

syn put up, raise, rear, set up; *compare* BUILD 1

rel elevate, heighten, hoist, lift, upraise, uprear; upend

4 *syn* see EXALT 1

idiom put on a pedestal

ant abase

5 to bring into existence as if by raising a building < *erect* social barriers along religious lines >

syn build up, construct, establish, hammer (out), set up

rel fabricate, fashion, forge, form, shape; bring about, effect

con break down, tear down; liquidate, purge; dispose (of), eliminate, remove

erection *n syn* see EDIFICE

eremitic *adj syn* see ANTISOCIAL

ergo *adv syn* see THEREFORE

erode *vb* 1 *syn* see EAT 3

rel crumble, decay, deteriorate, disintegrate; consume

2 *syn* see ABRADE 1

rel grate, rub (off *or* away), scrape (off *or* away)

erotic *adj* of, devoted to, affected by, or tending to arouse sexual love or desire < *erotic* art >

syn amative, amatory, amorous, aphrodisiac

rel ardent, fervent, fervid, impassioned, lovesome, passionate; earthy; carnal, epicurean, fleshly, voluptuous; bawdy, sexy, spicy; concupiscent, lecherous; lascivious, lewd, lickerish, prurient, salacious, sensual

eroticism *n syn* see LUST 2

err *vb* to depart from a standard (as of wisdom or morality) < the human tendency to *err* >

syn deviate, stray, wander

rel miscalculate; lapse, slip (up), stumble, trip; transgress, trespass; offend; sin

idiom go astray (*or* amiss *or* wrong), leave the straight and narrow

errable *adj syn* see FALLIBLE

errant *adj* 1 *syn* see ERRATIC 1

rel drifting, itinerant, meandering, rambling, ranging, roaming, roving, shifting, straying

con static, unmoving

2 deviating from an accepted pattern or standard < a parent scolding his *errant* child >

syn aberrant, devious, erring

rel deviating, straying, wandering; misbehaving, mischievous, naughty

idiom off the straight and narrow

3 *syn* see FALLIBLE

rel aberrant, erring; unreliable

con perfect, trustworthy

ant inerrant

erratic *adj* 1 moving about aimlessly or irregularly without a fixed course < an *erratic* breeze barely stirred the leaves of the tree >

syn devious, errant, stray, wandering

---

syn synonym(s)   *rel* related word(s)

ant antonym(s)   *con* contrasted word(s)

idiom idiomatic equivalent(s)

‖ use limited; if in doubt, see a dictionary

rel curving, meandering, roundabout, winding; shifting, undirected
con fixed, stable, unmoving; active, animated, brisk, lively, sprightly
ant static

2 *syn* see UNCERTAIN 1
rel doubtful, dubious
ant stable

3 *syn* see ARBITRARY 1
rel changeable, inconsistent, inconstant, unpredictable, variable; mercurial, unstable, volatile
con consistent, conventional, predictable, stable

4 *syn* see STRANGE 4
rel anomalous, irregular, unnatural
con natural, normal, regular, typical; customary, usual

erring *adj syn* see ERRANT 2

erroneous *adj* **1** *syn* see FALSE 1
rel amiss, askew, awry, off; defective; mistaken
idiom all off, all wrong, way off the mark
con right, true
ant accurate, correct

2 *syn* see MISTAKEN

erroneousness *n syn* see FALLACY 1
rel inaccurateness, mistakenness
con accuracy, accurateness, rightness
ant correctness

error *n* **1** an often unintentional deviation from truth or accuracy <made an *error* in adding the figures>
syn mistake, x
rel inaccuracy; miscalculation, miscomputation; oversight, slip

2 something (as an act, statement, or belief) that departs from what is or is generally held to be acceptable <spying on the opposing party proved to be a grave *error*>
syn blooper, blunder, boner, bull, bungle, fluff, lapse, miscue, misstep, mistake, rock, slip, slipup, trip; compare FAUX PAS
rel bevue, fault, misdoing, misjudgment, stumble; ‖boo-boo, botch, fumble, muff; howler, screamer; impropriety, indecorum

3 *syn* see FALLACY 1
rel misreading, misunderstanding; delusion, illusion

errorless *adj syn* see IMPECCABLE 1
con imprecise, inaccurate, incorrect, unexact, wrong

ersatz *adj syn* see ARTIFICIAL 2
rel factitious, synthetic; fake

ersatz *n syn* see IMITATION

erstwhile *adv syn* see BEFORE 2

erstwhile *adj syn* see FORMER 2

eruct *vb* **1** *syn* see BELCH 1
idiom bring up gas

2 *syn* see ERUPT 1

eructate *vb syn* see BELCH 1

erudite *adj syn* see LEARNED
rel lettered, well-read; studious
ant illiterate

eruditeness *n syn* see ERUDITION 2

erudition *n* **1** *syn* see EDUCATION 2

2 the quality or state of being erudite <a scholar of great cultivation and *erudition*>
syn eruditeness, learnedness, scholarliness, scholarship

rel cultivation, culture, education, intellectuality, literacy; bookishness, pedantry, studiousness
ant illiteracy

erupt *vb* **1** to give off or release (as something pent up) forcefully <the volcano *erupted* gouts of lava>
syn belch, disgorge, eject, eruct, expel, irrupt, spew
rel cast (out *or* up), hurl, throw off; boil, discharge, emit; jet, spout, spurt; extravasate

2 to break away or burst from limits or restraint <riots *erupted* in the ghetto>
syn break out, burst (forth), explode
rel detonate, touch off; go off

eruption *n* **1** *syn* see OUTBURST 1

2 *syn* see OUTBREAK 1

escalade *vb syn* see ASCEND 1
con clamber (down), climb (down); go (down)

escalate *vb* **1** *syn* see ASCEND 1

2 to increase in extent, volume, amount, number, intensity, or scope <a little war threatens to *escalate* into a huge, ugly one>
syn expand, grow
rel broaden, enlarge, heighten, increase, intensify, spread, widen
con decrease, limit, minimize; constrict, contract, narrow; collapse, shrink, shrivel
ant de-escalate

escapade *n* a usually adventurous action that runs counter to approved or conventional conduct <childish *escapades* on Halloween>
syn caper, lark, rollick; compare PRANK
rel antic, frolic, vagary; prank; fling, spree; mischief, roguery

escape *vb* **1** to run away especially from something that limits one's freedom and threatens one's well-being <trying to *escape* from prison>
syn abscond, break, ‖bunk, decamp, flee, fly, scape
rel get away, make off, mosey, run away; bail out, ‖ditch, double, duck out, flit, jump, skip; depart; disappear, vanish
idiom cut and run, cut loose, fly the coop, take it on the lam
con come back, return; abide, remain, stay; chase, follow, pursue, tag, trail

2 to get away or keep away from what one does not wish to incur, endure, or encounter <made every effort to *escape* suspicion>
syn avoid, bilk, double, duck, elude, eschew, evade, shun, shy; compare SHAKE 5, SKIRT 3
rel burke, bypass, circumvent; dodge, shake, shun, skit; miss
idiom fight shy of, give the slip
con catch, contract, incur; abide, bear, brook, endure, stand, suffer, tolerate; dare, face, meet

escape *n* **1** the act or fact of escaping or having escaped physically <succeeded in making his *escape* from the prison>
syn breakout, escapement, escaping, flight, getaway, lam, ‖scape, slip
rel departure; deliverance, liberation, release
con return; grasp, grip, hold, retention; imprisonment, incarceration

2 the act or fact of escaping or having escaped what one does not wish to incur, encounter, or endure <sought *escape* from responsibility>
syn avoidance, come-off, elusion, escaping, eschewal, evasion, runaround, shunning
rel bypassing, circumvention, dodging, ducking, sidestepping; elusiveness, evasiveness
con abidance, abiding, bearing, endurance, enduring, submission, submitting, toleration; facing
escapement *n syn see* ESCAPE 1
escaping *n* 1 *syn see* ESCAPE 1
2 *syn see* ESCAPE 2
eschew *vb* 1 *syn see* ESCAPE 2
idiom shy away from, steer clear of
con adopt, embrace, espouse
ant choose
2 *syn see* FORGO
rel abstain, refrain
idiom let well enough alone
eschewal *n syn see* ESCAPE 2
rel shirking; shying
escort *n* 1 a boy or man who goes on a date with a girl or woman <had her pick of *escorts* to the dance>
syn date
rel beau, boyfriend, fellow; cavalier, gallant, squire, vis-à-vis
2 a person who leads or directs another or others in a way or course (as through difficult terrain) <served as our *escort* when we drove through the desert>
syn guide
rel attendant, companion, guard
escort *vb* 1 *syn see* ACCOMPANY
2 *syn see* GUIDE
rel bring; squire
escritoire *n syn see* DESK
esculent *adj syn see* EDIBLE
esoteric *adj syn see* RECONDITE
especial *adj* 1 *syn see* SPECIAL 1
rel preeminent, supreme, surpassing; dominant, paramount, predominant, preponderant; exceptional, notable, singular, unusual
con unexceptional, usual
ant general
2 *syn see* EXPRESS 2
especially *adv* 1 in a special way <was *especially* good at math>
syn distinctively, particularly, special, specially, specifically
rel remarkably, unusually; exceptionally, markedly, peculiarly, singularly, uniquely; eminently, notably, preeminently, supremely
idiom before all else
2 *syn see* EXPRESSLY 2
espial *n syn see* DISCOVERY
espionage *n* systematic secret observation in order to accumulate information <agents engaged in industrial *espionage*>
syn spying
rel observation, reconnaissance, sleuthing, surveillance, watching

---

espousal *n* 1 *syn see* ENGAGEMENT 2
2 *often* **espousals** *pl syn see* WEDDING
3 *syn see* MARRIAGE
rel mating; union
idiom getting hitched, taking on the ball and chain, tying the knot
con estrangement, separation
4 ready acceptance of or the taking up of a cause or belief <his wholehearted *espousal* of left-wing philosophies worried his family>
syn adoption, embracement, embracing
rel acceptance, approval; advocacy; aid, promotion, support
con denial, rejection; disapproval, dislike, distaste; antipathy, aversion, intolerance
ant repudiation
espouse *vb* 1 *syn see* MARRY 1
2 *syn see* ADOPT
rel accept, approve; advocate, back, champion, support, uphold
con abandon, desert, forsake; deny, reject; disapprove, dislike
ant repudiate
esprit *n* 1 *syn see* SPIRIT 5
rel acumen, acuteness, brains, brightness, cleverness, intelligence, mind, quick-wittedness, sharpness, wit; courage, mettle, tenacity; fervor, passion
2 *syn see* MORALE
rel camaraderie, fellowship; devotion, loyalty; enthusiasm, fervor, passion
3 *syn see* WIT 5
esprit de corps *n syn see* MORALE
rel camaraderie, comradeship, fellowship; partisanism, partisanship; devotion, loyalty; enthusiasm, spirit
espy *vb* 1 *syn see* SEE 1
rel recognize, take in; sight, spot, spy; witness
idiom catch sight of, get a load of
2 *syn see* FIND 1
rel spy; make out; notice
essay *vb syn see* TRY 5
rel venture; labor, toil, travail, work
idiom give it a try (or fling or go), have at it, make a stab at, take a crack (or whack) at
essay *n* 1 *syn see* ATTEMPT
rel exertion; labor, toil, travail, work; go, venture
2 a relatively brief discourse written for others' reading or consideration <an *essay* on free will>
syn article, composition, paper, theme
rel discourse, discussion, explication, exposition, study; piece; tract, treatise; dissertation, thesis
essence *n* 1 a basic underlying or constituting entity, substance, or form <succeeds in conveying completely the cruel *essence* of loneliness>
syn being, essentia, essentiality, nature, texture
rel entity, form, substance
2 the most basic, significant, and indispensable element, attribute, quality, property, or aspect of a thing <the very *essence* of Machiavellianism is the belief that in politics there is neither good nor evil>
syn be-all and end-all, bottom, essentiality, marrow, pith, quintessence, quintessential, rock bottom, root, soul, stuff,

---

syn synonym(s)   *rel* related word(s)
ant antonym(s)   *con* contrasted word(s)
idiom idiomatic equivalent(s)

|| use limited; if in doubt, see a dictionary

substance, virtuality; *compare* BODY 3,
CENTER 2, SUBSTANCE 2
rel timber; element, fiber, property; aspect, attribute, quality, spirit; inwardness,
significance; crux, gist, kernel, nub, nubbin; distillate, distillation

essentia *n syn* see ESSENCE 1

essential *adj* 1 *syn* see INHERENT
con conditional, contingent, dependent
ant accidental
2 so important to the nature and essence
of a thing as to be indispensable <the
essential ingredient in this medicine is a
new drug>
syn cardinal, constitutive, fundamental,
vital
rel basal, basic, underlying; capital, chief,
foremost, leading, main, principal; primal,
primary, prime
con dependent, secondary, subordinate;
accessory, auxiliary, contributory, subsidiary
3 *syn* see ELEMENTAL 1
4 urgently required <raw materials *essential* to industry>
syn imperative, indispensable, necessary,
necessitous, prerequisite
rel needed, needful; required, requisite,
wanted; right-hand; vital
con dispensable, unnecessary, unneeded,
unrequired, unwanted
ant nonessential

essential *n* 1 something that forms part of
the minimal body, character, or structure
of a thing <prosperity is an *essential* of
the good life>
syn basic, element, fundamental, part and
parcel, rudiment
rel essence, stuff, substance; must, necessary, prerequisite, sine qua non
2 something necessary, required, or unavoidable <work was an *essential* to sur-
vival>
syn condition, must, necessity, precondition, prerequisite, requirement, requisite,
sine qua non
idiom name of the game

essentiality *n* 1 *syn* see ESSENCE 1
2 *syn* see ESSENCE 2

essentially *adv* 1 in regard to the essential
points <*essentially* the problem is this: he
is unreliable>
syn au fond, basically, fundamentally, in
essence
rel actually, really
idiom at bottom
2 *syn* see ALMOST 2
rel substantially, virtually
idiom in the main

establish *vb* 1 *syn* see SET 1
rel enroot, entrench, implant, inculcate,
infix, instill, root; set down, set up; moor,
rivet, secure; found, ground
con eradicate, exterminate, extirpate,
uproot, wipe (out)
ant abrogate
2 *syn* see BASE
idiom lay the foundation for (*or* of)
3 *syn* see ENACT 1
rel formulate; authorize, decree, legislate,
prescribe
ant repeal
4 *syn* see FOUND 2

rel endow, provide; originate; build
con disestablish; demolish, tear down
ant abolish
5 *syn* see ERECT 5
6 to make clear beyond a reasonable
doubt <*established* an alibi for the time of
the crime>
syn demonstrate, determine, make out,
prove, show
rel authenticate, confirm, corroborate,
document, substantiate, verify; attest;
clarify
idiom afford (*or* offer) proof of
con discredit, expose, show up; confute,
invalidate, parry, rebut, refute
ant disprove

established *adj syn* see FIRM 3

establishment *n* 1 *syn* see ENTERPRISE 3
rel workplace; institute, institution; foundation
2 *often cap* a group of influential leaders
who represent an established order of
society <the literary *establishment*>
syn Old Guard
rel conservative(s), diehard(s)
con liberal(s)

estate *n* 1 *syn* see ORDER 9
rel form, state
2 a class of people in a community distinguishable by social or political duties or
privileges <a party platform appealing to
people of every *estate*>
syn grade, rank
rel bracket, category; footing, level, order,
standing; place, position, station; caste,
class
3 an extensive landed property <spent
the weekend at his country *estate*>
syn acres, land, manor, quinta
rel farm, ranch; plantation; villa

esteem *n syn* see REGARD 4
rel approval, liking; appreciation, valuation
ant abomination

esteem *vb* 1 *syn* see APPRECIATE 1
rel idolize, revere, worship
idiom hold dear, think the world of
ant despise
2 *syn* see ADMIRE 2
rel revere, venerate
idiom hold in esteem (*or* high regard)
con abhor
ant abominate

estimable *adj* 1 *syn* see WORTHY 1
2 *syn* see RESPECTABLE 1
rel admired, esteemed, respected
con disreputable, unworthy; bad
3 *syn* see HONORABLE 1

estimate *vb* 1 to judge something with
respect to its worth <*estimated* the value
of the jewels>
syn appraise, assay, assess, evaluate, rate,
set (at), survey, valuate, value
rel adjudge, adjudicate, judge; ascertain,
determine, discover; price, prize; decide,
settle
2 *syn* see CALCULATE
rel cast, sum; count, enumerate
3 to fix some value (as size, distance, or
composition) more or less accurately <*estimated* the rainfall at over six inches>
syn approximate, call, judge, place, put,
reckon

rel round, round off; conjecture, guess, suppose, surmise; fancy, imagine; deduce, infer

con calculate, compute; measure

estimate *n* **1** the act of appraising or valuing the nature, character, quality, status, or worth of something <his influence as President is beyond *estimate*>

syn appraisal, appraisement, assessment, estimation, evaluation, valuation

rel calculation, measurement, reckoning; sizing up; projection

2 *syn* see ESTIMATION 1

idiom point of view

estimation *n* **1** the result of evaluating something <his *estimation* of the man's ability proved incorrect>

syn appraisal, appraisement, assessment, estimate, evaluation, judgment, stock

rel impression; opinion

2 *syn* see COMPUTATION

3 *syn* see ESTIMATE 1

4 *syn* see REGARD 4

estrange *vb* to cause one to break a bond or tie of affection or loyalty <her arrogance *estranged* her children and friends>

syn alien, alienate, disaffect, disunify, disunite, wean

rel break up, divide, divorce, part, separate, sever, split, sunder

idiom set at odds

con appease, conciliate, pacify, propitiate; associate, espouse, join, link, unite

ant reconcile

estrangement *n* the act of estranging or the condition of being estranged <a petty dispute resulted in total *estrangement*>

syn alienation, disaffection

rel division, divorce, schism; withdrawal

con appeasement, conciliation, propitiation

ant reconciliation

etceteras *n pl syn* see SUNDRIES

etch *vb* **1** *syn* see ENGRAVE 1

2 to set forth in a sharp, clear-cut manner with minute attention to detail <the most sharply *etched* character in the novel>

syn define, delineate

rel outline, set forth; depict, describe, picture, portray, represent

3 *syn* see ENGRAVE 2

eternal *adj syn* **1** *syn* see INFINITE 1

rel endless, interminable, unceasing, unending; lasting, permanent, perpetual; deathless, immortal, undying

con ephemeral, evanescent, momentary, passing, short-lived, temporary, transient

ant mortal

2 *syn* see EVERLASTING 1

rel deathless, undying

3 *syn* see CONTINUAL

con interrupted, sporadic

4 valid or existing unaltered at all times <right and wrong are *eternal* verities that cannot be changed>

syn ageless, dateless, intemporal, timeless

rel immemorial, lasting, perdurable, permanent, perpetual; immutable, inalterable, unalterable, unchangeable, unchanging

con alterable, changeable, changing, fluctuating, varying; debatable, questionable, suspect

eternalize *vb syn* see PERPETUATE

eternally *adv syn* see EVER 2

eternity *n* **1** a totality of infinite time <in *eternity* there is no change or passing away>

syn infinity, sempiternity

rel endlessness, infiniteness, infinitude, perpetuity, timelessness

con ephemerality, impermanence, transience; limitedness, restrictedness

ant finiteness

2 unending existence after death <belief in the *eternity* of our spiritual nature>

syn afterlife, everlastingness, eviternity, immortality, world-without-end

3 *syn* see AGE 2

idiom forever and a day, forever and ever

eternize *vb syn* see PERPETUATE

ethereal *adj syn* see AIRY 3

rel celestial, empyreal, empyrean, heavenly; vaporish, vaporlike, unsubstantial; filmy, gossamer; delicate, fragile, light

con heavy, thick

ant substantial

ethic *n* **1** ethics *pl but usu sing in constr* the discipline dealing with what is good and bad and with moral duty and obligation <*ethics* has been called the science of the ideal of human character>

syn morals

2 a group of moral principles or set of values <the Christian *ethic*>

syn morality, morals, mores

3 ethics *pl* the code of conduct or behavior governing an individual or a group (as the members of a profession) <medical *ethics*>

syn principles

rel moralities, morals, mores; criteria, standards

4 the complex of ideals, beliefs, or standards that characterizes or pervades a group, community, or people <the American work *ethic*>

syn ethos

rel belief, ideal, standard, value

ethical *adj syn* see MORAL 1

rel high-principled; elevated; upright, upstanding

con flagitious, iniquitous, nefarious; improper, indecent, indecorous, unbecoming, unseemly; immoral, low

ethnic *adj* **1** *syn* see HEATHEN

rel non-Christian, unchristian

2 of, relating to, or originating from the traits shared by members of a group as a product of their common heredity and cultural tradition <only a person thoroughly familiar with Yiddish can recognize the *ethnic* quality of the pun> <*ethnic* cookery>

syn racial

rel national; tribal

ethos *n syn* see ETHIC 4

etiquette *n* **1** *syn* see MANNER 5

2 *syn* see DECORUM 1

rel behavior, conduct, deportment, manners; amenities, civilities, formalities; convention, form, protocol

idiom social graces

---

syn synonym(s)   *rel* related word(s)
ant antonym(s)   *con* contrasted word(s)
idiom idiomatic equivalent(s)

‖ use limited; if in doubt, see a dictionary

eulogistic *adj* of, relating to, characterized by, or bestowing praise < the speaker made *eulogistic* remarks on the group's accomplishment >
syn encomiastic, laudative, laudatory, panegyrical, praiseful
rel approbatory, approving, commendatory, complimentary
con uncomplimentary; critical, disapproving, disparaging; abusive
ant dyslogistic

eulogize *vb syn* see PRAISE 2
rel applaud; belaud; bepraise
idiom praise to the skies, sing the praises of
ant vilify

eulogy *n syn* see ENCOMIUM
rel adulation, glorification
con calumny, slander
ant vilification

euphemism *n* an agreeable or inoffensive expression that is substituted for one that might offend or suggest unpleasantness < vandalism that goes under the *euphemism* of souvenir hunting >
syn nice Nelly, nice-nellyism
ant dysphemism

euphonic *adj syn* see MELODIOUS 1

euphonious *adj syn* see MELODIOUS 1

euphoria *n* 1 *syn* see ELATION 1
ant deflation, dysphoria
2 an often groundless or excessive feeling of well-being and happiness < drug-induced *euphoria* >
syn elation, exaltation, intoxication
rel ecstasy, frenzy; madness; glee
con anxiety, unease, uneasiness
ant depression

euphuistic *adj syn* see RHETORICAL
rel elaborate; colorful; verbose; elevated
con concise, simple, straightforward; lean

evacuee *n syn* see REFUGEE

evade *vb* 1 *syn* see ESCAPE 2
rel flee, fly, slip (away); foil, outwit, thwart
idiom keep (or know) one's distance
con accost, confront, dare, face
2 *syn* see EQUIVOCATE 2
rel bypass, circumvent, duck; parry, turn (aside)
idiom give (someone) the runaround
con confront, face; elucidate, explain

evaluate *vb* 1 *syn* see ESTIMATE 1
rel appreciate; class, gauge, rank; criticize
2 *syn* see CLASS 2

evaluation *n* 1 *syn* see ESTIMATE 1
rel interpreting; judging, rating
2 *syn* see ESTIMATION 1
rel appreciation; interpretation; decision

evanesce *vb syn* see VANISH
rel disintegrate, dispel, disperse, dissipate, dissolve, scatter
idiom go up in smoke, vanish into thin air
con appear; coalesce
ant materialize

evanescent *adj syn* see TRANSIENT
rel temporary; flying; dissolving, fading, melting; disappearing, vanishing

evangelical *adj* characterized by or reflecting a missionary, reforming, or redeeming impulse or purpose < a mood of *evangelical* nationalism >
syn crusading, evangelistic
rel ardent, fervid, impassioned, militant, zealous; missionary, propagandizing, proselytizing

evangelist *n syn* see MISSIONARY

evangelistic *adj syn* see EVANGELICAL
rel missionary, reforming

evangelize *vb syn* see PREACH 1

evanish *vb syn* see VANISH
idiom pass out of the picture

evaporate *vb syn* see VANISH
rel escape, pass (away or off); weaken; vaporize
idiom go pouf

evasion *n syn* see ESCAPE 2
rel dodging, equivocating, equivocation, evading, excuse, subterfuge; haggling, quibbling; escapism
con confrontation, confronting; daring
ant facing

evasive *adj* 1 tending to evade or avoid confrontation < his answers were ambiguous and *evasive* >
syn equivocating, prevaricative, prevaricatory, shifty, shuffling
rel ambiguous, equivocal, unclear, vague; sliding, slippery, sly
con categorical, definite, explicit, unambiguous, univocal; candid, forthright
ant direct
2 *syn* see ELUSIVE

even *adj* 1 *syn* see LEVEL
con bent, crooked, curved, twisted
ant uneven
2 *syn* see STEADY 2
rel equal, identical, same; consistent, continual, continuous, undeviating, unvaried
3 giving no advantage to either side < an *even* exchange >
syn equal, equitable, fair
rel balanced, fair and square; square; honest, straightforward, unprejudiced
con inequitable, unequal, unfair
ant uneven
4 being nicely in balance < his chances for success or failure are *even* >
syn equal, even-up, fifty-fifty
rel balanced, comparable, proportionate
con disproportionate, unbalanced
ant uneven
5 being neither more nor less than the named or understood amount, extent, or number < an *even* mile >
syn exact, square
con approximate, imprecise, inaccurate

even *adv* 1 in a like manner < they can learn *even* as others do >
syn as well, exactly, expressly, just, precisely
2 at the very time < perhaps *even* now the moment has come to consider a retreat >
syn already
3 not this merely but also — used as an intensive to emphasize the identity or character of something < a huge, *even* monstrous animal >
syn indeed, nay, truly, verily, yea
rel absolutely, positively; quite, really
4 — used as an intensive to indicate an extreme, hypothetical, or unlikely case or instance < refused *even* to look at her > < *even* if this were so, it should not change our plans >

syn so much as
idiom even so much as
5 *syn* see YET 1

even *vb* 1 to make (as a surface) smooth, even, level, or flat < *even* the soil with a spade>
syn flatten, flush, lay, level, plane, smooth, smoothen
rel grade, roll; align; symmetrize; uniform; pancake
con rough, roughen
2 to make even or balanced in advantage < hoped to *even* the odds by training>
syn equal, equalize
rel balance, square
con unbalance, unequalize, upset; derange, disarrange
3 *syn* see EQUALIZE 1

evening *n* 1 the closing part of day and the early part of night < the last light of *evening*>
syn ‖dimmet, ‖dimps, ‖dimpsy, dusk, ‖dusk dark, eventide, gloaming, nightfall, owl-light, twilight
rel afternoon; sundown, sunset; duskiness, duskiness
con sunrise; dawn
ant morning
2 a latter portion or a period of decline < in the *evening* of life>
syn sunset, twilight
3 a party taking place in the evening < their *evenings* were notable affairs>
syn soiree
rel reception; salon; party

evenly *adv* 1 in equal parts < a career divided *evenly* between stage and screen>
syn equally, fifty-fifty, squarely
rel commensurably, proportionately
con disproportionately, unequally
ant unevenly
2 in a just or fair manner < she was *evenly* polite to everyone>
syn equally, impartially
rel fairly, justly
con unfairly, unjustly
3 without variation or fluctuation < spread the paint *evenly*>
syn flatly, smooth, smoothly, uniformly
con irregularly, roughly
ant unevenly

event *n* 1 *syn* see OCCURRENCE
rel act, action, deed; achievement, exploit, feat; accident, chance, fortune
2 a matter worthy of remark < the trip was an *event* in their dull routine>
syn milepost, milestone, occasion
rel affair, landmark; delight, treat
idiom historic event
con insignificancy, trifle, triviality
3 *syn* see EFFECT 1
rel offshoot, outgrowth; product, resultant, sequent
idiom end result
4 a postulated outcome, condition, or contingency < in the *event* of rain, we will not meet>
syn case, eventuality

---

rel chance, fortuity, hap, happenstance
5 any of the contests in a sports program < track-and-field *events*>
syn match, meet
rel competition, contest
6 *syn* see FACT 2

eventide *n* *syn* see EVENING 1

eventual *adj* *syn* see LAST
rel consequent, ensuing, inevitable, succeeding; ending, endmost
con antecedent, beginning, inceptive, initial, original

eventuality *n* 1 *syn* see EVENT 4
rel contingency, possibility
2 *syn* see EFFECT 1
con antecedent, beginning, root

eventually *adv* *syn* see YET 2
idiom in the long run

even-up *adj* *syn* see EVEN 4

ever *adv* 1 *syn* see ALWAYS 1
2 through all or an indefinite time < a name that will *ever* be respected>
syn always, eternally, evermore, forever, forevermore, in perpetuum
3 in each and every case < war and suffering have *ever* gone hand in hand>
syn invariably
rel consistently, regularly, usually
4 at any time or on any occasion < he is seldom if *ever* absent>
syn anytime, at all
5 in any way < nor was it *ever* important>
syn anyway, anywise, at all, once
6 — used as an intensive after an inverted verb-subject construction < is he *ever* proud of himself>
syn confoundedly, consumedly, excessively, extremely, immensely, inordinately, over, overfull, overly, overmuch, super, too, unduly
rel annoyingly, plaguey; grievously, mortally; consummately,

ever and again *adv* *syn* see SOMETIMES

ever and anon *adv* *syn* see SOMETIMES

everlasting *adj* 1 lasting or enduring through all time < *everlasting* laws governing the physical universe>
syn amaranthine, ceaseless, endless, eternal, immortal, never-ending, unending, world-without-end; compare IMMORTAL 1
rel lasting, perdurable, permanent, perpetual; boundless, infinite, limitless, termless
con ephemeral, evanescent, momentary, short-lived, transitory
2 *syn* see CONTINUAL
con off-and-on, interrupted, periodic, sporadic

everlastingness *n* *syn* see ETERNITY 2

evermore *adv* *syn* see EVER 2

evert *vb* *syn* see DISPROVE 1

every *adj* *syn* see ALL 2

everybody *pron* every person < *everybody* must do what his conscience dictates>
syn all, everyman, everyone
idiom all and sundry
ant nobody

everyday *adj* 1 *syn* see COMMON 4
con distinctive, singular, unique; uncommon, unusual
ant exceptional
2 *syn* see PROSAIC 3
3 *syn* see ORDINARY 1

---

syn synonym(s)   *rel* related word(s)
ant antonym(s)   *con* contrasted word(s)
idiom idiomatic equivalent(s)
‖ use limited; if in doubt, see a dictionary

everymar *pron syn* see EVERYBODY
  idiom the man in the street

everyone *pron syn* see EVERYBODY
  ant no one

everyplace *adv syn* see EVERYWHERE 1
  idiom all over the place

everything *pron* the whole amount < lost *everything* in the fire >
  syn all
  idiom all in all, the lot, the whole bit (*or* shebang), the whole kit and kaboodle, the works

everywhere *adv* 1 in every place or in all places < poverty anywhere is a danger to peace and prosperity *everywhere* >
  syn all over, all round (*or* all around), everyplace, far and near, far and wide, high and low, overall, throughout
  idiom in all quarters, in every quarter
  2 *syn* see WHEREVER

evict *vb syn* see EJECT 1
  rel dislodge, dispossess, force (out), put out, shut out, turn out
  idiom turn (*or* put) out bag and baggage, turn out of doors, turn out of house and home
  con harbor, house, lodge, shelter

evidence *n* 1 *syn* see INDICATION 3
  2 *syn* see TESTIMONY

evidence *vb syn* see SHOW 2
  rel display, expose; attest, bespeak, betoken, confirm, indicate, prove, testify

evident *adj syn* see CLEAR 5
  rel noticeable, prominent, pronounced
  idiom as plain as the nose on one's face, plain as day
  con inconspicuous; ambiguous, unapparent, unrecognizable; concealed, hidden
  ant inevident

evidently *adv syn* see OSTENSIBLY

evil *n* 1 whatever is harmful, distressing, or disastrous < attempts to grasp the nature of *evil* >
  syn ill
  rel bad, badness, devilry, diablerie, diabolism, evilness, satanism, satanity, wickedness, wrong
  con goodness, virtue
  ant good
  2 whatever is morally unacceptable < return good for *evil* >
  syn debt, sin, wickedness, wrong
  rel evildoing, misconduct, sinfulness, wrongdoing
  con rectitude, righteousness, virtue
  ant good
  3 a particular thing (as an act) that is evil < choose the lesser of two *evils* >
  syn crime, diablerie, iniquity, sin, tort, wrong, wrongdoing
  rel badness, evilness, maleficence, vice, wickedness; misdeed, offense

evil *adj* 1 *syn* see WRONG 1
  rel base, low, vile; flagitious, nefarious; baneful, pernicious; black, damnable, execrable
  con high, noble; exemplary, salutary
  ant good
  2 *syn* see OFFENSIVE
  rel distasteful, repellent; fetid, putrid, stinking
  3 *syn* see MALICIOUS

  rel angry, disagreeable, ugly, unpleasant, wrathful; harmful, hurtful, injurious, mischievous; destructive
  4 *syn* see HARMFUL
  rel calamitous, destructive, disastrous
  con harmless, noninjurious
  ant innocuous
  5 reporting or predicting harm or misfortune < messengers bearing *evil* tidings >
  syn bad, ill, unfavorable; compare OMINOUS
  rel baleful, baneful, inauspicious; ill-boding, ill-omened, ominous
  con auspicious, favorable
  ant good
  6 marked by misfortune or calamity < the family fell upon *evil* times >
  syn bad, inauspicious
  rel unfavorable, unfortunate, unlucky; difficult, hard, trying; calamitous, disastrous
  con favorable; lucky; easy, prosperous; auspicious, halcyon, happy
  ant good

evince *vb* 1 *syn* see SHOW 2
  rel argue, attest, bespeak, betoken, confirm, indicate, prove; display, exhibit, expose, illustrate, signify
  con repress, suppress; conceal, hide
  2 *syn* see EDUCE 1
  rel bring (about), cause; provoke, stimulate

eviscerate *vb* to take out the entrails of < *eviscerate* a turkey >
  syn bowel, disembowel, draw, embowel, exenterate, gut, paunch

eviternity *n syn* see ETERNITY 2

evocative *adj* serving or tending to call something (as a mood) forth < conduct *evocative* of the utmost contempt >
  syn evocatory, suggestive
  rel meaningful, pregnant, weighty; arousing, moving, stimulating, stirring; causing, effecting, inducing, producing

evocatory *adj syn* see EVOCATIVE

evoke *vb syn* see EDUCE 1
  rel excite, provoke, stimulate; arouse, awaken, rally, rouse, stir, waken; call forth, call up, conjure (up), raise, summon (forth *or* up)

evolution *n syn* see DEVELOPMENT
  rel change, transformation

evolve *vb* 1 *syn* see DERIVE 1
  rel get (at), obtain; advance
  2 *syn* see UNFOLD 3
  rel advance, progress; mature, open (up), ripen

evolvement *n syn* see DEVELOPMENT
  rel metamorphosis, transformation

evulse *vb syn* see EXTRACT 1

exacerbate *vb* to cause to become increasingly bitter or severe < foolish words that only *exacerbated* the quarrel >
  syn acerbate, embitter, envenom
  rel annoy, exasperate, irritate, provoke; aggravate, heighten, intensify; inflame
  idiom add fuel to the flame, fan the flames, feed the fire, pour oil on the fire
  con appease, mollify, pacify, placate, quell; lessen, moderate
  ant assuage

exact *vb* 1 *syn* see EXTORT 1
  2 *syn* see LEVY

3 *syn* see DEMAND 1

rel coerce, compel, constrain, force, oblige; extort, extract, squeeze, wrest, wring

exact *adj* 1 *syn* see CORRECT 2

2 *syn* see EVEN 5

ant imprecise, inexact

3 *syn* see SAME 1

4 *syn* see CAREFUL 2

5 *syn* see PRECISE 4

exacting *adj syn* see ONEROUS

rel rigid, rigorous, severe, stern, strict, stringent; finicky, fussy, particular; critical, hypercritical

con laissez-faire, lenient

ant unexacting

exactitude *n syn* see PRECISION

exactly *adv* 1 *syn* see JUST 1

rel ‖plumb, plunk; specifically

idiom on the dot (*or* nose), right on the nail

con about, around, more or less, roughly

ant approximately

2 *syn* see ALL 1

rel absolutely, expressly, positively; completely

3 as you say or state — used to express agreement or concurrence < "You are accusing me of lying?" he asked. "*Exactly*," she replied.>

syn precisely, yes

idiom quite so, (that's) for sure (*or* certain)

4 *syn* see EVEN 1

exactness *n syn* see PRECISION

exaggerate *vb syn* see EMBROIDER

rel hyperbolize, overcolor, romance, romanticize

idiom blow up out of (all) proportion, draw the long bow, make the eagle scream

ant understate

exaggeration *n* an overstepping of the bounds of truth < the passage shows the author's penchant for grotesque *exaggeration* >

syn coloring, embellishment, embroidering, hyperbole, overstatement

rel aggrandizement, amplification, enlargement; overcoloring, overdrawing, romance, stretching

idiom flight of fancy, tall talk

con minimizing, underestimation

ant understatement

exalt *vb* 1 to enhance the status of < propaganda that *exalts* nationalism to the level of religion >

syn aggrandize, dignify, distinguish, ennoble, erect, glorify, honor, magnify, pedestal, stellify, sublime, uprear

rel boost, build up, elevate, lift, promote, raise, upgrade, uplift; enhance, heighten, intensify; acclaim, enhalo, extol, laud, praise; apotheosize

con debase, degrade, demean, humble, humiliate; belittle, decry, depreciate, derogate, detract, disparage, downgrade, minimize

---

syn synonym(s)   *rel* related word(s)

ant antonym(s)   *con* contrasted word(s)

idiom idiomatic equivalent(s)

‖ use limited; if in doubt, see a dictionary

---

ant abase

2 *syn* see FIRE 2

rel pique, stimulate, quicken; deepen, enhance, sharpen; encourage, inspirit, spirit (up), uplift

exaltation *n* 1 *syn* see APOTHEOSIS 2

rel upgrading, uplifting; extolment, laudation, praise

con debasement, degradation, demeanment, humiliation; belittlement, depreciation, derogation, disparagement, downgrading

ant abasement

2 *syn* see ELATION 1

rel delectation, delight; bliss, joy, rapture

ant deflation

3 *syn* see EUPHORIA 2

ant depression

exalted *adj* 1 raised to or having high rank < moved in *exalted* circles > < Alexander was *exalted* to the papal throne in 1492 >

syn astral, highest, highest-ranking, top-drawer, top-ranking

rel august, noble; eminent, illustrious, prominent; high, high-ranking; foremost, number one; first, leading, outstanding

con low, lowly, low-ranking, unimportant; minor; humble, plebeian

ant abject

2 *syn* see GRAND 3

ant abject

examination *n* a careful, detailed, and often formal study designed to uncover pertinent information < the doctor gave him a physical *examination* >

syn analysis, audit, check-over, checkup, inspection, perlustration, review, scan, scrutiny, survey, view

rel assay, breakdown, diagnosis, dissection; sifting, winnowing; canvass, catechization, inquiry, questioning, quizzing, testing

examine *vb* 1 *syn* see SCRUTINIZE 1

rel check (out), go (over), investigate, look (into); contemplate, look (at *or* over), observe

idiom give a going over, give the once-over, go over with a fine-toothed comb

2 *syn* see TRY 1

3 *syn* see ASK 1

rel cross-examine, grill; pump

idiom give the third degree to, put to the question

example *n* 1 *syn* see INSTANCE

2 *syn* see MODEL 2

idiom shining example

3 an instance that illustrates a rule or provides practice in its application < worked out his arithmetic *examples* >

syn ensample, illustration, problem

idiom case in point

exanimate *adj syn* see DEAD 1

exasperate *vb syn* see IRRITATE

rel agitate, work up

idiom try one's temper (*or* patience)

ant appease; mollify

exasperation *n* 1 *syn* see ANNOYANCE 2

rel irritation, vexation; displeasure; resentment

2 *syn* see ANNOYANCE 3

ex cathedra *adj syn* see OFFICIAL

excavate *vb* 1 *syn* see DIG 1

rel gouge (out), hollow (out), scoop (out), scrape (out), quarry (out)

2 *syn* see DIG 2

exceed *vb* **1** to go or be beyond a natural or set limit <the policeman *exceeded* his authority> <this task *exceeds* my powers>
  syn outstep, overrun, overstep, surpass
  rel outreach, overreach; dare, presume, venture

2 *syn* see SURPASS 1

exceedingly *adv syn* see VERY 1

excel *vb syn* see SURPASS 1

excellence *n* something that gives especial worth or value <the particular *excellence* of this cake is its lightness>
  syn arete, excellency, merit, perfection, quality, virtue
  rel value, worth; distinction, fineness, superiority; goodness, niceness, superbness; class
  con blemish, defect, flaw; failing, foible, frailty, vice
  ant fault

excellency *n syn* see EXCELLENCE

excellent *adj* meritoriously near the standard or model and eminently good of its kind <an *excellent* restaurant specializing in French cuisine>
  syn A1, bang-up, banner, blue-ribbon, ‖boss, bully, ‖bunkum, capital, champion, classic, classical, ‖dandy, famous, fine, first-class, first-rate, first-string, five-star, front-rank, Grade A, number one, par excellence, prime, quality, royal, skookum, ‖slap-up, sovereign, stunning, superior, ‖swinging, top, top-notch, whiz-bang; *compare* MARVELOUS 2; SUPREME
  rel high-class, high-grade, proper; ‖rum; distinguished, exceptional, premium; brag, incomparable, magnificent, nobby, sensational, smart, superb, superlative, terrific, tip-top, unsurpassed
  idiom all wool and a yard wide, beyond compare, out of this world
  con mediocre; bad, inadequate, inferior, low, low-grade, low-quality, substandard; fourth-rate, second-class, second-rate; poor, shoddy, sorry, unsatisfactory, wretched; commonplace, mediocre, ordinary
  ant execrable

except *vb* **1** *syn* see EXCLUDE
  rel omit, pass over; exempt; reject
  con incorporate, receive, work in
  ant admit

2 *syn* see OBJECT 1

except *prep* with the exclusion or exception of <*except* Christmas, we had no long holiday>
  syn apart from, aside from, bar, barring, bating, beside, besides, but, ‖cep, except for, excluding, exclusive of, outside, outside of, save, saving

except *conj* **1** on any other condition than that <wouldn't go near that woman *except* I had to>
  syn but, save, saving, unless, ‖without

2 *syn* see ONLY

except for *prep syn* see EXCEPT

exceptionable *adj syn* see OBJECTIONABLE
  con unimpeachable; exemplary
  ant unexceptionable

exceptional *adj* **1** being out of the ordinary <an *exceptional* opportunity>

syn extraordinary, phenomenal, rare, remarkable, singular, uncommon, uncustomary, unimaginable, unique, unordinary, unthinkable, unusual, unwonted; *compare* STRANGE 4
  rel infrequent, scarce; distinct, exceptional, notable, noteworthy
  con frequent; common, commonplace, familiar, ordinary, usual
  ant unexceptional

2 *syn* see SUPERIOR 4
  rel good; excellent, marvelous, outstanding, phenomenal, wonderful; extraordinary, singular, special
  con common, ordinary, run-of-the-mill
  ant average

exceptionally *adv syn* see VERY 1
  rel especially, particularly; extraordinarily, unusually; marvelously, phenomenally, stupendously, wonderfully

excerpt *vb* to select (passages or details) as typical of a larger store <quotations *excerpted* from many authors>
  syn extract
  rel cull, glean; choose, pick, pick out, select, single; cite, quote

excess *n* **1** whatever exceeds a limit, measure, bound, or accustomed degree <the proper balance between sufficiency and *excess*>
  syn fat, overabundance, overflow, overkill, overmuch, overplus, plethora, superfluity, surfeit, surplus, surplusage
  rel overbalance, overspill; oversupply; profusion; superabundance
  idiom enough and then some, enough and to spare, too much of a good thing
  con insufficiency, lack, scarcity
  ant deficiency; dearth

2 the amount or degree by which a thing or number exceeds another <an *excess* of 10 bushels over what was needed>
  syn overage, overstock, oversupply, plus, surplus, surplusage
  rel overproduction; overmeasure
  ant deficit, shortfall

3 *often* excesses *pl* undue or immoderate personal indulgence especially in eating and drinking <*excess* at table is seldom healthful> <his *excesses* led to his failure in business>
  syn immoderation, inordinateness, intemperance, overindulgence
  rel extravagance, overdoing; indulgence, self-indulgence; immoderacy, immoderateness; dissipation, prodigality, Saturnalia
  con moderation; sobriety, temperateness; restraint, self-discipline, self-restraint
  ant temperance

excess *adj syn* see SUPERFLUOUS
  rel redundant; unessential

excessive *adj* **1** going beyond a normal or acceptable limit <spend an *excessive* amount on clothes>
  syn dizzy, exorbitant, extravagant, extreme, immoderate, inordinate, sky-high, steep, stiff, stratospheric, supernatural, towering, unconscionable, undue, unmeasurable
  rel boundless, limitless, unbounded; over, overboard, overmuch, overweening; super
  idiom out of bounds
  con exiguous, meager, narrow, scant, scanty, skimpy, sparse, tight

ant deficient

2 given to personal excesses < an *excessive* drinker, often drunk and never quite sober >
syn immoderate, inordinate, intemperate, overindulgent, unrestrained, untempered
rel extravagant; indulgent, self-indulgent; dissipated, prodigal
con conservative, moderate, sober, temperate
ant restrained

excessively *adv syn* see EVER 6

exchange *vb* **1** *syn* see TRADE 1

2 to give up, taking in return something else < *exchanged* his uniform for civilian clothes >
syn change, substitute, swap, switch, trade; *compare* TRADE 1
rel displace, replace

3 to give and receive reciprocally < *exchanged* a few words with his neighbor >
syn bandy, interchange
rel pay back, reciprocate
idiom give as much as one takes, give tit for tat, return the compliment

exchangeable *adj syn* see INTERCHANGEABLE

exchequer *n syn* see TREASURY 2

excise *vb* to remove by or as if by dissecting < *excise* a tumor > < *excised* some wordy passages >
syn cut out, exsect, extirpate, resect
rel amputate, cut off; elide, remove, strike out; eradicate, root out; delete, expurgate, exscind; slash

excitable *adj* easily excited < an *excitable* child who needs a firm hand >
syn agitable, alarmable, combustible, edgy, skittery, skittish, startlish, volatile
rel high-strung, mercurial, temperamental, unstable; touchy
idiom like a bundle of nerves, likely to go off at half cock, on edge, on the ragged edge
con calm, collected, cool, easy, easygoing, phlegmatic, placid, quiet
ant unexcitable

excite *vb* **1** *syn* see PROVOKE 4
rel agitate, discompose, disquiet, disturb, perturb, stir up; impassion; charge (up), energize, touch off, turn on
idiom set astir, set on fire, stir the blood
con allay, placate, soothe
ant quiet

2 *syn* see ELATE
rel move; fire
con depress, dishearten

3 *syn* see INTEREST

excited *adj syn* see INTOXICATED 2
rel animated, atwitter; agitated, charged (up), inflamed, pink; delighted, enthusiastic
idiom all fired up, all of a twitter, beside oneself
con apathetic, unmoved; deflated
ant unexcited

exciting *adj* absorbingly interesting < the most *exciting* day of her life > < an *exciting* personality >

syn exhilarant, exhilarating, exhilarative, eye-popping, inspiring, intoxicating, rousing, stimulating, stirring
rel arresting, interesting, intriguing; moving, provocative; heady, thrilling
con blah, dull, uninteresting, unintriguing; humdrum, monotonous, tedious
ant unexciting

exclaim *vb* to speak or utter suddenly and usually sharply, vehemently, or passionately < *exclaimed* in delight at the sight of the toy >
syn blat, blurt (out), bolt, cry out, ejaculate
rel burst (out); roar, snort

exclude *vb* to prevent the participation, consideration, or inclusion of < *excluded* that subject from discussion >
syn bar, bate, count out, debar, eliminate, except, rule out, suspend
rel ban; close out, estop, obviate, preclude, prevent, prohibit, ward (off); blackball, blacklist, ostracize; block; disbar; lock out, put out, shut out
idiom close (*or* shut) the door on
con comprehend, involve; embrace, take in
ant admit; include

excluding *prep syn* see EXCEPT

exclusionary *adj syn* see EXCLUSIVE 1

exclusive *adj* **1** having or exercising the power to limit or exclude < a tangle of *exclusive* laws >
syn exclusionary, exclusory
rel barring, debarring, excluding; limitative, limiting, restrictive; preclusive, prohibitive
con free, unlimited, unrestricted, unrestrictive
ant admissive

2 *syn* see SELECT 1
rel aristocratic, elite, preferred, privileged, tony; aloof, clannish, cliquish, cliquy; high-hat, snobbish, standoffish
con catholic, cosmopolitan, universal; common, familiar, ordinary, popular, vulgar
ant inclusive

3 *syn* see STYLISH
con tasteless; frumpy, unfashionable

4 *syn* see SOLE 4
rel individual, lone, only
con common, general, public

5 *syn* see WHOLE 5
con divided, partial

exclusive *n syn* see SCOOP

exclusively *adv syn* see ONLY 1
rel completely, wholly; particularly

exclusive of *prep syn* see EXCEPT

exclusory *adj syn* see EXCLUSIVE 1

excogitate *vb* **1** *syn* see CONSIDER 1

2 *syn* see DERIVE 1
rel contrive, invent, think (up); develop, think (out)

excoriate *vb* **1** *syn* see CHAFE 3

2 *syn* see LAMBASTE 3
idiom tear into

excorticate *vb syn* see SKIN 2

excrescence *n syn* see OUTGROWTH 1

excrescency *n syn* see OUTGROWTH 1

excruciate *vb syn* see AFFLICT
rel inflame, irritate; hurt, pain, wound; convulse

---

syn synonym(s)   *rel* related word(s)
ant antonym(s)   *con* contrasted word(s)
idiom idiomatic equivalent(s)
‖ use limited; if in doubt, see a dictionary

idiom prolong the agony

excruciating *adj* intensely or unbearably painful < his suffering was *excruciating* >
syn agonizing, harrowing, racking, tearing, tormenting, torturing, torturous
rel acute, extreme; piercing, sharp, shooting, stabbing; consuming, rending

exculpate *vb* to free from alleged fault or guilt < the court *exculpated* him after a thorough investigation >
syn absolve, acquit, clear, disculpate, exonerate, vindicate
rel explain, justify, rationalize; condone, excuse, forgive, pardon, remit; amnesty, free, let off
idiom clear the (or one's) record, wipe the slate clean
con blame, censure, denounce, reprehend, reprobate; incriminate; accuse, charge; arraign, indict; impeach; convict
ant inculpate

excurse *vb syn* see DIGRESS 2

excursion *n* 1 a trip not involving a prolonged or definite separation from one's usual abode or way of life < an afternoon *excursion* to the city >
syn jaunt, junket, outing, roundabout, sally
rel expedition, journey, trek, trip, safari; circuit, tour; one-way trip, pleasure trip, round trip; ||pasear, paseo, walk, ||walkabout
2 *syn* see DIGRESSION

excursus *n syn* see DIGRESSION

excusable *adj* 1 *syn* see VENIAL
2 *syn* see JUSTIFIABLE

excuse *vb* 1 to exact neither punishment nor redress for or from < she was much too ready to *excuse* her children's faults >
syn condone, forgive, pardon, remit
rel alibi, apologize (for), explain, justify, pretext, rationalize; absolve, acquit, clear, exculpate, exonerate, vindicate; extenuate, gloss (over), gloze, overlook, palliate, pass over, shrug off, whitewash, wink (at)
con blame, censure, criticize, reprehend, reprobate; castigate, chasten, chastise, correct, discipline; admonish, chide, rebuke, reprimand
ant punish
2 *syn* see EXEMPT

excuse *n* 1 a justifying explanation of a fault or defect < what's your *excuse* for being late >
syn alibi, plea, pretext, ||right; *compare* APOLOGY 1, 2
rel defense; explanation, justification, rationalization; reason
2 *syn* see APOLOGY 2
3 an inferior example of a specified kind < this heap is a sorry *excuse* for a car >
syn apology
rel makeshift, shift, stopgap, substitute
idiom a sorry specimen
con nonpareil, paragon; gem, jewel, treasure

exec *n syn* see EXECUTIVE

execrable *adj* 1 so odious as to be utterly detestable < an *execrable* crime >
syn accursed, cursed, damnable
rel atrocious, heinous, horrific, horrifying, monstrous; base, despicable, foul, low, vile; detestable, loathsome, nauseating, repulsive, revolting

idiom beneath (or below) contempt, not to be put up with (or endured)
2 *syn* see DAMNED 2

execrate *vb* 1 to denounce violently < *execrated* those responsible for the concentration camps >
syn anathematize, curse, damn, objurgate
rel censure, condemn, denounce, reprehend, reprobate, reprove; ban; revile; accurse, imprecate
con applaud, commend, compliment; acclaim, extol, laud, praise; admire
ant eulogize
2 *syn* see HATE
3 *syn* see SWEAR 3

execration *n syn* see BLASPHEMY 1

execute *vb* 1 *syn* see PERFORM 2
rel act; bring about, cause; carry out, complete, discharge, transact
2 *syn* see ADMINISTER 1
rel discharge, dispatch, transact; conduct, handle
3 *syn* see FULFILL 1
rel put through
4 *syn* see MURDER 1
rel eliminate, purge
idiom put to death

executive *n* one who holds an administrative or managerial position < a senior sales *executive* >
syn administrator, exec, manager, officer, official
rel businessman, businesswoman; entrepreneur; higher-up; director, leader, supervisor

exegesis *n syn* see EXPLANATION 1

exegetic *adj syn* see EXPLANATORY

exemplar *n syn* see MODEL 2
rel soul; exponent, illustration; prototype

exemplary *adj* 1 *syn* see GOOD 11
rel ideal, model; admirable, commendable, praiseworthy, worthy
con evil, corrupt; unworthy
2 *syn* see TYPICAL 1

exemplify *vb* 1 to use examples in order to clarify < a good teacher *exemplifies* each complex point >
syn illustrate, instance
rel clarify, clear up, spell out; cite, quote; enlighten, illuminate
2 *syn* see EPITOMIZE 2
rel demonstrate; illustrate
3 *syn* see REPRESENT 2

exempt *vb* to free from a liability or requirement < *exempt* a man from military service >
syn absolve, discharge, dispense, excuse, let off, privilege (from), relieve, spare
rel except; free
idiom give (one) exemption

exemption *n* freeing or the state of being free or freed from a charge or obligation to which others are subject < received a tax *exemption* >
syn immunity, impunity
rel exception; discharge, freedom, release

exenterate *vb syn* see EVISCERATE

exercise *n* 1 the act of bringing into play or realizing in action < one can usually avoid accidents by the *exercise* of foresight >
syn application, employment, exercising, exertion, operation, use; *compare* USE 1

con dereliction, disregard, neglect; carelessness, heedlessness, inattention, laxity

2 regular or repeated appropriate use of a faculty, power, or bodily organ <muscular atrophy from lack of *exercise*>
syn activity, exercising, exertion
rel action, movement; practice, use, workout
con inactiveness, inactivity; idleness, unemployment

3 something practiced or performed in order to develop, improve, or display a specific power or skill <spelling *exercises*>
syn drill, drilling, practice

4 a performance having a strongly marked secondary or ulterior aspect <his writing is an *exercise* in confusion>
syn lesson, study

exercise *vb* 1 *syn* see USE 2
idiom put into practice

2 *syn* see EXERT

3 to use repeatedly in order to master or strengthen <beginning swimmers *exercising* their new skill> <games that *exercise* the muscles>
syn drill, practice, rehearse
rel break in, condition, groom, prepare, train; cultivate, develop, foster, improve; fix, set

4 *syn* see ANNOY 1

exercising *n* 1 *syn* see EXERCISE 1
2 *syn* see EXERCISE 2

exert *vb* to bring to bear especially with sustained effort or lasting effect <*exerted* tremendous influence over his son's development>
syn exercise, ply, put out, throw, wield
rel apply, employ, use
idiom put forth

exertion *n* 1 *syn* see EXERCISE 1
2 *syn* see EFFORT 1
rel strain, striving, struggle
idiom hard (or long) pull
con ease, leisure, relaxation, repose, rest; inactivity, idleness
ant inertia

3 *syn* see EXERCISE 2

exfoliate *vb* *syn* see SCALE 2

exhale *vb* to let or force out of the lungs <*exhaled* a cloud of cigarette smoke>
syn breathe (out), expire, outbreathe
rel emit, let (out); blow
ant inhale, inspire

exhaust *vb* 1 *syn* see DEPLETE
rel dispel, disperse, dissipate, scatter; run out
idiom suck dry
con conserve, preserve, save; renew, restore

2 *syn* see CONSUME 1

3 *syn* see GO 4

4 to tire utterly <the 14-hour flight *exhausted* everyone>
syn see ‖BUGGER compare TIRE 1
rel overdo, overdrive, overexert, overextend, overply, overwork; debilitate, enfeeble, weaken

---

syn synonym(s)   *rel* related word(s)
ant antonym(s)   *con* contrasted word(s)
idiom idiomatic equivalent(s)
‖ use limited; if in doubt, see a dictionary

idiom run one ragged, tire to death
con relax, rest, unlax

exhausted *adj* *syn* see EFFETE 2
rel run-down, weak, weakened; ‖beat, dog-tired, tired, ‖tucked up; limp; dead
idiom all done in (or for)

exhaustion *n* *syn* see FATIGUE
rel collapse, prostration

exhaustive *adj* testing all possibilities or considering all the elements of <an *exhaustive* investigation was soon under way>
syn complete, full-dress, thorough, thoroughgoing, whole-hog
rel all-encompassing, all-out, comprehensive, full-blown, full-scale, out-and-out, profound, total; intensive, radical, sweeping
con cursory, shallow; incomplete, partial; slipshod, unthorough
ant superficial

exhaustively *adv* 1 *syn* see HARD 3
con cursorily, superficially; incompletely, partially

2 *syn* see THOROUGHLY 2

exhibit *vb* 1 *syn* see SHOW 2
2 *syn* see LOOK 4
3 *syn* see SHOW 4
idiom parade one's wares, strut one's stuff

exhibit *n* *syn* see EXHIBITION 2

exhibition *n* 1 an act or instance of showing, evincing, or showing off <she gave an incredible *exhibition* of bad manners>
syn demonstration, display, show, spectacle
rel manifestation, sight

2 a public display of objects of interest <a trade *exhibition*>
syn exhibit, exposition, fair, show
rel demonstration, display, offering, presentation, showing

exhibitive *adj* *syn* see INDICATIVE

exhilarant *adj* *syn* see EXCITING

exhilarate *vb* *syn* see ELATE
rel animate, enliven, invigorate, vitalize; boost, buoy, exhalt, inspirit, lift, pep (up), uplift; cheer, delight, gladden, ‖send, thrill
idiom send into ecstasies
con deject, dishearten, dispirit, weigh down
ant depress

exhilarated *adj* *syn* see INTOXICATED 2
rel buoyed up, exalted, gladdened, pepped up, uplifted
idiom in ecstasies, on cloud nine
con blue, dispirited, down, low, unhappy, weighed down
ant depressed

exhilarating *adj* 1 *syn* see EXCITING
rel animating, animative, enlivening, inspiriting, invigorating, quickening; cheering, elevating, uplifting; breathtaking, electric
con deflating, disheartening, dispiriting
ant depressing

2 *syn* see INVIGORATING

exhilaration *n* *syn* see ELATION 1 compare ECSTASY
rel animation, enlivenment, firing, invigoration, quickening, stimulation, vitalization, vivification; electrification, excitation, excitement, galvanization; elevation, inspiration, uplift

exhilarative *adj* 1 *syn* see EXCITING
2 *syn* see INVIGORATING
exhort *vb syn* see URGE
rel admonish, plead; call upon, insist; stimulate
con block, deter, discourage, impede
ant inhume
exhumate *vb syn* see EXHUME
exhume *vb* to take out of a place of burial
< the body was *exhumed* and burned >
syn disinhume, disinter, exhumate, unbury, uncharnel
rel dig up, disentomb, unearth; disembalm
con bury, entomb, inter, ||plant
ant inhume
exigency *n* 1 *syn* see JUNCTURE 2
rel difficulty, hardship, rigor, vicissitude; dilemma, fix, jam, pickle, scrape; pressure, urgency
2 *syn* see NEED 4
rel demand, imperativeness, insistence, requirement; coercion, compulsion, constraint; duress, pressure, urgency
idiom matter of life and death
exigent *adj* 1 *syn* see PRESSING
rel acute; necessary; menacing, threatening
2 *syn* see ONEROUS
exiguous *adj syn* see MEAGER 2
rel diminutive, little, small, tiny; slender, slight, tenuous, thin; confined, limited, narrow, restricted, straitened
ant ample
exile *n* 1 forced removal from one's native country < a deposed king living in *exile* in Rome >
syn banishment, deportation, displacement, expulsion, ostracism, relegation
rel exclusion; extradition; expatriation; diaspora, dispersion, migration, scattering
con recall, restoration
2 *syn* see ÉMIGRÉ
rel nonperson, outcast, unperson
idiom man without a country
exile *vb syn* see BANISH
rel dispossess; evacuate; extradite; drive out
idiom turn out of house and home
con recall, restore
exist *vb* 1 *syn* see BE
2 *syn* see CONSIST 1
existence *n* 1 the state or fact of having independent reality < customs that have recently come into *existence* >
syn actuality, being
rel life; presence; reality; perseity
ant nonexistence
2 *syn* see ENTITY 1
rel essence; individuality
existent *adj* 1 *syn* see ACTUAL 1
rel existing; present
2 *syn* see EXTANT 1
3 *syn* see PRESENT
existent *n syn* see ENTITY 1
existing *adj syn* see EXTANT 1
exit *n* 1 *syn* see DEPARTURE 1
ant entry
2 *syn* see EGRESS 2
ant entrance, entry
exit *vb syn* see GO 2
idiom make an (*or* one's) exit
con arrive, come

ant enter
exiting *n syn* see DEPARTURE 1
ant entering
exodus *n syn* see DEPARTURE 1
rel emigration, migration; flight
con immigration; ingress
ant influx
ex officio *adj syn* see OFFICIAL
exonerate *vb syn* see EXCULPATE
rel disburden, free
ant incriminate
exorbitant *adj syn* see EXCESSIVE 1
rel overboard, overmuch; unwarranted; outrageous, preposterous; exacting, extortionate
idiom out of sight
con equitable, fair, just; rational, reasonable
exordium *n syn* see INTRODUCTION
rel preliminary
con afterword, conclusion, epilogue, postscript
exotic *adj* 1 not native to the place where found < *exotic* fish >
syn foreign
rel imported, introduced, naturalized; alien, extrinsic, strange
con aboriginal, autochthonous, endemic, native; domestic, local
ant indigenous
2 excitingly or enticingly different or unusual < he was moved by her *exotic* beauty >
syn romanesque, romantic, strange
rel different, unusual; alluring, enticing, fascinating, glamorous, mysterious
expand *vb* 1 *syn* see OPEN 4
2 *syn* see INCREASE 1
3 to increase or become increased in bulk, volume, or size < water *expands* when heated >
syn amplify, dilate, distend, inflate, swell
rel grow; bulk (up), enlarge, fill (out); bolster; mushroom, ||plim, puff (up)
con condense, decrease, deflate, shrink, shrivel; dwindle, lessen
ant contract
4 to express more fully and in greater detail < *expanded* his notes into an essay >
syn amplify, develop, elaborate, enlarge
rel detail, explicate; augment; discourse, expatiate
con compress, condense, contract
ant abridge
5 *syn* see INCREASE 2
6 *syn* see ESCALATE 2
rel prolong, protract
con de-escalate; circumscribe
ant limit, restrict
expanse *n* a significantly large area or range < a trackless *expanse* of moor >
syn amplitude, breadth, distance, expansion, space, spread, stretch
rel compass, extent, orbit, range, reach, scope, sweep; area, domain, field, sphere, territory; immensity, magnitude
expansion *n* 1 *syn* see EXPANSE
2 the act or process of increasing in some way < the recent *expansion* of science >
syn enlargement, extension, spread
con contraction, decrease, shrinking
expansive *adj* 1 *syn* see ELASTIC 2

rel communicative, demonstrative, extroverted, gregarious, unconstrained, unreserved, unrestrained; effusive, gushy, lavish; generous, liberal, openhanded
con austere, severe, stern; reserved, reticent, silent, taciturn
2 *syn* see DEMONSTRATIVE
ant withdrawn
3 *syn* see COMMUNICATIVE
4 *syn* see EXTENSIVE 1
rel ample, large; big, great
ant limited

expatiate *vb syn* see DISCOURSE 1
rel narrate, recite, recount, rehearse, relate; ramble

expatriate *vb syn* see BANISH
ant repatriate

expatriate *n syn* see ÉMIGRÉ
ant repatriate

expect *vb* **1** to anticipate in the mind <did not *expect* him for dinner>
syn await, count (on *or* upon), hope, look
rel anticipate, apprehend, divine, foreknow, foresee
idiom bargain on (or for), look for
ant despair (of)
2 *syn* see UNDERSTAND 3
rel feel, sense; presume, presuppose

expectancy *n* **1** the state of one who looks forward to something <had an air of wistful *expectancy*>
syn anticipation, expectation
rel presensation, presentiment
2 *syn* see EXPECTATION 2

expectant *adj* **1** characterized by expectation <an *expectant* crowd>
syn anticipant, anticipative, anticipatory, atiptoe, expecting
rel open-eyed, openmouthed; hopeful; eager; alert. watchful
con apathetic, indifferent, uninterested; unconcerned, unimpressed, unmoved
2 *syn* see PREGNANT 1
idiom anticipating a blessed event, waiting for the stork

expectation *n* **1** *syn* see EXPECTANCY 1
2 something that is expected <each had his own dreams and *expectations*>
syn expectancy
rel design, hope, intention, motive, notion; prospect

expecting *adj syn* see EXPECTANT 1
2 *syn* see PREGNANT 1

expediency *n* **1** *syn* see ORDER 11
rel propitiousness; convenience
2 *syn* see RESOURCE 3
rel design, strategy, tactic; measure, step
idiom card up one's sleeve, means to an end

expedient *adj* dictated by practical or prudential motives <decided it was not *expedient* to interfere yet>
syn advisable, politic, prudent, tactical, wise
rel advantageous, beneficial, convenient, practical, profitable, useful, utilitarian; opportune, seasonable, timely, well-timed; feasible, possible, practicable; appropriate, fit, fitting, suitable; judicious

con deleterious, detrimental; harmful, hurtful, injurious; fruitless, futile, vain; inappropriate, uncalled-for, unfitting, unsuitable; impolite, imprudent, inadvisable, injudicious, unwise
ant inexpedient

expedient *n syn* see RESOURCE 3
rel agency, instrument, instrumentality, means, medium

expedition *n* **1** *syn* see JOURNEY
rel campaign; entrada, exploration
2 *syn* see HASTE 1
rel alacrity, promptitude
con delay, retardation, slackening, slowing
ant procrastination
3 *syn* see ALACRITY
rel expeditiousness, speediness, swiftness; punctuality
con dawdling, delaying, faltering, hesitation

expeditious *adj syn* see FAST 3
rel effective, effectual, efficacious, efficient; prompt, ready
con ineffective, ineffectual, inefficacious, inefficient; dilatory, laggard, leisurely, slow
ant sluggish

expeditiously *adv syn* see FAST 2
rel effectively, efficaciously; punctually
con ineffectively; deliberately, dilatorily, leisurely, slowly
ant sluggishly

expeditiousness *n syn* see HASTE 1
expeditive *adj syn* see FAST 3

expel *vb* **1** *syn* see ERUPT 1
rel blow off, blow out, ejaculate, exhaust
2 *syn* see BANISH
rel drum out, read out; eliminate, turn out; ‖bounce
idiom give (one) the boot, give the bum's rush, give the old heave-ho, send to Coventry, throw out on one's ear
ant admit

expellee *n syn* see ÉMIGRÉ

expend *vb* **1** *syn* see SPEND 1
rel dispense, distribute; blow, exhaust, use up
idiom loose (or untie) the purse strings, open one's purse
con hoard, lay up, save
2 *syn* see GO 4

expenditure *n syn* see EXPENSE 1

expense *n* **1** something expended to secure a benefit or bring about a result <spared no *expense* in furnishing their home>
syn cost, disbursement, expenditure, outlay
2 a loss incurred in the course of gaining something <won the war at the *expense* of many lives>
syn cost, price, toll
rel decrement, forfeit, forfeiture, sacrifice; deprivation, loss

expensive *adj syn* see COSTLY 1
rel immoderate, uneconomical; big-ticket, high-priced
con economical, moderate; bargain, low-cost, low-priced, thrifty; cheap
ant inexpensive

experience *n syn* see ACQUAINTANCE 1
rel background; observation; know-how, practice, skill; savoir faire, sophistication; wisdom

---

syn synonym(s)   *rel* related word(s)
ant antonym(s)   *con* contrasted word(s)
idiom idiomatic equivalent(s)
‖ use limited; if in doubt, see a dictionary

ant inexperience

experience *vb* 1 to meet with directly (as through participation or observation) < *experience* pain > < trying to *experience* the problems of a different culture >
syn have, know, see, suffer, sustain, undergo
rel encounter, meet; accept, receive
2 *syn* see FEEL 2
rel behold, see, survey, view

experienced *adj* made skillful or wise through practice < an *experienced* sales executive >
syn old, old-time, practical, practiced, seasoned, skilled, versed, vet, veteran; *compare* PROFICIENT
rel broken in; accomplished, skillful; expert, qualified; old-line, wise
idiom having been around, knowing the score (*or* the ropes)
con apprentice, beginning, freshman, green, new, novice, raw, untested, untried
ant experienceless, inexperienced

experient *adj syn* see EMPIRICAL

experiential *adj syn* see EMPIRICAL

experiment *n* an operation or process carried out to resolve an uncertainty < *experiments* that added much to our understanding of nutritional needs >
syn experimentation, test, trial, trial and error, trial run
rel probe, research, search; examination, investigation; analysis, study

experiment *vb* to engage in experimentation < *experimenting* with regional solutions to urban problems >
syn experimentalize, experimentize, test (out), try (out), try on
rel investigate, probe, research, search; analyze, scrutinize, study, weigh
idiom play around with

experimental *adj* 1 *syn* see EMPIRICAL
2 of, relating to, or having the characteristics of experiment < *experimental* missile flights >
syn experimentative, test, trial
rel preliminary, preparatory; developmental; provisional, temporary, tentative
con tested, tried; permanent, proved, accepted, established, standard

experimentalize *vb syn* see EXPERIMENT

experimentation *n syn* see EXPERIMENT

experimentative *adj syn* see EXPERIMENTAL 2

experimentize *vb syn* see EXPERIMENT

expert *adj syn* see PROFICIENT
rel schooled, trained; adroit, deft, dexterous; pro, professional
con unpracticed; unschooled
ant amateur, inexpert

expert *n* one who has acquired special skill in or knowledge and mastery of something < a fingerprint *expert* >
syn adept, artist, artiste, authority, ‖dab, ‖dabster, doyen, master, master-hand, maven, passed master, past master, pro, professional, proficient, swell, virtuoso, whiz, wiz, wizard
rel ‖darb; specialist
con dabbler, dilettante, tyro; apprentice, novice, probationer
ant amateur

expertise *n* 1 *syn* see ABILITY 2

rel readiness; competence; skillfulness
2 *syn* see ART 1
rel quickness; cleverness, ingeniousness; finesse; savvy

expertism *n syn* see ABILITY 2

expertness *n syn* see ABILITY 2
rel prowess; facility

expiate *vb* to make amends or give satisfaction for wrong done < *expiated* his crime with his life >
syn atone
rel amend, compensate (for), correct, rectify, redress, remedy
idiom make up for, put right

expiative *adj syn* see PURGATIVE

expiatory *adj syn* see PURGATIVE

expire *vb* 1 *syn* see DIE 1
idiom draw one's last breath; give up the breath of life
con live, thrive
2 *syn* see PASS 3
3 *syn* see EXHALE
ant inspire

explain *vb* 1 to make something comprehensible or more comprehensible < a commentary that *explains* the allegory >
syn construe, explicate, expound, interpret, spell out; *compare* CLARIFY 2
rel decipher, disentangle, undo, unravel, unriddle, unscramble, untangle; analyze, break down; clear up, resolve, solve
idiom put into plain English
con confound, confuse, puzzle
ant obfuscate
2 *syn* see CLARIFY 2
3 to give the reason for or cause of < unable to *explain* his strange conduct >
syn account, explain away, justify, rationalize
rel condone, excuse; absolve, acquit, exculpate, exonerate, vindicate

explain away *vb syn* see EXPLAIN 3

explanation *n* 1 something that makes clear what is obscure < sought some *explanation* of the difficult passage >
syn construal, construction, exegesis, explication, exposé, exposition, interpretation
rel disentanglement, unscrambling; enlightenment, illumination; definition, meaning; resolution, solution; demonstration, example, exemplification, illustration
2 a statement of causes, grounds, or motives < refused an *explanation* for his act >
syn account, justification, rationale, rationalization, reason
rel grounds; motive

explanative *adj syn* see EXPLANATORY

explanatory *adj* serving to explain < *explanatory* notes in a book >
syn exegetic, explanative, explicative, explicatory, expositional, expositive, expository, interpretive
rel enlightening, illuminating; discursive; demonstrative, illustrative
con baffling, bewildering, confusing, misleading, mystifying, puzzling
ant obfuscatory

expletive *n syn* see SWEARWORD

explicate *vb syn* see EXPLAIN 1
rel amplify, develop, dilate, enlarge (upon), expand, expatiate; demonstrate

idiom dot the *i*'s (and cross the *t*'s)

explication *n syn* see EXPLANATION 1
  rel amplification, development, enlargement, expansion, expatiation

explicative *adj syn* see EXPLANATORY
  rel annotative, exemplificative, scholiastic

explicatory *adj syn* see EXPLANATORY

explicit *adj* characterized by full precise expression < gave the guard *explicit* orders about whom to admit >
  syn categorical, clean-cut, clear-cut, definite, definitive, express, specific, unambiguous
  rel certain, clear, distinct, lucid, perspicuous, plain, sure, understandable, unequivocal; accurate, correct, exact, precise
  con cryptic, dark, enigmatic, equivocal, obscure, unclear, vague; implicit, implied, inferred; imprecise, inaccurate, incorrect, inexact
  ant ambiguous

explicitly *adv syn* see EXPRESSLY 1

explode *vb* 1 to burst violently and noisily usually due to pressure within < the bomb *exploded* >
  syn blow up, burst, detonate, go off, mushroom
  rel blast, discharge
  idiom blow sky-high, blow to kingdom come
  con fail, fizzle, peter (out)
  2 *syn* see ERUPT 2
  rel flame (up), flare (up)
  idiom blow a fuse (or gasket)
  3 *syn* see DISCREDIT 2
  rel invalidate; deflate
  idiom shoot full of holes

exploit *n* 1 *syn* see ADVENTURE
  rel effort, job; maneuver
  2 *syn* see FEAT 2
  rel do, performance, stunt; blow, coup, stroke
  idiom bold stroke

exploit *vb* 1 *syn* see USE 2
  rel cultivate, work
  2 to take unfair advantage of < *exploits* his friend's good nature >
  syn abuse, impose (on *or* upon), use
  rel manipulate; bleed, fleece, skin, soak, stick
  3 *syn* see MANIPULATE 2

explore *vb* to search through or into < *explored* the possibilities of reaching an agreement >
  syn delve (into), dig (into), go (into), inquire (into), investigate, look (into), probe, prospect, sift
  rel burrow, mouse (out); quarry, search; examine, test, try; inquisite, question
  idiom nose around

explosion *n syn* see OUTBURST 1

exponent *n* one who actively promotes or backs something < an *exponent* of arbitration in labor disputes >
  syn advocate, champion, expounder, proponent, supporter
  rel backer, booster, partisan, promoter, protagonist; defender, upholder

---

con antagonist, enemy; opposition
  ant opponent

expose *vb* 1 to make accessible to something detrimental or dangerous < he needlessly *exposed* his troops to enemy fire >
  syn lay (open), subject, uncover
  rel endanger, hazard, imperil, jeopard, jeopardize, jeopardy, peril, risk
  idiom put (or leave) in harm's way
  con cover, shelter; guard, protect
  ant shield
  2 *syn* see OPEN 2
  rel unfold, unshroud
  3 *syn* see SHOW 4
  rel advertise, air, broadcast, publish
  4 to reveal the faults, frailties, unsoundness, or pretensions of < the monograph *exposed* the theory as being pure myth >
  syn debunk, discover, show up, uncloak, undress, unmask, unshroud
  rel disclose, reveal, uncover
  idiom lay bare

exposé *n syn* see EXPLANATION 1

exposed *adj syn* see OPEN 2
  rel apparent, evident, manifest; unconcealed, unhidden; revealed; visible
  idiom laid bare
  con covered, enveloped, sheathed
  2 *syn* see LIABLE 2
  rel likely; menaced, threatened
  con defended, guarded, protected, safeguarded, shielded

exposition *n* 1 *syn* see EXPLANATION 1
  rel presentation; discourse, discussion, disquisition, expounding; statement; delineation, enunciation
  2 *syn* see EXHIBITION 2
  rel display, production

expositional *adj syn* see EXPLANATORY

expositive *adj syn* see EXPLANATORY
  rel depictive, descriptive, graphic; illuminative; delineative

expository *adj syn* see EXPLANATORY
  rel disquisitional; critical

expostulate *vb syn* see OBJECT 1
  rel combat, fight, oppose, resist; argue, debate, discuss, dispute
  idiom raise one's voice against

exposure *n* the condition of being exposed to something detrimental < *exposure* to attack >
  syn liability, openness, vulnerability, vulnerableness
  rel susceptibility, susceptiveness, susceptivity; defenselessness, helplessness, unprotection; danger, jeopardy, peril, risk
  con bulwark, cover, protection, safeguard, shelter, shield, shielding

expound *vb syn* see EXPLAIN 1
  rel express, present, state; comment, discourse; clarify, delineate, describe, exemplify, illustrate

expounder *n syn* see EXPONENT
  rel explainer, expositor

express *adj* 1 *syn* see EXPLICIT
  rel expressed, uttered, voiced; out-and-out, unmistakable; unconditional, unqualified
  con unexpressed, unsaid, unstated; ambiguous, equivocal; conditional, qualified
  2 of a particular or exact sort < came for the *express* purpose of buying a car >
  syn especial, set, special, specific

rel individual; definite, particular; explicit; intended, intentional, premeditated
ant vague

express *vb* 1 *syn* see WORD
2 to give expression to (as a thought, an opinion, or an emotion) <*expressed* his views freely>
syn air, give, put, state, vent, ventilate; *compare* SAY 1, WORD
rel broach, circulate, put about; disclose; tell; frame; enunciate; phrase; announce, declare, proclaim, pronounce; discharge, drain
con hint, insinuate, intimate, suggest
ant imply
3 *syn* see MEAN 2
rel communicate, convey, impart
4 *syn* see PRESS 3

expression *n* 1 an act, process, or instance of expressing in words <his anger found *expression* in a string of oaths>
syn statement, utterance, vent, voice
rel issue; manifestation, representation; observation, reflection
con hint, insinuation, intimation, suggestion
2 *syn* see PHRASE 2
rel word; verbalism; idiom; clause
3 one thing that calls to mind another often symbolically <sent flowers as an *expression* of sympathy>
syn gesture, indication, reminder, sign, token
rel embodiment, manifestation, representation, symbol; demonstration, show
4 *syn* see ELOQUENCE
rel graphicness, vividness
5 *syn* see LOOK 2

expressionless *adj* lacking expression <cold *expressionless* eyes>
syn blank, deadpan, empty, inexpressive, unexpressive, vacant
rel dull, lackluster, lusterless, vacuous; impassive, inscrutable, stolid, wooden; dead
con lustrous; responsive; alive, vital
ant expressive

expressive *adj* clearly conveying or manifesting something <a forceful and *expressive* word>
syn eloquent, facund, meaningful, pregnant, rich, sententious, significant
rel revealing, revelatory, suggestive; graphic, pictorial, vivid; alive, demonstrative, lively, responsive, senseful, spirited
con banal, commonplace, drab, dull, flat, jejune, inane, insipid, vacuous, vapid; impassive, indifferent; austere, severe, stern, stiff, wooden; blank, deadpan, empty, expressionless, vacant; dead
ant inexpressive, unexpressive

expressiveness *n* *syn* see ELOQUENCE
ant inexpressiveness

expressivity *n* *syn* see ELOQUENCE

expressly *adv* 1 in direct and unmistakable terms <his beliefs *expressly* repudiate the church's teachings>
syn categorically, definitely, explicitly, specifically
rel directly; unmistakably
con ambiguously, equivocally; conditionally; likely, possibly, probably

2 for the express purpose <programs designed *expressly* to serve immediate political objectives>
syn especially, in specie, specially, specifically
3 *syn* see EVEN 1

expropriate *vb* *syn* see APPROPRIATE 1
rel dispossess; take (away)

expulse *vb* *syn* see BANISH
rel ||bounce; eject
con admit, receive

expulsion *n* *syn* see EXILE 1
rel driving out, forcing out; ejection, ousting; removal
idiom the boot, the old heave-ho

expunge *vb* *syn* see ERASE
rel discard, drop, exclude, omit; annihilate, eradicate

expurgate *vb* 1 *syn* see PURIFY 2
2 *syn* see CENSOR

expurgation *n* *syn* see PURIFICATION

expurgatorial *adj* *syn* see PURGATIVE

expurgatory *adj* *syn* see PURGATIVE

exquisite *adj* 1 *syn* see CHOICE
rel consummate, finished; faultless, flawless, impeccable
2 *syn* see IMPECCABLE 1
rel superb, superlative
con faulty, flawed, imperfect
3 *syn* see INTENSE 1
rel acute, extreme; consummate, transcending

exquisite *n* *syn* see FOP

exsect *vb* *syn* see EXCISE

exsiccate *vb* *syn* see DRY 1

extant *adj* 1 that is in existence <the most talented writer *extant*>
syn alive, around, existent, existing, living
con dead, defunct, destroyed, exterminated, extinct; departed, gone, lost
ant nonextant
2 *syn* see ACTUAL 1
rel current, immediate, present
con possible, potential
3 *syn* see PRESENT

extemporaneous *adj* composed, devised, or done at the moment rather than beforehand <made an *extemporaneous* speech after the dinner>
syn autoschediastic, extemporary, extempore, impromptu, improvised, offhand, spur-of-the-moment, unrehearsed, unstudied; *compare* UNINTENTIONAL
rel casual, informal; unprepared, unthought-out; impulsive, snap, spontaneous
idiom off the cuff, on the spur of the moment
con designed, planned, prepared, projected, schemed, thought-out; considered, deliberated, premeditated, studied

extemporary *adj* *syn* see EXTEMPORANEOUS

extempore *adj* *syn* see EXTEMPORANEOUS

extemporization *n* *syn* see IMPROVISATION

extemporize *vb* *syn* see IMPROVISE
rel dash off, knock off, toss off
idiom do offhand, play (it) by ear
con cook up, plan, prepare, think out

extend *vb* 1 *syn* see OPEN 4
con close, fold
2 *syn* see OFFER 1

rel allocate, allot; accord, advance, award, bestow, confer, grant; donate
idiom place at one's disposal
3 to make or become longer < *extended* his visit by a week >
syn draw, draw out, elongate, lengthen, prolong, prolongate, protract, spin (out), stretch
rel amplify, enlarge, expand, increase
con abridge; curtail
ant shorten
4 *syn* see INCREASE 1
5 *syn* see RUN 8
rel advance, proceed; continue
6 *syn* see RANGE 3
7 to reach a certain point < his education doesn't *extend* beyond elementary school >
syn go
rel reach, run; advance; attain
extended *adj* **1** *syn* see LONG 1
rel prolonged, protracted, spread out, stretched out (or forth)
ant contracted
2 *syn* see EXTENSIVE 1
rel far-flung, widespread
con narrow; inextensive
ant unextended
extension *n* **1** the act or state of extending or being extended < a one-month *extension* of the price freeze seems likely >
syn elongation, lengthening, production, prolongation, prolongment, protraction
rel continuation, continuing; drawing out, stretch, stretch-out
con abridgment, shortening; contraction, curtailment, shrinking
2 *syn* see EXPANSION 2
rel augmentation, increase; spreading out
con abridgment, curtailment; reduction
ant contraction
3 *syn* see RANGE 2
rel magnitude, size, spread; comprehensiveness
4 *syn* see ANNEX
extensity *n* *syn* see RANGE 2
extensive *adj* **1** widely ranging in scope or application < *extensive* privileges >
syn broad, expansive, extended, scopic, scopious, wide
rel comprehensive, general, inclusive; far-reaching, far-spreading, spacious, wide-ranging; all-encompassing, all-inclusive, blanket, boundless, indiscriminate, unrestricted, wholesale
con circumscribed, constricted, limited, narrow, restricted; unextended
2 *syn* see BIG 1
con little, small
extent *n* **1** *syn* see RANGE 2
rel domain, field, province, sphere
2 *syn* see SIZE 1
rel compass, extension, orbit, radius, reach, scope, sweep
3 *syn* see ORDER 4
extenuate *vb* **1** *syn* see THIN 1
rel mitigate; moderate, qualify, temper
con aggravate, enhance, heighten

---

syn synonym(s)   *rel* related word(s)
ant antonym(s)   *con* contrasted word(s)
idiom idiomatic equivalent(s)
|| use limited; if in doubt, see a dictionary

2 *syn* see PALLIATE
rel explain, justify, rationalize; apologize
idiom put a gloss on (or upon or over), put a good face upon
exterior *adj* *syn* see OUTER
rel outermost, outmost
con inner, ingrained, inherent, intrinsic
ant interior
exteriorize *vb* *syn* see EMBODY 1
ant interiorize
exterminate *vb* **1** *syn* see ANNIHILATE 2
rel finish off; execute; kill (off)
idiom do away with, put an end to, put out of the way
2 *syn* see SLAUGHTER 3
idiom wipe off the face of the earth, wipe off the map
external *adj* *syn* see OUTER
rel out, outermost, outmost, peripheral
con ingrained, inherent, intrinsic
ant internal
externalize *vb* *syn* see EMBODY 1
ant internalize
extinct *adj* **1** *syn* see DEAD 1
2 that has died out altogether < an *extinct* civilization >
syn bygone, dead, defunct, departed, gone, lost, vanished
rel nonexistent; collapsed, fallen, overthrown; disappeared
idiom gone from the face of the earth
con existent, existing, living; active; contemporary, current
ant extant
3 *syn* see OBSOLETE
rel antiquated, archaic, old-fashioned
con modern; contemporary
ant current
extinguish *vb* **1** to cause to cease burning < firemen *extinguishing* the blaze >
syn douse, ||dout, out, put out, quench, ||squench
rel blow out, snuff out; smother
con fire, kindle, start; torch
ant ignite
2 *syn* see ANNIHILATE 2
rel erase, expunge, obliterate
3 *syn* see CRUSH 5
rel check; smother, stifle; snuff (out); choke (out), trample (down)
idiom put the lid (or the kibosh) on
con encourage, fire (up)
ant inflame
extinguishment *n* *syn* see REPRESSION 1
extirpate *vb* **1** *syn* see ANNIHILATE 2
rel efface, erase, expunge, demolish, destroy, raze; kill off
con breed, engender, generate, propagate
2 *syn* see EXCISE
extol *vb* *syn* see PRAISE 2
idiom beat the drum for, make much of
ant decry
extort *vb* **1** to obtain something by pressure or intimidation < racketeers *extorting* protection money >
syn exact, gouge, pinch, screw, shake down, squeeze, wrench, wrest, wring; compare CHEAT, FLEECE 1
rel demand; coerce, force; extract, get, obtain, secure; bleed, fleece, skin
idiom bleed one white, make one pay through the nose, put the screws to
2 *syn* see EDUCE 1

extra *adj syn* see SUPERFLUOUS
rel added, additional, supplemental, supplementary

extra *adv* to a degree or extent beyond the usual < she was *extra* smart >
syn extremely, rarely, ||uncommon, uncommonly, unusually
rel especially; particularly; considerably, markedly, noticeably
con barely, scarcely

extract *vb* 1 to draw out forcibly or with effort < *extract* a confession > < *extract* a tooth >
syn evulse, pull, tear, yank
rel pry; avulse
2 *syn* see EKE OUT 3
3 *syn* see GLEAN
4 *syn* see EDUCE 1
5 *syn* see EXCERPT
rel abridge, condense, shorten

extraction *n syn* see ANCESTRY

extraneous *adj* 1 *syn* see EXTRINSIC
rel accidental, adventitious, incidental
con constitutional, ingrained, inherent; germane, material, pertinent
2 *syn* see IRRELEVANT
rel incidental; unessential; unrelated; pointless; inappropriate
idiom beside the point
ant relevant

extraordinary *adj syn* see EXCEPTIONAL 1
rel amazing; stupendous, terrific, wonderful
idiom out of the ordinary
con customary, normal, regular, usual
ant ordinary

extravagance *n* 1 *syn* see LUXURY
2 the quality, state, fact, or an instance of being extravagant < by living simply and avoiding *extravagance* they saved enough for the trip >
syn extravagancy, lavishness, overdoing, prodigality, squander, unthrift, waste, wastefulness
rel improvidence, spendthriftness; excess, indulgence, overindulgence
con moderation, temperateness; care, forehandedness, frugality, austerity
ant economy

extravagancy *n syn* see EXTRAVAGANCE 2

extravagant *adj* 1 grossly exaggerated < *extravagant* accusations >
syn fantastic, preposterous, wild
rel unbalanced, unrestrained; absurd, foolish, ludicrous, nonsensical, ridiculous, silly; bizarre, crazy; exaggerated, implausible
con plausible, sensible; restrained
ant reasonable
2 *syn* see EXCESSIVE 1
rel exuberant, lavish, profuse; prodigal, profligate, wasteful
con economical, frugal, sparing
ant restrained

extreme *adj* 1 very great < the project demanded *extreme* secrecy >
syn utmost, uttermost
2 *syn* see ARDENT 2
rel deep, moving
3 departing sharply from the traditional or usual < *extreme* political views >

syn extremist, fanatic, rabid, radical, revolutional, revolutionary, revolutionist, ultra, ultraist; *compare* OUTLANDISH 3
rel excessive, immoderate; desperate, drastic; extravagant, unreasonable; violent, wild
con conservative, moderate, restrained; reasonable, sensible
4 *syn* see EXCESSIVE 1
rel intolerable, unwarranted
5 most distant from a center < the *extreme* edge of the city >
syn farthest, furthermost, furthest, outermost, outmost, remotest, utmost, uttermost

extreme *n* 1 an extreme state or condition < an *extreme* of poverty >
syn extremity
rel excess, inordinancy
2 something situated at or marking one end or the other of a range < *extremes* of heat and cold >
syn extremity, limit
rel climax, consummation, culmination; ceiling, crest, crown, height; peak, pinnacle, summit, top; maximum, utmost, uttermost

extremely *adv* 1 *syn* see EVER 6
2 *syn* see VERY 1
3 *syn* see EXTRA

extremist *n syn* see RADICAL

extremist *adj syn* see EXTREME 3

extremity *n* 1 *syn* see EXTREME 2
rel acme, apex, apogee, vertex, zenith
2 *syn* see EXTREME 1

extricate *vb* 1 *syn* see KNOW 4
2 to free from an undesirable situation or condition < *extricate* himself from financial difficulties >
syn clear, clear away, discumber, disembarrass, disembroil, disencumber, disentangle, disentwine, unentangle, unscramble, untangle, untie, untwine
rel unravel; abstract, detach, disengage; disburden, disemburden; deliver, disinvolve, free, liberate, release, rescue; resolve
con embroil, entangle, tangle; clog, fetter, hog-tie, manacle, shackle, trammel; block, hamper, hinder, impede, obstruct

extrinsic *adj* not properly part of a thing < a point *extrinsic* to his basic thesis >
syn alien, extraneous, foreign
rel acquired, gained; exterior, external, outer, outside, outward
con native; inner, inside, interior, internal, inward; individual, personal
ant intrinsic

extrude *vb syn* see EJECT 1

exuberance *n syn* see EBULLIENCE
rel gayness; friskiness, life, liveliness, sprightliness, zest, zestfulness; abandon, ardor

exuberancy *n syn* see EBULLIENCE

exuberant *adj* 1 joyously unrestrained and enthusiastic < his warm *exuberant* personality >
syn brash, ebullient, effervescent, high-spirited, vivacious
rel gay, lively, spirited, sprightly, zestful; frolicsome; ardent, passionate
con constrained, inhibited, repressed, restrained, subdued; calm, impassive, quiet
ant austere

2 *syn* see PROFUSE

rel fecund, fertile, fruitful, prolific; rampant, rank; diffuse

con scant, scanty, spare

exude *vb* to flow slowly out < a sticky resin *exuded* from the bark >

syn bleed, ooze, percolate, ‖screeve, seep, ‖sew, ‖sicker, strain, sweat, transude, weep

rel emanate; discharge, emit; trickle

exult *vb* to rejoice especially with feelings or display of triumph or self-satisfaction < the team were *exulting* in their victory >

syn delight, glory, jubilate, triumph

rel rejoice; celebrate; boast, brag, crow, show off

con lament, mourn

ant bemoan

exultance *n* *syn* see EXULTATION

exultant *adj* manifesting proud elation < *exultant* over his successes >

syn cock-a-hoop, cock-a-whoop, exulting, jubilant, triumphal, triumphant

rel happy, joyous, overjoyed; delighting, rejoicing; elated, flushed

idiom in high feather

con depressed, mournful, unhappy

exultation *n* the act of exulting or the state of being exultant < the *exultation* of victory and the thrill of power >

syn exultance, jubilance, jubilation, triumph

rel delight, elation, satisfaction; celebration, rejoicing; gloating

exulting *adj* *syn* see EXULTANT

exuviate *vb* *syn* see SHED 2

eye *n* 1 an organ of sight < turned his *eyes* to the view >

syn lamp, ocular, oculus, ‖ogle, orb, peeper, winker

2 the faculty of seeing with or as if with the eyes < had a keen *eye* for details >

syn eyesight, seeing, sight, vision

3 very close watching or observation < kept an *eye* on him >

syn eagle eye, scrutiny, surveillance, tab, watch

4 often eyes *pl* a way of looking at something < in the *eyes* of the law, a man is innocent until proven guilty >

syn view, viewpoint; compare VIEWPOINT 2

rel attitude, position, thinking; conception, grasp; conclusion, judgment

5 *syn* see OPINION

6 *syn* see LOOP 1

7 *syn* see LOOP 2

‖8 *syn* see DETECTIVE

eye *vb* 1 to fix the eyes on < the child *eyed* the presents with delight >

syn consider, contemplate, gaze (upon), look (at or upon), view; compare LOOK 7

rel regard; stare (at)

2 to keep a close watch on < the detective *eyed* the suspect >

syn eyeball, scrutinize, watch; compare TAIL

rel stare (at); size up

idiom keep a close (or an eagle) eye on

3 *syn* see LOOK 7

eyeball *vb* *syn* see EYE 2

eye-catching *adj* *syn* see NOTICEABLE

eyeful *n* *syn* see BEAUTY

eyeless *adj* *syn* see BLIND 1

eye-popping *adj* *syn* see EXCITING

eyesight *n* *syn* see EYE 2

eyesore *n* something offensive to the sight < the old abandoned house was a neighborhood *eyesore* >

syn desight, fright, mess, monstrosity, sight

eyewash *n* *syn* see NONSENSE 2

eyewitness *n* *syn* see SPECTATOR

F

fable *n* 1 *syn* see FICTION

2 *syn* see ALLEGORY 2

fabric *n* 1 *syn* see BUILDING

2 *syn* see TEXTURE 2

fabricate *vb* *syn* see MAKE 3

rel turn out; create, formulate, invent; concoct, contrive, devise

fabrication *n* *syn* see FICTION

rel creation; deceit, fib; artifact, opus, product, production, work

fabulous *adj* *syn* see MYTHICAL

rel amazing, astonishing, astounding, incredible, marvelous, unbelievable, wonderful; exorbitant, extravagant, inordinate, outrageous, preposterous; monstrous, prodigious, stupendous

con believable, colorable, credible

---

facade *n* *syn* see MASK 2

face *n* 1 the front part of the head including the eyes, nose, mouth, cheeks, chin, and usually forehead < hid his *face* from the camera >

syn countenance, ‖dial, features, ‖kisser, ‖map, mug, ‖mush, muzzle, ‖pan, phiz, ‖puss, visage

rel lineaments, physiognomy

2 *syn* see LOOK 2

3 *syn* see APPEARANCE 2

4 *syn* see MASK 2

5 *syn* see EFFRONTERY

6 a distortion of the face usually as an expression of contempt or distaste < the old man made a *face* at the flat beer >

syn grimace, moue, mouth, mouthing, mow, mug

rel frown, glower, lower, pout, scowl

idiom wry face, wry mouth

con grin, simper, smile, smirk

7 *syn* see MAKEUP 3

8 *syn* see TOP 2

face vb 1 to have the face or front in a specified direction <the house *faces* toward the river>
syn front, look
rel border, meet
ant back

2 *syn* see MEET 6
rel watch; gaze, glare, stare; await, expect, look (for)

3 to confront with courage or boldness <ready to *face* his accusers>
syn ||banter, beard, brave, challenge, dare, defy, ||double-dog dare, front, outdare, outface, venture
rel confront, encounter, meet; oppose, resist, withstand; contend, fight
idiom brazen it out, face the music, face up to, take the bull by the horns
con elude, escape, eschew, evade, shun
ant avoid

4 *syn* see CONFRONT 1

5 *syn* see ACCOST 2
rel beard, brave, challenge, dare, defy
idiom stand up to

6 *syn* see ENGAGE 5

7 *syn* see SHEATHE

facet n *syn* see PHASE
rel face, front

facetious adj *syn* see WITTY
rel jesting, joking, quipping, wisecracking; blithe, jocund, jolly, jovial, merry; comic, comical, droll, funny, laughable, ludicrous
con grave, serious, sober, solemn, somber
ant lugebrious

facile adj *syn* see EASY 1
rel adroit, deft, dexterous; fluent, glib, voluble; cursory, shallow, superficial, uncritical
con awkward, clumsy, constrained, cumbersome, labored, maladroit; tongue-tied; deep, profound, thorough
ant arduous

facilely adv *syn* see EASILY 1
ant arduously

facilitate vb *syn* see EASE 3

facility n 1 *syn* see READINESS 3
rel skill, wit; aptitude, bent, leaning, propensity, turn; abandon, spontaneity, unconstraint; address, poise, tact; effortlessness, lightness, smoothness
con awkwardness, clumsiness, ineptness, maladroitness; rigidity, stiffness, woodenness; effort, exertion, pains

2 *syn* see AMENITY 2
rel accommodation, advantage, aid, fitting
con difficulty, hardship, inconvenience

facing prep 1 *syn* see AGAINST 1
con side by side

2 *syn* see BEFORE 2

facsimile n *syn* see REPRODUCTION
con archetype, model, original, pattern, prototype, standard

fact n 1 the quality of being actual <the realm of *fact* is distinct from fancy>
syn actuality, reality
rel authenticity, genuineness, truth
con fancy, fantasy, fiction

2 something that has actual existence <stubborn *facts* that cannot be confuted>
syn event, phenomenon

rel circumstance, detail, episode, particular; happening, incident, occurrence; observable
con contingency, eventuality, hope, possibility, potentiality, probability
ant illusion

faction n *syn* see COMBINATION 2
rel camp, offshoot, wing
idiom splinter group

factious adj *syn* see INSUBORDINATE
rel contending, fighting, warring; belligerent, contentious, quarrelsome; alienated, disaffected, estranged
con companionable, gregarious, social; acquiescent, compliant; faithful, loyal, true
ant cooperative

factitious adj *syn* see SYNTHETIC
rel affected, assumed, counterfeited, false, feigned, forced, pretended, sham, shammed, simulated
con authentic, bona fide, genuine, veritable; artless, naive, simple, spontaneous
ant natural

factor n 1 *syn* see ELEMENT 2
rel antecedent, cause, determinant; agency, agent, instrument, instrumentality, means

2 *syn* see AGENT 2
rel bailiff, majordomo, seneschal, steward; adjutant, aid, assistant, coadjutor, helper

factory n an establishment for the manufacturing of goods <a shoe *factory*>
syn manufactory, mill, plant, works

factual adj *syn* see ACTUAL 2
rel certain, undoubted, veritable; authentic, legitimate, unquestionable, valid
con erroneous, false, questionable, wrong
ant illusory

facultative adj *syn* see OPTIONAL

faculty n 1 *syn* see GIFT 2
rel instinct; property, quality; leaning, penchant, proclivity, propensity; predilection
con inability, incapability, incapacity, ineptness

2 *syn* see POWER 3

facund adj *syn* see EXPRESSIVE

facundity n *syn* see ELOQUENCE

fad n *syn* see FASHION 3
rel caprice, conceit, fancy, vagary, whim, whimsy
con custom, habit, practice, usage

fade vb 1 *syn* see FAIL 1

2 *syn* see DULL 1

3 *syn* see VANISH
rel deliquesce, dissolve, melt; abate, diminish, dwindle, ebb, lessen, moderate, wane; attenuate, rarefy, thin
idiom fade like a shadow
con intensify; eternalize, immortalize, perpetuate

faded adj *syn* see SHABBY 1
rel haggard, washed-out, wasted, worn; dim, murky; achromatic, colorless; ashen, pale, pallid, wan
con energetic, lusty, vigorous; colorful; vivid

fag n *syn* see CIGARETTE

fag vb *syn* see EXHAUST 4
con refresh, relax, rest, restore

fag n *syn* see HOMOSEXUAL

faggot n *syn* see HOMOSEXUAL

fail vb 1 to lose strength, power, vitality, or intensity <his health *failed* and he retired early>
syn decline, deteriorate, ||dwine, fade, flag, languish, weaken
rel jade, sink, slip, waste (away), worsen
idiom go downhill, hit the skids
con better, improve, strengthen
2 to become used up <food *failed* before they got back to civilization>
syn give out, run out
rel dwindle, shrink, wane
3 to be or become inadequate or deficient <the spring gradually *failed* as the drought persisted>
syn dwindle, shrink, wane, waste (away), weaken
rel decrease, diminish, lessen; give out, run out; short
idiom be found wanting
con appreciate, gain, grow, increase, wax
4 to be less than adequate or successful <the attack *failed*>
syn ||flop, flummox, wash out
rel bankrupt, bomb, deplete, drain, exhaust, impoverish; bust out, flunk, ||spin
idiom come to grief, fall flat (*or* short), go on the rocks, ||lay an egg, ||take the count
ant succeed
5 to be unable to meet financial engagements <the bank *failed*>
syn break, bust, crash, fold
rel gazette; close, end, finish, terminate
idiom be ruined, go bankrupt, go broke, go on the rocks, go to the wall, go under
con boom, prosper
6 **syn** see NEGLECT
idiom be found wanting, come (*or* fall) short of

failing n 1 **syn** see FAULT 2
rel imperfection, shortcoming
idiom weak point

failing adj **syn** see SHORT 3

failure n 1 omission of performance of an action or task <the mechanic's *failure* to adjust the brakes>
syn default, delinquency, dereliction, neglect, oversight
rel laxity, negligence, remissness, slackness; indifference, unconcern
con accomplishment, achievement, discharge, effectuation, fulfillment
2 lack of satisfactory performance or effect <the *failure* of the candidate in the election>
syn defeat, insuccess, nonsuccess, unsuccess, unsuccessfulness
rel failing, fault, imperfection, shortcoming
idiom no go
ant success
3 the fact or state of being inadequate <the crop *failure* brought on a near famine>
syn defalcation, deficiency, deficit, inadequacy, insufficience, insufficiency, lack, scantiness, shortage, underage; *compare* ABSENCE, SCARCITY

rel inferiority, meagerness, poorness, skimpiness; dearth, paucity
con abundance, adequacy, sufficiency
4 a marked weakening <felt a warning *failure* of physical strength>
syn declination, decline, deterioration, ebbing, waning
rel debilitation, enfeeblement, exhaustion, flagging, weakness
con improvement; invigoration, revitalization, strengthening
5 one that has failed <he is a *failure* in school because of inattention>
syn bomb, bust, dud, flop, lemon, loser
rel botch, fiasco, fizzle, hash, muddle, washout; might-have-been
ant success

fain adj **syn** see WILLING 1

faineant n **syn** see SLUGGARD

faineant adj **syn** see LAZY
rel apathetic, impassive, phlegmatic
con active, energetic, vigorous; busy, industrious

faint adj 1 **syn** see GENTLE 1
2 scarcely or imperfectly perceptible <he had only a *faint* idea of how he could help>
syn blear, bleary, dim, fuzzy, ill-defined, indistinct, obscure, shadowy, unclear, undefined, undetermined, undistinct, vague; *compare* OBSCURE 3
rel blurred, dusty, pale, wan, weak; hushed, inaudible, low, muffled, small, soft, stifled, thin
con bright, distinct, evident, obvious, patent, unmistakable; certain, sure
ant clear

faint n the act or condition of losing consciousness <was so frightened she fell into a *faint*>
syn blackout, coma, swoon, syncope
rel grayout, swim; dizziness, vertigo
idiom a dead faint

faint vb to lose consciousness <*fainted* at the sight of blood>
syn black out, ||crap out, pass out, ||swarf, ||swelt, swoon
rel gray out
idiom faint dead away, fall in a faint, go out like a light, pass out cold

faintly adv **syn** see SOTTO VOCE

fair adj 1 **syn** see BEAUTIFUL
rel dainty, delicate, exquisite; charming, enchanting; chaste, pure
con ill-favored, ugly
ant foul
2 not stormy <a *fair* day>
syn clarion, clear, cloudless, fine, pleasant, rainless, sunny, sunshine, sunshining, sunshiny, unclouded, undarkened
rel calm, placid, tranquil, unthreatening; balmy, clement, mild, pretty
con overcast, stormy, threatening
3 of light complexion <*fair* people often sunburn badly>
syn blond, light
rel ruddy, tawny
con brunet, dark, swarthy
4 characterized by honesty, justice, and freedom from improper influence <a *fair* decision by the judge>
syn candid, dispassionate, equal, equitable, impartial, impersonal, indifferent, just, nondiscriminatory, nonpartisan, objective,

---

square, unbiased, uncolored, undistinctive, unprejudiced, unprepossessed
rel detached, disinterested; balanced, rational, reasonable, sane; open-minded, straight
con biased, inequitable, partial, partisan, prejudiced, prepossessed, unjust
ant unfair
5 observing the rules < a *fair* fight >
syn clean, sportsmanlike, sportsmanly
rel decent, honest, lawful
con dirty, dishonest, fixed
ant unfair
6 *syn* see EVEN 3
7 *syn* see MEDIUM
rel common, ordinary
con choice, good, prime, right; bad, poor, wrong
fair *n* *syn* see EXHIBITION 2
rel carnival, festival
fair–haired *adj* *syn* see FAVORITE 1
fairish *adj* *syn* see MEDIUM
fairly *adv* 1 *syn* see ENOUGH 2
2 *syn* see SOMEWHAT 2
fairy *n* a benevolent mythical being < children who believe in *fairies* >
syn brownie, elf, fay, nisse, pixie, sprite
rel gremlin, imp, leprechaun, puck; dwarf, gnome, goblin, kobold
con ogre, troll
fairyland *n* *syn* see UTOPIA
faith *n* 1 *syn* see BELIEF 1
con dubiety, dubiosity, skepticism, uncertainty
2 *syn* see TRUST 1
con disbelief, incredulity, unbelief; apprehension, misgiving
3 *syn* see RELIGION 1
4 *syn* see RELIGION 2
rel doctrines, dogmas, tenets
faithful *adj* 1 firm in adherence to whatever one is bound to by duty or promise < a *faithful* public official, conscientious and above reproach >
syn allegiant, ardent, constant, ‖dinky-di, fast, liege, loyal, resolute, staunch, steadfast, steady, true
rel dependable, reliable, tried, trustworthy; affectionate, devoted, loving; dyed-in-the-wool
con disloyal, false, perfidious, traitorous, treacherous; fickle, inconstant, unstable
ant faithless
2 *syn* see TRUE 3
idiom at one with, on all fours with
3 *syn* see AUTHENTIC 1
faithfulness *n* 1 *syn* see ATTACHMENT 1
2 *syn* see FIDELITY 1
faithless *adj* not true to allegiance or duty < a *faithless* husband >
syn disloyal, false, perfidious, recreant, traitorous, treacherous, unfaithful, unloyal, untrue
rel capricious, fickle, inconstant, unstable; fluctuating, wavering; changeable, changeful
con constant, loyal, resolute, staunch, steadfast, true
ant faithful
faithlessness *n* 1 *syn* see TREACHERY
2 *syn* see INFIDELITY
fake *vb* *syn* see ASSUME 4
fake *n* *syn* see IMPOSTURE

2 *syn* see IMPOSTOR
fake *adj* 1 *syn* see COUNTERFEIT
rel fabricated, forged; concocted, framed, invented
con bona fide, genuine
2 *syn* see FICTITIOUS 2
faker *n* *syn* see IMPOSTOR
rel cheat, cheater, cozener, defrauder, swindler
fall *vb* 1 to pass downward < fruit *falling* off a tree > < the temperature *fell* sharply >
syn descend, drop, lower
rel decline, dip, plummet, sink; decrease, diminish, lessen; dangle, drag, droop, trail
ant rise
2 to come down suddenly and involuntarily < *fell* on the ice >
syn drop, go down, keel (over), pitch, plunge, slump, topple, tumble
rel slip, sprawl, stumble, trip
idiom come a cropper, take a header, take a spill
con ascend, climb
3 to suffer ruin, defeat, or failure < the city *fell* after a long siege >
syn go down, go under, submit, succumb, surrender
rel give up, yield
con endure, prevail, resist; conquer, triumph, vanquish, win
4 *syn* see ABATE 4
ant rise
5 *syn* see PLUMMET
fall (off *or* away) *vb* *syn* see SLIP 6
fall (on *or* upon) *vb* *syn* see ATTACK 1
fall *n* 1 *syn* see DESCENT 1
2 *syn* see DESCENT 3
3 *usu* **falls** *pl but sing or pl in constr* *syn* see WATERFALL
fallacious *adj* 1 *syn* see ILLOGICAL
ant valid, sound
2 *syn* see MISLEADING
ant veritable
fallaciousness *n* *syn* see FALLACY 1
rel ambiguity, equivocation; deception, deluding, misleading; faultiness, illogicality, unreasonableness
ant soundness, validity
fallacy *n* 1 a false or erroneous idea < his argument is based on a *fallacy* >
syn erroneousness, error, fallaciousness, falsehood, falseness, falsity, untruth
rel misconception, misconstrual, misinterpretation, misunderstanding
con comprehension, grasp, understanding; correctitude, correctness, truth
ant verity
2 unsound and misleading reasoning < the *fallacy* of his theory is clearly evident >
syn casuistry, deception, deceptiveness, delusion, equivocation, sophism, sophistry, speciousness, spuriousness
rel elusion, evasion, inconsistency, quibble, quibbling
fall back *vb* 1 *syn* see RETREAT 2
2 *syn* see RECEDE 1
fall flat *vb* *syn* see FAIL 4
fall guy *n* 1 *syn* see SCAPEGOAT
2 *syn* see POOL 3
fallible *adj* liable or inclined to error < a *fallible* rule >
syn errable, errant

rel careless, faulty, heedless
con careful, heedful; inerrable, inerrant, unerring; exact, perfect, precise
ant infallible

falling-out *n syn* see QUARREL

falloff *n syn* see DECLINE 3

fall out *vb* 1 *syn* see HAPPEN 1
   2 *syn* see QUARREL

fall to *vb syn* see PITCH IN 1

false *adj* 1 not in conformity with what is true < the information turned out to be *false* >
   syn counterfactual, erroneous, inaccurate, incorrect, specious, unsound, untrue, wrong; *compare* ILLOGICAL
   rel deceptive, delusive, delusory, distorted, fallacious, misleading; deceitful, dishonest, fraudulent, lying, mendacious, untruthful
   idiom contrary to fact, off the mark
   con accurate, correct, established, factual, truthful, veracious, veridical
   ant true
   2 *syn* see MISLEADING
   3 *syn* see FAITHLESS
   rel apostate, backsliding, renegade; crooked, devious; hollow
   ant true
   4 *syn* see COUNTERFEIT
   rel apparent, ostensible, seeming
   con bona fide, genuine
   ant real
   5 *syn* see ARTIFICIAL 2

false face *n syn* see MASK 2

false front *n syn* see MASK 2

falsehood *n syn* 1 *syn* see FALLACY 1
   2 *syn* see LIE
   rel fakery, feigning, pretense, sham; deceit, dissimulation, fraud
   ant truth
   3 *syn* see MENDACITY

falseness *n* 1 *syn* see FALLACY 1
   2 *syn* see INFIDELITY
   3 *syn* see DEFECTION

falsifier *n syn* see LIAR

falsify *vb* 1 *syn* see LIE
   2 *syn* see MISREPRESENT
   rel alter, change; cook, doctor; contort; contradict, contravene, deny, traverse

falsity *n* 1 *syn* see LIE
   2 *syn* see FALLACY 1
   rel bluff, fabrication, fake, sham; disingenuousness, hypocrisy, insincerity, uncandidness
   ant verity
   3 *syn* see INFIDELITY

falter *vb* 1 *syn* see TEETER
   2 *syn* see HESITATE
   rel blench, flinch, quail, recoil, shrink; quake, quaver, shake, shudder, tremble; tick over
   con persevere, persist; decide, determine, resolve

faltering *adj syn* see VACILLATING 2

fame *n* 1 *syn* see REPUTATION 2
   2 the state of being widely known for one's deeds < his *fame* was short-lived >
   syn celebrity, éclat, notoriety, renown, ‖rep, reputation, repute

---

syn synonym(s)   *rel* related word(s)
ant antonym(s)   *con* contrasted word(s)
idiom idiomatic equivalent(s)
‖ use limited; if in doubt, see a dictionary

---

rel acclaim, acclamation, applause; acknowledgment, recognition; conspicuousness, prominence; distinction, eminence, glory, greatness, honor, illustriousness, note, preeminence
   con disgrace, dishonor, disrepute, ignominy, obloquy, odium, opprobrium, shame
   ant obscurity; infamy

famed *adj syn* see FAMOUS 2
   ant obscure; ill-famed

familiar *n syn* see FRIEND

familiar *adj* 1 closely associated < time and interests have made them *familiar* >
   syn chummy, close, confidential, intimate, thick
   rel amicable, friendly, neighborly; affable, boon, cordial, genial, gracious, sociable; comfortable, cozy, easy, snug; forward, fresh, impertinent, intrusive, obtrusive, officious
   con detached, disinterested, incurious, indifferent, remote, unconcerned; ceremonial, ceremonious, conventional, formal
   ant aloof
   2 *syn* see COMMON 4
   rel accustomed, habitual, wonted; commonplace, prosaic
   con new, newfangled, new-fashioned, novel; rare, strange, uncommon; chimerical, fantastic
   ant unfamiliar
   3 well-informed especially through study or experience < *familiar* with what is being taught in the schools >
   syn abreast, acquainted, au courant, au fait, conversant, informed, up, versant, versed
   rel aware, cognizant, conscious, mindful
   con unacquainted, unconversant, uninformed, unversed; insensible, unaware, unconscious, unmindful; ignorant, unenlightened, unknowing
   ant unfamiliar

familiarity *n syn* see ACQUAINTANCE 1
   rel awareness, cognition, comprehension, knowledge, understanding
   ant unfamiliarity

familiarize *vb syn* see ACCUSTOM
   rel acquaint, adapt, adjust, condition, naturalize, season

family *n* 1 a group of persons of or regarded as of common ancestry < traditionally all men belong to the *family* of Noah >
   syn clan, folk, house, kindred, lineage, race, stock, tribe
   rel brood, dynasty, line, stirp, strain; issue, offspring, progeny
   idiom kith and kin, one's own flesh and blood
   2 a group of usually related persons living in one house and under one head < was the only child in her *family* >
   syn folks, house, household, ménage

family *adj syn* see DOMESTIC 1

family tree *n syn* see GENEALOGY

famished *adj syn* see HUNGRY

famous *adj* 1 *syn* see WELL-KNOWN
   2 widely known and honored for achievement < a *famous* physician >
   syn celebrated, celebrious, distinguished, eminent, famed, great, illustrious, notable,

prestigious, prominent, redoubtable, renowned; *compare* WELL-KNOWN
rel estimable, honorable, reputable, respectable, well-thought-of
idiom held in esteem
con humble, inconspicuous, undistinguished, unimportant, unknown
ant obscure; infamous
3 *syn* see EXCELLENT
ant wretched

fan *n* 1 *syn* see ADDICT
2 *syn* see AMATEUR 1
fan *vb* 1 *syn* see BLOW 1
‖2 *syn* see SEARCH 2
fan (out) *vb syn* see OPEN 4
fanatic *adj syn* see EXTREME 3
fanatic *n syn* see ENTHUSIAST
fancied *adj syn* see IMAGINARY 1
fancier *n syn* see AMATEUR 1
fanciful *adj* 1 *syn* see IMAGINARY 1
rel apocryphal, fabulous, fictitious, legendary, mythical; bizarre, fantastic, grotesque; absurd, preposterous; false, wrong
con matter-of-fact, prosaic; truthful, veracious
ant realistic
2 *syn* see FICTITIOUS 1
ant veridical
fancy *n* 1 *syn* see WILL 1
2 *syn* see CAPRICE
rel idea; irrationality, unreasonableness; contrariness, perverseness
3 *syn* see IMAGINATION
rel envisagement, envisioning, objectification
idiom flight of fancy
con awareness, experience, perception
4 an idea or image present in the mind but having no concrete or objective reality <unable to tell fact from *fancy*>
syn daydream, dream, fantasy (*or phantasy*), nightmare, phantasm, vision
rel fable, fabrication, fiction, figment, invention; concept, conception, idea, notion; chimera, delusion, illusion; fata morgana, hallucination, mirage
idiom figment of the imagination
con actuality, fact, reality
fancy *vb* 1 *syn* see LIKE
rel approve, endorse, sanction
idiom have a fancy (*or hankering*) for; have one's heart set on
con deprecate, disapprove; abhor, abominate, detest, dislike, hate, loathe
2 *syn* see THINK 1
con demonstrate, prove, test, try
fancy *adj syn* see ELABORATE 2
fancy–free *adj syn* see FREE 6
fancy house *n syn* see BROTHEL
fancy man *n* 1 *syn* see LOVER 1
2 *syn* see PIMP 1
fancy woman *n syn* see HARLOT 1
fanfare *n syn* see DISPLAY 2
fanny *n syn* see BUTTOCKS
fantastic *adj* 1 *syn* see FICTITIOUS 1
rel implausible, incredible, unbelievable; absurd, preposterous; irrational, unreasonable; deceptive, delusive, delusory, misleading
con common, commonplace, everyday, familiar, ordinary; customary, prevailing, universal, usual
2 conceived or made without reference to reality <their explanation was *fantastic*>

syn antic, bizarre, grotesque
rel adroit, clever, ingenious; eccentric, erratic, odd, queer, singular, strange; absurd, nonsensical, preposterous, ridiculous
con factual, solid, sound, valid, well-grounded; plausible, reasonable
3 *syn* see FOOLISH 2
4 *syn* see MONSTROUS 1
5 *syn* see EXTRAVAGANT 1
fantasy (*or phantasy*) *n* 1 *syn* see IMAGINATION
rel conceiving, envisioning, fancying, imagining; externalizing, objectifying
2 *syn* see FANCY 4
rel caprice, freak, vagary, whim, whimsy; bizarrerie, grotesquerie
con actuality, fact, reality
3 *syn* see PIPE DREAM
far *adv syn* see WELL 8
far *adj syn* see DISTANT 1
idiom a long day's journey
ant near
far and away *adv* by a considerable margin <he was *far and away* the best man for the job>
syn by all odds, by a long shot, by far, by long odds, by odds, out and away
rel decidedly, definitely; doubtless, unconditionally, undoubtedly, unequivocally, unquestionably; absolutely, positively; just, quite, very
con barely; slightly; possibly
far and near *adv syn* see EVERYWHERE 1
far and wide *adv syn* see EVERYWHERE 1
faraway *adj* 1 *syn* see DISTANT 1
ant near-at-hand
2 *syn* see ABSTRACTED
rel disregardful, heedless, oblivious, stargazing, unheeding, unmindful
idiom off one's guard
farce *n syn* see MOCKERY 2
farceur *n syn* see ZANY 2
farcical *adj syn* see LAUGHABLE
rel absurd, extravagant, nonsensical, outrageous, preposterous
fare *vb* 1 *syn* see GO 1
rel advance, progress
idiom make headway
con stay, stop
2 *syn* see SHIFT 5
farewell *interj syn* see GOOD-BYE
farewell *n syn* see PARTING
farewell *adj syn* see PARTING
farfetched *adj syn* see FORCED
rel bizarre, fantastic, grotesque; eccentric, erratic, queer, strange
con accustomed, usual, wonted
far–flung *adj syn* see DISTANT 1
far–gone *adj syn* see EFFETE 2
farming *n syn* see AGRICULTURE
rel cultivation, tillage; agronomy, geoponics, hydroponics
far–off *adj syn* see DISTANT 1
idiom behind the farthest range
ant nearby
far–out *adj syn* see OUTLANDISH 3
farther *adv syn* see BEYOND 1
farther *adj syn* see ADDITIONAL
farthest *adj syn* see EXTREME 5
ant nearest
fascinate *vb* 1 *syn* see ENTHRALL 2
2 *syn* see ATTRACT 1
rel affect, impress, influence, strike, sway, touch; delight, gladden, please, rejoice;

absorb, engage, engross, occupy, preoccupy

con disgust, horrify, repel; affront, insult, offend, outrage, shame

3 *syn* see INTEREST

fascinated *adj syn* see ENAMORED 3

fascinating *adj syn* see ATTRACTIVE 1

rel delectable, delightful; seducing

fascination *n syn* see CHARM 3

fashion *n* 1 *syn* see METHOD 1

rel custom, habit, practice, usage, wont

2 *syn* see VEIN 1

3 the prevailing or accepted custom <follow the *fashion*>

syn bandwagon, chic, craze, cry, dernier cri, fad, furore, mode, rage, style, thing, ton, trend, ||twig, vogue

rel drift, tendency; convention, form, usage

idiom the in thing, the last word, the latest thing

fashion *vb syn* see MAKE 3

rel contrive, devise; design, plan, plot; turn out

fashionable *adj syn* see STYLISH

rel current, popular, prevalent, up-to-the-minute

idiom all the rage

ant unfashionable

fast *adj* 1 *syn* see SURE 1

rel fixed, held, inextricable, stuck, wedged

con insecure, loose, shaky, unstable

2 *syn* see FAITHFUL 1

3 moving, proceeding, or acting with great celerity <a *fast* horse>

syn breakneck, expeditious, expeditive, fleet, harefooted, hasty, posthaste, quick, raking, rapid, snappy, speedy, swift

rel active, alert, brisk, keen, lively

idiom quick as lightning, quick as thought, swift as an arrow

con lethargic, logy, poky, sluggish, tardy, torpid; languid, languorous; deliberate, gradual

ant slow

4 persistent in adhering to something <a *fast* grip>

syn firm, fixed, secure, set, tenacious, tight; *compare* STABLE 4, SURE 1

idiom stuck fast

con insecure, loose, relaxed, unfirm, weak; free, unattached, unfixed

5 *syn* see WILD 7

6 *syn* see LICENTIOUS 2

7 sexually promiscuous—usually used of a woman <she's said to be *fast*>

syn easy, light, loose, ||riggish, unchaste, wanton, whorish

rel careless, heedless, lax, slack; bawdy, indecent; lascivious, lecherous, lewd, libertine, licentious, lickerish, riotous

idiom no better than one should be, of easy virtue

con chaste, decent, decorous, modest, moral, pure, virtuous

fast *adv* 1 *syn* see HARD 7

2 in a rapid manner <run up the hill as *fast* as you know how>

syn synonym(s)   *rel* related word(s)
ant antonym(s)   *con* contrasted word(s)
idiom idiomatic equivalent(s)
|| use limited; if in doubt, see a dictionary

syn apace, chop-chop, expeditiously, flatout, fleetly, full tilt, hastily, lickety-split, posthaste, presto, promptly, pronto, quick, quickly, rapidly, soon, speedily, swift, swiftly

idiom by leaps and bounds, in a flash, in a twinkling, in nothing flat, in short order, like a bat out of hell, like a blue streak, like a flash, like a house afire, like a shot, like a streak, like greased lightning, like wildfire

con deliberately, leisurely; apathetically, lethargically, sluggishly

ant slow

fasten *vb* 1 to cause one thing to hold to another <*fasten* a feather to a hat>

syn affix, attach, fix, rivet

rel connect, join, link, unite; adhere, cleave, cling, cohere, stick

con divide, divorce, part, separate, sever, sunder; loose, loosen

ant unfasten

2 to fix in place or in a desired position <*fasten* the door>

syn anchor, catch, fix, moor, secure

rel bed, implant, infix, lodge, set, settle; embed, join, wedge; establish; bar, hitch, hook

idiom make fast (*or* secure *or* sure)

con loose, undo, unloose, unloosen

ant unfasten

3 to direct (as attention or hope) directly and steadily <*fastened* his whole mind on the problem>

syn concenter, concentrate, fix, fixate, focus, put, rivet

rel address, apply, devote, direct, train, turn

con falter, vacillate, waver

fastidious *adj syn* see NICE 1

rel demanding, exacting; captious, critical, hypercritical

con cursory, uncritical

fastigium *n syn* see TOP 1

fastness *n syn* see FORT

rel retreat, shelter; defense, guard, protection; adytum, sanctum

fat *adj* 1 *syn* see FATTY 1

2 having excess adipose tissue <a *fat* woman overflowing her chair>

syn corpulent, fleshy, gross, heavy, obese, overblown, overweight, porcine, portly, pursy, stout, upholstered, weighty; *compare* ROTUND 2

rel beefy, bulky, chunky, dumpy, full-bodied, heavyset, squat, stocky, stubby, thick, thickset; paunchy, potbellied; brawny, burly; husky

idiom broad in the beam, fat as a pig

con angular, gaunt, lank, lanky, rawboned, scrawny, skinny, spare; slender, slight, slim, thin

ant lean

3 *syn* see LARGE 1

rel broad, deep, wide

con narrow, skinny

4 *syn* see RESONANT

||5 *syn* see REMOTE 4

fat *n* 1 *syn* see BEST

2 *syn* see EXCESS 1

fatal *adj* 1 *syn* see DEADLY 1

2 bringing on an adverse fate <to accept his word was a *fatal* mistake>

syn calamitous, cataclysmic, catastrophic, disastrous, fateful, ruinous

rel baneful, pernicious; baleful, malefic, maleficent, malign, sinister; ill-fated, ill-starred, unlucky

con advantageous, beneficial, profitable; auspicious, benign, favorable, propitious

fatal *n syn* see FATALITY 2

fatality *n* 1 the condition of causing death < the tuberculosis *fatality* remains high >
syn deadliness, lethality, mortality
rel malignancy, noxiousness, perniciousness, poisonousness, virulence
2 an instance of dying especially as the result of accident or disaster < two *fatalities* over the weekend >
syn casualty, death, fatal

‖**fat cat** *n syn* see NOTABLE 1

fate *n* whatever is destined or inevitably decreed for one < the *fate* of the bill has not been decided >
syn circumstance, destiny, doom, kismet, lot, moira, portion, weird
rel consequence, effect, issue, outcome, result, upshot; end, ending, termination; ineluctability, inescapableness, inevitability, inevitableness, unavoidability
con accident, chance, fortune, hazard, luck

fate *vb syn* see PREDESTINE

fateful *adj* 1 *syn* see OMINOUS
rel important, momentous, significant; conclusive, decisive, determinative; acute, critical, crucial
con inconclusive, insignificant, trivial, unimportant
2 *syn* see FATAL 2

fathead *n syn* see DUNCE

fatheaded *adj syn* see STUPID 1

father *n* 1 a male human parent < scarcely knew his *father* >
syn dad, dada, daddy, ‖governor, ‖old man, pa, ‖pap, papa, ‖pappy, ‖pater, pop, poppa; *compare* MOTHER 1
2 one that originates or institutes < the *father* of radiotelegraphy >
syn architect, author, creator, founder, generator, inventor, maker, originator, patriarch, sire
rel builder, encourager, motor, mover, organizer, prime mover, producer, promoter, promulgator, supporter; inaugurator, initiator, introducer
con disciple, follower

father *vb* 1 to be the male parent in reproduction < didn't know who *fathered* the child >
syn beget, breed, get, procreate, progenerate, sire
rel engender, generate, ingenerate; spawn
2 *syn* see GENERATE 1

fatherland *n syn* see COUNTRY

fatherless *adj syn* see ILLEGITIMATE 1

fathom *vb* 1 *syn* see SOUND
2 *syn* see KNOW 1
rel penetrate, pierce, probe; perceive, recognize; ‖dig, savvy

fathomable *adj syn* see UNDERSTANDABLE

fathomless *adj syn* see BOTTOMLESS 2

fatidic *adj syn* see PROPHETIC

fatigue *n* complete depletion of strength < suffering from *fatigue* >

syn exhaustion, lassitude, tiredness, weariness
rel enervation, ennui, languor, listlessness; debilitation, faintness, feebleness, weakness
con briskness, energy, liveliness, vigor, vitality; endurance, strength

fatigue *vb syn* see TIRE 1
rel deplete; exhaust, fag, tucker, wear out; debilitate, disable, weaken; annoy, bother, irk, vex
con refresh, rejuvenate, renew, restore; assuage, relieve

fatigued *adj syn* see TIRED 1

fatness *n syn* see OBESITY

‖**fatso** *n syn* see FATTY

fatty *adj* 1 containing fat especially in unusual amounts < a rather *fatty* steak >
syn adipose, fat
rel blubbery, lardy, suety
ant lean
2 having the qualities of fat < the constant frying left a *fatty* deposit on the kitchen woodwork >
syn greasy, oily, oleaginous, unctuous

fatty *n* a fat person < *fatties* trying to diet >
syn blimp, butterball, dumpling, ‖fatso, ‖tub
rel overweight; pudge, roly-poly, strapper; potbelly
idiom tons of fun
ant skinny

fatuous *adj syn* see SIMPLE 3
rel idiotic, imbecile, moronic; besotted, fond, infatuated, insensate; absurd, dumb, silly, stupid
con judicious, prudent, sage, sane, sapient, wise
ant sensible

faucet *n* a fixture for controlling the passage of fluid < turn off the *faucet* >
syn cock, gate, hydrant, petcock, spigot, stopcock, tap, valve
rel bung, spile

fault *n* 1 *syn* see IMPERFECTION
rel infirmity, weakness
con faultlessness, impeccability; meticulousness, preciseness, precision
2 an imperfection in character or an ingrained moral weakness < he has few *faults* >
syn failing, foible, frailty, vice
rel infirmity, weakness; blemish, defect, flaw
con excellence, perfection, virtue; desirability, goodness, rightness
ant merit
3 *syn* see BLAME
rel accountability, answerability, liability, responsibility; crime, error, offense, sin, transgression

faultfinder *n* 1 *syn* see CRITIC
2 *syn* see GROUCH

faultfinding *adj syn* see CRITICAL 1
rel particular, pernickety; ultracritical
con appreciative, cherishing, prizing, valuing

faultily *adv syn* see AMISS 1
rel erroneously, fallaciously, inaccurately, mistakenly, unfairly
con correctly, right

faultless *adj* 1 *syn* see IMPECCABLE 1
rel entire, intact, perfect, whole; blameless

con defective, deficient, imprecise, inaccurate, inexact, uncorrect

ant faulty

2 *syn* see INNOCENT 2

faulty *adj* marked by a fault or defect < a *faulty* mechanism >

syn amiss, defective, flawed, imperfect, sick

rel imprecise, inaccurate, inexact, uncorrect; deficient, inadequate, incomplete; erroneous, fallacious, fallible, specious, wrong; blemished, damaged, defaced, disfigured, marred

con accurate, correct, exact, nice, precise, right; complete, entire, intact, perfect, whole; excellent, good; unflawed, unimpaired

ant faultless

faux pas *n* a breach of etiquette or of social convention < hustled him out of the room before he could commit another *faux pas* >

syn blooper, boner, ‖boo-boo, break, gaffe, impropriety, indecorum, solecism; *compare* ERROR 2

rel bungle, misstep, stumble; howler, screamer; indiscretion, misjudgment, oversight, pratfall

favor *n* 1 *syn* see REGARD 4

ant disfavor

2 *syn* see APPROBATION 1

con depreciation, derogation, disparagement

ant disfavor

3 *syn* see GIFT 1

rel aid, assistance, backing, encouragement, help, support

4 a special privilege < willing to grant a *favor* to a good friend >

syn courtesy, dispensation, indulgence, kindness, service

rel aid, assistance, cooperation, help

favor *vb* 1 *syn* see APPROVE 1

rel endorse, OK (*or* okay), sanction; appreciate, prize, value

idiom set great store by

con decry, depreciate, disparage

ant disfavor

2 *syn* see OBLIGE 2

rel humor, indulge, pamper

idiom do one a favor (*or* service), do right by

con baffle, circumvent, foil, frustrate, thwart

3 *syn* see ENCOURAGE 2

4 *syn* see RESEMBLE

con contradict, differ

favorable *adj* 1 expressing approval < a *favorable* recommendation >

syn approbative, approbatory, approving

rel benignant, kind, kindly; recommendatory, well-disposed; commendatory, complimentary, laudatory, praiseful

idiom in one's favor

con depreciative, disapprobatory, disapproving, disparaging, uncomplimentary; censorious, condemnatory, critical, faultfinding

ant unfavorable

2 *syn* see PLEASANT 1

3 *syn* see GOOD 1

rel healthful, salutary, wholesome

con disadvantageous, unpropitious; damaging, hampering

ant unfavorable

4 *syn* see TIMELY 1

5 indicative of a successful outcome < *favorable* conditions for opening a new business >

syn auspicious, benign, bright, dexter, fortunate, propitious, white

rel advantageous, beneficial, profitable; happy, lucky, promising, providential; cheering, encouraging, reassuring

idiom full of promise

con calamitous, cataclysmic, catastrophic, disastrous, fatal, fateful, ruinous; baleful, malefic, maleficent, malign, sinister; illfated, ill-starred, unlucky; inauspicious, unpromising, unpropitious

ant unfavorable

favorably *adv syn* see WELL 5

favored *adj syn* see FAVORITE 2

favoring *adj syn* see GOOD 1

favorite *adj* 1 accorded special treatment or attention < a *favorite* daughter >

syn beloved, blue-eyed, darling, dear, fairhaired, loved, pet, precious, white-haired, white-headed

rel admired, adored, esteemed, revered; cherished, prized, treasured

idiom dear as the apple of one's eye, dear to one's heart, held dear

con contemned, despised, disdained; abhorrent, detested, hated

2 constituting a favorite < *favorite* melodies >

syn favored, popular, preferred, well-liked

rel laudable, pleasant, praiseworthy; cherished, prized, treasured

con despised, detested, disliked, hated, unpopular; eschewed, rejected

fawn *vb* to act or behave with abjectness in the presence of a superior < *fawn* on the master >

syn apple-polish, bootlick, ‖brownnose, cotton, cower, cringe, grovel, honey (up), kowtow, slaver, toady, truckle

rel blandish, cajole, coax, wheedle; batter (up), flatter, make up (to); cater (to), pander (to); crawl; abase, debase, demean; bow, cave, defer, submit, yield; court, invite, woo

idiom be at one's beck and call, curry favor, dance attendance, kiss one's feet, lick one's shoes (*or* boots), make a doormat of oneself, ‖suck up to

con contemn, despise, disdain, scorn, scout; reject, repudiate, spurn; flout, gibe, jeer, scoff; deride, mock, ridicule, taunt

ant domineer

fawning *adj* characteristic of one that fawns < sent *fawning* greetings >

syn bootlicking, cowering, cringing, groveling, kowtowing, parasitic, sycophant, sycophantic, sycophantical, sycophantish, toadying, truckling

rel flunkyish, obsequious, servile, slavish, subservient; compliant, deferential, humble, submissive, yielding; ingratiating; adulatory, flattering, mealy-mouthed; crawling, spineless; abject, ignoble, mean

---

syn synonym(s)   *rel* related word(s)
ant antonym(s)   *con* contrasted word(s)
idiom idiomatic equivalent(s)
‖ use limited; if in doubt, see a dictionary

con arrogant, disdainful, haughty, insolent, lordly, overbearing, proud, supercilious; contemptuous, insulting, scathing, scornful; authoritative, imperious, magisterial, masterful
ant domineering

fay *n syn* see FAIRY

faze *vb syn* see EMBARRASS
rel confound, dumbfound, mystify, nonplus, perplex, puzzle; confuse, muddle; appall, daunt, dismay, horrify; annoy, bother, irritate, vex
con calm, compose, quiet, relax, soothe; ease, relieve

fealty *n syn* see FIDELITY 1
rel faith, trueness, truth; dependability, reliability, trustworthiness; devotedness, support
con disloyalty, traitorousness, treacherousness
ant perfidy

fear *n* 1 agitation or dismay in the anticipation of or in the presence of danger < living in *fear* of what the future might hold >
syn alarm, cold feet, consternation, dismay, dread, fright, horror, panic, terror, trepidation, trepidity
rel apprehension, foreboding, misgiving, presentiment; angst, anxiety, concern, worry; agitation, discomposure, disquietude, perturbation; chickenheartedness, cowardice, cowardliness, faintheartedness, timidity, timorousness; funk, scare
idiom cold sweat
con boldness, bravery, courage, courageousness, dauntlessness, fortitude, gallantry, intrepidity, prowess, valiancy, valor
ant fearlessness
2 *syn* see REVERENCE 2
rel esteem, respect
con contempt, scorn

fearful *adj* 1 *syn* see AFRAID 1
rel agitated, alarmed, discomposed, disquieted, disturbed, perturbed
con audacious, bold, brave, courageous, dauntless, unafraid, valiant
ant fearless
2 inspired or moved by fear < *fearful* of loud noises >
syn afraid, apprehensive; *compare* AFRAID 1
rel alarmed, disquieted, disturbed; aflutter, agitated, jittery, nervous, perturbed, uneasy; anxious, concerned, solicitous, worried
con assured, confident, sanguine, sure; collected, composed, cool, imperturbable, nonchalant, unflappable, unperturbed
ant unafraid
3 causing fear < a *fearful* sight >
syn appalling, awful, dire, direful, dreadful, formidable, frightful, horrible, horrific, redoubtable, shocking, terrible, terrific, tremendous
rel alarming, frightening, terrifying; ghastly, grim, grisly, gruesome, lurid, macabre; baleful, malign, sinister; overwhelming, sublime
con attractive, charming, delightful, enchanting, pleasant, pleasing
ant reassuring

fearless *adj syn* see BRAVE 1

rel assured, confident, sanguine. sure
con afraid, frightened, scared, terrified
ant fearful

feasible *adj syn* see POSSIBLE 1
rel practical; advantageous, beneficial, profitable; appropriate, fit, fitting, suitable
con impossible, impracticable, unachievable, unattainable, unworkable; ambitious, pretentious, utopian
ant infeasible, unfeasible

feast *n syn* see DINNER
rel entertainment, festivity; refreshment, repast; meal

feat *n* 1 *syn* see ADVENTURE
idiom bold stroke, deed of derring-do
2 a remarkable act or performance < Washington's *feat* of tossing a dollar across the river >
syn achievement, deed, exploit, tour de force
rel act, action; accomplishment, consummation, execution, performance; conquest, triumph, victory
3 *syn* see TRICK 3

feather *n syn* see TYPE

featherbrain *n syn* see SCATTERBRAIN

featherbrained *adj syn* see GIDDY 1
rel capricious, fickle, impulsive, whimsical; shallow, superficial, unprofound

featherhead *n syn* see SCATTERBRAIN

featherlight *adj syn* see LIGHT 1

featherweight *n syn* see DUNCE

featherweight *adj syn* see LIGHT 1

feature *n* 1 *syn* see QUALITY 1
2 *syn* see CHARACTERISTIC 1
rel article, detail, item, particular; component, constituent, element, factor, ingredient; individuality, particularity, peculiarity, speciality, specialty; attribute, property, quality
3 features *pl syn* see FACE 1

feature *vb* ‖1 *syn* see RESEMBLE
2 *syn* see THINK 1
3 *syn* see EMPHASIZE

febrile *adj syn* see FEVERISH 1

feckless *adj* 1 having no real worth or purpose < after years of *feckless* negotiations >
syn fustian, good-for-nothing, meaningless, purposeless, unpurposed, useless, worthless
rel bootless, fruitless, futile, unavailing, vain; ineffective, ineffectual, inefficacious
con meaningful, purposeful, worthwhile; fruitful: effective, effectual, efficacious, consequential, important, momentous, significant, weighty
ant efficient, ‖feckful
2 *syn* see CARELESS 1
rel carefree, easygoing, happy-go-lucky, lackadaisical, nonchalant; remiss; irresponsible, undependable, unreliable, untrustworthy
con attentive, considerate, thoughtful; meticulous, punctilious, punctual, scrupulous; dependable, reliable, responsible, trustworthy
3 *syn* see IRRESPONSIBLE
ant ‖feckful

fecund *adj syn* see FERTILE
rel breeding, generating, propagating, reproducing
con infertile, sterile

ant barren

fecundity *n* 1 *syn* see FERTILITY
rel productiveness, productivity; exuberance, lavishness, lushness, luxuriance, prodigality, profuseness, profusion
con infertility, sterility, unproductiveness
ant barrenness, infecundity
2 *syn* see ELOQUENCE

federation *n syn* see ALLIANCE 2

fed up *adj* disgusted and completely out of patience < *fed up* with her bad behavior>
syn disgusted, sick, tired, weary
rel bored; glutted, sated, satiated, surfeited
idiom fed to the gills (*or* teeth), full up to here with, sick and tired of, sick (*or* tired) to death
con enchanted, enraptured, enthralled; delighted, excited, exhilarated, pleased, thrilled

fee *n syn* see WAGE
rel consideration; charge, cost, expense, price

‖**feeb** *n syn* see POOL 4

feeble *adj* 1 *syn* see WEAK 1
rel emasculated, enervated, unmanned, unnerved; helpless; aged, doddering, senile; ailing, sapless
con hale, healthy, sound; lusty, strenuous; strong
ant robust
2 *syn* see TENUOUS 3

feebleminded *adj syn* see RETARDED
ant strong-minded

feebleness *n syn* see INFIRMITY 1

feed *vb syn* see GIVE 3

feed (on) *vb syn* see EAT 1
idiom have (*or* take) a bite, ‖put on the feed bag (*or* nose bag)

feed *n* 1 *syn* see MEAL
2 *syn* see FOOD 1
rel banquet, feast, meal, repast

feel *vb* 1 *syn* see TOUCH 1
rel manipulate, ply, wield; explore, sound; fumble, grope
2 to have as an emotional response < *felt* pleasure in her company>
syn experience, know, savor, taste
rel apprehend; notice, observe, perceive; encounter, meet; endure, suffer, undergo
idiom be aware (*or* conscious) of, be sensible of
con disregard, ignore
3 to view as right or true <we *feel* that he should retire soon>
syn believe, consider, credit, deem, hold, sense, think; *compare* CONSIDER 3
rel assume, presume, suppose, suspect; conclude, deduce, gather, infer, judge; conjecture, guess, surmise; esteem, repute
idiom take (it) into one's head
con challenge, distrust, doubt, misdoubt, mistrust, question
4 *syn* see GROPE

feel (for) *vb syn* see COMPASSIONATE

feel *n syn* see TOUCH 1
2 *syn* see TOUCH 4
3 *syn* see AIR 3

syn synonym(s)   *rel* related word(s)
ant antonym(s)   *con* contrasted word(s)
idiom idiomatic equivalent(s)
‖ use limited; if in doubt, see a dictionary

con basis, essence, reality

feeler *n* an attempt to ascertain opinion <the letter was a *feeler* to see how they would react>
syn trial balloon
rel query, question; inquiry, probe, test; leader, leading question; sounding board; intimation, representation; prospectus; kiteflying

feeling *n* 1 *syn* see SENSATION 1
rel action, behavior, reaction; responsiveness; palpability, palpableness, perceptibility, perceptibleness, tangibility, tangibleness
con apathy, indifference, insensibility, numbness
2 *syn* see TOUCH 4
3 subjective response or reaction (as to a person or situation) <a *feeling* of sadness>
syn affection, affectivity, emotion, passion, sentiment
rel humor, mood, temper, vein; attitude, outlook; belief, opinion, view; concept, idea, impression, notion, thought
4 *syn* see OPINION
5 *syn* see AIR 3
rel impress, impression, imprint

feeling *adj syn* see EMOTIONAL 1
con numb, unmoved, unresponsive
ant unfeeling

feel out *vb syn* see PROBE 2

feign *vb syn* see ASSUME 4

feigned *adj syn* see ARTIFICIAL 3
rel counterfeit, false, sham
con heartfelt, hearty, sincere, wholehearted, whole-souled

feint *n syn* see TRICK 1
rel make-believe, pretense, pretension; befooling, hoax, hoodwinking; cheat, counterfeit, deceit, fake, humbug, imposture, sham; expedient, resort, shift

felicitate *vb syn* see CONGRATULATE
rel commend, compliment, recommend; salute
con comfort, console, solace; commiserate, condole (with), pity; gibe, jeer, scoff; deride, mock, ridicule, taunt; contemn

felicitous *adj syn* see FIT 1
rel convincing, telling; opportune, pat, seasonable, timely, well-timed; apposite, apropos, germane, pertinent, relevant
con awkward, clumsy, gauche, inept, maladroit; unfortunate, unhappy, unlucky
ant infelicitous

feline *adj syn* see STEALTHY 2

fell *vb* 1 to force an opponent off his feet < *felled* the heckler with a single blow>
syn bowl (down *or* over), bring down, down, drop, flatten, floor, ground, knock down, knock over, lay low, level, mow (down), prostrate, throw down, tumble
rel shoot, shoot down
idiom lay level with the ground
con pick up, raise
2 to bring down by cutting < *felled* the great oak by the driveway>
syn chop, cut, hew
rel flatten, level, raze; cleave, rive, split; sever, sunder; gash, hack, mangle, slash

fell *adj* 1 *syn* see FIERCE 1
rel baleful, malefic, maleficent, malign, sinister; implacable, relentless, unrelenting; fearful, horrible, horrific, terrific

con compassionate, sympathetic, tender; clement, forbearing, lenient, merciful; humane
2 *syn* see GRAVE 3

fell *n syn* see HIDE

fellow *n* 1 *syn* see PARTNER
2 *syn* see ACCOMPANIMENT 2
3 *syn* see MATE 5
4 *syn* see MAN 3

fellow feeling *n syn* see SYMPATHY 2

fellowship *n* 1 *syn* see COMPANY 1
2 *syn* see ASSOCIATION 2

felo-de-se *n syn* see SUICIDE

felon *n syn* see CRIMINAL

femme fatale *n syn* see SIREN

fen *n syn* see SWAMP

fence *n syn* see BAR 2

fence *vb* 1 *syn* see ENCLOSE 1
2 *syn* see DODGE 1
rel feint, maneuver; baffle, foil, outwit

fend *vb* 1 *syn* see DEFEND 1
2 *syn* see WARD 1

fend (off) *vb* to give a sharp check to < tried to *fend* off his attentions >
syn hold off, keep off, rebuff, rebut, repel, repulse, stave off, ward (off)
rel refuse, reject; snub, spurn; avert, avoid
idiom hold (*or* keep) at bay, keep at a distance, keep at arm's length
con allure, attract, captivate, charm, enchant, fascinate; embolden, hearten

feral *adj* 1 *syn* see BRUTISH
rel barbaric, barbarous, ferocious, fierce, inhuman, savage, vicious
con gentle, mild, tame
2 *syn* see SAVAGE 1

ferine *adj syn* see BRUTISH

ferment *vb syn* see SEETHE 4

ferment *n* 1 *syn* see UNREST
2 *syn* see COMMOTION 1

ferocious *adj* 1 *syn* see FIERCE 1
rel rapacious, ravening, ravenous, voracious; implacable, relentless
ant tender
2 *syn* see SAVAGE

ferret out *vb syn* see SEEK 1
rel elicit, extract; nose out, pry (out); penetrate, pierce, probe; chase, follow, pursue, trail; ascertain, determine, discover, learn
con conceal, hide, screen, secrete; camouflage, disguise; cover (up), hush (up), suppress
ant squirrel (away)

ferry *vb syn* see CARRY 1

fertile *adj* marked by abundant productivity < *fertile* soil > < a *fertile* mind >
syn childing, fecund, fruitful, productive, proliferant, prolific, rich, spawning
rel bearing, producing, yielding; abundant, bountiful, copious, exuberant, generous, lush, luxuriant, plenteous, plentiful, teeming; creative, ingenious, inventive, pregnant, resourceful; exciting, galvanizing, provoking, quickening, stimulating
con barren, impotent, unfruitful; dull, imitative, stupid, unproductive
ant sterile

fertility *n* the quality or state of being fertile < insure the *fertility* of the soil >
syn fecundity, fruitfulness, prolificacy

rel abundance, copiousness, plentifulness; creativity, ingenuity, inventiveness, resourcefulness
con barrenness, impotence, unfruitfulness
ant infertility, sterility

fervent *adj syn* see IMPASSIONED
rel devout, pious, religious; responsive, tender, warm, warmhearted; heartfelt, hearty, sincere, unfeigned, wholehearted, whole-souled; earnest, serious; eager, enthusiastic
con apathetic, impassive, phlegmatic; aloof, detached, indifferent, unconcerned

fervid *adj* 1 *syn* see IMPASSIONED
con collected, composed, cool, imperturbable, nonchalant
ant gelid
2 *syn* see FEVERISH 2

fervor *n syn* see PASSION 6
rel devoutness, piety, piousness; earnestness, seriousness, solemnity; heartiness, sincerity, wholeheartedness; empressement, warmth
con apathy, impassiveness, impassivity; aloofness, detachment, indifference, unconcern; languor, lethargy, torpor

fescennine *adj syn* see OBSCENE 2

fess (up) *vb syn* see ACKNOWLEDGE 1

fester *vb syn* see RANKLE

festive *adj syn* see MERRY

festivity *n syn* see MERRYMAKING

fetch *vb syn* see SELL 4

fetching *adj syn* see ENTICING

fetch up *vb* ‖ 1 *syn* see BRING UP 1
2 *syn* see STOP 4

fetid *adj syn* see MALODOROUS 1
rel loathsome, repugnant, repulsive, revolting
con aromatic, balmy, odorous, redolent
ant fragrant

fetish *n* 1 *syn* see CHARM 2
2 irrational reverence or attachment < had a *fetish* for red hair >
syn fixation, mania, obsession, thing
rel preoccupation, prepossession; bias, partiality, predilection, prejudice; leaning, penchant, proclivity, propensity
con antipathy, aversion, repugnance, repulsion; dislike, disrelish, distaste

fetter *n*, *usu* **fetters** *pl syn* see SHACKLE

fetter *vb syn* see HAMPER
con disembarrass, disencumber, disentangle, extricate, untangle; detach, disengage

fettle *n syn* see ORDER 10

feud *n* 1 *syn* see VENDETTA
2 *syn* see QUARREL
rel argument; combat, contest

fevered *adj* 1 *syn* see FEVERISH 1
ant afebrile
2 *syn* see FEVERISH 2

feverish *adj* 1 abnormally heated by fever < the child's forehead felt *feverish* >
syn febrile, fevered, fiery
rel burning, flushed, hectic, hot, inflamed, pyretic
ant afebrile
2 marked by intense emotion or activity < a *feverish* imagination >
syn burning, fervid, fevered, heated, hectic
rel excited, high-strung, nervous, overwrought; frenzied, furious, passionate
idiom keyed up

con calm, composed, cool, serene, tranquil; apathetic, languid, lethargic, listless, phlegmatic

few *adj syn* see INFREQUENT

few *n* a small quantity or number <sold a *few* of the books>
syn handful, scattering, smatch, smatter, smattering, spatter, spattering, sprinkling
con abundance, many, multitude, numbers

fiat *n syn* see SANCTION

fib *n syn* see LIE
rel equivocation, evasiveness; mendacity, untruthfulness
idiom tall tale

fib *vb syn* see LIE
rel concoct, fabricate, make up, trump up
idiom draw the long bow, stretch the truth

fibber *n syn* see LIAR

fibbery *n syn* see MENDACITY

fiber *n syn* see TEXTURE 2

fibrous *adj syn* see MUSCULAR 1

fibster *n syn* see LIAR

fickle *adj syn* see INCONSTANT 1
rel unfaithful; undependable, unreliable
con stable, unchanging
ant constant, true

fiction *n* a story, account, explanation, or conception which is an invention of the human mind <his belief was based on a *fiction*>
syn fable, fabrication, figment
rel concoction, fantasy, invention; falsehood, lie, misrepresentation, untruth; anecdote, narrative, story, tale, yarn; fish story
con actuality, reality
ant fact

fictional *adj syn* see FICTITIOUS 1

fictitious *adj* 1 suggestive of fiction especially in lacking a sound factual basis <*fictitious* values in logic>
syn chimerical, fanciful, fantastic, fictional, fictive, illusory, imaginary, suppositious, supposititious, unreal
rel concocted, created, invented, made; fabricated, fashioned; cooked-up, false, made-up, trumped-up, untrue; romantic
con actual, real, true; authentic, genuine; factual, veritable; truthful, veracious, verisimilar
2 not genuine <the gigolo wooed the heiress with *fictitious* ardor>
syn fake, mock, sham, simulated; compare ARTIFICIAL 2
rel deceptive, delusive, delusory, misleading; dishonest, unreal, untrue; artificial, ersatz, factitious, synthetic
con authentic, bona fide, veritable; actual, honest, real, true
ant genuine

fictive *adj syn* see FICTITIOUS 1

fiddle *vb* 1 to handle something nervously or absently <always *fiddling* with his tie>
syn fidget, play, trifle, twiddle
rel feel, handle, touch

2 to work aimlessly, fruitlessly, or pointlessly <*fiddled* around with the engine for hours>
syn doodle, mess, mess around, potter, puddle, putter, tinker
rel dabble, fool, monkey

fiddle-faddle *n syn* see NONSENSE 2

fiddlesticks *n pl syn* see NONSENSE 2

fidelity *n* 1 constancy to something to which one is bound by a pledge or duty <we must practice *fidelity* to our word>
syn allegiance, ardor, devotion, faithfulness, fealty, loyalty, piety
rel constancy, staunchness, steadfastness; dependability, reliability, trustworthiness
con disloyalty, falseness, falsity, perfidiousness, traitorousness, treacherousness; treachery; undependableness, unreliability, untrustworthiness
ant perfidy; faithlessness
2 *syn* see ATTACHMENT 1
ant infidelity

fidget *vb syn* see FIDDLE 1

fidgety *adj syn* see NERVOUS

field *n* a limited area of knowledge or endeavor to which pursuits, activities, and interests are confined <a lawyer eminent in his *field*>
syn bailiwick, champaign, demesne, domain, dominion, precinct, province, region, sphere, terrain, territory, walk
rel bounds, confines, limits; area, department; compass, orbit, purview, range, reach, scope, sweep
con terra incognita

fiend *n syn* see DEVIL 1
2 *syn* see DEVIL 2
3 *syn* see ENTHUSIAST

fiendish *adj* having or manifesting qualities associated with devils, demons, and fiends <inflicted *fiendish* tortures on his captive>
syn demoniac, demonian, demonic, devilish, diabolic, diabolonian, satanic, serpentine, unhallowed
rel hellish, infernal; baleful, malefic, maleficent, malign, sinister; malevolent, malicious, malignant; atrocious, heinous, monstrous, outrageous; barbarous, cruel, ferocious, inhuman, savage, vicious
con benign, benignant, kind, kindly; gentle, mild; compassionate, sympathetic, tender

fierce *adj* 1 displaying fury or malignity in looks or actions <*fierce* native tribes>
syn barbarous, cannibalic, cruel, fell, ferocious, grim, inhuman, inhumane, savage, truculent, wolfish
rel menacing, threatening; enraged, infuriated, maddened; aggressive, bellicose, belligerent, pugnacious; brutal, merciless, pitiless, ruthless, vicious, wild
con benign, benignant, gentle, kind, kindly; peaceful; subdued, submissive, tame
ant mild
2 *syn* see INTENSE 1
rel excessive, extreme, inordinate; penetrating, piercing; superlative, supreme, transcendent
con gentle, mild, subdued

fiercely *adv syn* see HARD 2

fiery *adj* 1 *syn* see BURNING 1

---

2 *syn* see HOT 1
ant frigid, icy
3 *syn* see FEVERISH 1
4 *syn* see SPIRITED 2
rel headlong, hotheaded, impetuous, madcap, precipitate; fervid, impassioned, perfervid; fierce, intense, vehement, violent; enthusiastic, excitable, impulsive, unrestrained; irascible, irritable
con deliberate, leisurely, slow; apathetic, dull, impassive, lethargic, phlegmatic, sluggish; enervated, listless, spiritless
5 *syn* see IMPASSIONED
ant icy

fifty–fifty *adv syn* see EVENLY 1
fifty–fifty *adj syn* see EVEN 4
fight *vb* 1 *syn* see CONTEND 1
rel strive, struggle; rowdy, scuffle, tussle; debate, dispute; altercate, bicker, quarrel, scrap, spat, squabble, tiff, wrangle
idiom ‖mix it, mix it up, put up a fight
con bow, capitulate, submit, succumb, yield
2 *syn* see RESIST
con abide, bear, endure, suffer; advocate, back, champion, support, uphold; defend, guard, protect, shield
fight *n* 1 *syn* see BRAWL 2
2 *syn* see QUARREL
3 *syn* see ATTACK 2
fighter *n syn* see SOLDIER
fighting man *n syn* see SOLDIER
figment *n syn* see FICTION
rel daydream, dream, fancy, nightmare; bubble, chimera, illusion; creation
figurant *n syn* see DANCER
figurante *n syn* see DANCER
figuration *n* 1 *syn* see OUTLINE
2 *syn* see ALLEGORY 1
figure *n* 1 *syn* see NUMBER
rel character, symbol
2 *syn* see FORM 1
rel delineation; appearance, build, frame, physique
3 a unit in a decorative composition (as in a fabric) <a rug with geometrical *figures* in blue and red>
syn design, device, motif, motive, pattern
rel decoration, embellishment, ornamentation
figure *vb* 1 *syn* see CALCULATE
2 *syn* see ADD 2
rel count, enumerate, number
3 *syn* see DECIDE
figure out *vb syn* see SOLVE 2
rel disentangle, unscramble, untangle; crack, decode
con obfuscate, obscure; conceal, hide, screen
figuring *n syn* see COMPUTATION
filch *vb syn* see STEAL 1
filcher *n syn* see THIEF
file *n syn* see LINE 5
filius nullius *n syn* see BASTARD 1
filius populi *n syn* see BASTARD 1
fill *vb* 1 to make full in a way or to a degree that prevents further entry or passage <*fill* a cavity in a tooth>
syn block, choke, clog, close, congest, obstruct, occlude, plug, stop, stopper
rel bar, dam, jam; ‖bung, pug
con clear, free
2 *syn* see LOAD 3

3 *syn* see SATISFY 5
4 *syn* see SATIATE
rel overfeed, overfill, overstuff
fille de joie *n syn* see PROSTITUTE
fillet *n syn* see STRIP 1
fill in *vb* 1 *syn* see INTRODUCE 6
2 *syn* see INFORM 2
fill-in *n syn* see SUBSTITUTE
film *n* 1 *syn* see HAZE 1
2 *syn* see MOVIE
filmy *adj* characterized by fineness and delicacy of texture <*filmy* curtains>
syn diaphanous, flimsy, gauzy, gossamer, sheer, tiffany, transparent
rel dainty, delicate, fine
con coarse, heavy, opaque, rough
filthy *adj* 1 *syn* see DIRTY 1
rel disheveled, slipshod, sloppy, slovenly, unkempt; loathsome, offensive, repulsive, revolting, verminous; coarse, gross, obscene, ribald, vulgar
con cleaned, cleansed; clean, cleanly; neat, shipshape, tidy, trig, trim
ant immaculate, spick-and-span
2 *syn* see OBSCENE 2
filthy lucre *n syn* see MONEY
finagle *vb syn* see ENGINEER
final *adj syn* see LAST
rel crowning, ending, finishing; conclusive, decisive, definitive, determinative; irrefutable, unanswerable, unappealable
con earliest, maiden, original, primary; beginning, incipient, introductory; inaugural
ant initial
finale *n* a final part or element (as of a sequence, series, or action) <the solution of the mystery forms the *finale* of the play>
syn close, conclusion, end, ending, finish, windup; *compare* END 2
rel climax, consummation, culmination; denouement, payoff; cessation, termination
con beginning, genesis, initiation, rise, start; inception, origin, root, source
ant prologue
finally *adv syn* see YET 2
idiom at last, at length, at long last, in the long run, when all is said and done
finance *vb* 1 *syn* see CAPITALIZE
idiom put up the money, raise the dough
2 *syn* see ENDOW 2
rel back, bank, bankroll, grubstake, stake, underwrite; patronize, promote, sponsor, support
financial *adj* of or relating to finance <the *financial* interests of the country>
syn fiscal, monetary, pecuniary, pocket
rel business, commercial, economic
find *vb* 1 to come upon <they soon *found* what they needed>
syn catch, descry, detect, encounter, espy, hit (on *or* upon), meet (with), spot, turn up
rel discern, discover, note, sight; distinguish, identify, recognize; dig up, scare up
idiom bring to light, come up with, fall in with, lay one's finger (on *or* upon), lay one's hand (on *or* upon)
con miss, overlook, pass (over)
ant lose
2 *syn* see GIVE 4
find *n* 1 one of unexpected worth or merit obtained or encountered more or less by

chance < the young understudy proved to be a remarkable *find* >
syn treasure, treasure trove
rel boast, gem, jewel, pride
idiom one in a thousand (*or* million)
2 *syn* see DISCOVERY

find out *vb syn* see DISCOVER 3

fine *n* a pecuniary penalty exacted by an authority < paid a *fine* of ten dollars >
syn amercement, forfeit, mulct, penalty
rel damages, reparation; punishment; assessment

fine *vb syn* see PENALIZE
rel distrain, exact, levy, tax; confiscate, sequestrate

fine *adj* 1 marked by subtlety of perception or discrimination < I cannot follow these *fine* distinctions >
syn delicate, finespun, hairline, hairsplitting, nice, refined, subtle
rel abstruse, esoteric, recondite; cryptic, enigmatic, obscure; minute, petty, trifling
con definite, explicit, express, specific; clear, lucid, perspicuous; broad, extensive, general, generic, indefinite, wide
2 consisting of small particles < *fine* sand >
syn impalpable, powdery, pulverized
rel light, loose, porous
ant coarse
3 *syn* see EXCELLENT
rel beautiful, splendid; enjoyable, pleasant
idiom fine and dandy
con miserable, wretched; atrocious, awful, objectionable, unpleasant
4 *syn* see FAIR 2

finecomb *vb syn* see SCOUR 2

finery *n* dressy clothing < decked out in all her *finery* >
syn ‖best bib and tucker, bravery, frippery, full dress, ‖glad rags, regalia, Sunday best, war paint
rel apparel, clothes; foofaraw, frill, gewgaw, ornament, trimming
con rags, tatters

finespun *adj syn* see FINE 1

finesse *vb syn* see MANIPULATE 2

fine-tooth-comb *vb syn* see SCOUR 2

finger *vb* 1 *syn* see TOUCH 1
2 *syn* see DESIGNATE 2
3 *syn* see IDENTIFY

finical *adj syn* see NICE 1
con slipshod, sloppy, slovenly; blowsy, dowdy, frowzy, slatternly

finicking *adj syn* see NICE 1

finicky *adj syn* see NICE 1

finish *vb* 1 *syn* see CLOSE 3
rel accomplish, achieve, effect, fulfill
idiom have done with
2 *syn* see GO 4
3 *syn* see KILL 1
4 *syn* see MURDER 1

finish *n* 1 *syn* see END 2
2 *syn* see FINALE
3 *syn* see ACQUIREMENT
rel correctness, discrimination, propriety, refinement; elegance, grace, polish; cultivation, taste

---

syn synonym(s)   *rel* related word(s)
ant antonym(s)   *con* contrasted word(s)
idiom idiomatic equivalent(s)
‖ use limited; if in doubt, see a dictionary

finished *adj* 1 *syn* see COMPLETE 4
2 *syn* see THROUGH 3
3 *syn* see CONSUMMATE 1
rel cultivated, cultured, refined; smooth, suave, urbane; elegant, exquisite; all-around, many-sided, versatile
con imperfect, incomplete
ant crude; unfinished

finish off *vb syn* see CLIMAX

finite *adj* having definite or definable limits or boundaries < a *finite* thickness >
syn bound, bounded, limited
rel confined, restricted; definable, defined, definite, determinate, fixed, terminable; exact, precise, specific
con boundless, unbounded, unlimited; absolute, complete, total
ant infinite

‖fink *n syn* see INFORMER

fire *n* 1 a destructive burning < the house was destroyed by *fire* >
syn conflagration, holocaust, inferno
rel blaze, flame, flare, glare; burning, charring, scorching, searing
idiom sea of flames, sheet of fire
2 *syn* see PASSION 6
rel animation, exhilaration, liveliness; dash, drive, energy, ginger, gusto, heartiness, pep, punch, snap, spirit, starch, verve, vigor, vim, zest, zing, zip
con languor, lassitude, lethargy, listlessness, stupor, torpidity, torpor; apathy, impassivity, phlegm

fire *vb* 1 *syn* see LIGHT 1
idiom set fire to, set on fire
con extinguish, quench, smother
2 to stimulate (as mental powers) to higher or more intense activity < a painting that *fired* the viewer's imagination >
syn animate, exalt, inform, inspire; compare PROVOKE 4
rel arouse, enliven, rouse, stir; electrify, excite; heighten, intensify; enthuse, thrill
con appall, dismay; alarm, frighten, terrify
ant daunt
3 *syn* see DISMISS 3
rel eject, expel, oust
idiom give the pink slip, give the sack, strike off the rolls
con engage; appoint, designate, elect, name
ant hire
4 *syn* see SHOOT 1
5 *syn* see THROW 1
6 to dry or harden by subjecting to heat < *fire* bricks >
syn bake, burn, kiln

firebug *n syn* see INCENDIARY

fire-new *adj syn* see BRAND-NEW

firewater *n syn* see LIQUOR 2

firm *adj* 1 *syn* see FAST 4
2 *syn* see STABLE 4
3 having a texture or consistency that resists deformation by external force < *firm* flesh >
syn hard, solid
rel close, compact, dense, thick; inelastic, inflexible, rigid, stiff, unyielding; sturdy, substantial, tough
con flaccid, flimsy, floppy, limp, loose, slack, sleazy, soft, squishy
ant flabby

4 that has been established and is not usually subject to change <a *firm* price>
syn certain, fixed, set, settled, stated, stipulated
rel established, going, prevailing; consistent, stable, steady, unwavering; definite, exact, explicit, specific, undeviating; flat
con changeable, fluctuating, shaky, shifting, unsteady, variable
5 **syn** see SURE 1
6 **syn** see SURE 2
firm *adv syn* see HARD 7
firm *n syn* see ENTERPRISE 3
firmament *n syn* see SKY
firmly *adv* 1 **syn** see HARD 7
2 **syn** see HARD 9
firmness *n* 1 **syn** see STABILITY
2 **syn** see GOOD 2
first *adj* 1 being number one in a series <the *first* day of the week>
syn foremost, headmost, inaugural, initial, leading
con final, terminal, ultimate; interjacent, intermediary, intermediate, intervenient, intervening
ant last
2 preceding all others <succeeded at his *first* try>
syn earliest, initial, maiden, original, pioneer, primary, prime
rel early, pristine; primal, primogenial, primordial
con derivative, imitative, secondary
ant final
3 exceeding all others <he was the *first* statesman of his era>
syn arch, champion, chief, foremost, head, leading, premier, principal
rel eminent, highest, preeminent, primary, prime, supreme; dominant, paramount, predominant, sovereign; main, outstanding
con ancillary, auxiliary, secondary, subsidiary
ant subordinate
4 most rudimentary <had not the *first* chance of success>
syn least, slightest, smallest
rel measly, slight, slim, trifling, trivial
con considerable, goodly, significant, substantial, tolerable, worthwhile
first *adv syn* see FIRSTLY
first-class *adj syn* see EXCELLENT
idiom in a class by itself
con fair, indifferent, middling; unexceptional, unnoteworthy, unremarkable
firsthand *adj syn* see DIRECT 4
firstly *adv* as the first thing to be mentioned <*firstly*, we wish to consider the economic problem>
syn first, initially
rel incipiently, originally, primarily
idiom before all (or anything) else, first of all, first off, to begin with
con ultimately
ant finally, lastly
first off *adv syn* see AWAY 3
first-rate *adj syn* see EXCELLENT
con fair, indifferent, middling, poor; unexceptional, unnoteworthy, unremarkable
first-string *adj syn* see EXCELLENT
firth *n syn* see INLET
fiscal *adj syn* see FINANCIAL
fish *n* 1 **syn** see POOL 3

‖2 **syn** see DOLLAR
fish *vb syn* see HINT 4
fishwife *n syn* see VIRAGO
fishy *adj syn* see DOUBTFUL 1
fissure *n* 1 **syn** see CRACK 3
rel abyss, chasm, gorge, ravine; breach, rent, rupture; gash, hole, opening
2 **syn** see BREACH 3
fist *n syn* see HANDWRITING
fisticuffs *n pl syn* see BOXING
fit *n syn* see ATTACK 3
fit *adj* 1 adapted to an end or use by nature or art <food *fit* for a king>
syn applicable, appropriate, apt, befitting, felicitous, fitting, happy, just, meet, proper, right, rightful, suitable; *compare* JUST 3
rel adapted, adjusted; congruous, consonant; decent, decorous; acceptable, adequate, tolerable
con improper, inadequate, inappropriate, unsuitable; false, wrong
ant unfit
2 **syn** see ELIGIBLE
rel able, competent
3 **syn** see GOOD 2
4 **syn** see HEALTHY 1
idiom fit as a fiddle
ant unfit
fit *vb* 1 **syn** see SUIT 4
2 **syn** see BELONG 1
3 **syn** see PREPARE 1
4 **syn** see ADAPT
fit (in) *vb syn* see AGREE 4
fitful *adj* lacking steadiness or regularity in course, movement, or succession <a *fitful* breeze>
syn catchy, desultory, on-again-off-again, spasmodic, sporadic, spotty
rel intermittent, interrupted, irregular, periodic, recurrent; haphazard, hit-or-miss, random; changeable, variable; capricious, inconstant, unstable
con equable, even, steady, uniform; methodical, orderly, regular, systematic
ant constant
fitly *adv syn* see WELL 1
fitness *n* 1 **syn** see ORDER 10
2 **syn** see ORDER 11
rel decency, decorum, harmony
ant unfitness
3 **syn** see USE 3
fit out *vb syn* see FURNISH 1
fitted *adj syn* see ASSORTED 2
fitting *adj* 1 **syn** see FIT 1
rel apposite, apropos, germane, pertinent, relevant, seemly; accordant, concordant, harmonious
2 **syn** see TRUE 7
fittingly *adv* 1 **syn** see WELL 1
2 **syn** see WELL 4
fivefold *adj syn* see QUINTUPLE
five-star *adj syn* see EXCELLENT
fix *vb* 1 **syn** see SET 1
rel stabilize, steady; decide, determine, rule; specify
con change, modify, vary
ant alter; abrogate
2 **syn** see ENTRENCH 1
rel inculcate, instill
con overthrow, overturn, subvert, upset
3 **syn** see FASTEN 1
4 **syn** see FASTEN 2

con dislodge, displace
5 *syn* see FASTEN 3
6 *syn* see PREPARE 1
7 *syn* see MEND 2
8 *syn* see ADJUST 2
rel mend, patch, rebuild, repair; amend, emend, revise
con disorganize, unsettle
9 *syn* see SOLVE 1
10 *syn* see STERILIZE
11 *syn* see BRIBE
fix *n syn* see PREDICAMENT
fixate *vb syn* see FASTEN 3
fixation *n syn* see FETISH 2
rel craze, fascination, infatuation
idiom bee in one's bonnet
fixed *adj* 1 *syn* see FAST 4
2 *syn* see IMMOVABLE 1
3 *syn* see DEFINITE 1
4 *syn* see INFLEXIBLE 3
5 *syn* see FIRM 4
con changing, variable, varying
6 *syn* see SURE 2
7 *syn* see WHOLE 5
con distracted, erratic, wandering
fixedly *adv syn* see HARD 7
rel stubbornly, tenaciously
fixture *n syn* see INSTITUTION
fix up *vb syn* see DRESS UP 1
fizz *vb syn* see HISS
fizzle *vb syn* see HISS
flabbergast *vb syn* see SURPRISE 2
rel overwhelm, shock
flabby *adj syn* see LIMP 1
rel soft, yielding; impotent, powerless; enervated, languid, listless; spiritless
con taut, tense, tight; strong, sturdy, tenacious, tough; gritty, plucky
ant firm
flaccid *adj syn* see LIMP 1
rel emasculated, enervated, unnerved; debilitated, enfeebled, sapped, weakened
con elastic, flexible, springy, supple; limber, lithe; energetic, lusty, nervous, vigorous
ant resilient
flag *n* a piece of fabric that is used as a symbol (as of a nation) or as a signaling device <we respect the *flag* of our fathers>
syn banderole, banner, bannerol, burgee, color, ensign, gonfalon, gonfanon, jack, oriflamme, pendant, pennant, pennon, standard, streamer
flag *vb syn* see SIGNAL
flag *vb* 1 *syn* see FAIL 1
2 *syn* see DROOP 3
rel abate, ebb, wane
flagellate *vb syn* see WHIP 1
flagitious *adj syn* see VICIOUS 2
rel criminal, scandalous, sinful, wicked; disgraceful, shameful; flagrant, glaring, gross
con good, upstanding, virtuous
flagrant *adj syn* see EGREGIOUS
rel bold, conspicuous, obvious, striking; heinous, flagitious, wicked; disgraceful, scandalous, shameful, shocking

syn synonym(s)   *rel* related word(s)
ant antonym(s)   *con* contrasted word(s)
idiom idiomatic equivalent(s)
‖ use limited; if in doubt, see a dictionary

con hidden, inconspicuous, obscure; excusable, unimportant
flagrante delicto *adv syn* see RED-HANDED
flag-waver *n syn* see PATRIOTEER
flair *n syn* see GIFT 2
flake (off) *vb syn* see SCALE 2
‖**flake out** *vb syn* see COLLAPSE 2
flam *n syn* see IMPOSTURE
flamboyant *adj* 1 *syn* see ORNATE
2 *syn* see SHOWY
flame *n* 1 *syn* see SWEETHEART 1
2 *syn* see GIRL FRIEND 1
3 *syn* see BOYFRIEND 2
flame *vb syn* see BLAZE
rel coruscate, glint; fire, ignite, kindle, light
flaming *adj syn* see BURNING 1
2 *syn* see IMPASSIONED
flammable *adj syn* see COMBUSTIBLE 1
ant incombustible, nonflammable
flap *n syn* see COMMOTION 2
flapdoodle *n syn* see NONSENSE 2
flare *vb syn* see BLAZE
rel dart, shoot; flicker, flutter
idiom burst into flame
ant gutter out
flare (up) *vb syn* see ANGER 2
idiom ‖blow one's stack (*or* top *or* lid), fly into a passion, fly off the handle
con calm (down), cool (off *or* down), simmer down
flare *n syn* see OUTBREAK 1
flare-up *n syn* see OUTBURST 1
flaring *adj syn* see BURNING 1
flash *vb* 1 to shoot forth light (as in rays or sparks) <lightning *flashed* in the sky>
syn coruscate, glance, gleam, glimmer, glint, glisten, glitter, scintillate, shimmer, spangle, sparkle, twinkle
rel dart, shoot; blare, blaze, burn, flame, flare, glare, glow, incandesce; blink, flicker, spark; dazzle; beam, radiate, shine
2 *syn* see BLINK 2
3 *syn* see SHOW 4
flash *n* 1 a sudden brief light <saw a *flash* sweep across the sky>
syn coruscation, glance, gleam, glimmer, glint, glisten, glitter, quiver, scintillation, shimmer, sparkle, twinkle
rel blare, blaze, flame, flare, glare, glow; flicker; beam, ray
2 *syn* see INSTANT 1
idiom half a second (*or* shake), twinkling of an eye
flashy *adj syn* see GAUDY
rel flamboyant, florid, ornate; flashing, glittering, sparkling
con dowdy, slatternly; natural, simple, unaffected; chic, modish, smart
flat *adj* 1 *syn* see LEVEL
idiom flat as a billiard table (*or* pancake)
con rugged, scabrous, uneven; hilly, mountainous
2 *syn* see PRONE 4
3 *syn* see DOWNRIGHT 2
4 *syn* see COLORLESS 2
5 *syn* see INSIPID 3
rel dull, lifeless; flavorless, stale, tasteless
6 *syn* see UNPALATABLE 1
7 *syn* see POOR 1
8 *syn* see DULL 7
flat *n syn* see APARTMENT 1

||flatfoot *n syn* see POLICEMAN

flatly *adv syn* see EVENLY 3

flat-out *adj syn* see UTTER

flat-out *adv syn* see FAST 2

flatten *vb* 1 *syn* see EVEN 1

2 *syn* see FELL 1

flatter *vb* to be becoming to <a neckline designed to *flatter* the stylishly stout>
syn become, enhance, suit
rel adorn, beautify, decorate, embellish, ornament; finish, perfect
idiom put in the best light
con deface, disfigure; distort; mar, spoil

flattery *n* flattering speech or attentions <*flattery* will get you nowhere>
syn adulation, blandishment, blarney, incense, oil, soft soap
rel compliments; laud, laudation, praise; cajolery, coaxing, wheedling; fulsomeness, unctuousness; bootlicking, fawning, ingratiation, obsequiousness, sycophancy, toadying, truckling
idiom honeyed words
con censure, condemnation, criticism, reprehension, reprobation; castigation, excoriation; aspersion, insult; contempt, disdain, scorn; belittling, depreciation, derogation, detraction, disparagement

flatulent *adj syn* see INFLATED
rel empty, hollow, vain; shallow, superficial
con weighty; cogent, compelling, convincing, telling; forceful, forcible, potent

flaunt *vb syn* see SHOW 4
rel boast, brag, gasconade, vaunt; disclose, discover, divulge, reveal; advertise, broadcast, declare, proclaim, publish; flourish, wave
idiom dangle before the (*or* one's) eyes
con camouflage, cloak, disguise, dissemble, mask; bury, conceal, hide, screen, secrete

flavor *n syn* see TASTE 3

flavorless *adj syn* see UNPALATABLE 1
ant flavorsome

flavorsome *adj syn* see PALATABLE
con flat, insipid, vapid, wishy-washy; bland, mild; displeasing, tasteless, unflavored, unpalatable, unpleasant, unsavory
ant flavorless

flaw *n syn* see BLEMISH
rel cleavage, rent, rip, riving, split, tear

flawed *adj* 1 *syn* see DAMAGED
ant flawless

2 *syn* see FAULTY
ant flawless

flawless *adj* 1 *syn* see WHOLE 1
ant flawed

2 *syn* see PERFECT 2

3 *syn* see IMPECCABLE 1
con defective, faulty, flawed, imperfect, unsound

4 *syn* see IDEAL 3

flaxen *adj syn* see BLOND 1

flay *vb syn* see LAMBASTE 3
rel assail, attack, berate, tongue-lash

fleckless *adj syn* see PERFECT 2

flection *n syn* see TURN 4

fledgling *n syn* see NOVICE

flee *vb* 1 *syn* see ESCAPE 1
rel avoid, elude, evade, shun
idiom take a (runout) powder

2 *syn* see RUN 2

con stand, stay

fleece *vb* 1 to obtain something valuable from by improper means <a corrupt mayor who *fleeced* the town treasury>
syn blood, milk, mulct, rook, stick, sweat; *compare* CHEAT, EXTORT 1
rel cheat, cozen, defraud, do, hustle, ||rope (in), swindle, take; pluck
idiom sell one a bill of goods, take for a sucker, take to the cleaner's

2 *syn* see OVERCHARGE 1

fleeceable *adj syn* see EASY 3

fleecy *adj syn* see HAIRY 1

fleer *vb* 1 *syn* see SNEER 1

2 *syn* see SCOFF
rel grin, smile, smirk
idiom cast in one's teeth, curl one's lip at, laugh one out of court

fleet *vb* 1 *syn* see WHILE
rel dally, fritter, idle, potter, squander, waste

2 *syn* see FLY 4
idiom go like the wind (*or* lightning), make (good) time

3 *syn* see HURRY 2

fleet *adj syn* see FAST 3
rel agile, brisk, nimble, spry; alert, animated, lively, spirited, sprightly, vivacious

fleeting *adj syn* see TRANSIENT
con abiding, enduring, persistent
ant lasting

fleetly *adv syn* see FAST 2

flesh *n syn* see MANKIND

fleshiness *n syn* see OBESITY

fleshliness *n syn* see ANIMALITY

fleshly *adj* 1 *syn* see BODILY

2 *syn* see CARNAL 2
rel epicurean, luxurious, sensuous, sybaritic, voluptuous; lay, profane, secular, temporal
con divine, religious, spiritual; intellectual, mental, psychic

fleshy *adj syn* see FAT 2
ant emaciated

flexible *adj syn* see ELASTIC 1
rel amenable, docile, manageable, tractable; acquiescent, compliant
con brittle, crisp, fragile, frangible; firm, hard, rigid, stiff, unyielding, wooden; intractable, recalcitrant, refractory, ungovernable; callous, hardened, indurated
ant inflexible

flexuous *adj syn* see WINDING

flexure *n syn* see TURN 4

flibbertigibbet *n syn* see SCATTERBRAIN

flick *n syn* see MOVIE

flicker *vb* 1 *syn* see FLIT 2

2 *syn* see BLINK 2
rel fluctuate, oscillate, swing, vibrate, waver; blaze, flame, flare, glare; coruscate, glance, gleam, glint, glitter, sparkle; quaver, quiver, tremble

flier *n syn* see PILOT 2

flight *n syn* see ESCAPE 1

flightiness *n syn* see LIGHTNESS
rel capriciousness, fickleness, inconstancy, instability, mercurialness
con constancy, equableness, steadfastness
ant steadiness

flighty *adj syn* see GIDDY 1
rel changeable, inconstant, mercurial, unstable; buoyant, effervescent, volatile; gay, lively, sprightly; irresponsible

con constant, dependable, reliable, responsible, trustworthy; stable; sedate
ant steady

flimflam *n* 1 *syn* see IMPOSTURE
2 *syn* see NONSENSE 2

flimflam *vb* 1 *syn* see DUPE
2 *syn* see CHEAT

flimflammer *n* *syn* see SWINDLER

flimsy *adj* 1 *syn* see FILMY
2 *syn* see IMPLAUSIBLE
ant substantial
3 *syn* see DELICATE 5
4 *syn* see WEAK 1
ant sturdy
5 *syn* see LIMP 1

flinch *vb* *syn* see RECOIL
rel avoid, elude, escape, eschew, evade, shun; retire, withdraw; recede, retreat

fling *vb* 1 *syn* see RUSH 1
2 *syn* see THROW 1
con catch, grab, receive

fling *n* 1 a casual attempt <I'm willing to take a *fling* at almost any job>
syn crack, go, pop, shot, slap, stab, ‖stagger, try, whack, whirl
rel attempt, effort, essay, trial
con best, limit, maximum
ant utmost
2 *syn* see SPREE 1

flip (through) *vb* *syn* see BROWSE

flippancy *n* *syn* see LIGHTNESS
rel archness, pertness, sauciness; impishness, mischievousness, playfulness, roguishness, waggishness; cheekiness, cockiness, freshness
con earnestness, gravity, soberness, solemnity
ant seriousness

flirt *vb* *syn* see TRIFLE 1
rel disport, play, sport; caress, fondle, pet

flirt *n* a woman who trifles amorously <a charming girl but an outrageous *flirt*>
syn coquette, vamp

flit *vb* 1 *syn* see HURRY 2
2 to move briskly, irregularly, and usually intermittently <the hummingbird *flitted* from flower to flower>
syn dance, flicker, flitter, flutter, hover
rel dart, float, fly, scud, skim
3 *syn* see FLY 4

flitter *vb* *syn* see FLIT 2
rel quaver, quiver, teeter

float *vb* 1 *syn* see DRIFT 1
2 *syn* see HANG 3
3 *syn* see FLY 1
rel drift, waft

floater *n* *syn* see VAGABOND

flock *n* 1 *syn* see MULTITUDE 1
2 *syn* see DROVE 2

flog *vb* *syn* see WHIP 1

flood *n* 1 *syn* see FLOW
2 a great or overwhelming flow of or as if of water <a *flood* of messages>
syn cataclysm, cataract, deluge, flooding, inundation, niagara, overflow, pour, spate, torrent
rel current, flow, stream, tide; excess, superfluity, surplus; outgushing, outpouring

con dribble, drip, dropping
ant trickle

flood *vb* 1 *syn* see DELUGE 1
2 *syn* see DELUGE 3

flooding *n* *syn* see FLOOD 2

floor *vb* *syn* see FELL 1

floozy *n* *syn* see DOXY 1

‖**flop** *vb* 1 *syn* see RETIRE 4
2 *syn* see FAIL 4
con come off, go over, succeed

flop *n* *syn* see FAILURE 5

floppy *adj* *syn* see LIMP 1

florid *adj* 1 *syn* see RHETORICAL
2 *syn* see ORNATE
rel ostentatious, pretentious, showy
con bald, bare, barren; austere, unadorned
3 *syn* see RUDDY
ant pallid

florilegium *n* *syn* see ANTHOLOGY

floss *n* *syn* see DOWN

flotsam *n* *syn* see DRIFTWOOD

flounce *vb* *syn* see SASHAY

flounder *vb* *syn* see WALLOW 2
rel strive, struggle; labor, toil, travail

flourish *vb* *syn* see SUCCEED 3
rel bloom, blossom, flower; augment, increase, multiply; amplify, expand; develop, grow, wax
con shrivel, wither; contract, shrink; abate, ebb, subside, wane
ant languish

flourishing *adj* enjoying a vigorous growth <a *flourishing* economy>
syn booming, prospering, prosperous, roaring, robust, thrifty, thriving; *compare* SUCCESSFUL
rel vigorous; rampant, rank; exuberant, lush, luxuriant, profuse
idiom going strong, in full swing
con decadent, declining, deteriorating; failing; decreasing, dwindling
ant languishing

flout *vb* *syn* see SCOFF
rel disregard, slight; repudiate, spurn; insult; defy
idiom thumb one's nose at
con admire, esteem, regard, respect
ant revere

flow *vb* 1 *syn* see POUR 2
rel cascade, jet, spout, spurt; well; course, ripple, run
2 *syn* see SPRING 1
3 *syn* see TEEM
4 *syn* see DISCHARGE 5

flow *n* something suggestive of running water <she expressed herself in a *flow* of words>
syn current, drift, flood, flux, rush, spate, stream, tide
rel progression, sequence, series, succession; continuance, continuation, continuity

flower *n* 1 the often showy part of a seed plant that bears reproductive organs <children picking *flowers* in the meadow>
syn bloom, blossom, posy
rel bud, floret; shoot, spray
2 *syn* see BEST
3 *syn* see ARISTOCRACY

flower *vb* *syn* see BLOSSOM

flowering *n* *syn* see DEVELOPMENT
ant fading

---

syn synonym(s)   *rel* related word(s)
ant antonym(s)   *con* contrasted word(s)
idiom idiomatic equivalent(s)
‖ use limited; if in doubt, see a dictionary

flowery *adj syn* see RHETORICAL
  rel diffuse, prolix, redundant, verbose, wordy
  con compendious, concise, laconic, pithy, succinct, summary, terse

flowing *adj syn* see EASY 9

flub *vb syn* see BOTCH

fluctuant *adj* 1 *syn* see WEAK 2
  2 *syn* see UNCERTAIN 1

flue *n syn* see DOWN

fluent *adj* 1 *syn* see VOCAL 3
  rel loquacious, talkative; easy, effortless, facile, smooth; apt, prompt, quick, ready
  con stammering, stuttering; tongue-tied; dumb; fettered, hampered, trammeled
  2 *syn* see EASY 9

fluff *n* 1 *syn* see DOWN
  2 *syn* see ERROR 2

fluff *vb syn* see BOTCH

fluid *adj syn* see CHANGEABLE 1

fluky *adj syn* see ACCIDENTAL

flummadiddle *n syn* see NONSENSE 2

flummox *vb syn* see FAIL 4

flurry *n syn* see STIR 1
  rel confusion, excitement, turbulence, turmoil; haste, hurry

flurry *vb syn* see DISCOMPOSE 1
  rel bewilder, distract, perplex; excite, galvanize, provoke, quicken, stimulate

flush *n* 1 *syn* see BLOOM 3
  2 *syn* see BLOOM 2

flush *vb* 1 *syn* see BLUSH
  2 *syn* see EVEN 1

flush *adj* 1 *syn* see RICH 1
  2 *syn* see RUDDY
  3 *syn* see LEVEL

flushed *adj syn* see RUDDY

fluster *vb* 1 *syn* see DISCOMPOSE 1
  rel bewilder, confound, distract, mystify, nonplus, perplex, puzzle; addle, confuse, fuddle, muddle
  ant steady
  2 *syn* see CONFUSE 2

flutter *vb syn* see FLIT 2
  rel quaver, quiver, shake, tremble, wobble; beat, palpitate, pulsate, throb; fluctuate, oscillate, swing, vibrate; flap

flux *n* 1 *syn* see DIARRHEA
  2 *syn* see FLOW

flux *vb syn* see LIQUEFY

fly *vb* 1 to pass lightly or quickly over or above a surface <clouds *flying* across the sky>
  syn dart, float, sail, scud, shoot, skim, skirr
  rel dance, flicker, flit, flitter, flutter, hover; arise, ascend, mount, rise, soar; glide, slide, slip
  2 *syn* see RUN 2
  rel hide; retreat, withdraw
  3 *syn* see ESCAPE 1
  4 to pass swiftly as if on wings <how time *flies* when we are happy>
  syn fleet, flit, sail, sweep, wing
  rel soar; hasten, hurry, speed; barrel, skim, whisk, zip; breeze, dart, dash, rush, tear
  idiom go like the wind (*or* lightning), outstrip the wind
  con dally, dawdle, dillydally, drift; lag, linger, loiter, trail; crawl, creep, poke
  ant drag
  5 *syn* see HURRY 2

fly-boy *n syn* see PILOT 2

fly-by-night *adj syn* see UNRELIABLE 1

flying colors *n pl syn* see SUCCESS

flyspeck *n syn* see POINT 11

foam *n* a mass of bubbles gathering in or on the surface of a liquid or something as insubstantial as such a mass <a *foam* of delicate lace at her throat>
  syn froth, lather, spume, suds, yeast

fob off *vb syn* see FOIST 3

focal point *n syn* see CENTER 2

focus *n syn* see CENTER 2
  idiom center of attraction (*or* interest), focus of attention

focus *vb* 1 *syn* see FASTEN 3
  2 *syn* see CONVERGE
  idiom come to a focus

foe *n syn* see ENEMY
  con associate, companion, comrade
  ant friend

fog *n syn* see HAZE 2

fog *vb* 1 *syn* see OBSCURE
  rel bewilder, distract, mystify, perplex, puzzle
  2 *syn* see CONFUSE 4
  rel addle, muddle

foggy *adj syn* see HAZY
  idiom in a fog

fogram *n syn* see FOGY

fogy *n* a person who is behind the times or overconservative <his father is an old *fogy*>
  syn antediluvian, fogram, fossil, fuddyduddy, mid-Victorian, mossback, square, stick-in-the-mud
  rel conservative, diehard; back number
  idiom regular old fogy
  ant modern

fogyish *adj syn* see CONSERVATIVE 1
  ant up-to-the-minute

foible *n syn* see FAULT 2
  rel imperfection, shortcoming

foil *vb syn* see FRUSTRATE 1
  rel discomfit, disconcert, embarrass, faze, rattle; curb, restrain

foist *vb* 1 *syn* see INSINUATE 3
  2 *syn* see IMPOSE 4
  3 to pass or offer (something spurious) as genuine or worthy <his theory was far more reasonable than many *foisted* on the public>
  syn fob off, palm (on *or* upon), palm off, pass off, work off; *compare* IMPOSE 4
  rel beguile, deceive, delude, mislead; bamboozle, dupe, gull, hoax, hoodwink, trick; cheat, defraud, overreach, swindle; impose, inflict, wish

fold *n syn* see WRINKLE

fold *vb* 1 *syn* see DOUBLE 2
  2 *syn* see FAIL 5

fold up *vb* 1 *syn* see GIVE 12
  2 *syn* see RUIN 3

foliage *n* the leaves of plants <a tree with handsome *foliage*>
  syn leafage, umbrage, verdure
  rel greenness, herbage; growth, vegetation

folk *n* 1 *syn* see FAMILY 1
  2 **folks** *pl syn* see FAMILY 2

folklore *n syn* see LORE 2

follow *vb* 1 to come after in time <a juggling act *followed* the singer>
  syn ensue, succeed, supervene
  rel displace, replace, supersede, supplant; postdate

con herald, lead, preface, usher (in); ante-date, predate

ant precede

2 to go after or on the track of < *followed* the boys to their hiding place>

syn chase, chivy, pursue, trail; *compare* TAIL

rel trace, track; hunt, search, seek; dog, hound, tag; accompany, attend, convoy; ape, copy, imitate; exercise, practice

con guide, lead, pilot, steer; elude, escape, evade; abandon, desert

ant precede; forsake

3 *syn* see OBEY

4 *syn* see APPREHEND 1

follower *n* one who attaches himself to another < he is a born *follower* >

syn adherent, cohort, disciple, henchman, partisan, satellite, sectary, sectator, supporter

rel addict, devotee, freak, habitué, votary; admirer, fan, fancier; advocate; bootlicker, hanger-on, lickspittle, parasite, sycophant, toady

ant leader

following *adj syn* see NEXT

following *n* 1 *syn* see ENTOURAGE

2 the body of persons who attach themselves to another especially as disciples, patrons, or admirers < he has a strong *following* in this country>

syn audience, clientage, clientele, public

following *prep syn* see AFTER 2

folly *n syn* see FOOLISHNESS

rel fatuity, stupidity

ant wisdom

foment *vb syn* see INCITE

rel goad, spur; cultivate, foster, nurse, nurture

con repress, suppress

ant quell

fomenter *n syn* see INSTIGATOR

fond *adj* 1 *syn* see OPTIMISTIC

2 *syn* see LOVING

rel responsive, romantic, sentimental, sympathetic, tender, warm; indulgent

idiom silly over

fondle *vb syn* see CARESS

rel clasp, embrace, hug; nestle, snuggle

fondness *n* 1 *syn* see LOVE 1

2 *syn* see APPETITE 3

rel partiality, predilection; relish

con disgust; hate

font name *n syn* see GIVEN NAME

food *n* 1 things that are edible < conserve a nation's supply of *food* >

syn bread, ‖chow, comestibles, ‖eats, edibles, feed, foodstuff, grub, meat, ‖muckamuck, nurture, provender, provisions, scoff, ‖tuck, viands, victuals, vivres

2 material which feeds and supports the mind or spirit < *food* for thought>

syn aliment, nourishment, nutriment, pabulum, pap, sustenance

foodstuff *n syn* see FOOD 1

foofaraw *n syn* see COMMOTION 3

fool *n* 1 a person lacking in judgment or prudence < stop acting like a *fool* >

syn ass, asshead, donkey, doodle, idiot, imbecile, jackass, jerk, madman, mooncalf, nincom, nincompoop, ninny, ninnyhammer, poop, ‖schmo, ‖schmuck, tomfool

rel blockhead, dimwit, dope, dumbbell, dummy, nitwit, numskull, pinhead; birdbrain, featherbrain, featherhead, rattlebrain, scatterbrain; goose, silly

2 a retainer formerly kept to provide casual entertainment < a king's *fool* >

syn idiot, jester, motley

rel buffoon, clown, comedian, comic, merry-andrew

3 one who is victimized or made to appear foolish < he's nobody's *fool* >

syn butt, chump, ‖come-on, ‖cull, dupe, easy mark, fall guy, fish, gudgeon, gull, mark, monkey, ‖mug, patsy, pigeon, sap, saphead, ‖schlemiel, simple, sucker, victim

rel pushover; laughingstock; loser; instrument, tool

4 one who is mentally deficient < a badly retarded child, little more than a *fool* >

syn ament, cretin, ‖feeb, half-wit, idiot, imbecile, moron, natural, simpleton, softhead, underwit, zany

fool *vb* 1 *syn* see TRIFLE 1

2 *syn* see MEDDLE

3 *syn* see BANTER

4 *syn* see DUPE

fool (around) *vb syn* see PHILANDER

fool (away) *vb syn* see WASTE 2

foolhardy *adj syn* see ADVENTUROUS

rel headlong, impetuous, precipitate

con calculating, cautious, circumspect; careful, prudent

ant wary

fooling *n syn* see HORSEPLAY

foolish *adj* 1 *syn* see SIMPLE 3

rel idiotic, imbecilic, moronic; daft, feebleminded, half-witted; ‖half-assed, half-cocked; irrational

con bright, clever, intelligent, quick-witted

ant smart

2 felt to be ridiculous because not exhibiting good or conventional sense < a *foolish* investment>

syn absurd, ‖balmy, crazy, ‖dilly, ‖dippy, donkeyish, dotty, fantastic, harebrained, idleheaded, insane, loony, loopy, lunatic, mad, ‖potty, preposterous, sappy, silly, tomfool, unearthly, wacky

rel laughable, ludicrous, ridiculous; halfbaked, headless, jerky, nonsensical; offbeat, unacceptable, unconventional, unorthodox

con judicious, sage, sapient; discreet, foresighted, prudent; canny, shrewd, slick

ant sensible; wise

foolishness *n* the quality or state of being foolish < the *foolishness* of so many of her schemes >

syn absurdity, craziness, dottiness, folly, inanity, insanity, lunacy, preposterousness, senselessness, silliness, witlessness

rel imprudence, indiscretion, injudiciousness, insensibility, unwiseness; irrationality, unreasonableness; impracticality; absurdness, ludicrousness, ridiculousness; bull, bunk, nonsense

con discretion, judiciousness, prudence, sensibility, wiseness; rationality, reason-

---

syn synonym(s)   *rel* related word(s)
ant antonym(s)   *con* contrasted word(s)
idiom idiomatic equivalent(s)
‖ use limited, if in doubt, see a dictionary

ableness; practicality; soundness; canniness, shrewdness
ant sense, wisdom

foot *n syn* see BOTTOM 3

foot *vb syn* see ADD 2

foot (it) *vb* 1 *syn* see DANCE 1
2 *syn* see WALK 1

footing *n* 1 *syn* see BASIS 1
2 *syn* see STATUS 1
3 *syn* see BASE 1
4 *syn* see TERM 5

footlicker *n syn* see SYCOPHANT

footlights *n pl syn* see DRAMA

footprint *n* the mark or impression made by a foot < *footprints* in the sand >
syn footstep, spoor, step, track, tract, vestige
rel sign, trace; pug, pugmark

footslog *vb syn* see PLOD 1

footstep *n syn* see FOOTPRINT

footstone *n syn* see TOMBSTONE

foozle *vb syn* see BOTCH

fop *n* a man who is conspicuously fashionable or elegant in dress or appearance < felt contempt for the mincing overdressed *fop* >
syn Beau Brummel, blood, buck, coxcomb, dandy, dude, exquisite, gallant, lounge lizard, macaroni, petit-maître, popinjay
rel fashion plate, silk stocking; blade, cavalier, man-about-town, spark, sport, swell; ladies' man, lady-killer, masher
idiom man of the world

for *prep* 1 *syn* see TO 5
2 on the side of < I'm *for* Smith all the way >
syn in favor of, pro, with
con anti, contra
ant against
3 *syn* see AFTER 1

for *conj syn* see BECAUSE

forage *vb syn* see SCOUR 2

forager *n syn* see MARAUDER

foray *vb* 1 *syn* see INVADE 1
2 *syn* see RAID 1

foray *n syn* see INVASION

forbear *vb* 1 *syn* see FORGO
rel bridle, curb, inhibit, restrain; avoid, escape, evade, shun; cease, desist
2 *syn* see REFRAIN 1
rel bear, endure, suffer, tolerate

forbearance *n* 1 *syn* see PATIENCE
rel restraint, temperance; endurance
2 the quality of being forbearing < she is known for her *forbearance* with children >
syn clemency, indulgence, lenience, leniency, mercifulness, tolerance, toleration; *compare* MERCY
rel longanimity, long-suffering, patience; charity, grace, lenity, mercy
con firmness, inflexibility, rigidity, sternness, strictness; austerity, harshness, inexorability
ant vindictiveness

forbearing *adj* disinclined to be severe or rigorous < *forbearing* toward her husband's weaknesses >
syn charitable, clement, easy, indulgent, lenient, merciful, tolerant
rel gentle, mild; longanimous, long-suffering, patient; considerate, thoughtful

con grim, implacable, merciless, relentless; impatient, nervous, restive; firm, inflexible, rigid, stern, strict; austere, harsh
ant unrelenting

forbid *vb* to debar one from using, doing, or entering or something from being used, done, or entered < smoking is *forbidden* here > < security regulations *forbid* the entry of unauthorized persons >
syn ban, enjoin, inhibit, interdict, outlaw, prohibit, taboo
rel debar, exclude, rule out, shut out; estop, obviate, preclude, prevent; forestall; proscribe, veto; check, curb, halt, restrain, stop; bar, block, hinder, impede, obstruct
con allow, let, suffer; authorize, license; approve, endorse, sanction; command, order; abide, bear, endure, tolerate
ant permit; bid

forbiddance *n syn* see TABOO

forbidden *adj* not permitted or allowed < accepting bribes is *forbidden* >
syn banned, prohibited, verboten
ant permitted

force *n* 1 *syn* see POWER 4
rel pressure, strain, stress, tension; headway, impetus, momentum, speed, velocity; vigor
2 *syn* see POINT 3
3 forces *pl syn* see TROOP 2
4 the exercise of power in order to impose one's will on a person or to have one's will with a thing < move a huge boulder by main *force* >
syn coercion, compulsion, constraint, duress, violence
rel fierceness, intensity, vehemence; effort, exertions, pains, trouble
con compliance, submission, yielding; impotence, powerlessness, weakness
ant forcelessness

force *vb* 1 *syn* see RAPE
2 to cause a person or thing to yield to pressure < hunger *forced* him to steal the food >
syn coerce, compel, concuss, constrain, make, oblige, shotgun
rel drive, impel, move; command, enjoin, order; demand, exact, require; press, pressure, sandbag; cause, occasion
con blandish, cajole, coax, wheedle; get, induce, persuade, prevail; entice, inveigle, lure, seduce, tempt

force (on *or* **upon)** *vb syn* see INFLICT 2

force *n syn* see WATERFALL

forced *adj* produced or kept up through effort < a *forced* laugh >
syn farfetched, labored, strained
rel coerced, compelled, constrained; artificial, factitious; unnatural; inflexible, rigid, stiff, wooden; exhausting, fatiguing
con easy, effortless, smooth; impulsive, instinctive, spontaneous; artless, natural, normal, unaffected, unsophisticated
ant unforced

forceful *adj* 1 *syn* see POWERFUL 2
rel compelling, constraining; manful, virile; cogent, telling
con decrepit, frail, infirm
ant feeble
2 *syn* see EMPHATIC

forcefully *adv syn* see HARD 1

forceless *adj syn* see WEAK 4

forcible *adj syn* see POWERFUL 2
  rel intense, vehement, violent; aggressive, assertive, militant, self-assertive; coercive
forcibly *adv syn* see HARD 1
forcing bed *n syn* see BREEDING GROUND
forcing house *n syn* see BREEDING GROUND
fore *adv syn* see BEFORE 1
forebear *n syn* see ANCESTOR 1
forebode *vb syn* see AUGUR 2
foreboding *n syn* see APPREHENSION 3
  rel augury, foretoken, omen, portent, prognostic; forewarning, warning
forecast *vb syn* see FORETELL
  rel conjecture, guess, surmise; conclude, gather, infer
forecast *n syn* see PREDICTION
forecaster *n syn* see PROPHET
foredestine *vb syn* see PREDESTINE 2
forefather *n syn* see ANCESTOR 1
forefeel *vb syn* see FORESEE
foregoer *n syn* see FORERUNNER 2
foregoing *adj syn* see PRECEDING
  ant following
forehandedness *n syn* see ECONOMY
forehead *n* the part of the face above the eyes < his broad noble *forehead* >
  syn brow, frons, front
foreign *adj* 1 *syn* see EXOTIC 1
  ant native
  2 *syn* see EXTRINSIC
  rel incompatible, incongruous, inconsistent, inconsonant; distasteful, obnoxious, repellent, repugnant; accidental, adventitious
  con applicable, apposite, apropos, material, pertinent, relevant; akin, alike, uniform
  ant germane
  3 *syn* see IRRELEVANT
foreigner *n syn* see STRANGER
foreknow *vb syn* see FORESEE
  rel conclude, gather, infer
foreland *n syn* see PROMONTORY
foremost *adj* 1 *syn* see FIRST 1
  2 *syn* see FIRST 3
forename *n syn* see GIVEN NAME
forenoon *n syn* see MORNING 2
forensic *n syn* see ARGUMENTATION
foreordain *vb* 1 *syn* see PREDESTINE 1
  2 *syn* see PREDESTINE 2
forerun *vb* 1 *syn* see PRECEDE 2
  2 *syn* see ANNOUNCE 2
forerunner *n* 1 one that goes before and in some way announces the coming of another < a coma is often a *forerunner* of death >
  syn harbinger, herald, outrider, precursor
  rel anticipator; advertiser, announcer; advertisement, announcement, augury, foretoken, omen, portent, presage, prognostic; forewarning, warning; mark, sign, symptom, token; foreshadow
  2 one belonging to an early developmental period of something contemporary or fully developed < the water-driven dynamo that was a *forerunner* of present-day giant atomic power plants >

syn synonym(s)   *rel* related word(s)
ant antonym(s)   *con* contrasted word(s)
idiom idiomatic equivalent(s)
‖ use limited; if in doubt, see a dictionary

  syn ancestor, antecedent, antecessor, foregoer, precursor, predecessor, prototype
  rel example, exemplar, model, pattern; pioneer; author, initiator, originator
  con consequence, result; effect, event, issue, outgrowth; conclusion, consummation, culmination
  ant end product
foresee *vb* to know or expect in advance that something will happen or come into existence or be made manifest < he had not *foreseen* his present problems >
  syn anticipate, apprehend, divine, forefeel, foreknow, preknow, previse, prevision, see, visualize
  rel forebode, forecast, foretell, predict, presage, prognosticate, prophesy; descry, discern, espy, perceive
  idiom look for, look forward to
foreseer *n syn* see PROPHET
foreshadow *vb* 1 *syn* see ADUMBRATE 1
  2 *syn* see AUGUR 2
foreshow *vb* 1 *syn* see AUGUR 2
  2 *syn* see ANNOUNCE 2
foresight *n syn* see PRUDENCE
  rel clairvoyance, discernment, perception
  ant hindsight
forest *n* a heavily wooded area
  syn timber, timberland, weald, wood(s), woodland
  rel coppice, copse, grove, thicket; wildwood, woodlot
  con field, meadow, plain, prairie
forestall *vb* 1 *syn* see PREVENT 2
  con court, invite, woo; advance, forward, further, promote
  2 *syn* see PREVENT 1
foretell *vb* to tell something before it happens through or as if through special knowledge or occult power < the prophet *foretold* the fall of the city >
  syn adumbrate, augur, call, forecast, portend, predict, presage, prognosticate, prophesy, soothsay, vaticinate
  rel anticipate, apprehend, divine, foreknow, foresee; announce, declare, proclaim; disclose, divulge, reveal; forewarn, warn; bode, forebode, foreshadow, foreshow, foretoken, promise; prefigure
foreteller *n syn* see PROPHET
foretelling *n syn* see PREDICTION
forethink *vb syn* see PREMEDITATE
forethought *n syn* see PRUDENCE 1
  rel deliberation, premeditation; gumption, judgment, sense
  ant rashness; impetuosity
foretime *n syn* see PAST
foretoken *n* something that serves as a sign of future happenings < they felt that his new job was a *foretoken* of good fortune >
  syn augury, bodement, boding, omen, portent, presage, prognostic
  rel badge, indication, mark, note, sign, symptom, token; forerunner, harbinger, herald, precursor; forewarning, shadow, warning; intimation, promise; ostent; hint, inkling, suggestion
foretoken *vb syn* see AUGUR 2
forever *adv syn* see EVER 2
forevermore *adv syn* see EVER 2
forewarn *vb syn* see WARN 1
forewarning *n syn* see WARNING

foreword *n syn* see INTRODUCTION

forfeit *n syn* see FINE

forfeit *vb syn* see LOSE 1

forfend *vb syn* see PREVENT 2

forgather *vb syn* see GATHER 6

forge *vb syn* see MAKE 3
rel beat, pound, turn out; copy, imitate

forget *vb* 1 to lose the remembrance of < I soon *forgot* his name>
syn disremember, ‖misremember, unknow
rel misrecollect; blow up, fluff; unlearn
idiom clean forget, draw a blank
con recall, recollect
ant remember
2 *syn* see NEGLECT
con bethink, mind, recall, recollect
ant remember

forgetful *adj* tending to lose or let go from one's mind something once known or learned <she is growing *forgetful*>
syn oblivious, unmindful, unwitting
rel lax, neglectful, negligent, remiss, slack; careless, heedless, thoughtless; absent, absentminded, abstracted, bemused
con alert, alive, awake, aware, cognizant, conscious, sensible; attentive, considerate, thoughtful

forgetfulness *n syn* see OBLIVION

forgivable *adj syn* see VENIAL

forgive *vb syn* see EXCUSE 1
idiom forgive and forget

forgo *vb* to deny oneself something for the sake of an end <he vowed to *forgo* all luxuries until the debt was paid>
syn eschew, forbear, sacrifice
rel abandon, relinquish, surrender, waive; abdicate, renounce, resign; forsake, give up

fork (out) *vb syn* see SPEND 1

forlorn *adj* 1 dejected and saddened especially by reason of being alone <a *forlorn* lost child>
syn lonely, lonesome, lorn
rel abandoned, deserted, desolate, forgotten, forsaken; miserable, wretched; friendless, homeless; defenseless, helpless; depressed, oppressed, weighed down; alone, solitary
2 *syn* see DESPONDENT
rel cynical, pessimistic; fruitless, futile, vain
con hopeful, optimistic, roseate, rose-colored

form *n* 1 outward appearance of something as distinguished from the substance of which it is made <the carefully graded *form* of the curves>
syn cast, configuration, conformation, figure, shape
rel contour, outline, profile, silhouette; anatomy, framework, skeleton, structure; economy, organism, scheme, system
2 conduct regulated by an external control (as custom or a formal protocol of procedure) <observing the *forms* of polite society>
syn ceremonial, ceremony, formality, liturgy, rite, ritual
rel procedure, proceeding, process; custom, habit, practice, usage; canon, law, precept, regulation, rule; method, mode; decorum, etiquette, propriety

3 a fixed or accepted way of doing or sometimes of expressing something <good *form* in swimming>
syn convenance, convention, usage
rel fashion, manner, mode, style, way

form *vb* 1 *syn* see MAKE 3
rel devise; create, invent; turn out; design, plan, plot, project, scheme; establish, found, organize
con demolish, destroy, ruin, wreck
2 *syn* see DEVELOP 4
3 *syn* see CONSTITUTE 1

formal *adj* 1 *syn* see CEREMONIAL
rel methodical, orderly, regular, systematic; decorous, proper, seemly; prim, unbending; distant, reserved
ant informal
2 *syn* see NOMINAL

formality *n* 1 *syn* see FORM 2
rel convenance, convention
ant informality
2 *syn* see RITE 2

formation *n syn* see MAKEUP 1

former *adj* 1 *syn* see PRECEDING
con following, succeeding, supervening
ant latter
2 having been such at some previous time <*former* friends>
syn bygone, erstwhile, late, old, once, onetime, past, quondam, sometime, whilom
con current, present; future, prospective

formerly *adv syn* see BEFORE 2

formidable *adj* 1 *syn* see FEARFUL 3
ant comforting
2 *syn* see HARD 6
ant simple

formless *adj* having no definite or recognizable form <a *formless* fear>
syn amorphous, inchoate, shapeless, unformed, unshaped
rel chaotic, orderless, unordered, unorganized; indistinct, obscure, unclear, vague; indefinite, indeterminate, undefined; crude, raw, rough, rude
con distinct, formed; definite, explicit, express, specific; ordered, organized

formulate *vb* 1 *syn* see WORD
2 *syn* see CONTRIVE 2
3 *syn* see DRAFT 3

‖**fornent** *prep adj syn* see BESIDE 1

for real *adv syn* see SERIOUSLY 1

forsake *vb syn* see ABANDON 1
rel spurn; leave; abdicate, resign
ant return to; revert (to)

forsaken *adj syn* see DERELICT 1

forswear *vb* 1 *syn* see ABJURE
2 *syn* see PERJURE

fort *n* a structure or place offering resistance to a hostile force <settlers fled to the *fort*>
syn citadel, fastness, fortress, redoubt, stronghold

forte *n* that in which one excels <cooking is her strongest *forte*>
syn eminence, long suit, medium, métier, oyster, strong suit
rel ableness, effectiveness, efficiency; ability, competence; bag, thing
idiom cup of tea, dish of tea, strong point
con inadequacy, incapability, incompetence, inefficiency; greenness, rawness

forth *adv* 1 *syn* see AHEAD 2

2 *syn* see ALONG 1

forthcome *vb syn* see LOOM 2

forthcoming *adj* being soon to appear or take place <the *forthcoming* holidays>
syn approaching, coming, nearing, on-coming, upcoming
rel future; imminent, impending, pending; anticipated, awaited, expected
con distant, far-off, remote; bygone, for-mer, gone, gone-by, past

forthright *adj* 1 *syn* see STRAIGHTFOR-WARD 2
con covert, secret, stealthy, surreptitious, underhand; deceitful, mendacious, un-truthful
ant furtive
2 *syn* see FRANK

forthwith *adv* 1 *syn* see AWAY 3
2 *syn* see SHORT 1

fortify *vb* 1 *syn* see STRENGTHEN 2
rel arouse, rally, rouse, stir; refresh, re-new, restore
con dilute, thin
ant enfeeble
2 *syn* see GIRD 3

fortitude *n* a quality of character combin-ing courage and staying power <she bore up under all her problems with admirable *fortitude*>
syn backbone, grit, guts, intestinal forti-tude, ‖moxie, nerve, sand, spunk; *compare* COURAGE
rel courage, mettle, pith, resoluteness, resolution, spirit, stick-to-itiveness, tenac-ity; boldness, bravery, courageousness, dauntlessness, fearlessness, intrepidity, valiancy, valor, valorousness; endurance, stamina, strength, constancy, determina-tion, perseverance; bottom
con cowardliness, fearfulness, timidity, timorousness; faintheartedness, milksoppi-ness, weakness; cowardice, yellowness
ant pusillanimity

fortress *n syn* see FORT

fortuitous *adj syn* see ACCIDENTAL
con activated, actuated, motivated; pro-jected, schemed
ant deliberate

fortuitously *adv syn* see INCIDENTALLY 1
ant deliberately

fortuity *n syn* see ACCIDENT 1
ant deliberation

fortunate *adj* 1 *syn* see FAVORABLE 5
ant disastrous
2 *syn* see LUCKY
ant unfortunate

fortunately *adv syn* see WELL 5

fortunateness *n syn* see LUCK 3
ant unfortunateness

fortune *n* 1 *syn* see CHANCE 2
rel destiny, doom, portion
con design, intent, intention
2 *syn* see LUCK 3
ant misfortune
3 *syn* see WEALTH 2
4 a very large amount of money <those furs must have cost a *fortune*>

syn ‖bomb, boodle, bundle, mint, packet, pile, pot, ‖roll, wad
idiom king's ransom, pretty penny, tidy sum

fortuneless *adj syn* see POOR 1

forty winks *n pl but sing or pl in constr* *syn* see NAP

forward *adj* 1 *syn* see PRESUMPTUOUS
2 *syn* see WISE 5
ant bashful
3 *syn* see PRECOCIOUS
con regressive, retrograde, retrogressive
ant backward

forward *adv* 1 *syn* see BEFORE 1
2 *syn* see AHEAD 2
ant backward
3 *syn* see ALONG 1

forward *vb* 1 *syn* see ADVANCE 1
rel back, champion, support, uphold
con baffle, circumvent, foil, frustrate, outwit, thwart
ant balk
2 *syn* see SEND 1

fossil *n syn* see FOGY

foster *vb* 1 *syn* see NURSE 2
rel back, champion, support, uphold; entertain, harbor, house, lodge, shelter; accommodate, assist, favor, help, oblige
con combat, fight, oppose, resist, with-stand; curb, inhibit, restrain; ban, forbid, interdict, prohibit; abuse, disregard, ne-glect
2 *syn* see ADVANCE 1

foul *adj* 1 *syn* see OFFENSIVE
2 *syn* see DIRTY 1
rel fetid, malodorous, noisome, putrid, stinking; loathsome, offensive, repulsive, revolting
ant fair; undefiled
3 *syn* see OBSCENE 2

foul *vb* 1 *syn* see SOIL 2
rel contaminate, defile, pollute; desecrate, profane
2 *syn* see CONTAMINATE 2

foul play *n syn* see MURDER

foul up *vb syn* see CONFUSE 5

found *vb* 1 *syn* see BASE
rel support, sustain; erect, raise, rear
2 to set going or to bring into existence <*founded* a new school for graduate studies>
syn constitute, create, establish, institute, organize, set up, start
rel begin, commence, inaugurate, initiate; fashion, form
con close, conclude, end, finish, termi-nate; arrest, check, halt, stay, stop

foundation *n* 1 *syn* see BASIS 1
2 *syn* see BASIS 3
3 *syn* see BASE 1

foundational *adj syn* see FUNDAMENTAL 1

foundationless *adj syn* see BASELESS

founder *n syn* see FATHER 2

founder *vb syn* see SINK 1

fount *n syn* see SOURCE

fountain *n syn* see SOURCE

fountainhead *n syn* see SOURCE

four *n syn* see QUARTET

fourberie *n syn* see DECEPTION 1

four-flush *vb syn* see DECEIVE

foursome *n syn* see QUARTET

foursquare *adj syn* see SQUARE 1

---

syn synonym(s)   *rel* related word(s)
ant antonym(s)   *con* contrasted word(s)
idiom idiomatic equivalent(s)
‖ use limited; if in doubt, see a dictionary

fourth n syn see QUARTER 1

foxiness n syn see CUNNING 2

foxy adj syn see SLY 2
rel deceitful, dishonest
con aboveboard, forthright, straightforward

foyer n syn see VESTIBULE

fracas n 1 syn see QUARREL
2 syn see BRAWL 2

fractional adj syn see INCOMPLETE 1

fractious adj 1 syn see UNRULY 1
ant orderly
2 syn see IRRITABLE
ant peaceable

fracturable adj syn see FRAGILE 1

fracture n syn see BREACH 3

fragile adj 1 easily broken < a *fragile* dish of the finest porcelain >
syn breakable, delicate, fracturable, frail, frangible, shatterable, shattery
rel brittle, crisp, crumbly, crunchy, friable, short
con infrangible, unbreakable; elastic, flexible, resilient; stout, strong, sturdy, tenacious
ant tough
2 syn see WEAK 1
ant durable

fragment n 1 syn see PARTICLE
2 syn see END 4

fragment vb syn see SHATTER 1

fragmentary adj syn see INCOMPLETE 1

fragrance n a sweet or pleasant odor < the *fragrance* of flowers >
syn aroma, balm, bouquet, incense, perfume, redolence, scent, spice
rel odor, smell
con fetidness, fetor, malodor, noisomeness, rancidness, rankness
ant stench, stink

fragrant adj syn see SWEET 2
rel delectable, delicious, delightful
ant fetid

frail adj 1 syn see WEAK 1
rel slender, slight, slim, tenuous, thin; petty, puny
con hale, healthy, sound
ant robust
2 syn see FRAGILE 1
con solid, substantial

frailty n syn see FAULT 2

frame vb 1 syn see CONTRIVE 2
2 syn see DRAFT 3
3 syn see MAKE 2

framework n syn see STRUCTURE 3

franchise n syn see SUFFRAGE

franchise vb syn see ENFRANCHISE

frangible adj syn see FRAGILE 1

frank adj marked by free, forthright, and sincere expression < a *frank* answer >
syn candid, direct, forthright, man-to-man, open, openhearted, plain, plainspoken, single, single-eyed, single-hearted, single-minded, straightforward, unconcealed, undisguised, undissembled, undissembling, unmannered, unreserved, unvarnished; *compare* COMMUNICATIVE, STRAIGHTFORWARD 2
rel ingenuous, naive, natural, simple, unsophisticated; bluff, blunt; heart-to-heart, sincere; honest, scrupulous, upright; dispassionate, fair, impartial, just, unbiased; barefaced, brazen, outspoken, uninhibited

con reserved, reticent, secretive, silent, taciturn, uncommunicative; covert, furtive, secret, sneaking, underhand; deceitful, deceptive, dishonest, evasive, false, lying, mendacious, tricky, untruthful; insincere
ant reticent

frank n syn see FRANKFURTER

frankfurter n a seasoned beef or beef and pork sausage
syn dog, frank, hot dog, wiener, wienerwurst, ‖wienie

frantic adj syn see FURIOUS 2

frantically adv syn see HARD 2

fraternity n syn see ASSOCIATION 2

fraud n 1 syn see DECEPTION 1
2 syn see IMPOSTURE
rel bamboozlement, bamboozling, dupery, duping, hoodwinking
3 syn see IMPOSTOR

fray n 1 syn see BRAWL 2
rel contention, discord, dissension, strife
2 syn see CLASH 2

frayed adj syn see RAGGED

frazzle vb syn see EXHAUST 4

frazzled adj syn see RAGGED

freak n 1 syn see CAPRICE
2 one that is physically abnormal < pitiful *freaks* displayed in sideshows >
syn abortion, lusus, miscreation, monster, monstrosity
rel aberration, chimera, malconformation, malformation, misshape, mosaic, mutation, sport; abnormality, anomaly, curiosity, oddity; rara avis, rarity; androgyne, hermaphrodite
idiom freak of nature
3 syn see ENTHUSIAST

freakish adj syn see ARBITRARY 1

freckle vb syn see SPECKLE 1

free adj 1 not subject to the rule or control of another < a *free* country >
syn autarchic, autarkic, autonomous, independent, separate, sovereign
rel free-born, unenslaved; delivered, emancipated, enfranchised, freed, liberated, released; democratic, self-directing, self-governing, self-ruling; sui juris; individualistic, unregimented
con coerced, compelled, constrained, forced, obliged; dependent, restricted, subject; inferior, subordinate, subservient; captive, enslaved, enthralled, subjugated
ant bond
2 not bound, confined, or detained by force < the prisoner was now *free* >
syn loose, unconfined, unrestrained
rel unbound, unchained, unfettered, unshackled, untied; clear, loose, scot-free; emancipated, freed, liberated; independent
idiom at liberty, free as a bird, free as air, free to come and go
con confined, restrained; impounded, imprisoned, incarcerated, interned, jailed; bound, chained, fettered, shackled, tied
3 syn see LIBERAL 1
ant close
4 syn see OUTSPOKEN
5 not costing or charging anything < a *free* public school >
syn chargeless, complimentary, costless, gratis, gratuitous
rel unpaid, unrecompensed, unremunerated

idiom for free, for love, for nothing, on the cuff, on the house
con charged, paid; costly, dear, expensive, high, high priced
6 not having the affections fixed on a particular object < she was happy to be *free* and in no hurry to fall in love again >
syn fancy-free, heart-whole

free *vb* to relieve from constraint or restraint < *free* an oppressed people >
syn discharge, disenthrall, disimprison, emancipate, liberate, loose, loosen, manumit, redeem, release, ||spring, unbind, unchain, unshackle
rel clear, detach, disencumber, disengage, disentangle; extricate; deliver, ransom, redeem, rescue; affranchise, enfranchise
idiom cut loose
con fetter, hamper, hog-tie, manacle, shackle, trammel; immure, imprison, incarcerate, intern, jail; circumscribe, confine, limit, restrict; curb, inhibit, restrain; enslave, enthrall, subjugate

freebooter *n* 1 *syn* see MARAUDER
2 *syn* see PIRATE

freedom *n* the power or condition of acting without compulsion < *freedom* of the press >
syn liberty, license
rel exemption, immunity; prerogative, privilege, right; compass, latitude, scope, sweep
con coercion, compulsion, constraint; restraint
ant necessity

free-for-all *n* *syn* see BRAWL 2
free hand *n* *syn* see CARTE BLANCHE
freehanded *adj* *syn* see LIBERAL 1
freeloader *n* *syn* see PARASITE
freely *adv* EASILY 1, effortlessly, facilely, lightly, readily, smoothly, well
free-minded *adj* *syn* see HAPPY-GO-LUCKY
free-spoken *adj* *syn* see OUTSPOKEN
freezer *n* *syn* see JAIL
freezing *adj* *syn* see COLD 1
ant scorching
freight *n* *syn* see LOAD 1
frenetic *adj* *syn* see FURIOUS 2
frenzied *adj* *syn* see FURIOUS 2
frenziedly *adv* *syn* see HARD 2
frenzy *n* *syn* see DELIRIUM
frenzy *vb* *syn* see MADDEN 1
frequent *adj* *syn* see COMMON 4
ant infrequent, rare
frequent *vb* to go to or be in often < he *frequents* the bar down the street >
syn affect, hang around, hang out, haunt, resort
rel attend, go (to), visit; infest, overrun
con avoid, miss, shun
ant shun
frequenter *n* *syn* see HABITUÉ 1
frequently *adv* 1 *syn* see OFTEN
ant infrequently
2 *syn* see USUALLY 2
fresh *adj* 1 *syn* see NEW 1

rel gleaming, glistening, sparkling; striking, vital, vivid; virginal, youthful; crude, green, raw, uncouth; artless, naive, natural, unsophisticated
con hackneyed, shopworn, stereotyped, threadbare, trite
ant stale
2 *syn* see ADDITIONAL
3 *syn* see INEXPERIENCED
4 *syn* see WISE 5
freshman *n* *syn* see NOVICE
freshness *n* *syn* see INEXPERIENCE
fret *vb* 1 *syn* see WORRY 3
rel chafe, fume; brood, mope
idiom eat one's heart out
2 *syn* see ANNOY 1
3 *syn* see CHAFE 3
4 *syn* see RIPPLE
fretful *adj* 1 *syn* see IRRITABLE
rel captious, carping, caviling, critical, faultfinding; contrary, perverse
con forbearing, long-suffering, patient, resigned; subdued, submissive, tame
2 *syn* see IMPATIENT 1
friable *adj* *syn* see SHORT 6
fribble *adj* *syn* see GIDDY 1
fribbling *adj* *syn* see GIDDY 1
fried *adj* *syn* see INTOXICATED 1
friend *n* a person with whom one is on good and, usually, familiar terms < he is one of my closest *friends* >
syn acquaintance, amigo, cater-cousin, confidant, familiar, intimate, mate; *compare* ASSOCIATE 3
rel alter ego, best friend, bosom friend; ally, colleague, partner; nodding acquaintance
con enemy; adversary, antagonist, opponent; competitor, rival
ant foe
friendliness *n* *syn* see GOODWILL 1
rel affability, amiability, congeniality, cordiality, neighborliness, sociability
ant unfriendliness
friendly *adj* 1 *syn* see AMICABLE 1
rel close, familiar, intimate; affectionate, devoted, loving
ant unfriendly; belligerent
2 *syn* see HARMONIOUS 3
3 *syn* see SYMPATHETIC 2
ant unfriendly
friendship *n* *syn* see GOODWILL 1
rel affinity, attraction; empathy; accord, concord, consonance, harmony; alliance, coalition, federation, fusion, league
con antagonism, antipathy, hostility, rancor; hate
ant animosity
fright *n* 1 *syn* see FEAR 1
2 *syn* see EYESORE
fright *vb* *syn* see FRIGHTEN
frighten *vb* to strike or to fill with fear or dread < the puppy was *frightened* by the unfamiliar noises >
syn affright, alarm, awe, fright, scare, ||spook, startle, terrify, terrorize
rel appall, astound, daunt, disconcert, dismay, faze, horrify, shock; demoralize, unman, unnerve; browbeat, bulldoze, cow, intimidate; agitate, discompose, disquiet, perturb, upset
idiom curdle the blood, curl the hair, frighten one out of one's wits, freeze the blood, give one a scare, give one a turn,

---

syn synonym(s)   *rel* related word(s)
ant antonym(s)   *con* contrasted word(s)
idiom idiomatic equivalent(s)
|| use limited; if in doubt, see a dictionary

make one's blood run cold, make one's flesh creep, make one's hair stand on end, make one's teeth chatter, make one tremble, put one's heart in one's mouth, scare hell out of, scare one spitless, scare one stiff, scare the life out of, scare the pants off of, scare to death, strike terror into, take one's breath away

con embolden, encourage, hearten, reassure

frightened *adj syn see* AFRAID 1
idiom in a fright
ant unfrightened

frightful *adj syn see* FEARFUL 3

frigid *adj* 1 *syn see* COLD 1
2 *syn see* COLD 2
3 free from or deficient in passion < claimed his wife was a *frigid* woman >
syn cold, inhibited, passionless, undersexed, unresponsive
idiom as cold as an iceberg
con affectionate, demanding, loving
ant ardent; amorous

frill *n syn see* LUXURY

fringe *n syn see* BORDER 1

fringe *vb syn see* BORDER 1

frippery *n syn see* FINERY

frisk *vb* 1 *syn see* GAMBOL
2 *syn see* SEARCH 2

frisky *adj syn see* PLAYFUL 1

fritter *vb syn see* WASTE 2

frivol away *vb syn see* WASTE 2

frivolity *n syn see* LIGHTNESS
rel coquetting, dallying, flirting, toying, trifling; fun, game, jest, play, sport
ant seriousness; staidness

frivolous *adj syn see* GIDDY 1
rel shallow, superficial, unprofound; gay, light, playful
ant serious

‖**frogskin** *n syn see* DOLLAR

frolic *vb* 1 *syn see* REVEL 1
2 *syn see* GAMBOL

frolic *n syn see* PRANK

frolicsome *adj* 1 *syn see* ANTIC 2
2 *syn see* PLAYFUL 1

from *prep* 1 *syn see* AFTER 1
2 in the face of < protect them *from* exploitation >
syn against

frondeur *n syn see* REBEL

frons *n syn see* FOREHEAD

front *n* 1 *syn see* FOREHEAD
2 *syn see* MASK 2
3 a person, group, or thing used to mask the identity or true character of a controlling agent < the export company was a *front* for illegal activities >
syn blind
rel disguise, facade, mask

front *vb* 1 *syn see* FACE 1
2 *syn see* FACE 3
3 *syn see* MEET 6
4 *syn see* ACCOST 2

frontier *n* 1 a region between two countries < lived on the *frontier* between Mexico and the U.S. >
syn border, borderland, march, marchland
2 a rural region that forms the margin of settled or developed territory < settlers found living on the *frontier* was a hard life >

syn backcountry, backland, ‖backveld, backwash, backwater, backwoods, ‖boondocks, ‖boonies, bush, hinterland, ‖outback, sticks, up-country
idiom the back of beyond

frontier *adj syn see* BACK 1

fronting *prep syn see* AGAINST 1

front-rank *adj syn see* EXCELLENT

frore *adj syn see* COLD 1

frosty *adj syn see* COLD 1

froth *n syn see* FOAM
rel flippancy, frivolity, levity, lightness

froward *adj syn see* CONTRARY 3

frown *vb* 1 to put on a dark or malignant countenance or aspect < he *frowned* at the naughty child >
syn gloom, glower, lower, scowl
rel glare; grimace; pout, sulk
idiom look black, look daggers
con grin, laugh
ant smile
2 *syn see* DISAPPROVE 1

frowsy *adj* 1 *syn see* SLATTERNLY
rel lax, neglectful, negligent, remiss, slack
ant trim; smart
2 *syn see* MALODOROUS 1

frugal *adj syn see* SPARING
rel careful, meticulous; discreet, prudent; conserving, preserving; cheeseparing, penny-pinching, scrimping, stinting
ant wasteful

frugality *n syn see* ECONOMY

‖**fruit** *n syn see* HOMOSEXUAL

fruitage *n syn see* HARVEST 2

fruitful *adj syn see* FERTILE
rel breeding, propagating, reproducing; abounding
con abortive, bootless, futile, vain
ant unfruitful; fruitless

fruitfulness *n syn see* FERTILITY

fruition *n syn see* PLEASURE 2
rel actualization, materialization, realization; accomplishment, fulfillment; achievement, attainment

fruitless *adj syn see* FUTILE
rel barren, infertile, sterile, unfruitful; foiled, frustrated, thwarted; infructuous, unprofitable
con fecund, fertile, prolific
ant fruitful

‖**fruity** *adj syn see* INSANE 1

‖**frumpish** *adj syn see* TACKY 2

frumpy *adj syn see* TACKY 2

frustrate *vb* 1 to come between a person and his aim or desire or to defeat another's plan < my efforts are *frustrated* at every turn >
syn baffle, balk, beat, bilk, buffalo, circumvent, dash, disappoint, foil, ruin, thwart; *compare* OUTWIT
rel annul, cancel, counteract, negative, neutralize, nullify; anticipate, forestall; conquer, defeat, lick, overcome; forbid, inhibit, prohibit; obviate, preclude, prevent; bar, block, hinder, impede, obstruct; arrest, check, halt, interrupt
idiom cut the ground from under one, dash one's hope, defeat expectation, throw a monkey wrench into the works, upset one's applecart
con accomplish, achieve, bring about, effect, perform; advance, forward, further, promote; abet, foment, incite, instigate

ant fulfill

2 *syn* see NEUTRALIZE

frying pan *n* a pan with a handle used for frying food <some still prefer the sturdy cast-iron *frying pan* >
syn skillet, spider

fuddle *vb syn* see CONFUSE 2
ant clarify, clear

fuddler *n syn* see DRUNKARD

fuddy-duddy *n* 1 *syn* see FOGY

2 *syn* see STUFFED SHIRT

3 *syn* see FUSSBUDGET

fudge *vb syn* see EMBROIDER

fudge *n syn* see NONSENSE 2

fugacious *adj syn* see TRANSIENT

fugitive *adj syn* see TRANSIENT

fugitive *n syn* see REFUGEE

fulfill *vb* 1 to do what is required by the terms of so as to make effective <found themselves unable to *fulfill* their contract >
syn complete, execute, implement, perform; *compare* EFFECT 2
rel effect, effectuate; discharge

2 *syn* see SATISFY 5

fulgent *adj syn* see BRIGHT 1

full *adj* 1 containing as much as is possible <the hamper is *full* >
syn awash, big, block and block, brimful, brimming, bung-full, chockablock, chock-full, cram-full, crammed, crowded, jam-full, jammed, jam-packed, loaded, packed, ‖packed out, replete, stuffed, ‖trig
rel abounding, teeming
idiom full to bursting (*or* overflowing), ready to burst
con blank, vacant, void; bare, barren
ant empty

2 *syn* see CIRCUMSTANTIAL
ant incomplete

3 *syn* see WHOLE 2
con denuded, dismantled, divested, stripped

4 *syn* see SATIATED

full-blooded *adj* 1 *syn* see PUREBRED

2 *syn* see RUDDY

full-blown *adj* 1 *syn* see MATURE 1

2 *syn* see TOTAL 5

full-bosomed *adj syn* see BUXOM

full-bodied *adj syn* see STRONG 3

full dress *n syn* see FINERY

full-dress *adj syn* see EXHAUSTIVE

full-fledged *adj syn* see MATURE 1

full-grown *adj syn* see MATURE 1

full-mouthed *adj syn* see LOUD 1

fullness *n syn* see BREADTH 2

full-out *adj syn* see TOTAL 5

full-scale *adj syn* see TOTAL 5

full tilt *adv syn* see FAST 2

fully *adv* 1 *syn* see DOWN 2

2 *syn* see WELL 3

fulsome *adj* too obviously extravagant or ingratiating to be accepted as genuine or sincere <offering sickeningly *fulsome* praise>
syn oily, oleaginous, slick, smarmy, soapy, unctuous, unctuous
rel canting, holier-than-thou, hypocritical, pecksniffian, pharisaical, sanctimonious;

bland, glib, honey-mouthed, honey-tongued, ingratiating, mealy-mouthed, oily-tongued, smooth, smooth-tongued, suave; buttery, flattering, wheedling; excessive, extravagant, exuberant, lavish, profuse; cloying, satiating, sating; bombastic, grandiloquent, magniloquent
con earnest, genuine, heartfelt, hearty, sincere, true, truthful, unfeigned, whole-hearted, whole-souled

fumble *vb* 1 *syn* see GROPE

2 *syn* see BOTCH
rel flounder, stumble

3 *syn* see MUMBLE

fume *n syn* see SNIT

fume *vb syn* see ANGER 2

fun *vb syn* see BANTER

fun *n* 1 action or speech intended to amuse or arouse laughter <you know he only said it in *fun*>
syn game, jest, joke, play, sport
rel amusement, diversion, entertainment, recreation; blitheness; jocundity, joviality, merriment; glee, hilarity, jollity, mirth; mischief, teasing
con soberness, thoughtfulness
ant earnestness, seriousness

2 *syn* see PLAY 1

function *n* 1 the acts or operations expected of a person or thing <fulfill one's *function* as a mother>
syn business, duty, office, province, role
rel affair, concern; job, task, work

2 *syn* see USE 4

3 *syn* see POWER 3
rel action, behavior, operation

function *vb* 1 *syn* see ACT 4

2 *syn* see ACT 5

3 to operate in the proper or expected manner <finally succeeded in getting the motor to *function*>
syn act, go, run, work
rel do, operate, perform

functional *adj syn* see PRACTICAL 2

functioning *adj syn* see ACTIVE 1

fund *n syn* see SUPPLY

fund *vb syn* see ENDOW 2

fundament *n syn* see BUTTOCKS

fundamental *adj* 1 forming or affecting the groundwork, roots, or lowest part of something <the *fundamental* rules of poetry>
syn basal, basic, bottom, foundational, primary, radical, underlying
rel primal, prime, primordial; elemental, elementary
con incidental

2 *syn* see ELEMENTAL 1

3 *syn* see ESSENTIAL 2
rel indispensable, necessary, needful, requisite; dominant, paramount

fundamental *n* 1 *syn* see PRINCIPLE 1
rel component, constituent, factor, element

2 *syn* see ESSENTIAL 1

3 *usu* **fundamentals** *pl syn* see ALPHABET 2

fundamentalist *n syn* see DIEHARD 1

fundamentally *adv syn* see ESSENTIALLY 1
ant superficially

funeral director *n syn* see MORTICIAN

funereal *adj syn* see GLOOMY 3

rel grave, solemn

con animated, gay, lively, sprightly, vivacious; blithe, jocund, jolly, jovial, merry

ant festive

fungible *adj syn* see INTERCHANGEABLE

funk *vb syn* see SMELL 3

funk *n syn* see COWARD

funker *n syn* see COWARD

funky *adj syn* see MALODOROUS 1

funnel *vb syn* see CONDUCT 4

funniness *n syn* see HUMOR 4

funny *adj syn* see LAUGHABLE

rel antic, bizarre, fantastic, grotesque

idiom too funny for words

con doleful, dolorous, lugubrious, melancholy, plaintive

ant unfunny

funnyman *n syn* see HUMORIST 2

fur *n* 1 *syn* see HIDE

2 *syn* see DOWN

furbish *vb syn* see POLISH 1

furious *adj* 1 *syn* see WILD 6

2 marked by uncontrollable excitement often under the stress of a powerful emotion < in a state of *furious* activity >

syn corybantic, delirious, frantic, frenetic, frenzied, mad, rabid, wild

rel excited, provoked, stimulated; enthusiastic, fanatic; desperate, feverish, hasty, impetuous; fierce, intense, vehement, violent; excessive, extravagant, extreme, inordinate; enraged, incensed, infuriated, maddened; hysterical, irrational, unreasonable; bewildered, distracted, upset; crazed, demented, insane, mad, maniac

con calm, composed, peaceful, placid, quiet, serene, subdued, tranquil; apathetic, impassive, imperturbable, inexcitable

3 *syn* see INTENSE 1

furiously *adv syn* see HARD 2

furl *vb syn* see ROLL 3

furnish *vb* 1 to supply one with what is needed (as for daily living or a particular activity) < *furnished* him the papers for his application >

syn accouter, appoint, arm, equip, fit out, gear, outfit, rig, turn out

rel dower, endow, endue; apparel, array, clothe; mount; give, provide, supply

con denude, dismantle, divest, strip; despoil, spoliate; relieve (of), take away

2 *syn* see GIVE 3

furor *n syn* see DELIRIUM

furore *n* 1 *syn* see STIR 1

2 *syn* see FASHION 3

3 *syn* see COMMOTION 3

furrow *n syn* see WRINKLE

rel channel, groove, rut

further *adv* 1 *syn* see BEYOND 1

2 *syn* see AGAIN 4

further *adj syn* see ADDITIONAL

further *vb syn* see ADVANCE 1

rel engender, generate, propagate

con bar, block, impede, obstruct; forestall, prevent

ant hinder; retard

furthermore *adv syn* see ALSO 2

furthermost *adj syn* see EXTREME 5

furthest *adj syn* see EXTREME 5

furtive *adj* 1 *syn* see SECRET 1

rel artful, crafty, cunning, foxy, guileful,

insidious, scheming, shifty, sly, sneaky, tricky, wily; calculating, cautious, circumspect, wary; cloaked, disguised, masked

con brash, impudent, presumptuous

ant forthright; barefaced, brazen

2 *syn* see STEALTHY 2

ant open

furtively *adv syn* see SECRETLY

ant openly

furuncle *n syn* see ABSCESS

fury *n syn* see ANGER

rel passion; furor; acerbity, acrimony, asperity

fuse *vb* 1 *syn* see LIQUEFY

2 *syn* see MIX 1

rel compact, consolidate, unify

fusillade *n syn* see BARRAGE

fusion *n syn* see MIXTURE

fuss *n* 1 *syn* see STIR 1

rel fluster, perturbation; bother, flap, stew; racket, rumpus; haste, hurry, speed

2 *syn* see COMMOTION 3

3 *syn* see QUARREL

fuss *vb* 1 *syn* see WORRY 3

idiom fret and fume

2 *syn* see COMPLAIN

3 *syn* see GRIPE

4 *syn* see NAG

fussbudget *n* one who becomes upset over trifles < he is the biggest *fussbudget* I know, always going into a tizzy over nothing >

syn fuddy-duddy, fusser, fusspot, granny, old lady, old maid

rel perfectionist, precisionist, stickler

fusser *n syn* see FUSSBUDGET

fusspot *n syn* see FUSSBUDGET

fussy *adj* 1 *syn* see BUSTLING

2 *syn* see CAREFUL 2

3 *syn* see NICE 1

rel fretful, irritable, querulous

fustian *n syn* see BOMBAST

fustian *adj syn* see FECKLESS 1

fusty *adj* 1 *syn* see MALODOROUS 1

rel close, moldy, dirty, filthy, squalid; disheveled, slipshod, sloppy, slovenly, unkempt

2 *syn* see OLD-FASHIONED

futile *adj* barren of results < efforts to convince him were *futile* >

syn abortive, bootless, fruitless, ineffective, ineffectual, unavailable, unavailing, unprevailing, unproductive, useless, vain

rel empty, hollow, idle, nugatory, otiose; inadequate, inefficacious, inefficient, insufficient; unsatisfactory, unsuccessful

idiom in vain, no dice, of no avail, to no effect

con effectual, efficacious, fruitful; advantageous, beneficial, profitable

ant effective

future *n* time that is to come < you must try to do better in the *future* >

syn aftertime, afterward, by-and-by, hereafter, offing, to-be; compare PRESENT

idiom time to come

ant past

fuzz *n* 1 *syn* see DOWN

‖2 *syn* see POLICEMAN

fuzzy *adj syn* see FAINT 2

G

gab *vb syn* see CHAT 1

gab *n syn* see CHATTER

gabber *n syn* see CHATTERBOX

gabble *vb* 1 *syn* see GIBBER
2 *syn* see BABBLE 2
3 *syn* see CHAT 1

gabble *n syn* see CHATTER

gabby *adj syn* see TALKATIVE

gad *vb syn* see WANDER 1

gadget *n* 1 a usually small and often novel mechanical or electronic device or contrivance <a new kitchen *gadget* for separating egg whites>
syn concern, gimmick, gizmo, jigger, widget; *compare* DEVICE 2, DOODAD, WHAT-DO-YOU-CALL-IT
rel apparatus, appliance, contraption, tool, utensil
2 *syn* see DOODAD

gaffe *n syn* see FAUX PAS

gaffer *n* a man of advanced years <doddering *gaffers* on the park benches>
syn graybeard, patriarch; *compare* BELDAM 1, OLDSTER
rel duffer, geezer, grandfather, old boy, veteran

gag *vb* 1 *syn* see RETCH
2 *syn* see DEMUR

gag *n syn* see JOKE 1
rel ruse, trick, wile

gaiety *n* 1 *syn* see MERRYMAKING
2 *syn* see MIRTH
rel cheerfulness, gladness, happiness, geniality, pleasantness, winsomeness; animation, conviviality, entertainment, exhilaration, liveliness, merrymaking, radiance, spiritedness, vivacity
con blues, cheerlessness, dismalness, dreariness, gloom, grief, infelicity, joylessness, misery, moodiness, moroseness, pensiveness, solemnity, somberness, sorrow, sullenness, uncheerfulness, wistfulness, woe

gain *n syn* see PROFIT
rel cut, rake-off, share, take, winnings
ant loss

gain *vb* 1 to arrive at a goal, point, or end <*gained* success in the theater>
syn accomplish, achieve, attain, rack up, reach, realize, score, win
rel complete, consummate, fulfill, perfect, produce; succeed
con falter, flop, flounder, flunk, lose
2 *syn* see IMPROVE 3
rel invigorate, renew, strengthen; cure, heal, remedy
3 *syn* see EARN 1
4 *syn* see GET 1
ant lose

5 *syn* see CLEAR 6
ant lose

gainful *adj syn* see ADVANTAGEOUS 1
rel fat, fruitful, generous, lush, productive, rich; satisfying, substantial

gainsay *vb syn* see DENY 4
rel combat, fight, oppose, resist, withstand
ant admit

gainsaying *n syn* see DENIAL 2
ant admission; admitting

gait *n syn* see SPEED 2

gal *n* 1 *syn* see GIRL 1
2 *syn* see GIRL FRIEND 1

gall *n syn* see EFFRONTERY
rel arrogance, conceit, haughtiness, loftiness, lordliness, overbearance, pomposity, pride, priggishness, self-importance, smugness
con bashfulness, humbleness, humility, lowliness, modesty, shyness
ant meekness

gall *vb* 1 *syn* see ABRADE 1
rel bark, burn, file, fray, frazzle, grate, graze, scrape, scratch, scuff, skin
2 *syn* see CHAFE 3
rel distress, pain; cut, score, wound
3 *syn* see ANNOY 1
4 *syn* see IRRITATE
rel chide, disturb, harass, harry, torment, worry; bedevil, needle, trouble

gallant *n* 1 *syn* see FOP
2 an individual who is amorously attracted to the opposite sex <his fiancee accused him of being a trifling *gallant*>
syn amorist, Casanova, Don Juan, lothario, paramour, Romeo
rel dirty old man, lecher, libertine, rake, satyr; admirer, adorer, beau, date, escort, lover, sparker, suitor, swain, wooer
idiom gay blade

gallant *adj* 1 *syn* see COURTLY
rel urbane, suave; attentive, considerate, thoughtful
con heedless, inattentive, indifferent, thoughtless, unconcerned
ant ungallant
2 *syn* see BRAVE 1
ant dastardly

gallantry *n* 1 *syn* see COURTESY 1
rel deference, duty, homage, honor; reverence, suavity, urbanity; address, poise, savoir faire, tact
con boorishness, churlishness, clownishness, loutishness; discourteousness
ant discourtesy
2 *syn* see HEROISM
rel bravery, dauntlessness; mettle, resolution, spirit
ant dastardliness

gallery *n syn* see MUSEUM

galley slave *n syn* see SLAVE 2

gallimaufry *n syn* see MISCELLANY 1

galling *adj syn* see BITTER 2

---

syn synonym(s)   *rel* related word(s)
ant antonym(s)   *con* contrasted word(s)
idiom idiomatic equivalent(s)
‖ use limited; if in doubt, see a dictionary

gallivant *vb syn* see WANDER 1

gallows *n pl syn* see SUSPENDERS

galluptious *adj syn* see MARVELOUS 2

galluses *n pl syn* see SUSPENDERS

galoot *n syn* see MAN 3

galumph *vb syn* see LUMBER

galvanize *vb syn* see PROVOKE 4
rel activate, energize, vitalize

gambit *n syn* see TRICK 1
rel design, plan, plot

gamble *vb* **1** to engage in a game of chance for something of value <swore he would never *gamble* for high stakes again>
syn bet, game, lay, play, put (on), set, stake, wager
rel chance, hazard, lot, risk, speculate, venture
idiom buck the odds, take a flyer (on), try one's luck
2 to take a chance on something <*gambled* on the train being late>
syn chance, hazard, risk, venture; *compare* VENTURE 1
rel brave, challenge, dare, defy, face; endanger, imperil, jeopardize
idiom go it blind, take a chance (*or* one's chances), tempt fortune, trust to luck

gambol *vb* to leap or tumble about playfully <young lambs *gamboling* in the meadow>
syn caper, cavort, frisk, frolic, rollick, romp
rel lark, revel, roister; bound, leap, spring
idiom kick up one's heels, let off steam

game *n* **1** *syn* see FUN 1
con business, duty, labor, study, toil
2 games *pl syn* see ATHLETICS
3 animals under pursuit <hunting big *game* is a risky and expensive sport>
syn chase, prey, quarry
rel kill, ravin, victim

game *vb syn* see GAMBLE 1

game *adj syn* see BRAVE 1

game plan *n syn* see PLAN 1

gamesome *adj syn* see PLAYFUL 1

gamin *n syn* see URCHIN

gamine *n syn* see TOMBOY

gammer *n syn* see BELDAM 1

gamy *adj syn* see MALODOROUS 2

gander *n syn* see PEEP

gangling *adj* being tall, thin, and usually loose-jointed <a *gangling* high-school boy>
syn gangly, lanky, rangy, spindling, spindly
rel bony, gaunt, lank, lean, scrawny, skinny, spare, tall, thin
con low, low-set, low-statured, short, squat, stocky, sturdy, thickset

gangly *adj syn* see GANGLING

gangrel *n syn* see VAGABOND

gap *n* **1** an open space in a barrier <the sheep got through a *gap* in the fence>
syn breach, break, discontinuity, hole, opening
rel fracture, rupture; chink, cleavage, cleft, crack, crevice, fissure, slit, slot; division, interspace, interval, separation; aperture, cranny, orifice
2 *syn* see RAVINE
3 a period of discontinuity <a *gap* of an hour between speakers>
syn breach, break, hiatus, interim, interruption, interval, lacuna; *compare* PAUSE

rel caesura, intermission, lull, pause, respite, rest

gape *vb* **1** *syn* see GAZE 1
2 *syn* see LOOK 7
3 *syn* see YAWN

gaping *adj syn* see CAVERNOUS 1

garb *vb syn* see CLOTHE

garbage *n syn* see REFUSE
rel dregs, rubble; filth, sewage, slop

garble *vb syn* see MISREPRESENT
rel becloud, conceal, hide, obfuscate, obscure

garden house *n syn* see SUMMERHOUSE

gargantuan *adj syn* see HUGE
ant lilliputian

garish *adj syn* see GAUDY
rel overdone, overwrought
con dark, dim, dreary, dull, dusky, murky; quiet, unpretentious
ant somber

garland *n* **1** *syn* see WREATH
2 *syn* see ANTHOLOGY

garment *vb syn* see CLOTHE

garner *vb* **1** *syn* see REAP
2 *syn* see GLEAN
3 *syn* see ACCUMULATE
rel gather, glean, harvest, reap; hoard, store
con disseminate, spread

garnish *vb syn* see ADORN

garrulous *adj syn* see TALKATIVE
rel blabbing, prattling, prolix, verbose, windy, wordy
con concise; terse; blunt, brusque, curt
ant taciturn

gas *n syn* see NONSENSE 2

gas *vb syn* see CHAT 1

gasbag *n syn* see BRAGGART

gasconade *vb syn* see BOAST

gash *vb syn* see CUT 1
rel carve, split; injure, wound; furrow, mark, notch; lance, nip

gasp *vb syn* see PANT 1

gasper *n syn* see CIGARETTE

gastronome *n syn* see EPICURE
rel aesthete, connoisseur, dilettante

gastronomer *n syn* see EPICURE

gastronomist *n syn* see EPICURE

gate *n syn* see FAUCET

gather *vb* **1** *syn* see GROUP 1
rel choose, cull, pick, select; accumulate, amass
idiom separate the wheat from the chaff (*or* the sheep from the goats)
con dispel, disperse, dissipate
ant scatter
2 *syn* see REAP
rel cull, pick, pluck; heap, mass, pile, stack
3 *syn* see GLEAN
4 *syn* see INFER
rel catch, fathom, follow, grasp, take in
idiom put two and two together
5 *syn* see UNDERSTAND 3
6 to bring or come together <a crowd *gathered* to watch the fight>
syn assemble, collect, congregate, congress, forgather, muster, raise, rendezvous; *compare* GROUP 1
rel aggregate, troop; affiliate, ally, associate, league; encounter, meet
con break up, disband, disperse, part, separate; disintegrate, disorganize, dissolve

ant scatter
7 *syn* see LOOM 2

gathering *n* 1 *syn* see CONCOURSE
2 a number of individuals come or
brought together <a *gathering* in the
town park>
syn aggregation, assemblage, assembly,
collection, company, congeries, congregation, crowd, group, muster, ruck; *compare*
GROUP 1
rel bunch, crew, crush, flock, gang,
horde, mass, press, rout, swarm, turnout
3 *syn* see HARVEST 1

gauche *adj syn* see AWKWARD 2
rel crude, green, unpolished
con bland, smooth, suave, urbane
ant adroit

gaudy *adj* cheaply or vulgarly showy
<*gaudy* sideshow posters>
syn blatant, brazen, chintzy, flashy, garish, glaring, loud, meretricious, tawdry,
tinsel
rel obtrusive, ostentatious, pretentious,
showy, tasteless; coarse, crude, gross,
vulgar; brummagem, fake, phony, sham
con restrained, tasteful, unobtrusive; factual, illuminating, informative
ant quiet

gauge *n syn* see STANDARD 3
rel check, mark, model, norm, pattern,
rule, type

gauge *vb syn* see MEASURE 2

||**gaum** *n syn* see OAF 2

gaunt *adj* 1 *syn* see LEAN
2 *syn* see EMACIATED
ant bloated

||**gaup** (or **gawp**) *vb* 1 *syn* see LOOK 7
2 *syn* see GAZE 1

gauzy *adj syn* see FILMY

gawk *vb syn* see GAZE 1

gawk *n syn* see OAF 2

gawky *adj syn* see CLUMSY 1

gay *adj* 1 *syn* see MERRY
2 *syn* see LIVELY 1
rel frolicsome, playful, sportive
con earnest, sedate, serious, solemn, somber, staid; quiet, silent, still
ant grave, sober
3 *syn* see COLORFUL
4 *syn* see WILD 7
5 *syn* see HOMOSEXUAL
6 *syn* see PRESUMPTUOUS

gaze *vb* 1 to look long and usually attentively <*gazed* out the window>
syn bore, gape, ||gaup (or gawp), gawk,
glare, gloat, goggle, peer, stare; *compare*
LOOK 7
rel look, see, watch; peek, peep; contemplate, inspect, observe, scrutinize, survey;
admire, ogle, regard
con glance, skim, skip
2 *syn* see LOOK 7

gaze (upon) *vb syn* see EYE 1

gazebo *n syn* see SUMMERHOUSE

gear *n syn* see EQUIPMENT
rel accessories, adjuncts, appendages,
appurtenances; belongings, effects, means,
possessions

---

syn synonym(s)   *rel* related word(s)
ant antonym(s)   *con* contrasted word(s)
idiom idiomatic equivalent(s)
|| use limited; if in doubt, see a dictionary

---

gear *vb syn* see FURNISH 1

||**gee** *n syn* see MAN 3

||**gee** *vb syn* see AGREE 4

Gehenna *n syn* see HELL

gel *vb syn* see COAGULATE

gelastic *adj syn* see LAUGHABLE

gelate *vb syn* see COAGULATE

gelatinize *vb syn* see COAGULATE

geld *vb syn* see STERILIZE

gelid *adj syn* see COLD 1
con ardent, burning, fervent, scorching,
sweltering, torrid
ant fervid

||**gelt** *n syn* see MONEY

gem *vb syn* see BEJEWEL

gendarme *n syn* see POLICEMAN

genealogy *n* an account often in chart
form recording a line of ancestors <de-
cided to prepare a *genealogy* of his fami-
ly>
syn ||begats, family tree, pedigree, stemma

general *adj* 1 conforming to what is expected in the ordinary course of events
<the *general* problems of everyday life>
syn common, commonplace, matter-of-
course, natural, normal, prevalent, regular,
run-of-the-mill, typic, typical, usual
rel everyday, popular; familiar, universal;
habitual, humdrum, routine, uneventful
con abnormal, extraordinary, irregular,
novel, strange, unexpected, unforeseeable,
unusual
2 belonging or relating to the whole <a
general change in the weather>
syn common, generic, universal
rel natural, normal, regular, typical;
broad, inclusive, wide
con individual, particular, special; characteristic, distinctive, peculiar
3 *syn* see ALL-AROUND 2
4 *syn* see PUBLIC 4

generally *adv* 1 in a reasonably inclusive
manner <the forest was *generally* conif-
erous>
syn chiefly, largely, mainly, mostly, overall, predominantly, primarily, principally
rel about, approximately, practically,
roughly, roundly
con altogether, totally, wholly
2 *syn* see ALTOGETHER 3
3 *syn* see USUALLY 2

generate *vb* 1 to bring into existence
<*generate* new business>
syn create, father, hatch, make, originate,
parent, procreate, produce, sire, spawn
rel bring about, effect, impose, occasion;
introduce; cause; found, inaugurate, institute, set up; develop, induce, whip (up)
idiom bring to pass, give birth to, give
rise to
con demolish, destroy, extinguish, ruin;
degenerate, deteriorate, impair, worsen
2 *syn* see PROCREATE 1
3 to be the cause or source of something
immaterial <actions that *generated* a
good deal of suspicion>
syn breed, cause, engender, get up, hatch,
induce, muster (up), occasion, produce,
provoke, work up
rel accomplish, achieve, perform
idiom give birth to, give rise to

generator *n syn* see FATHER 2

generic *adj syn* see GENERAL 2

ant specific

generous *adj* 1 marked by a noble or forbearing spirit < *generous* toward the weakness of others >
  syn benevolent, big, chivalrous, considerate, greathearted, lofty, magnanimous
  rel altruistic, charitable, kindhearted, kindly, thoughtful, ungrudging, unselfish; fair, honest; long-suffering, tolerant; helpful, willing
  con base, ignoble, mean, self-centered, selfish; grim, hard, harsh, intolerant
  ant ungenerous
  2 *syn* see LIBERAL 1
  ant stingy
  3 *syn* see PLENTIFUL
  rel lavish; luxuriant; affluent, wealthy
  con scant, scanty, sparse

generously *adv syn* see WELL 2

genesis *n syn* see BEGINNING
  rel provenance, provenience
  con cessation, conclusion, culmination, end, finish, termination

genial *adj* 1 *syn* see GRACIOUS 1
  rel amicable, friendly, neighborly; blithe, cheerful, jocund, jolly, jovial, merry
  con discourteous, rude, uncivil, ungracious; crabbed, morose, sullen; ironic, sarcastic, sardonic, satiric
  ant caustic (*remarks, comments*); saturnine (*manner, disposition, aspect*)
  2 *syn* see GENTLE 2

geniality *n syn* see AMENITY 1

genitalia *n pl* the external components of the reproductive system < the gradual adolescent differentiation of the *genitalia* >
  syn genitals, parts, private parts, privates, privities, privy parts, pudendum (*usu* pudenda *pl*), secrets

genitals *n pl syn* see GENITALIA

genius *n syn* see GIFT 2
  rel creativity, ingenuity, inventiveness, originality; astuteness, brains, grasp, intellect, intelligence, understanding

gent *n syn* see MAN 3

genteel *adj* 1 having characteristics or qualities befitting the upper classes < in those days croquet was a very *genteel* sport > < his manner was perfectly *genteel* >
  syn cultivated, cultured, distingué, polished, refined, urbane, well-bred
  rel elegant, fashionable, graceful, stylish; chivalrous, gentlemanly, knightly, ladylike, noble; mannerly, well-mannered
  con coarse, common, crude, ill-bred, rough, rude, uncouth, uncultured, unpolished, vulgar
  ant ungenteel
  2 *syn* see CIVIL 2
  rel well-behaved; aristocratic, cultured
  con crude, discourteous, inconsiderate, rough, rude
  3 involving or excessively preoccupied with the airs and forms of middle-class or upper-class proprieties < a shy *genteel* girl terrified of blundering socially >
  syn affected, la-di-da, ‖lardy-dardy, mincing, pretentious, stilted, too-too; *compare* PRECIOUS 4, PRIM 1
  rel artificial, formal, high-falutin
  con cultured, genuine, honest, refined; gracious, polished; gentlemanly, ladylike

4 *syn* see PRIM 1
  rel narrow; intolerant, uncharitable; confined, insular, parochial, provincial
  idiom nasty nice
  con charitable, tolerant, understanding; broad-minded, easy, relaxed

gentile *adj syn* see HEATHEN

gentility *n syn* see ARISTOCRACY

gentle *adj* 1 free from all harshness, roughness, or intensity < a *gentle* summer breeze >
  syn balmy, bland, faint, lenient, mild, smooth, soft
  rel delicate, mellow, tender; hushed, low, soothing; calm, halcyon, peaceful, placid, quiet, serene, tranquil
  con coarse, harsh, rough; exquisite, fierce, intense, savage, vehement, violent; forceful, forcible, powerful
  2 having a pleasant easygoing nature < a *gentle* person in everything she does >
  syn affable, amiable, genial
  rel kind, pleasant, pleasing, tender; agreeable, benign, mild; compassionate, kindly, softhearted, sympathetic, warmhearted
  con belligerent, cantankerous, contentious, ill-natured, petty, quarrelsome; aggressive, demanding, overbearing
  ant harsh, stern

gentleman *n* 1 a person of good or noble birth < the contributions of the country *gentleman* to social stability >
  syn aristo, aristocrat, blue blood, patrician
  rel Brahmin; chevalier; nob, swell
  con churl, clown, lout
  ant boor
  2 *syn* see MAN 3

gentleman friend *n syn* see BOYFRIEND 1

gentry *n syn* see ARISTOCRACY

genuine *adj* 1 *syn* see AUTHENTIC 2
  con artificial, ersatz, factitious; counterfeited, sham, simulated; sophisticated
  ant fraudulent
  2 *syn* see ACTUAL 2
  con uncommon, unordinary, unusual; alleged, apocryphal, apparent, fabulous, fictitious, mythical
  3 free from hypocrisy or pretense < a *genuine* love for his fellowman >
  syn heart-whole, honest, real, sincere, true, undesigning, undissembled, unfeigned; *compare* NATURAL 5, SINCERE 1
  rel reliable, trustworthy, unaffected, unimpeachable, veritable
  con affected, hypocritical
  ant insincere

genuinely *adv syn* see VERY 2

germ *n syn* see SEED 2

germane *adj syn* see RELEVANT
  con incompatible, incongruous, inconsonant
  ant foreign

gest *n syn* see ADVENTURE

gestapo *adj syn* see TERRORISTIC

gestation *n syn* see PREGNANCY

gesture *n syn* see EXPRESSION 3

gesture *vb syn* see SIGNAL

get *vb* 1 to come into possession of < hoped to *get* a fortune from his invention >

syn acquire, annex, chalk up, compass, gain, have, land, obtain, pick up, procure, pull, secure, win

rel educe, elicit, evoke, extort, extract, ‖promote; accept, receive; clutch, grab, grasp, take; accomplish, achieve, effect; capture, carry; draw

idiom come by

con abnegate, eschew, forbear, forgo, give up, sacrifice; abandon, forsake, renounce

2 *syn* see EARN 1

3 *syn* see BECOME 1

rel achieve, attain, effect, realize

idiom get to be, turn out to be

4 *syn* see CONTRACT 1

5 *syn* see FATHER 1

6 *syn* see PREPARE 1

rel arrange, order, right; adjust, coordinate, organize

7 *syn* see CATCH 1

8 *syn* see AFFECT

rel bend, bias, dispose, predispose, prompt

con benumb, deaden, numb; blunt, dull, harden

9 *syn* see NONPLUS 1

rel bother, distress, disturb, perturb, upset; discomfit, disconcert, embarrass

10 *syn* see IRRITATE

idiom try one's temper

con calm, compose, cool, lull, soothe, subdue

11 *syn* see LEARN 1

idiom get into one's head

12 *syn* see MEMORIZE

13 *syn* see INDUCE 1

rel provoke; beg, coax, press, pressure, urge

14 *syn* see REACH 4

15 *syn* see COME 1

get along *vb* 1 *syn* see ADVANCE 5

rel depart, go

con recede, regress, retreat, retrogress, reverse, revert

2 *syn* see SHIFT 5

rel flourish, prosper, succeed, thrive

get away *vb* *syn* see GO 2

getaway *n* *syn* see ESCAPE 1

get back *vb* *syn* see RECOVER 1

get by *vb* *syn* see SHIFT 5

get in *vb* *syn* see COME 1

get off *vb* 1 *syn* see GO 2

rel advance, progress

2 *syn* see BEGIN 1

get on *vb* 1 *syn* see DON 1

2 *syn* see ADVANCE 5

3 *syn* see SHIFT 5

get out *vb* 1 to go away quickly, immediately, and often secretly < had to *get out* before the police arrived >

syn begone, clear out, decamp, hightail, kite, scram, skedaddle, skiddoo, take off, ‖vamoose

rel depart, duck (out), egress, exit, go, leave, split

idiom beat it, be off, make tracks, take a powder, take a runout powder

con abide, remain, reside, stay

2 to become known < we can't let this story *get out* >

syn break, come out, leak, out, transpire

3 *syn* see PUBLISH 2

gettable *adj* *syn* see AVAILABLE 1

get up *vb* 1 *syn* see ROLL OUT

2 *syn* see RISE 1

3 *syn* see GENERATE 3

getup *n* 1 *syn* see COSTUME

2 *syn* see VIGOR 2

get-up-and-go *n* 1 *syn* see VIGOR 2

2 *syn* see ENTERPRISE 4

gewgaw *n* *syn* see KNICKKNACK

ghastly *adj* 1 disturbingly frightening or repellent in appearance or aspect < the *ghastly* sight of burned and rotting bodies >

syn grim, grisly, gruesome, hideous, horrible, horrid, horrifying, lurid, macabre, terrible, terrifying

rel appalling, awful, dreadful, frightening, frightful, shocking; disgustful, disgusting, nauseant, nauseating, sickening

con appealing, attractive, charming, pleasant, touching; acceptable, bearable; trivial, unimportant

2 resembling or suggestive of a ghost < a *ghastly* form slightly visible through the fog >

syn cadaverous, corpselike, deathlike, ghostlike, ghostly, shadowy, spectral

rel ashen, livid, lurid, pale; uncanny, weird; gruesome, haggard, macabre; dim, faint, weak; charnel, mortuary, sepulchral

ghost *n* *syn* see APPARITION

rel demon, devil

ghost *vb* *syn* see GHOSTWRITE

ghostlike *adj* *syn* see GHASTLY 2

ghostly *adj* *syn* see GHASTLY 2

ghostwrite *vb* to write for and in the name of another < a *ghostwritten* autobiography >

syn ghost, ‖spook

GI *n* *syn* see SOLDIER

giant *n* something of monstrous size, appearance, or power < a *giant* of a tractor >

syn behemoth, leviathan, mammoth, monster, whale

rel cyclops, polypheme

giant *adj* *syn* see HUGE

rel gross, hulking

con paltry, petty, puny, trifling, trivial

ant dwarf

gibber *vb* to utter or speak rapidly, inarticulately, and usually unintelligibly < a *gibbering* idiot >

syn babble, chatter, gabble, jabber

rel blather, drivel, prate, prattle, yammer; stammer, stutter; mumble, mutter; mow

idiom run off at the mouth

con articulate, enunciate, pronounce

gibberish *n* 1 unintelligible or meaningless talk < the *gibberish* of an imbecile >

syn babble, drivel, Greek, jabber, jabberwocky, nonsense, skimble-skamble; *compare* GIBBERISH 3

rel blather, bunkum, claptrap, twaddle; blabber, gabble, palaver, prattle

2 *syn* see GOBBLEDYGOOK

3 speech or actions that are esoteric in nature and suggest the magical, strange, or unknown < the shaman's strange *gibberish* >

---

syn synonym(s)   *rel* related word(s)
ant antonym(s)   *con* contrasted word(s)
idiom idiomatic equivalent(s)

‖ use limited; if in doubt, see a dictionary

syn abracadabra, hocus-pocus, mumbo jumbo, mummery

rel magic, sorcery, thaumaturgy

gibbet *vb syn see* HANG 2

gibble–gabble *n syn see* CHATTER

gibe *vb syn see* SCOFF

rel rail, rally, revile, scold, twit

giddy *adj* **1** having a lightheartedly silly nature <tried to teach a bunch of *giddy* Girl Scouts how to make a fire>

syn bird-witted, dizzy, empty-headed, featherbrained, flighty, fribble, fribbling, frivolous, harebrained, hoity-toity, light, lightheaded, rattlebrained, scatterbrained, silly, skittish, volage, yeasty

rel capricious, fickle, impulsive, whimsical; brainless, exuberant, thoughtless, witless

idiom giddy as a goose

con earnest, pensive, sedate, serious, sober, solemn, staid, thoughtful

2 *syn see* DIZZY 2

rel bemused, flustered

idiom going around in circles, like a chicken with its head cut off, seeing double

gift *n* **1** something freely given by one person to another for his benefit or pleasure <the watch was a graduation *gift*>

syn benevolence, boon, ‖compliment, favor, present

rel alms, benefaction, contribution, donation; award, bestowal, grant, presentation; legacy; offering, reward, tip; remembrance, souvenir, token

2 a natural or special facility or capableness <has a *gift* for electronics>

syn aptness, bent, bump, faculty, flair, genius, head, knack, nose, set, talent, turn; *compare* LEANING 2

rel ability, aptitude, capability; accomplishment, acquirement, attainment; instinct, numen, power; forte, leaning, propensity, specialty

con awkwardness, clumsiness, maladroitness

gigantean *adj syn see* HUGE

gigantesque *adj syn see* HUGE

gigantic *adj syn see* HUGE

rel hulking, stupendous

con paltry, petty, puny, trifling, trivial

giggle *vb syn see* LAUGH

gill *n syn see* CREEK 1

gimcrack *n syn see* KNICKKNACK

gimmick *n* **1** *syn see* GADGET 1

2 *syn see* TRICK 1

rel cheat, counterfeit, deceit, dodge, fake, humbug, imposture; fun, game, jest, method, sport

gimp *n syn see* SPIRIT 5

gingerly *adj syn see* CAUTIOUS

gingery *adj syn see* SPIRITED 2

con lethargic, listless, poky, slow; dead, dull, flat, insipid, stuffy, dreary; blasé, lackadaisical, nonchalant

‖**gin mill** *n syn see* BAR 5

gird *vb* **1** *syn see* BELT 1

ant ungird

2 *syn see* SURROUND 1

rel wrap, wreathe

3 to prepare oneself for action <*girded* himself for the coming trial>

syn brace, fortify, prepare, ready, steel, strengthen

rel bolster, buttress, support, sustain; harden, reinforce, shore (up); invigorate; dispose, forearm, prepare

idiom gird one's loins, whet the knife

gird *vb syn see* SCOFF

girdle *n syn see* BELT 1

girdle *vb* **1** *syn see* BELT

2 *syn see* SURROUND 1

girl *n* **1** a young unmarried female person <hired a *girl* to babysit>

syn damsel, gal, lass, lassie, maid, maiden, miss, missy, ‖quail, ‖quiff, wench

rel hoyden, tomboy; deb, debutante, subdeb, subdebutante; bobby-soxer; schoolgirl; gamine

2 *syn see* MAID 2

3 *syn see* GIRL FRIEND 1

girl Friday *n syn see* RIGHT-HAND MAN

girl friend *n* **1** a woman who is a man's usual or preferred companion <took his *girl friend* out every weekend>

syn best girl, ‖chick, ‖doney, gal, girl, lady friend, lass, mouse, popsy

2 a woman who shares with a man a strong and usually sexually oriented mutual attraction <his wife caught him with his *girl friend*>

syn ‖baby, beloved, flame, honey, inamorata, ladylove, steady, sweetheart, sweetie, truelove

3 *syn see* MISTRESS

gist *n syn see* SUBSTANCE 2

rel sap, soul, spirit; subject, theme, topic; bearing, drift, tenor

give *vb* **1** to provide gratuitously <*gave* their labor to rebuild the burned church>

syn bestow, devote, donate, give away, hand out, present; *compare* CONTRIBUTE 1

rel accord, award, confer, grant; hand; afford, contribute, furnish, provide; aid, assist, benefact, help

con keep, retain, withhold; lease, sell

2 to provide by or as if by formal action <he was *given* a diploma>

syn accord, award, confer, grant; *compare* GRANT 1

rel bestow, hand over, present; allocate, appropriate, assign

con decline, refuse; hold back, withhold

3 to put into the possession of another usually for use or consumption <*gave* the dog a drink of water>

syn deliver, dish out, dispense, feed, find, furnish, hand, hand over, provide, supply, transfer, turn over

rel administer, commit, offer; deal, disburse, disperse, distribute, divide, dole (out), lot (out); afford, lend

con have, hold, hold back, keep, keep back, reserve, retain, withhold

4 *syn see* OFFER 1

rel bestow, confer, render; administer, dispense, issue

5 *syn see* EXPRESS 2

6 *syn see* ALLOT

7 to furnish as a result or product <6 +6 *gives* 12>

syn produce, yield

rel be, equal, make; afford, furnish, offer, supply

8 *syn see* SPEND 1

9 *syn see* SELL 2

10 to bestow or dispense by some action < *gave* him a punch in the nose >
syn administer, deal, deliver, inflict, strike
rel bestow, dispense; fetch
11 *syn* see ADDRESS 3
12 to fail in response to physical stress < the bridge *gave* under the heavy load >
syn bend, break, cave, collapse, crumple, fold up, go, yield
rel fail, relax, relent, slacken, weaken
idiom cave in, give way
13 *syn* see HAPPEN 1

give away vb **1** *syn* see GIVE 1
2 *syn* see REVEAL 1

give back vb **1** *syn* see RETREAT 2
rel back out, backtrack, backwater; crumble, fail, falter, weaken
2 *syn* see RESTORE 5

given *adj syn* see APT 1

given name n the name that precedes one's surname < arguing over the baby's *given name* >
syn baptismal name, Christian name, font name, forename, personal name, prename
rel first name, middle name; appellation, appellative, compellation, denomination, style; praenomen; epithet, label, tag
con center, focus

give off vb **1** *syn* see EMIT 2
2 *syn* see DISCHARGE 5

give out vb **1** *syn* see EMIT 2
2 *syn* see COLLAPSE 2
3 *syn* see FAIL 2

give over vb *syn* see STOP 3

giver n *syn* see DONOR

give up vb **1** *syn* see RELINQUISH
2 *syn* see DESPAIR

gizmo n **1** *syn* see DOODAD
2 *syn* see GADGET

glabrous *adj syn* see HAIRLESS
rel beardless, shaven, smooth-shaven
con bristled, bristly, hairy, hirsute, stubbled, stubbly

glacial *adj* **1** *syn* see COLD 1
2 *syn* see COLD 2
rel aloof, distant, remote, reserved, standoffish, withdrawn; exclusive, inaccessible, seclusive, unapproachable
con affable, gregarious, sociable

glad *adj* **1** characterized by or expressing the mood of one who is pleased or delighted < he was *glad* to be on vacation >
syn happy, joyful, joyous, lighthearted
rel delighted, gratified, pleased, rejoiced, tickled; blithe, exhilarated, jocund, jolly, jovial, merry; gleeful, hilarious, mirthful
idiom filled with (or full of) delight
con blue, dejected, depressed, downcast, melancholy; despondent, dispirited, heavyhearted, sadhearted, unhappy; forlorn, joyless, sorrowful, woeful
ant sad
2 full of brightness and cheerfulness < a *glad* spring morning >
syn bright, cheerful, cheery, radiant
rel beaming, sparkling; beautiful; genial, pleasant
con dark, dim, dull, gloomy, somber

gladden vb *syn* see PLEASE 2

rel comfort, console, solace; animate, enliven, exhilarate, invigorate, liven, quicken, vivify
con depress, oppress, weigh; discourage, dishearten, dispirit; damp, dampen; bother, irk
ant sadden

gladiatorial *adj syn* see BELLIGERENT

‖**glad rags** n pl syn see FINERY

glamorous *adj syn* see ATTRACTIVE 1

glamour n *syn* see CHARM 3

glance vb **1** to strike a surface obliquely so as to go off at an angle < the bullet *glanced* off the stone wall >
syn carom, dap, graze, ricochet, skim, skip
rel brush, kiss, scrape, shave, slant; contact, hit, strike, touch; bounce, careen, rebound
con center, focus
2 *syn* see BRUSH 2
3 *syn* see FLASH 1

glance (at *or* over) vb *syn* see BROWSE

glance n **1** *syn* see FLASH 1
2 *syn* see PEEP

glance vb *syn* see POLISH 1

glare vb **1** *syn* see BLAZE
rel dazzle, flash, gleam, glisten, glitter
2 *syn* see GAZE 1
rel frown, glower, lower, scowl

glaring *adj* **1** *syn* see EGREGIOUS
rel conspicuous, noticeable, outstanding; excessive, extreme, inordinate; obtrusive
ant unnoticeable
2 *syn* see GAUDY
rel cheap, coarse, crude, gross
con elegant, tasteful

glass n *syn* see MIRROR 1

glass vb *syn* see REFLECT 1

‖**glasshouse** n *syn* see GREENHOUSE

glassy *adj syn* see SLEEK

glaze vb *syn* see POLISH 1

glaze n *syn* see LUSTER

gleam n *syn* see FLASH 1

gleam vb **1** *syn* see SHINE 1
2 *syn* see FLASH 1
rel burn

gleaming *adj syn* see LUSTROUS 1

glean vb to gather by effort and usually bit by bit < evidence *gleaned* from various testimonies >
syn cull, extract, garner, gather, pick up
rel sift, winnow; ascertain, conclude, deduce, learn
con amass, heap, pile

glee n *syn* see MIRTH
rel delectation, delight, enjoyment, joy, pleasure; blitheness; joyousness
ant gloom

gleeful *adj syn* see MERRY

glen n *syn* see VALLEY

glib *adj* characterized by very fluent often superficial address toward others < *glib* chatter >
syn silver-tongued, vocative, voluble, well-hung; compare TALKATIVE
rel articulate, eloquent, facile, fluent, vocal
con inarticulate, unfluent

glide vb **1** *syn* see SLIDE 1
rel float, fly, sail, scud, shoot, skim
2 *syn* see STEAL 3
3 *syn* see SNEAK

---

syn synonym(s)   **rel** related word(s)
ant antonym(s)   **con** contrasted word(s)
idiom idiomatic equivalent(s)
‖ use limited; if in doubt, see a dictionary

glimmer *vb syn* see FLASH 1

glimmer *n syn* see FLASH 1

glimpse *n syn* see PEEP

glint *vb syn* see FLASH 1

glint *n* 1 *syn* see FLASH 1

2 *syn* see LUSTER

glissade *vb syn* see SLIDE 1
rel float, fly, sail, scud, shoot, skim

glisten *vb syn* see FLASH 1

glisten *n syn* see FLASH 1

glistening *adj syn* see LUSTROUS 1

glitter *vb* 1 *syn* see FLASH 1

2 *syn* see SPANGLE 1

glitter *n syn* see FLASH 1

gloaming *n syn* see EVENING 1

gloat *vb syn* see GAZE 1
con begrudge, covet, envy, grudge

global *adj* 1 *syn* see UNIVERSAL 2
ant parochial

2 *syn* see ALL-ROUND 2
rel all-inclusive, blanket, catholic, grand, universal

globe *n* 1 *syn* see BALL

2 *syn* see EARTH 1

globule *n syn* see DROP 1

gloom *vb* 1 *syn* see FROWN 1
rel brood, mope
con smile; bubble, effervesce, enthuse, sparkle

2 *syn* see OBSCURE

gloom *n syn* see SADNESS
con hilarity, jollity, mirth; gaiety, gladness
ant glee

gloomy *adj* 1 *syn* see DARK 1
rel bleak, dismal, dreary
ant brilliant

2 *syn* see SULLEN
rel cheerless, dejected, depressed, downcast, joyless, melancholy, oppressed, solemn, unhappy, weary
con glad, happy, joyful, joyous, lighthearted; blithe, jocund, jovial, merry
ant cheerful

3 causing or marked by gloom <the *gloomy* atmosphere of the dungeon>
syn acheronian, acherontic, black, bleak, cheerless, cold, depressant, depressing, depressive, desolate, disconsolate, discouraging, disheartening, dismal, dispiriting, drear, dreary, dusky, funereal, joyless, lugubrious, morne, oppressive, somber, tenebrific, unhappy, woebegone
rel despondent, mirthless, pessimistic; melancholy, mournful, sad; drab, dull, muzzy
con bright, cheerful, happy; cheering, emboldening, encouraging, heartening, optimistic
ant gloomless

glorification *n syn* see APOTHEOSIS 2

glorify *vb* 1 *syn* see PRAISE 2

2 *syn* see EXALT 1

glorious *adj* 1 *syn* see SPLENDID 2
rel brilliant, effulgent, lustrous, radiant; imposing, impressive; majestic, noble; ravishing, stunning; beautiful
ant inglorious

2 *syn* see MARVELOUS 2

glory *vb syn* see EXULT

gloss *n syn* see LUSTER
rel glossiness, silkiness, sleekness, slickness; burnish

gloss *vb syn* see POLISH 1

gloss (over) *vb syn* see PALLIATE
rel account, explain, justify, rationalize; belie, falsify, miscolor, misrepresent

gloss *vb syn* see ANNOTATE

glossy *adj* 1 *syn* see LUSTROUS 1

2 *syn* see SLEEK

glow *vb* 1 *syn* see BLAZE
rel burn; ignite, kindle, light

2 *syn* see BLUSH

glow *n syn* see BLOOM 3

glower *vb syn* see FROWN 1
rel stare; look, watch

glowing *adj* 1 *syn* see RUDDY

2 *syn* see IMPASSIONED
rel enthusiastic; avid, desirous, eager, fierce, keen; burning, heated

gloze (over) *vb syn* see PALLIATE
rel account, explain, justify, rationalize; belie, falsify, miscolor, misrepresent

gluey *adj syn* see STICKY 1

glum *adj syn* see SULLEN
rel close-lipped, silent, taciturn, tight-lipped; depressed, oppressed, weighed down
con glad, happy, joyful, joyous, lighthearted
ant cheerful

glut *vb syn* see SATIATE
rel cram, feast, stuff
idiom make a pig of (oneself)
con scant, skimp
ant stint

glutted *adj syn* see SATIATED

gluttonous *adj syn* see VORACIOUS
rel hoggish, piggish; indulgent, intemperate
con sober, temperate; ascetic, austere; sparing
ant abstemious

gnaw *vb* 1 *syn* see WORRY 1
rel haunt, irritate, rankle

2 *syn* see EAT 3
rel abrade, fret; consume, crumble

gnome *n syn* see MAXIM

gnostic *adj syn* see WISE 1

go *vb* 1 to move on a course <they were glad to be *going* toward home>
syn ‖cruise, fare, hie, journey, pass, proceed, ‖process, push on, repair, travel, wend
rel advance; approach, near
idiom gain ground, get over the ground, make one's way
ant stay; stop

2 to move out of and away from where one is <it's time to *go* now>
syn ‖blow, depart, exit, get away, get off, leave, ‖mog, move, pop off, pull out, push off, quit, retire, run along, shove off, take off, withdraw
rel abscond, decamp, escape, flee, fly, hightail
idiom take a powder
con abide, remain, stay; arrive
ant come

3 *syn* see RUN 8

4 to be brought to or toward an end <his money will soon be *gone*>
syn consume, exhaust, expend, finish, run through, spend, use up, wash up
rel deplete, devour, dissipate, fritter (away), overspend, squander, waste

con conserve, preserve, save
5 *syn* see DIE 1
6 *syn* see PASS 3
7 *syn* see GIVE 12
8 *syn* see HAPPEN 1
9 *syn* see BECOME 1
10 *syn* see RANGE 3
11 *syn* see SUCCEED 3
12 *syn* see SUCCEED 2
13 *syn* see RESORT 2
14 *syn* see FUNCTION 3
15 *syn* see EXTEND 7
16 *syn* see AGREE 1
17 *syn* see BELONG 1
18 *syn* see BEAR 10
19 *syn* see ENJOY 1

go (for) *vb syn* see APPROVE 1
go (into) *vb syn* see EXPLORE
go (together *or* **with)** *vb syn* see SUIT 4
go *n* **1** *syn* see OCCURRENCE
2 *syn* see VIGOR 2
3 *syn* see ENERGY 2
4 *syn* see FLING 1
5 *syn* see SPELL 1
6 *syn* see SIEGE
7 *syn* see SUCCESS

goad *n syn* see STIMULUS
rel compulsion, drive, impulsion; desire, lust, passion, urge, zeal
ant curb
goad *vb syn* see URGE
rel impel, move: coerce, compel, force; instigate
go-ahead *adj syn* see ENTERPRISING 2
goal *n* **1** *syn* see AMBITION 2
2 *syn* see USE 4
goat *n syn* see SCAPEGOAT
goatish *adj syn* see LUSTFUL 2
gob *n* **1** *syn* see LUMP 1
2 *usu* **gobs** *pl syn* see SCAD
gob *n syn* see MOUTH 1
gobbet *n syn* see DROP 1
gobble *vb syn* see GULP
gobbledygook *n* wordy unintelligible language < *gobbledygook* of bureaucrats >
syn double-talk, gibberish
rel double Dutch, Greek, jabberwocky; ||bull, bunkum, claptrap, drivel, garbage, malarkey, nonsense, poppycock, twaddle
go-between *n* **1** *syn* see MARRIAGE BROKER
2 an intermediate agent between individuals or groups <served as *go-between* in the labor dispute>
syn broker, entrepreneur, interagent, interceder, intercessor, intermediary, intermediate, intermediator, mediator, middleman
rel agent, attorney, deputy, factor, proxy; emissary, envoy, messenger; delegate, representative; arbitrator, negotiator
godless *adj syn* see IRRELIGIOUS
rel agnostic, atheistic, infidel
ant godly
godlike *adj syn* see DIVINE 2
godly *adj* **1** *syn* see DIVINE 1
2 *syn* see SAINTLY
3 *syn* see DEVOUT

---

ant godless
go down *vb* **1** *syn* see FALL 2
rel droop, sag, sink; cave (in), collapse, crumple, fold
2 *syn* see SET 12
3 *syn* see SINK 1
4 *syn* see FALL 3
God's acre *n syn* see CEMETERY
godsend *n syn* see GOOD 1
go-getter *n syn* see HUSTLER 1
goggle *vb* **1** *syn* see LOOK 7
2 *syn* see GAZE 1
go in *vb syn* see ENTER 1
Golconda *n syn* see BONANZA
goldarn *adj* **1** *syn* see DAMNED 2
2 *syn* see UTTER
goldbrick *n syn* see SLACKER
goldbrick *vb syn* see IDLE
golden *adj* **1** *syn* see BLOND 1
2 *syn* see MELLIFLUOUS
golden-ager *n syn* see OLDSTER
gold mine *n syn* see BONANZA
golem *n syn* see ROBOT 2
gone *adj* **1** *syn* see EXTINCT 2
2 *syn* see ABSENT 1
3 *syn* see LOST 2
4 *syn* see PREGNANT 1
gonfalon *n syn* see FLAG
gonfanon *n syn* see FLAG
goo *n* **1** a sticky substance <slipped on a patch of greasy *goo* on the walk>
syn gook, goop, gumbo, gunk, muck; *compare* CRUD
rel dope
2 *syn* see CRUD
good *adj* **1** having a helpful or auspicious character <a *good* wind>
syn advantageous, benefic, beneficial, brave, favorable, favoring, helpful, propitious, toward, useful
rel convenient, suitable; desirable, needed; appropriate, proper, right
con disadvantageous, unfavorable; damaging, hampering, harmful; unwanted
ant ill
2 adapted to the end in view <they doubted that the fruit was *good* to eat>
syn appropriate, convenient, fit, meet, proper, suitable, useful
rel all right, apt, becoming, conformable, congruous, fitting, seemly
con inadequate, inappropriate, undesirable, unfit, unsuitable, useless
3 *syn* see WHOLE 1
con blemished, damaged, defective, flawed, impaired, imperfect, unsound
ant bad
4 *syn* see ADVANTAGEOUS 1
5 *syn* see PLEASANT 1
6 *syn* see HEALTHFUL
7 *syn* see CLEVER 5
8 *syn* see CONSIDERABLE 2
9 *syn* see WELL-FOUNDED
10 *syn* see DECENT 4
11 conforming to a high standard of morality or virtue <if you can't be *good*, be careful>
syn blameless, exemplary, guiltless, inculpable, innocent, irreprehensible, irreproachable, lily-white, pure, righteous, unblamable, virtuous
rel incorrupt, sound, uncorrupted, untainted

con blameworthy, impure, unrighteous; evil, iniquitous, reprobate, sinful
ant bad
12 *syn* see CHARITABLE 1
13 behaving in an acceptable or desirable manner < a *good* child >
syn decorous, well-behaved
rel polite, proper; considerate, kindly, thoughtful
con ill-behaved, indecorous, naughty; careless, heedless, inconsiderate, mischievous, thoughtless
ant bad
14 *syn* see SKILLFUL 2
ant bad
15 *syn* see ABLE
ant bad
good *n* **1** something that is desirable or beneficial < it's an ill wind that blows no *good* >
syn advantage, benediction, benefit, blessing, boon, godsend
con bane, harm, misfortune; detriment, jinx
ant evil, ill
2 *syn* see RIGHT 1
3 *syn* see WELFARE
4 **goods** *pl syn* see POSSESSION 2
5 **goods** *pl syn* see MERCHANDISE
good-bye *interj* — used as a conventional expression of good wishes at parting < the party was over; the time had come to say *good-bye* >
syn adieu, by, bye-bye, ||cheerio, farewell, so long, ||toodle-oo
rel good day, good evening, good morning, good night
idiom be good, be seeing you, fare you well, keep in touch, see you (later)
con hello, how do, howdy, hullo
good-bye *n syn* see PARTING
good-bye *adj syn* see PARTING
good faith *n* a state of mind characterizing one free from fraud, deceit, or misconduct < determined to act in *good faith* >
syn bona fides, sincereness, sincerity, uberrima fides
rel decency, decorum, propriety, seemliness; ethicality, morality, virtuousness
good-fellowship *n syn* see CAMARADERIE
good-for-nothing *n syn* see WASTREL 1
good-for-nothing *adj* **1** *syn* see FECKLESS 1
2 *syn* see WORTHLESS 1
ant precious
good-hearted *adj syn* see KIND
good-humored *adj syn* see AMIABLE 1
rel buoyant, cheerful, cheery, genial, smiling
ant ill-humored
good-looking *adj syn* see BEAUTIFUL
ant ill-looking
good-natured *adj syn* see AMIABLE 1
rel altruistic, benevolent, charitable; acquiescent, compliant
con choleric, cranky, cross, irascible, splenetic, touchy; crabbed, gloomy, glum, morose, splenetic
ant contrary; ill-natured
goodness *n* the quality or state of being morally excellent < that eternal *goodness* that burns away evil >
syn morality, probity, rectitude, righteousness, rightness, uprightness, virtue

rel honesty, honor, integrity; grace, merit, quality, superiority
ant badness, evil
good sense *n syn* see SENSE 6
good-tasting *adj syn* see PALATABLE
good-tempered *adj syn* see AMIABLE 1
con crabbed, surly; snappish, touchy; irascible
ant bad-tempered, ill-tempered
goodwill *n* **1** benevolent interest or concern < trying to promote interracial *goodwill* >
syn amity, benevolence, comity, friendliness, friendship, kindliness
rel altruism, charity, favor, generosity, helpfulness, kindness, rapport, sympathy, tolerance
con animus, disfavor, enmity, hatred, intolerance, malevolence
ant animosity, ill will
2 *syn* see ALACRITY
goody *n syn* see DELICACY
goody-goody *n syn* see PRUDE
gooey *adj* **1** *syn* see STICKY 1
2 *syn* see SENTIMENTAL
goof *n syn* see DUNCE
||**goof** (off) *vb syn* see IDLE
goof (up) *vb syn* see BOTCH
go off *vb syn* see EXPLODE 1
gook *n* **1** *syn* see GOO
2 *syn* see CRUD
3 *syn* see NONSENSE 1
go on *vb* **1** *syn* see PERSEVERE
2 *syn* see BEHAVE 1
||**goon** *n syn* see DUNCE
goop *n syn* see GOO 1
goose egg *n syn* see ZERO 1
goosey *adj* **1** *syn* see STUPID 1
2 *syn* see NERVOUS
go over *vb syn* see SUCCEED 2
gordian *adj syn* see COMPLEX 2
gore *n syn* see BLOOD 1
gorge *n syn* see RAVINE
gorge *vb syn* see SATIATE
rel bolt, devour, gobble, guzzle, raven, wolf; overeat, overindulge, stuff
idiom eat like a horse, eat one out of house and home
gorged *adj syn* see SATIATED
gorgeous *adj* **1** *syn* see SPLENDID 2
rel elegant, luxurious, opulent, plush, sumptuous; flamboyant, garish, gaudy, ostentatious, pretentious, showy; beautiful, colorful
2 *syn* see GRAND 2
||**gorilla** *n syn* see THUG 1
gory *adj syn* see BLOODY 1
gospel *n syn* see VERACITY 2
gossamer *adj syn* see FILMY
gossip *n* **1** a person who habitually retails private, scandalous, or sensational and often inaccurate information < her life ruined by a vicious old *gossip* >
syn carrytale, circulator, clack, gossiper, gossipmonger, ||long tongue, mumblenews, newsmonger, quidnunc, rumorer, rumormonger, scandalizer, scandalmonger, sieve, tabby, talebearer, telltale; *compare* BUSYBODY, INFORMER
2 *syn* see REPORT 1
rel account, chronicle, conversation, story, tale; babble, banter, chatter, prate
gossip *vb* to disclose something, often of questionable veracity, that is better kept

to oneself < *gossiped* about his neighbor's business>
syn blab, noise (about *or* abroad), rumor, talk, tattle
rel babble, chat, chatter, prate, prattle; hint, imply, insinuate, intimate, suggest
idiom dish the dirt, spill the beans, tell idle tales, tell tales out of school

gossiper *n syn* see GOSSIP 1

gossipmonger *n syn* see GOSSIP 1

Gothic *adj syn* see BARBARIAN 1
rel brutal, coarse, crude

gouge *vb syn* see EXTORT 1
rel cheat, con, swindle; overcharge

go under *vb* 1 *syn* see FALL 3
2 *syn* see SINK 1

gourmand *n syn* see EPICURE

gourmet *n syn* see EPICURE

govern *vb* 1 to exercise sovereign authority < a dictator may *govern* in a thoroughly enlightened manner>
syn overrule, reign, rule, sway
rel captain, command, head; administer, conduct, control, direct, manage, master; regulate, supervise
2 *syn* see ADMINISTER 1
3 to exercise a decisive role in influencing the actions and conduct of < parents who *govern* their children wisely>
syn control, direct, dominate, handle, manage
rel directionalize, guide, lead, shepherd, steer; boss, oversee, supervise
idiom be at the helm (*or* wheel), be in the driver's seat, hold the reins

‖**governor** *n syn* see FATHER 1

grab *vb syn* see SEIZE 2

grabble *vb syn* see GROPE

grabby *adj syn* see COVETOUS

grace *n* 1 a short prayer either asking a blessing before or giving thanks after a meal < taught each child a *grace* of his own>
syn benediction, blessing, thanks, thanksgiving
rel invocation, petition
2 *syn* see MERCY
rel compassionateness, responsiveness, tenderness; forbearance, indulgence, leniency; goodness
3 *syn* see ELEGANCE

graceless *adj* 1 *syn* see BARBARIC 1
2 *syn* see INFELICITOUS
ant graceful

gracious *adj* 1 marked by kindly courtesy < her *gracious* attitude toward those around her>
syn affable, congenial, cordial, genial, sociable, ‖sonsy
rel amiable, complaisant, easy, obliging; benign, benignant, kind, kindly; chivalrous, courteous, courtly; approachable, bonhomous, clubby, forthcoming, forthgoing, outgoing
con boorish, churlish; blunt, brusque, crabbed, crusty, curt, gruff, short, sullen, surly
ant ungracious

2 *syn* see COURTLY
rel mannered, starchy

gradation *n* the difference or variation between two things that are nearly alike < the *gradations* were too small to be seen with the unaided eye>
syn nuance, shade
rel difference, distinction, divergence; change, modification, variation

grade *n* 1 *syn* see DEGREE 1
2 *syn* see ESTATE 2
3 *syn* see CLASS 1
4 *syn* see QUALITY 3
5 *syn* see SLOPE

grade *vb syn* see CLASS 2
rel arrange, order; assort, sort

Grade A *adj syn* see EXCELLENT

gradient *n syn* see SLOPE

gradual *adj* proceeding slowly usually by minute or imperceptible steps or degrees < his health showed *gradual* improvement>
syn piecemeal, step-by-step
rel deliberate, dilatory, lagging, poky, sluggish
con acute, sharp, sudden
ant abrupt

gradually *adv* by small degrees or amounts < *gradually* he learned the new job>
syn bit by bit, little by little, piecemeal
idiom a little at a time, by degrees
con quickly, rapidly, speedily; at once, immediately, suddenly

grain *n syn* see PARTICLE

grainy *adj syn* see COARSE 1

grammar *n syn* see ALPHABET 2

grand *adj* 1 large and impressive in size, scope, extent, or conception < the platform provided a *grand* view of the canyon>
syn august, baronial, grandiose, imposing, lordly, magnific, magnificent, majestic, noble, princely, royal, stately; *compare* HUGE
rel monumental, prodigious, stupendous, tremendous; towering; gorgeous, splendid, sublime, superb
con measly, paltry, petty, puny, trifling, trivial
2 marked by great magnificence, display, and usually ceremony or formality < delighted to attend the *grand* presidential fete>
syn gorgeous, impressive, lavish, luxurious, splendid, sumptuous
rel magnificent, majestic; flashy, garish, gaudy, ornate, ostentatious, showy
con crude, meretricious, obtrusive, vulgar; flimsy, tawdry
3 noble in character or spirit < a *grand* outlook on life>
syn elevated, exalted, lofty, sublime, superb
rel magnificent, splendid
con average, common, commonplace, ordinary; base, lowly, mean, poor

grandam *n syn* see BELDAM 1

grande dame *n syn* see MATRIARCH

grandiloquent *adj syn* see RHETORICAL

grandiose *adj* 1 *syn* see GRAND 1
rel ostentatious, pretentious, showy; cosmic, overwhelming, unfathomable, vast

---

syn synonym(s)   **rel** related word(s)
ant antonym(s)   **con** contrasted word(s)
idiom idiomatic equivalent(s)
‖ use limited; if in doubt, see a dictionary

2 *syn* see AMBITIOUS 2

granny *n syn* see FUSSBUDGET

grant *vb* 1 to give as a favor or right < *granted* him an extension of payments >
syn accord, award, concede, vouchsafe
rel bestow, confer, donate, give, present; allow, permit; cede, relinquish, yield
con decline, refuse, turn down

2 *syn* see ACKNOWLEDGE 1
con differ, disagree, dissent; challenge, dispute, object, protest

3 *syn* see GIVE 2

grant *n syn* see APPROPRIATION
rel gift; assistance, benefaction, contribution, donation; alms, charity, dole, hand-out

granular *adj syn* see COARSE 1

grapevine *n syn* see REPORT 1

graph *n syn* see CHART 1
rel diagram, outline, sketch

graphic *adj* 1 giving a clear visual impression especially in words < gave a *graphic* description of the whole incident >
syn photographic, pictorial, picturesque, vivid
rel clear, lucid, perspicuous; clear-cut, incisive; cogent, compelling, convincing, telling; definite, explicit, precise, realistic, striking, visual
con confused, hazy, indistinct, obscure

2 *syn* see PICTORIAL 1

grapple *n syn* see HOLD

grapple *vb* 1 *syn* see SEIZE 2

2 *syn* see WRESTLE

grasp *vb* 1 *syn* see TAKE 4

2 *syn* see APPREHEND 1
rel envisage, fathom, perceive

3 *syn* see KNOW 1

grasp *n syn* see HOLD

graspable *adj syn* see UNDERSTANDABLE
ant ungraspable

grasping *adj syn* see COVETOUS
rel extorting, extortionate

grass *n syn* see MARIJUANA

grate *vb* 1 *syn* see SCRAPE 1
rel abrade, bark, chafe, fray, gall, scuff, skin

2 *syn* see IRRITATE

grateful *adj* 1 feeling or expressing gratitude < was *grateful* for the gift >
syn obliged, thankful
rel appreciative, beholden; gratified, pleased
idiom filled with gratitude
ant ungrateful

2 *syn* see PLEASANT 1
rel comforting, consoling, solacing; refreshing, rejuvenating, renewing, restorative, restoring; delectable, delicious, delightful
ant obnoxious

gratefulness *n syn* see AMENITY 1

gratify *vb* 1 *syn* see PLEASE 2
rel appease, baby, cater (to), coddle, favor, humor, indulge, oblige, pamper
con bother, irk; aggravate, exasperate, irritate, nettle, rile; agitate, disturb, perturb, upset

2 *syn* see SATISFY 3

3 *syn* see INDULGE 1
idiom do one proud

gratifying *adj syn* see PLEASANT 1
rel contenting, satisfying; delighting, gladdening, regaling, rejoicing

con invidious, obnoxious; offensive, revolting

grating *adj syn* see HARSH 3

gratis *adj syn* see FREE 5

gratuitous *adj* 1 *syn* see FREE 5
rel voluntary, willing

2 *syn* see SUPEREROGATORY

3 *syn* see BASELESS
rel indefensible, reasonless, unsupportable

gratuity *n* something given over and above what is due, generally in return for or expectation of good service < he found that an occasional *gratuity* smoothed his path >
syn cumshaw, lagniappe, largess, ‖palm grease, ‖palm oil, ‖perk(s), perquisite, pourboire, tip
rel alms, benefaction, contribution, donation; offering, reward

grave *vb* 1 *syn* see ENGRAVE 1

2 *syn* see IMPRESS 3

grave *n* a place of interment < his *grave* is in the church burial ground >
syn burial, ‖pit, sepulcher, sepulture, tomb
rel catacomb, crypt, vault; mausoleum; ossuary; cinerarium
idiom final resting place

grave *adj* 1 *syn* see SERIOUS 2

2 *syn* see SERIOUS 1
rel heavy, ponderous; grim, sad, saturnine; awful, dreadful, horrible, terrible
con flippant, light, light-minded
ant gay

3 involving marked risk of impairment or destruction < a *grave* illness >
syn dangerous, fell, grievous, major, serious, ugly; *compare* DANGEROUS 1
rel deadly, destructive, dire, fatal, killing, murderous; frightening, ghastly, terrible; afflicting, severe
con paltry, petty, trivial; harmless, innocuous; temporary, transitory

gravely *adv syn* see SERIOUSLY 2

grave marker *n syn* see TOMBSTONE

gravestone *n syn* see TOMBSTONE

graveyard *n syn* see CEMETERY

gravid *adj syn* see PREGNANT 1

gravidity *n syn* see PREGNANCY

graybeard *n syn* see GAFFER

gray matter *n syn* see MIND 1

graze *vb* 1 *syn* see BRUSH

2 *syn* see GLANCE 1

3 *syn* see ABRADE 1
rel harm, hurt, injure; bruise, contuse, wound

greasy *adj* 1 *syn* see FATTY 2

2 *syn* see SLICK 1

‖**greasy spoon** *n syn* see EATING HOUSE

great *adj* 1 *syn* see LARGE 1
con measly, paltry, petty, puny, trifling, trivial
ant little

2 *syn* see FAMOUS 2
rel superlative, supreme, surpassing, transcendent

great deal *n syn* see MUCH

greater *adj* 1 *syn* see BEST

2 *syn* see SUPERIOR 1

great gun *n syn* see NOTABLE 1

greathearted *adj* 1 *syn* see BRAVE 1

2 *syn* see GENEROUS 1

greatly *adv syn* see VERY 1

greatness *n syn* see SIZE 2

greed *n syn* see CUPIDITY
  rel gluttonousness, gluttony, rapaciousness, ravenousness, voraciousness

greedy *adj syn* see COVETOUS
  con bounteous, bountiful, generous, liberal, munificent, openhanded; exuberant, lavish, prodigal, profuse

Greek *n syn* see GIBBERISH 1

green *adj* 1 *syn* see YOUNG 1
  2 *syn* see INEXPERIENCED
  con grown-up, ripe, mature, matured; educated, instructed, trained; proficient, skilled, skillful
  ant experienced

green *n syn* see COMMON 2

‖greenbacks *n pl syn* see MONEY

green—eyed *adj syn* see ENVIOUS

greenhorn *n syn* see RUSTIC

greenhouse *n* a glass-enclosed structure for the cultivation and protection of tender plants <a small window *greenhouse* full of bloom>
  syn conservatory, ‖glasshouse
  rel coolhouse, hotbed, hothouse

greenness *n* 1 *syn* see YOUTH 1
  2 *syn* see INEXPERIENCE

greet *vb syn* see ADDRESS 7

greeting *n* the ceremonial words or acts of one who meets, welcomes, or formally addresses another <after the *greeting* the chairman called the roll>
  syn salutation, salute
  rel address, hail, hello, welcome
  con farewell, good-bye
  ant valediction

gregarious *adj syn* see SOCIAL 2

grief *n syn* see SORROW
  rel bemoaning, bewailing, deploring, lamenting
  con comfort, comforting, consolation, solace, solacing
  ant joy

grievance *n syn* see INJUSTICE 2
  rel hardship, rigor; affliction, cross, trial, tribulation

grieve *vb* 1 *syn* see DISTRESS 2
  2 to feel or express deep distress <*grieved* at the loss of so many lives>
  syn mourn, sorrow
  rel bear, endure, suffer; bemoan, bewail, deplore, lament; cry, keen, wail, weep
  ant rejoice
  3 *syn* see DEPLORE 1

grievous *adj* 1 *syn* see ONEROUS
  2 *syn* see BITTER 2
  3 *syn* see GRAVE 3
  4 *syn* see DEPLORABLE

‖grifter *n syn* see SWINDLER

grill *n syn* see CROSS-EXAMINATION

grilling *n syn* see CROSS-EXAMINATION

grim *adj* 1 *syn* see FIERCE 1
  rel foreboding, ominous
  2 forbidding in action or appearance <had a *grim* and determined expression on his face>
  syn austere, bleak, dour, hard, harsh, severe, stringent

rel cold, forbidding, ‖off-putting; fixed, rigid, set; determined, firm, stern
  con calm, mellow, mild, soft, warm; attractive, beautiful, pleasing
  ant pleasant
  3 being extremely obdurate or firm in action or purpose <fought with *grim* determination>
  syn implacable, ironfisted, merciless, mortal, relentless, ruthless, unappeasable, unflinching, unrelenting, unyielding
  rel adamant, inexorable, inflexible, obdurate, resolute, stubborn, unforgiving, vindictive; certain, inevitable; determined, dogged
  con considerate, gentle, mild; clement, forbearing, indulgent
  ant lenient
  4 *syn* see GHASTLY 1
  rel loathsome, offensive, repugnant, repulsive, revolting

grimace *n syn* see FACE 6

grimace *vb* to distort one's face by way of expressing a feeling <*grimaced* with pain>
  syn mop, mouth, mow, mug, ‖mump
  rel contort, deform, distort, misshape
  idiom make a face (*or* mouth), make a wry face (*or* mouth), pull a face, screw up one's face

grime *vb syn* see SOIL 2

grim reaper *n syn* see DEATH 1

grin *vb syn* see SMILE
  con frown, gloom
  ant grimace

grind *vb syn* see DRUDGE

grind *n* 1 *syn* see WORK 2
  2 *syn* see ROUTINE

grip *vb* 1 *syn* see TAKE 4
  2 *syn* see ENTHRALL 2

grip *n syn* see HOLD
  rel coercion, constraint, duress, restraint

gripe *vb* to complain emphatically and often petulantly <students *griping* about the cafeteria food>
  syn ‖beef, ‖bellyache, ‖bitch, bleat, ‖blow off, crab, ‖crib, fuss, squawk, yammer, yawp (*or* yaup); *compare* COMPLAIN
  rel brawl, kick, take on; croak, grouch, grouse, grumble, murmur, mutter
  con applaud, approve, cheer; rejoice; accept, bear, endure, tolerate

gripe *n* 1 *syn* see HOLD
  2 *usu* gripes *pl syn* stomachache, bellyache, colic, collywobbles

griper *n syn* see GROUCH

grisette *n syn* see DOXY 1

grisly *adj syn* see GHASTLY 1
  rel eerie, uncanny, weird

grit *n syn* see FORTITUDE
  con faltering, hesitation, vacillation, wavering
  ant faintheartedness

grobian *n syn* see BOOR 2

grog *n syn* see LIQUOR 2

‖groggery *n syn* see BAR 5

‖grogshop *n syn* see BAR 5

groove *n syn* see ROUTINE

groovy *adj syn* see MARVELOUS 2

grope *vb* to reach out or about blindly (as in testing or searching) <*groped* along the wall in search of a door>
  syn feel, fumble, grabble

---

syn synonym(s)   *rel* related word(s)
ant antonym(s)   *con* contrasted word(s)
idiom idiomatic equivalent(s)
‖ use limited; if in doubt, see a dictionary

rel poke, pry, root; examine, explore, search

gross *adj* 1 *syn* see EGREGIOUS
rel excessive, exorbitant, extreme, immoderate, inordinate
con paltry, trifling, trivial
ant petty
2 *syn* see UTTER
3 *syn* see FAT 2
4 *syn* see WHOLE 4
ant net
5 *syn* see MATERIAL 1
6 *syn* see COARSE 3
7 *syn* see OBSCENE 2
rel animal, carnal, fleshy, sensual; loathsome, offensive, repulsive, revolting; improper, unrefined
con decent, decorous, proper, refined

gross *n syn* see WHOLE 1

grotesque *adj syn* see FANTASTIC 2
rel baroque, flamboyant, rococo; eerie, uncanny, weird; extravagant, extreme; comic, comical, droll, ludicrous

grotto *n syn* see CAVE

grouch *n* an habitually irritable or complaining person <it's hard to live with a *grouch*>
syn ‖bellyacher, complainer, crab, crabber, crank, crosspatch, faultfinder, griper, grouser, growler, grumbler, grump, kicker, malcontent, sorehead, sourpuss
con optimist, Pollyanna

grouch *vb syn* see GRUMBLE 1

ground *n* 1 *syn* see BASIS 1
2 *syn* see BASE 1
3 *syn* see REASON 3
rel evidence, testimony; antecedent, cause, determinant; demonstration, test, trial
4 **grounds** *pl syn* see SEDIMENT
5 *syn* see EARTH 2

ground *vb* 1 *syn* see FELL 1
2 *syn* see BASE
rel buttress, support, sustain

grounded *adj syn* see AGROUND

groundless *adj syn* see BASELESS
ant well-founded, well-grounded

groundwork *n* 1 *syn* see BASIS 1
2 *syn* see BASE 1

group *n* 1 a usually comparatively small assemblage of individuals <people gathered in *groups* about the hall>
syn assembly, band, bevy, bunch, cluster, covey, crew, party; *compare* COMPANY 1, GATHERING
rel circle, clique, coterie, set
con crowd, crush, horde, mob, press, rout, throng
2 *syn* see GATHERING 2
3 an assemblage of things constituting a unit <a *group* of houses behind the church>
syn array, batch, battery, body, bunch, bundle, clot, clump, cluster, clutch, lot, parcel, passel, platoon, set, sort, suite
rel assemblage, collection, mess, shooting match
4 *syn* see SET 5
5 *syn* see SYNDICATE
6 *syn* see CLASS 1

group *vb* 1 to make into or bring together in a group <*grouped* the children according to age>
syn assemble, cluster, collect, gather, round up; *compare* GATHER 6

rel adjust, arrange, harmonize, organize, systematize; allocate, dispose, distribute, place; bunch, crowd, huddle
idiom bring together, get together
con disband, disperse, scatter, separate
2 *syn* see ASSORT

grouping *n syn* see CLASS 1

grouse *vb syn* see GRUMBLE 1

grouser *n syn* see GROUCH

grovel *vb syn* see FAWN
idiom lick the dust (*or* one's boots)

groveler *n syn* see SYCOPHANT

groveling *adj syn* see FAWNING

grow *vb* 1 to cause (something living) to exist or flourish <*grew* a crop of wheat>
syn breed, cultivate, produce, propagate, raise
rel care (for), foster, nurse, nurture, rear, tend
2 *syn* see MATURE
3 *syn* see ESCALATE 2
4 *syn* see BECOME 1

growl *vb syn* see RUMBLE

growler *n syn* see GROUCH

grown *adj* 1 *syn* see MATURE 1
2 *syn* see OVERGROWN

grown-up *adj syn* see MATURE 1
ant childish; callow

growth *n syn* see DEVELOPMENT

grow up *vb syn* see MATURE

grub *vb* 1 *syn* see DIG 1
rel burrow, poke, root
2 *syn* see SCOUR 2
3 *syn* see DRUDGE

grub *n* 1 *syn* see HACK 2
2 *syn* see FOOD 1

grubber *n syn* see HACK 2

grubby *adj syn* see DIRTY 1
ant immaculate

grubstake *vb syn* see CAPITALIZE

grudge *vb syn* see ENVY
rel deny; refuse

grudge *n syn* see MALICE
rel grievance, injury, injustice

gruesome *adj syn* see GHASTLY 1
rel appalling, daunting; horrendous, horrific; baleful, sinister

gruff *adj* 1 *syn* see BLUFF
rel crabbed, dour, morose, saturnine, sullen, surly; boorish, churlish; fierce, truculent
con bland, smooth, suave, urbane; fulsome, oily, slick, soapy, unctuous
2 *syn* see HOARSE 1

grumble *vb* 1 to complain in a low harsh voice and often in a surly manner <workers *grumbling* about the low wages>
syn croak, grouch, grouse, ‖grunt, murmur, mutter, scold; *compare* COMPLAIN
rel ‖beef, ‖bellyache, ‖bitch, brawl, crab, fuss, gripe, holler, squawk, whine; groan, moan; complain, kick
con applaud, cheer; rejoice
2 *syn* see RUMBLE

grumbler *n syn* see GROUCH

grump *n* 1 **grumps** *pl syn* see SULK
2 *syn* see GROUCH

grump *vb syn* see SULK

Grundy *n syn* see PRUDE

‖**grunt** *vb syn* see GRUMBLE 1

guarantee *n* 1 an assurance for the fulfillment of a condition <gave him a *guarantee* that the work would be done according to specifications>

syn bail, bond, guaranty, security, surety, warranty; *compare* PLEDGE 1
rel earnest, pledge, promise, token, undertaking, word; oath, vow
2 *syn* see WORD 8
guarantee *vb syn* see WARRANT 2
guarantor *n syn* see SPONSOR
guaranty *n syn* see GUARANTEE 1
rel bargain, contract
guaranty *vb syn* see WARRANT 2
guard *n* 1 *syn* see DEFENSE 1
2 a person or group on sentinel duty < posted six *guards* around the diamond necklace > < turned out the *guard* >
syn lookout, picket, sentinel, sentry, ward, watch, watchman
rel guardian, jailer, keeper, turnkey, warden, warder; patrolman; outguard, patrol
guard *vb syn* see DEFEND 1
rel attend, mind, tend, watch; accompany, chaperon, conduct, convoy, escort
guarded *adj* 1 *syn* see ULTERIOR
2 *syn* see CAUTIOUS
ant unguarded
guardian *n syn* see CUSTODIAN
guardianship *n syn* see CUSTODY
guardroom *n syn* see JAIL
gudgeon *n syn* see POOL 3
guerdon *n syn* see REWARD
guerdon *vb syn* see PAY 1
guerrilla *n syn* see PARTISAN 2
guess *vb* 1 *syn* see CONJECTURE
rel reason, speculate; deduce; estimate, reckon
idiom venture a guess
2 *syn* see PREDICT 2
guest *n* 1 *syn* see VISITOR 1
2 **guests** *pl syn* see COMPANY 2
guff *n* 1 *syn* see NONSENSE 2
2 *syn* see BACK TALK
guffaw *vb syn* see LAUGH
guide *vb* to put or lead on a course or into the way to be followed < *guided* them safely through the minefields >
syn conduct, direct, escort, lead, pilot, route, see, shepherd, show, steer
rel accompany, chaperon, convoy; control, manage; contrive, engineer, maneuver
idiom set one on one's way
con bewilder, distract, mystify, perplex, puzzle; beguile, deceive, delude, mislead
ant misguide
guide *n* 1 *syn* see LEADER 1
2 *syn* see ESCORT 2
rel conductor, director, leader, pilot
3 *syn* see HANDBOOK
guidebook *n syn* see HANDBOOK
guild *n syn* see ASSOCIATION 2
guile *n syn* see DECEIT 1
ant ingenuousness; candor
guileful *adj* 1 *syn* see SLY 2
ant guileless
2 *syn* see UNDERHAND
guileless *adj syn* see NATURAL 5
ant guileful
guillotine *vb syn* see BEHEAD
guilt *n syn* see BLAME
rel crime, offense, sin; responsibility

ant innocence; guiltlessness
guiltless *adj* 1 *syn* see GOOD 11
2 *syn* see INNOCENT 2
ant guilty
guilty *adj syn* see BLAMEWORTHY
rel accountable, answerable, responsible; impeached, incriminated, indicted
ant innocent; guiltless
guise *n* 1 *syn* see COSTUME
2 *syn* see APPEARANCE 2
3 *syn* see MASK 2
gulch *n syn* see RAVINE
gulf *n* 1 *syn* see INLET
2 a hollow place of vast width and depth < a *gulf* extending deep into the earth >
syn abysm, abyss, chasm
rel cave, cavity, hollow; crevasse, gulch, ravine; pit, shaft, well
gull *vb syn* see DUPE
gull *n syn* see POOL 3
gullible *adj syn* see EASY 3
ant astute
gulp *vb* to swallow hurriedly or greedily or in one swallow < *gulped* his lunch and ran off >
syn bolt, cram, englut, gobble, guzzle, ingurgitate, slop, slosh, wolf
rel devour, glut, stuff
con nibble, pick
gum (up) *vb syn* see BOTCH
gumbo *n syn* see GOO 1
gummy *adj syn* see STICKY 1
gumption *n syn* see SENSE 6
rel astuteness, perspicaciousness, perspicacity, sagaciousness, sagacity, shrewdness
gumptious *adj syn* see ENTERPRISING 2
gumshoe *n* 1 *syn* see DETECTIVE
2 *syn* see POLICEMAN
gumshoe *vb syn* see SNEAK
gun *n syn* see ASSASSIN
gung ho *adj syn* see ENTHUSIASTIC
gunk *n* 1 *syn* see GOO 1
2 *syn* see CRUD
gunman *n syn* see ASSASSIN
‖**gunsel** *n syn* see ASSASSIN
gunslinger *n syn* see ASSASSIN
gurge *vb syn* see SWIRL
gurgle *vb syn* see SLOSH 1
gush *vb syn* see POUR 2
rel flood, flush; emanate, issue, spring
gushing *adj syn* see EFFUSIVE
gushy *adj syn* see EFFUSIVE
gussy up *vb syn* see DRESS UP 1
gust *n syn* see OUTBURST 1
gusto *n syn* see TASTE 4
rel delectation, delight, enjoyment, pleasure; ardor, enthusiasm, fervor, passion, zeal
gusty *adj syn* see WINDY 1
‖**gusty** *adj syn* see PALATABLE
gut *n* 1 *usu* **guts** *pl syn* see ENTRAILS
‖2 *syn* see ABDOMEN
3 **guts** *pl syn* see COURAGE
4 **guts** *pl syn* see FORTITUDE
gut *vb* 1 *syn* see EVISCERATE
2 *syn* see DRESS 3
gut *adj syn* see INNER 2
gutless *adj syn* see COWARDLY
ant gutsy
‖**gutsy** *adj syn* see BRAVE 1
guy *n syn* see MAN 3
guzzle *vb* 1 *syn* see DRINK 3
2 *syn* see GULP

---

syn synonym(s)   rel related word(s)
ant antonym(s)   con contrasted word(s)
idiom idiomatic equivalent(s)
‖ use limited; if in doubt, see a dictionary

guzzler *n syn* see DRUNKARD
gyp *n* 1 *syn* see SWINDLER
   2 *syn* see IMPOSTURE
gyp *vb syn* see CHEAT
gypper *n syn* see SWINDLER
gyrate *vb* 1 *syn* see TURN 1

   2 *syn* see SPIN 1
gyration *n syn* see REVOLUTION 1
gyre *vb* 1 *syn* see TURN 1
   2 *syn* see SPIN 1
gyre *n syn* see REVOLUTION 1
gyve *n, usu* gyves *pl syn* see SHACKLE

H

habiliment *n* 1 habiliments *pl syn* see
EQUIPMENT
   2 *usu* habiliments *pl syn* see CLOTHES
habit *n* 1 a mode of behaving or doing
fixed by constant repetition <it was his
habit to rise early>
   syn consuetude, custom, habitude, manner, practice, praxis, trick, usage, use,
way, wont
   rel bent, disposition, inclination, proclivity, tendency, turn; convention, fashion,
form, mode, pattern, style; addiction;
groove, rote, routine, rut, set
   2 *syn* see PHYSIQUE
   rel carcass; framework; contour, outline
habitable *adj syn* see LIVABLE 1
   ant unhabitable, uninhabitable
habitant *n syn* see INHABITANT
habitat *n* the physical environment natural
to a kind of being <the watery *habitat* of
the eel>
   syn haunt, home, locality, range, site,
stamping ground
   rel environment, locale, surroundings,
territory
habitation *n* 1 the act of inhabiting or the
state of being inhabited <places suitable
for *habitation*>
   syn inhabitancy, inhabitation, occupancy,
occupation, residence, settlement
   rel colonization, domiciliation; peopling;
sojourning
   2 the place where one lives <habitations
unfit for human occupancy>
   syn abode, commorancy, domicile, dwelling, home, house, residence, residency
   rel apartment, flat, tenement; housing,
lodging, lodgment, quarters; haunt, haven,
homeplace, homestead, place, seat; ‖pad,
‖roost; astre, fireside,
hearth, hearthside, hearthstone, roof, roof-
tree
   idiom roof over one's head, where one
hangs one's hat
habitual *adj* 1 *syn* see USUAL 1
   rel constant, established, ingrained, inveterate, persistent, steady
   con infrequent, irregular, sporadic, uncommon
   ant occasional
   2 acting by force of habit <*habitual*
smokers who blue the air>
   syn accustomed, chronic, confirmed, habituated
   rel continual, inveterate, persistent, regular, steady; automatic, instinctive, involuntary; addicted; customary, wonted
   con conscious, deliberate, premeditative,
purposive, witting
habitually *adv syn* see USUALLY 1

   ant occasionally
habituate *vb* 1 *syn* see ACCUSTOM
   2 to make acceptable or desirable (as to
oneself) through use <*habituate* oneself to
poverty>
   syn addict, adjust, confirm (in), devote
(to), take (to)
   rel bear, endure, inure, support, tolerate;
condition, familiarize, season
   con balk (at), object (to), resist
habituated *adj syn* see HABITUAL 2
habitude *n syn* see HABIT 1
   rel attitude, position, stand; condition,
situation, state
   con humor, mood, temper; caprice, freak,
vagary, whim
habitué *n* 1 one who frequents a place
<an *habitué* of libraries>
   syn denizen, frequenter, haunter
   rel customer, devotee, patron, sojourner;
employer, user
   2 *syn* see ADDICT
habitus *n syn* see PHYSIQUE
hack *vb* to cut with repeated crude or ruthless blows <*hack* a path through the
jungle>
   syn hackle, haggle, slash
   rel gash, mangle; chop, cut, fell, hew
hack *n* 1 *syn* see TAXICAB
   2 one who surrenders intellectual or personal integrity for an assured reward (as a
regular income) <party *hacks* and hang-
ers-on>
   syn drudge, grub, grubber, hireling, mercenary, slavey
   rel grind, lackey, servant, slave; machine,
plodder; potboiler
hack *adj* 1 *syn* see INFERIOR 2
   rel commonplace, dull, ordinary, trite,
usual; inconsequential, petty, trivial
   con individual, original, uncommon, unusual
   2 *syn* see TRITE
   rel antiquated, old, outmoded, outworn
   con lively; unfamiliar
hackle *vb syn* see HACK
hackneyed *adj syn* see TRITE
   rel antediluvian, antiquated, archaic,
obsolete, outmoded, out-of-date; conventional, everyday, quotidian, stock; moth-
eaten
   ant unhackneyed
Hadean *adj syn* see INFERNAL 1
   rel gloomy, murky, stygian
hades *n syn* see HELL
hag *n* 1 *syn* see WITCH 1
   2 an ugly or evil-looking old woman <a
pitiful homeless *hag*>

syn ||bag, ||bat, beldam, biddy, crone, drab, trot, witch

rel gammer, grandam; ||battle-ax, fishwife, gorgon, harpy, harridan, shrew, slattern, virago, vixen

haggard *adj* thin and contracted by or as if by fatigue or inner distress < *haggard* from their long vigil >

syn careworn, drawn, pinched, worn

rel angular, gaunt, lank, lean, scraggy, scrawny, skinny, spare; ashen, faded, pale, pallid, wan; exhausted, fagged, fatigued, tired, wearied, worn-down

con energetic, lusty, strenuous, vigorous; easy, relaxed

haggle *vb syn* see HACK

2 to argue as to terms < *haggle* over prices >

syn bargain, chaffer, dicker, higgle, huckster, palter

rel barter, deal, horse-trade, trade; bicker, cavil, dispute, quibble, squabble, stickle, wrangle

hagridden *adj syn* see OBSESSED

hagride *vb syn* see WORRY 1

hail *n syn* see BARRAGE

hail *vb* 1 *syn* see ADDRESS 7

rel hallo, hallow, holler, shout

2 *syn* see COMMEND 2

con belittle, depreciate, disparage, downgrade; berate, censure, condemn, libel, rap; dismiss, reject

hail (from) *vb syn* see ORIGINATE 5

hair *n* a minute distance, degree, or margin < won the election by a *hair* >

syn ace, hairbreadth, whisker; compare HINT 2

rel bit, fraction, jot, mite, particle, trace, trifle

hairbreadth *n syn* see HAIR

haircutter *n syn* see BARBER

hairless *adj* lacking hair < he had a shining *hairless* head >

syn bald, glabrous, smooth

rel baldish; shaved, shaven, shorn, tonsured

ant hairy

hairline *adj syn* see FINE 1

hairsplitting *adj syn* see FINE 1

hair-trigger *adj syn* see INSTANTANEOUS

hairy *adj* 1 covered with or as if with hair < wore a *hairy* overcoat >

syn fleecy, hirsute, pileous, pilose, whiskered, woolly

rel bristly, bushy, downy, fluffy, fuzzy, lanate, nappy, pubescent, rough, shaggy, tomentose, tufted, unshorn, villous

con bald, barefaced, beardless, glabrous, shaved, shaven, shorn, smooth

ant hairless

2 *syn* see DANGEROUS 1

3 *syn* see ROUGH 1

halcyon *adj syn* see CALM 1

con blustery, fevered, foul, raging, rough, stormy, tempestuous, troubled, tumultuous, wild

hale *adj syn* see HEALTHY 1

rel husky, stout, strapping

idiom hale and hearty

ant infirm

haleness *n syn* see HEALTH

||**half-assed** *adj syn* see DEFICIENT 1

half-blind *adj syn* see PURBLIND

half blood *n syn* see HYBRID

ant full blood

half-breed *n syn* see HYBRID

ant full blood

halfhearted *adj syn* see TEPID 2

||**half-seas over** *adj syn* see INTOXICATED 1

halfway *adj syn* see MIDDLE 1

half-wit *n syn* see FOOL 4

half-witted *adj syn* see RETARDED

hall *n syn* see PASSAGE 4

hallo *vb syn* see CALL 1

hallow *vb* 1 *syn* see BLESS 1

2 *syn* see DEVOTE 1

con defile, desecrate, pollute, profane

hallowed *adj syn* see HOLY 1

hallucination *n syn* see DELUSION 1

rel apparition, fata morgana, phantom, wraith

hallway *n syn* see PASSAGE 4

halt *vb syn* see LIMP 1

halt *vb* 1 *syn* see STOP 4

ant proceed

2 *syn* see STOP 3

3 *syn* see ARREST 1

4 *syn* see HESITATE

5 *syn* see CLOSE 2

halting *adj* 1 *syn* see AWKWARD 2

2 *syn* see VACILLATING 2

ham-handed *adj syn* see AWKWARD 2

hammer *vb* 1 to strike or shape with or as if with a hammer < brass *hammered* into bowls and trays >

syn beat, malleate, pound

rel elaborate, fashion, form, shape

2 *syn* see BEAT 1

3 *syn* see IMPRESS 3

||4 *syn* see STAMMER 1

hammer (out) *vb syn* see ERECT 5

hammerhead *n syn* see DUNCE

hammerheaded *adj syn* see STUPID 1

hamper *vb* to impede in moving, progressing, or acting freely < the long dress *hampered* her escape >

syn clog, curb, entrammel, fetter, hobble, hog-tie, leash, shackle, tie, tie up, trammel; compare HINDER, RESTRAIN 1

rel cumber, encumber, handicap, hinder, impede, lumber, obstruct; baffle, balk, bar, block, foil, frustrate, thwart; restrain, restrict, retard; discomfit, embarrass; check, inconvenience, inhibit

idiom tie one's hands

con free, liberate, loose, release, unfetter, unleash, unshackle

ant aid, facilitate

hamper *n syn* see OBSTACLE 1

hams *n pl syn* see BUTTOCKS

hand *n syn* see SIDE 1

2 *syn* see PHASE

3 *syn* see HANDWRITING

4 *syn* see HELP 1

5 *syn* see WORKER

6 *syn* see TOUCH 6

hand *vb* 1 *syn* see GIVE 3

2 *syn* see PASS 9

handbill *n syn* see POSTER

handbook *n* a concise reference book < a *handbook* of wild flowers >

---

syn synonym(s)   *rel* related word(s)

ant antonym(s)   *con* contrasted word(s)

idiom idiomatic equivalent(s)

|| use limited; if in doubt, see a dictionary

syn Baedeker, compendium, enchiridion, guide, guidebook, manual, vade mecum
con cyclopedia, encyclopedia

hand down *vb* to convey in succession <a skill *handed down* from father to son>
syn bequeath, hand on, pass (on), transmit
con get, obtain, receive

handful *n* 1 *syn* see FEW

handicap *n* 1 *syn* see DISADVANTAGE
rel burden, encumbrance, load; embarrassment
ant asset
2 *syn* see ADVANTAGE 3

handicraft *n* *syn* see TRADE 1

hand in *vb* *syn* see SUBMIT 2

handkerchief *n* a small usually square piece of cloth used especially for blowing the nose <carry a pocket *handkerchief*>
syn hankie, kerchief, ||wipe, ||wiper

||**handle** *n* 1 *syn* see NAME 1
2 *syn* see NICKNAME

handle *vb* 1 *syn* see TOUCH 1
rel test, try; manipulate
2 to deal with or manage usually with dexterity or efficiency <*handles* his tools with great skill>
syn dispense, maneuver, manipulate, ply, swing, wield
rel direct, guide, manage, operate, run, work; brandish, flourish, shake, wave; aim, lay, level, point
3 *syn* see OPERATE 3
4 *syn* see TREAT 2
rel conduct, control, direct, manage
5 *syn* see GOVERN 3
6 *syn* see USE 2

handling *n* *syn* see OVERSIGHT 1

handmaid *n* *syn* see MAID 2

hand on *vb* *syn* see HAND DOWN

hand out *vb* *syn* see GIVE 1

hand over *vb* 1 *syn* see RELINQUISH
2 *syn* see GIVE 3
3 *syn* see COMMIT 1

hand running *adv* *syn* see TOGETHER 2

handsome *adj* 1 *syn* see LIBERAL 1
con economical, frugal, sparing; scrimpy, skimpy
2 *syn* see BEAUTIFUL
rel august, majestic, noble, stately; chic, dashing, fashionable, modish, smart, stylish
con inelegant, unsightly
ant unhandsome

handwriting *n* writing in which the letters are formed by a hand-guided implement (as a pen) <legible *handwriting*>
syn calligraphy, chirography, ductus, fist, hand, penmanship, script
rel longhand

handy *adj* 1 *syn* see CONVENIENT 2
idiom at one's hand (*or* elbow), ready to hand
ant unhandy
2 *syn* see PRACTICAL 2
rel adaptable, advantageous, beneficial, wieldy
con clumsy, cumbersome, cumbrous, unwieldy
ant unhandy
3 *syn* see DEXTEROUS 1

hang *vb* 1 to place or be placed so as to be supported at one point or side usually with the top <*hang* the washing on the line>

syn dangle, depend, sling, suspend
rel attach, hook; fix, pin, tack (up); adhere, cling, stick
2 to put to death by suspending by the neck <was *hanged* for stealing a sheep>
syn gibbet, noose, scrag, string (up), turn off
rel execute, lynch
idiom bring to the gallows, hang by the neck, make dance on air (*or* nothing)
3 to remain poised or stationary as if suspended in midair <clouds *hanging* in the west>
syn float, hover, poise
4 to project outward or incline downward <children *hanging* out the windows to watch a parade>
syn beetle, bend (over), jut, lean (over), overhang
rel drape, droop, loll, lop, sag, trail

hang (on *or* upon) *vb* *syn* see DEPEND (on *or* upon) 1

hang *n* the special method of doing, using, or dealing with something <can't get the *hang* of this gadget>
syn knack, swing, trick
rel art, craft, skill

hang around *vb* *syn* see FREQUENT

hanger-on *n* *syn* see PARASITE
rel bystander, follower, spectator, sycophant

hanging *adj* *syn* see SUSPENDED

hang on *vb* *syn* see PERSEVERE

hang out *vb* 1 *syn* see RESIDE 1
2 *syn* see FREQUENT

hangout *n* 1 *syn* see RESORT 2
2 *syn* see DIVE

hang up *vb* *syn* see DELAY 1

hanker *vb* *syn* see LONG
rel covet, desire, wish

hankie *n* *syn* see HANDKERCHIEF

hanky-panky *n* *syn* see DECEPTION 1

hap *n* *syn* see ACCIDENT 1
rel destiny, fate, lot, portion

hap *vb* *syn* see HAPPEN 1

||**hap** *vb* *syn* see BUNDLE UP

haphazard *adj* *syn* see RANDOM
rel accidental; careless, helter-skelter, slipshod; unorganized, unsystematic
con deliberate, designed, intentional, voluntary, willful
ant planned

haphazard *adv* *syn* see ABOUT 4
rel accidentally, aimlessly, carelessly, casually, promiscuously

haphazardly *adv* *syn* see ABOUT 4
rel accidentally, aimlessly, carelessly, casually, promiscuously

hapless *adj* *syn* see UNLUCKY
rel infelicitous; miserable, woeful, wretched

happen *vb* 1 to take place or come about <the incident *happened* at midnight>
syn befall, betide, break, chance, come, come off, develop, do, fall out, give, go, hap, occur, pass, rise, transpire
rel go off, turn out
idiom come to pass
2 to come by chance <he unexpectedly *happened* on a new method>
syn bump, chance, hit, light, luck, meet, stumble, tumble
rel befall

happening *n syn* see OCCURRENCE

happify *vb syn* see PLEASE 2

happily *adv syn* see WELL 5

happiness *n* a state of well-being or pleasurable satisfaction <felt *happiness* at her husband's success>
syn beatitude, blessedness, bliss, blissfulness
rel content, contentedness, satisfaction; cheer, cheerfulness, felicity, gladness; gaiety, jollity, joy; delectation, delight, enjoyment, pleasure
con discontent, dissatisfaction, vexation; cheerlessness, despair, desperation, despondency, hopelessness; distress, misery, wretchedness
ant unhappiness

happy *adj* 1 *syn* see LUCKY
rel accidental, casual, fortuitous, incidental; opportune, seasonable, timely
ant unhappy
2 *syn* see FIT 1
rel effective, effectual, efficacious, efficient; cogent, convincing, telling; pat, seasonable, well-timed; correct, nice, right
ant unhappy
3 *syn* see GLAD 1
rel content, contented, satisfied
ant unhappy; disconsolate

happy-go-lucky *adj* disposed to accept cheerfully whatever happens <enjoyed a *happy-go-lucky* existence without needlessly worrying>
syn carefree, free-minded, insouciant, lighthearted, lightsome; *compare* COOL 2
rel casual, easy, easygoing; blithe, careless, cheerful, feckless, heedless, lackadaisical; debonair, nonchalant, unconcerned; devil-may-care, reckless
con careful, cautious, circumspect, discreet, guarded, prudent

happy hunting ground *n syn* see HEAVEN 2

hara-kiri *n syn* see SUICIDE

harangue *n syn* see TIRADE

harangue *vb syn* see ORATE

harass *vb* 1 *syn* see RAID 1
2 *syn* see WORRY 1
rel badger, bait, bullyrag, chivy, devil, heckle, hector, hound, ride
idiom give a bad (*or* hard) time
3 *syn* see TRY 2

harassed *adj syn* see DISTRAUGHT

harasser *n syn* see BULLY 1

harassment *n syn* see ANNOYANCE 1
rel aggravation, disturbance, exasperation, irritation, perturbation

harbinger *n syn* see FORERUNNER 1

harbinger *vb syn* see ANNOUNCE 2

harbor *n* 1 *syn* see SHELTER 1
2 *syn* see INLET
3 a place where seacraft may ride secure <a yacht *harbor*>
syn anchorage, ‖chuck, harborage, haven, port, riding, road(s), roadstead

harbor *vb* 1 to provide with shelter or a refuge <*harbored* the refugees in our homes>

syn chamber, haven, house, roof, shelter, shield
rel cherish, foster, nurse, nurture; conceal, hide, secrete; guard, protect, safeguard, screen
idiom give shelter (*or* asylum) to
con eject, evict, expel, oust; banish, deport, exile; eliminate, exclude, shut out
2 to provide with a usually temporary place to live <the miners were *harbored* in camps>
syn accommodate, bestow, billet, board, bunk, domicile, domiciliate, entertain, house, hut, lodge, put up, quarter, room, roost
rel cabin, camp, encamp

harborage *n syn* see SHELTER 1
2 *syn* see REFUGE 1
3 *syn* see HARBOR 3

hard *adj* 1 *syn* see FIRM 2
rel compacted, compressed, concentrated, consolidated, packed; callous, hardened, indurate, indurated, set; adamantine, flinty, granitic, iron, ironhard
con fluid, liquid; flabby, limp; ductile, malleable, pliable, pliant, plastic; elastic, flexible, limber, resilient, supple
ant soft
2 *syn* see SPIRITUOUS
ant soft
3 *syn* see REALISTIC
4 *syn* see INSENSIBLE 5
5 *syn* see INTENSIVE
6 demanding great toil and effort <a *hard* but rewarding task>
syn arduous, difficile, difficult, effortful, formidable, heavy, knotty, labored, laborious, operose, rough, rugged, serious, severe, slavish, sticky, strenuous, terrible, toilful, toilsome, tough, uphill
rel burdensome, exacting, onerous; complex, complicated, intricate, involved, scabrous; backbreaking, distressing, exhausting, fatiguing, grinding, tiring, wearing, wearisome, wearying; bothersome, demanding, irksome, rocky, straining, troublesome, trying; merciless, unsparing
con effortless, facile, light, simple, smooth
ant easy
7 *syn* see ACTUAL 2
8 *syn* see GRIM 2
9 *syn* see SEVERE 3

hard *adv* 1 with great or utmost force <hit the nail *hard*>
syn energetically, forcefully, forcibly, hardly, might and main, mightily, powerfully, strongly, vigorously
rel actively, animatedly, briskly, snappily, spiritedly, sprightly, vivaciously; earnestly, intensely, keenly, seriously, urgently, wholeheartedly
idiom with all one's might
con faintly, feebly, nervelessly, softly, strengthlessly, unenergetically, weakly
ant easily, easy
2 in a violent manner <the wind blew *hard* all the next day>
syn fiercely, frantically, frenziedly, furiously, hardly, madly, stormily, tumultuously, turbulently, violently, wildly
rel boisterously, exuberantly, rowdily, uproariously; angrily, brutally, ferociously, savagely, viciously

---

syn synonym(s)　　*rel* related word(s)
ant antonym(s)　　*con* contrasted word(s)
idiom idiomatic equivalent(s)
‖ use limited; if in doubt, see a dictionary

idiom like a house afire, like fury, like mad

con gently, mildly, softly

3 with intentness and determination <made up his mind to study *hard*>

syn assiduously, dingdong, earnestly, exhaustively, intensely, intensively, painstakingly, thoroughly, unremittingly

rel conscientiously, meticulously, punctiliously

con carelessly, casually, desultorily, fitfully, haphazardly

4 in a fixed and intensive manner <stared *hard* at the offender>

syn closely, intently, searchingly, sharply

con casually, cursorily, idly, offhand

5 in such manner as to cause hardship, difficulty, or defeat <things will go *hard* with him if he doesn't reform>

syn badly, hardly, harshly, painfully, rigorously, roughly, severely; *compare* AMISS 2

rel cruelly; relentlessly; meanly, shabbily, unfairly

con comfortably, pleasantly, smoothly; acceptably, satisfactorily, satisfyingly

ant easily, easy

6 with great or excessive resentment or grief <don't take your setback so *hard*>

syn bitterly, hardly, keenly, rancorously, resentfully, sorely

con casually, lightly, nonchalantly, offhandedly

7 in a firm manner <hold on *hard*>

syn fast, firm, firmly, fixedly, solidly, steadfastly, tight, tightly

con easily, easy, loose, loosely, slackly

8 with difficulty <breathing *hard* after the climb>

syn arduously, burdensomely, difficultly, hardly, laboriously, onerously, toilsomely

rel exhaustingly, gruelingly, painfully, tiredly; awkwardly, cumbersomely, cumbrously, inconveniently, ponderously, unhandily, unwieldily

con effortlessly, evenly, handily, readily, smoothly

ant easily, easy

9 to the point of hardness <the pond is frozen *hard*>

syn firmly, hardly, solid, solidly

10 *syn* see CLOSE

hard—boiled *adj* 1 *syn* see UNFEELING 2

rel coarse, crude, rough; seasoned, sophisticated, worldly-wise

idiom not born yesterday

con artless, guileless, naive, simplehearted, unsophisticated; kindly, mild, soft

2 *syn* see REALISTIC

harden *vb* 1 to make or become physically hard or solid <this substance *hardens* immediately on exposure to air>

syn cake, concrete, congeal, dry, indurate, set, solidify

rel compact, consolidate, densify, firm, stiffen; anneal, caseharden, temper; calcify, fossilize, lithify, ossify, petrify

con deliquesce, dissolve, fuse, liquefy, melt

ant soften

2 to make proof against hardship, strain, or exposure <frontier life *hardened* most men quickly to rough conditions>

syn acclimate, acclimatize, climatize, season, toughen

rel accustom, habituate, indurate, inure; accommodate, adapt, adjust, conform

con emasculate, enervate; debilitate, devitalize, enfeeble, sap, undermine, weaken

ant soften

hardened *adj syn* see UNFEELING 2

hardfisted *adj syn* see STINGY

ant openhanded

hardhanded *adj syn* see STINGY

ant openhanded

hardheaded *adj syn* see OBSTINATE

2 *syn* see REALISTIC

hardhearted *adj syn* see UNFEELING 2

hardihood *n* 1 *syn* see TEMERITY

rel boldness, intrepidity; brazenness, cockiness; fortitude, grit, guts, pluck, sand

ant cowardice; timidity

2 *syn* see INSOLENCE

3 *syn* see ENERGY 2

hardiness *n syn* see TEMERITY

ant cowardice; timidity

hard—line *adj syn* see TOUGH 3

hardly *adv* 1 *syn* see HARD 1

2 *syn* see HARD 2

3 *syn* see HARD 5

4 *syn* see HARD 6

5 *syn* see HARD 8

6 *syn* see JUST 2

7 *syn* see HARD 9

hardly ever *adv syn* see SELDOM

hardness *n syn* see DIFFICULTY 1

ant easiness

hardpan *n syn* see BASE 1

hardscrabble *adj syn* see BARREN 2

hard—shell *adj syn* see INVETERATE 1

hardship *n syn* see DIFFICULTY 1

rel adversity, mischance, misfortune; danger, hazard, peril; affliction, trial, tribulation; drudgery, toil, travail; discomfort, distress

con comfort, ease

hardy *adj syn* see TOUGH 4

ant tender

harebrain *n* 1 *syn* see SCATTERBRAIN

2 *syn* see CRACKPOT

harebrained *adj* 1 *syn* see GIDDY 1

2 *syn* see FOOLISH 2

harefooted *adj syn* see FAST 3

hark *vb syn* see LISTEN

rel mark, mind, note, notice, remark

idiom be all ears, not miss a trick

harlequin *n syn* see CLOWN 3

harlot *n* 1 a woman who engages in unlawful or socially unacceptable sexual intercourse often for material gain <ply the trade of a *harlot*>

syn blowen, courtesan, demimondaine, demimonde, demirep, fancy woman, hetaera, kept woman, paphian, whore; *compare* DOXY, MISTRESS, PROSTITUTE, WANTON

2 *syn* see PROSTITUTE

harlotry *n syn* see PROSTITUTION

harm *n syn* see INJURY 1

rel deleteriousness; banefulness, noxiousness, perniciousness; mischance, misfortune, misuse; impairment, marring

con aid, help; accommodation, benefaction; charity, favor, service

ant benefit

harm *vb syn* see INJURE 1

rel abuse, ill-use, maltreat, mistreat, mis-use, molest; dilapidate, ruin; discommode, incommode, inconvenience; sabotage, sap, undermine

idiom do violence to

con ameliorate, better, improve; avail, profit

ant benefit

harmful *adj* inflicting or capable of inflicting injury <a *harmful* drug>

syn bad, damaging, deleterious, detrimental, evil, hurtful, ill, injurious, mischievous, nocent, nocuous, prejudicial, pernicious

rel baleful, baneful, malefic, malign, malignant, noisome, noxious, pernicious, toxic; insalubrious, unhealthful, unhealthy, unwholesome; dangerous, hazardous, risky, unsafe

con innocuous, inoffensive, nontoxic; beneficent, beneficial, benign, benignant, favorable, helpful, salutary, useful; safe, unhazardous

ant harmless

harmless *adj* not having hurtful or injurious qualities < *harmless* pastimes>

syn innocent, innocuous, innoxious, inobnoxious, inoffensive, unoffending, unoffensive; *compare* SAFE 3

rel guiltless; nontoxic, painless, safe

con baneful, dangerous, malignant, noxious, pernicious, toxic, virulent; damaging, detrimental, destructive, hurtful, injurious; deadly, fell, ruinous; improper, unsuitable, wrong

ant harmful

harmonic *adj syn* see HARMONIOUS 1

harmonious *adj* 1 musically concordant < a *harmonious* morning chorus of birds>

syn blending, chiming, consonant, harmonic, musical, symphonic, symphonious

rel canorous, dulcet, euphonious, melodious, mellifluous, mellisonant, musical, silvery, sonorous, sweet, tuneful; chordal, contrapuntal, counterpointed, polyphonic

idiom in concert, in tune

con clashing, discordant, dissonant, grating, harsh, jangling, jarring, raucous, shrill, strident, tuneless, unmusical, untuneful; atonal

ant disharmonious, inharmonious, unharmonious

2 having the parts agreeably related <a building with *harmonious* proportions>

syn accordant, concordant, congruous; *compare* CONSONANT 1

rel agreeable, pleasing, satisfying; concinnate, symmetrical

con clashing, incongruous, unsymmetrical; askew, distorted, skewed

ant inharmonious, unharmonious

3 marked by accord in sentiment or action <a *harmonious* effort to reach a practicable agreement>

syn amicable, amical, congenial, friendly

rel coactive, collaborative, cooperative; empathetic, empathic, simpatico, sympathetic; calm, irenic, pacific, peaceful

idiom of one accord

con incompatible, uncongenial, uncooperative, unfriendly, unsympathetic; belligerent, contentious, pugnacious

ant inharmonious, unharmonious

harmonize *vb* 1 *syn* see AGREE 3

rel cooperate, match, unite

con differ, disagree

ant clash; conflict

2 *syn* see AGREE 4

ant differ (from)

3 to bring into consonance or accord < *harmonize* the factions of a political party>

syn accommodate, attune, conform, coordinate, integrate, proportion, reconcile, reconciliate, tune

rel adapt, adjust, correlate; coapt, relate

con alienate, disrupt, estrange

ant disharmonize

4 to combine or adapt so as to achieve a desired effect < *harmonize* the elements of a story>

syn arrange, blend, integrate, orchestrate, symphonize, synthesize, unify

rel coordinate, correlate

harmonizing *n syn* see RECONCILIATION

harmony *n* 1 musical agreement of sounds < singing in *harmony*>

syn accord, chorus, concert, concord, consonance, tune

rel mellifluousness, melodiousness, melody, musicality, sonority, tunefulness; diapason, polyphony

con cacophony, discord, discordance, discordancy, dissonance, harshness, inharmoniousness, jangle, stridency, tunelessness, unharmoniousness, unmusicalness, untunefulness; atonality

ant disharmony, inharmony

2 the effect produced when different things come together without clashing or disagreement < goals that are in *harmony* with our capabilities>

syn accord, agreement, chime, concord, concordance, consonance, tune; *compare* CONSISTENCY

rel conformance, conformity, correspondence; articulation, coaptation, compatibility, congruity; concatenation, concurrence, integration, oneness, togetherness, unity

con disagreement, discord, disparity, dissidence, disunity, variance

ant conflict

3 the state of persons who are in full and perfect agreement < friends who live in *harmony*>

syn concord, rapport, unity

rel affinity, empathy, fellow-feeling, kinship; peace, tranquillity

idiom meeting of minds

con contention, dissension, strife

ant discord

4 *syn* see SYMMETRY

rel concinnity, consonance; dignity, elegance, grace; integrity, unity

con asymmetry, discordance, discordancy, imbalance

ant inharmony

harness *vb syn* see HITCH 2

‖**harness bull** (*or* **cop**) *n syn* see POLICEMAN

harpy *n syn* see VIRAGO

---

syn synonym(s)   *rel* related word(s)
ant antonym(s)   *con* contrasted word(s)
idiom idiomatic equivalent(s)
‖ use limited; if in doubt, see a dictionary

harrier *n syn* see BULLY 1

harrow *vb syn* see AFFLICT

rel fret, irritate, pester; badger, bait, bedevil, devil, heckle, hector, needle, tantalize, tease

harrowing *adj syn* see EXCRUCIATING

harry *vb* 1 *syn* see RAVAGE

2 *syn* see RAID 1

3 *syn* see WORRY 1

rel disturb, irk, perturb, upset; badger, irritate

harsh *adj* 1 *syn* see ROUGH 1

rel coarse, granular, loose; bristly, scraggly, scratchy, shaggy, stubbly

con glossy, satiny, silken, silky, sleek, slick, velvety

2 *syn* see ACRID

rel acerb, acerbic, biting, burning, mordant; pungent, tangy; dry, sour, tart

con mild, smooth, sweet, velvety

3 disagreeable to the ear < many birds have *harsh* cries >

syn dry, grating, hoarse, jarring, rasping, raucous, rough, rugged, rusty, squawky, strident, stridulous

rel discordant, dissonant, immelodious, ineuphonious, inharmonious, unmelodious, unmusical; grinding, jangling, scraping; blaring, brassy; ear-piercing, piercing, shrill, squeaky

con euphonious, harmonious, mellow, melodic, melodious, musical, sonorous, sweet; low, soft; agreeable, pleasing

4 *syn* see UNCOMFORTABLE

5 *syn* see GRIM 2

6 *syn* see SEVERE 3

ant mild

harshly *adv syn* see HARD 5

con considerately; gently, lightly, well; famously

ant smoothly

haruspex *n syn* see PROPHET

harvest *n* 1 the act, process, or occasion of gathering a crop < the time of *harvest* >

syn cropping, gathering, harvesting, ingathering, reaping

rel garnering, storing

con planting, seedtime, sowing

2 the gathered produce of land < a bountiful *harvest* saved the settlers >

syn crop, fruitage

rel yield; bearing, vintage

harvest *vb syn* see REAP

rel assemble, collect; accumulate, amass, bin, store (up), stow (away); cache, hide, hoard, squirrel, stash

harvesting *n syn* see HARVEST 1

hash *vb syn* see CHOP 2

hash *n* 1 *syn* see MISCELLANY 1

2 *syn* see CLUTTER 2

3 *syn* see MESS 3

‖**hashery** *n syn* see EATING HOUSE

‖**hash house** *n syn* see EATING HOUSE

hassle *n* 1 *syn* see QUARREL

2 *syn* see COMMOTION 4

3 *syn* see ATTEMPT

hassle *vb syn* see ARGUE 2

rel cavil; brawl, fight, spar, struggle

haste *n* 1 rapidity of motion or action < we finished our job with great *haste* >

syn celerity, dispatch, expedition, expeditiousness, hurry, hustle, rustle, speed, speediness, swiftness

rel fastness, fleetness, quickness, rapidity; pace, velocity; dash, drive

con languidness, languor, leisureliness, reluctance, slowness; lethargy, sluggishness, torpor

ant deliberateness, deliberation

2 rash or headlong action < oversights due to *haste* >

syn hastiness, hurriedness, precipitance, precipitancy, precipitateness, precipitation, rush

rel impetuosity, impetuousness, impulsiveness

con care, carefulness, circumspection, hastelessness, unhurriedness

ant deliberateness, deliberation

haste *vb syn* see HURRY 2

hasten *vb syn* see SPEED 3

2 *syn* see HURRY 2

hastily *adv syn* see FAST 2

rel agilely, nimbly; impetuously, impulsively, unpremeditatedly; carelessly, recklessly, thoughtlessly; precipitately, prematurely, suddenly

con carefully, designedly, studiedly, thoughtfully; gradually, leisurely, slowly, sluggishly

ant deliberately

hastiness *n syn* see WASTE 2

hasty *adj* 1 *syn* see FAST 3

rel agile, brisk, nimble; hurried, quickened

con dilatory, laggard, leisured, leisurely

2 *syn* see PRECIPITATE 1

ant deliberate

3 *syn* see RASH 1

rel devil-may-care, slambang, slapdash

hatch *vb* 1 *syn* see GENERATE 3

2 *syn* see GENERATE 1

hatch (up) *vb syn* see CONTRIVE 2

hatchet man *n syn* see ASSASSIN

hate *n* 1 *syn* see ABOMINATION 2

rel animosity, animus, antipathy, hostility, ill will, rancor; disgust, scorn, spite

con affection; toleration; adoration, veneration

ant love

2 *syn* see ABOMINATION 1

rel bother, grievance, gripe, irritant, nuisance, ‖pain, trouble

ant delight

hate *vb* to feel extreme enmity or dislike < Cain *hated* his brother > < *hate* to meet strangers >

syn abhor, abominate, detest, execrate, loathe

rel contemn, despise, disdain, dislike, scorn; deprecate, disapprove; resent

con cherish, enjoy, fancy, like, relish; favor, prefer, prize; esteem, respect, revere; dote; idolize, worship

ant love

hateable *adj syn* see HATEFUL 2

ant lovable

hateful *adj* 1 *syn* see MALICIOUS

rel acrimonious, ill-natured; bitter, resentful; mean

con benevolent, charitable, cordial, genial, good-humored, good-natured, kind, kindly, pleasant

2 deserving of or arousing hate < found himself in a *hateful* situation >

syn abhorrent, abominable, detestable, hateable, horrid, odious *rel* distasteful, distressing, obnoxious, repellent, repulsive; contemptible, despicable, execrable, opprobrious, reprehensible, scurvy; foul, infamous, vile; accursed, blasphemous, damnable, unspeakable

con compatible, congenial, consonant; alluring, appealing, attractive, charming, enchanting; agreeable, delectable, delightful, likable, pleasant, pleasing

ant lovable; sympathetic

hatred *n syn* see ABOMINATION 2

rel antipathy, dislike; animosity, enmity, hostility, rancor

con affability, benevolence, benignity, charitableness, cordiality

ant love; admiration

haughtiness *n syn* see PRIDE 3

ant lowliness

haughty *adj syn* see PROUD 1

rel aloof, detached, distant, indifferent, reserved; egotistic; contemptuous, scornful

con humble; obsequious, servile, subservient

ant lowly

haul *vb syn* see PULL 2

rel move, remove, shift; boost, elevate, hoist, lift, raise

haul *n syn* see LOAD 1

haul up *vb syn* see STOP 4

haunches *n pl syn* see BUTTOCKS

haunt *vb syn* see FREQUENT

haunt *n* 1 *syn* see RESORT 2

2 *syn* see HABITAT

3 *syn* see APPARITION

haunter *n syn* see HABITUÉ 1

hauteur *n syn* see PRIDE 3

ant lowliness

haut monde *n syn* see ARISTOCRACY

have *vb* 1 to keep, control, or experience as one's own <can't *have* your cake and eat it too>

syn enjoy, hold, own, possess, retain

idiom to be possessed of, have in hand

con lack, need, want

2 *syn* see INCLUDE

rel admit, compose, comprise

3 *syn* see BEAR 3

4 *syn* see GET 1

5 *syn* see EXPERIENCE 1

6 *syn* see LET 2

7 *syn* see KNOW 1

8 *syn* see OUTWIT

9 *syn* see BRIBE

10 *syn* see MUST 2

haven *n* 1 *syn* see HARBOR 3

2 *syn* see SHELTER 1

haven *vb syn* see HARBOR 1

haversack *n syn* see BACKPACK

havoc *n syn* see RUIN 3

rel calamity, cataclysm, catastrophe; despoiling, pillaging, ravaging; vandalism

havoc *vb syn* see RAVAGE

hawk *vb syn* see PEDDLE 2

hawker *n syn* see PEDDLER

hawk-eyed *adj syn* see SHARP-EYED

hawkshaw *n syn* see DETECTIVE

haymaker *n syn* see CUFF

hayseed *n syn* see RUSTIC

---

ant city slicker, slicker

hazard *n* 1 *syn* see CHANCE 2

2 *syn* see DANGER

hazard *vb* 1 *syn* see VENTURE 1

2 *syn* see GAMBLE 2

3 *syn* see ENDANGER

hazardous *adj syn* see DANGEROUS 1

ant safe; unhazardous

haze *vb syn* see OBSCURE

haze *n* 1 an atmospheric condition that is characterized by the presence of fine particulate material in the air and that deprives the air of its transparency <*haze* obscured the distant hills>

syn brume, film, mist, smaze

rel cloud, ||drisk, fog, murk, ||smeech, smog, smoke, vapor; cloudiness, mistiness, murkiness, smokiness

2 a state of mental vagueness or obtuseness <lived in a *haze* of pleasant memories>

syn befuddlement, daze, fog, ||maze, muddledness, muddleheadedness, muddlement

rel dream, reverie, stupor, trance; absentmindedness, abstraction, bemusement, preoccupation, woolgathering

con alertness, attentiveness, awareness

hazy *adj* obscured or made dim by or as if by haze <had only a *hazy* idea of where they were>

syn cloudy, foggy, misty, mushy, vague, vaporous, vapory

rel blurred, clouded, dim, indefinite, indistinct, murky, nebulous, obscure; bemused, dreamy, tranced, stuporous; dazed, ||mazed, muzzy

he *n syn* see MAN 3

head *n* 1 the upper division of the body that contains the brain, the chief sense organs, and the mouth <put your hat on your *head*>

syn ||bean, ||belfry, ||chump, ||coco, ||coconut, ||conk, ||dome, headpiece, noddle, noggin, noodle, ||nut, ||pallet, pate, poll, sconce

rel brainpan, cranium, crown, scalp

2 *syn* see MIND 1

3 *syn* see GIFT 2

4 *syn* see LEADER 2

con subordinate; aide, assistant, helper

5 *syn* see PROMONTORY

6 *syn* see TOILET

7 *syn* see HEADLINE

8 *syn* see SUBJECT 2

head *adj syn* see FIRST 3

head *vb* 1 *syn* see BEHEAD

2 *syn* see DIRECT 2

3 to commence to go in an indicated direction <the cowboys *headed* for town>

syn bear, light out, make, set out, strike out, take off

rel go, proceed, start

idiom make a beeline for

4 *syn* see SPRING 1

heading *n syn* see HEADLINE

headland *n syn* see PROMONTORY

headline *n* a word or group of words usually in large type introducing and summarizing a newspaper story <*headlines* that screamed the news of the president's death>

syn head, heading

rel banner, banner head, bannerline, scarehead, screamer, spreadhead

---

headlong adj syn see PRECIPITATE 1
 rel daredevil, daring, foolhardy, rash, reckless
headman n syn see LEADER 2
headmost adj syn see FIRST 1
headpiece n syn see HEAD 1
headshaker n syn see SKEPTIC
head start n syn see ADVANTAGE 3
headstone n syn see TOMBSTONE
headstrong adj syn see OBSTINATE
 con subdued, tame; amenable, biddable, docile, meek, obedient, tractable
headway n 1 syn see ADVANCE 2
heady adj syn see SHREWD
heal vb syn see CURE
healing adj syn see CURATIVE
health n the state of being sound in body or mind <the patient was nursed back to *health*>
 syn haleness, healthiness, soundness, wholeness
 rel stamina, vitality, well-being; euphoria
 con debility, decrepitude, feebleness; ill health, illness, sickliness
 ant disease, infirmity
healthful adj conducive or beneficial to the health or soundness of body or mind <regular exercise is a *healthful* practice>
 syn good, healthy, hygienic, salubrious, salutary, salutiferous, wholesome
 rel advantageous, beneficial, profitable, useful; corrective, curative, remedial; aiding, alleviative, helpful, mitigative, restorative, sanative
 con insalubrious, unhealthy, unhygienic, unwholesome; damaging, deleterious, detrimental, harmful, injurious, mischievous, pernicious
 ant unhealthful
healthiness n syn see HEALTH
 ant unhealthiness
healthy adj 1 enjoying or manifesting health <a *healthy* baby>
 syn ||bunkum, fit, hale, right, sane, sound, well, well-conditioned, well-liking, whole, wholesome
 rel hearty, iron, lusty, robust, thriving, vigorous; rugged, stalwart, strong, sturdy, tough; agile, chipper, spry; blooming, rosy, thriving
 idiom fit as a fiddle, in (top) condition, in fine fettle, in shape, in trim, sound as a dollar, up to snuff
 con decrepit, delicate, feeble, fragile, frail, weak; infirm, ||poorly, sickly
 ant unhealthy
 2 syn see HEALTHFUL
 ant unhealthful
 3 syn see SAFE 3
heap n 1 syn see PILE 1
 rel congeries, gathering
 2 syn see MUCH
 3 syn see SCAD
 4 syn see JALOPY
heap vb 1 to throw or collect in a pile <*heap* up leaves for a bonfire>
 syn bank, cock, drift, hill, mound, pile, stack
 rel cord, ||dess, rick, shock; bunch, clump, lumber, lump, mass; deposit, dump; accumulate, amass; assemble, collect, gather, group
 con broadcast, disperse, distribute, scatter, separate, spread, strew

 2 syn see LOAD 3
hear vb 1 syn see LISTEN
 idiom get wind of
 2 syn see DISCOVER 3
hearing n 1 syn see EARSHOT
 2 an opportunity to be heard <they finally obtained a *hearing* on their complaints>
 syn audience, audition
 rel conference, interview, meeting, parley; test, tryout; discussion, negotiation
hearken vb syn see LISTEN
hearsay n syn see REPORT 1
heart n 1 the seat or center of secret thoughts and emotions <in his *heart* he knew he was serious in the wrong>
 syn bosom, breast, soul
 idiom bottom of the heart, cockles of the heart
 2 syn see COURAGE
 3 syn see TASTE 4
 4 syn see CENTER 2
 5 syn see CENTER 3
heartache n syn see SORROW
 idiom aching heart, heavy heart
heartbreak n 1 syn see SORROW
 rel agony, bale, torment
 idiom bleeding heart
heartbreaking adj syn see DEPLORABLE
hearten vb syn see ENCOURAGE 1
 rel energize, enliven; arouse, rally, rouse, stir
 con damp, dampen; weigh
 ant dishearten
heartfelt adj syn see SINCERE 1
 rel bona fide, genuine, honest, true, unfeigned; deep, profound
 con hypocritical, insincere; false, pretended
heartless adj syn see UNFEELING 2
heartrending adj syn see DEPLORABLE
heart-searching n syn see INTROSPECTION
heartsick adj syn see DOWNCAST
heartsore adj syn see DOWNCAST
heartthrob n syn see SWEETHEART 1
heart-whole adj 1 syn see FREE 6
 2 syn see GENUINE 3
hearty adj syn see SINCERE 1
 rel responsive, warm, warmhearted; deep, profound; exuberant, profuse
 con cold, dispassionate, emotionless
 ant hollow
||**heat** n syn see POLICEMAN
heated adj 1 syn see HOT 1
 ant chilled
 2 syn see FEVERISH 2
 3 syn see ANGRY
heathen adj of or relating to people who do not acknowledge the God of the Bible <ancient *heathen* sacrificial rites>
 syn ethnic, gentile, infidel, infidelic, pagan, profane
 rel heathenish, paganish
heave vb 1 syn see THROW 1
 2 syn see TOSS 2
 3 syn see PANT 1
 4 syn see RETCH
 ||5 syn see VOMIT
heaven n 1 usu **heavens** pl syn see SKY
 2 an abode of blissful spiritual life after death <the religious conceptions of *heaven* and hell>

syn Abraham's bosom, bliss, Canaan, Civitas Dei, elysium, empyrean, happy hunting ground, kingdom come, New Jerusalem, nirvana, paradise, Zion
rel afterworld, eternity, glory, hereafter, promised land; everlastingness, immortality
idiom Beulah Land (*or* Land of Beulah), City of God, Kingdom of God, Kingdom of Heaven
con earth, world; Gehenna, hades, inferno, netherworld, perdition, pit, Sheol, Tartarus, Tophet, underworld
ant hell
3 *syn* see UTOPIA
4 *syn* see ECSTASY

heavenly *adj* 1 *syn* see CELESTIAL
con hadean, Tartarean
ant hellish
2 *syn* see DELIGHTFUL

heavy *adj* 1 having great or relatively great weight <a *heavy* load>
syn hefty, massive, ponderous, weighty; *compare* UNWIELDY
rel awkward, bulky, clumsy, lumbering, lumbersome; unhandy, unmanageable, unwieldy; cumbersome, cumbrous
con airy, buoyant, weightless; handy, manageable, wieldy
ant light
2 *syn* see FAT 2
3 *syn* see SERIOUS 2
4 *syn* see RECONDITE
5 *syn* see PREGNANT 1
6 *syn* see LETHARGIC
7 *syn* see OVERCAST
8 *syn* see HARD 6
9 *syn* see RICH 3

heavy-footed *adj* *syn* see PONDEROUS 2

heavy-handed *adj* 1 *syn* see AWKWARD 2
2 *syn* see PONDEROUS 2

heavyhearted *adj* *syn* see SAD 1
ant lighthearted

heavyheartedness *n* *syn* see SADNESS
ant lightheartedness

heavyset *adj* *syn* see STOCKY

heavyweight *n* *syn* see NOTABLE 1
con lightweight

hebetate *vb* *syn* see DULL 5

hebetude *n* *syn* see LETHARGY 1

hebetudinous *adj* *syn* see LETHARGIC

heckle *vb* 1 *syn* see BAIT 2
rel plague, worry; discomfit, disconcert, embarrass, faze, rattle; tease, torment
2 *syn* see MOLEST

hectic *adj* *syn* see FEVERISH 2

hector *n* *syn* see BULLY 1

hector *vb* 1 *syn* see INTIMIDATE
2 *syn* see BAIT 2

hedge *vb* 1 *syn* see EQUIVOCATE 2
2 *syn* see ENCLOSE 1

hedonist *n* one given to the zealous pursuit of pleasure <lead the life of a *hedonist*>
syn carpet knight, pleasuremonger, sybarite
rel bon vivant, man-about-town; epicure, epicurean, gourmand, gourmet; debauchee,

libertine, rake; sensualist, voluptuary; pleasure-seeker
ant ascetic

hedonistic *adj* *syn* see SYBARITIC
con austere, self-denying, self-disciplined, self-restricted
ant ascetic

heebie-jeebies *n pl* *syn* see JITTERS

heed *vb* *syn* see LISTEN
rel mark, mind, note; observe, see, watch
idiom give (*or* pay) heed to

heed *n* 1 *syn* see NOTICE 1
rel awareness, interest, mindfulness; audience, hearing
2 *syn* see ATTENTION 1
rel concern, interest
con inattention, unconcern
3 *syn* see CARE 4

heedful *adj* 1 *syn* see ATTENTIVE 1
ant heedless, unheeding
2 *syn* see MINDFUL 2
ant heedless, unheeding
3 *syn* see CAREFUL 2

heedfully *adv* *syn* see WELL 2
ant heedlessly, unheeding

heedfulness *n* *syn* see CARE 4
ant heedlessness

heedless *adj* *syn* see CARELESS 1
ant heedful, heeding

heedlessness *n* *syn* see APATHY 2
ant heedfulness

hee-haw *vb* *syn* see LAUGH

heel *n* 1 *syn* see REMAINDER
2 *syn* see VILLAIN 1

heel *vb* *syn* see SLANT 1

hefty *adj* 1 *syn* see HEAVY 1
2 *syn* see HUSKY 1
3 *syn* see BIG 1

height *n* the distance a thing rises above the level on which it stands <the *height* of a building>
syn altitude, elevation
rel highness, loftiness, rise, tallness, stature
con lowness, profundity
ant depth

heighten *vb* 1 *syn* see INCREASE 1
2 *syn* see INCREASE 2
rel elevate, lift, raise; better, improve; enlarge, increase
con diminish, lessen, shrink
3 *syn* see INTENSIFY

heinie (*or* hiney) *n* *syn* see BUTTOCKS

heinous *adj* *syn* see OUTRAGEOUS 2
con paltry, petty, trifling, trivial
ant venial

heinousness *n* *syn* see ENORMITY 1

heir *n* one who inherits <died without *heirs*>
syn heritor, inheritor

‖**heist** *vb* *syn* see STEAL 1

hell *n* a place or state of the dead or of the damned <went to *hell* for his sins>
syn abyss, barathrum, blazes, Gehenna, hades, inferno, netherworld, Pandemonium, perdition, pit, Sheol, Tophet
rel limbo, Styx, Tartarus
idiom the hot place, infernal regions, place of torment
ant heaven

hell *vb* *syn* see REVEL 1

hell-fired *adj* *syn* see UTTER

hellish *adj* *syn* see INFERNAL 2

helotry *n syn* see BONDAGE

help *n* 1 an act or instance of giving what will benefit or assist <the stranded travelers received *help* from passersby>
syn aid, assist, assistance, comfort, hand, lift, relief, secours, succor, support
rel benefit, cooperation, service
ant hindrance

2 something that is beneficial <the rain was a real *help* to late crops>
syn aid, support
rel benefit, use

3 *syn* see HELPER

help *vb* 1 to give assistance or support <*help* the children with their lessons>
syn abet, aid, assist, benefact, do for, help out, stead
rel back, bolster, boost, champion, second, support, uphold; avail, benefit, profit; advance, facilitate, forward, further, promote, serve; befriend, succor
idiom give a lift, lend a hand (*or* a helping hand), stand back of (*or* behind)
con bar, block, impede, obstruct, oppose; baffle, balk, foil, frustrate, thwart; discomfit, embarrass; damage, harm, hurt, injure
ant hinder

2 *syn* see IMPROVE 1
rel alleviate, mitigate, palliate, relieve
con harm, impair, worsen

helper *n* one that helps <was made boss and assigned a dozen *helpers*>
syn aid, ancilla, assistant, attendant, help, striker
rel helpmate, helpmeet; auxiliary, deputy, subordinate; associate, follower; employee, laborer, servant, worker
idiom helping hand, right-hand man

helpful *adj* 1 of service or assistance <*helpful* suggestions>
syn aidant, aiding, assistive, serviceable
rel beneficial, effective, profitable, salutary, usable; constructive, practical, useful
con timeserving, uncooperative, unreliable; impractical, ineffectual
ant unhelpful

2 *syn* see GOOD 1

helpless *adj* 1 lacking protection or support <*helpless* nestlings>
syn defenseless, unprotected
rel abandoned, desolate, forlorn, forsaken, friendless; feeble, weak

2 *syn* see POWERLESS

helplessly *adv syn* see WILLY-NILLY

help out *vb syn* see HELP 1

helter-skelter *adj* 1 *syn* see PELL-MELL

2 *syn* see ABOUT 4

hem *n syn* see BORDER 1

hem *vb* 1 *syn* see BORDER

2 *syn* see ENCLOSE 1

3 *syn* see SURROUND 1

hence *adv* 1 *syn* see AWAY 1

2 *syn* see THEREFORE

henceforth *adv* from this time forward <made up his mind to keep out of trouble *henceforth*>
syn henceforward, hereafter; *compare* THENCEFORTH
idiom from now on

henceforward *adv syn* see HENCEFORTH

henchman *n syn* see FOLLOWER
rel attendant; lackey, minion, stooge

henpeck *vb syn* see NAG

hep *adj syn* see WISE 4

herald *n syn* see FORERUNNER 1
rel courier, crier, messenger

herald *vb* 1 *syn* see ANNOUNCE 2

2 *syn* see TOUT

Herculean *adj syn* see HUGE

herd *n syn* see DROVE 2

herd *vb syn* see DRIVE 3

here *adv syn* see HITHERTO 2

hereafter *adv syn* see HENCEFORTH

hereafter *n* 1 *syn* see FUTURE

2 an existence or place of existence after this life <buried pots and tools with the dead for use in the *hereafter*>
syn afterlife, afterworld, beyond, otherworld
idiom great beyond (*or* hereafter), life after death, next world (*or* life), world beyond the grave, world to come
con here and now

here and there *adv syn* see SOMETIMES

heresy *n* defection from a dominant belief or ideology <the *heresy* of the flat-earth theory>
syn dissent, dissidence, heterodoxy, misbelief, nonconformism, nonconformity, schism, unorthodoxy
rel impiety, infidelity; apostasy, defection, revisionism; error, fallacy

heretic *n* one who is not orthodox in his beliefs <a *heretic* in religion>
syn dissenter, dissident, misbeliever, nonconformist, schismatic, schismatist, sectary, separatist
rel apostate, defector, iconoclast, recreant, recusant, renegade; infidel, unbeliever; deviationist, revisionist
ant orthodox

heretical *adj* of, relating to, or characterized by heresy <*heretical* beliefs>
syn dissident, heterodox, nonconformist, schismatic, sectarian, unorthodox
rel apostate, infidel, miscreant, revisionist; differing, disagreeing, dissentient, dissenting, dissentive, misbelieving, unbelieving
con conventional, established; agreeing, conforming, conformist
ant orthodox

heretofore *adv syn* see BEFORE 2

heritage *n* 1 something that one receives or is entitled to receive by succession (as from a parent) <the *heritage* of freedom>
syn birthright, heritance, inheritance, legacy, patrimony

2 *syn* see TRADITION 1

heritance *n syn* see HERITAGE 1

heritor *n syn* see HEIR

hermaphrodite *adj syn* see BISEXUAL

hermaphroditic *adj syn* see BISEXUAL

hermetic *adj* 1 *syn* see RECONDITE

2 *syn* see SECLUDED

hermit *n syn* see RECLUSE

heroic *adj* 1 *syn* see BRAVE 1
ant pusillanimous

2 *syn* see HUGE

heroism *n* conspicuous courage or bravery <received an award for *heroism*>
syn gallantry, prowess, valiance, valiancy, valor, valorousness
rel boldness, bravery, courage, doughtiness, fearlessness, intrepidity, spirit; chivalry, nobility

con cowardice, spiritlessness, timidity, timorousness, weakness
ant pusillanimity

hesitancy *n syn* see HESITATION

hesitant *adj* 1 *syn* see DISINCLINED
con resolute, staunch, steadfast
2 *syn* see VACILLATING 2

hesitate *vb* to show irresolution or uncertainty < *hesitate* to buy a new car just now>
syn dither, falter, halt, shilly-shally, stagger, vacillate, waver, whiffle, wiggle-waggle
rel balk, boggle, demur, scruple, stick, stickle; fluctuate, oscillate, swing; dawdle, delay, dillydally, hang back, procrastinate, stall, temporize; pause

hesitating *adj syn* see VACILLATING 2

hesitation *n* the act or action of hesitating < several persons volunteered without *hesitation*>
syn hesitancy, indecision, indecisiveness, irresolution, shilly-shally, to-and-fro, vacillation, wavering
rel doubt, dubiety, dubiosity, mistrust, uncertainty; dawdling, delay, procrastination; averseness, indisposition, reluctance
con alacrity, eagerness; courage, mettle, resolution, spirit, tenacity; aplomb, assurance, confidence

hetaera *n syn* see HARLOT 1

heteroclite *adj syn* see ABNORMAL 1

heterodox *adj syn* see HERETICAL
ant orthodox

heterodoxy *n syn* see HERESY
ant orthodoxy

heterogeneous *adj syn* see MISCELLANEOUS
ant homogeneous

hew *vb syn* see FELL 2

hex *vb syn* see BEWITCH 1

hex *n* 1 *syn* see JINX
2 *syn* see WITCH 1

hiatus *n syn* see GAP 3

hic jacet *n syn* see EPITAPH

hick *n syn* see RUSTIC

hick town *n syn* see BURG

hidden *adj syn* see ULTERIOR
ant open

hide *vb* to withdraw or withhold from sight or observation < they *hid* their loot in a cave>
syn bury, ‖bush up, cache, conceal, cover, ‖ditch, ensconce, occult, plant, screen, secrete, stash
rel mantle, mask, obscure, shade, shield; entomb, inter; cloak, curtain, shroud, veil; harbor, lodge, seclude, shelter
con bare, disclose, discover, display, exhibit, expose, reveal, show; uncover, unmask, unveil, unwrap; flaunt, parade, show off

hide *n* an animal skin < tanned *hides* for shoe leather>
syn fell, fur, jacket, pelt, skin

hide *vb syn* see WHIP 1

hideaway *n syn* see HIDEOUT

hidebound *adj syn* see ILLIBERAL

hideous *adj* 1 *syn* see UGLY 2
ant lovely
2 *syn* see OFFENSIVE
3 *syn* see GHASTLY 1

hideout *n* a place of retreat or concealment < a gangsters' *hideout*>
syn den, hideaway, lair
rel covert, haven, hermitage, refuge, retreat, sanctuary, shelter; robbers' roost

hie *vb syn* see GO 1

hierarch *n syn* see LEADER 2

hieratic *adj syn* see SACERDOTAL

higgle *vb syn* see HAGGLE 2

higgler *n syn* see PEDDLER

high *adj* 1 having a relatively great upward extension < a *high* building>
syn altitudinous, tall; *compare* LOFTY 6
rel aerial, eminent, lofty, soaring, towering; big, gigantic, grand, large, prominent
idiom tall (or high) as a steeple
con little, short, squat
ant low
2 *syn* see COSTLY 1
ant low
3 *syn* see MALODOROUS 1
4 *syn* see ELEVATED 4
5 *syn* see ACUTE 4
6 *syn* see DRUGGED

high and low *adv syn* see EVERYWHERE
1

high-and-mighty *adj syn* see PROUD 1

highball *vb syn* see HURRY 2

highbinding *n syn* see DECEPTION 1

highbrow *n syn* see INTELLECTUAL 2

highbrow *adj syn* see INTELLECTUAL 2

highbrowed *adj syn* see INTELLECTUAL 2
ant lowbrow, low-browed

higher *adj syn* see SUPERIOR 1

higher-up *n syn* see SUPERIOR

highest *adj* 1 *syn* see TOP 1
ant lowest
2 *syn* see EXALTED 1

highest-ranking *adj syn* see EXALTED 1

highfalutin *adj syn* see RHETORICAL
con down-to-earth, matter-of-fact

highfalutin *n syn* see BOMBAST

high-flown *adj syn* see RHETORICAL

high-handed *adj syn* see MASTERFUL 1

high hat *n syn* see SNOB

high-hat *adj syn* see SNOBBISH

high-hearted *adj syn* see SPIRITED 2

high jinks *n pl* 1 *syn* see HORSEPLAY
2 *syn* see REVELRY 2

highly *adv syn* see VERY 1

high-minded *adj syn* see ELEVATED 2
ant low-minded

high-muck-a-muck *n syn* see NOTABLE
1

high-principled *adj syn* see HONORABLE
1

high roller *n syn* see SPENDTHRIFT

high sign *n* 1 *syn* see SIGN 1
2 a private usually covert signal, warning, or cue < I gave him the *high sign* when I saw the police approaching>
syn ‖office
rel tip, tip-off, wink; nod; alarm, SOS, warning

high-sounding *adj syn* see PRETENTIOUS
3

high-spirited *adj* 1 *syn* see SPIRITED 2
rel jolly, lighthearted, merry, mirthful
ant low-spirited

---

syn synonym(s)   *rel* related word(s)
ant antonym(s)   *con* contrasted word(s)
idiom idiomatic equivalent(s)
‖ use limited; if in doubt, see a dictionary

2 *syn* see EXUBERANT 1

high-strung *adj* 1 *syn* see TENSE 3

2 *syn* see NERVOUS

hightail *vb syn* see GET OUT 1

highway *n syn* see WAY 1

high yellow *n syn* see MULATTO

hike *vb* 1 *syn* see RAISE 9

2 to travel about or through on foot
< *hiked* through the woods >
syn tramp, tromp
rel footslog; stroll, walk; ramble, rove,
wander; explore

hike *n* 1 *syn* see TRAMP 3

2 *syn* see RISE 3

hilarity *n syn* see MIRTH

hill *n syn* see PILE 1

hill *vb syn* see HEAP 1

hillbilly *n syn* see RUSTIC

hillman *n syn* see RUSTIC

hind *adj syn* see POSTERIOR 2

hind end *n syn* see BUTTOCKS

hinder *vb* to put obstacles in the way of
< their cause was *hindered* by the excesses
of overzealous supporters >
syn bar, block, brake, dam, impede, obstruct, overslaugh; compare HAMPER
rel arrest, check, interrupt, retard; clog,
entrammel, fetter, hamper, hog-tie, manacle, shackle, trammel; curb, deter, hamstring, inhibit, restrain, tie (down); embog,
mire; burden, handicap, lumber; baffle,
balk, frustrate, thwart
idiom bog down
con abet, advance, aid, assist, ease, encourage, facilitate, forward, promote; accelerate, hasten, quicken, speed
ant further, help

hinder *adj syn* see POSTERIOR 2

ant fore, front

hinder *n syn* see BUTTOCKS

hindmost *adj* 1 *syn* see POSTERIOR 2

con foremost, headmost

2 *syn* see LAST

hindrance *n syn* see ENCUMBRANCE

ant help

hinge (on *or* upon) *vb syn* see DEPEND (on
or upon) 1

hint *n* 1 a slight or indirect pointing out of
something and especially of the way to an
end < give me a *hint* on how you would
deal with the matter >
syn clue, cue, indication, inkling, intimation, notion, suggestion, telltale, wind
rel innuendo, insinuation; inspiration,
prompting; aiming, direction, pointing;
key, pointer, tip; advice, assistance
con command, directive, instruction, order

2 a very small amount or admixture
< add a *hint* of garlic to the salad >
syn breath, cast, dash, intimation, lick,
shade, shadow, smack, smatch, smell,
soupçon, spice, sprinkling, strain, streak,
suggestion, suspicion, taste, tincture, tinge,
touch, trace, trifle, twang, vein, whiff,
whisper, wink; compare HAIR
rel adumbration, taint, vestige; particle,
scintilla
con abundance, heap, lot
ant oodles

3 *syn* see ASSOCIATION 4

hint *vb* 1 *syn* see SUGGEST 1

2 *syn* see POINT 2

3 *syn* see ADUMBRATE 1

4 to seek to obtain by sly or indirect
means < kept *hinting* for an invitation to
the party >
syn angle, fish
rel beg, coax, plead; importune, press;
seek, solicit
con ask (for), demand, insist (on *or* upon)

hinterland *n syn* see FRONTIER 2

hipped *adj* 1 *syn* see DOWNCAST

2 *syn* see OBSESSED

hire *n syn* see WAGE

hire *vb* 1 to take or engage something or
grant the use of something for a stipulated
price or rate < *hire* a conveyance >
syn charter, lease, let, rent
rel contract (for); engage; sublease, sublet, subrent

2 *syn* see EMPLOY 2

ant fire

hired girl *n syn* see MAID 2

hireling *n syn* see HACK 2

hiring *n syn* see EMPLOYMENT 4

hirsute *adj syn* see HAIRY 1

ant hairless

hiss *vb* to make a sibilant sound < he
thought he heard a snake *hiss* >
syn buzz, fizz, fizzle, sibilate, sizz, sizzle,
swish, wheeze, whish, whisper, whiz,
whoosh

hiss *n syn* see RASPBERRY

history *n* 1 *syn* see ACCOUNT 7

2 a chronological record of events < a
history of the American Revolution >
syn annals, chronicle
rel account, recital, relation, report; diary,
journal, memoir; epic, saga, tale

histrionic *adj syn* see DRAMATIC 1

hit *vb* 1 *syn* see STRIKE 2

rel buffet, pound, stroke
idiom give one a clip

2 *syn* see OCCUR 2

3 *syn* see HAPPEN 2

hit (on *or* upon) *vb syn* see FIND 1

hit *n* 1 a stroke delivered with a part of the
body or an instrument < gave the disobedient boy a *hit* on the head with her ruler >
syn ‖conk, knock, lick, rap, swat, swipe,
wipe; compare BLOW 1, CUFF

2 *syn* see SMASH 6

hitch *vb* 1 *syn* see LIMP 1

2 to attach as a means of motive power
< *hitched* the team to a wagon >
syn couple, harness, yoke
idiom make fast
con free, release, unfasten; uncouple, un-
harness, unyoke
ant unhitch

‖3 *syn* see MARRY 2

4 *syn* see HITCHHIKE

hitchhike *vb* to travel by securing free
rides < *hitchhiked* to California >
syn hitch, thumb
idiom bum (*or* hook) a ride

hitherto *adv* 1 up to this particular point
or time < imposed order upon what was
hitherto haphazard >
syn as yet, earlier, so far, thus far, yet
rel before, formerly, heretofore, once,
previously
idiom up to now (*or* then)

2 to this place < the appointed delegate
shall come *hitherto* >

syn here

hit man *n syn* see ASSASSIN

hit-or-miss *adj syn* see RANDOM

hive *vb syn* see ACCUMULATE

hoard *n* 1 *syn* see ACCUMULATION

2 *syn* see RESERVE

hoard *vb* to store up beyond one's present or reasonable need < *hoarding* sugar during war>

syn squirrel, stash; *compare* ACCUMULATE, SAVE 4

rel garner, lay by, lay up

idiom take all one can lay one's hands on

hoarse *adj* 1 rough or dry in sound < developed a *hoarse* cough>

syn croaking, croaky, gruff, husky

rel coarse, dry, guttural, thick

2 *syn* see HARSH 3

con honeyed, mellifluent, mellifluous, smooth

hoary *adj syn* see ANCIENT 1

hoax *vb syn* see DUPE

hoax *n syn* see IMPOSTURE

hobble *vb* 1 *syn* see LIMP 1

2 *syn* see HAMPER

hobo *n syn* see VAGABOND

hoboism *n syn* see VAGRANCY

hock *vb syn* see PAWN

hocus-pocus *n syn* see GIBBERISH 3

‖**hodge** *n syn* see RUSTIC

hodgepodge *n syn* see MISCELLANY 1

hogback *n syn* see RIDGE 1

hogshead *n syn* see CASK

hog-tie *vb syn* see HAMPER

hogwash *n syn* see NONSENSE 2

hoi polloi *n syn* see RABBLE 2

hoist *vb syn* see LIFT 1

hoity-toity *adj syn* see GIDDY 1

hokum *n syn* see NONSENSE 2

hold *vb* 1 *syn* see KEEP 5

2 *syn* see ENTHRALL 2

3 *syn* see HAVE 1

4 *syn* see CONTAIN 2

5 *syn* see FEEL 3

hold (with) *vb syn* see APPROVE 1

hold *n* the act or manner of grasping or holding < lost his *hold* on the side of the boat>

syn clamp, clasp, clench, clinch, clutch, grapple, grasp, grip, gripe, tenure

rel handclasp, handhold; purchase

hold back *vb* 1 *syn* see RESTRAIN 1

2 *syn* see KEEP 5

3 *syn* see DENY 3

hold down *vb syn* see RESTRAIN 1

holder *n syn* see OWNER

hold in *vb syn* see RESTRAIN 1

hold off *vb* 1 *syn* see FEND (off)

2 *syn* see DEFER

hold out *vb syn* see OFFER 1

hold over *vb syn* see DEFER

hold up *vb syn* see DEFER

hole *n* 1 *syn* see APERTURE

2 *syn* see GAP 1

3 a space within the substance of a body or mass < buried their trash in a *hole* in the ground>

syn cavity, hollow, vacuity, void

rel gap, hiatus, lacuna; cranny, interstice, niche; fissure, rent, rift; vacancy, vacuum

4 *syn* see HOVEL

5 *syn* see PREDICAMENT

hole *vb syn* see OPEN 3

hole-and-corner *adj syn* see SECRET 1

holiday *n syn* see VACATION

holiness *n* a state of spiritual soundness and unimpaired virtue < the *holiness* of the saints>

syn saintliness, sanctity

rel blessedness, divineness, divinity, sacredness; consecration, devotion, devoutness, piety, piousness, spirituality

holler *vb syn* see CALL 1

hollo *vb syn* see CALL 1

hollow *adj* 1 having a muffled or reverberating quality < had a deep *hollow* gloomy voice>

syn cavernous, reverberant, sepulchral

rel echoing, resonant, resounding, reverberating, sounding

con dead, dull, flat, toneless

2 *syn* see VAIN 1

hollow *n* 1 *syn* see DEPRESSION 2

2 *syn* see HOLE 3

holocaust *n syn* see FIRE 1

holy *adj* 1 dedicated to the service of or set apart by religion < pilgrimages to *holy* places>

syn blessed, consecrated, hallowed, sacred, sanctified, unprofane; *compare* SACRED 2

rel adored, glorified, revered, reverenced, venerated, worshiped; divine, religious, spiritual

2 *syn* see SAINTLY

ant unholy

3 *syn* see DEVOUT

‖**Holy Joe** *n syn* see CLERGYMAN

holy place *n syn* see SHRINE

Holy Writ *n syn* see BIBLE

homage *n syn* see HONOR 1

home *n* 1 *syn* see HABITATION 2

2 *syn* see HABITAT

3 *syn* see COUNTRY

home *adj* 1 *syn* see DOMESTIC 1

2 *syn* see DOMESTIC 2

homeland *n syn* see COUNTRY

homely *adj* 1 *syn* see PLAIN 1

rel commonplace, familiar, intimate

2 *syn* see PLAIN 5

idiom homely as a mud (*or* hedge) fence, homely enough to sour milk

ant comely

homicidal *adj syn* see MURDEROUS

homicide *n* 1 *syn* see MURDERER

2 *syn* see MURDER

homilize *vb syn* see PREACH 1

hominine *adj syn* see HUMAN

hominoid *n syn* see ANTHROPOID

homo *n syn* see HOMOSEXUAL

homoerotic *adj syn* see HOMOSEXUAL

homophile *adj syn* see HOMOSEXUAL

Homo sapiens *n syn* see MANKIND

homosexual *adj* relating to or exhibiting sexual desire toward a member of one's own sex < *homosexual* acts between consenting adults>

syn gay, homoerotic, homophile, inverted, queer, uranian

rel androgynous, bisexual, epicene; transvestite; lesbian, sapphic; effeminate, swishy

---

syn synonym(s)　　*rel* related word(s)

ant antonym(s)　　*con* contrasted word(s)

idiom idiomatic equivalent(s)

‖ use limited; if in doubt, see a dictionary

homosexual *n* one who is inclined to or practices homosexuality < a bar frequented by *homosexuals* >
syn fag, faggot, ||fruit, homo, invert, queer, uranian, uranist
rel transvestite; fairy, nance, nancy, pansy, queen, ||swish; dike, lesbian, sapphist; pederast, sodomite

homunculus *n syn see* DWARF

honcho *n syn see* LEADER 2

hone *vb syn see* SHARPEN

honed *adj syn see* SHARP 1

honest *adj* 1 *syn see* GENUINE 3
rel reliable, unaffected, unimpeachable
2 *syn see* UPRIGHT 2
rel candid, forthright, frank, open, plain; dispassionate, objective; truthful, veracious
ant dishonest

honestness *n syn see* HONESTY
ant dishonesty

honesty *n* uprightness as evidenced in character and actions < he was generally known as a person of scrupulous *honesty* >
syn honestness, honor, honorableness, incorruption, integrity
rel conscientiousness, justness, probity, scrupulousness, uprightness; dependability, reliability, trustworthiness; goodness, morality, rectitude, virtue
con deceitfulness, mendaciousness, mendacity, untruthfulness; deceit, duplicity, guile
ant dishonesty

honey *n* 1 *syn see* SWEETHEART 1
2 *syn see* GIRL FRIEND 2

honey *vb syn see* SUGARCOAT 1

honey (up) *vb syn see* FAWN

honeybunch *n syn see* SWEETHEART 1

honeyed *adj syn see* MELLIFLUOUS

honky-tonk *n syn see* DIVE

honor *n* 1 respect or esteem shown one as his due or claimed by one as a right < received the *honor* his rank >
syn deference, homage, obeisance, reverence
rel admiration, esteem; adoration, adulation, devotion, veneration, worship; acknowledgment, compliment, recognition, regard, respect
con contempt, despite, disdain, scorn; disregard, neglect, slighting
ant dishonor
2 an evidence or symbol of distinction < received many *honors* for his devoted public service >
syn accolade, award, badge, bays, decoration, distinction, kudos, laurels
rel deference, esteem, respect; admiration, approval
3 *syn see* HONESTY
con disgrace, ignominy, shame
ant dishonor, dishonorableness

honor *vb syn see* EXALT 1
ant dishonor

honorable *adj* 1 deserving of or entitled to honor (as because of rank, achievements, or service) < medicine is an *honorable* profession >
syn estimable, high-principled, noble, sterling, worthy; *compare* VENERABLE 1
rel august, illustrious, reverend, venerable, worshipful

ant dishonorable
2 *syn see* UPRIGHT 2
ant dishonorable

honorableness *n syn see* HONESTY
ant dishonor, dishonorableness

||**hooch** *n* 1 *syn see* LIQUOR 2
2 *syn see* MOONSHINE 2

||**hood** *n syn see* THUG 1

hoodlum *n syn see* THUG 1

hoodoo *n syn see* JINX

hoodwink *vb syn see* DUPE

hooey *n syn see* NONSENSE 2

hoof *vb syn see* WALK 1

hoof (it) *vb syn see* DANCE 1

hoofer *n syn see* DANCER

hook *vb syn see* STEAL 1

||**hooker** *n syn see* PROSTITUTE

||**hookshop** *n syn see* BROTHEL

hookup *n syn see* ASSOCIATION 1

hooligan *n syn see* THUG 1

||**hoosegow** *n syn see* JAIL

hoosier *n syn see* RUSTIC

hoot *n* 1 *syn see* RASPBERRY
2 *syn see* PARTICLE

||**hootenanny** *n syn see* DOODAD

hop *vb* 1 *syn see* SKIP 1
2 *syn see* JUMP 1

||**hop** *n syn see* DRUG 2

hope *vb syn see* EXPECT 1

hope *n syn see* TRUST 1

hopeful *adj* 1 full of hope or inclined to hope < the candidate was *hopeful* of winning >
syn hoping; *compare* CONFIDENT 1, EXPECTANT 1, OPTIMISTIC
rel anticipative, assured, satisfied, secure; cheerful, content, easy, undisturbed; fond, optimistic, Pollyannaish, rose-colored, sanguine, upbeat
con doubtful, insecure, pessimistic, uncertain; discouraged, disheartened, gloomy, glum
ant hopeless
2 exhibiting qualities that inspire hope < a *hopeful* prospect for improvement >
syn couleur de rose, encouraging, likely, promiseful, promising, roseate, rose-colored, rosy
rel advantageous, auspicious, propitious; bright, cheering, cheery, golden, halcyon, happy, sunny; budding, up-and-coming
con discouraging, disheartening, dismal, dreary, gloomy, pessimistic
ant hopeless

hopeful *n syn see* CANDIDATE

hopeless *adj* 1 *syn see* DESPONDENT
rel gloomy, glum, morose
con cheerful; assured, confident, optimistic, sanguine, sure
ant hopeful
2 offering no prospect of change for the better < his case was *hopeless* and beyond all human aid >
syn cureless, immedicable, impossible, incurable, insanable, irremediable, irreparable, uncorrectable, uncurable, unrecoverable
rel insoluble; incorrigible, irredeemable
idiom beyond hope (*or* remedy *or* repair), beyond human aid
con correctable, curable, medicable, remediable, reparable
ant hopeful

hoper *n syn* see OPTIMIST

hoping *adj syn* see HOPEFUL 1

hop-o'-my-thumb *n syn* see DWARF

hopped-up *adj syn* see DRUGGED

hopping *adj syn* see BUSTLING

horde *n syn* see CROWD 1

horizon *n syn* see KEN

horn in *vb* 1 *syn* see MEDDLE
   2 *syn* see INTRUDE 1

horning *n* see SHIVAREE

hornswoggle *vb syn* see DUPE

horrible *adj* 1 *syn* see GHASTLY 1
   rel abhorrent, abominable, detestable, hateful; loathsome, obnoxious, offensive, repulsive, revolting
   con gratifying, pleasing, soothing
   2 *syn* see FEARFUL 3
   3 *syn* see OFFENSIVE

horrid *adj* 1 *syn* see GHASTLY 1
   2 *syn* see HATEFUL 2
   3 *syn* see OFFENSIVE

horrific *adj syn* see FEARFUL 3

horrify *vb syn* see DISMAY 1

horrifying *adj syn* see GHASTLY 1

horror *n* 1 *syn* see FEAR 1
   rel distress, pain, shock, throe, wrench
   3 *syn* see ABOMINATION 2

hors d'oeuvre *n syn* see APPETIZER

horse *n syn* see SAWHORSE

horse *vb syn* see CUT UP 2

horsefeathers *n pl syn* see NONSENSE 2

horse opera *n syn* see WESTERN

horseplay *n* rough or boisterous play < their friendly *horseplay* almost ended in tragedy >
   syn fooling, high jinks, roughhouse, roughhousing, rowdiness, skylarking
   rel buffoonery, clowning

horseplay *vb syn* see CUT UP 2

horse sense *n syn* see SENSE 6

hospice *n syn* see HOTEL

hospitable *adj syn* see SOCIAL
   ant inhospitable

host *n syn* see MULTITUDE 1

hostage *n syn* see PLEDGE
   rel guaranty, security, surety

hostel *n syn* see HOTEL

hostelry *n syn* see HOTEL

hostile *adj* 1 marked by lack of friendliness or by opposition < takes a *hostile* view of a tax increase > < *hostile* tribes >
   syn ill, inimicable, inimical, unfriendly
   rel argumentative, competitive, contrary, dim, disaffected, disapproving, opposed, opposite, unfavorable; dour, sour; bellicose, belligerent, contentious, pugnacious; militant, warlike
   con amicable, benign, friendly
   ant unhostile
   2 *syn* see BITTER 3

hostility *n syn* see ENMITY

hot *adj* 1 marked by a notable amount of heat < a *hot* day >
   syn ardent, baking, blistering, boiling, broiling, burning, fiery, heated, red-hot, scalding, scorching, sizzling, sultry, sweltering, sweltry, torrid, white-hot

---

syn synonym(s)   *rel* related word(s)
ant antonym(s)   *con* contrasted word(s)
idiom idiomatic equivalent(s)
‖ use limited; if in doubt, see a dictionary

---

   rel febrile, fevered, feverish, feverous, hectic; summery, tropic, tropical; mild, warm
   idiom hot as a firecracker (*or* furnace), hot as an oven, hot as hell
   con chilly, cool, frigid, icy
   ant cold
   2 *syn* see LUSTFUL 2
   3 *syn* see MARVELOUS 2
   4 *syn* see CONTRABAND

hot air *n syn* see NONSENSE 2

hotbed *n syn* see BREEDING GROUND

hot-blooded *adj syn* see IMPASSIONED
   con callous, hard, unfeeling
   ant cold-blooded

hotchpotch *n syn* see MISCELLANY 1

hot dog *n syn* see FRANKFURTER

hotel *n* an establishment for the lodging and entertainment especially of transients < spent their vacation at a resort *hotel* >
   syn auberge, caravansary, hospice, hostel, hostelry, inn, lodge, public house, roadhouse, tavern
   rel boardinghouse, lodging house, pension, rooming house, spa; bostel, motel, motor inn; ‖fleabag, ‖flophouse

hotfoot *adv syn* see PELL-MELL

hotfoot *vb syn* see HURRY 2

hotheaded *adj syn* see RASH 1
   ant cool

hothouse *n syn* see BREEDING GROUND

hot spot *n syn* see NIGHTCLUB

hot-tempered *adj* 1 *syn* see ILL-TEMPERED
   2 *syn* see IRASCIBLE

hot water *n* 1 *syn* see PREDICAMENT
   2 *syn* see TROUBLE 3

hound *n* 1 *syn* see DOG 1
   2 *syn* see ADDICT

hound *vb syn* see BAIT 2

house *n* 1 *syn* see HABITATION 2
   2 *syn* see FAMILY 2
   3 *syn* see FAMILY 1
   4 *syn* see ENTERPRISE 3

house *vb* 1 *syn* see HARBOR 1
   2 *syn* see HARBOR

housebreak *vb* to commit an act of breaking open and entering with a felonious purpose the dwelling of another by day or night < was arrested again in September for *housebreaking* >
   syn break in; *compare* BURGLARIZE, ROB 1
   rel knock over, rob; ransack, rifle
   idiom break and enter

household *n syn* see FAMILY 2

household *adj syn* see DOMESTIC 1

housemaid *n syn* see MAID 2

houseman *n syn* see BOUNCER 2

house of God *syn* see HOUSE OF WORSHIP

house of prayer *syn* see HOUSE OF WORSHIP

house of worship a building for religious exercises < there are many *houses of worship* in this city >
   syn church, house of God, house of prayer, tabernacle, temple
   rel abbey, basilica, bethel, cathedral, chantry, chapel, conventicle, ‖fane, ‖kirk, masjid, meetinghouse, minster, mosque, oratory, pagoda, sanctuary, shrine, stupa, synagogue

idiom the Lord's house

housing *n syn* see SHELTER 2

hovel *n* a small wretched dwelling place <*migrants* forced to live in *hovels*>
syn burrow, hole; *compare* HUT
rel hut, hutch, shack, shanty; pigpen, pigsty, sty

hover *vb* 1 *syn* see FLIT 2
2 *syn* see HANG 3

howbeit *adv syn* see HOWEVER

howbeit *conj syn* see THOUGH

however *conj syn* see ONLY

however *adv* in spite of that <I accept your decision; I cannot, *however*, approve of it>
syn after all, howbeit, nevertheless, nonetheless, notwithstanding, per contra, still, still and all, though, withal, yet
idiom all the same, be that as it may, for all that, on the other hand

howl *vb* 1 to utter or emit a loud sustained doleful sound or outcry <the dogs *howled* through the night>
syn bay, quest, ululate, wail
rel bark, growl, yelp; blubber, cry, keen, weep, whimper; bawl, squall, yowl
2 *syn* see YELL 2
3 *syn* see BAWL 2

howl *n syn* see RIOT 2

hoyden *n syn* see TOMBOY

hub *n syn* see CENTER 2

hubbub *n* 1 *syn* see DIN
2 *syn* see COMMOTION 4

║hubby *n syn* see HUSBAND

hubristic *adj syn* see PROUD 1

huckster *n syn* see PEDDLER

huckster *vb* 1 *syn* see HAGGLE 2
2 *syn* see PEDDLE 2

huddle *vb* 1 *syn* see CROUCH
2 *syn* see CONFER 2

huddle (on) *vb syn* see DON 1

huddle *n syn* see CONFUSION 3

hue *n syn* see COLOR 1

huff *vb* 1 *syn* see PANT 1
2 *syn* see IRRITATE

huff *n syn* see OFFENSE 2

huffy *adj* 1 *syn* see PROUD 1
2 *syn* see IRRITABLE

hug *vb syn* see EMBRACE 1

huge *adj* exceedingly or excessively large <*huge* corporations> <ate a *huge* dinner>
syn Antaean, behemothic, Brobdingnagian, Bunyanesque, colossal, cyclopean, dinosauric, elephantine, enormous, gargantuan, giant, gigantean, gigantesque, gigantic, Herculean, heroic, immense, jumbo, leviathan, lusty, mammoth, massive, massy, mastodonic, mighty, monster, monstrous, monumental, mountainous, planetary, prodigious, pythonic, ║swapping, Titan, titanic, tremendous, unfathomed, untold, vast, walloping, whacking, whaling, whopping; *compare* GRAND 1
rel bulky, extensive, great, immeasurable, magnificent, towering; outsize, oversize
con diminutive, little, miniature, minute, petite, small, teeny, tiny, wee, weeny

hugely *adv syn* see VERY 1

hugeness *n syn* see ENORMITY 2

hugger-mugger *n* 1 *syn* see SECRECY
2 *syn* see CLUTTER 2

hugger-mugger *adv syn* see SECRETLY

hugger-mugger *adj syn* see SECRET 1

hugger-muggery *n syn* see SECRECY

hull *n* an outer covering of a fruit or seed <peanut *hulls*>
syn case, husk, pod, ║shell, shuck, skin, ║slough
rel chaff; bark, peel, rind

hull *vb syn* see SHUCK

hullabaloo *n syn* see DIN

hum *vb* to make a low prolonged sound <the wind *hummed* in the chimney>
syn bombinate, ║bum, bumble, buzz, drone, ║sowf, strum, thrum
rel moan, murmur, purr, vibrate, whisper
con howl, roar, shriek

human *adj* of, relating to, or characteristic of mankind <problems of *human* relationships>
syn hominine, mortal
rel anthropological, ethnologic, ethological; anthropoid, hominid, hominoid
con angelic, divine, superhuman, animal, brute, subhuman

human *n* a member of the human race <every *human* has a right to live>
syn being, body, ║character, creature, individual, life, man, mortal, party, person, personage, soul, wight; *compare* MAN 3, MANKIND

humane *adj syn* see CHARITABLE 1
rel chickenhearted, compassionate, kindhearted, soft-hearted; benevolent, gentle, kind, kindly, mild
ant inhuman, inhumane

humanitarian *adj syn* see CHARITABLE 1

humanity *n syn* see MANKIND

humankind *n syn* see MANKIND

humanoid *n syn* see ANTHROPOID

humble *adj* 1 lacking all signs of pride, aggressiveness, or self-assertiveness <accepted his success with *humble* appreciation>
syn lowly, meek, modest, unassuming
rel simple, unobtrusive, unostentatious, unpretentious; acquiescent, compliant, resigned; quiet, subdued, submissive
con ostentatious, pretentious, showy; vain, vainglorious, arrogant, disdainful, haughty, lordly, overbearing, proud, toplofty
ant conceited
2 *syn* see IGNOBLE 1

humble *vb* to make lower in status, prestige, or esteem <his devotion to duty *humbled* his critics>
syn abase, bemean, cast down, debase, degrade, demean, humiliate, lower, sink
rel chagrin, mortify; abash, discomfit, embarrass
idiom bring low, take down a peg or two
con aggrandize, exalt, magnify

humbug *n* 1 *syn* see IMPOSTURE
2 *syn* see IMPOSTOR
3 *syn* see NONSENSE 2

humbug *vb syn* see DECEIVE

humdinger *n syn* ║DILLY, ║corker, crackerjack, ║daisy, dandy, jim-dandy, ║lulu, nifty, peach, ║pip

humdrum *adj syn* see DULL 9

humdrum *n syn* see MONOTONY

humid *adj* containing or characterized by an uncomfortable amount of atmospheric warmth and moisture <a *humid* climate>

syn mucky, muggy, soggy, sticky, sultry;
compare STIFLING 1, STUFFY 1

rel clammy, dank, sodden; close, oppressive, stuffy; sweltering

con arid, dry; cool, crisp, fresh

humilate *vb syn see* HUMBLE

humming *adj syn see* BUSTLING

humor *n* 1 *syn see* DISPOSITION 3

2 *syn see* MOOD 1

3 *syn see* CAPRICE

4 that quality or element which appeals to a sense of the ludicrous or incongruous < *see the* humor *in a situation* >

syn comedy, comicality, comicalness, drollery, drollness, funniness, humorousness, wittiness

rel jocosity, jocularity, jocundity, jocundness; flippancy, levity, lightness; banter, chaffing, jesting, joking, kidding

con earnestness, seriousness, solemnity; depth, profundity

5 something that is or is designed to be humorous < *his heavy* humor *fell flat* >

syn wit

rel banter, chitchat, pleasantry, repartee

6 *syn see* WIT 5

ant humorlessness

humor *vb* 1 *syn see* INDULGE 1

2 *syn see* BABY

humorist *n* 1 *syn see* WAG 1

2 a person noted for or specializing in humor < *a writer best known as a* humorist >

syn comedian, comic, droll, funnyman, jester, joker, jokester, quipster, wag, wit

rel buffoon, card, clown, cutup, gagman, gagster, jokesmith, merry-andrew, prankster, punster, zany; banterer, kidder

humorous *adj syn see* WITTY

humorousness *n syn see* HUMOR 4

humorsome *adj syn see* MOODY

‖**hump** *vb syn see* CARRY 1

hunch *vb syn see* CROUCH

hunch *n syn see* LUMP 1

hunger *vb syn see* LONG

hungry *adj* feeling distressed from lack of food < *a group of* hungry *children* >

syn famished, ‖peckish, ravenous, starved, starving

rel rapacious, voracious

con full, glutted, gorged, sated, satiated

ant surfeited

hunk *n syn see* LUMP 1

hunker (down) *vb syn see* SQUAT

hankers *n pl syn see* BUTTOCKS

hunks *n pl but sing or pl in constr syn see* MISER

hunky-dory *adj syn see* MARVELOUS 2

Hunnic *adj syn see* BARBARIAN 1

Hunnish *adj syn see* BARBARIAN 1

hunt *vb* 1 to search for or pursue (game or prey) for the purpose of capturing or killing < hunted *deer in bow-and-arrow season only* >

syn chase, run

rel dog, ferret, hawk, hound; course, drive, stalk, start, still-hunt, track; capture, kill, snare; gun, shoot

---

syn synonym(s)　　*rel* related word(s)
ant antonym(s)　　*con* contrasted word(s)
idiom idiomatic equivalent(s)
‖ use limited; if in doubt, see a dictionary

idiom go hunting

2 *syn see* SEEK 1

hunt (down *or* out *or* up) *vb syn see* RUMMAGE 3

hunting *n* the act or practice of seeking and taking wild and especially game animals < *lived by* hunting *and fishing* >

syn chase, venery

rel angling, coursing, falconry, fishing, gunning, hawking, shooting

hurdle *n syn see* OBSTACLE

hurdle *vb* 1 *syn see* CLEAR 8

2 *syn see* JUMP 1

3 *syn see* OVERCOME 1

hurl *vb syn see* THROW 1

hurly-burly *n syn see* COMMOTION 4

hurrah *n* 1 *syn see* PASSION 6

2 *syn see* COMMOTION 3

3 *syn see* ARGUMENT 2

hurricane *n* a violent rotating storm or system of winds originating in the tropics and often moving into temperate latitudes < *the* hurricane *struck the coast early today* >

syn tropical cyclone, tropical storm, typhoon, ‖willy-willy; *compare* TORNADO, WHIRLWIND 1

rel williwaw

hurried *adj syn see* PRECIPITATE 1

ant unhurried

hurriedness *n syn see* HASTE 2

hurry *vb* 1 *syn see* SPEED 3

2 to proceed or move with dispatch < hurry *home after school* >

syn barrel, barrelhouse, beeline, bucket, bullet, bustle, ‖dust, fleet, flit, fly, haste, hasten, highball, hotfoot, hustle, ‖nip, pelt, rock, rocket, run, rush, scoot, scour, ‖skeet, skin, smoke, speed, stave, ‖tatter, whirl, whish, whisk, whiz, zip; *compare* RUSH 1

rel jog, peg, skelp, trot; bowl (along), breeze; dig in; post

idiom get a move on, go (*or* move) like lightning, make tracks, step on it, step on the gas

con creep, dally, dawdle, drag, lag, linger, loiter, poke, saunter, stroll

hurry *n syn see* HASTE 1

hurry-scurry *adv syn see* PELL-MELL

hurt *vb* 1 *syn see* INJURE 1

rel abuse, afflict, mistreat, misuse

ant benefit

2 *syn see* INJURE 3

3 *syn see* DISTRESS 2

4 to experience or be the seat of sharp physical distress < *my arm still* hurts >

syn ache, pain, ‖suffer; *compare* SMART

hurt *n syn see* INJURY 1

hurtful *adj* 1 *syn see* HARMFUL

con harmless, innocuous

2 *syn see* PAINFUL 1

hurting *adj syn see* PAINFUL 1

husband *n* the male partner in a marriage < *neglected his responsibilities as a* husband >

syn ‖hubby, lord, man, ‖master, mister, Mr., ‖old man

rel consort, helpmate, helpmeet, mate, other half, spouse, benedict, bridegroom

husbanding *n syn see* CONSERVATION 1

ant squandering

husbandry *n* 1 *syn see* ECONOMY

2 *syn* see AGRICULTURE

hush *vb syn* see SILENCE

hush (up) *vb syn* see SUPPRESS 3

hush *adj syn* see STILL 3

hush *n* 1 *syn* see QUIET 1

2 *syn* see SECRECY

hushed *adj* 1 *syn* see CALM 1

2 *syn* see PRIVATE 2

hushful *adj syn* see STILL 3

hush–hush *adj syn* see SECRET 1

hush–hush *n syn* see SECRECY

husk *n syn* see HULL

husk *vb syn* see SHUCK

husky *adj syn* see HOARSE 1

husky *adj* 1 big and muscular <a *husky* man carried in the trunks>
syn beefy, burly, hefty
rel brawny, muscular, well-built; stalwart, stout, strapping, strong, sturdy; Herculean, mighty, powerful; Bunyanesque, gigantic
con delicate, fragile, frail; puny, scrawny, slight; elfin; mousey

2 *syn* see LARGE 1

hussy *n* 1 *syn* see WANTON

2 *syn* see MINX

hustle *vb* 1 *syn* see PUSH 2

2 *syn* see HURRY 2

hustle *n syn* see HASTE 1

hustler *n* 1 an alert enterprising individual <he's a *hustler*, eager to get ahead in the world>
syn dynamo, go-getter, live wire, peeler, rustler, self-starter
rel humdinger, hummer; new broom; doer, powerhouse
idiom busy bee
con dawdler, idler; slow coach, slowpoke, stick-in-the-mud

2 *syn* see PROSTITUTE

hustling *adj syn* see BUSTLING

hut *n* a small, simply constructed dwelling often for temporary or intermittent occupancy <the shepherds lived in *huts* in the summer>
syn box, cabin, caboose, camp, cot, cottage, lodge, shack, shanty; *compare* BUILDING, EDIFICE, HOVEL
rel cabana, chalet, crib, dacha, hovel, hutch, lean-to, shed, summer house

hut *vb syn* see HARBOR 2

Hyblaean *adj syn* see MELLIFLUOUS

hybrid *n* an offspring produced by parents of different strains, breeds, varieties, species, or genera <the mule is a *hybrid* of the ass and the horse>
syn bastard, cross, crossbred, crossbreed, half blood, half-breed, mongrel, mule
rel incross, incrossbred, outcross; combination, composite, mixture
con pureblood, purebred, thoroughbred

hybridize *vb syn* see CROSS 4

hydrant *n syn* see FAUCET

hydro *n syn* see SPA 1

hydroponics *n* the growing of plants in nutrient solution and without soil <tomatoes grown by *hydroponics*>
syn aquiculture, nutriculture
idiom soilless agriculture

hygienic *adj syn* see HEALTHFUL
ant unhygienic

hymeneal *adj syn* see MATRIMONIAL

hymn *n syn* see SONG 2

hymn *vb* 1 *syn* see PRAISE 2

2 *syn* see SING

hypaethral *adj syn* see OUTDOOR

hyperbole *n syn* see EXAGGERATION
con depreciation, minimization, understatement
ant litotes

hypercritical *adj syn* see CRITICAL 1

hypercriticize *vb syn* see QUIBBLE 1

hypnotic *adj syn* see SOPORIFIC 1

hypocorism *n syn* see NICKNAME

hypocrisy *n* the pretense or affectation of having virtues, principles, or beliefs that one does not actually have <political *hypocrisy*>
syn cant, hypocriticalness, pecksniffery, pharisaicalness, pharisaism, sanctimoniousness, sanctimony, sham, Tartuffery, Tartuffism
rel pietism, religiosity; casuistry, glibness, insincerity, self-righteousness, unctuousness; charlatanry, humbug, quackery
con candidness, fairness, openness; honesty, probity, truthfulness
ant sincerity

hypocrite *n* one who affects virtues, qualities, or attitudes he does not have <don't be a *hypocrite*—if you don't approve, say so>
syn dissembler, dissimulator, lip server, pharisee, Tartuffe, whited sepulcher
rel pietist; actor, attitudinizer, bluffer, charlatan, faker, four-flusher, fraud, humbug, impostor, masquerader, phony, poser, poseur, pretender, quack, sham

hypocritical *adj* 1 characterized by hypocrisy <*hypocritical* compliments>
syn canting, pecksniffian, pharisaic, pharisaical, sanctimonious, self-righteous
rel goody-goody, holier-than-thou, moralistic, pietistic, religiose; casuistic; affected, insincere; bland, glib, mealymouthed, oily, smooth, smooth-spoken, smooth-tongued, unctuous
con honest, open, straightforward
ant sincere

2 *syn* see INSINCERE

hypocriticalness *n syn* see HYPOCRISY
ant sincerity

hypostatize *vb syn* see MATERIALIZE 2

hypothesis *n syn* see THEORY 1

hypothetical *adj* 1 *syn* see SUPPOSED 1
rel doubtful, problematic

2 *syn* see ABSTRACT 1

I

icky *adj syn* see OFFENSIVE

iconographic *adj syn* see PICTORIAL 1

icy *adj* 1 *syn* see COLD 1
ant fiery
2 *syn* see COLD 2
ant fiery

idea *n* what exists in the mind as a representation (as of something comprehended) or as a formulation (as of a plan) <that's not my *idea* of a good time>
syn apprehension, conceit, concept, conception, image, impression, intellection, notion, perception, thought
rel assumption, belief, conclusion, conviction, estimation, feeling, inclination, judgment, opinion, persuasion, presumption, reaction, reflection, sentiment, view; conjecture, guess, hypothesis, speculation, supposition, surmise, suspicion, theory; caprice, fancy, fantasy, vagary, whim, whimsy; brainstorm, inspiration

ideal *adj* 1 *syn* see ABSTRACT 1
ant actual
2 *syn* see CONCEPTUAL
3 constituting a standard (as of perfection or excellence) <the *ideal* man of letters>
syn flawless, indefectible, model
rel archetypal, archetypical, prototypal, prototypical
con average, normal, representative, typical
4 *syn* see PERFECT 3
5 *syn* see TYPICAL 1

ideal *n* 1 *syn* see MODEL 2
2 *syn* see PARAGON

idealist *n syn* see DREAMER

idealist *adj syn* see IDEALISTIC

idealistic *adj* characterized by idealism <made an *idealistic* speech on human rights>
syn idealist, utopian, visionary
rel impractical, poetical, quixotic, romantic, starry, starry-eyed, unrealistic
con empirical, matter-of-fact, practical, pragmatic, rational, realistic
ant unidealistic

ideational *adj syn* see CONCEPTUAL

identic *adj syn* see SAME 2
ant nonidentical

identical *adj* 1 *syn* see SAME 1
2 *syn* see SAME 2
ant nonidentical

identicalness *n syn* see IDENTITY 1

identification *n syn* see RECOGNITION 1

identify *vb* to establish the identity of <the culprit was *identified* by his fingerprints>
syn determinate, diagnose, diagnosticate, distinguish, finger, pinpoint, place, recognize, spot

rel find; determine, establish, make out, pick out, select, separate (out)

identity *n* 1 the quality of being the same in all that constitutes the objective reality of separate things <the *identity* of the two texts is exact>
syn identicalness, oneness, sameness, selfsameness
rel agreement, likeness, resemblance, semblance, similarity, similitude; correspondence, equality, equivalence; uniformity
con dissimilarity, dissimilitude, unlikeness, unsimilarity
ant nonidentity
2 *syn* see INDIVIDUALITY 4

ideologue *n syn* see DREAMER

ideology *n* an overall view of or attitude toward life <an *ideology* based on tolerance>
syn credo, creed, weltanschauung
rel outlook, philosophy, view

idiom *n syn* see LANGUAGE 1

idiosyncratic *adj* 1 *syn* see CHARACTERISTIC
2 *syn* see STRANGE 4

idiot *n* 1 *syn* see FOOL 1
2 *syn* see FOOL 2
3 *syn* see FOOL 4
4 *syn* see DUNCE

idle *adj* 1 *syn* see VAIN 1
2 *syn* see VACANT 4
3 *syn* see INACTIVE
ant busy

idle *vb* to spend time in idleness <people *idling* in the park>
syn ‖brogue, bum, dawdle, diddle, diddle=daddle, drone, goldbrick, ‖goof (off), ‖lallygag, laze, lazy, loaf, loiter, loll, lounge
rel relax, repose, rest; amble, linger, mooch, mosey, saunter, stroll, tarry; hang around, sit around, sit back, sit by
idiom dog it, kill time, lie around, mark time

idleheaded *adj syn* see FOOLISH 2

idleness *n syn* see SLOTH 1

idler *n syn* see SLUGGARD

idolatry *n syn* see ADORATION

idolization *n syn* see ADORATION

idolize *vb syn* see ADORE 3
idiom worship the ground one walks on

iffy *adj syn* see UNCERTAIN 1

ignis fatuus *n syn* see DELUSION 1

ignitable *adj syn* see COMBUSTIBLE 1

ignite *vb syn* see LIGHT 1

ignited *adj syn* see BURNING 1

ignoble *adj* 1 belonging to or characteristic of socially or economically inferior classes <a person of *ignoble* antecedents>
syn base, baseborn, humble, low, lowborn, lowly, mean, plebeian, unennobled, unwashed

---

syn synonym(s)   *rel* related word(s)
ant antonym(s)   *con* contrasted word(s)
idiom idiomatic equivalent(s)
‖ use limited; if in doubt, see a dictionary

rel coarse, common, homely, inferior, inglorious, modest, ordinary, peasant, plain, poor, popular, simple, vulgar
con highborn, highbred, wellborn, well-bred; eminent, high, lofty, proud, superior
ant noble
2 *syn* see BASE 3
ant noble

ignominious *adj syn* see DISREPUTABLE 1

ignominy *n syn* see DISGRACE
rel contempt, despite, disdain, scorn; chagrin, mortification
con glory, honor; esteem, respect

ignoramus *n syn* see DUNCE

ignorance *n* 1 the state of being unlearned <the blight of *ignorance*>
syn benightedness, illiteracy
rel callowness, greenness, inexperience, naiveté, rawness, simpleness, simplicity, uncouthness, uncultivation, unsophistication; empty-headedness, unintelligence, witlessness; know-nothingism, philistinism
con education, enlightenment, erudition, learning, literacy
2 the state of being unaware or uninformed <*ignorance* of the law>
syn innocence, inscience, nescience, unacquaintance, unacquaintedness, unawareness, unfamiliarity, unknowingness
con acquaintance, acquaintanceship, experience; awareness, familiarity, knowledgeableness

ignorant *adj* 1 lacking knowledge or education <an *ignorant* boy with no taste for school>
syn benighted, empty-headed, illiterate, know-nothing, rude, uneducated, uninstructed, unlettered, unschooled, untaught, untutored
rel lowbrow, uncultured, unintellectual; callow, green, inexperienced; crude, gross, raw, uncouth; ingenuous, naive, simple, unsophisticated
con educated, erudite, learned, literate
2 lacking information on or awareness of something <was *ignorant* of the circumstances surrounding the affair>
syn incognizant, inconversant, oblivious, unacquainted, unaware, unfamiliar, uninformed, uninstructed, unknowing, unwitting
idiom in the dark
con aware, conscious, conversant, informed, knowing, knowledgeable
3 *syn* see BACKWARD 5

ignore *vb syn* see NEGLECT
rel avoid, evade

ilk *n syn* see TYPE

ill *adj* 1 *syn* see EVIL 5
ant good
2 *syn* see HARMFUL
3 *syn* see SICK 1
4 *syn* see RUDE 6
5 *syn* see HOSTILE 1

ill *n* 1 *syn* see EVIL 1
ant benefit
2 *syn* see DISEASE 1

ill-adapted *adj syn* see UNFIT 1

ill-advised *adj* 1 *syn* see RASH 1
2 *syn* see INADVISABLE
ant well-advised
3 *syn* see UNWISE
ant well-advised

illation *n* 1 *syn* see INFERENCE 1
2 *syn* see INFERENCE 2

ill-behaved *adj syn* see NAUGHTY 1

ill-boding *adj syn* see OMINOUS

ill-bred *adj* 1 *syn* see BOORISH
ant well-bred
2 *syn* see RUDE 6
ant well-bred, well-mannered

ill-chosen *adj syn* see INFELICITOUS

ill-defined *adj syn* see FAINT 2
ant well-defined

illegal *adj syn* see UNLAWFUL
rel banned, forbidden, interdicted, prohibited, proscribed, outlawed, unauthorized, unlicensed, unwarranted; felonious; contraband, hot; actionable, irregular
con authorized, lawful, licensed, licit, permitted, regular, right
ant legal

illegality *n* the quality or state of being illegal <the *illegality* of an act>
syn illegitimacy, illicitness, unlawfulness
rel badness, impropriety, wrongness
con lawfulness, legitimacy, licitness; propriety
ant legality

illegible *adj* incapable of being read or deciphered <an *illegible* signature>
syn indecipherable, undecipherable, unreadable
rel faint, indistinct, obscure, unclear
ant legible, readable

illegitimacy *n* 1 the state or condition of being born out of wedlock <he accepted the fact of his *illegitimacy*>
syn bastardy, illegitimateness, supposititiousness
rel bar sinister
ant legitimacy, legitimateness
2 *syn* see ILLEGALITY
ant legitimacy, legitimateness

illegitimate *adj* 1 not recognized by law as lawful offspring <an *illegitimate* child>
syn baseborn, bastard, fatherless, misbegotten, natural, spurious, supposititious, unfathered
rel birthless; adulterine
ant legitimate
2 *syn* see UNLAWFUL
ant legitimate

illegitimate *n syn* see BASTARD 1
ant legitimate

illegitimateness *n syn* see ILLEGITIMACY 1
ant legitimacy, legitimateness

ill-famed *adj syn* see INFAMOUS 1

ill-fated *adj syn* see UNLUCKY

ill-favored *adj* 1 *syn* see UGLY 2
ant well-favored
2 *syn* see OBJECTIONABLE

ill-flavored *adj syn* see UNPALATABLE 1

ill-humored *adj syn* see ILL-TEMPERED
ant good-humored, good-natured

illiberal *adj* unwilling or unable to grasp the point of view of others <had the *illiberal* outlook of an old-time schoolmaster>
syn bigoted, brassbound, hidebound, intolerant, narrow, narrow-minded, small-minded, unenlarged
rel biased, jaundiced, one-sided, opinionated, partial, partisan, prejudiced; grudging, little, mean, paltry, petty, small, un-

charitable, ungenerous; insular, parochial, provincial; rigid, rigorous, stringent
con broad-minded, open-minded, tolerant, unbigoted; advanced, progressive, radical
ant liberal

illicit *adj syn* see UNLAWFUL
ant licit

illicitness *n syn* see ILLEGALITY

illimitable *adj syn* see INFINITE 1
rel endless, interminable
ant limitable; limited

illiteracy *n syn* see IGNORANCE 1

illiterate *adj syn* see IGNORANT 1
ant literate; erudite

illiterate *n* one who cannot read or write
< the training of adult *illiterates* >
syn analphabet
rel functional illiterate, semiliterate, subliterate
ant literate

ill-judged *adj syn* see UNWISE

ill-kempt *adj syn* see SLOVENLY 1

ill-looking *adj syn* see UGLY 2
ant good-looking, ||well-looked

ill-mannered *adj syn* see RUDE 6
ant well-bred, well-mannered

ill-natured *adj syn* see ILL-TEMPERED
ant good-humored, good-natured

illness *n syn* see SICKNESS 1
ant health

illogical *adj* contrary to or devoid of logic
< came to an *illogical* conclusion from the facts presented >
syn fallacious, invalid, irrational, mad, nonrational, reasonless, sophistic, unreasonable, unreasoned; *compare* FALSE 1
rel inconsistent; plausible, specious; unscientific, unsound; absurd, meaningless, senseless
idiom without rhyme or reason
con rational, reasonable, sensible; sane, sound, valid
ant logical

ill-omened *adj syn* see OMINOUS
ant auspicious

ill-seasoned *adj syn* see UNSEASONABLE 1
ant seasonable

ill-starred *adj syn* see UNLUCKY
rel bodeful, fateful, foreboding, ominous, portentous; baleful, malefic, malign, sinister; unfavorable, unpromising, unpropitious

ill-suited *adj syn* see UNFIT 1

ill-tempered *adj* having a bad temper
< an *ill-tempered* old man >
syn bad-tempered, dyspeptic, hot-tempered, ill-humored, ill-natured, ||rusty, tempersome
rel crabbed, surly; fractious, huffy, irritable, peevish, petulant, querulous, snappish, sour, waspish; shrewish, vixenish
con calm, easy, placid, serene, tranquil; amiable, complaisant, considerate, good-natured, kindly, obliging, tolerant
ant good-tempered, sweet-tempered, well-tempered

ill-timed *adj syn* see UNSEASONABLE 1

---

syn synonym(s)   *rel* related word(s)
ant antonym(s)   *con* contrasted word(s)
idiom idiomatic equivalent(s)
|| use limited; if in doubt, see a dictionary

ant seasonable

2 *syn* see IMPROPER 1

ill-treat *vb syn* see ABUSE 4
rel aggrieve, harass, harry, molest
con befriend, relieve, succor; countenance, encourage, favor, patronize

illude *vb syn* see DECEIVE

illume *vb* **1** *syn* see ILLUMINATE 1
2 *syn* see ILLUMINATE 2

illuminant *adj syn* see ENLIGHTENING

illuminate *vb* **1** to supply with physical light < a room dimly *illuminated* by firelight >
syn illume, illumine, light, lighten
rel brighten; irradiate; floodlight, highlight, spotlight; fire, ignite, kindle
con blur, cloud, darken, dim, dull, obscure, pale
2 to supply with spiritual or intellectual light < the worth of a truly *illuminating* book >
syn edify, enlighten, illume, illumine, improve, irradiate, uplift
rel better, improve; ennoble, exalt, refine; finish, mature, perfect, polish
con becloud, cloud, darken, obfuscate, obscure, overshadow, shadow
3 *syn* see CLARIFY 2
rel construe, define, dramatize, expound, express, gloss, interpret
idiom shed light on (*or* upon)
con baffle, confound, confuse, mystify, pose, puzzle, stump

illuminati *n pl syn* see INTELLIGENTSIA

illuminating *adj syn* see ENLIGHTENING

illuminative *adj syn* see ENLIGHTENING

illumine *vb* **1** *syn* see ILLUMINATE 1
2 *syn* see ILLUMINATE 2

illumining *adj syn* see ENLIGHTENING

ill-use *vb syn* see ABUSE 4
con befriend, relieve, succor; countenance, encourage, favor, patronize

illusion *n* **1** *syn* see DELUSION 1
rel invention; bubble, chimera, dream, will-o'-the-wisp; appearance, seeming, semblance
2 *syn* see PIPE DREAM

illusionist *n syn* see MAGICIAN 2

illusive *adj syn* see APPARENT 2

illusory *adj* **1** *syn* see FICTITIOUS 1
ant factual
2 *syn* see APPARENT 2
rel chimerical, fanciful, fantastic, imaginary, unreal, visionary; deceptive, delusive, delusory, misleading
con actual, real, veritable; authentic, true, valid
ant factual

illustrate *vb* **1** *syn* see CLARIFY 2
rel display, exhibit, expose, show; disclose, discover, reveal
con cloak, conceal, enshroud, mask, screen, shroud, veil
2 *syn* see EXEMPLIFY 1
rel elucidate, explain, expound, interpret; demonstrate, manifest, show; enliven, vivify
3 *syn* see REPRESENT 2
4 *syn* see SHOW 2

illustration *n* **1** *syn* see EXAMPLE 3
2 *syn* see INSTANCE

illustrational *adj syn* see PICTORIAL 1

illustrative *adj syn* see PICTORIAL 1

illustratory *adj syn* see PICTORIAL 1

illustrious *adj syn* see FAMOUS 2
 rel glorious, resplendent, splendid, sublime; conspicuous, lofty, outstanding, signal, striking
 con abject, inglorious, mean; disgraceful, dishonorable, ignoble, ignominious, shameful
 ant infamous

illustriousness *n syn* see EMINENCE 1
 ant infamy

ill will *n syn* see MALICE
 rel hostility, rancor, venom
 ant goodwill

image *n* 1 one strikingly like another especially in appearance or manner < she was the *image* of her mother >
 syn double, picture, portrait, ringer, simulacrum, spit, spitting image
 rel counterpart, equal, equivalent, match
 idiom chip off the old block, dead ringer, speaking likeness, spit and image
 2 *syn* see IDEA

image *vb* 1 *syn* see REPRESENT 1
 2 *syn* see THINK 1
 3 *syn* see REFLECT 1

imaginable *adj syn* see THINKABLE 2
 ant unimaginable

imaginary *adj* 1 having no real existence but existing in imagination < elves are *imaginary* beings >
 syn fancied, fanciful, imagined, notional, shadowy
 rel imaginative; abstract, hypothetical, ideal, visionary; apparitional, chimerical, fantastic, figmental, hallucinatory, illusory, phantasmal, phantasmic, quixotic, spectral; unreal, unsubstantial
 con genuine, true, valid
 ant actual, real
 2 *syn* see FICTITIOUS 1
 ant actual, real

imagination *n* the power or function of the mind by which mental images are formed or the exercise of that power < children have great *imagination* >
 syn fancy, fantasy (*or* phantasy), imaginativeness
 rel creativity, inspiration, invention, inventiveness, visualization
 con literalness, matter-of-factness, prosaism, unimaginativeness

imaginativeness *n syn* see IMAGINATION
 ant unimaginativeness

imagine *vb* 1 *syn* see THINK 1
 2 *syn* see UNDERSTAND 3

imagined *adj syn* see IMAGINARY 1
 con known, recognized, seen

imbecile *adj syn* see RETARDED

imbecile *n* 1 *syn* see FOOL 4
 2 *syn* see FOOL 1

imbibe *vb* 1 *syn* see ABSORB 1
 2 *syn* see DRINK 1
 3 *syn* see DRINK 3

imbricate *vb syn* see OVERLAP

imbroglio *n syn* see QUARREL

imbrued *adj syn* see BLOODY 1

imbue *vb syn* see INFUSE 1

imitate *vb* 1 *syn* see COPY
 2 *syn* see MIMIC

imitation *adj syn* see ARTIFICIAL 2
 ant real

imitation *n* something made or produced as an often inferior likeness of something

else < usually wore *imitations* of her costly jewels >
 syn copy, ersatz, simulacrum
 rel counterfeit, fake, forgery, phony, sham, simulation; counterpart, duplicate, replica, reproduction; likeness, semblance
 ant original

imitative *adj* 1 *syn* see ONOMATOPOEIC
 2 *syn* see SLAVISH 3

immaculate *adj* 1 *syn* see CHASTE
 ant maculate
 2 *syn* see IMPECCABLE 1
 3 *syn* see CLEAN 1

immalleable *adj syn* see STIFF 1
 ant malleable

immaterial *adj* 1 not composed of matter < *immaterial* forces >
 syn asomatous, bodiless, disbodied, discarnate, disembodied, incorporeal, insubstantial, metaphysical, nonmaterial, nonphysical, spiritual, unbodied, ‖uncorporal, unembodied, unfleshly, unmaterial, unphysical, unsubstantial
 rel impalpable, imponderable; psychic, subjective; aerial, airy, ethereal; insensible, unearthly, unworldly; supernatural; celestial, heavenly; apparitional, ghostly, shadowy
 con bodily, corporeal, fleshly, incarnate; material, objective, palpable, physical, substantial; mundane, terrestrial, worldly
 ant material
 2 *syn* see IRRELEVANT
 ant material

immature *adj* 1 *syn* see YOUNG 1
 rel premature, precocious
 ant mature
 2 *syn* see CHILDISH
 ant mature

immeasurable *adj* 1 *syn* see INCALCULABLE 1
 2 *syn* see LIMITLESS

immediacy *n syn* see PROXIMITY

immediate *adj* 1 *syn* see DIRECT 4
 ant distant (*of relatives*)
 2 *syn* see INSTANTANEOUS
 3 *syn* see CLOSE 6

immediately *adv* 1 in direct connection without intermediary < *immediately* in front of the viewers >
 syn contiguously, directly
 2 *syn* see AWAY 3
 rel anon, shortly, soon
 idiom right now

immedicable *adj syn* see HOPELESS 2
 ant medicable

immense *adj syn* see HUGE

immensely *adv syn* see EVER 6

immensity *n syn* see ENORMITY 2

immerse *vb* 1 *syn* see DIP 1
 rel saturate, soak
 2 *syn* see BAPTIZE
 3 *syn* see ENGAGE 4

immersed *adj syn* see INTENT

immigrant *n syn* see EMIGRANT

imminent *adj* 1 about to take place < their departure is *imminent* >
 syn impending, proximate
 rel approaching, coming, nearing, upcoming; brewing, gathering; pending; likely, possible, probable; ineluctable, inescapable, inevasible, inevitable, unavoidable, unescapable

idiom in prospect, in store, in the cards, in the offing, in the wind, in view
con distant, far-off, remote
2 menacingly near <a thunderstorm was *imminent*>
syn lowering (*or* louring), lowery (*or* loury), menacing, overhanging, threatening
rel alarming, ominous, sinister; brewing, gathering; minatory

immingle *vb syn see* MIX 1

immix *vb syn see* MIX 1

immixture *n syn see* MIXTURE

immobile *adj* **1** *syn see* IMMOVABLE 1
ant mobile, movable
2 *syn see* STATIC

immobilize *vb syn see* PARALYZE 1

immoderate *adj* **1** *syn see* EXCESSIVE 1
ant moderate
2 *syn see* EXCESSIVE 2
ant moderate

immoderation *n syn see* EXCESS 3
ant moderation

immolate *vb syn see* SACRIFICE 1

immoral *adj* **1** *syn see* IMPURE 1
ant moral
2 *syn see* WRONG 1
ant moral

immorality *n syn see* VICE 1
ant morality

immortal *adj* **1** not subject to death <the *immortal* gods>
syn deathless, undying; *compare* EVERLASTING 1
rel endless, enduring, imperishable, indestructible, perpetual, sempiternal, timeless
con ephemeral, evanescent, fleeting, fugitive, passing, short-lived, transient, transitory
ant mortal
2 *syn see* EVERLASTING 1

immortality *n syn see* ETERNITY 2
ant mortality

immortalize *vb syn see* PERPETUATE

immotile *adj syn see* IMMOVABLE 1
ant motile

immotive *adj syn see* IMMOVABLE 1

immovable *adj* **1** incapable of moving or being moved <an *immovable* rock>
syn fixed, immobile, immotile, immotive, irremovable, ‖sitfast, steadfast, unmovable
rel adamant, fast, rooted, stable, stationary, stuck, unmoving, unyielding
con portable, removable, transferable, transportable
ant movable
2 *syn see* INFLEXIBLE 3

immunity *n syn see* EXEMPTION
ant susceptibility

immure *vb* **1** *syn see* ENCLOSE 1
2 *syn see* IMPRISON

immusical *adj syn see* DISSONANT 1
ant musical

immutable *adj syn see* INFLEXIBLE 3
ant mutable

imp *n* **1** a small demon, devil, or wicked spirit <the *imps* of hell>
syn deviling, devilkin

rel elf, gnome, goblin, gremlin, ‖hob, hobgoblin, kobold, ouph, pixie, puck, sprite, troll
2 *syn see* URCHIN

impact *n* a forcible or enforced contact between two or more things <a crater formed by the *impact* of a meteorite>
syn appulse, blow, bump, clash, collision, concussion, crash, impingement, jar, jolt, jounce, percussion, shock, smash, wallop
rel brunt; buffet, hit, pound, punch, rap, slap, smiting, strike, stroke; bounce, quake, quiver, rock, shake, tremble, tremor; encounter, meeting

impair *vb syn see* INJURE 1
rel sap, undermine, weaken
con ameliorate, better
ant improve; repair

impaired *adj syn see* DAMAGED

impale *vb* to pierce or fix with or as if with something pointed <an insect *impaled* on a pin>
syn lance, skewer, skiver, spear, spike, spit, transfix, transpierce
rel perforate, prick, punch, puncture, stab

impalpable *adj* **1** *syn see* IMPERCEPTIBLE
ant palpable
2 *syn see* FINE 2

imparity *n syn see* DISPARITY
ant parity

impart *vb syn see* COMMUNICATE 1

impartial *adj syn see* FAIR 4
ant partial

impartially *adv syn see* EVENLY 2

impassable *adj* **1** not allowing passage <an *impassable* barrier>
syn impenetrable, impermeable, impervious, unpierceable
con penetrable, permeable, pervious
ant passable
2 *syn see* INSUPERABLE

impasse *n* **1** *syn see* DEAD END
2 *syn see* PREDICAMENT

impassible *adj syn see* INSENSIBLE 5
rel cold, emotionless, passionless, unemotional, unfeeling; inert, unresponsive
ant passible

impassioned *adj* actuated by or showing intense feeling <*impassioned* oratory>
syn ardent, blazing, burning, dithyrambic, fervent, fervid, fiery, flaming, glowing, hot-blooded, overheated, passionate, perfervid, red-hot, torrid, white-hot
rel feverish, fierce, furious, intense, vehement, violent; deep, profound, warm, zealous; gushing, gushy, maudlin, melodramatic, mushy, overemotional, romantic, sentimental
con cold, cool, dispassionate, frigid, icy, unemotional; objective
ant unimpassioned

impassive *adj* **1** unresponsive to what might normally excite interest or emotion <*impassive* endurance of pain>
syn apathetic, dry, matter-of-fact, phlegmatic, stoic, stolid
rel calm, cold, cool; collected, composed, dispassionate, emotionless, imperturbable, inexcitable, unexcitable, unflappable; inexpressive, reserved, reticent, taciturn, unemotional, unexpressive; bovine, placid, passionless, spiritless, unconcerned, wooden; callous, hardened, indurated,

insensible; cold-blooded, coldhearted, heartless

con compassionate, sympathetic, tender, warm, warmhearted

ant responsive

2 *syn* see INSUSCEPTIBLE

impassivity *n syn* see APATHY 1

impatient *adj* 1 lacking power to endure hardship, distress, or opposition < married to an *impatient* self-centered man >

syn chafing, fretful, unpatient

rel abrupt, hasty, headlong, impetuous; anxious, edgy, itchy, nervous; irascible, irritable

idiom all of a stew

con enduring, forbearing, tolerant; self-controlled, Spartan, stoic

ant patient

2 *syn* see INTOLERANT 1

rel demanding, harsh

3 *syn* see EAGER

ant patient

impeach *vb syn* see ACCUSE

impeccable *adj* 1 absolutely correct and beyond criticism < *impeccable* manners >

syn errorless, exquisite, faultless, flawless, immaculate, irreproachable

rel accurate, clean, correct, exact, nice, perfect, precise, right; infallible, unerring

con defective, deficient, faulty; blameworthy, censurable, criticizable, culpable; cursory, shallow, superficial, uncritical

ant peccant

2 *syn* see PERFECT 2

impecunious *adj syn* see POOR 1

ant affluent; flush

impecuniousness *n syn* see POVERTY 1

ant affluence; flushness

impedance *n syn* see ENCUMBRANCE

impede *vb syn* see HINDER

rel discomfit, disconcert, embarrass, faze, rattle

ant aid, assist

impediment *n* 1 *syn* see ENCUMBRANCE

ant aid, assistance

2 *syn* see OBSTACLE

impel *vb syn* see MOVE 5

rel compel, constrain, force; foment, incite, instigate; goad, spur; inspire, motivate

con check, curb, inhibit

ant restrain

impend *vb syn* see LOOM 2

impending *adj syn* see IMMINENT 1

impenetrable *adj* 1 *syn* see IMPASSABLE 1

rel firm, solid, substantial

ant penetrable

2 *syn* see INCOMPREHENSIBLE 1

ant penetrable

3 *syn* see MYSTERIOUS

impenetrate *vb syn* see PERMEATE

impenitent *adj syn* see REMORSELESS

ant penitent

imperative *adj* 1 *syn* see MASTERFUL 1

rel bidding, commanding, ordering; harsh, stern

con begging, entreating, imploring; lenient, mild, soft

2 *syn* see PRESSING

rel acute, critical, crucial

3 *syn* see ESSENTIAL 4

rel basic, fundamental; claimed, demanded, exacted

4 *syn* see MANDATORY

imperceptible *adj* incapable of being apprehended by the senses or intellect < *imperceptible* changes in temperature >

syn impalpable, imponderable, inappreciable, indiscernible, insensible, intangible, invisible, unapparent, unappreciable, undiscernible, unobservable, unperceivable

rel faint, inconspicuous, indistinct, indistinguishable, insignificant, obscure, undistinguishable, unnoticeable, vague; ephemeral, evanescent, fugitive, momentary; slight, trivial

con apparent, appreciable, discernible, observable, palpable, ponderable, sensible, visible

ant perceptible, perceivable

imperceptive *adj* lacking perception or insight < *imperceptive* criticism >

syn impercipient, unperceiving, unperceptive

rel unappreciative, undiscerning, unobservant; cursory, shallow, slapdash, superficial

con astute, discerning, discriminating, judicious, perspicacious; delicate, nice, refined, sensitive, subtle

ant perceiving, perceptive, percipient

impercipient *adj syn* see IMPERCEPTIVE

ant perceiving, perceptive, percipient

imperfect *adj syn* see FAULTY

ant perfect

imperfection *n* an instance of failure to reach a standard of excellence or perfection < watch for *imperfections* in the cloth >

syn deficiency, demerit, fault, shortcoming, sin

rel blemish, defect, flaw; failing, foible, frailty

ant perfection

imperial *adj syn* see MASTERFUL 1

imperil *vb syn* see ENDANGER

imperious *adj syn* see MASTERFUL 1

rel heavy-handed, oppressive, strict, stringent; absolute, arbitrary

con considerate, easy, gentle, kindly

2 *syn* see MANDATORY

imperishable *adj syn* see INDESTRUCTIBLE

impermanent *adj syn* see TRANSIENT

ant permanent

impermeable *adj syn* see IMPASSABLE 1

ant permeable

impersonal *adj* 1 *syn* see NEUTRAL

2 *syn* see FAIR 4

3 *syn* see MATTER-OF-FACT 3

impersonate *vb syn* see ACT 1

impersonator *n syn* see ACTOR 1

impertinence *n syn* see INSOLENCE

impertinent *adj* 1 *syn* see IRRELEVANT

ant pertinent

2 going beyond what is proper or acceptable in thrusting oneself into the affairs of others < *impertinent* interference with her sister's family >

syn busy, intrusive, meddlesome, ‖nebby, obtrusive, officious, polypragmatic

rel arrogant, bold, brash, brazen, fresh, impudent, pert, presumptuous, saucy; inquisitive, interfering, meddling, nosy, prying; offensive, rude

con decent, decorous, proper, seemly; reserved, reticent, silent; apposite, germane, pertinent, relevant
3 *syn* see RUDE 6
4 *syn* see INSOLENT 2

imperturbability *n syn* see EQUANIMITY
imperturbable *adj syn* see COOL 2
rel complacent, self-satisfied, smug; unaffected, unmoved, untouched
con discomfited, disconcerted, fazed, rattled; irascible, splenetic, testy
ant choleric; touchy

impervious *adj syn* see IMPASSABLE 1
ant pervious

impervious *adj syn* see IMPASSABLE 1
ant pervious

impetuous *adj syn* see PRECIPITATE 1
rel spontaneous; restive; ardent, fervid, impassioned, passionate
con equable, even, steady; advised, considered, deliberate, planned, premeditated

impetuously *adv syn* see PELL-MELL
impetus *n syn* see STIMULUS
impignorate *vb syn* see PAWN
impingement *n syn* see IMPACT
impious *adj* 1 lacking reverence for holy or sacred matters <made *impious* remarks about the church>
syn irreverent, irreverential, profane, ungodly, unhallowed, unholy
rel godless, iconoclastic, irreligious, sacrilegious, scandalous, undevout
con devout, godly, religious, spiritual
ant pious
2 lacking due respect (as toward one's parents) <an *impious* son>
syn unduteous, undutiful
rel disobedient, froward, unfaithful, wayward; contrary, perverse, wrongheaded
con duteous, dutiful

impish *adj syn* see PLAYFUL 1
rel arch, pert, saucy; flippant, fresh, giddy; casual, devil-may-care, free and easy, offhand

impishness *n syn* see MISCHIEVOUSNESS
implacable *adj syn* see GRIM 3
con peaceable, tractable; kindly, tolerant
ant placable

implant *vb* to introduce into the mind <*implanted* worthy ideals in their children>
syn inculcate, infix, inseminate, instill
rel imbue, infuse, ingrain, inoculate, leaven, root; impenetrate, impregnate, penetrate, permeate, pervade, saturate; inspire

implausible *adj* not plausible or readily believable <an *implausible* explanation>
syn flimsy, improbable, inconceivable, incredible, thick, thin, unbelievable, unconceivable, unconvincing, unsubstantial, weak; *compare* TENUOUS 3
rel doubtful, dubious, fishy; problematic, puzzling, suspect
idiom a bit thick
con meaty, pithy; solid, sound, substantial; believable, conceivable, credible; likely, probable
ant plausible

implement *n* a usually relatively simple device for performing a mechanical or manual operation <spades, hoes, and other gardener's *implements*>
syn instrument, tool, utensil
rel apparatus, appliance; contrivance, device; contraption, gadget

implement *vb* 1 *syn* see FULFILL 1
2 *syn* see ENFORCE
rel actualize, materialize, realize

implemental *adj syn* see INSTRUMENTAL
impliable *adj syn* see STIFF 1
ant pliable

implicate *vb syn* see INVOLVE 1
rel affect, concern; incriminate
con absolve, acquit, exculpate, exonerate

implicated *adj syn* see INTERESTED
implication *n syn* see ASSOCIATION 4
implicit *adj* 1 *syn* see TACIT 1
idiom taken for granted
ant explicit
2 being such in essential character <our *implicit* freedom is better than your nominal liberty>
syn constructive, practical, virtual
rel absolute, complete, unqualified, wholehearted; genuine, real
ant spelled out

implied *adj syn* see TACIT 1
imploration *n syn* see PRAYER
implore *vb syn* see BEG
imply *vb* 1 *syn* see POINT 2
2 *syn* see SUGGEST 1
con state; express; affirm, assert, declare

impolite *adj syn* see RUDE 6
ant polite

impolitic *adj* 1 *syn* see UNWISE
ant politic
2 *syn* see INADVISABLE
ant politic
3 *syn* see TACTLESS

imponderable *adj syn* see IMPERCEPTIBLE
ant appreciable, ponderable

imponderous *adj syn* see LIGHT 1
ant ponderous

import *vb* 1 *syn* see MEAN 2
2 *syn* see MATTER

import *n* 1 *syn* see MEANING 1
rel construction, interpretation
2 *syn* see IMPORTANCE
rel value, worth; design, intent, object, objective, purpose; emphasis, stress

importance *n* the quality or state of being of notable worth or influence <persons of national and worldwide *importance*>
syn consequence, import, magnitude, moment, momentousness, pith, significance, ||signification, weight, weightiness
rel conspicuousness; distinction, eminence, mark, prominence, salience; notability, note, noteworthiness, reputation, standing; substance, value, worth, worthiness; gravity, seriousness
con inconsequence, insignificance, paltriness, pettiness, triviality
ant unimportance

important *adj* 1 marked by or indicative of notable worth or consequence <an *important* discovery> <his manner was grave and *important*>
syn big, consequential, considerable, material, meaningful, momentous, significant, substantial, weighty

---

syn synonym(s)   *rel* related word(s)
ant antonym(s)   *con* contrasted word(s)
idiom idiomatic equivalent(s)
|| use limited; if in doubt, see a dictionary

rel conspicuous, distinctive, exceptional, impressive, marked, memorable, notable, noteworthy, noticeable, outstanding, prominent, remarkable, salient, unusual; essential; valuable, worthwhile; worthy; effective, potent, powerful, telling; bigtime, first-class, first-rate, front-page, topnotch; distinguished, eminent, famous, noted

con inconsiderable, little, minor, paltry, petty, slight, trivial

ant unimportant

2 *syn* see POMPOUS 1

importunate *adj syn* see PRESSING

rel persevering, persistent; dogged, pertinacious

importune *vb syn* see BEG

impose *vb* 1 *syn* see DICTATE

rel charge, command, enjoin, order; demand, exact, require; compel, constrain, oblige

2 *syn* see LEVY

3 *syn* see INFLICT 2

4 to force another to accept < *imposed* all the dirty jobs on her sister>

syn foist, wish; *compare* FOIST 3, INFLICT 2

rel burden, lade, saddle; fob, fob off, palm off

idiom take advantage of

5 to take usually unwarranted advantage < did not wish to *impose* by turning up unannounced>

syn infringe, intrude, obtrude, presume

rel encroach, trespass

idiom make free, take liberties

impose (on *or* upon) *vb syn* see EXPLOIT 2

imposing *adj syn* see GRAND 1

rel impressive, moving; imperial, regal

ant unimposing

2 *syn* see PRETENTIOUS 3

impossible *adj* 1 not capable of being realized or attained < *impossible* goals>

syn impracticable, impractical, infeasible, irrealizable, unattainable, unfeasible, unrealizable, unworkable

rel absurd, inexecutable, unobtainable, unreasonable, unthinkable

idiom out of the question

con attainable, feasible, realizable; practicable, practical, rational, reasonable

ant possible

2 *syn* see HOPELESS 2

impost *n syn* see TAX 1

impostor *n* one who passes himself off as something or someone he is not < the presumed heir was discovered to be an *impostor*>

syn fake, faker, fraud, humbug, phony, pretender; *compare* CHARLATAN

rel imitator, mimic; beguiler, deceiver, misleader; cheat, pettifogger, shyster, trickster; hypocrite; charlatan, mountebank, quack; bluffer, dissembler, fourflusher, shammer

idiom wolf in sheep's clothing

imposture *n* the act, practice, or an instance of imposing on another by use of an assumed character or name < his claims were based on *imposture*>

syn cheat, counterfeit, deceit, deception, fake, flam, flimflam, fraud, gyp, hoax, humbug, mare's nest, phony, put-on, ||rig, sell, sham, spoof, swindle

rel copy, imitation; fabrication, forgery; artifice, feint, gambit, maneuver, ploy, ruse, sleight, stratagem, trick, wile; makebelieve, pretense, pretension

impotent *adj* 1 *syn* see POWERLESS

rel crippled, disabled, enfeebled

con able, capable, competent

ant potent

2 *syn* see WEAK 4

con forceful, powerful, puissant, strenuous, vigorous

ant potent

3 *syn* see STERILE 1

impoverish *vb* 1 *syn* see DEPLETE

ant enrich

2 *syn* see RUIN 3

impoverished *adj syn* see POOR 1

impoverishment *n syn* see POVERTY 1

impracticable *adj* 1 *syn* see IMPOSSIBLE 1

ant feasible, practicable

2 incapable of being successfully used or turned to account < a route through the mountains that is *impracticable* in winter>

syn impractical, nonfunctional, unfunctional, unserviceable, unusable, unworkable, useless

rel disadvantageous, unacceptable, undesirable, unsatisfactory; awkward, inconvenient, troublesome

con functional, practical, serviceable, usable, useful, workable

ant practicable

impractical *adj* 1 incapable of dealing prudently with practical matters < a very *impractical* person whose checkbook never balanced>

syn ivory-tower, ivory-towered, ivorytowerish, nonrealistic, unpractical, unrealistic, viewy

rel idealistic, otherworldly, quixotic, romantic, starry-eyed, visionary

con commonsensible, commonsensical, realistic, sensible, worldly-wise

ant practical

2 *syn* see IMPRACTICABLE 2

ant practical

3 *syn* see IMPOSSIBLE 1

imprecate *vb syn* see SWEAR 3

imprecation *n* 1 *syn* see BLASPHEMY 1

2 *syn* see PRAYER

3 *syn* see CURSE 1

con blessing

impregnable *adj syn* see INVINCIBLE 1

rel safe, secure; defended, guarded, protected, safeguarded, shielded

con exposed, open, susceptible

impregnate *vb* 1 *syn* see PERMEATE

rel inoculate, leaven

2 *syn* see SOAK 1

impress *vb* 1 *syn* see ENGRAVE 2

2 *syn* see AFFECT

rel enthuse, electrify, thrill; excite, galvanize, pique, provoke, stimulate

idiom make (*or* leave) one's mark

3 to fix in the mind or memory by emphasis or repetition < the speaker *impressed* his principal thesis upon his audience>

syn drive, grave, hammer, pound, stamp

rel establish, fix, set

idiom drive home to one, fix in one's mind, get into one's head

impress *n syn* see IMPRESSION 1

impressible *adj syn* see SENTIENT 3

impression *n* 1 the perceptible trace or traces left by pressure <the *impression* made by a die>
syn impress, imprint, indentation, print, stamp
rel dent, dint, hollow; trace, track, vestige; mark, sign
2 *syn* see IDEA
3 *syn* see EDITION

impressionable *adj syn* see SENTIENT 3
rel affectable, influenceable

impressive *adj* 1 *syn* see MOVING 2
rel august, grand, imposing, majestic, noble; splendid, superb; arresting, notable, striking
ant unimpressive
2 *syn* see GRAND 2

imprint *vb syn* see ENGRAVE 2

imprint *n syn* see IMPRESSION 1

imprison *vb* to shut up closely so that escape is impossible or unlikely <the offender was quickly sentenced and *imprisoned* >
syn bastille, confine, constrain, immure, incarcerate, intern, jail, jug, ||prison, ||quod
rel circumscribe, limit, restrict; check, curb, restrain
idiom put under lock and key
con free, liberate, release

improbable *adj* 1 not likely to be true or to occur <the immediate success of their plan is *improbable* >
syn doubtful, dubious, questionable, unlikely
ant probable
2 syn see IMPLAUSIBLE

impromptu *n syn* see IMPROVISATION

impromptu *adj syn* see EXTEMPORANEOUS
rel prompt, quick

improper *adj* 1 unsuited to the circumstances or the occasion <wore quite *improper* dress for such a formal reception>
syn ill-timed, inadmissible, inappropriate, inapt, inept, intempestive, malapropos, unapt, unbecoming, unbefitting, uncomely, undue, unfitting, unseasonable, unseemly, unsuitable, untimely
rel infelicitous, unhappy; inapplicable, inapposite; fresh, impertinent, sassy; crude, gauche, tactless
idiom out of place, out of season
con apposite, appropriate, apropos, apt, becoming, befitting, felicitous, fitting, germane, happy, opportune, pat, pertinent, seasonable, suitable, timely, well-timed
ant proper
2 *syn* see INDECOROUS
rel informal, unceremonious, unconventional
con correct, right
ant proper

impropriety *n* 1 the quality or state of being improper (as in social behavior) <was shocked by the *impropriety* of their actions>

syn incorrectness, indecorousness, indecorum, inelegance, unbecomingness, unmeetness, unseemliness, untowardness
rel inadmissibility, objectionableness, unacceptableness
con becomingness, decency, decorousness, decorum, meetness
ant propriety, seemliness
2 *syn* see FAUX PAS *compare* ERROR 2
3 *syn* see BARBARISM

improve *vb* 1 to make more acceptable or bring nearer to some standard <studied hard to *improve* his chances of success>
syn ameliorate, amend, better, help, meliorate
rel cultivate, develop, perfect; correct, emend, rectify, reform, remedy; edit, revise; enhance, enrich, refine, rub up, upgrade
con diminish, downgrade, lessen, lower
2 *syn* see ILLUMINATE 2
3 to grow or become better (as in health or well-being) <the invalid is steadily *improving* >
syn ameliorate, convalesce, gain, look up, mend, perk (up), recuperate
rel advance, better, progress; recover; rally, revive, strengthen
idiom gain ground, make progress
con decline, deteriorate, fail, flag, languish, run down, sink, weaken

improvident *adj* not foreseeing or providing for the future <an *improvident* way of life>
syn thriftless, unthrift, unthrifty
rel careless, heedless, imprudent; extravagant, prodigal, profligate, spendthrift; lavish, profuse, reckless; uneconomical, wasteful
con careful, economical, frugal, parsimonious, prudent, saving, sparing
ant provident, thrifty

improvisate *adj syn* see IMPROVISE

improvisation *n* something that is improvised <the pianist played several clever *improvisations* >
syn autoschediasm, extemporization, impromptu

improvise *vb* to perform or provide on the spur of the moment <*improvise* an excuse for being late>
syn ad-lib, extemporize, improvisate
rel concoct, contrive, devise, invent

improvised *adj syn* see EXTEMPORANEOUS

imprudent *adj* 1 *syn* see UNWISE
ant prudent
2 *syn* see INADVISABLE
ant prudent

impudence *n syn* see INSOLENCE

impudent *adj* 1 *syn* see WISE 5
2 *syn* see INSOLENT 2
3 *syn* see SHAMELESS

impugn *vb syn* see DENY 4
rel assail, attack
idiom call in (or into) question (or doubt), throw doubt on
con back, support, uphold
ant advocate; authenticate

impugnable *adj syn* see DOUBTFUL 1

impulse *n syn* see STIMULUS
rel excitant; lust, passion, urge; actuation, drive, impulsion

---

syn synonym(s)   *rel* related word(s)
ant antonym(s)   *con* contrasted word(s)
idiom idiomatic equivalent(s)
|| use limited; if in doubt, see a dictionary

inapproachable *adj syn see* INACCESSIBLE
  ant approachable

inappropriate *adj* 1 *syn see* UNFIT 1
  rel indecorous, unseemly; inconsonant
  con felicitous, fitting, happy, meet, proper; fit, suitable
  ant appropriate
  2 *syn see* IMPROPER 1

inapt *adj* 1 *syn see* UNFIT 1
  rel awkward, clumsy, gauche, maladroit; banal, flat, insipid, jejune
  con apposite, germane, pertinent, relevant
  ant apt
  2 *syn see* IMPROPER 1
  ant apt
  3 *syn see* UNSKILLFUL 1
  ant adept

inarguable *adj syn see* POSITIVE 3
  ant arguable

inarticulate *adj* 1 *syn see* DUMB 1
  ant articulate
  2 *syn see* TACIT 1
  3 failing to give or incapable of giving clear or effective verbal expression to one's ideas or feelings < made some *inarticulate* explanation for being late > < was completely *inarticulate* when it came to expressing affection >
  syn incoherent, maundering, tongue-tied, unvocal
  rel faltering, halting, hesitating, mumbling, stammered, stammering; blurred, indistinct
  con facile, glib, smooth
  ant articulate

inartificial *adj syn see* NATURAL 5
  ant artificial

inasmuch as *conj syn see* BECAUSE

inattentive *adj* not paying proper attention < an *inattentive* pupil dozing at his desk >
  syn inobservant, unheeding, unnoticing, unobservant, unobserving, unperceiving, unwatchful
  rel distracted, distrait, distraught; careless, heedless, thoughtless, undiscerning, unmindful, unthinking; bored, ennuyé
  ant attentive; observant

inaugural *adj syn see* FIRST 1

inaugural *n syn see* INITIATION

inaugurate *vb* 1 *syn see* INITIATE 3
  2 *syn see* BEGIN 1
  3 *syn see* INTRODUCE 3

inauguration *n syn see* INITIATION

inauspicious *adj syn see* OMINOUS
  ant auspicious
  2 *syn see* EVIL 6

in between *prep syn see* BETWEEN 2

inborn *adj* 1 *syn see* INNATE 1
  ant acquired
  2 *syn see* INHERENT

inbred *adj syn see* INHERENT

in brief *adv syn see* BRIEFLY

incalculable *adj* 1 being great beyond calculation < *incalculable* damage >
  syn immeasurable, inestimable, measureless, uncountable, unmeasurable, unmeasured, unreckonable

  rel countless, innumerable, unnumbered, untold; boundless, enormous, infinite, limitless, vast
  con minimal, slight, trivial
  ant infinitesimal
  2 *syn see* UNCERTAIN 1
  ant calculable

in camera *adv syn see* SECRETLY

incandescent *adj syn see* BRIGHT 1

incantation *n* 1 *syn see* SPELL
  2 *syn see* MAGIC 1

incapability *n syn see* INABILITY
  ant capability

incapable *adj* 1 *syn see* UNFIT 2
  ant capable
  2 *syn see* INEFFICIENT 2
  ant capable

incapacitate *vb* 1 *syn see* PARALYZE 1
  2 *syn see* DISQUALIFY
  ant capacitate

incapacity *n syn see* INABILITY
  ant capacity

incarcerate *vb syn see* IMPRISON

incarnadine *vb syn see* REDDEN 1

incarnate *vb syn see* EMBODY 1

incarnation *n syn see* EMBODIMENT

incautious *adj* 1 lacking in caution < made an *incautious* prediction >
  syn unalert, unguarded, unvigilant, unwary, unwatchful; *compare* CARELESS 1
  rel imprudent, indiscreet, injudicious; bold, brash, impetuous, rash, reckless; neglectful, negligent, regardless, thoughtless, unmindful; hasty
  idiom caught napping, off one's guard
  con careful, circumspect, judicious, wary, watchful; discreet, judicious, prudent; sensible, thoughtful, wise
  ant cautious
  2 *syn see* RASH 1
  ant cautious
  3 *syn see* IRRESPONSIBLE

incendiary *n* a person who deliberately and unlawfully sets fire to a building or other property < a fire set by an *incendiary* >
  syn arsonist, firebug, torch
  rel pyromaniac

incendiary *adj syn see* INFLAMMATORY

incense *n* 1 *syn see* FRAGRANCE
  2 *syn see* FLATTERY

incense *vb syn see* ANGER 1
  ant placate

incentive *n syn see* STIMULUS

inception *n syn see* SOURCE
  con closing, completion, conclusion
  ant termination

inceptive *adj syn see* INITIAL 1
  ant terminal

incertitude *n syn see* UNCERTAINTY
  ant certitude

incessant *adj* 1 *syn see* CONTINUAL
  ant intermittent

inchoate *adj* 1 *syn see* FORMLESS
  2 *syn see* INCOHERENT 1

incident *n syn see* OCCURRENCE

incident *adj* 1 *syn see* CONCOMITANT
  ant essential, fundamental
  2 *syn see* RELATED

incidental *adj syn see* ACCIDENTAL
  ant essential

incidentally *adv* 1 by chance < in this discussion grave questions were brought up *incidentally* >

---

syn synonym(s)   *rel* related word(s)
ant antonym(s)   *con* contrasted word(s)
idiom idiomatic equivalent(s)

‖ use limited; if in doubt, see a dictionary

impulsive *adj syn* see SPONTANEOUS
rel abrupt, hasty, headlong, impetuous, precipitate, sudden
con considered, designed, premeditated; calculating, cautious, circumspect
ant deliberate

impulsiveness *n syn* see ABANDON 2

impunity *n syn* see EXEMPTION

impure *adj* 1 morally or mentally unclean < *impure* thoughts >
syn dirty, immoral, unchaste, unclean, uncleanly
rel belowstairs, carnal, immodest, indecent, indecorous, lascivious, lewd, lustful, prurient, scarlet, sensual; filthy, vile
con chaste, clean, cleanly, decent, decorous, immaculate, modest, virtuous; moral
ant pure
2 *syn* see DIRTY 1
3 made unfit for ceremonial purposes < altars overturned and sacred vessels made *impure* by the touch of profane hands >
syn common, defiled, desecrated, polluted, profaned, unclean
rel unhallowed, unholy
con clean, consecrated, undefiled
ant pure
4 *syn* see UNREFINED 3

impute *vb syn* see ASCRIBE
rel accuse, indict; adduce; hint, insinuate, intimate

in *adj syn* see STYLISH

in *n syn* see PULL 2

inability *n* lack of sufficient power, resources, or capacity to perform < suffered from an *inability* to make quick decisions >
syn inadequacy, incapability, incapacity, incompetence, ineffectiveness, ineffectualness, inefficacy
rel inadeptness, inaptitude, inaptness, inefficiency, ineptitude, ineptness
con adequacy, capability, capacity; competence, efficiency
ant ability

inaccessible *adj* not capable of being achieved < an *inaccessible* goal >
syn inapproachable, unapproachable, unattainable, un-come-at-able, ungetatable, unobtainable, unreachable
rel distant, far, faraway, far-off, out-of-the-way, remote
ant accessible

inaccurate *adj syn* see FALSE 1
con right, true
ant accurate

inaction *n* lack of action or activity < the delay was due to the committee's *inaction* >
syn inactiveness, inactivity
rel drift, idleness, indolence, inertness, lethargy, quiescence, slackness, slothfulness, torpidity
con activeness, activity

inactive *adj* not characterized by or engaged in usual or normal activity < forced by illness to lead an *inactive* life >
syn asleep, idle, inert, passive, quiet, sleepy
rel abeyant, dormant, inoperative, latent, quiescent; do-nothing, indolent, lethargic, lymphatic, slack, slothful, sluggish, torpid; motionless, sedentary, static; disengaged,

jobless, unemployed, unoccupied, unworking; ossified
con busy, employed, engaged, occupied; energetic, strenuous, vigorous; animated, brisk, lively
ant active

inactiveness *n syn* see INACTION

inactivity *n syn* see INACTION
ant activity

in addition *adv syn* see AGAIN 4

inadept *adj syn* see UNSKILLFUL 1
ant adept

inadequacy *n* 1 *syn* see INABILITY
2 *syn* see FAILURE 3
ant adequacy

inadequate *adj* 1 *syn* see DEFICIENT 1
ant adequate
2 *syn* see SHORT 3
ant adequate
3 *syn* see MEAGER
ant adequate
4 *syn* see WEAK 4
ant adequate

inadmissible *adj* 1 *syn* see IMPROPER 1
2 *syn* see OBJECTIONABLE
ant admissible

in advance *adv syn* see BEFORE 1

in advance of *prep* 1 *syn* see BEFORE 1
2 *syn* see UNTIL

inadvertent *adj* 1 *syn* see CARELESS 1
ant advertent
2 *syn* see UNINTENTIONAL

inadvisable *adj* not likely to have a satisfactory outcome < it seemed *inadvisable* to go any farther because of threatening weather >
syn ill-advised, impolitic, imprudent, inexpedient, unadvisable, unexpedient
rel careless, inappropriate, incautious, rash, undesirable, unsensible; foolish, indiscreet, pointless, unwise; foolhardy, harebrained
con expedient, judicious, politic, prudent, sensible, wise
ant advisable

in all *adv syn* see ALTOGETHER 2

in all probability *adv syn* see PRESUMABLY

inalterable *adj syn* see INFLEXIBLE 3
ant alterable

inamorata *n* 1 *syn* see GIRL FRIEND 2
2 *syn* see MISTRESS

inamorato *n syn* see BOYFRIEND 2

in and out *adv syn* see THOROUGHLY 2

inane *adj syn* see INSIPID 3
rel asinine, fatuous, foolish, silly; idle, vain; blank, empty, hollow
con expressive, meaningful, pregnant, significant, weighty
ant deep, profound

inanimate *adj* 1 *syn* see INSENSATE 1
ant animate
2 *syn* see DEAD 1
ant animate; living

inanity *n syn* see FOOLISHNESS

inapplicable *adj syn* see IRRELEVANT
ant applicable

inapposite *adj syn* see IRRELEVANT
ant apposite

inappreciable *adj* 1 *syn* see IMPERCEPTIBLE
ant appreciable
2 *syn* see MEAGER

impress *n syn see* IMPRESSION 1

impressible *adj syn see* SENTIENT 3

impression *n* **1** the perceptible trace or traces left by pressure <the *impression* made by a die>
syn impress, imprint, indentation, print, stamp
rel dent, dint, hollow; trace, track, vestige; mark, sign
2 *syn see* IDEA
3 *syn see* EDITION

impressionable *adj syn see* SENTIENT 3
rel affectable, influenceable

impressive *adj* **1** *syn see* MOVING 2
rel august, grand, imposing, majestic, noble; splendid, superb; arresting, notable, striking
ant unimpressive
2 *syn see* GRAND 2

imprint *vb syn see* ENGRAVE 2

imprint *n syn see* IMPRESSION 1

imprison *vb* to shut up closely so that escape is impossible or unlikely <the offender was quickly sentenced and *imprisoned*>
syn bastille, confine, constrain, immure, incarcerate, intern, jail, jug, ‖prison, ‖quod
rel circumscribe, limit, restrict; check, curb, restrain
idiom put under lock and key
con free, liberate, release

improbable *adj* **1** not likely to be true or to occur <the immediate success of their plan is *improbable*>
syn doubtful, dubious, questionable, unlikely
ant probable
2 *syn see* IMPLAUSIBLE

impromptu *n syn see* IMPROVISATION

impromptu *adj syn see* EXTEMPORANEOUS
rel prompt, quick

improper *adj* **1** unsuited to the circumstances or the occasion <wore quite im*proper* dress for such a formal reception>
syn ill-timed, inadmissible, inappropriate, inapt, inept, intempestive, malapropos, unapt, unbecoming, unbefitting, uncomely, undue, unfitting, unseasonable, unseemly, unsuitable, untimely
rel infelicitous, unhappy; inapplicable, inapposite; fresh, impertinent, sassy; crude, gauche, tactless
idiom out of place, out of season
con apposite, appropriate, apropos, apt, becoming, befitting, felicitous, fitting, germane, happy, opportune, pat, pertinent, seasonable, suitable, timely, well-timed
ant proper
2 *syn see* INDECOROUS
rel informal, unceremonious, unconventional
con correct, right
ant proper

impropriety *n* **1** the quality or state of being improper (as in social behavior) <was shocked by the *impropriety* of their actions>

syn incorrectness, indecorousness, indecorum, inelegance, unbecomingness, unmeetness, unseemliness, untowardness
rel inadmissibility, objectionableness, unacceptableness
con becomingness, decency, decorousness, decorum, meetness
ant propriety, seemliness
2 *syn see* FAUX PAS *compare* ERROR 2
3 *syn see* BARBARISM

improve *vb* **1** to make more acceptable or bring nearer to some standard <studied hard to *improve* his chances of success>
syn ameliorate, amend, better, help, meliorate
rel cultivate, develop, perfect; correct, emend, rectify, reform, remedy; edit, revise; enhance, enrich, refine, rub up, upgrade
con diminish, downgrade, lessen, lower
2 *syn see* ILLUMINATE 2
3 to grow or become better (as in health or well-being) <the invalid is steadily *improving*>
syn ameliorate, convalesce, gain, look up, mend, perk (up), recuperate
rel advance, better, progress; recover; rally, revive, strengthen
idiom gain ground, make progress
con decline, deteriorate, fail, flag, languish, run down, sink, weaken

improvident *adj* not foreseeing or providing for the future <an *improvident* way of life>
syn thriftless, unthrift, unthrifty
rel careless, heedless, imprudent; extravagant, prodigal, profligate, spendthrift; lavish, profuse, reckless; uneconomical, wasteful
con careful, economical, frugal, parsimonious, prudent, saving, sparing
ant provident, thrifty

improvise *vb syn see* IMPROVISE

improvisation *n* something that is improvised <the pianist played several clever *improvisations*>
syn autoschediasm, extemporization, impromptu

improvise *vb* to perform or provide on the spur of the moment <*improvise* an excuse for being late>
syn ad-lib, extemporize, improvisate
rel concoct, contrive, devise, invent

improvised *adj syn see* EXTEMPORANEOUS

imprudent *adj* **1** *syn see* UNWISE
ant prudent
2 *syn see* INADVISABLE
ant prudent

impudence *n syn see* INSOLENCE

impudent *adj* **1** *syn see* WISE 5
2 *syn see* INSOLENT 2
3 *syn see* SHAMELESS

impugn *vb syn see* DENY 4
rel assail, attack
idiom call in (*or* into) question (*or* doubt), throw doubt on
con back, support, uphold
ant advocate; authenticate

impugnable *adj syn see* DOUBTFUL 1

impulse *n syn see* STIMULUS
rel excitant; lust, passion, urge; actuation, drive, impulsion

---

syn synonym(s)   *rel* related word(s)
ant antonym(s)   *con* contrasted word(s)
idiom idiomatic equivalent(s)
‖ use limited; if in doubt, see a dictionary

rel conspicuous, distinctive, exceptional, impressive, marked, memorable, notable, noteworthy, noticeable, outstanding, prominent, remarkable, salient, essential; valuable, worthwhile; worthy; effective, potent, powerful, telling; big-time, first-class, first-rate, front-page, top-notch; distinguished, eminent, famous, noted

con inconsiderable, little, minor, paltry, petty, slight, trivial

ant unimportant

2 *syn* see POMPOUS 1

importunate *adj syn* see PRESSING

rel persevering, persistent; dogged, pertinacious

importune *vb syn* see BEG

impose *vb* 1 *syn* see DICTATE

rel charge, command, enjoin, order; demand, exact, require; compel, constrain, oblige

2 *syn* see LEVY

3 *syn* see INFLICT 2

4 to force another to accept < *imposed* all the dirty jobs on her sister >

syn foist, wish; *compare* FOIST 3, INFLICT 2

rel burden, lade, saddle; fob, fob off, palm off

idiom take advantage of

5 to take usually unwarranted advantage < did not wish to *impose* by turning up unannounced >

syn infringe, intrude, obtrude, presume

rel encroach, trespass

idiom make free, take liberties

impose (on *or* **upon)** *vb syn* see EXPLOIT 2

imposing *adj syn* see GRAND 1

rel impressive, moving; imperial, regal

ant unimposing

2 *syn* see PRETENTIOUS 3

impossible *adj* 1 not capable of being realized or attained < *impossible* goals >

syn impracticable, impractical, infeasible, irrealizable, unattainable, unfeasible, unrealizable, unworkable

rel absurd, inexecutable, unobtainable, unreasonable, unthinkable

idiom out of the question

con attainable, feasible, realizable; practicable, practical, rational, reasonable

ant possible

2 *syn* see HOPELESS 2

impost *n syn* see TAX 1

impostor *n* one who passes himself off as something or someone he is not < the presumed heir was discovered to be an *impostor* >

syn fake, faker, fraud, humbug, phony, pretender; *compare* CHARLATAN

rel imitator, mimic; beguiler, deceiver, misleader; cheat, pettifogger, shyster, trickster; hypocrite; charlatan, mountebank, quack; bluffer, dissembler, four-flusher, shammer

idiom wolf in sheep's clothing

imposture *n* the act, practice, or an instance of imposing on another by use of an assumed character or name < his claims were based on *imposture* >

syn cheat, counterfeit, deceit, deception, fake, flam, flimflam, fraud, gyp, hoax, humbug, mare's nest, phony, put-on, ‖rig, sell, sham, spoof, swindle

rel copy, imitation; fabrication, forgery; artifice, feint, gambit, maneuver, ploy, ruse, sleight, stratagem, trick, wile; make-believe, pretense, pretension

impotent *adj* 1 *syn* see POWERLESS

rel crippled, disabled, enfeebled

con able, capable, competent

ant potent

2 *syn* see WEAK 4

con forceful, powerful, puissant, strenuous, vigorous

ant potent

3 *syn* see STERILE 1

impoverish *vb* 1 *syn* see DEPLETE

ant enrich

2 *syn* see RUIN 3

impoverished *adj syn* see POOR 1

impoverishment *n. syn* see POVERTY 1

impracticable *adj* 1 *syn* see IMPOSSIBLE 1

ant feasible, practicable

2 incapable of being successfully used or turned to account < a route through the mountains that is *impracticable* in winter >

syn impractical, nonfunctional, unfunctional, unserviceable, unusable, unworkable, useless

rel disadvantageous, unacceptable, undesirable, unsatisfactory; awkward, inconvenient, troublesome

con functional, practical, serviceable, usable, useful, workable

ant practicable

impractical *adj* 1 incapable of dealing prudently with practical matters < a very *impractical* person whose checkbook never balanced >

syn ivory-tower, ivory-towered, ivory-towerish, nonrealistic, unpractical, unrealistic, viewy

rel idealistic, otherworldly, quixotic, romantic, starry-eyed, visionary

con commonsensible, commonsensical, realistic, sensible, worldly-wise

ant practical

2 *syn* see IMPRACTICABLE 2

ant practical

3 *syn* see IMPOSSIBLE 1

imprecate *vb syn* see SWEAR 3

imprecation *n* 1 *syn* see BLASPHEMY 1

2 *syn* see PRAYER

3 *syn* see CURSE 1

con blessing

impregnable *adj syn* see INVINCIBLE 1

rel safe, secure; defended, guarded, protected, safeguarded, shielded

con exposed, open, susceptible

impregnate *vb* 1 *syn* see PERMEATE

rel inoculate, leaven

2 *syn* see SOAK 1

impress *vb* 1 *syn* see ENGRAVE 2

2 *syn* see AFFECT

rel enthuse, electrify, thrill; excite, galvanize, pique, provoke, stimulate

idiom make (*or* leave) one's mark

3 to fix in the mind or memory by emphasis or repetition < the speaker *impressed* his principal thesis upon his audience >

syn drive, grave, hammer, pound, stamp

rel establish, fix, set

idiom drive home to one, fix in one's mind, get into one's head

syn accidentally, casually, fortuitously
ant deliberately
2 by way of interjection or digression < another leading industry, *incidentally*, has quadrupled its business in four years >
syn by the bye, by the way, in passing, obiter, parenthetically
idiom in the bygoing

incipient *adj syn see* INITIAL 1

incise *vb* 1 *syn see* CUT 1
2 *syn see* ENGRAVE 1

incisive *adj* having, manifesting, or suggesting a keen alertness of mind < a man well known for his *incisive* wit >
syn biting, clear-cut, crisp, cutting, ingoing, penetrating, trenchant
rel acute, drilling, keen, sharp; acerb, acerbic, caustic, mordant, scathing, slashing, tart; concise, laconic, succinct, terse
con diffuse, prolix, verbose, wordy; feeble, limp, pithless, sapless
ant unincisive

incisiveness *n syn see* EDGE 2

incitation *n syn see* STIMULUS

incite *vb* to aid or promote the activity or development of < *incite* a riot >
syn abet, foment, instigate, provoke, raise, set, set on, stir (up), whip (up)
rel forward, further, promote, stimulate; set off, trigger; agitate, solicit; encourage, motivate, motive; excite, inflame, rouse
con check, curb, discourage, inhibit, restrain; calm, quiet, subdue

incitement *n syn see* STIMULUS
ant restraint; inhibition

inciter *n syn see* INSTIGATOR

incivil *adj syn see* RUDE 6
ant civil

inclement *adj syn see* SEVERE 3
ant clement

inclination *n* 1 *syn see* LEANING 2
ant disinclination
2 *syn see* WILL 1
ant disinclination
3 *syn see* APPETITE 3
ant disinclination
4 *syn see* SLOPE

incline *vb* 1 *syn see* TEND 1
2 *syn see* SLANT 1
rel deflect, turn
3 to have an attitude toward or to influence one to take an attitude < *inclined* to believe the story > < his argument *inclined* me to share his view >
syn bend, bias, dispose, predispose; *compare* PREJUDICE 2, TEND 1
rel affect, influence, prompt, sway; drive, impel, induce, move, persuade
ant disincline, indispose
4 *syn see* DIRECT 2

incline *n syn see* SLOPE

inclined *adj* 1 *syn see* WILLING 1
ant disinclined
2 *syn see* APT 1
ant disinclined
3 sloping from the horizontal or perpendicular < cars running on an *inclined* track >
syn declivate, declivitous, inclining, leaning, oblique, pitched, pitching, sloped, sloping, tilted, tilting, tipped; *compare* DIAGONAL

rel dipping, graded, raked

inclining *n syn see* LEANING 2

inclining *adj syn see* INCLINED 3

include *vb* to possess as an integral part of a whole < the park *includes* a zoo and a botanical garden >
syn comprehend, contain, embody, embrace, encompass, have, involve, subsume, take in
rel comprise, cover, encircle, enclose, hold; number; admit, receive
con leave out, omit; preclude, reject; debar; eliminate, rule out
ant exclude

inclusive *adj* 1 *syn see* ALL-AROUND 2
2 *syn see* ENCYCLOPEDIC

incogitable *adj syn see* INCREDIBLE 1
ant cogitable

incogitant *adj syn see* RASH 1

incognizable *adj syn see* INCOMPREHENSIBLE 1
ant cognizable

incognizant *adj syn see* IGNORANT 2
ant cognizant

incoherent *adj* 1 *syn see* LOOSE 3
2 lacking cohesion or continuity < an *incoherent* presentation >
syn disconnected, discontinuous, disjointed, disordered, inchoate, incohesive, muddled, unconnected, uncontinuous, unorganized
rel discordant, incompatible, incongruous, inconsistent, inconsonant, inharmonious
con ordered, orderly; connected; organized, planned, plotted
ant coherent
3 *syn see* INARTICULATE 3

incohesive *adj syn see* INCOHERENT 2
ant cohesive

incombustible *adj syn see* NONCOMBUSTIBLE
ant combustible

income *n syn see* REVENUE

incommode *vb syn see* INCONVENIENCE
rel block, hinder, impede, obstruct; annoy, bother, irk, vex
con favor, oblige; humor, indulge; gratify, please
ant accommodate

incommodious *adj* 1 *syn see* INCONVENIENT
ant commodious
2 *syn see* CRAMPED
ant commodious

incommunicable *adj* 1 *syn see* UNUTTERABLE
ant communicable
2 *syn see* RESERVED 1
ant communicable, communicative

incomparable *adj syn see* SUPREME
rel matchless
con common, commonplace, ordinary; indifferent, mediocre, medium, middling
ant average

incompatible *adj syn see* INCONSONANT 1
rel adverse, antagonistic, counter; antipathetic; antipodal, antipodean, antithetical, contradictory, contrary, opposite; irreconcilable, unadaptable, unconformable
ant compatible
2 *syn see* IRRECONCILABLE
ant compatible

incompetence n syn see INABILITY
incompetent adj 1 syn see UNFIT 2
    ant competent
    2 syn see INEFFICIENT 2
    ant competent
incomplete adj 1 lacking a part or parts
    <an *incomplete* text of a speech>
    syn fractional, fragmentary, part, partial
    rel broken, deficient, incoherent, lacking,
    short, wanting; bitty, composite, scrappy
    con intact, undamaged, whole
    ant complete
    2 syn see DEFICIENT 1
    ant complete
incompliant adj 1 syn see OBSTINATE
    ant compliant
    2 syn see STIFF 1
incomprehensible adj 1 lying above or
    beyond the reach of the human mind
    <the *incomprehensible* universe>
    syn impenetrable, incognizable, uncom-
    prehensible, unfathomable, ungraspable,
    unintelligible, unknowable
    rel inscrutable, mysterious, mystifying,
    unsearchable; cryptic, enigmatic, obscure,
    unclear; imperceptible, indistinguishable
    con cognizable, fathomable, graspable,
    intelligible, knowable; clear, lucid, plain,
    simple, straightforward; rational, reason-
    able
    ant comprehensible, understandable
    2 syn see INCONCEIVABLE 1
    ant comprehensible, graspable
inconceivable adj 1 impossible to compre-
    hend in the absence of actual experience
    or knowledge <color is *inconceivable* to
    those born blind>
    syn incomprehensible, unimaginable,
    unknowable, ununderstandable
    idiom beyond one's grasp
    con comprehensible, imaginable, know-
    able, understandable
    ant conceivable
    2 syn see INCREDIBLE 1
    ant conceivable
    3 syn see IMPLAUSIBLE
    con believable, convincing, credible, plau-
    sible
    ant conceivable
inconclusive adj leading to no conclusion
    or definite result <the report was *incon-
    clusive*>
    syn indecisive
    rel open, uncertain, undecided, unsettled;
    incomplete, unfinished
    con clarifying, illuminating; decisive
    ant conclusive
incondite adj syn see RUDE 6
inconformable adj syn see IRRECONCIL-
    ABLE
    ant conformable
incongruent adj syn see INCONSONANT 1
    ant congruent, congruous
incongruous adj syn see INCONSONANT 1
    rel alien, extraneous, foreign; bizarre,
    fantastic, grotesque
    idiom out of place
    con appropriate, fit, fitting, meet, seemly,
    suitable

---

syn synonym(s)   rel related word(s)
ant antonym(s)   con contrasted word(s)
idiom idiomatic equivalent(s)
‖ use limited; if in doubt, see a dictionary

    ant congruent, congruous
inconnu n syn see STRANGER
inconquerable adj 1 syn see INVINCIBLE
    1
    2 syn see INSUPERABLE
inconscient adj syn see ABSTRACTED
    ant conscient, conscious
inconscious adj syn see INSENSIBLE 2
    ant conscious
inconsequent adj syn see PETTY 2
inconsequential adj syn see PETTY 2
    ant consequential
inconsiderable adj 1 syn see LITTLE 3
    ant considerable
    2 syn see MEAGER
    ant considerable
    3 syn see PETTY 2
    ant considerable
inconsiderate adj 1 syn see RASH 1
    ant considerate
    2 syn see SHORT 5
    ant considerate
inconsistent adj 1 syn see INCONSTANT 1
    ant consistent
    2 syn see INCONSONANT 1
    ant consistent
    3 syn see IRRECONCILABLE
    ant consistent
inconsolable adj incapable of being con-
    soled <she was *inconsolable* over the loss
    of her child>
    syn desolate, disconsolate, unconsolable
    rel comfortless, dejected, forlorn, heart-
    sick
    ant consolable
inconsonant adj 1 not in agreement with
    one another or not agreeable one to the
    other <his actions are *inconsonant* with
    his words>
    syn conflicting, disconsonant, discordant,
    discrepant, dissonant, incompatible, incon-
    gruent, incongruous, inconsistent, unmix-
    able
    rel ill-matched, ill-suited, mismated, un-
    congenial; inappropriate, unsuitable
    con accordant, compatible, congenial,
    congruous, consistent
    ant consonant
    2 syn see INHARMONIOUS 2
    ant consonant
inconspicuous adj not readily noticeable
    <occupied an *inconspicuous* position>
    syn obscure, unconspicuous, unemphatic,
    unnoticeable
    rel indistinct, insignificant, unnoticeable,
    unobtrusive, vague
    con eye-catching, showy, striking; dis-
    tinct, noticeable
    ant conspicuous, prominent
inconstant adj 1 lacking firmness or
    steadiness (as in purpose or devotion)
    <depended too much on an *inconstant*
    friend>
    syn capricious, changeable, fickle, incon-
    sistent, lubricious, mercurial, temperamen-
    tal, ticklish, uncertain, unstable, variable,
    volatile; compare CHANGEABLE 1, MUTA-
    BLE 2, UNCERTAIN 1
    rel changeful, mutable, protean, unsettled,
    unsteady; elusive, erratic, vacillating, va-
    grant, wavering, wayward; irresolute,
    shifty, shilly-shally; undependable, unreli-
    able; disloyal, faithless, false, perfidious,

traitorous, treacherous, untrue; frivolous, light, light-minded
con dependable, reliable, trustworthy, trusty; faithful, loyal, resolute, staunch, steadfast, true
ant constant
2 *syn* see MUTABLE 2
ant constant

incontestable *adj syn* see POSITIVE 3
ant contestable

incontinent *adj syn* see LICENTIOUS 2
ant continent

incontinently *adv syn* see PELL-MELL

incontrovertible *adj syn* see POSITIVE 3
ant controvertible

inconvenience *n* the quality or state of being inconvenient < he hated the *inconvenience* of not having a telephone>
syn bother, bothersomeness, ‖disconvenience, troublesomeness
rel annoyance, aggravation, exasperation, trial; fuss, pother, stew
ant convenience

inconvenience *vb* to subject to disturbance or discomfort <was not seriously *inconvenienced* by the bad weather>
syn discommode, ‖disconvenience, disoblige, incommode, put about, put out, trouble
rel discompose, disturb; interfere, intermeddle, meddle; aggravate, exasperate, try
idiom put to trouble
ant convenience

inconvenient *adj* not conducive to physical, mental, or social ease and comfort <he came at an *inconvenient* time>
syn awkward, discommoding, discommodious, embarrassing, incommodious
rel bothersome, pestiferous, troublesome; inexpedient; detrimental, disadvantageous, prejudicial
con appropriate, becoming, fitting, suitable; acceptable, bearable, tolerable; advantageous, desirable, helpful
ant convenient

inconversible *adj syn* see SILENT 3
ant conversable

inconversant *adj syn* see IGNORANT 2
ant conversant

incorporate *vb* 1 *syn* see ABSORB 1
2 *syn* see EMBODY 2

incorporeal *adj syn* see IMMATERIAL 1
ant corporeal

incorrect *adj syn* see FALSE 1
ant correct

incorrectly *adv syn* see AMISS 1
ant correctly

incorrectness *n syn* see IMPROPRIETY 1
ant correctitude, correctness

incorruptible *adj syn* see INDESTRUCTIBLE
ant corruptible

incorruption *n syn* see HONESTY
ant corruption

increase *vb* 1 to make greater or more numerous < *increase* crops by good cultural practices>
syn aggrandize, augment, beef (up), boost, build, compound, enlarge, expand, extend, heighten, magnify, manifold, multiply, plus, push
rel aggravate, enhance, intensify; amplify, dilate, distend, inflate, swell; elongate,

lengthen, prolong, protract; reinforce, strengthen
con abate, abbreviate, condense, contract; depreciate, diminish, lessen, lower, reduce; curtail, shorten, shrink; minimize
ant decrease
2 to become greater or more numerous < his wealth *increased* over the years>
syn augment, build, burgeon, enlarge, expand, heighten, mount, multiply, rise, run up, snowball, upsurge, wax
rel dilate, distend, inflate, intensify, lengthen, strengthen, swell; pullulate, swarm, teem
con abate, condense, contract, diminish, lessen, lower, reduce, shorten, shrink; die off, die (out), end, terminate
ant decrease
3 *syn* see RAISE 9

increase *n* 1 *syn* see ADDITION
ant decrease
2 *syn* see RISE 3

increate *adj syn* see SELF-EXISTENT
ant created

incredible *adj* 1 too extraordinary or improbable to admit of belief <an *incredible* story of privations overcome>
syn incogitable, inconceivable, insupposable, unbelievable, unimaginable, unthinkable
rel absurd, outlandish, preposterous, ridiculous; impossible, untenable
idiom beyond belief, out of the question
con acceptable, believable, conceivable, likely, plausible, reasonable
ant credible
2 *syn* see IMPLAUSIBLE
ant credible

incredulity *n syn* see UNBELIEF
con gullibility, naïveté
ant credulity, credulousness

incredulous *adj* unwilling to admit or accept what is offered as true <his explanation met an *incredulous* response from his listeners>
syn aporetic, disbelieving, questioning, quizzical, show-me, skeptical, unbelieving
rel hesitant, suspicious, uncertain, wary; distrustful, distrusting, mistrustful; doubting, dubious, unconvinced, unsatisfied
con trustful, trusting; unsuspecting, unsuspicious, unwary; gullible, naive
ant credulous

increment *n syn* see ADDITION

incriminate *vb syn* see ACCUSE
rel implicate, involve
ant exonerate

incrustate *vb syn* see CAKE 1

inculcate *vb syn* see IMPLANT
rel educate, instruct, teach; communicate, impart

inculpable *adj* 1 *syn* see GOOD
ant culpable
2 *syn* see INNOCENT 2
ant culpable

inculpate *vb syn* see ACCUSE
ant exculpate

incult *adj syn* see COARSE 3

incur *vb* to bring (something usually unpleasant) upon oneself <he foolishly *incurred* debts beyond his ability to pay>
syn contract
rel acquire, get; bring on, induce

idiom bring down on (*or* upon)
con avoid, elude, escape, eschew, evade, shun; discharge, pay, settle

incurable *adj syn see* HOPELESS 2
  ant curable

incurious *adj syn see* INDIFFERENT 2
  rel absent, absentminded, abstracted, distraught, preoccupied
  con nosy, prying, snoopy; impertinent, intrusive, meddlesome; observant, observing
  ant curious, inquisitive

incursion *n syn see* INVASION

indebted *adj* owing gratitude or recognition (as for a favor or service rendered) <was *indebted* to the book for most of his information>
  syn beholden, obligated, obliged
  rel duty-bound, honor-bound

indebtedness *n* 1 a state of owing something <unable to escape from *indebtedness*>
  syn arrearage, debt, liability, obligation; *compare* DEBT 3
  rel delinquency, nonpayment; bankruptcy, failure, insolvency
  con discharge, liquidation, satisfaction; exoneration, freeing, release
  2 *syn see* DEBT 3

indecent *adj* 1 *syn see* INDECOROUS
  ant decent
  2 *syn see* OBSCENE 2
  ant decent

indecipherable *adj syn see* ILLEGIBLE
  ant decipherable

indecision *n syn see* HESITATION
  ant decision, decisiveness

indecisive *adj* 1 *syn see* INCONCLUSIVE
  ant decisive
  2 *syn see* DOUBTFUL 1
  con certain, incontrovertible, undebatable, unequivocal
  ant decisive
  3 *syn see* VACILLATING 2
  rel undecided, unsettled
  idiom of two minds
  con decided, determined, firm, positive, resolved, settled, unfaltering, unhesitant, unhesitating, unwavering
  ant decisive

indecisiveness *n syn see* HESITATION
  ant indecision, indecisiveness

indecorous *adj* not conforming with accepted standards of propriety or good taste <they regarded argument in public as *indecorous*>
  syn improper, indecent, indelicate, malodorous, ridiculous, rough, unbecoming, undecorous, ungodly, unseemly, untoward
  rel inappropriate, incorrect, unbefitting, unfit, unfitting; immodest, inelegant, undignified; coarse, gross, loose, offensive, shameful, tasteless, vulgar; discourteous, ill-mannered, impolite, rude, uncivil; irregular, unlawful
  idiom in bad form
  con becoming, courteous, decent, nice, proper, seemly; conventional, formal

---

ant decorous

indecorousness *n syn see* IMPROPRIETY 1
  ant decorousness

indecorum *n* 1 *syn see* FAUX PAS
  2 *syn see* IMPROPRIETY 1
  ant decorum

indeed *adv* 1 *syn see* WELL 7
  2 *syn see* EVEN 3

indefatigable *adj* capable of prolonged and arduous effort <a teacher who has *indefatigable* patience with slow learners>
  syn inexhaustible, tireless, unflagging, untiring, unweariable, unwearying, weariless
  rel assiduous, diligent, painstaking, sedulous; determined, dogged, patient, persevering, persistent, pertinacious, relentless, steadfast, stubborn, tenacious, unfaltering, unflinching, unrelenting, unwavering; energetic, strenuous, vigorous
  con dawdling, dilatory, laggard, lagging, procrastinating; faineant, indolent, lackadaisical, lazy, slothful, sluggish
  ant fatigable

indefectible *adj* 1 *syn see* PERFECT 2
  2 *syn see* IDEAL 3

indefensible *adj syn see* INEXCUSABLE
  ant defensible

indefinable *adj syn see* UNUTTERABLE
  ant definable

indefinite *adj* 1 having no exact limits <a region with *indefinite* boundaries>
  syn indeterminate, indistinct, inexact, undeterminable
  rel unclear, undefined, unfixed, unspecific; broad, loose, wide; general, obscure, vague
  con exact, measured; known
  ant definite
  2 *syn see* LIMITLESS
  ant definite

indelible *adj* that cannot be removed or erased <made an *indelible* impression on his hearers>
  syn ineffaceable, ineradicable, inerasable, inexpungible, inextirpable, uneradicable, unerasable
  rel indestructible, undestroyable; enduring, permanent
  con eradicable, effaceable, erasable, removable; ephemeral, evanescent, passing, temporary, transitory
  ant delible

indelicate *adj syn see* INDECOROUS
  rel callow, crude, rude, uncouth; lewd, wanton
  con chaste, modest, pure
  ant delicate

indemnification *n syn see* REPARATION

indemnify *vb syn see* COMPENSATE 3

indemnity *n syn see* REPARATION

indentation *n* 1 *syn see* NOTCH 1
  2 *syn see* IMPRESSION 1

indenture *n syn see* NOTCH 1

indentured *adj syn see* BOUND 2

independent *adj* 1 *syn see* FREE 1
  2 *syn see* SELF-SUFFICIENT
  ant dependent

independently *adv syn see* APART 1
  idiom on one's own

indescribable *adj syn see* UNUTTERABLE
  ant describable

indestructible *adj* incapable of being destroyed <*indestructible* idealism>

---

syn synonym(s)   *rel* related word(s)
ant antonym(s)   *con* contrasted word(s)
idiom idiomatic equivalent(s)
‖ use limited; if in doubt, see a dictionary

syn imperishable, incorruptible, inextermi-nable, inextinguishable, inextirpable, irre-fragable, irrefrangible, quenchless, unde-stroyable, unperishable

rel changeless, immutable, unalterable, unchangeable; deathless, immortal, perpet-ual, undying; durable, enduring, lasting, permanent; indelible, ineradicable; unex-tinguishable, unquenchable

con alterable, changeable, corruptible, impermanent, temporary, transient, unlast-ing; mortal, temporal; evanescent

ant destroyable, destructible, perishable

indeterminate *adj syn* see INDEFINITE 1
ant determinate

index *n syn* see INDICATION 3

Indian sign *n syn* see JINX

indicate *vb* 1 *syn* see POINT 2

2 to give evidence of or serve as ground for a valid or reasonable inference < sev-eral polls *indicate* a landslide for the incumbent >

syn announce, argue, attest, bespeak, betoken, testify, witness

rel denote, import, mean, signify; demon-strate, prove; evidence, evince, manifest, show; display, exhibit, express, illustrate; connote, hint, imply, suggest

3 *syn* see SHOW 5

indication *n* 1 *syn* see HINT 1

2 *syn* see EXPRESSION 3

3 something that is an outward manifesta-tion of something else < such *indications* of prosperity as second cars and color TVs >

syn evidence, index, indicia, mark, sign, significant, symptom, token; *compare* SYMBOL 1, TESTIMONY

rel expression, manifestation; hint, sug-gestion; proof; prefiguration; type

indicative *adj* serving to indicate < the roar of the crowd was *indicative* of its approval >

syn denotative, denotive, designative, exhibitive, indicatory, indicial, significative
rel characteristic, demonstrative, eviden-tial, evincive, expressive, suggestive, sym-bolic, symptomatic, testatory

indicatory *adj syn* see INDICATIVE

indicia *n pl syn* see INDICATION 3

indicial *adj syn* see INDICATIVE

indict *vb syn* see ACCUSE

indifference *n syn* see APATHY 2

indifferent *adj* 1 *syn* see FAIR 4

2 marked by a lack of interest or concern < was *indifferent* to suffering and pover-ty >

syn aloof, by-the-way, casual, detached, disinterested, incurious, numb, pococu-rante, remote, unconcerned, uncurious, uninterested, withdrawn; *compare* UNSO-CIABLE

rel apathetic, impassive, insensible; dis-passionate; careless, heedless, negligent, regardless, uncaring, unmindful; inatten-tive, unobserving

con attentive, considerate, heedful, inter-ested, mindful, regardful, sympathetic
ant concerned

3 *syn* see COLD 2

4 *syn* see MEDIUM

indigence *n syn* see POVERTY 1
ant affluence, opulence

indigency *n syn* see POVERTY 1
ant affluence, opulence

indigenous *adj* 1 *syn* see NATIVE 2
con alien, extraneous, foreign
ant exotic; naturalized

2 *syn* see INNATE 1

indigent *adj syn* see POOR 1
ant affluent, opulent

indignant *adj syn* see ANGRY
ant gratified

indignation *n syn* see ANGER
ant gratification

indignity *n syn* see AFFRONT
rel grievance, injury, injustice, wrong

indirect *adj* 1 deviating from a direct line or straightforward course < made *indirect* inquiries about the new neighbor >

syn circuitous, circular, collateral, ob-lique, roundabout

rel circumlocutory, crooked, devious; meandering, serpentine, sinuous, tortuous, twisting, winding; errant, vagrant, wander-ing

ant direct; forthright, straightforward

2 *syn* see UNDERHAND
ant straight

indirection *n syn* see DECEPTION 1

indiscernible *adj syn* see IMPERCEPTIBLE
ant discernible, distinguishable

indiscreet *adj syn* see UNWISE
ant discreet

indiscriminate *adj* 1 including all or nearly all within the range of choice, oper-ation, or effectiveness < her charity was *indiscriminate* but generous >

syn indiscriminating, indiscriminative, sweeping, undiscriminated, undiscriminat-ing, undistinguishing, wholesale

rel assorted, heterogeneous, miscella-neous, promiscuous; shallow, superficial, uncritical; broad, extensive, wide

con discretionary, discriminative; choosy, picky; critical, perfectionist

ant selective; discriminate, discriminated

2 *syn* see RANDOM

3 *syn* see MISCELLANEOUS

indiscriminating *adj syn* see INDISCRIMI-NATE 1
ant discriminating

indiscriminative *adj syn* see INDISCRIMI-NATE 1
ant discriminative

indispensable *adj syn* see ESSENTIAL 4
rel cardinal, fundamental
ant dispensable

indisposed *adj* 1 *syn* see UNWELL

2 *syn* see DISINCLINED

rel antagonistic, antipathetic, hostile, inimical

con amicable, neighborly; responsive, sympathetic

ant disposed

indisposition *n* 1 *syn* see DISLIKE

2 *syn* see SICKNESS 1

indisputable *adj* 1 *syn* see POSITIVE 3
ant disputable

2 *syn* see REAL 3

indistinct *adj* 1 *syn* see INDEFINITE 1
ant distinct

2 *syn* see FAINT 2
ant distinct

indistinguishable *adj syn* see SAME 2
ant distinguishable

indite vb syn see WRITE
individual adj 1 syn see PERSONAL 1
  ant common, popular
  2 syn see SPECIAL 1
  rel separate, single, sole
  con generic, universal
  ant general
  3 syn see CHARACTERISTIC
  ant common
  4 syn see SEVERAL 1
individual n 1 syn see ENTITY 1
  2 syn see THING 4
  3 syn see HUMAN
individualism n 1 syn see DISPOSITION 3
  2 syn see INDIVIDUALITY 3
individualist adj syn see EGOCENTRIC 1
individualistic adj syn see EGOCENTRIC 1
individuality n 1 syn see DISPOSITION 3
  2 syn see UNITY 1
  3 distinctive character < a person of marked *individuality* >
  syn distinctiveness, individualism, particularity, singularity
  rel character, personality
  4 individual identity < a teacher who respects children's *individualities* >
  syn identity, ipseity, personality, seity, selfdom, selfhood, selfness, singularity
  rel independence, separateness, uniqueness; difference, dissimilarity, unlikeness
  con likeness, resemblance, similarity
individualize vb syn see CHARACTERIZE 2
individually adv syn see APART 1
individuate vb syn see CHARACTERIZE 2
indocile adj syn see UNRULY 1
  ant docile
indolence n syn see SLOTH 1
  ant industry
indolent adj syn see LAZY
  con active, diligent, energetic, vigorous
  ant industrious
indomitable adj 1 syn see INVINCIBLE 1
  ant domitable
  2 syn see INSUPERABLE
  rel dogged, pertinacious, stubborn; resolute, staunch, steadfast
  ant domitable
  3 syn see UNRULY 1
indoors adv in or into a building < stayed *indoors* during the storm >
  syn inside, within, withindoors, withinside
  con outdoors, outside, without, withoutdoors
  ant outdoors
indubitable adj 1 syn see POSITIVE 3
  ant dubitable, questionable
  2 syn see AUTHENTIC 2
  ant doubtful, dubious
  3 syn see DOWNRIGHT 2
induce vb 1 to move another to do or agree to something < *induced* him to give up smoking for the sake of his health >
  syn argue (into), bring around, convince, draw, draw in, draw on, get, oversway, persuade, prevail (on *or* upon), procure, prompt, talk (into), win (over)

  rel influence, sway; abet, incite, lead; actuate, impel, move; activate, motivate
  con check, curb, hold back, restrain
  2 syn see GENERATE 3
inducible adj syn see INDUCTIVE
induct vb syn see INITIATE 3
induction n syn see INITIATION
inductive adj 1 derived or derivable by reasoning from a part to a whole, from particulars to generals, or from the individual to the universal < used an *inductive* approach to the problem >
  syn a posteriori, inducible
  rel Baconian, epagogic
  2 syn see PRELIMINARY
indulge vb 1 to give free rein to (as curiosity or a desire) < *indulged* their taste for gourmet foods >
  syn cater (to), gratify, humor
  rel favor, oblige, satisfy; delight, please, regale
  idiom give rein to
  con bridle, check, constrain, curb, restrain
  2 syn see BABY
  3 syn see WALLOW 3
indulgence n 1 syn see FORBEARANCE 2
  rel benignancy, benignity, benignness, kindliness, kindness; gentleness, mildness
  con rigor, severity, sternness, rigidity, rigorousness; harshness
  ant strictness
  2 syn see FAVOR 4
indulgent adj syn see FORBEARING
  rel cosseting, pampering, permissive; condoning, excusing, forgiving, pardoning; benign, benignant, kind, kindly
  con severe, stern; harsh, rigorous, stringent
  ant strict
indurate vb syn see HARDEN 1
industrious adj syn see ASSIDUOUS
  rel active, busy, live, dynamic; persevering, persistent
  con idle, inactive; lethargic, sluggish
  ant indolent, slothful; unindustrious
industry n syn see BUSINESS 4
indwell vb syn see BELONG 3
indweller n syn see INHABITANT
indwelling adj syn see INHERENT
inebriant n syn see LIQUOR 2
inebriate n syn see DRUNKARD
inebriated adj syn see INTOXICATED 1
inebrious adj syn see INTOXICATED 1
inedible adj not fit for food < an *inedible* plant >
  syn inesculent, uneatable
  rel indigestible, unwholesome; insipid, unappetizing; baneful, noxious, poisonous
  con eatable, esculent, digestible, wholesome; appetizing, savory, tasty; harmless, innocuous, innoxious, nonpoisonous
  ant edible
ineffable adj syn see UNUTTERABLE
  rel celestial, empyreal, empyrean, heavenly; ethereal; divine, holy, sacred, spiritual; abstract, ideal, transcendent, transcendental
  con expressible; utterable
ineffaceable adj syn see INDELIBLE
ineffective adj 1 syn see FUTILE
  ant effective
  2 syn see WEAK 4

---

syn synonym(s)   *rel* related word(s)
ant antonym(s)   *con* contrasted word(s)
idiom idiomatic equivalent(s)
‖ use limited; if in doubt, see a dictionary

3 not producing or not capable of producing a required result < *ineffective* remedies >
syn ineffectual, inefficacious, inefficient, useless, worthless
rel inadequate, incompetent, inferior; useless, worthless
con active, effectual, efficacious; esteemed, valuable
ant effective

ineffectiveness *n syn* see INABILITY
ant effectiveness

ineffectual *adj* 1 *syn* see FUTILE
ant effectual
2 *syn* see INEFFECTIVE 3
ant effectual
3 *syn* see WEAK 4
4 *syn* see LITTLE 2

ineffectualness *n syn* see INABILITY
ant effectualness

inefficacious *adj syn* see INEFFECTIVE 3
ant efficacious

inefficacy *n syn* see INABILITY
ant efficacy

inefficient *adj* 1 *syn* see INEFFECTIVE 3
ant efficient
2 incapable of the proper performance of duties < *inefficient* workmen >
syn incapable, incompetent, inept, inexpert, unexpert, unskilled, unskillful, unworkmanlike
rel careless, slipshod, slovenly; unfitted, unprepared, unqualified, untrained; unskilled, unskillful
con able, adept, capable, competent, expert, proficient, qualified, skilled, skillful, workmanlike
ant efficient

inelaborate *adj syn* see PLAIN 1
ant elaborate

inelastic *adj syn* see STIFF 1
ant elastic

inelegance *n syn* see IMPROPRIETY 1
ant elegance

inelegant *adj syn* see COARSE 3

ineligible *adj syn* see UNFIT 2
ant eligible

ineluctable *adj syn* see INEVITABLE
con doubtful, dubious, questionable; likely, possible, probable

ineludible *adj syn* see INEVITABLE

inenarrable *adj syn* see UNUTTERABLE

inept *adj* 1 *syn* see IMPROPER 1
ant apt
2 *syn* see INFELICITOUS
ant apropos, apt
3 *syn* see AWKWARD 2
ant apt; adept
4 *syn* see UNSKILLFUL 1
ant able
5 *syn* see INEFFICIENT 2
ant competent, efficient

inequable *adj syn* see INEQUITABLE
ant equable

inequality *n* 1 the quality of being uneven < hampered by the *inequality* of the ground >
syn asperity, irregularity, roughness, unevenness
rel cragginess, jaggedness, ruggedness, rugosity
con equality, evenness, levelness, smoothness
2 *syn* see DISPARITY

ant equality

inequitable *adj* not fair or just < an *inequitable* tax burden >
syn inequable, unequitable, unfair, unjust, unrighteous
rel undeserved, undue, unmerited; bad, wrong, wrongful; arbitrary, high-handed, oppressive
con fair, just
ant equitable

inequitableness *n syn* see INJUSTICE 1
ant equitableness

inequity *n syn* see INJUSTICE 1
ant equity

ineradicable *adj syn* see INDELIBLE
ant eradicable

inerasable *adj syn* see INDELIBLE
ant erasable

inerrable *adj syn* see INFALLIBLE 1
ant errable

inerrant *adj syn* see INFALLIBLE 1
rel accurate, correct, exact, precise; dependable, reliable, trustworthy
ant errant

inert *adj syn* see INACTIVE
rel impotent, powerless; apathetic, impassive, phleg- matic, stolid; dead, inanimate, lifeless
con animated, awake; alert, vigilant, watchful; live, operative
ant animated; dynamic

inerudite *adj syn* see UNSCHOLARLY
ant erudite, learned

inescapable *adj syn* see INEVITABLE
ant escapable

inescapably *adv syn* see WILLY-NILLY

inesculent *adj syn* see INEDIBLE
ant esculent

in essence *adv* 1 *syn* see ESSENTIALLY 1
2 *syn* see VIRTUALLY

inessential *adj syn* see UNNECESSARY
ant crucial, essential

inestimable *adj* 1 *syn* see INCALCULABLE 1
2 *syn* see PRECIOUS 1

inevasible *adj syn* see INEVITABLE

inevitable *adj* incapable of being avoided or escaped < the effect of the scandal on the election was *inevitable* >
syn certain, ineluctable, ineludible, inescapable, inevasible, necessary, returnless, unavoidable, unescapable, unevadable
rel ineliminable, sure, unpreventable; decided, settled; destined, foreordained; inexorable, inflexible
idiom as sure to follow as night follows day, in the cards
con eludible, escapable, evadable
ant avoidable, evitable

inevitably *adv syn* see WILLY-NILLY

inexact *adj syn* see INDEFINITE 1
ant exact

inexcusable *adj* being without excuse or justification < an *inexcusable* blunder >
syn indefensible, inexpiable, unforgivable, unjustifiable, unpardonable, untenable
rel blamable, blameworthy, censurable, criticizable; impermissible, unallowable, unpermissible; intolerable, reprehensible
con allowable, blameless, defensible, forgivable, justifiable, pardonable, venial
ant excusable

inexhaustible *adj syn* see INDEFATIGABLE

inexorable adj syn see INFLEXIBLE 2
rel resolute; immobile, immovable
con compassionate, responsive, sympathetic, tender; clement, forbearing, indulgent, lenient

inexpedient adj syn see INADVISABLE
ant expedient

inexpensive adj syn see CHEAP 1
ant expensive

inexperience n lack or serious deficiency of practical wisdom < his failure was due to his *inexperience* >
syn callowness, freshness, greenness, rawness
rel ignorance, naïveté; amateurishness; unfamiliarity; unsophistication, verdancy
con grasp, understanding; polish, sophistication; skill, training
ant experience

inexperienced adj lacking knowledge, skill, or practice based on direct observation and participation < hired *inexperienced* help >
syn callow, fresh, green, inexpert, raw, rude, unconversant, unexperienced, unfleshed, unpracticed, unseasoned, untried, unversed, young
rel ignorant, immature, inept, naive; prentice, unacquainted, unfamiliar, unskilled, untrained
con expert, old, practiced, seasoned, skilled, versed, veteran
ant experienced

inexpert adj 1 syn see INEXPERIENCED
ant expert
2 syn see UNSKILLFUL 1
ant expert
3 syn see INEFFICIENT 2
ant expert
4 syn see CRUDE 5

inexpiable adj syn see INEXCUSABLE
ant expiable

inexplainable adj syn see INEXPLICABLE
ant explainable, explicable

inexplicable adj not capable of being explained or accounted for < an *inexplicable* discrepancy in the accounts >
syn inexplainable, unaccountable, unexplainable; *compare* MYSTERIOUS
rel indecipherable, indescribable, inscrutable, undefinable, unfathomable, unsolvable; mysterious, odd, peculiar, strange
con clear, obvious, plain; comprehensible, graspable, intelligible
ant explainable, explicable

inexpressible adj syn see UNUTTERABLE
ant expressible

inexpressive adj syn see EXPRESSIONLESS
ant expressive

inexpugnable adj syn see INVINCIBLE 1
rel irresistible, unopposable
con assailable, attackable
ant expugnable

inexpungible adj syn see INDELIBLE

inexterminable adj syn see INDESTRUCTIBLE

inextinguishable adj syn see INDESTRUCTIBLE

ant extinguishable

inextirpable adj 1 syn see INDESTRUCTIBLE
2 syn see INDELIBLE

inextricable adj syn see INSOLUBLE
ant extricable

infallible adj 1 incapable of being in error < an *infallible* ear for pitch in music >
syn inerrable, inerrant, sure, unerring
rel faultless, flawless, impeccable, undeceivable; correct, exact, perfect
con deceivable, faulty, unsure; doubtful, dubious, questionable
ant fallible
2 not liable to mislead, deceive, or disappoint < an *infallible* remedy >
syn certain, sure, secure, unfailing
rel effective, efficacious, efficient; handy, helpful, useful; acceptable, agreeable, satisfying; satisfactory
con doubtful, questionable, uncertain, unsure; useless, worthless; unacceptable, unsatisfying; unsatisfactory
ant fallible

infamous adj 1 having an extremely and deservedly bad reputation < one of the most *infamous* of the dictator's henchmen >
syn ill-famed, notorious, opprobrious
rel abominable, atrocious, evil, hateful, heinous, iniquitous, odious, scandalous, vile, villainous; contemptible, despicable, scurvy, sorry
con distinguished, eminent, esteemed, honored, illustrious, notable, prestigious, reputable
2 syn see VICIOUS 2
rel disgraceful, disreputable, ignominious, shameful
con glorious, splendid, sublime
ant illustrious

infamy n syn see DISGRACE
rel notoriety, notoriousness

infancy n 1 early childhood < the helplessness of *infancy* >
syn babyhood, infanthood
rel childhood, immaturity, juvenility, nonage
con adulthood, maturity, old age, senescence
2 the state or period of being under the age established by law for the attainment of full civil rights < his heirs were still in *infancy* >
syn minority, nonage
rel immaturity, juniority, juvenility
con adulthood, adultness, maturity, seniority
ant majority

infant n syn see BABY 1

infant adj syn see YOUNG 1

infanthood n syn see INFANCY 1

infantile adj syn see CHILDISH
ant adult

infantine adj syn see CHILDISH
ant adult

infatuate adj syn see INFATUATED

infatuated adj possessed with or marked by a strong attachment or foolish or unreasoning love or desire < *infatuated* with a woman he can't have >
syn besotted, dotty, enamored, infatuate
rel bewitched, captivated, enraptured, obsessed; foolish, silly

con detached, dispassionate, objective, undazzled, unprepossessed

infatuation *n* a strong and unreasoning but transitory attachment <went through a series of *infatuations* before he settled down>
syn béguin, crush, ||pash, passion
rel ardor, craze, devotion, fascination, obsession, rage

in favor of *prep syn* see FOR 1

infeasible *adj syn* see IMPOSSIBLE 1
ant feasible

infectious *adj* 1 capable of causing infection <*viruses* and other *infectious* agents>
syn infective
rel mephitic, miasmic, noxious, pestilent, pestilential, poisonous, toxic, virulent
con healthful, hygienic, salutary, wholesome
2 transmissible by infection <*infectious* diseases>
syn catching, communicable, contagious
3 easily communicated or diffused <her enthusiasm was *infectious*>
syn catching, contagious, taking
rel irresistible, sympathetic

infective *adj syn* see INFECTIOUS 1

infecund *adj syn* see STERILE 1
ant fecund

infelicitous *adj* marked by a lack of appropriateness and grace of expression <made a very *infelicitous* remark>
syn awkward, graceless, ill-chosen, inept, unfortunate, unhappy
rel inappropriate, inapropos, inapt, malapropos, unapt; deplorable, gauche, regrettable
con fortunate, graceful, happy
ant felicitous

infer *vb* to arrive at by reasoning from evidence or from premises <we *inferred* from his questions that he was a stranger in the vicinity>
syn collect, conclude, deduce, deduct, derive, ||dope out, draw, gather, judge, make, make out; *compare* CONJECTURE
rel induce; conjecture, glean, guess, reckon, speculate, surmise, think; ascertain, construe, interpret, reason, understand
idiom come to (*or* draw *or* reach) a conclusion; read between the lines

inference *n* 1 the deriving of a conclusion by reasoning <the answer was obtainable by *inference*>
syn deduction, illation, judgment, ratiocination
rel conjecture, guessing, reckoning, supposition, surmise
2 a determination arrived at by reasoning <a wrong *inference* based on incomplete evidence>
syn conclusion, deduction, illation, judgment, ratiocination, sequitur
rel assumption, conjecture, guess, presumption, reckoning, supposition, surmise

inferior *adj* 1 being or regarded as being below the level of another thing <the *inferior* latitudes of the northern hemisphere>
syn lesser, low, lower, nether, subjacent, under

rel junior, minor, secondary, subaltern, subordinate
con greater, higher, over, overlying
ant superior
2 of little or less importance, value, or merit <sold *inferior* goods at high prices>
syn common, déclassé, hack, low-grade, mean, poor, second-class, second-drawer, second-rate; *compare* CHEAP 2
rel average, fair, indifferent, mediocre, middling, ordinary; bad, base, paltry, punk, shoddy, sleazy, sorry, tawdry, tinpot, wretched; good-for-nothing, lousy, ||no-account, no-good, unworthy, valueless, worthless
con choice, excellent, first-class, first-rate, high-grade, prime
ant superior

inferior *n* one lower than another (as in station or worth) <a man inclined to be disdainful of his social *inferiors*>
syn poor relation, scrub, secondary, subaltern, subordinate, underling, understrapper
rel attendant, auxiliary, deputy; retainer, satrap, subject, vassal; hanger-on, heeler, henchman, hireling, minion, satellite, sycophant; adherent, disciple, follower
con chief, head, leader, master, principal
ant superior

infernal *adj* 1 of or relating to a nether world of the dead <the *infernal* regions>
syn chthonian, chthonic, Hadean, plutonian, plutonic, sulphurous, Tartarean
con celestial, elysian, Hesperidean, paradisaic, paradisal, paradisiacal
ant supernal
2 resembling or appropriate to hell or its inhabitants <an *infernal* glow in the sky>
syn avernal, cimmerian, hellish, pandemoniac, plutonian, plutonic, stygian
rel demoniac, devilish, diabolic, fiendish; sulphurous
ant celestial, heavenly
3 *syn* see DAMNED 2
4 *syn* see UTTER

inferno *n* 1 *syn* see HELL
2 *syn* see FIRE 1

inferred *adj syn* see TACIT 1

infertile *adj* 1 *syn* see STERILE 1
rel depleted, drained, exhausted, impoverished
con breeding, generating, propagating, reproducing
ant fertile
2 *syn* see BARREN 2
ant fertile

infest *vb* 1 to spread or swarm over in a troublesome manner <lawns *infested* with weeds>
syn beset, overrun, overspread, overswarm
rel abound, crawl, swarm, teem; annoy, harass, harry, pester, plague, worry
2 to live in or on as a parasite <a dog *infested* by fleas>
syn parasite, parasitize

infidel *adj syn* see HEATHEN

infidelic *adj syn* see HEATHEN

infidelity *n* betrayal of a moral obligation <a leader guilty of *infidelity* to the responsibilities he had accepted>

syn disloyalty, faithlessness, falseness, falsity, perfidiousness, perfidy, unfaithfulness; *compare* TREACHERY
rel fickleness, inconstancy; treacherousness, treachery, treason
idiom bad faith
con devotion, faithfulness, fealty; constancy, loyalty, steadfastness
ant fidelity

infiltrate *vb syn see* INSINUATE 3

infinite *adj* 1 being without known limits < the idea of an *infinite* universe >
syn eternal, illimitable, perdurable, sempiternal, supertemporal
rel everlasting, perpetual
con bounded, circumscribed, limited, restricted
ant finite
2 *syn see* LIMITLESS
ant finite

infinity *n syn see* ETERNITY 1

infirm *adj syn see* WEAK 1
ant hale

infirmity *n* 1 the quality or state of being enfeebled and weakened in health < suffering from old age and attendant physical *infirmity* >
syn debility, decrepitude, disease, feebleness, infirmness, malaise, sickliness, unhealthiness; *compare* DISEASE 1, SICKNESS 1
rel debilitation, decay, enfeeblement, failing, frailty, weakening, weakness; diseasedness, unwellness; illness, indisposition, sickness, unhealth
ant haleness
2 *syn see* DISEASE 1
3 *syn see* SICKNESS 1

infirmness *n syn see* INFIRMITY 1

infix *vb* 1 *syn see* ENTRENCH 1
2 *syn see* IMPLANT

inflame *vb* 1 *syn see* LIGHT 1
ant extinguish
2 *syn see* IRRITATE

inflammable *adj syn see* COMBUSTIBLE 1
ant nonflammable, noninflammable

inflammatory *adj* exciting or tending to excite anger, animosity, or disorder < *inflammatory* speeches designed to spark rebellion >
syn incendiary
rel exciting, incitive, instigative, provocative; revolutionary, seditionary, seditious
con calming, moderating, soothing, temperate

inflate *vb syn see* EXPAND 3
ant deflate

inflated *adj* swollen with or as if with something insubstantial < had an *inflated* idea of his own importance >
syn dropsical, dropsied, flatulent, overblown, tumescent, tumid, turgid, windy
rel aureate, bombastic, flowery, grandiloquent, magniloquent, rhetorical; ostentatious, pretentious, showy; fustian, ranting, rhapsodical; diffuse, prolix, verbose, wordy
con compendious, concise, laconic, pithy, succinct, summary, terse

---

syn synonym(s)   *rel* related word(s)
ant antonym(s)   *con* contrasted word(s)
idiom idiomatic equivalent(s)
‖ use limited; if in doubt, see a dictionary

inflatus *n syn see* INSPIRATION

inflection *n* a particular manner of employing the sounds of the voice in speech < questions end on a rising *inflection* >
syn accent, intonation, tone
rel articulation, enunciation, pronunciation; timbre, tonality
idiom tone of voice

inflexible *adj* 1 *syn see* STIFF 1
rel immobile, immovable
con elastic, resilient, springy, supple; ductile, malleable, plastic, pliable, pliant; fluid, liquid
ant flexible
2 rigidly firm in will or purpose < a person of *inflexible* resolution >
syn adamant, adamantine, brassbound, dogged, inexorable, iron, obdurate, relentless, rigid, rockbound, rock-ribbed, single-minded, steadfast, stubborn, unbendable, unbending, uncompliant, uncompromising, unswayable, unyielding; *compare* STIFF 1
rel intractable, obstinate; indomitable, invincible, unconquerable; grim, hard, implacable, unrelenting; dyed-in-the-wool, fixed, set, ‖set
con agreeable, amenable, compliant, docile, pliant, responsive, swayable, yielding; mild, open
ant flexible
3 incapable of changing or being changed < *inflexible* rules >
syn constant, determinate, fixed, immovable, immutable, inalterable, invariable, ironclad, unalterable, unchangeable, unmodifiable, unmovable
rel strict, rigorous; established, set, settled; changeless, unchanging
con adaptable, adjustable, alterable, changeable, mutable, variable
ant flexible
4 *syn see* TOUGH 3

inflict *vb* 1 *syn see* GIVE 10
2 to cause one to endure (something damaging or painful) < *inflict* retribution >
syn force (on or upon), impose, visit, wreak, wreck; *compare* IMPOSE 4
rel expose, subject
idiom lay open to, put on the spot
con guard, protect, shelter, shield

inflow *n syn see* INFLUX
ant outflow, outflux

influence *n* 1 power exerted over the minds or behavior of others < a person of great *influence* in national politics >
syn authority, credit, prestige, weight; *compare* PULL 2
rel command, domination, dominion, mastery; ascendancy, dominance, eminence, predominance; consequence, importance, moment; ‖drag, in, pull
2 *syn see* PULL 2

influence *vb* 1 *syn see* AFFECT
2 *syn see* PREJUDICE 2

influenceable *adj syn see* RECEPTIVE 1

influx *n* a flowing in < anticipated an *influx* of immigrants >
syn inflow, influxion, inpour, inpouring, inrush
rel accession, augmentation, increase; illapse
con outpour, outpouring, outrush; efflux, effluxion, exodus

ant outflow, outflux

influxion *n syn see* INFLUX
ant effluxion

inform *vb* 1 *syn see* FIRE 2
  rel imbue, infuse, leaven, permeate; enlighten, illuminate; endow, endue
  2 to make aware or cognizant of something <was kept *informed* of developments>
  syn acquaint, advise, apprise, clue (*or* clew), fill in, notify, post, tell, warn, wise (up)
  rel educate, enlighten, instruct, teach; familiarize; caution, forewarn
  idiom keep posted
  3 to give information about someone especially as an informer <his suspicions aroused, he *informed* on his neighbor to the police>
  syn ‖nark, peach, ‖pimp, rat, ‖sing, snitch, squeak, squeal, ‖stool; *compare* TALK 6
  rel blab, tattle, tell; betray, give away, turn in

informal *adj* 1 conducted or carried out without rigidly prescribed procedure <carried on an *informal* investigation>
  syn irregular, unceremonious, unofficial
  rel casual, spontaneous; unauthorized; unconventional; private, special
  con authorized, ceremonious, conventional, official, regular
  ant formal
  2 *syn see* EASYGOING 3
  rel familiar, natural, simple
  con affected, mannered, prim, rigid, stiff, stilted
  ant formal

information *n* 1 *syn see* KNOWLEDGE 2
  2 *syn see* NEWS

informational *adj syn see* INFORMATIVE

informative *adj* imparting information <gave an *informative* talk>
  syn educational, educative, informational, informatory, instructional, instructive
  rel edifying, elucidative, enlightening, explanatory, illuminating
  ant uninformative

informatory *adj syn see* INFORMATIVE

informed *adj syn see* FAMILIAR 3
  ant uninformed

informer *n* one who informs against another <his arrest was brought about by an *informer*>
  syn betrayer, ‖canary, ‖fink, ‖nark, ‖pimp, snitch, squawker, ‖squeaker, squealer, stool, stoolie, stool pigeon, talebearer, tattler, tattletale, tipster; *compare* BUSYBODY, DETECTIVE, GOSSIP 1, SPY

infra *adv* 1 *syn see* BELOW 2
  ant above, supra
  2 *syn see* AFTER

infract *vb syn see* VIOLATE 1

infraction *n syn see* BREACH 1
  rel crime, offense, sin; error, faux pas, lapse, slip

infrastructure *n* 1 *syn see* BASE 1
  ant superstructure
  2 *syn see* BASIS 1

infrequent *adj* appearing, happening, or met with so seldom as to attract attention <held only *infrequent* press conferences>

syn few, occasional, rare, scarce, seldom, semioccasional, sporadic, uncommon, unfrequent
  rel isolated, scattered; meager, scant, scanty, sparse; exceptional, limited, unusual; odd, spasmodic, stray
  idiom few and far between
  con abundant, common, numerous, regular; ordinary, routine
  ant frequent

infrequently *adv* 1 *syn see* SELDOM
  ant frequently
  2 *syn see* OCCASIONALLY
  ant frequently

infringe *vb* 1 *syn see* TRESPASS 2
  2 *syn see* VIOLATE 1
  3 *syn see* IMPOSE 5

infringement *n syn see* BREACH 1

infuriate *vb syn see* ANGER 1

infuse *vb* 1 to introduce one thing into another so as to change or affect it <a teacher who *infused* her pupils with the desire to learn>
  syn imbue, ingrain, inoculate, invest, leaven, steep, suffuse
  rel animate, fire, inform, inspire; implant, inculcate, instill; impregnate, permeate, pervade, saturate; indoctrinate
  2 *syn see* INTERFUSE 1

ingather *vb syn see* REAP

ingathering *n syn see* HARVEST 1

ingeminate *vb syn see* REPEAT

ingenerate *adj syn see* INHERENT

ingenious *adj* 1 *syn see* INVENTIVE
  2 *syn see* CLEVER 4

ingenuous *adj syn see* NATURAL 5
  con covert, furtive, stealthy, surreptitious, underhand; artful, crafty, foxy, guileful, insidious, sly, tricky, wily
  ant disingenuous

ingest *vb syn see* EAT 1

inglorious *adj syn see* DISREPUTABLE 1
  ant glorious

ingoing *adj syn see* INCISIVE

ingot *n syn see* BAR 1

ingrain *vb* 1 *syn see* ENTRENCH 1
  rel engrave, etch, grave, incise
  2 *syn see* INFUSE 1

ingrained *adj syn see* INHERENT
  rel chronic, confirmed, deep-rooted, inveterate
  con exterior, external, outer, outside, outward

ingratiating *adj* intended or designed to gain favor <an *ingratiating* smile>
  syn deferential, disarming, ingratiatory, insinuating, insinuative, saccharine, silken, silky
  rel adulatory; fawning, sycophantic

ingratiatory *adj syn see* INGRATIATING

ingredient *n syn see* ELEMENT 2

ingress *n* 1 *syn see* ENTRANCE 1
  ant egress
  2 *syn see* DOOR 2
  ant egress

ingress *vb syn see* ENTER 1
  ant egress

ingression *n syn see* ENTRANCE 1
  ant egression

ingroup *n syn see* CLIQUE
  ant outgroup

ingurgitate *vb syn see* GULP

inhabit *vb* to dwell in as a place of settled residence <*islands* *inhabited* by Polynesians>
  syn occupy, people, tenant
  rel settle; abide, dwell, live

inhabitable *adj syn* see LIVABLE 1
  ant uninhabitable

inhabitancy *n syn* see HABITATION 1

inhabitant *n* one that occupies a particular place regularly <*inhabitants* of large cities>
  syn denizen, dweller, habitant, indweller, liver, occupant, resident, ‖residenter, resider
  rel aborigine, autochthon, indigene, native

inhabitation *n syn* see HABITATION 1

inhale *vb* to draw (as air) into the lungs <*inhaling* smoke>
  syn breathe (in), inspire
  ant exhale, expire

inharmonic *adj syn* see DISSONANT 1
  ant harmonic

inharmonious *adj* 1 *syn* see DISSONANT 1
  ant harmonious
2 lacking harmony especially in sentiment <the committee meeting was singularly *inharmonious*>
  syn discordant, inconsonant, uncongenial, unharmonious
  rel antagonistic, cat-and-dog, conflicting, conflictive, differing, disagreeing, incompatible, incongruous, quarrelsome
  con concordant, congenial, consonant; amiable, compatible; collaborative
  ant harmonious

inharmony *n syn* see DISCORD
  ant harmony

inhaust *vb syn* see ABSORB 1

inhere *vb* 1 *syn* see CONSIST 1
2 *syn* see BELONG 3

inherent *adj* being a part, element, or quality of a thing's inmost being <*inherent* rights of every citizen>
  syn born, built-in, congenital, connate, constitutional, deep-seated, elemental, essential, inborn, inbred, indwelling, ingenerate, ingrained, innate, intimate, intrinsic
  rel inner, internal, inward, resident; basic, elementary, fundamental, immanent, integral; characteristic, distinctive, individual, peculiar; natural, normal, regular, typical; bred-in-the-bone
  con shallow, superficial; accidental, fortuitous, incidental; alien, extraneous, extrinsic, foreign
  ant adventitious

inheritance *n* 1 *syn* see HERITAGE 1
2 *syn* see LEGACY 1

inherited *adj syn* see INNATE 1

inheritor *n syn* see HEIR

inhibit *vb* 1 *syn* see FORBID
  rel avert, ward
  ant allow
2 *syn* see RESTRAIN 1
  ant activate; animate

inhibited *adj syn* see FRIGID 3
  ant uninhibited

---

inhuman *adj syn* see FIERCE 1
  rel malicious, malign, malignant; implacable, relentless, unrelenting; devilish, diabolical, fiendish
  con altruistic, benevolent, charitable, eleemosynary, humanitarian, philanthropic; compassionate, tender
  ant humane

inhumane *adj syn* see FIERCE 1
  ant humane

inhumation *n syn* see BURIAL 2
  ant exhumation

inhume *vb syn* see BURY 1
  ant disinhume, exhume

inimicable *adj syn* see HOSTILE 1

inimical *adj syn* see HOSTILE 1

iniquitous *adj syn* see WRONG 1

iniquity *n syn* see EVIL 3

initial *adj* 1 marking a commencement or constituting a start <*initial* symptoms of the disease>
  syn beginning, inceptive, incipient, initiative, initiatory, introductory, nascent
  rel basic, elementary, first, fundamental; embryonic, germinal; early, infant; antecedent; earliest, introductory, primary
  con closing; concluding, conclusive; terminal, terminative; last, ultimate
  ant final
2 *syn* see FIRST 2
3 *syn* see FIRST 1
  ant final

initially *adv* 1 in the beginning <*initially* we were confused but soon enough we fully understood>
  syn originally, primarily, primitively
  rel first, firstly, incipiently
  idiom at first, at the first go-off, from the word go
  con lastly, ultimately
  ant finally
2 *syn* see FIRSTLY

initiate *vb* 1 *syn* see BEGIN 1
  ant terminate
2 *syn* see INTRODUCE 3
3 to put through the formalities for becoming a member or official <the club *initiated* four new members>
  syn inaugurate, induct, install, instate, invest
  rel institute; admit, enter, introduce, take in

initiation *n* the process or an instance of being formally introduced into an office or made a member of an organization <a fraternity *initiation*>
  syn inaugural, inauguration, induction, installation, investiture
  rel baptism; institution, introduction

initiative *adj syn* see INITIAL 1

initiative *n syn* see ENTERPRISE 4

initiatory *adj syn* see INITIAL 1

injudicious *adj syn* see UNWISE
  ant judicious

injunction *n syn* see COMMAND 1

injure *vb* 1 to deplete the soundness, strength, effectiveness, or perfection of something <*injured* his prestige by making rash statements>
  syn blemish, damage, harm, hurt, impair, mar, prejudice, spoil, tarnish, vitiate
  rel disserve; disadvantage; endamage, weaken; blight, queer; foul up, louse up; contort, deface, deform, disfigure, distort;

---

bespatter, foul, smirch; disable, incapacitate
con assist, help, succor; better, enhance, improve; benefit; strengthen
ant aid
2 *syn* see DISTRESS 2
idiom do dirt to
3 to inflict bodily hurt on <was *injured* in an auto accident>
syn hurt, wound
rel damage, harm; afflict, torment, torture; batter, cripple, maim, mangle, mutilate
idiom draw blood
injurious *adj syn* see HARMFUL
injury *n* 1 an act or the result of inflicting something that causes loss or pain <we cannot forgive his *injury* of the painting> <his falsehood caused grave *injury* to his brother's reputation>
syn damage, harm, hurt, mischief, outrage, ruin
rel agony, discomfiture, distress, misery, suffering; pain, pang; detriment, disservice, loss; bad, evil, ill
2 *syn* see INJUSTICE 2
injustice *n* 1 absence of justice <preached against *injustice*>
syn inequitableness, inequity, unfairness, unjustness, wrong
rel crime, malfeasance, malpractice, villainy, wrongdoing; favoritism, inequality, partiality, partisanship
con equity, fairness, right
ant justice, justness
2 an act or instance of unjustness <pointed out various *injustices* in the law> <you do him an *injustice* when you call him lazy>
syn grievance, injury, wrong
rel damage, harm, hurt, mischief, outrage, ruin; breach, infraction, infringement, tort, transgression, trespass, violation
ink *vb syn* see SIGN 1
inkling *n syn* see HINT 1
inky *adj syn* see BLACK 1
||**inland** *adj syn* see DOMESTIC 2
ant foreign
inlet *n* a recess in the shores of a body of water <*inlets* of lakes and rivers>
syn arm, bay, bayou, bight, cove, ||creek, firth, gulf, harbor, ||loch, ||lough, slough
inn *n syn* see HOTEL
innards *n pl syn* see ENTRAILS
innate *adj* 1 existing in or belonging to an individual inherently <*innate* vigor>
syn congenital, connate, connatural, inborn, indigenous, inherited, native, natural, unacquired
rel constitutional, deep-seated, essential, ingrained, inherent, intrinsic; hereditary; normal, regular, standard, typical
con accidental, adventitious, fortuitous, incidental; affected, assumed, feigned, simulated; cultivated, fostered, nurtured
ant acquired
2 *syn* see INHERENT
inner *adj* 1 situated further in <the *inner* layers were less worn>
syn ||innermore, inside, interior, internal, intestine, inward
rel central, focal, middle, nuclear; close, familiar, intimate; constitutional, essential, inherent, intrinsic

con exterior, external, outside, outward
ant outer
2 arising from one's inmost self <*inner* thoughts and feelings>
syn gut, interior, internal, intimate, visceral, viscerous
rel individual, personal, private; concealed, hidden, secret
con exterior, outer; open, public
||**innermore** *adj syn* see INNER 1
innervate *vb syn* see PROVOKE 4
innerve *vb syn* see PROVOKE 4
innholder *n syn* see SALOONKEEPER
innkeeper *n syn* see SALOONKEEPER
innocence *n syn* see IGNORANCE 2
innocent *adj* 1 *syn* see GOOD 11
rel unstained, unsullied, white, white-handed
2 free from legal guilt or fault <the defendant was found *innocent*>
syn blameless, clean, crimeless, faultless, guiltless, inculpable, unguilty
idiom in the clear
ant guilty
3 *syn* see LAWFUL
4 *syn* see DEVOID
5 *syn* see NATURAL 5
6 *syn* see HARMLESS
con harmful, injurious, mischievous
innocuous *adj* 1 *syn* see HARMLESS
con harmful, injurious; evil; troublesome
ant pernicious
2 *syn* see INSIPID 3
innominate *adj syn* see ANONYMOUS
innovation *n syn* see CHANGE 2
rel deviation, introduction, wrinkle
innovational *adj syn* see INVENTIVE
innovative *adj syn* see INVENTIVE
innovator *n* one who introduces something new <an *innovator* of bold ideas in the field of computers>
syn introducer, inventor, original, originator
rel author, creator, maker, producer; architect, builder, developer
innovatory *adj syn* see INVENTIVE
innoxious *adj syn* see HARMLESS
ant noxious
innuendo *n syn* see INSINUATION
innumerable *adj* too many to be counted <received *innumerable* requests for help>
syn countless, innumerous, numberless, uncountable, uncounted, unnumberable, unnumbered, untold
ant numerable
innumerous *adj syn* see INNUMERABLE
inobnoxious *adj syn* see HARMLESS
ant obnoxious
inobservant *adj syn* see INATTENTIVE
ant observant
inobtrusive *adj syn* see QUIET 4
ant obtrusive
inoculate *vb syn* see INFUSE 1
rel admit, enter, introduce
inodorous *adj syn* see ODORLESS
ant odorous; smelly
inoffensive *adj syn* see HARMLESS
con loathsome, repulsive, revolting; distasteful, obnoxious, repellent, repugnant
ant offensive
inopportune *adj syn* see UNSEASONABLE 1
ant opportune

inordinate adj 1 syn see EXCESSIVE 1
  rel irrational, unreasonable; gratuitous, supererogatory, uncalled-for, wanton; extra, superfluous, surplus
  con moderate, temperate; checked, curbed, inhibited, restrained
  2 syn see EXCESSIVE 2
inordinately adv syn see EVER 6
inordinateness n syn see EXCESS 3
in passing adv syn see INCIDENTALLY 2
in perpetuum adv syn see EVER 2
inpour n syn see INFLUX
  ant outpour, outpouring
inpouring n syn see INFLUX
  ant outpour, outpouring
inquest n syn see INQUIRY 1
inquietude n syn see UNREST
  rel anxiety, uneasiness
  ant quiet, quietness, quietude
inquire vb syn see ASK 1
  rel investigate, probe, search; scrutinize, study
inquire (into) vb syn see EXPLORE
inquiring adj syn see INQUISITIVE 1
inquiry n 1 the act or an instance of seeking truth, information, or knowledge about something <an exhaustive *inquiry* revealed no evidence of a conspiracy>
  syn delving, inquest, inquisition, investigation, probe, probing, quest, research
  rel catechizing, interrogation, questioning; audit, check, examination, inspection, scrutiny; hearing; inquirendo
  2 a request for information <addressed his *inquiry* to the personnel director>
  syn interrogation, interrogatory, query, question, questioning
inquisition n syn see INQUIRY 1
inquisitive adj 1 given to examination or investigation <an *inquisitive* child who was interested in everything around him>
  syn curious, disquisitive, inquiring, investigative, questioning
  rel nosy, prying, snoopy
  con indifferent, unconcerned, uninquisitive, uninterested
  ant incurious
  2 syn see CURIOUS 2
  ant incurious, uninquiring
inquisitorial adj syn see CURIOUS 2
inquisitory adj syn see CURIOUS 2
in re prep syn see APROPOS
in respect to prep syn see APROPOS
in reverse adv syn see ABOUT 6
inroad n syn see INVASION
inroad vb syn see INVADE 1
inrush n syn see INFLUX
  ant outrush
insalubrious adj syn see UNWHOLESOME 1
  ant salubrious, salutary
insalutary adj syn see UNWHOLESOME 1
  ant salubrious, salutary
insanable adj syn see HOPELESS 2
ins and outs n pl characteristic peculiarities or technicalities <soon learned the *ins and outs* of his job>
  syn minutiae, ropes

rel details, incidentals, particulars; ramifications; oddities, peculiarities, quirks
insane adj 1 being afflicted by or manifesting unsoundness of mind or an inability to control one's rational processes <adjudged *insane* after a period of observation>
  syn ‖batty, bedlamite, ‖bonkers, brainsick, ‖buggy, ‖bughouse, ‖bugs, crackbrained, cracked, ‖crackers, ‖cracky, ‖cranky, crazed, crazy, cuckoo, daffy, daft, demented, deranged, disordered, distraught, ‖fruity, ‖loco, lunatic, mad, maniac, ‖mental, mindless, non compos mentis, nuts, nutsy, nutty, reasonless, screwy, teched, unbalanced, unsane, unsound, wacky, witless, wrong
  rel irrational, unreasonable; bewildered, distracted; dotty, eccentric, off, rocky, strange, touched; ‖dippy
  idiom around the bend, crazy as a coot, not all there, not right in one's head, ‖off one's dot, off one's nut (or rocker), ‖off one's onion, out of (or off) one's head, out of one's mind, touched in the head
  con judicious, sapient, sensible, wise; rational, reasonable; balanced; logical, subtle; healthy, sound; clear, lucid
  ant sane
  2 syn see FOOLISH 2
  rel fanciful, fantastic, imaginary, visionary; impractical, unrealistic
  con feasible, possible, practicable, usable; rational, reasonable, sane, sensible; practical, realistic
insaneness n syn see INSANITY 1
  ant saneness, sanity
insanity n 1 grave disorder of mind that impairs one's capacity to function safely or normally in society <his *insanity* required confinement in a mental institution>
  syn aberration, alienation, derangement, distraction, insaneness, lunacy, madness, psychopathy, unbalance
  rel acromania; delirium, frenzy, hysteria; delusion, hallucination, illusion; irrationality, unreasonableness; dotage
  con judiciousness, sageness, sensibility, wiseness; rationality, reasonableness; healthiness, soundness, wholesomeness
  ant saneness, sanity
  2 syn see FOOLISHNESS
  rel asininity, fatuousness, stupidity; impracticality
insatiable adj incapable of being satisfied or appeased <an *insatiable* lust for glory>
  syn insatiate, quenchless, unappeasable, unquenchable, unsatiate, unsatisfiable
  rel unsatiated, unsatisfied; demanding, exigent, importunate, insistent, urgent; clamorous, crying, pressing, yearning
  con appeasable, quenchable, satisfiable; satiate, satiated, satisfied; controlled, curbed, restrained
  ant satiable
insatiably adv syn see VERY 1
insatiate adj syn see INSATIABLE
  ant satiate, satiated
inscience n syn see IGNORANCE 2
inscribe vb 1 syn see WRITE
  rel engrave, enscroll

2 *syn* see LIST 3

3 *syn* see ENGRAVE 2

inscrutable *adj syn* see MYSTERIOUS

insecure *adj* 1 not confident or sure <feels very *insecure* about his future>
syn unassured, unconfident, unsure
rel hesitant, questioning, uncertain
idiom in suspense, up in the air
con assured, confident, self-assured, self-confident, sure
ant secure

2 *syn* see WEAK 2
ant secure

inseminate *vb syn* see IMPLANT

insensate *adj* 1 lacking animate awareness or sensation <would often talk to stones and other *insensate* objects>
syn inanimate, insensible, insentient, senseless, unfeeling
rel exanimate, unanimated; anesthetic, insensitive
con aware, cognizant, conscious; feeling, sensible, sentient
ant sensate

2 *syn* see SIMPLE 3

3 *syn* see INSENSIBLE 5

insensibility *n syn* see APATHY 1
ant sensibility

insensible *adj* 1 *syn* see INSENSATE 1
ant sensible

2 deprived of consciousness <knocked *insensible* by a sudden punch>
syn cold, comatose, inconscious, senseless, unconscious
idiom out cold

3 *syn* see NUMB 1

4 *syn* see IMPERCEPTIBLE
ant sensible

5 devoid or insusceptible of emotion or passion <*insensible* to love or compassion>
syn anesthetic, bloodless, dull, hard, impassible, insensate, insensitive, rocky
rel blunt, obtuse; apathetic, impassive, phlegmatic, stoic, stolid; callous, hardened, indurated, pachydermatous, thickskinned; absorbed, engrossed, intent, rapt
con alert, alive, awake, aware, cognizant, conscious; affected, impressed, influenced, touched
ant sensible

insensitive *adj* 1 *syn* see INSENSIBLE 5
rel aloof, incurious, indifferent, unconcerned
con compassionate, responsive, tender
ant sensitive

2 *syn* see NUMB 1
ant sensitive

3 *syn* see INSUSCEPTIBLE
ant sensitive

insentient *adj* 1 *syn* see INSENSATE 1
ant sentient

2 *syn* see INSUSCEPTIBLE

insert *vb syn* see INTRODUCE 6
rel interlope, intrude, obtrude; implant, inculcate, instill; admit, enter
con detach, disengage
ant abstract, extract

in short *adv syn* see BRIEFLY

inside *n* 1 *syn* see INTERIOR
ant outside

2 **insides** *pl syn* see ENTRAILS

inside *adj* 1 *syn* see INNER 1

ant outside

2 *syn* see PRIVATE 2

inside *adv syn* see INDOORS
ant outside

inside out *adv syn* see THOROUGHLY 2

insidious *adj syn* see SLY 2
rel perfidious, treacherous; dangerous, perilous; gradual, subtle

insight *n* 1 *syn* see SAGACITY

2 *syn* see INTUITION

insighted *adj syn* see WISE 1

insightful *adj syn* see WISE 1
rel discriminating, penetrating; inseeing

insignia *n* a distinguishing mark of authority, office, or honor <wore a coronet with the strawberry leaf *insignia* of his ducal rank>
syn badge, emblem
rel decoration; regalia

insignificancy *n syn* see NONENTITY

insignificant *adj* 1 *syn* see SENSELESS 5
ant significant

2 *syn* see MINOR 2

3 *syn* see LITTLE 3
ant significant

insincere *adj* not being or expressing what one appears to be or express <an *insincere* person who could not be trusted>
syn ambidextrous, double, double-dealing, double-faced, doublehearted, doubleminded, double-tongued, hypocritical, lefthanded, mala fide
rel deceitful, dishonest, lying, mendacious, untruthful; shifty, slippery, tricky
con candid, frank, open, plain; direct, forthright, straight, straightforward
ant sincere

insinuate *vb* 1 *syn* see INTRODUCE 6

2 *syn* see SUGGEST 1
rel ascribe, impute
con affirm, assert, aver, avouch, avow, declare, profess; air, broach, express, state, voice

3 to introduce (as oneself) by stealthy, smooth, or artful means <*insinuated* himself into the confidence of others>
syn edge in, foist, infiltrate, work in, worm
rel insert, intercalate, interject, interpolate, interpose, introduce

insinuating *adj syn* see INGRATIATING

insinuation *n* a stealthy or indirect hinting or suggestion <*insinuations* about his opponent's probity>
syn innuendo, insinuendo
rel hint, hinting, implication, implying, intimation, suggestion; animadversion, aspersion, reflection; ascription, imputation

insinuative *adj syn* see INGRATIATING

insinuendo *n syn* see INSINUATION

insipid *adj* 1 *syn* see UNPALATABLE 1
rel bland, mild
con appetizing, flavorable, tasty
ant sapid, savory

2 *syn* see ARID 2
rel commonplace, ordinary, plain; mundane, prosaic, unimaginative

3 devoid of qualities that make for spirit and character <an *insipid* little story of teenage puppy love>
syn banal, bland, driveling, flat, inane, innocuous, jejune, milk-and-water, namby-

pambby, sapless, swashy, vapid, waterish, watery, wishy-washy
rel slight, tenuous, thin; feeble, weak; subdued, tame; mild, soft; pointless
con piquant, poignant, pungent, racy, spicy; fiery, gingery, high-spirited, mettlesome, peppery, spirited, spunky; exciting, piquing, provocative, provoking
ant sapid

insistent *adj* 1 *syn* see PERSISTENT 1
2 *syn* see EMPHATIC
rel persevering, persistent, pressing; obtrusive
3 *syn* see PRESSING

insociable *adj* *syn* see UNSOCIABLE
ant sociable

insolate *vb* *syn* see SUN

insolence *n* the quality, state, or an instance of being insulting or grossly lacking in respect <court-martialed because of *insolence* to an officer>
syn boldness, disrespect, hardihood, impertinence, impudence, insolency, insolentness; *compare* EFFRONTERY
rel brazenness; presumption; arrogance; rudeness; contempt
con deference; correctness, decency, decorum, decorousness, properness, seemliness
ant respect, respectfulness

insolency *n* *syn* see INSOLENCE
ant respect, respectfulness

insolent *adj* 1 *syn* see PROUD 1
rel imperative, peremptory; dictatorial, magisterial
ant deferential
2 exhibiting boldness or effrontery <an *insolent* child with no respect or regard for anyone>
syn audacious, bold, ‖boldacious, brazen, contumelious, impertinent, impudent, procacious, saucy
rel arrogant, disdainful, overbearing; discourteous, impolite, rude, uncivil, ungracious
con humble, lowly, meek, modest, unassertive; civil, courteous, polite
ant deferential

insolentness *n* *syn* see INSOLENCE
ant respect, respectfulness

insoluble *adj* admitting of no solution <seemingly *insoluble* problems faced the city council>
syn inextricable, insolvable, irresoluble, irresolvable, unsoluble, unsolvable
rel inexplicable, unexplainable; inconceivable, unaccountable; mysterious
con answerable, explicable, understandable; resolvable; clear, plain, straightforward
ant soluble, solvable

insolvable *adj* *syn* see INSOLUBLE
ant soluble, solvable

insomnia *n* prolonged inability to obtain adequate sleep <sleeping pills failed to relieve his *insomnia*>
syn insomnolence, sleeplessness
rel restlessness, wakefulness; stress, tension

insomnolence *n* *syn* see INSOMNIA

insorb *vb* *syn* see ABSORB 1

insouciance *n* *syn* see APATHY 2

insouciant *adj* *syn* see HAPPY-GO-LUCKY

inspect *vb* *syn* see SCRUTINIZE 1
rel notice, observe; catechize, inquire, interrogate, question; review

inspection *n* *syn* see EXAMINATION
rel inquest, inquiry, inquisition, investigation, probe, research; oversight, supervision, surveillance

inspiration *n* a divine or seemingly divine imparting of knowledge or power <*inspiration* is the only plausible explanation for his exquisite work>
syn afflation, afflatus, inflatus
rel animus, genius, muse, vision; enlightenment, illumination; brainstorm, brainwave

inspire *vb* 1 *syn* see INHALE
ant expire
2 *syn* see FIRE 2
rel quicken, stimulate; infect, infuse; endow, endue
3 *syn* see ELATE
4 *syn* see AFFECT

inspiring *adj* *syn* see EXCITING
ant uninspiring

inspirit *vb* *syn* see ENCOURAGE 1
rel exalt, fire, inform, inspire
ant dispirit

in spite of *prep* *syn* see AGAINST 4

instability *n* the state or quality of not being firm or fixed <the *instability* of the economy>
syn precariousness, shakiness, unfixedness, unsettledness, unstability, unstableness, unsteadfastness, unsteadiness
rel undependability, unreliability; inconstancy, insecurity
con firmness, soundness, stoutness, sturdiness; fixity, solidity
ant stability, stableness

install *vb* 1 *syn* see INITIATE 3
2 *syn* see ENSCONCE 2

installation *n* *syn* see INITIATION

instance *n* an individual that clearly belongs to an indicated class <their rescue was an *instance* of great courage>
syn case, case history, example, illustration, representative, sample, sampling, specimen
rel ground, proof, reason; detail, item, particular; exponent

instance *vb* 1 *syn* see EXEMPLIFY 1
2 *syn* see MENTION
rel exemplify, illustrate

instant *n* 1 an infinitesimal space of time <came not an *instant* too soon>
syn breathing, crack, flash, ‖jiff, jiffy, minute, moment, second, shake, split second, ‖tick, trice, twinkle, twinkling, wink
2 *syn* see POINT 7
3 *syn* see OCCASION 7

instant *adj* 1 *syn* see PRESSING
2 *syn* see PRESENT
3 *syn* see INSTANTANEOUS

instantaneous *adj* done, occurring, or acting without any perceptible duration of time <*instantaneous* answers to tough questions>
syn hair-trigger, immediate, instant; *compare* QUICK 2

---

syn synonym(s)   *rel* related word(s)
ant antonym(s)   *con* contrasted word(s)
idiom idiomatic equivalent(s)
‖ use limited; if in doubt, see a dictionary

rel spontaneous; fast, quick, rapid; momentary, transitory

con late, tardy; slow, sluggish

instanter *adv syn* see AWAY 3

instantly *adv syn* see AWAY 3

idiom in a flash, on a dime, on the spot

instate *vb syn* see INITIATE 3

instead *adv* as an alternative to something expressed or implied < longed *instead* for a quiet country life >

syn alternately, alternatively, in lieu, rather

insteep *vb syn* see SOAK 1

instigate *vb syn* see INCITE

rel activate, actuate; hint, insinuate, suggest; plan, plot, scheme; goad, urge; fire, inflame

instigation *n syn* see STIMULUS

instigator *n* one that goads or urges forward < the *instigator* of the riot >

syn agitator, fomenter, inciter, mover

rel firebrand, incendiary, inflamer, rabble-rouser

instill *vb syn* see IMPLANT

instinctive *adj* 1 prompted by natural instinct or propensity < was quite unable to control her *instinctive* fear of snakes >

syn instinctual, intuitive, visceral

rel congenital, inborn, innate; ingrained, inherent, intrinsic; natural

ant reasoned

2 *syn* see SPONTANEOUS

rel natural, normal, regular, typical

ant intentional

instinctual *adj syn* see INSTINCTIVE 1

institute *vb* 1 *syn* see FOUND 2

ant abrogate

2 *syn* see INTRODUCE 3

institute *n syn* see LAW 1

institution *n* something or someone well established in a customary relationship < he's been in the office so long that he has become an *institution* >

syn fixture

rel custom, habit; establishment, rite

instruct *vb* 1 *syn* see TEACH

rel acquaint, apprise, inform; engineer, guide, lead, pilot, steer

2 *syn* see COMMAND

rel assign, define, prescribe

instruction *n syn* see EDUCATION 1

instructional *adj syn* see INFORMATIVE

instructive *adj syn* see INFORMATIVE

rel didactic, moralistic, moralizing

instrument *n* 1 *syn* see MEAN 2

2 *syn* see IMPLEMENT

rel equipment, gear, machinery, paraphernalia, tackle

instrumental *adj* serving as a means, agent, or tool < was *instrumental* in organizing the strike >

syn implemental, ministerial

rel conducive, helpful; serviceable, useful

instrumentality *n syn* see MEAN 2

rel energy, force, might, power

instrumentation *n syn* see MEAN 2

insubordinate *adj* unwilling to submit to authority < *insubordinate* soldiers are court-martialed >

syn contumacious, factious, insurgent, mutinous, rebellious, seditious

rel intractable, recalcitrant, refractory, ungovernable, unruly; indocile, uncompliant, uncomplying; disaffected, dissentious

con amenable, biddable, docile, obedient, tractable; subdued, submissive, tame

ant subordinate

insubstantial *adj* 1 *syn* see IMMATERIAL 1

ant substantial

2 *syn* see WEAK 1

ant substantial

3 *syn* see TENUOUS 3

ant substantial

insuccess *n syn* see FAILURE 2

ant success, successfulness

insufferable *adj* incapable of being endured < that man is an *insufferable* bore >

syn insupportable, intolerable, unbearable, unbrookable, unendurable, unsufferable, unsupportable

rel distressing, painful; unacceptable

ant sufferable

insufficience *n* 1 *syn* see FAILURE 3

ant sufficiency

2 *syn* see SCARCITY

ant sufficiency

insufficiency *n* 1 *syn* see FAILURE 3

ant sufficiency

2 *syn* see SCARCITY

ant sufficiency

insufficient *adj* 1 *syn* see DEFICIENT 1

ant sufficient

2 *syn* see SHORT 3

ant sufficient

insular *adj* having the narrow and limited outlook characteristic of geographic isolation < the *insular* thinking of peasant communities >

syn local, ‖parish-pump, parochial, provincial, sectarian, small-town

rel regional, sectional; insulated, isolated, secluded; circumscribed, confined, limited, restricted; illiberal, narrow, narrow-minded

con broad-minded, liberal; cosmopolitan, metropolitan, urban

insulate *vb syn* see ISOLATE

insult *vb syn* see OFFEND 3

rel abase, debase, degrade, humble, humiliate; fleer, flout, gibe, gird, jeer, scoff, sneer; deride, mock, ridicule, taunt; rump

con admire, esteem, respect

ant honor

insult *n syn* see AFFRONT

rel abuse, invective, obloquy, vituperation; disgrace, ignominy, opprobrium, shame; disdainfulness, insolence, superciliousness; contempt, disdain, scorn; unpleasantry

con deference, homage, honor, obeisance, reverence

insuperable *adj* incapable of being surmounted, overcome, or passed over < they met with *insuperable* difficulties >

syn impassable, inconquerable, indomitable, insurmountable, invincible, unconquerable, unsurmountable

rel unachievable, unattainable; unsurpassable; impregnable, impenetrable, invulnerable

con surmountable; achievable, negotiable

ant superable

insupportable *adj syn* see INSUFFERABLE

ant bearable, supportable

insupposable *adj syn* see INCREDIBLE 1

ant supposable

insuppressible *adj* *syn* see IRREPRESS-IBLE
ant suppressible

insuppressive *adj* *syn* see IRREPRESSIVE

insure *vb* *syn* see ENSURE
rel guard, protect, safeguard, shield

insurgent *n* *syn* see REBEL

insurgent *adj* *syn* see INSUBORDINATE

insurmountable *adj* *syn* see INSUPER-ABLE
ant surmountable

insurrect *vb* *syn* see REVOLT 1

insurrectionist *n* *syn* see REBEL

insusceptible *adj* incapable of being moved, affected, or impressed < *insuscepti-ble* to flattery>
syn impassive, insensitive, insentient, unimpressible, unimpressionable, unresponsive, unsusceptible
con impressible, impressionable, responsive, sensitive, sentient
ant susceptible

intact *adj* 1 *syn* see WHOLE 1
ant defective
2 *syn* see VIRGIN 1
ant deflowered

intangible *adj* 1 *syn* see IMPERCEPTIBLE
rel rare, tenuous, thin; slender, slight; aerial, aeriform, airy, ethereal; eluding, elusive, evading, evasive; touchless
ant tangible
2 *syn* see ELUSIVE

integer *n* *syn* see NUMBER

integral *adj* *syn* see WHOLE 3

integral *n* *syn* see WHOLE 2

integrate *n* *syn* see WHOLE 2

integrate *vb* 1 *syn* see HARMONIZE 4
2 *syn* see HARMONIZE 3
3 to join together systematically < an economic system that successfully *inte-grates* private gain with public responsibility>
syn articulate, concatenate
rel combine, conjoin, link, unite; compact, concentrate, consolidate, unify; blend, coalesce, fuse, merge; organize, systematize
con disperse, dissipate, scatter; analyze, break down, resolve
ant disintegrate
4 *syn* see UNIFY 1
5 *syn* see EMBODY 2

integrative *adj* tending to integrate < *inte-grative* forces in a fragmented society>
syn centralizing, centripetal, compacting, concentrating, consolidating, unifying
ant disintegrative

integrity *n* 1 *syn* see HONESTY
rel forthrightness, straightforwardness
2 the quality or state of being complete or undivided < trying to maintain the *integ-rity* of the empire>
syn completeness, entireness, perfection, wholeness
rel soundness, stability; absoluteness, purity, simplicity

intellect *n* 1 *syn* see REASON 5

rel comprehension; intuition
2 a person with great intellectual powers < one of the great *intellects* of his time>
syn brain, intellectual, intelligence
rel genius; egghead, pundit; thinker

intellection *n* *syn* see IDEA

intellective *adj* *syn* see MENTAL 1

intellectual *adj* 1 *syn* see MENTAL 1
con animal, fleshly, sensual
ant carnal
2 devoted to or engaged in the creative use of the intellect < the play appealed to the *intellectual* members of the audience>
syn cerebral, highbrow, highbrowed, intellectualistic

intellectual *n* 1 *syn* see INTELLECT 2
2 a person who possesses or has pretensions of strong intellectual interest or superiority < accused of being an *intellectual* and a snob>
syn Brahmin, double-dome, egghead, highbrow
3 **intellectuals** *pl* *syn* see INTELLIGENTSIA

intellectualistic *adj* *syn* see INTELLEC-TUAL 2

intelligence *n* 1 the ability to learn and to cope < what he lacked in education, he made up in *intelligence*>
syn brain(s), brainpower, mentality, mother wit, sense, wit
rel acumen, discernment, insight, judgment; perspicacity, sagacity, wisdom
2 *syn* see INTELLECT 2
3 *syn* see NEWS

intelligent *adj* 1 *syn* see RATIONAL
con irrational, unreasonable
ant unintelligent
2 mentally keen or quick < quite *intelli-gent* for his age>
syn alert, brainy, bright, brilliant, clever, knowing, knowledgeable, quick-witted, ready-witted, sharp, smart; compare WISE 4
rel astute, perspicacious, sagacious, shrewd; acute, keen; adroit, cunning, ingenious
con foolish, idiotic, imbecilic, moronic; crass, dense, dull, dumb, slow, stupid
ant unintelligent

intelligentsia *n* a class of articulate persons devoted to intellectual, cultural, and social matters < the *intelligentsia* posed a threat to the new regime>
syn clerisy, illuminati, intellectuals, literati
rel avant-garde, vanguard"

intelligible *adj* *syn* see UNDERSTAND-ABLE
ant unintelligible

intemperance *n* *syn* see EXCESS 3
rel drunkenness, insobriety; debauchery
ant temperance

intemperate *adj* 1 *syn* see EXCESSIVE 2
rel bibacious, bibulous, crapulous, drunken; gluttonous
ant temperate, tempered
2 *syn* see SEVERE 3
ant temperate

intempestive *adj* *syn* see IMPROPER 1

intemporal *adj* *syn* see ETERNAL 4
ant temporal

intend *vb* 1 *syn* see MEAN 2
2 to have in mind as a purpose < *intended* to read the book>

---

syn aim, contemplate, design, mean, ‖mind, plan, propose, purpose
rel attempt, endeavor, essay, strive, try; plot, scheme; assign, designate, destine
idiom figure on, have in mind to, look forward to

intendance *n syn* see OVERSIGHT 1

intended *adj syn* see ENGAGED 2

intended *n syn* see BETROTHED

intendment *n* 1 *syn* see INTENTION
2 *syn* see MEANING 1

intensate *vb syn* see INTENSIFY

intense *adj* 1 extreme in degree, power, or effect < *intense* hatred >
syn concentrated, desperate, exquisite, fierce, furious, terrible, vehement, vicious, violent
rel aggravated, enhanced, heightened, intensified; accentuated, emphasized, stressed
ant subdued
2 *syn* see INTENSIVE
3 *syn* see ARDENT 2
ant slight

intensely *adv* 1 *syn* see HARD 3
rel fiercely, furiously, vehemently, viciously, violently
2 *syn* see SERIOUSLY 2

intensify *vb* to increase markedly in measure or degree < both companies *intensified* their efforts to win the contract > < the pain *intensified* sharply >
syn aggravate, deepen, enhance, heighten, intensate, magnify, mount, redouble, rise, rouse
rel accent, accentuate, emphasize, stress; aggrandize, exalt; sharpen
con moderate, qualify; alleviate, ease, lighten, relieve; decrease, diminish, lessen, reduce
ant abate; allay, mitigate; temper

intensive *adj* highly concentrated < an *intensive* study of the causes of the war >
syn blood-and-guts, deep, hard, intense, profound
con casual, shallow, superficial

intensively *adv syn* see HARD 3

intent *n* 1 *syn* see INTENTION
rel conation, volition, will
con chance, fortune, hap, hazard, luck
ant accident
2 *syn* see MEANING 1

intent *adj* 1 having one's mind or attention deeply fixed < the student was too *intent* on his work to hear the phone >
syn absorbed, deep, engaged, engrossed, immersed, preoccupied, rapt, wrapped, wrapped up
rel attending, attentive, minding, watching; concentrated, riveted
con absent, absent-minded, abstracted, bemused, faraway, preoccupied; daydreaming, napping, oblivious
ant distracted
2 *syn* see DECIDED 2

intention *n* 1 what one purposes to accomplish or do < his *intention* was to finish by noon >
syn animus, design, intendment, intent, meaning, plan, purpose; *compare* AMBITION 2
rel project, scheme; desire, hope, wish

intentional *adj syn* see VOLUNTARY

rel intended, meant, proposed, purposed; advised, considered, designed, designful, premeditated, studied
con accidental, casual, fortuitous; careless, heedless, inadvertent, thoughtless
ant unintentional

intentionally *adv* with intention < hurt her *intentionally* >
syn ‖apurpose, deliberately, designedly, on purpose, prepensely, purposedly, purposely, purposively
ant unintentionally

intentive *adj syn* see ATTENTIVE 1

intently *adv syn* see HARD 4

intentness *n syn* see EARNESTNESS

inter *vb syn* see BURY 1
ant disinter

interact *vb* to act upon one another < humor and pathos *interacted* to make a moving drama >
syn coact, interplay, interreact
rel collaborate, cooperate; combine, join, merge, unite

interagent *n syn* see GO-BETWEEN 2

interblend *vb syn* see MIX 1

interbreed *vb syn* see CROSS 4

intercalate *vb syn* see INTRODUCE 6

intercede *vb syn* see INTERPOSE 2

interceder *n syn* see GO-BETWEEN 2

intercept *vb* to stop, seize, or interrupt in progress or course < *intercept* a forward pass >
syn block, catch, cut off
rel grab, seize, take; check, curb
con fumble, miss; loose, release

intercessor *n syn* see GO-BETWEEN 2

interchange *vb syn* see EXCHANGE 3
rel reverse, transpose

interchangeable *adj* permitting mutual substitution < *interchangeable* parts >
syn commutable, exchangeable, fungible, interconvertible, substitutable
rel changeable, convertible; reciprocal, reciprocative

interchurch *adj syn* see NONSECTARIAN

intercommunication *n* 1 *syn* see COMMUNICATION 3
2 *syn* see CONTACT 2

intercomparable *adj syn* see LIKE

interconnect *vb syn* see INTERJOIN

interconvertible *adj syn* see INTERCHANGEABLE

intercourse *n* 1 *syn* see COMMERCE 2
2 *syn* see COMMUNICATION 3
3 *syn* see CONTACT 2

intercreedal *adj syn* see NONSECTARIAN

intercross *vb* 1 *syn* see INTERSECT
2 *syn* see CROSS 4

interdenominational *adj syn* see NONSECTARIAN

interdict *vb syn* see FORBID
ant sanction

interdiction *n syn* see TABOO
ant sanction

interest *n* 1 participation in advantage, profit, and responsibility < he owned a half *interest* in a furniture store >
syn claim, share, stake
2 *syn* see WELFARE
3 readiness to be concerned with or moved by something < had an *interest* in art >
syn concern, curiosity, interestedness, regard

rel enthusiasm, excitement, passion; attention, care, concernment; absorption, engrossment

con apathy, indifference, unconcern

ant disinterest

interest *vb* to engage the attention and interest of <his appeal failed to *interest* his listeners>

syn appeal, attract, excite, fascinate, intrigue

rel arouse, tantalize, titillate; lure, pull, snare, tempt; pique

ant bore

interested *adj* having a share or concern in some affair <all *interested* parties met for the reading of the will>

syn affected, concerned, implicated, involved

rel biased, partial, partisan, prejudiced

con aloof, incurious, indifferent, unconcerned; apathetic, bored, ennuyé

ant detached, disinterested

interestedness *n syn* see INTEREST 3

interfere *vb* 1 *syn* see INTERPOSE 2

rel bar, block, hinder, impede, obstruct

2 *syn* see MEDDLE

rel discommode, incommode, inconvenience, trouble; baffle, balk, foil, frustrate, thwart

interflow *vb syn* see MIX 1

interfuse *vb* 1 *syn* see MIX 1

2 to cause to pass into or through <*interfused* illuminating anecdotes with the informative text>

syn diffuse, infuse, interlard, intersow, intersperse, intersprinkle

rel impenetrate, impregnate, interpenetrate, penetrate, pervade, saturate

3 *syn* see PERMEATE

interfusion *n syn* see MIXTURE

interim *n syn* see GAP 3

interim *adj syn* see TEMPORARY

interior *adj* 1 *syn* see INNER 1

con extraneous, extrinsic, foreign

ant exterior

2 *syn* see INNER 2

interior *n* the internal or inner part <the *interior* of the house>

syn inside, inward(s), within

rel center, heart; belly, bosom; innards, internals

ant exterior, outside

interject *vb syn* see INTRODUCE 6

interjoin *vb* to join mutually <*interjoined* several stations into a new system>

syn anastomose, interconnect, interlink, intertie

rel interdigitate, interlace, interlock, interrelate

con disunite, part, separate, sunder

ant disjoin

interknit *vb syn* see INTERWEAVE

interlace *vb syn* see INTERWEAVE

interlard *vb syn* see INTERFUSE 2

interlink *vb syn* see INTERJOIN

interlope *vb* 1 *syn* see INTRUDE

2 *syn* see MEDDLE

interlude *n* an intervening or interruptive period or space <an *interlude* of happi-

ness in a tragic story> <woodland broken by *interludes* of meadow>

syn break, intermission, interregnum, interval, parenthesis

rel breather, lull, pause, respite, rest; episode, idyll; meantime, meanwhile, spell; entr'acte

intermeddle *vb syn* see MEDDLE

rel encroach, entrench, invade, trespass

intermeddler *n syn* see BUSYBODY

intermediary *adj syn* see MIDDLE 2

intermediary *n* 1 *syn* see GO-BETWEEN 2

2 *syn* see MEAN 2

intermediate *vb syn* see INTERPOSE 2

intermediate *adj* 1 *syn* see MIDDLE 2

2 *syn* see MEDIUM

intermediate *n syn* see GO-BETWEEN 2

intermediator *n syn* see GO-BETWEEN 2

interment *n syn* see BURIAL 1

ant disinterment

intermesh *vb syn* see ENGAGE 1

interminable *adj syn* see CONTINUAL

rel eternal, infinite; lasting, permanent

con intermittent, periodic; discontinued, stopped; closed, completed, ended, finished, terminated

intermingle *vb syn* see MIX 1

intermission *n* 1 *syn* see ABEYANCE

2 *syn* see INTERLUDE

intermit *vb syn* see DEFER

rel arrest, check, interrupt

con continue, persist; iterate, reiterate, repeat

intermittent *adj* occurring or appearing in interrupted sequence <they predict *intermittent* rain throughout the day>

syn alternate, isochronal, isochronous, periodic, periodical, recurrent, recurring

rel cyclic, cyclical, iterant, iterative, metrical, rhythmic, rhythmical, seasonal, serial; arrested, checked, interrupted; fitful, spasmodic; infrequent, occasional, sporadic; discontinuing, discontinuous

con constant, perpetual; everlasting, interminable

ant continual, continuous; incessant, unceasing

intermix *vb syn* see MIX 1

intermixture *n syn* see MIXTURE

intermutual *adj syn* see COMMON 1

intern *vb syn* see IMPRISON

internal *adj* 1 *syn* see INNER 1

ant external

2 *syn* see INNER 2

3 *syn* see DOMESTIC 2

ant external

internals *n pl syn* see ENTRAILS

internuncio *n syn* see MESSENGER

interpenetrate *vb syn* see PERMEATE

interplay *vb syn* see INTERACT

interpolate *vb syn* see INTRODUCE 6

rel admit, enter; interlope, intrude; add, annex, append, superadd

con cancel, delete, erase, expunge

interpose *vb* 1 *syn* see INTRODUCE 6

rel cast, throw, toss; push, shove, thrust

2 to come between disagreeing elements <forced to *interpose* when the argument grew heated>

syn intercede, interfere, intermediate, intervene, mediate, step in

rel butt in, interlope, intrude, obtrude; intermeddle, meddle; arbitrate, moderate, negotiate

syn synonym(s) *rel* related word(s)

ant antonym(s) *con* contrasted word(s)

idiom idiomatic equivalent(s)

‖ use limited; if in doubt, see a dictionary

interpret vb 1 syn see EXPLAIN 1
rel exemplify, illustrate; annotate, gloss; comment, commentate
con contort, deform, distort; garble, misrepresent; misconstrue, misunderstand
2 syn see REPRESENT 1
interpretation n 1 syn see EXPLANATION 1
2 manner of artistic presentation in performance or adaptation or an instance of this < interpretation involves a re-creative effort by the performer>
syn reading, rendering, rendition, version
interpretive adj syn see EXPLANATORY
interreact vb syn see INTERACT
interregnum n syn see INTERLUDE
interrogate vb syn see ASK 1
interrogation n 1 syn see CROSS-EXAMINATION
2 syn see INQUIRY 2
interrogatory n syn see INQUIRY 2
interrupt vb 1 syn see ARREST 1
rel defer, intermit, postpone, suspend
2 to ask questions or make remarks while another is speaking < a chatterbox who habitually interrupts everyone>
syn break in, chime in, chip in
rel cut in, put in
idiom break in on (or upon)
interruption n 1 syn see GAP 3
rel rent, rift, rupture, split
2 syn see ABEYANCE
intersect vb to divide by passing through or across < parallel lines can never intersect >
syn crisscross, cross, crosscut, decussate, intercross
rel traverse; bisect
intersow vb syn see INTERFUSE 2
intersperse vb syn see INTERFUSE 2
intersprinkle vb syn see INTERFUSE 2
intertangle vb syn see ENTANGLE 1
intertie vb syn see INTERJOIN
intertrude vb syn see INTRUDE 1
intertwine vb syn see INTERWEAVE
intertwist vb syn see INTERWEAVE
interval n 1 syn see PAUSE
2 syn see INTERLUDE
3 syn see GAP 3
intervene vb syn see INTERPOSE 2
rel divide, part, separate, sever
intervolve vb syn see INTERWEAVE
interweave vb to blend or unite intimately < joy and melancholy are often closely interwoven >
syn interknit, interlace, intertwine, intertwist, intervolve, interwind, interwork, interwreathe, inweave
rel associate, join, link; blend, fuse, mix
interwind vb syn see INTERWEAVE
interwork vb syn see INTERWEAVE
interwreathe vb syn see INTERWEAVE
intestinal fortitude n syn see FORTITUDE
intestine adj 1 syn see DOMESTIC 2
2 syn see INNER 1
intimacy n syn see ACQUAINTANCE 1
intimate vb syn see SUGGEST 1
rel attest, bespeak, betoken, indicate
con air, express, utter, vent, voice; affirm, assert, aver, avouch, declare, profess
intimate adj 1 syn see INHERENT
2 syn see INNER 2

3 syn see FAMILIAR 1
rel nearest, next; affectionate, devoted, fond, loving; privy, secret
con distant, remote
4 having or marked by a warm personal relation < intimate friends for many years > < an intimate friendship>
syn ||buddy-buddy, chummy, cozy, pally, ||palsy-walsy
idiom thick as thieves
intimate n syn see FRIEND
rel associate, companion, comrade, crony
con outsider, stranger
intimation n 1 syn see HINT 1
2 syn see HINT 2
intimidate vb to frighten or coerce into submission or obedience < refused to be intimidated by the manager>
syn bludgeon, bluster, ||bounce, browbeat, bulldoze, bully, bullyrag, cow, dragoon, hector, ||ruffle, strong-arm, terrorize
rel alarm, disquiet, frighten, scare, terrify; badger, bait, chivy, hound, ride; coerce, compel, constrain, force, oblige; ||ruffianize
con blandish, cajole, coax, wheedle; induce, persuade, prevail
intimidator n syn see BULLY 1
into prep syn see TO 1
intolerable adj syn see INSUFFERABLE
ant tolerable
intolerant adj 1 unwilling or unable to endure with composure < he was inclined to be very intolerant of interruption >
syn impatient, unforbearing, unindulgent
rel contemptuous, disdainful; fractious, irritable, snappish, waspish; indignant, irate, outraged, stuffy, upset, worked up
con forbearing, indulgent, long-suffering, patient; resigned, uncomplaining
ant tolerant
2 syn see ILLIBERAL
rel inflexible, obdurate; antipathetic, averse, unsympathetic
con forbearing, indulgent, lenient
ant tolerant
intonation n syn see INFLECTION
in to adv syn see ALL 1
intoxicant n syn see LIQUOR 2
intoxicated adj 1 significantly under the influence of alcoholic liquor < some people become intoxicated more easily than others>
syn alcoholized, ||bagged, blind, ||blotto, ||boiled, ||bombed, ||boozed, ||boozy, ||buffy, buzzed, ||canned, ||capernoited, cockeyed, ||crocked, cut, ||deleerit, disguised, drunk, drunken, fried, ||half-seas over, inebriated, inebrious, ||jagged, ||juiced, ||lit, ||lit up, ||loaded, looped, ||lushed, muddled, ||oiled, organized, ||pickled, ||pie-eyed, ||pipped, pissed, pixilated, ||plastered, polluted, ||potted, rum-dum, ||screwy, ||shick, shicker, ||shot, slewed, slopped, sloppy, ||smashed, soshed, sozzled, ||spifficated, squiffed, ||stewed, stiff, ||stinking, stinko, stoned, ||swacked, tanked, ||tiddly, tight, unsober, wet, zonked
rel befuddled, bemused, besotted, dazed, dopey, fuddled, loopy, maudlin, sodden, soppy, sotted, tipsy
idiom disguised with drink, full as a tick, in drink (or liquor), in one's cups, in the bag, stewed to the gills, the worse for drink, three sheets in (or to) the wind,

under the table, under the weather, with drink taken
con abstemious, abstinent, moderate, temperate
ant sober
2 profoundly and usually pleasantly moved < *intoxicated* with the beauty of the scene >
syn elated, excited, exhilarated, turned-on
rel affected, concerned, interested, moved; galvanized, piqued, quickened, stimulated
con disinterested, unconcerned; depressed, disheartened, distressed, saddened
intoxicating *adj syn* see EXCITING
intoxication *n syn* see EUPHORIA 2
intractable *adj* 1 *syn* see UNRULY 1
ant tractable
2 *syn* see OBSTINATE
ant tractable
intransigent *adj syn* see OBSTINATE
intrepid *adj syn* see BRAVE 1
ant craven
intricate *adj* 1 *syn* see COMPLEX 2
rel arduous, difficult, hard
2 *syn* see ELABORATE 2
intrigue *vb* 1 *syn* see INTEREST
2 *syn* see PLOT
intrigue *n* 1 *syn* see PLOT 2
2 *syn* see AMOUR 2
intrinsic *adj syn* see INHERENT
con added, annexed, appended, super-added
ant extrinsic
intrinsically *adv syn* see PER SE
introduce *vb* 1 *syn* see ENTER 2
rel inaugurate, induct, install; bring forward
2 *syn* see BROACH
3 to bring into practice or use < *introduce* reforms in the welfare system >
syn inaugurate, initiate, institute, launch, originate, set up, usher in
rel establish, found, organize; innovate, invent; unveil; pioneer
4 to cause to know each other personally < planned to *introduce* her to his mother >
syn acquaint, present, ‖quaint
5 *syn* see PRECEDE 3
6 to put among or between others < *introduced* several new lines of dialogue >
syn fill in, insert, insinuate, intercalate, interject, interpolate, interpose, throw in
rel inlay, inlet, inset; inject, instill; work in
con eject, evict, oust; eliminate, exclude
ant abstract; withdraw
introducer *n syn* see INNOVATOR
introduction *n* something that serves as a preliminary or antecedent < the crisis could be the *introduction* to a general war >
syn exordium, foreword, overture, preamble, preface, prelude, prelusion, proem, prolegomenon, prologue
introductory *adj* 1 *syn* see PRELIMINARY
ant closing, concluding
2 *syn* see INITIAL 1

---

syn synonym(s)   *rel* related word(s)
ant antonym(s)   *con* contrasted word(s)
idiom idiomatic equivalent(s)
‖ use limited; if in doubt, see a dictionary

introspection *n* the examination of one's own thought and feeling < a man much given to *introspection* >
syn heart-searching, self-contemplation, self-examination, self-observation, self-questioning, self-reflection, self-scrutiny, self-searching, soul-searching
rel contemplation, meditation, reflection; self-analysis
ant extrospection
intrude *vb* 1 to thrust or force in without permission, welcome, or fitness < constantly *intruded* himself into his sister's affairs >
syn butt in, chisel (in), cut in, horn in, intertrude, obtrude
rel encroach, entrench, infringe, invade, muscle, trespass; insinuate, intercalate, interject, interpolate, interpose, introduce; interfere, intervene; intermeddle, meddle; bother, disturb, pester
con retire, stand off, withdraw
2 *syn* see IMPOSE 5
intrusive *adj syn* see IMPERTINENT 2
rel butting in, intruding, obtruding
con bashful, coy, diffident, modest, retiring, shy
ant unintrusive
intuition *n* immediate apprehension or cognition < skeptical of the traditional woman's *intuition* >
syn anschauung, insight, intuitiveness
rel second sight, sixth sense
ant ratiocination
intuitive *adj syn* see INSTINCTIVE 1
rel direct, immediate, presentative
ant ratiocinative
intuitiveness *n syn* see INTUITION
inumbrate *vb syn* see SHADE
inundate *vb syn* see DELUGE 1
inundation *n syn* see FLOOD 2
inurbane *adj syn* see RUDE 6
ant urbane
inure *vb syn* see ACCUSTOM
rel discipline, train
inutile *adj syn* see WORTHLESS 1
ant utile
invade *vb* 1 to enter for conquest or plunder < the Danes *invaded* England >
syn foray, inroad, overrun, overswarm, raid
rel loot, pillage, plunder, ravage
2 *syn* see TRESPASS 2
rel impenetrate, interpenetrate, permeate, pervade
invalid *adj* 1 *syn* see ILLOGICAL
ant valid
2 *syn* see NULL
invalidate *vb syn* see ABOLISH 1
rel counteract, counterbalance, negative, neutralize, offset; discredit
ant validate
invaluable *adj syn* see PRECIOUS 1
ant worthless
invariable *adj* 1 *syn* see INFLEXIBLE 3
ant variable
2 *syn* see SAME 3
ant variable, varying
invariably *adv* 1 *syn* see ALWAYS 1
2 *syn* see EVER 3
invasion *n* a hostile entrance into the territory of another < Hitler's *invasion* of Poland >

syn foray, incursion, inroad, irruption, raid

rel aggression, attack, offense, offensive; breach, infraction, infringement, transgression, trespass, violation; encroachment, entrenchment

invective *adj syn see* ABUSIVE
rel censorious, condemnatory, damnatory, denunciatory, reproachful

invective *n syn see* ABUSE
rel diatribe, jeremiad, philippic, tirade

inveigh (against) *vb syn see* OBJECT 1

inveigle *vb syn see* LURE

inveiglement *n syn see* LURE 2

invent *vb syn see* CONTRIVE 2
rel conceive, envision, imagine; create, mint, produce, turn out; inaugurate, initiate

invention *n* a product of creative imagination < his most famous *invention* is the electric light bulb >
syn brainchild, coinage, contrivance
rel concoction, contraption, innovation, novelty; creation, opus, original

inventive *adj* adept or prolific at producing new things and ideas < had a very *inventive* turn of mind > < he was an *inventive* genius >
syn creative, demiurgic, deviceful, ingenious, innovational, innovative, innovatory, original, originative
rel fertile, fruitful, productive, teeming; causative, constructive, formative
con sterile, uncreative, unproductive
ant uninventive

inventor *n* 1 *syn see* INNOVATOR
2 *syn see* FATHER 2

inventory *n* 1 *syn see* SUPPLY
2 *syn see* RESERVE

inventory *vb* 1 to make an itemized report or record of < will *inventory* all office supplies >
syn catalog, itemize, tally
rel list, record, register; enumerate, tabulate
idiom take account (*or* stock) of
2 *syn see* ITEMIZE 1
3 *syn see* EPITOMIZE 1

inveracity *n syn see* LIE
ant veracity

inverse *vb syn see* REVERSE 1

inversion *n syn see* REVERSAL 1

invert *vb syn see* REVERSE 1
rel flip, turn down, turn over

invert *n syn see* HOMOSEXUAL

invertebrate *n syn see* WEAKLING

invertebrate *adj syn see* WEAK 4
rel disorganized, structureless

inverted *adj* 1 *syn see* UPSIDE-DOWN 1
2 *syn see* HOMOSEXUAL

invest *vb* 1 *syn see* INITIATE 3
rel endow, endue; consecrate, honor
ant divest, strip
2 to make a formal grant of power or authority < the Constitution *invests* the Congress with taxation powers >
syn authorize, empower, vest
rel bequeath, endow
con hold back, keep back, reserve, withhold
ant divest
3 *syn see* ENFOLD 1
4 *syn see* BESIEGE

5 *syn see* INFUSE 1

investigate *vb syn see* EXPLORE
rel muckrake, poke, pry

investigation *n syn see* INQUIRY 1
rel observation, observing; sounding, survey, surveying

investigative *adj syn see* INQUISITIVE 1

investigator *n syn see* DETECTIVE

investiture *n syn see* INITIATION

inveterate *adj* 1 firmly established or having something firmly established < the *inveterate* tendency to overlook the obvious >
syn bred-in-the-bone, confirmed, deepdyed, deep-rooted, deep-seated, dyed-inthe-wool, entrenched, hard-shell, irradicable, settled, sworn
rel accustomed, addicted, chronic, habituated; customary, habitual, usual; hardened, indurated; established, fixed, set; inbred, innate; abiding, enduring, persistent, persisting
2 *syn see* OLD 2

invidious *adj* 1 *syn see* LIBELOUS
2 *syn see* ENVIOUS
rel bitter; hateful
3 *syn see* REPUGNANT 1
rel abominable, detestable, hateful, odious
con agreeable, grateful, gratifying, pleasant, pleasing

invidiousness *n syn see* ENVY

invigorate *vb syn see* STRENGTHEN 2
rel refresh, rejuvenate, renew, restore; rally, rouse, stir; activate, animate, stimulate, vitalize, vitaminize
ant debilitate

invigorating *adj* having an enlivening effect < an *invigorating* discussion >
syn animating, bracing, exhilarating, exhilarative, quickening, stimulating, stimulative, tonic, vitalizing
rel brisk, lively; fascinating, interesting
con anesthetic, numbing, somniferous
ant deadening

invincible *adj* incapable of being conquered < the team proved to be *invincible* >
syn impregnable, inconquerable, indomitable, inexpugnable, invulnerable, unassailable, unbeatable, unconquerable, undefeatable
rel inviolable, untouchable; unattackable
con conquerable, subduable, surmountable, vanquishable
ant vincible
2 *syn see* INSUPERABLE
ant vincible

inviolable *adj syn see* SACRED 3
rel consecrated, hallowed; blessed, divine, holy; chaste, pure
ant violable

inviolate *adj syn see* SACRED 3
rel intact, perfect; faultless, flawless
con desecrated, profaned; defiled, polluted

invisible *adj syn see* IMPERCEPTIBLE
rel hidden, unseeable
ant visible

invitation *n syn see* PROPOSAL

invite *vb* to request the presence or participation of < *invited* guests to dinner > < *invited* the major nations to confer >
syn ask, bid
rel call, call in, summon; court, solicit, woo; entice, inveigle, lure, tempt

invoice n syn see BILL 1

invoke vb 1 syn see BEG
 2 syn see ENFORCE

involuntary adj syn see SPONTANEOUS
 rel unintended, unintentional, unwitting
 ant voluntary

involve vb 1 to bring a person or thing into circumstances or a situation from which extrication is difficult <nations *involved* in war>
 syn embroil, implicate, mire, tangle; compare ENTANGLE 3
 rel catch up; draw (into)
 2 syn see INCLUDE

involved adj 1 syn see COMPLEX 2
 rel confused, muddled
 con easy, facile, simple
 2 syn see INTERESTED
 rel enmeshed, entangled
 ant uninvolved

involvement n syn see ENTANGLEMENT 1

invulnerable adj syn see INVINCIBLE 1
 ant vulnerable

inward adj syn see INNER 1
 con alien, extraneous, extrinsic, foreign
 ant outward

inward n 1 often **inwards** pl syn see INTERIOR
 2 **inwards** pl syn see ENTRAILS

inwardness n syn see ACQUAINTANCE 1

inweave vb syn see INTERWEAVE

iota n syn see PARTICLE

ipseity n syn see INDIVIDUALITY 4

irascible adj easily aroused to anger <an *irascible* fellow and hard to get along with>
 syn choleric, cranky, cross, hot-tempered, ireful, passionate, peppery, quick-tempered, ratty, ‖stomachy, temperish, testy, tetchy, touchy; compare CANTANKEROUS, IRRITABLE
 rel fractious, huffy, irritable, peevish, petulant, querulous, snappish, waspish; impatient, jittery, jumpy, nervous, restive; bristly, crabbed, surly
 con amiable, complaisant, good-natured, obliging; calm, quiet, relaxed; long-suffering, patient, tolerant

irate adj syn see ANGRY

ire n syn see ANGER

ire vb syn see ANGER 1

ireful adj 1 syn see ANGRY
 2 syn see IRASCIBLE

irenic adj syn see PACIFIC
 ant acrimonious

irk vb 1 syn see ANNOY 1
 rel discommode, incommode, inconvenience, trouble
 2 syn see TRY 2

irking n syn see ANNOYANCE 1

irksome adj tending to cause boredom or tedium <an *irksome* task>
 syn boresome, boring, drudging, tedious, tiresome, tiring
 rel dull, stupid; exhausting, fagging, fatiguing, wearisome
 con exciting, inspiring, provocative, stimulative, stirring

---

syn synonym(s)   rel related word(s)
ant antonym(s)   con contrasted word(s)
idiom idiomatic equivalent(s)
‖ use limited; if in doubt, see a dictionary

---

ant absorbing, engrossing

iron n, usu **irons** pl syn see SHACKLE

iron adj syn see INFLEXIBLE 2

ironbound adj syn see ROUGH 1

ironclad adj syn see INFLEXIBLE 3

ironfisted adj 1 syn see STINGY
 2 syn see GRIM 3

ironhanded adj syn see RIGID 3

ironhead n syn see DUNCE

ironhearted adj syn see UNFEELING 2
 ant softhearted

ironic adj syn see SARDONIC
 rel biting, cutting, incisive, trenchant; caustic, mordant, scathing

ironman n syn see DOLLAR

irradiate vb syn see ILLUMINATE 2

irradicable adj syn see INVETERATE 1

irrational adj syn see ILLOGICAL
 rel crazy, demented, insane
 con logical, reasonable, sensible
 ant rational

irrealizable adj syn see IMPOSSIBLE 1
 ant realizable

irrebuttable adj syn see POSITIVE 3
 ant rebuttable

irreclaimable adj syn see IRRECOVERABLE
 ant reclaimable

irreconcilable adj incapable of being made consistent <the two versions of the story are completely *irreconcilable*>
 syn incompatible, inconformable, inconsistent
 rel discordant, discrepant, dissonant, inaccordant, incongruent, incongruous, inharmonious
 ant reconcilable

irrecoverable adj not capable of being recovered, regained, remedied, or rectified <suffered an *irrecoverable* loss in the fire>
 syn irreclaimable, irredeemable, irremediable, irreparable, irretrievable
 ant recoverable

irredeemable adj syn see IRRECOVERABLE
 ant redeemable

irreflective adj syn see CARELESS 1
 ant reflective

irrefragable adj syn see INDESTRUCTIBLE

irrefrangible adj syn see INDESTRUCTIBLE

irrefutable adj syn see POSITIVE 3
 ant refutable

irregular adj 1 not according with or explainable by law, rule, or custom <unusual problems require *irregular* solutions>
 syn abnormal, anomalous, deviant, divergent, off-key, unnatural, unregular
 rel aberrant, atypical; exceptional, odd, peculiar, queer, singular, strange, unique
 con natural, normal, typical; accustomed, customary, habitual, usual, wonted
 ant regular
 2 syn see INFORMAL 1
 3 syn see LOPSIDED
 ant regular
 4 syn see RANDOM
 rel occasional, sporadic; erratic, fitful, spasmodic; inconstant, uneven, unsteady
 5 syn see SPOTTY 1

irregular n syn see PARTISAN 2

irregularity n syn see INEQUALITY 1
  ant regularity
irregularly adv syn see OCCASIONALLY
  ant regularly
irrelative adj syn see IRRELEVANT
  ant relative
irrelevant adj not applicable or pertinent
  <age should be *irrelevant* to em-
  ployability>
  syn extraneous, foreign, immaterial, impertinent, inapplicable, inapposite, irrelative
  rel inconsequential, insignificant, unimportant
  idiom beside the point, neither here nor
  there, out of the question
  con applicable, appurtenant, germane,
  material, pertinent, significant
  ant relevant
irreligious adj lacking religious emotions,
  doctrines, or practices <an *irreligious*
  person but not openly hostile to organized
  religion>
  syn godless, nonreligious, unreligious
  rel indevout, undevout; ungodly, unholy,
  unsanctimonious; blasphemous, impious,
  profane, sacrilegious; amoral, unmoral
  con devout, pious
  ant religious
irremediable adj 1 syn see IRRECOVER-
  ABLE
  ant remediable
  2 syn see HOPELESS 2
irremovable adj syn see IMMOVABLE 1
  ant removable
irreparable adj 1 syn see IRRECOVER-
  ABLE
  ant reparable
  2 syn see HOPELESS 2
irreprehensible adj syn see GOOD 11
  ant reprehensible
irrepressible adj impossible to repress,
  restrain, or control <an *irrepressible* joy
  over his brother's good fortune>
  syn insuppressible, insuppressive, irrestrainable, uncontainable, uncontrollable,
  unrestrainable
  rel bubbling over, effervescent, enthusiastic, rhapsodical
  ant repressible
irreproachable adj 1 syn see GOOD 11
  2 syn see IMPECCABLE 1
irresoluble adj syn see INSOLUBLE
  ant resoluble
irresolute adj syn see VACILLATING 2
  ant resolute
irresolution n syn see HESITATION
  ant resolution
irresolvable adj syn see INSOLUBLE
  ant resolvable
irresponsible adj lacking in responsibility
  <*irresponsible* behavior>
  syn carefree, careless, feckless, incautious,
  reckless, uncareful, wild
  rel undependable, unreliable, untrustworthy; unaccountable, unanswerable
  con careful, cautious, discreet, heedful;
  dependable, reliable, trustworthy
  ant responsible
irrestrainable adj syn see IRREPRESSIBLE
  ant restrainable
irretrievable adj syn see IRRECOVER-
  ABLE

italicize   321

  ant retrievable
irreverent adj syn see IMPIOUS 1
  ant reverent
irreverential adj syn see IMPIOUS 1
  ant reverential
irreversible adj syn see IRREVOCABLE
  ant reversible
irrevocable adj incapable of being recalled
  or revoked <an *irrevocable* decision of the
  Supreme Court>
  syn irreversible, nonreversible, unrepealable
  rel constant, established, fixed; immutable, unchangeable, unmodifiable
  con repealable, reversible; alterable,
  changeable, modifiable
  ant revocable
irritable adj easily exasperated <the miserable weather made us all *irritable*>
  syn disagreeable, fractious, fretful, huffy,
  peevish, pettish, petulant, ‖pindling, prickish, prickly, querulent, querulential, querulous, raspish, raspy, snappish, snappy,
  twitty, waspish, waspy, whiny; compare
  CANTANKEROUS, IRASCIBLE
  rel cranky, cross, testy, touchy; choleric,
  irascible, splenetic
  con amiable, complaisant, good-natured,
  obliging; affable, cordial, genial, gracious,
  sociable
  ant easygoing
irritant n syn see ANNOYANCE 3
irritate vb to excite to angry annoyance
  <his rude interruptions really *irritated*
  her>
  syn aggravate, burn (up), exasperate, gall,
  get, grate, huff, inflame, nettle, peeve,
  pique, provoke, put out, rile, roil; compare
  ANNOY 1
  rel abrade, bother, ‖bug, chafe, exercise,
  fret, irk, ruffle, try, vex; anger, enrage,
  incense, infuriate, madden; affront, offend
  con appease, conciliate, mollify, pacify,
  placate, propitiate; delight, gladden, gratify, please
irrupt vb syn see ERUPT 1
irruption n syn see INVASION
Ishmael n syn see OUTCAST
Ishmaelite n syn see OUTCAST
island vb syn see ISOLATE
isochronal adj syn see INTERMITTENT
isochronous adj syn see INTERMITTENT
isolate vb to set apart from others <the
  jury was *isolated* for several days>
  syn close off, cut off, enisle, insulate,
  island, segregate, separate, sequester
  rel quarantine; block (off); abstract, detach, disengage, remove; divide, part,
  sever, sunder
  con associate, connect, join, link, unite
isolate adj syn see ALONE 1
isolated adj syn see ALONE 1
  rel retired, secluded, withdrawn; abandoned, deserted, forsaken, stranded
isolation n syn see SOLITUDE
issue n 1 syn see OFFSPRING
  2 syn see EFFECT 1
  3 syn see PROBLEM 2
  rel matter; subject, topic
issue vb 1 syn see SPRING 1
  2 syn see EMIT 2
  3 syn see PUBLISH 2
italicize vb syn see EMPHASIZE

itch *n* 1 *syn* see DESIRE 1
  2 *syn* see LUST 2
itch *vb syn* see LONG
itchy *adj syn* see COVETOUS
item *adv syn* see ALSO 2
item *n syn* see POINT 1
  rel component, piece; incidental, minutia
itemize *vb* 1 to set down in detail or by
  particulars < *itemize* deductions on a tax
  form >
  syn enumerate, inventory, list, particularize, specialize, specify; *compare* SPECIFY 3
  rel circumstantiate, document; count,
  number; cite, instance, mention; spell out
  ant summarize
  2 *syn* see INVENTORY
itemized *adj syn* see CIRCUMSTANTIAL
  ant summarized
iterate *vb syn* see REPEAT

itinerant *adj* traveling from place to place
  < *itinerant* preachers >
  syn ambulant, ambulatory, deambulatory,
  itinerate, nomadic, perambulant, perambulatory, peripatetic, roving, vagabond, vagrant, wandering, wayfaring
  rel rambling, ranging, roaming; moving,
  shifting
itinerate *adj syn* see ITINERANT
itsy–bitsy *adj syn* see TINY
itty–bitty *adj syn* see TINY
ivory *n often* ivories *pl syn* see DICE
ivory–tower *adj syn* see IMPRACTICAL 1
  ant down-to-earth
ivory–towered *adj syn* see IMPRACTICAL
  1
ivory–towerish *adj syn* see IMPRACTI-
  CAL 1

J

jab *vb syn* see POKE 1
jab *n* 1 *syn* see POKE 1
  2 *syn* see PRICK 1
jabber *vb syn* see GIBBER
jabber *n* 1 *syn* see GIBBERISH 1
  2 *syn* see CHATTER
jabberer *n syn* see CHATTERBOX
jabberwocky *n syn* see GIBBERISH 1
jack *n* 1 *syn* see MARINER
  2 *syn* see FLAG
  ‖3 *syn* see MONEY
jack (up) *vb syn* see RAISE 9
jackass *n* 1 *syn* see DONKEY 1
  2 *syn* see FOOL 1
jacket *n syn* see HIDE
jackleg *adj syn* see AMATEURISH
jackleg lawyer *n syn* see PETTIFOGGER
jackpot *n syn* see POT 3
jack–tar *n syn* see MARINER
jade *n* 1 *syn* see WANTON
  2 *syn* see MINX
jade *vb* 1 *syn* see TIRE 1
  rel cloy, pall, sate, satiate, surfeit; emasculate, enervate, unman, unnerve; depress,
  oppress, weigh
  con rejuvenate, renew, restore
  ant refresh
  2 *syn* see SATIATE
jaded *adj* 1 *syn* see TIRED 1
  ant refreshed
  2 *syn* see SATIATED
‖jag *n syn* see PRICK 1
jag *n syn* see BINGE 1
‖jag *vb syn* see CARRY 1
jagged *adj syn* see ROUGH 1
‖jagged *adj syn* see INTOXICATED 1
jail *n* a building or institution for the confinement of persons held in lawful custody
  < sent to *jail* for perjury >
  syn bastille, ‖big house, bridewell, ‖brig,

‖bucket, ‖caboose, ‖calaboose, ‖can, ‖car-
cel, ‖chokey, ‖clink, ‖college, cooler, coop,
freezer, guardroom, ‖hoosegow, jug, keep,
lockup, pen, penitentiary, ‖pokey, prison,
reformatory, rock pile, skookum-house,
slammer, ‖stir, stockade
  idiom house of correction
jail *vb syn* see IMPRISON
  ant release
jailbird *n syn* see CONVICT
jake *n syn* see RUSTIC
jakes *n pl but sing or pl in constr syn* see
  PRIVY 1
jalopy *n* a dilapidated old automobile
  < bought a *jalopy* for $50 >
  syn clunker, crate, dog, heap, junker,
  wreck
jam *vb* 1 *syn* see PRESS 1
  rel tamp, wad
  2 *syn* see CRAM 1
  3 *syn* see PRESS 2
jam *n syn* see PREDICAMENT
jam *n* a rich spread prepared by boiling
  fruit and sugar until the mixture thickens
  < enjoyed his mother's tasty berry *jams* >
  syn confiture, conserve, preserve
  rel jelly, marmalade
jam–full *adj syn* see FULL 1
jammed *adj syn* see FULL 1
jam–pack *vb syn* see CRAM 1
jam–packed *adj syn* see FULL 1
jangle *vb syn* see CLASH 2
jangle *n syn* see DIN
jape *n syn* see JOKE 1
jar *vb* 1 *syn* see CLASH 2
  2 *syn* see SHAKE 2
jar *n syn* see IMPACT
  rel fluctuation, sway, vibration; agitation,
  disturbance, upset
jargon *n* 1 *syn* see TERMINOLOGY
  2 *syn* see DIALECT 2
  rel idiom, speech; abracadabra, gibberish
jarring *adj syn* see HARSH 3
  ant soothing
jaundiced *adj syn* see BIASED 2
jaunt *n syn* see EXCURSION 1

---

syn synonym(s)   *rel* related word(s)
ant antonym(s)   *con* contrasted word(s)
idiom idiomatic equivalent(s)
‖ use limited; if in doubt, see a dictionary

‖**jaw** *n syn* see BACK TALK

jaw *vb* **1** *syn* see SCOLD 1

2 *syn* see CHAT 1

jay *n syn* see RUSTIC

‖**jazz** *n syn* see NONSENSE 2

jealous *adj* **1** intolerant of rivalry or unfaithfulness <her husband was *jealous* of her flirting with other men>
syn possessive, possessory
rel covetous, demanding; grasping, grudging; envious, green-eyed, invidious; mistrustful, suspicious; doubting, questioning
con tolerant, trusting, understanding

2 *syn* see ENVIOUS

3 *syn* see SUSPICIOUS 2

jealousy *n syn* see ENVY

jeer *vb syn* see SCOFF
con fawn, toady, truckle; approve, endorse, OK, sanction

jejune *adj syn* see INSIPID 3
rel slight, slim, tenuous, thin; arid, dry

jell *vb syn* see COAGULATE
rel stiffen, thicken; cohere, stick

jellify *vb syn* see COAGULATE

jelly *vb syn* see COAGULATE

jellyfish *n syn* see WEAKLING

jeopard *vb syn* see ENDANGER

jeopardize *vb syn* see ENDANGER

jeopardous *adj syn* see DANGEROUS 1

jeopardy *n syn* see DANGER
rel exposure; liability, openness, sensitiveness, susceptibility; accident, chance, hap
ant safety

jeopardy *vb syn* see ENDANGER

jeremiad *n syn* see TIRADE

jerk *vb* to act on with or make a sudden sharp quick movement <*jerked* to one side> <*jerk* a root from the ground>
syn lug, lurch, snap, twitch, vellicate, yank
rel drag, pull; fling, sling, throw, toss; wrench, wrest, wring

jerk *n syn* see FOOL 1

jerkwater town *n syn* see BURG

jerry-build *vb syn* see THROW UP 1

jest *n* **1** *syn* see JOKE 1
rel banter, chaff, jolly; derision, ridicule, twit

2 *syn* see FUN 1
con gravity, seriousness, soberness
ant earnest

3 *syn* see LAUGHINGSTOCK

jest *vb* **1** *syn* see SCOFF

2 *syn* see BANTER

jestee *n syn* see LAUGHINGSTOCK

jester *n* **1** *syn* see FOOL 2

2 *syn* see HUMORIST 2

jet *adj syn* see BLACK 1

jet *vb syn* see SQUIRT

jetsam *n syn* see DRIFTWOOD

jet set *n syn* see SMART SET

jettison *n syn* see DISPOSAL 2

jettison *vb syn* see DISCARD
ant salvage

jetty *n syn* see WHARF

jetty *adj syn* see BLACK 1

jewel *n syn* see PARAGON

jewel *vb syn* see BEJEWEL

jezebel *n syn* see WANTON

jib *vb syn* see DEMUR

jibe *vb syn* see AGREE 4

‖**jiff** *n syn* see INSTANT 1

jiffy *n syn* see INSTANT 1

jig *n syn* see TRICK 1

jigger *n* **1** *syn* see DOODAD

2 *syn* see GADGET 1

‖**jiggery-pokery** *n syn* see NONSENSE 2

jiggle *vb syn* see SHAKE 3

‖**jillion** *n syn* see SCAD

jim-dandy *n syn* see ‖DILLY

jimjams *n syn* see JITTERS

jimmies *n syn* see JITTERS

jimmy *vb syn* see PRY

jingle *vb* to make a repeated sharp light ringing sound <the coins *jingled* in his pocket>
syn chink, chinkle, clink, tingle, tinkle
rel clack, clatter, rattle

jinx *n* something that is felt or meant to bring bad luck <his continual bad luck seemed due to a *jinx*>
syn hex, hoodoo, Indian sign, voodoo, whammy
rel charm, enchantment, spell; curse, evil eye

jitters *n pl* a sense of panic or extreme nervousness <got the *jitters* whenever he thought of the money he had lost>
syn all-overs, dither, heebie-jeebies, ‖jimjams, ‖jimmies, jumps, shakes, shivers, whim-whams, willies

jittery *adj syn* see NERVOUS

‖**jive** *vb syn* see BANTER

job *n* **1** *syn* see TASK 1
rel affair, concern, matter, thing

2 a regular remunerative employment <held two *jobs* to make ends meet>
syn appointment, berth, billet, connection, office, place, position, post, situation, spot; *compare* WORK 1
rel assignment, engagement, posting; calling, employment, occupation, pursuit; profession, trade, vocation; niche, opening, slot

3 *syn* see WORK 1

4 *syn* see TASK 2

job *vb syn* see DUPE

jobless *adj syn* see UNEMPLOYED

jockey *vb syn* see MANIPULATE 2

jocose *adj syn* see WITTY
rel playful, roguish, sportive, waggish, whimsical; comic, comical, droll, laughable, ludicrous; blithe, jocund, jolly, jovial
con demure, earnest, grave, sedate, serious, sober, solemn, staid
ant lugubrious

jocular *adj syn* see WITTY
rel jolly, jovial, merry; playful, sportive; comic, comical, droll, laughable, ludicrous
con earnest, grave, serious, sober, solemn

jocularity *n syn* see MIRTH

jocund *adj syn* see MERRY
rel mischievous, playful, sportive
con dour, gloomy, glum, morose, saturnine, sullen; grave, sedate, serious, solemn, somber, staid

jocundity *n syn* see MIRTH

jog *vb syn* see POKE 1
rel agitate, shake

joggle *vb syn* see SHAKE 3

john *n syn* see TOILET

John Law *n syn* see POLICEMAN

johnny *n syn* see TOILET

join *vb* **1** to bring or come together into some manner of union <the couple were *joined* in marriage soon thereafter>

syn associate, bracket, coadunate, coagment, coalesce, combine, compound, concrete, conjoin, conjugate, connect, couple, link, marry, one, relate, unite, wed, yoke

rel agree, concur, cooperate; articulate, concatenate, integrate; affix, attach, fasten; knit, weave; bind, tie, tie up

con separate, sever, sunder; detach, disengage; disembarrass, disentangle, untangle

ant disjoin, part

2 *syn* see ADJOIN

join (up) *vb syn* see ENTER 3

joining *n syn* see JOINT 1

joint *n* 1 a place where two or more things are united <the leak was found at a *joint* in the pipeline>

syn connection, coupling, joining, junction, juncture, seam, union

rel crux, link, tie; interconnection; abutment, articulation, suture; concourse, confluence, meeting

2 *syn* see DIVE

joint *adj syn* see COMMON 1

jointly *adv syn* see TOGETHER 3

joke *n* 1 a remark, story, or action intended to evoke laughter <had a good memory for *jokes*>

syn crack, drôlerie, drollery, gag, jape, jest, quip, sally, waggery, wisecrack, witticism, ‖yak

rel antic, caper, dido, monkeyshine, prank; bijouterie, bon mot; burlesque, caricature, parody, quiz, rib; badinage, persiflage, raillery; facetiousness, humorousness, jocoseness, jocularity, wittiness; humor, repartee, sarcasm, wit

2 *syn* see FUN 1

3 *syn* see LAUGHINGSTOCK

joke *vb syn* see BANTER

joker *n* 1 *syn* see WAG 1

2 *syn* see HUMORIST 2

3 *syn* see ZANY 2

jokester *n* 1 *syn* see HUMORIST 2

2 *syn* see ZANY 2

jollity *n* 1 *syn* see MIRTH

rel blitheness; disport, frolic, gambol, play, rollick, romp, sport

con earnestness, gravity, sedateness, seriousness, solemnity, staidness

ant somberness

2 *syn* see MERRYMAKING

jolly *adj syn* see MERRY

rel frolicsome, mischievous, playful, roguish, sportive, waggish

con earnest, grave, sedate, serious, solemn, staid; doleful, dolorous, lugubrious, rueful

ant somber

jolly *vb syn* see BANTER

rel blandish, cajole

jolt *vb syn* see SHOCK 2

jolt *n* 1 *syn* see IMPACT

2 *syn* see DRAM

jongleur *n syn* see BARD 1

josh *vb syn* see BANTER

joskin *n syn* see RUSTIC

jostle *vb syn* see PUSH 2

jot *n syn* see PARTICLE

jounce *n syn* see IMPACT

journal *n* a publication that appears at regular intervals <a monthly scientific *journal*>

syn magazine, newspaper, organ, periodical, review

journey *n* passing or a passage from one place to another <at that time it was a four day *journey* from Boston to New York> <she was tired though their *journey* was barely begun>

syn expedition, peregrination(s), travel(s), trek, trip; *compare* TRIP 1

rel excursion, jaunt, junket, sally, tour; cruise, voyage; pilgrimage, progress, safari

journey *vb syn* see GO 1

jovial *adj syn* see MERRY

rel facetious, humorous, jocose, jocular; affable, genial, sociable; amiable, goodnatured; bantering, chaffing, jollying, joshing

con dour, gloomy, glum, morose, saturnine, sullen; grave, sedate, serious, solemn, staid

joviality *n syn* see MIRTH

joy *n syn* see PLEASURE 2

rel ecstasy, rapture, transport

ant sorrow; misery

joyance *n syn* see PLEASURE 2

joyful *adj syn* see GLAD 1

rel buoyant, effervescent, expansive

con despairing, desperate, despondent, forlorn, hopeless; depressed, oppressed, weighed down

ant joyless

joy girl *n syn* see PROSTITUTE

joyhouse *n syn* see BROTHEL

joy–juice *n syn* see LIQUOR 2

joyless *adj* 1 *syn* see SAD 2

2 *syn* see GLOOMY 3

joyous *adj syn* see GLAD 1

rel ecstatic, rapturous, transported

con doleful, dolorous, melancholy; miserable, wretched

ant lugubrious

jubilance *n syn* see EXULTATION

jubilant *adj syn* see EXULTANT

jubilate *vb syn* see EXULT

jubilation *n syn* see EXULTATION

judge *n* 1 a person who impartially decides unsettled questions or controversial issues <the *judge* declared the ruling invalid>

syn arbiter, arttitrator, referee, umpire

rel intermediary, mediator, negotiator; conciliator, peacemaker, reconciler

2 an official entrusted with administration of laws <the *judge* gave the defendant a suspended sentence>

syn ‖beak, court, justice, magistrate

judge *vb* 1 to decide something in dispute or controversy upon its merits and upon evidence <the committee will *judge* the truth of the testimony>

syn adjudge, adjudicate, arbitrate, referee, umpire

rel decide, determine, rule, settle

2 *syn* see INFER

rel demonstrate, prove, show; check, test, try

3 *syn* see ESTIMATE 3

judgmatic *adj syn* see WISE 2

judgment *n* 1 *syn* see INFERENCE 1

rel decision, determination, ruling; belief, conviction, opinion, persuasion, view

---

syn synonym(s)   *rel* related word(s)
ant antonym(s)   *con* contrasted word(s)
idiom idiomatic equivalent(s)
‖ use limited; if in doubt, see a dictionary

2 *syn* see INFERENCE 2

3 *syn* see ESTIMATION 1

4 *syn* see SENSE 6

rel astuteness, perspicacity, sagacity, shrewdness; acumen, discernment, insight, penetration

judicious *adj syn* see WISE 2

rel rational, reasonable; dispassionate, equitable, fair, objective

con irrational, thoughtless, unreasonable; ill-considered

ant injudicious; asinine

jug *n syn* see JAIL

jug *vb syn* see IMPRISON

juggle *vb syn* see DECEIVE

juice *n syn* see LIQUOR 2

juiced *adj syn* see INTOXICATED 1

juicy *adj syn* see SUCCULENT

juju *n syn* see CHARM 2

jumble *vb* 1 *syn* see CONFUSE 5

2 *syn* see DISORDER 1

jumble *n* 1 *syn* see CLUTTER 2

2 *syn* see MISCELLANY 1

jumbo *adj syn* see HUGE

jump *vb* 1 to move suddenly through space by or as if by muscular action <*jumped* across the open trench>

syn bounce, bound, hop, hurdle, leap, lop, saltate, spring, vault

2 *syn* see START 1

3 *syn* see RAISE 9

jump (in *or* into) *vb syn* see PITCH IN 1

jump (off) *vb syn* see BEGIN 1

jumps *n pl syn* see JITTERS

jumpy *adj syn* see NERVOUS

idiom on pins and needles

junction *n* 1 *syn* see CONCOURSE

2 *syn* see JOINT 1

juncture *n* 1 *syn* see JOINT 1

2 a critical or crucial time or state of affairs <was at a *juncture* where he had to make a decision>

syn contingency, crisis, crossroad(s), emergency, exigency, pass, pinch, strait, turning point, zero hour

rel condition, posture, situation, state, status; plight, predicament, quandary

3 *syn* see POINT 7

jungle *n* 1 *syn* see CLUTTER 2

2 *syn* see MAZE 1

junk *n syn* see REFUSE

junk *vb syn* see DISCARD

junker *n syn* see JALOPY

junket *n syn* see EXCURSION 1

junking *n syn* see DISPOSAL 2

Junoesque *adj syn* see CURVACEOUS

jurisdiction *n syn* see POWER 1

rel bounds, confines, limits; compass, range, reach, scope; bailiwick, domain, field, province, sphere, territory

just *adj* 1 *syn* see WELL-FOUNDED

2 *syn* see TRUE 3

3 being what is called for by circumstances or accepted standards <punishments once considered fair and *just* are now held to be cruel, excessive, and unreasonable>

syn appropriate, condign, deserved, due, merited, requisite, rhadamanthine, right, rightful, suitable; *compare* FIT 1

rel fit, fitting, meet, proper

con farfetched, irrelevant, remote, unconnected; improper, inapplicable, inapposite, inappropriate; abusive, cruel, harsh

ant unjust

4 *syn* see UPRIGHT 2

rel rigid, strict; dependable, reliable, tried, trustworthy

5 *syn* see FAIR 4

rel aloof; condign, due, rightful

ant unjust

6 *syn* see FIT 1

just *adv* 1 as stated or indicated without deviation <*just* six inches long>

syn accurately, bang, exactly, precisely, right, sharp, ‖smack-dab, spang, square, squarely

rel definitely, directly, expressly, unmistakably

con almost, nearly; approximately, imprecisely, inaccurately, inexactly, loosely

2 by a very small margin <*just* enough food for one meal>

syn barely, hardly, scarce, scarcely

rel almost, approximately, nearly

con copiously, fully, generously, lavishly, unstintedly, unstintingly

3 no more than <*just* a note to remind you>

syn but, merely, only, simply

idiom nothing but

4 *syn* see ALL 1

5 *syn* see EVEN 1

just about *adv syn* see NEARLY

justice *n* 1 the action, practice, or obligation of awarding each his just due <his *justice* was stern but absolutely fair>

syn equity

rel evenness, fairness, impartiality

con foul play, inequity, unjustness; bias, leaning, one-sidedness, partiality

ant injustice

2 *syn* see JUDGE 2

justifiable *adj* capable of being justified <thought her absence was not *justifiable*>

syn condonable, defensible, excusable, tenable, vindicable, warrantable

rel admissible, allowable, legitimate, reasonable; forgivable, pardonable, remissible

ant unjustifiable

justification *n* 1 *syn* see EXPLANATION 2

2 *syn* see APOLOGY 1

justified *adj syn* see WELL-FOUNDED

ant unjustified

justify *vb* 1 *syn* see MAINTAIN 2

rel demonstrate, prove; back, support, uphold

con confute, disprove, refute

2 *syn* see CONFIRM 2

3 *syn* see EXPLAIN 3

rel extenuate, gloss, gloze, palliate, whitewash

con accuse, arraign, incriminate, indict; blame, condemn, denounce

4 to constitute sufficient grounds <thought the storm warning *justified* his leaving early>

syn warrant

rel allow, permit; approve, authorize, sanction

justly *adv syn* see WELL 1

jut *vb* 1 *syn* see BULGE

rel elongate, extend, lengthen

2 *syn* see HANG 4

jut *n syn* see PROJECTION 1

juvenile *adj syn* see YOUNG 1

ant adult
juvenile *n syn* see CHILD 1

juvenility *n syn* see YOUTH 1
juxtaposed *adj syn* see ADJACENT 3

K

‖**kale** *n syn* see MONEY
‖**keck** *vb syn* see RETCH
keel (over) *vb syn* see FALL 2
keen *adj* 1 *syn* see SHARP 1
 2 *syn* see ENTHUSIASTIC
 3 *syn* see EAGER
 rel fervent, fervid, perfervid; fierce, intense, vehement; fired
 con apathetic, impassive, phlegmatic, stolid; languid, listless
 4 *syn* see SHARP 4
 5 *syn* see ACUTE 3
 con dull, obtuse
 6 *syn* see LIVELY 1
 ‖7 *syn* see MARVELOUS 2
keenly *adv syn* see HARD 6
keenness *n* 1 *syn* see EDGE 2
 2 *syn* see WIT 3
keep *vb* 1 *syn* see OBEY
 ant neglect
 2 to notice or honor a day, occasion, or deed <remember the Sabbath and *keep* it rightly>
 syn celebrate, commemorate, observe, solemnize
 rel regard, respect; bless, consecrate, sanctify; honor, laud, praise
 idiom keep the faith
 con disregard, forget, ignore, neglect, omit, overlook, slight; contravene, infringe, transgress, violate
 ant break
 3 *syn* see STOCK
 4 *syn* see RESTRAIN 1
 ant release
 5 to hold in one's possession or under one's control <*kept* all the money for himself>
 syn detain, hold, hold back, keep back, keep out, reserve, retain, withhold
 rel conserve, preserve, save; enjoy, have, own, possess; conduct, control, direct, manage
 con cast, discard, junk; refuse, reject, repudiate, spurn; abandon, resign, surrender, yield
 ant relinquish
 6 *syn* see REFRAIN 1
 7 *syn* see CONDUCT 3
keep *n* 1 *syn* see LIVING
 2 *syn* see JAIL
keep back *vb* 1 *syn* see KEEP 5
 2 *syn* see DENY 2
keeper *n syn* see CUSTODIAN
keeping *n* 1 *syn* see CUSTODY
 2 *syn* see PRESERVATION 1

keep off *vb syn* see FEND (off)
keep out *vb syn* see KEEP 5
keepsake *n syn* see REMEMBRANCE 3
keep up *vb syn* see MAINTAIN 1
keg *n syn* see CASK
‖**keister** *n syn* see BUTTOCKS
kelter *n syn* see REFUSE
ken *n* the extent of one's recognition, comprehension, perception, understanding, or knowledge <abstractions that are beyond the *ken* of small children>
 syn horizon, purview, range, reach
 rel comprehension, grasp, perception, understanding
kept woman *n syn* see HARLOT 1
kerchief *n* 1 a square of cloth used as a head covering or scarf <wore a *kerchief* around his neck>
 syn babushka, bandanna
 2 *syn* see HANDKERCHIEF
kernel *n syn* see SUBSTANCE 2
key *n syn* see PASSPORT
kibitzer *n syn* see BUSYBODY
kick *vb* 1 *syn* see OBJECT 1
 rel combat, fight, oppose, resist, withstand, anathematize, condemn, curse, damn, execrate
 idiom put up a fight (against)
 2 *syn* see COMPLAIN
kick *n syn* see THRILL
‖**kick around** *vb syn* see DISCUSS 1
kick back *vb syn* see BACKFIRE
kicker *n syn* see GROUCH
‖**kick in** *vb* 1 *syn* see CONTRIBUTE 1
 2 *syn* see DIE 1
kick off *vb* 1 *syn* see BEGIN 1
 ‖2 *syn* see DIE 1
kick out *vb* 1 *syn* see DISMISS 3
 2 *syn* see EJECT 1
kickshaw *n syn* see DELICACY
kid *n syn* see CHILD 1
kid *vb* 1 *syn* see DUPE
 2 *syn* see BANTER
kidnap *vb* to carry off a person surreptitiously for an illegal purpose <an ex-convict *kidnapped* the child for ransom>
 syn abduct, ‖snatch, spirit (away)
 rel shanghai, waylay; coax, decoy, entice, inveigh, lure, seduce
 idiom make off with
 con deliver, ransom, redeem, rescue; bring (back), give back, restore, return
kidney *n syn* see TYPE
kid stuff *n syn* see SNAP 1
kill *vb* 1 to deprive of life <found it hard to *kill* animals>
 syn carry off, cut off, destroy, dispatch, down, finish, lay low, put away, scrag, slay, take off; *compare* MURDER 1
 rel butcher, choke, drown, massacre, poison, shoot, slaughter, suffocate; knife, sacrifice, stifle; annihilate, exterminate, ruin

---

syn synonym(s)   *rel* related word(s)
ant antonym(s)   *con* contrasted word(s)
idiom idiomatic equivalent(s)
‖ use limited; if in doubt, see a dictionary

idiom do (*or* make) away with, do for, put out of the way, put (*or* do) to death, put to sleep, take one's life

2 *syn* see VETO

killer *n syn* see MURDERER

killing *n syn* see MURDER

kiln *vb syn* see FIRE 6

kilter *n syn* see ORDER 10

kin *n syn* see FAMILY

2 the members of one's immediate or extended family <all our *kin* gathered to celebrate great grandma's birthday>
syn cousinage, cousinhood, kinfolk, kinsmen

3 *syn* see RELATIVE

kind *n syn* see TYPE

kind *adj* showing or having a gentle considerate nature <mother was a *kind* person, always willing to help others>
syn benign, benignant, good-hearted, kindly
rel altruistic, benevolent, charitable, eleemosynary, humane, humanitarian, openhearted, philanthropic, propitious; compassionate, kindhearted, responsive, sympathetic, tender, warm, warmhearted; clement, forbearing, indulgent, lenient, merciful, tolerant; affable, amiable, cordial, genial, good-humored, good-natured, good-tempered, sweet-tempered; complaisant, obliging; gentle, good
con cruel, fell, fierce, inhuman, savage; hard, harsh, rough; grim, implacable, merciless, unrelenting
ant unkind

kindhearted *adj syn* see TENDER

kindle *vb* 1 *syn* see LIGHT 1
rel blaze, flame, flare, glow; excite, provoke, stimulate; arouse, foment, incite, instigate, rouse, stir
ant smother

2 *syn* see STIR 1
ant stifle

kindless *adj syn* see ANTIPATHETIC 2

kindliness *n syn* see GOODWILL 1
ant unkindliness

kindly *adj syn* see KIND
rel gracious, sociable; friendly, neighborly; attentive, considerate, thoughtful
con malevolent, malicious, malign, spiteful
ant unkindly; acrid (*of temper, attitudes, comments*)

kindly *adv syn* see WELL 2

kindness *n syn* see FAVOR 4

kind of *adv syn* see SOMEWHAT 2

kindred *n syn* see FAMILY 1

kindred *adj syn* see RELATED
ant alien

kinfolk *n pl syn* see KIN 2

king *n syn* see MAGNATE

kingdom come *n syn* see HEAVEN 2

kinglike *adj syn* see KINGLY

kingly *adj* of, relating to, or befitting a king <a *kingly* entourage>
syn kinglike, majestic, monarchal, monarchial, monarchical, regal, royal, sovereign
rel imperious, lordly, masterful, powerful, puissant; imperial, princely, queenly

kinky *adj syn* see OUTLANDISH 3

kinsman *n* 1 *syn* see RELATIVE

2 **kinsmen** *pl syn* see KIN 2

kinswoman *n syn* see RELATIVE

kismet *n syn* see FATE

kiss *vb* 1 to touch with the lips especially as a sign of affection <*kissed* his mother good night>
syn buss, lip, osculate, peck, smack, smooch, ||smoodge, ||smouch

2 *syn* see BRUSH

||**kisser** *n syn* see FACE 1

kiss off *vb syn* see DISMISS 5

kite *vb syn* see GET OUT 1

kittenish *adj syn* see PLAYFUL 1

kitty *n syn* see POT 3

klutz *n syn* see OAF 2

knack *n* 1 *syn* see GIFT 2
rel quickness, readiness
ant ineptitude

2 *syn* see ABILITY 2

3 *syn* see HANG

knapsack *n syn* see BACKPACK

knave *n syn* see VILLAIN 1

knavish *adj syn* see DISHONEST

knell *vb syn* see RING

knickknack *n* a small or trivial ornamental article <a collection of pretty *knickknacks* was displayed on the mantel>
syn bauble, bibelot, curio, dido, gewgaw, gimcrack, novelty, objet d'art, prettypretty, rattletrap(s), toy, trifle, trinket, whatnot, whigmaleerie
rel souvenir; bric-a-brac, virtu; miniature; kickshaw, notion; trumpery

knifelike *adj syn* see SHARP 8
ant dull

knobkerrie *n syn* see CUDGEL

knock *vb* 1 *syn* see TAP 1

2 *syn* see CRITICIZE
ant boost

knock *n syn* see HIT 1

knock about *vb syn* see MANHANDLE

knock down *vb* 1 *syn* see FELL 1

2 *syn* see EARN 1

knock-down-and-drag-out *n* 1 *syn* see BRAWL

2 *syn* see QUARREL

knocker *n syn* see CRITIC

knock off *vb* 1 *syn* see STOP 3

2 *syn* see DEDUCT 1

3 *syn* see MURDER 1

||4 *syn* see ROB 1

knock out *vb syn* see EXHAUST 4

knockout *n* 1 *syn* see ||DILLY

2 *syn* see BEAUTY

knock over *vb* 1 *syn* see FELL 1

2 *syn* see OVERTURN 1

3 *syn* see OVERWHELM 4

4 *syn* see ROB 1

knot *n* 1 *syn* see BOND 3

2 *syn* see BUMP 2

3 *syn* see MAZE 1

knothead *n syn* see DUNCE

knotty *adj* 1 *syn* see COMPLEX 2

2 *syn* see HARD 6

know *vb* 1 to possess an intellectual hold of <*knows* several languages>
syn appreciate, apprehend, cognize, comprehend, fathom, grasp, have, understand
rel apperceive; differentiate, discern, discriminate, distinguish, realize
idiom have at one's fingertips, see through

2 *syn* see EXPERIENCE 1

3 *syn* see FEEL 2

4 to recognize the differences between <*know* right from wrong>

syn difference, differentiate, discern, discrepate, discriminate, distinguish, extricate, separate, sever, severalize
con confound, mingle, mix
ant confuse, mix up
5 *syn* see RECOGNIZE 1

knowable *adj syn* see UNDERSTANDABLE
ant unknowable

know-how *n* 1 *syn* see ABILITY 2
2 *syn* see ART 1

knowing *adj* 1 *syn* see INTELLIGENT 2
rel vigilant, watchful; discerning, observant, perceptive
con blunt, obtuse
2 *syn* see WISE 1
3 *syn* see WISE 4
4 *syn* see AWARE
5 *syn* see SOPHISTICATED 2

know-it-all *n syn* see SMART ALECK

knowledge *n* 1 *syn* see EDUCATION 2
ant ignorance

2 the body of things known about or in science <made major contributions to scientific *knowledge*>
syn information, lore, science, wisdom
rel advice, intelligence, news; data, evidence, facts

knowledgeable *adj* 1 *syn* see INTELLIGENT 2
2 *syn* see WISE 1

know-nothing *adj syn* see IGNORANT 1

know-nothing *n syn* see DUNCE

knuckle *vb syn* see YIELD 2

knucklehead *n syn* see DUNCE

knuckle under *vb syn* see YIELD 2

kook *n syn* see CRACKPOT

kowtow *vb syn* see FAWN

kowtowing *adj syn* see FAWNING

kudize *vb syn* see COMMEND 2

kudo *n syn* see COMPLIMENT 1

kudos *n* 1 *syn* see EMINENCE 1
2 *syn* see HONOR 2

L

laager *vb syn* see CAMP

label *n syn* see TICKET 1
rel mark, marker

labor *n* 1 *syn* see WORK 2
rel endeavor, struggle
con ease, leisure, relaxation, repose, rest; amusement, diversion, entertainment, recreation; idleness, inactivity, inertia, inertness, passiveness
2 the physical activities involved in parturition <first *labors* are sometimes difficult>
syn birth pang(s), childbearing, childbirth, travail

labor *vb* 1 to exert one's powers of mind or body especially with painful or strenuous effort <*labored* all day to make a living>
syn drive, moil, strain, strive, toil, tug, work
idiom break one's neck
con idle, laze, loaf, lounge; goof (off), shirk; dawdle, poke, putter
||2 *syn* see TILL

labored *adj* 1 *syn* see HARD 6
2 *syn* see FORCED
rel heavy, ponderous, weighty; awkward, clumsy, inept, maladroit

laborer *n syn* see WORKER

laborious *adj syn* see HARD 6
ant easy, effortless

laboriously *adv syn* see HARD 8
ant easily, effortlessly

labyrinth *n syn* see MAZE 1

labyrinthine *adj syn* see COMPLEX 2

lacerated *adj* having jagged cuts or breaks <the *lacerated* area was badly swollen>
syn mangled, rent, torn

rel gashed, mutilated, ripped, slashed; jagged, ragged, saw-toothed, scalloped, scored; serrated

lachrymose *adj syn* see TEARFUL

lack *vb* to be without something and especially something essential or greatly needed <the building *lacks* a fire escape>
syn need, require, want
con enjoy, have, hold, own, possess

lack *n* 1 *syn* see ABSENCE
2 *syn* see FAILURE 3

lackadaisical *adj syn* see LANGUID
rel incurious, indifferent, unconcerned; fainéant, indolent, lazy, slothful; idle, passive; emasculated; romantic, sentimental
con energetic, lusty, strenuous, vigorous; active, dynamic, live

lacking *adj* 1 *syn* see ABSENT 1
2 *syn* see DEFICIENT 2

lacking *prep syn* see WITHOUT 2

lackluster *adj* 1 *syn* see DULL 7
2 *syn* see COLORLESS 2
rel dead, leaden, rusty, tarnished
con lustrous

lackwit *n syn* see DUNCE

laconic *adj syn* see CONCISE
rel brusque
con garrulous, glib, loquacious, talkative
ant verbose, wordy

laconically *adv syn* see BRIEFLY

lacuna *n syn* see GAP 3

lad *n syn* see BOY 1

laddie *n syn* see BOY 1

lade *vb* 1 *syn* see BURDEN
2 *syn* see DIP 2

la-di-da *adj* 1 *syn* see PRECIOUS 4
2 *syn* see GENTEEL 3

ladies' man *n syn* see WOLF

lading *n syn* see LOAD 1

ladle *vb syn* see DIP 2

lady *n syn* see WIFE

lady friend *n syn* see GIRL FRIEND 1

---

lady–killer *n syn see* WOLF

ladylove *n syn see* GIRL FRIEND 2

lag *vb syn see* DELAY 2

  rel retard, slacken, slow; stay

lag *adj syn see* LAST

‖**lag** *vb syn see* BANISH

‖**lag** *n syn see* CONVICT

laggard *adj syn see* SLOW 2

  rel dawdling, delaying, loitering, procrastinating; comatose, couch, lethargic, sluggish; apathetic, impassive, phlegmatic

  con alert, vigilant, watchful, wide-awake; expeditious, fast, fleet, speedy

  ant prompt, quick

laggard *n* one that delays unnecessarily or falls behind <no room for *laggards* on the expedition>

  syn dawdler, lingerer, loiterer, slow coach, slowpoke, straggler

  rel lazybones, loafer

  con dynamo, go-ahead, go-getter, hustler, live wire, rustler; eager beaver

lagniappe *n syn see* GRATUITY

lair *n* 1 a resting or living place of a wild animal <photographed the wolf at the entrance to his *lair*>

  syn burrow, couch, den, lodge

  2 *syn see* HIDEOUT

‖**lalapalooza** *n syn* ‖DILLY, ‖corker, crackerjack, ‖daisy, dandy, humdinger, jim-dandy, ‖lulu, peach, ‖pip

‖**lallygag** *vb syn see* IDLE

lam *vb syn see* BEAT 1

lam *n syn see* ESCAPE 1

lambaste *vb* 1 *syn see* BEAT 1

  2 *syn see* WHIP 2

  3 to assail with withering oral or written denunciation <the senator has been publicly *lambasted* for taking bribes>

  syn blister, castigate, ‖crawl, drub, excoriate, flay, lash (into), roast, scarify, scathe, scorch, score, scourge, slam, slap, slash, ‖slate; *compare* CRITICIZE, REPROVE, SCOLD 1

  rel censure, criticize, denounce, pan; berate, scold, tongue-lash; assail, attack, squabash

  idiom burn one's ears, ‖crawl all over, give (one) a roasting, pin one's ears back, rake (one) over the coals, read the riot act, rip into

  con applaud, extol, praise; approve, countenance, endorse

lambent *adj syn see* BRIGHT 1

lame–brain *n syn see* DUNCE

lament *vb syn see* DEPLORE 1

  ant exult; rejoice

lamentable *adj* 1 *syn see* DEPLORABLE

  2 *syn see* MELANCHOLY 2

lamia *n syn see* WITCH 1

lamp *n syn see* EYE 1

lampoonery *n syn see* SATIRE

lampooning *adj syn see* SATIRIC

lance *vb syn see* IMPALE

land *n* 1 *syn see* EARTH 2

  2 *syn see* COUNTRY

  3 *syn see* ESTATE 3

land *vb* 1 *syn see* DISEMBARK

  2 *syn see* ALIGHT

  3 *syn see* GET 1

lang syne *n syn see* PAST

language *n* 1 a body or system of words and phrases used by a large community or by a people, a nation, or a group of nations <the English and French *languages*>

  syn dialect, idiom, speech, tongue, vernacular

  rel argot, cant, jargon, lingo, patois, slang

  2 *syn see* TERMINOLOGY

languid *adj* lacking in vim or energy <doing the job in a slow and *languid* manner>

  syn die-away, enervated, lackadaisical, languishing, languorous, limp, listless, spiritless

  rel comatose, lethargic, sluggish, torpid; apathetic, impassive, phlegmatic; inactive, inert, supine

  con alert, awake, ‖fly, keen, lively, wide-awake

  ant vivacious; chipper

languish *vb syn see* FAIL 1

  ant flourish

languishing *adj syn see* LANGUID

  rel debilitated, enfeebled, weakened; faineant, indolent; longing, pining, yearning

  con hale, healthy, robust, sound; energetic, lusty, vigorous

  ant flourishing, thriving; unaffected

languor *n syn see* LETHARGY 1

  rel exhaustion, fatigue, weariness; blues, depression, dumps; doldrums, ennui, tedium

  con celerity, legerity; gusto, zest

  ant alacrity

languorous *adj syn see* LANGUID

  rel dilatory, laggard, leisurely, slow; faineant, indolent, slothful; passive; lax, loose, relaxed, slack; indulged, pampered

  ant vigorous; strenuous (*of times, seasons*)

lank *adj syn see* LEAN

  rel attenuated, extenuated

  con chubby

  ant burly

lanky *adj* 1 *syn see* GANGLING

  2 *syn see* LEAN

lap *vb syn see* OVERLAP

lap *vb* 1 *syn see* SLOSH 1

  2 *syn see* BATHE 2

lapse *n* 1 *syn see* ERROR 2

  rel crime, offense, sin, vice; failing, foible, frailty; breach, transgression, trespass, violation

  2 a temporary deviation or fall especially from a higher to a lower state <a *lapse* into nonproductiveness> <ashamed of his *lapse* from grace>

  syn backsliding, relapse

  rel decadence, declension, decline, degeneration, deterioration, devolution; recession, retrogradation; regression, retrogression

  con advance, progress; development, maturation; amendment; betterment, improvement

lapse *vb* to fall from a better or higher state into a lower or poorer one <*lapsed* into his old vulgar ways>

  syn backslide, recidivate, relapse

  rel return, revert; slide, slip; decline, degenerate, deteriorate; subside; descend; recede, retrograde; apostatize

  con advance, progress; develop, mature; amend, mend; better, improve

larcener *n syn see* THIEF

larcenist *n syn* see THIEF

larcenous *adj* prone to committing larceny
< *larcenous* employees were robbing the
company blind >
syn sticky-fingered, thieving, thievish
rel burglarious; light-fingered

larceny *n syn* see THEFT

lardy-dardy *adj syn* see GENTEEL 3

lares and penates *n pl syn* see POSSES-
SION 2

large *adj* 1 above the average of its kind in
magnitude < a *large* increase in the tax
rate >
syn big, bull, fat, great, husky, oversize
rel colossal, enormous, gigantic, huge,
immense, mammoth, vast, voluminous;
monstrous, monumental, prodigious, stupendous, tremendous; excessive, exorbitant, extravagant, extreme, immoderate,
inordinate
con diminutive, little, minute, tiny, wee;
slender, slight, slim, thin
ant small
2 *syn* see BIG 1

largely *adv syn* see GENERALLY 1

largeness *n syn* see SIZE 2

large-scale *adj syn* see BIG 1

largess *n* 1 *syn* see GIFT 1
2 *syn* see GRATUITY

largest *adj syn* see BEST

lark *n* 1 *syn* see ESCAPADE
2 *syn* see PRANK

larkish *adj syn* see PLAYFUL 1

‖**larrup** *vb* 1 *syn* see WHIP 1
2 *syn* see WHIP 2

‖**larruping** *adv syn* see VERY 1

lascivious *adj* 1 *syn* see LICENTIOUS 2
rel coarse, gross, obscene
2 *syn* see LUSTFUL 2

lash *vb* 1 *syn* see RUSH 1
2 *syn* see POUR 3
3 *syn* see WHIP 1
4 *syn* see WAG
5 *syn* see SCOLD 1

lash (into) *vb syn* see LAMBASTE 3

lashings *n pl syn* see MUCH

lass *n* 1 *syn* see GIRL 1
2 *syn* see GIRL FRIEND 1

lassie *n syn* see GIRL 1

lassitude *n* 1 *syn* see FATIGUE
2 *syn* see APATHY 2
3 *syn* see LETHARGY 1
rel doldrums, ennui, tedium; blues, depression, dumps; impotence, powerlessness
con energy, force, might, power, strength
ant vigor

last *vb syn* see CONTINUE 1

last *adj* following all relevant others (as in
time, order, or importance) < he was the
last one in line >
syn closing, concluding, eventual, final,
hindmost, lag, latest, latter, rearmost,
terminal, terminating, ultimate
rel bottommost, end, extreme, furthest,
outermost, remotest, utmost, uttermost
con beginning, inaugural, initial, introductory, original, primary, prime
ant first

---

syn synonym(s)   *rel* related word(s)
ant antonym(s)   *con* contrasted word(s)
idiom idiomatic equivalent(s)
‖ use limited; if in doubt, see a dictionary

---

lasting *adj* existing or continuing for so
long a time as to seem fixed or established
< his reading made a *lasting* impression
on him >
syn diuturnal, durable, enduring, perdurable, perduring, permanent, stable; *compare*
OLD 2
rel abiding, continuing, persisting; endless, everlasting, unceasing; continual,
continuous, incessant, perennial, unremitting; eternal, sempiternal; indelible, indis-
soluble, inexhaustible, inexpugnable, inexpungible
con ephemeral, evanescent, fugitive, momentary, passing, short-lived, transient,
transitory
ant fleeting

last word *n syn* see APOTHEOSIS 1

late *adj* 1 *syn* see TARDY
con opportune, seasonable, well-timed
ant early; prompt, punctual
2 *syn* see DEAD 1
3 *syn* see FORMER 2
4 *syn* see MODERN 1

lated *adj syn* see TARDY

lately *adv syn* see NEW

latency *n syn* see ABEYANCE

latent *adj* not now manifest or showing
signs of existence or activity < a *latent*
infection >
syn abeyant, dormant, lurking, potential,
prepatent, quiescent
rel concealed, hidden; idle, inactive, inert;
immature, unmatured, unripe
con active, dynamic, live, operative; activated, energized, vitalized
ant patent

later *adj syn* see SUBSEQUENT 1

later *adv syn* see AFTER
ant earlier

laterally *adv syn* see SIDEWAYS 1

latest *adj syn* see LAST
ant earliest

lather *n* 1 *syn* see FOAM
2 *syn* see COMMOTION 4
3 *syn* see COMMOTION 2

lather *vb syn* see WHIP 1

latitude *n syn* see ROOM 3

latrine *n syn* see TOILET

latter *adj syn* see LAST
ant former

latterly *adv syn* see AFTER

laud *vb syn* see PRAISE 2
rel adore, revere, reverence, venerate,
worship; admire; flatter
con blame, condemn; anathematize, curse,
damn, execrate, objurgate
ant revile

laudable *adj syn* see WORTHY 1
ant illaudable

laudative *adj syn* see EULOGISTIC

laudatory *adj syn* see EULOGISTIC

laugh *vb* to show mirth, joy, or scorn with
a smile and a usually explosive sound
< *laughed* at all the funny things that
happened >
syn chortle, chuckle, giggle, guffaw, hee-
haw, snicker, ‖sniggle, tehee, titter
rel cachinnate, cackle, crow, roar, whoop;
beam, grin, simper, smile, smirk

laughable *adj* provoking laughter or mirth
< the *laughable* antics of the clowns >
syn comic, comical, droll, farcical, funny,
gelastic, ludicrous, ridiculous, risible

rel amusing, diverting, entertaining, rich; facetious, humorous, jocose, jocular, witty; derisive, derisory, mocking
con grave, serious, solemn; boring, irksome, tedious, tiresome, wearisome; affecting, impressive, moving, pathetic, poignant, touching

laughingstock *n* an object of ridicule <totally unaware that he was the *laughingstock* of the entire office>
syn butt, derision, jest, jestee, joke, mock, mockery, pilgarlic, sport
rel gazingstock; mark, target

launch *vb* 1 *syn* see THROW 1
2 *syn* see BEGIN 1
3 *syn* see INTRODUCE 3

laurels *n pl syn* see HONOR 2

lavatory *n syn* see TOILET

lave *vb syn* see BATHE 2

lavish *adj* 1 *syn* see PROFUSE
con scant, scanty; economical, frugal, thrifty; discreet, provident, prudent; miserly, niggardly, parsimonious, penurious, stingy
ant sparing
2 *syn* see GRAND 2

lavishness *n syn* see EXTRAVAGANCE 2
ant sparingness

law *n* 1 a principle governing conduct, action, or procedure <found it hard to live by outdated *laws*>
syn assize, canon, decree, decretum, edict, institute, ordinance, precept, prescript, prescription, regulation, rule, statute
rel command, dictate, mandate
2 *syn* see PRINCIPLE 1
rel exigency, necessity
ant chance

lawbreaker *n syn* see CRIMINAL

lawcourt *n syn* see COURT 2

lawful *adj* being in accordance with law <obtained *lawful* custody of the child>
syn innocent, legal, legitimate, licit
rel condign, due, rightful; allowable, permissible; justifiable, warrantable; bona fide
idiom of right
con flagitious, iniquitous, nefarious; improper, unjustifiable, wrong; criminal, guilty, peccant; illegitimate, illicit
ant lawless, unlawful

lawless *adj syn* see UNLAWFUL
ant lawful

lawlessness *n syn* see ANARCHY 1
rel conflict, contention, difference, discord, dissension, strife, variance

lawsuit *n syn* see SUIT 1

lawyer *n* a person authorized to practice law in the courts or to serve clients in the capacity of legal agent or adviser <took the problem to his family *lawyer*>
syn attorney, attorney-at-law; *compare* PETTIFOGGER
rel advocate, ‖barrister, counsel, counselor, ‖mouthpiece, pleader, ‖solicitor; jurisconsult, jurisprudent, jurist; legist

lax *vb syn* see LOOSE 5

lax *adj* 1 *syn* see LOOSE 1
con firm, hard, solid; elastic, resilient, springy
ant rigid
2 *syn* see NEGLIGENT
rel forgetful, oblivious, unmindful
con austere, severe, stern; rigid, rigorous; conscientious, honest, upright, scrupulous

ant strict, stringent

lay *vb* 1 *syn* see SET 1
2 *syn* see GAMBLE 1
3 *syn* see EVEN 1
4 *syn* see ASCRIBE
5 *syn* see DIRECT 2
6 *syn* see SET 5
7 *syn* see ADDUCE

lay (for) *vb syn* see SURPRISE 1

lay (open) *vb syn* see EXPOSE 1

lay *n* 1 *syn* see MELODY
2 *syn* see SONG 2

lay *adj syn* see PROFANE 1
con professional

lay aside *vb* 1 *syn* see DISCARD
2 *syn* see SAVE 4

lay away *vb* 1 *syn* see SAVE 4
2 *syn* see BURY 1

lay by *vb syn* see SAVE 4

lay down *vb* 1 *syn* see RELINQUISH
2 *syn* see PRESCRIBE 2
3 *syn* see DICTATE

layer *n syn* see BOOKMAKER

lay in *vb syn* see SAVE 4

lay low *vb* 1 *syn* see FELL 1
2 *syn* see KILL 1

lay off *vb syn* see REST 3

lay out *vb* 1 *syn* see DESIGN 3
2 *syn* see SPEND 1

lay over *vb syn* see DEFER

lay up *vb* 1 *syn* see ACCUMULATE
2 *syn* see SAVE 4

laze *vb syn* see IDLE
con drudge, grind, labor, toil, travail, work

laze *n syn* see SLOTH 1

laziness *n syn* see SLOTH 1
ant industriousness

lazy *adj* not easily aroused to action or activity <the hot humid weather made them *lazy*>
syn drony, easygoing, faineant, indolent, slothful, slowgoing, work-shy
rel idle, inactive, inert, passive, supine, trifling; comatose, lethargic, sluggish, torpid; lackadaisical, languid, languorous, listless, unenergetic, unindustrious; lax, neglectful, negligent, remiss, shiftless, slack
con diligent, hardworking; brisk, chipper, energetic, vigorous; active, animated, lively, spry, vivacious; prompt, quick, ready
ant industrious

lazy *vb syn* see IDLE

lazybones *n syn* see SLUGGARD

lead *vb* 1 *syn* see GUIDE
rel get, induce, persuade, prevail
con drive, impel; coerce, compel, constrain, force, oblige
ant follow
2 *syn* see PRECEDE 3
3 *syn* see CONVERT 1

lead *n syn* see LEADER 1

leader *n* 1 one that takes the lead or initiative <each group selected its own *leader* for the tour>
syn ‖bell cow, bellwether, dean, doyen, guide, lead, pilot
rel pacemaker, pacesetter; forerunner, harbinger, herald, precursor; conductor, director, rector
con adherent, dependent, hanger-on, henchman, satellite

ant follower

2 a person in whom resides authority or ruling power < the company had only one *leader* >

syn boss, chief, chieftain, cock, dominator, head, headman, hierarch, honcho, master

rel captain, commander, general; director, principal, superintendent, superior; foreman, manager, straw boss

con inferior, subaltern, subordinate, underling, understrapper

3 *syn* see NOTABLE 1

leading *adj* 1 *syn* see FIRST 1

2 *syn* see FIRST 3

ant subordinate

3 *syn* see WELL-KNOWN

lead off *vb syn* see BEGIN 1

lead on *vb* 1 *syn* see LURE

2 *syn* see TRIFLE 1

leaf (through) *vb syn* see BROWSE

leafage *n syn* see FOLIAGE

league *n* 1 *syn* see ALLIANCE 2

2 *syn* see ASSOCIATION 2

3 *syn* see CLASS 1

4 a group of sports clubs or teams that play one another competitively < the new baseball *league* >

syn association, circuit, conference, loop, wheel

rel division

league *vb syn* see UNITE 2

leak *vb syn* see GET OUT 2

lean *vb* 1 *syn* see SLANT 1

rel bend, curve; deflect, divert, sheer, turn

2 *syn* see TEND 1

lean (over) *vb syn* see HANG 4

lean *n syn* see SLOPE

lean *adj* lean because of absence of superfluous flesh < a *lean* strong horse >

syn angular, bony, gaunt, lank, lanky, meager, rawboned, scraggy, scrawny, skinny, spare; *compare* THIN 1

rel slender, slight, slim, spare-set, stringy, thin; cadaverous, haggard, pinched, wasted, worn; wizened

con brawny, burly, husky, muscular, sinewy; stalwart, stout, strong, sturdy; corpulent, fat, fatty, flabby, obese, plump, portly, rotund

ant fleshy

leaning *n* 1 *syn* see SLOPE

2 an attraction to a particular activity, thing, or end < a strong *leaning* toward liberal views >

syn bent, bias, disposition, drift, inclination, inclining, lurch, partiality, penchant, predilection, predisposition, proclivity, propensity, sentiment, tendency; *compare* GIFT 2, PREJUDICE

rel favor, favoritism, odds

con avoidance, evasion, shunning; disdaining, scorning, scouting, spurning; disinterest, dislike, distaste

leaning *adj syn* see INCLINED 1

leap *vb* 1 *syn* see JUMP 1

rel arise, ascend, mount, rise, soar

con drop, fall, sink, slump

2 *syn* see CLEAR 8

learn *vb* 1 to acquire knowledge of or skill in by study and experience < *learn* a trade >

syn get, master, pick up

rel con, peruse, study

idiom make oneself master of

2 *syn* see MEMORIZE

3 *syn* see DISCOVER 3

learned *adj* possessing or manifesting unusually wide and deep knowledge < a most *learned* scholar in his field >

syn erudite, scholarly, scholastic

rel cultivated, cultured; academic, bookish, pedantic, professorial; abstruse, esoteric, polymath, recondite

con ignorant, illiterate, uneducated, unlearned, unlettered, untutored

learnedness *n syn* see ERUDITION 2

learning *n syn* see EDUCATION 2

lease *vb syn* see HIRE 1

leash *vb syn* see HAMPER

least *adj syn* see FIRST 4

leave *vb* 1 *syn* see WILL

rel commit, confide, consign, entrust; allot, apportion, assign

2 *syn* see LET 2

3 *syn* see GO 2

4 *syn* see QUIT 6

5 *syn* see RELINQUISH

leave *n* 1 *syn* see PERMISSION

rel assent

con refusal, rejection; forbiddance, interdiction, prohibition

2 *syn* see VACATION

leaven *vb syn* see INFUSE 1

rel moderate, qualify, temper; enliven, quicken, vivify

leave off *vb syn* see STOP 3

leave-taking *n syn* see PARTING

leaving *n, usu* leavings *pl syn* see REMAINDER

rel fragments, pieces, portions; discards, junk, scrap

lecherous *adj syn* see LICENTIOUS 2

lecture *n syn* see SPEECH 2

lecture *vb syn* see TALK 7

ledger *n syn* see TOMBSTONE

leech *n syn* see PARASITE

leer *vb syn* see SNEER 1

lees *n pl syn* see SEDIMENT

leeway *n syn* see ROOM 3

left-handed *adj syn* see INSINCERE

legacy *n* 1 a gift by will especially of money or personal property < received a *legacy* of $5,000 from her late uncle >

syn bequest, devise, inheritance

2 *syn* see HERITAGE 1

legal *adj syn* see LAWFUL

ant illegal

legal tender *n syn* see MONEY

legate *vb syn* see WILL

legend *n* 1 *syn* see MYTH 1

2 *syn* see CAPTION

3 *syn* see LORE 2

legendary *adj syn* see MYTHICAL

legerdemain *n syn* see MAGIC 1

legion *n syn* see MULTITUDE 1

legion *adj syn* see MANY

legitimate *adj* 1 *syn* see LAWFUL

rel cogent, sound, valid; acknowledged, recognized; customary, usual; natural, normal, regular, typical

---

syn synonym(s)　　*rel* related word(s)
ant antonym(s)　　*con* contrasted word(s)
idiom idiomatic equivalent(s)
‖ use limited; if in doubt, see a dictionary

ant illegitimate

2 *syn* see TRUE 8
ant arbitrary

leisure *n syn* see REST 1
con drudgery, grind, labor
ant toil

leisurely *adj syn* see SLOW 2
rel lax, relaxed, slack; delayed, retarded, slackened; comfortable, easy, restful
con fast, hasty, quick, rapid, speedy; headlong, impetuous, precipitate
ant hurried; abrupt

leitmotiv *n* a dominant recurring thematic element or feature (as in a work of art) < the *leitmotiv* of man against nature often appears in his paintings >
syn motif
rel motive, theme

lemon *n syn* see FAILURE 5

lend *vb* to give into another's keeping for temporary use on condition that the borrower return the same or its equivalent < I do not have another copy of the book to give, but I can *lend* you mine >
syn advance, loan
rel lease-lend, lend-lease; allow, furnish, give; accommodate, oblige

length *n* 1 *syn* see DISTANCE 1

2 *syn* see RANGE 2

lengthen *vb syn* see EXTEND 3
ant shorten; abbreviate

lengthening *n syn* see EXTENSION 1
ant shortening

lengthways *adv syn* see LENGTHWISE
ant widthways, width wise

lengthwise *adv* in the direction of the length < the students folded their papers *lengthwise* >
syn endways, endwise, lengthways, longitudinally, longways, longwise
con latitudinally, widthways; broadside, broadway, broadwise
ant widthways, widthwise

lengthy *adj* 1 *syn* see LONG 2
ant short

2 *syn* see LONG 1

lenience *n syn* see FORBEARANCE 2

leniency *n syn* see FORBEARANCE 2

lenient *adj* 1 *syn* see GENTLE 1
ant caustic

2 *syn* see FORBEARING
rel condoning, excusing, forgiving, pardoning; benign, benignant, kindly; compassionate, tender; humoring, indulging, pampering, mollycoddling, spoiling
con rigid, rigorous, stringent; austere, severe
ant stern; exacting

3 *syn* see AMIABLE 1

lenity *n syn* see MERCY
rel tenderness; benevolence, charitableness, humaneness
con rigidity, rigorousness, strictness, stringency; austerity, sternness
ant severity

leper *n syn* see OUTCAST

lessen *vb* 1 *syn* see ABRIDGE 1
rel amputate, clip, crop, truncate

2 *syn* see DECREASE
rel attenuate, dilute, thin, weaken

lesser *adj* 1 *syn* see INFERIOR 1

2 *syn* see MINOR 2

lesson *n syn* see EXERCISE 4

lesson *vb syn* see REPROVE

let *vb* 1 *syn* see HIRE 1

2 to neither forbid nor prevent < *let* the boy go to the movies >
syn allow, have, leave, permit, suffer
rel accredit, approve, certify, endorse, sanction; authorize, commission, license; concede, grant
con ban, enjoin, forbid, inhibit, interdict, prohibit; bar, block, hinder, impede, obstruct; circumvent, foil, frustrate, thwart

let down *vb syn* see LOWER 3

lethal *adj syn* see DEADLY 1
con renewing, restorative, restoring

lethality *n syn* see FATALITY 1

lethargic *adj* deficient in alertness or activity < became *lethargic* after taking the drug >
syn comatose, dopey, heavy, hebetudinous, sluggish, slumberous, stupid, torpid
rel dormant, idle, inactive, inert, passive, supine; apathetic, impassive, phlegmatic, spiritless, stolid; lackadaisical, languid, languorous, listless; dilatory, laggard, slow
con alert, aware, responsive; apt, prompt, quick, ready; brisk, gingery, peppery, spirited
ant energetic

lethargy *n* 1 physical and mental inertness < disgusted, he sank into a state of *lethargy* >
syn coma, dullness, hebetude, languor, lassitude, sleep, slumber, stupor, torpidity, torpidness, torpor
rel comatoseness, sluggishness; indolence, laziness, sloth, slothfulness; idleness, inactivity, inertia, inertness, passiveness, supineness; apathy, impassivity, inanition, phlegm
con aptness, promptness, quickness, readiness; alertness, quick-wittedness
ant vigor

2 *syn* see APATHY 2

lethe *n syn* see OBLIVION

let off *vb syn* see EXEMPT

let on *vb* 1 *syn* see ACKNOWLEDGE 1

2 *syn* see REVEAL 1

let out *vb* 1 *syn* see REVEAL 1

2 *syn* see DISMISS 3

letter *n* 1 letters *pl syn* see ALPHABET 1

2 a direct or personal written or printed message addressed to a person or organization < wrote several *letters* to his friends >
syn epistle, missive, note
rel dispatch, memorandum, message, report

lettuce *n syn* see MONEY

let up *vb syn* see ABATE 4

levee *n* 1 *syn* see WHARF

2 *syn* see RED-LIGHT DISTRICT

level *vb* 1 *syn* see EVEN 1

2 *syn* see DIRECT 2

3 *syn* see FELL 1

level *adj* having a surface without bends, curves, or irregularities < looked for a *level* spot to land the plane >
syn even, flat, flush, planate, plane, smooth
rel akin, alike, identical, like, parallel, similar, uniform; aligned; regular, equal, equivalent, same
con bumpy, irregular, lumpy, uneven; unaligned, unparallel; changing, varying;

fluctuating, rolling, swaying, undulating; coarse, rough

lever vb syn see PRY

leviathan n syn see GIANT

leviathan adj syn see HUGE

levity n syn see LIGHTNESS
  rel absurdity, folly, foolishness, silliness
  con collection, quietude, sobriety
  ant gravity

levy n syn see TAX 1

levy vb to determine and require satisfaction of (as a tax or obligation) <several broad-based taxes were levied>
  syn assess, exact, impose, put (on or upon)
  rel extort, wrest, wring; charge, lay (on or upon), place, set
  con remit; abate, diminish, lessen

lewd adj syn see LICENTIOUS 2
  rel coarse, gross, obscene; improper, indecent, indelicate
  con modest, proper, self-restrained; temperate
  ant chaste

lexicon n 1 syn see VOCABULARY 1
  2 syn see TERMINOLOGY

lexiphanicism n syn see BOMBAST

liability n 1 syn see DEBT 3
  ant asset
  2 syn see INDEBTEDNESS 1
  3 syn see EXPOSURE

liable adj 1 syn see RESPONSIBLE
  rel bound, tied
  con exempt, immune; free, independent
  2 being likely to be affected by some usually adverse contingency or action <without the heat shield he was liable to be burned>
  syn exposed, obnoxious, open, prone, sensitive, subject, susceptible
  rel assailable, penetrable, vulnerable; attackable, beatable, conquerable, vincible
  ant unliable
  3 syn see APT 1
  ant unliable

liaison n syn see AMOUR 2

liar n one that tells lies <he is a compulsive liar>
  syn Ananias, falsifier, fibber, fibster, perjurer, prevaricator, storyteller

libel vb syn see MALIGN
  rel burlesque, caricature, travesty

libelous adj injurious to reputation <the campaign degenerated into an exchange of libelous statements>
  syn backbiting, calumnious, defamatory, detracting, detractive, detractory, invidious, maligning, scandalous, slanderous, traducing, vilifying
  rel depreciative, depreciatory, derogative, disparaging, pejorative; contumelious, debasing, malevolent, vituperative
  con adulating, adulatory, applauding, commendatory, eulogistic, eulogizing, laudatory, praising

liberal adj 1 marked by generosity and openhandedness <a liberal allowance for his son>

syn bounteous, bountiful, free, freehanded, generous, handsome, munificent, openhanded, unsparing
  rel exuberant, lavish, prodigal, profuse; benevolent, charitable, eleemosynary, philanthropic
  con closefisted, miserly, niggardly, parsimonious, penurious, stingy, tight, tightfisted; meager, scanty
  ant close
  2 syn see PLENTIFUL
  3 not bound by authoritarianism, orthodoxy, or traditional forms <modern young people usually have a liberal attitude toward sex>
  syn advanced, broad, broad-minded, progressive, radical, tolerant, wide
  rel forbearing, indulgent, lenient
  con rigid, rigorous, strict, stringent; dictatorial, doctrinaire, dogmatic, oracular; conservative, reactionary
  ant authoritarian

liberate vb syn see FREE
  rel detach, unhook; untangle; disembarrass
  con bind, tie; ensnare, entrap, snare, trap; constrain, restrain, restrict

libertine adj syn see LICENTIOUS 2
  con ethical; continent, sober, temperate
  ant straitlaced

liberty n syn see FREEDOM
  rel autonomy, independence; delivery, emancipation, enfranchisement, liberation
  con circumscription, confinement, limitation, restriction
  ant restraint

libidinous adj 1 syn see LICENTIOUS 2
  rel coarse, gross, obscene
  2 syn see LUSTFUL 2

library n a place in which literary, musical, artistic, or reference materials (as books or films) are kept for use but not for sale <planned to study all evening in the library>
  syn archive(s), athenaeum
  rel reading room

license n syn see FREEDOM
  rel laxity, looseness, relaxation, slackness
  con duty, obligation; decency, propriety; continence, sobriety, temperance
  ant decorum

license vb syn see AUTHORIZE 1
  rel allow, let, permit, suffer; certify, sanction
  con check, curb, restrain
  ant ban

licentious adj 1 syn see ABANDONED 2
  2 disregarding sexual restraints <a coarse licentious man>
  syn fast, incontinent, lascivious, lecherous, lewd, libertine, libidinous, lustful, randy, salacious, satyric
  rel animal, carnal, fleshly, oversexed, sensual; abandoned, dissolute, profligate, reprobate; corrupt, debauched, depraved; scabrous; amoral, immoral, unmoral; lax, loose, relaxed
  con chaste, decent, pure; moral, virtuous; rigid, strict; ascetic, austere, severe
  ant continent

licit adj syn see LAWFUL
  rel approved, sanctioned; authorized, licensed

con banned, forbidden, inhibited, interdicted, prohibited
ant illicit

lick *vb* 1 *syn* see WHIP 2
2 *syn* see OVERCOME 1

lick *n* 1 *syn* see HINT 2
2 *syn* see HIT 1

lickerish *adj syn* see LUSTFUL 2

lickerishness *n syn* see LUST 2

lickety-split *adv syn* see FAST 2

licking *n syn* see DEFEAT 1

lickspit *n syn* see SYCOPHANT

lickspittle *n syn* see SYCOPHANT

lie *vb* 1 *syn* see REST 1
2 *syn* see REST 3

lie *vb* to be untruthful directly or indirectly < *lying* under oath is a crime >
syn equivocate, falsify, fib, palter, prevaricate
rel beguile, deceive, delude, misguide, misinform, misinstruct, mislead; distort, exaggerate, misstate

lie *n* a statement or declaration that is not true < was sued for printing *lies* about the candidate >
syn ‖bouncer, canard, cock-and-bull story, falsehood, falsity, fib, inveracity, misrepresentation, misstatement, prevarication, ‖rapper, story, tale, taradiddle, untruism, untruth
rel deceitfulness, dishonesty, distortion, fraudulence, inaccuracy, mendacity; fable, flam, myth; falsification, forgery, libel, perjury; fish story, song and dance
con veracity, verisimilitude, verity
ant truth

lie by *vb syn* see REST 3

lied *n syn* see SONG 2

lie down *vb syn* see REST 1

liege *adj syn* see FAITHFUL 1

lieutenant *n syn* see ASSISTANT 2

life *n* 1 *syn* see BIOGRAPHY
2 *syn* see HUMAN
3 *syn* see SPIRIT 5

lifeless *adj* 1 *syn* see DEAD 1
ant living
2 *syn* see COLORLESS 2
ant lifeful

lifelong *adj syn* see OLD 2

lifework *n syn* see MISSION

lift *vb* 1 to remove from a lower to a higher place or position < *lifted* the sack to his shoulder >
syn elevate, hoist, pick up, raise, rear, take up, uphold, uplift, upraise, uprear
rel arise, ascend, levitate, mount, rise, rocket, soar, surge, tower; aggrandize, exalt, magnify
con decrease, diminish, lessen, reduce; abase, debase, degrade, demean, humble, humiliate; depress, oppress, weigh
ant lower
2 *syn* see REVOKE 2
ant invoke
3 *syn* see STEAL 1
4 *syn* see RISE 4

lift *n* 1 *syn* see THEFT
2 *syn* see HELP 1

lifted *adj syn* see ELEVATED 1

ligament *n syn* see BOND 3

ligature *n syn* see BOND 3

light *n syn* see DAWN 1

light *adj syn* see FAIR 3

light *vb* 1 to cause something to start burning < *lighted* the fuse on the dynamite >
syn enkindle, fire, ignite, inflame, kindle
con douse, ‖dout, put out, quench, snuff; damp (down), smother, stamp (out)
ant extinguish
2 *syn* see ILLUMINATE 1

light *adj* 1 having little weight < the package was *light* >
syn featherlight, featherweight, imponderous, lightweight, unheavy, weightless
rel inconsequential, trifling, trivial; little, petty, small; flimsy, meager, slender, slight
idiom light as a feather
con bulky, burdensome, cumbersome, huge, massive, overweight, ponderous, portly, unwieldy, weighty
ant heavy
2 *syn* see EASY 1
ant arduous
3 *syn* see FAST 7
4 *syn* see GIDDY 1
5 *syn* see LITTLE 3
6 *syn* see DIZZY 2

light *vb* 1 *syn* see ALIGHT
2 *syn* see HAPPEN 2

lighted *adj syn* see BURNING 1
ant unlighted, unlit

lighten *vb syn* see ILLUMINATE 1
ant darken

lighten *vb syn* see RELIEVE 1
rel attenuate, dilute, extenuate, thin
con depress, oppress, weigh

light-headed *adj* 1 *syn* see GIDDY 1
2 *syn* see DIZZY 2

lighthearted *adj* 1 *syn* see HAPPY-GO-LUCKY
ant heavyhearted
2 *syn* see GLAD 1
rel buoyant, effervescent, expansive, resilient, volatile; high-spirited, spirited; gay, lively, sprightly, vivacious
con gloomy, glum, morose, sullen
ant despondent
3 *syn* see MERRY
ant heavyhearted

lighthouse *n* a building equipped to guide sea navigators by means of a powerful light < rowed out to the *lighthouse* >
syn beacon, pharos
rel direction, guidance

lightless *adj syn* see DARK 1
ant bright, ‖lightful

lightly *adv syn* see EASILY 1

light-mindedness *n syn* see LIGHTNESS

lightness *n* gaiety or indifference where seriousness and attention are called for < a crisis that allowed no room for *lightness* >
syn flightiness, flippancy, frivolity, levity, light-mindedness, volatility
rel buoyancy, effervescence, elasticity, expansiveness, resiliency; gaiety, liveliness, vivacity; cheerfulness, lightheartedness
con earnestness, gravity, sedateness, soberness, somberness, staidness
ant seriousness

light-o'-love *n syn* see DOXY 1

light out *vb syn* see HEAD 3

lightsome *adj* 1 *syn* see CHEERFUL 1
2 *syn* see HAPPY-GO-LUCKY

lightweight *adj syn* see LIGHT 1

like *vb* 1 *syn* see ENJOY 1

rel choose, elect, prefer, select; admire, esteem, regard, respect; approve, endorse; appreciate, comprehend, understand
ant dislike

2 *syn* see WILL

like *adj* being so similar as to appear to be the same or nearly the same (as in appearance, character, or quantity) < shirts of *like* design >
syn agnate, akin, alike, analogous, comparable, consonant, corresponding, equivalent, intercomparable, parallel, similar, such, suchlike, undifferenced, undifferentiated, uniform; *compare* SAME 2
rel equal, equivalent, identical, same, selfsame; allied, cognate, close, related, resembling; coextensive, commensurate
idiom of that ilk, on the order of
con different, disparate, divergent, diverse, dissimilar; distinct; discordant, discrepant, inconsistent, inconsonant
ant unlike

like *n syn* see EQUAL

likely *adj* 1 *syn* see PROBABLE
con problematic; certain, inevitable, necessary
ant unlikely

2 *syn* see APT 1
ant unlikely

3 *syn* see HOPEFUL 2

likely *adv syn* see PRESUMABLY

liken *vb syn* see EQUATE 2

likeness *n* agreement or correspondence in details (as of appearance, structure, or quality) < the remarkable *likeness* of the two cousins >
syn affinity, alikeness, analogy, comparison, resemblance, semblance, similarity, simile, similitude
rel equality, equivalence, identicalness, identity, sameness; agreement, conformity, correspondence; analogousness, comparableness, parallelism, uniformity
con difference, dissimilarity, distinction, divergence, divergency; disaffinity, opposition
ant unlikeness

likewise *adv* 1 *syn* see ALSO 1

2 *syn* see ALSO 2

liking *n* 1 *syn* see APPETITE 3
ant disliking

2 *syn* see WILL 1

lilliputian *adj* *syn* TINY, diminutive, minute, teensy, teensy-weensy, teenty, teeny, teeny-weeny, wee, weeny
ant Brobdingnagian

lilliputian *n syn* see DWARF

lily-livered *adj syn* see COWARDLY

lily-white *adj syn* see GOOD 11

limb *n* 1 a member of a woody plant that is an outgrowth from a main stem or from one of its divisions < hung the swing from a tree's *limb* >
syn bough, branch
rel shoot, spray, sprig, switch, twig; arm

2 *syn* see SCAMP

limber *adj syn* see SUPPLE 3
rel plastic, pliable, pliant; elastic, flexible, resilient, springy

---

syn synonym(s)   *rel* related word(s)
ant antonym(s)   *con* contrasted word(s)
idiom idiomatic equivalent(s)
‖ use limited; if in doubt, see a dictionary

con inflexible, rigid, stark, stiff, tense, wooden

limit *n* 1 a material or immaterial point beyond which something does not or cannot extend < there seemed no *limit* to the problems they faced >
syn bound, confine(s), end, limitation, term; *compare* ENVIRONS 1
rel circumscription, confinement, restriction, termination; border, brim, brink, edge, margin, rim, verge

2 **limits** *pl syn* see ENVIRONS 1

3 *syn* see EXTREME 2

limit *vb* 1 *syn* see DEMARCATE 1

2 to prescribe or serve as a restricting boundary < *limited* the naughty child to the house for three days > < ignorance that *limits* spiritual growth >
syn bar, circumscribe, confine, delimit, delimitate, prelimit, restrict
rel constrict, contract, lessen, narrow, pinch; check, curb, hinder, inhibit, restrain; appoint, assign, define, prescribe, set
con enlarge, expand, extend, increase, widen; develop, grow
ant broaden

limitation *n* 1 *syn* see LIMIT 1

2 *syn* see RESTRICTION 1

limited *adj* 1 *syn* see DEFINITE 1
rel inexhaustive, inextensive
con boundless, infinite
ant unlimited

2 *syn* see FINITE

3 *syn* see QUALIFIED 2

4 *syn* see LITTLE 2

limitless *adj* having no limits < the *limitless* black of deep space >
syn boundless, endless, immeasurable, indefinite, infinite, measureless, unbounded, unlimited, unmeasured
rel bottomless, countless, incalculable, incomprehensible, inexhaustible, innumerable, undrainable, unfathomable, vast, wasteless
con bound, bounded, finite, fixed, limited, measurable; comprehensible, fathomable; confined, restricted
ant limited

limn *vb syn* see REPRESENT 1

limp *vb* 1 to walk lamely < *limped* across the floor after his fall >
syn halt, hitch, hobble
rel toddle, totter, waddle; falter, stagger, stumble, wobble

2 *syn* see STUMBLE 6

limp *adj* 1 deficient in firmness of texture, substance, or structure < plants going *limp* from lack of water >
syn flabby, flaccid, flimsy, floppy, sleazy
rel lax, loose, relaxed, slack; limber, supple
con inflexible, rigid, stark, stiff, tense, wooden; firm, hard, solid; brittle, crisp

2 *syn* see LANGUID

limpid *adj syn* see TRANSPARENT 1

limpidity *n syn* see CLARITY

line *n* 1 *syn* see WAY 2

2 *syn* see COURSE 3

3 *syn* see WORK 1

‖ 4 *syn* see SPIEL

5 a series of things arranged in continuous or uniform order < a *line* of cars waiting at the light >

syn echelon, file, queue, rank, row, string, tier

rel column, progression, succession, train; sequence, series

6 *syn* see OUTLINE

7 *syn* see MERCHANDISE

line *vb* 1 to arrange in a line or lines < *lined* the bottles along the shelf >

syn align, allineate, line up, range

rel arrange, array, marshal, order, ordinate

con derange, disarrange, disorder, disturb; disperse, dissipate, scatter

2 *syn* see ADJOIN

lineage *n* 1 *syn* see ANCESTRY

2 *syn* see FAMILY 1

lineal *adj syn* see DIRECT 1

lineament *n syn* see OUTLINE

lineation *n syn* see OUTLINE

line up *vb syn* see LINE 1

linger *vb* 1 *syn* see STAY 2

2 *syn* see DELAY 1

3 *syn* see SAUNTER

lingerer *n syn* see LAGGARD

lingo *n syn* see DIALECT 2

link *n syn* see BOND 3

link up *vb syn* see JOIN 1

lint *n syn* see DOWN

lion *n syn* see NOTABLE 1

lionhearted *adj syn* see BRAVE 1

||**lip** *n syn* see BACK TALK

lip *vb* 1 *syn* see KISS 1

2 *syn* see BATHE 2

lip server *n syn* see HYPOCRITE

liquefy *vb* to convert or to become converted to a liquid state < *liquefy* a block of ice by heating >

syn deliquesce, dissolve, flux, fuse, liquesce, melt, run, thaw

rel soften; thin

con clot, coagulate, congeal; harden, set; gel, jellify, jelly; condense, inspissate, thicken

ant solidify

liquesce *vb syn* see LIQUEFY

liquid *adj syn* see MELLIFLUOUS

liquidate *vb* 1 *syn* see CLEAR 5

2 *syn* see PURGE 3

3 *syn* see MURDER 1

liquor *n* 1 *syn* see DRINK 1

2 an intoxicating beverage usually distilled after being fermented < belted down a slug of *liquor* >

syn alcohol, aqua vitae, booze, ||budge, drink, firewater, grog, ||hooch, inebriant, intoxicant, ||joy-juice, ||juice, ||lush, ||sauce, spirit(s), ||strunt, tipple

idiom Demon Rum, the bottle

liquor (up) *vb syn* see DRINK 3

lissome *adj syn* see SUPPLE 3

list *n* a series of items (as names) written down or printed expecially as a memorandum or record < all the people on the *list* were present >

syn catalog, register, roll, roll call, roster, schedule

rel checklist, handlist; index; inventory

list *vb* 1 *syn* see ENUMERATE 2

2 *syn* see ITEMIZE 1

3 to enter in a list < his name was not *listed* in the telephone book >

syn book, catalog, enroll, inscribe

rel file, index, note, post, schedule, tabulate; record, register, roster

4 *syn* see ENROLL 1

list *vb syn* see SLANT 1

listen *vb* to perceive by ear usually with careful or responsive attention < now hear me; *listen* to my words >

syn attend, hark, hear, hearken, heed

idiom give a hearing to, give ear to, hang upon the lips (*or* words) of, keep one's ears (*or* an) ear, prick up one's ears, strain one's ears

listless *adj syn* see LANGUID

rel careless, heedless, thoughtless

con agog, anxious, avid, keen; alert, vigilant, watchful; energetic, lusty, vigorous; prompt, quick, ready

ant eager

listlessness *n syn* see APATHY 2

||**lit** *adj syn* see INTOXICATED 1

literal *adj syn* see VERBATIM

literally *adv syn* see VERBATIM

literati *n pl syn* see INTELLIGENTSIA

literatim *adv syn* see VERBATIM

lithe *adj syn* see SUPPLE 3

rel slender, slight, slim, thin; lean, spare

con awkward, clumsy, gauche, inept, maladroit; inflexible, stiff, tense, wooden

lithesome *adj syn* see SUPPLE 3

litigious *adj syn* see CONTENTIOUS 2

litter *n* 1 *syn* see REFUSE

2 *syn* see CLUTTER 2

little *adj* 1 *syn* see SMALL 1

ant big

2 contemptibly limited < men with *little* minds picking at flaws in a great leader >

syn borné, ineffectual, limited, mean, narrow, paltry, set, small

rel bigoted, hidebound, illiberal, narrowminded, provincial; contemptible; niggard, niggardly, self-centered, selfish

ant great

3 lacking importance < the nagging *little* details of a job >

syn casual, inconsiderable, insignificant, light, minor, minute, petty, ||potty, shoestring, small, small-beer, trivial, unimportant; *compare* PETTY 2

rel fortuitous; incidental; collateral, secondary, subordinate, subsidiary

con consequential, meaningful, significant, substantial, weighty; basal, basic, essential, foundational, fundamental

ant important

little *adv syn* see SELDOM

ant much

little by little *adv syn* see GRADUALLY

||**little woman** *n syn* see WIFE

||**lit up** *adj syn* see INTOXICATED 1

liturgy *n* 1 *syn* see FORM 2

2 *syn* see RITE 2

livable *adj* 1 suitable for living < a very *livable* apartment >

syn habitable, inhabitable, lodgeable, occupiable, tenantable

rel cozy, homelike, homey, snug; acceptable, bearable, tolerable

ant unlivable

2 *syn* see BEARABLE

live *vb* 1 *syn* see BE

2 *syn* see RESIDE 1

live *adj syn* see ACTIVE 1

rel effective, effectual, efficacious, efficient

ant inactive, inert; dormant (*as a volcano*); defunct (*as an institution, journal*)

livelihood n syn see LIVING
rel art, craft, handicraft, profession, trade; emolument, fee, pay, salary, stipend, wage

lively adj 1 keenly alive and brisk <always thought of as a *lively* teacher>
syn alert, animate, animated, bright, ‖cant, ‖canty, chipper, ‖chirk, dashing, gay, keen, ‖peart, peppy, pert, rousing, spirited, ‖spirity, sprightful, sprightly, unpedantic, vivacious; compare CHEERFUL 1
rel agile, brisk, nimble, spry; buoyant, effervescent, elastic, expansive, resilient, volatile; blithe, cock-a-hoop, jocund, jolly, merry; gleeful, hilarious, mirthful; chirping, chirpy, chirrupy
con lethargic, sluggish, torpid; lackadaisical, languid, languorous, listless; apathetic, impassive, phlegmatic, stolid; boring, irksome, tedious
ant dull, unlively
2 syn see AGILE
idiom full of pep
3 syn see ENERGETIC 2
4 syn see BUSTLING
ant unanimated

liven vb syn see QUICKEN 1
liver n syn see INHABITANT
live wire n syn see HUSTLER 1
livid adj 1 syn see PALE 1
rel grisly; dusky, gloomy, murky
con bright, brilliant, effulgent, lucent, luminous, lustrous, radiant
2 syn see SENSATIONAL 2

living adj 1 having or showing life <the *living* things of a locality>
syn alive, animate, animated, vital, zoetic
rel being, existing, subsisting; active, dynamic, live, operative
con dead, deceased, defunct, demised, departed, gone, inanimate
ant lifeless
2 syn see EXTANT 1

living n supplies or resources needed to live <kept trying to earn a *living* the honest way>
syn alimenation, alimony, bread, bread and butter, keep, livelihood, maintenance, salt, subsistence, support, sustenance
rel sustainment, sustentation

load n 1 something which is carried, conveyed, or transported from one place to another <a *load* of grain just arrived>
syn burden, cargo, freight, haul, lading, payload
rel bale, pack, parcel, shipment
2 something heavy <could not lift the *load*>
syn weight
3 a burdensome or laborious responsibility <considered taking care of the children a heavy *load*>
syn burden, charge, deadweight, duty, millstone, onus, task, tax, weight
rel care, liability, obligation, responsibility; drag, drain, pressure
idiom millstone around one's neck
con breeze, child's play, cinch, duck soup, picnic, ‖pipe, pushover, snap

ant sinecure
4 usu loads pl syn see SCAD
load vb 1 syn see BURDEN
rel bear, carry, convey, transport
ant unload
2 syn see ADULTERATE
3 to make full or overfull <a basket *loaded* with fresh fruit>
syn charge, choke, fill, heap, pack, pile; compare CRAM 1
rel glut, gorge, surfeit; flood, oversupply, swamp
loaded adj 1 syn see FULL 1
‖2 syn see INTOXICATED 1
loaf vb syn see IDLE
con labor, toil, travail, work
loafer n syn see SLUGGARD
loan vb syn see LEND
loan shark n one who lends money to individuals at exorbitant rates of interest <got involved with *loan sharks*>
syn Shylock, usurer
rel lender, loaner, moneylender; shark
loath adj syn see DISINCLINED
ant anxious
loathe vb syn see HATE
rel decline, refuse, reject, repudiate, spurn
con covet, crave, desire, want, wish
ant tolerate
loathing n syn see ABOMINATION 2
ant tolerance
loathsome adj syn see OFFENSIVE
rel hateful, invidious, obnoxious
con bearable, endurable, sufferable, supportable; engaging, inviting; alluring, bewitching, charming, enchanting, fascinating
ant tolerable
lobby n syn see VESTIBULE
lobster n syn see OAF 2
local adj syn see INSULAR
ant cosmopolitan
locale n syn see SCENE 3
rel area, district, neighborhood, vicinage, vicinity
locality n 1 a more or less definitely circumscribed place or region <searched for the child in the *locality* of the waterfront>
syn area, district, neighborhood, vicinage, vicinity
rel belt, region, tract, zone; section, sector; bailiwick, domain, field, province, sphere, territory
idiom neck of the woods
2 syn see HABITAT
located adj syn see SITUATED
location n syn see PLACE 1
‖**loch** n syn see INLET
lockup n syn see JAIL
‖**loco** adj syn see INSANE 1
locum tenens n syn see SUBSTITUTE
locus n syn see PLACE 1
locution n syn see PHRASE 2
lodge vb 1 syn see HARBOR 2
rel accept, admit, receive, take; accommodate, contain, hold
2 syn see ENTRENCH 1
lodge n 1 syn see HUT
2 syn see HOTEL
3 syn see LAIR 1
lodgeable adj syn see LIVABLE 1
lodging n 1 syn see ACCOMMODATIONS

---

syn synonym(s)   rel related word(s)
ant antonym(s)   con contrasted word(s)
idiom idiomatic equivalent(s)
‖ use limited; if in doubt, see a dictionary

2 *usu* lodgings *pl syn see* APARTMENT 1

lodgment *n syn see* ACCOMMODATIONS

loftiest *adj syn see* TOP 1

loftiness *n syn see* PRIDE 3

lofty *adj* 1 *syn see* PROUD 1

2 *syn see* AMBITIOUS 2

3 *syn see* GRAND 3

4 *syn see* GENEROUS 1

5 *syn see* ELEVATED 4

6 extending or rising high in the air so as to have great or imposing height < a *lofty* monument to human aspiration >

syn aerial, airy, skyscraping, soaring, spiring, topless, towering, towery; *compare* HIGH 1

rel elevated, lifted, raised; aggrandized, exalted, magnified; august, imposing, majestic, stately

con humble, low, modest

logical *adj* 1 *syn see* RATIONAL

ant illogical

2 having or showing skill in thinking or reasoning < a *logical* argument >

syn analytic, analytical, ratiocinative, subtle

rel cogent, compelling, convincing, sound, telling, valid; clear, lucid, perspicuous; rational, reasonable; discriminating

con instinctive, intuitive; irrational, unreasonable; casuistical, sophistical

ant illogical

logo *n syn see* MARK 7

logotype *n syn see* MARK 7

loiter *vb* 1 *syn see* DELAY 2

2 *syn see* IDLE

loiterer *n syn see* LAGGARD

loll *vb* 1 *syn see* SLOUCH

2 *syn see* IDLE

‖**lollop** *vb syn see* SLOUCH

lone *adj* 1 having no company < a *lone* figure walking through the snow >

syn alone, lonely, lonesome, solitary

rel single, sole, unique; abandoned, deserted, forsaken; isolated, secluded

con attended, chaperoned, companioned, convoyed, escorted

ant accompanied

2 *syn see* ONLY 2

3 *syn see* SINGLE 2

lonely *adj* 1 *syn see* LONE 1

2 *syn see* FORLORN 1

loneness *n syn see* SOLITUDE

lonesome *adj* 1 *syn see* LONE 1

2 *syn see* FORLORN 1

3 *syn see* OBSCURE 2

long *adj* 1 having considerable extension in space or time < a *long* road > < it has been a *long* time since we have seen you >

syn elongate, elongated, extended, lengthy

rel extensive, longish, outstretched

con brief, curtailed

ant short

2 unduly extended < went through many *long* days of misery >

syn dragging, drawn-out, ‖dreich, lengthy, long-drawn-out, longsome, overlong, prolonged, protracted

rel diffuse, diffusive, long-winded, prolix; flatulent, verbose, wordy

con ephemeral, evanescent, fleeting, fugacious, fugitive, impermanent, passing, short-lived, transient, transitory; abbreviated, abridged, curtailed, shortened

ant brief

long *n syn see* AGE 2

long *vb* to desire urgently < *long* for peace >

syn ache, crave, dream, hanker, hunger, itch, lust, pine, sigh, suspire, thirst, yearn, yen

rel aim, aspire, want; miss

idiom have an appetite (*or* a longing) for

con abhor, detest, dread, fear, loathe

longanimity *n syn see* PATIENCE

long-drawn-out *adj syn see* LONG 2

ant short; curtailed

‖**long green** *n syn see* MONEY

longitudinally *adv syn see* LENGTHWISE

ant horizontally

long-lasting *adj syn see* OLD 2

ant ephemeral

long-lived *adj syn see* OLD 2

ant short-lived

longsome *adj syn see* LONG 2

long-suffering *n syn see* PATIENCE

rel subduedness; humility, lowliness, meekness

con impatience, uneasiness; irksomeness, tediousness, wearisomeness; boredom, ennui, tedium

long suit *n syn see* FORTE

rel specialism, specialization, specialty

longtimer *n syn see* VETERAN

con apprentice, neophyte, novice; newcomer, rookie, tenderfoot

‖**long tongue** *n syn see* GOSSIP 1

longways *adv syn see* LENGTHWISE

long-winded *adj syn see* WORDY

rel extended, lasting, lengthy, long, long-drawn-out, prolonged, protracted

con brief, close, compact

longwise *adv syn see* LENGTHWISE

loo *n syn see* TOILET

looby *n syn see* OAF 2

look *vb* 1 to make sure or take care (that something is or is not done) < *look* that you accuse no one unjustly >

syn mind, see, watch

rel attend, heed, tend; note, notice, observe; beware

2 *syn see* SEE 2

rel note, notice, observe, spot

idiom get a load of, take a gander at

3 *syn see* EXPECT 1

rel divine, forecast, foretell

ant despair (of)

4 to make apparent by the expression of the eyes or countenance < *looked* her annoyance at this interruption >

syn exhibit, show; *compare* SHOW 2

rel display, express, indicate, manifest

5 *syn see* SEEM

idiom strike one as

6 *syn see* FACE 1

7 to gaze in wonder or surprise < you should have seen them *look* >

syn eye, gape, ‖gaup (*or* gawp), gaze, goggle, ogle, rubberneck, stare; *compare* GAZE 1

rel gawk; glare, gloat, glower; peer

8 *syn see* TEND 1

look (at *or* upon) *vb syn see* EYE 1

look (into) *vb syn see* EXPLORE

look *n* 1 the directing of one's eyes in order to see < he wanted one last *look* before departing >

syn sight, view

rel glance, glimpse, peek, peep, squint; cast, slant; eye, ‖gander, ‖look-see, regard; eyeful, gaze, stare, survey

2 facial aspect especially as indicative of mood or feeling <you should have seen the *look* on her face>

syn cast, countenance, expression, face, visage

rel mug, physiognomy, ‖puss

3 *syn* see APPEARANCE 1

look down *vb* **1** *syn* see OVERLOOK 2

2 *syn* see DESPISE

3 *syn* see STARE DOWN

looker *n syn* see BEAUTY

looker-on *n syn* see SPECTATOR

look in *vb syn* see VISIT 2

look-in *n syn* see OPPORTUNITY

looking glass *n syn* see MIRROR 1

look out *vb syn* see BEWARE

lookout *n* **1** *syn* see GUARD 2

2 an elevated place affording a wide view for observation <guards posted at a *lookout* to watch for enemy troops entering the valley>

syn observatory, outlook, overlook

rel watchtower; crow's nest; cupola, widow's walk; firetower

3 a careful looking or watching <kept a constant *lookout* for new developments>

syn surveillance, tout, vigil, vigilance, watch, watch and ward

rel observance, observation

4 *syn* see VISTA

5 *syn* see BUSINESS 8

look up *vb* **1** *syn* see IMPROVE 3

2 *syn* see VISIT 2

loom *vb* **1** *syn* see APPEAR 1

2 to take shape as an impending occurrence <an international economic crisis *looms* ahead>

syn brew, forthcome, gather, impend

rel approach, come on, make up, near

con disappear, fade, pass, vanish; die (down *or* away), diminish, dwindle, wane; recede, retreat, withdraw

3 to appear in an impressively great or exaggerated form <the power of the enemy *loomed* in the soldiers' imagination>

syn bulk, stand out

rel lower, rear, threaten, tower

con die (down *or* away), diminish, dwindle, wane

loon *n syn* see LUNATIC 1

loony *adj syn* see FOOLISH 2

loony *n syn* see LUNATIC 1

loony bin *n syn* see ASYLUM 3

loop *n* **1** a curving or doubling of a line so as to form a closed or partly open curve <the transit makes a *loop* around town>

syn eye, ring

rel circlet, circuit, circumference, hoop, wreath; curve

2 a circular or curved piece used often to form a fastening or a handle <one of his belt *loops* is broken>

syn eye, ring, staple

rel hook

---

syn synonym(s)　　*rel* related word(s)
ant antonym(s)　　*con* contrasted word(s)
idiom idiomatic equivalent(s)
‖ use limited; if in doubt, see a dictionary

---

3 *syn* see LEAGUE 4

loop *vb syn* see SURROUND 1

rel arc, arch, bend, coil, curve

looped *adj syn* see INTOXICATED 1

loopy *adj syn* see FOOLISH 2

loose *adj* **1** not tightly bound, held, restrained, or stretched <*loose* rope>

syn lax, relaxed, slack

rel detached, free; flabby, flaccid, limp; desultory, negligent, remiss

con rigid, rigorous, stringent, taut, tense; exact, precise; bound, checked, curbed, inhibited, restrained, tied

ant strict; tight

2 *syn* see FREE 2

rel clear; disconnected, unattached, unconnected, undone, unfastened

con fast

3 not dense, close, or compact in structure <*loose* soil>

syn incoherent, nonadhesive

rel disconnected, disjointed, separate, unconnected

con compressed, condensed, contracted; concentrated; crammed, crowded, localized; close, compact, dense, thick

4 *syn* see FAST 7

rel capricious, extravagant, free, inconstant, reckless, unrestrained

loose *vb* **1** *syn* see FREE

2 *syn* see TAKE OUT (on)

3 to set free from a fastened or fixed condition <*loose* a knot>

syn disengage, unbind, undo, unfasten, unfix, unloose, unloosen

rel unbandage, unbar, unbolt, unbuckle, unbutton, unchain, unclasp, unglue, unhitch, unhook, unlace, unlash, unlatch, unlock, unpin, unscrew, unsnap, unstick, unstrap, untie

con bind, engage, fasten, fix, secure

4 *syn* see SHOOT 1

5 to make less rigid or tight <exercise *loosed* his muscles>

syn ease, ease off, lax, loosen, relax, slack, slacken, untighten

rel abate, alleviate, bate, lessen, let up, mitigate

con anchor, cement, clamp, clinch, fasten, knit, secure, set, tauten

ant tighten

loose-lipped *adj syn* see TALKATIVE

ant closemouthed

loosen *vb* **1** *syn* see LOOSE 5

ant tighten

2 *syn* see FREE

loosen up *vb syn* see RELAX 2

ant tighten (up)

loose-tongued *adj syn* see TALKATIVE

ant closemouthed

loot *n* **1** *syn* see SPOIL

rel lift, pillage, seizure

2 *syn* see MONEY

loot *vb syn* see ROB 1

looter *n syn* see MARAUDER

lop *vb* **1** *syn* see SLOUCH

2 *syn* see JUMP 1

lope *vb syn* see SKIP 1

rel run, sprint; romp, trip

‖**lopper** *vb syn* see CURDLE

lopsided *adj* lacking in balance, symmetry, or proportion <the arrangement of the furniture was *lopsided*>

syn asymmetric, difform, disproportional, disproportionate, irregular, nonsymmetrical, off-balance, overbalanced, proportionless, unbalanced, unequal, uneven, unproportionate, unsymmetrical

rel cockeyed, crooked, top-heavy, unsteady

con balanced, even, regular, symmetrical

loquacious *adj syn see* TALKATIVE

rel jabbering, overtalkative; prolix, verbose, wordy

con breviloquent, concise, succinct, taciturn, terse; abrupt, brusque, curt

lord *n syn see* HUSBAND

lord *vb* to affect an air of superiority and authority <nouveau riche love to *lord* it>

syn cock, peacock, pontificate, swagger, swank, swell

rel affect, pretend, put on; boss, order (about *or* around), overawe, overbear; tyrannize

idiom put on airs

lordly *adj* 1 *syn see* GRAND 1

2 *syn see* PROUD 1

rel egotistic, puffed; affected, snobbish, swollen; authoritarian, dictatorial, magisterial

con humble; abject, mean; subdued, submissive

lore *n* 1 *syn see* KNOWLEDGE 2

2 a body of traditions relating to a person, institution, or place <the Scottish highlands are rich in local *lore*>

syn folklore, legend, myth, mythology, mythos, tradition

rel custom, folkway, traditionalism; fable, old wives' tale, saga, superstition, tale

Lorelei *n syn see* SIREN

lorn *adj* 1 *syn see* DERELICT 1

2 *syn see* FORLORN 1

lose *vb* 1 to suffer deprivation of <*lost* all his savings in a poor investment>

syn drop, forfeit, sacrifice

rel mislay, misplace, miss; give up, relinquish, surrender, yield

con cash in, profit; clear, make, realize, take in; obtain, win

ant gain

2 to fail to win, gain, or obtain <*lost* every contest she entered>

syn drop, lose out

rel decline, fall, succumb, yield

ant win

3 *syn see* DEPRIVE 2

4 *syn see* SHAKE 5

5 *syn see* RID

lose out *vb syn see* LOSE 2

loser *n* 1 *syn see* FAILURE 5

rel also-ran, underdog

ant winner

2 *syn see* CONVICT

losing *n syn see* LOSS 1

loss *n* 1 the action of having something go out of one's control or possession <took precautions against *loss* or theft of his property>

syn losing, mislaying, misplacement, misplacing; *compare* PRIVATION 2

rel forfeit, forfeiture, sacrifice; bereavement, deprivation, deprivement, dispossession, divestiture, divestment, privation

2 *syn see* PRIVATION 2

3 *syn see* RUIN 3

lost *adj* 1 *syn see* DAMNED 1

rel incorrigible, irreclaimable, irredeemable, irreformable, unconverted, unregenerate; graceless

2 no longer possessed <earned his *lost* reputation by his outrageous behavior>

syn gone, missing

rel absent, lacking; passed; irrecoverable, irretrievable, irrevocable

con cherished, protected, treasured

3 *syn see* EXTINCT 2

4 *syn see* ABSTRACTED

rel absorbed; daydreamy, musing, unconscious

lot *n* 1 *syn see* SHARE 1

2 *syn see* FATE

rel decree, fortune; foreordination, predestination, predetermination

3 a measured portion of land having fixed boundaries <building *lots*>

syn parcel, plat, plot, tract

rel clearing, field, patch; part, plottage; block, frontage, real estate

4 *syn see* GROUP 3

rel aggregate, aggregation, conglomerate, conglomeration

5 *syn see* SET 5

6 *syn see* TYPE

7 *syn see* MUCH

lot *vb syn see* ALLOT

||**lot** (on *or* upon) *vb syn see* RELY (on *or* upon)

lot (out) *vb syn see* DISTRIBUTE 1

lothario *n syn see* GALLANT 2

loud *adj* 1 marked by intensity or volume of sound <a *loud* blast on a trumpet>

syn blaring, earsplitting, full-mouthed, piercing, roaring, stentorian, stentorious, stentorophonic

rel booming, deafening, ear-piercing, fulminating, pealing, ringing, thunderous; resonant, resounding, sonorous; harsh, hoarse, raucous, stertorous, strident

con dulcet, gentle, mellifluous, mellow, quiet, smooth

ant low, soft

2 *syn see* GAUDY

rel brassy, vulgar; obnoxious, offensive; obtrusive

loudmouthed *adj syn see* VOCIFEROUS

||**lough** *n syn see* INLET

lounge *vb syn see* IDLE

rel drift, vegetate; dally, slack; lie, lie down, recline

lounge *n syn see* BAR 5

lounge car *n syn see* PARLOR CAR

lounge lizard *n* 1 *syn see* POP

2 *syn see* PARASITE

louse *n syn see* SNOT 1

louse up *vb syn see* BOTCH

lout *n syn see* OAF 2

rel boor, bumpkin, churl, clodhopper, hayseed, hick, peasant, rube, rustic, yokel; dolt

lout *vb syn see* RIDICULE

loutish *adj syn see* BOORISH

rel awkward, bungling, clumsy, inept, maladroit, rusty; callow, crude, gauche, raw, rough, uncouth

lovable *adj* gifted with traits and qualities that attract affection <a *lovable* child>

syn adorable, lovesome

rel admirable, agreeable, attractive, desirable, genial, likable, pleasing, winning, winsome; alluring, appealing, bewitching, captivating, charming, enchanting, engaging, enthralling, entrancing, fetching, ravishing, seductive

con dislikable, displeasing, distasteful, unattractive, unlikable, unpleasing; odious, offensive; abhorrent, abominable, obnoxious, repellent; contemptible, despicable, detestable

ant hateful; unlovable

love *n* **1** the feeling which animates a person who is genuinely fond of someone or something <a mother's *love* for her child>

syn affection, attachment, devotion, fondness

rel like(s), liking, regard; adoration, idolatry, piety, worship; allegiance, fealty, fidelity, loyalty; emotion, sentiment; crush, infatuation, passion, yearning; ardency, ardor, enthusiasm, fervor, zeal

con antipathy, aversion; animosity, animus, enmity, hostility, rancor; abhorrence, detestation, hatred

ant hate

2 the affection and tenderness felt by lovers <the ability to distinguish between *love* and lust was the mark of her maturity>

syn amorousness, amour, passion

rel crush, infatuation; desire, lust, yearning; ardency, ardor, fervor

idiom (the) tender passion

3 *syn* see LOVE AFFAIR

4 *syn* see SWEETHEART 1

love *vb* **1** to like or desire actively <she *loves* her material possessions all too dearly>

syn adore, delight (in), ‖eat up

rel appreciate, cherish, prize, treasure, value; dote (on *or* upon), fancy

idiom hold dear

con abjure, give up, reject, relinquish

2 to feel a lover's passion, devotion, or tenderness for <in spite of all their misfortunes, they continued to *love* each other devotedly>

syn adore, affection, worship

rel deify, exalt, idolize, revere, venerate; cherish, dote (on *or* upon); admire, fancy, like

con avoid, disregard, ignore, neglect, overlook, shun, slight

3 *syn* see CARESS

love affair *n* a romantic attachment or episode between lovers <saddened by the end of a summer *love affair*>

syn affair, amour, love, romance

rel flirtation, intrigue; triangle, ménage à trois

love child *n* *syn* see BASTARD 1

loved *adj* *syn* see FAVORITE 1

love letter *n* a letter expressing a lover's affection <she had never received a *love letter*>

syn billet-doux, mash note

rel **valentine**

loveling *n* *syn* see SWEETHEART 1

lovely *adj* see BEAUTIFUL

rel alluring, bewitching, captivating, charming, enchanting, engaging, entrancing, lovesome; delectable, delightful; dainty, delicate, exquisite, rare; graceful

ant hideous; unlovely

lovely *n* *syn* see BEAUTY

lover *n* **1** a man who is a woman's regular partner in nonmarital sexual activity

syn boyfriend, fancy man, man, master, paramour

rel cavalier servente, sugar daddy

2 *syn* see BOYFRIEND 2

3 *syn* see ADDICT

4 *syn* see MISTRESS

lovesome *adj* **1** *syn* see LOVABLE

2 *syn* see LOVING

lovey-dovey *adj* *syn* see SENTIMENTAL

loving *adj* feeling or expressing love <his *loving* son unfailingly waited upon him during his last years>

syn affectionate, dear, devoted, doting, fond, lovesome

rel adoring, attached, benevolent, cordial, kind, tender, warmhearted; attentive, caring, considerate, solicitous; amatory, amorous, erotic; enamored, infatuated; ardent, fervent, impassioned, passionate; faithful; bound up

con aloof, detached, indifferent, unconcerned; chilly, cold, frigid

ant unloving

low *adj* ‖**1** *syn* see SHORT 2

rel squatty; unelevated

2 *syn* see INFERIOR 1

3 *syn* see POOR 1

4 *syn* see IGNOBLE 1

rel lowbred, rude

5 *syn* see BASE 3

rel scrubby, scruffy; miserable, woebegone, woeful

con decent, decorous, proper, seemly; ethical, moral, noble; high, lofty

6 *syn* see COARSE 3

7 *syn* see UNWELL

rel declining, weak; dizzy, faint, feverish

8 *syn* see DOWNCAST

9 of lesser degree, size, or amount than average or ordinary <the energy crisis resulted in *lower* speed limits for all vehicles>

syn subaverage, subnormal

rel fallen, reduced; brief, short; mediocre, moderate; atypical

10 *syn* see CHEAP 1

rel economical; moderate, nominal; cut, cut-rate, marked down, slashed

con elevated, enhanced, increased, raised

lowborn *adj* *syn* see IGNOBLE 1

ant highborn

lowbred *adj* *syn* see BOORISH

ant highbred

low-cost *adj* *syn* see CHEAP 1

low-down *adj* *syn* see BASE 3

lower *vb* *syn* see FROWN 1

rel peer, stare; intimidate, menace, threaten

lower *adj* *syn* see INFERIOR 1

ant higher

lower *vb* **1** *syn* see FALL 1

ant rise

2 *syn* see DEPRECIATE 1
rel demote; de-escalate, deflate
con raise

3 to cause or allow to descend < *lowered* the landing gear of the aircraft>
syn couch, demit, depress, droop, let down, sink
rel detrude, submerge; debase, reduce
con elevate, hoist, lift, pull up, raise

4 *syn* see REDUCE 2
ant raise

5 *syn* see HUMBLE
ant elevate

lowering (*or* **louring**) *adj* 1 *syn* see IMMINENT 2
rel frowning, gloomy, sullen; black, dark; foreboding, impending, portentous

2 *syn* see OVERCAST

lowermost *adj syn* see BOTTOMMOST
ant uppermost

lowery (*or* **loury**) *adj syn* see IMMINENT 2

lowest *adj syn* see BOTTOMMOST
ant highest

low-grade *adj syn* see INFERIOR 2

low-key *adj syn* see SUBDUED 2

low-keyed *adj syn* see SUBDUED 2

lowlife *n* 1 *syn* see WRETCH 1
2 *syn* see VILLAIN 1

lowly *adj* 1 *syn* see HUMBLE 1
rel retiring, withdrawing; deferential, obeisant, reverential; obsequious, servile
ant haughty

2 *syn* see IGNOBLE 1

3 *syn* see PROSAIC 3

low-pressure *adj syn* see EASYGOING 3
ant high-pressure

low-priced *adj syn* see CHEAP 1

low-rate *vb syn* see DECRY 2

low-set *adj syn* see SHORT 2

low-spirited *adj syn* see DOWNCAST
ant high-spirited

low-statured *adj syn* see SHORT 2

loyal *adj syn* see FAITHFUL 1
con faithless; alienated, disaffected, estranged; contumacious, factious, insubordinate, mutinous, rebellious, seditious
ant disloyal

loyalist *n syn* see PATRIOT 1

loyalty *n* 1 *syn* see FIDELITY 1
rel trueness, truth
ant disloyalty

2 *syn* see ATTACHMENT 1

lubber *n syn* see OAF 2

lubberland *n syn* see UTOPIA

lubberly *adj syn* see BOORISH

lubricate *vb syn* see BRIBE

lubricious *adj* 1 *syn* see INCONSTANT 1
2 *syn* see SLICK 1

lucent *adj* 1 *syn* see BRIGHT 1
2 *syn* see CLEAR 4

lucid *adj* 1 *syn* see BRIGHT 1
2 *syn* see SANE 2
3 *syn* see UNDERSTANDABLE
4 *syn* see CLEAR 4
con dusky, gloomy, murky; muddy, turbid

lucidity *n* 1 *syn* see CLARITY
rel comprehensibility, intelligibility, understandability; distinctness, explicitness
ant ambiguity

2 *syn* see WIT 2

Lucifer *n syn* see DEVIL 1

luck *n* 1 *syn* see CHANCE 2

rel break, occasion, opportunity

2 *syn* see ACCIDENT 1

3 success dependent on chance < he had all the *luck* in the world and was greatly envied by every one of his associates>
syn fortunateness, fortune, luckiness
rel advantage, break, fluke, godsend, opportunity, windfall; weal; hap, kismet
ant ill-fortune

4 *syn* see CHARM 2

luck *vb syn* see HAPPEN 2

luckiness *n syn* see LUCK 3

luckless *adj syn* see UNLUCKY
rel miserable, wretched
ant lucky

lucky *adj* having a favorable outcome or an unforeseen or unpredictable success < he can only be described as *lucky*, as his success and fame are unearned>
syn fortunate, happy, providential, ‖sonsy, well
rel auspicious, benign, favorable, propitious; advantageous, beneficial, profitable; felicitous
idiom in luck
con baleful, malefic, maleficent, malign, sinister
ant luckless, unlucky

lucrative *adj syn* see ADVANTAGEOUS 1

lucre *n* 1 *syn* see PROFIT
2 *syn* see MONEY

luculent *adj syn* see CLEAR 4

ludicrous *adj syn* see LAUGHABLE
rel absurd, foolish, preposterous, silly; antic, bizarre, fantastic, grotesque
con doleful, dolorous, lugubrious, melancholy

lug *vb* 1 *syn* see PULL 2
2 *syn* see CARRY 1
3 *syn* see JERK

lug *n syn* see OAF 2

‖**lugs** *n pl syn* see POSE 2

lugubrious *adj* 1 *syn* see MELANCHOLY 2
rel depressing, oppressing, oppressive; dour, glum, morose, saturnine, sullen
con blithe, jocund, jolly, jovial, merry; cheerful, glad, joyful
ant facetious

2 *syn* see GLOOMY 3

lukewarm *adj* 1 *syn* see TEPID 1
2 *syn* see TEPID 2
rel irresolute, irresolved, uncommitted, unresolved; hesitant, indecisive, uncertain, undecided; cool; wishy-washy
ant icy; boiling

lull *vb* 1 *syn* see CALM
rel moderate, qualify, temper
ant agitate

2 *syn* see ABATE 4

lull *n* 1 *syn* see QUIET 1
2 *syn* see PAUSE
rel abeyance, quiescence

lullaby *n* a song to quiet children or lull them to sleep < sang a *lullaby* to the baby every night>
syn berceuse, cradlesong

‖**lulu** *n syn* see ‖DILLY

lumber *vb* to tread heavily or clumsily < the tired old man slowly *lumbered* home>
syn barge, clump, galumph, stumble, stump
rel plod, trudge; shamble, slog

lumber *vb syn* see BURDEN

lumbering *adj* 1 *syn* see CLUMSY 1
rel cumbersome, cumbrous, ponderous; hulking, hulky

2 *syn* see AWKWARD 2

luminary *n* 1 *syn* see CELEBRITY 2
rel leading light

2 *syn* see NOTABLE 1

luminous *adj* 1 *syn* see BRIGHT 1

2 *syn* see CLEAR 4

3 *syn* see UNDERSTANDABLE

lummox *n syn* see OAF 2

lump *n* 1 a compact mass of indefinite size and shape < dropped a large *lump* of butter into the steaming chowder >
syn chunk, clod, clump, gob, hunch, hunk, nugget, wad
rel particle, piece, portion; batch, bunch, ‖swad; bit, chip, crumb, morsel, scrap; wedge; block, bulk

2 *syn* see MUCH

3 *syn* see BUMP 2
rel bulge, protuberance, swelling

4 *syn* see OAF 2

5 **lumps** *pl syn* see DUE 1

lump *vb syn* see BEAR 10

lumpish *adj* 1 *syn* see BOORISH

2 *syn* see CLUMSY 1

lumpkin *n syn* see OAF 2

lumpy *adj syn* see RUDE 1

lunacy *n* 1 *syn* see INSANITY 1
rel absurdity, folly, foolery, foolishness; asininity, fatuity, inanity, ineptitude, stupidity

2 *syn* see FOOLISHNESS

lunatic *adj* 1 *syn* see INSANE 1

2 *syn* see FOOLISH 2

lunatic *n* 1 a person who is insane or of unsound mind < Bedlam was a famous old English asylum for *lunatics* >
syn bedlamite, dement, loon, loony, madling, madman, maniac, non compos, nut, Tom o' Bedlam
rel demoniac, energumen; raver; neuropath, neurotic, paranoid, psycho, psychoneurotic

2 *syn* see CRACKPOT

lunch counter (*or* bar) *n syn* see EATING HOUSE

luncheonette *n syn* see EATING HOUSE

lunchroom *n syn* see EATING HOUSE

lunch wagon (*or* cart) *n syn* see EATING HOUSE

lunge *vb syn* see PLUNGE 2

lunk *n syn* see DUNCE

lunkhead *n syn* see DUNCE

lupanar *n syn* see BROTHEL

lurch *vb* 1 *syn* see LEANING 2

lurch *vb* 1 *syn* see SEESAW

2 to move forward unsteadily while swaying from side to side < the sodden drunk *lurched* uncertainly toward the door >
syn careen, stagger, ‖stoit, ‖stoiter, ‖stot, sway, swing, weave, wobble; *compare* TEETER
rel reel, rock, roll, swag, toss, totter, whirl; bob; wave, waver
con march, stride

3 *syn* see TEETER
rel pitch, plunge

4 *syn* see JERK

5 *syn* see WALLOW 2

6 *syn* see STUMBLE 3

lure *n* 1 *syn* see ATTRACTION 1

2 something that leads an individual into a place or situation from which escape is difficult < used her charm as a *lure* to trap the unsuspecting youth >
syn allurement, bait, come-on, decoy, enticement, inveiglement, seducement, siren song, snare, ‖stale, temptation, trap
rel appeal, attraction, incentive, inducement; con game, gimmick, suck-in, trick; ambush, blind, camouflage, delusion, fake, illusion
con caution, caveat, warning

lure *vb* to draw from a usual, desirable, or proper course or situation into one felt as unusual, undesirable, or wrong < the promise of money *lured* him away from his steady job >
syn allure, bait, decoy, entice, entrap, inveigle, lead on, seduce, tempt, toll, train
rel bag, capture, catch, draw in, ensnare, rope, snare, suck in; attract, beguile, bewitch, captivate, charm, enchant, fascinate, invite; draw, draw on; blandish, cajole, wheedle
idiom bait the hook, give the come-on
con drive (away *or* off), rebuff, repulse
ant repel

lurid *adj* 1 *syn* see PALE 1

2 *syn* see GHASTLY 1
rel ashen, ashy, livid, pale, pallid, wan; baleful, malefic, maleficent, malign, sinister

3 *syn* see SENSATIONAL 2

luring *adj syn* see ENTICING
ant repellent, repelling

lurk *vb syn* see SNEAK

lurking *adj syn* see LATENT

luscious *adj* 1 *syn* see DELIGHTFUL
rel appetizing, flavorsome, nectarious, palatable, piquant; choice, distinctive, exquisite, rare, rich
ant austere

2 *syn* see LUXURIOUS 3

3 *syn* see SENSUOUS

4 *syn* see ORNATE

lush *adj* 1 *syn* see PROFUSE
rel luxurious, sumptuous

2 *syn* see DELIGHTFUL

3 *syn* see SENSUOUS

4 *syn* see LUXURIOUS 3

lush *n* ‖1 *syn* see LIQUOR 2

2 *syn* see DRUNKARD

lush (up) *vb syn* see DRINK 3

‖**lushed** *adj syn* see INTOXICATED 1

‖**lusher** *n syn* see DRUNKARD

lust *n* 1 *syn* see DESIRE 1
rel coveting, yearning, yen

2 sexual appetency < they mistakenly thought that *lust* was lasting love >
syn aphrodisia, concupiscence, desire, eroticism, itch, lickerishness, lustfulness, passion, prurience, pruriency
rel nymphomania, priapism, satyriasis, satyrism; excitement, heat, hunger, libido, rut; fervor; carnality, lasciviousness, lecherousness, lechery, lubricity, salacity

lust *vb syn* see LONG

rel desire, wish

luster *n* the quality or condition of shining by reflected light < the satiny *luster* of fine pearls >
syn glaze, glint, gloss, polish, sheen, shine
rel iridescence, opalescence; brilliance, brilliancy, effulgence, luminosity, radiance, refulgence; afterglow, gleam, glow; candescence, incandescence

lusterless *adj* 1 *syn* see DULL 7
ant lustrous
2 *syn* see COLORLESS 1

lustful *adj* 1 *syn* see LICENTIOUS 2
2 sexually excited < *lustful* old man >
syn concupiscent, goatish, hot, lascivious, libidinous, lickerish, passionate, prurient, ruttish, rutty, satyric
rel burning, hot-blooded, itching; lecherous, salacious

lustfulness *n* *syn* see LUST 2

lustral *adj* *syn* see PURGATIVE

lustrate *vb* *syn* see PURIFY 2

lustration *n* *syn* see PURIFICATION

lustratory *adj* *syn* see PURGATIVE

lustrous *adj* 1 having a high gloss or shine < a *lustrous* star sapphire >
syn burnished, gleaming, glistening, glossy, polished, sheeny, shining, shiny
rel gleamy, glimmering, glinting, sparkling; radiant
con dull, flat, lackluster, mat
ant lusterless
2 *syn* see BRIGHT 1
rel glorious, resplendent, splendid

lusty *adj* 1 *syn* see VIGOROUS
rel hale, healthy
ant effete
2 *syn* see STRONG 3
3 *syn* see HUGE

lusus *n* *syn* see FREAK 2

luxuriant *adj* 1 *syn* see PROFUSE
rel fecund, fertile, fruitful, prolific; rampant, rank

con barren, infertile, sterile, unfruitful
2 *syn* see LUXURIOUS 3

luxuriate *vb* *syn* see WALLOW 3
rel overindulge, overdo; eat up, enjoy, feast, love, riot

luxurious *adj* 1 *syn* see SENSUOUS
rel self-indulging, self-pampering; languishing, languorous
con self-abnegating, self-denying; austere, severe, stern
ant ascetic
2 *syn* see GRAND 2
rel imposing, majestic, stately
3 ostentatiously rich or magnificent < the robber barons built *luxurious* homes which rivaled the palaces of Europe >
syn Capuan, deluxe, luscious, lush, luxuriant, opulent, palace, palatial, plush, plushy, sumptuous, upholstered
rel extravagant, grandiose, ostentatious, posh, pretentious, showy; awful, grand, imposing, magnificent, majestic, stately; Lucullan; elaborate, fancy; costly, expensive, precious
con economical, frugal, sparing, thrifty; exiguous, meager, scant, scanty, scrimpy, skimpy, spare

luxury *n* something adding to pleasure but not absolutely necessary < the poor cannot even afford the essentials, let alone occasional *luxuries* >
syn amenity, extravagance, frill, luxus, superfluity
rel comfort; embellishment, redundancy, self-indulgence; dainty, delicacy
con basics, essential(s), fundamental(s)

luxus *n* *syn* see LUXURY

lying *adj* *syn* see DISHONEST
rel false, wrong; deceptive, delusive, delusory, misleading

lying-in *n* *syn* see CONFINEMENT 2

lyncean *adj* *syn* see SHARP-EYED

lynx-eyed *adj* *syn* see SHARP-EYED

ma *n* *syn* see MOTHER 1

macabre *adj* *syn* see GHASTLY 1
rel deadly, deathlike, deathly; ghostlike, ghostly

macaroni *n* *syn* see FOP

mace *n* *syn* see CUDGEL

‖**mace** *n* *syn* see SWINDLER

‖**mace** *vb* *syn* see CHEAT

machinate *vb* 1 *syn* see ENGINEER
2 *syn* see PLOT

machination *n* *syn* see PLOT 2

machine *n* 1 *syn* see CAR
2 *syn* see ROBOT 2

machinery *n* *syn* see EQUIPMENT
rel agency, agent, channel, instrument, instrumentality, means, medium, organ, vehicle; contraption, contrivance, device, gadget; appliance, implement, instrument, tool, utensil

‖**mack** *n* *syn* see PIMP 1

macquereau *n* *syn* see PIMP 1

macrocosm *n* *syn* see UNIVERSE
ant microcosm

macrocosmos *n* *syn* see UNIVERSE
ant microcosm

mad *adj* 1 *syn* see INSANE 1
rel delirious, frantic, frenetic, furious, rabid, wild
2 *syn* see FOOLISH 2
3 *syn* see ILLOGICAL
4 *syn* see ANGRY
rel sore, worked up; affronted, offended, outraged
5 *syn* see FURIOUS 2

mad *vb* *syn* see ANGER 1

mad *n* *syn* see ANGER

mad-brained *adj* *syn* see RASH 1

madcap *adj* *syn* see RASH 1

madden *vb* 1 to make insane < prolonged solitary confinement had *maddened* the prisoners >
syn craze, derange, distract, frenzy, unbalance, unhinge

rel shatter; possess
idiom drive insane (*or* mad *or* crazy)
2 *syn* see ANGER 1
con allay, assuage, mitigate, relieve
made-to-order *adj syn* see CUSTOM-MADE
madhouse *n syn* see ASYLUM 3
madid *adj syn* see WET 1
madling *n syn* see LUNATIC 1
madly *adv syn* see HARD 2
rel foolishly, insanely, irrationally; hastily, rashly
madman *n* 1 *syn* see LUNATIC 1
2 *syn* see FOOL 1
madness *n syn* see INSANITY 1
maelstrom *n syn* see EDDY
rel commotion, confusion, fury, storm, turmoil
magazine *n* 1 *syn* see DEPOT 2
rel cache, lumber room
2 *syn* see ARMORY
3 *syn* see JOURNAL
rel publication; digest, gazette; annual, bimonthly, biweekly, daily, monthy, quarterly, semiweekly, weekly
mage *n syn* see MAGICIAN 1
maggot *n syn* see CAPRICE
magian *n syn* see MAGICIAN 1
magian *adj syn* see MAGIC
magic *n* 1 the use of means (as charms or spells) believed to have supernatural power over natural forces < the practice of *magic* >
syn bewitchment, conjuring, conjury, enchantment, ensorcellment, incantation, magicking, necromancy, sorcery, thaumaturgy, witchcraft, witchery, witching, wizardry
rel abracadabra, alchemy, augury, charm, divining, exorcism, fortune-telling, mumbo jumbo, occultism, soothsaying, sortilege, voodooism; devilry, deviltry, diablerie, diabolism, satanism; wicca
2 the art of producing mysterious effects by illusion and sleight of hand < the club presented a program of clever *magic* to raise funds >
syn conjuring, legerdemain
idiom sleight of hand
magic *adj* having seemingly supernatural qualities or powers < modern medicine has developed a host of *magic* drugs >
syn magian, magical, mystic, necromantic, sorcerous, thaumaturgic, witchy, wizardry
rel extraordinary, marvelous, prodigious, remarkable, stupendous, unbelievable, unprecedented
magical *adj syn* see MAGIC
magician *n* 1 one who practices magical arts < a *magician* cast a spell over the child >
syn archimage, charmer, conjurer, enchanter, mage, magian, magus, necromancer, sorcerer, voodoo, voodooist, warlock, wizard; *compare* WITCH 1
rel augurer, brujo, diviner, exorciser, exorcist, invocator, thaumaturge, thaumaturgist; medicine man, shaman; prophet,

seer, soothsayer; fortune-teller, medium; diabolist, satanist
2 one who practices tricks of illusion and sleight of hand < a *magician* performed tricks for the children at the party >
syn conjurer, illusionist, trickster
magicking *n syn* see MAGIC 1
magisterial *adj* 1 *syn* see DICTATORIAL
rel disdainful, insolent, lordly, supercilious
2 *syn* see MASTERFUL 1
3 *syn* see POMPOUS 1
magistrate *n syn* see JUDGE 2
magnanimous *adj syn* see GENEROUS 1
rel altruistic, liberal, unselfish; great, highminded, knightly, noble, nobleminded, princely
con measly, paltry, petty, picayunish, picayune
magnate *n* a businessman of exceptional wealth, influence, or power < the oil and steel *magnates* who controlled whole nations >
syn baron, czar, king, merchant prince, mogul, prince, tycoon
rel figure, name, personage; ‖biggie, big gun, big-timer, ‖big wheel, fat cat, lion, nabob; plutocrat
idiom captain of industry
magnetic *adj syn* see ATTRACTIVE 1
rel arresting, irresistible; charismatic
con repellent, repugnant, repulsive
magnetism *n syn* see CHARM 3
magnetize *vb syn* see ATTRACT 1
magnific *adj syn* see GRAND 1
magnificent *adj* 1 *syn* see GRAND 1
rel glorious, resplendent, splendid, sublime, superb; luxurious, opulent, sumptuous
con abject, ignoble, mean, sordid; humble, lowly, meek; paltry
ant modest
2 *syn* see SPLENDID 2
3 *syn* see SUPERB 3
magnify *vb* 1 *syn* see PRAISE 2
2 *syn* see EXALT 1
rel augment, enlarge, increase; amplify, dilate, distend, expand, inflate, swell
ant belittle, minimize
3 *syn* see INCREASE 1
ant minify
4 *syn* see INTENSIFY 1
5 *syn* see OVERPLAY 2
6 *syn* see EMBROIDER
magniloquent *adj syn* see RHETORICAL
magnitude *n* 1 *syn* see ENORMITY 2
2 *syn* see SIZE 1
3 *syn* see SIZE 2
4 *syn* see ORDER 4
5 *syn* see IMPORTANCE
magnum opus *n syn* see MASTERPIECE 1
magpie *n syn* see CHATTERBOX
magus *n syn* see MAGICIAN 1
mahogany *n syn* see TABLE 1
maid *n* 1 *syn* see GIRL 1
2 a woman hired to do housework < in addition to her other duties the *maid* was expected to care for the baby >
syn biddy, girl, handmaid, hired girl, housemaid, maidservant
rel au pair girl; chambermaid, nursemaid, parlormaid; handmaiden; domestic, factotum, ‖muchacha, servant

syn synonym(s)   *rel* related word(s)
ant antonym(s)   *con* contrasted word(s)
idiom idiomatic equivalent(s)
‖ use limited; if in doubt, see a dictionary

idiom maid of all work

maiden *n syn* see GIRL 1

maiden *adj* 1 *syn* see VIRGIN 1
rel husbandless; old-maidish, spinsterish, spinsterly
2 *syn* see FIRST 2

maidenhead *n syn* see VIRGINITY

maidenhood *n syn* see VIRGINITY

maiden lady *n syn* see SPINSTER

maidservant *n syn* see MAID 2

maim *vb* to wound so severely as to deprive of the use of or to cause loss of a limb or member <an arm hanging useless, *maimed* in an auto accident>
syn cripple, dislimb, dismember, mayhem, mutilate; *compare* PARALYZE 1
rel disable, disfigure, hamstring; batter, break, bung up, mangle, massacre, maul
con rehabilitate, restore, salvage; cure, fix, heal, mend, remedy, repair

main *n syn* see OCEAN

main *adj syn* see CHIEF 2
rel foremost, head, leading, paramount; cardinal, controlling, essential, fundamental, vital; prevailing

‖**main** *adv syn* see VERY 1

‖**mainline** *vb syn* see SHOOT UP 2

mainly *adv syn* see GENERALLY 1

mainstay *n* a chief reliance <the *mainstay* of the organization held things together>
syn backbone, pillar, sinew(s)
rel brace, buttress, crutch, maintainer, prop, staff, standby, stay, support, supporter, sustainer, upholder

maintain *vb* 1 to keep in a state of repair, efficiency, or validity <he followed a careful regimen to *maintain* his good health>
syn keep up, preserve, save, sustain; *compare* SAVE 3
rel husband, manage; care (for), cultivate; guard, protect
con disregard, ignore, neglect, omit, overlook, slight
2 to uphold as true, right, proper, or acceptable often in the face of challenge or indifference <I *maintain* that his actions were justified by the circumstances>
syn argue, assert, claim, contend, defend, justify, vindicate, warrant
rel affirm, aver, avouch, avow, declare, profess, protest; emphasize, insist, persist, stress; correct, rectify, right
con contradict, deny, gainsay, traverse; challenge, query, question
3 *syn* see SUPPORT 3

maintenance *n syn* see LIVING

majestic *adj* 1 *syn* see GRAND 1
rel courtly, dignified; ceremonious; imperial
2 *syn* see KINGLY

major *adj* 1 *syn* see CHIEF 2
rel better, greater, higher, superior
2 *syn* see BIG 1
3 *syn* see GRAVE 3

make *vb* 1 *syn* see EFFECT 1
rel initiate, originate, start
2 *syn* see GENERATE 1
rel brew
3 to bring something into being by forming, shaping, combining, or altering materials <*made* a dress from odd bits of material>

syn assemble, build, construct, erect, fabricate, fashion, forge, form, frame, manufacture, mold, produce, put together, shape; *compare* BUILD 1
4 *syn* see DRAFT 3
5 *syn* see CONSTITUTE 1
6 *syn* see PREPARE 1
7 *syn* see DESIGNATE 2
8 *syn* see ENACT 1
9 *syn* see INFER
10 *syn* see EARN 1
rel harvest, reap
11 *syn* see CLEAR 6
12 *syn* see FORCE 2
13 *syn* see HEAD 3
rel break (for)
‖14 *syn* see MEDDLE
15 *syn* see RUN 8

make—believe *n syn* see PRETENSE 2

make off *vb syn* see RUN 2
rel depart, go, leave, quit, retire, withdraw; abscond, decamp, escape

make out *vb* 1 *syn* see APPREHEND 1
2 *syn* see ESTABLISH 6
3 *syn* see INFER
‖4 *syn* see SHIFT 5
5 *syn* see SUCCEED 3

make over *vb syn* see TRANSFER 4

make–peace *n syn* see PEACEMAKER

maker *n syn* see FATHER 2
rel executor, operator; manufacturer

makeshift *n syn* see RESOURCE 3

makeshift *adj* serving as a temporary expedient <forced to make *makeshift* plans>
syn provisional, rough-and-ready, rough-and-tumble, stopgap

make up *vb* 1 *syn* see CONTRIVE 2
2 *syn* see MIX 1
3 *syn* see PREPARE 1
4 *syn* see CONSTITUTE 1
5 *syn* see COMPENSATE 1

make up (to) *vb syn* see ADDRESS 8

makeup *n* 1 the way in which parts or constituents are related in an organized whole <the complex *makeup* of the eye>
syn architecture, composition, constitution, construction, design, formation
rel arrangement, ordering, organization, plan, setup; form, shape, style
2 *syn* see DISPOSITION 3
rel cast, fiber, grain, mold, stamp, stripe, vein; constitution, frame
3 cosmetics used to color and beautify the face or body <with *makeup* on, she didn't look bad>
syn face, maquillage, paint, war paint
rel powder; blackface, grease paint

maladroit *adj* 1 *syn* see AWKWARD 2
rel blundering, floundering, stumbling, ungraceful; left-handed, unskilled
con deft, dexterous, handy; clever, cunning, ingenious
ant adroit
2 *syn* see TACTLESS

malady *n syn* see DISEASE 1

mala fide *adj syn* see INSINCERE
ant bona fide

malaise *n syn* see INFIRMITY 1

malapert *adj syn* see SAUCY 1

malapert *n syn* see MINX

malapropos *adj* 1 *syn* see IMPROPER 1
ant apropos

2 *syn* see UNSEASONABLE 1

malarkey *n syn* see NONSENSE 2

malconformation *n syn* see DEFORMITY

malcontent *n* 1 *syn* see GROUCH

2 *syn* see REBEL

malcontent *adj syn* see DISCONTENTED
rel alienated, disaffected, estranged; disobedient, ungovernable, unruly; restless; contumacious, factious, insubordinate, mutinous, rebellious, seditious

malcontented *adj syn* see DISCONTENTED

male *adj syn* see VIRILE 2

malediction *n syn* see CURSE 1
ant benediction

malefactor *n syn* see CRIMINAL
rel blackguard, knave, miscreant, rascal, rogue, scoundrel; evildoer, sinner, wrongdoer

malefic *adj syn* see SINISTER
ant benefic

maleficent *adj syn* see SINISTER
ant beneficent

malevolence *n syn* see MALICE
rel antagonism, hostility; abhorrence, abomination, detestation
ant benevolence

malevolent *adj syn* see MALICIOUS
rel baleful, malefic, maleficent, sinister
con benign, benignant, kind, kindly
ant benevolent

malformation *n syn* see DEFORMITY

malice *n* a desiring or wishing pain, injury, or distress to another < they sought to ruin his reputation out of pure *malice* >
syn despite, despitefulness, grudge, ill will, malevolence, maliciousness, malignancy, malignity, spite, spitefulness, spleen
rel bane, poison, venom; bile; animosity, animus, antipathy, down, enmity; hate, hatefulness, hatred, invidiousness, meanness; bitterness, resentment, unbrage
con benevolence, benignancy, benignity, charity, kindliness, kindness

malicious *adj* having, showing, or indicative of intense often vicious ill will < the helpless victim of *malicious* rumors >
syn bitchy, catty, despiteful, evil, hateful, malevolent, malign, malignant, nasty, rancorous, spiteful, spitish, vicious, wicked
rel poisonous, poison-pen, venomous, virulent; baneful, deleterious, detrimental, noxious, pernicious; envious, green, green-eyed, jealous; mean, petty
con benevolent, charitable, friendly, kind, kindly; considerate, thoughtful

maliciousness *n syn* see MALICE

malign *adj* 1 *syn* see SINISTER
rel baneful, deleterious, detrimental, injurious, noxious, pernicious
con auspicious, favorable, propitious; fortunate, happy, lucky, providential
ant benign

2 *syn* see MALICIOUS
rel antagonistic, antipathetic, hostile, inimical
con benignant, kind, kindly
ant benign

malign *vb* to speak evil of for the purpose of injuring and without regard for the truth < the candidates increasingly *maligned* each other as the campaign degenerated >
syn asperse, befoul, bespatter, blacken, calumniate, defame, denigrate, libel, ‖scandal, scandalize, slander, slur, smear, spatter, tear down, traduce, vilify, villainize
rel decry, depreciate, derogate, detract, disparage; opprobriate, revile, vituperate; backbite, besmirch, defile, pollute, smirch, soil, stain, sully, taint, tarnish
idiom blow upon, cast aspersion(s) on (or upon)
con acclaim, applaud, eulogize, extol, laud, praise; defend, justify, maintain, vindicate

malignancy *n syn* see MALICE

malignant *adj syn* see MALICIOUS
rel devilish, diabolical, fiendish
con altruistic, benevolent, charitable, humane
ant benignant

maligning *adj syn* see LIBELOUS

malignity *n syn* see MALICE
rel revengefulness, vengefulness, vindictiveness
ant benignity

malison *n syn* see CURSE 1
ant benison

‖malkin *n syn* see SLATTERN 1

malleable *adj syn* see PLASTIC
rel governable, manageable; transformable
con intractable, recalcitrant, ungovernable, unmanageable, unruly
ant refractory

malleate *vb syn* see HAMMER 1

malodorous *adj* 1 having an unpleasant smell < *malodorous* cheeses >
syn fetid, frowsy, funky, fusty, gamy, high, mephitic, musty, nidorous, noisome, olid, putrid, rancid, rank, reeking, reeky, ‖smellful, smelly, stale, stenchful, stenchy, stinking, stinky, strong, whiffy; compare ODOROUS
rel bad, foul, offensive, nauseating, vile; decayed, decomposed, fuggy, off, rotten, spoiled, tainted; nasty, noxious, pestilential, poisonous, polluted
con clean, deodorized, fresh
ant fragrant, sweet

2 *syn* see INDECOROUS

maltreat *vb syn* see ABUSE 4

‖mam *n syn* see MOTHER 1

mama (or **mamma**) *n syn* see MOTHER 1

‖mammock *vb syn* see DISORDER 1

mammoth *n syn* see GIANT

mammoth *adj syn* see HUGE

mammy *n syn* see MOTHER 1

man *n* 1 *syn* see HUMAN

2 *syn* see MANKIND

3 a male human being < just an average *man* trying to get by >
syn ‖bloke, boy, buck, ‖cat, chap, cuss, fellow, galoot, ‖gee, gent, gentleman, guy, he, ‖mun, skate, snap, ‖stirra; compare HUMAN

4 *syn* see HUSBAND

5 *syn* see LOVER 1

6 *syn* see POLICEMAN

manage *vb* 1 *syn* see CONDUCT 3
rel superintend; guide

2 *syn* see GOVERN 3

3 *syn* see SHIFT 5

---

syn synonym(s)   *rel* related word(s)
ant antonym(s)   *con* contrasted word(s)
idiom idiomatic equivalent(s)

‖ use limited; if in doubt, see a dictionary

rel bring about, carry out, contrive, effect, execute; accomplish, achieve, succeed
idiom sink or swim on one's own
con collapse, fail, fall down; give up, poop (out)

management *n syn* see OVERSIGHT 1

manager *n syn* see EXECUTIVE
rel handler, impresario, producer

man-at-arms *n syn* see SOLDIER

mancipium *n syn* see SLAVE 1

mandarin *n syn* see BUREAUCRAT

mandate *n syn* see COMMAND 1
rel decree, fiat, imperative; authority, authorization

mandatory *adj* containing or constituting a command < *mandatory* entrance examinations >
syn compulsory, compulsory, imperative, imperious, obligatory, required
rel essential, indispensable, irremissible, necessary, needful, requisite; binding, commanding, compelling, de rigueur; forced, involuntary
con discretionary, elective, voluntary
ant optional

maneuver *n* 1 *syn* see MEASURE 7
2 *syn* see TRICK 1
rel contrivance, device; intrigue, machination, manipulation, plot; demarche, movement, plan; finesse, subterfuge

maneuver *vb* 1 *syn* see ENGINEER
rel navigate; finesse; design
2 *syn* see HANDLE 2
rel navigate
3 *syn* see MANIPULATE 2

man Friday *n syn* see RIGHT-HAND MAN

manful *adj syn* see BRAVE 1

mangle *vb syn* see BATTER 1
rel damage, impair, injure, mar; deface, disfigure; contort, deform, distort; butcher, hack

mangled *adj syn* see LACERATED

mangy *adj syn* see SHABBY 1

manhandle *vb* to treat roughly < riot police *manhandled* innocent bystanders >
syn knock about, mishandle, rough (up), roughhouse, slap around
rel abuse, maltreat, mistreat; batter, ||bung up, mangle, maul

mania *n syn* see FETISH 2
rel craze, enthusiasm, fancy, fascination, infatuation, passion; compulsion, fixed idea, hangup, idée fixe

maniac *adj syn* see INSANE 1
rel berserk, delirious, frantic, frenetic, frenzied, furious, rabid, raging, ranting, violent, wild

maniac *n* 1 *syn* see LUNATIC 1
2 *syn* see ENTHUSIAST

manifest *adj syn* see CLEAR 5
rel disclosed, divulged, revealed, told; evidenced, evinced, shown; noticeable, prominent
con implicit; obscure

manifest *vb* 1 *syn* see EMBODY 1
2 *syn* see SHOW 2
rel display, expose; express, utter, vent, voice
con adumbrate, shadow
ant suggest

manifold *adj* comprehending or uniting various features < a *manifold* operation >

syn diverse, diversiform, multifarious, multifold, multiform, multiplex, multivarious
rel multiphase, polymorphic, polymorphous
con homogeneous, pure, uniform; plain, simple, straightforward, uncomplex, uncomplicated

manifold *vb syn* see INCREASE 1

manikin *n syn* see DWARF

manipulate *vb* 1 *syn* see HANDLE 2
2 to control or play upon by artful, unfair, or insidious means < the sycophant cleverly *manipulated* his master >
syn beguile, exploit, finesse, jockey, maneuver, play; *compare* ENGINEER
rel machinate, use; conduct, control, direct, engineer, manage

mankind *n* the human race < all *mankind* will benefit from this new discovery >
syn flesh, Homo sapiens, humanity, humankind, man, mortality; *compare* HUMAN

manlike *adj* 1 *syn* see ANTHROPOID
2 *syn* see VIRILE 2

manly *adj* 1 *syn* see VIRILE 2
2 *syn* see BRAVE 1

man-made *adj syn* see SYNTHETIC

manner *n* 1 *syn* see HABIT 1
2 *syn* see METHOD 1
rel custom, habit, habitude, practice, usage, use, wont; form, style
3 *syn* see STYLE 4
4 *syn* see VEIN 1
rel form, turn; affectation, affectedness, mannerism; idiosyncrasy, peculiarity
5 **manners** *pl* habitual conduct or deportment in social intercourse evaluated according to some conventional standard of politeness or civility < a person with impeccable *manners* >
syn amenities, civilities, decorum(s), etiquette, mores, proprieties
rel formalities, protocol; elegancies; bearing, behavior, demeanor, deportment, mien, p's and q's; mannerliness
idiom conduct becoming a gentleman
con mannerlessness, unmannerliness

mannered *adj syn* see SELF-CONSCIOUS

mannerism *n syn* see POSE 2
rel eccentricity, idiosyncrasy; oddness, peculiarity, queerness, singularity

mannerless *adj syn* see RUDE 6
ant mannerly

mannerly *adj syn* see CIVIL 2
ant mannerless, unmannerly

manor *n* 1 *syn* see MANSION
2 *syn* see ESTATE 3

mansion *n* a large imposing residence < the governor's *mansion* >
syn castle, chateau, manor, villa
rel estate, hall, house

manslaughter *n syn* see MURDER

manslayer *n syn* see MURDERER

mantic *adj syn* see PROPHETIC

mantle *vb syn* see BLUSH

man-to-man *adj syn* see FRANK

manual *n syn* see HANDBOOK
rel abecedarium, hornbook, primer; text, textbook

manufactory *n syn* see FACTORY

manufacture *vb syn* see MAKE 3

manumit *vb syn* see FREE

ant enslave

many *adj* consisting of a goodly but indefinite number < *many* lives were lost in the flood>
syn legion, multifarious, multitudinal, multitudinous, numerous, populous, ‖several, sundry, various, voluminous
rel divers, manifold, multiple, multiplicate, multiplied, myriad; abounding, abundant, bounteous, bountiful, copious, plentiful
con meager, scant, scanty, sparse; only, sole
ant few

many *pron syn* see SUNDRY

many-sided *adj* 1 *syn* see MULTILATERAL
2 *syn* see VERSATILE

map *n* 1 *syn* see CHART 1
rel picture, portrayal; delineation, design, diagram, draft, outline, sketch, tracing
‖2 *syn* see FACE 1

map (out) *vb syn* see DESIGN 3

maquillage *n syn* see MAKEUP 3

mar *vb syn* see INJURE 1
rel bruise, scar, scratch, warp; ruin, wreck
con adorn, beautify, decorate, embellish; mend, patch, repair; amend, correct, emend, rectify, reform, revise

maraud *vb syn* see RAID 1

marauder *n* one who raids in search of plunder < *marauders* sacked village after village>
syn bandit, brigand, bummer, cateran, depredator, despoiler, forager, freebooter, looter, pillager, plunderer, raider, ravager, ravisher, sacker, spoiler, spoliator
rel buccaneer, desperado, pirate; wrecker

marblehearted *adj syn* see UNFEELING 2
ant softhearted

marbles *n pl syn* see WIT 1

march *n syn* see FRONTIER 1
rel boundary, periphery; territory; outlands, provinces

march *vb syn* see ADJOIN
rel fringe, hem, rim, skirt; extend; parallel

march *vb* 1 *syn* see AGREE 4
2 *syn* see STRIDE 1
3 *syn* see ADVANCE 5

march *n syn* see ADVANCE 2

marchland *n syn* see FRONTIER 1

mare's nest *n syn* see IMPOSTURE
rel babel, clamor, din, hubbub, hullabaloo, racket, uproar

margin *n* 1 *syn* see BORDER 1
rel frame, trimming; shore; side
2 *syn* see ROOM 3
3 *syn* see MINIMUM

margin *vb syn* see BORDER 1
rel abut, connect, join, line, neighbor, touch

marijuana *n* the dried leaves and flowering tops of the pistillate hemp plant sometimes smoked for their intoxicating effect < *marijuana* was smoked by several students at the party>
syn boo, cannabis, grass, ‖Mary Jane, moocah, pot, ‖tea, weed

---

syn synonym(s)   *rel* related word(s)
ant antonym(s)   *con* contrasted word(s)
idiom idiomatic equivalent(s)

‖ use limited; if in doubt, see a dictionary

---

rel joint, reefer; hash, hashish

marine *adj* 1 of or relating to the sea < *marine* biology>
syn maritime, oceanic, thalassic
rel hydrographic oceanographic; abyssal, bathyal, bathybic, bathysmal, benthic, dipsey, neritic, pelagic; aquatic, fluvial, fluviatile, lacustrine
2 of or relating to the navigation of the sea < *marine* charts and maps>
syn maritime, nautical, navigational
rel naval; seamanlike, seamanly; deep-sea, ocean-going, seafaring, seagoing

mariner *n* one engaged in sailing or handling a ship < the tanker crew was made up mostly of experienced *mariners*>
syn jack, jack-tar, sailor, sailorman, salt, seaman, tar, tarpaulin
rel bluejacket, gob, rating, ‖swab, ‖swabbie; ‖lascar, ‖limey; old salt, sea dog, shellback

marital *adj syn* see MATRIMONIAL

maritime *adj* 1 *syn* see MARINE 2
2 *syn* see MARINE 1

mark *n* 1 *syn* see AMBITION 2
2 *syn* see TARGET 1
3 *syn* see USE 4
4 *syn* see POOL 3
5 *syn* see INDICATION 3
rel attribute, emblem, symbol, type; character, property, quality
6 *syn* see QUALITY 1
7 a device (as a word) pointing distinctly to the origin or ownership of merchandise to which it is applied and legally reserved to the exclusive use of the owner < the company was brought to court for illegally using the *mark* of its rival>
syn brand, logo, logotype, trademark
rel label, stamp
idiom brand name
8 *syn* see CHARACTER 1
9 *syn* see NOTICE 1

mark *vb* 1 *syn* see CHOOSE 1
2 *syn* see SHOW 5
3 *syn* see SHOW 2
4 *syn* see CHARACTERIZE 2
rel bespeak, betoken, denote, signify
idiom set apart
5 *syn* see SEE 1
rel record, register; attend, heed, regard

mark (out) *vb syn* see DEMARCATE 1
rel lay off, mark off; chart, lay out, map

mark down *vb* 1 *syn* see REDUCE 2
ant mark up
2 *syn* see DEPRECIATE 1

marked *adj syn* see NOTICEABLE
rel distinguished, noted; considerable

market *n syn* see STORE 4

market *vb* 1 *syn* see SELL 3
rel wholesale
2 *syn* see SELL 2

marketable *adj* capable of being sold < *marketable* commodities>
syn merchandisable, merchantable, salable, sellable, trafficable, vendible
rel commercial; profitable, selling; fit, good, sound, wholesome
con unmerchantable, unsalable
ant unmarketable

‖maroon *vb syn* see CAMP

marred *adj syn* see DAMAGED
rel banged-up, battered, bruised, mutilated; ruined, wrecked

ant unmarried

marriage *n* 1 the state of being united to a person of the opposite sex as husband or wife < *marriage* was not in the plans of this couple >
syn conjugality, connubiality, matrimony, wedlock
rel match, union
2 *syn* see WEDDING

marriage broker *n* one who arranges marriages < the old widow served as the town's *marriage broker* >
syn go-between, matchmaker
rel shadchan

marriage portion *n syn* see DOWRY

married *adj syn* see MATRIMONIAL

marrow *n syn* see ESSENCE 2
rel core, heart, kernel, meat

marrowy *adj syn* see PITHY

marry *vb* 1 to take as spouse < he *married* her for her money >
syn catch, espouse, wed
rel wive
idiom get hitched, get married, tie the knot
con annul, divorce, separate
2 to join in wedlock < the minister *married* all three daughters in one ceremony >
syn ‖hitch, mate, splice, tie, wed
idiom tie the knot, unite in marriage
3 *syn* see JOIN 1

marsh *n syn* see SWAMP

marshal *vb* 1 *syn* see ORDER 1
rel distribute, space; escort, guide, shepherd, usher
2 *syn* see MOBILIZE 3

marshland *n syn* see SWAMP

martial *adj* belonging to, engaged in, or appropriate to the affairs of war < the reviewing officer saw the company standing in *martial* array >
syn military, warlike
rel bellicose, belligerent, combative, pugnacious; aggressive, militant; high-spirited, mettlesome, spirited
con civil, civilian; irenic, pacific, peaceable, peaceful
ant unmartial

martyr *vb syn* see AFFLICT

martyrize *vb syn* see AFFLICT

marvel *n syn* see WONDER 1

marveling *n syn* see WONDER 2
rel surprise

marvelous *adj* 1 causing or exciting wonder < the way in which he could bring together opposing forces was truly *marvelous* >
syn amazing, astonishing, astounding, miraculous, prodigious, spectacular, staggering, strange, stupendous, surprising, wonderful, wondrous
rel awe-inspiring, awesome, awful, awing; incomprehensible, inconceivable, incredible, unimaginable; fabulous, phenomenal, supernatural; exceptional, extraordinary; bewildering, confounding, striking, stunning
con commonplace, ordinary, routine; blah, unexciting, uninteresting
2 superior or outstanding of its kind < had a *marvelous* weekend >
syn ‖cool, ‖dandy, divine, dreamy, ‖galluptious, glorious, groovy, hot, hunkydory, ‖keen, ‖neat, nifty, peachy, ripping,

sensational, super, swell, terrific, wonderful; exquisite EXCELLENT, SUPERIOR 4, SUPREME
rel agreeable, enjoyable, pleasant, pleasurable; rewarding, satisfying
con dreary, dull, humdrum, monotonous, tedious; inferior, low-grade, mean, poor, punk

‖**Mary Jane** *n syn* see MARIJUANA

mascot *n syn* see CHARM 2

masculine *adj syn* see VIRILE 2
ant effeminate, unmasculine

mash *n syn* see CLUTTER 2

mash *vb* 1 *syn* see CRUSH 2
‖2 *syn* see PRESS 1

mashed *adj syn* see ENAMORED 1

masher *n syn* see WOLF

mash note *n syn* see LOVE LETTER

mask *n* 1 a cover or partial cover for the face that has openings for the eyes and is used especially for disguise < on Halloween he wore a pirate's *mask* >
syn domino, doughface, false face, visor, vizard
rel disguise, masquerade; veil
2 an outward appearance that seeks to obscure an underlying true character < he was able to maintain a *mask* of dignity and tranquillity in his time of anxiety >
syn cloak, color, coloring, cover, disguise, disguisement, facade, face, false front, front, guise, masquerade, muffler, pretense, pretext, put-on, semblance, show, veil, veneer, window dressing; *compare* APPEARANCE 2
rel affectation, air, pose, posture; fakery, sham; dissembling, dissimulation, seeming, simulation; appearance, aspect

mask *vb syn* see DISGUISE
rel screen, secrete, veil; blur; defend, guard, protect, safeguard, shield

masquerade *n syn* see MASK 2

masquerade *vb syn* see POSE 4

mass *n* 1 *syn* see BODY 4
2 *syn* see PILE 1
3 *syn* see BULK 1
rel aggregate, aggregation, conglomerate, conglomeration; sum, whole
4 *syn* see BODY 3
5 *syn* see MUCH
6 *usu* masses *pl syn* see RABBLE 2

massacre *vb syn* see SLAUGHTER 3

massacre *n* the act or an instance of killing a considerable number of human beings under circumstances of atrocity or cruelty < the *massacre* of the Indians by the soldiers and settlers >
syn bloodbath, bloodshed, butchery, carnage, slaughter
rel blood purge, decimation, genocide, pogrom; internecion; assassination, killing, murder, slaying

massive *adj* 1 *syn* see HEAVY 1
rel hulking, hulky, massy
2 *syn* see HUGE
3 *syn* see MONSTROUS 1

massy *adj syn* see HUGE

master *n* 1 *syn* see EXPERT
rel maestro, savant; genius, mastermind; guru, swami
2 *syn* see LEADER 2
rel overlord, overman, overseer
3 *syn* see VICTOR 1

‖4 *syn* see HUSBAND

5 *syn* see LOVER 1

master *vb* 1 *syn* see OVERCOME 1

2 *syn* see DOMESTICATE

rel dominate, govern, predominate, rule

3 *syn* see CONQUER 2

4 *syn* see LEARN 1

master *adj* 1 *syn* see DOMINANT 1

2 *syn* see PROFICIENT

masterdom *n syn* see SUPREMACY

masterful *adj* 1 disposed to exercise or flaunt dictatorial authority in a way to override any protestation <the royal favorite was pompous and *masterful* when dealing with subordinates>

syn bossy, domineering, high-handed, imperative, imperial, imperious, magisterial, overbearing, peremptory

rel absolute, arbitrary, authoritarian, authoritative, dictative, dictatorial, doctrinaire, dogmatic; autocratic, despotic, tyrannical; high-and-mighty, self-willed

con humble, modest, unpretentious; indecisive, irresolute; submissive, yielding; feeble, weak

2 *syn* see PROFICIENT

rel adroit, deft, dexterous; preeminent, superlative, supreme, transcendent

master-hand *n syn* see EXPERT

masterly *adj syn* see PROFICIENT

rel preeminent, superlative, supreme, transcendent

masterpiece *n* 1 something done or made with extraordinary skill or brilliance <his latest work is unquestionably a *masterpiece*>

syn chef d'oeuvre, classic, magnum opus, masterwork, tour de force

rel objet d'art, masterstroke

con botch, disaster, fiasco

2 *syn* see SHOWPIECE

mastership *n syn* see ABILITY 2

masterwork *n syn* see MASTERPIECE 1

mastery *n* 1 *syn* see POWER 1

2 *syn* see ABILITY 2

masticate *vb syn* see CHEW 1

rel bruise, crush, macerate, mash, pulp, pulpify, smash, squash

mastodonic *adj syn* see HUGE

mat *adj syn* see DULL 7

matador *n syn* see BULLFIGHTER

match *n* 1 *syn* see OPPONENT

2 *syn* see EQUAL

rel analogue, parallel

3 *syn* see MATE 5

4 *syn* see PARALLEL

5 *syn* see EVENT 5

rel bout, engagement, game

match *vb* 1 *syn* see OPPOSE 1

2 *syn* see EQUATE 2

3 *syn* see AMOUNT 2

rel complement, supplement

4 *syn* see EQUAL 3

rel compare, stack up

idiom hold a candle to

matched *adj syn* see ASSORTED 2

rel balanced, equated, evened, similar; coordinated, harmonized; coupled, joined, mated, paired, yoked

ant unmatched

matchless *adj syn* see ALONE 3

ant matchable

matchmaker *n syn* see MARRIAGE BROKER

mate *n* 1 *syn* see PARTNER

2 *syn* see ACCOMPANIMENT 2

3 *syn* see FRIEND

rel bedmate, classmate, co-mate, helpmate, playmate, roommate, schoolmate, teammate

4 *syn* see SPOUSE

rel match, parti

5 one of a pair matched in one or more qualities <the *mate* of a shoe>

syn companion, coordinate, double, duplicate, fellow, match, reciprocal, twin

rel alter ego, complement, sosie; compeer, equal, equivalent, peer

mate *vb syn* see MARRY 2

rel breed, crossbreed, pair; generate, procreate

‖**mater** *n syn* see MOTHER 1

material *adj* 1 of or belonging to actuality <for him the *material* world is the only world>

syn corporeal, gross, objective, phenomenal, physical, sensible, substantial, tangible

rel actual, real, true; appreciable, palpable, perceptible; earthly, worldly; animal, carnal, fleshly, sensual

con impalpable, imperceptible, intangible, unsubstantial; spiritual

ant immaterial, nonmaterial

2 *syn* see IMPORTANT 1

ant immaterial

3 *syn* see RELEVANT

rel consequential, important, momentous, significant; cardinal, essential, fundamental, vital

ant immaterial

material *n* 1 *syn* see THING 4

rel component, constituent, element, ingredient; apparatus, equipment, machinery

2 *usu* **materials** *pl syn* see EQUIPMENT

materialistic *adj* of or relating to a preoccupation with or stress upon material rather than intellectual or spiritual things <*materialistic* values characterize the modern age>

syn banausic, earthy, mundane, sensual, temporal, worldly

rel carnal, profane; earthly, terrestrial; secular, unspiritual

con intellectual, mental; spiritual, unfleshly, unworldly; heavenly

materiality *n syn* see ACTUALITY 2

materialize *vb* 1 *syn* see EMBODY 1

rel appear, emerge, loom, show; issue, rise, spring

2 to convert mentally into something concrete <with the help of graphs and figures abstract ideas can be *materialized*>

syn entify, hypostatize, reify

rel actualize, pragmatize, realize; corporealize; symbolize, typify

matériel *n syn* see EQUIPMENT

matriarch *n* a dignified, usually elderly woman of some rank or authority <the local *matriarchs* controlled the town's social functions>

syn dame, dowager, grande dame, matron

rel materfamilias, mother

matrimonial adj of, relating to, or characteristic of marriage <the *matrimonial* bond between husband and wife>
syn conjugal, connubial, hymeneal, marital, married, nuptial, spousal, wedded
rel bridal, epithalamic

matrimony n syn see MARRIAGE 1

matron n syn see MATRIARCH

matter n 1 syn see SUBJECT 2
2 syn see AFFAIR 1
rel complication, grievance, to-do, worry; circumstance, predicament
3 syn see SUBSTANCE 2
4 syn see THING 4
5 syn see ORDER 7

matter vb to be of importance <being your own self is what really *matters*>
syn count, import, mean, signify, weigh
idiom carry weight

matter-of-course adj syn see GENERAL 1

matter-of-fact adj 1 syn see REALISTIC
rel objective, sound
2 syn see PROSAIC 1
3 involving no display of emotion <the *matter-of-fact* reading of the judge masked his inner anguish>
syn cold, cold-blooded, emotionless, impersonal, unimpassioned
rel unaffected, unsentimental; prosaic
con emotional, impassioned, personal
4 syn see IMPASSIVE 1

maturate vb syn see MATURE

mature adj 1 having attained the normal peak of natural growth and development <*mature* plants ready to bear fruit>
syn adult, full-blown, full-fledged, full-grown, grown, grown-up, matured, ripe, ripened
rel developed, ready
idiom of age
con childish, childlike; boyish, green, juvenile, maiden, puerile, youthful
ant immature
2 syn see DUE 2
3 syn see UNPAID 2

mature vb to become fully developed or ripe <she *matured* as an actress after several years of summer stock>
syn age, develop, grow, grow up, maturate, mellow, ‖ripe, ripen
rel blossom, flower; advance, progress, round; season; decline, deteriorate, olden, wane
idiom come of age

matured adj 1 syn see MATURE 1
rel completed, finished; advised, considered, deliberate, designed, premeditated, studied
con callow, crude, green, raw, rough, rude, uncouth
ant premature, unmatured
2 syn see RIPE 3

maudlin adj syn see SENTIMENTAL
rel addled, befuddled, confused, fuddled, muddled; silly

maul n syn see BRAWL 2

maul vb syn see BATTER 1
rel flagellate, flail, lash, whip; bang, bash, buffet, pound; abuse, maltreat, manhandle, molest, rough (up)

maunder vb syn see WANDER 1

maundering adj syn see INARTICULATE 3

maven n syn see EXPERT

maverick n syn see BOHEMIAN

mawkish adj syn see SENTIMENTAL
rel banal, flat; cloying, nauseating, sickening

maxim n a general truth or fundamental principle usually expressed sententiously <Francis Bacon is noted for his fondness for *maxims*>
syn aphorism, apothegm, axiom, brocard, dictum, gnome, moral, rule, truism
rel commonplace, motto, platitude; law, precept, prescript; theorem; proverb
idiom rule of thumb

maximal adj syn see MAXIMUM
ant minimal

maximize vb syn see OVERPLAY 2
ant minimize

maximum adj greatest in quantity or highest in degree attainable or attained <apply *maximum* pressure above the point of injury>
syn maximal, outside, top, topmost, utmost; compare SUPREME
rel greatest, highest, largest
con least, lowest, slightest, smallest
ant minimum

maybe adv syn see PERHAPS

mayhem vb syn see MAIM

maze n 1 something intricately or confusingly elaborate or complicated <the landscape soon became a *maze* of superhighways>
syn jungle, knot, labyrinth, mesh, mizmaze, morass, skein, snarl, tangle, web
rel fog, haze; gordian knot; conglomeration, hodgepodge, miscellany, mishmash
‖2 syn see HAZE 2

‖**mazuma** n syn see MONEY

MD n syn see PHYSICIAN

meager adj 1 syn see LEAN
2 being smaller than what is normal, necessary, or desirable <the remains of dinner provided only a *meager* meal that evening>
syn exiguous, poor, scant, scanty, scrimp, scrimpy, skimp, skimpy, spare, sparse; compare SHORT 3
rel deficient, inadequate, insufficient; inappreciable, inconsiderable, slight; bare, mere, minimum; miserable, shabby
con adequate, enough, sufficient; appreciable, considerable; copious, plentiful
ant ample

meal n the portion of food taken at one time to satisfy appetite <the noonday dinner was the big *meal* of the day in those times>
syn ‖chow, feed, refection, repast
rel feast, spread; refreshment, regalement; collation, snack; fare, grub, meat, mess, victuals; board, table

meal vb syn see EAT 1

mean adj 1 syn see IGNOBLE 1
ant wellborn
2 syn see INFERIOR 2
3 syn see LITTLE 2
4 syn see CONTEMPTIBLE
5 syn see CHEAP 2
6 syn see STINGY
7 syn see TROUBLESOME

rel difficult, formidable, rough, rugged, tough

8 *syn* see UNWELL

mean *vb 1 syn* see INTEND 2
rel desire, want, wish
2 to convey (as an idea) to the mind < your answer *means* nothing to me>
syn add up (to), connote, denote, express, import, intend, signify, spell
rel designate, name; attest, betoken, indicate; hint, imply, intimate, suggest
3 *syn* see MATTER

mean *n 1 syn* see AVERAGE
2 *usu means sing or pl in constr* one by which work is accomplished or an end effected < careful planning is a major *means* of improving output > < use any *means* to secure peace>
syn agency, agent, channel, instrument, instrumentality, instrumentation, intermediary, medium, ministry, organ, vehicle
rel fashion, manner, method, mode, system, way; apparatus, equipment, machinery, paraphernalia
3 *means pl* one's total property including real property and intangibles < people of moderate *means* are feeling the effects of inflation worse>
syn assets, capital, resources, wealth
rel finances, fortune, funds, moneybags, pocket, purse; ||bundle, nest egg, pile, reserves, savings; estate, holdings, possessions; intangibles

mean *adj 1 syn* see MIDDLE 2
2 *syn* see MEDIUM

meander *vb syn* see WANDER 1
rel snake, turn, twist, wind

meanderer *n syn* see ROVER

meandering *adj syn* see WINDING

meandrous *adj syn* see WINDING

meaning *n 1* the idea that something conveys to the mind < critics have endlessly debated the *meaning* of the poem >
syn acceptation, import, intendment, intent, message, purport, sense, significance, significancy, signification, sum and substance, understanding; *compare* SUBSTANCE 2, TENOR 1
rel drift, effect, essence, tenor; force, point, value; hint, implication, intimation, suggestion; connotation, denotation, definition
2 *syn* see INTENTION

meaningful *adj 1 syn* see EXPRESSIVE
ant meaningless
2 *syn* see IMPORTANT 1

meaningless *adj 1 syn* see SENSELESS 5
rel blank, empty, vacant
ant meaningful
2 *syn* see FECKLESS 1

measly *adj syn* see PETTY 2

measure *n 1 syn* see RATION
2 *syn* see TEMPERANCE 1
3 *syn* see SIZE 1
4 *syn* see MELODY
5 *syn* see RHYTHM
6 *syn* see STANDARD 3

7 an action planned or taken toward the accomplishment of a purpose < developed a new set of safety *measures*>
syn maneuver, move, procedure, proceeding, step
rel effort, project, proposal, proposition; expedient, makeshift, resort, resource, shift, stopgap

measure *vb 1 syn* see DEMARCATE 1
2 to ascertain the quantity, mass, extent, or degree of in terms of a standard unit or fixed amount < *measure* the depth of the water>
syn gauge, scale
rel size, size up; calculate, compute, estimate, figure, reckon

measure (out) *vb syn* see DISTRIBUTE 1

measureless *adj 1 syn* see INCALCULABLE 1
ant measurable
2 *syn* see LIMITLESS
ant measurable

measure up *vb syn* see EQUAL 3

meat *n 1 syn* see FOOD 1
2 *syn* see SUBSTANCE 2

meathead *n syn* see OAF 2

meaty *adj syn* see PITHY

mechanical *adj syn* see PERFUNCTORY

meddle *vb* to concern oneself with officiously, impertinently, or indiscreetly < continually *meddling* in other people's affairs>
syn busybody, butt in, fool, horn in, interfere, interlope, intermeddle, ||make, mess around, monkey (with), ||tamper (with)
rel intervene, intrude, invade, obtrude; pry, snoop, trespass
idiom put (or shove *or* stick) one's oar in, stick one's nose into
con disregard, ignore, neglect, omit, overlook, slight; avoid, eschew, shun

meddler *n syn* see BUSYBODY

meddlesome *adj syn* see IMPERTINENT 2

Meddlesome Mattie *n syn* see BUSYBODY

medial *adj 1 syn* see MIDDLE 1
2 *syn* see MIDDLE 2
3 *syn* see MEDIUM

median *n syn* see AVERAGE
rel center, middle

median *adj 1 syn* see MIDDLE 1
2 *syn* see MIDDLE 2

mediate *vb syn* see INTERPOSE 2

mediator *n 1 syn* see GO-BETWEEN 2
rel arbitrator, judge; conciliator, peacemaker; negotiator, troubleshooter
2 *syn* see MODERATOR

medical *n syn* see PHYSICIAN

medicament *n syn* see REMEDY 1

medicant *n syn* see REMEDY 1

medication *n syn* see REMEDY 1

medicinal *n syn* see DRUG 1

medicine *n syn* see REMEDY 1

mediciner *n syn* see PHYSICIAN

medico *n syn* see PHYSICIAN

mediocre *adj syn* see MEDIUM
rel bad, inferior, poor; common, commonplace, ordinary, unexceptional
idiom no great shakes, nothing to write home about

meditate *vb syn* see PONDER 2

meditative *adj 1 syn* see THOUGHTFUL 1

---

syn synonym(s)   *rel* related word(s)
ant antonym(s)   *con* contrasted word(s)
idiom idiomatic equivalent(s)
|| use limited; if in doubt, see a dictionary

rel musing, ruminant; wistful

2 *syn* see PENSIVE 2

medium *adj* midway between the extremes of a scale, measurement, or evaluation < bought a suit of *medium* quality >
syn average, fair, fairish, indifferent, intermediate, mean, medial, mediocre, middle= rate, middling, moderate, run-of-mine, run-of-the-mill, so-so
rel median, par; passable, tolerable; neutral; popular, vulgar; normal, standard
idiom fair to middling
con inferior, low-grade, poor; excellent, first-class, high-grade, prime, superior

medium *n* 1 *syn* see MEAN 2
rel intermediate, intermedium

2 *syn* see ENVIRONMENT

3 *syn* see FORTE

medley *n* *syn* see MISCELLANY 1

||**meech** *vb* *syn* see SNEAK

meed *n* 1 *syn* see REWARD
rel recompensing, satisfaction

2 *syn* see RATION
rel desert, due, merit

meek *adj* *syn* see HUMBLE 1
rel gentle, mild; tame; forbearing, lenient, tolerant; long-suffering, patient
con high-spirited, mettlesome, spirited, spunky; contumacious, insubordinate, rebellious
ant arrogant

meet *vb* 1 *syn* see HAPPEN 2

2 *syn* see CONFRONT 1

3 *syn* see ENGAGE 5
rel brave, oppose

4 *syn* see EQUAL 3

5 *syn* see SATISFY 5
rel approach, equal, match, rival, tie, touch

6 to come together face-to-face or as if face-to-face < the two leaders agreed to *meet* in a series of summit talks >
syn close, encounter, face, front; *compare* CONFRONT 1
rel accost, greet, salute; bump, clash, collide, cross; grapple, tussle, wrestle; experience, suffer, sustain, undergo
con elude, escape, evade, shun
ant avoid

7 *syn* see CONVERGE

8 *syn* see CONVENE 1

meet (with) *vb* *syn* see FIND 1

meet *n* 1 *syn* see EVENT 5

2 *syn* see CONTEST 2

meet *adj* 1 *syn* see FIT 1
rel accommodated, conformed, reconciled; good, right; equitable, fair, just
ant unmeet

2 *syn* see GOOD 2
ant unmeet

meeting *n* 1 *syn* see CONTEST 2

2 *syn* see CONCOURSE

3 *syn* see TALK 4
rel congress, moot

meetness *n* *syn* see ORDER 11
ant unmeetness

megacosm *n* *syn* see UNIVERSE
ant microcosm

megrim *n* *syn* see CAPRICE
rel impulse, urge

melancholic *adj* *syn* see SAD 2

melancholy *n* *syn* see SADNESS

rel miserableness, misery, wretchedness; despair, desperation; boredom, ennui, tedium
con hopefulness, optimism
ant exhilaration

melancholy *adj* 1 *syn* see SAD 1

2 expressing or suggesting sorrow or mourning < the gloomy day led him to a *melancholy* train of thought >
syn doleful, dolesome, dolorous, lamentable, lugubrious, moanful, mournful, plaintive, rueful, sighful, sorrowful, wailful, woeful; *compare* SAD 1, SAD 2
rel pensive, reflective, thoughtful; discomposing, disquieting, disturbing, perturbing; dismal, dreary, funereal, gloomy, lachrymose, somber, sombrous
con cheerful, glad, happy, joyful, joyous, lighthearted; gay, lively, vivacious

3 *syn* see SAD 2

mélange *n* *syn* see MISCELLANY 1

meld *vb* *syn* see MIX 1

melding *n* *syn* see UNIFICATION

melee *n* 1 *syn* see CLASH 2
rel dogfight, scuffle

2 *syn* see BRAWL 2

3 *syn* see MISCELLANY 1

meliorate *vb* *syn* see IMPROVE 1

melisma *n* *syn* see MELODY

mellay *n* 1 *syn* see BRAWL 2

2 *syn* see CLASH 2

mellifluent *adj* *syn* see MELLIFLUOUS

mellifluous *adj* having a smooth rich flow < his *mellifluous* voice held his audience in a trance >
syn golden, honeyed, Hyblaean, liquid, mellifluent, mellow; *compare* MELODIOUS 1
rel accordant, canorous, euphonic, euphonious, harmonious, mellisonant, silvery; golden-tongued, silver-tongued; dulcet; sweet; resonant, sonorous
con blatant, boisterous, clamorous, obstreperous, strident, vociferous; discordant, grating, harsh

mellisonant *adj* *syn* see MELODIOUS 1

mellow *adj* 1 *syn* see RIPE 3

2 *syn* see MELLIFLUOUS

mellow *vb* *syn* see MATURE

melodia *n* *syn* see MELODY

melodic *adj* 1 *syn* see MELODIOUS 2

2 *syn* see MELODIOUS 1

melodious *adj* 1 pleasing to the ear < *melodious* sounds of the forest >
syn dulcet, euphonic, euphonious, mellisonant, melodic, sweet, tuneful; *compare* MELLIFLUOUS
rel canorous, harmonious
con discordant, grating, harsh
ant unmelodious

2 containing, constituting, or characterized by melody < his voice shows marked improvement and a new richly *melodious* quality >
syn melodic, musical, songful, tuned, tuneful
rel cantabile, lyric, melic

melody *n* a rhythmic succession of single tones organized as an aesthetic whole < took out his flute and played a simple *melody* >
syn air, descant, diapason, lay, measure, melisma, melodia, strain, tune, warble; *compare* SONG 2

rel song; bel canto, canto, vocalise; lyrics

melt *vb* 1 *syn* see LIQUEFY
rel heat, warm
con coagulate, harden, set
ant freeze; solidify
2 *syn* see BURN 3
rel perspire, sweat

member *n syn* see PART 1

memento *n* 1 *syn* see REMEMBRANCE 3
2 *syn* see VESTIGE 2

memo *n* 1 *syn* see NOTE 2
2 *syn* see MEMORANDUM 2

memoir *n* 1 *syn* see BIOGRAPHY
rel anecdote; memory, recollection, remembrance, reminiscence
2 *syn* see DISCOURSE 2

memoirist *n syn* see BIOGRAPHER

memorable *adj syn* see NOTEWORTHY
rel momentous, rememberable; deathless, unfadable, unforgettable
ant unmemorable

memorandum *n* 1 *syn* see NOTE 2
2 a communication that contains directive, advisory, or informative matter < the *memorandum* announced the holiday schedule >
syn directive, memo, notice
rel announcement, dispatch, minute; epistle, letter, missive, note; reminder, tickler; message; diary

memorial *adj* serving to preserve remembrance < a *memorial* plaque >
syn commemorative, commemoratory
rel celebrative, consecrative, dedicatory, enshrining

memorial *n* 1 *syn* see REMEMBRANCE 3
2 *syn* see MONUMENT 2

memorialize *vb* 1 *syn* see ADDRESS 4
2 to record or honor the memory of by or as if by a monument < the new library *memorializes* the late President >
syn commemorate, monument, monumentalize
rel etch, grave, impress, imprint; jog, nudge, remind
idiom bring to mind, fix in the (or one's) mind (or memory), impress on one's mind, treasure in one's heart
con forget, neglect, overlook

memorial park *n syn* see CEMETERY

memorize *vb* to commit to memory < the actors hadn't even *memorized* their lines >
syn con, get, learn
rel study
idiom get (or learn) by heart, get (or learn) word for word
con forget

memory *n* 1 the power or process of reproducing or recalling what has been learned < blessed with a good *memory* >
syn recollection, remembrance, reminiscence
rel reflection, retrospection; retention, retentiveness; mind, recall; mind's eye; awareness, cognizance, consciousness
con forgetfulness, obliviousness, unmindfulness; lethe, oblivion
2 a particular act of recalling < her *memory* of her wedding day remains vivid >

syn anamnesis, recall, recollection, remembrance, reminiscence
rel memento, souvenir

menace *vb* 1 *syn* see THREATEN
rel alarm, frighten, scare; endanger, torment; loom, lower
2 *syn* see ENDANGER

menacing *adj syn* see IMMINENT 2

ménage *n syn* see FAMILY 2
rel ménage à trois

mend *vb* 1 *syn* see CORRECT 1
2 to put into good shape or working order again < *mends* garments in her spare time >
syn doctor, do up, fix, overhaul, patch, rebuild, recondition, reconstruct, repair, revamp, ‖right, ‖rightle, vamp
rel condition, ready, service; refurbish, rejuvenate, renew, renovate, restore; correct, emend, rectify, redress, reform; heal
3 *syn* see IMPROVE 3

mendacious *adj syn* see DISHONEST
rel false, wrong; erroneous, fallacious, spurious; equivocating, fibbing, paltering, prevaricating
ant veracious

mendaciousness *n syn* see MENDACITY
ant veraciousness, veracity

mendacity *n* the practice or an instance of lying < he was ultimately caught by his own outrageous *mendacity* >
syn falsehood, fibbery, mendaciousness, truthlessness, untruthfulness, unveracity
rel boggling, caviling, dodging, equivocation, hedging, quibbling, shifting, sidestepping
ant veraciousness, veracity

mendicancy *n* the practice or act of begging < the city passed an ordinance against *mendicancy* >
syn beggary, bumming, cadging, mendicity, mooching, panhandling
rel sponging

mendicity *n syn* see MENDICANCY

menial *adj syn* see SUBSERVIENT 2

mental *adj* 1 of or relating to the mind < the *mental* aspects of the problem >
syn cerebral, intellective, intellectual, psychic, psychical, psychological
rel immaterial, inner, spiritual; telepathic; intelligent, rational, reasoning, thinking; ideological
con bodily, corporal, corporeal, physical, somatic; perceptive; sensual, sensuous
‖2 *syn* see INSANE 1

mentality *n syn* see INTELLIGENCE 1

mention *vb* to refer to someone or something in a clear unmistakable manner < several donors were *mentioned* in the article >
syn cite, instance, name, specify
rel denominate, designate; detail; advert, allude, refer; quote
idiom make mention of
con disregard, ignore, neglect, overlook, pass by, pass over, slight

menu *n* a list of the dishes that may be ordered (as at a restaurant) or that are to be served (as at a banquet) < hoped to find something tasty on the *menu* > < he saved the elaborate *menu* as a souvenir of the awards banquet >
syn card, carte du jour

---

idiom bill of fare

Mephistophelian *adj syn* see SATANIC 1

mephitic *adj* 1 *syn* see MALODOROUS 1
2 *syn* see POISONOUS

mercenary *n syn* see HACK 2

mercenary *adj syn* see CORRUPT 2
ant unmercenary

merchandisable *adj syn* see MARKET-
ABLE
ant unmerchantable, unsalable

merchandise *n* the products that are
bought and sold in business < *merchandise* of inferior quality >
syn commodities, goods, line, vendible(s),
wares
rel effects; job lot, stock; staples

merchandise *vb syn* see SELL 3
rel advertise, publicize

merchandiser *n syn* see MERCHANT

merchant *n* a buyer and seller of commodities for profit <a *merchant* of dry
goods >
syn businessman, dealer, merchandiser,
trader, tradesman, trafficker
rel jobber, retailer, wholesaler

merchantable *adj syn* see MARKETABLE
ant unmerchantable, unsalable

merchant prince *n syn* see MAGNATE

merciful *adj syn* see FORBEARING
rel compassionate, pitiful, softhearted;
benign, kind, kindly; condoning, forgiving,
pardoning
ant merciless, unmerciful

mercifulness *n syn* see FORBEARANCE 2
rel commiseration, pity, ruth
con severeness, severity, sternness
ant mercilessness, unmercifulness

merciless *adj* 1 *syn* see PITILESS
ant merciful
2 *syn* see GRIM 3
rel compassionless, cutthroat, pitiless;
gratuitous, uncalled-for, wanton
con charitable, lenient, tolerant; easy,
easygoing
ant merciful

mercurial *adj syn* see INCONSTANT 1
rel buoyant, effervescent, elastic, expansive, resilient; mobile, movable; adroit,
clever, cunning, ingenious
ant saturnine

mercy *n* a show of or a disposition to
show kindness or compassion <the *mercy*
of the Lord knows all seasons >
syn caritas, charity, clemency, grace,
lenity; *compare* FORBEARANCE 2
rel commiseration, compassion, pity,
ruth; benevolence, benignancy, benignity,
kindliness, kindness; generosity, goodwill
con reprisal, retaliation, retribution, revenge, vengeance; castigation, chastening,
chastisement, punishment

mere *adj syn* see VERY 4

merely *adv syn* see JUST 3

meretricious *adj syn* see GAUDY
rel deceptive, delusive, delusory, misleading, spurious; insincere

meretrix *n syn* see PROSTITUTE

merge *vb syn* see MIX 1

mergence *n syn* see UNIFICATION

merger *n* 1 *syn* see CONSOLIDATION 2
2 *syn* see UNIFICATION

merging *n syn* see UNIFICATION

meridian *n syn* see APEX 2

merit *n* 1 *syn* see EXCELLENCE
ant fault
2 *syn* see QUALITY 2
3 *syn* see DUE 1
rel gaining(s), winning(s)

merit *vb syn* see EARN 2
rel award, reward; recompense, repay,
requite; entitle, justify, warrant

meritable *adj syn* see WORTHY 1
ant meritless

merited *adj syn* see JUST 3
rel entitled, justified, warranted
ant unmerited

meritorious *adj syn* see WORTHY 1

merriment *n* 1 *syn* see MIRTH
2 *syn* see MERRYMAKING

merry *adj* indicative of or marked by high
spirits or lightheartedness <the *merry* life
of the town folk was a joy to see>
syn blithe, blithesome, boon, festive, gay,
gleeful, jocund, jolly, jovial, lighthearted,
mirthful, riant
rel animated, lively, sprightly, vivacious;
cheerful, glad, happy, joyful, joyous; hilarious, mad, unconstrained, wild
con gloomy, glum, melancholy; grave,
sober, somber; earnest, sedate, serious,
staid

merry-andrew *n syn* see CLOWN 3

merrymaking *n* gay or festive activity <a
night of *merrymaking* >
syn festivity, gaiety, jollity, merriment,
revel, reveling, revelment, revelry,
whoopee
rel enjoyment, indulgence, pleasure, self-
indulgence

mesh *n* 1 *usu* meshes *pl syn* see WEB 2
2 *syn* see MAZE 1
rel net, network

mesh *vb syn* see ENGAGE 1

meshuggaas *n syn* see NONSENSE 2

mesmeric *adj syn* see ATTRACTIVE 1

mesmerize *vb syn* see ENTHRALL 2
rel entrance, hypnotize

mess *n* ‖1 *syn* see MUCH
2 *syn* see EYESORE
3 a confused or disordered state, condition, or situation <upon becoming president, he proceeded to make a *mess* of the
government>
syn botch, botchery, hash, mess-up, mix-
up, muddle, mull, muss, shambles; *compare* MISCELLANY 1
rel confusion, disorder; wreck, wreckage
idiom kettle of fish

mess *vb* 1 *syn* see BOTCH
rel confuse, disorder, jumble
idiom make a mess of
2 *syn* see FIDDLE 2

mess (up) *vb syn* see DISORDER 1
rel damage, mar, ruin, spoil; ‖muck,
mucker, muff

message *n* 1 something (as information)
conveyed by writing, speech, or signals
<left a *message* before he went out >
syn communication, directive, word
rel communiqué, dispatch, report; memo,
memorandum; epistle, letter, missive, note
2 *syn* see MEANING 1

mess around *vb* 1 *syn* see FIDDLE 2
2 *syn* see MEDDLE
3 *syn* see PHILANDER

messenger *n* one who bears a message or
does an errand < blamed the *messenger*
for the bad news he brought >
  syn bearer, carrier, courier, emissary,
envoy, internuncio
  rel herald; go-between, intermediary,
mediator; dispatcher, post
mess–up *n syn* see MESS 3
messy *adj* 1 *syn* see SLOVENLY 1
  rel dirty, grimy, grubby
  con clean
  ant neat
  2 *syn* see SLIPSHOD 3
metagrobolize *vb syn* see PUZZLE
metamorphize *vb syn* see TRANSFORM
metamorphose *vb syn* see TRANSFORM
  rel age, develop, mature, ripen
metanoia *n syn* see CONVERSION 1
metaphor *n syn* see ANALOGY 2
  rel comparison, trope; allegory, personification
  idiom figure of speech
metaphysical *adj* 1 *syn* see IMMATERIAL
1
  rel supernatural, transcendent, transcendental
  2 *syn* see SUPERNATURAL 1
mete (out) *vb* 1 *syn* see ADMINISTER 2
  rel measure
  2 *syn* see ALLOT
meter *n syn* see RHYTHM
method *n* 1 the means or procedures used
in attaining an end < he claimed that his
ends justified his *methods* >
  syn fashion, manner, mode, modus, system, technique, way, wise
  rel design, plan, schema, scheme; form,
style; course, line; modus operandi, practice, procedure, process, routine; wrinkle
  2 *syn* see ORDER 8
methodic *adj syn* see ORDERLY 1
  ant desultory, unmethodical
methodical *adj syn* see ORDERLY 1
  rel methodized, organized, systematized;
analytical, logical; careful, meticulous,
scrupulous
  con casual, hit-or-miss, random; confused,
jumbled
  ant desultory, unmethodical
methodize *vb syn* see ORDER 1
  rel establish, fix, set, settle
meticulous *adj syn* see CAREFUL 1
  rel fastidious, pernickety, picky; cautious,
strict, thorough; microscopic
métier *n* 1 *syn* see TRADE 1
  2 *syn* see FORTE
metropolitan *adj syn* see COSMOPOLITAN
1
mettle *n syn* see COURAGE
mettlesome *adj syn* see SPIRITED 2
  rel edgy, excitable, high-strung, skittish,
startlish
mew *vb syn* see ENCLOSE 1
Mickey Mouse *adj syn* see PETTY 2
mid *adj* 1 *syn* see MIDDLE 2
  2 *syn* see MIDDLE 1
mid *prep* 1 *syn* see AMID 1
  2 *syn* see AMONG 1

3 *syn* see DURING
middle *adj* 1 equally distant from the extremes < the *middle* finger >
  syn center, centermost, equidistant,
halfway, medial, median, mid, middlemost, midmost
  2 being at neither extreme < paid a *middle* price for it >
  syn center, central, intermediary, intermediate, mean, medial, median, mid
middle *n syn* see CENTER 1
middlebrow *n syn* see PHILISTINE
middleman *n syn* see GO-BETWEEN 2
middlemost *adj syn* see MIDDLE 1
middle-of-the-road *adj syn* see MODER-
ATE 4
middle–rate *adj syn* see MEDIUM
middle–road *adj syn* see MODERATE 4
middling *adj syn* see MEDIUM
  rel inferior, poor, second-rate
midge *n syn* see DWARF
midget *n syn* see DWARF
midget *adj syn* see TINY
midmost *adj syn* see MIDDLE 1
midpoint *n syn* see CENTER 1
midst *n syn* see CENTER 1
midst *prep* 1 *syn* see AMID 1
  2 *syn* see AMONG 1
  3 *syn* see DURING
mid–Victorian *n syn* see FOGY
  rel bluenose, goody-goody, Mrs. Grundy,
prig, prude, puritan; Victorian
mien *n* 1 *syn* see BEARING 1
  rel expression, manner, mannerism
  2 *syn* see APPEARANCE 1
miff *n* 1 *syn* see OFFENSE 2
  rel conniption, fit
  2 *syn* see QUARREL
might *n* 1 *syn* see POWER 1
  2 *syn* see POWER 4
  rel energeticness, lustiness, strenuousness,
vigor, vigorousness; forcefulness, forcibleness, powerfulness
  3 *syn* see ABILITY 1
  4 *syn* see MUSCLE 1
might and main *adv syn* see HARD 1
mightily *adv* 1 *syn* see HARD 1
  rel arduously, laboriously, strenuously,
toilsomely
  2 *syn* see VERY 1
mighty *adj* 1 *syn* see POWERFUL 2
  2 *syn* see STRONG 1
  3 *syn* see HUGE
  rel eminent, illustrious, renowned; august,
grand, imposing, impressive, moving
mighty *adv syn* see VERY 1
migrant *adj syn* see MIGRATORY
migrant *n syn* see EMIGRANT
  rel in-migrant, out-migrant; drifter,
mover, nomad, traveler, wanderer
migrate *vb* to move from one country,
place, or locality to another < his father
had *migrated* to the Far West years before >
  syn emigrate, transmigrate
  rel immigrate, in-migrate, out-migrate,
remigrate; drift, trek; nomadize, range,
roam, rove, wander
migrative *adj syn* see MIGRATORY
  ant nonmigratory
migratorial *adj syn* see MIGRATORY
  ant nonmigratory

---

syn synonym(s)   *rel* related word(s)
ant antonym(s)   *con* contrasted word(s)
idiom idiomatic equivalent(s)
‖ use limited; if in doubt, see a dictionary

migratory *adj* moving habitually or occasionally from one region or climate to another <the study of *migratory* birds>
syn migrant, migrative, migratorial, mobile, transmigratory
rel errant, nomad, nomadic, ranging, roving, wandering
ant nonmigratory

mild *adj* 1 *syn* see GENTLE 1
rel choice, dainty, delicate, exquisite; moderate, temperate; benign, benignant
con intense, severe, sharp, vehement
ant fierce, harsh
2 *syn* see AMIABLE 1
rel docile, meek; subdued, submissive; deferential, obeisant, subservient

milepost *n syn* see EVENT 2

milestone *n syn* see EVENT 2

milieu *n syn* see ENVIRONMENT

militant *adj* 1 *syn* see BELLIGERENT
rel martial, military
2 *syn* see AGGRESSIVE

military *adj syn* see MARTIAL
rel chauvinistic, jingoistic, militaristic, warmongering; soldierlike, soldierly
ant unmilitary

military *n syn* see TROOP 2

militate *vb syn* see WEIGH 3

milk *vb* 1 *syn* see FLEECE 1
rel exact, exploit, extort; drain, empty, exhaust, pump, suck, wring
2 *syn* see EDUCE 1

milk-and-water *adj syn* see INSIPID 3

milk-livered *adj syn* see COWARDLY

milksop *n syn* see WEAKLING
rel effeminate; coward

milk-warm *adj syn* see TEPID 1

mill *n syn* see FACTORY

million *n syn* see SCAD

millstone *n syn* see LOAD 3

Milquetoast *n syn* see WEAKLING

mime *n syn* see ACTOR 1

mimic *n syn* see ACTOR 1

mimic *vb* to copy or exaggerate (as manner or gestures) often by way of mockery <*mimicked* her halting speech>
syn ape, burlesque, imitate, mock, parody, take off, travesty
rel hit off, mime, mum; act, do, enact, impersonate, perform, personate, play; copycat; pantomime

mimicry *n* the art or practice of closely imitating another in speech, gestures, or manners <engaged in *mimicry* of café society>
syn apery
rel imitation, mimesis, mimetism; mock, mockery; caricature, parody

miminy-piminy *adj syn* see NICE 1

mince *vb* 1 *syn* see CHOP 2
2 *syn* see SASHAY

mincing *adj syn* see GENTEEL 3
rel dainty, delicate, fastidious, finical, finicking, finicky, fussy, nice, particular, pernickety, persnickety, squeamish

‖**mincy** *adj syn* see NICE 1

mind *n* 1 an element or complex of elements in an individual that feels, perceives, thinks, wills, and especially reasons <sad to see such a *mind* dulled by drink and drugs>
syn brain, gray matter, head, ‖upper story, ‖upperworks, wit

rel brainpower, intellect, intelligence; consciousness, mentality; faculty, function, power
2 *syn* see WILL 1
rel disposition, temper, temperament
con aversion, disinclination, indisposition
3 *syn* see WIT 2
4 *syn* see OPINION
5 *syn* see MOOD 1
‖6 *syn* see NOTICE 1

mind *vb* ‖1 *syn* see REMEMBER
‖2 *syn* see ENJOY 1
3 *syn* see SEE 1
‖4 *syn* see INTEND 2
5 *syn* see OBEY
6 *syn* see LOOK 1
7 *syn* see BEWARE
8 *syn* see TEND 2
rel oversee, superintend, supervise; discipline, govern
con forget, slight
9 *syn* see CONSIDER 1

minded *adj syn* see WILLING 1
rel contemplating, intending, planning, purposing

mindful *adj syn* see AWARE
ant unmindful
2 inclined to be aware <*mindful* of the ever-changing social scene>
syn heedful, observant, observative, observing, regardful, thoughtful
rel attentive, conscientious; aware, cognizant, conscious, conversant, sensible; alert, vigilant, watchful
con heedless, inattentive
ant mindless, unmindful

mindless *adj* 1 *syn* see SIMPLE 3
2 *syn* see INSANE 1

mine *n syn* see BONANZA
rel lode, quarry, vein; spring, well, wellspring

mine *vb* to dig into for the purpose of obtaining items of use or value <*mined* manuscripts looking for undiscovered masterpieces>
syn delve, quarry
rel burrow, drill, excavate, sap, scoop; work

mingle *vb* 1 *syn* see MIX 1
2 *syn* see SOCIALIZE

mingle-mangle *n syn* see MISCELLANY 1

mingy *adj syn* see STINGY

miniature *n syn* see MODEL 1

miniature *adj syn* see TINY
rel small-scale, subminiature
con large-scale

minify *vb syn* see ABRIDGE 1
rel dwarf, miniaturize, shrink

minikin *adj syn* see TINY

minim *n syn* see PARTICLE

minimal *adj* constituting the least possible <*minimal* differences of opinion>
syn minimum
rel littlest, lowest, slightest, smallest; basal, basic, essential, fundamental
con maximum, topmost, utmost; greatest, highest, largest, most
ant maximal

minimize *vb syn* see DECRY 2
rel dwarf, reduce
ant magnify, maximize

minimum *n* the least quantity assignable, admissible, or possible <testing the use of a *minimum* of security at the prison>

syn margin
rel dab, hair, iota, jot, modicum, particle, pittance, smidgen, speck, whit
con abundance, bushel(s), gob(s), ‖lashings, load(s), lot(s), mass(es), much, oodles, profusion, scads, slather(s), ton(s), world(s)
ant maximum

minimum *adj syn* see MINIMAL
ant maximum

minion *n syn* see SYCOPHANT

minister *n syn* see CLERGYMAN

minister (to) *vb* to attend to the wants and comforts of someone <*minister* to the sick and dying>
syn care (for), mother, nurse, serve, wait (on)
rel cure, heal, remedy; doctor, treat; pander

ministerial *adj syn* see INSTRUMENTAL

minister plenipotentiary *n syn* see ENVOY 1

ministry *n syn* see MEAN 2

minor *adj* 1 *syn* see LITTLE 3
rel dependent; inferior, piddling, trifling; junior, lower
con meaningful, significant
ant major

2 lower in standing or reputation than others of the same class <a *minor* poet of the late eighteenth century>
syn dinky, insignificant, lesser, minor-league, secondary, small, small-fry, small-time
rel average, fair, indifferent, mediocre, medium, middling, second-rate, undistinguished, unnoticeable; trivial, unimportant
con chief, foremost, leading, principal
ant major

minor *n syn* see INFANT 2

minority *n syn* see INFANCY 2
ant majority

minor–league *adj syn* see MINOR 2

minstrel *n syn* see BARD 1
rel balladist, singer, wait

mint *n syn* see FORTUNE 4

mint *adj syn* see BRAND-NEW
rel intact, original, perfect, unmarred

minus *prep syn* see WITHOUT 2
ant plus

minute *n syn* see INSTANT 1

minute *adj* 1 *syn* see TINY
2 *syn* see LITTLE 3
3 *syn* see CIRCUMSTANTIAL
rel careful, meticulous, punctilious, scrupulous
con abstract; general, universal; comprehending, comprehensive, embracing, embracive, including, inclusive

minutely *adj syn* see CONTINUAL

minutia *n, usu* minutiae *pl* 1 *syn* see INS AND OUTS
2 *syn* see TRIVIA

minx *n* a pert girl <her rivals called her a brazen *minx*>
syn hussy, jade, malapert, saucebox, slut, snip
rel broad, brat, upstart; baggage, chippy, drab, floozy, strumpet, tart, trollop, trull

miracle *n syn* see WONDER 1

miraculous *adj* 1 *syn* see SUPERNATURAL 1
2 *syn* see MARVELOUS 1
con natural, normal

mirage *n syn* see DELUSION 1

mire *n syn* see SWAMP
rel muck

mire *vb* 1 *syn* see DELAY 1
rel bemire, sink; adhere, cleave, cling, cohere, stick; enmesh, ensnare, entangle, entrap, involve, snare, trap
2 *syn* see INVOLVE 1

mirror *n* 1 a polished or smooth surface (as of glass) that forms images by reflection <spent hours looking at herself in the *mirror*>
syn glass, looking glass, ‖seeing glass
rel cheval glass, pier glass, reflector, speculum
2 *syn* see MODEL 2

mirror *vb* 1 *syn* see REFLECT 1
2 *syn* see REPRESENT 2

mirth *n* a mood or temper characterized by joy and high spirits and usually manifested in laughter and merrymaking <a man of contentment, but seldom of *mirth*>
syn glee, hilarity, jocularity, jocundity, jollity, joviality, merriment
rel cheer, cheerfulness, joyfulness, lightheartedness; gladness, happiness; frivolity, levity
con blues, dejection, depression, dumps, gloom, sadness; boredom, ennui, tedium; anguish, misery, woe; infelicity, wretchedness
ant melancholy

mirthful *adj syn* see MERRY
ant mirthless

miry *adj syn* see MUDDY 1

misadventure *n* 1 *syn* see DISASTER
2 *syn* see ACCIDENT 2
rel blunder, boner, bull, error, faux pas, howler, lapse, slip

misanthropic *adj syn* see ANTISOCIAL
rel misogynic
con altruistic, benevolent, charitable, humane, humanitarian
ant philanthropic

misapply *vb syn* see ABUSE 2
rel misappropriate, misdirect, mismanage

misapprehend *vb* 1 *syn* see MISUNDERSTAND 1
ant apprehend
2 *syn* see MISUNDERSTAND 2
ant apprehend

misappropriate *vb syn* see EMBEZZLE

misbegotten *adj syn* see ILLEGITIMATE 1

misbehaving *adj syn* see NAUGHTY 1
ant well-behaved

misbehavior *n syn* see MISCONDUCT

misbelief *n syn* see HERESY

misbeliever *n syn* see HERETIC

miscalculate *vb* to calculate wrongly <*miscalculate* the distance> <he seriously *miscalculated* the effect of his remark>
syn misestimate, misjudge, misreckon
rel discount, disregard, overlook; misconstrue, misinterpret, misunderstand; overestimate, overprize, overrate, overvalue; understimate, underprize, underrate, undervalue

---

syn synonym(s)   *rel* related word(s)
ant antonym(s)   *con* contrasted word(s)
idiom idiomatic equivalent(s)
‖ use limited; if in doubt, see a dictionary

miscarry *vb* to go wrong or amiss < his plans *miscarried* almost from the start >
syn misfire, miss
rel abort; fail, flop
idiom fall through, miss fire, miss the mark
con come off, prevail, succeed

miscellaneous *adj* consisting of diverse things or members < gathered together a *miscellaneous* lot of books for sale >
syn assorted, chowchow, conglomerate, heterogeneous, indiscriminate, mixed, motley, multifarious, promiscuous, unassorted, unsorted, varied
rel different, disparate, divergent, diverse, various; divers, many, sundry; odd; commingled, jumbled, mingled, scrambled
con akin, alike, identical, like, parallel, similar, uniform

miscellany *n* 1 an unorganized mixture of various dissimilar items or elements < sold a *miscellany* of old household effects >
syn assortment, brew, chowchow, colluvies, gallimaufry, hash, hodgepodge, hotchpotch, jumble, medley, mélange, melee, mingle-mangle, mishmash, mixed bag, motley, odds and ends, olio, olla podrida, omnium-gatherum, pasticcio, pastiche, patchwork, porridge, potpourri, rumble-bumble, salad, salmagundi, smorgasbord, stew
rel mess, muddle; accumulation, aggregation, congeries, conglomeration, cumulation; combination, mix, mixture
2 *syn* see ANTHOLOGY

mischance *n* 1 *syn* see MISFORTUNE
2 *syn* see ACCIDENT 2

mischief *n* 1 *syn* see INJURY 1
rel difficulty, hardship, trouble
2 *syn* see SCAMP
3 *syn* see MISCHIEVOUSNESS
4 *syn* see DISCORD

||**mischieful** *adj* *syn* see PLAYFUL 1

mischief-maker *n* *syn* see TROUBLEMAKER

mischievous *adj* 1 *syn* see HARMFUL
rel dangerous, hazardous, perilous, precarious, risky
2 *syn* see NAUGHTY 1
rel annoying, bothering, bothersome, irking, irksome, vexatious, vexing
3 *syn* see PLAYFUL 1
rel artful, foxy, insidious, sly, tricky

mischievousness *n* action or conduct that annoys or irritates without causing or meaning serious harm < a wag who was forever engaging in *mischievousness* >
syn devilment, devilry, deviltry, diablerie, impishness, mischief, roguery, roguishness, sportiveness, waggery, waggishness
rel doggery, odiousness, offensiveness; evil, harm, hurt, injury; annoying, pestering, teasing

miscolor *vb* *syn* see MISREPRESENT

miscomprehend *vb* *syn* see MISUNDERSTAND 1

misconceive *vb* *syn* see MISUNDERSTAND 2

misconduct *n* improper behavior < was charged with *misconduct* >
syn misbehavior, misdoing, wrongdoing
rel impropriety; malfeasance, malversation, misfeasance

misconstrue *vb* *syn* see MISUNDERSTAND 2

miscreant *adj* *syn* see VICIOUS 2

miscreant *n* *syn* see VILLAIN 1

miscreation *n* *syn* see FREAK 2
rel deformation, deformity

miscue *n* *syn* see ERROR 2

misdate *n* *syn* see ANACHRONISM 1

misdating *n* *syn* see ANACHRONISM 1

misdeed *n* *syn* see CRIME 1

misdeem *vb* 1 *syn* see MISJUDGE 2
2 *syn* see MISTAKE 1

misdoing *n* *syn* see MISCONDUCT

misdoubt *vb* *syn* see DISTRUST
rel apprehend, dread, fear

mise-en-scène *n* 1 *syn* see SCENE 1
2 *syn* see SCENE 3
3 *syn* see ENVIRONMENT

misemploy *vb* *syn* see ABUSE 2

miser *n* a mean grasping person < an old *miser* who loved only his bank account >
syn cheapskate, cheeseparer, chuff, hunks, moneygrubber, muckworm, nabal, niggard, ||nipcheese, penny pincher, piker, scrooge, skin, skinflint, stiff, tightwad
rel glutton, hog, pig

miserable *adj* *syn* see WOEFUL 1
rel despairing, despondent, forlorn, hopeless; piteous, pitiable, pitiful; melancholy
con cheerful, glad, happy, joyful, joyous, lighthearted

miserly *adj* *syn* see STINGY
rel avaricious, covetous, grasping, greedy; abject, ignoble, sordid
con bounteous, generous; altruistic, benevolent, charitable

misery *n* 1 a state of suffering and want that is the result of poverty or conditions beyond one's control < the poor learn to live with *misery* > < the utter *misery* in which the flood victims survived >
syn unhappiness, woe, wretchedness
rel agony, anguish; despondency, grief, sorrow; desolation, squalor
con beatitude, blessedness, bliss, felicity, happiness; content, ease, satisfaction
2 *syn* see DISTRESS
rel adversity, misfortune; dejection, depression, melancholy, sadness
ant blessedness
||3 *syn* see PAIN 1

misesteem *vb* *syn* see MISJUDGE 2

misestimate *vb* *syn* see MISCALCULATE

misfire *vb* *syn* see MISCARRY

misfortunate *adj* *syn* see UNLUCKY
ant fortunate

misfortune *n* adverse fortune or an instance of this < his hopes and dreams soon ended in *misfortune* > < unable to grasp why he had been struck by such a *misfortune* >
syn adversity, contretemps, ||dole, mischance, mishap, tragedy, ||unluck
rel calamity, cataclysm, catastrophe, disaster; accident, casualty; affliction, cross, trial, tribulation, visitation
con break, chance, luck, opportunity
ant fortune

misgiving *n* *syn* see APPREHENSION 3
rel doubt, fear, qualm, suspicion; distrust, mistrust

misguided *adj* *syn* see MISTAKEN

mishandle *vb* 1 *syn* see MANHANDLE

2 *syn* see ABUSE 2

mishap *n* 1 *syn* see MISFORTUNE

2 *syn* see ACCIDENT 2

mishmash *n* 1 *syn* see MISCELLANY 1

2 *syn* see CLUTTER 2

misidentify *vb* *syn* see MISTAKE 1

misimprove *vb* *syn* see ABUSE 2

misinterpret *vb* *syn* see MISUNDERSTAND 2

misjudge *vb* 1 *syn* see MISCALCULATE

2 to have a mistaken opinion of < her first impression led her to *misjudge* the girl >

syn misdeem, misesteem, mistake

rel misapprehend, miscomprehend, misconceive, misconstrue, misinterpret, misunderstand

con catch on (to), penetrate, tumble (to), wise (up)

misknow *vb* *syn* see MISUNDERSTAND 1

mislaying *n* *syn* see LOSS 1

mislead *vb* *syn* see DECEIVE

rel lie, misguide, misinform; entice, inveigle, lure, seduce, tempt

misleading *adj* having an appearance or character that leads one astray or into error < the president made several *misleading* statements to the people >

syn beguiling, deceiving, deceptive, deluding, delusive, delusory, fallacious, false

rel casuistical, sophistical, specious; wrong; bewildering, confounding, distracting, perplexing, puzzling; deceitful, inaccurate

con clarifying, elucidative, explanatory, illuminating

‖**mismannered** *adj* *syn* see RUDE 6

mismatch *vb* *syn* see CLASH 2

misorder *n* *syn* see CONFUSION 3

misplacement *n* *syn* see LOSS 1

misplacing *n* *syn* see LOSS 1

misread *vb* *syn* see MISUNDERSTAND 2

misreckon *vb* *syn* see MISCALCULATE

‖**misremember** *vb* *syn* see FORGET 1

misrepresent *vb* to give a false, imperfect, or misleading representation of < the summary totally *misrepresents* the facts of the case >

syn belie, color, confuse, distort, falsify, garble, miscolor, misstate, pervert, twist, warp, wrench, wrest

rel dress, embellish, embroider, gild, gloss, varnish; camouflage, cloak, disguise, dissemble, mask; counterfeit, feign, simulate; equivocate, lie, palter, prevaricate, weasel

idiom give a false coloring, put a false construction (*or* appearance) on

misrepresentation *n* *syn* see LIE

misrule *n* *syn* see DISORDER 2

miss *vb* 1 *syn* see NEGLECT

2 *syn* see MISUNDERSTAND 1

3 *syn* see MISCARRY

‖**miss** *n* *syn* see ABSENCE

miss *n* *syn* see GIRL 1

misshape *vb* *syn* see DEFORM

misshape *n* *syn* see DEFORMITY

missing *adj* *syn* see ABSENT 1

---

2 *syn* see LOST 2

mission *n* a continuing task or responsibility that one is destined or fitted to do or specially called upon to undertake < his *mission* in life was to serve humanity >

syn calling, lifework, vocation

rel goal, purpose; business, profession, trade

missionary *n* one who attempts to convert others to a specific way of life, set of ideas, or course of action < served as a *missionary* for the feminist cause >

syn apostle, colporteur, evangelist, missioner, propagandist

rel revivalist; promoter

missioner *n* *syn* see MISSIONARY

missish *adj* *syn* see PRIM 1

missive *n* *syn* see LETTER 2

Miss-Nancyish *adj* *syn* see EFFEMINATE

misstate *vb* *syn* see MISREPRESENT

misstatement *n* *syn* see LIE

misstep *n* *syn* see ERROR 2

‖**missus** *n* *syn* see WIFE

missy *n* *syn* see GIRL 1

mist *n* *syn* see HAZE 1

mist *vb* *syn* see OBSCURE

mistake *vb* 1 to take one thing to be another < he *mistakes* sarcasm for wit >

syn confound, confuse, misdeem, misidentify, mix, mix up

rel misconceive, misknow; addle, jumble, muddle, tumble

con discern, distinguish, grasp, perceive; differentiate, separate

ant recognize

2 *syn* see MISUNDERSTAND 2

3 *syn* see MISJUDGE 2

mistake *n* 1 *syn* see ERROR 2

rel confounding, confusion, mistaking; inadvertence; disregarding, neglect, neglecting, omission, omitting, slight, slighting

2 *syn* see ERROR 1

mistaken *adj* acting, thinking, or judging in a manner at variance with truth or the facts < he is *mistaken* in his evaluation of the crisis >

syn erroneous, misguided, wrong

rel confounded, confused; deceived, deluded, misinformed

idiom all wet, off base, off the track

con accurate, correct, right, unerring; exact, precise

mister *n* *syn* see HUSBAND

mistimed *adj* *syn* see UNSEASONABLE 1

ant well-timed

mistiming *n* *syn* see ANACHRONISM 1

mistreat *vb* *syn* see ABUSE 4

mistress *n* a woman who is a man's regular partner in nonmarital sexual activity < gave up his *mistress* when he married >

syn ‖doxy, girl friend, inamorata, lover, paramour, woman; *compare* HARLOT 1

rel bedmate; concubine; kept woman; dulcinea

mistrust *n* *syn* see UNCERTAINTY

rel apprehension, foreboding, misgiving, presentiment

con dependence, faith, reliance

ant assurance, trust

mistrust *vb* 1 *syn* see DISTRUST

rel anticipate, apprehend, foresee; alarm, frighten, scare; appall, dismay

---

syn synonym(s)   *rel* related word(s)

ant antonym(s)   *con* contrasted word(s)

idiom idiomatic equivalent(s)

‖ use limited; if in doubt, see a dictionary

ant trust

2 *syn* see QUESTION 2

mistrustful *adj syn* see SUSPICIOUS 2

ant trustful, trusting

mistrustfully *adv syn* see ASKANCE 2

ant trustfully, trustingly

misty *adj syn* see HAZY

misunderstand *vb* 1 to fail to understand < he *misunderstood* the full meaning of the novel>

syn misapprehend, miscomprehend, misknow, miss

rel misconceive, misconstrue, misinterpret, misread, mistake

con apprehend, conceive, know, realize; fathom, follow, grasp, seize, take in

ant comprehend, understand

2 to interpret incorrectly < *misunderstood* the instructions>

syn misapprehend, misconceive, misconstrue, misinterpret, misread, mistake

rel misexplain, mistranslate; miscomprehend, misknow

con fathom, follow, take in

ant understand

misuse *vb* 1 *syn* see ABUSE 2

2 *syn* see ABUSE 4

mite *n syn* see PARTICLE

mitigate *vb syn* see RELIEVE 1

rel extenuate, palliate

con aggravate, enhance, heighten; augment, increase

ant intensify

mitigation *n syn* see EASE 3

mix *vb* 1 to combine or be combined into a more or less uniform whole < *mixed* the ingredients to make a thick sauce>

syn admix, amalgamate, blend, comingle, commingle, commix, compound, fuse, immingle, immix, interblend, interflow, interfuse, intermingle, intermix, make up, meld, merge, mingle

rel associate, combine, conjoin, inosculate, join, link, unite; braid, lump, work in; coalesce; blunge

con divide, part, separate, sever, sunder

2 *syn* see MISTAKE 1

mix *n syn* see MIXTURE

mixed *adj syn* see MISCELLANEOUS

rel amalgamated, blended, fused, merged, mingled

mixed bag *n syn* see MISCELLANY 1

mixologist *n syn* see BARTENDER

mixture *n* a product formed by the combination of two or more things < the tea is actually a *mixture* of several varieties>

syn admixture, alloy, amalgam, amalgamation, blend, commixture, composite, compost, compound, fusion, immixture, interfusion, intermixture, mix, mix-up

rel brew, concoction, confection, mélange

mix up *vb* 1 *syn* see CONFUSE 2

ant straighten (out)

2 *syn* see CONFUSE 5

3 *syn* see MISTAKE 1

4 *syn* see DISORDER 1

ant straighten (out *or* up)

mix-up *n* 1 *syn* see MESS 3

2 *syn* see MIXTURE

mizmaze *n syn* see MAZE 1

‖**mizzle** *vb syn* see SPRINKLE 5

‖**mizzle** *vb syn* see CONFUSE 2

moan *vb syn* see DEPLORE 1

moanful *adj syn* see MELANCHOLY 2

mob *n* 1 *syn* see RABBLE

2 a large disorderly crowd of people usually bent on riotous or destructive action < the *mob* screamed for a lynching>

syn rabble, rout

rel posse; crowd, crush, horde, press, push, throng; herd, swarm

3 *syn* see CLIQUE

‖**mob** *vb syn* see SCOLD 1

mobile *adj* 1 *syn* see MOVABLE

rel fluid, liquid; protean; capricious, fickle, inconstant, mercurial

con immutable, invariable, unchangeable

ant immobile

2 *syn* see CHANGEABLE 1

ant immobile, stable

3 *syn* see VERSATILE

4 *syn* see MIGRATORY

mobilize *vb* 1 to put into movement or circulation < an increase in prices *mobilizes* the whole cycle of inflation>

syn actuate, circulate, set off

rel activate; impel, propel

idiom set in motion

con inactivate, slow (down *or* up)

ant immobilize

2 *syn* see MOVE 5

3 to assemble (as resources) and make ready for use or action < the president tried to *mobilize* support for the new proposal>

syn marshal, muster, organize, rally

mobocracy *n syn* see ANARCHY 1

mock *vb* 1 *syn* see RIDICULE

rel buffoon, burlesque, caricature, parody, travesty

2 *syn* see DECEIVE

3 *syn* see MIMIC

rel affect, assume, counterfeit, feign, simulate

mock *n* 1 *syn* see LAUGHINGSTOCK

2 *syn* see MOCKERY 2

mock *adj* 1 *syn* see ARTIFICIAL 2

rel pseudo, quasi, so-called

2 *syn* see FICTITIOUS 2

rel bogus, phony

mockery *n* 1 *syn* see LAUGHINGSTOCK

2 an insincere, contemptible, or impertinent imitation of something worthwhile < arbitrary methods that make a *mockery* of justice>

syn burlesque, caricature, farce, mock, sham, travesty

rel derision, ridicule, sport; parody, satire, take-off; joke, laughingstock

mode *n* 1 *syn* see VEIN 1

2 *syn* see METHOD 1

3 *syn* see STATE 1

mode *n syn* see FASHION 3

model *n* 1 a miniature representation of something < a *model* of the dam that was accurate down to the last detail>

syn miniature, pocket edition

rel copy, mock-up, replica, reproduction; dummy, effigy

2 something set or held before one for guidance or imitation < Samuel Johnson's literary style is often used as a *model* for writers seeking precision and clarity>

syn archetype, beau ideal, ensample, example, exemplar, ideal, mirror, paradigm, pattern, standard; *compare* PARAGON *rel* apotheosis, nonesuch, nonpareil, paragon; emblem, symbol, type; embodiment, epitome, quintessence; criterion, gauge, touchstone

model *adj* 1 *syn* see IDEAL 3
rel commendable, exemplary
2 *syn* see PERFECT 3
3 *syn* see TYPICAL 1

moderate *adj* 1 *syn* see SOBER 3
2 not excessive in degree, amount, or intensity <the new proposals were met with only *moderate* enthusiasm> <the snowfall is expected to be no more than *moderate*>
syn modest, reasonable, temperate
rel bland, gentle, mild, soft; inconsequential, inconsiderable, slight, small; paltry, piddling, trifling, trivial
con excessive, extreme, inordinate, intemperate, radical, unreasonable
ant immoderate
3 *syn* see MEDIUM
rel constant, equable, even, steady
4 avoiding extreme political or social measures <party policy became increasingly *moderate*>
syn middle-of-the-road, middle-road, softshell
con conservative, right, tory; left, radical, red; extremist, fanatical, ultra
5 *syn* see CONSERVATIVE 2

moderate *vb* 1 to modify as to avoid an extreme or keep within bounds <actors *moderate* their voices and gestures to fit the size of the theatre>
syn modulate, restrain, temper
rel abate, decrease, diminish, lessen, reduce; alleviate, cushion, lighten, mitigate, mollify, relieve, slacken, slow; constrain, control, qualify; chasten, cool, subdue, tone (down)
con aggravate, enhance, heighten, intensify; augment, increase
2 *syn* see ABATE 4

moderately *adv* 1 *syn* see ENOUGH 2
2 *syn* see SOMEWHAT 2
ant extremely, immoderately

moderateness *n* *syn* see TEMPERANCE 1
ant immoderateness, immoderation

moderation *n* *syn* see TEMPERANCE 1
ant immoderateness, immoderation

moderator *n* one who arbitrates <the labor dispute was finally referred to a *moderator*>
syn arbitrator, mediator
rel arbiter, judge; conciliator, negotiator, peacemaker

modern *adj* 1 having taken place, existed, or developed in times close to the present <*modern* concepts of engineering made the bridge possible>
syn late, recent
rel contemporary, present-day; latter
con antiquated, old-fashioned, old hat, outdated, outmoded, outworn
ant old-time
2 *syn* see NEW 1

---

syn synonym(s)   *rel* related word(s)
ant antonym(s)   *con* contrasted word(s)
idiom idiomatic equivalent(s)
‖ use limited; if in doubt, see a dictionary

rel coincident, concomitant, concurrent, contemporaneous, contemporary; current, prevailing, prevalent
ant ancient, antique

modernistic *adj* *syn* see NEW 1
rel futuristic
ant antiquated

modernize *vb* *syn* see RENEW 1

modest *adj* 1 *syn* see HUMBLE 1
rel moderate, temperate; retiring, withdrawing; unboastful; unpresuming, unpresumptuous, unpretending
con barefaced, brazen, impudent, shameless
ant ambitious
2 *syn* see SHY 1
rel reticent, silent; nice, proper, seemly
3 *syn* see CHASTE
rel priggish, prim, prissy, prudish, puritanical, straitlaced, stuffy
con improper, indecent, indecorous, indelicate, unseemly
ant immodest
4 *syn* see MODERATE 2
5 *syn* see PLAIN 1

modicum *n* *syn* see PARTICLE

modification *n* *syn* see CHANGE 1
rel conversion, metamorphosis, transformation, transmogrification; qualification, tempering

modified *adj* *syn* see QUALIFIED 2

modify *vb* *syn* see CHANGE 1
rel modulate, restrain, temper; qualify

modish *adj* *syn* see STYLISH
rel voguish

modulate *vb* *syn* see MODERATE 1

modus *n* *syn* see METHOD 1

‖**mog** *vb* *syn* see GO 2

mogul *n* *syn* see MAGNATE

moiety *n* *syn* see PART 1

moil *vb* 1 *syn* see LABOR 1
‖2 *syn* see SEETHE 4

moil *n* 1 *syn* see WORK 2
2 *syn* see COMMOTION 4

moira *n* *syn* see FATE

moist *adj* 1 *syn* see DAMP
2 *syn* see SENTIMENTAL

moistureless *adj* *syn* see DRY 1
ant moist

moisty *adj* *syn* see DAMP

‖**moke** *n* *syn* see DONKEY 1

mold *n* *syn* see TYPE

mold *vb* *syn* see MAKE 3

moldable *adj* *syn* see PLASTIC

molder *vb* *syn* see DECAY

moldy *adj* *syn* see OLD-FASHIONED

mole *n* *syn* see BIRTHMARK 1

molecule *n* *syn* see PARTICLE

molest *vb* to annoy or disturb with hostile intent or injurious effect <he was specifically warned by the court not to *molest* his former wife>
syn bait, beckle, persecute, torment
rel annoy, badger, bother, irk, pester; pother, tease; bedevil, beset, devil, trouble; harass, harry, vex

moll *n* *syn* see PROSTITUTE

mollify *vb* 1 *syn* see PACIFY
rel lighten; temper; abate, decrease, lessen, reduce
ant exasperate
2 *syn* see RELIEVE 1

‖**molly** *n* *syn* see WEAKLING

mollycoddle n syn see WEAKLING
 rel ‖mollycot
mollycoddle vb syn see BABY
 ant neglect; abuse
molt vb syn see SHED 2
mom n syn see MOTHER 1
‖**momble** vb syn see CONFUSE 2
moment n 1 syn see INSTANT 1
 ant eternity
 2 syn see POINT 7
 3 syn see OCCASION 5
 4 syn see IMPORTANCE
 rel advantage, avail, profit, use
momentaneous adj syn see TRANSIENT
momentary adj syn see TRANSIENT
 rel brief, quick, short; impulsive
 ant agelong
momentous adj 1 syn see IMPORTANT 1
 ant trivial
 2 syn see EPOCHAL
momentousness n syn see IMPORTANCE
 ant triviality
mommy n syn see MOTHER 1
momus n syn see CRITIC
monarchal adj syn see KINGLY
monarchial adj syn see KINGLY
monarchical adj syn see KINGLY
mondaine adj syn see SOPHISTICATED 2
monetary adj syn see FINANCIAL
 rel numismatic
money n something (as pieces of stamped
 metal or paper certificates) customarily
 and legally used as a medium of exchange
 <the only thing that he liked about his
 job was the *money* >
 syn ‖blunt, ‖brass, ‖bread, ‖cabbage, cash,
 ‖chink, ‖chips, ‖coin, currency, ‖dibs,
 dinero, ‖do-re-mi, dough, filthy lucre,
 gelt, ‖greenbacks, ‖jack, ‖kale, legal tender, ‖lettuce, ‖long green, loot, lucre,
 mazuma, ‖moolah, ‖mopus, needful,
 ooftish, pelf, rhino, rocks, ‖scratch, ‖shek-
 els, ‖smash, stuff, ‖stumpy, ‖sugar, swag,
 ‖wampum
 rel bankroll, capital, coinage, finances,
 funds, mammon, resources, riches, treasure, wealth, wherewithal; boodle, hay;
 ‖stiff
moneyed adj syn see RICH 1
 ant penniless, unmoneyed
moneygrubber n syn see MISER
moneymaking adj syn see ADVANTA-
 GEOUS 1
monger n syn see PEDDLER
monger vb syn see PEDDLE 2
mongerer n syn see PEDDLER
mongrel n syn see HYBRID
‖**moniker** n 1 syn see NAME 1
 2 syn see NICKNAME
monish vb syn see REPROVE
monition n syn see WARNING
monitorial adj syn see MONITORY
monitory adj giving a warning <the parents wrote their son a *monitory* letter>
 syn admonishing, admonitory, cautionary,
 cautioning, monitorial, warning
 rel advisory, counseling; critical, expostu-
 latory, remonstratory; exhortatory, horta-
 tory; moralistic, moralizing, preachy
monkey n 1 syn see FOOL 3
 2 syn see URCHIN
monkey adj syn see SMALL 1
monkey (with) vb syn see MEDDLE

monkeyshine n syn see PRANK
monocratic adj syn see ABSOLUTE 4
 con democratic
monogram n a sign of identity usually
 formed of the combined initials of a name
 <everything he owned had his *monogram*
 on it>
 syn cipher
 rel device, initials; John Hancock, signature
monograph n syn see DISCOURSE 2
monography n syn see DISCOURSE 2
monopolize vb to take up completely <he
 would attempt to *monopolize* every con-
 versation>
 syn absorb, consume, engross, sew up
 rel corner, hog; devour; have, hold, own,
 possess; employ, use, utilize; control, manage
 con contribute, participate, share
monopolizing adj syn see ENGROSSING
monopoly n exclusive possession <neither
 party has a *monopoly* on morality>
 syn corner
 rel cartel, consortium, pool, syndicate,
 trust; copyright; ownership, possessorship,
 proprietorship
monotone n syn see MONOTONY
monotone adj syn see DULL 9
monotonous adj syn see DULL 9
 rel samely, uniform, unvaried; repetitious;
 jogtrot, singsong
 con changing, varying; fresh, new, novel;
 absorbing, engrossing, interesting
monotonousness n syn see MONOTONY
monotony n a tedious sameness or reiteration <the *monotony* of his job finally got
 to him>
 syn humdrum, monotone, monotonousness
 rel ennui, boredom, tedium; dryness,
 flatness, uniformity
 con variability, variation; diversification,
 diversity, multifariousness, variety
monster n 1 syn see FREAK 2
 rel demon, devil, fiend, hellhound; ban-
 dersnatch
 2 syn see GIANT
monster adj syn see HUGE
monstrosity n 1 syn see FREAK 2
 2 syn see EYESORE
monstrous adj 1 extremely impressive
 <the traditional burial ceremonies turned
 into a *monstrous* spectacle>
 syn cracking, fantastic, massive, monumental, mortal, prodigious, stupendous,
 towering, tremendous
 rel grandiose, impressive, magnificent,
 showy, splendid, superb; colossal, enormous, huge, immense, mammoth, vast
 con mean, petty, picayune, poky, small-
 time
 2 syn see HUGE
 3 syn see OUTRAGEOUS 2
 rel glaring, rank; fateful, ominous, portentous; flagitious, infamous
‖**monstrous** adv syn see VERY 1
monstrousness n syn see ENORMITY 1
monument n 1 syn see DOCUMENT 2
 2 a lasting evidence or reminder of someone or something notable <the whole
 body of students who learned from him
 form his *monument*>

syn memorial, testimonial
rel memento, tribute
3 *syn* see TOMBSTONE
monument *vb syn* see MEMORIALIZE 2
monumental *adj* 1 *syn* see HUGE
2 *syn* see MONSTROUS 1
3 *syn* see TOWERING 4
monumentalize *vb syn* see MEMORIALIZE
2
moocah *n syn* see MARIJUANA
mooch *vb syn* see WANDER 1
moocher *n syn* see BEGGAR 1
mooching *n syn* see MENDICANCY
mood *n* 1 a state of mind in which an
emotion or set of emotions gains ascendancy < a melancholy *mood* induced by
the sight of ancient ruins >
syn humor, mind, strain, temper, tone,
vein
rel character, disposition, individuality,
personality, temperament; soul, spirit;
affection, emotion, feeling, response
2 *syn* see TEMPER 1
3 *syn* see AIR 3
moody *adj* subject to moods < a *moody*
person whose behavior was erratic and
whose actions were unpredictable >
syn humorsome, temperamental
rel capricious, fickle, inconstant, mercurial, unstable, whimsical; broody
con calm, dispassionate, stable, steady,
unexcitable; bovine, impassive, stolid
‖**mooish** *n syn* see MONEY
mooncalf *n syn* see FOOL 1
‖**moonraker** *n syn* see DUNCE
moonshine *n* 1 *syn* see NONSENSE 2
2 illegally distilled liquor < his death was
caused by bad *moonshine* >
syn bathtub gin, ‖blockade, bootleg,
‖busthead, ‖hooch, mountain dew, white
lightning
rel homebrew; ‖bug juice, grappa, ‖jake,
smoke, squareface
moor *vb syn* see FASTEN 2
moot *vb* 1 *syn* see BROACH
2 *syn* see DISCUSS 1
moot *adj* open to question < it is a *moot*
point whether he would have been tried
and convicted >
syn arguable, debatable, disputable,
doubtful, dubious, mootable, problematic,
questionable, uncertain; compare DOUBT-
FUL 1
rel controversial, suspect; unsettled
con confirmed, established, settled; inarguable, indisputable, undebatable, unproblematic, unquestionable; certain, sure
mooting *n syn* see ARGUMENTATION
mootable *adj syn* see MOOT
mop *vb syn* see GRIMACE
mop (up) *vb syn* see WHIP 2
mope *vb* 1 to become listless or dejected
< *moped* for several days after the di-
vorce >
syn brood, despond
rel ache, grieve, grump, pout, sulk
2 *syn* see SAUNTER
mopes *n pl syn* see SADNESS

mopey *adj syn* see DOWNCAST
moppet *n syn* see CHILD 1
‖**mopus** *n syn* see MONEY
moral *adj* 1 conforming to a standard of
what is right and good < *moral* goodness
may be distinguished from intellectual
goodness >
syn ethical, moralistic, noble, principled,
righteous, right-minded, virtuous
rel good, right; conscientious, honest,
honorable, just, scrupulous, upright;
chaste, decent, modest, pure
con amoral, nonmoral, unmoral
ant immoral
2 *syn* see DIDACTIC
3 *syn* see ELEVATED 2
moral *n syn* see MAXIM
morale *n* a sense of common purpose or a
degree of dedication to a common task
regarded as characteristic of or dominant
in a group < *morale* was high among the
troops >
syn esprit, esprit de corps
rel drive, spirit, vigor; assurance, confidence, self-confidence, self-possession
con enervation; aimlessness, purposelessness; egoism, egotism, self-centeredness
moralistic *adj syn* see MORAL 1
rel didactic
morality *n* 1 *syn* see GOODNESS
rel godliness, saintliness
2 *syn* see ETHIC 2
moralize *vb* to make moral reflections
usually in an officious or tiresome manner
< people avoided him as he was always
moralizing >
syn preach, preachify, sermonize
rel lecture, pontificate
moralizing *adj syn* see DIDACTIC
morally *adv syn* see VIRTUALLY
morals *n pl* 1 *syn* see ETHIC 1
2 *syn* see ETHIC 2
rel conduct, habits, standards
morass *n* 1 *syn* see SWAMP
2 *syn* see MAZE 1
rel dunghill
moratorium *n syn* see SUSPENSION 2
morbid *adj* abnormally susceptible to or
characterized by gloomy or unwholesome
feelings < his *morbid* poetry is the product
of his lifelong frustrations >
syn morose, sick, sickly
rel gloomy, melancholic; psychotic; dark,
moody, saturnine, sullen
con healthy, sound, well, wholesome;
solid, stable, stolid, sturdy
mordacious *adj syn* see CAUSTIC 1
mordancy *n syn* see ACRIMONY
rel incisiveness, pungency, trenchancy;
acidity, acridity, causticity, mordacity
mordant *adj syn* see CAUSTIC 1
more *adj syn* see ADDITIONAL
more *adv syn* see ALSO 2
2 to a greater or higher degree < were
more evenly matched >
syn better
more or less *adv* 1 *syn* see SOMEWHAT 2
2 *syn* see NEARLY
moreover *adv syn* see ALSO 2
mores *n pl* 1 *syn* see ETHIC 2
2 *syn* see MANNER 5
morgue *n syn* see PRIDE 3

---

syn synonym(s)   *rel* related word(s)
ant antonym(s)   *con* contrasted word(s)
idiom idiomatic equivalent(s)
‖ use limited; if in doubt, see a dictionary

moribund *adj* approaching death or a final end <found lying *moribund* in her bed> <fox hunting is a *moribund* sport>
syn dying
rel expiring, fading, going; decadent, deteriorating, regressing
idiom at death's door, on one's last legs, with one foot in the grave
con booming, flourishing, prospering, thriving; lively, viable

morn *n* 1 *syn* see DAWN 1
2 *syn* see MORNING 2

morne *adj syn* see GLOOMY 3

morning *n* 1 *syn* see DAWN 1
con sundown, sunset
2 the time before noon <it rained most of the *morning*>
syn forenoon, morn
con afternoon, evening; day, night

moron *n* 1 *syn* see FOOL 4
2 *syn* see DUNCE

moronic *adj syn* see RETARDED

morose *adj* 1 *syn* see SULLEN
rel choleric, cranky, irascible, splenetic, testy; irritable, waspish; brusque, gruff
con jocund, jolly, jovial, merry
ant blithe
2 *syn* see MORBID

morsel *n* 1 a small piece or quantity of food <tossed a *morsel* of meat to the dog>
syn bit, bite, mouthful
rel taste; tidbit; crumb, ort, scrap
2 *syn* see SNACK
3 *syn* see DELICACY

mort *n syn* see CORPSE

‖**mortacious** *adv syn* see VERY 1

mortal *adj* 1 *syn* see DEADLY 1
rel implacable, relentless, unrelenting
2 *syn* see GRIM 3
3 *syn* see MONSTROUS 1
4 *syn* see HUMAN
rel finite, temporal; frail, weak
5 *syn* see PROBABLE

mortal *n syn* see HUMAN

mortality *n* 1 *syn* see FATALITY 1
2 *syn* see MANKIND

mortally *adv syn* see VERY 1

mortgage *vb syn* see PAWN

mortician *n* one whose business is to prepare the dead for burial and to arrange and manage funerals <*morticians* must be certified>
syn funeral director, undertaker
rel embalmer

mortiferous *adj syn* see DEADLY 1

mortified *adj* 1 *syn* see SEVERE 1
2 *syn* see ASHAMED
rel annoyed, harassed, harried, worried

mortuary *adj syn* see SEPULCHRAL 1

mosey *vb syn* see SAUNTER

‖**moss** *n syn* see SWAMP

mossback *n* 1 *syn* see RUSTIC
2 *syn* see FOGY

most *adj syn* see BEST
rel greatest, highest, maximum, utmost, uttermost

most *adv syn* see VERY 1

most *adv syn* see NEARLY

mostly *adv syn* see GENERALLY 1
idiom for the most part

mote *n syn* see POINT 11

moth-eaten *adj* 1 *syn* see SHABBY 1

2 *syn* see OLD-FASHIONED

mother *n* 1 a female human parent <the *mother* of seven children>
syn ma, ‖mam, mama (*or* mamma), mammy, ‖mater, mom, mommy, ‖mum, mummy, ‖old lady, ‖old woman; *compare* FATHER 1
2 *syn* see SOURCE

mother *vb syn* see MINISTER (to)

mother country *n syn* see COUNTRY

motherland *n syn* see COUNTRY

mother-naked *adj syn* see NUDE 2

mother wit *n syn* see INTELLIGENCE 1

motif *n* 1 *syn* see LEITMOTIV
2 *syn* see SUBJECT 2
3 *syn* see FIGURE 3

motion *n* 1 the act or an instance of moving <the *motion* of the planets>
syn move, movement, stir, stirring
rel agitation, fluctuation, oscillation, sway, swing, wavering; locomotion
con inertia, inertness, passivity
2 an impulse or inclination of the mind or will <a *motion* of the will toward what appears good>
syn movement
rel goad, impulse, incentive, inducement, motive, spring, spur
con inertia, stagnation, vegetation

motion *vb syn* see SIGNAL

motionless *adj* being without motion <stood *motionless* so that he would remain undiscovered>
syn still, stock-still, stone-still
rel stagnant, static, stationary, unmoving; fixed, immobile, immotile, immotive, immovable, irremovable, ‖sitfast, steadfast, unmovable
con active, changing, mobile, moving

motion picture *n syn* see MOVIE

motivate *vb syn* see PROVOKE 4

motivation *n syn* see STIMULUS

motive *n* 1 the object influencing a choice or prompting an action <trying to discover what was his *motive* in killing the girl>
syn cause, consideration, reason, spring; *compare* STIMULUS
rel antecedent, determinant; emotion, feeling, passion; aim, end, intent, intention, purpose
2 *syn* see FIGURE 3
3 *syn* see SUBJECT 2

motley *adj* 1 *syn* see VARIEGATED
2 *syn* see MISCELLANEOUS
rel discrepant, incompatible, incongruous, uncongenial

motley *n* 1 *syn* see FOOL 2
2 *syn* see MISCELLANY 1

motor *n syn* see CAR

motor *vb* 1 *syn* see RIDE 5
2 *syn* see DRIVE 5

motorcar *n syn* see CAR

motorist *n* a person who travels by automobile <the roads were crowded with *motorists* going to work>
syn autoist, automobilist, driver, operator

mottle *vb syn* see SPLOTCH

motto *n syn* see BATTLE CRY
rel byword, catchphrase, catchword, shibboleth, slogan, watchword, word

moue *n syn* see FACE 6

mound *vb syn* see HEAP 1

mound *n syn* see PILE 1
mount *n syn* see MOUNTAIN 1
mount *vb* 1 *syn* see INCREASE 2
2 *syn* see ASCEND 1
con descend, fall, lower
ant drop
3 *syn* see RISE 4
ant drop
4 *syn* see INTENSIFY
5 to get on (something) as a means of
conveyance < *mount* a horse>
syn back, bestride
rel seat, settle
ant dismount
‖6 *syn* see TESTIFY 2
7 *syn* see STAGE
mountain *n* 1 a relatively steep and high
elevation of land < why are *mountains* in
New England considered no more than
hills in Colorado >
syn alp, mount, peak
rel butte, mesa; bald, dome; hill; bluff;
volcano; sierra
con bottom, bottomland, dale, dell, vale,
valley
2 *syn* see PILE 1
3 *syn* see MUCH
4 *syn* see OBSTACLE
mountain dew *n syn* see MOONSHINE 2
mountaineer *n syn* see RUSTIC
mountainous *adj syn* see HUGE
mountebank *n* 1 *syn* see CHARLATAN
2 *syn* see SWINDLER
mourn *vb syn* see GRIEVE 2
con delight, gladden, please, rejoice
mournful *adj* 1 *syn* see SAD 1
2 *syn* see SAD 2
3 *syn* see MELANCHOLY 2
4 *syn* see DEPLORABLE
mournfulness *n syn* see SADNESS
mouse *n* 1 *syn* see GIRL FRIEND 1
2 *syn* see BLACK EYE 1
mouse *vb* 1 *syn* see SNOOP
2 *syn* see STEAL 3
mousehole *n syn* see CUBBYHOLE
mousetrap *n syn* see PITFALL
mouth *n* 1 the opening through which food
passes into the body of an animal < the
mouth in vertebrates is one of the features
of the face>
syn ‖bazoo, gob, ‖mush, ‖row, ‖trap, ‖yap
rel mug, muzzle
2 *syn* see FACE 6
3 *syn* see SPOKESMAN
4 *syn* see BACK TALK
5 the place where a tributary enters a
larger stream or body of water < the
mouth of the Mississippi river is in the
Gulf of Mexico>
syn embouchement, embouchure
rel estuary; delta
mouth *vb* 1 *syn* see ORATE
2 *syn* see BOAST
3 *syn* see REVEAL 1
4 *syn* see GRIMACE
mouthful *n syn* see MORSEL 1
mouthing *n syn* see FACE 6
mouthpiece *n syn* see SPOKESMAN

mouth-watering *adj syn* see PALATABLE
‖**mouthy** *adj* 1 *syn* see TALKATIVE
2 *syn* see RHETORICAL
movable *adj* capable of moving or of being
moved < a device with a *movable* attach-
ment>
syn mobile, moving, unstable, unsteadfast, unsteady
rel remotive, removable; motile; changeable, changeful, mutable, variable; roving
con immobile, immotile, immotive, irremovable, steadfast; established, fixed, set,
settled; stagnant, static, unmoving
movables *n pl syn* see POSSESSION 2
move *vb* 1 *syn* see GO 2
2 *syn* see ADVANCE 5
3 *syn* see BE
4 to change or cause to change from one
place to another < he *moved* quickly
down the staircase > < *move* the chair
across the room>
syn dislocate, disturb, remove, shift, ship,
transfer
rel displace, replace, supersede, supplant;
bear, carry, convey, transmit, transport
5 to set or keep in motion or action < the
mechanism that *moves* the locomotive >
syn actuate, drive, impel, mobilize, propel
rel activate, motivate
con bring up, draw up, fetch up, halt,
haul up, pull up, stop
6 *syn* see PROVOKE 4
7 *syn* see AFFECT
rel induce, persuade, prevail
8 *syn* see CONVERT 1
9 *syn* see BEHAVE 1
move *n* 1 *syn* see MEASURE 7
2 *syn* see MOTION 1
rel alteration, change, modification, variation
movement *n* 1 *syn* see MOTION 1
rel action, act, deed; activity, dynamism,
liveness, operation, operativeness
2 *syn* see MOTION 2
mover *n syn* see INSTIGATOR
movie *n* a representation (as of a story) by
means of motion pictures < tired old *movies* that appear on TV>
syn cine, ‖cinema, film, flick, motion
picture, moving picture, photoplay, picture, picture show, show
rel cinematics, cinematography
moving *adj* 1 *syn* see MOVABLE
2 having the power to excite deep and
usually somber emotion < made a *moving*
appeal for help for the orphaned chil-
dren>
syn affecting, impressive, poignant, touching; compare EMOTIONAL 2
rel eloquent, expressive, facund, meaningful, pregnant, sententious, significant;
arousing, awakening, rallying, rousing,
stirring; exciting, provoking, quickening,
stimulating; breathless, gripping
con unaffecting, unimpressive, untouch-
ing; casual, cold, formal
ant unmoving
3 *syn* see EMOTIONAL 2
moving picture *n syn* see MOVIE
mow *n syn* see PILE 1
mow *vb* to cut down standing grass or
grain with a tool or a machine < *mowed*
the lawn every week>

syn synonym(s)   *rel* related word(s)
ant antonym(s)   *con* contrasted word(s)
idiom idiomatic equivalent(s)
‖ use limited; if in doubt, see a dictionary

syn clip, crop, cut

rel reap; pare, trim

mow (down) *vb syn* see FELL 1

mow *n syn* see FACE 6

mow *vb syn* see GRIMACE

moxie *n* 1 *syn* see ENERGY 2

2 *syn* see COURAGE

3 *syn* see FORTITUDE

‖**mozo** *n syn* see WORKER

Mr. *n syn* see HUSBAND

Mrs. *n syn* see WIFE

Mrs. Grundy *n syn* see PRUDE

much *adv* 1 *syn* see VERY 1

2 *syn* see OFTEN

3 *syn* see NEARLY

much *n* a great quantity, amount, extent, or degree <learned *much* worth remembering from his experiences in the army>

syn barrel, great deal, heap, lashings, lot, lump, mass, ‖mess, mountain, multiplicity, pack, peck, pile, plenty, ‖power, ‖sight; *compare* MULTITUDE 1, SCAD

rel excess, overage, oversupply, plethora, superfluity

idiom all kinds of

con bit, crumb, modicum, trifle; deficiency, inadequacy, insufficiency, undersupply

ant little

‖**much** *vb syn* see BABY

much as *conj syn* see THOUGH

muck *n* 1 *syn* see SLIME

2 *syn* see REFUSE

3 *syn* see GOO 1

muck *vb* 1 *syn* see SOIL 2

‖2 *syn* see BOTCH

‖3 *syn* see COMPLICATE

‖4 *syn* see DRUDGE

‖5 *syn* see SAUNTER

‖**muckamuck** *n syn* see FOOD 1

muckamuck *n syn* see NOTABLE 1

mucker *vb syn* see BOTCH

mucker *n* 1 *syn* see BOOR

2 *syn* see WRETCH 1

3 *syn* see TOUGH

mucking *adj syn* see DAMNED 2

muckworm *n syn* see MISER

mucky *adj* 1 *syn* see DIRTY 1

2 *syn* see MURKY 3

3 *syn* see HUMID

‖**mucky** *vb syn* see SOIL 2

mucronate *adj syn* see POINTED 1

mud *vb syn* see ROIL 1

muddle *vb* 1 *syn* see ROIL 1

2 *syn* see MUMBLE

3 *syn* see CONFUSE 2

4 *syn* see CONFUSE 2

5 *syn* see CONFUSE 5

6 *syn* see COMPLICATE

7 *syn* see STUMBLE 6

muddle (away) *vb syn* see WASTE 2

muddle *n* 1 *syn* see CONFUSION 3

2 *syn* see MESS 3

3 *syn* see CLUTTER 2

muddled *adj* 1 *syn* see INCOHERENT 2

2 *syn* see INTOXICATED 1

muddiedness *n syn* see HAZE 2

muddlehead *n syn* see DUNCE

muddleheadedness *n syn* see HAZE 2

muddlement *n syn* see HAZE 2

muddle through *vb syn* see SHIFT 5

muddy *adj* 1 having a great deal of mud <playing in the wet field, he got his shoes all *muddy*>

syn bemired, ‖claggy, ‖clarty, miry, oozy

rel black, dirty, dungy, filthy, foul, grubby, impure, nasty, soily, sordid, squalid, unclean, uncleanly; bedraggled, draggled

con clean, cleanly, immaculate, spotless, taintless, unsoiled, unsullied

ant mudless

2 *syn* see TURBID

rel gloomy, murky; addled, confused, muddled

3 *syn* see DULL 8

muddy *vb* 1 *syn* see SOIL 2

2 *syn* see ROIL 1

3 *syn* see DULL 1

4 *syn* see CONFUSE 4

rel conceal, hide, screen

con illuminate, illumine, light, lighten

mudhole *n* 1 *syn* see POTHOLE

2 *syn* see BURG

muff *vb syn* see BOTCH

muffle *vb* 1 *syn* see BUNDLE UP

rel cover, envelop, overspread, shroud, veil

2 to dull the sound of <closed the door to *muffle* the outside noises>

syn dampen, deaden, mute, stifle

rel mellow, soften, soft-pedal, subdue, tone (down); smother

con amplify, enhance, heighten, magnify, reinforce, strengthen

3 *syn* see SUPPRESS 2

muffler *n syn* see MASK 2

mug *n* 1 *syn* see FACE 1

2 *syn* see FACE 6

3 *syn* see DUNCE

‖4 *syn* see FOOL 3

5 *syn* see TOUGH

mug *vb syn* see GRIMACE

‖**mug (up)** *vb syn* see CRAM 4

muggins *n syn* see DUNCE

muggy *adj syn* see HUMID

rel damp, dampish, moist, moisty, wettish

con dry

mughouse *n syn* see ALEHOUSE

mug-up *n syn* see SNACK

mugwump *n syn* see NOTABLE 1

mulatto *n* a person of mixed Caucasian and Negro ancestry <the special conflicts faced by *mulattoes* with both whites and blacks>

syn high yellow

rel mulatta, mulattress; octoroon, quadroon; sambo, zambo; mustee; half-breed

mulct *n syn* see FINE

mulct *vb* 1 *syn* see PENALIZE

rel claim, demand, exact, require

2 *syn* see FLEECE 1

mule *n syn* see HYBRID

muleheaded *adj syn* see OBSTINATE

muley *adj syn* see OBSTINATE

mulish *adj syn* see OBSTINATE

rel ungovernable, unruly; fixed, set

mull *n syn* see MESS 3

mull *vb* 1 *syn* see DEADEN 1

2 *syn* see CONFUSE 2

3 *syn* see DELAY 2

mull (over) *vb syn* see PONDER 2

mulligrubs *n pl syn* see SULK

rel blues, dejection, depression, (the) dismals, dumps, gloom, heavyheartedness, melancholy, mournfulness, sadness, unhappiness

‖mullock n 1 syn see REFUSE
2 syn see CONFUSION 3
multeity n syn see VARIETY 1
multicolor adj syn see VARIEGATED
ant monotone
multicolored adj syn see VARIEGATED
ant monotone
multifarious adj 1 syn see MANY
2 syn see MANIFOLD
3 syn see MISCELLANEOUS
multifariousness n syn see VARIETY 1
multifold adj syn see MANIFOLD
multiform adj syn see MANIFOLD
ant uniform
multiformity n syn see VARIETY 1
ant uniformity
multihued adj syn see VARIEGATED
ant monotone
multilateral adj having many sides < multilateral figures>
syn many-sided
ant one-sided, unilateral
multiloquent adj syn see TALKATIVE
multiloquious adj syn see TALKATIVE
multiplex adj syn see MANIFOLD
multiplicity n 1 syn see VARIETY 1
ant unity
2 syn see MUCH
multiply vb 1 syn see INCREASE 1
2 syn see INCREASE 2
3 syn see PROCREATE 1
multitude n 1 a very large number of
individuals or things < that child always
asks a multitude of questions>
syn army, cloud, crowd, flock, host, legion, rout, scores; compare CROWD 1,
MUCH, SCAD
rel numbers, oodles, quantities
con few, handful, scattering, smatter,
smattering, sprinkling
ant none
2 syn see CROWD 1
multitudinal adj syn see MANY
rel countless, innumerable, innumerous,
numberless, uncountable, uncounted, unnumberable, unnumbered, untold
multitudinous adj syn see MANY
rel countless, innumerable, innumerous,
numberless, uncountable, uncounted, unnumberable, unnumbered, untold
multivarious adj syn see MANIFOLD
multivocal adj syn see VOCIFEROUS
mum adj syn see SILENT 2
‖mum n syn see MOTHER 1
mumble vb to utter with a low inarticulate
voice < embarrassed, he mumbled an
apology>
syn ‖chunter, fumble, muddle, ‖mump,
murmur, mutter, swallow
rel maunder, limp, shuffle, stumble;
‖hammer, stammer, ‖stut, stutter; speak,
talk, utter, verbalize, vocalize, voice
idiom speak with mush in one's mouth
con speak out, speak up; clamor, cry out,
shout, vociferate
mumble n syn see MURMUR 1
mumblenews n pl but sing or pl in constr
syn see GOSSIP 1

syn synonym(s)   rel related word(s)
ant antonym(s)   con contrasted word(s)
idiom idiomatic equivalent(s)
‖ use limited; if in doubt, see a dictionary

mumbo jumbo n syn see GIBBERISH 3
‖mumchance adj syn see SILENT 2
mummer n syn see ACTOR 1
mummery n syn see GIBBERISH 3
mummify vb syn see WITHER
mummy n syn see MOTHER 1
mummy vb syn see WITHER
‖mump vb 1 syn see MUMBLE
2 syn see GRIMACE
3 syn see SULK
‖mump vb syn see CHEAT
mumpish adj syn see SULLEN
mumps n pl syn see SULK
‖mun vb syn see MUST 2
‖mun n syn see MAN 3
munch vb syn see CHEW 1
mundane adj 1 syn see EARTHLY 1
rel profane, secular, temporal
ant eternal
2 syn see MATERIALISTIC
rel animal, carnal, fleshly
3 syn see PROSAIC 3
municipal adj 1 syn see DOMESTIC 2
2 syn see URBAN
munificent adj syn see LIBERAL 1
con close, mean, niggard, ungiving
murder n the crime of killing a person < a
murder occurred during a gang shoot-
out>
syn blood, ‖bump-off, foul play, homicide, killing, manslaughter
murder vb 1 to kill (a human being) unlawfully and with premeditated malice
< planned a safe way to murder his ri-
val>
syn assassinate, ‖bump off, cool, do in,
‖dust off, execute, finish, knock off, liquidate, put away, rub out, scrag, slay; compare KILL 1
rel asphyxiate, behead, decapitate, elec-
trocute, garrote, guillotine, hang, lynch,
smother, strangle
idiom take for a ride
2 syn see ANNIHILATE 2
murderer n one who kills a human being
< a murderer who wouldn't hesitate to
kill in cold blood>
syn homicide, killer, manslayer, slayer;
compare ASSASSIN
rel butcher, slaughterer
murdering adj syn see MURDEROUS
murderous adj characterized by or of a
kind to cause murder or bloodshed
< made a murderous assault on his former
friend>
syn bloodthirsty, bloody, homicidal, murdering, sanguinary, sanguine, sanguineous
rel deadly; destructive, devastating, ruinous
con harmless, innocuous, trivial
mure vb syn see ENCLOSE 1
murk vb 1 syn see OBSCURE
2 syn see SOIL 2
murky adj 1 syn see DARK 1
rel glooming, glowering, lowering
con bright, brilliant, effulgent, radiant
2 syn see OBSCURE 3
3 having visible material in suspension < a
murky liquid>
syn cloudy, mucky
rel muddy, roily, turbid
con clear, limpid, lucent, translucent,
transparent; clean, fresh, pure, unpolluted

4 *syn* see DULL 8

5 *syn* see DIRTY 1

murmur *n* 1 a low indistinct but often continuous sound (as of voices) <could hear the *murmur* of the audience throughout the entire performance>
syn mumble, mutter, rumor, susurration, undertone, whisper
rel murmuration; buzz, drone, hum, purr; brool

2 *syn* see REPORT 1

murmur *vb* 1 *syn* see GRUMBLE 1

2 *syn* see COMPLAIN

3 *syn* see MUMBLE

muscle *n* 1 muscular strength <loading cargo calls for real *muscle*>
syn beef, brawn, might, sinew, thew
rel power, strength
con impotence

2 *syn* see POWER 4

muscle-bound *adj syn* see STIFF 1

muscular *adj* 1 marked by good well-developed musculature <his arms were lean but *muscular*>
syn fibrous, ropy, sinewy, stringy, wiry
rel flexible, elastic, resilient, springy, supple
con flabby, flaccid, flimsy, floppy, limp, sleazy; feeble, weak

2 strong and powerful in build or action <a *muscular* lad who could wield an ax like a man>
syn athletic, brawny, sinewy; compare STRONG 1
rel stalwart, stout, strong, sturdy; well-built, well-knit, well-set; beefy, burly, husky; Herculean, mighty, powerful
con faint, fragile, frail; delicate, feeble, weak; ||pindling, puny, slight

muse *vb syn* see PONDER 2
rel excogitate, study

muse *n syn* see REVERIE

muse *n syn* see POET

museum *n* a room, building, or locale where a collection of objects is put on exhibition <an art *museum* with a famous collection of jade>
syn gallery
rel salon; picture gallery, pinacotheka

||**mush** *n* 1 *syn* see MOUTH 1

2 *syn* see FACE 1

||**mush** (up) *vb syn* see CRUSH 2

mushroom *vb syn* see EXPLODE 1

mushy *adj* 1 *syn* see SOFT 6

2 *syn* see HAZY

3 *syn* see SENTIMENTAL

music *n syn* see DIN

musical *adj syn* see HARMONIOUS 1
ant unmusical; musicless

2 *syn* see MELODIOUS 2
ant unmusical; musicless

musician *n* one skilled in music <the one playing the sax is a real *musician*>
syn musicianer, ||musicker, musico, virtuoso
rel performer, player

musicianer *n syn* see MUSICIAN

||**musicker** *n syn* see MUSICIAN

musico *n syn* see MUSICIAN

muskeg *n syn* see SWAMP

muss *n* ||1 *syn* see BRAWL 2

2 *syn* see MESS 3

muss (up) *vb syn* see DISORDER 1

rel dishevel, rumple, wrinkle

mussy *adj syn* see SLOVENLY 1

must *verbal auxiliary* 1 *syn* see WANT 3

2 — used to indicate requirement by immediate or future need or purpose <we *must* hurry if we want to catch the bus>
syn have, ||mun, need
rel ought, should want
idiom have got to, must needs

must *n* 1 *syn* see OBLIGATION 2

2 *syn* see ESSENTIAL 2

master *vb* 1 *syn* see ENTER 3

2 *syn* see MOBILIZE 3

3 *syn* see GATHER 6

muster (up) *vb syn* see GENERATE 3

muster *n* 1 *syn* see GATHERING 2

2 *syn* see ROSTER 1

muster out *vb syn* see DISCHARGE 7
ant call up, draft

muster roll *n syn* see ROSTER 1

musty *adj* 1 *syn* see MALODOROUS 1
rel dirty, filthy, squalid

2 *syn* see TRITE

mutable *adj* 1 *syn* see CHANGEABLE 1
rel fluctuating, swaying, swinging, wavering; fickle, inconstant, unstable
con equable, even, steady, uniform; durable, lasting, permanent, stable
ant immutable

2 liable to change or to be changed <a flexible and perhaps too *mutable* policy>
syn changeable, inconstant, shifty, slippery, uncertain, unstable, unsteady, variable; compare CHANGEABLE 1, INCONSTANT 1
rel changeful, protean, unsettled; capricious, fickle, inconsistent, lubricious, mercurial, temperamental, ticklish, volatile; fluctuating, shilly-shally, vacillating, wavering
con constant, established, fixed, immovable, inalterable, invariable, set, unalterable, unchangeable, unmodifiable, unmovable
ant immutable

mutate *vb* 1 *syn* see TRANSFORM

2 *syn* see CHANGE 1

mutation *n* 1 *syn* see CHANGE 1

2 *syn* see CHANGE 2

mute *adj* 1 *syn* see DUMB 1

2 *syn* see SILENT 2
con articulate, eloquent, fluent, glib, vocal, voluble

mute *vb syn* see MUFFLE 2

muted *adj syn* see DULL 7

mutedly *adv syn* see SOTTO VOCE

mutilate *vb* 1 *syn* see MAIM
rel damage, hurt, injure, mar, spoil; deface

2 *syn* see STERILIZE

mutineer *n syn* see REBEL

mutinous *adj syn* see INSUBORDINATE
rel alienated, disaffected

mutiny *vb syn* see REVOLT 1

mutt *n syn* see DUNCE

mutter *vb* 1 *syn* see MUMBLE

2 *syn* see GRUMBLE 1
rel repine, wail

mutter *n syn* see MURMUR 1

muttonchops *n pl syn* see SIDE-WHISKERS

muttonhead *n syn* see DUNCE

mutual *adj syn* see COMMON 1
rel partaken, participated; associated, connected, related, united

mutually *adv syn* see TOGETHER 3

||**mux** *vb syn* see DISORDER 1

muzzle *n syn* see FACE 1

myopic *adj* affected by a condition in which the visual images come to a focus in front of the retina of the eye resulting especially in defective vision of distant objects < so *myopic* that he used glasses even to read >
syn nearsighted, shortsighted
rel presbyopic; astigmatic
ant farsighted, hyperopic, longsighted

myriad-minded *adj syn* see VERSATILE

mysterial *adj syn* see MYSTERIOUS

mysterious *adj* being beyond one's powers to discover, understand, or explain < he had a *mysterious* sense of humor, laughing when other people did not >
syn arcane, cabalistic, impenetrable, inscrutable, mysterial, mystic, numinous, unaccountable, unexaminable, unguessed, unknowable; *compare* INEXPLICABLE, STRANGE 4
rel impenetrable, incognizable, incomprehensible, uncomprehensible, ungraspable, unintelligible, unknowable; abstruse, esoteric, occult, recondite; ambiguous, cryptic, enigmatic, equivocal, obscure
con explainable, explicable; apprehensible, comprehendible, comprehensible, fathomable, graspable, intelligible, knowable, lucid, scrutable; candid, frank, honest, straightforward
ant unmysterious

mystery *n* something which baffles or perplexes < the *mystery* of his disappearance has never been solved >
syn Chinese puzzle, closed book, conundrum, enigma, mystification, puzzle, puzzlement, riddle, why
rel poser, problem, stumper; perplexity; brainteaser, brain twister
con open book

mystic *adj* 1 *syn* see MYSTICAL 1
rel imaginary, visionary; quixotic
2 *syn* see MYSTERIOUS
3 *syn* see MAGIC

mystical *adj* 1 having a spiritual meaning or reality that is neither apparent to the senses nor obvious to the intelligence < the *mystical* food of the sacrament >
syn anagogic, mystic, telestic
rel abysmal, deep, profound; absolute, categorical, ultimate; divine, holy, sacred, spiritual; miraculous, supernatural, supranatural
2 *syn* see SECRET 1

mystification *n syn* see MYSTERY

mystifying *adj syn* see CRYPTIC

myth *n* 1 a traditional story of ostensibly historical content whose origin has been lost < the various Greek *myths* that have come down to us >
syn legend, mythos, mythus; *compare* ALLEGORY 2
rel saga; fable, fabrication, fiction, figment; creation, invention
2 *syn* see ALLEGORY 2
3 *syn* see LORE 2

mythical *adj* lacking factual basis or historical validity < a *mythical* account attributes the founding of the city to Noah >
syn fabulous, legendary, mythological
rel fictional, fictitious, fictive, imaginary, supposititious, unreal; fanciful, fantastic, visionary; created, invented
con actual, real, true; authentic, genuine, veritable; truthful, veracious, verisimilar
ant historical

mythological *adj syn* see MYTHICAL

mythology *n syn* see LORE 2

mythos *n* 1 *syn* see MYTH 1
2 *syn* see LORE 2

mythus *n syn* see MYTH 1

N

nab *vb* 1 *syn* see ARREST 2
2 *syn* see SEIZE 2
3 *syn* see STEAL 1

||**nab** *n* 1 *syn* see POLICEMAN
2 *syn* see ARREST

nabal *n syn* see MISER

nabob *n syn* see NOTABLE 1

nada *n syn* see NOTHINGNESS

nadir *n syn* see BOTTOM 3
con acme, climax, culmination; peak, summit
ant apex, zenith

nag *vb* to find fault incessantly < stop *nagging* her over nothing >
syn carp (at), fuss, henpeck, peck (at)
rel annoy, harass, harry, pester, plague,

tease, worry; bother, irk, vex; badger, bait, chivy, heckle, hector, hound, ride; egg, goad, needle, prod, urge
idiom give a bad (*or* hard) time, pick at (*or* on), take it out on
con commend, compliment, praise; acclaim, applaud, hail

nail *vb* 1 *syn* see CATCH 1
||2 *syn* see SEIZE 2
3 *syn* see STEAL 1
4 *syn* see STRIKE 2

naïve *adj* 1 *syn* see NATURAL 5
rel fresh, original
ant sophisticated
2 *syn* see EASY 3

naked *adj* 1 *syn* see BARE 1
2 *syn* see NUDE 2
3 *syn* see OPEN 2
rel disclosed, discovered, revealed; evident, manifest, obvious, palpable; colorless, uncolored; pure, sheer, simple

namby-pamby *adj* 1 *syn* see INSIPID 3
2 *syn* see CHARACTERLESS

---

syn synonym(s)   *rel* related word(s)
ant antonym(s)   *con* contrasted word(s)
idiom idiomatic equivalent(s)
|| use limited; if in doubt, see a dictionary

namby-pamby *n syn* see WEAKLING

name *n* 1 the word or combination of words by which something is called and by means of which it can be distinguished or identified < the *name* always given to the eldest son> <what is the *name* of that bird?>
syn appellation, appellative, cognomen, compellation, denomination, designation, ‖handle, ‖moniker, nomen, rubric, style, title
rel baptismal name, Christian name, font name, forename, personal name, prename; byname, byword, hypocorism, nickname, pet name, sobriquet; epithet, label, tag; alias, incognito, nom de guerre, nom de plume, pen name, pseudonym
2 *syn* see REPUTATION 2
3 *syn* see CELEBRITY 2

name *vb* 1 to give a name to < *named* the child for his grandfather>
syn baptize, call, christen, denominate, designate, dub, entitle, style, term, title
rel label, tag, ticket; nickname
idiom give a handle, pin a moniker on
2 *syn* see DESIGNATE 2
rel advertise, announce, declare, publish
3 *syn* see MENTION
rel identify, recognize

nameable *adj syn* see NOTEWORTHY

nameless *adj* 1 *syn* see OBSCURE 5
2 *syn* see ANONYMOUS
ant named

namely *adv* that is to say <understandably his wife disapproves of his bad habits, *namely* gambling and fornication>
syn scilicet, to wit, videlicet
rel especially, expressly, particularly, specially, specifically

nana *n syn* see NURSEMAID

‖**nanny** *n syn* see NURSEMAID

nap *n* a short sleep <generally took an hour's *nap* after lunch>
syn catnap, dog nap, ‖dover, forty winks, siesta, snooze; *compare* DOZE, SLEEP 1
rel dogsleep; break, interlude, intermission, let up, pause, respite, rest

nap *vb* to sleep briefly < *napped* for an hour after lunch>
syn catnap, ‖caulk (off), siesta, snooze; *compare* DOZE, SLEEP
rel drowse; relax, rest, unlax
idiom catch a wink of sleep, catch forty winks, take a nap (*or* siesta *or* snooze)

narcissism *n syn* see CONCEIT 2

narcissistic *adj syn* see VAIN 3

narcotic *n* 1 *syn* see DRUG 2
2 *syn* see ANODYNE 2

narcotic *adj syn* see SOPORIFIC 1

‖**nark** *n syn* see INFORMER

‖**nark** *vb syn* see INFORM 3

narrate *vb syn* see RELATE 1
rel descant, dilate, discourse, expatiate

narration *n* 1 *syn* see DESCRIPTION 2
2 *syn* see STORY 2

narrative *n* 1 *syn* see STORY 2
2 *syn* see ACCOUNT 7

narrow *adj* 1 *syn* see DEFINITE 1
2 *syn* see LITTLE 2
3 *syn* see ILLIBERAL
rel inexorable, inflexible, obdurate
con forbearing, indulgent, lenient, tolerant
ant broad

‖4 *syn* see STINGY

narrow *vb syn* see CONSTRICT 2

narrow-fisted *adj syn* see STINGY
ant openhanded

narrowhearted *adj syn* see STINGY
ant openhearted

narrow-minded *adj syn* see ILLIBERAL
ant broad-minded

nascent *adj syn* see INITIAL 1

nasty *adj* 1 *syn* see DIRTY 1
rel coarse, gross, obscene, ribald, vulgar; improper, indecent, indecorous, indelicate, unseemly
2 *syn* see OFFENSIVE
3 *syn* see OBSCENE 2
4 *syn* see MALICIOUS

nates *n pl syn* see BUTTOCKS

national *adj* 1 *syn* see PUBLIC 1
2 *syn* see DOMESTIC 2

national *n syn* see CITIZEN 2

native *adj* 1 *syn* see INNATE 1
2 belonging to a locality by birth or origin < a *native* tradition> <delighted with the tasty *native* fruits>
syn aboriginal, autochthonous, endemic, indigenous
rel domestic, local
con adopted, introduced, naturalized
ant alien, foreign, nonnative
3 *syn* see DOMESTIC 2
4 *syn* see WILD 1
5 *syn* see UNREFINED 3

Nativity *n syn* see CHRISTMAS

‖**natter** *vb syn* see CHAT 1

‖**natty** *adj syn* see DAPPER

natural *adj* 1 *syn* see ILLEGITIMATE 1
2 *syn* see INNATE 1
ant abnormal, unnatural
3 *syn* see GENERAL 1
4 *syn* see WILD 1
5 free from pretension or calculation <he spoke in a perfectly *natural* manner>
syn artless, guileless, inartificial, ingenuous, innocent, naive, simple, simplehearted, unaffected, unartful, unartificial, unschooled, unsophisticated, unstudied, untutored, unworldly; *compare* GENUINE 3
rel impulsive, instinctive, spontaneous; easy, unlabored; constitutional, ingrained, inherent; folksy, homespun, unpretentious; ignorant, primitive, undesigning; unconstrained, unembarrassed; candid, frank, open, plain; sincere, unfeigned; provincial, rustic
con ceremonial, ceremonious, conventional, formal; ostentatious, pretentious, showy; assumed, contrived, counterfeited, feigned, pretended; artful, sophisticated, studied
ant affected; artificial, unnatural

natural *n syn* see FOOL 4

natural child *n syn* see BASTARD 1

naturalness *n syn* see UNCONSTRAINT
ant unnaturalness

nature *n* 1 *syn* see TYPE
rel anatomy, framework, structure; conformation, figure, shape
2 *syn* see ESSENCE 1
3 *syn* see DISPOSITION 3
4 *syn* see UNIVERSE

naught (*or* **nought**) *n* 1 *syn* see NOTHING 1

2 *syn* see ZERO

naughty *adj* 1 guilty of misbehavior <a *naughty* boy who teased the cat and upset the milk>
syn bad, ill-behaved, misbehaving, mischievous, paw; *compare* DISOBEDIENT
rel contrary, froward, perverse, wayward; headstrong, intractable, recalcitrant, refractory, ungovernable, unruly, willful; disorderly, rowdy, ruffianly; evil, indecorous, wicked
con decorous, good, well-behaved; amenable, docile, obedient, tractable; amiable, complaisant, good-natured, obliging; polite, proper; considerate, kindly, thoughtful
2 *syn* see DISOBEDIENT

nausea *n* a stomach distress with an urge to vomit <overcome with *nausea* as the boat continued to pitch and wallow>
syn qualmishness, queasiness, squeamishness

nauseate *vb syn* see DISGUST

nauseated *adj* affected with nausea <was *nauseated* after taking the drug>
syn nauseous, squeamish; *compare* SQUEAMISH 1
rel choking, gagging; heaving; barfing, upchucking, vomiting
idiom ready (*or* about) to lose one's cookies

nauseating *adj syn* see OFFENSIVE
ant appetizing

nauseous *adj syn* see NAUSEATED

nautical *adj syn* see MARINE 2

navigable *adj syn* see PASSABLE
ant unnavigable

navigational *adj syn* see MARINE 2

nawob *n syn* see NOTABLE 1

nay *adv* 1 *syn* see NO
2 *syn* see EVEN 3

naze *n syn* see PROMONTORY

neanderthal *adj syn* see OLD-FASHIONED

near *adv* 1 *syn* see CLOSE
ant far
2 *syn* see ABOUT 5

near *prep* 1 *syn* see ABOUT 1
2 not far distant from <kept the boy *near* him>
syn ‖aside, beside, by, nearby, nigh, round
idiom close to, hard by, within earshot, within reach, within sight

near *adj* 1 *syn* see CLOSE 6
ant far
2 *syn* see COMPARATIVE

near *vb syn* see APPROACH 1
rel equal, match, rival, touch
con alter, change, modify, vary; differ

‖**nearabout** *adv syn* see NEARLY

near-at-hand *adj* 1 *syn* see NEIGHBORING
2 *syn* see CLOSE 6
3 *syn* see CONVENIENT 2

near-at-hand *adv syn* see ABOUT 5

nearby *adv* 1 *syn* see CLOSE
2 *syn* see ABOUT 5

nearby *prep* 1 *syn* see NEAR 2

2 *syn* see ABOUT 1

nearby *adj* 1 *syn* see CLOSE 6
2 *syn* see NEIGHBORING
3 *syn* see CONVENIENT 2

nearing *adj syn* see FORTHCOMING

nearly *adv* very close to <our work is *nearly* done for today>
syn about, all but, almost, approximately, as good as, just about, more or less, most, much, ‖nearabout, nigh, practically, roughly, round, roundly, rudely, say, some, somewhere, well-nigh
rel virtually
idiom as near as never mind(s), in effect, in essence, in substance, in the main, nigh on (*or* onto *or* upon), to all (practical) intents and purposes

nearsighted *adj syn* see MYOPIC

neat *adj* 1 *syn* see STRAIGHT 3
2 manifesting care and orderliness <always kept a *neat* house>
syn chipper, orderly, prim, shipshape, snug, spick-and-span, tidy, trig, trim, uncluttered, well-groomed; *compare* DAPPER
rel clean, immaculate, spotless; dainty, fastidious, finicky, nice; methodical, regular, systematic; accurate, correct, exact, precise
idiom in good order, neat as a pin (*or* bandbox), neat as can be, neat as wax
con disheveled, disordered, slipshod, sloppy, slovenly, unkempt, untidy; dirty, filthy, foul, nasty; lax, negligent, remiss, slack
ant disorderly, messy
‖3 *syn* see MARVELOUS 2

neat-handed *adj syn* see DEXTEROUS 1

neb *n syn* see BILL 1

‖**nebby** *adj syn* see IMPERTINENT 2

‖**necessary** *n syn* see PRIVY 1

necessary *adj* 1 *syn* see ESSENTIAL 4
rel compelling, compulsory, constraining, mandatory, obligatory; important, momentous, significant; cardinal, fundamental
con insignificant, unessential, unimportant
ant unnecessary
2 *syn* see INEVITABLE
rel inerrable, inerrant, infallible, unerring

necessitate *vb syn* see DEMAND 2

necessitous *adj* 1 *syn* see POOR 1
rel depleted, drained, exhausted
2 *syn* see ESSENTIAL 4

necessity *n* 1 *syn* see NEED 4
rel coercion, compulsion, constraint, duress, obligation; indispensableness, needfulness, requisiteness
2 *syn* see OCCASION 3
3 *syn* see ESSENTIAL 2

neck *vb syn* see BEHEAD

necrology *n syn* see OBITUARY

necromancer *n syn* see MAGICIAN 1

necromancy *n syn* see MAGIC 1

necromantic *adj syn* see MAGIC

necropolis *n syn* see CEMETERY

necropsy *n syn* see AUTOPSY

‖**neddy** *n syn* see DONKEY 1

need *n* 1 *syn* see OBLIGATION 2
2 *syn* see REQUIREMENT 1
3 opportunity or requirement to employ <found little *need* for his rifle>
syn demand, occasion, use

---

syn synonym(s)   *rel* related word(s)
ant antonym(s)   *con* contrasted word(s)
idiom idiomatic equivalent(s)
‖ use limited; if in doubt, see a dictionary

rel call, claim, exaction

4 a pressing lack of something essential < he is in *need* of food >
syn exigency, necessity
rel deficiency, deficit, lack, shortage, want
con adequacy, enough, sufficiency
5 *syn* see POVERTY 1

need *vb* **1** *syn* see LACK
rel claim, demand, exact; hanker, hunger, long, pine, thirst, yearn; covet, crave, desire, wish
2 *syn* see MUST 2

needed *adj syn* see NEEDFUL
ant unneeded

needful *adj* necessary for supply or relief < provided them with everything *need-ful* >
syn needed, required, requisite
rel essential, imperative, indispensable, necessary; lacked, wanted; cardinal, fundamental, vital
con excess, redundant, superfluous; nonessential, unessential; uncalled-for, unnecessary, unneeded
ant needless

needful *n syn* see MONEY

neediness *n syn* see POVERTY 1

needle *vb syn* see WORRY 1

needless *adj syn* see UNNECESSARY
ant needful

needy *adj syn* see POOR 1

ne'er *adv syn* see NEVER

ne'er-do-well *n syn* see WASTREL 1

nefarious *adj syn* see VICIOUS 2
rel atrocious, heinous, monstrous, outrageous; flagrant, glaring, gross, rank
ant exemplary

negate *vb* **1** *syn* see DENY 4
ant affirm
2 *syn* see ABOLISH 1
3 *syn* see NEUTRALIZE

negation *n syn* see DENIAL 2
ant affirmation

negative *adj syn* see ADVERSE 2

negative *vb* **1** *syn* see VETO
2 *syn* see DENY 4
ant affirm
3 *syn* see NEUTRALIZE
rel abrogate, invalidate, nullify

neglect *vb* to pass over without giving due attention < *neglected* his family for the sake of his mistress >
syn blink (at *or* away), discount, disregard, elide, fail, forget, ignore, miss, omit, overleap, overlook, overpass, pass, pass by, pass over, pretermit, slight, slough over, slur (over)
rel brush (off *or* aside), disdain, dismiss, reject, scant, scorn, shrug away, shrug off
idiom pay no attention to, pay no heed (*or* mind), think little of
con appreciate, prize, treasure, value; cultivate, foster, nurse, nurture
ant cherish

neglect *n syn* see FAILURE 1

neglected *adj* not properly or sufficiently attended to or cared for < the whole property had a *neglected* appearance >
syn run-down, uncared-for, untended
rel disregarded, ignored, overlooked, slighted, unheeded
con prized, treasured; fostered, tended; guarded, supervised, watched

ant cherished

neglectful *adj syn* see NEGLIGENT
ant attentive

negligent *adj* failing to give proper attention or care < *negligent* in taking care of the children > < a *negligent* man, prone to forgetfulness >
syn behindhand, careless, delinquent, derelict, disdnct, disregardful, lax, neglectful, regardless, remiss, slack
rel heedless, inadvertent, inattentive, inconsiderate, thoughtless, unheedful, unthinking; incurious, indifferent, unconcerned; slipshod, slovenly
con rigid, rigorous, strict; attentive, considerate, heedful, thoughtful; careful, exact, fussy, meticulous, punctilious, punctual, scrupulous
ant attentive

negligible *adj syn* see REMOTE 4
ant significant

negotiable *adj syn* see PASSABLE
ant nonnegotiable

negotiate *vb* **1** to bring about by mutual agreement < *negotiate* a treaty >
syn arrange, concert, settle
rel adjust, compose, transact; agree, bargain, contract, covenant
con break off, intermit, interrupt, suspend; differ, disagree, dissent
2 *syn* see CLEAR 8

neigh *vb* to make the cry typical of a horse < the frightened horse *neighed* and stamped >
syn nicker, whicker, ||whinner, whinny

neighbor *vb syn* see ADJOIN

neighborhood *n* **1** *syn* see LOCALITY 1
2 *syn* see ORDER 4

neighboring *adj* not distant < the need for understanding between *neighboring* countries >
syn adjacent, close-at-hand, close-by, contiguous, near-at-hand, nearby; *compare* CLOSE 6
rel abutting, adjoining, bordering, conterminous, touching; close, near
con distant, far, faraway, far-off, remote, removed; parted, separated

neighborly *adj syn* see AMICABLE
rel cooperative, gregarious, hospitable, social; cordial, gracious, sociable
ant unneighborly; ill-disposed

neonate *n syn* see BABY 1

neophyte *n syn* see NOVICE

neoteric *adj syn* see NEW 1

nepenthe *n syn* see ANODYNE 2

ne plus ultra *n syn* see APEX 2

nerve *n* **1** *syn* see FORTITUDE
2 *syn* see TEMERITY
3 *syn* see EFFRONTERY

nerve *vb syn* see ENCOURAGE 1

nerve center *n syn* see CENTER 2

nervous *adj* easily upset or irritated < a *nervous* fretful woman >
syn fidgety, goosey, high-strung, jittery, jumpy, nervy, spooky, twittery, unrestful
rel agitated, edgy, excitable, skittish, volatile; fretful, irritable, querulous, snappish, waspish
con calm, placid, serene, steady, tranquil; collected, composed, cool, imperturbable, inexcitable, poised, unflappable, unruffled
ant nerveless

nervous breakdown *n* an emotional disorder often characterized by depression, tenseness, irritability, headache, and susceptibility to fatigue < worked and worried himself into a *nervous breakdown* >
syn breakdown, collapse, crack-up, nervous prostration
rel neurasthenia; prostration

nervous prostration *n syn* see NERVOUS BREAKDOWN

nervy *adj* 1 *syn* see WISE 5
2 *syn* see NERVOUS
rel excitable, fidgety, jerky, tense, twitchy
idiom tied up in knots
con composed, easy, relaxed
ant phlegmatic
3 *syn* see TENSE 2

nescience *n syn* see IGNORANCE 2

nest egg *n syn* see RESERVE

nestle *vb syn* see SNUGGLE

net *vb syn* see CLEAR 6

nether *adj syn* see INFERIOR 1

nethermost *adj syn* see BOTTOMMOST
ant uppermost

netherwards *adv syn* see DOWN 1
ant upwards

netherworld *n syn* see HELL

nettle *vb syn* see IRRITATE
rel agitate, discompose, disturb, perturb, upset

nettlesome *adj syn* see THORNY

neuter *vb syn* see STERILIZE

neutral *adj* not experiencing or generating a strong emotional commitment or response < made a *neutral* response to his challenge >
syn abstract, colorless, detached, disinterested, dispassionate, impersonal, poker-faced, unpassioned
rel clinical, collected, composed, cool, nonchalant; calm, easy, relaxed; aloof, indifferent
con intemperate, loaded; fervent, impassioned, passionate, vehement

neutralize *vb* to make inoperative or ineffective usually by means of an opposite force, influence, or effect < attacked by the kind of propaganda that is difficult to *neutralize* >
syn annul, cancel (out), counteract, countercheck, frustrate, negate, negative, redress
rel balance, compensate, counterbalance, counterpoise, countervail, offset; abrogate, invalidate, nullify; conquer, defeat, overcome, subdue; override, overrule
con activate, animate, dynamize, vitalize

never *adv* not at any time < they had *never* seen him before >
syn ne'er
idiom never in all one's born days, never in one's life, never in the world, never on earth
con constantly, continuously, ever, invariably, perpetually
ant always

never-ending *adj syn* see EVERLASTING 1

ant ended; transitory

never-failing *adj syn* see SURE 2

nevertheless *adv syn* see HOWEVER

nevus *n syn* see BIRTHMARK 1

new *adj* 1 recently come into existence or use or a particular state or relation < *new* styles that flatter stout figures >
syn fresh, modern, modernistic, neoteric, newfangled, new-fashioned, new-sprung, novel, recent
rel first-hand, independent, primary
con dated, outdated, outmoded, out-of-date; shabby, worn; hackneyed, old hat, trite
ant old
2 *syn* see UNFAMILIAR 1
3 *syn* see ADDITIONAL
4 *syn* see REFRESHED

new *adv* within recent time < the scent of *new-*mown grass >
syn afresh, anew, lately, newly, of late, recently
con aforetime, before, earlier, formerly; heretofore, hitherto
ant once

newborn *n syn* see BABY 1

newcomer *n syn* see NOVICE

newfangled *adj syn* see NEW 1
ant oldfangled

new-fashioned *adj syn* see NEW 1
ant old-fashioned

New Jerusalem *n syn* see HEAVEN 2

newly *adv syn* see NEW

news *n pl but sing in constr* a report of events or conditions not previously known < her friend gave her the bad *news* >
syn advice, information, intelligence, speerings, tidings, word
rel announcement, report; dope, lowdown, ||poop; gossip, rumor, tattle

newsmonger *n syn* see GOSSIP 1

newspaper *n syn* see JOURNAL

new-sprung *adj syn* see NEW 1

next *adj* being the one that comes immediately after another < the *next* day >
syn coming, ensuing, following; *compare* CONSECUTIVE
rel proximate

next *adv syn* see AFTER

next *prep syn* see AFTER 2

next to *prep syn* see BESIDE 1

nexus *n syn* see BOND 3

niagara *n syn* see FLOOD 2

nib *n syn* see BILL 1

||nibby *adj syn* see CURIOUS 2

nice *adj* 1 having or displaying exacting standards < too *nice* about his food to like camp cooking >
syn ||choicy, choosy, clerkish, dainty, delicate, fastidious, finical, finicking, finicky, fussy, miminy-piminy, ||mincy, niminy-piminy, old-maidish, old-womanish, particular, pernickety, persnickety, picksome, picky, precious, squeamish, squeamy
rel discerning, discriminating, penetrating; overparticular; queasy; careful, meticulous, punctilious, scrupulous; judicious, sage, sapient, wise
con coarse, gross, vulgar; callow, crude, green, raw, uncouth; lax, neglectful, negligent, remiss, slack; careless, sloppy, slovenly

---

syn synonym(s)   *rel* related word(s)
ant antonym(s)   *con* contrasted word(s)
idiom idiomatic equivalent(s)
|| use limited; if in doubt, see a dictionary

2 *syn* see FINE 1

3 *syn* see PLEASANT 1

4 *syn* see CORRECT 2

  rel rigid, strict, stringent; exquisite, rare

  con haphazard, happy-go-lucky, hit-or-miss, random; careless, heedless, inadvertent

5 *syn* see DECOROUS 1

nicely *adv syn* see WELL 1

nice Nelly *n* 1 *syn* see PRUDE

2 *syn* see EUPHEMISM

nice-nellyism *n syn* see EUPHEMISM

niche *n syn* see NOOK

nick *n syn* see NOTCH 1

‖**nick** *vb syn* see STEAL 1

nicker *vb syn* see NEIGH

nickname *n* a descriptive or familiar name that is used instead of or in addition to one's proper name <because he was a redhead his friends gave him the *nickname* "Red">

  syn byname, byword, ‖handle, hypocorism, ‖moniker, sobriquet

  rel first name, middle name; appellation, appellative, compellation, denomination, style; epithet, label, tag

nictate *vb syn* see WINK

nictitate *vb syn* see WINK

nidorous *adj syn* see MALODOROUS 1

nifty *adj syn* see MARVELOUS 2

nifty *n syn* see ‖DILLY

niggard *n syn* see MISER

niggard *adj syn* see STINGY

niggardly *adj syn* see STINGY

  ant bounteous, bountiful

niggling *adj syn* see PETTY 2

nigh *adv* 1 *syn* see CLOSE

2 *syn* see NEARLY

nigh *adj syn* see CLOSE 6

nigh *prep* 1 *syn* see NEAR 2

2 *syn* see ABOUT 1

nigh *vb syn* see APPROACH 1

night *n* the time from dusk to dawn <stayed up all *night*>

  syn nighttide, nighttime

  con day, daytime

night *adj syn* see NIGHTLY

night and day *adv syn* see TOGETHER 2

nightclub *n* a restaurant serving liquor and providing entertainment <Las Vegas *nightclubs*>

  syn bistro, cabaret, café, discotheque, hot spot, nightery, night spot, nitery, supper club, watering hole, watering place

nightery *n syn* see NIGHTCLUB

nightfall *n syn* see EVENING 1

nightly *adj* of, relating to, or associated with the night <*nightly* noises>

  syn night, nocturnal

  con daily, diurnal; matutinal, morning; evening, twilight, vespertine

nightmare *n syn* see FANCY 4

night spot *n syn* see NIGHTCLUB

nightstick *n syn* see CUDGEL

nighttide *n syn* see NIGHT

nighttime *n syn* see NIGHT

nightwalker *n syn* see PROSTITUTE

nihility *n syn* see NOTHINGNESS

nil *n syn* see NOTHING 1

nim *vb syn* see STEAL 1

nimble *adj* 1 *syn* see AGILE

  rel light, lightsome; alert, vigilant, watchful, wide-awake

2 *syn* see DEXTEROUS 1

nimble-witted *adj syn* see WISE 4

  ant slow-witted

niminy-piminy *adj syn* see NICE 1

nimmer *n syn* see THIEF

nincom *n syn* see FOOL 1

nincompoop *n syn* see FOOL 1

ninny *n syn* see FOOL 1

ninnyhammer *n syn* see FOOL 1

nip *vb* 1 *syn* see BLAST 1

  rel arrest, check; press, squeeze; balk, frustrate, thwart

2 *syn* see STEAL 1

‖3 *syn* see HURRY 2

nip *n syn* see DRAM

nip *vb syn* see DRINK 3

‖**nipcheese** *n syn* see MISER

‖**nipper** *n syn* see CHILD 1

nipping *adj syn* see COLD 1

nippy *adj syn* see COLD 1

nirvana *n syn* see HEAVEN 2

nisse *n syn* see FAIRY

nit *adv syn* see NO

nitery *n syn* see NIGHTCLUB

nitwit *n syn* see DUNCE

nitwitted *adj syn* see SIMPLE 3

nix *n syn* see NOTHING 1

‖**nix** *adv syn* see NO

nix *vb syn* see VETO

no *adv* — used as a function word to express negation, dissent, denial, or refusal <*no*, you can't come with me>

  syn nay, ‖nit, ‖nix, ‖nope

  idiom by no manner of means, by no means, in no case, no dice, not at any price, not for love or money, not for the life of me, not for the world, nothing doing, not on your life, on no account, on no condition, under no circumstances

  ant yes

‖**no-account** *adj syn* see WORTHLESS 1

Noachian *adj syn* see ANCIENT 1

noble *adj* 1 *syn* see GRAND 1

  rel eminent, illustrious

  con beggarly, contemptible, despicable, scurvy, sorry

  ant cheap, ignoble, unnoble

2 *syn* see ELEVATED 2

  ant base

3 *syn* see HONORABLE 1

  ant ignoble

4 *syn* see MORAL 1

nobody *pron syn* see NO ONE

  ant everybody; somebody

nobody *n syn* see NONENTITY

  ant somebody

nocent *adj syn* see HARMFUL

  ant innocent

nocturnal *adj syn* see NIGHTLY

  con daily, diurnal

nocuous *adj syn* see HARMFUL

  ant innocuous

nodding *adj syn* see SLEEPY 1

noddle *n syn* see HEAD 1

noddy *n syn* see DUNCE

noel *n syn* see CHRISTMAS

noggin *n syn* see HEAD 1

no-good *adj syn* see WORTHLESS 1

no-good *n* 1 *syn* see WASTREL 1

2 *syn* see WRETCH 1

noise *n syn* see SOUND 1

  rel babel, clamor, din, hubbub, pandemonium, racket, uproar *con* quiet, silence, stillness

noise (about *or* abroad) *vb syn* see GOSSIP

noiseful *adj syn* see NOISY
ant noiseless, silent

noiseless *adj syn* see STILL 3
con boisterous, clamorous, strident, vociferous
ant noiseful, noisy

noiselessness *n syn* see SILENCE 1
ant noisiness

noisome *adj* 1 *syn* see UNWHOLESOME 1
ant wholesome

2 *syn* see MALODOROUS 1
rel dirty, filthy, squalid; loathsome, revolting
ant balmy

3 *syn* see OFFENSIVE

noisy *adj* making noise < the *noisiest* car you ever heard >
syn clangorous, clattery, noiseful, rackety, sonorous, uproarious
rel blatant, boisterous, clamorous, obstreperous, strepitous, strident, vociferous; tumultuous, turbulent
con quiet, silent, still, stilly
ant noiseless

nomadic *adj syn* see ITINERANT

no man *pron syn* see NO ONE
ant everybody, everyman

nom de guerre *n syn* see PSEUDONYM

nomen *n syn* see NAME 1

nominal *adj* being something in name or form only < the *nominal* head of his party >
syn formal, so-called, titular
rel apparent, ostensible, seeming; alleged, pretended, professed
idiom in name only
con genuine, real, true
ant actual

nominate *vb syn* see DESIGNATE 2
rel intend, mean, propose, purpose; offer, present, proffer, tender

nonadhesive *adj syn* see LOOSE 3

nonage *n syn* see INFANCY 2
ant age

nonchalant *adj syn* see COOL 2
rel cheerful, glad, lighthearted; easy, effortless, light, smooth
con anxious, careful, concerned, solicitous, worried

noncombustible *adj* incapable of being burned < *noncombustible* material was used whenever possible >
syn apyrous, incombustible, nonflammable, noninflammable, uninflammable
rel fireproof, fire-resistant, fire-resistive, fire-retardant, flameproof
con flammable, inflammable
ant combustible

noncommittal *adj syn* see RESERVED 1

noncompos *n syn* see LUNATIC 1

non compos mentis *adj syn* see INSANE 1

nonconformism *n syn* see HERESY
ant conformism

nonconformist *n* 1 *syn* see HERETIC
ant conformist

2 *syn* see BOHEMIAN
ant conformist

nonconformist *adj syn* see HERETICAL

nonconformity *n syn* see HERESY
ant conformity

noncreative *adj syn* see UNORIGINAL
ant creative

nondiscriminatory *adj syn* see FAIR 4
ant discriminatory

none *pron syn* see NO ONE

nonentity *n* an utterly insignificant person < tired of dealing with subordinates and *nonentities* >
syn cipher, insignificancy, nobody, nothing, nullity, rushlight, whiffet, whippersnapper, whipster, zero, zilch
rel lightweight, obscurity, sad sack, small beer, small fry
idiom blank space in the rear rank, man in the street, no great shakes

nonesuch *n syn* see PARAGON
idiom one in a million

nonessential *adj syn* see DISPENSABLE
ant essential

nonetheless *adv syn* see HOWEVER

nonexistence *n syn* see NOTHINGNESS
ant existence; reality

nonflammable *adj syn* see NONCOMBUSTIBLE
ant flammable, inflammable

nonfunctional *adj syn* see IMPRACTICABLE 2
ant functional

noninflammable *adj syn* see NONCOMBUSTIBLE
ant flammable, inflammable

nonliterate *adj syn* see PRIMITIVE 6

nonmaterial *adj syn* see IMMATERIAL 1
ant material

nonobligatory *adj syn* see OPTIONAL
ant obligatory

no-nonsense *adj syn* see SERIOUS 1

nonpareil *n syn* see PARAGON

nonpartisan *adj syn* see FAIR 4
ant partisan

nonphysical *adj syn* see IMMATERIAL 1
ant physical

non-placet *vb syn* see VETO

nonplus *vb* 1 to cause to be at a total loss as to how to act or decide < was totally *nonplussed* by the economic problems >
syn beat, buffalo, get, stick, stump; *compare* PUZZLE
rel baffle, frustrate, stymie, thwart; confound, perplex; mystify; dumbfound; overcome, throw; paralyze; confuse, flurry, fluster, muddle, rattle
idiom put (*or* drive) to one's wit's end, put up a tree (*or* stump), throw on one's beam end

2 *syn* see STAGGER 5
rel faze, rattle; baffle, balk, frustrate

nonprofessional *n syn* see AMATEUR 2
ant professional

nonrational *adj syn* see ILLOGICAL
ant rational

nonrealistic *adj syn* see IMPRACTICAL 1
ant realistic

nonreligious *adj syn* see IRRELIGIOUS
rel lay, profane, secular, temporal
ant religious

nonresistant *adj syn* see PASSIVE 2
ant resistant, resisting

---

syn synonym(s)   *rel* related word(s)
ant antonym(s)   *con* contrasted word(s)
idiom idiomatic equivalent(s)

‖ use limited; if in doubt, see a dictionary

nonresisting adj syn see PASSIVE 2
ant resistant, resisting
nonreversible adj syn see IRREVOCABLE
ant reversible
nonsectarian adj not affiliated with or restricted to a particular religious group <the problems facing *nonsectarian* colleges>
syn interchurch, intercreedal, interdenominational, undenominational, unsectarian
con denominational
ant sectarian
nonsense n 1 syn see GIBBERISH 1
2 something uttered or proposed that seems senseless or absurd <his theories are mere *nonsense*>
syn ||applesauce, balderdash, ||baloney, bilge, blague, blah, blather, blatherskite, bosh, ||bull, ||bunk, bunkum, bushwa, claptrap, ||cock, ||crap, double-talk, ||drip, drivel, drool, eyewash, fiddle-faddle, fiddlesticks, flapdoodle, flimflam, flummadiddle, fudge, ||gas, gook, guff, hogwash, hokum, hooey, ||horsefeathers, hot air, humbug, jazz, ||jiggery-pokery, malarkey, meshuggaas, moonshine, piffle, pishposh, poppycock, punk, rot, rubbish, slipslop, tomfoolery, tommyrot, tosh, trash, trumpery, twaddle, whangdoodle, windbaggery
idiom stuff and nonsense
nonsuccess n syn see FAILURE 2
ant success, successfulness
nonsymmetrical adj syn see LOPSIDED
ant symmetrical
nonviolent adj syn see PACIFIC
ant violent
noodle n 1 syn see DUNCE
2 syn see HEAD 1
nook n a secluded or sheltered place <resting in a shady *nook*>
syn byplace, cranny, niche
rel alcove, recess; cubbyhole, hole
noon n syn see APEX 2
no one pron no person <*no one* will be allowed to leave early>
syn nobody, no man, none
idiom never a one, nobody on earth, nobody under the sun, not a blessed soul, not a soul
con all, everyman; many, some
ant everybody, everyone
noontide n syn see APEX 2
noose vb syn see HANG 1
||**nope** adv syn see NO
ant ||yep, ||yup
norm n syn see AVERAGE
normal adj 1 syn see SANE 2
2 syn see GENERAL 1
nose n 1 the prominent part of the human face that bears the nostrils and covers the nasal passage <had a large *nose*>
syn beak, ||beezer, ||boko, ||conk, pecker, proboscis, ||schnozzle, smeller, ||sneezer, ||snitch, snoot, snout
2 syn see BUSYBODY
3 syn see GIFT 2
nose vb 1 syn see SMELL 1
2 syn see SNOOP
nose-dive vb syn see PLUMMET
nosegay n syn see BOUQUET 1
nosey Parker n syn see BUSYBODY
Nostradamus n syn see PROPHET
nostrum n syn see PANACEA

nosy adj syn see CURIOUS 2
notability n 1 syn see NOTABLE 1
2 syn see CELEBRITY 2
notable adj 1 syn see NOTEWORTHY
2 syn see FAMOUS 2
notable n 1 a person of consequence or prominence <*notables* of Congress and the diplomatic corps>
syn big, big boy, ||big bug, ||big cheese, ||big chief, ||biggie, big gun, ||big noise, big shot, big-timer, ||big wheel, bigwig, character, chief, dignitary, eminence, ||fat cat, great gun, heavyweight, high-muck-a-muck, leader, lion, luminary, muckamuck, mugwump, nabob, nawob, notability, personage, personality, pooh-bah, pot, somebody, VIP
rel figure; baron, czar, king, magnate, mogul, prince; light, star; power
idiom big-time operator, his nibs, Mr. Big
con cipher, nobody, nonentity; functionary, underling
2 syn see CELEBRITY 2
notably adv syn see VERY 1
notandum n syn see NOTE 2
notation n syn see NOTE 2
notch n 1 a usually V-shaped depression in an edge or surface <a *notch* in the table>
syn indentation, indenture, nick; compare DEPRESSION 2
rel cut, gash, incision, score, scratch; cleft, gap, nock
2 syn see DEGREE 1
note vb syn see SEE 1
note n 1 syn see CALL 1
2 a written reminder <made a *note* to return the call>
syn chit, memo, memorandum, notandum, notation
3 syn see REMARK 2
rel reminder
4 syn see LETTER 2
5 syn see NOTICE 1
noted adj syn see WELL-KNOWN
ant unnoted
note-perfect adj syn see PERFECT 2
noteworthy adj having a quality that attracts one's attention <a *noteworthy* event>
syn ||bodacious, memorable, nameable, notable, observable, red-letter, rubric
rel conspicuous, noticeable, outstanding, prominent, remarkable; evident, manifest, patent; exceptional, extraordinary
con blah, common, commonplace, inconsequential, insignificant, ordinary, quotidian, unimportant, unremarkable
ant unnoteworthy
nothing n 1 something that does not exist <his hopes were based on *nothing*>
syn naught (or nought), nil, ||nix, wind
idiom nothing at all, nothing whatever
con something
2 syn see ZERO 1
3 syn see NONENTITY
idiom (the) little end of nothing whittled down to a point
nothing adj syn see WORTHLESS 1
nothingness n the quality or state of being nothing <the house was blown into *nothingness* by the force of the explosion>
syn nada, nihility, nonexistence, nullity, vacuity

rel emptiness; vacuum, void
con concreteness, solidity, substantiality; materiality, reality
ant somethingness

notice *n* **1** a noting of or concerning oneself with something <take *notice* of the gathering clouds>
syn attention, cognizance, ear, heed, mark, ‖mind, note, observance, observation, regard, remark
rel care, concern, consideration, thought; apprehension, grasp, understanding
con disinterest, disregard, indifference, unconcern; carelessness, heedlessness, unmindfulness; insouciance, negligence, recklessness
2 *syn* see MEMORANDUM 2
3 *syn* see CRITICISM

notice *vb syn* see SEE 1
rel acknowledge, recognize; advert, allude, refer
con disregard, ignore, neglect, overlook, slight

noticeable *adj* attracting or compelling notice or attention <they both showed a *noticeable* aversion to his company>
syn arresting, arrestive, conspicuous, eye-catching, marked, outstanding, pointed, prominent, remarkable, salient, sensational, signal, striking
rel notable, noteworthy; evident, manifest, obvious, palpable, patent; spectacular
con obscure, vague; concealed, hidden, shrouded; insignificant, undistinguished
ant unnoticeable

notify *vb syn* see INFORM 2
rel announce, broadcast, declare, proclaim, promulgate, publish; disclose, discover, divulge, reveal

notion *n* **1** *syn* see IDEA
2 *syn* see CAPRICE
3 *syn* see HINT 1

notional *adj* **1** *syn* see CONCEPTUAL
2 *syn* see IMAGINARY 1
ant real

notoriety *n syn* see FAME 2
rel ballyhoo, promotion, propaganda, publicity

notorious *adj* **1** *syn* see WELL-KNOWN
2 *syn* see INFAMOUS 1

notwithstanding *prep syn* see AGAINST 4

notwithstanding *adv syn* see HOWEVER

nourish *vb* **1** *syn* see NURSE 1
2 *syn* see NURSE 2

nourishing *adj syn* see NUTRITIOUS
ant unnourishing

nourishment *n syn* see FOOD 2
rel keep, living, maintenance, support

nouveau riche *n syn* see UPSTART

novel *adj syn* see NEW 1
rel different, odd, peculiar, singular, special, strange, uncommon, unfamiliar, unique, unusual
con customary, habitual, usual; common, familiar, ordinary

novelty *n* **1** *syn* see CHANGE 2
con old story
2 *syn* see KNICKKNACK

---

syn synonym(s)   *rel* related word(s)
ant antonym(s)   *con* contrasted word(s)
idiom idiomatic equivalent(s)
‖ use limited; if in doubt, see a dictionary

---

novice *n* one who is just entering a field in which he has no previous experience <a *novice* in the theater —had never even had a walk-on role>
syn apprentice, beginner, boot, colt, fledgling, freshman, neophyte, newcomer, novitiate, prentice, punk, recruit, rookie, tenderfoot, tyro
rel amateur; cub; postulant, probationer; greenhorn, greeny; learner, student, trainee, undergraduate
con expert, pro, professional
ant doyen, old hand, old-timer, veteran

novitiate *n syn* see NOVICE

now *adv* **1** *syn* see TODAY
ant then
2 *syn* see AWAY 3

now *conj syn* see BECAUSE

now *n syn* see PRESENT

nowadays *adv syn* see TODAY

now and again *adv syn* see SOMETIMES

now and then *adv syn* see SOMETIMES

noxious *adj* **1** *syn* see UNWHOLESOME 1
ant wholesome; sanitary
2 *syn* see PERNICIOUS
rel fetid, putrid, noisome, stinking
ant innocuous, innoxious

nuance *n syn* see GRADATION
rel dash, soupçon, suggestion, suspicion, tinge, touch; nicety, refinement, subtlety

nub *n syn* see SUBSTANCE 2

nubbin *n syn* see SUBSTANCE 2

nubilous *adj* **1** *syn* see OVERCAST
2 *syn* see OBSCURE 3

nucleus *n syn* see SEED 2

nude *adj* **1** *syn* see BARE 1
con covered
2 not wearing any clothes <all the boys liked to swim *nude*>
syn au naturel, buff-bare, mother-naked, naked, raw, stark, stark-naked, stripped, unclad, unclothed, undressed
rel peeled, uncovered; dishabille, garmentless, unattired, unrobed
idiom ‖buck naked, in a state of nature, in one's birthday suit, in one's skin, in the altogether, in the buff, in the raw, stripped to the buff, without a stitch on, without a stitch to one's name
con attired, robed; decent; covered
ant clad, clothed, dressed

nudge *vb syn* see POKE 1

nudnick *n syn* see PEST 2

nugatory *adj syn* see VAIN 1

nugget *n syn* see LUMP 1

nuisance *n* **1** *syn* see PEST 2
2 *syn* see ANNOYANCE 3

null *adj* having no legal or binding force or validity <a *null* ballot>
syn bad, invalid, null and void, void
rel ineffective, ineffectual, inefficacious, useless, worthless
con acceptable, good, valid

null and void *adj syn* see NULL

nullify *vb syn* see ABOLISH 1
rel counteract, neutralize; compensate, counterbalance, countervail, offset; confine, limit, restrict

nullity *n* **1** *syn* see NOTHINGNESS
2 *syn* see NONENTITY

numb *adj* **1** devoid of sensation or feeling <my arm is *numb*>

syn anesthetized, asleep, benumbed, dead, deadened, insensible, insensitive, numbed, senseless, unfeeling
rel insensate, insentient, stupefied; comatose, unconscious
con alert; aware, conscious; sensitive
2 *syn* see INDIFFERENT 2

numb *vb syn* see DEADEN 1
rel chill, freeze, frost

numbed *adj syn* see NUMB 1

number *n* a character by which an arithmetical value is designated <you must add the *numbers* of the first column>
syn chiffer, cipher, digit, figure, integer, numeral, whole number

number *vb* **1** *syn* see COUNT 1
2 *syn* see AMOUNT 1

numberless *adj syn* see INNUMERABLE
ant numberable

number one *adj* **1** *syn* see CHIEF 2
2 *syn* see EXCELLENT

numeral *n syn* see NUMBER

numerate *vb* **1** *syn* see ENUMERATE 2
2 *syn* see COUNT 1

numerous *adj syn* see MANY
rel big, great, large

numinous *adj* **1** *syn* see SUPERNATURAL 1
2 *syn* see SACRED 2
3 *syn* see SPIRITUAL 4
4 *syn* see MYSTERIOUS

numskull *n syn* see DUNCE

numskulled *adj syn* see STUPID 1

nuptial *adj syn* see MATRIMONIAL

nuptial *n, usu* nuptials *pl syn* see WEDDING

nurse *n syn* see NURSEMAID

nurse *vb* **1** to feed from the breast <decided to *nurse* her baby>
syn breast-feed, nourish, suckle
rel bottle-feed
2 to promote the growth, development, or progress of <*nursed* the flame into a blaze>
syn cherish, cultivate, foster, nourish, nursle, nurture
rel feed; advance, forward, further, promote; humor, indulge, pamper
con check, hold back, retard, slow
3 *syn* see MINISTER (to)

nursemaid *n* one who is regularly employed to look after children <the *nursemaid* had three children in her charge>

syn ‖amah, ‖ayah, nana, ‖nanny, nurse, nurserymaid
rel babysitter, ‖minder, sitter; chaperon; governess

nurserymaid *n syn* see NURSEMAID

nursle *vb syn* see NURSE 2

nurture *n syn* see FOOD 1

nurture *vb syn* see NURSE 2
rel bring up, raise, rear; discipline, educate, school, train; back, bolster, support, sustain, uphold
con disregard, ignore, neglect, overlook, pass over, slight

nut *n* **1** *syn* see PROBLEM 2
‖**2** *syn* see HEAD 1
3 *syn* see CRACKPOT
4 *syn* see LUNATIC 1
5 *syn* see ENTHUSIAST

‖**nuthouse** *n syn* see ASYLUM 3

nutriculture *n syn* see HYDROPONICS

nutrient *adj syn* see NUTRITIOUS

nutriment *n syn* see FOOD 2
rel bread, bread and butter, keep, livelihood, living, maintenance, subsistence, support

nutrimental *adj syn* see NUTRITIOUS

nutritional *adj syn* see NUTRITIVE 1

nutritious *adj* promoting growth and repairing natural waste <*nutritious* food>
syn nourishing, nutrient, nutrimental, nutritive
rel good, healthful, salubrious, salutary, wholesome; balanced
con indigestible; bad, insalubrious, unhealthful, unwholesome
ant innutritious

nutritive *adj* **1** relating to or concerned with nutrition <*nutritive* organs of the body>
syn alimentary, alimentative, nutritional
rel digestive, metabolic; constructive, creative, formative, productive
2 *syn* see NUTRITIOUS

nuts *adj syn* see INSANE 1

nutshell *vb syn* see EPITOMIZE 1

nutsy *adj syn* see INSANE 1

nutty *adj* **1** *syn* see ENTHUSIASTIC
2 *syn* see INSANE 1

nuzzle *vb syn* see SNUGGLE

nymph *n syn* see DOXY 1

nymphet *n syn* see DOXY 1

O

oaf *n* **1** *syn* see DUNCE
2 a big clumsy, usually slow-witted person <an *oaf* who bumped into everything he passed>
syn bohunk, ‖gaum, gawk, klutz, lobster, looby, lout, lubber, ‖lug, lummox, lump, lumpkin, meathead, palooka, slouch
rel ‖baboon, beast, bruiser, brute, bull, gorilla, hulk, missing link, ox; clod, clown, dub, galoot, slob; blunderbuss, blunderer, blunderhead

oar *vb syn* see ROW

oater *n syn* see WESTERN

oath *n syn* see SWEARWORD

obdurate *adj* **1** *syn* see UNFEELING 2
con tender
2 *syn* see INFLEXIBLE 2
rel mulish, stiff-necked; immovable
con relenting, submitting

obedient *adj* submissive to the will, guidance, or control of another <children should always be *obedient* to their parents>
syn amenable, biddable, docile, ‖docious, tractable
rel acquiescent, compliant, sheeplike, submissive, yielding; duteous, dutiful, loyal; law-abiding; obeisant, subservient
con insubordinate, rebellious; contrary, froward, perverse, wayward, willful; headstrong, intractable, recalcitrant, refractory, uncontrollable, ungovernable, unruly
ant contumacious, disobedient

obeisance *n syn* see HONOR 1
rel allegiance, fealty, loyalty

obeisant *adj syn* see SUBSERVIENT 2

obese *adj syn* see FAT 2
ant skinny

obesity *n* a condition characterized by excessive bodily fat <could barely walk because of his *obesity*>
syn adiposity, corpulence, fatness, fleshiness
rel chubbiness, chunkiness, embonpoint, grossness, plumpness, portliness, pudginess, rotundity, stockiness, stoutness, tubbiness
con lankiness, leanness, scrawniness, slenderness, slimness
ant skinniness

obey *vb* to act or behave in conformity with (as an order) or in duty to (as a parent) <*obey* a superior's order>
syn comply, conform, follow, keep, mind, observe
rel bow, defer, submit, yield; accede, acquiesce, agree, assent; fulfill, satisfy; carry out; heed, regard
idiom abide by

---

syn synonym(s)　　*rel* related word(s)
ant antonym(s)　　*con* contrasted word(s)
idiom idiomatic equivalent(s)
‖ use limited; if in doubt, see a dictionary

---

con break, disregard, transgress, violate; command, order
ant disobey

obfuscate *vb syn* see OBSCURE
ant clarify

obit *n syn* see OBITUARY

obiter *adv syn* see INCIDENTALLY 2

obiter dictum *n syn* see REMARK 2

obituary *n* a notice of a person's death usually with a short biographical account <always read the *obituaries* in the paper>
syn necrology, obit

object *n* **1** *syn* see THING 3
rel doodad; gadget
2 *syn* see THING 4
3 *syn* see BODY 4
4 *syn* see VIEW 6
5 *syn* see USE 4

object *vb* **1** to oppose by arguing against <*objecting* because the evidence was unclear>
syn except, expostulate, inveigh (against), kick, protest, remonstrate
rel balk, boggle, demur, dissent, jib, stickle; complain; criticize; challenge; spurn; rail, rant, rave, storm
con accede, agree, assent, consent; accredit, approve, sanction
ant acquiesce
2 *syn* see DISAPPROVE 1

objectify *vb syn* see EMBODY 1

objection *n syn* see DEMUR 2

objectionable *adj* arousing or likely to arouse objection <the language in that movie is *objectionable*>
syn exceptionable, ill-favored, inadmissible, unacceptable, undesirable, unwanted, unwelcome
rel abhorrent, loathsome, offensive, repellent, repugnant, repulsive, revolting; disagreeable, distasteful, invidious, obnoxious, unpleasant; unfit, unsuitable; censurable, reprehensible
con acceptable, agreeable, gratifying, pleasant, pleasing, welcome
ant unobjectionable

objective *adj* **1** *syn* see MATERIAL 1
rel external, outer, outside, outward
ant subjective
2 *syn* see FAIR 4
ant subjective

objective *n* **1** *syn* see AMBITION 2
2 *syn* see USE 4

objectless *adj syn* see RANDOM

objet d'art *n syn* see KNICKKNACK

objurgate *vb syn* see EXECRATE 1
rel castigate, censure

obligated *adj syn* see INDEBTED

obligation *n* **1** *syn* see OCCASION 3
2 something one is bound to do or forbear <it is our *obligation* to obey the law>
syn charge, commitment, committal, devoir, duty, must, need, ought, ‖right

rel compulsion, constraint, restraint; burden, requirement, responsibility; business, part, place
con choice, discretion, free will, option; decision, determination, pleasure, will
3 *syn* see INDEBTEDNESS 1

obligatory *adj syn* see MANDATORY
ant nonobligatory

oblige *vb* 1 *syn* see FORCE 2
2 to do a service or courtesy <you will *oblige* me greatly if you will get there on time>
syn accommodate, convenience, favor
rel gratify, please; avail, benefit, profit; aid, assist, contribute, help
con bother, discommode, incommode, inconvenience, trouble
ant disoblige

obliged *adj* 1 *syn* see GRATEFUL 1
2 *syn* see INDEBTED

obliging *syn* see AMIABLE 1
ant disobliging

oblique *adj* 1 *syn* see INCLINED 3
2 *syn* see INDIRECT 1
ant straight

obliquely *adv syn* see ASIDE 1
ant straight

obliterate *vb syn* see ERASE

oblivion *n* a state of forgetting or the fact of having forgotten <the *oblivion* of sleep>
syn forgetfulness, lethe, obliviousness
rel nirvana; insensibleness
con alertness, awareness, consciousness; memory, recall, recalling, recollection, remembrance

oblivious *adj* 1 *syn* see FORGETFUL
rel absorbed, unaware, unconscious
idiom turned off
2 *syn* see IGNORANT 2

obliviousness *n syn* see OBLIVION

obloquy *n* 1 *syn* see ABUSE
2 *syn* see ANIMADVERSION
3 *syn* see DISGRACE

obnoxious *adj* 1 *syn* see LIABLE 2
ant unobnoxious
2 *syn* see REPUGNANT 1
con congenial, likable, simpatico
ant grateful; unobnoxious

obscene *adj* 1 *syn* see OFFENSIVE
2 marked by the use of words regarded as taboo in polite usage <knew all the *obscene* expressions for the genitalia>
syn barnyard, coarse, crude, crusty, dirty, fescennine, filthy, foul, gross, indecent, nasty, paw, profane, rank, raunchy, ‖raw, rocky, scatological, scurrilous, smutty, vulgar; *compare* RISQUÉ
rel bawdy, ribald, smoking-room; impure, lascivious, lewd, warm; lurid, pornographic, salacious, scabrous, sultry; earthy, rich; unprintable; foulmouthed
con acceptable, proper, tolerable; appropriate, fit, suitable; clean, decent, decorous, seemly

obscure *adj* 1 *syn* see DARK 1
rel clouded, cloudy, fuliginous; shadowy, shady, umbrageous
con clear, lucid; bright, brilliant, luminous
2 withdrawn from the main centers of human activity <was exiled to an *obscure* Siberian village>

syn devious, lonesome, out-of-the-way, remote, removed, retired, secret
rel distant, far, far-off; close, hidden, odd, secluded, sequestered, solitary; blind; inaccessible
idiom back of beyond, off the beaten track (*or* path), in the boondocks (*or* sticks)
con central; urban; populous
3 not readily understood or grasped <an *obscure* textual reference>
syn ambiguous, amphibological, double-edged, double-faced, dusky, equivocal, murky, nubilous, opaque, sibylline, tenebrous, uncertain, unclear, unexplicit, unintelligible, vague; *compare* CRYPTIC, FAINT 2
rel difficult, incomprehensible, inexplicable, puzzling, unfathomable; illegible; abstruse, Delphian, enigmatic, esoteric, inscrutable, mysterious, mystic, mystical; inconclusive, indecisive, indefinite
con definite, explicit, obvious; clear, express, unambiguous, unequivocal
ant lucid
4 *syn* see INCONSPICUOUS
rel humble, lowly, minor, unimportant
5 lacking the prominence, showiness, or worth by which attention might be attracted <an *obscure* Roman poet>
syn nameless, uncelebrated, unfamed, unheard-of, unknown, unnoted, unrenowned
rel inconspicuous; minor, undistinguished, unimportant
con celebrated, distinguished, named, notable, noted, noteworthy, renowned, well-known
ant famed, famous
6 *syn* see FAINT 2
ant clear

obscure *vb* to make dark, dim, or indistinct <fog *obscured* our view>
syn adumbrate, becloud, bedim, befog, cloud, darken, dim, dislimn, eclipse, fog, gloom, haze, mist, murk, obfuscate, overcast, overcloud, overshadow, shadow
rel blear, blur, fuzz; blind, conceal, dim out, hide, screen, shade, shroud; bemask, camouflage, cloak, cover, disguise, mask, veil; belie, falsify, misrepresent
con brighten, light (up), lighten; clarify, enlighten; elucidate, exemplify, explain
ant illuminate, illumine

obscured *adj syn* see ULTERIOR

obsequious *adj syn* see SUBSERVIENT 2
rel deferential; parasitic, sycophantic, toadying
con self-assertive

observable *adj* 1 *syn* see PERCEPTIBLE
ant unobservable
2 *syn* see NOTEWORTHY

observance *n* 1 *syn* see RITE 2
2 *syn* see NOTICE 1
ant nonobservance, unobservance

observant *adj* 1 *syn* see ATTENTIVE 1
rel awake
ant unobservant
2 *syn* see MINDFUL 2

observation *n* 1 *syn* see NOTICE 1
2 *syn* see REMARK 2

observative *adj syn* see MINDFUL 2

observatory *n syn* see LOOKOUT 2

observe *vb* **1** *syn* see OBEY
2 *syn* see KEEP 2
rel revere, reverence, venerate
ant break, violate
3 *syn* see SEE 1
4 *syn* see REMARK 2

observer *n syn* see SPECTATOR

observing *adj syn* see MINDFUL 2
ant unobserving

obsessed *adj* preoccupied intensely or abnormally < *obsessed* with cleanliness >
syn hagridden, hipped, queer
rel bewitched, dominated, gripped, held, possessed, prepossessed; bedeviled, beset, dogged, harassed, haunted, plagued, troubled; overcome
idiom have on the brain
con detached, unconcerned, uninterested; indifferent, neutral; cool, easy-going

obsession *n syn* see FETISH 2

obsolesce *vb syn* see OUTDATE

obsolete *adj* no longer active or in use < *obsolete* social customs >
syn dead, disused, extinct, outmoded, outworn, passé, superseded; *compare* ANCIENT 1
rel old-fashioned, old hat, old-time, old-timey, out-of-date, unfashionable; dusty, fusty, moldy, moth-eaten, musty, stale, timeworn
idiom behind the times
con contemporary, modern, new-fashioned, up-to-date, up-to-the-minute; novel, original, unique
ant current

obsolete *vb syn* see OUTDATE

obstacle *n* something that seriously hampers action or progress < lack of education is an *obstacle* to advancement >
syn bar, Chinese wall, crimp, hamper, hurdle, impediment, mountain, obstruction, rub, snag, stumbling block, traverse
rel clog, encumbrance, handicap, hindrance; bump, difficulty, hardship, vicissitude; catch, hitch; disincentive
con aid, assist, assistance, help
ant advantage

obstinate *adj* unwilling to submit (as to reason or control) < he had an *obstinate* determination to live as he pleased >
syn bullheaded, closed-minded, deaf, hardheaded, headstrong, incompliant, intractable, intransigent, muleheaded, muley, mulish, pertinacious, perverse, pervicacious, pigheaded, refractory, self-willed, ‖sot, stiff, stiff-necked, stubborn, tough, unpliable, unpliant, unyielding, willful, wrongheaded; *compare* UNRULY 1
rel resistant, unsubmissive, withstanding; contrary, crabbed, recalcitrant; renitent; inexorable, inflexible, obdurate; opinionated; resolute, staunch, steadfast, unbudging
con acquiescent, complaisant, compliant; submissive, yielding; agreeable, cooperative, willing
ant pliable, pliant

obstipated *adj syn* see CONSTIPATED

---

syn synonym(s)　　　*rel* related word(s)
ant antonym(s)　　　*con* contrasted word(s)
idiom idiomatic equivalent(s)
‖ use limited; if in doubt, see a dictionary

obstreperous *adj* **1** *syn* see VOCIFEROUS
2 *syn* see DISOBEDIENT

obstruct *vb* **1** *syn* see FILL 1
2 *syn* see HINDER
3 *syn* see SCREEN 3

obstruction *n syn* see OBSTACLE

obtain *vb syn* see GET 1

obtainable *adj* **1** *syn* see AVAILABLE 1
rel derivable
2 *syn* see PURCHASABLE 1

obtrude *vb* **1** *syn* see IMPOSE 5
2 *syn* see INTRUDE 1

obtrusive *adj syn* see IMPERTINENT 2
ant unobtrusive

obtund *vb syn* see DULL 3

obtuse *adj syn* see DULL 6

obviate *vb syn* see PREVENT 2
rel anticipate; interfere, interpose, intervene

obvious *adj syn* see CLEAR 5
ant abstruse, obscure; unobvious

occasion *n* **1** *syn* see OPPORTUNITY
2 *syn* see CAUSE 1
3 something that provides a reason for something else < there is no *occasion* for alarm >
syn call, cause, necessity, obligation
rel basis, foundation, ground, warrant; justification, right; excuse
4 *syn* see OCCURRENCE
5 a particular point of time at which something takes place < we always spoke, but on that *occasion* we didn't >
syn instant, moment, time, while
idiom point in time
6 *syn* see NEED 3
7 occasions *pl syn* see BUSINESS 8
8 *syn* see EVENT 2

occasion *vb syn* see GENERATE 3

occasional *adj syn* see INFREQUENT
rel incidental; casual, random
con accustomed, habitual, usual; constant, continual, continuous
ant customary

occasionally *adv* on a few occasions < *occasionally* she'll walk instead of drive >
syn infrequently, irregularly, on occasion, sporadically, uncommonly; *compare* SOMETIMES
rel off and on, once or twice
idiom every now and then, from time to time, ‖once in a way, once in a while
con continually, continuously, frequently; commonly, customarily, habitually, often; hardly ever, rarely, scarcely, seldom; never
ant constantly

occlude *vb syn* see FILL 1

occult *vb syn* see HIDE

occult *adj syn* see RECONDITE
rel arcane, mysterious; cabalistic, mystical, supernatural; eerie, unearthly, weird

occupancy *n syn* see HABITATION 1

occupant *n syn* see INHABITANT

occupation *n* **1** *syn* see WORK 1
2 *syn* see HABITATION 1

occupiable *adj syn* see LIVABLE 1

occupied *adj syn* see BUSY 1
ant unoccupied

occupy *vb* **1** *syn* see ENGAGE 4
2 *syn* see INHABIT

occur *vb* **1** *syn* see HAPPEN 1
2 to enter one's mind < it just *occurred* to me: she can't drive >

syn hit, strike

idiom come into one's head, come to mind, cross one's mind, flash across one's mind, go through one's head

occurrence *n* something that happens or takes place <the chance encounter turned out to be a fortunate *occurrence*>
syn circumstance, episode, event, go, happening, incident, occasion, thing
rel contingency, emergency, exigency, juncture, pass; condition, situation, state; adventure, experience

ocean *n* the body of water that covers nearly three-fourths of the earth <pulled the downed pilot from the *ocean*>
syn blue, brine, ||briny, deep, drink, main, sea

oceanic *adj syn see* MARINE 1

ochlocracy *n syn see* ANARCHY 1

ocular *adj* 1 *syn see* VISUAL 2
2 *syn see* VISUAL 1

ocular *n syn see* EYE 1

oculus *n syn see* EYE 1

odd *adj* 1 being without a corresponding mate <had only an *odd* glove; the other was lost>
syn unmatched, unpaired
rel lone, only, single
con matched, paired
2 *syn see* ACCIDENTAL
3 *syn see* STRANGE 4

oddball *n syn see* ECCENTRIC

oddball *adj syn see* STRANGE 4

oddity *n* 1 *syn see* ECCENTRIC
2 *syn see* CURIOSITY 2

oddments *n pl syn see* SUNDRIES

odds *n pl syn see* ADVANTAGE 3

odds and ends *n pl* 1 *syn see* SUNDRIES
2 *syn see* MISCELLANY 1

odiferous *adj syn see* ODOROUS

odious *adj syn see* HATEFUL 2

odium *n* 1 *syn see* DISGRACE
rel hate, hatred
ant honor
2 *syn see* STIGMA

odor *n syn see* SMELL 1

odoriferous *adj syn see* ODOROUS

odorize *vb syn see* SCENT 2

odorless *adj* having no odor <*odorless* castor oil>
syn inodorous, scentless, smell-less
rel deodorant, deodorizing; unscented
con scented, smelly
ant odorous

odorous *adj* having or emitting an odor <*odorous* chemicals are often malodorous>
syn odiferous, odoriferous, scented; *compare* MALODOROUS 1, SWEET 2
rel redolent, reeking, smelling, smelly; heady, pungent, strong; olfactive, olfactory
ant inodorous, odorless, scentless

o'er *prep syn see* OVER 1

oeuvre *n* a substantial body of work constituting the lifework of a writer, composer, or artist <one of the more popular operas in the Mozart *oeuvre*>
syn corpus, opera omnia
rel output

off *adv syn see* AWAY 2

off *adj* 1 *syn see* REMOTE 4
2 *syn see* SLOW 3

offal *n syn see* REFUSE

off-balance *adj syn see* LOPSIDED

off-center *adj syn see* ECCENTRIC 1

off-color *adj* 1 *syn see* UNWELL
2 *syn see* RISQUÉ

offend *vb* 1 *syn see* TRESPASS 1
2 *syn see* VIOLATE 1
3 to cause hurt feelings or deep resentment <*offended* her by his cruel remark>
syn affront, insult, outrage
rel aggrieve, hurt, sting, wound; exasperate, gall, irritate, nettle; excite, provoke; appall, horrify, scandalize, shock; disoblige, displease, distress, disturb, miff, pique, upset
idiom hurt one's feelings, ruffle one's feathers, step (or tread) on one's toes
con delight, gratify, please, tickle; captivate, charm, enchant; flatter

offender *n syn see* CRIMINAL

offense *n* 1 *syn see* ATTACK 1
2 an emotional response to a slight or indignity <he is so sensitive that he takes *offense* at the slightest criticism>
syn dudgeon, huff, miff, pique, resentment, ||snuff, umbrage
rel affront, indignity, insult; anger, indignation; displeasure, pet, tizzy; explosion, flare-up, outburst, scene
con delight, pleasure
3 *syn see* CRIME 1

offensive *adj* utterly unpleasant or distasteful to the senses or sensibilities <the *offensive* odor of stale garbage> <her arrogant assurance was more than a little *offensive*>
syn atrocious, disgusting, evil, foul, hideous, horrible, horrid, icky, loathsome, nasty, nauseating, noisome, obscene, repellent, repugnant, repulsive, revolting, sickening, ungrateful, unwholesome, vile
rel abhorrent, bad, disagreeable, objectionable, uncongenial, unpleasant; abominable, detestable, fulsome, odious; rank; appalling, awful, beastly, dreadful, frightful, ghastly, grim, grisly, gruesome, lurid, shocking, terrible; unappetizing, unpalatable, unsavory
con agreeable, appealing, attractive, pleasant, pleasing; favorable, unobjectionable, welcome; appetizing, palatable, savory; divine
ant inoffensive, unoffensive

offensive *n syn see* ATTACK 1

offer *vb* 1 to put something before another for acceptance or consideration <he was soon *offered* another job>
syn extend, give, hold out, pose, present, proffer, tender
rel display, exhibit, show
con accept, receive, take; decline, refuse, reject
2 *syn see* ADDUCE
3 *syn see* TRY 5
4 *syn see* SHOW 1

offering *n* 1 *syn see* VICTIM 1
2 *syn see* DONATION

offgoing *n syn see* DEPARTURE 1

offhand *adj syn see* EXTEMPORANEOUS

office *n* 1 *syn see* JOB 2
2 *syn see* FUNCTION 1
||3 *syn see* PRIVY 1

‖4 *syn* see HIGH SIGN 2

officer *n* 1 *syn* see POLICEMAN

2 *syn* see EXECUTIVE

official *n* *syn* see EXECUTIVE

official *adj* derived from the proper office, officer, or authority <the mayor's office issued an *official* statement>

syn authoritative, ex cathedra, ex officio

rel approved, authorized, certified, cleared, endorsed, OK'd, sanctioned; canonical, cathedral

ant officious (*in diplomatic use*), unofficial

officially *adv* *syn* see OSTENSIBLY

officiate *vb* *syn* see ACT 4

officious *adj* *syn* see IMPERTINENT 2

offing *n* *syn* see FUTURE

offish *adj* 1 *syn* see UNSOCIABLE

2 *syn* see UNWELL

off-key *adj* *syn* see IRREGULAR 1

off-load *vb* *syn* see UNLOAD

off-lying *adj* *syn* see DISTANT 1

offscouring *n* *syn* see OUTCAST

offset *vb* *syn* see COMPENSATE 1

rel check, stop

offshoot *n* *syn* see OUTGROWTH 2

offspring *n* *pl* those who follow in direct parental line <a mother of numerous *offspring*>

syn ‖begats, brood, children, descendants, issue, posterity, progeniture, progeny, scions, seed

rel hatch, swarm; produce, spawn, young

con antecedents, ascendants, forebears, forefathers, progenitors

ant ancestors

offstage *adj or adv* *syn* see BACKSTAGE

ant onstage

of late *adv* *syn* see NEW

oft *adv* *syn* see OFTEN

often *adv* many times <we called *often* but still could not reach you>

syn again and again, frequently, much, oft, oftentimes, ofttimes, over and over, repeatedly, time and again

idiom a number of times, many a time, many times over, time and time again

con infrequently, rarely; now and then, occasionally

ant seldom

oftentimes *adv* *syn* see OFTEN

ofttimes *adv* *syn* see OFTEN

ogle *vb* *syn* see LOOK 7

‖**ogle** *n* *syn* see EYE 1

ogress *n* *syn* see VIRAGO

oil *n* *syn* see FLATTERY

‖**oiled** *adj* *syn* see INTOXICATED 1

oily *adj* 1 *syn* see FATTY 2

2 *syn* see FULSOME

ointment *n* a semisolid medicinal or cosmetic preparation for application to the skin <put *ointment* on the burned skin>

syn balm, cerate, chrism, cream, salve, unction, unguent

rel embrocation, liniment; demulcent, emollient; lotion; dressing

OK (*or* okay) *adv* *syn* see YES 1

OK (*or* okay) *vb* *syn* see APPROVE 2

OK (*or* okay) *n* *syn* see APPROBATION

---

syn synonym(s)	*rel* related word(s)
ant antonym(s)	*con* contrasted word(s)
idiom idiomatic equivalent(s)	
‖ use limited; if in doubt, see a dictionary	

‖**okeydoke** *adv* *syn* see YES 1

old *adj* 1 *syn* see ANCIENT 1

con contemporary, current, recent; advanced

ant new

2 of long standing <the ending of such an *old* friendship was tragic>

syn continuing, enduring, inveterate, lifelong, long-lasting, long-lived, perennial; compare LASTING

rel constant, perpetual, staying; established, firm, solid, steady

con newfound, recent; brief, short-lived; casual, temporary, transitory, weak

ant new

3 *syn* see OLD-FASHIONED

rel primitive; traditional

con newish

ant modern, new

4 *syn* see AGED 1

idiom along in years, getting on

con juvenile, young

ant youthful

5 *syn* see EXPERIENCED

con young

ant new

6 *syn* see FORMER 2

old age *n* the final stage of the normal life span <spent his *old age* in a nursing home>

syn age, caducity, elderliness, senectitude, senescence, years; compare DOTAGE

rel decrepitude, feebleness; infirmity

idiom advanced years, declining years, winter of life

ant youth

olden *adj* 1 *syn* see ANCIENT 1

2 *syn* see AGED 1

oldest profession *n* *syn* see PROSTITUTION

oldfangled *adj* *syn* see OLD-FASHIONED

ant newfangled

old-fashioned *adj* typical of an earlier time and often replaced by something more modern or fashionable <*old-fashioned* high-buttoned shoes>

syn antiquated, antique, archaic, belated, bygone, dated, démodé, demoded, dowdy, fusty, moldy, moth-eaten, neanderthal, old, oldfangled, old hat, old-time, old-timey, outdated, outmoded, out-of-date, passé, rococo, unmodern, vintage

rel aged, ancient; discarded, disused, obsolete; outworn, unfashionable; crusty, fogyish, fuddy-duddy, fusty, moss-backed, moss-grown, mossy, stodgy, Victorian; old-line

con modernistic, modish, newfangled, stylish, ‖trendy; current, recent, timely; new-fashioned, up-to-date, up-to-the-minute

ant contemporary; modern

Old Gooseberry *n* *syn* see DEVIL 1

Old Guard *n* *syn* see ESTABLISHMENT 2

old hand *n* *syn* see VETERAN

old hat *adj* 1 *syn* see OLD-FASHIONED

2 *syn* see TRITE

old lady *n* ‖1 *syn* see WIFE

‖2 *syn* see MOTHER 1

3 *syn* see FUSSBUDGET

old-line *adj* *syn* see CONSERVATIVE 1

old liner *n* *syn* see DIEHARD 1

old maid *n* 1 *syn* see SPINSTER

2 *syn* see FUSSBUDGET

old-maidish *adj syn* see NICE 1

‖**old man** *n* 1 *syn* see HUSBAND

2 *syn* see FATHER 1

Old Nick *n syn* see DEVIL 1

Old Scratch *n syn* see DEVIL 1

oldster *n* a person of advanced years <an *oldster* long retired from the business world>

syn ancient, elder, golden-ager, old-timer, senior, senior citizen; *compare* BELDAM 1, GAFFER

ant youngster, youth

old-time *adj* 1 *syn* see OLD-FASHIONED

2 *syn* see EXPERIENCED

old-timer *n* 1 *syn* see VETERAN

2 *syn* see OLDSTER

old-timey *adj syn* see OLD-FASHIONED

‖**old woman** *n* 1 *syn* see WIFE

2 *syn* see MOTHER 1

old-womanish *adj syn* see NICE 1

oleaginous *adj syn* see FATTY 2

2 *syn* see FULSOME

olid *adj syn* see MALODOROUS 1

olio *n syn* see MISCELLANY 1

olla podrida *n syn* see MISCELLANY 1

omen *n syn* see FORETOKEN

omen *vb syn* see AUGUR 2

ominous *adj* indicative of future misfortune or calamity <dark *ominous* clouds preceded the storm>

syn apocalyptic, baleful, baneful, dire, direful, doomful, fateful, ill-boding, ill-omened, inauspicious, threatening, unlucky, unpropitious; *compare* EVIL 5, SINISTER

rel portentous; malefic, maleficent, malign, sinister; comminatory, forbidding, grim, lowering, menacing; hostile, inhospitable, unfriendly

con auspicious, benign, favorable, promising, propitious; beneficial

omission *n* something omitted or missing <several *omissions* in the list>

syn blank, chasm, overlook, oversight, preterition, pretermission, skip

rel inadvertence, inadvertency, lapse, slip; break, gap, hiatus, lacuna

con inclusion; accession, addition, augmentation, increase, reinforcement; superaddition

omit *vb syn* see NEGLECT

omitted *adj syn* see ABSENT 1

ant included

omnibus *n syn* see ANTHOLOGY

omnipotent *adj* having virtually unlimited authority or influence <an *omnipotent* leader>

syn all-powerful, almighty

rel divine, godlike; unlimited, unrestricted

con impotent, powerless; limited, restricted

omnipresent *adj* present at all places at all times <*omnipresent* God>

syn allover, ubiquitous, universal

rel boundless, endless, immeasurable, infinite, limitless, unending

con bounded, finite, limited, restricted; cramped, strained; narrow, strait

omnium-gatherum *n syn* see MISCELLANY 1

on *prep* 1 *syn* see OVER 4

2 *syn* see OVER 3

on *adv syn* see ALONG 1

on-again-off-again *adj syn* see FITFUL

onanism *n syn* see SELF-GRATIFICATION

onanistic *adj syn* see SYBARITIC

once *adv* 1 *syn* see EVER 5

2 *syn* see BEFORE 2

once *adj syn* see FORMER 2

once and again *adv syn* see SOMETIMES

once more *adv syn* see OVER 7

oncoming *adj syn* see FORTHCOMING

on-dit *n syn* see REPORT 1

one *adj syn* see SINGLE 2

one *vb syn* see JOIN 1

one by one *adv syn* see APART 1

one-horse town *n syn* see BURG

oneness *n* 1 *syn* see UNITY 1

ant multiplicity

2 *syn* see UNIQUENESS

3 *syn* see ENTIRETY 1

4 *syn* see IDENTITY 1

oner *n syn* see DOLLAR

onerous *adj* imposing great hardship or strain <found the care of his old mother an *onerous* burden>

syn burdensome, demanding, exacting, exigent, grievous, oppressive, superincumbent, taxing, tough, trying, weighty

rel arduous, difficult, hard, laborious; heavy, hefty, ponderous; cumbersome, unruly, unwieldy; driving, heavy-handed

con easy, effortless; facile, light, simple, smooth, unexacting, untaxing

onerously *adv syn* see HARD 8

one-sided *adj syn* see BIASED 2

rel lopsided, weighted

con many-sided

one-sidedness *n syn* see PREJUDICE

con manysidedness

onetime *adj syn* see FORMER 2

onfall *n syn* see ATTACK 1

ongoing *n syn* see ADVANCE 2

rel development, growth

onlooker *n syn* see SPECTATOR

only *adj* 1 *syn* see ALONE 3

2 being one or more of which there exist no others <the *only* survivors of the wreck>

syn alone, lone, singular, sole, solitary, solo, unexampled, unique, unrepeatable

rel incomparable, inimitable, matchless, peerless, transcendent, unequaled, unparalleled, unrivaled; companionless, separate, unaccompanied, unattended, uncompanied, uncompanioned

con divers, many, multifarious, numerous, sundry, various

3 *syn* see SINGLE 2

only *adv* 1 to the exclusion of any alternative or competitor <he will confess *only* to you>

syn alone, but, entirely, exclusively, solely

2 *syn* see JUST 3

only *conj* in spite of which <it looks delicious, *only* I'm not hungry>

syn but, except, however, save, yet

on occasion *adv syn* see OCCASIONALLY

on offer *adj syn* see PURCHASABLE 1

onomatopoeic *adj* formed in imitation of a natural sound <*buzz* is an *onomatopoeic* word to describe the sound of bees>

syn echoic, imitative, onomatopoetic

rel emulative, simulative; mimetic, mimic, mimical

onomatopoetic *adj syn see* ONOMATOPO-
EIC
on purpose *adv syn see* INTENTIONALLY
onset *n* 1 *syn see* ATTACK 1
  2 *syn see* BEGINNING
onslaught *n syn see* ATTACK 1
on the whole *adv syn see* ALTOGETHER 3
onus *n* 1 *syn see* LOAD 3
  2 *syn see* BLAME
  3 *syn see* STIGMA
onward *adv* 1 *syn see* AHEAD 2
  2 *syn see* ALONG 1
onyx *adj syn see* BLACK 1
oodles *n pl but sometimes sing in constr*
  syn see SCAD
∥**ooftish** *n syn see* MONEY
∥**oofy** *adj syn see* RICH 1
ooid *adj syn see* OVAL
oomph *n syn see* SPIRIT 5
ooze *vb syn see* EXUDE
oozy *adj syn see* MUDDY 1
opaque *adj syn see* OBSCURE 3
  ant transparent, transpicuous
ope *vb syn see* OPEN 1
open *adj* 1 not closed or obstructed < escaped through the *open* gate >
  syn patent, unclosed, unobstructed
  rel agape, dehiscent, gaping, patulous,
  ringent, wide, yawning; ajar; unbarred,
  unbolted, unfastened, unlocked, unsealed;
  clear, unimpeded
  con blocked, obstructed; constricted,
  cramped, narrow, strait
  ant closed, shut
  2 lacking a cover or covering < an *open*
  wound that continued to ooze blood >
  < his chest *open* to the sun >
  syn bare, denuded, exposed, naked,
  peeled, stripped, uncovered
  3 *syn see* LIABLE 2
  ant closed
  4 not restricted to a particular group or
  situation < favored *open* enrollment in the
  schools >
  syn accessible, open-door, public, unrestricted
  rel attainable, available, obtainable,
  reachable, securable
  idiom to be had, within reach
  con limited, restricted; inaccessible, private
  ant closed
  5 available for use or consideration or
  decision < there are only two courses *open*
  to us >
  syn accessible, employable, operative,
  practicable, usable
  rel appropriate, fit, proper, suitable; acceptable, agreeable, pleasing
  idiom within reach
  con inaccessible, inoperative, unusable
  ant closed
  6 *syn see* DOUBTFUL 1
  7 *syn see* FRANK
  ant close; clandestine
open *vb* 1 to change from a closed to an
  open condition < *open* the window >
  syn ope, unblock, unclose, undo, unshut,
  unstop

syn synonym(s)   *rel* related word(s)
ant antonym(s)   *con* contrasted word(s)
idiom idiomatic equivalent(s)
∥ use limited; if in doubt, see a dictionary

  rel clear, free, release; bare, disclose,
  expose, reveal
  idiom lay open, swing open, throw open
  con block, occlude, stop
  ant close, shut
  2 to make physically or mentally visible
  < dawn *opened* a surprising scene to his
  startled eyes >
  syn disclose, display, expose, reveal, unclothe, uncover, unveil
  rel adumbrate, hint, shadow, suggest
  idiom bring to light, bring to (or into)
  view, lay bare, make plain, show forth
  con cloak, conceal, hide, screen, secrete,
  shroud
  3 to make an opening in < decided to
  open a can of beans >
  syn breach, disrupt, hole, rupture
  rel break, broach, tap, undo; cut, gash,
  slash; perforate, pierce
  idiom lay open
  con occlude, shut; fasten, secure
  ant close
  4 to spread out < the falcon slowly
  opened her mighty wings >
  syn expand, extend, fan (out), outspread,
  outstretch, spread, unfold
  rel billow, dilate, distend, swell; cover,
  mantle, overspread
  con collect, concentrate, contract, gather
  (in)
  ant close
  5 *syn see* BEGIN 1
  ant close
  6 *syn see* CONVENE 1
open *n syn see* OUTDOORS
open air *n syn see* OUTDOORS
open–air *adj syn see* OUTDOOR
  con indoor, inside; enclosed
open–and–shut *adj syn see* CLEAR 5
open–door *adj syn see* OPEN 4
open–eyed *adj syn see* WATCHFUL
openhanded *adj* 1 *syn see* LIBERAL 1
  ant closefisted, tightfisted
  2 *syn see* CLEAR 5
openhearted *adj syn see* FRANK
opening *n* 1 *syn see* BEGINNING
  ant closing
  2 *syn see* APERTURE
  3 *syn see* GAP 1
  4 *syn see* OPPORTUNITY
opening gun *n syn see* BEGINNING
openmouthed *adj syn see* VOCIFEROUS
openness *n syn see* EXPOSURE
open sesame *n syn see* PASSPORT
open up *vb syn see* OPERATE 2
opera omnia *n syn see* OEUVRE
operate *vb* 1 *syn see* ACT 5
  2 to perform surgery < *operated* on him to
  remove a brain tumor >
  syn cut, open up
  3 to cause to function < knew how to
  operate earth-moving equipment >
  syn handle, run, use, work
  rel play; manage, maneuver; drive, pilot,
  steer; ply, wield
  idiom make go
  4 *syn see* CONDUCT 3
operation *n* 1 *syn see* EXERCISE 1
  2 *syn see* USE 1
operative *adj* 1 *syn see* ACTIVE 1
  ant inoperative
  2 *syn see* OPEN 5

operative *n* **1** *syn* see WORKER

2 *syn* see PRIVATE DETECTIVE

operator *n* *syn* see MOTORIST

operose *adj* **1** *syn* see HARD 6

2 *syn* see ASSIDUOUS

opiate *adj* *syn* see SOPORIFIC 1

opiate *n* **1** *syn* see DRUG 2

2 *syn* see ANODYNE 2

opine *vb* to form or express an opinion < he *opined* that the story was true>

syn ‖opinion, opinionate

rel accept, believe, consider, hold, judge, regard, think, view; speculate

con deny, disclaim, disown, reject, repudiate; disbelieve, discredit, doubt

opinion *n* an idea or judgment held as true or valid < seek an expert *opinion* on the authenticity of the painting>

syn belief, conviction, eye, feeling, mind, persuasion, sentiment, view

rel attitude, impression, notion, think, thought; conclusion, estimate, estimation, judgment, reaction; assumption, conjecture, speculation, supposition, theory

idiom point of view

con disbelief, discredit, doubt, unbelief; distrust, mistrust, questioning, skepticism

‖**opinion** *vb* *syn* see OPINE

opinionate *vb* *syn* see OPINE

opponent *n* one who expresses or manifests opposition < his *opponent* in the debate>

syn adversary, antagonist, anti, con, match, opposer, oppugnant

rel enemy, foe; competitor, rival; assailant, combatant; counteragent

con ally, colleague, comrade, confederate, partner; advocate, champion

ant exponent, pro, proponent

opportune *adj* *syn* see TIMELY 1

rel appropriate, felicitous, happy

ant inopportune

opportunity *n* a state of affairs or combination of circumstances favorable to some end < all he asked was an *opportunity* to show what he could do>

syn break, chance, look-in, occasion, opening, shot, show, squeak, time

rel room, space; leisure, liberty; relief, spell, turn; juncture, pass; dog's chance, hope, prayer

oppose *vb* **1** to place over against something to provide resistance or counterbalance < *oppose* one military force to another>

syn counter, match, pit, play (off), vie

rel array, confront, face

idiom set over against

2 *syn* see RESIST

opposed *adj* *syn* see ADVERSE 1

opposer *n* *syn* see OPPONENT

opposing *adj* *syn* see ADVERSE 1

opposite *n* something that is exactly opposed or contrary < virtue and vice are *opposites*>

syn antipode, antipole, antithesis, contra, contradictory, contrary, converse, counter, counterpole, reverse

rel contrast, counterpoint, foil; contrapositive, inverse, obverse; antonym

idiom the other extreme, the other side of the coin

con analogon, analogue, counterpart, like, parallel, similar; equal, equivalent; correlate, correlative; carbon copy, duplicate, replica

ant same

opposite *adj* being so far apart as to be or to seem irreconcilable < held *opposite* views on the solution of the problem>

syn antipodal, antipodean, antithetical, contradictory, contrary, converse, counter, diametric, polar, reverse

rel contrasting; contrapositive, inverse, obverse; antonymous; different, dissimilar, divergent, opposed, unalike, unlike, unsimilar; independent, separate, unconnected, unrelated

con alike, analogous, equivalent, like, parallel, similar; equal; correlative

ant same

opposite *prep* *syn* see TO 6

oppositely *adv* *syn* see AGAIN 5

opposite number *n* one holding an equivalent or parallel position < the Secretary of State and his *opposite number*, the Foreign Minister>

syn coordinate, counterpart, vis-à-vis; *compare* EQUAL

rel complement, cousin, equal, equivalent, like, match, tally

opposition *n* *syn* see ANTAGONISM 2

opposure *n* *syn* see ANTAGONISM 2

oppress *vb* **1** *syn* see WRONG

rel harass, harry; afflict, torment, torture; conquer, overcome, overthrow, subjugate

2 *syn* see DEPRESS 2

rel burden, distress, trouble

oppressive *adj* **1** *syn* see ONEROUS

ant unoppressive

2 *syn* see GLOOMY 3

oppressor *n* *syn* see TYRANT

opprobriate *vb* *syn* see DECRY 2

opprobrious *adj* **1** *syn* see ABUSIVE

2 *syn* see INFAMOUS 1

opprobrium *n* *syn* see DISGRACE

rel abuse, scurrility, vituperation

con credit, prestige

oppugn *vb* *syn* see CONTEND 1

oppugnant *adj* *syn* see ADVERSE 1

oppugnant *n* *syn* see OPPONENT

opt (for) *vb* *syn* see CHOOSE 1

optate *vb* *syn* see CHOOSE 1

optic *adj* *syn* see VISUAL 1

optical *adj* *syn* see VISUAL 1

optimacy *n* *syn* see ARISTOCRACY

optimism *n* an inclination to put the most favorable construction on actions and events or to anticipate the best possible outcome < was a practitioner of *optimism* in his everyday life>

syn Pollyannaism, rose-colored spectacles, sanguineness, sanguinity

rel brightness, buoyancy, happiness; idealism, positivism

con hopelessness; despair, gloom, melancholy; malism; defeatism, fatalism; cynicism

ant pessimism

optimist *n* one given to optimism < was a jaunty *optimist*>

syn hoper, Pollyanna

rel dreamer, idealist, positivist

con defeatist, fatalist; cynic, doubter, skeptic

ant pessimist

optimistic *adj* anticipating only the best to happen and minimizing all other possibili-

ties < was *optimistic* about book sales that
year >
syn fond, Pollyannaish, sanguine, upbeat;
compare HOPEFUL 1
rel bright, cheerful, merry, sunny; hopeful, hoping; assured, confident
idiom feeling on top of the world, looking
on the bright side, riding (*or* sitting) on
cloud nine
con cynical; doubtful, uncertain
ant pessimistic

option *n syn* see CHOICE 1
rel prerogative, privilege, right

optional *adj* not compulsory < attendance
at the meeting is *optional* >
syn discretionary, elective, facultative,
nonobligatory
rel free, voluntary; alternative
con demanded, imperative; enforced,
involuntary; essential, necessary
ant compulsory, mandatory, obligatory,
required

opulent *adj* 1 **syn** see RICH 1
rel lavish, prodigal, profuse; extravagant,
ostentatious, pretentious, showy; plush,
swank
con modest, simple, unpretentious
2 **syn** see LUXURIOUS 3
3 **syn** see PROFUSE

oracle *n syn* see REVELATION

oracular *adj syn* see PROPHETIC

oral *adj* 1 **syn** see VOCAL 1
2 expressed or transmitted vocally < stories of folk heroes kept alive in *oral* tradition >
syn spoken, traditional, unwritten, verbal,
word-of-mouth
rel narrated, recounted, related, told
con chronicled, recorded, written, written
down

orate *vb* to talk in a declamatory, grandiloquent, or impassioned manner < *orated* to
the crowd about the flag and patriotism >
syn bloviate, declaim, harangue, mouth,
perorate, rant, rave, soapbox
rel elocute; bombast, rodomontade, sermonize, speechify; blah-blah

oratorical *adj syn* see RHETORICAL

oratory *n* the art of speaking in public
eloquently and effectively < a politician
who was a master at *oratory* >
syn elocution, rhetoric, speechcraft

orb *n* 1 **syn** see BALL
2 **syn** see EYE 1

orbit *n syn* see RANGE 2

orchestra *n* a usually large group of musi-
cians who perform together < a string
orchestra played at the reception >
syn band, philharmonic, symphony
rel combo, ensemble

orchestrate *vb syn* see HARMONIZE 4

orchidaceous *adj syn* see SHOWY

orchids *n pl syn* see COMPLIMENT 1

ordain *vb* 1 **syn** see CONDUCT 3
2 **syn** see DICTATE

ordeal *n syn* see TRIAL 1

order *n* 1 **syn** see ASSOCIATION 2
2 **syn** see TYPE

rel bracket, branch, pigeonhole, set; estate, grade, rank, status
3 sequential occurrence in space or time
< changed the *order* of the books on the
shelf >
syn arrangement, disposal, disposition,
distribution, ordering, sequence
rel array, arrayal, collocation; allocation,
allotment, apportionment, arrayment,
proration
con disarrangement, disordering; chaos,
confusion, disorder, mix-up, muddle
4 general or approximate size or amount
< a loss on the *order* of seven million
dollars >
syn extent, magnitude, matter, neighborhood, range, tune, vicinity
rel approach, approximation, closeness,
nearness, proximity
5 manner of being arranged in space or of
occurring in time < tell everything in the
order in which it happened >
syn consecution, procession, sequence,
succession
rel consecutiveness, following, successiveness; chain, progression, series, train
6 **syn** see SUCCESSION 2
7 orderly conduct < about to call the
meeting to *order* when the interruption
occurred >
syn correctitude, correctness, decorousness, decorum, orderliness, properness,
propriety, seemliness
rel goodness, niceness, rightness; fitness,
suitability; integrity, probity, rectitude,
uprightness
con impropriety, indecorousness, indecorum, unseemliness
ant disorder
8 orderly arrangement or disposition
< troubled by the lack of *order* in their
daily lives >
syn method, orderliness, pattern, plan,
system
con anarchy, chaos, confusion, muddle,
||snafu
ant disorder
9 state with respect to quality, functioning, or status < the equipment was in very
poor *order* >
syn case, condition, estate, repair, shape
rel fettle, fitness, kilter, trim
10 a state of soundness < had his car put
in *order* for spring >
syn condition, fettle, fitness, kilter, repair,
shape, trim
rel adjustment, amendment, correction,
gear, rectification
idiom working order
con disrepair
11 the state of being appropriate to or
required by the circumstances < that remark is definitely out of *order* >
syn appositeness, appropriateness, aptness, expediency, fitness, meetness, propriety, rightness, suitability, suitableness
rel opportuneness, seasonableness, timeli-
ness; auspiciousness, favorableness; felicity, grace
con inappropriateness, unfitness, unsuitability, unsuitableness
12 **syn** see COMMAND 1
rel authorization, permission

---

syn synonym(s)   **rel** related word(s)
ant antonym(s)   **con** contrasted word(s)
idiom idiomatic equivalent(s)
|| use limited; if in doubt, see a dictionary

order *vb* 1 to bring about an orderly disposition of individuals, units, or elements < *ordered* his affairs in preparation for marriage>
syn arrange, array, dispose, marshal, methodize, organize, systematize
rel adjust, fix, regulate, right; align, line, line up, range; classify, codify, hierarchize; regiment, routine, routinize; streamline
idiom put (*or* set) in order, put in shape, put (*or* set) to rights, reduce to order, whip into shape (*or* order)
ant disorder
2 *syn* see COMMAND

ordering *n* *syn* see ORDER 3

orderliness *n* 1 *syn* see ORDER 7
ant disorderliness
2 *syn* see ORDER 8
ant disorderliness

orderly *adj* 1 following a set arrangement, design, or pattern < work out an *orderly* procedure and stick to it > < an *orderly* row of houses surrounded the village green >
syn methodic, methodical, regular, systematic
rel accurate, correct, exact, precise; alike, uniform; businesslike; conventional, formal
idiom in apple-pie order
con haphazard, irregular, unmethodical, unsystematic; careless, casual, free and easy
ant chaotic, disorderly
2 *syn* see NEAT 2
rel picked up
ant disordered; disorderly

order up *vb* *syn* see CALL UP

ordinance *n* *syn* see LAW 1

ordinarily *adv* *syn* see USUALLY 2

ordinary *adj* 1 of the customary or common type encountered in the normal course of events < *ordinary* traffic had been stopped to let the marchers pass >
syn everyday, plain, plain Jane, quotidian, routine, unremarkable, usual, workaday
rel commonplace, natural, normal, regular; customary, familiar, frequent
con infrequent, rare, uncommon; accidental, casual, chance, fortuitous
ant extraordinary
2 *syn* see COMMON 6

organ *n* 1 *syn* see MEAN 2
2 *syn* see JOURNAL

organize *vb* 1 *syn* see FOUND 2
rel construct, put together
2 *syn* see ORDER 1
rel coordinate, integrate
3 *syn* see MOBILIZE 3

‖**organized** *adj* *syn* see INTOXICATED 1

orgulous *adj* *syn* see PROUD 1

orgy *n* 1 *syn* see BINGE 1
2 an act or occasion of excessive indulgence in sex < the house detective investigated an *orgy* in the penthouse suite >
syn bacchanal, bacchanalia, debauch, party, saturnalia
3 *syn* see SPREE 1

orifice *n* *syn* see APERTURE

oriflamme *n* *syn* see FLAG

origin *n* 1 *syn* see ANCESTRY
rel maternity, parentage, paternity
2 *syn* see SOURCE

original *n* 1 a first form from which copies or reproductions can be produced < students copying the da Vinci *original* >
syn archetype, protoplast, prototype
rel forerunner, mother, precursor; model, pattern; precedent
con dummy, imitation, simulacrum; counterfeit, fake, forgery
ant copy, reproduction
2 *syn* see INNOVATOR
3 *syn* see ECCENTRIC

original *adj* 1 *syn* see FIRST 2
rel archetypal, prototypal
2 *syn* see PRIMARY 5
3 *syn* see INVENTIVE
con banal, trite; derivative, initative
ant unoriginal

originally *adv* *syn* see INITIALLY 1

originate *vb* 1 *syn* see GENERATE 1
2 *syn* see INTRODUCE 3
3 *syn* see SPRING 1
4 *syn* see BEGIN 2
5 to have one's origin or home base in < he *originates* from Ohio >
syn come (from), hail (from)
rel derive (from), spring (from), stem (from)

originative *adj* *syn* see INVENTIVE
ant unoriginative

originator *n* 1 *syn* see FATHER 2
2 *syn* see INNOVATOR

orison *n* *syn* see PRAYER

ornament *vb* *syn* see ADORN
rel enrich; embroider

ornate *adj* elaborately and often pretentiously decorated or designed < a very *ornate* room—all marble, gilt, and brocade >
syn baroque, flamboyant, florid, luscious, rich, rococo
rel elaborate, high-wrought, resplendent; labored, overdone, overelaborated, overembellished, overworked, overwrought; luxuriant, luxurious, opulent, sumptuous; aureate, gilded
con natural, plain, quiet, simple; severe, unembellished, unornamented, unostentatious, unpretentious; restrained, subdued
ant austere; chaste

ornery *adj* ‖1 *syn* see CHEAP 2
2 *syn* see CANTANKEROUS
3 *syn* see CONTRARY 3

orotund *adj* 1 *syn* see RESONANT
rel loud, stentorian
2 *syn* see RHETORICAL

orphan *adj* deprived by death of one and usually both parents < seeking homes for the countless *orphan* children from the disaster area >
syn orphaned, parentless, unparented
rel alone, solitary; abandoned, cast-off, forsaken, lost; disregarded, ignored, neglected, slighted

orphaned *adj* *syn* see ORPHAN

orphic *adj* *syn* see RECONDITE

orthodox *adj* 1 conforming to doctrines or practices that are held to be right or true by an authority, standard, or tradition < those who still hold an *orthodox* view about evolution >
syn accepted, authoritative, canonical, received, sanctioned, sound

rel acknowledged, admitted, approved; customary, official, recognized, standard, traditional; correct, proper, right
con heretical, heterodox, unauthoritative, uncanonical
ant unorthodox
2 *syn* see CONVENTIONAL 1
3 *syn* see CONSERVATIVE 1
ant unorthodox

oscillate *vb syn* see SWING 2
osculate *vb syn* see KISS 1
ostend *vb syn* see SHOW 1
ostensible *adj* 1 *syn* see APPARENT 2
2 *syn* see ALLEGED
ostensibly *adv* to all outward appearances <*ostensibly* it was a business trip but actually it was all pleasure>
syn apparently, evidently, officially, outwardly, professedly, seemingly
rel externally, superficially; sensibly
idiom on the face of it, on the surface, to the eye
con genuinely, really, truly; au fond, basically

ostentatious *adj syn* see SHOWY
ant unostentatious
ostracism *n syn* see EXILE 1
ostracize *vb* 1 *syn* see BANISH
con accept, entertain, receive, welcome; harbor, haven, refuge, shelter
2 *syn* see CUT 7
other *adj* 1 *syn* see DIFFERENT 1
2 *syn* see ADDITIONAL
‖**othergates** *adv syn* see OTHERWISE 1
other half *n syn* see RABBLE 2
otherness *n syn* see DISSIMILARITY
‖**otherways** *adv syn* see OTHERWISE 2
‖**otherwhile** *adv syn* see SOMETIMES
otherwise *adv* 1 in a different way or manner <he could not act *otherwise*>
syn differently, diversely, ‖othergates, variously
ant likewise
2 under different conditions <might *otherwise* have left>
syn else, ‖elseways, elsewise, ‖otherways
otherwise *adj syn* see DIFFERENT 1
otherworld *n syn* see HEREAFTER 2
otherworldly *adj* 1 of or relating to a world other than the actual world <believed in the existence of *otherworldly* phenomena>
syn transcendental, transmundane
rel exterrestrial, extramundane, extraterrestrial; unearthly, unworldly
2 *syn* see DREAMY 1
otiose *adj syn* see VAIN 1
rel purposeless, useless; inexcusable; superfluous, supernumerary, surplus
oubliette *n syn* see DUNGEON
ought *vb syn* see WANT 3
ought *n syn* see OBLIGATION 2
ounce *n syn* see PARTICLE
oust *vb* 1 *syn* see DEPRIVE 2
2 *syn* see BANISH
out *adv syn* see OUTDOORS
out *vb* 1 *syn* see EJECT 1
2 *syn* see EXTINGUISH 1

3 *syn* see GET OUT 2
out *n syn* see SHOWING 1
out and away *adv syn* see FAR AND AWAY
out-and-out *adj syn* see UTTER
‖**outback** *n syn* see FRONTIER 2
outbalance *vb syn* see OUTWEIGH 1
outbloom *vb syn* see BLOSSOM
outbreak *n* 1 a sudden or violent beginning of activity <an *outbreak* of new housing starts>
syn burst, eruption, flare, outburst; *compare* EPIDEMIC
rel beginning, commencement, dawn, onset, outset
2 *syn* see EPIDEMIC
outbreathe *vb syn* see EXHALE
outburst *n* 1 a violent expression of emotion <an *outburst* of anger>
syn access, burst, eruption, explosion, flare-up, gust, sally
rel scene, storm, tantrum; frenzy, rapture, transport(s)
2 *syn* see OUTBREAK 1
outcast *n* one who is cast out by society <a political *outcast*>
syn castaway, derelict, Ishmael, Ishmaelite, leper, offscouring, pariah, untouchable
rel hobo, tramp, vagabond, vagrant; displaced person; exile, expatriate; reprobate
con big name, bigwig, celebrity, lion, luminary, name, notable, personage, somebody
outcome *n syn* see EFFECT 1
outcomer *n syn* see STRANGER
out-country *adj syn* see RURAL
outcrier *n syn* see PEDDLER
outcry *n syn* see COMMOTION 1
outdare *vb syn* see FACE 3
outdate *vb* to make obsolete or out-of-date <the automobile *outdated* the horse and buggy>
syn antiquate, obsolesce, obsolete, outmode, superannuate
rel age, date, fossilize; replace, supersede
outdated *adj syn* see OLD-FASHIONED
ant up-to-the-minute
outdistance *vb syn* see OUTSTRIP 1
outdo *vb* 1 *syn* see SURPASS 1
idiom out-Herod Herod, steal (*or* get) a march on
2 *syn* see DEFEAT 1
outdoor *adj* taking place, done, or existing in the open air <an *outdoor* restaurant>
syn alfresco, hypaethral, open-air, out-of-door, outside
ant indoor, inside
outdoors *adv* in or into the open air <went *outdoors* for some fresh air>
syn out, out of doors, outside, without, withoutdoors
ant indoors, inside, withindoors
outdoors *n pl but sing in constr* the space where air is unconfined <every night he let the dog run in the *outdoors*>
syn open, open air, out-of-doors, outside, without
idiom God's good (*or* green) earth
outer *adj* being or located outside something <the sheep's thick *outer* coat of wool>
syn exterior, external, outside, outward, over

---

syn synonym(s)   *rel* related word(s)
ant antonym(s)   *con* contrasted word(s)
idiom idiomatic equivalent(s)
‖ use limited; if in doubt, see a dictionary

rel extraneous, extrinsic, superficial, surface; outlying, remote
con inside, interior, internal, inward
ant inner

outermost *adj syn* see EXTREME 5
ant inmost, innermost

outface *vb syn* see FACE 3

outfit *n* 1 *syn* see EQUIPMENT
2 *syn* see COSTUME
3 *syn* see COMPANY 4
4 *syn* see ENTERPRISE 3

outfit *vb syn* see FURNISH 1

outfox *vb syn* see OUTWIT

outgeneral *vb syn* see OUTWIT
rel outfight, outflank, outgame
idiom steal a march

outgo *vb syn* see SURPASS 1

outgoing *adj syn* see DEMONSTRATIVE
ant aloof

outgrowth *n* 1 a projecting part of an organism < a warty *outgrowth* on the skin >
syn excrescence, excrescency, process, processus
rel enlargement, prolongation, swelling; offshoot, shoot
2 something that develops or grows directly out of something else < the new TV series was an *outgrowth* of a popular play >
syn by-product, derivative, descendant, offshoot, spin-off
rel branch, member; child, offspring, product; aftereffect, consequence, effect, issue, outcome, result
con origin, root, source; antecedent, cause, determinant

outhouse *n syn* see PRIVY 1

outing *n syn* see EXCURSION 1

outjockey *vb syn* see OUTWIT

outland *adj syn* see RURAL

outlander *n syn* see STRANGER

outlandish *adj* 1 *syn* see BARBARIC 1
rel foreign, strange
2 *syn* see STRANGE 4
rel monstrous; outré
con commonplace, everyday
3 marked by sharp departure from the traditional or usual < men who wear beads, feathers, and other *outlandish* gear >
syn far-out, kinky, outré, ultra; *compare* EXTREME 3
rel bizarre, extravagant, outrageous, wild; unconventional, unorthodox
con conservative, conventional; compliant, conformable; moderate
4 *syn* see BACK 1

outlast *vb syn* see OUTLIVE

outlaw *n* a criminal of the American western frontier < *outlaws* held up stagecoaches >
syn badman, ‖bandido, bandit, desperado
rel gunman, gunslinger
idiom bad guy

outlaw *vb syn* see FORBID

outlay *vb syn* see SPEND 1

outlay *n syn* see EXPENSE 1

outlet *n* 1 *syn* see APERTURE
2 *syn* see EGRESS 2
rel escape; release
3 *syn* see STORE 4

outline *n* the line that gives form or shape to a body or a figure < saw only a dark *outline* of the house through the gloom >
syn contour, delineation, figuration, line, lineament, lineation, profile, silhouette
rel configuration, conformation, figure, form, shape; skyline
con bulk, bulk, mass

outline *vb* 1 *syn* see BORDER 1
2 *syn* see SKETCH

outlive *vb* to remain in existence longer than < the committee has *outlived* its usefulness >
syn outlast, outwear, survive
rel outstand, outstay

outlook *n* 1 *syn* see LOOKOUT 2
2 *syn* see VISTA
3 *syn* see VIEW 4
4 *syn* see VIEWPOINT 2

outlying *adj syn* see DISTANT 1

outmaneuver *vb syn* see OUTWIT
idiom steal a march (on)

outmatch *vb syn* see SURPASS 1

outmode *vb syn* see OUTDATE

outmoded *adj* 1 *syn* see OLD-FASHIONED
2 *syn* see OBSOLETE
3 *syn* see TACKY 2

outmost *adj syn* see EXTREME 5
ant inmost, innermost

out-of-date *adj* 1 *syn* see OLD-FASHIONED
ant up-to-date
2 *syn* see TACKY 2

out-of-door *adj syn* see OUTDOOR

out-of-doors *n pl but sing in constr syn* see OUTDOORS

out of doors *adv syn* see OUTDOORS

out-of-the-way *adj syn* see OBSCURE 2

outpace *vb syn* see OUTSTRIP 1

outplace *vb syn* see REPLACE 3

output *n* the amount of something produced < an annual *output* of 3,000,000 units >
syn outturn, product, production, turnout, yield
rel gain, get, profit, take; crop, harvest
con input; raw material

outrage *n syn* see INJURY 1

outrage *vb* 1 *syn* see RAPE
2 *syn* see ABUSE 4
3 *syn* see WRONG
4 *syn* see OFFEND 3

outrageous *adj* 1 exceeding the limits of what is normal or tolerable < *outrageous* prices that threaten our way of life >
syn barbarous, unchristian, uncivilized, unconscionable, ungodly, unholy, wicked
rel abominable, awful, beastly, dreadful, ghastly, horrible, horrid, impossible, intolerable, terrible, unreasonable; scandalous, shocking
con normal, reasonable, tolerable; acceptable, bearable, endurable, supportable
2 enormously or flagrantly bad or horrible < *outrageous* treatment of prisoners >
syn atrocious, crying, desperate, heinous, monstrous, scandalous, shocking
rel enormous, flagrant, gross; egregious, nefarious, notorious, villainous
con condonable, excusable, forgivable, pardonable; defensible, justifiable; legitimate, reasonable; comprehensible, plausible, understandable

outrank *vb syn* see PRECEDE 1

outré *adj syn* see OUTLANDISH 3

outreach *vb syn* see OUTWIT

outrecuidance *n syn* see CONCEIT 2

outrider *n syn* see FORERUNNER 1

outright *adj* 1 *syn* see UTTER
2 *syn* see WHOLE 4

outrun *vb syn* see OUTSTRIP 1

outset *n syn* see BEGINNING

outshine *vb syn* see SURPASS 1

outside *n syn* see OUTDOORS

outside *adj* 1 *syn* see OUTER
rel alien, foreign
ant inside
2 *syn* see OUTDOOR
3 *syn* see MAXIMUM
4 *syn* see REMOTE 4

outside *adv syn* see OUTDOORS

outside *prep* 1 *syn* see BEYOND 1
2 *syn* see EXCEPT

outside of *prep syn* see EXCEPT

outsider *n syn* see STRANGER
con insider

outskirt *n usu* outskirts *pl syn* see ENVIRONS 2

outslick *vb syn* see OUTWIT

outsmart *vb syn* see OUTWIT

outspeed *vb syn* see OUTSTRIP 1

outspoken *adj* speaking without fear or
reserve < quite *outspoken* in her views on
child rearing >
syn free, free-spoken, round, vocal
rel candid, direct, forthright, frank, open,
plain, plainspoken, straightforward, unreticent; bluff, blunt; explicit, point-blank,
unequivocal; strident
con reserved, restrained, reticent; private,
retiring, shrinking; unassertive

outspread *vb syn* see OPEN 4
ant folded *(of wings or a fan)*

outstanding *adj* 1 *syn* see UNPAID 2
2 *syn* see NOTICEABLE
3 *syn* see CHIEF 2
4 *syn* see SUPERB 3

outstare *vb syn* see STARE DOWN

outstart *n syn* see BEGINNING

outstep *vb syn* see EXCEED 1

outstretch *vb syn* see OPEN 4

outstrip *vb* 1 to go faster than < could
outstrip even the fastest horse >
syn distance, outdistance, outpace, outrun, outspeed
rel outfly, outsoar, outwing; outfoot,
outrace, outride; outsail; outtravel; lose,
shake off
con follow, trail; drag, hang back, lag
2 *syn* see SURPASS 1

outsweepings *n pl syn* see REFUSE

outthink *vb syn* see OUTWIT

outthrust *n syn* see PROJECTION 1

outtire *vb syn* see EXHAUST 4

outturn *n syn* see OUTPUT

outward *adj syn* see OUTER
ant inward

outwardly *adv syn* see OSTENSIBLY
ant inwardly

outwear *vb* 1 *syn* see EXHAUST 4
2 *syn* see OUTLIVE

outweigh *vb* 1 to exceed in weight, value,
or importance < her brother *outweighed*
her by nearly fifty pounds > < the facts
outweigh his argument >
syn outbalance, overbalance, overweigh,
overweight
rel overbear
2 *syn* see COMPENSATE 1

outweighing *adj syn* see DOMINANT 1

outwit *vb* to defeat or get the better of by
superior cleverness or ingenuity < *outwitted* the enemy by taking a different
route >
syn have, outfox, outgeneral, outjockey,
outmaneuver, outreach, outslick, outsmart,
outthink, overreach; undo; *compare* FRUS-
TRATE 1
rel bamboozle, befool, dupe, gull, hoax,
hoodwink, outtrick, outtrump, trick;
outdo; outguess

outworn *adj syn* see OBSOLETE

oval *adj* having the shape of a longitudinal
section of an egg < an *oval* pond >
syn ooid, ovate, oviform, ovoid
rel ovaloid; ellipsoidal, elliptic

ovate *adj syn* see OVAL

over *adv* 1 from one point to another
across intervening space < sailed *over* to
the island >
syn across, athwart, beyond, transversely
2 *syn* see AWAY 2
3 *syn* see EVER 6
4 at a higher point < the plane was directly *over* >
syn above, aloft, overhead
idiom on high
ant under
5 at or to an end < it's all *over* between
them >
syn by, through
6 *syn* see THROUGH 1
7 yet another time < do the work *over* >
syn afresh, again, anew, de novo, once
more
idiom over again

over *prep* 1 at a higher level < clouds hung
over the town >
syn above, o'er
ant under
2 *syn* see ACROSS
3 with respect to < children squabbling
over toys >
syn about, on, upon, with
4 so as to make contact with < hit him
over the head >
syn on, upon
5 *syn* see DURING
6 as the result of < quarreled *over* money
matters >
syn because of, due to, owing to, through

over *adj* 1 *syn* see SUPERIOR 1
ant under
2 *syn* see OUTER

over *vb syn* see CLEAR 8

overbounding *adj syn* see SUPERABUN-
DANT

overabundance *n syn* see EXCESS 1

overabundant *adj syn* see SUPERABUN-
DANT

overact *vb* to exaggerate in acting especially on the stage or screen < was criticized for *overacting* the part >

---

syn synonym(s)   *rel* related word(s)
ant antonym(s)   *con* contrasted word(s)
idiom idiomatic equivalent(s)

‖ use limited; if in doubt, see a dictionary

syn overplay

rel ham, mug; declaim, rant, spout

idiom chew the scenery

ant underact, underplay

over against *prep* **1** *syn* see AGAINST 1

2 *syn* see VERSUS 2

overage *n syn* see EXCESS 2

ant shortage, underage

overall *adv* **1** *syn* see EVERYWHERE 1

2 *syn* see GENERALLY 1

overall *adj syn* see ALL-AROUND 2

over and above *prep syn* see BESIDES 1

over and over *adv syn* see OFTEN

overbalance *vb syn* see OUTWEIGH 1

overbalanced *adj syn* see LOPSIDED

overbalancing *adj syn* see DOMINANT 1

overbearing *adj* **1** *syn* see MASTERFUL 1

2 *syn* see DOMINANT 1

3 *syn* see PROUD 1

rel absolute, autocratic, despotic, tyrannical

con passive, unassertive; acquiescent, compliant, unresisting

ant subservient

overblown *adj* **1** *syn* see FAT 2

2 *syn* see INFLATED

3 *syn* see RHETORICAL

4 *syn* see PRETENTIOUS 3

overbold *adj syn* see SHAMELESS

overbrim *vb syn* see OVERFLOW 2

overburden *vb syn* see OVERLOAD

overcast *vb* **1** *syn* see OBSCURE

2 *syn* see COVER 3

overcast *adj* clouded over <a gray *overcast* March day>

syn cloudy, ||dowly, dull, heavy, lowering (*or* louring), nubilous, overclouded

rel brooding, dirty, oppressive, sullen

ant clear, cloudless

overcharge *vb* **1** to charge excessively for service or goods <a clip joint well known for *overcharging* customers>

syn clip, fleece, skin, soak, stick

ant undercharge

2 *syn* see OVERLOAD

3 *syn* see EMBROIDER

overcloud *vb syn* see OBSCURE

overclouded *adj syn* see OVERCAST

overcome *vb* **1** to get the better of <*overcome* a bad habit>

syn conquer, down, hurdle, lick, master, surmount, throw; *compare* CONQUER 2

rel beat, defeat; outlive, prevail

con adopt, embrace, take up; indulge

2 *syn* see CONQUER 2

3 *syn* see OVERWHELM 4

4 *syn* see WIN 1

overconfident *adj syn* see PRESUMPTUOUS

overcritical *adj syn* see CRITICAL 1

overdo *vb* to make excessive use or application of <he has *overdone* that joke to the point that it is no longer funny>

syn overplay, overuse, overwork

idiom go overboard, go to extremes, run into the ground

overdoing *n syn* see EXTRAVAGANCE 2

overdraw *vb syn* see EMBROIDER

overdue *adj* **1** *syn* see UNPAID 2

2 *syn* see TARDY

ant early

overearly *adj syn* see EARLY 2

overemphasize *vb syn* see OVERPLAY 2

ant underemphasize

overesteem *vb syn* see OVERVALUE

overestimate *vb syn* see OVERVALUE

ant underestimate

overfill *vb syn* see OVERFLOW 2

overflow *vb* **1** *syn* see DELUGE 1

2 to flow over the brim <the river *overflowed* its banks>

syn overbrim, overfill, overrun, run over, spill, well over

rel brim, cascade, slop, slosh

con drop, recede, withdraw

overflow *n* **1** *syn* see FLOOD 2

2 *syn* see EXCESS 1

overflowing *adj* **1** *syn* see ALIVE 5

2 *syn* see SUPERABUNDANT

overfull *adv syn* see EVER 6

overgrown *adj* covered with growth or herbage <a vacant lot *overgrown* with weeds>

syn grown, rank

rel braky, brambly, brushy, copsy, jungly, thicketed, thickety; dense, overrun, thick; lush

||**overhand** *n syn* see ADVANTAGE 3

overhang *vb* **1** *syn* see BULGE

2 *syn* see HANG 4

overhanging *adj syn* see IMMINENT 2

overhaul *vb* **1** *syn* see MEND 2

2 *syn* see CATCH 7

overhead *adv syn* see OVER 4

ant underfoot

overheated *adj syn* see IMPASSIONED

overindulgence *n syn* see EXCESS 3

overindulgent *adj syn* see EXCESSIVE 2

overkill *n syn* see EXCESS 1

overlade *vb syn* see OVERLOAD

overlap *vb* to extend over and cover a part of <each course of shingles should *overlap* the preceding course by several inches>

syn imbricate, lap, overlie, override, ride, shingle

overlay *vb syn* see COVER 3

overleap *vb* **1** *syn* see CLEAR 8

2 *syn* see NEGLECT

overlie *vb syn* see OVERLAP

overload *vb* to load to excess <*overload* a ship>

syn overburden, overcharge, overlade, overtax, overweigh, overweight

con lighten

overlong *adj syn* see LONG 2

overlook *vb* **1** *syn* see SURVEY 3

2 to rise above and afford a view of <the tower *overlooks* the city>

syn dominate, look down, overtop, tower (above *or* over)

rel oversee

3 *syn* see NEGLECT

4 *syn* see SUPERVISE

overlook *n* **1** *syn* see OMISSION

2 *syn* see LOOKOUT 2

overly *adv syn* see EVER 6

overlying *adj syn* see SUPERIOR 1

ant underlying

overmuch *n syn* see EXCESS 1

overmuch *adv syn* see EVER 6

overnice *adj syn* see PRECIOUS 4

overpaint *vb syn* see EMBROIDER

overpass *vb syn* see NEGLECT

overpeopled *adj syn* see OVERPOPULATED

ant underpeopled

overplay *vb* 1 *syn* see OVERACT

  ant underact, underplay

  2 to give undue attention or emphasis to < *overplaying* the ephemeral at the expense of the significant >

  syn magnify, maximize, overemphasize, overstress

  rel accent, accentuate, point up; dramatize, exaggerate, hyperbolize, overdraw, overstate, stretch; overvalue

  idiom lay it on thick

  con downgrade, downplay; minimize

  3 *syn* see OVERDO

overplus *n* *syn* see EXCESS 1

overpopulated *adj* populated too densely < *overpopulated* cities >

  syn overpeopled

  rel congested, dense, overcrowded

  con empty, vacant, void; unpopulated

  ant underpopulated

overpower *vb* 1 *syn* see CONQUER 1

  2 *syn* see OVERWHELM 4

overpress *vb* *syn* see PRESSURE

overprize *vb* *syn* see OVERVALUE

  ant underprize, undervalue

overrate *vb* *syn* see OVERVALUE

  ant underrate

overreach *vb* 1 *syn* see CHEAT

  2 *syn* see OUTWIT

overreckon *vb* *syn* see OVERVALUE

overrefined *adj* *syn* see PRECIOUS 4

override *vb* *syn* see OVERLAP

overriding *adj* *syn* see CENTRAL 1

  rel primary, principal

overripe *adj* *syn* see EFFETE 3

overrule *vb* *syn* see GOVERN 1

overruling *adj* *syn* see CENTRAL 1

overrun *vb* 1 *syn* see WHIP 2

  2 *syn* see INVADE 1

  3 *syn* see INFEST 1

  4 *syn* see EXCEED 1

  5 *syn* see OVERFLOW 2

oversea *adj* *syn* see OVERSEAS

oversea *adv* beyond or across the sea < served *oversea* for two years >

  syn abroad

  con stateside

overseas *adj* situated, originating in, or relating to lands overseas < attempting to tap the potential of *overseas* markets >

  syn oversea, transmarine, ultramarine

  rel alien, exotic, foreign, strange

  con domestic, home; stateside

oversee *vb* 1 *syn* see SURVEY 3

  2 *syn* see SUPERVISE

overset *vb* 1 *syn* see OVERTURN 1

  2 *syn* see OVERTHROW 2

overshadow *vb* *syn* see OBSCURE

oversight *n* 1 the function or duty of watching or guarding for the sake of proper direction or control < had *oversight* of the children as they played >

  syn care, charge, conduct, handling, intendance, management, running, superintendence, superintendency, supervision

  rel custody, guard, guardianship; keeping, maintenance; surveillance; aegis, tutelage; ciceronage; chaperonage; check, control

---

  2 *syn* see FAILURE 1

  3 *syn* see OMISSION

oversize *adj* *syn* see LARGE 1

  ant undersized

overslaugh *vb* *syn* see HINDER

oversoon *adj* *syn* see EARLY 2

oversoon *adv* *syn* see EARLY 2

overspread *vb* 1 *syn* see COVER 3

  2 *syn* see INFEST 1

overstate *vb* *syn* see EMBROIDER

  ant understate

overstatement *n* *syn* see EXAGGERATION

  ant understatement

overstep *vb* *syn* see EXCEED 1

  rel infringe, transgress, trespass

overstock *n* *syn* see EXCESS 2

  ant understock

overstress *vb* *syn* see OVERPLAY 2

oversupply *n* *syn* see EXCESS 2

  ant undersupply

overswarm *vb* 1 *syn* see INFEST 1

  2 *syn* see INVADE 1

oversway *vb* *syn* see INDUCE 1

overtake *vb* *syn* see CATCH 7

overtax *vb* *syn* see OVERLOAD

overthrow *vb* 1 *syn* see OVERTURN 1

  2 to cause the downfall of < *overthrow* the government >

  syn overset, overturn, topple, tumble, unhorse; *compare* CONQUER 1

  rel depose, dethrone, oust, remove, unseat; liquidate, purge; conquer, defeat, destroy, ruin

  con create, establish, found, set up

overthrow *n* *syn* see DEFEAT 1

overtone *n* *syn* see ASSOCIATION 4

overtop *vb* *syn* see OVERLOOK 2

overture *n* 1 action intended to attract favorable attention < made friendly *overtures* to the new member of the class >

  syn advance, approach

  rel bid, proposal, proposition, tender

  2 *syn* see INTRODUCTION

overturn *vb* 1 to turn from an upright or level position < the embarrassed boy backed into the table and *overturned* a lamp >

  syn knock over, overset, overthrow, tip (over), topple, turn over, upset

  rel capsize, keel (over *or* up), upend, upturn; prostrate; down; roll (over)

  con erect, right, set up, straighten (up)

  2 *syn* see OVERTHROW 2

overturn *n* *syn* see SHAKE-UP

overuse *vb* *syn* see OVERDO

  ant underuse

overvalue *vb* to set too high a value on < inclined to *overvalue* his own charm >

  syn overesteem, overestimate, overprize, overrate, overreckon

  rel cherish, prize, treasure; adore, idolize, worship

  con belittle, depreciate

  ant underprize, undervalue

overweening *adj* *syn* see PRESUMPTUOUS

overweigh *vb* 1 *syn* see OUTWEIGH 1

  2 *syn* see OVERLOAD

overweighing *adj* *syn* see DOMINANT 1

overweight *vb* 1 *syn* see OUTWEIGH 1

  2 *syn* see OVERLOAD

overweight *adj* *syn* see FAT 2

  ant underweight

overwhelm *vb* 1 *syn* see DELUGE 1

---

syn synonym(s)   *rel* related word(s)

ant antonym(s)   *con* contrasted word(s)

idiom idiomatic equivalent(s)

‖ use limited; if in doubt, see a dictionary

2 *syn* see DELUGE 3

3 *syn* see WHIP 2

4 to subject to the grip of something overpowering and usually distressing or damaging < *overwhelmed* by the death of his only child > < human wants that tend to *overwhelm* environmental realities >

syn drown, knock over, overcome, overpower, prostrate, whelm

rel demoralize, devastate, dumbfound, shatter; floor, sink; disturb, upset; destroy, ruin, wreck; downgrade, lower, subordinate

overwhelmed *adj syn* see AGHAST 2

overwhelming *adj syn* see TOWERING 4

overwork *vb syn* see OVERDO

oviform *adj syn* see OVAL

ovoid *adj syn* see OVAL

owing *adj syn* see UNPAID 2

owing to *prep syn* see OVER 6

owl-light *n syn* see EVENING 1

own *vb* 1 *syn* see HAVE 1

2 *syn* see ACKNOWLEDGE 1

con deny, disclaim

ant disown, repudiate

owner *n* one that has the legal or rightful title < *owner* of the shop >

syn holder, possessor, proprietor

rel lord, master

con lessee, renter, tenant; squatter; interloper, intruder, trespasser

ownership *n* lawful claim or title < would soon have *ownership* of the house >

syn dominion, possession, possessorship, property, proprietary, proprietorship

rel hand

own up *vb syn* see ACKNOWLEDGE 1

oyster *n syn* see FORTE

P

pa *n syn* see FATHER 1

pablum *n syn* see PAP 2

pabulum *n syn* see FOOD 2

pace *n* 1 *syn* see TEMPO

2 *syn* see SPEED 2

3 *syn* see ROUTINE

pace *vb* 1 *syn* see WALK 1

2 *syn* see PRECEDE 2

pacific *adj* affording or promoting peace < a *pacific* policy >

syn irenic, nonviolent, pacificatory, pacifist, peaceable, peaceful

rel appeasing, conciliating, conciliatory, pacifying, propitiating, propitiatory; dovelike, gentle, inoffensive

con belligerent, combative, contentious, pugnacious, quarrelsome; unpeaceable, unpeaceful; hawkish, violent, warlike

ant bellicose, unpacific

pacificator *n syn* see PEACEMAKER

pacificatory *adj syn* see PACIFIC

pacificist *n syn* see PACIFIST

idiom man of peace

pacifist *n* one who opposes war or violence as a means of settling disputes < *pacifists* who fight war with argument and propaganda >

syn dove, pacificist

rel satyagrahi; ||conchie, conscientious objector; peacemonger

con belligerent, combatant; chauvinist, hawk, jingo, jingoist, warmonger

ant bellicist

pacifistic *adj syn* see PACIFIC

ant combative

pacify *vb* to allay anger or agitation < saw his mounting rage and tried to *pacify* him >

syn appease, assuage, conciliate, mollify, placate, propitiate, sweeten

rel dulcify, soften; allay, alleviate, mitigate, relieve; moderate, qualify, smooth (over), temper

idiom pour balm into, pour oil on (the) troubled waters

con arouse, stir (up)

ant anger

pack *n* 1 *syn* see BACKPACK

2 *syn* see MUCH

pack *vb* 1 *syn* see STOW

2 *syn* see LOAD 3

3 *syn* see CARRY 1

packed *adj syn* see FULL 1

idiom packed like sardines (or herrings)

||**packed out** *adj syn* see FULL 1

packet *n syn* see FORTUNE 4

packman *n syn* see PEDDLER

packsack *n syn* see BACKPACK

pact *n* 1 *syn* see CONTRACT

rel settlement

2 *syn* see TREATY

||**pad** *n syn* see PROTECTION 2

pad *vb syn* see EMBROIDER

paddle *vb syn* see ROW

||**paddy** *n syn* see POLICEMAN

pagan *adj syn* see HEATHEN

pageant *n syn* see PRETENSE 2

pagoda *n syn* see SUMMERHOUSE

pain *n* 1 a bodily sensation that causes acute discomfort or suffering < suffering from chest *pains* >

syn ache, ||misery, pang, stitch, throe, twinge

rel discomfort, distress, hurt, suffering; agony, torment, torture

2 **pains** *pl syn* see EFFORT 1

rel assiduousness, diligence, industry, sedulousness

pain *vb* 1 *syn* see HURT 4

rel agonize, convulse, crucify, excruciate, harrow, lacerate

2 *syn* see DISTRESS 2

rel afflict; distress, upset; wound; anguish

idiom ||hit one where one lives

3 *syn* see TRY 2

painful *adj* 1 causing, marked by, or affected with pain < a *painful* wound >

syn aching, afflictive, algetic, hurtful, hurting, sore

rel raw; acute, piercing, sharp, shooting, stabbing, stinging; agonizing, excruciating, harrowing, racking, tormenting, torturous *ant* painless, unpainful

2 *syn* see BITTER 2
   rel unappetizing, unsavory
   ant painless

painfully *adv syn* see HARD 5
   ant painlessly

pain–killer *n syn* see ANODYNE 1

painstaking *adj syn* see CAREFUL 2

painstakingly *adv syn* see HARD 3
   rel carefully, meticulously; lovingly

paint *n syn* see MAKEUP 3

pair *n syn* see COUPLE

paired *adj syn* see TWIN

pal *n syn* see ASSOCIATE 3

palace *adj syn* see LUXURIOUS 3

palace car *n syn* see PARLOR CAR

palatable *adj* agreeable or pleasant especially to the sense of taste <a *palatable* meal>
   syn aperitive, appetizing, flavorsome, good-tasting, ‖gusty, mouth-watering, relishing, sapid, saporous, savorous, savorsome, savory, tasteful, tasty, toothsome, toothy
   rel delectable, delicious, delightful, luscious, scrumptious, yummy; tempting; saporific
   con bad-tasting, disagreeable, distasteful, ill-flavored, unappetizing
   ant unpalatable

palate *n syn* see TASTE 4

palatial *adj syn* see LUXURIOUS 3
   rel noble, regal; monumental; impressive; rich, splendid

palaver *n* 1 *syn* see CONFERENCE 2
   rel dialogue, discussion; parley
   2 *syn* see CHATTER
   rel gas, guff, hot air
   3 *syn* see TERMINOLOGY
   4 *syn* see BUSINESS 8

palaverous *adj syn* see WORDY

pale *adj* 1 deficient in color or in intensity of color <a *pale* face>
   syn ashen, ashy, blanched, colorless, complexionless, doughy, livid, lurid, pallid, paly, wan, waxen
   rel sallow, sick, sickly; gray, pasty, pasty-faced, waxlike; white, whitened; deathlike, ghastly
   con flushed, ruddy; bright, colorful, florid
   2 being weak and thin in substance or in vital qualities <a *pale*, inadequate foreign policy>
   syn anemic, bloodless, pallid, waterish, watery
   rel inane, insipid, jejune, wishy-washy; insubstantial, unsubstantial; ineffective, ineffectual; faint, feeble, weak
   con strong, substantial; effective, effectual; bright, colorful
   ant brilliant

pale *vb syn* see DULL 1

Pale Horse *n. used with* the *syn* see DEATH 1

palinode *vb syn* see ABJURE

pall *vb* 1 *syn* see BORE
   2 *syn* see SATIATE
   rel disgust, weary

pallet *n syn* see HEAD 1

palliate *vb* to give a speciously fine appearance to what is erroneous, base, or evil <did not try to conceal or *palliate* his errors>
   syn blanch (over), extenuate, gloss (over), gloze (over), prettify, sugarcoat, varnish, veneer, white, whiten, whitewash
   rel alleviate, lighten, mitigate; condone, excuse; moderate, qualify, soften, temper; camouflage, cloak, conceal, cover up, disguise, dissemble, mask; hush (up)
   idiom paper over the cracks, put a good face on (*or* upon)

pallid *adj* 1 *syn* see PALE 1
   2 *syn* see PALE 2

pally *adj syn* see INTIMATE 4

palm (on *or* **upon)** *vb syn* see FOIST 3

‖palm grease *n syn* see GRATUITY

palm off *vb syn* see FOIST 3

‖palm oil *n syn* see GRATUITY

palooka *n syn* see OAF 2

palpable *adj* 1 *syn* see TANGIBLE 1
   2 *syn* see PERCEPTIBLE
   rel apparent, ostensible, seeming; believable, colorable, credible, plausible
   3 *syn* see CLEAR 5
   rel certain, positive, sure; arresting, noticeable, remarkable, striking
   con doubtful, dubious, problematic, questionable
   ant impalpable

palpate *vb syn* see TOUCH 1

palpation *n syn* see TOUCH 2

palpitate *vb syn* see PULSATE
   rel pitter-patter

‖palsy–walsy *adj syn* see INTIMATE 4

palter *vb* 1 *syn* see LIE
   rel evade, fence
   idiom play false, play fast and loose
   2 *syn* see HAGGLE 2

paltry *adj* 1 *syn* see CHEAP 2
   rel beggarly, shabby; pitiful
   2 *syn* see LITTLE 2
   rel base, low, low-down, vile
   3 *syn* see PETTY 2
   rel insignificant, unimportant

paly *adj syn* see PALE 1

pamper *vb syn* see BABY
   rel regale, tickle; caress, dandle, fondle, pet; overindulge

‖pan *n syn* see FACE 1

pan *vb syn* see CRITICIZE

panacea *n* a remedy for all ills or difficulties <bicycles are not a *panacea* for the traffic problem>
   syn catholicon, cure-all, elixir, nostrum
   rel relief; remedy
   idiom universal (*or* sovereign) remedy

pandect *n syn* see COMPENDIUM 1

pandemoniac *adj syn* see INFERNAL 2

pandemonium *n* 1 *cap* **Pandemonium** *syn* see HELL
   2 *syn* see SINK 1
   3 *syn* see DIN

pander *n syn* see PIMP 1

panegyric *n syn* see ENCOMIUM

panegyrical *adj syn* see EULOGISTIC

panegyrize *vb syn* see PRAISE 2

pang *n syn* see PAIN 1
   rel prick, stab, ‖stang

‖pang *vb syn* see CRAM 1

panhandler *n syn* see BEGGAR 1

panhandling *n syn* see MENDICANCY

panic *n* 1 *syn* see FEAR 1
 rel frenzy, hysteria; stampede
 con composure, equanimity, sangfroid, self-possession
 ||2 *syn* see RIOT 2

||**pank** *vb syn* see PANT 1

panoply *n syn* see DISPLAY 2

panorama *n syn* see RANGE 2

pan out *vb syn* see SUCCEED 2

pansified *adj syn* see EFFEMINATE

pant *vb* 1 to breathe quickly, spasmodically, or in a labored manner <was *pant-ing* after running up the stairs>
 syn blow, gasp, heave, huff, ||pank, ||pegh, puff
 rel gulp; wheeze; wind; chuff
 idiom be out of breath
 2 *syn* see AIM 2
 rel hunger, long, pine, thirst; desire, want, wish
 idiom be consumed with desire (for)

pantywaist *n syn* see WEAKLING

pantywaist *adj syn* see CHARACTERLESS

pap *n* 1 *syn* see FOOD 2
 2 something (as reading matter) lacking in solid value or substance <the sentimental *pap* that he offered his readers>
 syn pablum, rubbish, slop
 rel garbage, trash

||**pap** *n syn* see FATHER 1

papa *n syn* see FATHER 1

paper *n syn* see ESSAY 2

paphian *n syn* see HARLOT 1

pappy *adj syn* see SOFT 6

||**pappy** *n syn* see FATHER 1

par *n* 1 *syn* see EQUIVALENCE
 2 *syn* see AVERAGE
 rel standard

parable *n syn* see ALLEGORY 2
 rel comparison, similitude

parachronism *n syn* see ANACHRONISM 1

parade *n syn* see DISPLAY 2
 rel exhibition

parade *vb syn* see SHOW 4
 rel disclose, divulge, reveal; advertise, declare, proclaim, publish; boast, brag, gasconade
 idiom parade one's wares
 con camouflage, cloak, disguise, dissemble, mask

paradigm *n syn* see MODEL 2

paradigmatic *adj syn* see TYPICAL 1

paradise *n* 1 *syn* see HEAVEN 2
 idiom the next world (*or* life)
 2 *syn* see UTOPIA

paragon *n* an individual of unequaled excellence often serving as a model <she is a *paragon* of a housewife>
 syn ideal, jewel, nonesuch, nonpareil, phoenix; *compare* MODEL 2
 rel apotheosis, epitome, last word, quintessence, ultimate; archetype, beau ideal, exemplar, pattern; ||beaut, beauty, crackerjack, gem, love, lovely, peach, trump; champ, champion; cream, pick, tops

paragon *vb syn* see EQUATE 2

parallel *adj syn* see LIKE
 ant nonparallel, unparallel

parallel *n* one that corresponds to or closely resembles another <we seek in vain a *parallel* for this situation>

syn analogue, correlate, correspondent, counterpart, countertype, match; *compare* COUNTERPART 1, EQUAL
 rel equivalent; double, duplicate, duplication

parallel *vb* 1 *syn* see EQUATE 2
 2 to place (something) so as to be parallel with another <machines that combed and *paralleled* the fibers>
 syn collimate, collocate, parallelize
 rel align, line up

parallelize *vb syn* see PARALLEL 2

paralyze *vb* 1 to render completely powerless, ineffective, or inert <a general strike that *paralyzed* the nation>
 syn cripple, disable, disarm, immobilize, incapacitate, prostrate; *compare* MAIM, WEAKEN 1
 rel deaden, enfeeble, weaken; close, shut (down); freeze; demolish, destroy, knock out
 idiom bring to a grinding halt, tie hand and foot
 2 *syn* see DAZE 2
 rel appall, daunt, dismay, horrify; cripple, disable, enfeeble, weaken; astound, flabbergast, nonplus
 con animate, enliven, pep (up), stimulate
 ant galvanize

paramount *adj syn* see DOMINANT 1
 rel capital, headmost; commanding, controlling; cardinal, crowning

paramour *n* 1 *syn* see GALLANT 2
 2 *syn* see LOVER 1
 3 *syn* see MISTRESS

parapet *n syn* see BULWARK

paraphernalia *n pl but sometimes sing in constr syn* see EQUIPMENT 1

paraphrase *n syn* see VERSION 1

paraphrase *vb* to express or interpret something (as a text or passage) in other words <*paraphrased* the complicated document>
 syn rephrase, restate, reword, translate (into)
 rel summarize; transcribe
 con quote, reproduce

parasite *n* a person who is supported or seeks support from another without making an adequate return <lived as a *parasite* in his father's house>
 syn barnacle, bloodsucker, freeloader, hanger-on, leech, lounge lizard, ||spiv, sponge, sponger, sucker; *compare* SYCOPHANT
 rel dependent; smell-feast; deadbeat, idler, laze

parasite *vb syn* see INFEST 2

parasitic *adj syn* see FAWNING
 rel freeloading, leechlike, sponging

parasitize *vb syn* see INFEST 2

parboil *vb syn* see BOIL 2

parcel *n* 1 *syn* see PART 1
 2 *syn* see LOT 3
 3 *syn* see GROUP 3

parcel *vb syn* see APPORTION 2
 rel allocate, allot, assign; deal, disburse, disperse; dole (out), lot (out)

parch *vb syn* see DRY 1

||**pard** *n syn* see PARTNER

pardon *n* a remission of penalty or punishment <the governor granted the prisoner a *pardon*>

syn absolution, amnesty
rel acquittal, exculpation, exoneration, indemnification, indemnity; forgiveness, remission; justification, vindication
con conviction; condemnation
ant punishment

pardon *vb syn* see EXCUSE 1
rel justify; accept, tolerate; free, liberate, release
idiom let bygones be bygones, wipe the slate clean
con amerce, fine, mulct, penalize
ant punish

pardonable *adj syn* see VENIAL
ant unpardonable

pare *vb* 1 *syn* see CUT 6
rel flay, scalp, skin, strip
2 *syn* see REDUCE 2

parent *vb syn* see GENERATE 1

parenthesis *n* 1 *syn* see DIGRESSION
2 *syn* see INTERLUDE

parenthetically *adv syn* see INCIDENTALLY

parentless *adj syn* see ORPHAN
ant parented

par excellence *adj syn* see EXCELLENT

pariah *n syn* see OUTCAST
rel déclassé

‖**parish–pump** *adj syn* see INSULAR

parity *n syn* see EQUIVALENCE
rel analogy, parallelism, similitude; approximation, closeness, nearness
ant disparity, imparity

parlance *n syn* see WORDING

parley *vb* 1 *syn* see SPEAK 3
2 *syn* see CONFER 2

parley *n* 1 *syn* see TALK 4
rel rap session
2 *syn* see CONVERSATION 1

parlor car *n* a railroad passenger car equipped with individual revolving and reclining chairs and providing the services of an attendant
syn chair car, club car, lounge car, palace car, tavern car

parlor house *n syn* see BROTHEL
idiom flesh factory

parlous *adj syn* see DANGEROUS 1

parlous *adv syn* see VERY 1

Parnassian *n syn* see POET

parochial *adj syn* see INSULAR
rel prejudiced; bigoted
con unprejudiced; uncircumscribed, unlimited; cosmic, universal
ant catholic

parody *n syn* see CARICATURE 2
rel spoof, spoofery, rib, ridicule

parody *vb syn* see MIMIC

paronomasia *n syn* see PUN

parous *adj syn* see PREGNANT 1

parry *vb* 1 *syn* see DODGE 1
rel preclude, prevent; anticipate, forestall
2 *syn* see WARD 1

parsimonious *adj syn* see STINGY
idiom penny-wise and pound-foolish
ant prodigal

parson *n syn* see CLERGYMAN

---

syn synonym(s)   *rel* related word(s)
ant antonym(s)   *con* contrasted word(s)
idiom idiomatic equivalent(s)
‖ use limited; if in doubt, see a dictionary

---

part *n* 1 something less than the whole to which it belongs < a *part* of the road was paved >
syn cut, division, member, moiety, parcel, piece, portion, section, segment
rel component, constituent, element, ingredient; detail, fraction, fragment; bit, chip, scrap
con aggregate, total; combination, complex; entirety, entity, totality, unity
ant whole
2 **parts** *pl syn* see GENITALIA
3 *syn* see RATION
4 *syn* see SHARE 1
rel chunk
5 *syn* see SIDE 4

part *vb syn* see SEPARATE 1
ant unite

part *adj syn* see INCOMPLETE 1

partage *n syn* see SHARE 1

partake *vb syn* see SHARE 2
rel accept, receive, take
idiom take part in

partake (of) *vb* 1 *syn* see EAT 1
2 *syn* see AMOUNT 2
idiom bear resemblance (to)

partaker *n syn* see PARTICIPANT

part and parcel *n syn* see ESSENTIAL 1

partial *adj* 1 *syn* see BIASED 2
ant impartial
2 *syn* see INCOMPLETE 1
rel halfway
ant whole

partiality *n* 1 *syn* see PREJUDICE
2 *syn* see LEANING 2

participant *n* one that takes part in something < were *participants* in the uprising >
syn actor, partaker, participator, party, sharer
rel aide, assistant, helper; colleague, confrere, fellow, partner
con bystander, looker-on, nonparticipant, observer, onlooker, spectator, watcher

participate *vb syn* see SHARE 2
rel enter (into), join (in)
idiom be a party to, be in on, be (*or* get) in the act, have to do with
con observe, watch; retire, withdraw

participator *n syn* see PARTICIPANT

particle *n* a tiny or insignificant amount, part, or piece < not a *particle* of sense >
syn ace, atom, bit, crumb, damn, ‖dite, doit, dram, drop, fragment, grain, hoot, iota, jot, minim, mite, modicum, molecule, ounce, ray, ‖rissom, scrap, scruple, shred, smidgen, smitch, snap, speck, spot, syllable, tittle, whit, whoop
rel morsel; snip; dribbet, dribble; dot

parti–color *adj syn* see VARIEGATED

parti–colored *adj syn* see VARIEGATED
ant unicolor, unicolorous

particular *adj* 1 *syn* see SINGLE 2
ant general
2 *syn* see CIRCUMSTANTIAL
rel careful, meticulous, punctilious, scrupulous
3 *syn* see SPECIAL 1
rel appropriate; distinct; singular
ant universal
4 *syn* see SEVERAL 1
5 *syn* see NICE 1

particular *n syn* see POINT 1
rel speciality, specific

con entirety

ant universal

particularity *n syn* see INDIVIDUALITY 3

particularize *vb* 1 *syn* see SPECIFY 3

idiom draw it fine

2 *syn* see ITEMIZE 1

particularized *adj syn* see CIRCUMSTAN-TIAL

ant generalized

particularly *adv syn* see ESPECIALLY 1

parting *n* a mutual separation of two or more persons <saddened by their approaching *parting* >

syn adieu, congé, farewell, good-bye, leave-taking

rel separation; departure

con joining, meeting; return

ant reunion

parting *adj* given, taken, or performed during leave-taking <remembered his father's *parting* advice>

syn departing, farewell, good-bye, valedictory

rel final, last

partisan *n* 1 *syn* see FOLLOWER

rel backer, champion, upholder; die-hard, stalwart

con adversary, antagonist, opponent

2 an irregular soldier who operates behind enemy lines <a train blown up by *partisans*>

syn guerrilla, irregular, patriot

partisan *adj syn* see BIASED 2

rel denominational, factional, sectarian; blind, devoted, die-hard, fanatic, unreasoning

con impartial, indifferent, unbiased, unprejudiced

ant nonpartisan

partition *n syn* see SEPARATION 1

partition *vb syn* see DISTRIBUTE 1

partner *n* one that is associated in any action with another <*partners* in crime>

syn associate, cohort, confrere, consociate, copartner, fellow, mate, ||pard

rel assistant, helper, sidekick; bedfellow, buddy, chum, companion, comrade, crony, pal

partnership *n syn* see ASSOCIATION 1

rel consociation, fellowship

parturient *adj syn* see PREGNANT 1

parturition *n syn* see BIRTH 1

party *n* 1 *syn* see COMBINATION 2

rel alliance, union; side

2 *syn* see PARTICIPANT

3 *syn* see HUMAN

4 *syn* see GROUP 1

5 *syn* see COMPANY 4

6 *syn* see ORGY 2

party girl *n* 1 *syn* see DOXY 1

2 *syn* see PROSTITUTE

parvenu *n syn* see UPSTART

idiom codfish aristocrat, pig in clover

||**pash** *vb syn* see SHATTER 1

||**pash** *n syn* see INFATUATION

pass *vb* 1 *syn* see GO 1

rel jog, ||mog

2 *syn* see DIE 1

idiom pass on to the Great Beyond

con linger

3 to move or come to a termination or end <as time *passes*, the pain too will *pass* >

syn see ELAPSE

rel slip (by); roll (on); fade (away), peter (out); cease, close, discontinue, end, stop, terminate

con continue; linger

4 *syn* see HAPPEN 1

idiom come to pass

5 *syn* see SURPASS 1

idiom leave way behind, shoot ahead of

6 *syn* see SPEND 3

7 *syn* see NEGLECT

8 *syn* see PROMISE 1

9 to transfer by hand from one person to another <*pass* the salt >

syn buck, hand, reach, ||shoot

rel give; fork (over)

pass (as *or* for) *vb syn* see POSE 4

pass (on) *vb syn* see HAND DOWN

pass (over) *vb syn* see TRAVEL 2

pass *n syn* see JUNCTURE 2

passable *adj* capable of being passed, crossed, or traveled <*passable* roads>

syn navigable, negotiable, travelable

rel open, unblocked; ||motorable; accessible, attainable, reachable

con blocked, closed; unnavigable; inaccessible, unattainable, unreachable

ant impassable

passably *adv syn* see ENOUGH 2

passage *n* 1 movement or transference from one place or point to another <air *passage* from New York to London> <the *passage* of current through a wire>

syn transit, travel

rel traject, trajet, traverse, traversing; transfer, transference, transmission, transmittal, transmittance

2 *syn* see TRANSITION

3 *syn* see WAY 2

4 a typically long narrow way connecting parts of a building <the office building contained endless *passages*>

syn corridor, couloir, hall, hallway, passageway

rel areaway

passageway *n syn* see PASSAGE 3

pass away *vb* 1 *syn* see DIE 1

2 *syn* see PASS 3

pass by *vb syn* see NEGLECT

passé *adj* 1 *syn* see OBSOLETE

2 *syn* see OLD-FASHIONED

ant a la mode

passed master *n syn* see EXPERT

passel *n syn* see GROUP 3

passing *n syn* see DEATH 1

passing *adj syn* see TRANSIENT

con lingering

passion *n* 1 *syn* see DISTRESS

2 *syn* see DESIRE 1

rel coveting; aiming, aspiring, panting

3 *syn* see FEELING 3

ant dispassion

4 *syn* see TEMPER 4

rel outbreak, outburst

5 *syn* see LOVE 2

rel heartthrob

6 intense, high-wrought emotion that compels to action <the *passion* of an evangelist >

syn ardor, calenture, enthusiasm, fervor, fire, hurrah, zeal

rel dedication, devotion; eagerness, lust; lyricism; ecstasy, rapture, transport; fury, rage

7 *syn* see LUST 2
rel amorousness; sensuality, sensuousness
8 *syn* see INFATUATION
passionate *adj* 1 *syn* see IRASCIBLE
2 *syn* see IMPASSIONED
rel excited, quickened, stimulated; high-powered, high-pressure, steamed up; headlong, impetuous, precipitate
ant dispassionate
3 *syn* see LUSTFUL 2
rel steamy, sultry
ant passionless
passionless *adj* *syn* see FRIGID 3
rel detached, impassive, unsusceptible; unaffected, unmoved; apathetic, indifferent, uncaring, unconcerned, unfeeling; cold-blooded, coldhearted, frozen, heartless
ant passionate, passionful
passive *adj* 1 *syn* see INACTIVE
rel apathetic, impassive, phlegmatic, stolid
ant active
2 receiving or enduring without resistance < a *passive* acceptance of her fate >
syn acquiescent, nonresistant, nonresisting, resigned, submissive, unresistant, unresisting, yielding
rel bearing, enduring, patient; compliant, docile, tractable; nonviolent
con resistant, resisting, unresigned, unsubmissive, unyielding
pass off *vb* 1 *syn* see FOIST 3
2 *syn* see POSE 4
pass on *vb* *syn* see COMMUNICATE 1
pass out *vb* 1 *syn* see FAINT
2 *syn* see DIE 1
pass over *vb* *syn* see NEGLECT
passport *n* a means of entry into a desirable group, society, or condition of life < his skill at sports was a *passport* to fame and fortune >
syn key, open sesame, password, ticket
password *n* 1 a word or phrase that must be spoken by a person before he may pass a guard < give the *password* before entering the fort >
syn countersign, watchword, word
rel tessera
2 *syn* see PASSPORT
3 something (as a short phrase) used as a sign of recognition among members of the same society, class, or group < a fraternity that has secret handshakes and passwords >
syn watchword, word
past *adj* 1 *syn* see PRECEDING
2 *syn* see FORMER 1
rel bypast, gone-by; late, previous
ant present
past *prep* 1 *syn* see BEYOND 1
rel by
ant before
2 *syn* see BEYOND 2
past *n* former time < reminisced about the past >
syn foretime, ||lang syne, yesterday, yesteryear, yore; *compare* PRESENT

rel antiquity
idiom bygone days (*or* times), days gone by, the good old days
con here and now; tomorrow
ant present; future
paste *vb* *syn* see BEAT 1
idiom give one a pasting
||**paste** *n* *syn* see CUFF
pasticcio *n* *syn* see MISCELLANY 1
pastiche *n* *syn* see MISCELLANY 1
past master *n* *syn* see EXPERT
pastoral *adj* *syn* see RURAL
rel agrarian
patch *vb* *syn* see MEND 2
patchwork *n* *syn* see MISCELLANY 1
patchy *adj* *syn* see SPOTTY 1
pate *n* *syn* see HEAD 1
patent *adj* 1 *syn* see OPEN 1
2 *syn* see CLEAR 5
rel prominent; flagrant, glaring, gross, rank
idiom patently obvious
con impalpable, imperceptible, insensible; concealed, hidden, secreted
ant latent
||**pater** *n* *syn* see FATHER 1
path *n* 1 *syn* see TRAIL
2 *syn* see WAY 1
3 *syn* see WAY 2
pathetic *adj* *syn* see PITIFUL 1
pathos *n* a quality that moves one to pity and sorrow < the *pathos* of the play was rarely offset by moments of comedy >
syn poignance, poignancy
rel bathos
pathway *n* *syn* see TRAIL
patience *n* the power or capacity to endure without complaint something difficult or disagreeable < it took a lot of *patience* to put up with him >
syn forbearance, longanimity, long-suffering, patientness, resignation, uncomplainingness
rel composure, cool, equanimity, imperturbability, self-control; endurance, sufferance, suffering, tolerance, toleration; nonresistance, passiveness, passivity, submission, submissiveness
con fretfulness; restiveness, restlessness; hastiness; rebellion, resistance
ant impatience
patientness *n* *syn* see PATIENCE
patois *n* 1 *syn* see VERNACULAR 3
2 *syn* see DIALECT 2
patriarch *n* 1 *syn* see FATHER 2
2 *syn* see GAFFER
patriarchal *adj* *syn* see VENERABLE 1
patrician *n* *syn* see GENTLEMAN
ant plebeian
patriciate *n* *syn* see ARISTOCRACY
ant plebs
patrimony *n* *syn* see HERITAGE 1
patriot *n* 1 a person who loves his country and supports its interests < *patriots* who asked what they could do for their country >
syn loyalist
rel nationalist
ant traitor
2 *syn* see PATRIOTEER
3 *syn* see PARTISAN 2
patrioteer *n* one who is ostentatiously and chauvinistically patriotic < bloodthirsty

---

syn synonym(s)   *rel* related word(s)
ant antonym(s)   *con* contrasted word(s)
idiom idiomatic equivalent(s)
|| use limited; if in doubt, see a dictionary

patrioteers immersed in political witch-hunts >
syn flag-waver, patriot, superpatriot
rel jingo, jingoist

patrolman *n syn see* POLICEMAN

patron *n* 1 *syn see* PATRON SAINT
2 *syn see* SPONSOR
ant client; protégé
3 *syn see* CUSTOMER

patronage *n* 1 *syn see* BACKING
rel benefaction, guardianship, protection; subsidy
2 commercial transactions of customers and patrons < developed a large *patronage* by offering fair prices and courteous service >
syn business, custom, trade, traffic
rel clientage, clientele
3 the power to make appointments to government jobs on a basis other than merit alone < ousted his enemies from office and used *patronage* to support his policies >
syn pork-barreling
rel cronyism

patron saint *n* a saint to whose protection and intercession a person, society, church, or place is dedicated < Saint Christopher is the *patron saint* of travelers >
syn avowry, patron
rel titular; guardian angel

patsy *n* 1 *syn see* SCAPEGOAT
2 *syn see* FOOL 3

patter *vb syn see* CHAT 1

patter *n syn see* DIALECT 2

pattern *n* 1 *syn see* MODEL 2
rel original
2 *syn see* FIGURE 3
rel patterning
3 *syn see* ORDER 8
rel arrangement, constellation

paucity *n syn see* SCARCITY
rel fewness

Paul Pry *n syn see* BUSYBODY

paunch *n* 1 *syn see* ABDOMEN
2 *syn see* POTBELLY

paunch *vb syn see* EVISCERATE

pauper *n* a person having no financial resources except those derived from charity
syn beggar, down-and-out
rel have-not, indigent; ||casual; almsman, lazarus
con millionaire, plutocrat

pauper *vb syn see* RUIN 3

pauperism *n syn see* POVERTY 1

pauperize *vb syn see* RUIN 3

pausation *n syn see* PAUSE

pause *n* a temporary cessation of activity or of an activity < a *pause* in the conversation >
syn comma, interval, lull, pausation; *compare* BREAK 4, GAP 3
rel caesura, hush, lapse, letup, suspension; interlude, intermission, recess, respite; wait; break, gap, interruption; cessation, ||deval
con continuation, progression

paw *vb syn see* TOUCH 1

paw *adj* 1 *syn see* NAUGHTY 1
2 *syn see* OBSCENE 2

pawn *n syn see* PLEDGE 1

pawn *vb* to give or deposit as security for the payment of a loan or debt or for the fulfillment of an obligation < had to *pawn* all her jewels >
syn ||dip, hock, impignorate, mortgage, pledge, ||pop, ||spout
ant redeem

pawn *n syn see* TOOL 2

pay *vb* 1 to discharge an obligation to usually with money < *paid* the doctor for his services >
syn compensate, guerdon, remunerate
rel indemnify, recompense, satisfy; cough (up), plunk down, pony (up), pungle (up), remit, render, tender; pay off
2 *syn see* CLEAR 5
3 *syn see* SPEND 1
4 *syn see* COMPENSATE 3
idiom make up for
5 *syn see* YIELD 5

pay *n syn see* WAGE

payable *adj* 1 *syn see* DUE 2
ant unpayable
2 *syn see* UNPAID 2

pay envelope *n syn see* WAGE

paying *adj syn see* ADVANTAGEOUS 1
rel productive; sound; solvent

payload *n syn see* LOAD 1

pay up *vb syn see* CLEAR 5

PDQ *adv syn see* AWAY 3

peaceable *adj syn see* PACIFIC
rel amicable, friendly, neighborly; amiable, complaisant
ant acrimonious; contentious; warlike

peaceful *adj syn see* PACIFIC
rel collected, composed, cool, unruffled; constant, equable, steady
con agitated, discomposed, disquieted, disturbed, perturbed, upset

peacemaker *n* one that makes or seeks to make peace < a president who was remembered as a great *peacemaker* >
syn make-peace, pacificator
rel arbitrator, mediator, negotiator; placater; appeaser, peacemonger; peacekeeper
con chauvinist, jingo, jingoist, militarist, war dog, warmonger; peacebreaker

peace officer *n syn see* POLICEMAN

peach *n syn* ||DILLY, crackerjack, ||daisy, dandy, humdinger, jim-dandy, ||lalapalooza, ||lulu, nifty, ||pip
rel pearl

peach *vb syn see* INFORM 3

peachy *adj syn see* MARVELOUS 2

peacock *vb syn see* LORD

peacockish *adj syn see* SHOWY

peacocky *adj syn see* SHOWY

peak *n* 1 *syn see* VISOR 1
2 *syn see* TOP 1
3 *syn see* MOUNTAIN 1
4 *syn see* APEX 2

peak (out) *vb syn see* DECREASE

peaked *adj syn see* POINTED 1

peaked *adj syn see* SICKLY 2

||peaking *adj syn see* SICKLY 2

peaky *adj syn see* POINTED 1

peaky *adj syn see* SICKLY 2

peal *vb syn see* RING

peanut *adj syn see* PETTY 2

||peart *adj syn see* LIVELY 1

||pearten (up) *vb syn see* ENCOURAGE 1

peasant *n syn see* RUSTIC

peck *n syn see* MUCH

peck *vb* 1 to strike at or pick up with the beak < a hen *pecking* the scattered grain from the ground >

syn beak, pick

2 *syn* see KISS 1

peck (at) *vb syn* see NAG

pecker *n* 1 *syn* see BILL 1

2 *syn* see NOSE 1

||**peckish** *adj syn* see HUNGRY

pecksniffery *n syn* see HYPOCRISY

pecksniffian *adj syn* see HYPOCRITICAL

peculate *vb syn* see EMBEZZLE

peculiar *adj* 1 *syn* see CHARACTERISTIC

rel unique

2 *syn* see STRANGE 4

rel uncustomary

con normal

peculiarity *n syn* see QUALITY 1

pecuniary *adj syn* see FINANCIAL

pedantic *adj* too narrowly concerned with scholarly matters < intellectual life that was *pedantic* rather than broad and humane >

syn academic, bookish, book-learned, booky, quodlibetic, scholastic

rel erudite, learned; didactic, donnish, inkhorn, schoolish, schoolteacherish; arid, dry, dryasdust, dull

ant unpedantic

peddle *vb* 1 *syn* see PUSH 6

2 to sell or offer for sale from place to place < *peddled* fish from a pushcart >

syn hawk, huckster, monger, vend

rel sell; push

peddler *n* one who travels about with merchandise to sell < *peddlers* were once common in rural areas >

syn ||arab, cheap-jack (*or* cheap-john), ||duffer, hawker, higgler, huckster, monger, mongerer, outcrier, packman, piepoudre, roadman, vendor

rel colporteur, costermonger; pusher

peddling *adj syn* see PETTY 2

pedestal *vb syn* see EXALT 1

pedestrian *adj syn* see DULL 9

rel commonplace, platitudinous, truistic; banal, inane, jejune, wishy-washy; heavy

pedigree *n* 1 *syn* see GENEALOGY

2 *syn* see ANCESTRY

pedigree *adj syn* see PUREBRED

pedigreed *adj syn* see PUREBRED

peek (*in or* out) *vb syn* see PEEP

peek *n syn* see PEEP

peel *vb* 1 *syn* see SKIN 2

2 *syn* see SCALE 2

peeled *adj syn* see OPEN 2

peeler *n* 1 *syn* see STRIPTEASER

2 *syn* see HUSTLER

||**peeler** *n syn* see POLICEMAN

peep *vb syn* see CHIRP

rel pip

peep *vb* to peer through or as if through a hole or crevice < *peeped* cautiously under the bed >

syn peek (in *or* out)

rel glance; look; peer, stare

idiom take a peep (*or* peek)

peep *n* a brief and sometimes furtive look < take a *peep* at the new neighbors >

syn ||gander, glance, glimpse, peek

rel look-over, look-see; oeillade, ogle; stare

---

syn synonym(s)   *rel* related word(s)

ant antonym(s)   *con* contrasted word(s)

idiom idiomatic equivalent(s)

|| use limited; if in doubt, see a dictionary

---

peeper *n* 1 *syn* see PEEPING TOM

2 *syn* see EYE 1

peeping tom *n* a pruriently prying person < a *peeping tom* spying on the couple >

syn peeper, voyeur

rel prowler, snoop, snooper

idiom porch climber, window (*or* transom) peeper

||**peepy** *adj syn* see SLEEPY 1

peer *vb syn* see GAZE 1

rel eye, rubberneck; pry, snoop

peerless *adj syn* see ALONE 3

rel dominant, paramount, predominant, sovereign

peery *adj syn* see CURIOUS 2

peeve *vb syn* see IRRITATE

rel disturb; miff

idiom make one hot under the collar

peevish *adj syn* see IRRITABLE

rel captious, carping, caviling, critical, faultfinding

idiom being in a peeve

peewee *n syn* see DWARF

peewee *adj syn* see TINY

||**peg** *n syn* see DRINK 3

||**pegh** *vb syn* see PANT 1

peg out *vb* 1 *syn* see COLLAPSE 2

2 *syn* see DIE 1

pejorative *adj syn* see DEROGATORY

con acclaiming, extolling, lauding, praising; aggrandizing, exalting, magnifying

pelf *n* 1 *syn* see MONEY

||**2** *syn* see REFUSE

pell—mell *adv* in or as if in confused haste < barged in *pell-mell* without thinking >

syn helter-skelter, hotfoot, hurry-scurry, impetuously, incontinently

rel hurriedly; indiscreetly; carelessly, heedlessly, rashly, thoughtlessly

idiom on the spur of the moment

pell—mell *n syn* see CONFUSION 3

pell—mell *vb syn* see STAMPEDE 2

pellucid *adj* 1 *syn* see TRANSPARENT 1

rel sheer

con muddy, roily, turbid

2 *syn* see CLEAR 4

pelt *n syn* see HIDE

pelt *vb* 1 *syn* see BEAT 1

2 *syn* see HURRY 2

pen *vb syn* see ENCLOSE 1

ant unpen

pen *n syn* see JAIL

penalize *vb* to inflict a penalty on < *penalize* a delinquent taxpayer with a stiff fine >

syn amerce, fine, mulct

rel castigate, chasten, chastise, correct, discipline, punish; condemn; judge

penalty *n syn* see FINE

penance *n syn* see PENITENCE

penchant *n syn* see LEANING 2

||**pend** *vb syn* see DEPEND (on *or* upon) 1

pendant *n* 1 *syn* see FLAG

2 *syn* see COUNTERPART 1

pendent *adj* 1 *syn* see SUSPENDED

2 *syn* see PENDING

pending *adj* not yet settled or decided < a claim still *pending* >

syn pendent, undecided, undetermined, unsettled

idiom hanging in the balance, in suspense, up in the air

con decided, determined, settled

ant closed

pendulant *adj syn* see SUSPENDED

pendulate *vb syn* see SWING 2

pendulous *adj* 1 *syn* see SUSPENDED
2 *syn* see VACILLATING 2

penetrable *adj syn* see PERMEABLE
ant impenetrable

penetrate *vb* 1 *syn* see ENTER 1
rel encroach, invade, trespass
2 to enter or go through by or as if by
overcoming resistance <the icy wind
penetrated the heavy parka>
syn pierce
rel bore, perforate, prick, puncture; jab,
knife, stab; drill, drive
3 *syn* see PERMEATE
rel insert, insinuate, interpolate, introduce

penetrating *adj* 1 *syn* see INCISIVE
rel penetrant, penetrative
2 *syn* see SHARP 4

penetration *n syn* see WIT 3
rel penetrativeness

penetrative *adj syn* see SHARP 4

penitence *n* regret for sin or wrongdoing
<forgiveness following true *penitence*>
syn attrition, compunction, contriteness,
contrition, penance, penitency, remorse,
remorsefulness, repentance, rue, ruth
rel qualm, scruple; self-accusation, self-
castigation, self-punishment, self-reproach,
self-reproof; anguish, distress, grief, regret,
sadness, sorrow; debasement, degradation,
humbling, humiliation
con adamancy, inexorableness, obduracy,
obdurateness, stubbornness

penitency *n syn* see PENITENCE

penitent *adj syn* see REMORSEFUL

penitential *adj syn* see REMORSEFUL

penitentiary *n syn* see JAIL
Idiom correctional institution

penmanship *n syn* see HANDWRITING

pennant *n syn* see FLAG

pennilessness *n syn* see POVERTY 1

pennon *n syn* see FLAG

penny dreadful *n syn* see DIME NOVEL

penny pincher *n syn* see MISER

penny-pinching *adj syn* see STINGY

penny-wise *adj syn* see STINGY

pennyworth *n syn* see BARGAIN

pensile *adj syn* see SUSPENDED

pension (off) *vb syn* see RETIRE 2

pensive *adj* 1 *syn* see THOUGHTFUL 1
rel musing, ruminating
2 being musingly sad and thoughtful
<gazed out the window with a *pensive*
expression on her face>
syn meditative, ‖pensy, wistful
rel absorbed, abstracted, contemplative,
musing, preoccupied, thoughtful, withdrawn; blue, melancholy, sad, saddened
con alert, aware, interested, outgoing

‖**pensy** *adj* 1 *syn* see PENSIVE 2
2 *syn* see THOUGHTFUL 1
3 *syn* see SQUEAMISH 1

penumbra *n syn* see SHADE 1

penurious *adj* 1 *syn* see POOR 1
2 *syn* see STINGY

penury *n syn* see POVERTY 1
ant luxury

peon *n syn* see SLAVE 2

peonage *n syn* see BONDAGE

people *n* 1 *syn* see SOCIETY 3
2 *syn* see COMMONALTY

people *vb syn* see INHABIT

pep *n* 1 *syn* see ENERGY 2
2 *syn* see VIGOR 2

pepper *vb syn* see SPECKLE

peppery *adj* 1 *syn* see PUNGENT
2 *syn* see IRASCIBLE
3 *syn* see SPIRITED 2
rel pepperish; alert, keen, lively, peppy

peppy *adj syn* see LIVELY 1

per *prep syn* see VIA 2

‖**per** *adv syn* see APIECE

perambulant *adj syn* see ITINERANT

perambulate *vb syn* see TRAVERSE 5

‖**perambulator** *n syn* see BABY CAR-
RIAGE

perambulatory *adj syn* see ITINERANT

per capita *adv syn* see APIECE

per caput *adv syn* see APIECE

perceive *vb syn* see SEE 1
rel divine, identify, realize, recognize;
grasp, seize, take; apprehend

perceptible *adj* apprehensible as real or
existent <a *perceptible* change in at-
titude>
syn appreciable, detectable, discernible,
observable, palpable, sensible, tangible;
compare TANGIBLE 1
rel distinguishable, recognizable; cognizable, understandable; clear, lucid, perspicuous; conspicuous, noticeable, signal
con impalpable, indiscernible, intangible,
invisible, unappreciable, undetectable,
undiscernible, unnoticeable, unobservable
ant imperceptible

perception *n syn* see IDEA

perceptive *adj* 1 *syn* see ACUTE 3
rel responsive
ant imperceptive, unperceptive
2 *syn* see WISE 1
rel prehensile, prehensive, prehensorial
ant imperceptive, unperceptive

perch *vb syn* see ALIGHT

perchance *adv syn* see PERHAPS

percipience *n syn* see WIT 3

percolate *vb* 1 *syn* see PERMEATE
2 *syn* see EXUDE

per contra *adv syn* see HOWEVER

percussion *n syn* see IMPACT
rel percussiveness

perdition *n syn* see HELL

perdurable *adj* 1 *syn* see LASTING
ant fleeting
2 *syn* see INFINITE 1

perdure *vb syn* see CONTINUE 1

perduring *adj syn* see LASTING
ant fleeting

peregrination *n, usu* peregrinations *pl syn*
see JOURNEY

peremptory *adj syn* see MASTERFUL 1
rel certain, positive; decided, decisive;
absolute, fixed, uncompromising; obstinate

perennial *adj syn* see OLD 2
rel durable, perdurable

perfect *adj* 1 *syn* see WHOLE 1
ant imperfect
2 being entirely without flaw and meeting
supreme standards of excellence <a ballerina whose technique was *perfect*>
syn absolute, flawless, fleckless, impeccable, indefectible, note-perfect, unflawed;
compare CONSUMMATE 1
rel excellent; consummate; expert, finished, masterful, masterly

con defective, faulty, flawed; deficient, inadequate, wanting; unfinished, unpolished; unsound
ant imperfect

3 precisely appropriate or right <found the *perfect* gift for him>
syn ideal, model, very
rel needed, required, requisite; appropriate, fit, proper, right, suitable; exact, express, precise
idiom being just the thing
con foolish, inappropriate, undesirable, unsuitable

4 **syn** see PURE 2

5 **syn** see WHOLE 3
rel consummate

6 **syn** see UTTER

perfect vb syn see POLISH 2

perfected adj syn see CONSUMMATE 1
ant unperfected

perfectibilian n syn see PERFECTIONIST
perfectibilist n syn see PERFECTIONIST
perfection n 1 syn see INTEGRITY 2
2 syn see EXCELLENCE
ant imperfection

perfectionist n one that demands or works to achieve perfection <a *perfectionist* who rehearsed one scene fifty times>
syn perfectibilian, perfectibilist, perfectist
rel precisian, precisionist, stickler

perfectist n syn see PERFECTIONIST
perfectly adv syn see WELL 3
perfervid adj syn see IMPASSIONED
rel enhanced, heightened, intensified

perfidious adj syn see FAITHLESS
rel mercenary, venal; alienated, estranged, disaffected; deceitful, dishonest

perfidiousness n 1 syn see INFIDELITY
2 syn see TREACHERY

perfidy n 1 syn see TREACHERY
rel foul play
idiom Judas' kiss
ant fealty
2 syn see INFIDELITY
rel betrayal, sellout

perforate vb to pierce through so as to leave a hole <*perforate* a sheet of postage stamps>
syn bore, drill, prick, ||pritch, punch, puncture
rel pit; probe; drive, penetrate, pierce

perforce adv syn see WILLY-NILLY

perform vb 1 syn see FULFILL 1
2 to carry something (as a process) to a successful conclusion <*perform* a surgical procedure>
syn achieve, do, execute; *compare* EFFECT 2
rel accomplish, bring off; complete, end, finish, wind up
idiom carry to completion (*or* a successful conclusion), do to a turn, do up brown
3 syn see ACT 1
4 syn see ACT 5

performance n syn see EFFICIENCY 1
performer n syn see ACTOR 1
perfume n syn see FRAGRANCE

perfume vb syn see SCENT 2
perfumed adj syn see SWEET 2
perfumy adj syn see SWEET 2
perfunctory adj characterized by routine and often done merely as a duty <gave her his usual *perfunctory* nod>
syn automatic, mechanical
rel cursory, superficial; involuntary, unaware; routine, usual; standard, stock; cool, impersonal, indifferent; wooden; unconcerned, uninterested
con cordial, friendly, genial, hearty, warm

pergola n syn see ARBOR

perhaps adv conceivably but not certainly so <*perhaps* this is true, but I think it's debatable>
syn maybe, perchance, possibly
rel conceivably, feasibly, imaginably
idiom as it may be, as the case may be, for all one knows
con certainly, definitely, doubtlessly, surely, undoubtedly, unquestionably

perhaps n syn see THEORY 2
periapt n syn see CHARM 2
peril n syn see DANGER
rel exposure, liability, openness, subjection; endangerment
idiom cause for alarm, rocks (*or* breakers) ahead

peril vb syn see ENDANGER
perilous adj syn see DANGEROUS 1
rel shaky, tottery, unstable, unsteady; delicate, ticklish, touchy

perimeter n 1 syn see CIRCUMFERENCE
2 syn see BORDER 1

period n 1 syn see END 2
2 an extent of time set off or typified by someone or something <the Victorian *period*> <a *period* of expansion>
syn age, day(s), epoch, era, time

periodic adj syn see INTERMITTENT
rel on-again-off-again
periodical adj syn see INTERMITTENT
periodical n syn see JOURNAL
peripatetic adj syn see ITINERANT
periphery n 1 syn see CIRCUMFERENCE
2 syn see BORDER 1

periphrase n syn see VERBIAGE 1
periphrasis n syn see VERBIAGE 1
perish vb 1 syn see DIE 1
2 to suffer spiritual or moral death <nations *perishing* for lack of true leaders>
syn die
rel decline; collapse, go under; expire, succumb; disappear, vanish; cease, end
con flourish, prosper, thrive
ant endure
||3 syn see DECAY

perishing adj syn see DAMNED 2

perjure vb to make a false swearer of oneself by violating one's oath to tell the truth <a *perjured* witness>
syn forswear
rel equivocate; deceive, delude, mislead, trick; lie, prevaricate
idiom commit perjury, lie under oath, swear falsely

perjurer n syn see LIAR
perk (up) vb syn see IMPROVE 3
||**perk** n, usu perks pl syn see GRATUITY
perlustrate vb syn see SCRUTINIZE 1
perlustration n syn see EXAMINATION

---

syn synonym(s)   **rel** related word(s)
ant antonym(s)   **con** contrasted word(s)
idiom idiomatic equivalent(s)
|| use limited; if in doubt, see a dictionary

permanent *adj syn* see LASTING
rel imperishable, invariable
ant temporary

permeable *adj* capable of being permeated especially by fluids <a *permeable* membrane>
syn penetrable, pervious, porose, porous
rel passable
con impassable, impenetrable, impervious
ant impermeable

permeate *vb* to pass or cause to pass through every part of a thing <air *permeated* with cigar smoke>
syn charge, compenetrate, impenetrate, impregnate, interfuse, interpenetrate, penetrate, percolate, pervade, saturate, transfuse
rel invade; imbrue, imbue, infiltrate, infuse, ingrain; diffuse, suffuse; drench, soak, steep; fill

permissible *adj* that may be permitted <a *permissible* error>
syn admissible, allowable
rel unforbidden, unprohibited; allowed, permitted, tolerated; approved, authorized, endorsed, sanctioned; acceptable, bearable, tolerable
con banned, forbidden, disallowed, prohibited, unpermitted, verboten; unacceptable, unbearable
ant impermissible

permission *n* a sanctioning to act or do something that is granted by one in authority <received *permission* to leave work early>
syn allowance, authorization, consent, leave, permit, sanction, sufferance
rel acceptance, acquiescence; approbation, approval; endorsement
ant prohibition

permit *vb syn* see LET 2
rel tolerate
idiom give one his head
ant forbid, prohibit

permit *n syn* see PERMISSION

permutation *n syn* see CHANGE 2
rel alteration, modification

pernicious *adj* exceedingly harmful or destructive <*pernicious* gossip>
syn baneful, deadly, noxious, pestiferous, pestilent, pestilential; *compare* DEADLY 1
rel damaging, deleterious, detrimental, harmful, hurtful; baleful, malefic, maleficent, malign, sinister; miasmatic, miasmic, poisonous, toxic, venomous; malignant, swart, virulent; destructive, devastating, ruinous; fatal, killing, lethal, mortal
con harmless, uninjurious; nonmalignant, nonpoisonous, nontoxic
ant innocuous

pernickety *adj syn* see NICE 1

perorate *vb syn* see ORATE

perpend *vb syn* see CONSIDER 1

perpendicular *adj syn* see VERTICAL
rel stand-up, straight
ant horizontal

perpendicularity *n syn* see VERTICALITY
rel erectness, uprightness
ant horizontality

perpetrate *vb syn* see COMMIT 2
rel effect; inflict, wreak
idiom ‖up and do

perpetual *adj syn* see CONTINUAL

ant ephemeral, transient

perpetually *adv syn* see ALWAYS 1

perpetuate *vb* to make perpetual or cause to last indefinitely <*perpetuate* his memory for future generations>
syn eternalize, eternize, immortalize
rel bolster, conserve, keep, maintain, preserve, secure, support, sustain
con annihilate, blot out, erase, expunge
ant obliterate

perplex *vb* 1 *syn* see PUZZLE
rel discompose, perturb; balk, thwart; astonish, astound, surprise
idiom put (*or* drive) to one's wit's end
2 *syn* see COMPLICATE
3 *syn* see ENTANGLE 1

perquisite *n* 1 *syn* see GRATUITY
2 *syn* see RIGHT 2

per se *adv* by, of, or in itself or oneself or themselves <a lover of language *per se*>
syn as such, intrinsically
rel alone, independently, solely

persecute *vb* 1 *syn* see WRONG
rel dragoon, rack, torment, torture
con back, champion, support, uphold
2 *syn* see MOLEST
rel worry; hound, ride
con humor, indulge, pamper; accommodate, favor, oblige

perseverant *adj syn* see PERSISTENT 1

perseverative *adj syn* see PERSISTENT 1

persevere *vb* to continue in a state, enterprise, or undertaking in spite of counter influences, opposition, or discouragement <*persevered* in his unpopular economic policy>
syn carry on, go on, hang on, persist
rel continue, get on, press (on), proceed
idiom ‖hang in there, keep at it, keep driving, never say die, stick (*or* tough) it out
con falter, hesitate, vacillate, waver; renounce, surrender, yield
ant give up

persevering *adj syn* see PERSISTENT 1

persiflage *n syn* see BANTER

persist *vb* 1 *syn* see PERSEVERE
con cease, discontinue, quit, stop
ant desist
2 *syn* see CONTINUE 1
rel go on; linger; obtain, prevail
ant desist

persistence *n* 1 *syn* see CONTINUATION 1
2 *syn* see RUN 2
rel course

persistent *adj* 1 continuing in a course of action without regard to discouragement, opposition, or previous failure <a *persistent* suitor>
syn dogged, insistent, perseverant, perseverative, persevering, persisting, persistive
rel determined, steadfast, tenacious, unshakable; relentless, unremitting
con malleable, pliant, tractable, yielding; infirm, invertebrate, spineless; vacillating, wavery, wobbling
2 *syn* see PRIMITIVE 3

persisting *adj syn* see PERSISTENT 1

persistive *adj syn* see PERSISTENT 1

persnickety *adj syn* see NICE 1

person *n syn* see HUMAN
rel chap, ‖cookie, coot, fellow, galoot, guy, specimen, stick

personage n 1 syn see NOTABLE 1
2 syn see HUMAN
personal adj 1 of, relating to, or affecting a particular person < owed his *personal* allegiance to his wife >
syn individual
rel particular, peculiar, special
con general, universal; common, joint, mutual, shared; commonplace, everyday, ordinary
2 syn see PRIVATE 1
personal effects n pl privately owned items (as clothing and toilet articles) normally worn or carried on the person < packed his *personal effects* in a small bag >
syn ||plunder, stuff, things, traps, tricks
rel belongings, goods, possessions
idiom personal belongings
personality n 1 syn see INDIVIDUALITY 4
2 syn see DISPOSITION 3
3 syn see NOTABLE 1
personalize vb 1 syn see EMBODY 1
rel anthropomorphize
2 syn see REPRESENT 2
personal name n syn see GIVEN NAME
personate vb 1 syn see ACT 1
2 syn see REPRESENT 2
personification n syn see EMBODIMENT
personify vb 1 syn see EMBODY 1
rel reincarnate
2 syn see REPRESENT 2
personize vb syn see EMBODY 1
perspective n syn see VISTA
perspicacious adj syn see SHREWD
rel quick-sighted, sharp-sighted, sharp=witted
perspicacity n syn see WIT 3
perspicuity n syn see CLARITY
rel intelligibility; explicitness
perspicuous adj syn see CLEAR 4
perspiring adj syn see SWEATY
perspiry adj syn see SWEATY
persuadable adj syn see RECEPTIVE 1
ant unpersuadable
persuade vb 1 syn see INDUCE 1
rel affect, impress, touch; reason; convert
con discourage, hinder, prevent
ant dissuade
2 syn see CONVERT 1
3 syn see ASSURE 2
ant dissuade
persuasible adj syn see RECEPTIVE 1
ant unpersuasible
persuasion n 1 syn see OPINION
rel bias, partiality, predilection, prejudice, prepossession
2 syn see RELIGION 1
3 syn see RELIGION 2
rel affiliation; order
4 syn see TYPE
pert adj 1 syn see SAUCY 1
rel bold, daring; audacious, brazen
con shy
ant coy
2 syn see WISE 5
rel disrespectful, rude
3 syn see LIVELY 1

syn synonym(s)   rel related word(s)
ant antonym(s)   con contrasted word(s)
idiom idiomatic equivalent(s)
|| use limited: if in doubt, see a dictionary

pertain vb 1 syn see BELONG 2
2 syn see BEAR (on or upon)
rel associate, combine, connect, join
idiom be pertinent (or relevant) to
pertinacious adj syn see OBSTINATE
rel fixed, unshakable; dogged, tenacious
pertinent adj syn see RELEVANT
rel pertaining
ant impertinent
perturb vb syn see DISCOMPOSE 1
rel trouble; unsettle
ant compose
pervade vb syn see PERMEATE
idiom spread through and through
perverse adj 1 syn see VICIOUS 2
2 syn see OBSTINATE
rel cranky, irritable, unreasonable
3 syn see CONTRARY 3
pervert vb 1 syn see DEBASE 1
rel abuse, maltreat, mistreat, misuse, outrage; ruin
2 syn see ABUSE 2
rel ill-treat
3 syn see MISREPRESENT
perverted adj syn see DEBASED
rel defiled, polluted, tainted; contorted, distorted, warped; abused, misused, outraged
pervicacious adj syn see OBSTINATE
pervious adj syn see PERMEABLE
ant impervious
pesky adj syn see TROUBLESOME
pesky adv syn see VERY 1
pessimist n one who emphasizes adverse aspects or conditions and expects the worst < *pessimists* predicting another depression >
syn calamity howler, Cassandra, crepe-hanger, worrywart
rel fussbudget; Job's comforter; defeatist; killjoy; cynic, misanthrope
con positivist; idealist; Pollyanna
ant optimist
pest n 1 syn see ANNOYANCE 3
rel bane, trouble, vexation, worry
idiom pain in the neck, pea in the shoe, thorn in the flesh
2 one who pesters or annoys < a little *pest* who constantly asked questions >
syn nudnick, nuisance, pesterer
rel badgerer, heckler, tormentor
idiom pain in the neck
pester vb syn see WORRY 1
rel ride
idiom drive (one) crazy, drive (one) up the wall, pester to death
pester n syn see ANNOYANCE 3
pesterer n syn see PEST 2
||**pesterment** n syn see ANNOYANCE 3
pesticide n a chemical agent used to destroy pests < the need to control indiscriminate use of *pesticides* >
syn biocide, economic poison
rel bactericide, fungicide, germicide, insecticide, microbicide, rodenticide, vermicide
pestiferous adj syn see PERNICIOUS
pestilence n syn see PLAGUE 1
pestilent adj 1 syn see DEADLY 1
2 syn see PERNICIOUS
pestilential adj 1 syn see DEADLY 1
2 syn see PERNICIOUS
pet adj syn see FAVORITE 1

pet *vb syn* see CARESS
rel embrace, hug

pet *vb syn* see SULK

petcock *n syn* see FAUCET

peter (out) *vb syn* see DECREASE

Peter Funk *n syn* see SWINDLER

petite *adj syn* see SMALL 1
rel diminutive, dwarf, lilliputian, miniature, wee

petition *n syn* see PRAYER
rel request

petition *vb* to make an earnest, formal, and often written request < *petitioned* for a hearing before the labor board >
syn appeal, sue (for or to)
rel ask, request; beg, beseech, entreat, implore, plead, pray, supplicate
con claim, demand, exact, press (for)

petitioner *n syn* see SUPPLIANT

petit-maître *n syn* see FOP

petrify *vb syn* see DAZE 2
rel alarm, frighten, startle, terrify; appall, dismay, horrify; numb
idiom turn to stone

pettifogger *n* an unscrupulous lawyer < done out of his rights by a slick *pettifogger* >
syn jackleg lawyer, shyster; *compare* LAWYER
rel ambulance chaser, Philadelphia lawyer; ‖bush lawyer

pettifogging *adj syn* see PETTY 2

pettish *adj syn* see IRRITABLE

petty *adj* 1 *syn* see LITTLE 3
2 being often contemptibly insignificant or unimportant < *petty* quarrels and intrigues >
syn inconsequent, inconsequential, inconsiderable, measly, Mickey Mouse, niggling, paltry, peanut, peddling, pettifogging, picayune, picayunish, piddling, piffling, pimping, puny, small, trifling, trivial, unconsequential, unconsidered, ungenerous, unvital; *compare* LITTLE 3
rel negligible, unimportant; hair-drawn, hairsplitting; impertinent, irrelevant
con consequential, considerable; big, gross; significant, vital
ant important, momentous

petulant *adj syn* see IRRITABLE
rel grouchy, sulky

phantasm *n* 1 *syn* see DELUSION 1
rel fabrication, fiction, invention
2 *syn* see APPARITION
3 *syn* see FANCY 4

phantom *n syn* see APPARITION

pharisaic *adj syn* see HYPOCRITICAL

pharisaical *adj syn* see HYPOCRITICAL

pharisaicalness *n syn* see HYPOCRISY

pharisaism *n syn* see HYPOCRISY

pharisee *n syn* see HYPOCRITE

pharmaceutic *n syn* see DRUG 1

pharmaceutical *n syn* see DRUG 1

pharmacist *n syn* see DRUGGIST

pharmacon *n syn* see REMEDY 1

pharos *n syn* see LIGHTHOUSE

phase *n* one of the possible ways of viewing or being presented to view < the moral *phase* of the problem >
syn angle, aspect, facet, hand, side
rel condition, situation, state; position, posture, view, viewpoint; appearance, look, semblance; color, complexion

phenomenal *adj* 1 *syn* see MATERIAL 1
con ontic
ant noumenal
2 *syn* see EXCEPTIONAL 1

phenomenon *n* 1 *syn* see FACT 2
rel experience; actuality, reality
2 *syn* see WONDER 1
rel abnormality; anomaly, paradox; peculiarity, singularity, uniqueness, unusualness

philander *n syn* see WOLF
idiom ‖skirt chaser

philander *vb* to have many love affairs < his reputation for *philandering* with married women >
syn fool (around), mess around, play (around), wolf, womanize
rel dally, flirt, trifle; chase, pursue; ‖tomcat (around)
idiom ‖chase skirts, play Don Juan, play the femmes

philanderer *n syn* see WOLF

philanthropic *adj syn* see CHARITABLE 1
rel bighearted, freehearted, greathearted, kindhearted, largehearted, openhearted; contributing, donating, freehanded, giving, magnanimous; civic-minded, public-spirited
ant misanthropic

philharmonic *n syn* see ORCHESTRA

philippic *n syn* see TIRADE

philistine *n* a crass, prosaic, often priggish individual guided by material rather than artistic or intellectual values < *philistines* who opposed everything new and creative in art >
syn Babbitt, boeotian, boob, middlebrow
rel bourgeois; capitalist; materialist; boor, clown, lout, vulgarian
ant aesthete

phiz *n syn* see FACE 1

phlegm *n* 1 *syn* see APATHY 1
2 *syn* see EQUANIMITY
rel nonchalance, unconcern

phlegmatic *adj syn* see IMPASSIVE 1
rel calm, undemonstrative; aloof, incurious, indifferent, unconcerned; lethargic, sluggish

phoebus *n syn* see SUN 1

phoenix *n syn* see PARAGON

phonate *vb syn* see ARTICULATE 2

phone *vb syn* see TELEPHONE

phony *adj syn* see COUNTERFEIT

phony *n* 1 *syn* see IMPOSTURE
2 *syn* see IMPOSTOR

photo *vb syn* see PHOTOGRAPH
idiom take a photo (of)

photog *n syn* see PHOTOGRAPHER

photograph *vb* to use a camera to make a picture, image, or likeness of < *photographed* the whole family >
syn photo, shoot
rel cinematize, ‖cinematograph, cinemize, film, filmize, picture; kodak, snap, snapshoot, snapshot; mug
idiom capture on film, take a picture (or photograph)

photographer *n* one who takes photographs < a newspaper *photographer* >
syn cameraman, camerist, photog, photographist, photoist
rel snapshooter, ‖snapshotter; shutterbug

photographic *adj syn* see GRAPHIC 1

rel accurate, detailed, exact

photographist *n syn* see PHOTOGRAPHER

photoist *n syn* see PHOTOGRAPHER

photoplay *n syn* see MOVIE

phrase *n* **1** *syn* see WORDING
   rel styling
   2 a group of words which, taken together, express a notion and may constitute part of a sentence <an adverbial *phrase* > <a trite *phrase* >
   syn expression, locution
   rel phrasing; idiom; catchword, slogan
   3 *syn* see CATCHWORD

phrase *vb syn* see WORD

phraseology *n syn* see WORDING
   idiom choice of words

phrasing *n syn* see WORDING

phthisis *n syn* see TUBERCULOSIS

phylactery *n syn* see CHARM 2

physic *n syn* see REMEDY 1

physical *adj* **1** *syn* see MATERIAL 1
   rel natural; elemental, elementary
   ant spiritual
   2 *syn* see BODILY
   rel visceral; lusty; brute
   ant mental

physician *n* a doctor of medicine <the shortage of *physicians* in rural areas>
   syn ||croaker, doc, doctor, MD, medical, mediciner, medico, ||sawbones
   rel medic; general practitioner, practitioner; surgeon; specialist
   idiom medical doctor, medical man

physique *n* bodily makeup or type <a muscular *physique* >
   syn build, constitution, habit, habitus
   rel anatomy, structure; configuration, shape; body, figure, form, frame

picaroon *n syn* see PIRATE

picayune *adj syn* see PETTY 2

picayunish *adj syn* see PETTY 2

pick *vb* **1** *syn* see CHOOSE 1
   idiom pick and choose
   ant reject
   2 *syn* see PECK 1

pick *n syn* see BEST

pick *adj syn* see SELECT 1

picked *adj syn* see SELECT 1

picket *n syn* see GUARD 2

pickle *n syn* see PREDICAMENT
   idiom pretty pickle, ||sticky wicket, tight spot

||**pickled** *adj syn* see INTOXICATED 1

pick out *vb syn* see CHOOSE 1

pickpocket *n* one who steals from pockets <his wallet was lifted by a *pickpocket* >
   syn ||cannon, cutpurse, ||dip, ||diver, purse cutter, ||wire
   rel ||ganef, thief; ||mobsman, ||swell-mobsman
   idiom pocket prowler

picksome *adj syn* see NICE 1

pick up *vb* **1** *syn* see LIFT 1
   2 *syn* see GLEAN
   3 *syn* see GET 1
   4 *syn* see LEARN 1
   5 *syn* see ARREST 2
   rel book

idiom ||take (someone) downtown
   6 *syn* see RESUME 2
   idiom pick up the thread again

pickup *n syn* see ARREST
   rel booking

picky *adj syn* see NICE 1

picnic *n syn* see SNAP 1

pictorial *adj* **1** consisting of or relating to pictures <a collection of *pictorial* materials>
   syn graphic, iconographic, illustrational, illustrative, illustratory, pictoric
   rel photographic, pictographic
   2 *syn* see GRAPHIC 1

pictoric *adj syn* see PICTORIAL 1

picture *n* **1** *syn* see REPRESENTATION
   2 *syn* see IMAGE 1
   3 *syn* see MOVIE

picture *vb syn* see REPRESENT 1
   rel draw

picture show *n syn* see MOVIE

picturesque *adj syn* see GRAPHIC 1

piddling *adj syn* see PETTY 2

pie *n syn* see SNAP 1

piece *n* **1** *syn* see PART 1
   ||**2** *syn* see SNACK

pièce de résistance *n syn* see SHOWPIECE

piecemeal *adv syn* see GRADUALLY

piecemeal *adj syn* see GRADUAL

pie-eyed *adj syn* see INTOXICATED 1

piepoudre *n syn* see PEDDLER

pier *n* **1** *syn* see WHARF
   rel pierage, wharfage
   2 *syn* see PILLAR 1

pierce *vb* **1** *syn* see CUT 1
   rel penetrate, perforate
   2 *syn* see PENETRATE 2
   rel run through

piercing *adj* **1** *syn* see SHARP 8
   2 *syn* see LOUD 1
   3 *syn* see ACUTE 4

pietistic *adj syn* see DEVOUT
   rel reverencing, reverential

piety *n syn* see FIDELITY 1
   rel docility, obedience; enthusiasm, fervor, passion, zeal; holiness, sanctity

piffle *n syn* see NONSENSE 2

piffling *adj syn* see PETTY 2

pig *n* **1** *syn* see WANTON
   2 *syn* see POLICEMAN

pigeon *n syn* see FOOL 3

pigeon *vb syn* see DUPE

pigeonhole *n* **1** *syn* see CUBBYHOLE
   2 *syn* see CLASS 1
   rel niche, slot

pigeonhole *vb syn* see ASSORT
   rel identify, label, name; place, rank, rate; catalog; break down, subdivide

pigeon house *n syn* see DOVECOTE

pigeonry *n syn* see DOVECOTE

pigheaded *adj syn* see OBSTINATE
   idiom not to be moved (or budged)

pigment *n syn* see COLOR 6

pigpen *n syn* see STY 1

pigsty *n syn* see STY 1

piked *adj syn* see POINTED 1

piker *n syn* see VAGABOND

piker *n syn* see MISER

pilaster *n syn* see PILLAR 1

pile *n* **1** a quantity of things heaped or stacked together <a *pile* of dirty clothes>

syn synonym(s)   *rel* related word(s)
ant antonym(s)   *con* contrasted word(s)
idiom idiomatic equivalent(s)
|| use limited; if in doubt, see a dictionary

syn bank, ‖bing, cock, drift, heap, hill, mass, mound, mountain, mow, pyramid, rick, ‖rickle, ‖ruck, shock, stack, stockpile, windrow

rel barrow, pyre, tumulus; ‖dess, haycock, hayrick, haystack; accumulation, aggregate, aggregation, amassment, assemblage, collection, conglomeration, glomeration, hoard, jumble

2 *syn* see MUCH
3 *syn* see EDIFICE
4 *syn* see FORTUNE 4
idiom a pile of money

pile *vb* 1 *syn* see HEAP 1
2 *syn* see LOAD 3

pile (in) *vb syn* see RETIRE 4

pile (out) *vb syn* see ROLL OUT
idiom ‖get the lead out, ‖shake it out

pile *n syn* see DOWN

pileous *adj syn* see HAIRY 1
con bare; pileless

pile up *vb syn* see SHIPWRECK 1

pileup *n syn* see CRASH 3

pilfer *vb syn* see STEAL 1

pilferer *n syn* see THIEF

pilgarlic *n syn* see LAUGHINGSTOCK

‖**pill** *n syn* see CIGARETTE

pillage *vb* 1 *syn* see RAVAGE
rel encroach, invade, trespass; appropriate, arrogate, confiscate, usurp
idiom lay waste
2 *syn* see STEAL 1

pillager *n syn* see MARAUDER

pillar *n* 1 a firm upright support for a superstructure <stone *pillars* supported the ceiling>
syn column, pier, pilaster
rel prop; pedestal; post
2 *syn* see MAINSTAY

pilose *adj syn* see HAIRY 1

pilot *n* 1 *syn* see LEADER 1
2 one who flies or is qualified to fly an airplane <jet *pilots*>
syn airman, aviator, birdman, flier, flyboy
rel aerialist

pilot *vb* 1 *syn* see GUIDE
2 *syn* see DRIVE 5

pimp *n* 1 a man who solicits for a prostitute, lives off her earnings, and often lives with her <after dark, the *pimp* appeared on the street seeking clients for his girls>
syn bully, cadet, ‖easy rider, fancy man, ‖mack, macquereau, pander
rel procurer; white slaver
‖2 *syn* see INFORMER

‖**pimp** *vb syn* see INFORM 3

pimping *adj syn* see PETTY 2

pimple *n syn* see ABSCESS
rel ‖plouk

pimple *vb syn* see SPOT 2

pin *n syn* see BROOCH

pinch *vb* 1 *syn* see EXTORT 1
2 *syn* see STEAL 1
3 *syn* see ARREST 2
4 *syn* see SCRIMP

pinch *n* 1 *syn* see JUNCTURE 2
2 *syn* see THEFT
3 *syn* see ARREST

pinchbeck *adj syn* see COUNTERFEIT

pinched *adj syn* see HAGGARD
con stalwart, stout, strong, sturdy; healthy, robust

pinching *adj syn* see STINGY

pinch hitter *n syn* see SUBSTITUTE

pinchpenny *adj syn* see STINGY

‖**pindling** *adj syn* see IRRITABLE

pine *vb syn* see LONG
rel brood, fret, mope; grieve, mourn; agonize

pinhead *n syn* see DUNCE

pinhead *adj syn* see STUPID 1

pinheaded *adj syn* see STUPID 1

pink *vb syn* see BLUSH

pinken *vb syn* see BLUSH

Pinkerton *n syn* see PRIVATE DETECTIVE

pin money *n syn* see POCKET MONEY

pinnacle *n syn* see APEX 2

pinpoint *vb syn* see IDENTIFY

pint-size *adj syn* see TINY

pioneer *adj syn* see FIRST 2
rel pilot

pious *adj syn* see DEVOUT
rel priestlike, priestly
ant impious

pip *vb* ‖1 *syn* see DEFEAT 2
2 *syn* see DIE 1

‖**pip** *n* *syn* ‖DILLY, ‖corker, crackerjack, ‖daisy, dandy, humdinger, jim-dandy, ‖lalapalooza, ‖lulu, nifty

pipe *n* 1 *syn* see CASK
‖2 *syn* see PIPE DREAM
3 *syn* see SNAP 1

pipe *vb* ‖1 *syn* see CRY 2
2 *syn* see CONDUCT 4

pipe down *vb syn* see SHUT UP 1

pipe dream *n* an illusory or fantastic plan or hope <*pipe dreams* of universal peace>
syn bubble, chimera, dream, fantasy (*or* phantasy), illusion, ‖pipe, rainbow
rel expectation, hope, prospect

pipeline *n* a person through whom information is transmitted <she was his news *pipeline* from the mayor's office>
syn channel, conduit
rel grapevine; origin, source, wellspring; supplier; connection, contact

piping *adj syn* see ACUTE 4

‖**pipped** *adj syn* see INTOXICATED 1

pippin *n* *syn* ‖DILLY, ‖corker, crackerjack, dandy, ‖dinger, ‖doozer, humdinger, jim-dandy, ‖lalapalooza, ‖pip

piquant *adj syn* see PUNGENT
rel high-flavored, well-flavored; appetizing, sparkling
con inane, jejune
ant banal

pique *n syn* see OFFENSE 2
rel annoyance, irk, irking, vexation; exasperation, irritation, provocation

pique *vb* 1 *syn* see IRRITATE
2 *syn* see PROVOKE 4
rel prick, punch; ignite
3 *syn* see PRIDE

pirate *n* a robber on the high seas <little boys dreaming of sailing as *pirates*>
syn buccaneer, corsair, freebooter, picaroon, rover, sea dog, sea robber, sea rover, sea wolf
rel viking; privateer; looter, marauder, pillager, plunderer, raider

‖**pirl** *vb syn* see SPIN 1

‖**piroot** *vb syn* see SNOOP

pirouette *vb syn* see SPIN 1

pishposh *n syn* see NONSENSE 2

‖**piss away** *vb* *syn* see WASTE 2

‖**pissed** *adj* 1 *syn* see ANGRY

   2 *syn* see INTOXICATED 1

‖**pissed off** *adj* *syn* see ANGRY

pit *n* ‖1 *syn* see GRAVE

   2 *syn* see HELL

pit *vb* *syn* see OPPOSE 1

pitch *vb* 1 *syn* see THROW 1

  rel hoist, raise; move

   2 *syn* see THROW 2

  ‖3 *syn* see PLANT 1

   4 *syn* see FALL 2

  idiom take a pitch

   5 *syn* see PLUNGE 2

  rel drop, fall, sink

   6 *syn* see TOSS 2

   7 *syn* see SEESAW

pitch *n* *syn* see SPIEL

  rel persuasion

pitch-black *adj* *syn* see BLACK 1

pitch-dark *adj* *syn* see BLACK 1

pitched *adj* *syn* see INCLINED 3

pitch in *vb* 1 to set about doing something energetically <had a lot to do and decided to *pitch in*>

  syn buckle (down), fall to, jump (in *or* into), set to, wade (in *or* into)

  rel attack, tackle; launch, tee off; begin, commence, start (off *or* out *or* up)

  idiom fall to it, fall to work, get busy (*or* cracking), get down to it, get going, get (*or* have) with it, go to it, hop (*or* jump) to it

  con dally, dawdle, procrastinate, stall; vacillate

   2 *syn* see CONTRIBUTE 1

pitching *adj* *syn* see INCLINED 3

pitchy *adj* *syn* see BLACK 1

piteous *adj* *syn* see PITIFUL 1

  rel beseeching, entreating, imploring, supplicating; doleful, dolorous, melancholy, plaintive; ruined

pitfall *n* a hidden or obscure source of danger, error, or harm <*pitfalls* that trap the unwary investigator>

  syn booby trap, deadfall, mousetrap, springe, trapfall

  rel danger, hazard, peril, risk; cobweb, entanglement, mesh(es), toil(s), web; bait, lure, snare, trap

pith *n* 1 *syn* see ESSENCE 2

  rel center, focus, nucleus; meaning, meaningfulness

   2 *syn* see SUBSTANCE 2

  idiom the long and (the) short

   3 *syn* see CENTER 3

  rel fulcrum; hub

   4 *syn* see IMPORTANCE

pithy *adj* being rich in meaning and tersely cogent in expression <a *pithy* summary>

  syn compact, epigrammatic, marrowy, meaty; *compare* CONCISE

  rel brief, concise, lean, short, short and sweet, succinct; crisp, curt, terse; effective, forceful; meaningful, significant, substantial

  idiom brief and to the point, down to brass tacks, right to the point

  con flatulent, inflated, tumid, turgid; prolix, verbose, wordy

  ant diffuse

pitiable *adj* 1 *syn* see PITIFUL 1

   2 *syn* see CONTEMPTIBLE

  rel miserable, wretched; deplorable, lamentable

pitiful *adj* 1 arousing or deserving pity <*pitiful* refugees driven from their homes>

  syn commiserable, pathetic, piteous, pitiable, poor, rueful

  rel affecting, moving, touching; miserable, woeful, wretched; heartrending

   2 *syn* see CONTEMPTIBLE

pitiless *adj* devoid of or unmoved by pity <a *pitiless* concentration camp guard>

  syn merciless, unmerciful, unpitying; *compare* UNFEELING 1

  rel coldhearted, hardhearted, heartless, ironhearted, marblehearted, stony, stonyhearted, uncompassionate, unfeeling; barbarous, brutal, cruel, cutthroat, inhuman, savage

  idiom lacking bowels of compassion, without an ounce of pity

  con compassionate, humane, sympathetic; clement, merciful; tender, warmhearted

  ant pitying

pittance *n* a small, often barely sufficient amount or allowance <a *pittance* of an education> <worked for a mere *pittance*>

  syn dribble, driblet, ‖scrimption

  rel bit, mite, scrap, smidgen, trace; inadequacy, insufficiency

  idiom a drop in the bucket, cheeseparings and candle ends, ‖pinchgut money

  con abundance, opulence, plenty, wealth

pity *n* sympathetic feeling for one suffering, distressed, or unhappy <felt the deepest *pity* for the prisoners>

  syn commiseration, compassion, rue, ruth, sympathy

  rel dejection, distress, melancholy, sadness, sorrow; charity, clemency, lenity, mercy

  con contempt, disdain, disgust, scorn

pity *vb* *syn* see COMPASSIONATE

pivot *vb* *syn* see TURN 6

pivotal *adj* *syn* see CENTRAL 1

  rel essential, vital; momentous; capital, principal

pixie *n* 1 *syn* see FAIRY

   2 *syn* see SCAMP

pixie *adj* *syn* see PLAYFUL 1

pixieish *adj* *syn* see PLAYFUL 1

pixilated *adj* 1 *syn* see PLAYFUL 1

   2 *syn* see INTOXICATED 1

placard *n* *syn* see POSTER

placard *vb* *syn* see POST

placate *vb* *syn* see PACIFY

  rel comfort; tranquilize

  idiom lay the dust

  con anger, incense, infuriate, madden; excite, pique, provoke, stimulate

  ant enrage

place *n* 1 the portion of space occupied by or chosen for something <the *place* where we'll meet>

  syn location, locus, point, position, site, situation, spot, station, where

  rel district, locality, vicinity; area, region, tract, zone; field, province, territory

---

syn synonym(s)   *rel* related word(s)

ant antonym(s)   *con* contrasted word(s)

idiom idiomatic equivalent(s)

‖ use limited; if in doubt, see a dictionary

2 *syn* see STATUS 1

3 *syn* see JOB 2

place *vb* 1 *syn* see SET 1

2 *syn* see ESTIMATE 3

3 *syn* see IDENTIFY

rel know, tell; nail, peg

idiom put one's finger on

placed *adj syn* see SITUATED

ant displaced

placid *adj syn* see CALM 1

rel irenic, peaceful, serene, unagitated, unstirring

ant roiled

2 *syn* see CALM 2

rel detached, inexcitable, unmoved

con fidgety, jittery, jumpy, skittery; agitated

ant choleric

plague *n* 1 an epidemic disease causing a high mortality rate <smallpox finally ceased to be a *plague* in those nations>

syn curse, pestilence, scourge

rel infestation, invasion; affliction, disease; epidemic; ravage

2 *syn* see ANNOYANCE 3

rel bane, curse

3 *syn* see EPIDEMIC

plague *vb syn* see WORRY 1

rel chafe, gall; badger, bait, hassle, hector, hound, ride; afflict, torment

plain *adj* 1 free from all ostentation or superficial embellishment <just give the *plain* facts>

syn discreet, dry, homely, inelaborate, modest, simple, unadorned, unbeautified, undecorated, unelaborate, unembellished, unembroidered, ungarnished, unornamented, unostentatious, unpretentious

rel muted, restrained; austere, bald, bare, severe, spartan, stark, unluxurious; homespun

con adorned, beautified, elaborate, embellished, embroidered, exaggerated; highflown, ostentatious, pretentious; flamboyant, rococo

ant rich

2 *syn* see STRAIGHT 3

3 *syn* see CLEAR 5

rel broad, unmistakable; legible

ant abstruse

4 *syn* see FRANK

rel unfeigned; abrupt

idiom plain and open

5 lacking allure without being positively ugly <a *plain* woman, drably dressed>

syn homely, unalluring, unattractive, unbeauteous, unbeautiful, uncomely, unhandsome, unpretty

rel plain-featured; inelegant; ordinary, plain Jane, unremarkable; ill-favored

idiom not much for looks, not much to look at, short on looks

con alluring, attractive, beautiful, comely, handsome; elegant; striking; knockout, sensational

6 *syn* see ORDINARY 1

plainclothesman *n syn* see DETECTIVE

plain dealing *adj syn* see STRAIGHTFORWARD 2

plain Jane *adj syn* see ORDINARY 1

plainness *n syn* see CLARITY

ant abstruseness

plainspoken *adj syn* see FRANK

plaintive *adj syn* see MELANCHOLY 2

rel deploring, lamenting, wailing; piteous, pitiful; sad, saddening

plan *n* 1 a method devised for making or doing something or attaining an end <each company had a *plan* for increasing profits>

syn blueprint, design, game plan, project, scheme, strategy

rel conception, idea, notion; ground plan, projection, projet; intent, intention, platform, purpose; means, method, way

idiom course (*or* plan) of action

2 *syn* see INTENTION

rel policy

3 *syn* see ORDER 8

plan *vb* 1 *syn* see DESIGN 3

2 to formulate a plan for arranging, realizing, or achieving something <*planned* next year's program>

syn arrange, blueprint, cast, chart, design, devise, ‖dope out, project; *compare* DESIGN 3

rel contemplate, meditate; cut out, draft, outline, sketch; figure (out), think (out); formulate, work out; organize

3 *syn* see INTEND 2

idiom be planning (*or* counting) on, have all intentions of, have every intention of

planate *n syn* see LEVEL

plane *vb syn* see EVEN 1

plane *adj syn* see LEVEL

planet *n,* used with the *syn* see EARTH 1

planetary *adj* 1 *syn* see HUGE

2 *syn* see UNIVERSAL 2

plangent *adj syn* see RESONANT

plant *vb* 1 to put or set into the ground for growth <*plant* corn>

syn ‖pitch, put in, seed, sow

rel drill; broadcast, dust, scatter; seed down

con crop, gather, harvest, reap

2 *syn* see HIDE

3 *syn* see BURY 1

plant *n syn* see FACTORY

plash *vb syn* see SPLASH

plaster *vb syn* see SMEAR 1

‖plastered *adj syn* see INTOXICATED 1

plastic *adj* susceptible of being modified in form or nature <the *plastic* quality of modeling clay> <the *plastic* affections of children>

syn adaptable, ductile, malleable, moldable, pliable, pliant, supple

rel elastic, flexible, resilient, supple, workable; impressionable, influenceable, suggestible, susceptible; amenable, bending, giving, tractable, yielding

con inflexible, rigid, stiff; accepted, customary, prevailing, set, standard, wonted

plat *n syn* see LOT 3

plateau *n* a usually extensive level land area raised sharply above adjacent land on at least one side <the *plateaus* of central Bolivia>

syn table, tableland, upland

rel mesa

con dale, glen, vale, valley; bottom, bottomland, lowland

platitude *n syn* see COMMONPLACE

rel inanity, insipidity, vapidity; mawkishness, sentimentality

platoon *n syn* see GROUP 3

plaudit n. usu **plaudits** pl syn see AP-PLAUSE
rel kudos

plausibility n syn see VERISIMILITUDE

plausible adj syn see BELIEVABLE
rel likely, possible, probable; presumable
con impossible, improbable, unlikely
ant implausible

play n 1 activity engaged in for amusement <children need periods of work and play>
syn disport, diversion, fun, recreation, sport
rel amusement, entertainment; frolic, gambol, romp; delectation, delight, enjoyment, pleasure
con business, duty, obligation; labor; drudgery
ant work
2 syn see FUN 1
rel sportiveness
ant earnest
3 syn see TRICK 1
4 syn see USE 1
5 syn see ROOM 3

play vb 1 to engage in an activity for amusement or recreation <played outside for hours>
syn disport, recreate, sport
rel amuse, divert, engage, entertain; frolic, gambol, rollick, romp
con labor, toil, travail; drudge, fag, slave
ant work
2 syn see FIDDLE 1
3 syn see TREAT 2
4 syn see MANIPULATE 2
5 syn see ACT 1
6 syn see GAMBLE 1

play (around) vb syn see PHILANDER

play (down) vb syn see SOFT-PEDAL
rel restrain; mute, soften
ant play (up)

play (off) vb syn see OPPOSE 1

play (up) vb syn see EMPHASIZE
idiom make a (big) production of
ant play (down)

playact vb syn see ACT 1

playactor n syn see ACTOR 1

player n syn see ACTOR 1

playful adj 1 given to or characterized by play, jests, or tricks <in a playful mood>
syn antic, coltish, elvish, frisky, frolicsome, gamesome, impish, kittenish, larkish, ||mischieffui, mischievous, pixie, pixieish, pixilated, prankful, prankish, pranky, puckish, roguish, sportive, waggish, wicked
rel gay, lighthearted, whimsical; dashing, larking, lively, sprightly; blithe, jocund, jolly, jovial, merry, gleeful, hilarious, mirthful
idiom as playful as a kitten (or colt), feeling one's oats
con grim, stern, stolid; grave, serious
2 syn see ANTIC 2

||**play-pretty** n syn see TOY 2

plaything n syn see TOY 2

---

syn synonym(s)   rel related word(s)
ant antonym(s)   con contrasted word(s)
idiom idiomatic equivalent(s)
|| use limited; if in doubt, see a dictionary

---

playwright n one who writes plays <a famous Broadway playwright>
syn dramatist, dramatizer, dramaturge
rel librettist; scenarist

plaza n syn see COMMON 2

plea n 1 syn see EXCUSE 1
rel extenuation, mitigation, palliation; apology; out; vindication
2 syn see PRAYER
rel overture; call, cry
idiom solemn entreaty (or plea)

plead vb syn see BEG

pleasance n syn see AMENITY 1

pleasant adj 1 highly acceptable to the mind or senses <a pleasant personality> <a pleasant respite>
syn agreeable, congenial, favorable, good, grateful, gratifying, nice, pleasing, pleasurable, pleasureful, welcome
rel cheerful, cheering, cheery, glad, joyful, joyous; alluring, attractive, charming, pretty; convivial, engaging
con displeasing, distasteful; harsh; obnoxious, repellent, repelling, repugnant, repulsive
ant unpleasant
2 syn see FAIR 2

pleasantness n syn see AMENITY 1
rel goodness, niceness
ant unpleasantness

please vb 1 syn see WILL
2 to give or be a source of pleasure to <her work pleased him>
syn arride, delectate, delight, gladden, gratify, happify, pleasure
rel content, satisfy, suit; amuse, tickle, titillate; regale, rejoice; overjoy
con vex; annoy; anger
ant displease
3 syn see SUIT 6

pleasing adj syn see PLEASANT 1
rel satisfactory, suitable; enchanting, winning; adorable, darling, delightful
ant displeasing, repellent

pleasurable adj syn see PLEASANT 1
ant unpleasurable

pleasure n 1 syn see WILL 1
2 the agreeable emotion accompanying the expectation, acquisition, or possession of something good or desirable <the pleasures and pains of growing up>
syn delectation, delight, enjoyment, fruition, joy, joyance; compare ENJOYMENT 1
rel bliss, felicity, happiness; kick, thrill
con vexation; annoyance; anger; affliction, distress, sorrow, trouble
ant displeasure
3 syn see ENJOYMENT 1
ant displeasure

pleasure vb syn see PLEASE 2

pleasure dome n syn see RESORT 3

pleasureful adj syn see PLEASANT 1

pleasuremonger n syn see HEDONIST

pleb n plebs pl syn see COMMONALTY

plebeian adj syn see IGNOBLE 1
ant patrician

plebeians n pl syn see COMMONALTY
ant patricians

plebs n plebes pl syn see COMMONALTY
rel peasantry, peasants
ant patricians, patriciate

pledge n 1 something given or held as a sign of another's good faith or intentions

< the new school is the *pledge* given by the community to its children >
syn earnest, pawn, security, token, warrant; *compare* GUARANTEE 1, PROMISE
rel bail, bond, guarantee, guaranty, surety, warranty; promise; word; oath, vow
2 *syn* see WORD 8
pledge *vb* 1 *syn* see PAWN
2 *syn* see DRINK 2
3 *syn* see PROMISE 1
rel bind, tie; commit, confide, consign, entrust
idiom give (*or* make) a solemn pledge, pledge one's honor
4 *syn* see VOW
plenteous *adj syn* see PLENTIFUL
rel full, hearty; fruitful, galore, prolific; luxuriant, opulent, sumptuous; lavish, prodigal, profuse, profusive, rampant, rife
plentiful *adj* being more than sufficient without being excessive <a *plentiful* harvest >
syn abundant, ample, bounteous, bountiful, copious, generous, liberal, plenteous, plenty
rel enough, sufficient; fulsome, rich, unstinted; excessive, extravagant, overabundant, overflowing, superabundant; abounding, bumper, bursting, swarming, swimming, teeming
con deficient, exiguous, meager, skimpy; inadequate, insufficient
ant scant, scanty
plenty *n syn* see MUCH
rel abundance, cornucopia
plenty *adj syn* see PLENTIFUL
pleonasm *n syn* see VERBIAGE 1
plethora *n syn* see EXCESS 1
rel much, plenty; many; deluge, flood
pliable *adj syn* see PLASTIC
rel manipulable, manipulatable
con unadaptable, unflexible, unmalleable, unpliant
ant unpliable
pliant *adj syn* see PLASTIC
rel spongy
ant unpliant
plica *n syn* see WRINKLE
plight *vb syn* see VOW
idiom plight one's honor
plight *n syn* see PROMISE
plight *n syn* see PREDICAMENT
rel quandary
plighted *adj syn* see ENGAGED 2
plink *vb syn* see TINKLE 1
plod *vb* 1 to walk laboriously and heavily < slowly *plodded* across the sodden field >
syn footslog, ||plodge, plunther, slog, slop, stodge, toil, ||trash, trudge; *compare* TRAMP 1
rel tramp, trample, tromp; stamp, stomp, stump; flounder, wallow
2 *syn* see DRUDGE
idiom plug away at it
plodding *adj syn* see DULL 9
||**plodge** *vb syn* see PLOD 1
plot *n* 1 *syn* see LOT 3
2 a secret plan for accomplishing a usually evil or unlawful end <an assassination *plot* >
syn cabal, conspiracy, covin, intrigue, machination, practice, scheme

rel design, plan; connivance, conniving; collusion, complicity; contraption, contrivance, device; artifice, maneuver, ruse, stratagem, trick
plot *vb* to work out a plan especially for something unlawful or wrong < *plotted* the overthrow of the government >
syn cogitate, ||collogue, collude, connive, conspire, contrive, devise, intrigue, machinate, scheme (out)
rel lay; brew, concoct, cook (up), hatch, set up; finagle, maneuver
plow *vb* to cut into and work the surface of (soil) < *plow* a field >
syn break, plow up, turn, turn over
rel cultivate, till; fallow; ||backset; furrow, list, ridge, trench; harrow, rake
plow up *vb syn* see PLOW
rel plow out
ploy *n syn* see TRICK 1
pluck *n syn* see COURAGE
||**plucked** *adj syn* see BRAVE 1
plucky *adj syn* see BRAVE 1
idiom full of pluck (*or* spunk)
con feeble, weak
ant pluckless
plug *n syn* see PUFF 3
plug *vb* 1 *syn* see FILL 1
rel pack; cork
2 *syn* see PROMOTE 3
plugging *n syn* see WORK 2
plug-ugly *n syn* see TOUGH
plum *n syn* see REWARD
rel catch, find
||**plumb** *adv syn* see WELL 3
plumb *vb syn* see SOUND
plumb *adj syn* see VERTICAL
plumbless *adj syn* see BOTTOMLESS 2
con plumbable
plumb-line *vb syn* see SOUND
plumbness *n syn* see VERTICALITY
plume *n syn* see PRIDE
plummet *vb* to decrease suddenly and sharply in financial value or price < the stock *plummeted* 60 points when the story broke >
syn dip, drop, fall, nose-dive, plunge, skid, tumble
rel decline, decrease, descend, sink; dump; precipitate; collapse, crash
idiom take a sudden downturn (*or* downtrend)
con increase; rise; shoot up
ant skyrocket, soar
plummetless *adj syn* see BOTTOMLESS 2
plump *adj syn* see ROTUND 2
rel fleshy, portly
idiom plump as a partridge
ant skinny
plumpish *adj syn* see ROTUND 2
idiom like a butterball
plumpy *adj syn* see ROTUND 2
plunder *vb syn* see ROB 1
plunder *n* 1 *syn* see SPOIL
||2 *syn* see PERSONAL EFFECTS
plunderage *n syn* see SPOIL
plunderer *n syn* see MARAUDER
plunge *vb* 1 *syn* see THRUST 2
2 to thrust or cast oneself or something into or as if into deep water < *plunged* into the crowd >
syn burst, dive, drive, lunge, pitch, ||splunge; *compare* RUSH 1

rel dip, immerse, submerge; plump, plunk; propel, push, shove, thrust; boil, charge, fling, rush, tear
idiom plunge headlong
con ease, glide, slide, slip
3 *syn* see FALL 2
idiom take a plunge
4 *syn* see PLUMMET
idiom drop like a rock, take a downward plunge
plunther *vb syn* see PLOD 1
plus *n syn* see EXCESS 2
plus *vb syn* see INCREASE 1
plush *adj syn* see LUXURIOUS 3
idiom fit for the gods
plushy *adj syn* see LUXURIOUS 3
plutonian *adj* 1 *syn* see INFERNAL 1
2 *syn* see INFERNAL 2
plutonic *adj* 1 *syn* see INFERNAL 1
2 *syn* see INFERNAL 2
ply *vb* 1 *syn* see HANDLE 2
rel exercise; function
2 *syn* see EXERT
pneuma *n syn* see SOUL 1
pneumatic *adj syn* see AIRY 1
pocket *n syn* see DEAD END
pocket *vb* 1 *syn* see STEAL 1
2 *syn* see ACCEPT 2
pocket *adj* 1 *syn* see TINY
2 *syn* see CONDENSED
3 *syn* see FINANCIAL
pocket edition *n syn* see MODEL 1
pocket money *n* money for small personal expenses or incidentals <he had spent all his *pocket money* on candy and snacks>
syn pin money, spending money
rel petty cash; change, small change
con fortune, resources; income
pocket-size *adj syn* see TINY
pococurante *adj syn* see INDIFFERENT 2
pod *n* 1 *syn* see HULL
2 *syn* see POTBELLY
podex *n syn* see BUTTOCKS
podgy *adj syn* see ROTUND 2
Podunk *n syn* see BURG
poem *n* a particular example of metrical writing <recited a *poem* by Robert Frost>
syn poesy, poetry, rhyme, rune, verse
poesy *n* 1 *syn* see POEM
2 *syn* see POETRY 1
poet *n* a writer of verse <a *poet* to stir men's souls>
syn bard, muse, Parnassian
rel jongleur, rhapsodist, trouvère, trouveur; balladist, elegist, idyllist, lyricist, lyrist, odist, satirist, sonneteer, sonnetist
poetaster *n* a writer of mediocre or inferior verse <*poetasters* who churn out tasteless verse>
syn balladmonger, bardlet, bardling, poeticule, poetling, rhymer, rhymester, verseman, versemonger, verser, versesmith, versificator, versifier
poeticule *n syn* see POETASTER
poetling *n syn* see POETASTER
poetry *n* 1 metrical language or writing <studied the *poetry* of Milton>

syn poesy, rhyme, song, verse
2 *syn* see POEM
poignance *n syn* see PATHOS
poignancy *n syn* see PATHOS
poignant *adj* 1 *syn* see PUNGENT
ant dull
2 *syn* see MOVING 2
rel agitating, disturbing, perturbing
point *n* 1 one unitary part of a whole made up of two or more parts <listened to each *point* of his opponent's argument>
syn article, detail, element, item, particular, thing; *compare* ELEMENT 2
rel characteristic, feature, trait; constituent, material, part; circumstantial, circumstantiality
con aggregate, sum, total, whole
2 *syn* see CHARACTERISTIC 1
3 the quality of an utterance that arouses interest and produces an effect <a book that lacks *point*>
syn cogency, effectiveness, force, punch, validity, validness
rel appositeness, convincement, significance, suggestiveness; appeal, attraction, charm, fascination, interest
4 *syn* see SUBJECT 2
5 *syn* see TIP
6 *syn* see PLACE 1
7 a particular limited and often critical interval of time <at that *point* he was interrupted>
syn instant, juncture, moment
rel brink, threshold, verge
8 *syn* see VERGE 1
9 a sharp or slender and tapering terminal part <the *point* of a sword>
syn apex, cusp, tip
rel awn, barb, jag, nib, prong, snag, spike, tag, tine
10 *syn* see PROMONTORY
11 a tiny mark or spot <saw a distant *point* of light>
syn dot, flyspeck, mote, speck
rel bit, fleck, iota, minim, mite, particle, scrap, tittle, trace
point *vb* 1 *syn* see PUNCTUATE
2 to tend to show something as probable <all signs *point* to an economic recovery>
syn hint, imply, indicate, suggest; *compare* SUGGEST 1
idiom make (or give) promise of, lead one to expect, offer a good prospect of
3 *syn* see DIRECT 2
point (out) *vb syn* see REFER 3
point (to) *vb syn* see TESTIFY 1
pointed *adj* 1 tapering to a thin tip <a *pointed* rock>
syn acicular, aciculate, acuminate, acuminous, acute, cuspidate, mucronate, peaked, peaky, piked, pointy, sharp
con dull, rounded
ant blunt
2 *syn* see NOTICEABLE
pointer *n syn* see TIP
pointful *adj syn* see RELEVANT
pointless *adj syn* see SENSELESS 5
‖**pointsman** *n syn* see POLICEMAN
pointy *adj syn* see POINTED 1
poise *vb* 1 *syn* see STABILIZE
rel back, support, uphold
con agitate, disturb, upset; overthrow, overturn, subvert

---

syn synonym(s)   *rel* related word(s)
ant antonym(s)   *con* contrasted word(s)
idiom idiomatic equivalent(s)
‖ use limited; if in doubt, see a dictionary

2 *syn* see HANG 3

poise *n* 1 *syn* see BALANCE 1

2 *syn* see TACT

rel aplomb, assurance, confidence, self-possession; calmness, serenity, tranquillity; dignity, elegance, grace

poised *adj syn* see CALM 2

poison *n* something that harms, interferes with, or destroys the activity, progress, or welfare of something else < the publicity was *poison* to them >

syn bane, contagion, venom, virus

rel adulteration, contamination, corruption, sophistication

con catholicon, elixir, panacea

ant antidote

poison *vb syn* see DEBASE 1

poison *adj syn* see POISONOUS

poisonous *adj* having the properties or effect of poison < *poisonous* propaganda >

syn mephitic, poison, toxic, toxicant, venomous, virulent

rel miasmal, miasmatic, miasmic, pestilent, pestilential; deadly, fatal, lethal, mortal; baneful, deleterious, detrimental, nocuous, noxious, pernicious

con corrective, countervailing, emendatory, healing, remedial

ant antidotal

‖**poke** *n syn* see BAG 1

poke *vb* 1 to thrust something into so as to stir up, urge on, or attract attention < he *poked* the man in front of him to get his attention >

syn dig, jab, jog, nudge, prod, punch

rel push, shove, thrust; arouse, awaken, rouse, stir; excite, galvanize, provoke, quicken, stimulate

2 *syn* see SNOOP

3 *syn* see DELAY 2

4 *syn* see BULGE

poke *n* 1 a quick thrust with or as if with the hand < gave him a *poke* in the ribs with my finger >

syn dig, jab, punch, stab

rel bunt, butt; boost, push, shove

2 *syn* see CUFF

3 *syn* see DUNCE

poker-faced *adj* 1 *syn* see SERIOUS 1

2 *syn* see NEUTRAL

‖**pokey** *n syn* see JAIL

poky *adj syn* see DULL 9

polar *adj syn* see OPPOSITE

polemical *adj syn* see CONTENTIOUS 2

polestar *n syn* see CENTER 2

police *n syn* see POLICEMAN

‖**police constable** *n syn* see POLICEMAN

policeman *n* a member of a police force < ask the *policeman* for directions >

syn ‖bluebottle, bluecoat, ‖bobby, ‖bull, ‖constable, cop, ‖copper, Dogberry, ‖flatfoot, ‖fuzz, ‖gendarme, gumshoe, ‖harness bull (*or* cop), ‖heat, John Law, man, ‖nab, officer, ‖paddy, patrolman, peace officer, ‖peeler, ‖pig, ‖pointsman, police, ‖police constable, police officer, ‖rozzer, ‖trap

police officer *n syn* see POLICEMAN

policy *n syn* see COURSE 3

polish *vb* 1 to make smooth or glossy usually by friction < *polished* the silver >

syn buff, burnish, furbish, glance, glaze, gloss, rub, shine

rel brighten, scour, scrub

con roughen

2 to give an elegant finish to < attended classes to *polish* his manners >

syn perfect, refine, round, sleek, slick, smooth

rel better, improve, mend; brush up, furbish, touch up; mature, perfect

polish *n* 1 *syn* see LUSTER

2 *syn* see CULTURE

polished *adj* 1 *syn* see LUSTROUS 1

2 *syn* see SLEEK

3 *syn* see GENTEEL 1

polish off *vb* 1 *syn* see CONSUME 5

2 *syn* see EAT UP 1

polite *adj syn* see CIVIL 2

rel attentive, considerate, thoughtful

ant impolite

politic *adj* 1 *syn* see EXPEDIENT

rel astute, perspicacious, sagacious, shrewd

2 *syn* see TACTFUL

rel judicious, wise

polity *n syn* see COURSE 3

poll *n syn* see HEAD 1

pollard *vb syn* see TOP 1

polloi *n syn* see RABBLE 2

pollute *vb* 1 *syn* see CONTAMINATE 1

2 *syn* see CONTAMINATE 2

polluted *adj* 1 *syn* see IMPURE 3

2 *syn* see INTOXICATED 1

Pollyanna *n syn* see OPTIMIST

rel daydreamer, wishful thinker

Pollyannaish *adj syn* see OPTIMISTIC

Pollyannaism *n syn* see OPTIMISM

‖**polly-fox** *vb syn* see SKIRT 3

poltroon *n syn* see COWARD

poltroon *adj syn* see COWARDLY

poltroonish *adj syn* see COWARDLY

polyandrium *n syn* see CEMETERY

polychromatic *adj syn* see VARIEGATED

polychrome *adj syn* see VARIEGATED

polypragmatic *adj syn* see IMPERTINENT 2

polypragmatist *n syn* see BUSYBODY

pomp *n syn* see DISPLAY 2

rel ceremonial, ceremony, form, formality, liturgy, ritual

pom-pom girl *n syn* see PROSTITUTE

pompous *adj* 1 characterized by or exhibiting self-importance < a *pompous* old fool >

syn arrogant, bloated, important, magisterial, pontifical, puffy, self-important, stuffy, wiggy; *compare* EGOCENTRIC 2, PROUD 1

rel conceited, narcissistic, self-conceited, stuck-up, vain, vainglorious; affected, highfalutin, hoity-toity, pretentious; presumptuous, self-centered, selfish; flaunting, flossy, ostentatious

con natural, unaffected, unpretentious; humble, meek, plain, simple; modest, unassuming

2 *syn* see RHETORICAL

ponder *vb* 1 *syn* see CONSIDER 1

rel appraise, evaluate

2 to consider or examine attentively or deliberately < *ponder* the best way to do it >

syn ‖chaw, deliberate, meditate, mull (over), muse, revolve, roll, ruminate, turn over

rel cogitate, reason, reflect, speculate, think; brood, debate, dwell

pondering *adj syn* see THOUGHTFUL 1

ponderous *adj* 1 *syn* see HEAVY 1
  rel substantial; burdensome, onerous, oppressive
  2 lacking all lightness and grace <a *ponderous* prose style>
  syn elephantine, heavy-footed, heavy-handed, uninspired
  rel dreary, dry, dull, humdrum, lifeless, monotonous, pedestrian, plodding, stodgy, stuffy; arid, barren; flat, insipid, savorless, vapid; buckram, cardboard, muscle-bound, stiff, stilted, wooden
  con sparkling, vivid; easy, natural, relaxed, supple, unlabored
  3 *syn* see UNWIELDY

pontifical *adj syn* see POMPOUS 1

pontificate *vb syn* see LORD

pony *n* a literal translation of a foreign language text used especially surreptitiously by students in rendering a lesson <had his *pony* hidden in his lap>
  syn crib, trot

‖**pooch** *n syn* see DOG 1

pooh *n syn* see RASPBERRY

pooh-bah *n syn* see NOTABLE 1

pooh-pooh *n syn* see RASPBERRY

pooh-pooh *vb syn* see DISMISS 5

pool *n* a small body of standing liquid <saw the *pool* of blood on the floor>
  syn puddle

pool *n* 1 *syn* see POT 3
  2 *syn* see SYNDICATE

poop *n syn* see FOOL 1

‖**poop** *vb syn* see EXHAUST

poor *adj* 1 lacking money or material possessions <they were so *poor* that the children had no winter coats>
  syn beggared, broke, destitute, dirt poor, flat, fortuneless, impecunious, impoverished, indigent, low, necessitous, needy, penurious, poverty-stricken, stone-broke, stony, strapped, unprosperous
  rel distressed, embarrassed, pinched, reduced, straitened; bankrupt, bankrupted, insolvent; hardscrabble; moneyless, penceless, penniless, unmoneyed; beggarly, down-and-out, pauperized; underprivileged
  idiom down to one's bottom dollar, flat broke, hard up, in need, in penury, in rags, in want, on one's beam-ends, on one's uppers, out at elbows, out of pocket, poor as a church mouse, unable to keep the wolf from the door, unable to make ends meet
  con affluent, comfortable, moneyed, ‖oofy, opulent, pecunious, prosperous, wealthy, well-fixed, well-heeled, well-off, well-to-do
  ant rich
  2 *syn* see MEAGER 2
  3 *syn* see PITIFUL 1
  4 *syn* see CHEAP 2
  5 *syn* see INFERIOR 2
  6 *syn* see BAD 1

poorly *adj syn* see UNWELL

poorness *n syn* see POVERTY 1

poor relation *n syn* see INFERIOR

poor-spirited *adj syn* see COWARDLY

pop *vb* 1 *syn* see STRIKE 2
  ‖2 *syn* see PAWN

pop *n syn* see FLING 1

pop *n syn* see FATHER 1

pop (in) *vb syn* see VISIT 2

popinjay *n syn* see POP

pop off *vb* 1 *syn* see GO 2
  2 *syn* see DIE 1

poppa *n syn* see FATHER 1

popping *adj syn* see BUSTLING

poppycock *n syn* see NONSENSE 2

popsy *n syn* see GIRL FRIEND 1

populace *n syn* see COMMONALTY

popular *adj* 1 *syn* see PUBLIC 4
  2 *syn* see DEMOCRATIC
  3 *syn* see CHEAP 1
  4 *syn* see PREVAILING
  5 *syn* see FAVORITE 2
  ant unpopular
  6 *syn* see WELL-KNOWN
  ant unpopular

populate *vb syn* see INHABIT

populous *adj syn* see MANY

porcine *adj syn* see FAT 2

pork-barreling *n syn* see PATRONAGE 3

porky *adj syn* see FATTY 2

porose *adj syn* see PERMEABLE

porous *adj syn* see PERMEABLE

porridge *n syn* see MISCELLANY 1

port *n* 1 *syn* see HARBOR 3
  2 *syn* see SHELTER 1

port *n syn* see BEARING 1

portable *adj* capable of being carried or moved about <a *portable* TV>
  syn carriageable, portative, transportable
  rel convenient, handy, manageable, wieldy
  con fixed, stationary

portal *n syn* see DOOR 1

portative *adj syn* see PORTABLE

portend *vb* 1 *syn* see AUGUR 2
  2 *syn* see FORETELL

portent *n* 1 *syn* see FORETOKEN
  2 *syn* see WONDER 1

porter *n syn* see BEARER 2

portion *n* 1 *syn* see SHARE 1
  2 *syn* see FATE
  3 *syn* see PART 1
  4 *syn* see RATION

portion *vb syn* see APPORTION 2

portion (out) *vb syn* see ADMINISTER 2

portly *adj syn* see FAT 2

portrait *n syn* see IMAGE 1

portraiture *n syn* see REPRESENTATION

portray *vb syn* see REPRESENT 1
  rel photograph; copy, duplicate, reproduce

portrayal *n syn* see REPRESENTATION

pose *vb* 1 *syn* see OFFER 1
  2 *syn* see PROPOSE 1
  rel ask, query, question; confound, puzzle; baffle
  3 to assume a particular physical posture <they *posed* for a family portrait>
  syn posture, sit
  rel peacock, strut
  4 to assume an artificial or pretended attitude or character usually to deceive or impress <*posed* as a salesman>
  syn attitudinize, masquerade, pass (as *or* for), pass off, posture
  rel fake, feign, pretend, sham; profess, purport; grandstand, show off

pose *n* 1 *syn* see POSTURE 1
2 an adopted way of speaking or acting
< his reticence is just a *pose* >
syn affectation, air(s), lugs, mannerism,
prettyism
rel dog, prettiness; fake, pretense, pretension
pose *vb syn* see OFFER 1
pose *vb syn* see PUZZLE
posh *adj syn* see STYLISH
posit *vb syn* see PRESUPPOSE
posit *n syn* see ASSUMPTION 2
position *n* 1 a firmly held point of view or
way of regarding something < took a
conservative *position* on educational issues >
syn attitude, color, stance, stand; *compare*
SIDE 4
rel belief, judgment, opinion, view; angle,
slant, standpoint, viewpoint
2 *syn* see PLACE 1
3 *syn* see STATUS 1
4 *syn* see STATUS 2
5 *syn* see JOB 2
positioned *adj syn* see SITUATED
positive *adj* 1 expressed clearly and usually
peremptorily < her answer was a *positive*
no >
syn categorical, decided, definite, unequivocal
rel clear, unmistakable; decisive, emphatic, energetic, firm, forceful, forcible;
explicit, express, specific, unambiguous
con irresolute, uncertain, undecided, unsure
2 *syn* see SURE 5
ant doubtful
3 not subject to being disputed or called in
question < gave *positive* proof that he
had been there >
syn certain, inarguable, incontestable,
incontrovertible, indisputable, indubitable,
irrebuttable, irrefutable, sure, uncontestable, uncontrovertible, undeniable, undisputable, undoubtable, unequivocal, unquestionable; *compare* DOWNRIGHT 1
rel assured, clear, decisive
con contestable, controvertible, debatable,
disputable, doubtful, dubious, inconclusive, questionable, unconvincing
4 *syn* see UTTER
5 *syn* see ACTUAL 2
6 capable of being constructively applied
< *positive* proposals for improving the
city >
syn affirmative
rel practical, reasonable, sound
con impractical, unsound, unusable
ant negative
7 *syn* see RIGHT-HANDED
positively *adv syn* see EASILY 2
positure *n syn* see POSTURE 1
possess *vb* 1 *syn* see HAVE 1
2 *syn* see BEAR 3
possessed *adj syn* see CALM 2
possession *n* 1 *syn* see OWNERSHIP
2 possessions *pl* things one owns usually
excluding real property and intangibles
< lost all their *possessions* in the fire >
syn belongings, chattels, effects, goods,
lares and penates, movables, things,
rel appointments, fixtures, furnishings,
furniture; accessories, appurtenances, bag-
gage, ||duds, duffle, equipment, impedi-

menta, paraphernalia, trappings, tricks;
havings; tangibles
possessive *adj syn* see JEALOUS 1
possessor *n syn* see OWNER
possessorship *n syn* see OWNERSHIP
possessory *adj syn* see JEALOUS 1
possibilities *n pl syn* see POTENTIAL
possible *adj* 1 capable of being realized
< a cure is still *possible* >
syn doable, feasible, practicable, viable,
workable
rel advisable, expedient; achievable, attainable, available
con futile, hopeless, impracticable
ant impossible
2 *syn* see PROBABLE
rel dormant, latent, potential
3 *syn* see POTENTIAL 1
possibly *adv syn* see PERHAPS
post *vb* to affix to a usual place (as a wall)
for public notices < *posted* the notice on
the bulletin board >
syn placard, poster
post *vb syn* see INFORM 2
post *n syn* see JOB 2
post *vb syn* see STATION
||**post** *n syn* see AUTOPSY
poster *n* a notice or announcement for
posting in a public place < nailed the
poster to the side of the building >
syn affiche, bill, handbill, placard
rel advertisement, announcement, banner,
broadside, notice, sign; billboard, sign-
board
poster *vb syn* see POST
posterior *adj* 1 *syn* see SUBSEQUENT 1
2 situated at or toward the back < the
posterior part of the animal >
syn after, back, hind, hinder, hindmost,
rear, retral
con fore, front
ant anterior
posterior *n* 1 *syn* see BACK 1
2 *syn* see BUTTOCKS
posterity *n syn* see OFFSPRING
ant ancestry
posthaste *adv syn* see FAST 2
posthaste *adj syn* see FAST 3
posthumous *adj* occurring after one's
death < *posthumous* fame >
syn postmortal, postmortem, post-obit,
post-obituary
rel delayed, late, retarded
con opportune, seasonable, timely
ant antemortem
postliminary *adj syn* see SUBSEQUENT 1
postmortal *adj syn* see POSTHUMOUS
postmortem *adj syn* see POSTHUMOUS
ant antemortem
postmortem *n syn* see AUTOPSY
postmortem examination *n syn* see
AUTOPSY
post-obit *adj syn* see POSTHUMOUS
post-obituary *adj syn* see POSTHUMOUS
postpone *vb syn* see DEFER
postulate *vb* 1 *syn* see DEMAND 1
2 *syn* see PRESUPPOSE
rel affirm, assert, aver, predicate
postulate *n syn* see ASSUMPTION 2
postulation *n syn* see ASSUMPTION 2
posture *n* 1 the position or bearing of the
body < erect *posture* >
syn attitude, carriage, pose, positure,
stance

rel bearing, deportment, mien
2 *syn* see STATE 1
rel promptness, quickness, readiness
posture *vb* **1** *syn* see POSE 3
2 *syn* see POSE 4
posy *n* **1** *syn* see FLOWER 1
2 *syn* see BOUQUET 1
3 *syn* see ANTHOLOGY
pot *n* **1** *syn* see FORTUNE 4
2 *syn* see BET
3 the total of the bets at stake at one time <lost track of how much was in the *pot*>
syn jackpot, kitty, pool
4 *syn* see POTSHOT
‖**5** *syn* see POTBELLY
6 *syn* see NOTABLE 1
7 *syn* see MARIJUANA
‖**8** *syn* see TOILET
potable *adj* suitable for drinking <*potable* water>
syn drinkable
rel clean, fresh, pure, uncontaminated, unpolluted
con dirty, foul, impure, polluted, unclean
ant impotable
potable *n* *syn* see DRINK 1
potbelly *n* an enlarged, swollen, or protruding abdomen <he had the biggest *potbelly* we had ever seen>
syn bay window, corporation, paunch, pod, ‖pot
potency *n* **1** *syn* see POWER 4
ant impotence
2 *syn* see EFFICACY 1
3 *syn* see ENERGY 2
ant impotence
potent *adj* **1** *syn* see POWERFUL 2
ant impotent
2 *syn* see STRONG 3
3 able to copulate <a *potent* male>
syn virile
ant impotent
potential *adj* **1** existing in possibility <a *potential* site for the new factory>
syn possible
rel conceivable, imaginable, likely, plausible, probable, thinkable
idiom within the realm (*or* range) of possibility
con existent, extant; doubtful, impossible, questionable; impracticable, unsuitable
ant actual
2 *syn* see LATENT
potential *n* something that can develop or become actual <industrial *potential*>
syn possibilities, potentiality
ant actuality, reality
potentiality *n* *syn* see POTENTIAL
ant actuality
pother *n* **1** *syn* see COMMOTION 4
2 *syn* see STIR 1
3 *syn* see ANNOYANCE 2
4 *syn* see COMMOTION 2
pother *vb* *syn* see WORRY 3
pothole *n* a hole, depression, or rut in a road surface <*potholes* all over that stretch of highway>

syn chuckhole, mudhole
pothouse *n* *syn* see BAR 5
potpourri *n* *syn* see MISCELLANY 1
potshot *n* a critical remark made in a random or sporadic manner <took a few *potshots* at his neighbor's argument>
syn pot, shy, sideswipe
rel cut, crack, dig; gibe, jeer; aspersion, criticism, insult
potted *adj* **1** *syn* see CONDENSED
‖**2** *syn* see INTOXICATED 1
potter *vb* *syn* see FIDDLE 2
potter (away) *vb* *syn* see WASTE 2
potter's field *n* *syn* see CEMETERY
potty *adj* ‖**1** *syn* see LITTLE 3
‖**2** *syn* see FOOLISH 2
3 *syn* see SNOBBISH
‖**potty** *n* *syn* see TOILET
pouch *n* *syn* see BAG 1
pouch *vb* *syn* see BULGE
pouf *n* *syn* see QUILT
poule *n* *syn* see PROSTITUTE
poultice *n* a soft, usually heated, and sometimes medicated mass spread on cloth and applied to sores or other lesions <slapped a bread *poultice* over the boil>
syn cataplasm
rel plaster; compress; dressing
pound *vb* **1** *syn* see HAMMER 1
2 *syn* see BEAT 1
3 *syn* see IMPRESS 3
pound *n* *syn* see BLOW 1
pour *vb* **1** *syn* see DISCHARGE 5
2 to send forth or come forth abundantly <medical supplies *poured* into the stricken area>
syn flow, gush, roll, sluice, stream, surge
rel issue, proceed, spring; course, rill, run, rush, swarm; cascade, cataract; deluge, flood, inundate
3 to rain heavily <it *poured* for two solid days>
syn drench, lash, teem
rel beat; deluge, flood, stream
idiom come down in buckets (*or* torrents), rain cats and dogs
pour *n* *syn* see FLOOD 2
pourboire *n* *syn* see GRATUITY
pout *vb* **1** *syn* see SULK
2 *syn* see BULGE
pouts *n pl* *syn* see SULK
poverty *n* **1** the state of one with insufficient resources <repeated crop failures had reduced the farmers to *poverty*>
syn beggary, borasca, destituteness, destitution, impecuniousness, impoverishment, indigence, indigency, need, neediness, pauperism, pennilessness, penury, poorness, privation, unprosperousness, want
rel exigency, necessity; juncture, pass, pinch, strait; difficulty, distress, embarrassment; hardship, suffering; mendicancy
idiom hand-to-mouth existence, straitened circumstances
con affluence, comfort, luxury, opulence, prosperity, richness, wealth
ant riches
2 *syn* see SCARCITY
poverty–stricken *adj* *syn* see POOR 1
powder *vb* **1** *syn* see SPRINKLE 1
2 *syn* see PULVERIZE 1
powdering *n* *syn* see DUSTING
powdery *adj* *syn* see FINE 2

---

syn synonym(s)   *rel* related word(s)
ant antonym(s)   *con* contrasted word(s)
idiom idiomatic equivalent(s)
‖ use limited; if in doubt, see a dictionary

power *n* **1** the right or prerogative of determining, ruling, or governing or the exercise of that right or prerogative < party in *power* >
syn authority, command, control, domination, jurisdiction, mastery, might, strings, sway
rel birthright, prerogative, privilege, right; direction, management; ascendancy, dominance, dominion, masterdom, sovereignty, supremacy; superiority; influence, prestige, weight; force, strength
con forcelessness, impotence, weakness
ant impuissance, powerlessness
‖ *syn see* MUCH
3 the ability of a living being to perform in a given way or a capacity for a particular kind of performance < the *power* to think clearly >
syn faculty, function
rel ability, capability, capacity; aptitude, bent, turn; endowment, gift, talent
con inability, incapability, incapacity; inaptness, ineptitude
4 the ability to exert effort for a purpose < raised the productive *power* of the nation >
syn arm, beef, dint, energy, force, might, muscle, potency, puissance, sinew, steam, strength, strong arm, vigor, virtue
rel ability, capability, capacity; effectiveness; dynamism, powder, voltage; dynamis, potentiality; competence, qualification
con inability, incapability, incapacity; ineffectiveness; incompetence
powerful *adj* **1** *syn see* STRONG 1
2 having or manifesting power to effect great or striking results < a *powerful* leader >
syn forceful, forcible, mighty, potent, puissant
rel able, capable, competent; effective, effectual, efficacious, efficient; dynamic, energetic, strenuous, vigorous; convincing, great, invincible; authoritative, dominant, influential, weighty
con faulty, feeble, flawed; impotent, inadequate, incompetent, weak
ant powerless
powerfully *adv syn see* HARD 1
powerless *adj* unable to effect one's purpose, intention, or end < *powerless* to leave >
syn helpless, impotent
rel inactive, inert, passive, supine; decrepit, feeble, infirm, weak; incapable, incompetent, ineffective, unfit
con effective, effectual, efficient; able, capable, competent; potent, puissant
ant powerful
powwow *syn see* TALK 4
powwow *vb syn see* CONFER 2
‖ **prabble** *n syn see* QUARREL
practic *adj syn see* REALISTIC
practicable *adj* **1** *syn see* POSSIBLE 1
ant impracticable
2 *syn see* PRACTICAL 2
3 *syn see* OPEN 5
ant impracticable
practical *adj* **1** *syn see* IMPLICIT 2
2 capable of being turned to use or account < had a *practical* rather than a theoretical acquaintance with mechanics >

syn functional, handy, practicable, serviceable, useful, utile
con abstract, academic, theoretical
ant impractical, unpractical
3 *syn see* REALISTIC
ant impractical, unpractical
4 *syn see* EXPERIENCED
practically *adv* **1** *syn see* VIRTUALLY
2 *syn see* ALMOST 2
3 *syn see* NEARLY
practice *vb syn see* EXERCISE 3
rel execute, fulfill, perform; follow, pursue; iterate, repeat
practice *n* **1** *syn see* HABIT 1
rel procedure, proceeding, process; method, mode, system
2 *syn see* PLOT 2
3 *syn see* EXERCISE 3
rel use, usefulness, utility; convenance, convention, form, usage
ant theory; precept
practiced *adj syn see* EXPERIENCED
ant unpracticed
praetorian *adj syn see* CORRUPT 2
praetorian *n syn see* DIEHARD 1
pragmatic *n syn see* BUSYBODY
pragmatic *adj syn see* REALISTIC
pragmatical *adj syn see* REALISTIC
pragmatist *n syn see* BUSYBODY
praisable *adj syn see* WORTHY 1
praise *vb syn see* COMMEND 2
ant censure, criticize
2 to glorify and exalt expecially in song or writing < *praised* God for all his blessings >
syn bless, celebrate, cry up, eulogize, extol, glorify, hymn, laud, magnify, panegyrize, psalm, psalmody, resound
rel aggrandize, dignify, distinguish, ennoble, erect, exalt, honor, sublime, uprear; enhance, heighten, intensify; apotheosize; proclaim
idiom sing the praises of
con asperse, calumniate, defame, libel, malign, traduce, vilify; belittle, decry, depreciate, derogate, detract (from), discount, disparage, minimize, opprobriate; censure, criticize, denounce, reprehend, reprobate; abuse, reproach, revile
ant dispraise; blame
praiseful *adj syn see* EULOGISTIC
praiseworthy *adj syn see* WORTHY 1
ant despicable
‖ **pram** *n syn see* BABY CARRIAGE
prance *vb* **1** *syn see* SASHAY
2 *syn see* DANCE 1
‖ **prang** *vb syn see* BUMP 1
prang *n syn see* CRASH 3
prank *n* a mischievous or roguish act < he was always playing *pranks* on his sister >
syn antic, caper, dido(es), frolic, lark, monkeyshine, ‖rig, shenanigan, shine(s), ‖skite, tomfoolery, trick, wheeze; *compare* ESCAPADE, TRICK 1
rel fooling, high jinks, horseplay, roughhouse, roughhousing, roughness, skylarking; gambol, play, rollick, sport; frivolity, levity, lightness; caprice, conceit, fancy, freak, vagary, whim, whimsy
prank *vb* **1** *syn see* ADORN
2 *syn see* DRESS UP 1
prankful *adj syn see* PLAYFUL 1
prankish *adj syn see* PLAYFUL 1

pranky adj syn see PLAYFUL 1
‖**prat** n syn see TRICK 1
prate vb 1 syn see CHAT 1
  2 syn see BOAST
  3 syn see BABBLE 2
prate n syn see CHATTER
prater n syn see CHATTERBOX
prattle vb 1 syn see CHAT 1
  2 syn see BABBLE 2
prattle n syn see CHATTER
prattler n syn see CHATTERBOX
praxis n syn see HABIT 1
pray vb syn see BEG
prayer n an earnest and usually a formal request for something <the *prayer* in a bill in equity is the part that specifies the kind of relief sought>
  syn appeal, application, entreaty, imploration, imprecation, orison, petition, plea, suit, supplication
  rel begging, beseeching, imploring, pleading; adoration, worship
  con claim, demand, exaction
prayer n syn see SUPPLIANT
prayerful adj syn see DEVOUT
preach vb 1 to discourse publicly on a religious subject <*preached* at Sunday services>
  syn evangelize, homilize, sermonize
  rel minister, mission, missionary; prophesy; address, lecture, speak, talk
  2 syn see MORALIZE
preach n syn see SERMON
preacher n syn see CLERGYMAN
preachify vb syn see MORALIZE
preaching n syn see SERMON
preachment n syn see SERMON
preachy adj syn see DIDACTIC
preamble n syn see INTRODUCTION
precarious adj 1 syn see DOUBTFUL 1
  2 syn see DELICATE 7
precariousness n syn see INSTABILITY
precaution n syn see PRUDENCE 1
precede vb 1 to go before in rank, dignity, or importance <the small countries at the conference were *preceded* by the large wealthy ones> <those who still feel that age should *precede* beauty>
  syn outrank, rank
  2 to go before in time <all-out war was *preceded* by many small raids>
  syn antecede, antedate, forerun, pace, predate
  rel announce, herald, foreshadow, harbinger, presage
  con ensue, supervene
  ant follow, succeed
  3 to cause to be preceded <*preceded* his address with a welcome to the visitors>
  syn introduce, lead, preface, usher
  ant follow
precedence n syn see PRIORITY
precedency n syn see PRIORITY
precedent adj syn see PRECEDING
precedently adv syn see BEFORE 1
preceding adj being before especially in time or in arrangement <the *preceding* day>

syn antecedent, anterior, foregoing, former, past, precedent, previous, prior
  rel other; preexistent, precursive, precursory; erstwhile, heretofore, hitherto
  con coming, ensuing, next, sequent, sequential, subsequent, successive
  ant following, succeeding
preceding prep syn see BEFORE 1
precept n syn see LAW 1
  rel axiom, fundamental, principle; doctrine, dogma, tenet; behest, bidding, injunction
  ant practice; counsel
précieux adj syn see PRECIOUS 4
precinct n 1 syn see QUARTER 2
  2 syn see FIELD
  3 **precincts** pl syn see ENVIRONS 1
precious adj 1 of such great value that a suitable price is hard to estimate <a *precious* twelfth century painting>
  syn costly, inestimable, invaluable, priceless, valuable; *compare* COSTLY 1
  rel choice, exquisite, rare, recherché; treasurable; rich; prizable
  idiom of price
  con base, common, mean, paltry, poor, rubbishy, shabby, trashy; contemptible, despicable, miserable; claptrap, gimcrack, trumpery
  ant cheap; worthless
  2 syn see FAVORITE 1
  3 syn see NICE 1
  4 excessively refined <too *precious* to mingle with the common people>
  syn affected, alembicated, chichi, la-di-da, overnice, overrefined, précieux; *compare* GENTEEL 3
  rel ostentatious, pretentious, showy; artful, sophisticated, studied
  con artless, ingenuous, naive, natural, simple, unaffected, unartful, unschooled, unsophisticated, unstudied, untutored; down-to-earth, matter-of-fact, practical, pragmatic, rational
precipitance n syn see HASTE 2
precipitancy n syn see HASTE 2
precipitant adj syn see PRECIPITATE 1
precipitate n 1 syn see SEDIMENT
  2 syn see EFFECT 1
precipitate adj 1 characterized by impetuous or unexpected haste <beat a *precipitate* retreat>
  syn abrupt, hasty, headlong, hurried, impetuous, precipitant, precipitous, rushing, subitaneous, sudden
  rel breakneck, headstrong, hotheaded, impatient, impulsive, madcap, refractory, uncontrolled, willful; unanticipated, unexpected, unforeseen, unlooked-for; overhasty
  con leisurely, slow, unhurried
  ant deliberate
  2 syn see STEEP 1
precipitateness n syn see HASTE 2
precipitation n 1 syn see HASTE 2
  2 syn see SEDIMENT
precipitous adj 1 syn see PRECIPITATE 1
  2 syn see STEEP 1
précis n syn see COMPENDIUM 1
precise adj 1 syn see DEFINITE 1
  2 syn see CORRECT 2
  rel rigid, stringent
  con careless, heedless; lax, slack

---

syn synonym(s)   *rel* related word(s)
ant antonym(s)   *con* contrasted word(s)
idiom idiomatic equivalent(s)
‖ use limited; if in doubt, see a dictionary

ant imprecise; loose
3 *syn* see PRIM 1
4 distinguished from every other <arrived just at the *precise* moment when he was needed>
  syn exact, very
  rel specific; individual; particular
  con general, inexact, nonspecific
  ant imprecise
precisely *adv* 1 *syn* see JUST 1
  idiom on the button
  ant imprecisely; approximately
2 *syn* see EVEN 1
3 *syn* see EXACTLY 3
preciseness *n* *syn* see PRECISION
  ant impreciseness
precisian *n* *syn* see PURIST
precision *n* the quality or character of what is precise <the *precision* involved in close-tolerance machining>
  syn accuracy, correctness, definiteness, definitiveness, definitude, exactitude, exactness, preciseness
  rel care, carefulness; attention, heed
  con inaccuracy, incorrectness, indefiniteness, inexactness; obscurity, unclearness, vagueness; unreliability, untrustworthiness
  ant imprecision
precisionist *n* *syn* see PURIST
preclude *vb* *syn* see PREVENT 2
  rel cease, discontinue, quit, stop
precocious *adj* exceptionally early in development <a *precocious* child, smart beyond his years>
  syn advanced, forward; *compare* EARLY 2
  rel ahead, early, overearly, oversoon, premature, previous, ǁsoon; developed, mature
  con backward, undeveloped; dull, slow, slow-witted, sluggish
  ant retarded
precogitate *vb* *syn* see PREMEDITATE
preconception *n* an attitude, belief, or impression formed beforehand <had a lot of *preconceptions* about a man she'd never met>
  syn prejudgment, prepossession; *compare* PREJUDICE
  rel illusion; delusion
  idiom preconceived notion (*or* idea *or* opinion)
precondition *n* *syn* see ESSENTIAL 2
precursor *n* 1 *syn* see FORERUNNER 1
2 *syn* see FORERUNNER 2
predacious *adj* *syn* see RAPACIOUS 1
predate *vb* *syn* see PRECEDE 2
predative *adj* *syn* see RAPACIOUS 1
predatorial *adj* *syn* see RAPACIOUS 1
pre-latory *adj* *syn* see RAPACIOUS 1
predecessor *n* *syn* see FORERUNNER 2
predestinate *vb* *syn* see PREDESTINE 2
predestine *vb* 1 to fix the future of in advance <his treasured scribblings were *predestined* to light a kitchen fire>
  syn destine, determine, doom (to), fate, foreordain, predetermine, preform, preordain
  rel predecide; prejudge; preestablish
2 to determine by or as if by divine decree or eternal purpose <some believe that God *predestines* individuals to eternal life or to eternal death>
  syn foredestine, foreordain, predestinate, predetermine, preordain

predetermine *vb* 1 *syn* see PREDESTINE 2
2 *syn* see PREMEDITATE
3 *syn* see PREDESTINE 1
predicament *n* a difficult, perplexing, or trying situation <was in a *predicament*, trying to decide whether or not to take the job>
  syn box, corner, deep water, dilemma, fix, hole, hot water, impasse, jam, pickle, plight, quagmire, scrape, soup, spot
  rel emergency, exigency, juncture, pass, pinch, strait; asperity, difficulty, hardness, hardship, rigor, vicissitude; Dutch, trouble; condition, posture, situation, state
  idiom ǁin a bind
predicate *vb* 1 *syn* see ASSERT 1
2 *syn* see BASE
predict *vb* 1 *syn* see FORETELL
2 to conjecture correctly <*predicted* the turn of the market months in advance>
  syn call, guess
  rel conjecture, presume, suppose, surmise, think; conclude, gather, infer, judge
  idiom hazard a conjecture (*or* guess)
prediction *n* something that is predicted <the *prediction* was for a good outcome>
  syn cast, forecast, foretelling, prevision, prognosis, prognostication, prophecy, weird
  rel conjecture, guess, surmising
predictor *n* *syn* see PROPHET
predilection *n* *syn* see LEANING 2
predispose *vb* *syn* see INCLINE 3
  rel impress, strike, sway
  con disaffect, disincline, disinterest, indispose
predisposed *adj* *syn* see WILLING 1
  ant indisposed
predisposition *n* *syn* see LEANING 2
  ant indisposition
predominant *adj* 1 *syn* see DOMINANT 1
  ant subordinate
2 *syn* see CHIEF 2
predominantly *adv* *syn* see GENERALLY 1
predominate *adj* *syn* see DOMINANT 1
predominate *vb* *syn* see RULE 2
preeminence *n* 1 *syn* see SUPREMACY
2 *syn* see EMINENCE 1
preeminent *adj* 1 *syn* see SUPREME
2 *syn* see CHIEF 2
preempt *vb* 1 *syn* see APPROPRIATE 1
2 *syn* see ARROGATE 1
preen *vb* *syn* see PRIDE
preengage *vb* 1 *syn* see RESERVE 2
2 *syn* see PREPOSSESS 1
preface *n* *syn* see INTRODUCTION
preface *vb* *syn* see PRECEDE 3
prefatial *adj* *syn* see PRELIMINARY
prefatorial *adj* *syn* see PRELIMINARY
prefatory *adj* *syn* see PRELIMINARY
prefer *vb* 1 *syn* see ADVANCE 2
2 *syn* see CHOOSE 1
3 *syn* see PROPOSE 1
preferable *adj* *syn* see BETTER 2
preference *n* 1 *syn* see CHOICE 1
  rel partiality, predilection, prepossession
2 *syn* see ADVANCEMENT 1
preferment *n* *syn* see ADVANCEMENT 1
preferred *adj* *syn* see FAVORITE 2
prefigurate *vb* *syn* see ADUMBRATE 1
prefigure *vb* *syn* see ADUMBRATE 1

preform *vb syn* see PREDESTINE 1

pregnance *n syn* see PREGNANCY

pregnancy *n* the condition of containing unborn young within the body <she was in the last trimester of her *pregnancy*>
syn gestation, gravidity, pregnance, situation

pregnant *adj* 1 containing unborn young within the body <she was *pregnant* with her second child>
syn big, childing, enceinte, expectant, expecting, gone, gravid, heavy, parous, parturient
idiom in an interesting condition, in the family way, with child (*or* young)
con barren, infertile; delivered; postpartum
2 *syn* see EXPRESSIVE
rel consequential, important, momentous, significant, weighty

prehend *vb syn* see CATCH 1

prehensile *adj syn* see COVETOUS

preindicate *vb syn* see ANNOUNCE 2

prejudgment *n syn* see PRECONCEPTION

prejudice *n* the inclination to take a stand (as in a conflict) usually without just grounds or sufficient information <could not review his competitor's work without *prejudice*>
syn bias, one-sidedness, partiality; *compare* LEANING 2, PRECONCEPTION
rel partisanship
idiom jaundiced eye
con detachment, dispassion, impartiality, indifference, neutrality
ant objectivity

prejudice *vb* 1 *syn* see INJURE 1
2 to cause to have opinions formed without due knowledge or examination <*prejudice* a man against his neighbor by innuendo>
syn bias, influence, prepossess; *compare* INCLINE 3, SLANT 3
rel bend, dispose, incline, predispose; angle, skew, slant; prejudge

prejudiced *adj syn* see BIASED 2
ant unprejudiced; disinterested

prejudicial *adj* 1 *syn* see HARMFUL
2 *syn* see DISCRIMINATORY

prejudicious *adj syn* see HARMFUL

prekindergarten *adj syn* see CHILDISH

preknow *vb syn* see FORESEE

prelation *n syn* see ADVANCEMENT 1

prelect *vb syn* see TALK 7

∥prelim *adj syn* see PRELIMINARY

preliminary *adj* serving to make ready the way for something that follows <held a *preliminary* discussion to set up the agenda of the conference>
syn inductive, introductory, prefatial, prefatorial, prefatory, ∥prelim, preludial, prelusive, preparative, preparatory, proemial
rel primal, primary; elemental, elementary; basic, fundamental; fitting, preparing, readying
ant postliminary

prelimit *vb syn* see LIMIT 2

preliterate *adj syn* see PRIMITIVE 6

prelude *n syn* see INTRODUCTION

preludial *adj syn* see PRELIMINARY

prelusion *n syn* see INTRODUCTION

prelusive *adj syn* see PRELIMINARY

premature *adj syn* see EARLY 2

prematurely *adv syn* see EARLY 2

premeditate *vb* to think on and revolve in the mind beforehand <carefully *premeditating* each step of his plan of campaign>
syn forethink, precogitate, predetermine
rel prearrange, preplan, set up; predecide; prepare

premeditated *adj syn* see DELIBERATE 1
ant unpremeditated; spontaneous

premier *adj syn* see FIRST 3

premise *n syn* see ASSUMPTION 2

premise *vb syn* see PRESUPPOSE

premium *n syn* see REWARD

premium *adj syn* see SUPERIOR 4

premonition *n syn* see APPREHENSION 3

prename *n syn* see GIVEN NAME

prenotion *n syn* see APPREHENSION 3

prentice *n syn* see NOVICE

prentice *adj syn* see CRUDE 5

preoccupied *adj* 1 *syn* see INTENT
2 *syn* see ABSTRACTED
rel absorbed; forgetful
ant unpreoccupied

preoccupy *vb syn* see PREPOSSESS 1

preordain *vb* 1 *syn* see PREDESTINE 1
2 *syn* see PREDESTINE 2

preparative *adj syn* see PRELIMINARY

preparatory *adj syn* see PRELIMINARY

prepare *vb* 1 to make ready in advance usually for a particular use or disposition <*prepared* rooms for the expected guests>
syn fit, fix, get, make, make up, ready
rel furnish, provide, supply; dower, endow, endue; equip, outfit; dispose, incline, predispose; prime
idiom set the stage (for)
ant unprepare
2 *syn* see DRAFT 3
3 *syn* see GIRD 3

prepared *adj syn* see READY 1
ant unprepared

prepatent *adj syn* see LATENT

prepense *adj syn* see DELIBERATE 1

prepensely *adv syn* see INTENTIONALLY

preponderance *n syn* see SUPREMACY

preponderancy *n syn* see SUPREMACY

preponderant *adj syn* see DOMINANT 1

preponderate *vb syn* see RULE 2

preponderation *n syn* see SUPREMACY

prepossess *vb* 1 to influence or affect strongly beforehand <was *prepossessed* with the notion of his own superiority>
syn preengage, preoccupy
rel busy, engage, engross, immerse, occupy, soak; absorb, imbue, involve
2 *syn* see PREJUDICE 2

prepossessed *adj syn* see BIASED 2
ant unprepossessed

prepossessing *adj syn* see ATTRACTIVE 1

prepossession *n syn* see PRECONCEPTION

preposterous *adj* 1 *syn* see FOOLISH 2
rel irrational, unreasonable
2 *syn* see EXTRAVAGANT 1

preposterousness *n syn* see FOOLISHNESS

prepotence *n syn* see SUPREMACY

---

syn synonym(s)   *rel* related word(s)
ant antonym(s)   *con* contrasted word(s)
idiom idiomatic equivalent(s)
∥ use limited; if in doubt, see a dictionary

prepotency n syn see SUPREMACY
prerequisite n syn see ESSENTIAL 2
prerequisite adj syn see ESSENTIAL 4
prerogative n syn see RIGHT 2
　rel exemption, immunity
presage n syn see FORETOKEN
　2 syn see APPREHENSION 3
presage vb 1 syn see AUGUR 2
　rel bespeak, indicate
　2 syn see ANNOUNCE 2
　3 syn see FORETELL
prescribe vb 1 syn see DICTATE
　2 to fix arbitrarily or authoritatively for
　the sake of order or of a clear understand-
　ing < the Constitution *prescribes* the con-
　ditions under which it may be amend-
　ed >
　syn assign, define, lay down
　rel establish, fix, set, settle; decide, deter-
　mine; choose, pick out, select
prescript n syn see LAW 1
prescription n syn see LAW 1
presence n syn see BEARING 1
　rel appearance, aspect, look, seeming
present n syn see GIFT 1
present vb 1 syn see INTRODUCE 4
　2 syn see GIVE 1
　3 syn see OFFER 1
　4 syn see ADDUCE
　5 syn see DIRECT 2
present adj now existing or in progress
　< the *present* state of the economy seems
　to be shaky from all reports >
　syn contemporary, current, existent, ex-
　tant, instant, present-day, todayish
　rel contemporaneous, modern; newfash-
　ioned, up-to-date, up-to-the-minute
　con bygone, erstwhile, late, old, once,
　onetime, quondam, sometime, whilom
　ant past
present n the present time < the course
　covers U.S. history from 1900 to the *pres-
　ent* >
　syn now, today; compare FUTURE, PAST
　idiom here and now, this day and age
　ant past; future
presentable adj syn see RESPECTABLE 5
present-day adj syn see PRESENT
presenter n syn see DONOR
presentiment n syn see APPREHENSION 3
　rel discomposing, discomposure, disquie-
　tude, disturbance, perturbation
presently adv 1 without undue time lapse
　< the results will be evident *presently* >
　syn anon, by and by, directly, shortly,
　soon
　2 syn see TODAY
presentment n syn see REPRESENTATION
preserval n syn see CONSERVATION 1
preservation n the act of preserving or
　the state of being preserved < the *preser-
　vation* of peace in the world >
　syn conservation, keeping, safekeeping,
　salvation, saving, sustentation
　rel defense, guard, protection, safeguard,
　shield; care, guardianship, ward
　2 syn see CONSERVATION 1
preserve vb 1 syn see SAVE 3
　2 syn see MAINTAIN 1
preserve vb syn see JAM
preside vb to occupy the place of authority
　(as in an assembly) < the chief justice
　presides over the supreme court > < the
　presiding elders of the church >

　syn chair
　rel carry on, conduct, control, direct,
　keep, manage, operate, ordain, run; ad-
　minister, handle, head, oversee, supervise
press n syn see CROWD 1
press vb 1 to act upon through steady
　pushing or thrusting force exerted in
　contact < *pressed* his nose against the
　window >
　syn bear, compress, constrain, crowd,
　crush, jam, ||mash, push, ||squab, squash,
　squeeze, squish, squush
　rel propel, shove, thrust; drive, impel,
　move
　2 syn see DEPRESS 2
　3 to squeeze out the juice or con-
　tents of < *press* grapes >
　syn crush, express
　rel compress, squeeze
　4 syn see PUSH 2
　5 syn see PRESSURE
　6 syn see EMBRACE 1
　7 to crowd closely against or around
　someone or something < hundreds *pressed*
　around the performer after the show >
　syn cram, crowd, crush, jam, squash,
　squeeze; compare CRAM 1
　rel pack, ram, stuff, tamp; mass, pile;
　assemble, collect, congregate, gather
　8 to force or push one's way (as through
　a crowd or against obstruction) < had to
　press through the traffic to get to the
　other side of town >
　syn bear, squeeze
　rel force, push, shove
press-agent vb syn see PUBLICIZE
press-agentry n syn see PUBLICITY
pressing adj demanding or claiming espe-
　cially immediate attention < he was barely
　able to pay his most *pressing* debts >
　syn burning, clamant, clamorous, crying,
　dire, exigent, imperative, importunate,
　insistent, instant, urgent
　rel direct, immediate; claiming, demand-
　ing, exacting, requiring; compelling, con-
　straining, forcing, obliging; acute, critical,
　crucial
pressure n syn see STRESS 1
pressure vb to insist upon unduly < *pres-
　sured* him into making the wrong move >
　syn overpress, press, push
　rel drive, impel; rush
prestige n 1 syn see STATUS 2
　2 syn see INFLUENCE 1
　rel power, sway
　3 syn see EMINENCE 1
prestigious adj syn see FAMOUS 2
presto adv syn see FAST 2
presumably adv by reasonable assumption
　< *presumably* the best qualified for the job
　should get it >
　syn assumably, doubtless, likely, pre-
　sumptively, probably
　con indubitably, surely, undoubtedly,
　unquestionably
presume vb 1 syn see CONJECTURE
　2 syn see PRESUPPOSE
　3 syn see IMPOSE 5
presuming adj syn see PRESUMPTUOUS
　ant unassuming, unpresuming
presumption n 1 syn see EFFRONTERY
　2 syn see PRESUPPOSITION 1
　3 syn see ASSUMPTION 2

presumptively *adv syn* see PRESUMABLY

presumptuous *adj* marked by or based on bold and excessive self-confidence < in such company his demand for attention was utterly *presumptuous* >
syn brash, brassbound, confident, forward, gay, overconfident, overweening, presuming, pushful, pushing, ‖pushy, self-asserting, self-assertive, uppish, uppity
rel pretentious, self-assured, self-conceited; lofty, pompous, supercilious; complacent, self-satisfied, smug; inexcusable, outrageous
idiom above one's britches
con deferential, dutiful, respectful, submissive; appropriate, proper

presuppose *vb* to take something for granted or as true or existent especially as a basis for action or reasoning < a lecturer who talks above the heads of his listeners *presupposes* too extensive a knowledge on their part >
syn assume, posit, postulate, premise, presume
rel conjecture, guess, surmise; deduce, infer, judge; believe, expect, gather, imagine, reckon, suppose, suspect, take, think, understand; preconceive

presupposition *n* 1 an act of presupposing < going on his *presupposition* that they would succeed >
syn assumption, presumption
rel conjecture, guess, surmise; deduction, inference, judgment; belief, conviction, opinion, view
2 *syn* see ASSUMPTION 2

pretend *vb* 1 *syn* see ASSUME 4
rel beguile, deceive, delude, mislead; profess, purport
idiom make believe
2 *syn* see CONJECTURE

pretended *adj syn* see ALLEGED

pretender *n syn* see IMPOSTOR

pretense *n* 1 *syn* see CLAIM 1
2 the offering of something false as real or true < there is too much *pretense* in his piety >
syn charade, disguise, make-believe, pageant, pretension, pretentiousness
rel deceit, deception, fake, fraud, humbug, imposture, sham; affectation, air, mannerism, pose
con sincereness; reality, soundness, substantiality, validity; fairness, honesty
ant sincerity
3 *syn* see MASK 2

pretension *n* 1 *syn* see CLAIM 1
2 *syn* see AMBITION 1
3 *syn* see PRETENSE 2

pretentious *adj* 1 *syn* see SHOWY
ant unpretentious
2 *syn* see GENTEEL 3
ant unpretentious
3 flamboyant, turgid, or bombastic in manner or content < a *pretentious* literary style >
syn arty, arty-crafty, big, high-sounding, imposing, overblown

rel affected, feigned, put-on; pompier; aureate, bombastic, euphuistic, flowery, grandiloquent, magniloquent, rhetorical; inflated, tumid, turgid
con heartfelt, hearty, sincere, unfeigned, wholehearted, whole-souled; artless, genuine, natural, simple, unaffected
ant unpretentious
4 *syn* see AMBITIOUS 2

pretentiousness *n syn* see PRETENSE 2
ant unpretentiousness

preterition *n syn* see OMISSION

pretermission *n syn* see OMISSION

pretermit *vb syn* see NEGLECT

preternatural *adj* 1 *syn* see SUPERNATURAL 1
rel anomalous, unnatural; nonnatural
2 *syn* see ABNORMAL 1
ant natural

pretext *n* 1 *syn* see EXCUSE 1
2 *syn* see MASK 2

prettify *vb syn* see PALLIATE

pretty *adj* 1 *syn* see SKILLFUL 2
2 *syn* see BEAUTIFUL
rel darling, ducky; cunning, cute
ant unpretty

pretty *adv syn* see SOMEWHAT 2
idiom pretty much

‖**pretty** *n syn* see TOY 2

prettyism *n syn* see POSE 2

pretty-pretty *n syn* see KNICKKNACK

preux *adj syn* see COURTLY

prevail *vb* 1 *syn* see CONQUER 2
2 *syn* see WIN 1
3 *syn* see RULE 2

prevail (on *or* upon) *vb syn* see INDUCE 1
rel affect, impress

prevailing *adj* general (as in circulation, acceptance, or use) in a given place or at a given time < the *prevailing* point of view among farmers >
syn current, popular, prevalent, rampant, regnant, rife, ruling, widespread
rel dominant, predominant, preponderant; common, familiar, ordinary; general, universal
con exceptional, uncommon, unusual

prevalent *adj* 1 *syn* see DOMINANT 1
2 *syn* see PREVAILING
3 *syn* see GENERAL 1
rel accustomed, customary, wonted

prevaricate *vb syn* see LIE
rel belie, garble, misrepresent

prevarication *n syn* see LIE

prevaricative *adj syn* see EVASIVE 1

prevaricator *n syn* see LIAR

prevaricatory *adj syn* see EVASIVE 1

prevent *vb* 1 to be or get ahead of or to deal with beforehand < many problems are *prevented* easily if one plans wisely >
syn anticipate, forestall
rel baffle, balk, foil, frustrate, thwart; arrest, check, interrupt
2 to stop from advancing or occurring < take steps to *prevent* war > < measures designed to *prevent* the spread of disease >
syn avert, deter, forestall, forfend, obviate, preclude, rule out, stave off, ward
rel bar, block, dam, hinder, impede, obstruct; debar, shut out; forbid, inhibit, interdict, prohibit
con allow, leave, let, suffer
ant permit

---

syn synonym(s)   *rel* related word(s)
ant antonym(s)   *con* contrasted word(s)
idiom idiomatic equivalent(s)
‖ use limited; if in doubt, see a dictionary

previous adj 1 syn see PRECEDING
ant subsequent; consequent
2 syn see EARLY 2
previous adv syn see BEFORE 1
previously adv syn see BEFORE 2
ant subsequently; consequently
previousness n syn see PRIORITY
previse vb syn see FORESEE
prevision n syn see PREDICTION
prevision vb syn see FORESEE
prey n 1 syn see GAME 3
2 syn see VICTIM 2
‖**pribble** n syn see QUARREL
price n 1 the quantity of one thing that is
exchanged or demanded in barter or sale
for another < what is the *price* of this
book>
syn charge, cost, price tag, rate, tab, tariff
2 syn see EXPENSE 2
priceless adj syn see PRECIOUS 1
rel cherished, prized, treasured, valued
idiom without price
price tag n syn see PRICE 1
prick n 1 a mark or shallow hole made by
or as if by a pointed tool < a needle *prick*
in his arm>
syn jab, ‖jag, puncture, stab
rel prickle; hole
‖2 syn see SNOT 1
prick vb syn see PERFORATE
rel enter; cut, slash, slit
2 syn see URGE
rel excite, pique, stimulate
‖**prick (up)** vb syn see DRESS UP 1
prickish adj syn see IRRITABLE
prickly adj 1 syn see THORNY
rel annoying, bothersome
2 syn see IRRITABLE
pride n 1 syn see CONCEIT 2
rel bighead, cockiness, overconfidence,
self-assurance
idiom overweening pride
ant humility
2 a reasonable or justifiable sense of one's
worth or position < inhumane treatment
in prison caused him to lose his *pride* >
syn amour propre, self-esteem, self-regard,
self-respect
rel dignity, face, pridefulness, self-confidence, self-trust
con humiliation, mortification; shame-
facedness
ant shame
3 proud or disdainful behavior or actions
< her snobbishness and overbearing *pride*
were offensive>
syn arrogance, disdain, disdainfulness,
haughtiness, hauteur, loftiness, morgue,
superbity, superciliousness
rel condescension, snobbishness; contempt, scorn; insolence; smugness; pretentiousness
idiom haughty airs
con humbleness, modesty, unpretentiousness
ant humility
4 syn see BEST
idiom pride of the herd
pride vb to congratulate (oneself) for something one is, has, or has done or achieved
< he *prides* himself on his ancestry >
syn pique, plume, preen
rel boast, brag, crow, gasconade, vaunt;
congratulate, felicitate

ant efface
‖**pridy** adj syn see PROUD 1
prier (*or* pryer) n syn see BUSYBODY
priestal adj syn see SACERDOTAL
priestish adj syn see SACERDOTAL
priestlike adj syn see SACERDOTAL
priestly adj syn see SACERDOTAL
‖**prig** vb syn see STEAL 1
prig n syn see THIEF
prig n syn see PRUDE
prig adj syn see PRIM 1
priggish adj 1 syn see COMPLACENT
rel self-righteous; self-esteeming, self-
loving
2 syn see PRIM 1
prim adj 1 excessively concerned with what
one regards as proper or right < a *prim*
woman, easily shocked by vulgar lan-
guage>
syn bluenosed, genteel, missish, precise,
prig, priggish, prissy, proper, prudish,
puritanical, straitlaced, stuffy, tight-laced,
Victorian; *compare* GENTEEL 3
rel correct, nice, precise; decorous; rigid,
stiff, wooden; ceremonial, ceremonious,
conventional, formal, straight
idiom prim and proper
con lax, loose, slack; easy, easygoing, free
2 syn see NEAT 2
prima facie adj syn see SELF-EVIDENT
primarily adv 1 syn see GENERALLY 1
2 syn see INITIALLY 1
primary adj 1 syn see FIRST 2
2 syn see PRIMITIVE 4
3 syn see FUNDAMENTAL 1
4 syn see DIRECT 3
5 not based on or derived from something
else < the *primary* studies in nuclear phy-
sics>
syn original, prime, primitive, underivative, underived
rel first, firsthand; basic, foundational,
fundamental, principal, underlying
con derivate, derivational, derivative,
derived; borrowed, secondhand
ant secondary
prime n 1 syn see MORNING 1
2 syn see YOUTH 1
3 syn see BEST
prime adj 1 syn see FIRST 2
2 syn see EXCELLENT
3 syn see PRIMARY 5
prime vb syn see PROVOKE 4
primeval adj syn see PRIMITIVE 4
primevous adj syn see PRIMITIVE 4
primitial adj syn see PRIMITIVE 4
primitive adj 1 syn see PRIMARY 5
2 syn see EARLY 1
3 closely approximating an early ancestral type < the opossums are *primitive*
mammals>
syn archaic, persistent, undeveloped, unevolved
ant advanced
4 of or relating to earlier ages of the
world or of human history < archaeology
is concerned especially with the study of
primitive man>
syn primary, primeval, primevous, primitial
ant unprimitive
5 syn see ELEMENTAL 1

6 characterized by a lack of written language, simple technology, and a relatively simple social organization
syn nonliterate, preliterate
rel barbarian, uncivilized, uncultivated
con advanced, civilized, cultivated
primitively *adv syn see* INITIALLY 1
primogenitor *n syn see* ANCESTOR 1
primordial *adj* 1 *syn see* EARLY 1
2 *syn see* FIRST
primp *vb syn see* DRESS UP 1
primrose *n syn see* BEST
prince *n syn see* MAGNATE
princely *adj syn see* GRAND 1
principal *adj* 1 *syn see* CHIEF 2
2 *syn see* FIRST 3
principally *adv syn see* GENERALLY 1
principium *n syn see* PRINCIPLE 1
principle *n* 1 a comprehensive and fundamental rule, doctrine, or assumption <the *principle* of free speech>
syn axiom, fundamental, law, principium, theorem
rel basis, foundation, ground; canon, precept, rule; convention, form, usage
2 *principles pl syn see* ETHIC 3
3 *principles pl syn see* ALPHABET 2
principled *adj syn see* MORAL 1
ant unprincipled
‖**prink** *vb syn see* SASHAY
prink (up) *vb syn see* DRESS UP 1
print *n* 1 *syn see* IMPRESSION 1
2 printed state or form <to see his name in *print*>
syn black and white, writing
printing *n syn see* EDITION
prior *adj syn see* PRECEDING
rel ahead, before, forward
con after, behind
priority *n* the act, the fact, or the right of preceding another <the right to inherit a title is dependent mainly on *priority* of birth>
syn antecedence, precedence, precedency, previousness
rel arrangement, order, ordering; ascendancy, supremacy; preeminence, transcendence
prior to *prep* 1 *syn see* BEFORE 1
2 *syn see* UNTIL
prison *n syn see* JAIL
‖**prison** *vb syn see* IMPRISON
prison bird *n syn see* CONVICT
prissy *adj* 1 *syn see* PRIM 1
rel fastidious, finicky, squeamish
2 *syn see* EFFEMINATE
‖**pritch** *vb syn see* PERPORATE
private *adj* 1 belonging to or concerning an individual person, company, or interest <*private* property>
syn personal, privy
rel intimate
con common, general, shared
ant public
2 known only to a select few <the group had *private* information about the strike>
syn closet, confidential, hushed, inside
rel secret; discreet; concealed, hidden

con common, general, open
ant public
private detective *n* a person concerned with the maintenance of lawful conduct or the investigation of crime either as a regular employee of a private interest (as a hotel) or as a contractor for fees <obtained a *private detective* to report on his wife's associates>
syn operative, Pinkerton, ‖private eye, ‖shamus; *compare* DETECTIVE
‖**private eye** *n syn see* PRIVATE DETECTIVE
privately *adv syn see* SECRETLY
private parts *n pl syn see* GENITALIA
privates *n pl syn see* GENITALIA
privation *n* 1 *syn see* ABSENCE
2 the state of one deprived of something previously or normally possessed <suffered great *privation* during the famine>
syn deprivation, deprivement, dispossession, divestiture, loss; *compare* LOSS 1
rel distress, misery, suffering; losing, mislaying, misplacement, misplacing
3 *syn see* POVERTY 1
privilege *n syn see* RIGHT 2
rel allowance, concession; boon, favor
privilege (from) *vb syn see* EXEMPT
privities *n pl syn see* GENITALIA
privy *adj* 1 *syn see* PRIVATE 1
2 *syn see* ULTERIOR
privy *n* 1 an outdoor toilet <in less settled areas, *privies* often take the place of indoor plumbing>
syn backhouse, ‖biffy, ‖closet, jakes, ‖necessary, ‖office, outhouse
2 *syn see* TOILET
privy parts *n pl syn see* GENITALIA
prize *n* 1 *syn see* REWARD
2 *syn see* BEST
prize *vb syn see* APPRECIATE 1
prize *n syn see* SPOIL
prize *vb syn see* PRY
prizefighting *n syn see* BOXING
pro *prep syn see* FOR 2
ant anti, con
pro *n syn see* EXPERT
pro and con *vb syn see* DISCUSS 1
probable *adj* being such as may become true or actual <seems to be a *probable* candidate>
syn conceivable, earthly, likely, mortal, possible
rel believable, colorable, credible, plausible; rational, reasonable; apparent, illusory, ostensible, seeming
con doubtful, dubious, questionable, unlikely
ant improbable, unprobable
probably *adv syn see* PRESUMABLY
ant improbably
probe *n syn see* INQUIRY 1
probe *vb* 1 *syn see* EXPLORE
2 to try to find out (as by discreet questioning) the views or intentions of <*probed* the neighbors on the subject of political reform>
syn feel out, sound (out)
rel ask, catechize, examine, inquire, interrogate, query, quiz
idiom feel the pulse, put out a feeler, see how the land lies, see which way the wind blows

---

syn synonym(s)   *rel* related word(s)
ant antonym(s)   *con* contrasted word(s)
idiom idiomatic equivalent(s)
‖ use limited; if in doubt, see a dictionary

3 *syn* see SCOUT

probing *n syn* see INQUIRY 1

probity *n syn* see GOODNESS

problem *n* 1 *syn* see EXAMPLE 3
2 something requiring thought and skill to arrive at a proper conclusion or decision < what to do now is a *problem* >
syn issue, nut, question
rel enigma, mystery, puzzle; bugaboo, bugbear; count, point
idiom a hard nut to crack

problematic *adj* 1 *syn* see DOUBTFUL 1
ant unproblematic
2 *syn* see MOOT
ant unproblematic

proboscis *n syn* see NOSE 1

procacious *adj* 1 *syn* see INSOLENT 2
2 *syn* see WISE 5

procedure *n* 1 *syn* see COURSE 3
2 *syn* see MEASURE 7
3 *syn* see PROCESS 1

proceed *vb* 1 *syn* see SPRING 1
2 *syn* see GO 1
3 *syn* see ADVANCE 5
ant recede

proceeding *n* 1 *syn* see MEASURE 7
2 *syn* see PROCESS 1

proceeds *n pl syn* see PROFIT

process *n* 1 the series of actions, operations, or motions involved in the accomplishment of an end < the *process* of making sugar from sugarcane >
syn procedure, proceeding
rel fashion, manner, method, mode, modus, system, technique, way, wise; routine; operation
2 *syn* see OUTGROWTH 1

‖**process** *vb syn* see GO 1

procession *n syn* see ORDER 5

processus *n syn* see OUTGROWTH 1

proclaim *vb* 1 *syn* see DECLARE 1
rel utter, vent, ventilate, voice
2 *syn* see SHOW 2

proclamation *n syn* see DECLARATION

proclivity *n syn* see LEANING 2

procrastinate *vb syn* see DELAY 1
rel defer, postpone, stay, suspend; prolong, protract

procreate *vb* 1 to produce offspring < *procreate* children >
syn bear, beget, breed, generate, multiply, produce, propagate, reproduce
rel mother; engender; hatch, spawn; proliferate
idiom give birth to, multiply the earth
2 *syn* see GENERATE 1
3 *syn* see FATHER 1

procumbent *adj syn* see PRONE 4

procurable *adj syn* see AVAILABLE 1

procure *vb* 1 *syn* see GET 1
2 *syn* see INDUCE 1

prod *vb* 1 *syn* see POKE 1
2 *syn* see URGE
rel instigate; excite, pique, provoke, stimulate

prodigal *adj syn* see PROFUSE
ant parsimonious; frugal

prodigal *n syn* see SPENDTHRIFT

prodigality *n syn* see EXTRAVAGANCE 2
ant parsimoniousness

prodigalize *vb syn* see WASTE 2

prodigious *adj* 1 *syn* see MARVELOUS 1
2 *syn* see MONSTROUS 1

3 *syn* see HUGE

prodigy *n syn* see WONDER 1

produce *vb* 1 *syn* see PROCREATE 1
2 *syn* see STAGE
3 *syn* see EFFECT 1
4 *syn* see GENERATE 1
5 *syn* see GENERATE 3
6 *syn* see MAKE 3
7 *syn* see BEAR 9
8 *syn* see GIVE 7
9 *syn* see GROW 1

produce *n syn* see PRODUCT 1

product *n* 1 something produced by physical labor or intellectual effort < the literary *products* of the Age of Reason >
syn produce, production
rel handiwork; consequence, effect, offshoot, outcome, outgrowth, result; fruit, harvest
2 *syn* see OUTPUT

production *n* 1 *syn* see PRODUCT 1
2 *syn* see EXTENSION 1
3 *syn* see OUTPUT

productive *adj syn* see FERTILE
ant unproductive

proem *n syn* see INTRODUCTION

proemial *adj syn* see PRELIMINARY

profanation *n* a violation or misuse of something normally held sacred < the *profanation* of a religious ritual >
syn blasphemy, desecration, sacrilege, violation
rel contamination, defilement, pollution; corruption, debasement, perversion, vitiation; transgression, trespass
con glorification, hallowing, sanctification
ant purification; consecration

profane *adj* 1 not concerned with religion or religious purposes < he was speaking of *profane* history, not the history found in the Bible >
syn lay, secular, temporal, unsacred
rel earthly, mundane, terrestrial, worldly
con consecrated, hallowed, holy, sanctified; divine, religious, spiritual
ant sacred
2 *syn* see HEATHEN
3 *syn* see IMPIOUS 1
4 *syn* see SACRILEGIOUS
5 *syn* see OBSCENE 2

profaned *adj syn* see IMPURE 3
ant unprofaned

profanity *n syn* see BLASPHEMY 1

profess *vb syn* see ASSERT 1

professed *adj syn* see ALLEGED

professedly *adv syn* see OSTENSIBLY

profession *n syn* see TRADE 1

professional *n syn* see EXPERT
ant amateur

proffer *vb syn* see OFFER 1

proffer *n syn* see PROPOSAL

proficiency *n syn* see ADVANCE 2

proficient *adj* having or manifesting the knowledge, skill, and experience needed for success in a particular field or endeavor < a *proficient* glider pilot >
syn adept, crack, crackerjack, expert, master, masterful, masterly, skilled, skillful; compare EXPERIENCED, SKILLFUL 2
rel checked-out, drilled, exercised, practiced; effective, effectual, efficient; able, capable, competent, qualified; accomplished, consummate, finished

con ignorant, untaught, untrained; inexperienced; unskilled
ant incompetent

proficient *n syn see* EXPERT

profile *n syn see* OUTLINE

profit *n* the excess of returns over expenditure in a transaction or a series of transactions < his *profits* from the business venture were rewarding >
syn earnings, gain, lucre, proceeds, return
rel cleaning, cleanup, killing; receipt(s); output, outturn, product, production, turnout, yield
con cost, expenditure, expense, outgo
ant loss

profit *vb syn see* BENEFIT
ant lose

profitable *adj syn see* ADVANTAGEOUS 1
ant profitless, unprofitable

profligate *adj syn see* ABANDONED 2

profligate *n* 1 *syn see* WASTREL 1
2 *syn see* SPENDTHRIFT

profound *adj* 1 *syn see* RECONDITE
2 *syn see* DEEP 1
3 *syn see* INTENSIVE

profoundness *n syn see* DEPTH 2

profundity *n syn see* DEPTH 2

profuse *adj* proffered in or characterized by great abundance < a *profuse* flow of blood >
syn exuberant, lavish, lush, luxuriant, opulent, prodigal, profusive, riotous
rel abundant, copious; abounding, swarming, teeming; excessive, extravagant, immoderate; bounteous, bountiful, generous, liberal, munificent, openhanded
con exiguous, meager, scrimpy, skimpy, slight, small, sparse
ant scant, scanty

profusive *adj syn see* PROFUSE

progenerate *vb syn see* FATHER 1

progenitor *n syn see* ANCESTOR 1

progeniture *n syn see* OFFSPRING

progeny *n syn see* OFFSPRING

prognosis *n syn see* PREDICTION

prognostic *n syn see* FORETOKEN

prognosticate *vb syn see* FORETELL

prognostication *n syn see* PREDICTION

prognosticator *n syn see* PROPHET

program *n* 1 a formulated plan listing things to be done or to take place especially in their time order < the *program* of a concert >
syn agenda, calendar, card, docket, programma, schedule, sked, timetable
rel bill; slate; plan
idiom order of the day
2 *syn see* COURSE 3

programma *n syn see* PROGRAM 1

progress *n* 1 *syn see* ADVANCE 2
ant regression, retrogression
2 a movement onward (as in time or space) < the *progress* of a disease > < they made slow *progress* toward their destination >
syn advance, course, progression
rel passage
3 *syn see* DEVELOPMENT

progress *vb syn see* ADVANCE 5
ant retrogress

progression *n* 1 *syn see* PROGRESS 2
2 *syn see* SUCCESSION 2
3 *syn see* DEVELOPMENT
ant regression, retrogression

progressive *adj syn see* LIBERAL 3
ant reactionary

prohibit *vb syn see* FORBID
ant permit

prohibited *adj syn see* FORBIDDEN

prohibition *n syn see* TABOO
ant permission

project *n* 1 *syn see* PLAN 1
2 something (as a business operation) that one engages in or attempts < large-scale *projects* involving large sums of money >
syn enterprise, undertaking
rel affair, business, concern, matter, proposition, thing; adventure, emprise, exploit, feat, gest, venture

project *vb* 1 *syn see* PLAN 2
rel intend, propose, purpose; delineate, diagram
2 *syn see* THINK 1
|| 3 *syn see* WANDER 1
4 *syn see* BULGE
rel extend, lengthen, prolong

projection *n* 1 something which extends beyond a level or a normal outer surface < buttresses are *projections* which serve to support a wall >
syn bulge, jut, outthrust, protrusion, protuberance
rel bump, bunch, swelling; extension, prolongation; hook, knob, point, spine, spur
ant depression
2 *syn see* EMINENCE 3

prolegomenon *n syn see* INTRODUCTION

proletariat *n syn see* RABBLE 2

proliferant *adj syn see* FERTILE

prolific *adj syn see* FERTILE
rel abounding, swarming; breeding, generating, propagating, reproducing, reproductive
ant barren, unfruitful

prolificacy *n syn see* FERTILITY
ant barrenness, unfruitfulness

prolix *adj syn see* WORDY
rel irksome, tedious, tiresome, wearisome; prolonged, protracted

prolixity *n syn see* VERBOSITY

prolixness *n syn see* VERBOSITY

prologue *n syn see* INTRODUCTION
ant epilogue

prolong *vb syn see* EXTEND 3
rel continue, endure, last, persist
con abbreviate, retrench, shorten
ant curtail

prolongate *vb syn see* EXTEND 3

prolongation *n syn see* EXTENSION 1

prolonged *adj syn see* LONG 2
ant curtailed

prolongment *n syn see* EXTENSION 1

prominence *n* 1 *syn see* EMINENCE 1
2 *syn see* EMINENCE 3

prominency *n syn see* EMINENCE 1

prominent *adj* 1 *syn see* NOTICEABLE
ant inconspicuous
2 *syn see* FAMOUS 2
3 *syn see* WELL-KNOWN

promiscuous *adj* 1 *syn see* MISCELLANEOUS

---

syn synonym(s)   rel related word(s)
ant antonym(s)   con contrasted word(s)
idiom idiomatic equivalent(s)
|| use limited; if in doubt, see a dictionary

2 *syn* see RANDOM

promise *vb* 1 to give one's word to do, bring about, or provide < *promised* to render all possible assistance to the flood victims >
syn engage, pass, pledge, undertake; *compare* VOW
rel accede, agree, assent, consent; bargain, compact, contract; covenant, plight, swear, vow; assure, ensure, insure; guarantee
idiom give (*or* make) a promise, pass one's word

2 *syn* see AUGUR 2

promise *n* a declaration that one will do or refrain from doing something specified < never gave a *promise* that he did not intend to keep >
syn engagement, plight, word; *compare* PLEDGE 1, WORD 8
rel earnest, guarantee, pawn, pledge, security, token; covenant, swear, vow; assurance, warrant
idiom word of honor

‖**promised** *adj syn* see ENGAGED 2

promised land *n syn* see UTOPIA

promiseful *adj syn* see HOPEFUL 2

promising *adj syn* see HOPEFUL 2
ant unpromising

promontory *n* a high point of land or rock projecting into a body of water beyond the line of coast < stood on the *promontory* watching boats come in with the tide >
syn beak, bill, cape, foreland, head, headland, naze, point

promote *vb* 1 *syn* see ADVANCE 2
con break, bust, declass, degrade, demerit, disgrade, disrate, downgrade, reduce
ant bump, demote

2 *syn* see ADVANCE 1

3 to encourage public acceptance of (as a policy or merchandise) through publicity < official attempts to *promote* energy conservation > < television helped *promote* the new smaller cars >
syn advertise, boost, plug, push; *compare* PUBLICIZE
rel ballyhoo, propagandize; build up, cry, press-agent, publicize, puff; communicate, impart
idiom make much of
con belittle, decry, depreciate, discredit, knock, run down
ant disparage

promotion *n* 1 *syn* see ADVANCEMENT 1
ant demotion

2 *syn* see PUBLICITY
rel advertisement

prompt *vb* 1 *syn* see INDUCE 1

2 *syn* see URGE

prompt *adj* 1 *syn* see QUICK 2
rel alert, vigilant, watchful, wide-awake; expeditious, speedy, swift
con lax, remiss, slack; dilatory

2 *syn* see PUNCTUAL 2

promptitude *n syn* see ALACRITY

promptly *adv* see FAST 2

promulgate *vb syn* see DECLARE 1

promulgation *n syn* see DECLARATION

prone *adj* 1 *syn* see WILLING 1

2 *syn* see LIABLE 2

3 *syn* see APT 1

4 lying down < lying *prone* on the floor >
syn decumbent, flat, procumbent, prostrate, reclining, recumbent
rel resupine, supine; level
con arrect, raised, stand-up, straight-up, upright, upstanding
ant erect

pronounce *vb syn* see ARTICULATE 2

pronounced *adj syn* see DECIDED 1

pronouncement *n syn* see DECLARATION

‖**pronto** *adv syn* see FAST 2

pronunciamento *n syn* see DECLARATION

proof *n* 1 *syn* see REASON 3

2 *syn* see TESTIMONY

prop *n syn* see SUPPORT 3

prop *vb* 1 *syn* see SUPPORT 1

2 *syn* see SUPPORT 5

propagandist *n syn* see MISSIONARY

propagate *vb* 1 *syn* see PROCREATE 1

2 *syn* see GROW 1

3 *syn* see SPREAD 1

propel *vb* 1 *syn* see PUSH 1

2 *syn* see MOVE 5

3 *syn* see URGE

propellant *n syn* see STIMULUS

propensity *n syn* see LEANING 2
ant antipathy

proper *adj* 1 *syn* see FIT 1
ant improper

2 *syn* see TRUE 7
ant improper

3 *syn* see DECOROUS 1
ant improper

4 *syn* see ABLE

5 *syn* see GOOD 2
ant improper

6 *syn* see CHARACTERISTIC

‖7 *syn* see UTTER

8 *syn* see CORRECT 2

9 *syn* see PRIM 1

properly *adv* 1 *syn* see WELL 4
ant improperly

2 *syn* see WELL 1
idiom by rights
ant improperly

properness *n syn* see ORDER 7
ant improperness

property *n* 1 *syn* see QUALITY 1

2 *syn* see WEALTH 2

3 *syn* see OWNERSHIP

prophecy *n* 1 *syn* see REVELATION

2 *syn* see PREDICTION

prophesier *n syn* see PROPHET

prophesy *vb syn* see FORETELL

prophet *n* one who predicts events or developments < there have been many *prophets* foretelling the end of the world >
syn augur, auspex, forecaster, foreseer, foreteller, haruspex, Nostradamus, predictor, prognosticator, prophesier, seer, soothsayer

prophetic *adj* of, relating to, or characteristic of a prophet or prophecy < the old woman seemed to have *prophetic* powers >
syn apocalyptic, Delphian, fatidic, mantic, oracular, prophetical, sibylline, vatic, vaticinal
rel revelatory; interpretive; mysterious, mystic, strange, unexplainable
ant unprophetic

prophetical *adj syn* see PROPHETIC

propinquity *n syn* see PROXIMITY
propitiate *vb syn* see PACIFY
  rel adapt, adjust, conform, reconcile; content, satisfy; intercede, mediate
propitiatory *adj syn* see PURGATIVE
propitious *adj* 1 *syn* see FAVORABLE 5
  ant unpropitious; adverse
  2 *syn* see TIMELY 1
  ant unpropitious
  3 *syn* see GOOD 1
  ant unpropitious; adverse
||**propone** *vb syn* see PROPOSE 1
proponent *n syn* see EXPONENT
  ant opponent
proportion *n* 1 *syn* see DEGREE 2
  2 *syn* see SYMMETRY
  ant disproportion
  3 *syn* see SIZE 1
proportion *vb syn* see HARMONIZE 3
proportional *adj* being in proportion <his weight is *proportional* to his size>
  syn commensurable, commensurate, equal, symmetrical
  rel correlative, corresponding, reciprocal; contingent, dependent, relative
  con asymmetrical, disproportionate, irregular, lopsided, nonsymmetrical, off-balance, overbalanced, unbalanced, unequal, uneven, unsymmetrical
  ant disproportional
proportionless *adj syn* see LOPSIDED
proposal *n* something which is proposed to another for consideration <his *proposal* for a new bussing plan>
  syn invitation, proffer, proposition, suggestion
  rel motion; recommendation; idea, plan, project; outline, scheme
propose *vb* 1 to set before the mind for consideration <he *proposed* Mr. Smith for secretary of the club>
  syn pose, prefer, ||propone, proposition, propound, put, suggest
  rel move (for); offer, present, submit, tender; ask, request, solicit
  idiom put forth (*or* forward)
  ant withdraw
  2 *syn* see INTEND 2
proposition *n syn* see PROPOSAL
proposition *vb syn* see PROPOSE 1
propound *vb syn* see PROPOSE 1
proprietary *n syn* see OWNERSHIP
proprietor *n syn* see OWNER
proprietorship *n syn* see OWNERSHIP
propriety *n syn* see ORDER 11
  2 *syn* see DECORUM 1
  ant impropriety
  3 *syn* see ORDER 7
  ant impropriety
  4 **proprieties** *pl syn* see MANNER 5
prorate *vb syn* see APPORTION 2
prorogate *vb syn* see ADJOURN 2
prorogue *vb* 1 *syn* see DEFER
  2 *syn* see ADJOURN 2
prosaic *adj* 1 belonging to or characteristic of prose as distinguished from poetry <his poetry is far more fanciful than his *prosaic* writings>

  syn matter-of-fact, prose, prosing, prosy
  rel actual, factual; literal
  con figurative, metaphorical, symbolic; fanciful, florid, flowery, ornate
  ant poetic
  2 *syn* see COLORLESS 2
  3 belonging to or suitable to the everyday world <the *prosaic* business of day-to-day housekeeping>
  syn commonplace, everyday, lowly, mundane, workaday, workday
  rel practicable, practical; boring, irksome, tedious
  4 *syn* see COMMON 6
prosaicism *n syn* see COMMONPLACE
prosaism *n syn* see COMMONPLACE
proscribe *vb syn* see SENTENCE
proscription *n syn* see TABOO
prose *n syn* see CHAT 2
prose *adj syn* see PROSAIC 1
prosing *adj syn* see PROSAIC 1
prospect *n syn* see VISTA
prospect *vb syn* see EXPLORE
prosper *vb syn* see SUCCEED 3
  rel augment, increase, multiply; bear, produce, turn out, yield
prospering *adj syn* see FLOURISHING
prosperity *n* 1 *syn* see SUCCESS
  2 a state of good fortune and especially of financial success <his wise investments finally brought him a life of *prosperity*>
  syn abundance, ease, easy street, prosperousness, thriving, well-being
  rel affluence, riches, wealth
  idiom bed of roses, comfortable (*or* easy) circumstances, life of ease, the good life
  con misery, suffering; distress, embarrassment, indigence, poverty, straits
  ant adversity
  3 *syn* see WELFARE
  4 a state of high general economic activity marked by relatively full employment <a war economy often generates *prosperity*>
  syn boom, prosperousness
  rel expansion; growth; inflation
  con recession, slump, stagnation; bust
  ant depression
prosperous *adj* 1 *syn* see TIMELY 1
  rel appropriate, convenient, desirable; felicitous, fortunate, happy, lucky
  con ill-seasoned, ill-timed, inauspicious, inopportune, unpropitious, unseasonable, untimely
  ant unprosperous
  2 *syn* see SUCCESSFUL
  3 enjoying or marked by economic well-being <in *prosperous* circumstances>
  syn comfortable, easy, ||snug, substantial, well, well-fixed, well-heeled, well-off, well-to-do
  rel affluent, opulent, rich, wealthy; halcyon
  idiom comfortably off, comfortably situated, in (the) clover, in good case
  con impecunious, necessitous, needy, poor; failing, unfortunate, unsuccessful
  ant unprosperous
  4 *syn* see FLOURISHING
  rel lusty, strong
  con decrepit, feeble, spindling, weak
prosperously *adv syn* see WELL 5
  ant unprosperously
prosperousness *n* 1 *syn* see PROSPERITY 2

---

syn synonym(s)   *rel* related word(s)
ant antonym(s)   *con* contrasted word(s)
idiom idiomatic equivalent(s)
|| use limited; if in doubt, see a dictionary

ant unprosperousness

2 *syn* see PROSPERITY 4

prostitute *vb syn* see ABUSE 2

rel corrupt, debase, debauch, deprave, vitiate

prostitute *n* a woman who engages in promiscuous sexual intercourse especially for money < streets haunted by *prostitutes* >

syn bawd, ‖callet, call girl, camp follower, cocotte, ‖cruiser, drab, fille de joie, harlot, ‖hooker, hustler, ‖joy girl, meretrix, moll, nightwalker, party girl, pom-pom girl, poule, quean, sporting girl, street girl, streetwalker, ‖tomato, whore; *compare* DOXY, HARLOT 1, WANTON

rel bar girl, B-girl, pickup; V-girl, victory girl; cocodette

idiom lady of pleasure, lady of the evening, woman of the street (*or* streets), woman of the town

prostitution *n* the act or practice of engaging in promiscuous sexual intercourse especially for money < the problem of *prostitution* around military installations >

syn harlotry, oldest profession, (the) social evil, streetwalking, whoredom

prostrate *adj syn* see PRONE 4

prostrate *vb* 1 *syn* see FELL 1

2 *syn* see PARALYZE 1

3 *syn* see OVERWHELM 4

4 *syn* see EXHAUST 4

prosy *adj* 1 *syn* see PROSAIC 1

2 *syn* see COLORLESS 2

protean *adj syn* see CHANGEABLE 1

protect *vb syn* see DEFEND 1

rel conserve, preserve, save; harbor, shelter

protection *n* 1 *syn* see DEFENSE 1

2 money paid under threat of depredation < offered *protection* to keep his store from being vandalized >

syn ‖pad

rel extortion, shakedown, squeeze; graft; bribe

pro tem *adj syn* see TEMPORARY

pro tempore *adj syn* see TEMPORARY

protest *n syn* see DEMUR 2

protest *vb* 1 *syn* see ASSERT 1

2 *syn* see OBJECT 1

rel demonstrate; combat, fight, oppose, resist

ant agree

protoplast *n syn* see ORIGINAL 1

prototypal *adj syn* see TYPICAL 1

prototype *n* 1 *syn* see ORIGINAL 1

2 *syn* see FORERUNNER 2

prototypical *adj syn* see TYPICAL 1

protract *vb syn* see EXTEND 3

ant curtail

protracted *adj syn* see LONG 2

ant curtailed

protraction *n syn* see EXTENSION 1

rel dallying, dawdling, delay, lag; stay, suspension

ant curtailment

protrude *vb syn* see BULGE

protrusion *n syn* see PROJECTION 1

protuberance *n syn* see PROJECTION 1

protuberate *vb syn* see BULGE

proud *adj* 1 showing or feeling superiority toward others < a woman who was too *proud* to do her share of menial tasks >

syn arrogant, cavalier, disdainful, dismissive, haughty, high-and-mighty, hubristic, huffy, insolent, lofty, lordly, orgulous, overbearing, ‖pridy, proudhearted, supercilious, superior, toploftical, toplofty; *compare* POMPOUS 1, VAIN 3

rel contemptuous, scornful; misproud; ostentatious, pretentious; bloated, important, pompous, self-important, stuffy, wiggy; conceited, narcissistic, self-conceited, stuck-up, vain, vainglorious; domineering, high-handed, imperious, masterful

con lowly, meek, modest, unassuming; chagrined, mortified

ant humble

2 *syn* see SPLENDID 2

proudhearted *adj syn* see PROUD 1

prove *vb* 1 to establish a point by appropriate objective means < gathered evidence that *proved* the need for better controls >

syn demonstrate, test, try

rel confirm, corroborate, substantiate, verify; argue, attest, bespeak, betoken, indicate

ant disprove; refute

2 *syn* see TRY 1

3 *syn* see ESTABLISH 6

provenance *n syn* see SOURCE

provender *n syn* see FOOD 1

provenience *n syn* see SOURCE

prove out *vb syn* see SUCCEED 2

proverb *n syn* see SAYING

provide *vb syn* see GIVE 3

provide (for) *vb syn* see SUPPORT 3

providence *n* 1 *syn* see ECONOMY

ant improvidence

2 *syn* see PRUDENCE 1

ant improvidence

provident *adj syn* see SPARING

ant improvident

providential *adj syn* see LUCKY

rel benignant, kind, kindly

province *n* 1 *syn* see FUNCTION 1

rel calling, pursuit, work

2 *syn* see FIELD

provincial *n syn* see RUSTIC

provincial *adj* 1 *syn* see RURAL

2 *syn* see INSULAR

rel bigoted, hidebound

con cosmic, universal; progressive

ant catholic

provision *n syn* see CONDITION 1

provisional *adj* 1 *syn* see CONDITIONAL 1

rel temporary; contingent, dependent

ant definitive

2 *syn* see MAKESHIFT

provisionary *adj syn* see CONDITIONAL 1

provisions *n pl syn* see FOOD 1

proviso *n syn* see CONDITION 1

provisory *adj syn* see CONDITIONAL 1

provocation *n syn* see ANNOYANCE 1

provocative *adj syn* see STIMULUS

provoke *vb* 1 *syn* see IRRITATE

rel insult, outrage

ant gratify

2 *syn* see ANNOY 1

rel anger, incense, madden

3 *syn* see INCITE

rel perturb, upset

4 to lead one into doing or feeling or to produce by so leading a person < was *provoked* into finding a solution to the

problem> <this foolish answer *provoked* an outburst of rage>
syn excite, galvanize, innervate, innerve, motivate, move, pique, prime, quicken, rouse, ||roust, stimulate, suscitate; *compare* FIRE 2, STIR 1
rel arouse, awaken, bestir, build up, challenge, kindle, rally, stir, wake, waken, whet; animate, exalt, fire, inform, inspire; electrify, enthuse, thrill; titillate, titivate
idiom bring (one) to one's feet
con calm, relax, soothe
5 *syn* see GENERATE 3
provoking *n* 1 *syn* see ANNOYANCE 1
prowess *n* 1 *syn* see HEROISM
2 *syn* see ADDRESS 1
proximate *adj* 1 *syn* see CLOSE 6
2 *syn* see IMMINENT 1
3 *syn* see RUDE 3
ant exact
proximity *n* the quality or state of being near <the two houses are in close *proximity*>
syn appropinquity, contiguity, contiguousness, immediacy, propinquity
rel togetherness; closeness, nearness; adjacency, juxtaposition
con farness, remoteness
ant distance
proxy *n* *syn* see AGENT 2
prude *n* a person who is excessively or priggishly attentive to propriety or decorum <in that narrow atmosphere she hardened into a rigid, inhibited, censorious person—a thorough *prude*>
syn bluenose, comstock, goody-goody, Grundy, Mrs. Grundy, nice Nelly, prig, puritan, ||wowser
rel spoilsport, stick-in-the-mud, wet blanket; fuddy-duddy, old fogy, stuffed shirt; fussbudget, old maid
con freethinker, latitudinarian, libertarian
prudence *n* 1 a quality in a person that allows him to choose the sensible course <displayed *prudence* in setting up his business>
syn canniness, caution, discreetness, discretion, foresight, forethought, precaution, providence; *compare* WIT 3
rel acumen, astucity, astuteness, clearsightedness, discrimination, keenness, penetration, percipience, perspicacity, shrewdness, wit; insight, sagaciousness, sagacity, sageness, sapience, wisdom; advisableness, expediency; calculation, circumspection
con indiscretion, unreasonableness, unwiseness
ant imprudence
2 *syn* see ECONOMY
prudent *adj* 1 *syn* see WISE 2
ant imprudent
2 *syn* see EXPEDIENT
prudish *adj* *syn* see PRIM 1
rel strict; austere, severe, stern
prune *n* *syn* see DUNCE
prune *vb* *syn* see CUT 6
rel brash, lop; thin; eliminate, exclude

prurience *n* *syn* see LUST 2
pruriency *n* *syn* see LUST 2
prurient *adj* *syn* see LUSTFUL 2
rel bawdy, erotic, lewd; sensual
pry *vb* *syn* see SNOOP
idiom nose into
pry *vb* to raise, move, or pull apart with or as if with a pry <*pry* up a floorboard>
syn jimmy, lever, prize
rel elevate, hoist, lift, pick up, raise, rear, take up, uphold, uplift, upraise, uprear; turn, twist; disengage, disjoin, divide, separate
prying *adj* *syn* see CURIOUS 2
rel obtrusive, officious
psalm *vb* *syn* see PRAISE 2
psalmody *vb* *syn* see PRAISE 2
pseudo *adj* *syn* see COUNTERFEIT
rel wrong
pseudonym *n* a fictitious or assumed name <used a *pseudonym* in many of his adventures>
syn alias, anonym, nom de guerre
rel ananym; nom de plume, pen name; stage name; incognito
psychal *adj* *syn* see PSYCHIC 1
psyche *n* *syn* see SOUL 1
psychic *adj* 1 sensitive to nonphysical forces and influences <because he foretold many things correctly, people regarded him as *psychic*>
syn psychal, psychical, supersensible, supersensory
rel telepathic; spiritual; impressible, impressionable, responsive, sensible, sensile, sensitive, sentient, susceptible, susceptive
2 *syn* see MENTAL 1
psychical *adj* 1 *syn* see PSYCHIC 1
2 *syn* see MENTAL 1
psychological *adj* *syn* see MENTAL 1
psychopathy *n* *syn* see INSANITY 1
pub *n* *syn* see BAR 5
puberty *n* *syn* see YOUTH 1
pubescence *n* *syn* see YOUTH 1
public *adj* 1 of, relating to, or affecting the people as an organized community <*public* affairs>
syn civic, civil, national
rel government, governmental; community; state; municipal, urban
2 *syn* see OPEN 4
rel common, general, universal
con private
3 *syn* see COMMON 1
con private
4 held by or applicable to the majority of the people <*public* opinion>
syn general, popular, vulgar
rel prevalent, usual, widespread
ant private
public *n* 1 *syn* see SOCIETY 3
2 *syn* see FOLLOWING 2
rel hangers-on, suite
||**publican** *n* *syn* see SALOONKEEPER
publication *n* *syn* see DECLARATION
rel dissemination
public house *n* 1 *syn* see HOTEL
||2 *syn* see BAR 5
publicity *n* information with news value issued to gain public attention or support <$100,000 was allocated for new-product *publicity*>
syn advertising, buildup, press-agentry, promotion, puffery

rel broadcasting, promulgation, skywriting; réclame; announcement, write-up; blurb, commercial, plug, puff; ballyhoo, hoopla; propaganda; hard sell

publicize *vb* to give publicity to < *publicize* a new book>
syn advertise, build up, cry, press-agent, puff; compare PROMOTE 3
rel announce, broadcast, headline, promulgate, skywrite; advance, boost, plug, push; extol; bruit, tout, trumpet; propagandize
idiom bring into the limelight, throw the spotlight on

publish *vb* 1 *syn* see DECLARE 1
rel broach, express, utter, vent, ventilate
idiom bring to public notice, lay before the public, publish (*or* noise *or* spread) abroad, put forth
2 to produce for publication and allow to be distributed and sold < *published* a newspaper>
syn get out, issue, put out
rel produce; bring out; market; distribute

puckfist *n syn* see BRAGGART

puckish *adj syn* see PLAYFUL 1

pudding *n, usu* **puddings** *pl syn* see ENTRAILS

puddle *n syn* see FOOL

puddle *vb syn* see FIDDLE 2

puddy *adj syn* see ROTUND 2

pudendum *n, usu* **pudenda** *pl syn* see GENITALIA

pudgy *adj syn* see ROTUND 2
rel ‖chuffy, ‖chumpy, squab, squdgy, ‖stuggy, stumpy, thick-bodied

puerile *adj syn* see CHILDISH

puff *vb* 1 *syn* see PANT 1
idiom huff and puff, pant and blow
2 *syn* see BOAST
3 *syn* see PUBLICIZE

puff *n* 1 *syn* see DRAW 1
rel inhalation, inhaling
2 *syn* see QUILT
3 a commendatory and often extravagant publicity notice or review < this book fails to deliver what the *puff* promises>
syn blurb, plug, puffing, write-up
rel boost, buildup, push; laudation, praise

puffery *n syn* see PUBLICITY

puffing *n syn* see PUFF 3

puffy *adj syn* see POMPOUS 1

‖puggy *adj syn* see SWEATY

pugilism *n syn* see BOXING

pugnacious *adj syn* see BELLIGERENT
rel pushing, pushy, self-assertive; defiant, rebellious; brawling
idiom itching for a fight, itching (*or* ready) to fight, ready to fight at the drop of a hat
con bland, easygoing, mild; calm, peaceful; quiet
ant pacific

pugnacity *n syn* see ATTACK 2

puissance *n syn* see POWER 4
rel clout, influence, sway
con powerlessness, weakness
ant impuissance

puissant *adj syn* see POWERFUL 2
rel influential; commanding, ruling
con ineffectual, inefficacious, powerless
ant impuissant

puke *n syn* see SNOT 1

pukka *adj syn* see AUTHENTIC 2

pulchritudinous *adj syn* see BEAUTIFUL

pule *vb syn* see WHIMPER

pull *vb* 1 *syn* see EXTRACT 1
2 to cause to move toward or after an applied force < *pull* a trunk across the floor>
syn drag, draw, haul, lug, tow, tug
rel strain; heave; jerk, wrench, yank; drive, impel, push, shove
3 *syn* see STRAIN 2
4 *syn* see ROW
idiom pull on the oar (*or* oars)
5 *syn* see COMMIT 1
idiom ‖go and do
6 *syn* see DON 2
7 *syn* see GET 1

pull *n* 1 *syn* see DRAW 1
2 the power or ability to secure special favor or partiality < had lots of *pull* with the government>
syn clout, ‖drag, in, influence; compare INFLUENCE 1
rel persuasion; wire-pulling
idiom backstairs influence
3 *syn* see ATTRACTION 1

pullback *n syn* see DIEHARD 1

pull down *vb syn* see DESTROY 1

pull in *vb* 1 *syn* see RESTRAIN 1
2 *syn* see ARREST 1

pull out *vb syn* see GO 2
ant pull in

pull through *vb syn* see SURVIVE 2

pullulate *vb syn* see TEEM

pull up *vb syn* see STOP 4

pulp *vb syn* see CRUSH 2

pulpitarian *n syn* see CLERGYMAN

pulpiteer *n syn* see CLERGYMAN

pulpiter *n syn* see CLERGYMAN

pulpous *adj syn* see SOFT 6

pulpy *adj syn* see SOFT 6

pulsate *vb* to course or move with or as if with rhythmic strokes < blood *pulsating* through his veins>
syn beat, palpitate, pulse, throb
rel fluctuate, oscillate, vibrate; pump; drum, pound, roar, thrum

pulse *vb syn* see PULSATE

pulverize *vb* 1 to reduce (as by crushing, beating, or grinding) to minute particles < *pulverized* the ore in a stamp mill>
syn bray, buck, comminute, contriturate, crush, powder, triturate; compare SHATTER 1
rel break up; abrade, grate, grind; crumble, crunch, mull; levigate; atomize, fragment, fragmentalize, fragmentize, micronize; beat, shatter, smash, smatter, splinter; flour, mill
2 *syn* see DESTROY 1

pulverized *adj syn* see FINE 2
rel pulverous, pulverulent; dusty, granular, splintery
ant unpulverized

pummel *vb syn* see BEAT 1

pump *vb syn* see DRAIN 1

pumpkin head *n syn* see DUNCE

‖pumpknot *n syn* see BUMP 2

pun *n* the humorous use of a word so as to suggest different meanings, or of words having the same or similar sound but different meanings < "mourning shall come with approaching day" is a *pun*>

syn calembour, paronomasia
rel double entendre
idiom play on words

punch *vb* 1 *syn* see POKE 1
rel hit, slap, strike
2 *syn* see PERFORATE

punch *n* 1 *syn* see CUFF
2 *syn* see POKE 1
3 *syn* see POINT 3
4 *syn* see VIGOR 2

punctilious *adj* *syn* see CAREFUL 2
rel conventional, formal, observant; over-conscientious, overscrupulous

punctual *adj* 1 *syn* see CAREFUL 2
ant unpunctual
2 marked by exact adherence to an appointed time < a *punctual* arrival >
syn prompt, timely
rel quick, ready
idiom on the dot, on time
con late, tardy
ant unpunctual

punctuate *vb* to mark or divide (written matter) with punctuation marks < *punctuated* the sentence >
syn point
rel divide, separate

puncture *n* *syn* see PRICK 1
rel perforation

puncture *vb* 1 *syn* see PERFORATE
rel riddle
2 *syn* see DISCREDIT 2
idiom shoot full of holes

pungent *adj* sharp and stimulating to the mind or senses < his *pungent* wit >
syn peppery, piquant, poignant, racy, snappy, spicy, zesty
rel acute, keen, salt, salty, sharp; biting, bitter, cutting, hot, incisive, trenchant; exciting, provocative, stimulating; rich
con banal, corny, dull, flat, hackneyed, insipid, old hat, platitudinous, prosaic, prosy, stale, stodgy, tasteless, unimaginative, uninteresting
ant bland

punish *vb* 1 to inflict a penalty on in requital for a wrongdoing < *punished* the child for misbehaving >
syn castigate, chasten, chastise, correct, discipline
rel criticize, reprove; amerce, fine, mulct, penalize; avenge, fix, revenge; lambaste, scourge
con overlook; absolve, acquit, exculpate, exonerate, vindicate; let off, release
ant excuse, pardon
2 *syn* see CONSUME 5

punishing *adj* *syn* see PUNITIVE

punishment *n* the act or an instance of punishing < a spanking was his *punishment* >
syn castigation, chastisement, correction, discipline, punition, rod
rel criticism, reproof; amercement, fine, mulct, penalty; avengement, revenge
idiom carrot-and-stick treatment, disciplinary action, dose of strap oil, what for
con overlooking; acquittal, exculpation, exoneration, vindication

ant excuse, pardon

punition *n* *syn* see PUNISHMENT
idiom punitive measures

punitive *adj* inflicting, involving, or constituting punishment < took *punitive* action against him >
syn castigating, disciplinary, punishing, punitory
rel correctional, penal

punitory *adj* *syn* see PUNITIVE

punk *n* 1 *syn* see NONSENSE 2
2 *syn* see NOVICE
3 *syn* see TOUGH

∥**punk** *adj* *syn* see BAD 1

puny *adj* 1 *syn* see PETTY 2
rel feeble, weak
2 *syn* see WEAK 1

pup *n* *syn* see TWERP

puppet *n* *syn* see TOOL 2
rel dupe; slave

puppy *n* *syn* see TWERP

purblind *adj* partly blind < *purblind* with cataracts >
syn dim-sighted, half-blind
rel myopic, nearsighted, shortsighted; dim; blind, dark, sightless

purchasable *adj* 1 capable of being bought < *purchasable* goods >
syn available, obtainable, on offer
rel marketable, salable
idiom on (or for) sale, on the market, to be had
con rare; unavailable, unobtainable
ant unpurchasable
2 *syn* see VENAL 1
rel undependable, unreliable; slippery, tricky; treacherous

purchase *vb* *syn* see BUY 1
idiom make a purchase
ant sell

purchaser *n* one to whom something is sold < instruction booklets for new-car *purchasers* >
syn buyer, emptor, vendee
rel marketer, shopper; client, customer, patron; consumer, user
con seller, vendor

pure *adj* 1 *syn* see STRAIGHT 3
ant impure
2 being such and no other < his solution of the problem was *pure* genius >
syn absolute, perfect, pure and simple, sheer, simple, unadulterated, unalloyed, undiluted, unmitigated, unmixed, unqualified; *compare* UTTER
rel complete, plenary, total; authentic, genuine; classic; out-and-out, plain, utter
con mixed, qualified; doubtful, dubious, questionable, uncertain
3 *syn* see UTTER
4 *syn* see GOOD 11
ant impure
5 *syn* see CHASTE
rel fresh, inviolate, unblighted, unprofaned
idiom as pure as the driven snow
con contaminated, dirty, sullied
ant immoral, impure

∥**pure** *adv* *syn* see VERY 1

pure and simple *adj* *syn* see PURE 2

pureblood *adj* *syn* see PUREBRED

purebred *adj* being of unmixed ancestry < a *purebred* collie >

---

syn full-blooded, pedigree, pedigreed, pureblood, thoroughbred
rel registered
con bastard, hybrid, lowbred, mixed
ant mongrel

‖**puredee** (*or* pure–D) *adj syn see* UTTER
purely *adv syn see* ALL 1
purgation *n syn see* PURIFICATION
purgative *adj* cleansing or purifying especially from sin <confession as a *purgative* ritual>
syn expiative, expiatory, expurgatorial, expurgatory, lustral, lustratory, propitiatory, purgatorial

purgatorial *adj syn see* PURGATIVE
‖**purgatory** *n syn see* SWAMP
purge *vb* 1 *syn see* DISABUSE
rel absolve, cleanse; clear, rid
2 *syn see* PURIFY 2
3 to get rid of often by exile, imprisonment, or murder <Stalin *purged* all the Party dissidents>
syn eliminate, liquidate, remove
rel debar, exclude, shut out; dismiss, eject, expel, oust; erase, expunge, wipe (out); exterminate
con rehabilitate; reinstate; repatriate; accept, bear (with), tolerate
ant depurge

purification *n* a freeing from something morally harmful, offensive, or sinful <sought *purification* through repentance>
syn catharsis, cleansing, expurgation, lustration, purgation
rel atonement, expiation; absolution, forgiveness; grace, redemption, salvation; rebirth, regeneration; sanctification
con contamination, defilement

purify *vb* 1 to free from material impurities or noxious matter <*purify* the water for drinking>
syn clarify, clean, cleanse, depurate
rel elutriate; filter; refine
con dirty, foul, soil
ant contaminate, pollute
2 to free from guilt or moral blemish (often ceremonially) <*purify* one's heart through confession>
syn cleanse, expurgate, lustrate, purge
rel atone, expiate; absolve, remit
con defile, sully, tarnish

purist *n* one who adheres strictly and often excessively to a tradition <*purists* who believe in prescriptive grammar>
syn precisian, precisionist, traditionalist
rel Atticist, classicist; bitter-ender, conservative, diehard, Puritan
con liberal, radical, young Turk
ant revisionist

puritan *n syn see* PRUDE
puritanical *adj syn see* PRIM 1
rel rigorous, strict; bigoted, hidebound, illiberal, intolerant, narrow, narrow-minded
con liberal, tolerant; modern

purl *vb syn see* SWIRL
‖**purl** *vb syn see* SPIN 1
purlieu *n* 1 *syn see* RESORT 2
2 **purlieus** *pl syn see* ENVIRONS 1
3 **purlieus** *pl syn see* ENVIRONS 2
purloin *vb syn see* STEAL 1
purloiner *n syn see* THIEF

purloining *n syn see* THEFT
purple *adj* 1 *syn see* RISQUÉ
2 *syn see* RHETORICAL
purport *n* 1 *syn see* MEANING 1
2 *syn see* TENOR 1
rel connotation; implication
3 *syn see* SUBSTANCE 2
purported *adj syn see* ALLEGED
rel postulated, presupposed; suppositional, suppositive; academic, speculative, theoretical; reputed, rumored; suspected
purportless *adj syn see* SENSELESS 5
purpose *n* 1 *syn see* INTENTION
rel destination, direction; aim, goal, mission, objective, point; ambition, aspiration; proposal, proposition
2 *syn see* USE 4
rel mission
purpose *vb syn see* INTEND 2
rel meditate, ponder; consider; conclude, decide, determine; resolve
purposedly *adv syn see* INTENTIONALLY
purposefulness *n syn see* DECISION 2
rel certainty, confidence, sureness
con indecision, irresoluteness, irresolution, vacillation, waffling, wavering, weakness; aimlessness, indirection
ant purposelessness
purposeless *adj* 1 *syn see* FECKLESS 1
rel unhelpful, unprofitable; purportless, senseless; nonsensical
con helpful, profitable
ant purposeful
2 *syn see* RANDOM
ant purposeful
purposely *adv syn see* INTENTIONALLY
rel expressly; explicitly
con unintentionally
ant accidentally
purposively *adv syn see* INTENTIONALLY
purposiveness *n syn see* DECISION 2
purse cutter *n syn see* PICKPOCKET
pursual *n syn see* PURSUIT 2
pursuance *n syn see* PURSUIT 2
pursue *vb* 1 *syn see* FOLLOW 1
rel persevere, persist; oppress, persecute; badger, bait, hound, ride
idiom go in pursuit (of)
2 *syn see* ADDRESS 8
pursuing *n syn see* PURSUIT 2
pursuit *n* 1 *syn see* WORK 1
2 a following with a view to reach, accomplish, or obtain <the *pursuit* of happiness>
syn pursual, pursuance, pursuing, quest, search, seeking
rel following; reaching; obtaining; accomplishing, accomplishment
idiom a going all out (after)
pursy *adj syn see* FAT 2
purview *n* 1 *syn see* RANGE 2
2 *syn see* KEN
push *vb* 1 to use force so as to cause to move ahead or aside <*push* a wheelbarrow across the yard>
syn drive, propel, shove, thrust
rel launch; impel, move; force, ram
con brake, check, stay
ant pull
2 to do, effect, or accomplish by forcing aside obstacles or opposition <*pushed* his way through the crowd> <*pushed* the measure through congress>

syn bulldoze, elbow, hustle, jostle, press, ‖shog, shoulder, shove
rel dig, nudge; hunch; drive, force, thrust; bump, butt, ram
con ease, facilitate, slide (by), slip (through); expedite, help (along)
3 *syn* see INCREASE 1
4 *syn* see PRESSURE
5 *syn* see PROMOTE 3
rel oversell
6 to engage in the illicit sale of (narcotics) < *pushing* drugs to teenagers>
syn peddle, shove
7 *syn* see PRESS 1
push *n* 1 *syn* see ENTERPRISE 4
2 *syn* see VIGOR 2
3 *syn* see STIMULUS
4 *syn* see CROWD 1
5 *syn* see SET 5
push around *vb syn* see BAIT 2
pushful *adj* 1 *syn* see AGGRESSIVE
2 *syn* see PRESUMPTUOUS
rel imposing, intrusive, obtruding, obtrusive, officious; assured, confident, self-confident
pushing *adj* 1 *syn* see AGGRESSIVE
idiom ‖not backward in going forward
2 *syn* see PRESUMPTUOUS
push off *vb syn* see GO 2
push on *vb syn* see GO 1
pushover *n syn* see SNAP 1
pushy *adj* 1 *syn* see AGGRESSIVE
‖2 *syn* see PRESUMPTUOUS
pusillanimous *adj syn* see COWARDLY
puss *n syn* see CHILD 1
‖**puss** *n syn* see FACE 1
pussyfoot *vb* 1 *syn* see SNEAK
2 *syn* see EQUIVOCATE 2
pustule *n syn* see ABSCESS
put *vb* 1 *syn* see SET 1
2 *syn* see FASTEN 3
3 *syn* see PROPOSE 1
4 *syn* see WORD
5 *syn* see TRANSLATE 1
6 *syn* see EXPRESS 2
7 *syn* see ESTIMATE 3
put (back) *vb syn* see RESTORE 5
put (on) *vb syn* see GAMBLE 1
put (on *or* upon) *vb syn* see LEVY
put *n syn* see DUNCE
put about *vb syn* see INCONVENIENCE
putative *adj syn* see SUPPOSED 1
put away *vb* 1 *syn* see DIVORCE 2
2 *syn* see CONSUME 5
3 *syn* see MURDER 1
4 *syn* see BURY 1
5 *syn* see KILL 1
put by *vb syn* see SAVE 4
put down *vb* 1 *syn* see CRUSH 5
2 *syn* see DEGRADE 1
3 *syn* see CONSUME 5
put in *vb syn* see PLANT 1
put off *vb* 1 *syn* see DELAY 2
idiom drag one's feet
2 *syn* see DEFER

idiom lay on the table, let the matter stand
3 *syn* see REMOVE 3
ant put on
put on *vb* 1 *syn* see DON 1
ant put off
2 *syn* see DON 2
rel affect, feign, sham, simulate; masquerade, pose
idiom make as if (*or* as though)
3 *syn* see ASSUME 4
idiom put on a (false) front, put on an act
4 *syn* see EMPLOY 2
5 *syn* see STAGE
put-on *adj syn* see ARTIFICIAL 3
rel mannered, posed; faked, sham
put-on *n* 1 *syn* see IMPOSTURE
2 *syn* see MASK 2
put out *vb* 1 *syn* see EXERT
2 *syn* see EXTINGUISH 1
3 *syn* see PUBLISH 2
4 *syn* see IRRITATE
5 *syn* see INCONVENIENCE
rel displease, dissatisfy; annoy, irritate
idiom put out of the way, put to it
put over *vb syn* see DEFER
putrefy *vb syn* see DECAY
putresce *vb syn* see DECAY
putrid *adj* 1 *syn* see BAD 5
2 *syn* see MALODOROUS 1
3 *syn* see VICIOUS 2
putter *vb syn* see FIDDLE 2
rel boondoggle; dawdle
‖**put to** *vb syn* see CLOSE 1
put together *vb syn* see MAKE 3
put up *vb* 1 *syn* see HARBOR 2
2 *syn* see BUILD 1
rel forge, make, put together, shape
3 *syn* see ERECT 1
4 *syn* see RAISE 9
rel elevate, escalate
‖**puxy** *n syn* see SWAMP
puzzle *vb* to baffle and disturb mentally < a persistent fever that *puzzled* her doctor>
syn befog, bewilder, ‖cap, confound, confuse, metagrobolize, perplex, pose, stumble; *compare* NONPLUS 1
rel baffle, foil, frustrate; befuddle, ‖bumfuzzle, fuddle; disconcert, distract, disturb, upset; addle, muddle; mystify; amaze, dumbfound, flabbergast
con enlighten, inform
puzzle *n syn* see MYSTERY
puzzlement *n syn* see MYSTERY
puzzle out *vb syn* see SOLVE 2
idiom find the key to, pick the lock
pygmy *n syn* see DWARF
ant giant
pygmy *adj syn* see TINY
pyramid *n syn* see PILE 1
Pyrrhonian *n syn* see SKEPTIC
Pyrrhonist *n syn* see SKEPTIC
pythonic *adj syn* see HUGE

---

syn synonym(s)   *rel* related word(s)
ant antonym(s)   *con* contrasted word(s)
idiom idiomatic equivalent(s)
‖ use limited; if in doubt, see a dictionary

Q

quack *n syn* see CHARLATAN
  rel counterfeiter, pretender, shammer, simulator
‖**quackle** *vb syn* see SUFFOCATE
quacksalver *n syn* see CHARLATAN
quackster *n syn* see CHARLATAN
quad *n syn* see COURT 1
quadrangle *n syn* see COURT 1
quadrate *adj syn* see SQUARE 1
quadrate *vb* 1 *syn* see AGREE 4
  2 *syn* see ADAPT
quadratic *adj syn* see SQUARE 1
quadratical *adj syn* see SQUARE 1
quaesitum *n syn* see AMBITION 2
quaff *vb syn* see DRINK 1
quag *n syn* see SWAMP
quaggy *adj syn* see SOFT 6
quagmire *n* 1 *syn* see SWAMP
  2 *syn* see PREDICAMENT
quail *n syn* see GIRL 1
quail *vb syn* see RECOIL
  rel cower, cringe
quaint *adj syn* see STRANGE 4
  rel droll, funny, laughable; antiquated, antique, archaic
‖**quaint** *vb syn* see INTRODUCE 4
quake *vb* 1 *syn* see SHAKE 2
  rel fluctuate, waver
  2 *syn* see SHAKE 1
quake *n syn* see EARTHQUAKE
‖**quaker** *n syn* see EARTHQUAKE
quaking *adj syn* see TREMULOUS
quaky *adj syn* see TREMULOUS
qualification *n syn* see ABILITY 1
qualified *adj* 1 *syn* see ABLE
  rel disciplined, instructed, trained; catechized, examined, quizzed; proved, tested, tried
  con incapable, incompetent, unequipped, unfit
  ant disqualified, unqualified
  2 not unlimited and complete <gave only a *qualified* endorsement to the project>
  syn limited, modified, reserved
  rel circumscribed, definite, determined, fixed, restricted; partial
  con complete, entire, full, total, utter, whole; unlimited, unrestricted
  ant absolute, unqualified
qualifiedness *n syn* see ABILITY 1
qualify *vb* 1 *syn* see CHARACTERIZE 2
  rel ascribe, assign, attribute, impute; predicate
  2 *syn* see ENTITLE 2
quality *n* 1 something inherent and distinctive <learned the special *qualities* of the native herbs>
  syn affection, attribute, character, characteristic, feature, mark, peculiarity, property, savor, trait, virtue; *compare* CHARACTERISTIC 1
  rel individuality; affirmation, predication; element, factor, parameter
  2 a usually high level of merit or superiority <merchandise of *quality*>

  syn caliber, merit, stature, value, virtue, worth
  rel arete, excellence, excellency, perfection, superbness, superiority
  con inferiority, meanness, mediocrity, poorness; inadequacy; deficiency
  3 degree of excellence <upgrading the *quality* of incoming students>
  syn caliber, class, grade
  rel capacity, character, footing, place, position, rank, situation, standing, state, station, status
  4 *syn* see STATUS 1
  5 *syn* see ARISTOCRACY
  6 *syn* see EXCELLENCE
quality *adj syn* see EXCELLENT
qualm *n* a misgiving about what one is going to do <had *qualms* about the secret meeting>
  syn compunction, conscience, demur, scruple, squeam
  rel apprehension, foreboding, misgiving, presentiment; doubt, mistrust, suspicion, uncertainty; agitation, insecurity, perturbation; objection, remonstrance; reluctance, unwillingness; impatience, nervousness, unease, uneasiness
  con aplomb, assurance, confidence, self-assurance, self-confidence, self-possession; certainty, certitude, conviction
qualmish *adj syn* see SQUEAMISH 1
qualmishness *n syn* see NAUSEA
qualmy *adj syn* see SQUEAMISH 1
quantity *n* 1 *syn* see BODY 5
  2 quantities *pl syn* see SCAD
quantum *n* 1 *syn* see BODY 5
  2 *syn* see RATION
quarrel *n* a usually verbal dispute marked by anger or discord <a *quarrel* over who would drive the car>
  syn altercation, ‖barney, beef, bickering, brabble, brannigan, brawl, controversy, difficulty, dispute, dust, dustup, embroilment, falling-out, feud, fight, fracas, fuss, hassle, imbroglio, knock-down-and-drag-out, miff, ‖prabble, ‖pribble, rhubarb, row, ruckus, run-in, set-to, spat, squabble, squall, tiff, to-and-fro, word(s), wrangle; *compare* BRAWL 2
  rel battle royal, catfight; affray, bobbery, broil, donnybrook, fray, free-for-all, melee, ruction, rumpus, scrap, scrimmage, scuffle; conflict, contention, difference, discord, dissension, strife, variance; disagreement, misunderstanding
  idiom ‖pribbles and prabbles
  con accord, concord, harmony; agreement, likemindedness, understanding, unity
quarrel *vb* to contend noisily or captiously <with his belligerent personality he was always *quarreling* with someone>
  syn altercate, bicker, brabble, brawl, ‖cast out, caterwaul, fall out, row, scrap, spat, squabble, tiff, wrangle; *compare* ARGUE 2

rel differ, disaccord, dissent, divide, vary;
bump, clash, collide, conflict, thwart;
battle, contend, fight, war
idiom have words with, pull caps
con agree, coincide, concur

quarrelsome *adj* 1 *syn* see BELLIGERENT
rel adverse, antagonistic, counter; antipathetic, hostile, inimical, rancorous
idiom having a chip on one's shoulder
2 apt or disposed to quarrel < when he's
in a bad mood he becomes so *quarrelsome* >
syn battlesome, brawling, brawlsome,
brawly, scrappy; *compare* BELLIGERENT
rel argumentative; disputatious; cankered,
crabbed, irascible, irritable
con conciliatory, propitiatory

quarry *n* 1 *syn* see GAME 3
quarry *vb* *syn* see MINE
quarter *n* 1 one of four equal parts < ate
one *quarter* of the pie >
syn fourth, quartern
rel quadrant
2 a division or part of a town or city
< the market *quarter* in Paris >
syn district, precinct, section, sector
rel division, part; area; locality; barrio
quarter *vb* 1 *syn* see HARBOR 2
2 *syn* see BILLET 1
quarterage *n* *syn* see SHELTER 2
quarterback *vb* *syn* see SUPERVISE
quartern *n* *syn* see QUARTER 1
quarter–witted *adj* *syn* see RETARDED
quartet *n* a group consisting of four individuals < a singing *quartet* >
syn four, foursome, quartetto, quatre,
quatuor, tetrad
rel quadruplet
quartetto *n* *syn* see QUARTET
quash *vb* 1 *syn* see ANNUL 4
2 *syn* see ABOLISH 1
3 *syn* see CRUSH 5
quashing *n* *syn* see REPRESSION 1
‖**quat** *vb* *syn* see SQUAT
quaternion *n* *syn* see QUARTET
quatuor *n* *syn* see QUARTET
quaver *vb* *syn* see SHAKE 1
rel falter, hesitate, vacillate, waver
‖**quawk** *vb* *syn* see SQUALL 1
‖**quay** *n* *syn* see WHARF
‖**queak** *vb* *syn* see SQUEAK 1
‖**quean** *n* *syn* see PROSTITUTE
queasiness *n* *syn* see NAUSEA
queasy *adj* 1 *syn* see DOUBTFUL 1
2 *syn* see SQUEAMISH 1
queer *adj* 1 *syn* see STRANGE 4
rel doubtful, dubious, questionable; droll,
funny, laughable
2 *syn* see OBSESSED
3 *syn* see HOMOSEXUAL
4 *syn* see SQUEAMISH 1
queer *n* *syn* see HOMOSEXUAL
‖**quelch** *vb* *syn* see SUPPRESS 2
quell *vb* *syn* see CRUSH 5
rel conquer, overcome, subjugate, vanquish
con abet, incite, instigate
ant foment

---

syn synonym(s)   *rel* related word(s)
ant antonym(s)   *con* contrasted word(s)
idiom idiomatic equivalent(s)
‖ use limited; if in doubt, see a dictionary

quench *vb* 1 *syn* see EXTINGUISH 1
2 *syn* see CRUSH 5
rel end, terminate
3 *syn* see DESTROY 1
4 to bring (as thirst) to an end with or as
if with a refreshing drink < after being in
the hot sun, he found it difficult to *quench*
his thirst >
syn slake, ‖squench
rel appease, content, gratify, satisfy; sate,
satiate; allay, alleviate, assuage, lighten,
mitigate, relieve; decrease, diminish,
lessen, reduce
quenching *n* *syn* see REPRESSION 1
quenchless *adj* 1 *syn* see INSATIABLE
2 *syn* see INDESTRUCTIBLE
querulent *adj* *syn* see IRRITABLE
querulential *adj* *syn* see IRRITABLE
querulous *adj* *syn* see IRRITABLE
rel blubbering, crying, wailing, weeping,
whimpering; bemoaning, deploring, lamenting
query *n* 1 *syn* see INQUIRY 2
2 *syn* see UNCERTAINTY
query *vb* *syn* see ASK 1
quest *n* 1 *syn* see INQUIRY 2
2 *syn* see PURSUIT 2
quest *vb* 1 *syn* see HOWL 1
2 *syn* see SEEK 1
question *n* 1 *syn* see INQUIRY 2
2 *syn* see PROBLEM 2
3 *syn* see DEMUR 2
question *vb* 1 *syn* see ASK 1
2 to express doubt about < *questioned* his
decision to take a new job >
syn challenge, dispute, doubt, mistrust
rel suspect, ‖suspicion; hesitate (over),
puzzle (over), wonder (about)
questionable *adj* 1 *syn* see IMPROBABLE
1
ant unquestionable
2 *syn* see MOOT
rel refutable; equivocal, obscure, vague
con dependable, true, trustworthy, trusty;
genuine, indubitable, real, undoubted,
undubitable, veritable, very
ant authoritative; unquestionable, unquestioned
3 *syn* see UNRELIABLE 1
questioning *n* *syn* see INQUIRY 2
questioning *adj* 1 *syn* see INCREDULOUS
ant questionless, unquestioning
2 *syn* see INQUISITIVE 1
questionless *adj* *syn* see AUTHENTIC 2
queue *n* *syn* see LINE 5
quibble *vb* 1 to find fault with something
usually on minor grounds < was a peevish
critic, always ready to *quibble* >
syn cavil, chicane, hypercriticize
rel carp, criticize
idiom split hairs
con applaud, commend, compliment,
recommend; approve, endorse, sanction
2 *syn* see ARGUE 2
quick *adj* 1 *syn* see FAST 3
rel agile, brisk, nimble; abrupt, impetuous
idiom quick on the trigger
con dilatory, laggard, leisurely, slow,
unhasty, unhurried; comatose
ant sluggish
2 able to respond without delay or hesitation or indicative of such ability < very
quick in perception > < his *quick* eye spotted the trouble >

syn apt, prompt, ready; *compare* INSTANTANEOUS

rel clever, intelligent, quick-witted, smart; adroit, deft, dexterous; acute, keen, sharp; able, capable, competent, effective, effectual

con comatose, lethargic, logy, poky, torpid; crass, dense, dull, dumb, stupid

ant slow; sluggish

3 *syn* see WISE 4

quick *adv syn* see FAST 2

quick *n syn* see CENTER 3

quicken *vb* 1 to make alive or lively < warm spring days that *quicken* the earth >

syn animate, enliven, liven, vivificate, vivify

rel activate, energize, vitalize; arouse, awaken, rouse, stir, wake

con blunt, dull; slow (down)

ant deaden

2 *syn* see PROVOKE 4

rel activate, actuate, motivate; goad, induce, spur

con check, halt, interrupt, stall, stay; curb, inhibit, restrain

ant arrest

3 *syn* see SPEED 3

con bog (down), detain, embog, hang up, mire

ant slacken

quickening *adj syn* see INVIGORATING

quick–lunch *n syn* see EATING HOUSE

quickly *adv syn* see FAST 2

quickness *n syn* see SPEED 2

ant slowness

quick–sighted *adj syn* see SHARP 4

quick–tempered *adj syn* see IRASCIBLE

quick–witted *adj* 1 *syn* see SHARP 4

2 *syn* see INTELLIGENT 2

rel apt, prompt, quick, ready

3 *syn* see WISE 4

rel acute, keen; facetious, humorous, witty

ant slow-witted

quidnunc *n* 1 *syn* see BUSYBODY

2 *syn* see GOSSIP 1

quiescence *n syn* see ABEYANCE

quiescency *n syn* see ABEYANCE

quiescent *adj syn* see LATENT

rel calm, halcyon, hushed, placid, quiet, still, stilly, untroubled

quiet *n* 1 a period of intensified silence < the *quiet* before the storm >

syn calm, hush, lull

rel cessation, stop, termination

con din, hubbub, racket, uproar

2 *syn* see SILENCE 1

quiet *adj* 1 *syn* see CALM 1

con harsh, rough; disquieted, disturbed, perturbed, upset

ant unquiet

2 *syn* see INACTIVE

3 *syn* see STILL 3

con blatant, boisterous, clamorous, strident, vociferous

4 not showy or obtrusive < always dressed in *quiet* good taste >

syn inobtrusive, restrained, subdued, tasteful, tasty, unobtrusive

rel homely, plain, simple, unpretentious

con blatant, brazen, flashy, garish, glaring, meretricious, tawdry, tinsel; elaborate

ant gaudy, loud

quiet *vb* 1 *syn* see SILENCE 1

rel abate, decrease, lessen

con excite, provoke, quicken, stimulate; awaken, rally, stir

2 *syn* see CALM

con agitate; unhinge, untune

ant disquiet; excite

‖**quieten** *vb* 1 *syn* see SILENCE 1

2 *syn* see CALM

ant arouse; excite

quietive *adj syn* see SEDATIVE

quietness *n syn* see SILENCE 1

quietude *n syn* see SILENCE 1

quietus *n syn* see DEATH 1

‖**quiff** *n syn* see GIRL 1

quilt *n* a bed coverlet made of two layers of cloth with a stuffing (as of cotton, wool, or feathers) between < a warm *quilt* is nice on a winter night >

syn ‖comfortable, comforter, pouf, puff

rel bedcover, bedspread, counterpane; eiderdown

quinary *adj syn* see QUINTUPLE

quinta *n syn* see ESTATE 3

quintessence *n* 1 *syn* see ESSENCE 2

2 *syn* see APOTHEOSIS 1

quintessential *adj syn* see TYPICAL 1

quintessential *n syn* see ESSENCE 2

quintuple *adj* consisting of five < the problem is viewed as having *quintuple* aspects >

syn fivefold, quinary

rel quintuplicate

quip *n syn* see JOKE 1

quip (at) *vb syn* see SCOFF

quipster *n syn* see HUMORIST 2

quit *vb* 1 *syn* see CLEAR 5

2 *syn* see BEHAVE 1

3 *syn* see GO 2

4 *syn* see ABANDON 1

rel relinquish, resign, surrender

5 *syn* see STOP 3

6 to give up (as a habit, activity, or employment) especially with finality < *quit* a job > < determined to *quit* smoking >

syn drop, leave, resign, terminate

rel retire, secede, withdraw

idiom draw one's time, give notice

con hire on, hire out

quite *adv* 1 *syn* see WELL 3

2 *syn* see ALTOGETHER 2

3 *syn* see ALL 1

4 *syn* see WELL 8

quittance *n syn* see REPARATION

quitter *n syn* see COWARD

quiver *n syn* see FLASH 1

quiver *vb syn* see SHAKE 1

rel beat, palpatate, pulsate, pulse, throb

quivering *adj syn* see TREMULOUS

quivery *adj syn* see TREMULOUS

quiz *n syn* see ECCENTRIC

quiz *vb* 1 *syn* see RIDICULE

2 *syn* see ASK 1

quizzical *adj syn* see INCREDULOUS

rel curious, inquisitive; probing, searching

‖**quod** *vb syn* see IMPRISON

quodlibetic *adj syn* see PEDANTIC

quondam *adj syn* see FORMER 2

quota *n* 1 *syn* see SHARE 1

2 *syn* see RATION

quota *vb syn* see APPORTION 2

quotidian *adj* 1 *syn* see DAILY

2 *syn* see ORDINARY 1

R

rabbity *adj syn* see SHY 1
rabble *n* 1 *syn* see MOB 2
   2 the lowest class of people < the *rabble*
   of the city >
   syn canaille, doggery, dreg(s), hoi polloi,
   mass(es), mob, other half, polloi, prole-
   tariat, raff, ||ragabash, ragtag, ragtag and
   bobtail, riffraff, roughscuff, rout, scum,
   scurf, tag and rag, tagrag and bobtail,
   trash, unwashed
   rel bourgeoisie, commonalty, many, people, populace, public, rank and file
   idiom the great unwashed, the scum of
   the earth, the submerged tenth
   con aristocracy, aristoi, elite, Four Hundred, gentility, nobility, upper class, upper
   crust, upper ten, upper ten thousand
rabble-rouser *n syn* see DEMAGOGUE
rabid *adj* 1 *syn* see FURIOUS 2
   rel crazed, crazy, demented, deranged,
   insane
   2 *syn* see EXTREME 3
   rel enthusiastic, keen, obsessed, zealous
race *n syn* see CREEK 2
race *vb* 1 *syn* see RUSH 1
   2 *syn* see COURSE
race *n syn* see FAMILY 1
   rel culture, nation, nationality, people;
   breed, type, variety
rachis *n syn* see SPINE
rachitic *adj syn* see RICKETY
racial *adj syn* see ETHNIC 2
racialism *n syn* see RACISM
racism *n* racial prejudice or discrimination
   < an act of overt *racism* >
   syn racialism
   rel discrimination, prejudice; illiberality,
   unfairness; bias, one-sidedness, partiality
   con broad-mindedness, liberalness, open-
   mindedness, tolerance; indifference, neutrality
rack *vb syn* see AFFLICT
   rel distress, pain; oppress, persecute
||rack back *vb syn* see REPROVE
racket *n* 1 *syn* see DIN
   ||2 *syn* see WORK 2
racketry *n syn* see DIN
rackety *adj* 1 *syn* see NOISY
   2 *syn* see RICKETY
racking *adj syn* see EXCRUCIATING
   rel barbarous, cruel, ferocious, fierce,
   inhuman, savage
rack up *vb syn* see GAIN 1
racy *adj* 1 *syn* see PUNGENT
   rel fiery, gingery, mettlesome, spirited
   con banal, inane, jejune
   2 *syn* see RISQUÉ
radiant *adj* 1 *syn* see BRIGHT 1

   2 *syn* see GLAD 2
radiate *vb* 1 *syn* see SHINE 1
   2 *syn* see SPREAD 1
   rel diverge
radical *adj* 1 *syn* see FUNDAMENTAL 1
   rel cardinal, essential, vital; constitutional, inherent, intrinsic
   ant superficial
   2 *syn* see EXTREME 3
   3 *syn* see LIBERAL 3
radical *n* one who favors rapid and sweeping changes < the *radicals* advocated overthrow of the government >
   syn extremist, revolutionary, revolutionist,
   ultraist; *compare* REACTIONARY
   rel liberal, progressive, reformer; agitator,
   insurgent, insurrectionist, rebel; anarchist,
   nihilist, red, subversive; out-and-outer;
   secessionist, separatist
   con bitter-ender, diehard, fogy, intransigent, mossback, reactionary, rightist,
   standpatter
   ant conservative
radius *n syn* see RANGE 2
raff *n syn* see RABBLE 2
raffish *adj syn* see WILD 7
rag *vb* 1 *syn* see SCOLD 1
   2 *syn* see BANTER
||ragabash *n syn* see RABBLE 2
ragamuffin *n* a person dressed in ragged
   clothing < a poor *ragamuffin* found begging >
   syn ragshag, scarecrow, tatterdemalion
   rel hobo, tramp, vagabond, vagrant; bum,
   loafer, wastrel; orphan, waif
   con buck, coxcomb, dandy, dude, fop
rage *n* 1 *syn* see ANGER
   rel acerbity, acrimony, asperity; frenzy,
   hysteria, mania; agitation, perturbation,
   upset
   2 *syn* see FASHION 3
   rel caprice, conceit, crotchet, fancy, freak,
   vagary, whim
rage *vb syn* see ANGER 2
ragged *adj* torn or worn to tatters < never
   saw such *ragged* clothes >
   syn frayed, frazzled, shreddy, tattered
   rel rent, torn; battered, patched; dilapidated, dingy, faded, seedy, shabby,
   threadbare, worn-out
raging *adj syn* see WILD 6
rags *n pl* 1 poor or ragged clothing < a
   beggar in *rags* >
   syn ||duds, tatters
   rel odds and ends, ribbons, shreds
   2 *syn* see CLOTHES
ragshag *n syn* see RAGAMUFFIN
ragtag *n syn* see RABBLE 2
ragtag and bobtail *n syn* see RABBLE 2
raid *n* 1 *syn* see INVASION
   rel assault, onset, onslaught
   2 a sudden attack by officers of the law
   < a *raid* on a gambling joint >
   syn ||bust

---

syn synonym(s)   *rel* related word(s)
ant antonym(s)   *con* contrasted word(s)
idiom idiomatic equivalent(s)

|| use limited; if in doubt, see a dictionary

raid *vb* 1 to make a raid on < Indians *raided* the settlers frequently >
syn foray, harass, harry, maraud
rel despoil, devastate, ravage, sack, spoliate, waste; loot, plunder, rifle, rob
2 *syn* see INVADE 1

raider *n syn* see MARAUDER

rail *n syn* see RAILING

rail *vb syn* see SCOLD 1

railing *n* a usually protective barrier consisting essentially of an elongated raised member < a staircase without a *railing* >
syn balustrade, banister, rail

raillery *n syn* see SATIRE

railroad station *n* a building containing accommodations for railroad passengers or freight < an old *railroad station* fallen into disrepair >
syn depot, station, station house

raiment *n syn* see CLOTHES

raiment *vb syn* see CLOTHE

rainbow *n syn* see PIPE DREAM

rainless *adj syn* see FAIR 2
ant rainy

raise *vb* 1 *syn* see LIFT 1
ant lower
2 *syn* see INCITE
3 *syn* see RESURRECT 1
4 *syn* see ERECT 3
5 *syn* see BUILD 1
6 *syn* see BRING UP 1
7 *syn* see GROW 1
8 *syn* see GATHER 6
9 to make larger in amount < *raised* the rent >
syn boost, hike, increase, jack (up), jump, put up, up
rel inflate
idiom send through the roof
con cut back, decrease, drop, lessen, reduce, roll back; minimize
ant lower

raise *n syn* see ADDITION

raised *adj syn* see ELEVATED 1
2 *syn* see ERECT

rake *vb syn* see SCOUR 2

rakehell *adj syn* see WILD 7

raking *adj syn* see FAST 3

rakish *adj syn* see WILD 7

rally *vb* 1 *syn* see MOBILIZE 3
2 *syn* see STIR 1
rel fire; refresh, renew, restore
3 *syn* see RECOVER 2
rel brace (up), enliven, invigorate, perk (up), pick up

rally *vb syn* see RIDICULE
rel harass, harry, tantalize, tease, worry

rallying cry *n syn* see BATTLE CRY

ram *vb* 1 *syn* see THRUST 2
2 *syn* see CRAM 1

ramble *vb* 1 *syn* see WANDER 1
2 *syn* see DIGRESS 2
3 *syn* see SPRAWL 2

ramble *n syn* see WALK 1

rambler *n syn* see ROVER

rambunctious *adj syn* see TURBULENT 1

rampage *n syn* see SPREE 1
rel turmoil, uproar

rampant *adj* 1 *syn* see RANK 1
rel excessive, immoderate, inordinate
con moderate, temperate; checked, curbed, restrained
2 *syn* see PREVAILING

rampart *n syn* see BULWARK

rancid *adj syn* see MALODOROUS 1
rel ‖reasty; loathsome, repulsive
ant sweet

rancor *n syn* see ENMITY
rel bitterness, vindictiveness, virulence

rancorous *adj* 1 *syn* see MALICIOUS
2 *syn* see BITTER 3

rancorously *adv syn* see HARD 6

random *adj* lacking a definite plan, purpose, or pattern < a *random* choice >
syn aimless, designless, desultory, haphazard, hit-or-miss, indiscriminate, irregular, objectless, promiscuous, purposeless, slapdash, spot, unaimed, unconsidered, unplanned; *compare* ACCIDENTAL
rel contingent, fluky, fortuitous, incidental, odd
con arranged, organized, planned; methodical, systematic; deliberate, purposeful
ant purposive

random *adv syn* see ABOUT 4
ant orderly

randomly *adv syn* see ABOUT 4
ant orderly

randy *adj syn* see LICENTIOUS 2

range *vb* 1 *syn* see LINE 1
rel assort, classify, sort; bias, dispose, incline, predispose
2 *syn* see WANDER 1
3 to change or differ within limits < discounts *range* from 10% to 40% >
syn extend, go, run, vary
rel differ, fluctuate

range *n* 1 *syn* see HABITAT
2 sphere of action, expression, or influence < a political movement worldwide in its *range* and power >
syn ambit, circle, compass, confine(s), dimension(s), extension, extensity, extent, length, orbit, panorama, purview, radius, reach, realm, scope, stretch, sweep, width
rel area, space, span; horizon, field, province, sphere, territory; amplitude, expanse, gamut, spread
3 *syn* see KEN
rel compass
idiom range of comprehension
4 *syn* see ORDER 4

rangy *adj syn* see GANGLING
ant compact

rank *adj* 1 growing or increasing at an immoderate rate < *rank* weeds >
syn rampant
rel exuberant, lavish, lush, luxuriant, profuse
con scanty, sparse, thin
2 *syn* see OVERGROWN
3 *syn* see OBSCENE 2
4 *syn* see EGREGIOUS
rel conspicuous, noticeable, outstanding
5 *syn* see UTTER
6 *syn* see MALODOROUS 1
rel dank, humid; loathsome, repulsive

rank *n* 1 *syn* see LINE 5
2 *syn* see ESTATE 2
3 *syn* see STATUS 1
4 *syn* see STATUS 2

rank *vb* 1 *syn* see CLASS 2
rel arrange, order; assort, sort
2 *syn* see PRECEDE 1

rank and file *n syn* see COMMONALTY

rankle *vb* to produce continual or progressive anger, irritation, or bitterness < this

decision has long *rankled* as an act of injustice>
syn fester
rel annoy, bother, irk, vex; aggravate, exasperate, irritate; harass, obsess, plague, torment

ransack *vb* 1 *syn* see SCOUR 2
2 *syn* see ROB 1

ransom *vb* to liberate by paying a price <*ransomed* the king>
syn buy, redeem
rel recover, regain, retrieve; emancipate, free, liberate; extricate, release

rant *vb* 1 *syn* see ORATE
rel bluster, huff; rage, storm
2 *syn* see SCOLD 1

rant *n* *syn* see BOMBAST

ran-tan *n* *syn* see BINGE 1

rantankerous *adj* *syn* see CANTANKEROUS

rap *n* 1 *syn* see HIT 1
2 *syn* see REBUKE

rap *vb* 1 *syn* see TAP 1
2 *syn* see CRITICIZE

rap *n* 1 *syn* see CHAT 2
2 *syn* see CONFERENCE 1

rapacious *adj* 1 subsisting on prey <the *rapacious* wolf seized the lamb>
syn predacious, predative, predatorial, predatory, raptorial, vulturine, vulturish, vulturous
2 *syn* see VORACIOUS
rel ferocious, fierce

rapacity *n* *syn* see CUPIDITY
rel claim, demand, exaction

rape *vb* to have sexual intercourse with a woman without her consent and chiefly by force or deception <*rape* a young girl>
syn defile, deflorate, deflower, force, outrage, ravish, spoil, violate
rel debauch, devirginate, dishonor, ruin; betray, deceive, mislead; entice, lure, seduce, tempt; compromise, shame, wrong

rapid *adj* *syn* see FAST 3
rel agile, brisk, nimble; hurried, quickened
ant deliberate; leisurely

rapidity *n* *syn* see SPEED 2

rapidly *adv* *syn* see FAST 2

rapidness *n* *syn* see SPEED 2

||**rapper** *n* *syn* see LIE

rapport *n* *syn* see HARMONY 3

rapprochement *n* *syn* see RECONCILIATION

rapscallion *n* *syn* see SCAMP

rap session *n* *syn* see CONFERENCE 2

rapt *adj* *syn* see INTENT

raptorial *adj* *syn* see RAPACIOUS 1

rapture *n* *syn* see ECSTASY

rare *adj* 1 *syn* see THIN 2
2 *syn* see CHOICE
rel excellent, fine, unique
3 *syn* see INFREQUENT
con accustomed, customary, habitual, usual, wonted; abounding, profuse
4 *syn* see EXCEPTIONAL 1

rarefied *adj* *syn* see THIN 2

rarefy *vb* *syn* see THIN 2

rarely *adv* 1 *syn* see SELDOM
2 *syn* see EXTRA

raring *adj* *syn* see EAGER

rascal *n* 1 *syn* see VILLAIN 1
2 *syn* see SCAMP

rash *adj* 1 acting, done, or expressed with undue haste or disregard for consequences <don't do anything *rash*> <that was a very *rash* statement>
syn brash, hasty, hotheaded, ill-advised, incautious, incogitant, inconsiderate, madbrained, madcap, reckless, thoughtless, unadvised, unconsidered, unwary; *compare* CARELESS 1
rel abrupt, headlong, impetuous, precipitate, precipitous, sudden; foolhardy, foolish, impulsive, silly; careless, heedless, imprudent, indiscreet, injudicious, unthinking, unwise
con careful, cautious, chary, circumspect, wary; advised, considered, deliberate, designed, premeditated, studied; calm, cool, level-headed
ant calculating
2 *syn* see ADVENTUROUS

rash *n* *syn* see EPIDEMIC

rasp *vb* *syn* see SCRAPE 1

raspberry *n* a sound of disapproval, contempt, or derision <the crowd gave the umpire a *raspberry*>
syn bazoo, bird, boo, ||Bronx cheer, catcall, hiss, hoot, pooh, pooh-pooh, ||razz

rasping *adj* *syn* see HARSH 3

raspish *adj* *syn* see IRRITABLE

raspy *adj* *syn* see IRRITABLE

rat *n* 1 *syn* see RENEGADE
2 *syn* see SNOT 1

rat *vb* 1 *syn* see DEFECT
2 *syn* see INFORM 3

rate *vb* *syn* see SCOLD 1

rate *n* 1 *syn* see PRICE 1
2 *syn* see DEGREE 2

rate *vb* 1 *syn* see ESTIMATE 1
2 *syn* see CLASS 2
3 *syn* see EARN 2

rather *adv* 1 *syn* see ENOUGH 2
2 *syn* see INSTEAD
3 *syn* see SOMEWHAT 2
4 *syn* see WELL 8

ratherish *adv* *syn* see SOMEWHAT 2

ratify *vb* to make something legally valid or operative usually by formal approval or sanctioning <agreed to *ratify* the treaty>
syn confirm
rel accredit, authorize, commission, license; approve, endorse, sanction; authenticate, validate
con disown, reject, repudiate

ratio *n* *syn* see DEGREE 2

ratiocination *n* 1 *syn* see INFERENCE 1
ant intuition
2 *syn* see INFERENCE 2

ratiocinative *adj* *syn* see LOGICAL 2

ration *n* an amount allotted or made available especially from a limited supply <saved up their gasoline *ration* for a vacation trip>
syn allotment, allowance, apportionment, measure, meed, part, portion, quantum, quota, share; *compare* SHARE 1
rel assignment, consignment, distribution, division

---

syn synonym(s)   *rel* related word(s)
ant antonym(s)   *con* contrasted word(s)
idiom idiomatic equivalent(s)
|| use limited; if in doubt, see a dictionary

ration *vb syn* see APPORTION 2
  rel allocate, allot, assign, mete (out)
rational *adj* agreeable to reason < offered a *rational* explanation >
  syn consequent, intelligent, logical, reasonable, sensible, sound
  rel calm, cool, level-headed, sober, stable; circumspect, judicious, prudent; lucid, normal, sane
  con rash, reckless, wild; groundless, illogical, unreasonable, unreasoning, unsound; crazy, demented, deranged
  ant animal, irrational; absurd
rationale *n syn* see EXPLANATION 2
rationalization *n syn* see EXPLANATION 2
rationalize *vb syn* see EXPLAIN 3
rattle *vb* 1 to make a rapid succession of short sharp noises < the window *rattled* in the wind >
  syn bicker, clack, clatter, clitter, ‖ruttle, shatter
  2 *syn* see CHAT 1
  3 *syn* see EMBARRASS
  rel addle, muddle; disturb, upset; bewilder, distract, perplex
rattlebrain *n syn* see SCATTERBRAIN
rattlebrained *adj syn* see GIDDY 1
rattlehead *n syn* see SCATTERBRAIN
rattletrap *n, usu* rattletraps *pl syn* see KNICKKNACK
rattletrap *adj syn* see RICKETY
rattling *adv syn* see VERY 1
ratty *adj syn* see IRASCIBLE
raucous *adj* 1 *syn* see HARSH 3
  rel brusque, gruff
  2 *syn* see TURBULENT 1
raunchy *adj* 1 *syn* see SLOVENLY 1
  2 *syn* see OBSCENE 2
ravage *vb* to lay waste (as by plundering or destroying) < the countryside was *ravaged* by the invading soldiers >
  syn deflower, depredate, desecrate, desolate, despoil, devast, devastate, devour, harry, havoc, pillage, sack, scourge, spoil, spoliate, strip, waste
  rel demolish, destroy, raze; loot, plunder, ransack, rob; ruin, wreck; encroach, invade, trespass; crush, overpower, overrun, overthrow, overwhelm
  idiom lay in ruins, lay waste
  con build, improve, rehabilitate
ravager *n syn* see MARAUDER
rave *vb* 1 *syn* see ORATE
  2 *syn* see ENTHUSE 2
ravel *vb syn* see COMPLICATE
raven *adj syn* see BLACK 1
ravening *adj syn* see VORACIOUS
ravenous *adj* 1 *syn* see VORACIOUS
  2 *syn* see HUNGRY
ravine *n* a small narrow steep-sided valley < followed the *ravine* high up into the hills >
  syn arroyo, chasm, cleft, clough, clove, gap, gorge, gulch
  rel cut, notch; defile, pass; abyss, gulf; crevasse, crevice, fissure; ‖dry wash, gully, gutter, ‖wash; canyon
raving *adj syn* see DELIRIOUS 1
ravish *vb* 1 *syn* see TRANSPORT 2
  2 *syn* see RAPE
ravisher *n syn* see MARAUDER
raw *adj* 1 not cooked < a *raw* egg >

syn uncooked
  2 *syn* see UNREFINED 3
  3 *syn* see RUDE 1
  4 *syn* see NUDE 2
  5 *syn* see INEXPERIENCED
  rel untaught, untutored; unmatured, unripe
  con drilled, exercised; hardened; adult, grown-up, mature, matured, ripe
  6 *syn* see COARSE 3
  ‖7 *syn* see OBSCENE 2
rawboned *adj syn* see LEAN
rawhider *n syn* see SLAVE DRIVER
rawness *n syn* see INEXPERIENCE
ray *n* 1 one of the lines of light that appear to radiate from a bright or luminous object < the *rays* of the sun >
  syn beam, shaft, shoot
  rel raylet; pencil, streak, stream; moonbeam, sunbeam
  con gleam, glow, incandescence, shine
  2 *syn* see PARTICLE
raze *vb syn* see DESTROY 1
razor-sharp *adj syn* see SHARP 1
‖razz *n syn* see RASPBERRY
razz *vb* 1 *syn* see BANTER
  2 *syn* see RIDICULE
re *prep syn* see APROPOS
reach *vb* 1 *syn* see COME 1
  2 *syn* see GAIN 1
  3 to get into contact with especially intellectually or emotionally < there was no common ground on which she could *reach* him >
  syn approach
  rel affect, influence, sway; get, move, touch
  idiom establish contact with, find a common denominator, get through to, get to, have a meeting of minds, make advances to, make overtures to, make up to, reach (or share) common ground
  4 to communicate with < you can *reach* me at this number >
  syn contact, get
  idiom get in touch (or contact) with, get through to, get to, keep in touch (or contact) with, maintain connections with
  5 *syn* see PASS 9
  6 *syn* see RUN 8
reach *n* 1 *syn* see RANGE 2
  2 *syn* see KEN
react *vb* 1 *syn* see ACT 5
  2 *syn* see RETURN 1
reactionarist *n syn* see REACTIONARY
reactionary *adj syn* see CONSERVATIVE 1
reactionary *n* one who strongly resists change and often favors a prior condition < he is a staunch political *reactionary* >
  syn blimp, Bourbon, diehard, reactionarist, reactionist, royalist, ultraconservative, white; *compare* DIEHARD 1, RADICAL
  rel bitter-ender, conservative, intransigent, rightist, right-winger, standpatter; fogy, mossback
  con extremist, radical, revolutionary, revolutionist, ultraist; liberal, progressive, reformer
reactionist *n syn* see REACTIONARY
reactivate *vb syn* see REVIVE 3
read *vb syn* see SHOW 5
readily *adv syn* see EASILY 1

readiness n 1 syn see ALACRITY
2 syn see ADDRESS 1
3 the power of doing something without
evidence of effort < his *readiness* in repartee >
syn ease, facility
rel eloquence, fluency, volubility
con effort, exertions, pains, trouble

reading n syn see INTERPRETATION 2

readjust vb syn see REORGANIZE

ready adj 1 in a state of mental or physical
fitness for some experience or action
< *ready* to leave at a moment's notice >
syn prepared, set
rel adjusted, fit, qualified; primed
idiom all ready, all set, champing at the
bit
con unprepared, unqualified
ant unready
2 syn see WILLING 1
3 syn see QUICK 2
rel adept, expert, masterly, proficient,
skilled, skillful; active, dynamic, live

ready vb 1 syn see PREPARE 1
2 syn see GIRD 3

ready-made adj made for general sale or
use rather than prepared according to
individual specifications < *ready-made*
clothing >
syn bought, ||boughten, ready-to-wear,
store, store-bought, ||store-boughten
idiom off the rack
con custom-built, made-to-order, tailor-
made; handmade
ant custom-made

ready-to-wear adj syn see READY-MADE

ready-witted adj syn see INTELLIGENT 2

real adj 1 syn see AUTHENTIC 2
ant bogus
2 syn see GENUINE 3
3 corresponding to known facts < discovered the *real* reason for his hasty departure >
syn actual, indisputable, true, undeniable,
unfabled, veridical
rel being, existing, subsisting; certain,
inevitable, necessary; sound, valid, well-
grounded
idiom deniable, disputable, doubtful,
questionable; improbable, uncertain, unlikely
ant unreal; apparent; imaginary

realistic adj having no illusions and facing
reality squarely < he made a *realistic* appraisal of his chances for advancement >
syn down-to-earth, earthy, hard, hard-
boiled, hardheaded, matter-of-fact, practic,
practical, pragmatic, pragmatical, sober,
unfantastic, unidealistic, unromantic, unsentimental, utilitarian
rel rational, reasonable, sane, sensible,
sound; astute, prudent, shrewd; nonaca-
demic
con dreamy, fantastic, imaginative; idealistic, impractical, irrational, romantic,
visionary; theoretical
ant unrealistic; fanciful

reality n 1 syn see FACT 1

2 syn see ACTUALITY 2

realize vb 1 syn see GAIN 1
2 syn see THINK 1

really adv 1 syn see VERY 2
2 syn see WELL 7

realm n syn see RANGE 2

ream n, usu reams pl syn see SCAD

ream vb syn see CHEAT

||**ream out** vb syn see SCOLD 1

reanimation n syn see REVIVAL

reap vb to do the work of collecting ripened crops < storms hampered his *reaping* >
syn garner, gather, harvest, ingather
rel glean

reaping n syn see HARVEST 1

reappearance n syn see RECURRENCE

rear vb 1 syn see BUILD 1
2 syn see ERECT 3
3 syn see LIFT 1
4 syn see BRING UP 1
rel foster, nurse, nurture; breed, propagate

rear n 1 syn see BACK 1
ant front
2 syn see BUTTOCKS

rear adj syn see POSTERIOR 2
ant front

rear end n syn see BUTTOCKS

rearmost adj syn see LAST

rearrange vb syn see REORGANIZE

rearward n syn see BACK 1

reason n 1 syn see EXPLANATION 2
2 syn see MOTIVE 1
3 a point or points that support something open to question < he soon gave
sensible *reasons* for the proposed change >
syn argument, ground, proof, wherefore,
why, whyfor
rel explanation, justification, rationalization
4 syn see CAUSE 1
5 the power of the mind by which man
attains truth or knowledge < we all must
use *reason* to solve this problem >
syn intellect, understanding
rel inference, ratiocination
6 syn see WIT 2

reason vb syn see THINK 5

reasonable adj 1 syn see CONSERVATIVE
2
2 syn see MODERATE 2
3 syn see CHEAP 1
ant extravagant
4 syn see RATIONAL
ant unreasonable

reasoned adj syn see DEDUCTIVE

reasonless adj 1 syn see INSANE 1
2 syn see ILLOGICAL

reassume vb syn see RESUME 1

rebate vb syn see DECREASE

rebate n syn see DEDUCTION 1

rebel n one who breaks with or opposes
constituted authority or the established
order < he is a *rebel* among educators >
syn anarch, anarchist, frondeur, insurgent, insurrectionist, malcontent, mutineer,
revolter
rel adversary, antagonist, opponent; assailant, attacker; extremist, radical, revolutionary, revolutionist, ultraist; debunker,
iconoclast
con authoritarian, intransigent, traditionalist; conservative, reactionary, white

---

syn synonym(s)   rel related word(s)
ant antonym(s)   con contrasted word(s)
idiom idiomatic equivalent(s)
|| use limited; if in doubt, see a dictionary

rebel *vb syn* see REVOLT 1

rebellious *adj syn* see INSUBORDINATE
rel alienated, disaffected, estranged
con acquiescent, resigned; submissive

rebirth *n* 1 *syn* see CONVERSION 1
2 *syn* see REVIVAL

rebound *vb syn* see RECOVER 3

rebuff *vb syn* see FEND (off)
idiom give the cold shoulder

rebuild *vb syn* see MEND 2

rebuke *vb syn* see REPROVE

rebuke *n* an expression of strong disapproval < his bad behavior earned him a sharp *rebuke* >
syn admonishment, admonition, chiding, rap, reprimand, reproach, reproof, wig
rel dressing down, earful, lecture, lesson, scolding, talking-to, tongue-lashing
idiom a flea in one's ear, slap on the wrist
con applause, compliment, praise

rebut *vb* 1 *syn* see FEND (off)
2 *syn* see DISPROVE 1

recalcitrance *n syn* see DEFIANCE 2

recalcitrant *adj syn* see UNRULY 1
rel obstinate, stubborn; opposing, resisting, withstanding
ant amenable

recall *vb* 1 *syn* see REMEMBER
rel educe, elicit, evoke, extract; arouse, awaken, rouse, stir, waken
2 *syn* see ABJURE
3 *syn* see REVOKE 2
4 *syn* see RESTORE 1

recall *n syn* see MEMORY 2

recant *vb syn* see ABJURE

recapitulation *n syn* see SUMMARY

recede *vb* 1 to move backward < they will return after the floodwaters *recede* >
syn back, fall back, retract, retreat, retrocede, retrograde
rel regress, retrogress; depart, retire, withdraw
ant proceed; advance
2 *syn* see DECREASE

receipts *n pl syn* see REVENUE

receive *vb syn* see TAKE 10

received *adj syn* see ORTHODOX 1

recension *n syn* see REVISION 1

recent *adj* 1 *syn* see NEW 1
2 *syn* see MODERN 1

recently *adv syn* see NEW

receptive *adj* open to ideas, impressions, or suggestions < he has a most *receptive* mind >
syn acceptant, acceptive, influenceable, persuadable, persuasible, responsive, suasible, swayable
rel open, open-minded; accessible, amenable, suggestible
con closed, closed-minded, inhospitable
ant unreceptive
2 *syn* see SYMPATHETIC 2

recess *vb syn* see ADJOURN 2

recession *n syn* see DEPRESSION 3

recherché *adj syn* see CHOICE
rel fresh, new, novel, original; exotic, uncommon, unusual
ant commonplace

recidivate *vb syn* see LAPSE

reciprocal *n syn* see MATE 5

reciprocate *vb* to give back, usually in kind or quantity < they were glad of the chance to *reciprocate* her kindness >
syn recompense, requite, retaliate, return
rel exchange, interchange; compensate, repay; retort, serve out
con accept, acquire, pocket, take

recital *n syn* see DESCRIPTION 2
rel discourse, story; enumeration

recite *vb syn* see RELATE 1
rel count, enumerate, number, tell

reckless *adj* 1 *syn* see ADVENTUROUS
rel desperate, hopeless
2 *syn* see RASH 1
ant calculating
3 *syn* see IRRESPONSIBLE

reckon *vb* 1 *syn* see CALCULATE
rel count, enumerate, number; add, cast, foot, sum, total
2 *syn* see CONSIDER 3
rel conjecture, guess, surmise
3 *syn* see ESTIMATE 3
4 *syn* see UNDERSTAND 3

reckon (on) *vb syn* see RELY (on *or* upon)

reckoning *n* 1 *syn* see BILL 1
2 *syn* see COMPUTATION

reclaim *vb syn* see RESTORE 3

recline *vb* 1 *syn* see SLANT 1
2 *syn* see REST 1

reclining *adj syn* see PRONE 4

recluse *adj syn* see SECLUDED

recluse *n* a person who leads a secluded or solitary life < a man who led the life of a *recluse* although living in a busy city >
syn hermit, solitary
rel anchorite, cenobite, eremite

reclusion *n syn* see SECLUSION

reclusive *adj syn* see ANTISOCIAL

recognition *n* 1 a learning process that relates a perception of something new to knowledge already possessed < *recognition* of a genuine diamond >
syn apperception, assimilation, identification
rel cognizance, realization; awareness, consciousness, sensibility
ant irrecognition
2 *syn* see CREDIT 4
ant unrecognition

recognize *vb* 1 to make out as or perceive to be something previously known < said they would *recognize* that face anywhere >
syn know
rel recall, recollect, remember
2 *syn* see IDENTIFY
3 *syn* see ACKNOWLEDGE 2
rel note, notice, observe, remark

recoil *vb* to draw back usually through fear or disgust < *recoiled* from the snake >
syn blanch, blench, flinch, quail, shrink, squinch, start, wince
rel falter, hesitate, waver; balk, shy, stick, stickle; dodge, duck, swerve; quake, shake, shudder, tremble; reel (back)
con advance, approach, near
ant confront; defy

re-collect *vb syn* see COMPOSE 4

recollect *vb syn* see REMEMBER
rel arouse, awaken, rally, rouse, stir, waken

recollection *n* 1 *syn* see MEMORY 2
2 *syn* see MEMORY 1

recommence *vb syn* see RESUME 2

recommend *vb* 1 *syn* see COMMEND 2
ant discommend
2 *syn* see COUNSEL

recommendation *n* *syn* see CREDEN-
TIALS
  rel approval, endorsement; commendation
recompense *vb* 1 *syn* see COMPENSATE 3
  rel accord, award, grant, vouchsafe; balance, offset
  2 *syn* see RECIPROCATE
recompense *n* *syn* see REPARATION
reconcile *vb* 1 *syn* see HARMONIZE 3
  idiom bury the hatchet, make peace
  ant estrange
  2 *syn* see ADAPT
reconcilement *n* *syn* see RECONCILIA-
TION
reconciliate *vb* *syn* see HARMONIZE 3
reconciliation *n* establishment of harmony
  <a *reconciliation* between the two
  countries was effected after ten years>
  syn harmonizing, rapprochement, reconcilement
  rel appeasement, conciliation, mollification, propitiation, satisfying
  ant disagreement
recondite *adj* beyond the reach of the
  average intelligence <a *recondite* sub-
ject>
  syn abstruse, acroamatic, deep, esoteric,
heavy, hermetic, occult, orphic, profound,
secret
  rel erudite, learned, scholarly; academic,
pedantic; difficult, hard; dark, enigmatic,
obscure; anagogic, cabalistic, mystic, mystical; cryptic, runic, sibylline
  con easy, facile, simple, straightforward
recondition *vb* 1 *syn* see RESTORE 3
  2 *syn* see MEND 2
reconnoiter *vb* *syn* see SCOUT
reconsider *vb* to consider again with a
  view to changing or reversing <was asked
  to *reconsider* his decision>
  syn reevaluate, reexamine, rethink, retreat, review, reweigh, think (over)
  rel draw off; sleep (on); amend, correct,
revise
  idiom revise one's thoughts, think better
of, view in a new light
reconsideration *n* *syn* see REVIEW 5
reconstitute *vb* *syn* see REORGANIZE
reconstruct *vb* 1 *syn* see MEND 2
  2 *syn* see REORGANIZE
  3 *syn* see RESTORE 3
record *vb* *syn* see SHOW 5
record *n* *syn* see DOCUMENT 2
recount *vb* *syn* see RELATE 1
recountal *n* *syn* see DESCRIPTION 2
recounting *n* *syn* see DESCRIPTION 2
recoup *vb* *syn* see RECOVER 1
recourse *n* *syn* see RESOURCE 3
recover *vb* 1 to obtain again <*recover* a
  lost watch>
  syn get back, recoup, recruit, regain,
repossess, retrieve
  rel reclaim, redeem; reacquire, recapture,
retake, rewin; reoccupy, resume; redis-
cover; balance, compensate, offset
  con lose, mislay, misplace; forfeit, sacrifice
  2 to regain health <*recovering* from a
  bout of pneumonia>

syn synonym(s)   *rel* related word(s)
ant antonym(s)   *con* contrasted word(s)
idiom idiomatic equivalent(s)
‖ use limited; if in doubt, see a dictionary

syn come round, rally
  rel convalesce, improve, mend, recuperate; perk (up), revive; heal; refresh, rejuvenate, renew, restore
  idiom get back in shape, get better, sit up
and take nourishment, take a turn for the
better
  con decline, fail, weaken, worsen; die,
expire, perish
  3 to regain a former or normal state <the
  textile industry was *recovering* quickly
  from the depression>
  syn bounce (back), rebound, snap back
  rel rally, revive
  con decline, fail
  ant worsen
  4 *syn* see RESTORE 3
recreancy *n* *syn* see DEFECTION
recreant *adj* *syn* see FAITHLESS
recreant *n* *syn* see RENEGADE
recreate *vb* 1 *syn* see AMUSE
  rel refresh, rejuvenate, renew, restore
  2 *syn* see PLAY 1
recreation *n* 1 *syn* see ENTERTAINMENT
  rel ease, relaxation, repose; frolic, rollick;
hilarity, jollity, mirth
  2 *syn* see PLAY 1
recrementitious *adj* *syn* see SUPER-
FLUOUS
recrudesce *vb* *syn* see RETURN 1
  rel refurbish, renew, renovate
  con repress, suppress; cease, discontinue,
stop
recruit *n* *syn* see NOVICE
recruit *vb* *syn* see RECOVER 1
  rel refresh, renew, renovate, restore;
mend, rebuild, repair
rectify *vb* *syn* see CORRECT 1
  rel rebuild, repair
rectitude *n* *syn* see GOODNESS
  rel conscientiousness, justness, scrupulousness
recumbent *adj* *syn* see PRONE 4
  ant erect, upright
recuperate *vb* *syn* see IMPROVE 3
recur *vb* 1 *syn* see RETURN 1
  rel iterate, reiterate, repeat
  2 *syn* see RESORT 2
recurrence *n* a periodic or frequent return-
ing <the *recurrence* of the nightmare
upset him>
  syn reappearance, reoccurrence, return
  rel repetition, reproduction; crebrity,
frequency
recurrent *adj* *syn* see INTERMITTENT
recurring *adj* *syn* see INTERMITTENT
Red *n* *syn* see COMMUNIST
red-blooded *adj* *syn* see VIGOROUS
redden *vb* 1 to make red <blood soon
  reddened the bandage>
  syn incarnadine, rubify, rubric, ruby, rud,
ruddle, ruddy
  2 *syn* see BLUSH
redeem *vb* 1 *syn* see RANSOM
  2 *syn* see FREE
  3 *syn* see COMPENSATE 1
red-handed *adv* in the act of committing
  a misdeed <caught *red-handed*>
  syn dead to rights, flagrante delicto
  rel blatantly, openly
red-hot *adj* 1 *syn* see HOT 1
  2 *syn* see IMPASSIONED
  3 *syn* see UP-TO-DATE

red-letter *adj syn* see NOTEWORTHY

red-light district *n* a district characterized by brothels < sailors frequented the
red-light district >
syn levee, stew(s), tenderloin
idiom street of fallen women

red-neck *n syn* see RUSTIC

redolence *n syn* see FRAGRANCE

redolent *adj* **1** *syn* see SWEET 2
2 *syn* see REMINISCENT

redouble *vb syn* see INTENSIFY

redoubt *n syn* see FORT

redoubtable *adj* **1** *syn* see FEARFUL 3
2 *syn* see FAMOUS 2

redound *vb* **1** *syn* see CONTRIBUTE 2

redraft *n syn* see REVISION 1

redraft *vb syn* see REVISE

redraw *vb syn* see REVISE

redress *vb* **1** *syn* see AVENGE
2 *syn* see NEUTRALIZE

redress *n syn* see REPARATION
rel balancing, offsetting; retaliation, vengeance

reduce *vb* **1** *syn* see DECREASE
2 to decrease in amount < they decided to
reduce prices to stimulate sales >
syn clip, cut, cut back, cut down, lower,
mark down, pare, shave, slash
rel curtail, decrease, diminish, lessen;
deflate, depreciate; scale (down), step
down; roll back
con boost, hike, jack (up), jump, put up,
raise, up
ant increase
3 *syn* see CONQUER 1
rel cripple, disable, enfeeble, undermine,
weaken; debase, degrade, humble, humiliate
4 *syn* see DEGRADE 1
ant advance
5 to lose body weight especially by dieting
< ate no cake while *reducing* >
syn slenderize, slim (down)
rel bant, diet
idiom lose flesh, take off weight
ant fatten

reduction *n* **1** *syn* see DEDUCTION 1
2 *syn* see DEMOTION

redundancy *n syn* see VERBIAGE 1
rel flatulence, inflatedness, inflation, tumidity, turgidity

redundant *adj syn* see WORDY
rel extra, spare, superfluous, supernumerary, surplus; iterating, reiterating, repetitious
ant concise

reduplicate *vb syn* see COPY

reduplication *n syn* see REPRODUCTION

reedy *adj syn* see THIN 1

reek *vb syn* see SMELL 3

reeking *adj syn* see MALODOROUS 1

reeky *adj syn* see MALODOROUS 1

reel *vb* **1** *syn* see SPIN 2
2 to move uncertainly or uncontrollably
(as in intoxication) < *reeled* down the
street >
syn stagger, titubate, totter, wheel
rel careen, lurch, ||swaver, sway, swing,
weave, wobble; falter, ||stammer, stumble,
teeter, topple; bob, waver

reestablish *vb syn* see RESTORE 1

reevaluate *vb syn* see RECONSIDER

reexamination *n syn* see REVIEW 5

reexamine *vb syn* see RECONSIDER

refashion *vb syn* see CHANGE 1

refection *n syn* see MEAL

refer *vb* **1** *syn* see ASCRIBE
2 *syn* see SUBMIT 2
3 to call or direct attention to something
< no one *referred* to his recent divorce >
syn advert, allude, bring up, point (out)
rel insert, interpolate, introduce; cite,
quote; instance, mention, name, specify;
glance, touch
idiom make an allusion to
4 *syn* see RESORT 2
rel advise, commune, confer, consult

referee *n syn* see JUDGE 1

referee *vb syn* see JUDGE 1

reference *n syn* see CREDENTIALS

refine *vb syn* see POLISH 2

refined *adj* **1** *syn* see GENTEEL 1
ant earthy
2 *syn* see FINE 1

refinement *n syn* see CULTURE
rel finish, suavity, urbanity; civility, courtesy, politeness; dignity, elegance, grace
ant vulgarity

reflect *vb* **1** to reproduce or show as a
mirror does < the trees on the shore were
reflected in the water >
syn glass, image, mirror
rel repeat, reproduce
2 *syn* see THINK 5
rel study, weigh

reflecting *adj syn* see THOUGHTFUL 1

reflection *n* **1** *syn* see ANIMADVERSION
rel assault, attack, onset, onslaught; depreciation, derogation, disparagement
2 *syn* see THOUGHT 1

reflective *adj syn* see THOUGHTFUL 1

reformatory *n syn* see JAIL

refractory *adj syn* see OBSTINATE
ant malleable

refrain *vb* **1** to hold oneself back from
doing or indulging in something < re-
frained from speaking out of turn >
syn abstain, forbear, keep, withhold
rel arrest, check, halt, interrupt, stop;
curb, inhibit, restrain
2 *syn* see DENY 3

refresh *vb syn* see RENEW 1
rel animate, enliven, quicken, vivify; recover, recruit, regain; amuse, divert, recreate
con exhaust, tire
ant addle; jade

refreshed *adj* made or become fresh
< awoke a *refreshed* man >
syn new, regenerated, reinvigorated, renewed, revived
rel recreated, renovated; animated, exhilarated, invigorated, stimulated
con exhausted, fagged, fatigued, jaded,
tired, tuckered, wearied, worn-down,
worn-out

refuge *n* **1** the state of being covered or
protected < exiles seeking *refuge* in neutral countries >
syn asylum, harborage, sanctuary, shelter;
compare SHELTER 1
rel protection, shield; immunity
con exposure, liability, openness; vulnerability
2 *syn* see SHELTER 1
3 *syn* see RESOURCE 3

refugee *n* one who flees for safety < the
villagers fed and housed the *refugees* from
the bombed city >
  syn displaced person, DP, émigré, evacuee, fugitive
  rel exile; emigrant, expatriate
  idiom stateless person

refulgent *adj syn see* BRIGHT 1

refurbish *vb syn see* RENEW 1

refusal *n syn see* DENIAL 1

refuse *vb* 1 *syn see* DECLINE 4
  2 *syn see* DENY 2

refuse *n* matter that is regarded as worthless and fit only for throwing away
< heaps of *refuse* left by the former ten-
ant >
  syn ‖collateral, debris, dreck, ‖dust, garbage, junk, kelter, litter, ‖muck, ‖mullock,
offal, outsweepings, ‖pelf, riffraff, rubbish,
‖sculch, spilth, sweepings, swill, trash,
waste
  rel dump, dustheap; rejectamenta, scraps;
lumber; offscouring(s)

refute *vb syn see* DISPROVE 1

regain *vb syn see* RECOVER 1
  rel achieve, attain, compass, gain; reach;
reclaim, redeem, save; renew, restore

regal *adj syn see* KINGLY
  rel august, imposing, magnificent, stately;
glorious, resplendent, splendid, sublime

regale *n syn see* DINNER

regalia *n pl syn see* FINERY

regard *n* 1 *syn see* NOTICE 1
  2 *syn see* CONSIDERATION 3
  ant disregard
  3 *syn see* INTEREST 3
  4 a feeling of deferential approval and
liking < held in high *regard* by his neighbors >
  syn account, admiration, consideration,
esteem, estimation, favor, respect
  rel deference, homage, honor, reverence;
appreciation, cherishing, prizing, valuing;
approbation, approval, satisfaction
  con deprecation, disapproval; disfavor,
disgust, dislike, distaste; contempt, disdain, scorn; detestation, hate, hatred
  ant despite
  5 *syn see* CARE 4

regard *vb* 1 *syn see* ADMIRE 2
  con reject, repudiate, scorn
  ant despise
  2 *syn see* CONSIDER 3
  rel assay, assess, estimate, rate, value

regardful *adj* 1 *syn see* ATTENTIVE 1
  2 *syn see* MINDFUL 2
  3 *syn see* RESPECTFUL

regarding *prep syn see* APROPOS

regardless *adj syn see* NEGLIGENT

regardless of *prep syn see* AGAINST 4

regenerated *adj syn see* REFRESHED

region *n* 1 *syn see* AREA 1
  rel neighborhood, vicinity; division, part,
section, sector
  2 *syn see* FIELD

register *n syn see* LIST

register *vb* 1 *syn see* ENROLL 1
  2 *syn see* SHOW 5

---

syn synonym(s)   *rel* related word(s)
ant antonym(s)   *con* contrasted word(s)
idiom idiomatic equivalent(s)
‖ use limited; if in doubt, see a dictionary

regnant *adj* 1 *syn see* DOMINANT 1
  2 *syn see* PREVAILING

regress *vb syn see* REVERT 2

regret *vb* to be very sorry for < *regrets* his
mistakes > < *regret* the problems facing
minorities >
  syn deplore, repent, rue
  rel bemoan, bewail, lament; grieve,
mourn, sorrow; deprecate, disapprove

regret *n* 1 *syn see* SORROW
  rel compunction, contrition, penitence;
remorse, repentance; demur, qualm, scruple
  2 regrets *pl syn see* APOLOGY 2

regretful *adj syn see* REMORSEFUL

regretless *adj syn see* REMORSELESS

regrettable *adj syn see* DEPLORABLE

regular *adj* 1 *syn see* GENERAL 1
  rel customary, ordinary
  ant irregular
  2 *syn see* ORDERLY 1
  rel fixed, set, settled; constant, equable,
even, steady, uniform
  ant irregular; sporadic
  3 *syn see* UTTER

regulate *vb syn see* ADJUST 2
  rel arrange, methodize, order, organize,
systematize; moderate, temper

regulation *n syn see* LAW 1

rehabilitate *vb syn see* RESTORE 3

rehearse *vb* 1 *syn see* RELATE 1
  rel iterate, reiterate, repeat
  2 *syn see* EXERCISE 3
  rel run through

reify *vb syn see* MATERIALIZE 2

reign *vb* 1 *syn see* GOVERN 1
  idiom sit on the throne
  2 *syn see* RULE 2

reimburse *vb syn see* COMPENSATE 3
  rel recover; balance, compensate, offset
  con default, dishonor, repudiate; welsh

rein *vb syn see* COMPOSE 4

reinforce *vb syn see* STRENGTHEN 2
  rel augment, enlarge, increase, multiply;
bolster, buttress, pillar, prop, sustain
  ant undermine

reinstate *vb* 1 *syn see* RESTORE 5
  2 *syn see* RESTORE 1

reintroduce *vb* 1 *syn see* RESTORE 1

reinvigorated *adj syn see* REFRESHED

reissue *n syn see* EDITION

reiterate *vb syn see* REPEAT

reject *vb* 1 *syn see* DECLINE 4
  rel debar, eliminate, exclude, shut out
  ant accept; choose, select
  2 *syn see* DISCARD

rejection *n syn see* DENIAL 1

rejoin *vb syn see* ANSWER 1

rejoinder *n syn see* ANSWER 1

rejuvenate *vb* 1 *syn see* RENEW 1
  2 *syn see* RESTORE 3

rekindle *vb syn see* REVIVE 3

relapse *n syn see* LAPSE 2

relapse *vb syn see* LAPSE

relate *vb* 1 to tell orally or in writing the
details or circumstances of a situation
< *related* the story of his life >
  syn describe, narrate, recite, recount,
rehearse, report, state
  rel disclose, divulge, reveal, tell; detail,
itemize, particularize; depict, express,
render; pronounce
  idiom make public

2 *syn* see JOIN 1

rel ascribe, assign, credit, impute, refer

3 *syn* see BEAR (on *or* upon)

related *adj* connected by or as if by family ties < persons *related* in the first degree > < physics and mathematics are closely *related* >

syn affiliated, agnate, akin, allied, cognate, connate, connatural, consanguine, incident, kindred

rel associated, connected; complementary, convertible, correlative, corresponding, reciprocal; alike, analogous, identical; germane, pertinent, relevant

con different, dissimilar, divergent, unconnected, unlike

ant unrelated

relation *n syn* see RELATIVE

relative *n* a person connected with another by blood < all of his *relatives* live out of state >

syn kin, kinsman, kinswoman, relation

rel brother, half brother, half sister, sib, sibling, sister; father, mother, parent; child, daughter, son; grandfather, grandmother, grandparent; grandchild, granddaughter, grandson; aunt, half aunt, half uncle, uncle; half nephew, half niece, nephew, niece; cousin, cross-cousin, half cousin, ortho-cousin; agnate, cognate

relative *adj* 1 *syn* see DEPENDENT 1

2 *syn* see COMPARATIVE

relax *vb* 1 *syn* see LOOSE 5

2 to become less tense or reserved < couldn't *relax* in crowds >

syn ease off, loosen up, unbend, unlax, unwind

rel calm (down), collect (oneself), compose (oneself), cool (off), simmer down

idiom be at ease, breathe easily, feel at home, make oneself at home

con rack (oneself), tense (up)

3 *syn* see REST 2

relaxation *n syn* see REST 1

rel amusement, diversion, recreation; alleviation, assuagement, mitigation, relief

ant tension

relaxed *adj* 1 *syn* see LOOSE 1

rel flexuous, sinuous; gentle, lenient, mild, soft

ant stiff

2 *syn* see EASYGOING 3

con ascetic, austere, severe, stern

ant tense

release *vb* 1 *syn* see FREE

rel acquit, exculpate, exonerate; relinquish, resign, surrender, yield

idiom cast loose, set at large

ant detain

2 *syn* see EMIT 2

3 *syn* see TAKE OUT (on)

ant check

relegate *vb* 1 *syn* see BANISH

2 *syn* see COMMIT 1

rel accredit, charge, credit, refer

relegation *n* 1 *syn* see EXILE 1

2 *syn* see DISPOSAL 2

relent *vb syn* see ABATE 4

relentless *adj* 1 *syn* see GRIM 3

rel rigorous, strict, stringent; cruel, ferocious, fierce, inhuman

con submissive, yielding

2 *syn* see INFLEXIBLE 2

relevance *n syn* see USE 3

relevant *adj* relating to or bearing upon the matter in hand < *relevant* testimony >

syn ad rem, applicable, applicative, applicatory, apposite, apropos, germane, material, pertinent, pointful

rel allied, cognate, related; appropriate, apt, fit, fitting, proper, suitable; important, significant, weighty; admissible, allowable

idiom in point, in question, to the point

con impertinent, inadmissible, inapplicable, inapposite, inappropriate; unallied, unassociated, unconnected, unrelated; alien, extrinsic, foreign

ant irrelevant; extraneous

reliable *adj* 1 having qualities that merit confidence or trust < a *reliable* friend >

syn dependable, secure, tried, tried and true, trustworthy, trusty

rel safe; inerrable, inerrant, infallible, unerring; apposite, cogent, compelling, convincing, meaningful, significant, sound, telling, valid; attested, authenticated, circumstantiated, confirmed, proven, validated, verified; unimpeachable, unquestionable

con doubtful, dubious, problematic, questionable, suspect; independable, undependable, untried, untrustworthy; unattested, unauthenticated, unconfirmed, unvalidated

ant unreliable

2 *syn* see CERTAIN 3

reliance *n syn* see TRUST 1

reliant *adj syn* see DEPENDENT 1

relic *n* 1 *syn* see REMEMBRANCE 3

2 *syn* see VESTIGE 1

relief *n* 1 *syn* see EASE 3

rel lightening, softening; allayment, appeasement, assuagement, mollification

ant anguish

2 *syn* see HELP 1

relieve *vb* 1 to make less grievous or more tolerable < drugs that *relieve* pain >

syn allay, alleviate, assuage, ease, lighten, mitigate, mollify

rel comfort, console, solace; appease, palliate, relieve, soften; quiet, soothe, subdue; moderate, qualify, temper; decrease, diminish, lessen, reduce; aid, benefit, help

con aggravate, enhance, heighten, sharpen; reinforce

ant intensify

2 *syn* see ROB 1

3 to take the place of for a time < sent to *relieve* the sentry >

syn spell, take over

rel fill in, sub, substitute; replace, supply

4 *syn* see EXEMPT

religion *n* 1 a system of religious belief < tolerant of all *religions* >

syn creed, cult, faith, persuasion

rel belief, doctrine

2 the body of persons who accept a system of religious belief < all the members of my *religion* strive for tolerance >

syn church, communion, connection, creed, cult, denomination, faith, persuasion, sect

religious *adj syn* see DEVOUT

rel faithful, staunch, steadfast, true; ethical, moral, noble, righteous, virtuous; honest, honorable, just, upright

con godless, ungodly
ant irreligious

relinquish *vb* to let out of one's possession or control completely < few leaders willingly *relinquish* power >
syn abandon, cede, give up, hand over, lay down, leave, resign, surrender, ‖turn up, waive, yield; *compare* ABDICATE 1
rel lay aside; quit, throw up; abdicate, renounce; desert, forsake; abnegate, forbear, forgo, sacrifice; cast, discard, shed
ant keep

relish *n* 1 *syn* see TASTE 3
2 *syn* see TASTE 4
rel enjoying, liking, loving; bias, prejudice; flair, leaning, penchant, propensity
3 *syn* see ENJOYMENT 1

relish *vb* 1 *syn* see ENJOY 1
2 to eat or drink with pleasure < so hungry that he will *relish* plain food >
syn savor
3 *syn* see ADMIRE 1

relishing *adj syn* see PALATABLE
rel delighting, gratifying, pleasing, regaling, rejoicing, tickling
con banal, flat, inane, insipid, jejune

reluct *vb syn* see DISGUST

reluctant *adj syn* see DISINCLINED
rel calculating, cautious, chary, circumspect, wary

rely (on *or* upon) *vb* to place full confidence < *relied* on the doctor for an accurate diagnosis >
syn bank (on *or* upon), build (on), calculate (on *or* upon), count (on), depend (on *or* upon), ‖lot (on *or* upon), reckon (on), trust (in *or* to)
rel commit, confide, entrust; await, expect, hope, look
idiom put faith in, swear by
con distrust, mistrust

remain *vb syn* see STAY 2
ant depart

remainder *n* a remaining group, part, or trace < he spent the *remainder* of his life in prison >
syn balance, heel, leavings, remains, remanet, remnant, residual, residue, residuum, rest
rel excess, surplus; hangover, leftover

remains *n pl* 1 *syn* see REMAINDER
2 *syn* see CORPSE

remanet *n syn* see REMAINDER

remark *vb* 1 *syn* see SEE 1
2 to make observations and pass on one's judgment < he *remarked* on the lack of modern paintings at the gallery >
syn animadvert, comment, commentate, observe
rel mention, note

remark *n* 1 *syn* see NOTICE 1
2 an expression of opinion or judgment < a *remark* that led to a vehement argument >
syn comment, commentary, note, obiter dictum, observation
rel assertion, reflection, saying, statement, utterance; clarification, elucidation, explanation, explication, exposition, interpreta-

tion; annotation, exegesis, gloss, postil, scholium

remarkable *adj* 1 *syn* see NOTICEABLE
rel exceptional; important, momentous, significant, weighty; peculiar, singular, strange, unique
2 *syn* see EXCEPTIONAL 1

remarkably *adv syn* see VERY 1

remedial *adj syn* see CURATIVE

remedy *n* 1 something used for the treatment of disease < a cold *remedy* >
syn cure, medicament, medicant, medication, medicine, pharmacon, physic
rel biologic, drug, medicinal, pharmaceutical
2 something that corrects or counteracts < no easy *remedy* for discontent >
syn antidote, corrective, counteractant, counteractive, counteragent, countermeasure, counterstep, cure
rel cure-all, elixir, panacea; nostrum

remedy *vb syn* see CURE

remedying *adj syn* see CURATIVE

remember *vb* to bring an image or idea from the past into the mind < *remembers* the old days >
syn bethink, cite, ‖mind, recall, recollect, remind, reminisce, retain, retrospect, revive, revoke
rel look back (on *or* upon), think (of), treasure; relive; educe, elicit, evoke, extract
con disregard, ignore, neglect, overlook; disremember, lose
ant forget

remembrance *n* 1 *syn* see MEMORY 1
2 *syn* see MEMORY 2
3 something that serves to keep a person or thing in mind < wanted to give her a small *remembrance* >
syn keepsake, memento, memorial, relic, remembrancer, reminder, souvenir, token, trophy
rel favor, gift, present

remembrancer *n syn* see REMEMBRANCE 3

remind *vb syn* see REMEMBER
rel hint, imply, intimate, suggest; admonish, advise, warn; jog, prompt
idiom put in mind

reminder *n* 1 *syn* see EXPRESSION 3
2 *syn* see REMEMBRANCE 3
rel memo, memorandum, note, notice; hint, intimation, suggestion; admonition, warning

remindful *adj syn* see REMINISCENT

reminisce *vb syn* see REMEMBER

reminiscence *n* 1 *syn* see MEMORY 1
2 *syn* see MEMORY 2

reminiscent *adj* tending to remind < shoes *reminiscent* of those worn fifty years ago >
syn redolent, remindful
rel evocative, suggestive
idiom bringing to mind

remise *vb syn* see TRANSFER 4

remiss *adj syn* see NEGLIGENT
rel faineant, indolent, lazy, slothful
ant scrupulous

remit *vb* 1 *syn* see EXCUSE 1
2 *syn* see DEFER
3 *syn* see SEND 1

remittable *adj syn* see VENIAL

remnant *n syn* see REMAINDER

remonstrance *n syn* see DEMUR 2

remonstrate *vb syn* see OBJECT 1

rel combat, fight, oppose, resist, withstand

remonstration *n syn* see DEMUR 2

remorse *n syn* see PENITENCE

remorseful *adj* motivated or marked by remorse <a *remorseful* confession>

syn apologetic, attritional, compunctious, contrite, penitent, penitential, regretful, repentant, sorry

rel mournful, rueful, sorrowful

con impenitent, regretless, unregretful; hard, obdurate

ant remorseless

remorsefulness *n syn* see PENITENCE

remorseless *adj* having no remorse <a *remorseless* villain>

syn impenitent, regretless, uncontrite, unregretful, unremorseful, unrepentant, unsorry

rel compassionless, merciless, pitiless, ruthless, uncompassionate, unmerciful

con penitent, regretful, sorry

ant remorseful

remote *adj* 1 *syn* see DISTANT 1

ant close; adjacent

2 *syn* see BACK 1

3 *syn* see OBSCURE 2

4 small in degree <a *remote* possibility>

syn ||fat, negligible, off, outside, slender, slight, slim, small

con great, large; important, significant, weighty

5 *syn* see INDIFFERENT 2

remotest *adj syn* see EXTREME 5

remove *vb* 1 *syn* see MOVE 4

2 to take something from a place or position <*removed* the book from the shelf>

syn take away, take off, take out, withdraw

rel move, shift, transfer; extract

3 to take (as a hat) from one's person <*removed* her coat when she entered the house>

syn doff, douse, put off, take off

rel cast off, throw off

idiom off with

con don, put on, replace

4 to get rid of <*remove* the causes of poverty>

syn clear away, eliminate, take out

rel dispose (of), eradicate, exterminate, extirpate; blot out, efface, erase, expunge, obliterate

idiom do away with

5 *syn* see PURGE 3

removed *adj* 1 *syn* see DISTANT 1

ant adjoining

2 *syn* see OBSCURE 2

3 *syn* see ALONE 1

remunerate *vb* 1 *syn* see PAY 1

rel accord, award, grant, vouchsafe

2 *syn* see COMPENSATE 3

remunerative *adj syn* see ADVANTAGEOUS 1

renaissance *n syn* see REVIVAL

renascence *n syn* see REVIVAL

rencontre *n syn* see CONTEST 2

rend *vb syn* see TEAR 1

rel divide, separate

render *vb* 1 *syn* see RETURN 3

2 *syn* see REPRESENT 1

3 *syn* see TRANSLATE 1

4 *syn* see ADMINISTER 1

rendering *n* 1 *syn* see INTERPRETATION 2

2 *syn* see VERSION 1

rendezvous *n* 1 *syn* see ENGAGEMENT 3

2 *syn* see RESORT 2

rendezvous *vb syn* see GATHER 6

rendition *n syn* see INTERPRETATION 2

renegade *n* a person who forsakes his faith, party, cause, or allegiance and aligns himself with another <the *renegade* derided his former beliefs>

syn apostate, defector, rat, recreant, runagate, tergiversator, turnabout, turncoat

rel iconoclast, insurgent, rebel; abandoner, deserter, forsaker; heretic, schismatic

con liege man; disciple, follower

ant adherent

renege *vb syn* see BACK DOWN

renew *vb* 1 to make like new <rested to *renew* their strength>

syn modernize, refresh, refurbish, rejuvenate, renovate, restore, update

rel make over, remodel; mend, rebuild, repair; correct, rectify, reform, revise

con bankrupt, deplete, drain, exhaust, impoverish; consume

ant wear out

2 *syn* see RESTORE 1

3 *syn* see REVIVE 3

4 *syn* see REPEAT

5 *syn* see RESUME 2

renewed *adj syn* see REFRESHED

renounce *vb* 1 *syn* see ABDICATE 1

ant arrogate

2 *syn* see ABANDON 1

idiom wash one's hands of

3 *syn* see DEFECT

renouncement *n syn* see RENUNCIATION

renovate *vb* 1 *syn* see REVIVE 3

2 *syn* see RENEW 1

rel clean, cleanse

renown *n* 1 *syn* see FAME 2

2 *syn* see EMINENCE 1

renowned *adj syn* see FAMOUS 2

rel acclaimed, extolled, lauded, praised; outstanding, signal

rent *vb syn* see HIRE 1

rent *adj syn* see LACERATED

rent *n syn* see BREACH 3

rental *n syn* see APARTMENT 1

renunciation *n* voluntary surrender or putting aside of something desired or desirable <led a life of total *renunciation* as a monk>

syn abnegation, denial, renouncement, self-abnegation, self-denial, self-renunciation

rel abjurement, eschewing, forbearing, forgoing, forswearing, sacrifice, self-sacrifice; rejection, repudiation, surrender, yielding

con gripping, holding, keeping

ant retention

reoccupy *vb syn* see RESUME 1

reoccurrence *n syn* see RECURRENCE

reopen *vb syn* see RESUME 2

reorder *vb syn* see REORGANIZE

reorganization *n syn* see SHAKE-UP

reorganize *vb* to arrange in a different way <*reorganize* a bankrupt company>

syn readjust, rearrange, reconstitute, reconstruct, reorder, reorient, reorientate, reshuffle, retool *rel* reestablish, refound, resettle; rebuild, regenerate, renovate

con disarrange, disorder, disorganize

reorient *vb syn* see REORGANIZE

reorientate *vb syn* see REORGANIZE

||**rep** *n* 1 *syn* see FAME 2

2 *syn* see REPUTATION 2

repair *vb* 1 *syn* see GO 1

2 *syn* see RESORT 2

repair *vb syn* see MEND 2

repair *n* 1 *syn* see ORDER 9

2 *syn* see ORDER 10

reparation *n* a return for something lost or suffered, usually through the fault of another < war *reparations* >

syn amends, compensation, indemnification, indemnity, quittance, recompense, redress, reprisal, restitution

rel atonement, expiation; remuneration, requital, retribution, reward; adjustment, settlement

repartee *n* 1 *syn* see RETORT 2

2 *syn* see BANTER

rel humor, irony, sarcasm, satire, wit; rejoinder, response, retort

repast *n syn* see MEAL

repay *vb syn* see COMPENSATE 3

rel balance, offset; accord, award

repeal *vb syn* see REVOKE 2

ant establish; enact

repeat *vb* to say or do again < *repeat* a command >

syn ingeminate, iterate, reiterate, renew, reprise, resay

rel recite, recount, rehearse, relate; hash over, recapitulate, rehash, restate, retell; chime, din, echo, harp, ring; duplicate, reproduce; copy, ditto, imitate; recrudesce, recur, return, revert

repeatedly *adv syn* see OFTEN

idiom day after day, day by day, day in and day out

repel *vb* 1 *syn* see FEND (off)

2 *syn* see RESIST

3 *syn* see DISGUST

ant allure; attract

repellent *adj* 1 *syn* see REPUGNANT 1

con alluring, bewitching, captivating, charming; enticing, luring, seductive, tempting

ant attractive; pleasing

2 *syn* see OFFENSIVE

3 *syn* see ANTIPATHETIC 2

repent *vb syn* see REGRET

repentance *n syn* see PENITENCE

con complacency, self-complacency, self-satisfaction

repentant *adj syn* see REMORSEFUL

rephrase *vb syn* see PARAPHRASE

repine *vb syn* see COMPLAIN

replace *vb* 1 *syn* see RETURN 4

2 *syn* see RESTORE 5

3 to put out of a usual or proper place or into the place of another < the old bridge was *replaced* by a new one last year >

syn outplace, supersede, supplant

rel renew, restore; alter, change; recoup, recover, regain, retrieve

4 *syn* see CHANGE 5

replacement *n syn* see SUBSTITUTE

replete *adj* 1 *syn* see ALIVE 5

2 *syn* see FULL 1

replica *n syn* see REPRODUCTION

replicate *vb syn* see COPY

replication *n syn* see REPRODUCTION

reply *vb syn* see ANSWER 1

con accuse, charge, impeach, indict; address, greet, salute

reply *n syn* see ANSWER 1

con argument, dispute; greeting, salute

report *n* 1 common talk or an instance of it that spreads rapidly < spread a false *report* >

syn buzz, cry, gossip, grapevine, hearsay, murmur, on-dit, rumble, rumor, scuttlebutt, talk, tattle, tittle-tattle, whispering, word

rel conversation, speech; chat, chatter, chitchat, prating, small talk; canard, dirt, scandal; advice, intelligence, news, tidings

2 *syn* see REPUTATION 2

3 *syn* see ACCOUNT 7

rel declaration, statement; comment, notice, review; brief, bulletin

report *vb syn* see RELATE 1

rel communicate, impart

repose *vb syn* see REST 1

repose *n syn* see REST 1

rel refreshment, renewal, restoration

con strain, stress; agitation, discomposure, perturbation

repository *n syn* see DEPOT 2

repossess *vb* 1 *syn* see RECOVER 1

2 *syn* see RESUME 1

3 to resume possession of (an item purchased on installment) in default of payments due < *repossessed* the car >

syn take back

rel get back, reclaim, recover, retrieve

reprehend *vb syn* see CRITICIZE

rel admonish, chide, rebuke, reprimand, reproach, reprove; berate, rate, scold, upbraid

reprehensible *adj syn* see BLAMEWORTHY

represent *vb* 1 to present an image or lifelike imitation of (as in art) < the painting *represents* a spring scene >

syn delineate, depict, describe, image, interpret, limn, picture, portray, render

rel express, realize, show; display, exhibit; hint, suggest; draft, outline, sketch; narrate, relate

con color, distort, falsify, garble, misinterpret, pervert, twist, warp

2 to serve as the counterpart or image of < a movie hero who *represents* the ideals of the culture >

syn body (forth), emblematize, embody, epitomize, exemplify, illustrate, mirror, personalize, personate, personify, symbolize, typify; *compare* EMBODY 1

rel denote, mean, signify; impersonate, substitute; copy, imitate, reproduce

con belie, distort, garble, twist, warp

ant misrepresent

representant *n syn* see DELEGATE

representation *n* the act of delineating < an exponent of *representation* in art >

syn delineation, depiction, description, picture, portraiture, portrayal, presentment

---

syn synonym(s)   *rel* related word(s)
ant antonym(s)   *con* contrasted word(s)
idiom idiomatic equivalent(s)
|| use limited; if in doubt, see a dictionary

rel demonstration, exemplification, illustration

representative *adj syn* see TYPICAL 1
ant atypical

representative *n* 1 *syn* see INSTANCE
2 *syn* see DELEGATE

repress *vb* 1 *syn* see SUPPRESS 2
2 *syn* see COMPOSE 4

repression *n* 1 the action or process of putting down by authority or force < *repression* of unpopular opinions >
syn choking, extinguishment, quashing, quenching, smothering, squashing, squelching, stifling, strangling, suppression, throttling
rel check, control, curb, restraint; crushing, quelling, subdual
con emboldening, encouragement, support
2 an instance of putting down by authority or force < racial *repressions* >
syn clampdown, crackdown, suppression
rel crushing, extinction, smothering; limitation, repression, restriction

reprieve *n syn* see RESPITE 1

reprimand *n syn* see REBUKE

reprimand *vb syn* see REPROVE

reprinting *n syn* see EDITION

reprisal *n* 1 *syn* see REPARATION
2 *syn* see RETALIATION

reprise *vb syn* see REPEAT

reproach *n syn* see REBUKE
rel blame, censure, discredit

reproach *vb syn* see REPROVE

reprobate *vb* 1 *syn* see CRITICIZE
2 *syn* see DECLINE 4

reprobate *adj* 1 *syn* see ABANDONED 2
2 *syn* see WRONG 1

reprobate *n syn* see VILLAIN 1

reproduce *vb* 1 *syn* see PROCREATE 1
2 *syn* see COPY

reproduction *n* one thing which closely or essentially resembles another that has already been made, produced, or written < printed *reproductions* of the great masters >
syn carbon, carbon copy, copy, ditto, duplicate, facsimile, reduplication, replica, replication
ant original

reproof *n syn* see REBUKE

reprove *vb* to criticize adversely, especially in order to warn of or to correct a fault < *reproved* him for talking in class >
syn admonish, call down, chide, lesson, monish, ||rack back, rebuke, reprimand, reproach, ||sncap, tick off; *compare* CRITICIZE, LAMBASTE 3, SCOLD 1
rel counsel, warn; blame, censure, criticize, reprehend, reprobate; chasten, correct, discipline, punish
idiom haul over the coals, slap one's wrist, take to task

reptile *n syn* see SYCOPHANT

repudiate *vb* 1 *syn* see DECLINE 4
con acknowledge, admit, avow, confess, own
ant adopt
2 *syn* see DEFECT
3 *syn* see DISCLAIM
rel abandon, desert, forsake; cast, discard
con allow, concede, grant
ant own

repugnance *n syn* see ABOMINATION 2

repugnancy *n syn* see ABOMINATION 2

repugnant *adj* 1 so alien or unlikable as to arouse antagonism and aversion < the idea of moving again became *repugnant* to her >
syn abhorrent, invidious, obnoxious, repellent, revulsive
rel alien, extraneous, extrinsic, foreign; incompatible, incongruous, inconsonant, uncongenial
con acceptable, bearable, tolerable; agreeable, gratifying, pleasant, pleasing, pleasurable
ant congenial
2 *syn* see OFFENSIVE
3 *syn* see ANTIPATHETIC 2

repulse *vb* 1 *syn* see FEND (off)
2 *syn* see DISGUST
ant captivate

repulsion *n syn* see ABOMINATION 2

repulsive *adj syn* see OFFENSIVE
ant alluring

reputable *adj syn* see RESPECTABLE 1

reputation *n* 1 *syn* see FAME 2
rel authority, credit, influence, prestige, weight
2 the estimation in which one is generally held < a good *reputation* >
syn character, fame, name, ||rep, report, repute

repute *n* 1 *syn* see FAME 2
ant disrepute
2 *syn* see REPUTATION 2

reputed *adj* 1 *syn* see RESPECTABLE 1
2 *syn* see SUPPOSED 1

request *vb syn* see ASK 2
rel appeal, petition, pray, sue

requiescence *n syn* see REST 1

require *vb* 1 *syn* see DEMAND 1
2 *syn* see DEMAND 2
3 *syn* see LACK

required *adj* 1 *syn* see NEEDFUL
2 *syn* see MANDATORY
ant optional

requirement *n* 1 something wanted or needed < production was not sufficient to satisfy *requirements* for cars >
syn demand, need, want
2 *syn* see ESSENTIAL 2

requisite *adj syn* see NEEDFUL
2 *syn* see JUST 3

requisite *n syn* see ESSENTIAL 2

requisition *vb syn* see DEMAND 1

requital *n syn* see RETALIATION

requite *vb* 1 *syn* see RECIPROCATE
rel content, satisfy; revenge
2 *syn* see COMPENSATE 1

resay *vb syn* see REPEAT

rescind *vb syn* see REVOKE 2

rescript *n syn* see REVISION 1

rescue *vb* to set free (as from confinement or risk) < *rescue* a drowning child >
syn deliver, save
rel emancipate, free, liberate, manumit, release; conserve, preserve; disembarrass, disentangle, extricate; recover, regain, retrieve; buy, ransom, redeem

research *n syn* see INQUIRY 1

resect *vb syn* see EXCISE

resemblance *n syn* see LIKENESS
rel parallel
ant dissemblance

resemble *vb* to be like or similar to < he *resembles* his father >

syn favor, ‖feature, simulate

idiom be a dead ringer for, bear a resemblance to, be the spit and image of, be the very image of, bring to mind, have all the earmarks of, look like, put one in mind of, remind one of, take after

con differ, vary

resentfully *adv syn* see HARD 6

resentment *n syn* see OFFENSE 2

rel animosity, animus, antagonism, antipathy, rancor; ill will, malice, malignancy, malignity, spite

reservation *n syn* see CONDITION 1

rel circumscription

reserve *vb* 1 *syn* see KEEP 5

2 to set or have set aside or apart <*reserve* a hotel room>

syn bespeak, book, preengage

rel contract, engage, retain

reserve *n* something stored or kept available for future use or need <keep a *reserve* of canned foods on hand>

syn backlog, hoard, inventory, nest egg, reservoir, stock, stockpile, store

rel fund, supply

idiom something for a rainy day, something in the sock

reserved *adj* 1 inclined to cautious restraint in the expression of knowledge or opinions <too *reserved* to offer a spontaneous criticism>

syn constrained, incommunicable, noncommittal, restrained

rel bashful, diffident, modest, shy; ceremonious, conventional, formal

con demonstrative, expansive, unconstrained, unrestrained; boisterous, loud, ostentatious; extroverted, open, outgoing

ant unreserved

2 *syn* see SILENT 3

ant effusive

3 *syn* see UNSOCIABLE

ant affable

4 *syn* see ANTISOCIAL

5 *syn* see QUALIFIED 2

reservoir *n syn* see RESERVE

reshuffle *vb syn* see REORGANIZE

reside *vb* 1 to have as one's habitation or domicile <he *resides* in Boston>

syn abide, bide, ‖dig, dwell, hang out, live

rel inhabit, occupy, people, tenant; continue, endure

2 *syn* see CONSIST 1

residence *n* 1 *syn* see HABITATION 1

2 *syn* see HABITATION 2

residency *n syn* see HABITATION 2

resident *n syn* see INHABITANT

‖**residenter** *n syn* see INHABITANT

resider *n syn* see INHABITANT

residual *n syn* see REMAINDER

residue *n syn* see REMAINDER

residuum *n syn* see REMAINDER

resign *vb* 1 *syn* see RELINQUISH

2 *syn* see ABDICATE 1

3 *syn* see QUIT 6

resignation *n syn* see ACQUIESCENCE

rel humbleness, lowliness, meekness, modesty

2 *syn* see PATIENCE

resigned *adj syn* see PASSIVE 2

ant rebellious

resile *vb syn* see BACK DOWN

resilient *adj* 1 *syn* see ELASTIC 1

2 *syn* see ELASTIC 2

ant flaccid

resist *vb* to stand firm against a person or influence <the criminal *resisted* the police> <we must learn to *resist* temptation>

syn buck, combat, contest, dispute, duel, fight, oppose, repel, traverse, withstand

rel assail, assault, attack; contradict, contravene, gainsay, impugn; baffle, balk, foil, frustrate, thwart; check, counter, hinder, obstruct, stem

con bow, capitulate, surrender

ant submit, yield

resolute *adj* 1 *syn* see DECIDED 2

rel obstinate, pertinacious, stubborn

2 *syn* see FAITHFUL 1

resoluteness *n syn* see DECISION 2

resolution *n* 1 *syn* see ANALYSIS 1

2 *syn* see DECISION 1

3 *syn* see DECISION 2

4 *syn* see COURAGE

resolve *vb* 1 *syn* see ANALYZE

ant blend

2 *syn* see SOLVE 1

3 *syn* see SOLVE 2

rel dispel, disperse, dissipate; clear, disabuse, purge, rid

4 *syn* see DECIDE

resolve *n syn* see DECISION 2

resolved *adj syn* see DECIDED 2

resonant *adj* marked by conspicuously full and rich sounds or tones (as of speech or music) <a deep *resonant* voice rang out>

syn consonant, fat, orotund, plangent, resounding, ringing, rotund, round, sonorant, sonorous, vibrant

rel full, mellow, rich; deep, profound; enhanced, heightened, intensified; earsplitting, loud, powerful, stentorian, strident; beating, pulsating, pulsing, throbbing; booming, clangorous, noisy, reverberant, reverberating, sounding, thundering, thunderous; electrifying, thrilling

con faint, low, murmurous, muted, smothered, soft, weak; flat, toneless, unmusical; cacophonous, discordant, inharmonious, off-key

resort *n* 1 *syn* see RESOURCE 3

2 a place that is habitually frequented <a favorite *resort* of teenagers>

syn hangout, haunt, purlieu, rendezvous, stamping ground, watering hole

rel harbor, haven, refuge, retreat; den, nest

3 a place providing recreation and entertainment especially to vacationers <returned to the same *resort* every year>

syn pleasure dome, spa, watering place

rel hotel, inn, lodge; bath(s), hot spring(s), mineral spring(s), spring(s), thermal spring(s)

resort *vb* 1 *syn* see FREQUENT

ant avoid

2 to betake oneself or to have recourse when in need of help or relief <they were unwilling to *resort* to her parents for aid>

syn apply, go, recur, refer, repair run, turn

---

syn synonym(s)   *rel* related word(s)

ant antonym(s)   *con* contrasted word(s)

idiom idiomatic equivalent(s)

‖ use limited; if in doubt, see a dictionary

rel address, devote, direct, employ, use, utilize

idiom avail oneself of, fall back on (*or* upon)

resound *vb syn* see PRAISE 2

resounding *adj* 1 *syn* see RESONANT

2 *syn* see EMPHATIC

resource *n* 1 resources *pl syn* see MEAN 3

2 resources *pl syn* see WEALTH 2

3 something to which one turns for assistance in difficulty or need in the absence of a usual means or source of supply < has exhausted every *resource* he can think of >
syn dernier ressort, expediency, expedient, makeshift, recourse, refuge, resort, shift, stopgap, string, substitute, surrogate
rel contraption, contrivance, device, lash-up; creation, invention; fashion, manner, method, mode, system, way; means, measure, step; artifice, dodge, stratagem, subterfuge; hope, opportunity, possibility, relief

respect *n syn* see REGARD 4
rel awe, fear, reverence; adoration, veneration, worship
ant scorn

respect *vb syn* see ADMIRE 2
rel reverence, venerate
ant abuse; misuse; scorn

respectable *adj* 1 worthy of esteem or deference < a *respectable* scientist >
syn creditable, estimable, reputable, reputed, well-thought-of
rel honorable, worthy
ant disreputable, unrespectable

2 *syn* see DECOROUS 1

3 *syn* see DECENT 4

4 *syn* see CONSIDERABLE 2

5 acceptable in appearance or standing < wore old but *respectable* clothes >
syn decent, presentable, tolerable; *compare* DECENT 4
rel adequate, satisfactory; acceptable, appropriate, proper, suitable
ant disreputable

respectful *adj* marked by or showing respect or deference < a *respectful* glance >
syn deferential, duteous, dutiful, regardful
rel reverent, reverential, venerating; attentive, civil, courteous, gracious, polite
con abusive, insolent, insulting, offensive; contemptuous, impudent, irreverent, rude
ant disrespectful

respecting *prep syn* see APROPOS

respective *adj syn* see SEVERAL 1

respire *vb syn* see BREATHE 3

respite *n* 1 a temporary suspension of the execution of a capital offender < the murderer won a *respite* >
syn reprieve

2 *syn* see BREAK 4
rel intermission, lull, pause, recess; ease, leisure, rest

resplendent *adj syn* see SPLENDID 2
rel blazing, flaming, glowing

respond *n syn* see ANSWER 1

respond *vb syn* see ANSWER 1
rel act, behave, react

response *n syn* see ANSWER 1

responsible *adj* subject to an authority which may exact redress in case of default < he is *responsible* for the safe delivery of the goods >

syn accountable, amenable, answerable, liable
rel exposed, open, subject
con clear, exempt, immune; irresponsible, unaccountable, unanswerable, unliable
ant irresponsible

responsive *adj* 1 *syn* see RECEPTIVE 1
ant unresponsive

2 *syn* see SENTIENT 3
rel answering, replying, responding

3 *syn* see TENDER
con cold, cool, indifferent

rest *n* 1 freedom from toil or strain < enjoyed his well-deserved *rest* >
syn ease, leisure, relaxation, repose, requiescence
rel deferring, intermission, suspension; quiet, silence, stillness; calm, peace, peacefulness, placidity, restfulness, serenity, tranquillity
con action, work; restlessness, strain

2 *syn* see BASE 1

rest *vb* 1 to dispose oneself at ease in order to relieve or avoid fatigue < she is *resting* in the bedroom after a hard day's work >
syn lie, lie down, recline, repose, stretch (out)
rel doze, nap, nod, sleep, slumber, snooze

2 to refrain from labor or exertion < planned to do nothing but *rest* during his vacation >
syn relax, rest up, unbend, unlax
rel loaf, loll, lounge; ease off, ease up, let down, let up, slacken, slack off
idiom take it easy, take life easy
con labor, toil, work; drudge, grind, slave

3 to allow an interval of rest from exertion < they *rested* for ten minutes before going back to work >
syn breathe, lay off, lie by, spell
idiom lie (*or* rest) on one's oars, stop for breath, take a break (*or* rest), take five (*or* ten), take time out

4 *syn* see BASE

rest *n syn* see REMAINDER
rel excess, overplus, superfluity, surplus, surplusage

restart *vb syn* see RESUME 2

restate *vb syn* see PARAPHRASE

restatement *n syn* see VERSION 1

restitute *vb* 1 *syn* see RESTORE 3

2 *syn* see RETURN 4

restitution *n syn* see REPARATION

restive *adj* 1 *syn* see CONTRARY 3

2 *syn* see TENSE 2

restiveness *n syn* see UNREST

restless *adj* lacking rest or giving no rest < the patient was *restless* from pain > < *restless* sleep >
syn uneasy, unpeaceful, unquiet, unrestful, unsettled, untranquil
rel agitated, disturbed, perturbed, troubled; fidgety, jittery, jumpy, nervous, restive; fitful, intermittent, spasmodic
con easy, peaceful, quiet, tranquil
ant restful

restlessness *n syn* see UNREST

restorative *adj* 1 *syn* see CURATIVE

2 *syn* see TONIC 1

restore *vb* 1 to put or bring back (as into existence or use) < *restore* peace in the world >

syn recall, reestablish, reinstate, reintroduce, renew, revive

rel get back, recover, regain, retrieve, win (back)

2 *syn* see RENEW 1

3 to put into a previous good state < made plans to *restore* slum areas >

syn reclaim, recondition, reconstruct, recover, rehabilitate, rejuvenate, restitute

rel redeem, rescue, save; amend, reform, revise; recoup, recruit, regain, retrieve; better, improve; correct, rectify, remedy, right; return

ant deteriorate

4 to help or cause to regain signs of life and vigor < *restore* him to health >

syn resuscitate, revive, revivify

rel cure, heal, remedy; arouse, rally, rouse, stir

5 to put again in possession of something < *restore* the king to his throne >

syn give back, put (back), reinstate, replace, return

6 *syn* see RETURN 4

restrain *vb* 1 to prevent from or control in doing something < *restrained* the child from picking all the flowers >

syn bit, bridle, check, coarct, constrain, crimp, curb, hold back, hold down, hold in, inhibit, keep, pull in, withhold; *compare* HAMPER

rel arrest, interrupt, stop; prevent; forbear, refrain; block, hinder, impede, obstruct; gag, muzzle

idiom keep in line, put (*or* lay) under restraint

con countenance, encourage; incline, induce, move, prompt; persuade; allow, permit

ant impel; incite

2 *syn* see COMPOSE 4

ant abandon

3 *syn* see MODERATE 1

restrained *adj* 1 *syn* see QUIET 4

ant unrestrained

2 *syn* see UNDEMONSTRATIVE

3 *syn* see RESERVED 1

4 *syn* see CONSERVATIVE 2

ant extravagant

restraint *n* *syn* see RESTRICTION 2

restrict *vb* *syn* see LIMIT 2

rel bind, tie; shrink

restricted *adj* *syn* see DEFINITE 1

restriction *n* 1 something that restricts or restrains < they both wanted to be free of the *restriction* of the school >

syn ‖ball and chain, circumscription, cramp, limitation, stint, stricture

rel brake, check, control, curb

2 an act of restricting or the condition of being restricted < undue *restriction* of children >

syn circumscription, confinement, constrainment, constraint, cramp, restraint

rest up *vb* *syn* see REST 2

restyle *vb* *syn* see REVISE

result *n* 1 *syn* see EFFECT 1

rel close, conclusion, end, finish, termination; product, production

---

syn synonym(s)   *rel* related word(s)
ant antonym(s)   *con* contrasted word(s)
idiom idiomatic equivalent(s)
‖ use limited; if in doubt, see a dictionary

con origin, root, source

2 *syn* see ANSWER 2

resume *vb* 1 to assume or take again < *resumed* her place in society >

syn reassume, reoccupy, repossess, retake

rel reclaim, recoup, recover, regain, retrieve

2 to return to or begin again after interruption < *resumed* her work >

syn continue, pick up, recommence, renew, reopen, restart, take up

rel carry on, go on, keep up

con cease, discontinue, end, halt, postpone, quit, stop; check, intermit, interrupt

résumé *n* *syn* see SUMMARY

resurgence *n* *syn* see REVIVAL

resurrect *vb* 1 to restore to life < believed that his body would be literally *resurrected* >

syn raise

idiom raise from the dead

2 *syn* see REVIVE 3

resurrection *n* *syn* see REVIVAL

resuscitate *vb* 1 *syn* see RESTORE 4

2 *syn* see REVIVE 3

resuscitation *n* *syn* see REVIVAL

retail *vb* *syn* see SELL 3

retain *vb* 1 *syn* see HAVE 1

2 *syn* see KEEP 5

con abdicate, resign; abjure, forswear, recant, renounce, retract

3 *syn* see REMEMBER

retake *vb* *syn* see RESUME 1

retaliate *vb* *syn* see RECIPROCATE

rel avenge, revenge

idiom even the score, get back at, get even with, give in kind, give one a dose of his own medicine, give one tit for tat, pay one in his own coin, settle (*or* square) accounts, turn the tables on

retaliation *n* the act of inflicting or the intent to inflict injury in return for injury < they had no opportunity for *retaliation* >

syn avengement, avenging, counterblow, reprisal, requital, retribution, revanche, revenge, vengeance

rel correction, discipline, punishment; indemnification, recompense, repayment; amends, indemnity, redress, reparation, restitution

idiom an eye for an eye, blow for blow, measure for measure, tit for tat

con clemency, grace, lenity, mercy; forgiveness, pardon, remission

retard *vb* *syn* see DELAY 1

rel decrease, lessen, reduce; clog, fetter, hamper; baffle, balk

ant accelerate; advance

retarded *adj* limited in intellectual or emotional development < a *retarded* child >

syn backward, dim-witted, dull, feebleminded, half-witted, imbecile, moronic, quarter-witted, simple, simpleminded, slow, slow-witted; *compare* SIMPLE 3, STUPID 1

rel dim, ‖dough-baked, ‖dunny, opaque; exceptional, underachieving; touched

idiom not all there, soft in the head

con bright, capable, intelligent

retch *vb* to make an effort to vomit < started to *retch* after drinking it >

syn gag, heave, keck

rethink *vb syn* see RECONSIDER

reticent *adj syn* see SILENT 3
con candid, open, plain
ant frank, unreticent

retinue *n syn* see ENTOURAGE

retire *vb* 1 *syn* see RETREAT 2
2 *syn* see GO 2
rel recede, retreat; abandon, relinquish, surrender, yield
ant advance
3 to cause to withdraw from one's position or occupation < all employees are automatically *retired* at age sixty-five >
syn pension (off), superannuate
rel discharge, dismiss; drop, leave, quit, resign, terminate, vacate
4 to go to bed < youngsters should always *retire* before midnight >
syn bed, ‖flop, pile (in), roll in, turn in
idiom go beddie-bye, go night-night, hit the hay (or sack)
con arise, get out, get up, pile (out), roll out, turn out, uprise
ant rise

retired *adj syn* see OBSCURE 2

retirement *n syn* see SECLUSION

retiring *adj* 1 *syn* see SHY 1
ant assertive
2 *syn* see UNDEMONSTRATIVE
ant forward

retool *vb syn* see REORGANIZE

retort *vb syn* see ANSWER 1

retort *n* 1 *syn* see ANSWER 1
2 a quick, witty, or cutting reply < he made a very clever *retort* >
syn back answer, comeback, repartee, riposte
rel reprisal, retaliation, revenge; crack, gag, jape, jest, joke, quip, sally, wisecrack, witticism

retouch *vb syn* see TOUCH UP

retract *vb* 1 *syn* see RECEDE 1
ant protract
2 *syn* see ABJURE
rel eliminate, exclude, rule out, suspend

retral *adj* 1 *syn* see POSTERIOR 2
2 *syn* see BACKWARD 1

retreat *n syn* see SHELTER 1

retreat *vb* 1 *syn* see RECEDE 1
rel quail, recoil, shrink
ant advance
2 to draw back from action or danger < the army *retreated* in disarray >
syn fall back, give back, retire, withdraw
rel abandon, depart, evacuate, go, leave, pull out, quit, vacate; decamp, escape, flee, fly; back down, back out, bow out, climb down
idiom beat a retreat, drop back, give ground, give way, sound a retreat
con advance, move, proceed, progress
ant attack

re-treat *vb syn* see RECONSIDER

retrench *vb syn* see SHORTEN

retribution *n syn* see RETALIATION
rel affliction, trial, tribulation, visitation

retrieve *vb* 1 *syn* see RECOVER 1
2 *syn* see REVIVE 3

retrocede *vb syn* see RECEDE 1

retrograde *adj syn* see BACKWARD 1

retrograde *vb* 1 *syn* see RECEDE 1
rel retire, revert; invert, reverse; backslide, lapse, relapse

2 *syn* see DETERIORATE 1

retrogress *vb syn* see REVERT 2

retrospect *n syn* see REVIEW 5

retrospect *vb syn* see REMEMBER

retrospection *n syn* see REVIEW 5

return *vb* 1 to go or come back (as to a person, place, or condition) < the converted sinner soon *returned* to his old ways >
syn react, recrudesce, recur, revert, turn back
rel advert; revolve, rotate, turn; renew, restore; recover, regain; rebound, reflect, repercuss, reverberate
con abandon, depart, leave, quit
ant forsake
2 *syn* see ANSWER 1
3 to bring back (as a writ or verdict) to an office or tribunal < return a verdict of not guilty >
syn render
4 to bring, send, or put back to a former or proper place < return the gun to its holster >
syn replace, restitute, restore, take back
ant remove
5 *syn* see RESTORE 5
6 *syn* see YIELD 5
7 *syn* see RECIPROCATE
rel bestow, give

return *n* 1 *syn* see RECURRENCE
2 *syn* see ANSWER 1
3 *syn* see PROFIT
ant outlay

returnless *adj syn* see INEVITABLE

revamp *vb* 1 *syn* see MEND 2
2 *syn* see REVISE

revanche *n syn* see RETALIATION

reveal *vb* 1 to make known what has been or should be concealed < he solemnly promised he would not *reveal* the truth >
syn betray, blab (out), disclose, discover, divulge, give away, let on, ‖let out, mouth, spill, tell, unbosom, unclose, uncover, uncurtain, unveil
rel break, communicate, impart; announce, blow (about or abroad), broadcast, declare, give out, publish, vent; breathe, whisper; leak; acknowledge, admit, avow, confess, let on; peach, rat, ‖split, squeak, squeal (on), ‖stool, talk
idiom let slip, let the cat out of the bag, spill the beans
con cover (up), hide, obscure, veil
ant conceal
2 *syn* see OPEN 2

revel *vb* 1 to be festive in a noisy or riotous manner < they *reveled* all night long >
syn carouse, frolic, hell, riot, roister, spree, wassail
idiom blow off steam, cut loose, kick up one's heels, let go, let loose, paint the town red, whoop it up
2 *syn* see WALLOW 3

revel *n* 1 *syn* see MERRYMAKING
2 *syn* see REVELRY 2

revelation *n* disclosure or something disclosed by or as if by divine or preternatural means < a *revelation* closely guarded by members of the sect >
syn apocalypse, oracle, prophecy, vision
ant adumbration

reveling *n syn* see MERRYMAKING

revelment *n* 1 *syn* see MERRYMAKING
2 *syn* see REVELRY 2

revelry *n* 1 *syn* see MERRYMAKING
2 boisterous partying < they were exhausted after the night of *revelry* >
syn high jinks, revel, revelment, skylarking, wassail, whoop-de-do, whoopee, whoopla, whoop-up

revenant *n syn* see APPARITION

revenge *vb syn* see AVENGE
rel defend, justify
idiom get one's own back, have one's revenge, take an eye for an eye

revenge *n syn* see RETALIATION

revengeful *adj syn* see VINDICTIVE
rel adamant, inexorable, inflexible, obdurate

revenue *n* amount received or gained usually measured in money < still holds property that yields a good *revenue* >
syn coming(s) in, income, receipts
rel earnings, gains, salary, wages; proceeds, profit, returns, yield
con expenditure, expense(s), outgoings, outlay

reverberant *adj syn* see HOLLOW 1

revere *vb* to honor and admire profoundly and respectfully < he is *revered* for his wisdom >
syn adore, reverence, venerate, worship
rel admire, esteem, regard, respect; appreciate, cherish, prize, treasure, value; exalt, magnify; enjoy, love
con contemn, despise, disdain, scorn, scout; insult, mock, scoff
ant flout

revered *adj syn* see VENERABLE 1

reverence *n* 1 *syn* see HONOR 1
rel devotion, fealty, loyalty, piety
2 the emotion inspired by what arouses one's deep respect or veneration < a deep *reverence* for honesty >
syn awe, fear
con contempt, despite, disdain, hatred, scorn; insult, mockery

reverence *vb syn* see REVERE
idiom hold in reverence

reverend *adj syn* see VENERABLE 1

reverend *n syn* see CLERGYMAN

reverential *adj syn* see VENERABLE 1

reverie *n* the condition of being lost in thought < spent the day in *reverie* before the fire >
syn brown study, muse, study, trance
rel absorption, abstraction, preoccupation; contemplation, meditation, thought; castle-building, daydreaming, dreaming

reversal *n* 1 a causing to move or face in an opposite direction or to appear in an inverted position < a *reversal* in policy > < the *reversal* of objects seen through a simple lens >
syn about-face, changeabout, inversion, reverse, reversement, reversion, right-about, right-about-face, turn, turnabout, turning, volte-face
rel bouleversement, overturning

2 *syn* see SETBACK

reverse *adj syn* see OPPOSITE

reverse *vb* 1 to change to the contrary or opposite side or position < the chairman *reversed* the order in which they would speak >
syn change, inverse, invert, revert, transplace, transpose, turn
rel capsize, overturn, upset; exchange, interchange; shift, transfer
2 *syn* see REVOKE 2

reverse *n* 1 *syn* see OPPOSITE
2 *syn* see REVERSAL 1
3 *syn* see SETBACK

reversement *n syn* see REVERSAL 1

reversion *n* 1 a return to an ancestral type or condition or an instance of such a return < the law was a shocking *reversion* to earlier times >
syn atavism, throwback
rel backsliding, lapse, relapse
con advance, amendment, bettering, betterment, improvement; reform
2 *syn* see REVERSAL 1

revert *vb* 1 *syn* see RETURN 1
2 to come or go back to a lower or worse condition < *reverted* to savagery >
syn regress, retrogress, throw back
rel backslide, lapse, relapse; decline, degenerate, deteriorate, retrograde
con advance, progress
3 *syn* see REVERSE 1

review *n* 1 *syn* see REVISION 1
2 *syn* see EXAMINATION
3 *syn* see CRITICISM
4 *syn* see JOURNAL
5 a retrospective view of or meditation on past events < an occurrence that in *review* did not surprise him >
syn afterlight, reconsideration, reexamination, retrospect, retrospection, revision
rel reflection, study; second thought
con anticipation, contemplation, foreseeing

review *vb syn* see RECONSIDER

reviewal *n syn* see CRITICISM

revile *vb syn* see SCOLD 1
rel asperse, calumniate, defame, libel, malign, slander, traduce, vilify
con acclaim, eulogize, extol, praise
ant laud

revisal *n syn* see REVISION 1

revise *vb* to make a new, amended, improved, or up-to-date version of < the many problems involved in *revising* a dictionary >
syn redraft, redraw, restyle, revamp, rework, rewrite, work over
rel overhaul, reorganize; perfect, polish, upgrade
con discard, disregard

revise *n syn* see REVISION 1

revision *n* 1 an act of revising < the *revision* of a manuscript >
syn recension, redraft, rescript, review, revisal, revise
rel amendment, correction, emendation, rectification
2 *syn* see REVIEW 5

revitalize *vb syn* see REVIVE 3

revival *n* a renewal of life, activity, or prominence < a *revival* of weaving >
syn reanimation, rebirth, renaissance, renascence, resurgence, resurrection, resus-

---

syn synonym(s)   *rel* related word(s)
ant antonym(s)   *con* contrasted word(s)
idiom idiomatic equivalent(s)
‖ use limited; if in doubt, see a dictionary

citation, revivification, reviviscence, risorgimento

rel regeneration, rejuvenation, renewal, restoration

revive *vb* 1 *syn* see RESTORE 4

rel gain, improve, recuperate

2 *syn* see RESTORE 1

3 to restore from a depressed, inactive, or unused state < *revived* his hope of escape>

syn reactivate, rekindle, renew, renovate, resurrect, resuscitate, retrieve, revitalize, revivify

rel reanimate, regenerate, reinvigorate, rejuvenate; arouse, galvanize, quicken, stimulate; activate, energize, vitalize

con extinguish, put down, put out, quell, quench, suppress; inhibit

4 *syn* see REMEMBER

revived *adj* *syn* see REFRESHED

revivification *n* *syn* see REVIVAL

revivify *vb* 1 *syn* see REVIVE 3

2 *syn* see RESTORE 4

reviviscence *n* *syn* see REVIVAL

revoke *vb* 1 *syn* see REMEMBER

2 to annul by recalling or taking back < *revoke* a privilege>

syn dismantle, lift, recall, repeal, rescind, reverse

rel abrogate, annul, void; cancel, erase, expunge; invalidate, nullify; countermand, counterorder; abjure, forswear, recant, retract

ant confirm

revolt *vb* 1 to renounce allegiance or subjection < *revolted* against the king>

syn insurrect, mutiny, rebel, rise (against)

rel defy, oppose, resist; break, renounce, turn (against); boycott, strike; overthrow, overturn, riot

idiom kick over the traces, take up arms against

con obey, submit; aid, assist, help, succor, support; bolster, prop (up), sustain, uphold

2 *syn* see DISGUST

revolter *n* *syn* see REBEL

revolting *adj* *syn* see OFFENSIVE

revolute *vb* *syn* see REVOLUTIONIZE

revolution *n* 1 the action or an act of moving around an orbit or circular course < the *revolution* of the earth around the sun>

syn circuit, circulation, circumvolution, gyration, gyre, revolve, rotation, round, turn, wheel, whirl

rel cycle, pirouette, reel, roll, spin, twirl

2 *syn* see SHAKE-UP

revolution *vb* *syn* see REVOLUTIONIZE

revolutional *adj* *syn* see EXTREME 3

revolutionary *adj* *syn* see EXTREME 3

revolutionary *n* *syn* see RADICAL

revolutionist *n* *syn* see RADICAL

revolutionist *adj* *syn* see EXTREME 3

revolutionize *vb* to change fundamentally or completely < he *revolutionized* manufacturing processes>

syn revolute, revolution

rel alter, change, modify; recast, refashion, reform, remodel; redraw, restyle, revamp, revise; metamorphose, transfigure, transform, transmogrify; overthrow, overturn

idiom break with the past, make a clean sweep, make a radical change

revolve *vb* 1 *syn* see PONDER 2

2 *syn* see TURN 1

revolve *n* *syn* see REVOLUTION 1

revulsion *n* *syn* see ABOMINATION 2

revulsive *adj* *syn* see REPUGNANT 1

reward *n* something that is offered or given for some service or attainment < the miner received a *reward* for his hard work >

syn carrot, dividend, guerdon, meed, plum, premium, prize

rel compensation, recompense, remuneration, requital

reweigh *vb* *syn* see RECONSIDER

reword *vb* *syn* see PARAPHRASE

rework *vb* *syn* see REVISE

rewrite *vb* *syn* see REVISE

rhadamanthine *adj* *syn* see JUST 3

rhapsodize *vb* *syn* see ENTHUSE 2

rel acclaim, extol, praise

con blame, condemn, denounce; decry, derogate, detract, minimize

rhapsody *n* 1 *syn* see BOMBAST

2 *syn* see ECSTASY

rhapsody *vb* *syn* see ENTHUSE 2

rhetoric *n* 1 *syn* see ORATORY

2 *syn* see BOMBAST

rhetorical *adj* emphasizing style often at the expense of thought < the candidate was given to windy *rhetorical* speeches>

syn aureate, bombastic, declamatory, euphuistic, florid, flowery, grandiloquent, highfalutin, high-flown, magniloquent, ||mouthy, oratorical, orotund, overblown, pompous, purple, sonorous, stilted, swelling, swollen, tumescent, tumid, turgid

rel chichi, orchidaceous, ostentatious, pretentious, showy; gassy, inflated, windy; exaggerated, overdone, overwrought; grand, grandiose, high-sounding, imposing; flamboyant, ornate; embellished; articulate, eloquent, fluent, glib, vocal, voluble

con homely, literal, plain, simple, unpretentious; unadorned, undecorated, unembellished, ungarnished, unornamented

ant unrhetorical

rhino *n* *syn* see MONEY

rhubarb *n* *syn* see QUARREL

rhyme *n* 1 *syn* see POETRY 1

2 *syn* see POEM

3 *syn* see RHYTHM

rhyme *vb* *syn* see AGREE 4

rhymer *n* *syn* see POETASTER

rhymester *n* *syn* see POETASTER

rhythm *n* the regular rise and fall in intensity of sounds that is associated chiefly with poetry and music < the *rhythm* of the music made it easy to dance to>

syn beat, cadence, cadency, measure, meter, rhyme, rhythmus, swing

rel lilt; accent

rhythmus *n* *syn* see RHYTHM

riant *adj* *syn* see MERRY

||**rib** *n* *syn* see WIFE

rib *vb* *syn* see BANTER 1

ribald *n* *syn* see SCAMP

ribbon *n* *syn* see STRIP 1

rich *adj* 1 having goods, property, and money in abundance < he was a *rich* man, having accumulated his wealth in business>

syn affluent, moneyed, ‖oofy, opulent, wealthy

rel comfortable, easy, independent, prosperous, well-fixed, well-heeled, well-off, well-to-do; fat, flush

idiom flush with money, having money to burn, in the money, rich as Croesus, rolling in money

con destitute, indigent, penurious, poverty-stricken

ant poor

2 *syn* see ORNATE

3 highly seasoned and fatty, oily, or sweet < ate *rich* desserts every day >

syn heavy

rel cloying, oversweet; filling, satiating, sating; fat

con natural, simple, unseasoned

ant plain

4 *syn* see FERTILE

5 *syn* see EXPRESSIVE

richen *vb syn* see ENRICH

riches *n pl syn* see WEALTH 2

rick *n syn* see PILE 1

‖**rick** *vb syn* see SPRAIN

rickety *adj* likely to give way or break down < a *rickety* old chair >

syn rachitic, rackety, rattletrap, shaky, wobbly; *compare* WEAK 2

rel unsound, unsteady

con firm, rugged, solid, sturdy, substantial, well-made

ant stable

‖**rickle** *n syn* see PILE 1

ricochet *vb syn* see GLANCE 1

rel bound, rebound, recoil

rid *vb* to set a person or thing free of something that encumbers < *rid* himself of his troubles >

syn clear, lose, shake (off), throw off, unburden

rel free, liberate, release; disembosom, unbosom; eradicate, exterminate, extirpate, remove, uproot; abolish, extinguish

con burden, charge, clog, cumber, encumber, lade, load, lumber, saddle, task, tax, weigh, weight

ant weigh down

riddance *n syn* see DISPOSAL 2

riddle *n syn* see MYSTERY

ride *vb* 1 to travel by automobile < often *rode* out to the countryside >

syn auto, motor

idiom go for a spin

2 *syn* see DRIFT 1

3 *syn* see BAIT 2

rel oppress, persecute; torment, torture

4 *syn* see OVERLAP

ride (out) *vb syn* see SURVIVE 2

ride *n syn* see DRIVE 1

rel excursion, expedition, journey, tour, trip

rider *n syn* see APPENDIX 1

ridge *n* 1 a top or upper part especially when long and narrow < topped the mountain *ridge* >

syn chine, crest, hogback

2 *syn* see WRINKLE

‖**ridge runner** *n syn* see RUSTIC

ridicule *vb* to make an object of laughter < *ridiculed* him for his inability to perform the feat >

syn deride, lout, mock, quiz, rally, razz, scout, taunt, twit

rel ‖barrack, flout, gibe, jape, jeer, scoff, sneer; burlesque, caricature, mimic, travesty; haze, ride, roast

idiom laugh out of court, make fun (*or* game *or* sport) of, poke fun at

ridiculous *adj* 1 *syn* see LAUGHABLE

rel absurd, foolish, preposterous, silly; antic, bizarre, fantastic, grotesque

2 *syn* see INDECOROUS

riding *n* 1 *syn* see SHIVAREE

2 *syn* see HARBOR 3

rife *adj* 1 *syn* see PREVAILING

2 *syn* see ALIVE 5

riff (through) *vb syn* see BROWSE

riffle *vb syn* see RIPPLE

riffle (through) *vb syn* see BROWSE

riffraff *n* 1 *syn* see RABBLE 2

2 *syn* see REFUSE

rifle *vb syn* see ROB 1

rift *n* 1 *syn* see CRACK 3

2 *syn* see BREACH 3

rel gap, hiatus, interruption, interval

rig *vb syn* see FURNISH 1

rig *n syn* see COSTUME

‖**rig** *n* 1 *syn* see IMPOSTURE

2 *syn* see PRANK

‖**rig** *vb syn* see DUPE

rigamajig *n syn* DOODAD, business, dingus, dofunny, doohickey, gadget, gizmo, thingum, thingumajig, thingumbob

rigging *n syn* see CLOTHES

‖**riggish** *adj syn* see FAST 7

right *adj* 1 *syn* see UPRIGHT 2

2 *syn* see DECOROUS 1

3 *syn* see JUST 3

4 *syn* see TRUE 3

con specious, unsound; misguided, mistaken

ant unright, wrong

5 *syn* see CORRECT 2

6 *syn* see FIT 1

7 *syn* see AUTHENTIC 2

8 *syn* see SANE 2

9 *syn* see HEALTHY 1

10 *syn* see CONSERVATIVE 1

11 *syn* see DECENT 4

right *n* 1 qualities (as adherence to duty or obedience to lawful authority) that together constitute the ideal of moral propriety or merit moral approval < the *right* is not all on one side >

syn good, straight

rel correctitude, correctness, properness, propriety, rightness

con debt, sin, wickedness; improperness, impropriety, incorrectness, unrightness

ant unright, wrong

2 something to which one has a just claim < the *right* to life, liberty, and the pursuit of happiness >

syn appanage, birthright, perquisite, prerogative, privilege

rel claim, interest, title; freedom, liberty, license

3 *usu* **rights** *pl syn* see DUE 1

4 *syn* see DIEHARD 1

‖5 *syn* see OBLIGATION 2

‖6 *syn* see EXCUSE 1

right *adv* 1 *syn* see JUST 1
‖2 *syn* see WELL 4
ant wrong, wrongly
3 *syn* see DIRECTLY 1
4 *syn* see WELL 3
5 *syn* see AWAY 3
6 *syn* see VERY 1

right *vb* 1 *syn* see CORRECT 1
‖2 *syn* see MEND 2

right-about *n* *syn* see REVERSAL 1

right-about-face *n* *syn* see REVERSAL 1

right away *adv* *syn* see AWAY 3

righteous *adj* 1 *syn* see MORAL 1
con corrupt, flagitious, nefarious; bad, evil, immoral, reprobate, sinful, vicious, wicked, wrong
ant iniquitous, unrighteous
2 *syn* see GOOD 11
ant unrighteous

righteousness *n* *syn* see GOODNESS
ant unrighteousness

rightful *adj* 1 *syn* see JUST 3
rel equitable, fair, impartial
ant unrightful
2 *syn* see TRUE 8
ant unrightful
3 *syn* see FIT 1

right hand *n* *syn* see RIGHT-HAND MAN

right-handed *adj* having the same direction or course as the movement of the hands of a watch viewed from in front <a *right-handed* propeller>
syn clockwise, dextrorotatory, positive

right-hand man *n* a reliable or indispensable person <the boss viewed his efficient assistant as his *right-hand man*>
syn girl Friday, man Friday, right hand

rightist *n* *syn* see DIEHARD 1
ant leftist

‖**rightle** *vb* *syn* see MEND 2

rightly *adv* *syn* see WELL 3

right-minded *adj* *syn* see MORAL 1

rightness *n* 1 *syn* see GOODNESS
2 *syn* see ORDER 11

right off *adv* *syn* see AWAY 3

‖**right smart** *adj* *syn* see CONSIDERABLE 2

‖**right smart** *adv* *syn* see VERY 1

right wing *n* *syn* see DIEHARD 1

right-winger *n* *syn* see DIEHARD 1
ant left-winger

rigid *adj* 1 *syn* see STIFF 1
rel firm, hard, solid
ant elastic
2 *syn* see INFLEXIBLE 2
3 extremely severe or stern <was regarded as a *rigid* disciplinarian>
syn draconian, ironhanded, rigorist, rigorous, strict, stringent, unpermissive
rel austere, severe, stern; hard-line, inflexible, tough, uncompromising, unyielding; adamant, adamantine, inexorable, obdurate
con humoring, indulgent, pampering; loose, relaxed; easy, gentle, mild
ant lax

rigor *n* *syn* see DIFFICULTY 1
rel austerity, severity, sternness; harshness, roughness; affliction, trial, tribulation, visitation
ant amenity

rigorist *adj* *syn* see RIGID 3

rigorous *adj* 1 *syn* see RIGID 3
rel inflexible, stiff; ascetic; burdensome, exacting, onerous, oppressive
con easy, effortless, facile, light, smooth
ant mild
2 *syn* see SEVERE 3
rel drastic
con bland, faint, lenient, smooth
3 *syn* see CORRECT 2

rigorously *adv* *syn* see HARD 5

rile *vb* 1 *syn* see ROIL 1
2 *syn* see IRRITATE

riley *adj* *syn* see TURBID

rim *n* *syn* see BORDER 1

rim *vb* *syn* see BORDER 1

rima *n* *syn* see CRACK 3

rimation *n* *syn* see CRACK 3

rime *n* *syn* see CRACK 3

rime *vb* *syn* see CAKE 1

rimple *n* *syn* see WRINKLE

rimple *vb* *syn* see CRUMPLE 1

‖**rimption** *n*, *usu* **rimptions** *pl* *syn* see SCAD

‖**rindle** *n* *syn* see CREEK 2

ring *n* 1 *syn* see LOOP 2
2 *syn* see LOOP 1
3 *syn* see BOXING
4 *syn* see CLIQUE
5 *syn* see COMBINATION 2

ring *vb* *syn* see SURROUND 1

ring *vb* to sound clearly and resonantly <the church bells were *ringing*>
syn bell, bong, chime, knell, peal, toll
rel resound, reverberate, sound

‖**ring (up)** *vb* *syn* see TELEPHONE

ringer *n* *syn* see IMAGE 1

ringing *adj* *syn* see RESONANT

ring off *vb* *syn* see SHUT UP 2

riot *n* 1 *syn* see DISORDER 2
2 something or someone wildly amusing <the new comedy is a *riot*>
syn howl, ‖panic, scream, sidesplitter
rel sensation, smash, wow

riot *vb* *syn* see REVEL 1

riot (away) *vb* *syn* see WASTE 2

riotous *adj* *syn* see PROFUSE

rip *vb* *syn* see TEAR 1

rip (out) *vb* *syn* see SPUTTER 1

ripe *adj* 1 *syn* see MATURE 1
rel seasonable, timely, well-timed; overdue
con callow, crude, raw, rude; immature, unmatured, unmellow
ant unripe; green
2 *syn* see CONSUMMATE 1
3 brought to full flavor or the best state <*ripe* cheese>
syn aged, matured, mellow, ripened
rel ready
ant unripe

ripe *vb* *syn* see MATURE

ripen *vb* *syn* see MATURE
rel better, improve; enhance, heighten, intensify, season

ripened *adj* 1 *syn* see MATURE 1
ant unripened
2 *syn* see RIPE 3

riposte *n* *syn* see RETORT 2

ripper *n* *syn* see DILLY, ‖corker, crackerjack, dandy, ‖dinger, humdinger, jim-dandy, ‖lulu, nifty, peach

ripping *adj* *syn* see MARVELOUS 2

ripple *vb* to become fretted or lightly ruffled on the surface (as water) < the pond was *rippled* by rain >
syn cockle, dimple, fret, riffle

ripsnorter *n* *syn* ‖DILLY, ‖corker, crackerjack, ‖daisy, dandy, ‖dinger, ‖doozer, humdinger, jim-dandy, ‖lulu

rise *vb* 1 to assume an upright or standing position < he *rose* from his chair >
syn get up, stand up, uprise, upspring
rel sit up; straighten up
idiom come to one's feet
con lie, lounge, recline, sit; loll, sprawl
2 *syn* see ROLL OUT
ant retire
3 *syn* see ADJOURN 2
ant sit
4 to move or come up from a lower to a higher level < smoke *rose* from the chimneys >
syn arise, ascend, aspire, lift, mount, soar, up, uprear
rel surge, tower; climb, scale; elevate, raise, rear
con descend, drop, lower; dip, plummet, sink
ant fall; decline
5 *syn* see INTENSIFY
6 *syn* see SURFACE
7 *syn* see INCREASE 2
ant abate; fall
8 *syn* see HAPPEN 1
9 *syn* see SPRING 1

rise (against) *vb* *syn* see REVOLT 1
rise (to) *vb* *syn* see APPLAUD 2
rise *n* 1 *syn* see ASCENT
ant fall
2 *syn* see ADDITION
3 an increment in amount, number, or volume < crime is on the *rise* >
syn boost, breakthrough, hike, increase, upgrade, wax
con declension, decline, lessening, letup, reduction, slump; decrement, loss
ant drop

rise and shine *vb* *syn* see ROLL OUT
risible *adj* *syn* see LAUGHABLE
ant lachrymose, larmoyant
rising *n* *syn* see ASCENT
ant falling
risk *n* *syn* see DANGER
rel accident, chance, fortune, luck; exposedness, exposure, liability, liableness, openness
risk *vb* 1 *syn* see ENDANGER
rel beard, brave, dare, defy, face; confront, encounter, meet
idiom go out of one's depth
2 *syn* see VENTURE 1
3 *syn* see GAMBLE 2
riskless *adj* *syn* see SAFE 2
risky *adj* 1 *syn* see DANGEROUS 1
rel delicate, precarious, sensitive, ticklish, touchy; speculative
idiom on thin ice
2 *syn* see RISQUÉ
risorgimento *n* *syn* see REVIVAL
risqué *adj* verging on impropriety or indecency < blushed at his *risqué* stories >

---

syn blue, broad, off-color, purple, racy, risky, salty, sexy, shady, spicy, suggestive, wicked; *compare* OBSCENE 2
rel naughty, warm; coarse, crude, earthy, gross, lewd, obscene, raunchy, raw, ribald, vulgar; dirty, foul; indecent, indecorous, indelicate, inelegant, unrefined
con clean, decent, proper; restrained; euphemistic

‖**rissom** *n* *syn* see PARTICLE
rite *n* 1 *syn* see FORM 2
2 forms (as religious rites) appropriate to a particular event < the marriage *rites* >
syn ceremonial, ceremony, formality, liturgy, observance, ritual, service
rel celebration, occasion, solemnity; sacrament, sacramental; form

‖**rithe** *n* *syn* see CREEK 2
ritual *n* 1 *syn* see RITE 2
2 *syn* see FORM 2
rival *n* one of two or more striving for what only one can possess < political *rivals* for the nomination >
syn competition, competitor, corrival
rel contender, contestant, entrant; adversary, antagonist, opponent
rival *vb* 1 *syn* see COMPETE 1
2 to strive to equal or surpass < *rivaling* each other for the most work done >
syn compete, emulate, rivalize
rel attempt, strive, struggle, try; contend, fight
3 *syn* see EQUAL 3
4 *syn* see AMOUNT 2
rivalize *vb* *syn* see RIVAL 2
rivalry *n* *syn* see CONTEST 1
rive *vb* 1 *syn* see TEAR 1
rel divide, separate; chop, hew
2 *syn* see SHATTER 1
rivel *n* *syn* see WRINKLE
rivet *vb* 1 *syn* see FASTEN 1
2 *syn* see FASTEN 3
rivulet *n* *syn* see CREEK 2
road *n* 1 *often* roads *pl* *syn* see HARBOR 3
2 *syn* see WAY 1
3 *syn* see WAY 2
roadblock *n* *syn* see BAR 2
roadhouse *n* *syn* see HOTEL
roadman *n* *syn* see PEDDLER
roadstead *n* *syn* see HARBOR 3
roadster *n* *syn* see VAGABOND
roam *vb* *syn* see WANDER 1
roamer *n* *syn* see ROVER
roar *vb* to make a very loud and often a continuous or protracted noise < the crowd *roared* their disapproval of the speech >
syn bawl, bellow, bluster, clamor, rout; *compare* BAWL 2
rel rebound, repercuss, reverberate; shout, vociferate, yell; din
con breathe, murmur, mutter, whisper
roaring *adj* 1 *syn* see LOUD 1
2 *syn* see FLOURISHING
roast *vb* 1 *syn* see BURN 3
2 *syn* see LAMBASTE 3
rob *vb* 1 to take possessions unlawfully < *rob* a bank > < he was mugged and *robbed* >
syn knock off, knock over, loot, plunder, ransack, relieve, rifle, stick up; *compare* BURGLARIZE, HOUSEBREAK
rel ‖heist, hold up; jackroll; roll; strongarm; filch, hijack, lift, pilfer, purloin, steal,

---

syn synonym(s)   *rel* related word(s)
ant antonym(s)   *con* contrasted word(s)
idiom idiomatic equivalent(s)
‖ use limited; if in doubt, see a dictionary

thieve; cheat, defraud, hustle, swindle; despoil, pillage, ravage, sack

2 *syn* see DEPRIVE 2

robber *n* one who commits the crime of robbery <only one *robber* was involved in the holdup>

syn yegg; *compare* THIEF

rel hijacker; sandbagger; crook, swindler; cat burglar, cat man, housebreaker, raffles, second-story man; rifler; holdup man, stickup man; ‖bushranger, highwayman, ‖sticker-up

roborant *adj syn* see TONIC 1

robot *n* 1 a machine that looks like a human being and performs various complex acts (as walking or talking) of a human being <a *robot* that performed household chores>

syn android, automaton

rel golem

2 an efficient, insensitive, often brutalized person <working on an assembly line can often turn a man into a *robot*>

syn automaton, golem, machine

robust *adj* 1 *syn* see FLOURISHING

2 *syn* see STRONG 3

robustious *adj syn* see BOORISH

rock *vb* 1 *syn* see SHAKE 4

rel oscillate, sway, swing, undulate; quake, totter, tremble

2 *syn* see TOSS 2

3 *syn* see HURRY 2

rock *n* 1 *syn* see ERROR 2

2 *syn* see DOLLAR

3 rocks *pl syn* see MONEY

rock bottom *n syn* see ESSENCE 2

rock-bottom *adj syn* see BOTTOMMOST

rockbound *adj* 1 *syn* see ROCKY 1

2 *syn* see INFLEXIBLE 2

rocket *vb* 1 *syn* see SKYROCKET

rel arise, ascend, levitate, mount, surge, tower

2 *syn* see HURRY 2

rock pile *n syn* see JAIL

rock-ribbed *adj* 1 *syn* see ROCKY 1

2 *syn* see INFLEXIBLE 2

rocky *adj* 1 abounding in or consisting of rocks <a *rocky* shore>

syn rockbound, rock-ribbed

rel bebouldered, bouldery; stony

2 *syn* see INSENSIBLE 5

rocky *adj* 1 *syn* see UNSTABLE 2

2 *syn* see OBSCENE 2

‖**Rocky Mountain canary** *n syn* see DONKEY 1

rococo *adj* 1 *syn* see OLD-FASHIONED

2 *syn* see ORNATE

rod *n* 1 *syn* see BAR 1

2 *syn* see PUNISHMENT

idiom rod in pickle

rodomont *n syn* see BRAGGART

rodomontade *n* 1 *syn* see BOMBAST

rel boasting, bragging, vaunting; pride, vainglory, vanity

2 *syn* see BRAGGART

rodomontade *vb syn* see BOAST

rodomontade *adj syn* see BOASTFUL

rogue *n* 1 *syn* see VILLAIN 1

rel culprit, delinquent

2 *syn* see SWINDLER

3 *syn* see SCAMP

roguery *n syn* see MISCHIEVOUSNESS

roguish *adj* 1 *syn* see DISHONEST

2 *syn* see PLAYFUL 1

3 *syn* see COY 2

roguishness *n syn* see MISCHIEVOUSNESS

roil *vb* 1 to make turbid <*roiled* the brook with his splashings>

syn mud, muddle, muddy, rile

rel befoul, contaminate, dirty, pollute

con clear, purify, settle

2 *syn* see IRRITATE

roily *adj syn* see TURBID

roister *vb syn* see REVEL 1

role *n* 1 characteristic exterior properties and aspects, style, and atmosphere in which something intangible is discerned <the moral *role* of the legislature>

syn character, clothing

rel appearance, face, guise, seeming, semblance, show; aspect, look

2 *syn* see FUNCTION 1

roll *n* 1 *syn* see LIST

2 *syn* see ROSTER 1

‖3 *syn* see FORTUNE 4

roll *vb* 1 *syn* see PONDER 2

2 *syn* see SWATHE

3 to wrap around on itself or something else <this cloth *rolls* unevenly>

syn furl

4 *syn* see WALLOW 3

5 *syn* see TURN 1

6 *syn* see WANDER 1

7 *syn* see POUR 2

8 *syn* see RUMBLE

9 *syn* see TOSS 2

roll call *n syn* see LIST

rollick *vb* 1 *syn* see GAMBOL

2 *syn* see WALLOW 3

rollick *n syn* see ESCAPADE

rollicking *adj syn* see ANTIC 2

rel cheerful, glad, happy, joyful, joyous, lighthearted

roll in *vb syn* see RETIRE 4

ant roll out

rolling stone *n syn* see ROVER

roll out *vb* to leave one's bed <*rolled* out at dawn>

syn arise, get up, pile (out), rise, rise and shine, turn out, uprise

ant roll in

roll up *vb syn* see ACCUMULATE

roly-poly *adj syn* see ROTUND 2

romance *n syn* see LOVE AFFAIR

romanesque *adj syn* see EXOTIC 2

romantic *adj syn* see EXOTIC 2

2 *syn* see SENTIMENTAL

rel fanciful, fantastic, imaginary, quixotic, visionary; created, invented

ant unromantic; matter-of-fact

Romeo *n syn* see GALLANT 2

romp *n syn* see RUNAWAY

romp *vb syn* see GAMBOL

idiom cut capers, horse around

rondure *n syn* see BALL

roof *n syn* see TOP 1

roof *vb syn* see HARBOR 1

rook *vb syn* see FLEECE 1

rookie *n syn* see NOVICE

room *n* 1 space in a building enclosed or set apart by a partition <the house had seven *rooms*>

syn apartment, chamber

2 rooms *pl syn* see APARTMENT 1

3 enough space or range for free movement <no *room* for hope>

syn elbowroom, latitude, leeway, margin, play, scope

rel clearance; license, range, rein, sway; rope

room *vb syn* see HARBOR 2

room and board *n syn* see ACCOMMODATIONS

roomy *adj syn* see SPACIOUS

ant cramped

‖**roose** *vb syn* see COMMEND 2

roost *vb* 1 *syn* see ALIGHT

2 *syn* see HARBOR 2

root *n* 1 *syn* see SOURCE

rel basis, foundation, ground

2 *syn* see BASIS 1

3 *syn* see CENTER 3

4 *syn* see ESSENCE 2

root *vb syn* see ENTRENCH 1

ant uproot

root *vb syn* see APPLAUD 2

rootage *n syn* see SOURCE

rootless *adj syn* see WEAK 2

root out *vb syn* see ANNIHILATE 2

rel demolish, destroy, raze

ant enroot

rootstock *n syn* see SOURCE

roperipe *n syn* see VILLAIN 1

ropes *n pl syn* see INS AND OUTS

ropy *adj syn* see MUSCULAR 1

rose *vb syn* see BLUSH

roseate *adj syn* see HOPEFUL 2

rose-colored *adj syn* see HOPEFUL 2

rose-colored spectacles *n pl syn* see OPTIMISM

roster *n* 1 a list of officers or enlisted men <an army *roster*>

syn muster, muster roll, roll

2 *syn* see LIST

rosy *adj syn* see HOPEFUL 2

rot *vb* 1 *syn* see DECAY

rel corrupt, debase, vitiate

2 *syn* see DETERIORATE 1

3 *syn* see DEBASE 1

rot *n syn* see NONSENSE 2

rotate *vb* 1 *syn* see TURN 1

2 to succeed or cause to succeed each other in turn <the drivers in the car pool *rotated* each week>

syn alternate

rel bandy, exchange, interchange; ensue, follow, succeed; relieve, spell

rotation *n syn* see REVOLUTION 1

rote *n syn* see ROUTINE

rotten *adj* 1 *syn* see BAD 5

rel foul; tainted, touched; sour

2 *syn* see VICIOUS 2

3 *syn* see BAD 8

4 *syn* see BAD 1

rotter *n syn* see CAD

rotund *adj* 1 *syn* see RESONANT

2 rounded or swollen with fat <a wheezing *rotund* man lumbered by>

syn chubby, plump, plumpish, plumpy, podgy, puddy, pudgy, roly-poly, round, roundabout, spuddy, tubby; *compare* FAT 2

rel beefy, chunky, dumpy, heavyset, squat, stocky, stubby, thick, thickset; paunchy, potbellied; buxom, ‖crummy

idiom on the plump side

con angular, gaunt, lank, lanky, lean, rawboned, scrawny, skinny, spare; slender, slight, slim, thin

roturier *n syn* see UPSTART

rouge *vb syn* see BLUSH

rough *adj* 1 not smooth or even <a *rough* undressed block of stone>

syn asperous, cragged, craggy, hairy, harsh, ironbound, jagged, rugged, scabrous, scraggy, uneven, unlevel, unsmooth

rel bumpy, choppy; burred; firm, hard, solid; coarse, gross

con flat, flush, level, plain, plane

ant smooth

2 *syn* see WILD 6

con calm, halcyon, peaceful, placid, serene, tranquil

3 *syn* see TOUGH 2

4 *syn* see TIGHT 4

5 *syn* see INDECOROUS

6 *syn* see RUDE 1

idiom in the rough

7 *syn* see RUDE 3

8 *syn* see HARSH 3

9 *syn* see COARSE 3

rel discourteous, impolite, uncivil, ungracious

10 *syn* see BLUFF

11 *syn* see HARD 6

rough *n syn* see TOUGH

rough (out) *vb syn* see SKETCH

rough (up) *vb syn* see MANHANDLE

rough-and-ready *adj syn* see MAKESHIFT

rough-and-tumble *n syn* see BRAWL 2

rough-and-tumble *adj syn* see MAKESHIFT

roughhewn *adj syn* see RUDE 1

roughhouse *n syn* see HORSEPLAY

roughhouse *vb syn* see MANHANDLE

roughhousing *n syn* see HORSEPLAY

roughly *adv* 1 *syn* see HARD 5

ant smoothly

2 *syn* see NEARLY

roughneck *n syn* see TOUGH

roughness *n syn* see INEQUALITY 1

ant smoothness

roughscuff *n syn* see RABBLE 2

round *adj* 1 having every part of the circumference equally distant from a center within <flowers crowded in stiff *round* beds>

syn circular

rel annular, globular, orbed, orbicular, rounded, spherical, spiral

2 *syn* see CURVED

3 *syn* see ROTUND 2

4 *syn* see OUTSPOKEN

5 *syn* see RESONANT

round *adv* 1 *syn* see ABOUT 1

2 *syn* see NEARLY

3 *syn* see THROUGH 1

4 *syn* see ABOUT 3

round *prep* 1 *syn* see NEAR 2

2 *syn* see ABOUT 4

round *n* 1 *syn* see BALL

2 *syn* see REVOLUTION 1

3 *syn* see TOUR 2

4 *syn* see CYCLE 1

5 *syn* see CURVE

round *vb* 1 *syn* see BALL

2 *syn* see SURROUND 1

---

syn synonym(s)   *rel* related word(s)

ant antonym(s)   *con* contrasted word(s)

idiom idiomatic equivalent(s)

‖ use limited; if in doubt, see a dictionary

3 *syn* see POLISH 2
4 *syn* see CURVE
round about *adv* 1 *syn* see ABOUT 1
2 *syn* see ABOUT 6
3 *syn* see ABOUT 2
roundabout *n* 1 *syn* see DETOUR
2 *syn* see VERBIAGE 1
3 *syn* see TOUR 2
4 *syn* see EXCURSION 1
round up *vb* *syn* see GROUP 1
roundabout *adj* 1 *syn* see INDIRECT 1
2 *syn* see ROTUND 2
rounded *adj* 1 *syn* see CURVED
2 *syn* see CURVACEOUS
rounder *n* *syn* see WASTREL 1
roundheel *n* *syn* see DOXY 1
roundly *adv* 1 *syn* see WELL 3
2 *syn* see NEARLY
round off *vb* *syn* see CLIMAX
round trip *n* *syn* see TOUR 2
round up *vb* *syn* see GROUP 1
rouse *vb* 1 *syn* see WAKE 1
rel animate, enliven, quicken, vivify; excite, provoke, stimulate; foment, incite,
instigate
con calm, compose, lull, quiet, quieten,
settle, soothe, still, tranquilize
2 *syn* see INTENSIFY
3 *syn* see PROVOKE 4
4 *syn* see STIR 1
rouser *n* *syn* see ||DILLY
rousing *adj* 1 *syn* see EXCITING
2 *syn* see LIVELY 1
||**roust** *vb* *syn* see PROVOKE 4
roustabout *n* *syn* see WORKER
rout *n* 1 *syn* see MOB 2
2 *syn* see RABBLE 2
3 *syn* see MULTITUDE 1
rout *vb* *syn* see ROAR
rout *vb* *syn* see RUMMAGE 3
rout *n* 1 *syn* see DEFEAT 1
2 *syn* see RUNAWAY
rout *vb* 1 to put to precipitate flight < the
army regrouped and *routed* the enemy >
syn derout, stampede
rel chase, dispel, drive, expel
idiom put to flight
2 *syn* see WHIP 2
route *n* *syn* see WAY 2
route *vb* 1 *syn* see SEND 1
2 *syn* see GUIDE
routine *n* habitual or mechanical and
sometimes monotonous performance of an
established procedure < settled into the
routine of factory work >
syn grind, groove, pace, rote, rut, treadmill
rel squirrel cage; ||drill
idiom the beaten path, the drab monotony of habit
routine *adj* 1 *syn* see ORDINARY 1
2 *syn* see USUAL 1
rove *vb* *syn* see WANDER 1
rover *n* *syn* see PIRATE
rover *n* one who roams habitually < he
spent most of his life as a *rover* always on
the move >
syn drifter, meanderer, rambler, roamer,
rolling stone, wanderer
rel gad, gadabout, gadder, runabout;
itinerant, peripatetic; floater
idiom bird of passage
con homebody
ant stay-at-home

roving *adj* *syn* see ITINERANT
row *vb* to propel a boat by means of oars
< *rowed* across the lake >
syn oar, paddle, pull
rel scull; punt; sail, scud
row *n* 1 *syn* see LINE 5
2 *syn* see SUCCESSION 2
row *n* 1 *syn* see BRAWL 2
2 *syn* see QUARREL
3 *syn* see MOUTH 1
row *vb* ||1 *syn* see SCOLD 1
2 *syn* see QUARREL
rowdiness *n* *syn* see HORSEPLAY
rowdy *adj* *syn* see TURBULENT 1
rowdy *n* *syn* see TOUGH
rowdydow *n* 1 *syn* see COMMOTION 4
2 *syn* see BRAWL 2
3 *syn* see BINGE 1
rowdydowdy *adj* *syn* see TURBULENT 1
rowdyish *adj* *syn* see TURBULENT 1
royal *adj* 1 *syn* see KINGLY
rel glorious, resplendent, splendid, superb; august, imposing, stately
2 *syn* see EASY 1
3 *syn* see GRAND 1
4 *syn* see EXCELLENT
royalist *n* *syn* see REACTIONARY
||**rozzer** *n* *syn* see POLICEMAN
rub *vb* 1 *syn* see ABRADE 1
2 *syn* see CHAFE 3
rel aggravate, exasperate, nettle, peeve,
provoke, rile; annoy, bother, irk, vex
3 *syn* see POLISH 1
rub *n* *syn* see OBSTACLE
rubber *n* *syn* see BUSYBODY
rubberneck *n* 1 *syn* see BUSYBODY
2 *syn* see TOURIST
rubberneck *vb* *syn* see LOOK 7
rubber stamp *n* *syn* see COMMONPLACE
rubbish *n* 1 *syn* see REFUSE
2 *syn* see NONSENSE 2
3 *syn* see PAP 2
rubbishing *adj* *syn* see CHEAP 2
rubbishly *adj* *syn* see CHEAP 2
rubbishy *adj* *syn* see CHEAP 2
rube *n* *syn* see RUSTIC
rubicund *adj* *syn* see RUDDY
rubify *vb* *syn* see REDDEN 1
rub out *vb* 1 *syn* see DESTROY 1
2 *syn* see MURDER 1
rubric *n* *syn* see NAME 1
rubric *adj* *syn* see NOTEWORTHY
rubric *vb* *syn* see REDDEN 1
ruby *vb* *syn* see REDDEN 1
ruck *n* ||1 *syn* see PILE 1
2 *syn* see GATHERING 2
ruck *n* *syn* see WRINKLE
ruck (up) *vb* *syn* see CRUMPLE 1
||**ruckle** *vb* *syn* see CRUMPLE 1
rucksack *n* *syn* see BACKPACK
ruckus *n* 1 *syn* see COMMOTION 3
rel brawl, broil, melee, scrap
2 *syn* see QUARREL
ruction *n* 1 *syn* see BRAWL 2
2 *syn* see COMMOTION 4
||**ructious** *adj* *syn* see BELLIGERENT
rud *vb* *syn* see REDDEN 1
ruddle *vb* *syn* see REDDEN 1
ruddy *adj* having a healthy reddish color
< has a *ruddy* complexion after being out
in the cold >
syn florid, flush, flushed, full-blooded,
glowing, rubicund, sanguine

rel bronzed; blooming; blowsy

con ashen, ashy, livid, pale, pallid, wan, waxy; anemic, bloodless

ruddy *vb syn* see REDDEN 1

rude *adj* **1** lacking in craftsmanship or artistic finish < a *rude* sketch >

syn angular, crude, lumpy, raw, rough, roughhewn, undressed, unfashioned, unfinished, unformed, unhewn, unpolished, unworked, unwrought

rel unlicked; unprocessed; primitive, rudimental, rudimentary

con dressed, fashioned, finished, formed, hewn, polished, worked, wrought

2 *syn* see DISSONANT 1

3 hastily executed and admittedly imperfect or imprecise < *rude* estimates for the cost of building the house >

syn approximate, proximate, rough

rel crude, imperfect, imprecise, inexact

idiom ‖in the ball park

con accurate, correct; faultless, perfect; exact, precise; meticulous, scrupulous

4 *syn* see COARSE 3

5 *syn* see IGNORANT 1

6 lacking in social refinement < gave a *rude* reply to a polite question >

syn discourteous, disgracious, disrespectful, ill, ill-bred, ill-mannered, impertinent, impolite, incivil, incondite, inurbane, mannerless, ‖mismannered, uncalled-for, uncivil, uncourteous, uncouth, ungracious, unhandsome, unmannered, unmannerly, unpolished

rel brusque, crusty, curt, gruff; harsh; intrusive, meddlesome; crabbed, surly; boorish, churlish, clownish, loutish

con courteous, genteel, mannerly, polite, well-mannered; bland, diplomatic, politic, smooth, suave; affable, considerate, gracious

ant civil; urbane

7 *syn* see BARBARIAN 1

8 *syn* see INEXPERIENCED

rudely *adv syn* see NEARLY

rudiment *n* **1** *syn* see ESSENTIAL 1

2 rudiments *pl syn* see ALPHABET 2

rudimental *adj syn* see ELEMENTARY 1

rudimentary *adj syn* see ELEMENTARY 1

rue *vb syn* see REGRET 1

rue *n* **1** *syn* see SORROW

2 *syn* see PENITENCE

3 *syn* see PITY

rueful *adj* **1** *syn* see PITIFUL 1

2 *syn* see WOEFUL 1

3 *syn* see MELANCHOLY 2

rel depressed, oppressed, weighed down; piteous, pitiful; despairing, despondent, hopeless

ruffian *n* **1** *syn* see TOUGH

2 *syn* see THUG 1

ruffle *vb* **1** *syn* see BLOW 1

2 *syn* see ABRADE 1

3 *syn* see ANNOY 1

‖**4** *syn* see INTIMIDATE

rugged *adj* **1** *syn* see ROUGH 1

2 *syn* see SEVERE 3

rel arduous, difficult

---

syn synonym(s)   *rel* related word(s)
ant antonym(s)   *con* contrasted word(s)
idiom idiomatic equivalent(s)
‖ use limited; if in doubt, see a dictionary

---

3 *syn* see HARSH 3

4 *syn* see BOORISH

5 *syn* see TOUGH 4

rel brawny, burly, husky, muscular

ant fragile

6 *syn* see HARD 6

ruin *n* **1** *syn* see DETERIORATION 1

2 *syn* see DOWNFALL 2

3 the bringing about of or the results of disaster < met *ruin* at the hands of the enemy >

syn confusion, destruction, devastation, havoc, loss, ruination

rel crumbling, disintegration; break up, dissolution; disrepair; wreck

con rebuilding, reconstruction, re-creation

4 *syn* see INJURY 1

ruin *vb* **1** *syn* see DESTROY 1

rel deface, disfigure; maim, mangle, mutilate; depredate, desecrate, desolate, despoil, devastate, devour, pillage, sack, spoliate, waste

ant restore

2 to subject to forces that are destructive of soundness, worth, or usefulness < in danger of being *ruined* by prosperity >

syn bankrupt, dilapidate, do in, shipwreck, wreck

rel corrupt, debase, degenerate, vitiate

idiom play hob (*or* the devil) with

con rebuild, renew, restore; reclaim, redeem, retrieve, salvage

3 to overthrow the fortunes of < was *ruined* during the great crash >

syn bankrupt, break, bust, fold up, impoverish, pauper, pauperize

rel beggar, clean out, deplete, drain, draw, draw down, exhaust, use up; wipe (out); reduce

idiom go under, lose one's shirt (*or* pants), take to the cleaners

4 *syn* see FRUSTRATE 1

‖**ruinate** *vb syn* see DESTROY 1

ruination *n* **1** *syn* see RUIN 3

2 *syn* see DOWNFALL 2

ruinator *n syn* see VANDAL

ruiner *n syn* see VANDAL

ruinous *adj* **1** *syn* see DESTRUCTIVE

2 *syn* see FATAL 2

rule *n* **1** *syn* see LAW 1

rel order; axiom, fundamental, principle; decorum, etiquette, propriety

2 *syn* see MAXIM

rel fundamental, principle

rule *vb* **1** *syn* see GOVERN 1

rel guide, lead

2 to hold preeminence in (as by ability, strength, or position) < an actor who rightfully *rules* the Shakespearian stage >

syn dominate, domineer, predominate, preponderate, prevail, reign

rel guide, lead; preside

idiom be number one, take first place (in *or* on)

3 *syn* see DECIDE

rel deduce, gather, infer, judge

rule out *vb* **1** *syn* see EXCLUDE

2 *syn* see PREVENT 2

ruling *n syn* see EDICT 1

ruling *adj* **1** *syn* see CENTRAL 1

con peripheral

2 *syn* see PREVAILING

‖**rum** *adj syn* see STRANGE 4

rumble *vb* to make a low heavy rolling sound <thunder *rumbling* in the distance>
syn growl, grumble, roll
rel boom, roar, thunder; peal, resound; blast, burst, clap, crack, crash

rumble *n syn* see REPORT 1

rumble–bumble *n syn* see MISCELLANY 1

rumbustious *adj syn* see TURBULENT 1

rum–dum *adj syn* see INTOXICATED 1

rumdum *n syn* see DRUNKARD

‖**rum–hole** *n syn* see BAR 5

ruminate *vb* 1 *syn* see PONDER 2
rel consider, excogitate, weigh
2 *syn* see CHEW 1

ruminative *adj syn* see THOUGHTFUL 1

rummage *n syn* see CLUTTER 2
rel conglomeration, hash, hotchpotch, miscellany, patchwork, potpourri

rummage *vb* 1 *syn* see DISORDER 1
2 *syn* see SCOUR 2
3 to produce by searching <*rummaged* an old dress out of the attic>
syn dig out, hunt (down or out or up), rout
rel ferret (out), find; fish, search (out), spy (out); poke

rummery *n syn* see BAR 5

‖**rum–mill** *n syn* see BAR 5

rummy *adj syn* see STRANGE 4

rummy *n syn* see DRUNKARD

rumor *n* 1 *syn* see REPORT 1
2 *syn* see MURMUR 1

rumor *vb syn* see GOSSIP

rumorer *n syn* see GOSSIP 1

rumormonger *n syn* see GOSSIP 1

rump *n syn* see BUTTOCKS

rumple *vb syn* see CRUMPLE 1

‖**rumpot** *n syn* see DRUNKARD

rumpus *n* 1 *syn* see COMMOTION 3
2 *syn* see ARGUMENT 2

rumshop *n syn* see BAR 5

run *vb* 1 to move at a fast springing gait in which both feet are momentarily off the ground in the course of each pace <the boy *ran* down the walk>
syn dash, scamper, scoot, scurry, shin, sprint; *compare* SCUTTLE
rel career, course, race; bustle, hurry, hustle, rush, speed; scorch
con crawl, creep, drag, inch, mosey, poke, saunter, stroll, toddle
2 to hasten away from something that frightens or perturbs <afraid to fight but ashamed to *run* >
syn bolt, flee, fly, make off, scamper, scoot, ‖screw, skedaddle, skip, skirr
idiom ‖dog it, make a break, run for it, show a clean pair of heels, take flight, take French leave, take to one's heels
3 *syn* see HURRY 1
idiom go all out, go like (greased) lightning
4 *syn* see RESORT 1
5 *syn* see FUNCTION 3
6 *syn* see BECOME 1
7 *syn* see LIQUEFY
8 to lie in or take a certain course <the path *runs* along the crest of the hill>
syn extend, go, make, reach, stretch
9 *syn* see RANGE 3
10 *syn* see HUNT 1
11 *syn* see DRIVE 3

12 *syn* see THRUST 2
13 *syn* see SMUGGLE
14 *syn* see OPERATE 3
15 *syn* see CONDUCT 3

run (through or over) *vb syn* see BROWSE

run (to or into) *vb syn* see AMOUNT 1

run *n* 1 ‖*syn* see CREEK 2
2 an uninterrupted course of occurrence or repetition especially of like things or events <the play had a long *run* >
syn continuance, continuation, duration, persistence
rel continuity, endurance, prolongation
3 *syn* see TENDENCY 1
rel course, set; bearing, direction, line, swing
4 *syn* see TRIP 1
‖5 **runs** *pl* but *sing or pl in constr syn* see DIARRHEA

runagate *n* 1 *syn* see RENEGADE
2 *syn* see VAGABOND

run along *vb syn* see GO 2

runaround *n* 1 *syn* see DETOUR
2 *syn* see ESCAPE 2

run away *vb syn* see ELOPE

runaway *n* a one-sided or overwhelming victory <the game was a *runaway*, the home team winning by 30 points>
syn cakewalk, romp, rout, walkaway, walkover
rel breather, cinch, duck soup, pushover; setup; shutout; conquest, triumph, victory, win
con photo finish, tossup

run down *vb syn* see DECRY 2

run–down *adj* 1 *syn* see SHABBY 1
2 *syn* see NEGLECTED
rel abandoned, derelict, deserted, desolate, forsaken, lorn

rune *n* 1 *syn* see SPELL
2 *syn* see POEM

rung *n syn* see DEGREE 1

run in *vb* 1 *syn* see ARREST 2
2 *syn* see VISIT 2

run–in *n* 1 *syn* see ENCOUNTER
2 *syn* see QUARREL

runnel *n syn* see CREEK 2

running *n syn* see OVERSIGHT 1

running *adj* 1 *syn* see ACTIVE 1
2 *syn* see EASY 9

running *adv syn* see TOGETHER 2

running mate *n syn* see ASSOCIATE 2

run–of–mine *adj* 1 *syn* see UNREFINED 3
2 *syn* see MEDIUM

run–of–the–mill *adj* 1 *syn* see MEDIUM
rel uncommon, unexceptional
2 *syn* see GENERAL 1

run on *vb syn* see CHAT 1

run out *vb* 1 *syn* see FAIL 2
2 *syn* see BANISH

run over *vb syn* see OVERFLOW 2

runt *n syn* see DWARF

runted *adj syn* see STUNTED

run through *vb syn* see GO 4

runtish *adj syn* see STUNTED

runty *adj syn* see STUNTED

run up *vb* 1 *syn* see INCREASE 2
2 *syn* see THROW UP 1

rupture *n* 1 *syn* see BREACH 3
rel division, divorce, parting
2 *syn* see SEPARATION 1

rupture *vb syn* see OPEN 3
rel divide, divorce, part, separate, sunder; cleave, rend, rive, split

2 *syn* see SEPARATE 1

rural *adj* relating to or characteristic of the country <a peaceful *rural* scene>
syn agrestic, bucolic, campestral, countrified, country, out-country, outland, pastoral, provincial, rustic
rel arcadian, idyllic; natural, simple, unsophisticated
con metropolitan, municipal, oppidan; crammed, crowded, packed, populous; bustling, busy, hustling; artificial, mundane, sophisticated, worldly
ant urban; citified

ruse *n syn* see TRICK 1

rush *vb* 1 to move or cause to move quickly, impetuously, and often heedlessly <*rushed* around madly trying to get things done>
syn boil, bolt, charge, chase, dash, fling, lash, race, shoot, ||swither, tear; *compare* COURSE. HURRY 2, PLUNGE 2, STAMPEDE 2
rel hasten, hurry, speed; dart, fly, scud; break
idiom go off half-cocked, not look before one leaps
2 *syn* see HURRY 2
3 *syn* see COURSE

rush *n* 1 *syn* see HASTE 2
2 *syn* see FLOW

rushing *adj syn* see PRECIPITATE 1

rushlight *n syn* see NONENTITY

rustic *adj syn* see RURAL

rustic *n* an inhabitant of a rural or remote area who is usually characterized by an utter lack of sophistication and cultivation <an unbelieving *rustic* gawking at the skyscrapers>
syn ||apple knocker, ||backwoodser, backwoodsman, bucolic, bumpkin, chawbacon, clodhopper, clown, country jake, countryman, greenhorn, hayseed, hick, hillbilly, hillman, ||hodge, hoosier, jake, jay, joskin, mossback, mountaineer, peasant, provincial, redneck, ||ridge runner, rube, ||wayback, woodsy, yap, ||yob, yokel
rel rural; exurbanite, suburbanite; agriculturalist, farmer, granger, husbandman
con burgher, oppidan, townsman; cityite, urbanite; cosmopolitan, cosmopolite
ant city slicker

rustle *n syn* see HASTE 1

rustler *n syn* see HUSTLER 1

rusty *adj syn* see HARSH 3

||**rusty** *adj syn* see ILL-TEMPERED

rut *n syn* see ROUTINE

ruth *n* 1 *syn* see PITY
2 *syn* see PENITENCE

ruthful *adj syn* see WOEFUL 1

ruthless *adj syn* see GRIM 3

ruttish *adj syn* see LUSTFUL 2

||**ruttle** *vb syn* see RATTLE 1

rutty *adj syn* see LUSTFUL 2

S

sable *adj syn* see BLACK 1
rel dark, dusky, murky; gloomy, somber

sabotage *n* willful effort by indirect means to hinder, prevent, undo, or discredit (as a plan or activity) <*sabotage* of the project by disgruntled officials>
syn subversion, undermining, wreckage, wrecking
rel subversiveness, subversivism; damage, impairment, injury

sabotage *vb* to practice sabotage on <*sabotaged* his opponent's campaign with rumors and smears>
syn subvert, undermine, wreck
rel frustrate, hamper, hinder; block, obstruct; damage; break up, destroy
idiom throw a monkey wrench into
con assist, back, support

saccharine *adj syn* see INGRATIATING
rel candied, cloying, honeyed, oversweet, sugar-candy, sugar-coated, sugared, sugary, sweet, syrupy

sacerdotal *adj* of, relating to, or belonging to priests or priesthood <*sacerdotal* vestments>
syn hieratic, priestal, priestish, priestlike, priestly, sacerdotical

---

rel churchly, ecclesiastical, religious; clerical, ministerial; apostolic, papal

sacerdotical *adj syn* see SACERDOTAL

sack *n syn* see BAG 1
rel container; pocket

sack *vb syn* see DISMISS 3
rel expel, ship; ||bump, ||chuck
idiom give one the sack, send packing

sack *vb syn* see RAVAGE
rel forage, raid; strip

sacker *n syn* see MARAUDER

sacred *adj* 1 *syn* see HOLY 1
rel sacramental; angelic, godly, saintly; cherished
con lay, secular, temporal; earthly; unhallowed
ant profane
2 dedicated to or hallowed by association with a deity <*sacred* songs>
syn numinous, spiritual; *compare* HOLY 1
rel hallowed, sanctified
3 protected (as by law, custom, or human respect) against abuse <a fund *sacred* to charity>
syn inviolable, inviolate, sacrosanct
rel defended, guarded, protected, shielded; immune, untouchable

Sacred Writ *n syn* see BIBLE
idiom Good Book

sacrifice *n syn* see VICTIM 1
rel burnt offering, oblation; sacrification; hecatomb; sin offering

sacrifice *vb* 1 to offer as a victim in sacrifice <Abraham about to *sacrifice* Isaac>

---

syn immolate, victimize
rel offer (up); consecrate, dedicate, devote; donate, give, yield
2 *syn* see LOSE 1
idiom kiss good-bye
3 *syn* see FORGO
rel cede, yield
idiom part with

sacrilege *n syn* see PROFANATION
rel irreverence; heresy; crime, impiety, offense, sin

sacrilegious *adj* involving or marked by debasement or defilement of what is sacred < *sacrilegious* despoilers of ancient churches >
syn blasphemous, profane
rel impious, irreverent, ungodly; evil, sinful, wicked; irreligious
con godly, pious, reverent; religious

sacrosanct *adj syn* see SACRED 3
rel esteemed, regarded, respected

sad *adj* 1 affected with or expressing sadness < was *sad* to see him go >
syn heavyhearted, melancholy, mournful, saddened, sorry, unhappy; *compare* DOWNCAST, MELANCHOLY 2
rel blue, dejected, dispirited, down, downbeat, downcast, drear, dumpish, dumpy; grieving, unenjoying; depressed, morose; depressing, dismal, joyless, mirthless, saddening, triste; desolate
con happy, joyful, joyous; blithe, gay, lighthearted; exalted, fired, inspired, uplifted
ant glad
2 causing sadness < felt miserable after listening to that *sad* song >
syn depressing, joyless, melancholic, melancholy, mournful, saddening, triste; *compare* MELANCHOLY 2
rel dismal, gloomy; afflicting, doleful, dreary, lamentable, sorrowful; pathetic, tear-jerking
con bright, gay, lively; exhilarating, heartwarming, stimulating, stirring
ant happy

sadden *vb syn* see DEPRESS 2
idiom make blue, ‖put into a funk
ant gladden

saddened *adj syn* see SAD 1

saddening *adj syn* see SAD 2

saddle *vb syn* see BURDEN
rel hamper, impede, restrict; impose, inflict
idiom hang like a millstone around one's neck

sadness *n* the quality, state, or an instance of being sad < her feelings of *sadness* and longing persisted long after he left >
syn blues, dejection, depression, dinge, (the) dismals, (the) dolefuls, dumps, dysphoria, gloom, heavyheartedness, melancholy, mopes, mournfulness, suds, unhappiness
rel dispiritedness, doldrums, downcastness, downheartedness, downs, ‖funk, listlessness, moodiness; anguish, grief, sorrow, sorrowfulness, woe; desolation, disconsolateness, disconsolation, forlornness, misery, mourning; blue devils, despondency, hopelessness, megrims, melancholia
idiom slough of despond

con happiness, joy, joyfulness, joyousness; cheerfulness, cheeriness, gayness, lightheartedness, liveliness; exhilaration, ups
ant gladness

safe *adj* 1 having been freed from risk, danger, harm, or injury < refugees who found themselves *safe* at last in a neutral country >
syn scatheless, unharmed, unscathed
rel unhurt, uninjured; intact
idiom in (or with) a whole skin, out of harm's way, safe and sound
con damaged, harmed, hurt, injured
ant unsafe
2 affording security from threat of harm, injury, risk, or loss < found a *safe* place to hide >
syn riskless, secure
rel guarding, protecting, safeguarding, sheltering, shielding; defended, guarded, protected, sheltered, shielded; unthreatened; impregnable, inviolable, invulnerable, unassailable
idiom safe as a bank vault
con insecure, undefended, unguarded, unprotected, vulnerable; threatened; hazardous, risky
ant dangerous, unsafe
3 not threatening danger < it's *safe* to go there only in the daytime >
syn healthy, uninjurious, wholesome; *compare* HARMLESS
rel innocent, innocuous, inoffensive
con hazardous, perilous, precarious, risky; harmful, injurious, unhealthy
ant dangerous, unsafe
4 *syn* see CAUTIOUS

safeguard *n syn* see DEFENSE 1
rel palladium; buffer, screen

safeguard *vb syn* see DEFEND 1
rel conserve, preserve, save; assure, ensure, insure

safekeeping *n* 1 *syn* see CUSTODY
2 *syn* see PRESERVATION 1

safeness *n syn* see SAFETY

safety *n* the quality, state, or condition of being safe < there's *safety* in numbers >
syn assurance, safeness, security
rel cover, protection, shelter; defense; impregnability, inviolability, invulnerability
con hazard, jeopardy, peril, risk, threat; instability, vulnerability
ant danger

sag *vb* 1 *syn* see SLIP 6
2 *syn* see DROOP 3
rel bend, decline; dangle, flap, flop
idiom ‖have a case of the sags
ant tauten

sag *n* 1 *syn* see DEPRESSION 2
rel settling, sinking
2 *syn* see DECLINE 3

sagacious *adj* 1 *syn* see WISE 1
rel clever, intelligent, smart; far-seeing; judicious, prudent, sapient
idiom wise as an owl
con dumb, stupid, unintelligent; ignorant, unlearned, untaught; unperceptive; unwise
2 *syn* see SHREWD
rel critical, discerning, discriminating
idiom wise in the ways of the world

sagaciousness *n syn* see SAGACITY

rel judgment, wiseness

sagacity *n* intelligent application of knowledge < *sagacity* acquired from years of learning and experience>
syn insight, sagaciousness, sageness, sapience, wisdom
rel discernment, penetration, perception, perceptiveness, sensitivity; understanding; judiciousness, prudence; comprehension, grasp

sage *adj* 1 *syn* see WISE 1
rel philosophic; learned; profound
2 *syn* see WISE 2
rel acute, penetrating, probing

sage *n* one distinguished for his breadth of knowledge, experience, wisdom, and sound judgment <was one of the renowned *sages* of constitutional law>
syn savant, scholar, wise man
rel expert, master

sageness *n* *syn* see SAGACITY

said *adj* *syn* see SUCH 1

sail *vb* 1 *syn* see FLY 1
2 *syn* see FLY 4

sailor *n* *syn* see MARINER

sailorman *n* *syn* see MARINER

saintliness *n* *syn* see HOLINESS
rel righteousness, worthiness

saintly *adj* being of deeply religious and wholly upright character <a *saintly* old couple>
syn angelic, godly, holy
rel righteous, upright, upstanding, virtuous, worthy; devout, God-fearing, pious; sainted; seraph, seraphic, seraphlike
idiom pure in mind and heart

salable *adj* *syn* see MARKETABLE
ant unsalable

salacious *adj* *syn* see LICENTIOUS 2

salad *n* *syn* see MISCELLANY 1

salary *n* *syn* see WAGE

salient *adj* *syn* see NOTICEABLE
rel important, pertinent, significant, weighty; impressive, moving; obvious, pronounced; intrusive, obtrusive

saliferous *adj* *syn* see SALTY 1

saline *adj* *syn* see SALTY 1

saliva *n* a liquid secreted into the mouth and helpful to digestion <*saliva* drooled down the baby's chin>
syn slaver, spit, spittle, water
rel sputum

salivate *vb* *syn* see DROOL 2

sally *n* 1 *syn* see OUTBURST 1
2 *syn* see JOKE 1
3 *syn* see EXCURSION 1

salmagundi *n* *syn* see MISCELLANY 1

salon *n* 1 a spacious elegant apartment or living room (as in a fashionable house) <her *salon* was decorated à la Louis XV>
syn drawing room, saloon
rel parlor; suite
2 a fashionable assemblage of notables held by custom at the home of a prominent person <was famous for her literary *salons*>
syn saloon

---

syn synonym(s)   *rel* related word(s)
ant antonym(s)   *con* contrasted word(s)
idiom idiomatic equivalent(s)
‖ use limited; if in doubt, see a dictionary

rel at home; reception; levee; evening, soiree

saloon *n* 1 *syn* see SALON 1
rel gallery; hall
2 *syn* see SALON 2
rel gathering, party
3 *syn* see BAR 5

saloonist *n* *syn* see SALOONKEEPER

saloonkeeper *n* one who owns or manages a bar <the traditional image of the fat cigar-smoking *saloonkeeper*>
syn barkeeper, boniface, innholder, innkeeper, ‖publican, saloonist, taverner; *compare* BARTENDER
rel victualler

salt *n* 1 *syn* see LIVING
2 *syn* see MARINER

salt *adj* *syn* see SALTY 1

saltate *vb* *syn* see JUMP 1

salt away *vb* *syn* see SAVE 4

saltimbanque *n* *syn* see CHARLATAN
rel impostor, pretender; cheat, fraud

salty *adj* 1 of, relating to, or containing salt < *salty* deposits>
syn saliferous, saline, salt
rel brackish, briny, saltish; salted
ant saltless
2 *syn* see RISQUÉ
3 *syn* see CAUSTIC 1

salubrious *adj* *syn* see HEALTHFUL
rel bracing, invigorating, stimulating
ant insalubrious

salutary *adj* *syn* see HEALTHFUL
rel restorative, sanative, sanatory, tonic
con debilitating, enfeebling, weakening; bad, evil
ant deleterious; unsalutary

salutation *n* 1 *syn* see GREETING
2 *syn* see ENCOMIUM

salute *vb* *syn* see ADDRESS 7

salute *n* *syn* see GREETING

salutiferous *adj* *syn* see HEALTHFUL

salvage *vb* to rescue and save from wreckage, destruction, or loss < *salvaged* the torpedoed vessel>
syn salve
rel deliver, redeem, rescue, save; reclaim, recover, regain, retrieve; ransom
con dump, jettison

salvation *n* 1 *syn* see PRESERVATION 1
2 *syn* see CONSERVATION 1

salve *n* *syn* see OINTMENT
rel emollient, lubricant; counterirritant; aid, remedy

salve *vb* *syn* see SALVAGE

salvo *n* 1 *syn* see BARRAGE
rel discharge; spray
2 *syn* see TESTIMONIAL 3

same *adj* 1 being one rather than another or more <went to the *same* hotel each summer>
syn exact, identical, selfsame, very
rel comparable, like, similar
ant different
2 agreeing fundamentally or absolutely <all the family have the *same* dark eyes>
syn duplicate, equal, equivalent, identic, identical, indistinguishable, tantamount; *compare* LIKE
rel comparable, like, similar; coequal
ant different
3 not changing or fluctuating <treated everyone with the *same* courtesy>

syn consistent, constant, invariable, unchanging, unfailing, unvarying

con changeable, fluctuant, inconsistent, inconstant, irregular, variable, varying

sameness *n* 1 *syn* see IDENTITY 1
rel alikeness; uniformity, uniformness, unity

2 *syn* see EQUIVALENCE
rel analogy; resemblance, similarity

sample *n syn* see INSTANCE
rel indication, sign; fragment, part, piece, portion, segment; constituent, element; individual, unit

sampling *n syn* see INSTANCE

sanative *adj syn* see CURATIVE
rel healthful, hygienic, salutary, sanitary

sanatory *adj syn* see CURATIVE

sanctified *adj syn* see HOLY 1
rel canonized, deified, sainted
ant unsanctified

sanctify *vb syn* see BLESS 1

sanctimonious *adj syn* see HYPOCRITICAL
rel deceiving, false; snuffling
ant unsanctimonious

sanctimoniousness *n syn* see HYPOCRISY
idiom odor of sanctity
ant unsanctimoniousness

sanctimony *n syn* see HYPOCRISY

sanction *n* 1 explicit authoritative permission or recognition that gives validity to acts of a subordinate <a colonial governor acting under the *sanction* of the king>
syn endorsement, fiat
rel approval, authorization, consent, permission; approbation, confirmation, encouragement, ratification, recommendation, support
con restraint; debarment; interdict, prohibition; disapprobation, disapproval, objection
ant interdiction

2 *syn* see PERMISSION

sanction *vb syn* see APPROVE 2
rel authorize, commission, license
con ban, disallow, forbid, prohibit
ant interdict

sanctioned *adj syn* see ORTHODOX 1
ant unsanctioned

sanctity *n syn* see HOLINESS
rel godliness; righteousness, uprightness

sanctorium *n syn* see SHRINE

sanctuary *n* 1 *syn* see SHRINE

2 *syn* see SHELTER 1
rel bamah; oasis

3 *syn* see REFUGE 1

sanctum *n syn* see SHRINE

sand *n syn* see FORTITUDE
rel chutzpah, gall
idiom true (or clear) grit

sandwich shop *n syn* see EATING HOUSE

sane *adj* 1 *syn* see HEALTHY 1

2 free from mental disorder <a thoroughly *sane* and well-balanced man>
syn all there, compos mentis, lucid, normal, right
rel balanced, oriented; levelheaded, rational, sensible, sober, sound
idiom of sound mind
con abnormal, unbalanced; neurotic, paranoid, psychopathic, psychotic, schizophrenic; balmy, crazy, ||cuckoo, non com-

pos, non compos mentis, nuts, screwy; deranged, lunatic, mad, wild
ant insane

3 *syn* see WISE 2
rel logical, rational, reasonable; good, right; cogent, compelling, convincing, sound
con imprudent, injudicious, unwise

saneness *n syn* see WIT 2
rel clear-mindedness, perception; comprehension, ||smarts, understanding

sangfroid *n syn* see EQUANIMITY
rel self-containment, self-control; aloofness, coolheadedness, indifference, unconcern

sanguinary *adj* 1 *syn* see MURDEROUS

2 *syn* see BLOODY 1
ant unsanguinary

sanguine *adj* 1 *syn* see BLOODY 1

2 *syn* see MURDEROUS

3 *syn* see RUDDY

4 *syn* see CONFIDENT 1
rel expectant; hopeful, undespairing
idiom full of hope
ant hopeless

5 *syn* see OPTIMISTIC
ant unsanguine

sanguineness *n syn* see OPTIMISM

sanguineous *adj* 1 *syn* see BLOODY 1

2 *syn* see MURDEROUS

sanguinity *n syn* see OPTIMISM

sanity *n syn* see WIT 2
rel intelligence; comprehension
idiom sound mind
ant insanity

sans *prep syn* see WITHOUT 2

sap *n syn* see FOOL 3

sap *vb syn* see WEAKEN 1
rel deplete, drain, exhaust, knock out; ruin, wreck; destroy

saphead *n syn* see FOOL 3
rel ||boob, jerk

sapid *adj syn* see PALATABLE
idiom fit for a king
con bland, tasteless; repulsive, unpalatable
ant insipid

sapidity *n syn* see TASTE 3
ant insipidity

sapience *n syn* see SAGACITY

sapient *adj syn* see WISE 2
rel erudite, learned, scholarly; thinking; discriminating, sapiential

sapless *adj syn* see INSIPID 3

sapor *n syn* see TASTE 3

saporous *adj syn* see PALATABLE

sappy *adj syn* 1 *syn* SUCCULENT, juicy

2 *syn* see SENTIMENTAL

3 *syn* see FOOLISH 2

sarcasm *n* a savage bitter form of humor usually intended to hurt or wound <a speech full of personal jabs and *sarcasm*>
syn acerbity, causticity, corrosiveness, sarcasticness
rel humor, irony, raillery, satire, wit; jest, repartee; gibe, lampooning; mockery, ridicule, scorn, sneering; acrimony, invective; rancor, sharpness
con playfulness, waggishness, whimsicality

sarcastic *adj* marked by, expressive of, or given to sarcasm <a critic noted for his

sarcastic comments on actors' performances >
syn acerb, acerbic, archilochian, caustic, corrosive, ‖sarky; compare CAUSTIC 1
rel dry; cynical, ironic, sardonic, satiric; jeering, mocking, scornful; biting, cutting, incisive; mordant, scathing, sharp, stinging; pungent, tart, trenchant
con droll, playful, sportive, waggish, whimsical

sarcasticness *n syn* see SARCASM
rel bitingness, cuttingness, incisiveness, trenchancy; derision, mocking, taunting

sardonic *adj* characterized by or expressing disdainful, skeptical humor < had a *sardonic* smile that mirrored his fixed expectation of the worst from everyone >
syn cynical, ironic, wry
rel contemptuous, disdainful, scornful; derisive, jeering, mocking, saturnine, sneering; caustic, corrosive, sarcastic, satiric

‖**sarky** *adj syn* see SARCASTIC

sash *n syn* see BELT 1

sashay *vb* to move about often self-consciously and usually in a conspicuous manner < *sashaying* around, trying to walk like a model >
syn flounce, mince, prance, ‖prink, strut
rel swagger

sass *n syn* see BACK TALK
rel impertinence, insolence, sassiness

sassy *adj* 1 *syn* see WISE 5
rel brazen, unabashed; audacious
2 *syn* see DAPPER

Satan *n* 1 *syn* see DEVIL 1
rel deuce; Mephistopheles; devil-god
idiom fallen angel, lord of the underworld, prince of darkness
2 *syn* see DEVIL 2
rel renegade, villain; beast, viper

satanic *adj* 1 of, relating to, or characteristic of Satan < *Satanic* rites >
syn devilish, diabolic, Mephistophelian
rel saturnine
2 *syn* see FIENDISH
rel evil, wicked

satanism *n* the worship of Satan usually marked by the travesty of Christian rites < interpreted *satanism* as an offshoot of the belief in two coequal and coeternal principles of good and evil >
syn diabolism
rel Black Mass

sate *vb* 1 *syn* see SATIATE
rel overfill, overstuff, stuff
idiom have (or give) a bellyful of, have (or give) an overdose of

sated *adj syn* see SATIATED
ant unsated

satellite *n syn* see FOLLOWER
rel favorite, minion

satellite *adj syn* see CONCOMITANT

satiate *adj syn* see SATIATED
idiom stuffed to the gills
con insatiable, unsatiable
ant insatiate, unsatiate

satiate *vb* to satisfy fully or to repletion < tried to titillate rather than *satiate* his readers' interest >
syn cloy, fill, glut, gorge, jade, pall, sate, ‖stall, stodge, surfeit; compare SATISFY 3
rel content, fulfill, gratify, indulge, satisfy; overdose, stuff
con coax, court, invite, pique, tantalize, tempt, titillate

satiated *adj* filled to repletion < the mob, *satiated* with violence, finally dispersed >
syn full, glutted, gorged, jaded, sated, satiate, surfeited
rel fulfilled, gratified, indulged, satisfied
con avid, greedy, ravening; craving, hungering, hungry, lusting, thirsting, thirsty
ant unsatiated

satiny *adj syn* see SOFT 3

satire *n* humorous ridicule often used to convey rebuke or criticism or to expose folly or vice < a brilliant writer noted for his *satire* >
syn lampoonery, raillery, satiricalness
rel banter, chaffing; causticity, irony; mockery, ridicule; pasquinade, persiflage, squib; parody, spoof, spoofery, takeoff

satiric *adj* of, relating to, characterized by, or based on satire < witty, eloquent, and *satiric* sermons >
syn lampooning, satirizing
rel bantering, chaffing; caustic, ironic; mocking, ridiculing; parodying, spoofing; farcical; Rabelaisian

satiricalness *n syn* see SATIRE

satirizing *adj syn* see SATIRIC

satisfactorily *adv syn* see WELL 4
rel competently, sufficiently
ant unsatisfactorily

satisfactory *adj* 1 *syn* see SUFFICIENT 1
ant unsatisfactory
2 *syn* see VALID
ant unsatisfactory
3 *syn* see DECENT 4
rel fair, goodish, passable
ant unsatisfactory

satisfy *vb* 1 *syn* see CLEAR 5
2 *syn* see SUIT 6
3 to satiate desires or longings < strove to *satisfy* his lust for money and power >
syn appease, content, gratify; compare SATIATE
rel gladden, humor, indulge, please; sate, satiate; pacify, placate
con tantalize, tease; excite, pique, provoke, stimulate; arouse
4 *syn* see ASSURE 2
rel induce, inveigle, win (over)
5 measure up to a set of criteria or requirements < courses taken to *satisfy* requirements for graduation >
syn answer, fill, fulfill, meet
rel comply (with), conform (to), serve; do, suffice
idiom fill the bill, make good

satisfying *adj syn* see VALID
ant unsatisfying

satisfyingly *adv syn* see WELL 5
rel gratifyingly, pleasingly
ant unsatisfyingly

saturate *vb* 1 *syn* see SOAK 1
rel bathe, douche, wash; imbue, infuse, suffuse
2 *syn* see PERMEATE

---

syn synonym(s)   *rel* related word(s)
ant antonym(s)   *con* contrasted word(s)
idiom idiomatic equivalent(s)
‖ use limited; if in doubt, see a dictionary

rel pierce, probe; inoculate, instill

saturate *adj syn* see WET 1

saturated *adj syn* see WET 1

saturnalia *n syn* see ORGY 2

saturnine *adj syn* see SULLEN

rel grave, serious, solemn, somber, staid; moping; dark, funereal; reserved, silent, taciturn, uncommunicative

con cheerful, cheery, happy; cordial, polite

ant genial

satyric *adj* 1 *syn* see LICENTIOUS 2

2 *syn* see LUSTFUL 2

sauce *n* 1 *syn* see BACK TALK

rel pertness, sauciness

||2 *syn* see LIQUOR 2

saucebox *n syn* see MINX

saucy *adj* flippant and bold in manner or attitude <a *saucy* little flirt>

syn arch, bantam, ||cocket, malapert, pert

rel flippant, frivolous, light-minded, volatile, bold, brash, combative; impertinent, impudent, insolent; intrusive, meddlesome, obtrusive; smart, smart-alecky, wise

con gentle, meek, mild, quiet, subdued

ant deferential

2 *syn* see INSOLENT 2

sault *n syn* see WATERFALL

saunter *vb* to walk slowly in an idle or leisurely manner <*sauntered* about the streets, stopping in at various shops>

syn amble, bummel, drift, linger, mope, mosey, ||muck, stroll; *compare* WANDER 1

rel meander, ramble, roam, rove, spatiate, ||stravage, wander; loiter, tarry

con bustle, chase, hustle, scurry, tear

saunter *n syn* see WALK 1

savage *adj* 1 being undomesticated and often destructive or ferocious through lack of restraints or human control <*savage* dogs>

syn feral, vicious, wild; *compare* WILD 1

rel uncivilized, undomesticated, unsocialized; unbroken, unsubdued, untamed; bestial, brutal, brute; ferocious, fierce

con civilized, domesticated, socialized; broken, subdued, tamed; domestic, tame

2 *syn* see FIERCE 1

rel coldhearted, heartless, implacable, relentless, unrelenting; rapacious, ravenous, voracious; bloodthirsty, bloody, butcherly, murderous, rabid

3 *syn* see BARBARIAN 1

rel primeval, primitive; uncontrolled, unharnessed; harsh, rough, rugged

savant *n syn* see SAGE

save *vb* 1 *syn* see RESCUE

rel unchain, unshackle

idiom snatch from the jaws of death

con desert, leave; condemn, damn

2 *syn* see MAINTAIN 1

3 to keep secure or maintain intact from injury, decay, or loss <regular painting helps *save* the wood>

syn conserve, preserve; *compare* MAINTAIN 1

rel defend, guard, protect, safeguard, shield

con draw (out), withdraw; consume, spend, use up

4 to accumulate and store up (a supply) for future use <*saved* his money for college>

syn lay aside, lay away, lay by, lay in, lay up, put by, salt away, ||spare; *compare* HOARD

rel accumulate, cache, collect, stockpile, store (up); hoard, squirrel, stash (away), conserve, husband, manage; keep, reserve, set by; deposit, stow

idiom feather one's nest, keep as a nest egg, save for a rainy day, save to fall back on

con lose, squander, use up, waste

ant consume, spend

5 *syn* see ECONOMIZE

save *prep syn* see EXCEPT

save *conj* 1 *syn* see ONLY

2 *syn* see EXCEPT 1

save-all *adj syn* see STINGY

saving *n* 1 *syn* see PRESERVATION 1

2 *syn* see CONSERVATION 1

saving *prep syn* see EXCEPT

saving *conj syn* see EXCEPT 1

saving *adj syn* see SPARING

savoir faire *n syn* see TACT

rel manners; dignity, elegance, grace; refinement, savoir vivre, taste; aplomb, confidence, self-assurance, self-possession; experience, blaséness, sophistication

con awkwardness, clumsiness, gaucherie, ineptness, maladroitness

savor *n* 1 *syn* see TASTE 3

rel scent, tinge

2 *syn* see QUALITY 1

savor *vb* 1 *syn* see SMACK

2 *syn* see FEEL 2

3 *syn* see RELISH 2

savorless *adj syn* see UNPALATABLE 1

rel bland; thin, watery, weak; unpleasing

con appetizing, pleasing, tempting; piquant, spicy

ant savory

savorous *adj syn* see PALATABLE

savorsome *adj syn* see PALATABLE

savory *adj* 1 *syn* see PALATABLE

rel pleasing, tempting; gustful

con acrid, sharp, strong

ant unsavory

2 *syn* see SWEET 2

||**savvy** *adj syn* see SHREWD

saw *n syn* see SAYING

||**sawbones** *n syn* see PHYSICIAN

sawbuck *n syn* see SAWHORSE

saw-edged *adj syn* see SERRATE

sawhorse *n* a rack on which something (as a board) is laid for sawing <*sawhorses* in the carpentry shop>

syn buck, horse, sawbuck, trestle, workhorse

sawtooth *adj syn* see SERRATE

saw-toothed *adj syn* see SERRATE

say *vb* 1 to express in words <learn to *say* what you mean>

syn bring out, chime in, come out (with), declare, deliver, state, tell, throw out, utter; *compare* EXPRESS 2

rel breathe; articulate, enunciate, pronounce; announce, proclaim; animadvert, comment, give, remark; cite, quote, recite, repeat; affirm, assert, aver, avow, protest

idiom out with, put in (or into) words, put it

2 *syn* see ARTICULATE 2

rel speak, talk

3 *syn* see SHOW 5

say *n syn* see VOICE 2
    rel authority; decision
say *adv syn* see NEARLY
saying *n* an oft-repeated statement usually
    involving common experience or observa-
    tion < the old *saying* that ignorance is
    bliss >
    syn adage, byword, proverb, saw, word
    rel dictum, maxim; truism
say-so *n syn* see VOICE 2
scabrous *adj syn* see ROUGH 1
    rel scabby, scaly, scurfy; downy; knobby,
    knotty; bristly, prickly, thorny
    con bald, glabrescent
    ant glabrous, smooth
scad *n, usu* **scads** *pl* a great number or
    abundance < *scads* of opportunities >
    syn gob(s), heap, jillion, load(s), million,
    oodles, quantities, ream(s), ‖rimption(s),
    slather(s), slew, thousand, trillion, wad(s);
    compare MUCH, MULTITUDE 1
    rel great deal, lot
    con few, handful, scattering, sprinkle,
    sprinkling
scalawag *n syn* see SCAMP
scalding *adj syn* see HOT 1
    ant freezing
scale *vb* 1 *syn* see SKIN 2
    2 to shed scales or fragmentary surface
    matter < *scaling* skin >
    syn desquamate, exfoliate, flake (off), peel
    rel chip (off), spall (off)
scale *n syn* see DEGREE 2
scale *vb* 1 *syn* see ASCEND 1
    2 *syn* see MEASURE 2
‖**scamble** *vb syn* see SPRAWL 1
scamp *n* a pleasantly mischievous person
    < what have those little *scamps* done
    now >
    syn devil, enfant terrible, limb, mischief,
    pixie, rapscallion, rascal, ribald, rogue,
    scalawag, skeezicks, slyboots, villain
    rel bird, chap, dog, ‖duck; ‖bleeder;
    joker, prankster
    con sobersides
scamper *vb* 1 *syn* see RUN 2
    rel hasten (off), hurry (away *or* off), light
    out, speed (away); dash (off), rush (off),
    shoot, tear (off), whip (off), whiz (off)
    2 *syn* see RUN 1
    rel scud, scuddle, scuttle
scan *vb syn* see BROWSE
    idiom pass one's eye over
scan *n syn* see EXAMINATION
    rel perusal; observation, reconnaissance
scandal *n syn* see DETRACTION
    rel aspersion; reproach; discredit, disre-
    pute
‖**scandal** *vb syn* see MALIGN
scandalize *vb* 1 *syn* see MALIGN
    2 *syn* see SHOCK 1
scandalizer *n syn* see GOSSIP 1
    rel blabber, blabbermouth, talker
scandalmonger *n syn* see GOSSIP 1
    rel meddler, snoop; backbiter; muckraker
scandalous *adj* 1 *syn* see LIBELOUS
    2 *syn* see OUTRAGEOUS 2
‖**scant** *n syn* see SCARCITY

---

syn synonym(s)   *rel* related word(s)
ant antonym(s)   *con* contrasted word(s)
idiom idiomatic equivalent(s)
‖ use limited: if in doubt, see a dictionary

scant *adj* ‖1 *syn* see STINGY
    2 *syn* see SHORT 3
    3 *syn* see MEAGER 2
    ant ample
scant *vb syn* see SPARE 3
scantiness *n syn* see FAILURE 3
    rel scarceness, scarcity; sparseness, spar-
    sity
    con excess, overage, surplus
scanty *adj* 1 *syn* see MEAGER 2
    rel scarce, wanting
    con ample, enough; profuse
    ant plentiful
    2 *syn* see SHORT 3
scape *vb syn* see ESCAPE 1
‖**scape** *n syn* see ESCAPE 1
scape *n syn* see VISTA
scapegoat *n* one that bears the blame for
    another or others < was made the *scape-
    goat* for his boss's errors >
    syn fall guy, goat, patsy, whipping boy
    rel mark, target; victim
scapegrace *n syn* see WASTREL 1
scar *n* a mark left by the healing of injured
    tissue < still had *scars* from the opera-
    tion >
    syn cicatrix, scarification
    rel blemish, defect, flaw; blister, pock-
    mark, scab; disfigurement
scar *vb* to mark with a scar < burns that
    had *scarred* his face >
    syn cicatrize, scarify
    rel cut, score, scratch; blemish, disfigure,
    flaw, mar; damage, deface
scarce *adj* 1 *syn* see SHORT 3
    rel curtailed, shortened, truncated
    con adequate, sufficient, unwanting
    ant abundant
    2 *syn* see INFREQUENT
    idiom scarce as ice water in hell, scarcer
    than hen's teeth, seldom met with
scarce *adv syn* see JUST 2
scarcely *adv syn* see JUST 2
    idiom just barely, only just
scarceness *n syn* see SCARCITY
scarcity *n* smallness of supply, quantity,
    or number in proportion to demand < a
    serious *scarcity* of grain >
    syn insufficience, insufficiency, paucity,
    poverty, ‖scant, scarceness; *compare* FAIL-
    URE 3
    rel deficiency, shortage, underage; mea-
    gerness; rareness, uncommonness; absence,
    dearth, lack
    con sufficiency; great deal, much; over-
    abundance, overage, oversupply, surplus
    ant abundance
scare *vb syn* see FRIGHTEN
    rel panic, shake up; freeze, paralyze, pet-
    rify
    idiom give a scare to, strike terror into
    the heart of, throw a scare into
scarecrow *n syn* see RAGAMUFFIN
scared *adj syn* see AFRAID 1
    rel startled; panicked, panicky, terror=
    stricken
    con emboldened, heartened, reassured;
    aggressive, bold
    ant unafraid, unscared
scarification *n syn* see SCAR
scarify *vb* 1 *syn* see SCAR
    rel deform, disfigure, maim, mar
    2 *syn* see LAMBASTE 3

scary *adj syn* see AFRAID 1

scathe *vb syn* see LAMBASTE 3
  idiom ‖give holy hell, give the business, rip (someone) up one side and down the other

scatheless *n syn* see SAFE 1

scathing *adj syn* see CAUSTIC 1
  rel brutal; burning, scorching, searing, sulphurous

scatological *adj syn* see OBSCENE 2

scatter *vb* 1 to cause to separate or break up < the rain *scattered* the crowd >
  syn dispel, disperse, dissipate
  rel break up, shatter; disband; diverge, divide, part, separate, sever
  con assemble, congregate, convene; accumulate, amass, collect, concentrate, crowd
  ant gather
  2 *syn* see STREW 1
  rel dispense, distribute; cast, discard, shed; besprinkle, sprinkle
  con accumulate, amass, concentrate
  ant collect

scatterbrain *n* a flighty thoughtless person < his wife is a *scatterbrain* >
  syn birdbrain, featherbrain, featherhead, flibbertigibbet, harebrain, rattlebrain, rattlehead, shatterbrain
  rel fool, goose, silly, simpleton

scatterbrained *adj syn* see GIDDY 1

scattergood *n syn* see SPENDTHRIFT

scattering *n syn* see FEW

scene *n* 1 the total arrangement of the objects that form the scenic environment in which a drama is enacted < spectacle plays that attempt a realistic, three-dimensional *scene* >
  syn mise-en-scène, scenery, set, setting, stage set, stage setting
  rel hangings, scene cloth; ‖back cloth, backdrop, background; tableau
  2 *syn* see VIEW 4
  3 the place of an occurrence or action < the *scene* of the crime >
  syn locale, mise-en-scène, site
  rel locality, location, place, spot
  4 a sphere of activity, interest, or controversy < the drug *scene* >
  syn arena
  rel compass, field, setting, sphere; culture, environment, milieu

scenery *n syn* see SCENE 1
  rel decor; furnishings, furniture; properties, props

scent *vb syn* see SMELL 1
  2 to imbue or fill with an odor < air *scented* with herbs >
  syn aromatize, odorize, perfume

scent *n* 1 *syn* see SMELL 1
  rel essence, whiff
  2 *syn* see FRAGRANCE

scented *adj* 1 *syn* see SWEET 2
  2 *syn* see ODOROUS
  ant scentless, unscented

scentless *adj syn* see ODORLESS

schedule *n* 1 *syn* see LIST
  rel chart, table
  2 *syn* see PROGRAM 1

schedule *vb* 1 to place in a schedule < *schedule* a new train >
  syn card, sked
  rel list, record, slate
  2 *syn* see TIME 1

scheme *n* 1 *syn* see PLAN 1
  rel presentation, proposal, proposition, suggestion; arrangement, order, ordering; contrivance, device, expedient
  2 *syn* see PLOT 2

scheme (out) *vb syn* see PLOT

schism *n* 1 *syn* see BREACH 3
  2 *syn* see HERESY
  3 a division of a group into two discordant groups < a *schism* within a political party >
  syn chasm, cleavage, cleft, split; *compare* BREACH 3
  rel divergence, division, separation; breach, break, rupture; estrangement
  con unification, unity; reconciliation

schismatic *n syn* see HERETIC
  rel protester; skeptic, radical, Young Turk

schismatic *adj syn* see HERETICAL
  rel rebellious; unconventional

schismatist *n syn* see HERETIC

‖**schlemiel** *n syn* see FOOL 3

‖**schmo** *n syn* see FOOL 1

‖**schmuck** *n syn* see FOOL 1

‖**schnook** *n syn* see DUNCE

‖**schnorrer** *n syn* see BEGGAR 1

‖**schnozzle** *n syn* see NOSE 1

scholar *n syn* see SAGE
  rel pupil, student; bookman; polymath

scholarliness *n syn* see ERUDITION 2
  ant unscholarliness

scholarly *adj syn* see LEARNED
  rel studious; intellectual, long-hair; educated, taught, trained
  con untaught, untrained
  ant unscholarly

scholarship *n* 1 *syn* see EDUCATION 2
  2 *syn* see ERUDITION 2

scholastic *adj* 1 *syn* see PEDANTIC
  rel lettered, literary; scholarly; formal
  2 *syn* see LEARNED
  rel conversant, versed
  con unconversant, unscholarly

school *vb syn* see TEACH
  rel inform; guide, lead, show; advance, cultivate; control, direct, manage

schooling *n syn* see EDUCATION 1
  rel knowledge; book learning, booklore

schoolmasterish *adj syn* see DIDACTIC

science *n* 1 *syn* see KNOWLEDGE 2
  2 *syn* see EDUCATION 2

scilicet *adv syn* see NAMELY

scintillate *vb syn* see FLASH 1

scintillating *adj syn* see CLEVER 5

scintillation *n syn* see FLASH 1

scions *n pl syn* see OFFSPRING

scoff *vb* to show contempt by derision or mockery < heard his tale and *scoffed* at it >
  syn fleer, flout, gibe, gird, jeer, jest, quip (at), scout (at), sneer
  rel pooh-pooh; deride, mock, rally, ridicule, taunt, twit; contemn, despise, disdain, scorn; boo
  con accept, approve, commend; compliment; acclaim, laud, praise

scoff *n syn* see FOOD 1

scold *n syn* see VIRAGO

scold *vb* 1 to reproach angrily and abusively < loudly *scolded* him for staying out late >
  syn baste, bawl out, berate, ‖bless out, ‖cample, ‖carpet, ‖chew, ‖chew out, dress

down, jaw, lash, ║mob, rag, rail, rant, rate, ║ream out, revile, ║row, tell off, tongue, tongue-lash, ║tongue-walk, upbraid, vituperate, wig; *compare* CRITICIZE, LAMBASTE 3, REPROVE

rel blame, censure, criticize, denounce, reprehend, reprobate; admonish, chide, rebuke, reprimand, reproach, reprove; execrate, objurate; brace, grill, harass, hound; blister, excoriate

idiom jump down one's throat, rake over the coals, read one the riot act, walk into

2 *syn* see GRUMBLE 1

sconce *n syn* see HEAD 1

scoop *n* a news story first obtained and reported by only one source (as a newspaper) < the story was a *scoop* by just a few hours >

syn beat, exclusive

scoop *vb* 1 *syn* see DIP 2

rel gather; lift, pick up

2 *syn* see DIG 2

rel gouge, grub

3 to report a news item in advance of competitors < CBS *scooped* NBC on that story >

syn beat

scoot *vb* 1 *syn* see HURRY 2

2 *syn* see RUN 1

3 *syn* see RUN 2

scope *n* 1 *syn* see ROOM 3

2 *syn* see RANGE 2

3 *syn* see BREADTH 2

scopic *adj syn* see EXTENSIVE 1

scopious *adj syn* see EXTENSIVE 1

scorch *vb* 1 *syn* see LAMBASTE 3

2 *syn* see BURN 3

rel seethe, simmer, stew; ║plot

scorching *adj syn* see HOT 1

idiom scorching hot, sizzling hot

score *n* 1 *scores pl syn* see MULTITUDE 1

2 a slight cut or line made with or as if with a sharp instrument < cut *scores* on the ham before baking it >

syn scotch, scratch

rel line, mark; nick, notch, serration; cut, slit; cleft, furrow, groove, indentation; gash

3 *syn* see BILL 1

4 an obligation or injury kept in mind for future reckoning < had a *score* to settle with him >

syn account

rel grudge

5 the number of points gained by contestants in a game or contest < a record *score* of 263 for 72 holes >

syn tally

rel account, record; summary, total

idiom the final count

score *vb* 1 *syn* see LAMBASTE 3

rel ream out

idiom tear to pieces

2 *syn* see GAIN 1

3 *syn* see SUCCEED 3

scorn *n syn* see DESPITE 1

rel flouting, gibing, jeering, scoffing; derision, mockery, ridicule, taunt, taunting

---

syn synonym(s)   *rel* related word(s)
ant antonym(s)   *con* contrasted word(s)
idiom idiomatic equivalent(s)
║ use limited; if in doubt, see a dictionary

con consideration, respectfulness

ant respect

scorn *vb syn* see DESPISE

rel flout, gibe, jeer, scoff; mock, ridicule, taunt

idiom hold in utter contempt

con accept, acknowledge, welcome

ant respect

scotch *n syn* see SCORE 2

scotch *adj syn* see SPARING

Scotch *adj syn* see SPARING

scoundrel *n syn* see VILLAIN 1

scour *vb* 1 *syn* see HURRY 2

2 to make a thorough search or examination of < *scoured* the neighborhood for the lost child >

syn beat, comb, finecomb, fine-tooth-comb, forage, grub, rake, ransack, rummage, search

rel rout; look (for), seek; fan, range; rifle; ferret (out), find

idiom beat the bushes, leave no stone unturned, look high and low, look up and down, turn inside out, turn upside down

scour *vb* 1 *syn* see SCRUB 1

2 *syn* see EAT 3

scour *n, usu scours pl syn* see DIARRHEA

scourge *n syn* see PLAGUE 1

scourge *vb* 1 *syn* see WHIP 1

rel hit; knout; frail, whop

idiom whip to ribbons

2 *syn* see RAVAGE

3 *syn* see LAMBASTE 3

scout *vb* to explore in order to obtain information < forward observers *scouted* the terrain before the attack >

syn probe, reconnoiter

rel look (over), survey; observe; check out, examine; ║case, inspect

idiom run reconnaissance

scout *vb* 1 *syn* see RIDICULE

2 *syn* see DESPISE

rel mock, ridicule

scout (at) *vb syn* see SCOFF

scowl *vb syn* see FROWN 1

idiom look black as thunder, pull a face (or scowl)

scrabble *vb* 1 *syn* see SCRIBBLE

2 *syn* see SCRAMBLE 1

scrag *vb* 1 *syn* see HANG 2

2 *syn* see KILL 1

3 *syn* see MURDER 1

scraggy *adj* 1 *syn* see ROUGH 1

2 *syn* see LEAN

rel gangling, spindling, spindly; skeletal; dwarfed, scrubby, stunted, undersize

scram *vb syn* see GET OUT 1

idiom ║beat it, ║cheese it, ║get the hell out

scramble *vb* 1 to move or climb hastily on all fours < *scrambled* across the rocks >

syn clamber, scrabble, ║spartle, ║sprauchle

rel scurry, scuttle

2 *syn* see SPRAWL 2

scramble *n syn* see CLUTTER 2

rel conglomeration

scrap *n* 1 *syn* see END 4

rel chip, cutting; scrappage, waste

2 *syn* see PARTICLE

scrap *vb syn* see DISCARD

idiom consign to the scrap heap

scrap *n syn* see BRAWL 2

scrap *vb syn* see QUARREL

scrape *vb* 1 to rub or slide against something that is often harsh, rough, or sharp < chalk *scraping* on the blackboard >

syn grate, rasp, scratch
rel graze, rub, scuff; abrade, chafe, grind
2 syn see SCRIMP
3 to make one's way with great difficulty or succeed by a narrow margin < the student barely *scraped* through the exam >
syn shave
rel struggle; get along, get by
idiom cut it (or the corner) pretty close, have a close shave
scrape n syn see PREDICAMENT
rel trouble; discomfiture, embarrassment
scrapping n syn see DISPOSAL 2
scrappy adj 1 syn see QUARRELSOME 2
2 syn see BELLIGERENT
scratch vb 1 syn see SCRAPE 1
rel squeak, squeal
2 syn see SCRIBBLE
scratch n 1 syn see SCORE 2
‖2 syn see MONEY
scrawl vb syn see SCRIBBLE
rel inscribe; doodle
scrawny adj syn see LEAN
idiom just (or nothing but) skin and bones
ant brawny
screak vb syn see SQUEAL 2
scream vb 1 to voice a sudden piercing loud cry often in shock, terror, or pain < *screamed* at the sight of the accident and then fainted >
syn screech, shriek, shrill, squeal; compare SHOUT 1
rel screak, squeak; cry, yell; bellow, roar; caterwaul, howl, wail, ‖yawl
idiom let out a scream (or shriek or screech)
2 syn see SQUEAL 2
3 syn see YELL 2
rel complain, grumble, protest; blare
idiom raise a howl
4 to produce a vivid, blatant, or startling effect < clothes and furnishings that *screamed* nouveau riche >
syn blare, shout, shriek
scream n syn see RIOT 2
screech vb 1 syn see SCREAM 1
rel penetrate, pierce; vent, voice
2 syn see SQUEAL 2
screen vb 1 syn see DEFEND 1
2 syn see SHADE
3 to cut off from view by interposing something resembling a screen < *screen* a view with a tall hedge >
syn block out, close, obstruct, shroud, shut off, shut out
rel conceal, hide; separate, wall off; protect, seclude; embosk
idiom throw up a screen
con bare, disclose, expose, open, reveal
4 syn see HIDE
rel defend, guard, protect, safeguard, shield; camouflage, cloak, cover up, disguise
5 to examine carefully and methodically in order to separate, select, or eliminate < the personnel department *screened* seventy candidates for ten jobs >
syn sieve, sift; compare SORT 2
rel choose, pick out, select; extract, filter (out), riddle, sort (out), winnow (out)
6 syn see CENSOR

‖**screeve** vb syn see EXUDE
‖**screw** n syn see SHAFT 3
screw vb 1 syn see CRUMPLE 1
2 syn see EXTORT 1
‖3 syn see CHEAT
4 syn see SCRIMP
‖5 syn see RUN 2
‖**screw** (up) vb syn see BOTCH
rel confuse, muddle, snafu; spoil
screwball n syn see CRACKPOT
‖**screwing** n syn see SHAFT 3
screwy adj ‖1 syn see INTOXICATED 1
2 syn see INSANE 1
idiom having a screw loose
scribble vb to write or draw hastily or roughly < *scribbled* a quick note to her on his way out >
syn scrabble, scratch, scrawl, squiggle
rel jot (down); scribe, write
scribe vb syn see WRITE
scrimmage n 1 syn see CLASH 2
rel scuffle; fight; free-for-all
2 syn see BRAWL 2
scrimp adj syn see MEAGER 2
scrimp vb to be extremely frugal and parsimonious in an effort to economize < *scrimped* all year to buy that fur coat >
syn pinch, scrape, screw, skimp, ‖skinch, spare, stint; compare SPARE 3
rel scamp; scratch; save (up)
idiom pinch pennies
‖**scrimption** n syn see PITTANCE
scrimpy adj 1 syn see MEAGER 2
2 syn see SHORT 3
3 syn see STINGY
scrimy adj syn see STINGY
script n syn see HANDWRITING
Scripture n syn see BIBLE
scrooch (down) vb syn see CROUCH
scrooge n syn see MISER
scrub n syn see INFERIOR
scrub vb 1 to clean by abrasive action < *scrubbed* the pots and pans >
syn scour
rel brush; rub; cleanse, wash; buff, polish
2 syn see CANCEL 2
scrubby adj syn see SHABBY 1
scruffy adj syn see SHABBY 1
scrumptious adj syn see DELIGHTFUL
scrunch vb 1 syn see CHEW 1
2 syn see CRUMPLE 1
‖**scrunty** adj syn see STUNTED
scruple n syn see PARTICLE
scruple n syn see QUALM
rel faltering, hesitancy, hesitation, pause; reconsideration, second thought
scruple vb syn see DEMUR
rel question; fret, worry
scrupulous adj 1 syn see UPRIGHT 2
rel fair-minded; strict; upstanding
con questionable; shifty, slippery; dishonorable, unprincipled; dishonest
ant unscrupulous
2 syn see CAREFUL 2
rel critical, fastidious
con careless; undiscriminating, unparticular
ant remiss
scrutinize vb 1 to look at or over critically and searchingly < the jeweler *scrutinized* the diamonds to see if they were fakes >
syn canvass, ‖case, check over, check up, con, examine, inspect, perlustrate, study, survey, vet, view

rel look over, overlook, peruse, pore
(over), scan; consider, contemplate, weigh;
penetrate, pierce, probe; analyze, dig
(into), dissect; comb
idiom turn a careful (*or* heedful) eye to
(*or* on)
2 *syn* see EYE 2

scrutiny *n* 1 *syn* see EXAMINATION
rel look-in, lookover, look-see
2 *syn* see EYE 3

scud *vb syn* see FLY 1

scuddle *vb syn* see SCUTTLE

scuff *vb syn* see SHUFFLE 3

scuffle *vb* 1 *syn* see WRESTLE
rel cuff, scuff
2 *syn* see SHUFFLE 3

scuffle *n syn* see BRAWL 2

‖sculch *n syn* see REFUSE

sculp *vb syn* see SCULPTURE

sculpt *vb syn* see SCULPTURE

sculpture *vb* to form an image or representation from solid material (as wood or
stone) < *sculptured* a colossal statue of a
horse>
syn carve, chisel, sculp, sculpt
rel cast, form; model, mold, shape

scum *n* 1 *syn* see RABBLE 2
idiom scum of the earth
2 *syn* see SNOT 1

scummy *adj syn* see CONTEMPTIBLE

scurf *n syn* see RABBLE 2

scurrile *adj syn* see ABUSIVE

scurrility *n syn* see ABUSE
rel scurrilousness; maligning, traducing,
vilification

scurrilous *adj* 1 *syn* see ABUSIVE
rel coarse, gross; filthy, foul; insulting,
offending, offensive, outrageous, outraging
2 *syn* see OBSCENE 2

scurry *vb* 1 *syn* see SCUTTLE
2 *syn* see RUN 1
rel shoot, tear; dart, fly; scuffle, skelter

scurvy *adj syn* see CONTEMPTIBLE
rel base, low, vile

scutter *vb syn* see SCUTTLE
rel hasten, hurry, run, speed

scuttle *vb* to move with or as if with short
rapidly alternating steps < armies of fid-
dler crabs *scuttled* across the road >
syn scuddle, scurry, scutter; *compare* RUN
1
rel scoot; scramble; scud

scuttlebutt *n syn* see REPORT 1

sea *n syn* see OCEAN

sea dog *n syn* see PIRATE

seal *n* an adhesive-backed device bearing a
symbolic, pictorial, or official design < the
seal on a diploma >
syn stamp, sticker

seam *n syn* see JOINT 1
rel bond

seaman *n syn* see MARINER

sear *vb* 1 *syn* see DRY 1
2 to burn or scorch with a sudden application of intense heat < *seared* the steaks
in the broiler >
syn sizzle
rel scorch, shrivel, parch; burn (up)

---

syn synonym(s)   *rel* related word(s)
ant antonym(s)   *con* contrasted word(s)
idiom idiomatic equivalent(s)
‖ use limited; if in doubt, see a dictionary

search *vb* 1 *syn* see SCOUR 2
rel run down, scout (around), scrimmage,
skirmish
idiom search high and low
2 to subject (a person) to a thorough
check for concealed or contraband articles
< police *searching* the suspects for
weapons >
syn ‖fan, frisk, shake down
rel check, examine; inspect, look over,
scan, scrutinize, study

search (for *or* out) *vb syn* see SEEK 1
rel pry (out), scout (out)

search *n syn* see PURSUIT 2

searchingly *adv syn* see HARD 4

sea robber *n syn* see PIRATE

sea rover *n syn* see PIRATE

season *n* a particular period of the year
< the Christmas *season* >
syn time
rel period, term

season *vb syn* see HARDEN 2
rel discipline, school, train; fit, prepare;
case harden, steel

seasonable *adj syn* see TIMELY 1
rel apropos, pertinent, relevant; appropriate, apt; convenient
con irrelevant; inappropriate, inapt; ill-
timed, inconvenient, inopportune
ant unseasonable

seasonably *adv syn* see EARLY 1
ant unseasonable

seasoned *adj syn* see EXPERIENCED
rel acclimated, acclimatized, hardened,
toughened; case-hardened, steeled
con inexperienced, unpracticed, unskilled,
unversed; unacclimated, unacclimatized,
unsteeled, untempered, untried
ant unseasoned

seat *n* 1 *syn* see BUTTOCKS
2 *syn* see CENTER 2
rel fulcrum
3 *syn* see BASE 1

seat *vb* to cause to be seated < an usher
seated her in the third row>
syn sit
rel establish, place, put

seating *n syn* see BASE 1

sea wolf *n syn* see PIRATE

seclude *vb* to remove or separate (oneself
or another) from external influences < in
the convent she was *secluded* from secular
life>
syn cloister, sequester
rel retire, separate, withdraw; closet,
confine, enclose, immure, isolate; screen,
shut off

secluded *adj* disposed to, living in, or
characterized by seclusion < *secluded*
monks > < they enjoyed *secluded* country
living >
syn cloistered, hermetic, recluse, secluse,
seclusive, sequestered
rel retired, withdrawn; close, hidden,
private, screened, shy, alone, isolated,
solitary
con communal, public

secluse *adj syn* see SECLUDED

seclusion *n* the act or condition of seclud-
ing or of being secluded < the queen went
into *seclusion* when her husband died >
syn reclusion, retirement, sequestration;
compare SOLITUDE

rel detachment, separation, withdrawal; reclusiveness, seclusiveness; privacy, privateness; aloneness, isolation, separateness, solitude

seclusive *adj syn* see SECLUDED

second *n syn* see INSTANT 1
idiom the flash of an eyelid

secondary *adj* 1 *syn* see SUBORDINATE
rel accessory, subservient
con major, prime; first, first-ranking, first-string
ant primary
2 formed from something original, primary, or basic <a *secondary* historical analysis based on original archives>
syn derivate, derivational, derivative, derived
rel borrowed, secondhand; consequent, resultant, subsequent
con basic, principle; first, firsthand, original, uncopied, underived
ant primary
3 *syn* see MINOR 2

secondary *n syn* see INFERIOR
rel second fiddle, second-in-command

second childhood *n syn* see DOTAGE

second-class *adj syn* see INFERIOR 2

second-drawer *adj syn* see INFERIOR 2

second-rate *adj syn* see INFERIOR 2
ant first-rate

secours *n syn* see HELP 1

secrecy *n* the practice or policy of keeping secrets or maintaining concealment <*secrecy* is an inherent feature of intelligence operations>
syn hugger-mugger, hugger-muggery, hush, hush-hush, secretiveness, secretness, silence
rel clandestineness, covertness, furtiveness; concealment, stealth, subterfuge; censorship, suppression
ant openness

secret *adj* 1 existing or done in such a way as to maintain concealment <was involved in *secret* negotiations with the enemy>
syn clandestine, covert, furtive, hole-and-corner, hugger-mugger, hush-hush, mystical, sneak, stealthy, sub-rosa, surreptitious, undercover, ‖underneath, under-the-table; *compare* STEALTHY 2, UNDERHAND
rel underhand, underhanded; unacknowledged, unavowed, undeclared; concealed, hidden, screened; classified, confidential, ‖eyes-only, restricted, top secret
con acknowledged, avowed, declared, revealed; aboveboard, straightforward, unconcealed; declassified, unclassified, unrestricted; clear, evident, manifest, obvious, patent, plain
ant open, public
2 *syn* see OBSCURE 2
3 *syn* see RECONDITE

secret *n* secrets *pl syn* see GENITALIA

secretaire *n syn* see DESK

secretary *n syn* see DESK

secrete *vb syn* see HIDE
rel deposit; withhold

secretiveness *n syn* see SECRECY

secretly *adv* in a secret manner <negotiated *secretly* with both sides>

syn by stealth, clandestinely, covertly, furtively, hugger-mugger, in camera, privately, stealthily, sub rosa, surreptitiously
rel confidentially; privatim, privily
idiom behind closed doors, on the qt, on the quiet, under the rose, under the table
con forthrightly, plainly, publicly; manifestly, overtly
ant openly

secretness *n syn* see SECRECY

sect *n syn* see RELIGION 2

sectarian *adj* 1 *syn* see HERETICAL
rel splinter
con unified, united
ant nonsectarian
2 *syn* see INSULAR

sectary *n* 1 *syn* see HERETIC
rel beatnik, Bohemian, hippie; maverick; liberal, radical, Young Turk; rebel, revolutionary
con advocate, conformist, follower
2 *syn* see FOLLOWER
rel bigot

sectator *n syn* see FOLLOWER

section *n* 1 *syn* see PART 1
rel district, locality, subdivision, vicinity; area, belt, zone; region, tract; field, sphere, territory
2 *syn* see QUARTER 2

section *vb* to divide into sections <*sectioned* the class on the basis of ability>
syn sectionalize, sectionize; *compare* SEGMENT
rel break up, divide, separate, slice, split; sector, segment

sectionalize *vb syn* see SECTION

sectionize *vb syn* see SECTION

sector *n syn* see QUARTER 2

secular *adj syn* see PROFANE 1
rel nonclerical, nonreligious
con clerical, ecclesiastical, ministerial, priestly, regular; eternal
ant religious

securable *adj syn* see AVAILABLE 1
rel convenient, handy, reachable, ready
idiom at one's disposal
con unavailable, unreachable

secure *adj* 1 *syn* see CONFIDENT 1
2 *syn* see SAFE 1
rel firm, stable, strong
con open, wide-open; assailable, weak; dangerous, precarious
ant insecure
3 *syn* see RELIABLE 1
4 *syn* see FAST 4
rel strong; iron
5 *syn* see STABLE 4
6 *syn* see SURE 1
rel established, settled; balanced
con precarious; unbalanced; unstable, wobbly
ant insecure

secure *vb* 1 *syn* see DEFEND 1
2 *syn* see ENSURE
rel underwrite
3 *syn* see CATCH 1
4 *syn* see FASTEN 2
rel batten (down), clamp, clinch, pinion, rivet, tie down; cement
con unfasten, untie
5 *syn* see GET 1
6 *syn* see EFFECT 1

security *n* 1 *syn* see SAFETY

ant insecurity

2 *syn* see STABILITY

3 *syn* see PLEDGE 1

4 *syn* see GUARANTEE 1

rel assurance; certification; pledge

5 *syn* see DEFENSE 1

sedate *adj syn* see SERIOUS 1

rel calm, placid, serene, tranquil; collected, composed, dispassionate, imperturbable, unruffled; decorous, dignified, proper, seemly

con indecorous, undignified, unseemly; airy, flippant, light

ant flighty

sedative *n* an agent or drug that relieves irritability, nervousness, or excitement <took a *sedative* to help her sleep>

syn calmant, calmative, quietive

rel balm; pacifier, tranquilizer; sleeping pill, sleeping tablet; depressant; ‖dowser

con energizer; stimulant; ‖upper

sediment *n* matter which settles to the bottom of a liquid <rocks hidden by *sediment* spoiled the cove for diving>

syn deposit, dreg(s), grounds, lees, precipitate, precipitation, settlings

rel bottoms, dross, recrement, scoria, slag; draff, heeltap

sedition *n* an offense against official ruling authority (as a government or sovereign) to which one owes allegiance <considered the defense industry strike to be overt *sedition*>

syn seditiousness, treason

rel alienation, disaffection, estrangement; action, protest, strike; coup, coup d'etat, putsch; insurrection, mutiny, rebellion, revolt, revolution, uprising; quislingism

con allegiance, fealty, fidelity, loyalty; duty, respect, responsibility

seditious *adj syn* see INSUBORDINATE

rel alienated, disaffected, dissident; faithless, disloyal, perfidious, traitorous, treacherous; lawless, violent

con faithful, loyal, patriotic

seditiousness *n syn* see SEDITION

seduce *vb* **1** *syn* see LURE

rel coax, tease; betray, deceive, delude, mislead; enslave, entrance; overpower, overwhelm

2 to persuade or entice into sexual partnership <lechers who *seduce* silly young girls>

syn debauch, undo

rel deflower; rape, ravish, violate; corrupt, degrade, pervert, ruin

seducement *n* **1** *syn* see SEDUCTION 1

rel undoing

2 *syn* see LURE 2

seduction *n* **1** the act or an instance of seducing or being seduced into a sexual relationship <women who lay themselves open to *seduction*>

syn seducement

rel deflowering; rape, ravishment, violation; corruption, degradation, perversion, ruin

2 *syn* see ATTRACTION 1

---

rel lorelei, siren song, temptation

seductive *adj syn* see ATTRACTIVE 1

rel desirable, mouth-watering, provocative

seductress *n syn* see SIREN

sedulous *adj syn* see ASSIDUOUS

rel active; busy; hustling, persevering, persistent, unremitting

see *vb* **1** to take cognizance of by physical or mental vision <*saw* that the boat was being driven ashore> <the only one who *saw* the truth>

syn behold, descry, discern, distinguish, espy, mark, mind, note, notice, observe, perceive, remark, view

rel sight; make out; examine, inspect, scan, scrutinize; penetrate, pierce, probe; consider, study; appraise, ponder, weigh

idiom fix one's eyes (*or* mind *or* thoughts) on, occupy oneself with, pay heed (*or* attention) to, take notice of

2 to perceive something by means of the eyes <she *sees* clearly with her new glasses>

syn ‖dekko, look, watch

rel gape, gaze, glare, peek, peep, peer, stare

idiom give the eye, hold in view, keep one's eye on, lay eyes on, turn one's eyes to

3 *syn* see EXPERIENCE 1

4 *syn* see DISCOVER 3

5 *syn* see THINK 1

6 *syn* see APPREHEND 1

rel discern, discriminate, recognize

7 *syn* see FORESEE

idiom see the day when

8 *syn* see LOOK 1

rel look out, watch out

idiom see to it that

9 *syn* see VISIT 2

10 *syn* see DATE

11 *syn* see GUIDE

rel accompany, go (with); attend

seeable *adj syn* see VISUAL 2

ant unseeable

seed *n* **1** *syn* see OFFSPRING

2 a beginning or source from which something (as a conception) may later develop <the growing *seeds* of suspicion in her mind>

syn bud, embryo, germ, nucleus, spark

rel rudiment; core, kernel; conceit, concept, conception, image, impression, notion

seed *vb syn* see PLANT 1

seedy *adj syn* see SHABBY 1

rel drooping, droopy, flagging, sagging, wilted, wilting; messy, slovenly, unkempt, untidy; neglected, overgrown

idiom gone to seed

con manicured, polished, shined

seeing *n syn* see EYE 2

seeing *conj syn* see BECAUSE

idiom ‖being as how, in that

‖seeing glass *n syn* see MIRROR 1

seek *vb* **1** to look for <has gone to *seek* a doctor>

syn cast about, ferret out, hunt, quest, search (for *or* out)

rel bird-dog, delve, dig, fish, mouse, nose, root, smell out, sniff

idiom go in quest (*or* search) of

2 *syn* see TRY 5

---

syn synonym(s)   *rel* related word(s)

ant antonym(s)   *con* contrasted word(s)

idiom idiomatic equivalent(s)

‖ use limited; if in doubt, see a dictionary

seeker n syn see CANDIDATE
  rel bidder; petitioner; solicitant; claimant
seeking n syn see PURSUIT 2
seem vb to give the impression of being
  without necessarily being so in fact
  < things are not always the way they
  seem >
  syn appear, look, sound
  rel resemble, suggest; hint, imply, insinuate, intimate
  idiom have (or show) every sign of, have
  the earmarks of
seeming n 1 syn see APPEARANCE 2
  rel feigning, pretense, sham; facade; illusion
  idiom false face (or front), outward show
  2 syn see APPEARANCE 1
  rel bearing, demeanor, posture; image,
  style; effect, impression
seeming adj syn see APPARENT 2
seemingly adv syn see OSTENSIBLY
seemliness n 1 syn see ORDER 7
  2 syn see DECORUM 1
  ant unseemliness
seemly adj syn see DECOROUS 1
  rel compatible, congenial, congruous,
  consistent, consonant; pleasing
  con inappropriate, unfit, unseasonable,
  unsuitable, untimely; incompatible, uncongenial; displeasing, unpleasing
  ant unseemly
seep vb syn see EXUDE
  rel drip; leak; flow
seer n syn see PROPHET
seesaw vb to move backward and forward
  or up and down from a central axis usually in a swaying often unsteady way
  < planes landing on the seesawing flight
  deck >
  syn lurch, pitch, swag, tilt, tilter, yaw;
  compare TEETER, TOSS 2
  rel cant, incline, lean, list; rock, roll,
  sway
seethe vb 1 syn see BOIL 2
  2 syn see SOAK 1
  3 syn see ANGER 2
  idiom ‖do a slow burn
  con calm (down), simmer (down)
  ant cool (down)
  4 to be in a state of internal and especially mental agitation, excitement, or
  turmoil < his brain seethed with unan-
  swered questions >
  syn boil, bubble, churn, ferment, ‖moil,
  simmer, smolder, stir
  rel abound, swarm, teem; fret, fume,
  sizzle, steam; bubble over, erupt, overflow
see-through adj syn see TRANSPARENT 1
segment n syn see PART 1
segment vb to separate into segments
  < tried to segment the poem into understandable units >
  syn segmentalize, segmentize; compare
  SECTION
  rel categorize, compartmentalize; divide,
  separate; isolate, seclude, set off
segmentalize vb syn see SEGMENT
segmentize vb syn see SEGMENT
segregate vb syn see ISOLATE
  rel disconnect; choose, select, single
  con mix
  ant desegregate
segregation n the quality, state, or condition of being socially or racially excluded

or separated < fought against racial segregation in the schools >
  syn apartheid, separateness, separation,
  separatism
  rel discrimination, jim crowism; ghetto-
  ization; isolation, seclusion
  ant desegregation
seity n syn see INDIVIDUALITY 4
seize vb 1 syn see APPROPRIATE 1
  rel occupy; usurp
  2 to take possession or control of
  usually suddenly and forcibly < the
  cat seized the fish and made off >
  < seized the rope and dragged the boat
  ashore >
  syn catch, clutch, ‖cotch, grab, grapple,
  nab, ‖nail, snatch, take; compare CATCH 1
  rel fasten (onto), grasp, latch (onto), snap
  (at); apprehend, arrest; capture, secure,
  take over; abduct, carry off, kidnap, spirit
  (away or off)
  idiom get into one's clutches, get one's
  hands (or paws) on, lay hold (on or of)
  con free, loose, release
  3 to affect especially as if by laying
  hold of < was seized with a coughing
  fit >
  syn catch, strike, take
  rel overtake; afflict
seizure n syn see ATTACK 3
  rel convulsion; breakdown
seldom adv in few instances < she seldom
  writes home anymore >
  syn hardly ever, infrequently, little,
  rarely, unfrequently, unoften
  rel occasionally; semioccasionally; irregularly, sporadically; hardly, scarcely
  idiom once in a blue moon
  con regularly; frequently; usually
  ant often
seldom adj syn see INFREQUENT
select adj 1 singled out from a number or
  group by fitness or preference < this hotel
  caters to a select clientele >
  syn chosen, elect, exclusive, pick, picked,
  selected
  rel culled, screened, weeded (out), win-
  nowed (out); favored, preferred; best, elite
  con random; indiscriminate; average,
  commonplace, mediocre, run-of-the-mill
  2 syn see CHOICE
  rel blue-chip, fine; best; top
  3 syn see ECLECTIC 1
select vb syn see CHOOSE 1
  idiom make a choice (or selection)
  con ignore, pass (over); drop
  ant reject
selected adj syn see SELECT 1
  rel singled (out); appointed, tagged,
  tapped
selection n syn see CHOICE 1
  rel choosing, culling, draft, drafting, picking; acumen, discernment, discrimination,
  insight
  ant rejection
selective adj syn see ECLECTIC 1
  rel particular, scrupulous
self-abandoned adj syn see ABANDONED
  2
self-abnegating adj syn see SELF-SAC-
  RIFICING
self-abnegation n syn see RENUNCIA-
  TION

rel abandonment, relinquishment, resignation

self–absorbed *adj syn* see EGOCENTRIC 2
rel arrogant, cocky, self-important

self–abuse *n syn* see SELF-REPROACH

self–accusation *n syn* see SELF-RE-PROACH

self–admiration *n syn* see CONCEIT 2

self–asserting *adj syn* see PRESUMPTU-OUS
rel aggressive, militant
con meek, modest, unassuming; docile, passive
ant self-effacing

self–assertive *adj* 1 *syn* see AGGRESSIVE
rel impertinent, intrusive, meddlesome, obtrusive, officious; audacious, bold; cocksure, sure
2 *syn* see PRESUMPTUOUS

self–assurance *n syn* see CONFIDENCE 2
rel collectedness, coolness, imperturbability; composure, equanimity, sangfroid
con insecurity, uncertainness

self–assured *adj syn* see CONFIDENT 1
rel self-satisfied, smug

self–assuredness *n syn* see CONFIDENCE 2

self–centered *adj* 1 *syn* see SELF-SUFFI-CIENT
2 *syn* see EGOCENTRIC 2
idiom wrapped up in oneself

self–centeredness *n syn* see SELFISHNESS

self–command *n syn* see WILL 3
rel self-containment, uncommunicativeness

self–complacency *n syn* see CONCEIT 2

self–complacent *adj syn* see COM-PLACENT

self–composed *adj syn* see CALM 2

self–conceit *n syn* see CONCEIT 2

self–conceited *adj syn* see VAIN 3

self–concern *n syn* see SELFISHNESS

self–concerned *adj syn* see EGOCENTRIC 2

self–confidence *n syn* see CONFIDENCE 2
rel sanguineness, sureness; cockiness, overconfidence
con diffidence, shyness; self-distrust; doubt, uneasiness
ant self-doubt

self–confident *adj syn* see CONFIDENT 1

self–conscious *adj* aware of the scrutiny of others to the point of not appearing natural or spontaneous < felt *self-conscious* about wearing platform shoes>
syn affected, conscious, mannered
rel self-aware; anxious, ill at ease, uncomfortable, uneasy; formal, stiff, stilted; artificial; ||mim, prim; exhibitionist, flaunty, ostentatious
con unaware, unconcerned; blithe, easy; natural, spontaneous, unaffected

self–consequence *n syn* see CONCEIT 2

self–contained *adj syn* see SELF-SUF-FICIENT

self–contemplation *n syn* see INTRO-SPECTION

self–contented *adj syn* see COMPLACENT

---

syn synonym(s)   *rel* related word(s)
ant antonym(s)   *con* contrasted word(s)
idiom idiomatic equivalent(s)

|| use limited; if in doubt, see a dictionary

---

self–control *n syn* see WILL 3
rel constraint, reserve, self-containedness; balance, stability; dignity
idiom presence of mind
ant self-abandonment

self–criticism *n syn* see SELF-REPROACH

self–deceit *n syn* see SELF-DECEPTION

self–deception *n* the act or an instance of deceiving oneself or of being so deceived < to presume agreement where none exists is a dangerous form of *self-deception* >
syn self-deceit, self-delusion
rel misconception, misinterpretation, misunderstanding; deception, delusion, illusion
idiom kidding oneself

self–defense *n* an act, instance, or means of defending oneself, one's property, or a close relative < sought some measure of *self-defense* against society's lawless elements >
syn self-protection
rel self-preservation

self–delusion *n syn* see SELF-DECEPTION

self–denial *n syn* see RENUNCIATION
rel abstaining, abstemiousness, abstinence; asceticism, selflessness, self-sacrifice, self-sacrificing; self-forgetful, self-forgetting
ant self-indulgence

self–denying *adj syn* see SELF-SAC-RIFICING

self–dependence *n syn* see SELF-RELI-ANCE

self–destruction *n syn* see SUICIDE

self–discipline *n syn* see WILL 3

selfdom *n syn* see INDIVIDUALITY 4

self–educated *adj syn* see SELF-TAUGHT

self–effacing *adj syn* see SHY 1

self–esteem *n* 1 *syn* see PRIDE 2
rel self-content, self-contentment; self-satisfaction
con self-distrust, self-doubt; self-contempt
ant self-hate
2 *syn* see CONCEIT 2
rel self-flattery, self-glorification
con self-distrust, self-doubt; self-hate
ant self-contempt

self–evidencing *adj syn* see SELF-EVI-DENT

self–evident *adj* evident in itself without need of argument or proof < *self-evident* truths >
syn prima facie, self-evidencing
rel clear, manifest, obvious, plain; unmistakable, unquestionable
con enigmatic, hidden, mysterious, obscure; doubtable, doubtful, questionable, uncertain

self–exaltation *n syn* see CONCEIT 2

self–examination *n syn* see INTROSPEC-TION

self–existent *adj* existing of or by itself and having no antecedent cause < argues backward to a first great cause, which is itself *self-existent* >
syn increate, self-existing, unbegotten, uncaused, uncreated, unoriginated
rel self-generated, self-originated, self-produced
con consequent, resultant, sequential
ant derivative

self–existing *adj syn* see SELF-EXISTENT

self–explaining *adj syn* see SELF-EX-PLANATORY

self–explanatory *adj* capable of being understood without explanation <his actions are *self-explanatory:* he wants to resign>
  syn self-explaining; *compare* CLEAR 5
  rel clear, evident, obvious, manifest, plain, self-evident; comprehensible, understandable
  con equivocal, obscure, uncertain, unclear, vague; complex; incomprehensible, mysterious; inexplicable, unexplainable

self–forgetful *adj syn see* SELFLESS

self–forgetting *adj syn see* SELFLESS

self–giving *adj syn see* SELF-SACRIFICING

self–glorifying *adj syn see* BOASTFUL

self–glory *n syn see* CONCEIT 2
  rel self-aggrandizement, self-glorification

self–governing *adj syn see* DEMOCRATIC

self–government *n syn see* WILL 3

self–gratification *n* the act of pleasing oneself or of satisfying one's desires <human beings driven by unconscious forces toward *self-gratification*>
  syn onanism, self-indulgence
  rel self-abandonment; self-pleasing; self-satisfaction; autotheism, narcissism, self-worship

selfhood *n* 1 *syn see* INDIVIDUALITY 4
  2 *syn see* SELFISHNESS

self–importance *n* 1 *syn see* CONCEIT 2
  2 *syn see* EGOTISM 1
  rel arrogance, pomposity

self–important *adj syn see* POMPOUS 1

self–imposed *adj* imposed by oneself or itself <insists on working under *self-imposed* handicaps>
  syn self-inflicted
  rel self-generated, self-produced

self–indulgence *n syn see* SELF-GRATIFICATION
  rel indulgence; excess, intemperance, overindulgence
  ant abstinence

self–indulgent *adj syn see* SYBARITIC

self–inflicted *adj syn see* SELF-IMPOSED
  rel self-determined; accepted; voluntary

self–instructed *adj syn see* SELF-TAUGHT

self–interest *n syn see* SELFISHNESS

self–interested *adj syn see* EGOCENTRIC 2

self–involved *adj syn see* EGOCENTRIC 2

selfish *adj syn see* EGOCENTRIC 2
  idiom ‖looking out for number one
  con self-denying, selfless, self-sacrificing; altruistic, benevolent, charitable, generous, magnanimous
  ant unselfish

selfishness *n* a concern for one's own welfare at the expense of or in disregard of others <his *selfishness* was consummate: he cared for no one but himself>
  syn self-centeredness, self-concern, selfhood, self-interest, self-regard, self-seeking
  rel egoism, egotism, self-absorption; self, selfism, selfness; autotheism, self-worship
  con self-denial, selflessness, self-sacrificing; benevolence, charity, generosity
  ant unselfishness

self–knowledge *n* knowledge or understanding of one's own character, motivations, and capabilities <a poet whose verse reflected deep *self-knowledge* and honesty>

  syn autognosis, self-understanding
  rel self-awareness; introspection; self-examination, self-observation

selfless *adj* having no concern for oneself <*selfless* service to community, state, and nation>
  syn self-forgetful, self-forgetting, unselfish
  rel self-giving, self-sacrificing; self-renouncing; elevated, generous, high-minded, magnanimous
  con self-devoted, self-loving, self-serving
  ant self-centered, selfish

self–love *n syn see* CONCEIT 2
  idiom the sixth insatiable sense
  con self-abuse, self-accusation, self-reproach; self-forgetfulness, selflessness
  ant self-hate

self–mastery *n syn see* WILL 3

self–murder *n syn see* SUICIDE

selfness *n syn see* INDIVIDUALITY 4

self–observation *n syn see* INTROSPECTION

self–opinion *n syn see* CONCEIT 2

self–pleased *adj syn see* COMPLACENT

self–possessed *adj syn see* CALM 2
  rel aloof, reserved; self-contained, self-controlled; self-assured

self–possession *n syn see* EQUANIMITY

self–pride *n syn see* CONCEIT 2

self–proclaimed *adj syn see* SELF-STYLED

self–protection *n syn see* SELF-DEFENSE

self–questioning *n syn see* INTROSPECTION

self–recrimination *n syn see* SELF-REPROACH

self–reflection *n syn see* INTROSPECTION

self–regard *n* 1 *syn see* SELFISHNESS
  2 *syn see* PRIDE 2

self–reliance *n* reliance on one's own resources, efforts, and ability <a strong people characterized by bravery and *self-reliance*>
  syn self-dependence
  rel confidence, self-assurance, self-confidence; self-sufficiency, self-support

self–renouncing *adj syn see* SELF-SACRIFICING

self–renunciation *n syn see* RENUNCIATION

self–reproach *n* an act or instance of reproaching oneself <experienced both guilt and *self-reproach* after the quarrel>
  syn self-abuse, self-accusation, self-criticism, self-recrimination, self-reproof
  rel contrition, regret, remorse; self-castigation, self-condemnation, self-flagellation, self-punishment; self-contempt
  con self-contentment, self-satisfaction; self-applause
  ant self-approbation

self–reproof *n syn see* SELF-REPROACH

self–respect *n syn see* PRIDE 2

self–restraining *adj syn see* ABSTEMIOUS

self–restraint *n syn see* WILL 3
  ant abandon

self–righteous *adj syn see* HYPOCRITICAL

self–ruling *adj syn see* DEMOCRATIC

self–sacrificing *adj* sacrificing or denying oneself for others <a *self-sacrificing* love>
  syn self-abnegating, self-denying, self-giving, self-renouncing

rel selfless, unselfish; charitable, generous, kindly, philanthropic
con self-centered, selfish, self-seeking

selfsame *adj syn* see SAME 1
rel alike, like
idiom (the) very same
con different, unlike
ant diverse

selfsameness *n syn* see IDENTITY
ant diverseness

self-satisfied *adj syn* see COMPLACENT

self-scrutiny *n syn* see INTROSPECTION

self-searching *n syn* see INTROSPECTION

self-seeking *n syn* see SELFISHNESS

self-seeking *adj syn* see EGOCENTRIC 2

self-serving *adj syn* see EGOCENTRIC 2

self-slaughter *n syn* see SUICIDE

self-starter *n syn* see HUSTLER 1

self-styled *adj* given a specified designation or title by oneself often without justification <a department cluttered with *self-styled* experts>
syn self-proclaimed, soi-disant
rel self-appointed, self-created, self-given; so-called; quasi; would-be

self-sufficient *adj* maintaining or able to maintain oneself without outside aid <organisms are not *self-sufficient*, closed systems>
syn closed, independent, self-centered, self-contained, self-sufficing, self-supported, self-supporting, self-sustained, self-sustaining
rel self-dependent, self-reliant; self-subsistent, self-subsisting; individual, one-man, unit
idiom one's own man, sufficient unto oneself (or itself)
con dependent

self-sufficing *adj syn* see SELF-SUFFICIENT

self-supported *adj syn* see SELF-SUFFICIENT

self-supporting *adj syn* see SELF-SUFFICIENT

self-sustained *adj syn* see SELF-SUFFICIENT

self-sustaining *adj syn* see SELF-SUFFICIENT

self-taught *adj* having knowledge or skills acquired by one's own efforts without formal instruction <a *self-taught* painter>
syn autodidactic, self-educated, self-instructed

self-trust *n syn* see CONFIDENCE 2

self-understanding *n syn* see SELF-KNOWLEDGE

self-violence *n syn* see SUICIDE

self-willed *adj syn* see OBSTINATE
con weak, weak-willed, wishy-washy; spineless

sell *vb* 1 *syn* see BETRAY 2
2 to give up (property) to another for money or other valuable consideration <can *sell* you the house now>
syn give, market, vend
ant buy, purchase

3 to deal in or offer (articles) for sale on a regular basis <he *sells* small appliances>
syn market, merchandise, retail
rel barter, deal (in), exchange, trade, traffic; hawk, peddle; vend
ant buy

4 to command a specified price <that coat *sells* for $300>
syn bring, bring in, fetch
rel command, draw; realize, return, yield; gross, net

sell *n syn* see IMPOSTURE

sellable *adj syn* see MARKETABLE

sell off *vb syn* see SELL OUT 1

sell out *vb* 1 to dispose of entirely by selling <*sold out* his share of the business>
syn close out, sell off, ‖sell up
rel dump, move, unload; sacrifice
2 *syn* see DECEIVE
3 *syn* see BETRAY 2

‖**sell up** *vb syn* see SELL OUT 1

selvage *n syn* see BORDER 1

semblance *n* 1 *syn* see AIR 3
rel aspect, look
2 *syn* see LIKENESS
3 *syn* see APPEARANCE 2
rel air, pose
4 *syn* see MASK 2

semblant *adj syn* see APPARENT 2

seminar *n syn* see CONFERENCE 2

semioccasional *adj syn* see INFREQUENT

sempiternal *adj syn* see INFINITE 1

sempiternity *n syn* see ETERNITY 1

send *vb* 1 to cause to go or be taken from one place, person, or condition to another <*send* a messenger to the bank> <his cold *sent* him to bed>
syn address, consign, dispatch, forward, remit, route, ship, transmit
rel allocate, assign, commit, delegate; advance, launch; expedite, rush
ant receive
2 *syn* see THRILL

senectitude *n syn* see OLD AGE

senescence *n syn* see OLD AGE

senile *adj* exhibiting the weakness and loss of mental faculties often associated with old age <a *senile* professor now unable to lecture coherently>
syn doddering, doddery, ‖doted, doting
rel aging, senescent; aged, ancient, old; enfeebled, feeble, weak; decrepit, doddered, shattered
idiom in one's second childhood

senility *n syn* see DOTAGE
rel decline; senescence

senior *n* 1 *syn* see OLDSTER
2 one older than another <he was her *senior* by eight years>
syn elder
ant junior
3 *syn* see SUPERIOR
con inferior, subordinate, underling

senior citizen *n syn* see OLDSTER

sensation *n* 1 the power to respond or an act of responding to stimuli <the stage of *sensation* precedes that of rational comprehension>
syn feeling, sense, sensibility, sensitivity
rel susceptibility; consciousness; sensitiveness, sensitivity; impression, perception, response
2 *syn* see WONDER 1

---

syn synonym(s)   *rel* related word(s)
ant antonym(s)   *con* contrasted word(s)
idiom idiomatic equivalent(s)
‖ use limited; if in doubt, see a dictionary

rel bomb, bombshell

sensational *adj* 1 *syn* see SENSORY
2 arousing or designed to arouse a quick, intense, and usually superficial emotional response < *sensational* crime reporting >
syn livid, lurid, sensationalistic, sensationist, sultry, tabloid
rel juicy, piquant, pungent; colored, extravagant; coarse, vulgar
con exact, factual; dignified, formal, proper, restrained
3 *syn* see NOTICEABLE
rel impressive, stunning
4 *syn* see MARVELOUS 2
rel boffo, crashing, rousing, slambang, smash, smashing, superfine

sensationalistic *adj* *syn* see SENSATIONAL 2

sensationist *adj* *syn* see SENSATIONAL 2

sensatory *adj* *syn* see SENSORY

sense *n* 1 *syn* see MEANING 1
rel gist, pith, substance; center, core, focus, nucleus
2 *syn* see SUBSTANCE 2
3 *syn* see SENSATION 1
rel awareness, cognizance; discernment, discrimination, penetration; appreciation; recognition
4 *usu* senses *pl* *syn* see WIT 2
rel consciousness
5 *syn* see INTELLIGENCE 1
6 ability to make intelligent choices and to reach intelligent conclusions or decisions < had enough *sense* to study something practical >
syn common sense, good sense, gumption, horse sense, judgment, wisdom
rel discretion, foresight, prudence; appreciation, comprehension, understanding; brains, intelligence, ||smarts, wit
ant folly

sense *vb* *syn* see FEEL 3
rel anticipate; know, realize

senseless *adj* 1 *syn* see NUMB 1
rel oblivious, unaware; inanimate, wooden
2 *syn* see INSENSATE 1
3 *syn* see INSENSIBLE 2
4 *syn* see SIMPLE 3
rel irrational, surd
5 having no meaning < an ancient custom, now outdated and *senseless* >
syn insignificant, meaningless, pointless, purportless, unmeaning
rel purposeful; trivial, unimportant
idiom without rhyme or reason
con purposeful; important, meaning, meaningful, significant

senselessness *n* *syn* see FOOLISHNESS
rel illogicality, stupidity

sensibility *n* *syn* see SENSATION 1
rel discernment, discrimination, insight, keenness, penetration, responsiveness; affection, emotion, heart
con apathy, indifference, insensibleness, insentience, unfeelingness, unresponsiveness
ant insensibility

sensibilize *vb* *syn* see SENSITIZE

sensible *adj* 1 *syn* see MATERIAL 1
rel concrete, solid
con immaterial, insubstantial; unreal
2 *syn* see PERCEPTIBLE

rel imaginal, perceptual, sensational; weighable; evident, manifest, obvious, patent
con imperceptible; cloudy, unclear
ant insensible
3 *syn* see CONSIDERABLE 2
4 *syn* see SENTIENT 3
5 *syn* see AWARE
rel sensitive, susceptible; noting, observing, perceiving, remarking, seeing; appreciating, comprehending, understanding; intelligent, knowing
con anesthetic, insensate, insensitive
ant insensible
6 *syn* see RATIONAL
rel sensemaking
7 *syn* see WISE 2
rel rational, reasonable; down-to-earth, matter-of-fact
con unreasonable, unsound, unwise; asinine, fatuous
ant absurd, foolish

sensile *adj* *syn* see SENTIENT 3

sensitive *adj* 1 *syn* see SENTIENT 3
rel hypersensitive, supersensitive
con impervious, insensible, unfeeling, unimpressionable, unresponsive; wooden
ant insensitive, unsensitive
2 *syn* see EMOTIONAL 1
rel high-strung, irritable, nervous, tense; insultable, oversensitive, umbrageous; unstable
con impervious, insensate, insensible, unaffected, unemotional
ant insensitive, unsensitive
3 *syn* see ACUTE 3
rel perceiving, seeing; aware, cognizant, conscious; knowing, understanding
4 *syn* see LIABLE 2
rel affected, impressed, influenced; disposed, inclined, predisposed
ant insensitive
5 *syn* see DELICATE 7
6 *syn* see SENSORY

sensitivity *n* *syn* see SENSATION 1

sensitize *vb* to cause to become sensitive or more sensitive < *sensitizing* corporate officers to social and environmental problems >
syn sensibilize
rel animate, excite, quicken, sharpen, stimulate, whet
ant desensitize

sensorial *adj* *syn* see SENSORY

sensory *adj* of or relating to sensation or the senses < *sensory* perception >
syn sensational, sensatory, sensitive, sensorial, sensual
rel sensate; receptive

sensual *adj* 1 *syn* see SENSORY
2 *syn* see CARNAL 2
rel irreligious, unspiritual
3 *syn* see SENSUOUS
4 *syn* see MATERIALISTIC

sensualistic *adj* *syn* see SENSUOUS

sensuous *adj* producing or characterized by gratification of the senses < *sensuous* pleasures >
syn epicurean, luscious, lush, luxurious, sensual, sensualistic, voluptuous; compare CARNAL 2, SYBARITIC
rel bacchic, dionysiac, Dionysian, hedonistic, pleasure-loving, pleasure-seeking;

self-indulgent, sybaritic; carnal, fleshly, fleshy

con ascetic, disciplined, restrained

sentence *vb* to decree the fate or punishment of one adjudged guilty, unworthy, or unfit < was *sentenced* to exile >

syn condemn, damn, doom, proscribe

rel adjudge, adjudicate, judge; ordain, rule; blame, denounce; penalize, punish; devote

idiom pass sentence on

con absolve, acquit, exculpate, exonerate, vindicate; discharge, free, liberate, release

sententious *adj syn* see EXPRESSIVE

rel aphoristic, concise, crisp, epigrammatic, piquant, pithy, terse

sentient *adj* 1 *syn* see AWARE

2 *syn* see EMOTIONAL 1

3 capable of receiving and of being readily affected by external stimuli < deeply disturbed in the most *sentient* reaches of his mind >

syn impressible, impressionable, responsive, sensible, sensile, sensitive, susceptible, susceptive

rel sensate; open, receptive, susceptive; reactive

con insensate; closed, unreceptive; unreactive

sentiment *n* 1 *syn* see LEANING 2

2 *syn* see OPINION

rel leaning, predilection, propensity; position, posture

idiom way of thinking

3 *syn* see FEELING 3

rel conception; sensation; emotionalism, sentimentality

sentimental *adj* unduly or affectedly emotional < *sentimental* love stories >

syn bathetic, drippy, gooey, lovey-dovey, maudlin, mawkish, moist, mushy, romantic, sappy, slushy, sobby, sobful, soft-boiled, ||soppy, soupy, sticky, syrupy, tear-jerking

rel dreamy, misty-eyed, moonstruck, nostalgic, oversentimental; inane, insipid, jejune, namby-pamby, schoolgirlish, vapid; rosewater, saccharine, soft, sugar-candy, sugary, sweet; loving, tender; affectionate, demonstrative, effusive; gushing, gushy; passionate

con unaffectionate, undemonstrative; dispassionate, emotionless, unemotional, unresponsive; unfeeling, unloving; dry

ant unsentimental

sentinel *n syn* see GUARD 2

sentry *n syn* see GUARD 2

separate *vb* 1 to become or cause to become disunited or disjoined < forces that *separate* families >

syn break up, dichotomize, disjoin, disjoint, dissect, dissever, disunite, divide, divorce, part, rupture, sever, split (up), sunder, uncombine

rel alienate, discontinue, disunify, estrange; dislink, uncouple, unjoin, unlink; disaggregate, disassemble, disgregate, dispel, disperse, dissolve, scatter; detach,

disengage, disrelate, dissociate; halve, quarter

con assemble, associate, blend, mingle, mix; connect, couple, join, link; unify, unite; agglutinate, bind, cement, fuse, weld

ant combine

2 *syn* see KNOW 4

3 *syn* see SORT 2

rel compartment, compartmentalize

4 *syn* see DISCHARGE 7

5 *syn* see ISOLATE

separate *adj* 1 *syn* see SINGLE 2

rel distinctive, peculiar; detached, disconnected, disengaged

2 *syn* see FREE 1

3 *syn* see DISTINCT 1

rel free, independent

separately *adv syn* see APART 1

rel distinctly; solely

con conjointly, jointly

ant together

separateness *n syn* see SEGREGATION

ant togetherness

separation *n* 1 the act, process, or an instance of separating or of being separated < *separation* of church and state > < their *separation* was a sad occasion >

syn detachment, dissolution, disunion, division, divorce, divorcement, partition, rupture, split-up

rel disrelation, dissociation, disunity, parting, shedding; disconnection, disjointedness, disjointure; breakup, disjunction, dissection, sequestration; diffluence, dispersal; dichotomy, diremption, trichotomy

con combination; unification

ant union

2 *syn* see SEGREGATION

separatism *n syn* see SEGREGATION

separatist *n syn* see HERETIC

sepulcher *n syn* see GRAVE

sepulcher *vb* 1 *syn* see ENTOMB 1

2 *syn* see BURY 1

sepulchral *adj* 1 of, relating to, or serving as a sepulcher or a memorial to the dead < *sepulchral* inscriptions >

syn mortuary, tumulary

rel exequial, funebrial, funeral, funerary, funereal

2 *syn* see HOLLOW 1

sepulture *n* 1 *syn* see BURIAL 2

2 *syn* see GRAVE

sepulture *vb* 1 *syn* see ENTOMB 1

2 *syn* see BURY 1

sequel *n* 1 *syn* see SUCCESSION 2

2 *syn* see EFFECT 1

rel end, ending, termination; close, closing, finish, finishing

3 *syn* see EPILOGUE 2

rel continuation, development; aftermath, outcome, result

sequence *n* 1 *syn* see SUCCESSION 2

rel arrangement, disposition, ordering; procession

2 *syn* see ORDER 3

rel classification, grouping; placement

3 *syn* see EFFECT 1

4 *syn* see ORDER 5

sequent *adj syn* see CONSECUTIVE

sequential *adj syn* see CONSECUTIVE

sequester *vb* 1 *syn* see ISOLATE

2 *syn* see SECLUDE

---

syn synonym(s)   *rel* related word(s)
ant antonym(s)   *con* contrasted word(s)
idiom idiomatic equivalent(s)
|| use limited; if in doubt, see a dictionary

rel hide, secrete
3 *syn* see APPROPRIATE 1
rel attach; impound; dispossess
sequestered *adj syn* see SECLUDED
rel sheltered; closeted
sequestration *n syn* see SECLUSION
rel retreat
sequitur *n syn* see INFERENCE 2
seraglio *n syn* see BROTHEL
sere *adj syn* see DRY 1
serene *adj syn* see CALM 2
rel noiseless, quiet, still; quiescent, resting; undisturbed
con agitated, disquieted, upset
serfage *n syn* see BONDAGE
serfdom *n syn* see BONDAGE
serial *adj syn* see CONSECUTIVE
series *n syn* see SUCCESSION 2
rel continuance, continuation, run; category, group, set; column, tier; gradation, scale
serious *adj* **1** not light or frivolous (as in disposition, appearance, or manner) < he was disturbed by her stern, *serious* look >
syn earnest, grave, no-nonsense, poker-faced sedate, sober, sobersided, solemn, somber, staid, weighty
rel businesslike, ‖dern, determined, steady, steady-going; intent, serious-minded; contemplative, meditative, pensive, reflective, thoughtful; austere, severe, stern; humorless, unhumorous; grim
idiom serious as a judge
con flighty, ‖flip, flippant, frivolous, volatile; casual, easy, relaxed
ant light, unserious
2 expressing, involving, or characterized by seriousness or gravity (as of consequence) < a *serious* economic situation >
syn grave, heavy, severe, weighty
rel important, significant; sobering; unamusing, unfunny; unhumorous; grim
idiom no joke, no laughing matter
con inconsequential, insignificant, unimportant, unserious
ant trifling, trivial
3 *syn* see HARD 6
4 *syn* see GRAVE 3
rel menacing, threatening
seriously *adv* **1** in a serious manner < at last settled *seriously* to work >
syn actively, down, earnestly, for real
rel gravely, soberly, solemnly; intently; vigorously, zealously; determinedly, purposefully, resolutely; fervently, passionately
idiom all joking aside, in all seriousness, in earnest
con airily, casually, flippantly, lightly, unconcernedly; carelessly, haphazardly
2 to a serious extent < the cities are *seriously* overcrowded >
syn gravely, intensely, severely
rel decidedly, quite, very; dangerously; critically, deplorably, regrettably
serious–mindedness *n syn* see EARNEST-
NESS
rel thoughtfulness; sober-mindedness
seriousness *n syn* see EARNESTNESS
rel sedateness, sobriety, solemnity, staidness
con gaiety, jollity; lightness
ant flippancy, frivolity

sermon *n* a religious discourse delivered in public by a clergyman as part of a worship service < preached his first *sermon* on Sunday >
syn preach, preaching, preachment, sermonizing
rel preachification; sermonary, sermonology; sermonette; exhortation, harangue, lecture, tirade
sermonic *adj syn* see DIDACTIC
sermonize *vb* **1** *syn* see PREACH 1
2 *syn* see DISCOURSE 1
3 *syn* see MORALIZE
sermonizer *n syn* see CLERGYMAN
sermonizing *n syn* see SERMON
sermonizing *adj syn* see DIDACTIC
serpent *n syn* see DEVIL 1
serpentine *adj* **1** *syn* see FIENDISH
2 *syn* see WINDING
rel serpentiform, serpentile, serpentlike, snakelike; crooked, devious
serrate *adj* notched or toothed on the edge < jagged peaks and *serrate* ridges >
syn denticulate, saw-edged, sawtooth, saw-toothed, serrated, serried
rel indented, notched, scored, toothed; serrulate
serrated *adj syn* see SERRATE
serried *adj syn* see SERRATE
serve *vb* **1** *syn* see BENEFIT
2 *syn* see ACT 4
3 to prove adequate or sufficient < will not *serve* as a true translation >
syn do, suffice, suit
rel service; function, work; fit; satisfy; make
idiom fill the bill
4 *syn* see MINISTER (to)
5 to put in (a term of imprisonment) < *served* ten years for armed robbery >
syn do
rel put in, spend; undergo
idiom do a hitch (or stretch), serve (out) a sentence, serve time, ‖take a vacation
6 *syn* see ADVANCE 1
7 *syn* see TREAT 2
service *n* **1** the performance of military duty in wartime and especially in a combat zone < saw a year's *service* in Vietnam >
syn action, combat
rel active duty, duty; fighting
2 *syn* see FAVOR 4
3 *syn* see RITE 2
4 *syn* see USE 3
serviceability *n syn* see USE 3
rel serviceableness; durability
serviceable *adj* **1** *syn* see HELPFUL 1
ant unserviceable
2 *syn* see PRACTICAL 2
ant unserviceable
serviceman *n* **1** *syn* see SOLDIER
2 servicemen *pl syn* see TROOP 2
servile *adj* **1** *syn* see SUBSERVIENT 2
rel obedient, submissive; passive, unresisting; bootlicking, groveling, toadish
con aggressive
ant authoritative
2 *syn* see BASE 3
servility *n syn* see BONDAGE
servitude *n syn* see BONDAGE
con freedom, independence
set *vb* **1** to position (something) in a specified place < *set* the lamp on the table >

syn establish, fix, lay, place, put, settle, stick

rel bestow, deposit, park; emplace, ensconce, install; affix, anchor, wedge

con displace, replace, supplant; remove, take (away); uproot

2 *syn* see DIRECT 2

idiom set one's sights on

3 *syn* see STATION

4 *syn* see DICTATE

rel designate, direct, instruct, specify, stipulate; establish; make, name

5 to put in order for a meal <she quickly *set* the table for dinner>

syn lay, spread

rel fix, prepare, ready; arrange

ant clear

6 *syn* see GAMBLE 1

7 *syn* see INCITE

‖8 *syn* see SIT 1

9 *syn* see BELONG 1

10 *syn* see COAGULATE

11 *of a fowl* to incubate eggs by crouching upon them <a chicken house filled with hens *setting* on eggs>

syn brood, ‖clock, cover, sit

rel hatch, incubate; hover

12 *of a celestial body* to pass below the horizon <the sun *set* at seven o'clock>

syn decline, dip, go down, sink

rel descend, drop

con ascend, climb, come up

ant rise

13 *syn* see HARDEN 1

rel crystallize, granulate; fix

set (at) *vb syn* see ESTIMATE 1

set *adj* 1 *syn* see SITUATED

2 *syn* see DECIDED 2

3 *syn* see FIRM 4

rel confirmed, entrenched, established, inveterate, rooted, well-set, well-settled; prescribed, specified

4 *syn* see LITTLE 2

rel diehard, inflexible, obstinate, pigheaded, rigid, unbending, unyielding

5 *syn* see FAST 4

rel fastened; close; sound

6 *syn* see EXPRESS 2

7 *syn* see READY 1

set *n* 1 *syn* see GIFT 2

2 *syn* see BEARING 1

3 *syn* see SCENE 1

4 *syn* see GROUP 3

rel assortment, gaggle; kit, pack

5 a number of people having something (as habit, interest, occupation, or age) in common <the horsey *set* was gathered at the bar>

syn bunch, circle, crowd, group, lot, push; *compare* CLIQUE

rel clan, clique, crew, gang, mob; cénacle; camp, faction; company

set back *vb syn* see DELAY 1

setback *n* a checking of progress <loss of his fellowship was a serious *setback* to his education>

syn backset, check, reversal, reverse; *compare* COMEDOWN

---

syn synonym(s)　　*rel* related word(s)

ant antonym(s)　　*con* contrasted word(s)

idiom idiomatic equivalent(s)

‖ use limited; if in doubt, see a dictionary

rel delay, retardation, slowdown; hindrance, impediment, obstacle, stumbling block; disappointment; rebuff; defeat; regress, regression

idiom reverse of fortune

con advancement, forwarding, progressing

set down *vb syn* see ALIGHT

set off *vb* 1 *syn* see COMPENSATE 1

2 *syn* see MOBILIZE 1

set on *vb syn* see INCITE

set out *vb* 1 *syn* see DESIGN 3

2 *syn* see HEAD 3

idiom set one's course for

setout *n* 1 *syn* see COSTUME

2 *syn* see BEGINNING

setting *n syn* see SCENE 1

setting-out *n syn* see DEPARTURE 1

settle *vb* 1 *syn* see ENSCONCE 2

2 *syn* see CALM

rel assure, reassure

ant unsettle

3 *syn* see SET 1

rel found, ground, lodge, seat

con dislodge, uproot, unseat

ant unsettle

4 *syn* see DECIDE

rel fix, seal

idiom come to a decision (*or* conclusion), form a judgment, make a decision

5 *syn* see NEGOTIATE 1

rel mediate, reconcile, straighten (out)

idiom bring to terms (*or* agreement)

6 *syn* see CLEAR 5

idiom settle the score, settle up (*or* square) accounts

7 to put in order for final disposal <waiting to *settle* an estate>

syn clean up, wind up

8 *syn* see ALIGHT

rel flop (down), plop (down)

settled *adj* 1 *syn* see FIRM 4

rel decided, determined

con uncertain, undecided

ant unsettled

2 *syn* see INVETERATE 1

3 *syn* see DECIDED 2

rel certain, fixed

con irresolute, undecided, undetermined, unresolved, vacillating, wavering

ant unsettled

settlement *n* 1 *syn* see HABITATION 1

2 *syn* see DECISION 1

rel showdown; quietus

settlings *n pl syn* see SEDIMENT

set to *vb* 1 *syn* see BEGIN 1

2 *syn* see PITCH IN 1

set-to *n* 1 *syn* see BRAWL 2

2 *syn* see QUARREL

3 *syn* see ENCOUNTER

set up *vb* 1 *syn* see ERECT 5

ant tear down

2 *syn* see ELATE

3 *syn* see ERECT 3

con disassemble, take down

4 *syn* see FOUND 2

rel generate, originate; start up; open

5 *syn* see INTRODUCE 3

6 *syn* see TREAT 3

setup *n syn* see SNAP 1

seventh heaven *n syn* see ECSTASY

rel exhilaration; bliss, paradise

con sadness, unhappiness; blues, doldrums, dumps

sever *vb* **1** *syn* see SEPARATE 1

2 *syn* see KNOW 4

3 *syn* see CUT 5

several *adj* **1** possessed by or attributed to a specific individual <the debaters expressed their *several* opinions>
syn individual, particular, respective, singular
rel independent; personal, special, specific
2 *syn* see DISTINCT 2
3 consisting of an indefinite number more than two and less than many <*several* days passed>
syn divers, some, sundry, various
rel particular, separate, single; few; considerable; many, numerous
idiom not a few
‖**4** *syn* see MANY

‖**several** *pron syn* see SUNDRY

severalize *vb syn* see KNOW 4

severally *adv syn* see APART 1
rel discretely; exclusively
idiom one at a time

severe *adj* **1** given to or characterized by strict discipline and firm restraint <treated all the students with *severe* impartiality>
syn ascetic, astringent, austere, mortified, stern
rel exacting, heavy-handed, onerous, oppressive; disciplined, iron-willed, self-disciplined; inflexible, restrictive, rigid, rigorous, strict, stringent, uncompromising, unyielding
con easy, easygoing, gentle, mild, soft; clement, forbearing, indulgent, lax, lenient, merciful
ant tender, tolerant
2 *syn* see GRIM 2
rel serious, sober, stern
3 of a kind to cause discomfort or hardship <a *severe* winter storm>
syn bitter, brutal, hard, harsh, inclement, intemperate, rigorous, rugged
rel crimpy, unpleasant; forbidding, hostile, inhospitable; bleak, disagreeable, grim; painful, raw, sharp, smart; blistering, extreme, intense, savage; blustering, blustery, stormy, wintry
con balmy, calm, equable, gentle, moderate, soft, temperate
ant mild
4 *syn* see HARD 6
5 *syn* see SERIOUS 2
rel consequential; dear, sore

severely *adv* **1** *syn* see HARD 5
2 *syn* see SERIOUSLY 2
rel markedly

‖**sew** *vb syn* see EXUDE

sew up *vb* ‖**1** *syn* see EXHAUST 4
2 *syn* see MONOPOLIZE

sexy *adj syn* see RISQUÉ

shabby *adj* **1** being ill-kept and showing signs of wear and tear <a *shabby* neighborhood full of depressing tenements>
syn bedraggled, broken-down, decrepit, dilapidated, dingy, disreputable, down-at-heel, faded, mangy, moth-eaten, run-down, scrubby, scruffy, seedy, shoddy, sleazy, slipshod, squalid, tacky, tagrag, tattered, threadbare, tired
rel disfigured, dog-eared; decaying, deteriorated, deteriorating; ramshackle, ratty, rickety; bare, miserable, neglected, poor,

poverty-stricken; sordid; worm-eaten; outworn, worn-out; abandoned, desolate, ruined, ruinous, wrecked
idiom gone to seed
con neat, spick-and-span, tidy, trig, trim, well-kept; brand-new, fresh, new; unused
ant spruce
2 *syn* see CONTEMPTIBLE
3 *syn* see DISREPUTABLE 1

‖**shack** *n syn* see VAGABOND

shack *n syn* see HUT

shackle *n, usu* **shackles** *pl* something that confines the legs or arms so as to prevent free movement <slaves in *shackles*>
syn bond(s), chains, fetter(s), gyve(s), iron(s)
rel anklet, bilbo, leg-iron, trammel; bracelet, handcuff, manacle; straitjacket; collar, garrote

shackle *vb syn* see HAMPER
rel lash, rope, strap; chain, enchain, manacle; handcuff; pinion, secure
con unchain, unfetter, untie
ant unshackle

shade *n* **1** comparative darkness or obscurity due to interception of light rays <trees providing *shade* from the sunlight>
syn adumbration, penumbra, shadow, umbra, umbrage
rel blackness, darkness, dimness, obscuration, obscurity; cover, shelter
con brightness, brilliancy, effulgence, radiance; blaze, glare, glow
2 *syn* see APPARITION
3 *syn* see COLOR 1
rel intensity, saturation
4 *syn* see GRADATION
rel difference, distinction, variation
5 *syn* see HINT 2

shade *vb* to cast into shadow by intercepting light rays <avenues *shaded* by large trees>
syn inumbrate, screen, shadow, umbrage
rel shelter; cover
con roast, scorch, swelter; expose

shaded *adj syn* see SHADY 1
ant unshaded

shadow *n* **1** *syn* see SHADE 1
2 *syn* see APPARITION
3 *syn* see VESTIGE 1
4 *syn* see HINT 2

shadow *vb* **1** *syn* see SHADE
2 *syn* see OBSCURE
3 *syn* see TAIL

shadow (forth) *vb* **1** *syn* see SUGGEST 5
2 *syn* see ADUMBRATE 1
rel forecast, foretell, predict

shadow *adj syn* see SHADY 1

shadowed *adj syn* see SHADY 1
ant unshadowed

shadowy *adj* **1** *syn* see IMAGINARY 1
2 *syn* see GHASTLY 1
3 *syn* see FAINT 2
rel amorphous; foggy
4 *syn* see SHADY 1
ant bright

shady *adj* **1** producing, affording, or abounding in shade <a *shady* day> <cool, *shady* streets>
syn shaded, shadow, shadowed, shadowy, umbrageous, umbrous
rel bosky, screened, sheltered; dusky; dark

con exposed, unshaded, unshadowed; unsheltered; bright, light
ant sunny
2 *syn* see DOUBTFUL 1
3 *syn* see DISREPUTABLE 1
rel subreputable
4 *syn* see RISQUÉ
rel disreputable, shameful

shaft *n* 1 *syn* see RAY 1
2 a scornful, cutting, or pithily critical remark <the target of his latest *shaft* is the president himself>
syn barb, dart
rel cut, jab, thrust; potshot
3 harsh or unfair treatment <he really got the *shaft*: he was fired without notice>
syn ‖screw, ‖screwing
rel short end
idiom ‖a royal screwing, the dirty end of the stick, ‖the royal shaft

shake *vb* 1 to move irregularly to and fro or up and down often in a wavering or oscillating manner <was so frightened that her hands *shook*>
syn ‖didder, dither, quake, quaver, quiver, shiver, shudder, tremble, tremor, twitter
rel palpitate, quail, waver; flicker, flit, flitter, flutter; fluctuate, oscillate; chatter, shimmy, vibrate
idiom shake like an aspen leaf
2 to undergo strong vibration especially as the result of a physical blow or shock <the platform *shook* as the train passed>
syn jar, quake, tremble, tremor, vibrate
rel bounce, jounce; chatter, quiver, shimmy; rock, stagger
3 to cause to move in a quick, jerky manner <rattling and *shaking* the latch>
syn jiggle, joggle
rel bounce, ‖chounse, jounce; jostle; rattle; jerk
4 to cause to move to and fro or up and down violently <an earthquake that *shook* the whole coast>
syn agitate, concuss, convulse, rock
rel jog, jostle, rattle, ‖shog; commove, discompose, disorder, jar, jolt, unsettle; disquiet, disturb, perturb, upset; churn, roil, ruffle, stir up, whip
5 to get or keep away from (a pursuer) <tried unsuccessfully to *shake* the man tailing him>
syn lose, slip, throw off; *compare* ESCAPE 2
rel avoid, elude; outwit
idiom get rid of, give (someone) the shake (*or* slip), slip from under the eye of
6 *syn* see DISMAY 1
rel disturb, jar, rattle, unsettle, upset; bother, worry; unstring
shake (off) *vb* *syn* see RID
shake *n* 1 *syn* see EARTHQUAKE
2 **shakes** *pl syn* see JITTERS
3 *syn* see INSTANT 1
4 *syn* see DEAL 2
shake down *vb* 1 *syn* see EXTORT 1
2 *syn* see SEARCH 2

shake up *vb* *syn* see SPEED 3
shake–up *n* an extensive and often drastic rearrangement <a personnel *shake-up* effected by new management>
syn overturn, reorganization, revolution, turnover
rel liquidation, purge; cleanout, cleanup, clearing out, clear-up; removal, riddance
idiom break with the past, clean sweep
shakiness *n syn* see INSTABILITY
shaking *adj syn* see TREMULOUS
rel unsettled, unstable, unsteady; tottering
con unshakable, unshaken
shaky *adj* 1 *syn* see WEAK 2
rel unsettled; infirm, unsound, unsteady; precarious, tottering, tottery
2 *syn* see DOUBTFUL 1
3 *syn* see TREMULOUS
4 *syn* see RICKETY
shallow *adj* 1 lacking physical depth <buried in a *shallow* grave>
syn shoal, superficial
rel shallowish; surface
idiom as deep as a mud puddle, no deeper than a heavy dew, not deep enough to float a match
con bottomless, unfathomable
ant deep
2 *syn* see SUPERFICIAL 2
rel paltry, petty, trifling, trivial; empty, hollow, idle, vain; bird-witted, feather-brained, flighty
con heavy, profound; discerning, penetrating
ant deep
shallow *n syn* see SHOAL
ant deep
sham *n* 1 *syn* see IMPOSTURE
rel facade, fakery, false front, Potemkin village
2 *syn* see HYPOCRISY
3 *syn* see MOCKERY 2
sham *vb syn* see ASSUME 4
rel ape, copy, imitate, mock; create, invent; lie, mislead
sham *adj* 1 *syn* see FICTITIOUS 2
rel affected, assumed, feigned; pseudo, so-called; make-believe, pretend
2 *syn* see COUNTERFEIT
3 *syn* see ARTIFICIAL 2
rel plaster, synthetic; adulterated; bogus
shamble *vb syn* see SHUFFLE 3
shambles *n pl but usu sing in constr syn* see MESS 3
shame *n syn* see DISGRACE
rel chagrin, embarrassment; guilt, mortification, self-reproach, self-reproof
con pride, self-admiration, self-love, self-respect
ant glory
shamed *adj syn* see ASHAMED
rel crestfallen; shamefaced, shamefast; crushed, disgraced
idiom loaded (*or* bowed down) with shame
ant proud
shameful *adj syn* see DISREPUTABLE 1
shameless *adj* characterized by or exhibiting boldness and a lack of shame <a *shameless* hussy>
syn arrant, barefaced, blatant, brassy, brazen, brazenfaced, impudent, overbold, unabashed, unblushing

rel audacious, bold. cheeky, presumptuous; baldfaced, high-handed; abandoned, dissolute, profligate; immodest, lewd; disgraceful, outrageous

idiom bold as brass, dead (*or* lost) to shame

con bashful, diffident, mousy, shy; chaste, decent, modest, pure

‖**shamus** *n syn* see PRIVATE DETECTIVE

Shangri—la *n syn* see UTOPIA

shanty *n syn* see HUT

shape *vb syn* see MAKE 3

rel devise, plan, work up; tailor

shape *n* 1 *syn* see FORM 1

rel appearance, aspect, look, semblance

2 *syn* see ORDER 9

3 *syn* see ORDER 10

rel state, whack

shapeful *adj syn* see SHAPELY

ant shapeless

shapeless *adj syn* see FORMLESS

rel unshapely; deformed, misshapen

con proportional, proportionate, proportioned, shapeful, symmetrical

ant shapeful, shapely

shapely *adj* having a regular or pleasing shape <a *shapely* girl>

syn clean-limbed, shapeful, statuesque, trim, well-proportioned, well-turned; *compare* CURVACEOUS

rel balanced, clean-cut, proportioned, regular, symmetrical; comely, pleasing; ‖built, full-figured, rounded, ‖stacked; buxom

con dumpy, squat, stumpy; angular, lank, lean; ill-favored, ill-looking

ant shapeless, unshapely

share *n* 1 something belonging to, assumed by, or falling to one (as in division or apportionment) <wanted his *share* of the prize money>

syn allotment, allowance, bite, cut, lot, part, partage, portion, quota, slice; *compare* RATION

rel proportion, quotient, quotum; commission, percentage; divide, ‖divvy; rakeoff

idiom piece of the action, slice of the melon

2 *syn* see RATION

3 *syn* see INTEREST 1

share *vb* 1 *syn* see APPORTION 2

rel assign, deal (out), dispense, dole (out), give out, mete (out)

idiom ‖go snucks, share and share alike

con retain, withhold; combine, unite

2 to have, get, or use in common with another or others <she *shared* her husband's fate>

syn partake, participate

rel experience

idiom have a share (*or* part) in, have (*or* take) a hand in

shared *adj syn* see COMMON 1

ant unshared

share out *vb syn* see ADMINISTER 2

sharer *n syn* see PARTICIPANT

sharp *adj* 1 having a fine edge <a *sharp* knife makes a clean cut>

syn honed, keen, razor-sharp, unblunted, whetted

rel acute

idiom sharp as a razor blade

con blunted, dulled; unsharpened

ant blunt, dull

2 *syn* see POINTED 1

3 *syn* see INTELLIGENT 2

4 possessing or indicative of alert competence and clear understanding <people of *sharp* judgment and refined sensibilities>

syn acute, keen, penetrating, penetrative, quick-sighted, quick-witted, sharp-sighted, sharp-witted; *compare* SHREWD

rel alert, bright; clever, cute, ingenious, original, resourceful; fast, quick

idiom sharp as a knife (*or* tack)

con dull-witted; unintelligent; foolish, simple, slow, stupid

ant dull

5 *syn* see ACUTE 3

6 *syn* see WISE 4

rel adroit, nimble; clever, cute; sly, unethical

idiom nobody's fool

7 *syn* see SHORT 5

rel acrimonious, biting, double-edged, incisive, penetrating, piercing, stabbing, stinging; caustic, virulent, vitriolic

8 causing intense mental or physical distress <a *sharp* pain>

syn acute, knifelike, piercing, shooting, stabbing

rel intense, severe, smart; biting, drilling, stinging; penetrating; agonizing, excruciating; paralyzing

9 *syn* see ACRID

rel odorous; strong-scented, strong-smelling; suffocating

10 *syn* see ACUTE 4

11 *syn* see STYLISH

‖**sharp** *vb syn* see SHARPEN

sharp *adv syn* see JUST 1

sharpen *vb* to give a keen edge to <*sharpen* an ax>

syn edge, hone, ‖sharp, whet

rel dress, file, grind, stroke

idiom hone to a razor edge, hone to razor sharpness

ant blunt, dull

sharper *n syn* see SWINDLER

sharp—eyed *adj* having keen vision <the *sharp-eyed* child found all the Easter eggs>

syn eagle-eyed, hawk-eyed, lyncean, lynx-eyed, sharp-sighted

rel alert, attentive, aware, keen, lynxlike, observant, sharp, vigilant, watchful

con myopic, nearsighted, shortsighted; dim-sighted, purblind; blind

sharpie *n syn* see SWINDLER

sharply *adv syn* see HARD 4

rel intensely, penetratingly, piercingly

sharpness *n syn* see EDGE 2

ant bluntness, dullness

sharp practice *n syn* see DECEPTION 1

sharp—sighted *adj* 1 *syn* see SHARP-EYED

2 *syn* see SHARP 4

sharp—witted *adj* 1 *syn* see SHARP 4

2 *syn* see WISE 4

shatter *vb* 1 to break into small pieces by or as if by a blow <*shatter* a windowpane with a rock>

syn burst, fragment, ‖pash, rive, shiver, smash, ‖smatter, splinter, splinterize, splitter; *compare* PULVERIZE 1

rel break, crack, rend, snap, ‖spalt, split; crunch, crush; crash, dash; fragmentalize,

fragmentize, pulverize; demolish, destroy, disintegrate, ruin, ||total, wreck
idiom smash to smithereens (*or* bits)
2 *syn* see DESTROY 1
3 *syn* see RATTLE 1
shatterable *adj syn* see FRAGILE 1
ant shatterproof
shatterbrain *n syn* see SCATTERBRAIN
shattering *adj syn* see DESTRUCTIVE
shattery *adj syn* see FRAGILE 1
idiom as delicate as an eggshell
shave *vb* 1 *syn* see SLIVER
2 *syn* see CUT 6
rel shingle
3 *syn* see REDUCE 2
4 *syn* see BRUSH
idiom cut (*or* shave) it close
5 *syn* see SCRAPE 3
shaveling *n syn* see BOY 1
shear *vb syn* see CUT 6
rel mow; barb, barber; manicure, snip
sheath *n syn* see SKIN 3
sheathe *vb* to cover (a surface) with something that protects <a house *sheathed* with aluminum siding>
syn clad, face, side, skin
rel envelop, surround, wrap; case, cover, encase, jacket; panel
con bare, expose, strip
sheathing *n syn* see SKIN 3
shed *vb* 1 *syn* see DISCARD
rel drop; divest
2 to cast off (a body covering) in a periodic process of growth or renewal <a snake *shedding* its skin>
syn exuviate, molt, slip, slough
rel cast off, discard; doff, take off
sheen *n syn* see LUSTER
rel finish; shininess
sheeny *adj syn* see LUSTROUS 1
sheepheaded *adj syn* see SIMPLE 3
sheer *adj* 1 *syn* see FILMY
rel airy, chiffon, thin; see-through
2 *syn* see UTTER
3 *syn* see PURE 2
rel arrant, bald-faced, complete, outright
4 *syn* see STEEP 1
sheer *vb* 1 *syn* see TURN 6
2 *syn* see SWERVE 1
||**shekels** *n pl syn* see MONEY
shell *n syn* see HULL
shell *vb* 1 *syn* see SHUCK
2 *syn* see BOMBARD
rel pepper; rake
idiom open fire on
shellac *vb syn* see WHIP 2
shellacking *n syn* see DEFEAT 1
rel ||clobbering, whipping
shell out *vb syn* see SPEND 1
shelter *n* 1 something (as a structure or place) that covers or affords protection <a bomb *shelter*>
syn asylum, cover, covert, harbor, harborage, haven, port, refuge, retreat, sanctuary; *compare* REFUGE 1
rel buen retiro, den, hermitage, hide, hideaway, hideout, hidey-hole, retirement, tower

2 dwellings provided for numbers of people or for a community <*shelter* for the aged>
syn housing, quarterage
rel dwellings, lodging; roof
3 *syn* see REFUGE 1
shelter *vb syn* see HARBOR 1
shelve *vb syn* see DEFER
rel dish, drop, give up
idiom put on the shelf
shenanigan *n* 1 *syn* see TRICK 1
rel fast one, game, legerdemain
2 *syn* see PRANK
rel frolic; goings-on, mischievousness; stunt
Sheol *n syn* see HELL
shepherd *vb syn* see GUIDE
Sherlock *n syn* see DETECTIVE
Sherlock Holmes *n syn* see DETECTIVE
shibboleth *n* 1 *syn* see CATCHWORD
rel platitude, truism
2 *syn* see COMMONPLACE
||**shick** *adj syn* see INTOXICATED 1
||**shicker** *adj syn* see INTOXICATED 1
||**shicker** *n syn* see DRUNKARD
shield *n syn* see DEFENSE 1
rel buffer, bumper, screen
shield *vb* 1 *syn* see HARBOR 1
idiom give cover (*or* shelter) to; take (*or* shield) under one's wing
ant expose
2 *syn* see DEFEND 1
shift *vb* ||1 *syn* see APPORTION 2
2 *syn* see CHANGE 5
3 *syn* see MOVE 4
rel alter, change, vary; budge, stir; shuffle; relocate
idiom shift place
4 *syn* see CONSUME 5
5 to carry on one's affairs independently and self-sufficiently often under difficult circumstances <had to *shift* for his own maintenance on very meager pay>
syn do, fare, get along, get by, get on, ||make out, manage, muddle through, stagger (on *or* along)
rel contrive, survive; freelance; progress, succeed
idiom fend for oneself, make do, make it alone, make shift, paddle one's own canoe, stand on one's own two feet
shift *n* 1 *syn* see CONVERSION 2
2 *syn* see RESOURCE 3
rel gambit, maneuver, ploy, strategy
3 *syn* see SPELL 1
4 *syn* see TRANSITION
5 *syn* see TURN 2
shifty *adj* 1 *syn* see EVASIVE 1
rel dodging, elusive; cagey, collusive, conniving, crafty, cunning; furtive, shifty-eyed, sneaky, tricky; insidious, shady; deceitful, dishonest, fraudulent; treacherous
idiom shifty as the sand
2 *syn* see DISHONEST
3 *syn* see UNDERHAND
4 *syn* see MUTABLE 2
shill *n syn* see DECOY 2
shillaber *n syn* see DECOY 2
||**shillelagh** *n syn* see CUDGEL
shilling shocker *n syn* see DIME NOVEL
shilly-shally *adj syn* see VACILLATING 2
shilly-shally *n syn* see HESITATION

---

syn synonym(s)   *rel* related word(s)
ant antonym(s)   *con* contrasted word(s)
idiom idiomatic equivalent(s)
|| use limited; if in doubt, see a dictionary

shilly-shally *vb syn* see HESITATE
shilly-shallying *adj syn* see VACILLAT-
ING 2
rel halfhearted, lukewarm
shimmer *vb syn* see FLASH 1
shimmer *n syn* see FLASH 1
rel blinking; spangle; spark, sparking
shin *vb syn* see RUN 1
shindig *n* 1 a large, festive, and often
overly lavish party < threw the *shindig* of
the year for the debs >
syn bash, ‖blowout, shindy
rel fête, gala; ball, dance; party; affair,
shebang; ‖shivoo
2 *syn* see COMMOTION 3
shindy *n* 1 *syn* see SHINDIG 1
2 *syn* see COMMOTION 3
shine *vb* 1 to emit rays of light < the
storm is over and the sun is *shining* >
syn beam, burn, gleam, radiate
rel glimmer, glow; incandesce, luminesce;
flash, sparkle, twinkle; flare; glare
2 *syn* see POLISH 1
shine *n* 1 *syn* see DISPLAY 2
2 *syn* see LUSTER
rel finish
3 *usu* shines *pl syn* see PRANK
shiner *n syn* see BLACK EYE 1
shingle *vb syn* see OVERLAP
shining *adj syn* see LUSTROUS 1
shiny *adj syn* see LUSTROUS 1
ship *vb* 1 *syn* see SEND 1
rel direct; freight; export
ant receive
2 *syn* see MOVE 4
shipshape *adj syn* see NEAT 2
shipwreck *vb* 1 to destroy, disable, or
seriously damage a ship (as by running
aground or causing to founder) < the
typhoon *shipwrecked* the entire fishing
fleet >
syn beach, cast away, pile up, strand,
wreck
rel break up; scuttle; founder; capsize; go
down, sink
idiom go aground, go to the bottom (*or*
Davy Jones's locker), run on the rocks
2 *syn* see RUIN 1
shirk *vb* 1 *syn* see SNEAK
2 *syn* see DODGE 1
rel bilk, burke; bypass, double, eschew,
get around; shuffle off, shun
shirker *n syn* see SLACKER
shirty *adj syn* see ANGRY
shivaree *n* a noisy mock serenade to a
newly married couple < *shivarees* and
other such disappearing rural customs>
syn ‖belling, ‖bull band, ‖callithump,
charivari, ‖horning, ‖riding, ‖skimmelton
rel entertainment, reception, welcome
shiver *vb syn* see SHATTER 1
shiver *vb syn* see SHAKE 1
‖**shivereens** *n pl syn* see SMITHEREENS
shivering *adj syn* see TREMULOUS
shivers *n pl syn* see JITTERS
shivery *adj* 1 *syn* see TREMULOUS
2 *syn* see COLD 1
shoal *adj syn* see SHALLOW 1
shoal *n* a place where a body of water (as
a sea or river) is not deep < dangerous
shoals in uncharted waters >
syn shallow
rel barrier, barrier reef, coral reef, fring-
ing reef, reef, sand reef; bank, bar, sand-

bank, sandbar, tombolo; hook, spit; sea-
mount
con abyss, deep, depth
shock *n syn* see PILE 1
shock *n* 1 *syn* see IMPACT
2 *syn* see EARTHQUAKE
3 *syn* see TRAUMA
rel prostration, stupefaction
shock *vb* 1 to offend the moral sense of
< were *shocked* by pornography >
syn scandalize
rel astonish, astound, startle, surprise;
jar, jolt, shake up; insult, offend, outrage;
appall, horrify; floor, knock out; disgust,
nauseate, sicken
idiom stink in one's nostrils, turn one's
stomach
2 to cause to undergo a physical or psychological shock < his slap *shocked* her
out of hysterics >
syn jolt, startle
rel shake; jar; electrify
shocked *adj syn* see AGHAST 1
rel jarred, jolted, shaken up, ‖shook up;
offended, outraged; appalled, horrified
shocker *n* 1 *syn* see THRILLER
2 *syn* see DIME NOVEL
shocking *adj* 1 *syn* see FEARFUL 3
rel heinous, monstrous
2 *syn* see OUTRAGEOUS 2
rel burning, glaring; disgraceful, shameful; unspeakable
shoddy *adj* 1 *syn* see CHEAP 2
rel makeshift, scambling
2 *syn* see SHABBY 1
3 *syn* see DISREPUTABLE 1
shoeless *adj syn* see BAREFOOT 1
ant shod
shoestring *adj syn* see LITTLE 3
‖**shog** *vb syn* see PUSH 2
shoo-in *n syn* see SURE THING
‖**shool** *vb syn* see SHUFFLE
shoot *vb* 1 to cause (a weapon) to drive a
projectile forward < *shoot* an arrow at a
target >
syn discharge, fire, loose
rel trigger; launch, project; expel; blast;
poop
idiom let fly
2 *syn* see DESTROY 1
3 *syn* see DISCREDIT 2
‖4 *syn* see DISCARD
5 *syn* see VOMIT
‖6 *syn* see PASS 9
7 *syn* see SHOOT UP 2
8 *syn* see FLY 1
9 *syn* see RUSH 1
rel gallop, highball, hotfoot; spurt
10 *syn* see PHOTOGRAPH
shoot *n syn* see RAY 1
shooting *adj syn* see SHARP 8
ant stationary
shooting match *n syn* see AFFAIR 1
shoot up *vb* 1 *syn* see SKYROCKET
2 to take (a drug) by hypodermic needle
< had been *shooting up* heroin for weeks >
syn ‖mainline, shoot
shop *n syn* see STORE 4
rel boutique
shoplift *vb* to steal displayed goods from a
store < the manager caught them *shoplift-
ing* records >
syn ‖boost

rel bag, cop, ‖nick, palm, pilfer, pinch, rip off, snitch, swipe

shopworn *adj syn* see TRITE
rel overused, overworked, overworn

shore *n* the land bordering a usually large body of water < watched the ships while walking along the *shore* >
syn bank, beach, coast, strand
rel coastline, shoreline, waterfront, waterside; coastland, seacoast, seashore; foreshore, littoral, shoreface, shoreside; brink, embankment, riverbank, riverside

shore (up) *vb syn* see SUPPORT 4

shore *n syn* see SUPPORT 3

short *adj* 1 having little length in space or time < a *short* visit >
syn brief
rel abbreviate, abbreviated, abridged, curtailed, decreased, diminished, lessened, shortened; curtate, decurtate
con extensive, lengthy; drawn-out, overlong; extended, prolonged, protracted
ant long
2 having small physical stature < he was the *shortest* boy present >
syn ‖low, low-set, low-statured
rel chunky, dumpy, squat, squatty, stubby, thick, thickset
con gangling, gangly, lanky, rangy; elevated, high, lofty, spiring, towering
ant tall
3 not coming up to a measure or need < fuel was very *short* that year >
syn deficient, failing, inadequate, insufficient, scant, scanty, scarce, scrimpy, shy, skimpy, slender, unsufficient, wanting; *compare* MEAGER 2
rel lacking, needing; exiguous, meager, sparse
con abounding, overflowing, teeming; abundant, ample, copious, plenteous, plentiful
ant long
4 *syn* see BLUFF
ant expansive
5 lacking in graciousness or consideration < his manner was *short* and abrupt >
syn inconsiderate, sharp, thoughtless, unceremonious, ungracious
rel bluff, blunt, brusque, crusty, curt; short-spoken; gruff, irascible
con considerate, gracious, kindly; bland, smooth; ceremonious
6 readily breaking or crumbling < a rich *short* pastry >
syn brittle, crisp, crumbly, ‖crump, crunchy, friable
rel delicate, fragile
con soggy, tough
7 *syn* see CONCISE
rel compact; pointed
idiom to the point
con extended, protracted, spun-out
ant lengthy, long-drawn-out

short *adv* 1 without hesitation or delay < stopped *short* >
syn abruptly, asudden, forthwith, sudden, suddenly

con hesitantly; gradually, slowly
2 *syn* see UNAWARES

short *n syn* see SUBSTANCE 2

short *vb syn* see SPARE 3

shortage *n syn* see FAILURE 3
rel curtailment, pinch, tightness; shortfall
ant overage

short and sweet *adj syn* see CONCISE

shortcoming *n syn* see IMPERFECTION
idiom weak point
con forte, long suit

shortcut *n* a route shorter or more direct than the one ordinarily taken < they took a *shortcut* down the back roads >
syn cutoff
rel bypass
ant detour

shorten *vb* to reduce in extent (as of length or duration) < decided to *shorten* their visit > < *shorten* a skirt for summer wear >
syn abbreviate, abridge, curtail, cut, cut back, retrench, slash
rel decrease, diminish, elide, excerpt, lessen, reduce; compress, condense, contract, shrink; bobtail, clip, dock; minimize
idiom cut short
con draw out, protract
ant elongate; lengthen; extend, prolong

shorthanded *adj* short of the necessary number of people < the office was critically *shorthanded* >
syn underhanded, undermanned, understaffed
rel short, wanting
con overmanned, overstaffed

short-lived *adj syn* see TRANSIENT
rel short-haul, short-run, short-term
con long-run, long-term
ant agelong; long-lived

shortly *adv* 1 *syn* see BRIEFLY
2 *syn* see PRESENTLY 1
rel pronto, quickly

short-range *adj syn* see TACTICAL 1
ant long-range

shortsighted *adj syn* see MYOPIC
ant farsighted, longsighted

short-spoken *adj syn* see BLUFF
ant windy

shot *n* 1 *syn* see FLING 1
2 *syn* see OPPORTUNITY
3 *syn* see DRAM

‖**shot** *adj syn* see INTOXICATED 1

shotgun *vb syn* see FORCE 2

should *vb syn* see WANT 3

shoulder *vb syn* see PUSH 2

shout *vb* 1 to utter a sudden loud cry (as to express joy or triumph or to attract attention) < the mob *shouted* for a speech >
syn cry, whoop, yell; *compare* CALL 1, SCREAM 1
rel exclaim; howl, scream, shriek; bawl, bellow, clamor, roar, vociferate
con murmur, whisper
2 *syn* see SCREAM 4
3 *syn* see CALL 1
rel bark; bray
4 *syn* see TREAT 3

shove *vb* 1 *syn* see PUSH 1
rel cram, jam; dig, jab, poke, prod
idiom push and shove
2 *syn* see PUSH 2

---

syn synonym(s)   *rel* related word(s)
ant antonym(s)   *con* contrasted word(s)
idiom idiomatic equivalent(s)
‖ use limited; if in doubt, see a dictionary

3 *syn* see PUSH 6

shove (off) *vb syn* see GO 2
ant pull in

shovel *vb* 1 *syn* see DIG 1

2 *syn* see DIG 2

shovel *vb syn* see SHUFFLE

show *vb* 1 to set out or place on view for customers < we're *showing* lots of long dresses this fall >
syn display, offer
rel afford, supply; exhibit; present, proffer, submit; deal (in), sell

2 to reveal outwardly or make apparent < asked a question or two to *show* his intelligence >
syn demonstrate, evidence, evince, exhibit, illustrate, manifest, mark, ostend, proclaim; *compare* LOOK 4
rel disclose, discover, divulge, lay out, reveal, unveil; present, project
con camouflage, conceal, dissemble, hide, obscure
ant disguise

3 *syn* see STAGE

4 to present in such a way as to invite notice, attention, and admiration < she loved to *show* her jewels to everyone >
syn brandish, display, disport, exhibit, expose, flash, flaunt, parade, show off, trot out
rel air, lay out, set out, spread; blazon, flourish, sport, vaunt
con belittle, deprecate, depreciate, minimize

5 to give an exact and usually automatic reading or indication of < the speedometer *shows* 70 MPH >
syn indicate, mark, read, record, register, say
rel point (to); ring up

6 *syn* see LOOK 4
rel lay out, reveal, unveil

7 *syn* see GUIDE

8 *syn* see ESTABLISH 6
rel present; plead; allege

9 *syn* see APPEAR 1
rel come, show up; materialize

10 *syn* see COME 1
idiom ‖make the scene, put in an appearance, show one's face

11 *syn* see TURN UP 3

show *n syn* see APPEARANCE 2
rel likeness; effect, impression
idiom outward show

2 *syn* see MASK 2

3 *syn* see DISPLAY 2

4 *syn* see OPPORTUNITY

5 *syn* see EXHIBITION 1

6 *syn* see EXHIBITION 1

7 *syn* see MOVIE

8 *syn* see SHOWING 1

shower *n syn* see BARRAGE
rel shatter, spatter, spray

shower *vb syn* see BATHE 1

showing *n* 1 performance in a test of skill, power, or effectiveness < he made a good *showing* in the race >
syn out, show
rel record

2 *syn* see APPEARANCE 2

show-me *adj syn* see INCREDULOUS

show off *vb syn* see SHOW 4
rel boast, brag, swagger

---

showpiece *n* a prime or outstanding example used or suitable for exhibition < a Fabergé Easter egg was the *showpiece* of the collection >
syn chef d'oeuvre, masterpiece, pièce de résistance
rel gem, jewel; prize
con claptrap, rubbish, trash, trivia, truck

showroom *n syn* see STORE 4

show up *vb syn* see EXPOSE 4
rel discredit; invalidate

2 *syn* see TURN UP 3

3 *syn* see COME 1

showy *adj* given to or marked by excessive outward display < *showy* decorations >
syn chichi, flamboyant, orchidaceous, ostentatious, peacockish, peacocky, pretentious, splashy, swank
rel sporty; flashy, garish, gaudy, jazzy, meretricious, tawdry; gorgeous, resplendent; luxurious, opulent, ornate, sumptuous; overdone, overwrought; sensational
con muted, quiet, restrained, subdued; elegant, graceful, restrained; appropriate, seemly
ant unshowy

shred *n syn* see PARTICLE

shred *vb syn* see SLIVER

shreddy *adj syn* see RAGGED

shrew *n syn* see VIRAGO
rel she-devil, spitfire

shrewd *adj* marked by clever discerning awareness and hardheaded acumen < the captain was a *shrewd* judge of character >
syn argute, astucious, astute, cagey, heady, perspicacious, sagacious, ‖savvy; *compare* SHARP 4, WISE 2, 4
rel canny, crafty, foxy, ingenious, ‖pawky, slick, ‖sly, tidy; clever, intelligent, knowing, quick-witted, smart; polite, smooth; judicious, prudent, sensible, wise; penetrating, piercing, probing; acute, keen, sharp; farsighted, foresighted
con green, naive, simple, soft; foolable, gullible, slow

shrewdness *n syn* see WIT 3
rel canniness, foxiness

shriek *vb* 1 *syn* see SCREAM 1
rel squawk, ‖yarm

2 *syn* see SQUEAL 4

3 *syn* see SCREAM 4

shrill *vb syn* see SCREAM 1

shrill *adj syn* see ACUTE 4

shrine *n* a structure or place considered sacred by a religious group < pilgrims going to the *shrine* at Lourdes hoping to be healed >
syn holy place, sanctorium, sanctuary, sanctum
rel reliquary; enshrinement

shrink *vb* 1 *syn* see CONTRACT 3
rel shrivel (up), wither
con amplify, expand
ant swell

2 *syn* see FAIL 3
idiom shrink (*or* dwindle) down to nothing

3 *syn* see RECOIL
rel cower, cringe, crouch, huddle, slink; draw (back), recede, retire, retreat, withdraw; boggle, demur, scruple

shrinking *adj* *syn* see UNDEMONSTRATIVE

shrivel vb syn see WITHER
rel parch; fossilize

shroud vb 1 syn see ENFOLD 1
2 syn see SCREEN 3

shrouded adj syn see ULTERIOR

shuck n syn see HULL

shuck vb to strip, break off, or remove the enclosing case or cover of < *shuck* corn >
syn hull, husk, shell; compare SKIN 2
rel decorticate, peel, skin, strip

shuck (off) vb syn see DISCARD

shudder vb syn see SHAKE 1
rel gyrate, shimmy

shuffle vb 1 syn see DISORDER 1
2 syn see EQUIVOCATE 2
3 to walk awkwardly in a sliding, dragging way without lifting the feet < an old drunk *shuffling* along in filthy bedroom slippers >
syn scuff, scuffle, shamble, ||shool, shovel
rel drag, pad, scrape, slipper, slip-slop, slur; draggle, straggle, trail (along)
4 syn see STUMBLE 6

shuffle n syn see CLUTTER 2

shuffling adj syn see EVASIVE 1

shun vb syn see ESCAPE 2
rel decline, refuse, reject; snub; despise, disdain, scorn
idiom have nothing to do with, keep away from, stand aloof from, steer clear of, turn away from, turn one's back upon
con accept, adopt, welcome

shunning n syn see ESCAPE 2

shunt vb 1 to push or turn off to one side < *shunt* a railroad car onto a siding >
syn sidetrack, switch; compare TURN 6
rel change, move, shift, transfer; avert, deflect, divert, head off
idiom push aside (or to the side)
2 syn see SHUTTLE

shush vb 1 syn see SILENCE
2 syn see SUPPRESS 2

shut vb syn see CLOSE 1
rel lock, seal; batten (down)
ant open

||shut-eye n syn see SLEEP 1

shut in vb syn see ENCLOSE 1
ant shut out

shut-in adj syn see UNSOCIABLE

shut-mouthed adj syn see SILENT 3
ant openmouthed

shut off vb syn see SCREEN 3

shut out vb syn see SCREEN 3

shuttle vb to travel back and forth frequently < *shuttled* between New York and Washington every week >
syn shunt
rel shuttlecock; alternate

shut up vb 1 syn see SILENCE
2 to cease speaking < told the boy to sit down and *shut up* >
syn dry up, dumb (up), ||dummy (up), pipe down, ||ring off
rel hush, quiet (down), shush, soft-pedal
idiom button (or seal) one's lips, keep quiet

shy adj 1 disinclined to obtrude oneself < *shy* in the presence of strangers >

syn backward, bashful, coy, demure, diffident, modest, rabbity, retiring, self-effacing, timid, unassertive, unassured
rel backhanded, hesitant, reluctant; conscious, self-conscious, self-distrustful, shamefaced, sheepish; introversive, introvert, introverted, inturned; circumspect, reserved; cautious, chary, suspicious, wary; apprehensive, fearful, nervous, skittish, timorous
con brash, forward; aggressive, audacious, intrusive, obtruding, pushing, pushy; blunt, crass
ant bold, obtrusive
2 syn see DISINCLINED
3 syn see SHORT 3
4 syn see excess, over, surplus

shy vb 1 syn see DEMUR
rel blench, quail, recoil, shrink
2 syn see ESCAPE 2

shy n syn see POTSHOT

Shylock n syn see LOAN SHARK

shyster n syn see PETTIFOGGER

||sib adj syn see SYMPATHETIC 2

sibilate vb syn see HISS

sibylline adj 1 syn see PROPHETIC
2 syn see OBSCURE 3

sic vb syn see URGE
rel agitate, catalyze, inspirit, instigate; abet, aid, countenance, favor

sick adj 1 affected with illness or disease < was *sick* with pneumonia >
syn down, ill; compare UNWELL
rel diseased, disordered, fevered; ailing, ||cronk, ||crook, funny, indisposed, unwell; debilitated, sickly, unhealthy; rocky, tottering, wobbly; confined, laid up; lousy, mean, rotten
idiom ||on the sick list, sick as a dog
con healthy, strong
ant well
2 syn see MORBID
3 syn see FED UP
idiom ||up to here with
4 syn see FAULTY
5 syn see SICKLY 2

sick (up) vb syn see VOMIT

sicken vb 1 syn see UPSET 5
2 syn see DISGUST

sicken (with or of) vb syn see CONTRACT 1

sickening adj syn see OFFENSIVE

||sicker vb syn see EXUDE

sickliness n syn see INFIRMITY 1

sickly adj 1 syn see UNWELL
rel ||cranky, down
con hale, hearty; healthy, well
ant robust
2 accompanying, indicating, or suggesting sickness < a *sickly* complexion >
syn peaked, ||peaking, peaky, sick
rel ||pimping, puny, sickish, weak; diseased; unhealthy
con healthy, hearty
3 syn see UNWHOLESOME 1
4 syn see MORBID

sickness n 1 the condition of being ill < finally recovered from her *sickness* >
syn affliction, diseasedness, disorder, illness, indisposition, infirmity, unhealth; compare DISEASE 1, INFIRMITY 1
rel indisposedness, unhealthfulness, unhealthiness, unwellness; affection, ailment, ill

idiom ill health
con haleness, healthiness, heartiness
ant health
2 *syn* see DISEASE 1
side *n* 1 a place, space, or direction with
respect to a center or a line of division
<lived on the north *side* of the
street> <the morning *side* of the hill>
<turned to one *side*>
syn hand
rel direction, flank, sector
2 *syn* see PHASE
3 *syn* see VIEWPOINT 2
4 the attitude, position, or action of one
person or group as opposed to another
<could understand her *side* as well as his
in the quarrel>
syn part; *compare* POSITION 1
rel attitude, disposition; posture, stance,
stand; position, standpoint, viewpoint
side *vb syn* see SHEATHE
side (with) *vb syn* see SUPPORT 2
side action *n syn* see SIDE EFFECT
sideboards *n pl syn* see SIDE-WHISKERS
sideburns *n pl syn* see SIDE-WHISKERS
side effect *n* a secondary and usually
adverse effect (as of a drug) <drowsiness
is a common *side effect* of antihistimines>
syn side action, side reaction
rel effect; reaction, response
side–glance *n* a look or glance directed to
one side <she shot an impatient *side-
glance* at him>
syn side-look
rel glance; stare
sideling *adv syn* see SIDEWAYS 1
sideling *adj syn* see STEEP 1
‖**sidelings** *adv syn* see SIDEWAYS 1
sidelong *adv syn* see SIDEWAYS 1
side–look *n syn* see SIDE-GLANCE
side reaction *n syn* see SIDE EFFECT
sidereal *adj syn* see STELLAR 1
sidesplitter *n syn* see RIOT 2
sidestep *vb* 1 *syn* see EQUIVOCATE 2
2 *syn* see SKIRT 3
3 *syn* see DODGE 1
sideswipe *n syn* see POTSHOT
sidetrack *vb syn* see SHUNT 1
sideward *adv syn* see SIDEWAYS 1
sideways *adv* 1 to, toward, or at one side
<slipped *sideways* on the ice>
syn crabwise, laterally, sideling, ‖side-
lings, sidelong, sideward, sidewise; *compare* ASIDE 1
rel obliquely; indirectly
con straight; directly
2 *syn* see ASIDE 1
side–whiskers *n pl* the usually shaped
growth of whiskers on both sides of a
man's face <grew *side-whiskers* and a
moustache in order to look older>
syn burnsides, dundrearies, muttonchops,
sideboards, sideburns
sidewise *adv* 1 *syn* see SIDEWAYS 1
2 *syn* see ASIDE 1
sidle *vb* to move sideways or obliquely
especially in an unobtrusive or furtive
manner <a suspicious-looking man *sidled*
up to her>
syn edge, ‖slive
rel ease, slip
siege *n* a sometimes prolonged period of
disorder or stress (as of body or mind)
<endured a three-week *siege* of flu>

syn bout, go; *compare* ATTACK 3
rel attack, onslaught, seizure, spell
siesta *n syn* see NAP
siesta *vb syn* see NAP
sieve *n syn* see GOSSIP 1
sieve *vb syn* see SCREEN 5
sift *vb* 1 *syn* see SCREEN 5
2 *syn* see SORT 2
3 *syn* see EXPLORE
sigh *vb* 1 to take in and let out a deep
audible breath (as in weariness, grief, or
relief) <flopped down in the chair and
sighed deeply>
syn ‖sock, sough, suspire
rel breathe, respire; exhale; gasp, pant,
wheeze; groan, moan; sob
idiom heave a sigh
2 to make a sound like sighing <the wind
sighed in the branches>
syn sough
rel blow; murmur, whisper; moan; whine;
whistle; howl, roar
3 *syn* see LONG
sighful *adj syn* see MELANCHOLY 2
sight *n* 1 *syn* see EYESORE
‖2 *syn* see MUCH
3 *syn* see EYE 2
4 *syn* see LOOK 1
5 *syn* see VIEW 4
6 *syn* see VIEW 5
sightless *adj syn* see BLIND 1
ant sighted
sightseer *n syn* see TOURIST
sign *n* 1 a motion, action, gesture, or word
by which a command, thought, or wish is
expressed <put a finger to her lips as a
sign to keep quiet>
syn high sign, signal
rel gesticulation, gesture, motion; hint,
indication, suggestion, warning
2 *syn* see CHARACTER 1
3 *syn* see EXPRESSION 3
rel symbolization; attestation, evidence,
proof
4 *syn* see INDICATION 3
rel earmark, exponent, indicator; exhibit,
show
sign *vb* 1 to affix a signature to <he refused to *sign* a confession>
syn autograph, ink, signature, subscribe
idiom put one's John Hancock on, put
one's John Henry down (*or* on)
2 *syn* see SIGNAL
sign (over) *vb syn* see TRANSFER 4
signal *n syn* see SIGN 1
rel alarm, alert, tocsin; movement
signal *vb* to notify by or as if by a signal
<*signaled* his wife to keep quiet>
syn flag, gesture, motion, sign, signalize
idiom give the high sign (to)
signal *adj syn* see NOTICEABLE
rel characteristic, distinctive, individual,
peculiar, significative; eminent, famous,
illustrious, renowned
signalize *vb* 1 *syn* see CHARACTERIZE 2
2 *syn* see SIGNAL
signature *vb syn* see SIGN 1
significance *n* 1 *syn* see MEANING 1
2 *syn* see IMPORTANCE
rel authority, credit, influence, merit,
prestige; excellence, perfection, virtue
con indifference; triviality, unimportance,
worthlessness; irrelevance

ant insignificance

significancy *n syn* see MEANING 1

significant *adj* 1 *syn* see EXPRESSIVE
  rel cogent, compelling, convincing, sound, telling, valid; forceful, powerful; important, momentous, weighty
  con meaningless, unexpressive; unimportant
  ant insignificant
  2 *syn* see IMPORTANT 1
  con inconsequential, meaningless, unimportant
  ant insignificant

significant *n syn* see INDICATION 3

significantly *adv syn* see WELL 8
  ant insignificantly

signification *n* 1 *syn* see MEANING 1
  rel implying, signifying; construction, implication; essence, gist, substance
  ‖**2** *syn* see IMPORTANCE

significative *adj syn* see INDICATIVE

signify *vb* 1 *syn* see MEAN 2
  rel bear, carry, convey; bespeak, purport
  2 *syn* see MATTER

sign on *vb syn* see ENTER 3

sign up *vb syn* see ENTER 3

silence *n* 1 absence of sound or noise
  < the heavy *silence* of the night >
  syn noiselessness, quiet, quietness, quietude, soundlessness, still, stillness
  rel calm, hush, lull
  con din, uproar
  ant noise
  2 *syn* see SECRECY
  3 *syn* see DEATH 1

silence *vb* to compel or reduce to silence
  < *silenced* the courtroom chatter by pounding his gavel >
  syn choke (off), hush, quiet, ‖quieten, shush, shut up, still
  rel dampen, deaden, dumb, lull, muffle, mute; quash, quell, squash, squelch, suppress; gag, muzzle

silent *adj* 1 *syn* see DUMB 1
  2 characterized by absence of speech
  < was *silent* as he faced the altar >
  syn dumb, mum, ‖mumchance, mute, speechless, wordless; *compare* DUMB 1
  rel inarticulate, muted, tongue-tied, voiceless
  con speaking, talking
  3 showing marked restraint in speaking
  < a stern, *silent* man >
  syn close, close-lipped, closemouthed, close-tongued, dumb, inconversable, reserved, reticent, shut-mouthed, silentious, speechless, taciturn, tight-lipped, tight-mouthed, uncommunicative, wordless
  rel checked, curbed, inhibited, restrained; unconversational, unsociable; inarticulate, incoherent; mute, voiceless; mum, secretive
  con articulate, fluent, glib, vocal, voluble; babblative, garrulous, loquacious, windy; blabbering, blabbery, chattering
  ant talkative
  4 *syn* see STILL 3
  idiom silent as a post (*or* stone), silent as the grave (*or* tomb)

---

syn synonym(s)   *rel* related word(s)
ant antonym(s)   *con* contrasted word(s)
idiom idiomatic equivalent(s)
‖ use limited; if in doubt, see a dictionary

---

ant noisy
  5 *syn* see UNSPOKEN 1

silentious *adj syn* see SILENT 3

silhouette *n syn* see OUTLINE
  rel ‖shade, shadow

silken *adj* 1 *syn* see SOFT 3
  2 *syn* see INGRATIATING

silky *adj* 1 *syn* see SOFT 3
  2 *syn* see INGRATIATING

silliness *n syn* see FOOLISHNESS
  rel illogicality
  con logic, logicality, logicalness, sanity, sensibleness; wisdom

silly *adj* 1 *syn* see SIMPLE 3
  rel empty, empty-headed, vacuous; irrational, unreasonable; ignorant, unintelligent, unwise
  ant sensible
  2 *syn* see GIDDY 1
  rel ‖balmy, crazy, ‖dippy, irrational, off, ‖wacked-out
  idiom silly as a goose
  con level-headed, practical, rational, serious
  ant sensible
  3 *syn* see FOOLISH 2
  rel funny, senseless

silvern *adj syn* see SILVERY

silver-tongued *adj syn* see GLIB

silvery *adj* relating to, containing, or resembling silver < repeated polishings gave the wood a *silvery* sheen >
  syn argent, argentate, argenteous, argentine, silvern
  rel silver; brilliant, glittering, shimmering, shining

similar *adj syn* see LIKE
  rel complementary, correlative; reciprocal
  idiom much of a muchness, much the same
  con antithetical, antonymous, contradictory, contrary, opposite
  ant dissimilar

similarity *n syn* see LIKENESS
  rel approximation; collation, correlation; association, interrelation; parallel; closeness, coincidence, synonymity
  con unlikeness, variance
  ant dissimilarity

similarly *adv syn* see ALSO 1
  idiom by the same token

simile *n* 1 *syn* see ANALOGY 2
  2 *syn* see LIKENESS

similitude *n* 1 *syn* see LIKENESS
  rel copy, image, replica
  ant dissimilitude
  2 *syn* see ANALOGY 2

simmer *vb* 1 *syn* see BOIL 2
  2 *syn* see SEETHE 4

simmer down *vb syn* see COMPOSE 4
  rel quiet (down), subside
  idiom ‖cool it, take it easy
  con boil, seethe; explode, fulminate
  ant boil over

Simon Legree *n syn* see SLAVE DRIVER

simon-pure *adj syn* see AUTHENTIC 2

simp *n syn* see DUNCE

simper *vb syn* see SMIRK

simple *adj* 1 *syn* see NATURAL 5
  rel childish, childlike; amateur, green, unexperienced; trusting; ‖square
  2 *syn* see PLAIN 1
  ant elaborate

3 actually or apparently deficient in intelligence <a poor *simple* woman easily duped >
  syn asinine, brainless, ||buffle-headed, fatuous, foolish, insensate, ||mindless, nit-witted, senseless, sheepheaded, silly, soft, spoony, unintelligent, unwitty, weak-headed, weak-minded, witless; *compare* RETARDED, STUPID 1
  rel amateur, green, inexperienced, inexpert; credulous, gullible; childish, child-like, naive; ignorant, illiterate, uneducated, unschooled, untaught; crass, dense, dopey, dull, dumb, slow, stupid; doting, feeble-minded, idiotic, retarded, simpleminded
  con able, competent; alert, clever, keen; bright, intelligent, understanding
  ant wise

4 *syn* see RETARDED

5 *syn* see PURE 2
  rel inelaborate, stark; bald, bare, mere; fundamental, uncompounded

6 *syn* see EASY 1
  rel incomplex, incomplicate
  idiom simple as ABC
  ant complex, complicated

simple *n syn* see FOOL 3

simplehearted *adj syn* see NATURAL 5

simpleminded *adj syn* see RETARDED

simplest *adj syn* see ELEMENTARY 1

simpleton *n* 1 *syn* see FOOL 4

2 *syn* see DUNCE
  rel bungler, ||clot

simplify *vb* to make simple or simpler <*simplify* a manufacturing process >
  syn boil down, streamline
  rel clarify, clean up, disentangle, disin-volve, straighten (out), unscramble; abridge, cut down, reduce, shorten; over-simplify
  ant complicate

simply *adv syn* see JUST 3

simulacrum *n* 1 *syn* see IMAGE 1

2 *syn* see IMITATION

3 *syn* see APPEARANCE 2

simulate *vb* 1 *syn* see ASSUME 4
  rel ape, copy, imitate, mimic; play-act, pose
  idiom ||make out like (*or* as if)

2 *syn* see RESEMBLE

simulated *adj* 1 *syn* see FICTITIOUS 2
  ant genuine

2 *syn* see ARTIFICIAL 2
  ant genuine

simultaneous *adj syn* see CONTEMPORARY 1
  rel agreeing, concurring, coinciding

simultaneously *adv syn* see TOGETHER 1
  idiom in one breath

sin *n* 1 *syn* see EVIL 3

2 *syn* see EVIL 2

3 *syn* see IMPERFECTION

sin *vb syn* see TRESPASS 1

since *prep syn* see AFTER 2
  ant before

since *conj syn* see BECAUSE

sincere *adj* 1 genuine in feeling or expression <had a *sincere* dislike for politics >
  syn heartfelt, hearty, unfeigned, whole-hearted, whole-souled; *compare* GENUINE 3
  rel candid, frank, frankhearted, open, plain; faithful, honest, truthful; above-board, forthright, pretensionless, straight-

forward, unpretentious; dear, devout, heartful; meant, unaffected
  con affected, artificial, feigned, put-on, unmeant
  ant insincere

2 *syn* see GENUINE 3
  rel authentic, bona fide; serious; actual
  idiom honest to God
  ant insincere

sincereness *n syn* see GOOD FAITH

sincerity *n syn* see GOOD FAITH
  rel heart; goodwill; singleness, straightfor-wardness
  con cunning, deceit, guile; ill will
  ant insincerity

sine qua non *n syn* see ESSENTIAL 2

sinew *n* 1 *syn* see POWER 4

2 *usu* sinews *pl syn* see MAINSTAY

sinewy *adj syn* see MUSCULAR 1
  rel strong, sturdy, tenacious, tough
  ant flabby

2 *syn* see MUSCULAR 2

sinful *adj* 1 *syn* see WRONG 1
  rel base, low, vile; disgraceful, shameful; culpable, damnable

2 *syn* see BLAMEWORTHY
  ant sinless

sing *vb* 1 to utter words in musical tones and with musical inflections and modula-tions <children often can *sing* before they converse >
  syn chant, tune, vocalize
  rel descant; carol, serenade, troll; croon, hum, lull, lullaby; cantillate, hymn, in-tone; singsong; roar

2 *syn* see TALK 6

||3 *syn* see INFORM 3

single *adj* 1 being without a spouse <en-joying life as a *single* girl >
  syn sole, spouseless, unmarried, unwed
  rel free, unattached, unfettered; celibate; maiden, virgin
  idiom footloose and fancy-free
  con attached; united; wed
  ant married

2 one as distinguished from two or more or all others <a *single* instance of dishon-esty has been cited >
  syn lone, one, only, particular, separate, sole, solitary, unique
  rel individual, singular; especial, special, specific; distinguished, singled-out; distinct
  con several; manifold, many, numerous
  ant multiple

3 *syn* see FRANK

4 *syn* see SOLE 4

single (out) *vb syn* see CHOOSE 1
  rel screen, winnow (out); accept, admit, receive

single-eyed *adj syn* see FRANK

single-hearted *adj syn* see FRANK

single-minded *adj* 1 *syn* see INFLEXIBLE 2

2 *syn* see INFLEXIBLE 2
  rel diehard; bigoted

singleness *n* 1 *syn* see UNIQUENESS

2 *syn* see UNITY 1
  ant multifariousness

singly *adv syn* see APART 1
  ant together

singular *adj* 1 *syn* see SEVERAL 1
  rel discrete; certain, definite; exclusive

2 *syn* see EXCEPTIONAL 1
  ant usual

3 *syn* see ONLY 2
idiom first and last, one and only, one only

4 *syn* see STRANGE 4
idiom passing strange

singularity *n* 1 *syn* see INDIVIDUALITY 4
2 *syn* see INDIVIDUALITY 3
3 *syn* see UNITY 1
ant multiplicity

singularize *vb syn* see CHARACTERIZE 2

singularness *n syn* see UNITY 1
ant multifariousness

sinister *adj* seriously threatening disaster
< a *sinister* plot >
syn baleful, malefic, maleficent, malign;
compare OMINOUS
rel fateful, ill-omened, inauspicious, ominous, portentous, unpropitious; apocalyptic, dire, doomful, ill-boding, threatening; lowering, menacing; evil, malicious
con harmless, innocent, innocuous

sink *vb* 1 to become submerged < the overloaded raft *sank* below the surface >
syn founder, go down, go under, submerge, submerse
rel capsize, overturn, tip (over); dive, plunge; scuttle; shipwreck, wreck
idioms go to Davy Jones's locker, go to the bottom, sink like a rock
con come up, rise
ant float

2 *syn* see SET 12
3 *syn* see DETERIORATE 1
ant rise
4 *syn* see STOOP 2
5 *syn* see LOWER 3
6 *syn* see THRUST 2
7 *syn* see HUMBLE
ant uplift

sink *n* 1 a place marked by a staggering amount of corruption and filth < that area of the city was a *sink* of vice and crime >
syn Augean stable, cesspit, cesspool, den, pandemonium, Sodom, sty
rel hellhole; fleshpot
idiom Alsatian den, den of iniquity, sink of corruption

2 *syn* see DEPRESSION 2

sinkage *n syn* see DEPRESSION 2

sinkhole *n syn* see DEPRESSION 2

sinuous *adj syn* see WINDING
rel twisted; snake-shaped
idiom twisting and turning

sip *vb syn* see DRINK 1

siphon *vb* 1 *syn* see CONDUCT 4
2 *syn* see DRAIN 1

sire *n syn* see FATHER 2

sire *vb* 1 *syn* see FATHER 1
2 *syn* see GENERATE 1

siren *n* an enticingly attractive woman who lures men into dangerous or compromising situations < a slinky *siren* of the silent screen era >
syn femme fatale, Lorelei, seductress, temptress
rel charmer, vamp

siren *adj syn* see ATTRACTIVE 1

rel sirenic

siren song *n syn* see LURE 2

sissified *adj syn* see EFFEMINATE

sissy *n syn* see WEAKLING

sissy *adj syn* see EFFEMINATE

sissy-pants (*or* **sissy-britches**) *n pl but sing or pl in constr syn* see WEAKLING

sit *vb* 1 to rest on the buttocks or haunches
< she was *sitting* in a chair >
syn ∥set
rel perch, rest; ∥plop (down), seat, sit down; squat
con arise, get up, rise, stand, stand up
2 *syn* see CONVENE 1
3 *syn* see POSE 3
4 *syn* see SET 11
5 *syn* see SEAT
rel ensconce, install, settle

sit down *vb syn* see ALIGHT

site *n* 1 *syn* see PLACE 1
2 *syn* see SCENE 3
3 a place where an archaeological excavation is made < a burial *site* >
syn dig
4 *syn* see HABITAT

sited *adj syn* see SITUATED

∥**sitfast** *adj syn* see IMMOVABLE 1

sitting duck *n syn* see TARGET 1
rel sitter

situate *adj syn* see SITUATED

situated *adj* having a site, situation, or location < a town *situated* on a hill >
syn located, placed, positioned, set, sited, situate

situation *n* 1 *syn* see PLACE 1
2 *syn* see PREGNANCY
3 *syn* see JOB 2
4 *syn* see STATUS 1
5 *syn* see STATE 1
rel bargain

sizable *adj* 1 *syn* see CONSIDERABLE 2
2 *syn* see BIG 1
rel man-sized; giant-sized

sizableness *n syn* see SIZE 2

size *n* 1 the amount of measurable space or area occupied by or comprising a thing
< the *size* of the card is 3"x 5" >
syn admeasurement, dimension(s), dimensionality, extent, magnitude, measure, proportion
rel area; body, bulk, mass, volume; height; extension, length; amplitude, breadth, expanse, spread, stretch, width; measurement

2 considerable amount, proportion, volume, character, or importance < left an estate of some *size* >
syn amplitude, bigness, greatness, largeness, magnitude, sizableness
rel dimension, extent
con littleness, smallness; minuteness, tininess

sizz *vb syn* see HISS

sizzle *vb* 1 *syn* see SEAR 2
2 *syn* see HISS

sizzling *adj syn* see HOT 1

∥**skag** *n syn* see CIGARETTE

skate *n syn* see MAN 3

sked *n syn* see PROGRAM 1

sked *vb syn* see SCHEDULE 1

skedaddle *vb* 1 *syn* see RUN 2
rel ∥split; cut out
2 *syn* see GET OUT 1

---

syn synonym(s)   *rel* related word(s)
ant antonym(s)   *con* contrasted word(s)
idiom idiomatic equivalent(s)
∥ use limited; if in doubt, see a dictionary

idiom lift them up and set them down,
‖take off like a bat out of hell

‖**skeet** *vb syn* see HURRY 2

skeezicks *n syn* see SCAMP

skein *n syn* see MAZE 1

skeletal *adj syn* see EMACIATED

skeleton *vb syn* see SKETCH

skeletonize *vb syn* see SKETCH

‖**sken** *vb syn* see SQUINT

skeptic *n* a doubting or incredulous person
<men of long experience are often *skeptics* >
  syn doubter, doubting Thomas, head-shaker, Pyrrhonian, Pyrrhonist, unbeliever, zetetic
  rel questioner; agnostic, pessimist; scoffer; cynic, misanthrope; disbeliever
  con accepter; apostle, disciple, follower; devotee, diehard
  ant believer

skeptical *adj syn* see INCREDULOUS
  rel freethinking; dissenting; suspicious; cynical
  idiom ‖from Missouri
  ant believing

skeptically *adv syn* see ASKANCE 2
  idiom with a grain of salt, with a note of skepticism, with a skeptical eye
  con trustingly
  ant gullibly

skepticism *n syn* see UNCERTAINTY
  rel qualm, qualmishness
  idiom question in one's mind, shadow of doubt
  con belief, trust
  ant gullibility

sketch *n syn* see COMPENDIUM 1

sketch *vb* to present succinctly <let's *sketch* our plan of action>
  syn adumbrate, block (out), chalk (out), characterize, draft, outline, rough (out), skeleton, skeletonize
  rel depict; diagram, diagrammatize; blueprint, delineate, line; draw, plot, trace; design, develop; detail, lay out, map (out)

sketchy *adj syn* see SUPERFICIAL 2

skew *vb* 1 *syn* see SLANT 3
  2 *syn* see SWERVE 1
  rel skid, slide, slip

skewer *vb syn* see IMPALE

skid *vb* 1 *syn* see SLIDE 3
  rel sheer, skew, slue, veer
  idiom go into a skid
  2 *syn* see PLUMMET

skiddoo *vb syn* see GET OUT 1
  idiom go (*or* take) off like a shot

skid road *n syn* see SKID ROW

skid row *n* a city street or district notorious for cheap bars, flophouses, and homeless derelicts <boozy old men wandering the *skid row* >
  syn bowery, skid road

skill *n* 1 *syn* see ABILITY 2
  2 *syn* see ART 1
  3 *syn* see ADDRESS 1
  rel ease, skillfulness

skilled *adj* 1 *syn* see PROFICIENT
  con skill-less, unproficient
  ant unskilled, unskillful
  2 *syn* see EXPERIENCED
  rel prepared, primed, trained
  con unfit, unqualified, untrained
  ant unskilled

skillet *n syn* see FRYING PAN

skillful *adj* 1 *syn* see PROFICIENT
  rel learned, versant, well-versed
  ant unskillful
  2 accomplished or done with proficiency or skill <his answer was a very *skillful* evasion>
  syn adroit, clever, good, pretty, ‖skilly, wicked, workmanlike, workmanly; *compare* CLEVER 4, PROFICIENT
  rel expert, masterful
  con clumsy; unskilled
  ant inept, unskillful

‖**skilly** *adj syn* see SKILLFUL 2

skim *vb* 1 *syn* see BRUSH
  2 *syn* see GLANCE 1
  3 *syn* see FLY 1

skim (through) *vb syn* see BROWSE
  con examine, inspect, scrutinize

skimble-skamble *n syn* see GIBBERISH 1

‖**skimmelton** *n syn* see SHIVAREE

skimp *adj syn* see MEAGER 2

skimp *vb* 1 *syn* see SCRIMP
  2 *syn* see SPARE 3

skimpy *adj* 1 *syn* see MEAGER 2
  2 *syn* see SHORT 3

skin *n* 1 *syn* see HIDE
  2 *syn* see HULL
  3 a usually thin casing forming the outside surface of a structure or thing <aircraft *skins* made of aluminum alloys>
  syn sheath, sheathing
  rel facing, siding; case, casing, cover, jacket; shell
  4 *syn* see MISER
  5 *syn* see SWINDLER
  ‖6 *syn* see DOLLAR

skin *vb* 1 *syn* see SHEATHE
  2 to remove the surface, skin, or thin outer covering of <*skin* a Bermuda onion>
  syn decorticate, excorticate, peel, scale, strip; *compare* SHUCK
  rel cut off, pull off; pare, shave (off), trim; hull, husk, shuck; bark, rind; excoriate, flay, gall
  3 *syn* see OVERCHARGE 1
  4 *syn* see CRITICIZE
  5 *syn* see HURRY 2

‖**skinch** *vb* 1 *syn* see SCRIMP
  2 *syn* see SPARE 3

skinflint *n syn* see MISER

‖**skinhead** *n syn* see BALDHEAD

skinny *adj syn* see LEAN
  rel twiggy, weedy; emaciated; skeletal
  idiom mere skin and bones, skinny as a rail
  ant fleshy

skip *vb* 1 to move or proceed with a light bounding step <children *skipping* home from school>
  syn hop, lope, skitter, spring, trip
  rel caper, cavort, curvet, frisk, gambol; bounce, hippety-hop; jump; leap; bound
  con hobble, shamble, shuffle; hitch, limp, stagger, totter
  2 *syn* see GLANCE 1
  3 *syn* see RUN 2
  idiom ‖split the scene

skip *n syn* see OMISSION

skirmish *n* 1 *syn* see CLASH 2
  rel assault, attack; ambush
  con pitched battle

2 *syn* see ENCOUNTER

skirr *vb* 1 *syn* see RUN 1

2 *syn* see FLY 1

skirt *n syn* see BORDER 1

rel skirting

skirt *vb* 1 *syn* see BORDER 1

2 to make a detour or circuit (as around a congested area) < *skirted* the city to avoid traffic >

syn bypass, circumnavigate, circumvent, detour

idiom go around

3 to avoid (as a topic or question) because of difficulty, complexity, controversy, or danger < *skirted* all touchy issues >

syn burke, bypass, circumvent, ||polly-fox, sidestep; *compare* EQUIVOCATE 2, ESCAPE 2

rel avoid, dodge, duck, evade, hedge; elude, escape; ignore, skip

idiom get around

con confront, face, meet, take on

||**skite** *n syn* see PRANK

skitter *vb syn* see SKIP 1

skittery *adj syn* see EXCITABLE

skittish *adj* 1 *syn* see GIDDY 1

rel irresponsible, undependable, unreliable

2 *syn* see EXCITABLE

rel restive; nervous

skive *vb syn* see CUT 6

skiver *vb syn* see IMPALE

skookum *adj syn* see EXCELLENT

skookum-house *n syn* see JAIL

skulk *vb syn* see SNEAK

skunk *n syn* see SNOT 1

skunk *vb syn* see WHIP 2

sky *n* the expanse of space surrounding the earth < blue *sky* crisscrossed with jet trails >

syn empyrean, firmament, heaven(s), welkin

rel azure; celestial sphere

idiom the wild blue yonder

sky-high *adv syn* see APART 3

sky-high *adj syn* see EXCESSIVE 1

skylarking *n* 1 *syn* see HORSEPLAY

idiom ||making whoopee

2 *syn* see REVELRY 2

sky pilot *n syn* see CLERGYMAN

rel chaplain; padre

skyrocket *vb* to rise abruptly and rapidly (as to an unprecedented level or amount < when the election was over taxes and prices *skyrocketed* >

syn rocket, shoot up, soar

rel climb, rise; upsoar, upspring

con slide; fall; drop

ant crash, plummet

skyscraping *adj syn* see LOFTY 6

slab *n syn* see BAR 1

rel chunk, lump

||**slab** *n syn* see SLIME

slabber *vb syn* see DROOL 2

slack *adj* 1 *syn* see NEGLIGENT

rel dilatory, lackadaisical, lethargic, sluggish; faineant, indolent, lazy, slothful; inert, stagnant

con assiduous, busy, diligent, industrious, sedulous

---

syn synonym(s)   *rel* related word(s)
ant antonym(s)   *con* contrasted word(s)
idiom idiomatic equivalent(s)
|| use limited; if in doubt, see a dictionary

---

2 *syn* see LOOSE 1

rel feeble, infirm, soft, unsteady, weak; inactive, inert, passive, supine; laggard, leisurely, slow

con tensed, tightened; constant, equable, even, steady, uniform; firm, hard

ant taut, tight

3 *syn* see SLOW 3

slack *vb syn* see LOOSE 5

idiom ||cut some slack, make slack

ant tighten

slack *n syn* see SLOWDOWN 1

slacken *vb* 1 *syn* see DELAY 1

idiom keep back

ant quicken

2 *syn* see ABATE 4

3 *syn* see LOOSE 5

ant tighten

slackening *n syn* see SLOWDOWN 1

slacker *n* one who shirks work, responsibility, or an obligation < didn't want any *slackers* in his office >

syn goldbrick, shirker, slinker, ||spiv

rel idler, loafer; slugabed, sluggard

slack-spined *adj syn* see WEAK 4

slake *vb syn* see QUENCH 4

slam *n* 1 *syn* see BLOW 1

2 *syn* see BANG 2

3 *syn* see ANIMADVERSION

rel fling, swipe; crack, potshot; rap, slap; dig, jab

slam *vb* 1 to strike with extreme force or violence < *slammed* the ball out of the park > < the car *slammed* into the fence >

syn belt, blast, clobber, slug, smash, wallop; *compare* STRIKE 2

rel bang, bat, hit, knock, slap, swat, thwack; cudgel, hammer, mace; batter, beat, pound

2 *syn* see LAMBASTE 3

||**slam** *adv syn* see WELL 3

slammer *n syn* see JAIL

slander *n syn* see DETRACTION

rel black wash, muckraking, mud-slinging, roorback, scandal-mongering

slander *vb syn* see MALIGN

rel assail, attack; damage, hurt, injure; blackwash, muckrake; belie, strumpet

idiom dish the dirt, run a smear campaign, sling the mud

ant panegyrize

slanderous *adj syn* see LIBELOUS

rel blackwashing, muckraking, scandalmongering

ant panegyrical

slang *n syn* see DIALECT 2

rel slanginess, slanguage

slangism *n syn* see BARBARISM

slant *adv syn* see ASIDE 1

slant *vb* 1 to set or be set at an angle < *slanted* the ladder against the wall >

syn cant, heel, incline, lean, list, recline, slope, tilt, tip

rel bank, decline, descend; bend, deviate, diverge, splay, swerve, veer

2 to direct (written or spoken material) to the interests of a particular audience or group < a magazine *slanted* to farm families >

syn aim, angle

rel direct, orient, point, train; concentrate, focus; spoon-feed; bias, skew, warp

3 to orient (material) from objective presentation so as to favor a particular bias

<accused the media of *slanting* the news against the president>
syn angle, bias, skew; *compare* PREJUDICE 2

rel influence, prejudice; color, distort, twist, warp

ant objectify, objectivize

slant *n* 1 **syn** *see* SLOPE

2 **syn** *see* VIEWPOINT 2

rel predilection, predisposition, prejudice

slanted *adj* **syn** *see* DIAGONAL

slanting *adj* **syn** *see* DIAGONAL

slantingly *adv* **syn** *see* ASIDE 1

slantingways *adv* 1 **syn** *see* ASIDE 1

2 **syn** *see* DIAGONALLY

slantly *adv* **syn** *see* ASIDE 1

slantways *adv* 1 **syn** *see* ASIDE 1

2 **syn** *see* DIAGONALLY

slantwise *adv* 1 **syn** *see* ASIDE 1

2 **syn** *see* DIAGONALLY

slap *n* 1 **syn** *see* CUFF

2 **syn** *see* AFFRONT

3 **syn** *see* FLING 1

slap *vb* 1 to strike quickly and sharply with the hand <*slapped* the hysterical girl>
syn blip, box, buffet, cuff, smack, spank, ||wherret; *compare* STRIKE 2

rel ||biff, ding, hit, sock, swat, whack; ||wap, wham; bash

2 **syn** *see* LAMBASTE 3

||**slap** *adv* **syn** *see* WELL 3

slap around *vb* **syn** *see* MANHANDLE

slapdash *adj* 1 **syn** *see* RANDOM

2 **syn** *see* SLIPSHOD 3

||**slap-up** *adj* **syn** *see* EXCELLENT

slash *vb* 1 **syn** *see* CUT 1

2 **syn** *see* HACK

3 **syn** *see* LAMBASTE 3

idiom ||light into

4 **syn** *see* REDUCE 2

5 **syn** *see* SHORTEN

slate *n* **syn** *see* TICKET 3

||**slate** *vb* **syn** *see* LAMBASTE 3

slather *n*, *often* **slathers** *pl* **syn** *see* SCAD

slattern *n* 1 an untidy slovenly woman <two blowsy *slatterns* gossiping at the bar>
syn dowd, dowdy, drab, draggle-tail, ||malkin, slut, ||streel, traipse

rel frump; slob, ||slommack, sloven; crone, gammer, hag, witch

2 **syn** *see* WANTON

rel prostitute, whore

slattern *adj* **syn** *see* SLATTERNLY

slatternly *adj* being habitually untidy and very dirty especially in dress or appearance <a filthy, *slatternly* old woman>
syn blowsy, dowdy, draggletailed, frowsy, slattern, sordid; *compare* SLOVENLY 1

rel careless, disordered, neglected, poky; bedraggled, disheveled, draggled, draggly, messy, mussy, slipshod, sloppy, slovenly, unkempt, untidy; dirty, filthy, foul, grimy, squalid

con clean, fresh, neat, tidy, trim; smart; immaculate, spotless

ant bandbox

slaughter *n* **syn** *see* MASSACRE

rel slaughtery; annihilation, destruction

slaughter *vb* 1 to kill (animals) for food <*slaughtered* a beef for the winter>
syn butcher, slay

rel stick

2 to kill (a person) in an especially bloody or barbarous manner <Jack the Ripper *slaughtered* his victims with a knife>
syn butcher, slay

rel kill, murder, ||total, ||waste; maim, mangle, mutilate, torture

3 to kill (people) in large numbers <millions *slaughtered* in death camps>
syn annihilate, decimate, exterminate, massacre, wipe (out)

||**slaunchways** *adv* 1 **syn** *see* DIAGONALLY

2 **syn** *see* ASIDE 1

slave *n* 1 a person held in servitude or bondage <plantations worked by *slaves*>
syn bondman, bondslave, bondsman, chattel, mancipium

rel help, menial, retainer, servant; helot, serf, thrall, vassal

con freedman, freedwoman; ||deditician

ant freeman

2 one who works at a hard, monotonous, usually menial task <*slaves* working all night on a senator's speech>
syn dray horse, drudge, galley slave, peon, slavey, toiler, workhorse

rel ||coolie

slave *vb* **syn** *see* DRUDGE

idiom work like a slave

slave driver *n* a person in authority who exacts extreme effort from his subordinates <the chief proofreader was a real *slave driver*>
syn rawhider, Simon Legree, taskmaster

rel martinet

idiom a hard taskmaster

slaver *vb* 1 **syn** *see* DROOL 2

2 **syn** *see* FAWN

slaver *n* **syn** *see* SALIVA

slavery *n* 1 **syn** *see* WORK 2

2 **syn** *see* BONDAGE

idiom involuntary servitude, the yoke (*or* chains) of slavery

slavey *n* 1 **syn** *see* SLAVE 2

2 **syn** *see* HACK 2

slavish *adj* 1 **syn** *see* HARD 6

2 **syn** *see* SUBSERVIENT 2

rel spineless, subdued, tame; miserable, wretched

ant independent

3 copying obsequiously something superior <the painting was a *slavish* copy of an old master>
syn apish, emulative, imitative

rel uninspired; unoriginal

con fresh, new, novel, original; fanciful, imaginative, ingenious, inspired; extravagant, high-flown

slay *vb* 1 **syn** *see* KILL 1

2 **syn** *see* MURDER 1

3 **syn** *see* SLAUGHTER 2

4 **syn** *see* SLAUGHTER 1

slayer *n* **syn** *see* MURDERER

sleazy *adj* 1 **syn** *see* LIMP 1

rel slight, tenuous, thin; gossamery

2 **syn** *see* CHEAP 2

3 **syn** *see* SHABBY 1

sleek *vb* **syn** *see* POLISH 2

sleek *adj* having a very smooth or lustrous surface or texture <the car's *sleek* new paint job>
syn glassy, glossy, polished, ||sleekit, sleeky, smarmy

rel smooth; glistening, lustrous

||**sleekit** *adj syn* see SLEEK

sleeky *adj syn* see SLEEK

sleep *n* 1 the natural periodic suspension of consciousness during which the powers of the body are restored <needed eight hours of *sleep* to function efficiently>
syn ||doss, ||shut-eye, slumber; *compare* DOZE, NAP
rel repose, rest; slumberland
idiom land of Nod, the arms of Morpheus
con wakefulness
2 *syn* see LETHARGY 1
3 *syn* see DEATH 1

sleep *vb* to rest in a state of sleep <slept for over eight hours>
syn ||doss, slumber; *compare* DOZE, NAP
rel relax, repose, rest; oversleep, sleep in
idiom be in the land of Nod, be sunk in sleep, pound one's ear, rest in the arms of Morpheus, sleep like a top (*or* log)
con arouse, awaken, wake (up)

sleeplessness *n syn* see INSOMNIA

sleepy *adj* 1 having an inclination for or affected by sleep <was *sleepy* after the long day>
syn dozy, drowsy, nodding, ||peepy, ||sloomy, slumberous, slumbery, snoozy, somnolent, soporific
rel heavy, heavy-eyed, lethargic, sluggish, torpid; dazed, dopey, listless, oscitant, yawning; asleep, sleeping, slumbering; nepenthean, poppied; comatose, ||out
con awake, conscious; restless, sleepless, unsleeping; alert, wide-awake
ant wakeful
2 *syn* see INACTIVE
3 *syn* see SOPORIFIC 1

||**sleer** *vb syn* see SNEER 1

sleight *n* 1 *syn* see ADDRESS 1
2 *syn* see TRICK 1

||**sleighty** *adj syn* see CLEVER 4

slender *adj* 1 *syn* see THIN 1
rel slenderish, slimmish; lithe, svelte, trim
idiom slender as a reed
2 *syn* see SHORT 3
3 *syn* see REMOTE 4

slenderize *vb syn* see REDUCE 5

sleuth *n syn* see DETECTIVE

slew *n syn* see SCAD

slewed *adj syn* see INTOXICATED 1

slice *n syn* see SHARE 1
rel segment
idiom a slice of the pie (*or* melon)

slice *vb* 1 *syn* see CUT 1
2 *syn* see CUT 5

slick *vb* 1 *syn* see POLISH 2
2 *syn* see DRESS UP 1
3 *syn* see SLIDE 1

slick *adj* 1 having a glassy surface that often offers insecure footing <a floor *slick* with wax>
syn greasy, lubricious, ||sliddery, ||slipper, slippery, slippy, slithery
rel oily; ||slape, smooth; soapy
idiom slick as a greased pig
con coarse, gritty, rough, uneven

---

syn synonym(s)   *rel* related word(s)
ant antonym(s)   *con* contrasted word(s)
idiom idiomatic equivalent(s)
|| use limited; if in doubt, see a dictionary

2 *syn* see FULSOME
rel glossy; slippery
3 *syn* see WISE 4

slicker *n syn* see SWINDLER

||**slidder** *vb* 1 *syn* see SLIDE 3
2 *syn* see SLITHER 2

||**sliddery** *adj syn* see SLICK 1

slide *vb* 1 to go or progress with a smooth continuous motion <goldfish *slid* across the pool>
syn glide, glissade, slick, slip, slither
rel flow, stream
2 *syn* see SLIP 6
3 to fall or nearly fall because of loss of balance or footing <stumbled and *slid* on the ice>
syn skid, ||slidder, slip, ||slur
idiom take a slide (*or* a skid)
4 to shift or be shifted out of place or away from one's grasp <the packages *slid* from her arms>
syn slip
rel shift; move; fall, spill, tumble
5 *syn* see CREEP 1
6 to take a natural course <preferred to let the matter *slide* for a while>
syn coast, drift
rel glide
idiom run its course
7 *syn* see STEAL 3
8 *syn* see SNEAK

slide *n syn* see DECLINE 3

slight *adj* 1 *syn* see THIN 1
rel slightish, ||slighty; smallish; pint-sized
2 *syn* see DELICATE 5
rel gossamery, sleazy
3 *syn* see REMOTE 4

slight *vb syn* see NEGLECT
rel skip; contemn, despise; flout, scoff

slightest *adj syn* see FIRST 4
rel ||fat, negligible

slighting *adj syn* see DEROGATORY

slim *adj* 1 *syn* see THIN 1
rel lissome, lithe, lithesome, svelte
ant chubby
2 *syn* see CLEVER 4
3 *syn* see REMOTE 4

slim (down) *vb syn* see REDUCE 5

slime *n* a viscous and usually dirty or offensive substance <a layer of *slime* formed in the bottom of the pool>
syn muck, ||slab, slum
rel ooze, ||sleech, sludge; scum

sling *vb* 1 *syn* see THROW 1
rel catapult; sock
2 *syn* see STRIDE 1

sling *vb syn* see HANG 1

slink *vb syn* see SNEAK

slink *n syn* see SNEAK

slinker *n syn* see SLACKER

slip *vb* 1 *syn* see SLIDE 1
2 *syn* see SNEAK
3 *syn* see STEAL 3
4 *syn* see SLIDE 4
5 *syn* see SLIDE 3
6 to decline gradually from a standard or accustomed level <sales in some lines *slipped*>
syn drop (off), fall (off *or* away), sag, slide, slump
rel erode, soften; decline, go down, sink; dip, drop; nose-dive, plummet, topple; crash

con better, gain, improve, rally, rebound; ascend, climb, rise; skyrocket, soar

7 *syn* see SHAKE 5

8 *syn* see SHED 2

slip (on) *vb syn* see DON 1

ant slip (off)

slip *n* **1** *syn* see WHARF

2 *syn* see ESCAPE 1

3 *syn* see ERROR 2

4 *syn* see DECLINE 3

‖**slipper** *adj syn* see SLICK 1

slippery *adj* **1** *syn* see SLICK 1

2 *syn* see MUTABLE 2

slippy *adj syn* see SLICK 1

slipshod *adj* **1** *syn* see SHABBY 1

2 see SLOVENLY 1

3 marked by indifference to exactness, precision, and accuracy < a *slipshod* piece of research >

syn botchy, careless, messy, slapdash, sloppy, slovenly, unthorough, untidy

rel neglected, negligent; haphazard, slaphappy, unmeticulous; botched-up, fouled-up, messed-up, ‖screwed-up; faulty, imperfect, inaccurate, inexact

con fastidious, meticulous, neat; accurate, exact, precise; methodical, orderly, systematic; thorough

slipslop *n syn* see NONSENSE 2

slipup *n syn* see ERROR 2

slit *vb syn* see CUT 1

slither *vb* **1** *syn* see SLIDE 1

rel ‖sluther

2 to walk or move in a sinuous way < a slinky blonde *slithered* over from the bar >

syn ‖slidder, snake, undulate

rel creep, glide, sidle, steal; lurk, prowl, slink, sneak

slithery *adj syn* see SLICK 1

‖**slive** *vb syn* see SIDLE 1

‖**sliver** *vb* to cut into very thin slices < *slivered* cheese >

syn shave, shred

rel carve, haggle, slice

con chop, dice, mince; comminute, powder, pulverize; crush, mash

slobber *vb syn* see DROOL 2

slobbering *adj syn* see EFFUSIVE

slobbery *adj* **1** *syn* see EFFUSIVE

2 *syn* see SLOVENLY 1

slog *vb* **1** *syn* see STRIKE 2

2 *syn* see PLOD 1

3 *syn* see DRUDGE

slogan *n syn* see CATCHWORD

rel expression, idiom, locution

slogging *n syn* see WORK 2

‖**stommacky** *adj syn* see SLOVENLY 1

‖**sloom** *n syn* see DOZE

‖**sloom** *vb syn* see DOZE

‖**sloomy** *adj syn* see SLEEPY 1

slop *n syn* see PAP 2

slop *vb* **1** *syn* see SPILL 1

2 *syn* see SPLASH

3 *syn* see GULP

4 *syn* see PLOD 1

slope *vb syn* see SLANT 2

slope *n* a natural or artificial inclined surface < the steep *slope* of the hill >

syn grade, gradient, inclination, incline, lean, leaning, slant, tilt

rel acclivity, ascent, rise; declivity, descent; deflection, deviation, obliqueness,

obliquity; pitch, swag, sway, tip; bend, skew

con champaign, flat, flatland, mesa, plain(s), plateau, tableland

ant level

sloped *adj syn* see INCLINED 3

slopeways *adv syn* see ASIDE 1

sloping *adj syn* see INCLINED 3

slopped *adj syn* see INTOXICATED 1

sloppy *adj* **1** *syn* see SLIPSHOD 3

rel amateurish; mediocre; awkward, clumsy; poor

ant exact, precise

2 *syn* see SLOVENLY 1

3 *syn* see EFFUSIVE

rel soft; oversentimental

4 *syn* see INTOXICATED 1

slosh *n syn* see BLOW 1

slosh *vb* **1** *of a liquid* to move with a gentle lapping motion or sound < heard water *sloshing* in the bottom of the boat >

syn bubble, burble, gurgle, lap, swash, wash

rel babble; ripple; dash, plash, splash, tumble; bespatter, spatter; churn, whirl; gush, rush; roar

2 *syn* see SPLASH

3 *syn* see GULP

‖**4** *syn* see STRIKE 2

sloth *n* **1** disinclination to action or labor < a bland *sloth*-provoking summer day >

syn idleness, indolence, laze, laziness, slothfulness, slouch, sluggishness

rel ergophobia, faineancy, idling, lazing, loafing; apathy, heaviness, languidness, languor, lassitude, lethargy, listlessness, torpidity; shiftlessness

con assiduity, assiduousness, busyness, diligence, sedulity, sedulousness

ant industriousness, industry

2 sluggishness and apathy in the practice of virtue < the deadly sin of *sloth* >

syn acedia

rel heedlessness, inattention, inattentiveness

con assiduity

slothful *adj syn* see LAZY

con assiduous, busy, diligent, sedulous

ant industrious

slothfulness *n syn* see SLOTH 1

slouch *n* **1** *syn* see OAF 2

2 *syn* see SLUGGARD

3 *syn* see SLOTH 1

slouch *vb* to assume, have, or move with an awkwardly drooping posture, carriage, or gait < three drunks *slouched* across the room >

syn droop, loll, ‖lollop, lop, slump, trollop

rel loaf, lounge, saunter, shamble, shuffle; bend, lean, stoop; sag, wilt

con erect, straighten (up); sit up, stand up

slough *n* **1** *syn* see SWAMP

2 *syn* see INLET

‖**slough** *n syn* see HULL

slough *vb* **1** *syn* see SHED 2

2 *syn* see DISCARD

idiom ‖get shut (or shed) of

slough over *vb syn* see NEGLECT

sloven *adj syn* see SLOVENLY 1

slovenly *adj* **1** negligent of or marked by lack of neatness and order especially in appearance or dress < *slovenly* attire >

syn careless, disheveled, ill-kempt, messy, mussy, raunchy, slipshod, slobbery, ||slommacky, sloppy, sloven, uncombed, unfastidious, unkempt, sloven, untidy; *compare* SLATTERNLY

rel down-at-heel, shabby, sleazy, sluttish, slutty; blowsy, dowdy, frowsy, frumpish

con fastidious, neat, tidy, trim; combed, groomed, well-groomed; immaculate

ant neat

2 *syn* see SLIPSHOD 3

slow *adj* 1 *syn* see RETARDED

rel limited; ||dunch

2 moving, flowing, or proceeding at less than the usual, desirable, or required speed <a *slow* advance toward mutual understanding>

syn deliberate, dilatory, laggard, leisurely, unhasty, unhurried

rel measured, slowish, steady; unhasting, unhurrying; slow-footed, slow-going, slow-paced; plodding, poky, rusty; dragging, flagging, halting, lagging, straggling; dawdling, delaying, postponing, procrastinating; leaden, sluggish; crawling, snaillike, snail-paced, ultra-slow

idiom as slow as a swamp turtle, as slow as molasses in January

con blitz, lightning, quick, rapid, swift; fast-going, fast-moving, fast-paced, rapid-paced

ant fast

3 marked by reduced economic activity (as in sales or patronage) <trading was *slow* on the commodity exchange today>

syn down, off, slack, sluggish

rel moderate; reduced; low; inactive, stagnant

con active; up; heavy

slow (up *or* down) *vb syn* see DELAY 1

rel moderate, qualify, temper; abate, decrease, lessen, reduce

ant speed

slow coach *n syn* see LAGGARD

slowdown *n* 1 a slowing or gradual decrease in activity <a *slowdown* in car sales this quarter>

syn slack, slackening, slow-up

rel decline, downtrend, downturn; drop, drop-off, falloff; inactivity, stagnation; freeze

con increase, rise, upswing, upturn; acceleration, quickening

ant speedup

2 a deliberate slowing down by workers in the rate and quantity of production <air traffic snarled by a controllers' *slowdown*>

syn ||ca' canny

rel action; protest; slow-up; sit-down; strike, walkout; stoppage

ant speedup

slowgoing *adj syn* see LAZY

slowpoke *n syn* see LAGGARD

slow-up *n syn* see SLOWDOWN 1

slow-witted *adj syn* see RETARDED

ant quick-witted

||slubberdegullion *n syn* see VILLAIN 1

---

slue *vb syn* see SWERVE 1

slug *n syn* see SLUGGARD

rel slacker, sloven

slug *n syn* see DRAM

slug *vb syn* see SLAM 1

slugabed *n syn* see SLUGGARD

sluggard *n* an habitually lazy, shiftless, and inactive person <a *sluggard* who wanted to sleep all day>

syn bum, dolittle, do-nothing, faineant, idler, lazybones, loafer, slouch, slug, slugabed

rel lie-abed, sleepyhead; dawdler, laggard, slow coach, slowpoke; goldbrick, shirker

idiom ||his idleship, ||Weary Willie

con go-getter, hustler, live wire

ant dynamo

sluggish *adj* 1 *syn* see LETHARGIC

rel dragging, draggy, leaden, lumpish; costive, stiff; apathetic, stupefied

con go-getting, hustling, vigorous; expeditious

ant brisk

2 *syn* see SLOW 3

sluggishness *n syn* see SLOTH 1

sluice *vb syn* see POUR 2

rel flush, wash; douse, drench, soak

slum *n* a densely populated usually urban area marked by run-down housing, poverty, and social disorganization <a *slum* full of vagrants, junkies, pimps, and pushers>

syn stew

rel slumdom, slumland; tobacco road; tenderloin; skid row; ghetto; hive, kennel, rookery, warren

idiom desolation row, the wrong side of the tracks

slum *n syn* see SLIME

slumber *vb* 1 *syn* see DOZE

2 *syn* see SLEEP

slumber *n* 1 *syn* see SLEEP 1

2 *syn* see DOZE

3 *syn* see LETHARGY 1

slumberous *adj* 1 *syn* see SLEEPY 1

2 *syn* see SOPORIFIC 1

3 *syn* see LETHARGIC

slumbery *adj syn* see SLEEPY 1

slump *vb* 1 *syn* see FALL 2

rel droop, flag, sag

idiom come down like a rock (*or* a ton of bricks)

2 *syn* see SLOUCH

rel cave in, collapse

3 *syn* see SLIP 6

slump *n* 1 *syn* see DECLINE 3

2 *syn* see DEPRESSION 3

slup *vb syn* see SLURP

||slur *vb syn* see SLIDE 3

slur *vb syn* see MALIGN

slur (over) *vb syn* see NEGLECT

slur *n* 1 *syn* see ANIMADVERSION

2 *syn* see STIGMA

slurp *vb* to eat or drink noisily <*slurping* soup with a large spoon>

syn slup

rel guzzle, lap (up), slosh, swill; suck; wolf (down); smack

con nibble, pick (at); sip

slushy *adj syn* see SENTIMENTAL

slut *n* 1 *syn* see SLATTERN 1

2 *syn* see WANTON

3 *syn* see MINX

---

syn synonym(s)   *rel* related word(s)
ant antonym(s)   *con* contrasted word(s)
idiom idiomatic equivalent(s)
|| use limited; if in doubt, see a dictionary

sly *adj* 1 *syn* see CLEVER 4
rel smart; cagey; masterful
2 attaining or seeking to attain one's ends by devious means <a *sly* way of upping sales>
syn artful, astute, crafty, cunning, deep, ‖downy, foxy, guileful, insidious, subdolous, subtle, tricky, vulpine, wily; *compare* UNDERHAND
rel disingenuous, unfrank; calculating, designing, Machiavellian, scheming; cagey, devious, shady, shifty, ‖slanter, slick, slippery, smooth; clandestine, covert, furtive, stealthy; underhand, underhanded, unscrupulous; predatory; crooked, dishonest
idiom crazy like a fox, cunning as a fox (*or* serpent), sly as a fox
con candid, forthright, frank, honest, open, sincere, straightforward

sly *vb syn* see SNEAK

slyboots *n pl but sing in constr syn* see SCAMP

slyness *n syn* see CUNNING 2

smack *n* 1 *syn* see TASTE 3
2 *syn* see HINT 2

smack *vb* to have a trace, vestige, or suggestion of something <that plan *smacks* of radicalism>
syn savor, smell
rel resemble, suggest; reek, stink

smack *vb* 1 *syn* see KISS 1
idiom ‖plant a juicy kiss on
2 *syn* see SLAP 1

smack *n* 1 *syn* see CUFF
2 *syn* see BLOW 1

‖**smack-dab** *adv syn* see JUST 1

‖**smacker** *n syn* see DOLLAR

‖**smackeroo** *n syn* see DOLLAR

small *adj* 1 being the opposite of large <a *small* white house>
syn bantam, little, monkey, petite, smallish; *compare* TINY
rel cramped, limited, narrow, two-by-four; puny, undersized; paltry, petty, piddling, trivial
con big, great; considerable, sizable; enormous, huge, immense, vast
ant large
2 *syn* see MINOR 2
3 *syn* see LITTLE 2
4 *syn* see LITTLE 3
5 *syn* see PETTY 2
6 *syn* see REMOTE 4

small beer *n syn* see TRIVIA

small-beer *adj syn* see LITTLE 3

small change *n syn* see TRIVIA

smallest *adj syn* see FIRST 4

small-fry *adj syn* see MINOR 2

smallish *adj syn* see SMALL 1
ant largish

small-minded *adj syn* see ILLIBERAL
ant large-minded

small potato *n, usu* **small potatoes** *pl but sing or pl in constr syn* see TRIVIA

small talk *n* light or casual conversation <had to make *small* talk at the cocktail party>
syn bavardage, by-talk, chitchat, chitter-chatter, trifling
rel badinage, banter, repartee; babble, babbling, bibble-babble, chatter, prattle, prattling, prittle-prattle

small-time *adj syn* see MINOR 2

ant big-time

small-town *adj syn* see INSULAR

‖**smarm** *vb syn* see SMEAR 1

smarmy *adj* 1 *syn* see SLEEK
2 *syn* see FULSOME

smart *vb syn* see HURT 4

smart *vb* to cause or produce a sharp stinging and usually localized pain <gave him a slap that was hard enough to *smart*>
syn bite, burn, ‖stang, sting; *compare* HURT 4
rel prick; tingle; hurt

smart *adj* 1 *syn* see INTELLIGENT 2
ant stupid
2 *syn* see WISE 4
idiom knowing the score, on the ball
ant dull, dumb
3 *syn* see CLEVER 5
rel pert, saucy
4 *syn* see WISE 5
5 *syn* see STYLISH
rel dapper, ‖dinky, spruce
ant dowdy
‖6 *syn* see CONSIDERABLE 2

smart aleck *n* an obnoxiously conceited and self-assertive person with pretensions to smartness or cleverness <was heckled by a *smart aleck* in the back row>
syn know-it-all, smarty, smarty-pants, wiseacre, wisecracker, wise guy, wisehead, wisenheimer
rel blowhard, boaster, braggadocio, braggart, gasbag, windbag; exhibitionist, grandstander, show-off
idiom hot-air artist

smart-alecky *adj syn* see WISE 5

smarten (up) *vb syn* see DRESS UP 1

smart set *n* ultrafashionable often international society <the *smart set* that suns in Cannes and skis in St. Moritz>
syn beautiful people, jet set, ton
rel aristocracy, aristoi, blue bloods, bon ton, elite, Four Hundred, society, upper crust, who's who

smarty *n syn* see SMART ALECK

smarty-pants *n pl but sing in constr syn* see SMART ALECK

smash *vb* 1 *syn* see SHATTER 1
2 *syn* see SLAM 1
3 *syn* see DESTROY 1

smash *n* 1 *syn* see BLOW 1
2 *syn* see BANG 2
3 *syn* see IMPACT
4 *syn* see CRASH 3
5 *syn* see COLLAPSE 2
6 a striking success <the new musical was a box-office *smash*>
syn bang, bell ringer, hit, succès fou, ten-strike, wow
rel sensation; knockout
idiom howling (*or* roaring) success, smash hit
con disaster, dud, failure
ant flop

smash *n syn* see MONEY

‖**smashed** *adj syn* see INTOXICATED 1

smashup *n* 1 *syn* see COLLAPSE 2
2 *syn* see CRASH 3

smatch *n* 1 *syn* see HINT 2
2 *syn* see FEW

smatter *vb* ‖1 *syn* see SHATTER 1
2 *syn* see CHAT 1

smatter *n syn* see FEW

smatterer *n syn* see AMATEUR 2

smattering *n syn* see FEW

smaze *n syn* see HAZE 1

smear *vb* 1 to overspread with something unctuous, viscous, or adhesive < *smeared* the crack with wet concrete>
syn bedaub, besmear, dab, daub, plaster, ‖smarm, smudge
rel rub, coat, cover, overlay, overspread, spread; smirch, soil
2 *syn* see TAINT 1
3 *syn* see MALIGN
idiom use smear tactics (on *or* against)
4 *syn* see WHIP 2
rel foil, frustrate; repulse
idiom mop up the floor (*or* earth) with

smell *vb* 1 to perceive by means of the olfactory organs < *smelled* a dead skunk>
syn nose, scent, sniff, ‖snift, snuff
rel detect, perceive, sense; whiff; ‖snaffle, snuffle
idiom get a whiff of
2 *syn* see SMACK
3 to have or emit an offensive odor < the canal *smells* today>
syn funk, reek, stench, stink
idiom offend the nostrils, smell (*or* stink) to high heaven

smell *n* 1 a quality that makes a thing perceptible to the olfactory sense < the *smell* of a ham cooking>
syn aroma, odor, scent
rel bouquet, fragrance, incense, perfume, redolence, spice; flavor, savor, stench, stink
2 *syn* see HINT 2

smeller *n syn* see NOSE 1

‖**smelliful** *adj syn* see MALODOROUS 1
ant odorless, smell-less

smellfungus *n syn* see CRITIC

smell-less *adj syn* see ODORLESS
ant ‖smelliful, smelly

smelly *adj syn* see MALODOROUS 1
con odorless, scentless, smell-less; fragrant, fresh, sweet

smidgen *n syn* see PARTICLE

smile *vb* to express amusement, satisfaction, or pleasure by brightening one's eyes and curving the corners of one's mouth upward < *smiled* as she greeted him>
syn beam, grin
rel simper, smirk
idiom break into a smile, crack a smile
con grimace; glare, glower, lower, scowl
ant frown

smirch *vb syn* see SOIL 2
rel discolor; smear

smirk *vb* to smile in an affected manner < *smirking* children imitating their teacher>
syn simpler, ‖smirkle; *compare* SNEER 1
rel grin, smile; fleer, leer, sneer

‖**smirkle** *vb syn* see SMIRK

smitch *n syn* see PARTICLE

smite *vb* 1 *syn* see STRIKE 2
rel bat, belt, clobber; dash

idiom smite a blow
2 *syn* see AFFLICT

smithereens *n pl syn* see SMITHEREENS

smithereens *n pl* very small particles or fragments < a house blown to *smithereens* by a bomb>
syn ‖shivereens, smithers
rel fragments, particles, pieces

smithers *n pl syn* see SMITHEREENS

smitten *adj syn* see ENAMORED 1
idiom bitten by the love bug

smoke *n syn* see CIGARETTE

smoke *vb syn* see HURRY 2

smolder *vb syn* see SEETHE 4
rel burst, erupt, explode; fulminate

smooch *vb syn* see SOIL 2

smooch *vb syn* see KISS 1
idiom ‖plant a smooch on

‖**smoodge** *vb syn* see KISS 1

smooth *adj* 1 *syn* see LEVEL
rel glossy, sleek, slick; rippleless, unbroken, unwrinkled
con harsh, rugged, scabrous, uneven
ant rough
2 *syn* see HAIRLESS
3 *syn* see EASY 9
4 *syn* see EASY 1
rel smooth-running
idiom smooth and easy
ant labored
5 *syn* see SUAVE
rel courteous, courtly, polite; smooth-faced, smooth-tongued
con bluff, blunt, brusque, crusty, curt, gruff, harsh
6 *syn* see GENTLE 1
rel agreeable, soothing

smooth *vb* 1 *syn* see EVEN 1
con corrugate; roughen; wrinkle
ant unsmooth
2 *syn* see POLISH 2

smooth *adv syn* see EVENLY 3

smoothen *vb syn* see EVEN 1

smoothly *adv* 1 *syn* see EVENLY 3
con unevenly, ununiformly
ant roughly
2 *syn* see EASILY 1
ant unsmoothly

smooth-spoken *adj syn* see VOCAL 3
ant rough-spoken

smorgasbord *n syn* see MISCELLANY 1

smother *vb* 1 *syn* see SUFFOCATE
2 *syn* see COMPOSE 4
rel hush up, muffle; cork; quash, quell, squelch; quench
3 *syn* see WHIP 2

smothering *adj syn* see STIFLING 1

smothering *n syn* see REPRESSION 1

smothery *adj syn* see STIFLING 1

‖**smouch** *vb syn* see STEAL 1

smouch *vb syn* see KISS 1

smudge *vb* 1 *syn* see SOIL 2
rel smear; blotch, splotch
2 *syn* see SMEAR 1
3 *syn* see TAINT 1

‖**smudgy** *adj syn* see STIFLING 1

smug *adj syn* see COMPLACENT
idiom pleased with oneself

smug *vb syn* see DRESS UP 1

smuggle *vb* to import or export secretly and in violation of the law < *smuggling* weapons into the country>
syn bootleg, contraband, run
idiom run contraband

---

syn synonym(s)   *rel* related word(s)
ant antonym(s)   *con* contrasted word(s)
idiom idiomatic equivalent(s)
‖ use limited; if in doubt, see a dictionary

smut *vb* 1 *syn* see STAIN 1
2 *syn* see TAINT 1

smutch *vb* 1 *syn* see SOIL 2
2 *syn* see TAINT 1

smutty *adj* *syn* see OBSCENE 2

snack *n* food served or taken informally and usually in small amounts and typically under other circumstances than a regular meal < a milk-and-cookie *snack* after school >
syn ‖bait, ‖bever, bite, ‖chack, morsel, mug-up, ‖piece, tapa
rel collation, refreshment, tea
idiom bite to eat

snack bar (*or* **counter**) *n* *syn* see EATING HOUSE

‖**snaffle** *vb* *syn* see STEAL 1

‖**snafu** *vb* *syn* see CONFUSE 5

snag *n* *syn* see OBSTACLE
rel brake, clog, curb, drag; hold-up
idiom snags and sawyers

snake *n* *syn* see SNOT 1

snake *vb* ‖1 *syn* see STEAL 1
2 *syn* see CREEP 1
3 *syn* see SLITHER 2
‖4 *syn* see SNEAK

snaky *adj* *syn* see WINDING

snap *vb* 1 to speak in a curt, biting tone < *snapped* at his subordinates for inefficiency >
syn bark, snarl
rel growl, grumble, grunt, snort; roar, yell
idiom bite one's head off, snap off one's head (*or* nose)
2 *syn* see JERK
rel clutch, grab, grasp, seize, snaffle, snatch

snap *n* 1 something easily managed or accomplished < that exam was a *snap* >
syn breeze, child's play, cinch, duck soup, kid stuff, picnic, pie, ‖pipe, pushover, setup, ‖snip, soft touch
rel sinecure
idiom a simple twist of the wrist, simplicity itself, soft snap
con difficulty, headache, problem, trouble; bother, inconvenience, pain
ant chore
2 *syn* see PARTICLE
3 *syn* see MAN 3
4 *syn* see VIGOR 2

snap back *vb* *syn* see RECOVER 3

‖**snapper** *vb* *syn* see STUMBLE 3

snapping *adv* *syn* see VERY 1

snappish *adj* *syn* see IRRITABLE
rel curt, short, ungracious; crabbed, morose, surly

snappy *adj* 1 *syn* see IRRITABLE
2 *syn* see FAST 3
3 *syn* see PUNGENT
rel animated, lively, vivacious; prompt, quick, ready
4 *syn* see STYLISH

snare *n* *syn* see LURE 2
rel chicane, chicanery, deception; ensnarement, entrapment

snare *vb* *syn* see CATCH 3
rel seduce, tempt; involve; embrangle, enmesh, ensnarl, trammel

‖**snark** *vb* *syn* see SNORE

snarl *n* 1 *syn* see CONFUSION 3

rel entanglement, tangle; complexity, complication, intricacy, intricateness; labyrinth, maze; mishmash, swarm; jam
idiom tangled skein, wheels within wheels
2 *syn* see MAZE 1

snarl *vb* 1 *syn* see ENTANGLE 1
2 *syn* see COMPLICATE

snarl *vb* *syn* see SNAP 1

snarl up *vb* *syn* see CONFUSE 5

snatch *vb* 1 *syn* see SEIZE 2
rel jerk, wrench, yank; nip (up), whip (up)
‖2 *syn* see KIDNAP

sneak *vb* to move or go stealthily and furtively < *sneaked* into the garage and stole the car >
syn creep, glide, gumshoe, lurk, ‖meech, pussyfoot, shirk, skulk, slide, slink, slip, sly, ‖snake, ‖snook, steal; *compare* STEAL 3
rel crawl, slither, worm, prowl
idiom go on (little) cat's feet, move under cover
con barge, strut, swagger; clump, stamp, stump; stride; march, parade

sneak *n* a person who behaves in a stealthy, furtive, or shifty manner < found out that he was a liar, a cheat, and a *sneak* >
syn slink, sneaker, sneaksby, weasel
rel blackguard, knave, scoundrel; cur, heel, louse, reptile, skunk, snake; toad
idiom Jerry Sneak

sneak *adj* *syn* see SECRET 1

sneaker *n* *syn* see SNEAK

sneaking *adj* *syn* see UNDERHAND
ant forthright

sneaksby *n* *syn* see SNEAK

sneaky *adj* *syn* see UNDERHAND

‖**sneap** *vb* *syn* see REPROVE

sneer *vb* 1 to smile with attendant facial contortions expressing scorn or contempt < *sneered* haughtily at the beggar >
syn fleer, leer, ‖sleer; *compare* SMIRK
rel grin, smile
idiom curl one's lip, make a scornful (*or* mocking) face
2 *syn* see SCOFF
rel belittle, detract, disparage, underrate
idiom cock a snook at, give the Bronx cheer to, give the raspberry, sneeze at, thumb one's nose at

‖**sneezer** *n* *syn* see NOSE 1

snicker *vb* *syn* see LAUGH
idiom have a case of the snickers

snide *adj* 1 *syn* see COUNTERFEIT
2 *syn* see CROOKED 2

sniff *vb* *syn* see SMELL 1

‖**snift** *vb* *syn* see SMELL 1
rel ‖snifter

snifter *n* *syn* see DRAM

‖**sniggle** *vb* *syn* see LAUGH

snip *n* 1 *syn* see MINX
‖2 *syn* see SNAP 1

snippety *adj* *syn* see BLUFF
rel impolite, insolent, rude

snippy *adj* *syn* see BLUFF

snip-snap *n* *syn* see BANTER

snit *n* a state of agitation or excited irritation especially over a trivial matter < was in a *snit* because his secretary was one minute late >
syn fume, stew, sweat, swivet, tizzy

rel huff, pique; conniption, fit, frenzy, seizure, taking; dither, flap, panic, ‖swither

snitch *vb 1 syn* see INFORM 3
2 *syn* see STEAL 1

snitch *n* ‖1 *syn* see NOSE 1
2 *syn* see INFORMER

snob *n* one inclined to rebuff or ignore people or things that he regards as inferior (as in culture or social status) <appeals to real lovers of music rather than musical *snobs*>
syn high-hat, snoot, snot
rel name-dropper, snobbling; bootlicker, hanger-on, lickspittle, sycophant, toady

snob *vb syn* see CUT 7

snobbish *adj* of, relating to, or characteristic of a snob <a *snobbish* group of jet-set sophisticates>
syn ‖dicty, high-hat, potty, snobby, snooty
rel aloof, remote; high-flown, pretentious, snotty, supercilious; haughty, hoity-toity, pompous, ritzy; condescending, patronizing; insecure, uncertain, unconfident, unselfconfident, unsure
con certain, confident, secure, self-confident

snobby *adj syn* see SNOBBISH
rel snubbing, snubby

‖**snook** *vb 1 syn* see SNOOP
2 *syn* see SNEAK

snoop *vb* to look, inquire, or search impertinently or intrusively <he knew he had no right to *snoop* into her private life>
syn busybody, mouse, nose, ‖piroot, poke, pry, ‖snook
rel peek, peep, peer, stare; interfere, intrude, meddle, mess
idiom stick (*or* poke) one's nose into

snoop *n syn* see BUSYBODY

snoopy *adj syn* see CURIOUS 2

snoot *n 1 syn* see NOSE 1
2 *syn* see SNOB

snooty *adj syn* see SNOBBISH

snooze *vb syn* see NAP

snooze *n syn* see NAP

‖**snoozle** *vb syn* see DOZE

snoozy *adj syn* see SLEEPY 1

snore *vb* to breathe during sleep with a rough hoarse noise due to vibration of the soft palate <driven to distraction by her sister's *snoring*>
syn ‖snark
rel wheeze; snuffle; snort, ‖snotter
idiom ‖drive pigs to market, ‖saw logs (*or* wood)

snort *n syn* see DRAM

snorter *n syn* see DRAM

snot *n 1* an utterly contemptible person <a despicable *snot* whom everyone shunned>
syn ‖bugger, cur, dog, louse, ‖prick, puke, rat, scum, skunk, snake, sod, stinkard, stinkaroo, stinker, toad, wretch; *compare* VILLAIN 1
rel ‖creep, ‖crumb, lowlife; knave, rogue, scoundrel, ‖skite; pig, reptile
2 *syn* see SNOB

---

snout *n syn* see NOSE 1

snowball *vb syn* see INCREASE 2

snub *vb syn* see CUT 7
rel high-hat, ‖ritz, swank; put down
idiom look coldly upon, turn a cold shoulder (on *or* upon)

‖**snudge** *vb syn* see SNUGGLE

‖**snuff** *n syn* see OFFENSE 2

snuff *vb syn* see SMELL 1

‖**snuff** (out) *vb syn* see DIE 1

snug *adj 1 syn* see NEAT 2
2 *syn* see COMFORTABLE 2
idiom snug as a bug in a rug
‖3 *syn* see PROSPEROUS 3

snug *vb syn* see SNUGGLE

snuggle *vb* to assume or be in a warm comfortable position usually near another person or thing <a baby *snuggling* close to his mother>
syn burrow, ‖croodle, cuddle, nestle, nuzzle, ‖snudge, snug, ‖snuzzle
rel curl up; huddle; spoon
idiom snuggle up like a bug in a rug
con flinch, recoil, shrink

‖**snuzzle** *vb syn* see SNUGGLE

sny *vb syn* see TEEM

so *adv 1 syn* see ALSO 1
2 *syn* see THUS 1
3 *syn* see VERY 1
4 *syn* see THEREFORE

so *conj* with the purpose that <repeated it aloud *so* there'd be no mistake>
syn so as, so that
idiom in order that, to the end that, with the intent that

soak *vb 1* to permeate or be permeated with or as if with water <*soak* a sponge with water> <rain *soaked* her to the skin>
syn drench, ‖drouk, impregnate, insteep, saturate, seethe, sodden, ‖sog, sop, souse, steep, waterlog; *compare* WET
rel dip, immerse, submerge; draw, infuse; infiltrate, penetrate, permeate, pervade; water-soak; drown
2 *syn* see WET 1
3 *syn* see ENGAGE 4
4 *syn* see OVERCHARGE 1
5 *syn* see DRINK 3
idiom ‖soak it up like a sponge

soak *n 1 syn* see DRUNKARD
2 *syn* see BINGE 1

soaked *adj syn* see WET 1

soaker *n syn* see DRUNKARD

soaking *adj syn* see WET 1
idiom soaking wet

so-and-so *n syn* see DAMNED 2

soapbox *vb syn* see ORATE

soapy *adj syn* see FULSOME

soar *vb 1 syn* see RISE 4
rel climb; shoot
2 *syn* see SKYROCKET
ant plummet

soaring *adj syn* see LOFTY 6
idiom high as the sky

so as *conj syn* see SO

sob *vb syn* see CRY 2

sobby *adj syn* see SENTIMENTAL

sober *adj 1 syn* see ABSTEMIOUS
rel controlled, restrained; self-possessed
con indulgent, overindulgent; uncontrolled, unrestrained; immoderate, intemperate; excessive; profligate

---

syn synonym(s)   *rel* related word(s)
ant antonym(s)   *con* contrasted word(s)
idiom idiomatic equivalent(s)
‖ use limited; if in doubt, see a dictionary

2 *syn* see SERIOUS 1
rel decorous, proper; calm, placid, serene, tranquil
con flippant, light, light-minded; unstable, volatile
ant gay

3 having or exhibiting self-control and avoiding extremes of behavior <his bearing was *sober*, his comments judicious>
syn moderate, temperate, unimpassioned; *compare* ABSTEMIOUS
rel rational, reasonable; calm, collected, composed, cool, imperturbable; constrained, disciplined, inhibited, reserved, restrained, self-controlled, self-disciplined; abstaining, forbearing, refraining; abnegating, eschewing, forgoing
con irrational, unreasonable; emotional, hotheaded, impassioned, overemotional, passionate; intemperate, uncontained, uncontrolled; excited; drunk, intoxicated; abandoned
ant unsober

4 *syn* see SUBDUED 2

5 *syn* see REALISTIC
rel sober-eyed, sober-minded

sobersided *adj syn* see SERIOUS 1

sobful *adj syn* see SENTIMENTAL

sobriety *n syn* see TEMPERANCE 2
rel gravity, sedateness, seriousness, soberness
con excitement; drunkenness, intoxication; abandonment
ant insobriety

sobriquet *n syn* see NICKNAME

so-called *adj syn* see NOMINAL

2 *syn* see ALLEGED

sociable *adj* 1 *syn* see SOCIAL 2
ant nonsocial

2 *syn* see GRACIOUS 1
rel companionable, convivial; gregarious, close, familiar, intimate; good-natured
ant unsociable

3 *syn* see SOCIAL 1
ant unsociable, unsocial

social *adj* 1 conducive to, marked by, or passed in pleasant companionship with one's friends or associates <a relaxed, *social* evening>
syn companionable, convivial, sociable
rel amusing, entertaining, pleasant, pleasurable; cordial, friendly, genial, gracious, hospitable
con unfriendly, unhospitable, unsociable; eremitic, solitary
ant unsociable, unsocial

2 inclined by nature to association or community life with others of the same species <man is a *social* animal>
syn gregarious, sociable
rel social-minded; intersocial
con eremitic, solitary, unsociable; antisocial, asocial, unsocial; remote, withdrawn
ant nonsocial

social evil *n*, used with the *syn* see PROSTITUTION

socialize *vb* to participate actively in a social group <*socializes* with his colleagues>
syn mingle
rel associate, mix

society *n* 1 *syn* see COMPANY 1

2 *syn* see ASSOCIATION 2

3 an organized aggregate of persons who are responsible for a prevailing social order <rules made in the interests of *society* rather than for the chosen few>
syn community, people, public
rel masses, populace
idiom people in general, society at large, the general public

4 *syn* see ARISTOCRACY
idiom high society (or life)

sock *vb syn* see STRIKE 2

sock *n* 1 *syn* see BLOW 1

2 *syn* see CUFF

‖**sock** *vb syn* see SIGH 1

sod *n syn* see SNOT 1

sodality *n syn* see ASSOCIATION 2

sodden *adj syn* see WET 1

sodden *vb syn* see SOAK 1

Sodom *n syn* see SINK 1
rel Babylon

so far *adv syn* see HITHERTO 1
idiom up till now

soft *adj* 1 *syn* see GENTLE 1
rel moderate, temperate

2 *syn* see SUBDUED 2
ant loud

3 smooth or delicate in texture, grain, or fiber <the dog's fur was *soft*>
syn cottony, satiny, silken, silky, velvety
rel smooth; sleek
con coarse, rough
ant harsh

4 *syn* see COMFORTABLE 2
ant rough

5 *syn* see SIMPLE 3
idiom ‖soft in the head

6 giving way easily to physical touch or pressure <a *soft* cheese>
syn mushy, pappy, pulpous, pulpy, quaggy, spongy, squashy, squelchy, squishy, squushy, yielding
rel softish; compressible, malleable, pliable, pliant, workable; doughy, formless; flabby, fleshy
idiom soft as butter
con firm, solid; resistant, rigid, tough, unyielding; nail-hard, rock-hard
ant hard

soft (on) *adj syn* see ENAMORED 1

soft-boiled *adj syn* see SENTIMENTAL
ant hard-boiled

soften *vb syn* see DEPRECIATE 1

softened *adj syn* see SUBDUED 2

softhead *n syn* see FOOL 4

softhearted *adj syn* see TENDER
ant hardhearted

soft-pedal *vb* to reduce the emphasis, importance, or effect of something (as an issue) <tried to *soft-pedal* military spending>
syn de-emphasize, play (down)
rel tone (down), tune (down); cushion, dampen, muffle, subdue; hush (up), silence, suppress; conceal, disguise
con emphasize, play (up); focus (on), spotlight

soft-shell *adj syn* see MODERATE 4

soft soap *n syn* see FLATTERY
rel ‖snow job

soft-soap *vb syn* see COAX

soft spot *n* 1 *syn* see APPETITE 3

2 a vulnerable point <the major *soft spot* in the West's armor>

syn Achilles' heel
rel vulnerability, vulnerableness, weakness; chink, loophole
idiom heel of Achilles, weak link (*or* point), weak link in the chain
con impregnability, invulnerability; invincibility

soft touch *n* 1 someone who can be easily talked into giving help (as a loan) <recognized him as a *soft touch* when she was broke>
syn easy mark
rel softy; dupe, fool, pushover; sucker; mark, sitting duck, target
con cynic, doubting Thomas, hard case, skeptic
2 **syn** see SNAP 1

‖**sog** *vb* **syn** see SOAK 1
‖**sog** *vb* **syn** see DOZE
soggy *adj* **syn** see HUMID
soi-disant *adj* **syn** see SELF-STYLED
soil *vb* 1 **syn** see CONTAMINATE 1
ant purify
2 to make or become unclean <a shirt *soiled* with grease and grime>
syn begrime, besoil, dirty, foul, grime, muck, ‖mucky, muddy, murk, smirch, smooch, smudge, smutch, tarnish; *compare* STAIN 1
rel ‖beccom, ‖benasty, ‖nasty; bedaub, daub, smear; drabble, draggle; mess, spoil
con brighten, cleanse, freshen, renew; purify
ant clean
3 **syn** see TAINT 1
soil *n* 1 **syn** see EARTH 2
2 **syn** see COUNTRY
soily *adj* **syn** see DIRTY 1
soiree *n* **syn** see EVENING 3
sojourn *n* a temporary but sometimes extended stay <a summer *sojourn* in Nice>
syn stopover, tarriance, visit
rel stay, stop; layover
sojourn *vb* **syn** see VISIT 3
rel linger, abide
Sol *n* **syn** see SUN 1
solace *vb* **syn** see COMFORT
idiom offer (*or* give) solace to, wipe one's tears away
soldier *n* a person engaged in military service <*soldiers* fighting and dying in futile wars>
syn fighter, fighting man, GI, man-at-arms, serviceman, swad, ‖swaddy, ‖sweat, warrior
rel dogface, doughboy, ‖doughfoot, infantryman; trooper; guerrilla, partisan; condottiere, free companion, free lance, mercenary, soldier of fortune
soldierly *adj* **syn** see BRAVE 1
rel martial; aggressive, combative, militant, pugnacious, warlike
con unsoldierly
sole *n* **syn** see BOTTOM 1
sole *adj* 1 **syn** see SINGLE 1
2 **syn** see SINGLE 2
3 **syn** see ONLY 2

idiom one and only
4 belonging, granted, or attributed to the one person or group <*sole* rights of publication>
syn exclusive, single, unshared
con multiple; shared
solecism *n* 1 **syn** see ANACHRONISM 2
2 **syn** see BARBARISM
3 **syn** see FAUX PAS
solely *adv* **syn** see ONLY 1
solemn *adj* 1 **syn** see CEREMONIAL
rel full, plenary; august, grand, impressive, magnificent, majestic, overwhelming; ostentatious
2 **syn** see SERIOUS 1
idiom as solemn as an owl, grave as an undertaker
solemnize *vb* **syn** see KEEP 2
rel dignify, honor, solemnify, venerate
solicit *vb* 1 to seek (as advertising, orders, or votes) especially on a large scale <*solicited* contributions all over the district>
syn canvass, drum, drum up
rel ask, request; beg, beseech, implore; claim, demand, exact
2 **syn** see ASK 2
rel apply, go, refer, resort, turn
3 **syn** see DEMAND 1
solicitous *adj* **syn** see EAGER
solicitude *n* 1 **syn** see CARE 2
rel attention, heed, watchfulness; presentiment; compunction, qualm, scruple
con carelessness, heedlessness, indifference, neglect, negligence
ant unmindfulness
2 **syn** see CONSIDERATION 3
solid *adj* 1 **syn** see FIRM 2
rel compacted, concentrated, consolidated
con spongy; disintegrated; fluid, liquid
2 **syn** see STABLE 4
3 **syn** see VALID
rel firm, hard
ant insubstantial
4 **syn** see UNANIMOUS
solid *adv* **syn** see HARD 9
solidarism *n* **syn** see SOLIDARITY
solidarity *n* a feeling of unity (as in interests, standards, and responsibilities) that binds members of a group together <*solidarity* among union members is essential in negotiations>
syn cohesion, solidarism, togetherness
rel cohesiveness; oneness, singleness, undividedness; integrity, solidity, union, unity; esprit, esprit de corps; firmness, fixity
con separation; discord, dissension, schism; confusion, disorder, disorganization
ant division
solidify *vb* **syn** see HARDEN 1
rel compress, contract
idiom make (*or* become) hard as a rock
con soften; disintegrate, dissolve
ant liquefy
solidly *adv* 1 **syn** see HARD 9
2 **syn** see HARD 7
solitariness *n* **syn** see SOLITUDE
solitary *adj* 1 **syn** see ANTISOCIAL
ant gregarious
2 **syn** see UNSOCIABLE
3 **syn** see DERELICT 1
4 **syn** see LONE 1

---

syn synonym(s)   **rel** related word(s)
ant antonym(s)   **con** contrasted word(s)
idiom idiomatic equivalent(s)
‖ use limited; if in doubt, see a dictionary

rel companionless, unaccompanied, unattended

ant accompanied

5 *syn* see SINGLE 2

6 *syn* see ONLY 2

solitary *n syn* see RECLUSE

solitude *n* the state of one who is alone <a very social person who could not bear *solitude*>

syn aloneness, isolation, loneness, solitariness; *compare* SECLUSION

rel detachment, separateness; retirement, withdrawal; confinement, quarantine; loneliness, lonesomeness

con companionship, company

solo *adj syn* see ONLY 2

so long *interj syn* see GOOD-BYE

solution *n syn* see ANSWER 2

solve *vb* **1** to find an answer or solution for (a problem or difficulty) <mass transit partially *solved* the traffic problem>

syn fix, resolve, work, work out

rel decide, determine, settle

idiom hit upon a solution

2 to find an explanation or solution for something obscure, mysterious, or incomprehensible <the mystery of the missing cookies has been *solved*>

syn break, ||cipher, clear up, decipher, dissolve, ||dope out, figure out, puzzle out, resolve, unfold, unravel, unriddle

rel enlighten, illuminate, construe, elucidate, explain, interpret

idiom get to the bottom of, have it, put two and two together

somatic *adj syn* see BODILY

somber *adj* **1** *syn* see DARK 1

2 *syn* see GLOOMY 3

3 *syn* see SERIOUS 1

idiom as somber as an undertaker

some *adj* **1** *syn* see CERTAIN 2

2 *syn* see SEVERAL 3

some *adv* **1** *syn* see NEARLY

2 *syn* see SOMEWHAT 2

somebody *pron* one or some individual of no certain or known identity <*somebody* should be home>

syn someone

rel anybody, one

con none

ant nobody, no one

somebody *n* **1** *syn* see NOTABLE 1

ant nobody

2 *syn* see CELEBRITY 2

someday *adv syn* see YET 2

||**somegate** *adv syn* see SOMEHOW

somehow *adv* in some way not yet known or specified <this thing must be done *somehow*>

syn ||somegate, someway, somewise

rel anyhow, anyway, anywise

idiom by hook or by crook, in one way or another, in some such way, somehow or other (or another)

con nohow, noway, nowise

someone *pron syn* see SOMEBODY

someplace *adv syn* see SOMEWHERE 1

ant no place

something *adv syn* see SOMEWHAT 2

something *n syn* see ENTITY 1

sometime *adv syn* see YET 2

idiom one of these days

sometime *adj syn* see FORMER 2

sometimes *adv* at intervals <illustrated by beautiful and *sometimes* outstanding photographs>

syn at times, ||betimes, ever and again, ever and anon, here and there, now and again, now and then, once and again, ||otherwhile; *compare* OCCASIONALLY

rel intermittently, periodically, recurrently; frequently; consistently, constantly

idiom every now and then (or again), every once in a while, every so often, from time to time

con continually, continuously, unceasingly, uninterruptedly; endlessly, ever, interminably

someway *adv syn* see SOMEHOW

somewhat *adv* **1** *syn* see WELL 8

2 to some extent or in some degree <felt *somewhat* better but not fine>

syn fairly, kind of, moderately, more or less, pretty, rather, ratherish, some, something, sort of

rel adequately, bearably, tolerably; insignificantly, slightly

idiom rather more than less

somewhen *adv syn* see YET 2

somewhere *adv* **1** to, at, or in some unknown or unspecified location <lived on a farm *somewhere* in the Midwest>

syn someplace, ||somewheres

rel somewhither; elsewhere, otherwhere

idiom someplace or other

con anyplace, anywhere, ||anywheres; no place, ||nowheres

ant nowhere

2 *syn* see NEARLY

||**somewheres** *adv syn* see SOMEWHERE 1

ant ||nowheres

somewise *adv syn* see SOMEHOW

somnifacient *adj syn* see SOPORIFIC 1

somniferous *adj syn* see SOPORIFIC 1

somnific *adj syn* see SOPORIFIC 1

somnolent *adj* **1** *syn* see SOPORIFIC 1

2 *syn* see SLEEPY 1

rel inactive, passive, supine

somnorific *adj syn* see SOPORIFIC 1

so much as *adv syn* see EVEN 4

son *n syn* see BOY 1

rel sonny; junior

sonance *n syn* see SOUND 1

sonant *adj syn* see VOCAL 1

song *n* **1** *syn* see POETRY 1

2 music or a piece of music intended for vocal expression <played and sang a *song*>

syn aria, descant, ditty, hymn, lay, lied; *compare* MELODY

rel lyric; piece

3 *syn* see CALL 1

song and dance *n syn* see SPIEL

songful *adj syn* see MELODIOUS 2

sonorant *adj syn* see RESONANT

sonorous *adj* **1** *syn* see RESONANT

2 *syn* see RHETORICAL

3 *syn* see NOISY

||**sonsy** *adj* **1** *syn* see LUCKY

2 *syn* see GRACIOUS 1

3 *syn* see EASYGOING 3

soon *adv* **1** *syn* see PRESENTLY 1

rel forthwith, instantly, pronto, quickly

idiom in the near future

2 *syn* see FAST 2

3 *syn* see EARLY 1

‖**soon** adj syn see EARLY 2
sooner adv syn see BEFORE 3
sooner or later adv syn see YET 2
soothe vb syn see CALM
  rel comfort, console; hush, subdue
  con annoy, irritate, vex
  ant excite
‖**soother** n syn see CALM
soothsay vb syn see FORETELL
soothsayer n syn see PROPHET
sop n 1 syn see WEAKLING
  2 a conciliatory or propitiatory gift or
  advance <provided the $400 raise as a
  sop> <the new office was a sop to his
  wounded feelings>
  syn sugarplum
  rel douceur, gratuity; ‖baksheesh, ‖boo-
  dle, bribe, ‖palm oil
  idiom sop in the pan, sop to Cerberus
sop vb 1 syn see WET
  2 syn see SOAK 1
  3 syn see BRIBE
sophic adj syn see WISE 1
sophism n syn see FALLACY 2
  rel illogicality, irrationality; invalidity,
  unsoundness; claptrap
sophistic adj syn see ILLOGICAL
sophisticate adj syn see SOPHISTICATED
  2
sophisticate vb syn see ADULTERATE
sophisticated adj 1 syn see COMPLEX 2
  ant unsophisticated
  2 being experienced in the ways of the
  world <a sophisticated, well-traveled
  man>
  syn blasé, disenchanted, disentranced,
  disillusioned, knowing, mondaine, sophisticate, worldly, worldly-wise, world-wise;
  compare COSMOPOLITAN 1
  rel adult, mature; experienced, practiced,
  schooled, seasoned; salty, uncelestial;
  couth, well-bred; smooth, suave, svelte,
  urbane; bored, jaded, world-weary; brittle;
  cynical, skeptical
  con artless, gee-whiz, ingenuous, natural;
  green, inexperienced, unseasoned, virginal;
  unworldly
  ant naive, unsophisticated
sophistry n syn see FALLACY 2
  rel ambiguity, tergiversation
soporiferous adj syn see SOPORIFIC 1
soporific adj 1 tending to induce sleep <a
  soporific drug> < soporific prose>
  syn hypnotic, narcotic, opiate, sleepy,
  slumberous, somnifacient, somniferous,
  somnific, somnolent, somnorific, soporiferous, soporifical
  rel calming, quietening, sedative, tranquil-
  izing; anesthetic, deadening, numbing
  con arousing, waking; invigorating, stimulating
  2 syn see SLEEPY 1
soporifical adj syn see SOPORIFIC 1
sopping adj syn see WET 1
soppy adj 1 syn see WET 1
  ‖2 syn see SENTIMENTAL
sorcerer n syn see MAGICIAN 1
sorceress n syn see WITCH 1

sorcerous adj syn see MAGIC
sorcery n syn see MAGIC 1
sordid adj 1 syn see DIRTY 1
  2 syn see SLATTERNLY
  3 syn see BASE 3
  rel foul, nasty, seamy, sodden
sore adj syn see PAINFUL 1
sorehead n syn see GROUCH
sorely adv syn see HARD 6
sorrow n distress of mind <felt great
  sorrow at the loss of her friend>
  syn affliction, anguish, care, ‖dole, grief,
  heartache, heartbreak, regret, rue, woe
  rel mournfulness, sadness, sorrowfulness,
  unhappiness; grieving, lamentation,
  mourning, sorrowing; dejection, depression, melancholy; agony, distress, dolor,
  misery, suffering, wretchedness
  con cheerfulness, gaiety, gladness, happiness, joyfulness; ecstasy
  ant joy
sorrow vb syn see GRIEVE 2
  rel groan, moan, sob
  idiom break one's heart over, eat one's
  heart out
  ant rejoice
sorrowful adj 1 syn see WOEFUL 1
  rel sorrow-laden, sorrow-stricken, sorrow-
  struck
  idiom full of (or filled with) sorrow
  con sorrowless
  ant joyful
  2 syn see MELANCHOLY 2
  ant gay
sorry adj 1 syn see SAD 1
  rel bad, regretful, remorseful; miserable,
  wretched
  ant glad
  2 syn see REMORSEFUL
  3 syn see CONTEMPTIBLE
  rel inadequate, paltry, poor, trifling;
  cheesy, scruffy, shoddy; disgraceful
sort n 1 syn see TYPE
  2 syn see GROUP 3
sort vb 1 syn see ASSORT
  2 to analyze and assort (as individuals or
  things) to obtain those desired or required
  <he knew he must sort out facts from
  fancy>
  syn comb, separate, sift, winnow; compare
  SCREEN 5
  rel riddle, screen; choose, cull, pick, select
  con consolidate, join, lump, merge; aggregate, amalgamate, blend, fuse, mix; unify
sort of adv syn see SOMEWHAT 2
SOS n syn see ALARM 1
soshed adj syn see INTOXICATED 1
so-so adj syn see ENOUGH 2
so-so adj syn see MEDIUM
sot n syn see DRUNKARD
‖**sot** adj syn see OBSTINATE
so that conj syn see SO
sotto voce adv in an inaudible or barely
  audible voice <made a snide remark to
  her sotto voce>
  syn faintly, mutedly, weakly
  rel low, quietly, softly, muffledly; mutter-
  ingly; aside, privately
  idiom below one's breath, between one's
  teeth, in an aside, in an undertone, in a
  whisper, out of earshot, under one's
  breath
  con aloud, out, out loud

---

syn synonym(s)   rel related word(s)
ant antonym(s)   con contrasted word(s)
idiom idiomatic equivalent(s)
‖ use limited; if in doubt, see a dictionary

sough *vb* 1 *syn* see SIGH 2
2 *syn* see SIGH 1

soul *n* 1 an animating essence or principle held to be inseparably associated with life or living beings < philosophers who teach that life is a manifestation of *soul* >
syn anima, animus, élan vital, pneuma, psyche, spirit, vital force
rel life, vitality
idiom breath of life
2 the immortal part of man believed to have permanent individual existence < into God's hands I commit my *soul* >
syn spirit
rel life; noumenon
idiom one's immortal soul
con flesh
ant body
3 *syn* see HEART 1
rel character, personality, psyche; conscience; spirit
idiom heart of hearts, heart's core, one's inmost soul (or mind), one's secret (or inner) self, (the) secret recesses of the heart
4 *syn* see ESSENCE 2
5 *syn* see HUMAN

soul-searching *n* *syn* see INTROSPECTION

soul-sick *adj* *syn* see DOWNCAST

sound *adj* 1 *syn* see HEALTHY 1
rel intact, unimpaired; perfect
idiom sound as a bell (or whistle), sound of mind and body
con impaired; unfit
ant unsound
2 *syn* see WHOLE 1
3 *syn* see STABLE 4
ant unsound
4 *syn* see VALID
rel errorless, faultless, flawless, impeccable; accurate, correct, exact, precise; rational, reasonable; well-founded, well-grounded
con questionable, shaky; invalid
ant unsound
5 *syn* see ORTHODOX 1
6 *syn* see RATIONAL
rel right-minded, sober, sober-minded, sound-minded
ant unsound

sound *n* 1 a sensation or effect resulting from stimulation of the auditory receptors < the *sound* of thunder >
syn noise, sonance
rel vibration; resonance; sonancy; reverberation
con quiet, soundlessness
ant silence
2 *syn* see EARSHOT

sound *vb* 1 *syn* see SEEM
2 *syn* see DECLARE 1

sound *vb* to measure the depth of (as a body of water) typically with a weighted line < *sounding* the distance to the bottom >
syn fathom, plumb, plumb-line
idiom ‖cast (or sling) the lead, make a sounding, take soundings

sound (out) *vb* *syn* see PROBE 2

soundless *adj* *syn* see BOTTOMLESS 2
ant soundable

soundless *adj* *syn* see STILL 3

soundlessness *n* *syn* see SILENCE 1

soundness *n* 1 *syn* see HEALTH
ant unsoundness
2 *syn* see STABILITY
3 *syn* see WIT 2
rel level-headedness, sensibleness
idiom sound mind, soundness of mind
ant unsoundness

sound off *vb* *syn* see SPEAK UP

soup *n* *syn* see PREDICAMENT

soupçon *n* *syn* see HINT 2

soupy *adj* *syn* see SENTIMENTAL

sour *adj* 1 causing or characterized by the one of the basic taste sensations produced chiefly by acids < *sour* pickles >
syn acerb, acerbic, acetose, acid, acidulous, dry, tart
rel keen, sharp, tangy; ‖blinky, sourish; fermented, soured, turned; acrid, bitter, vinegary
ant sweet
2 *syn* see BAD 8

source *n* the point at which something begins its course or existence < the *source* of his wisdom was long practical experience >
syn derivation, fount, fountain, fountainhead, inception, mother, origin, provenance, provenience, root, rootage, rootstock, spring, well, wellhead, wellspring, whence
rel birthplace; beginning, commencement, dawn, dawning, onset, opening, start, starting; authorship, origination, rise, rising; antecedent, cause, determinant; parent, paternity
con end, ending, terminus
ant termination; outcome

sourpuss *n* *syn* see GROUCH
rel killjoy

souse *vb* 1 *syn* see DIP 1
2 *syn* see WET
3 *syn* see SOAK 1

souse *n* *syn* see BINGE 1

soused *adj* *syn* see WET 1

souvenir *n* *syn* see REMEMBRANCE 3
idiom token of remembrance

sovereign *adj* 1 *syn* see FREE 1
rel self-determined, self-governed
2 *syn* see DOMINANT 1
rel commanding, directing, guiding; highest, loftiest
3 *syn* see EXCELLENT
4 *syn* see KINGLY

sovereignty *n* *syn* see SUPREMACY

sow *vb* 1 *syn* see PLANT 1
2 *syn* see STREW 1
rel fling, toss; drill

‖sowf *vb* *syn* see HUM

sozzled *adj* *syn* see INTOXICATED 1

spa *n* 1 a locality featuring mineral springs or water cures < hoped a week at a *spa* would help his arthritis >
syn baths, ‖hydro, springs, watering place, wells
rel waters
idiom health spa
2 *syn* see RESORT 3

space *n* 1 *syn* see WHILE 1
rel lapse; interval, term; duration
2 *syn* see EXPANSE
rel room, roomage; spaciousness

spaced-out *adj* *syn* see DRUGGED

spacious *adj* larger in extent or capacity than the average <a mansion with *spacious* rooms and gardens>
syn ample, capacious, commodious, roomy, wide
rel big, generous, great, large, spacy; enormous, immense, vast; expansive, extended, extensive; boundless, spaceless
con circumscribed, confined, cramped, limited, narrow, restricted; small, tiny
ant strait

spade *vb* 1 *syn* see DIG 2
    2 *syn* see DIG 1

span *n* *syn* see TERM 2
rel interval; space

spang *adv* *syn* see JUST 1

spangle *vb* 1 to adorn with small brilliant objects <a tutu *spangled* with sequins>
syn bespangle, glitter
rel adorn, decorate, ornament, trim
    2 *syn* see FLASH 1

spang-new *adj* *syn* see BRAND-NEW

spaniel *n* *syn* see SYCOPHANT

spank *vb* *syn* see SLAP 1

spank *n* *syn* see CUFF
idiom a sound spank

spanking *adv* *syn* see VERY 1

spanking-new *adj* *syn* see BRAND-NEW

span-new *adj* *syn* see BRAND-NEW

spare *vb* 1 *syn* see EXEMPT
    2 *syn* see SAVE 4
    3 to refrain from the free use or consumption of <don't *spare* the syrup on my pancakes>
syn scant, short, skimp, ‖skinch, stint; *compare* SCRIMP
rel pinch
    4 *syn* see SCRIMP

spare *adj* 1 *syn* see SUPERFLUOUS
idiom enough and to spare, more than enough
    2 *syn* see LEAN
ant corpulent
    3 *syn* see MEAGER 2
ant profuse

sparing *adj* careful in the use of money, goods, or resources <was *sparing* in his expenditures>
syn canny, chary, economical, frugal, provident, saving, Scotch, stewardly, thrifty, unwasteful, wary; *compare* STINGY
rel parsimonious, ‖scant, tight, tightfisted, ungiving
con exuberant, liberal, prodigal, profuse
ant lavish, unsparing

spark *n* *syn* see SEED 2

spark *n* *syn* see SUITOR 2

spark *vb* *syn* see ADDRESS 8

sparker *n* *syn* see SUITOR 2

sparkish *adj* *syn* see DAPPER

sparkle *vb* *syn* see FLASH 1

sparkle *n* *syn* see FLASH 1

sparse *adj* *syn* see MEAGER 2
rel dispersed, scattered; infrequent, occasional, sporadic; rare, scarce, uncommon
con close, compact, thick

‖spartle *vb* *syn* see SCRAMBLE 1

spasmodic *adj* *syn* see FITFUL

---

syn synonym(s)   *rel* related word(s)
ant antonym(s)   *con* contrasted word(s)
idiom idiomatic equivalent(s)
‖ use limited; if in doubt, see a dictionary

---

rel spurtive
con continual, continuous, uninterrupted

spat *n* 1 *syn* see QUARREL
    ‖2 *syn* see CUFF

spat *vb* *syn* see QUARREL

spate *n* 1 *syn* see FLOOD 2
rel progression, series, succession; rain, river, spurt
    2 *syn* see FLOW

spatter *vb* 1 *syn* see SPLASH 1
rel sparge
    2 *syn* see SPOT 1
    3 *syn* see MALIGN
    4 *syn* see SPUTTER 2

spatter *n* *syn* see FEW

spattering *n* *syn* see FEW

spawn *vb* *syn* see GENERATE 1

spawning *adj* *syn* see FERTILE

speak *vb* 1 to articulate words in order to express thoughts <always *speak* clearly>
syn talk, utter, verbalize, vocalize, voice
rel drawl, gasp, mouth, mumble, murmur, mutter, shout, splutter, spout, whisper; descant, dilate (on *or* upon), expatiate, perorate; converse, discourse; allege, assert, aver, convey, declare, tell
idiom break silence, give voice (*or* tongue *or* utterance) to, let fall, make public (*or* known), open one's mouth (*or* lips), put in (*or* into) words, say one's say, speak one's piece
con gabble, gibber, jabber; maunder, mumble, mutter; mispronounce, misspeak
    2 *syn* see TALK 7
    3 to have oral command of (a language) <he *speaks* fluent German>
syn converse (in), parley, talk, use
idiom be at ease in
con falter, hesitate, stumble

speaker *n* *syn* see SPOKESMAN

speaking *n* *syn* see SPEECH 1

speak out *vb* *syn* see SPEAK UP

speak up *vb* to speak strongly, boldly, or vigorously <we'll never know how you feel if you don't *speak up*>
syn sound off, speak out
idiom come out with it, have one's say, let one's voice be heard, make oneself heard, speak one's mind, stand up and be counted

spear *vb* *syn* see IMPALE
rel stick; bore, drill, penetrate, pierce; gouge, ream

special *adj* 1 of or relating to one thing or class <*special* soap for infants>
syn especial, individual, particular, specific
rel characteristic, distinctive, peculiar; exceptional, occasional, rare, uncommon; unique
con common, familiar, ordinary; customary, habitual, usual
    2 *syn* see EXPRESS 2
rel defined, determinate; designated, earmarked

special *adv* *syn* see ESPECIALLY 1

specialize *vb* *syn* see ITEMIZE 1

specially *adv* 1 *syn* see ESPECIALLY 1
    2 *syn* see EXPRESSLY 2

species *n* *syn* see TYPE

specific *adj* 1 *syn* see SPECIAL 1
rel limited, reserved, restricted, specialized

con general, generic
ant nonspecific, unspecific
2 *syn see* EXPLICIT
con ambiguous, cloudy, indefinite, uncertain, unexplicit, unspecified, vague
ant nonspecific, unspecific
3 *syn see* EXPRESS 2
ant nonspecific, unspecific
specifically *adv* 1 *syn see* EXPRESSLY 2
2 *syn see* ESPECIALLY 1
3 *syn see* EXPRESSLY 1
specificate *vb syn see* SPECIFY 3
specificize *vb syn see* SPECIFY 3
specify *vb* 1 *syn see* MENTION
2 *syn see* ITEMIZE 1
3 to make something (as a condition or requirement) specific <his will *specified* how the money would be divided>
syn detail, particularize, specificate, specificize, stipulate; *compare* ITEMIZE 1
rel determine, establish, fix, settle; condition, limit, set; pin (down); enumerate, list; precise
specimen *n syn see* INSTANCE
rel sort, species, type, variety
specious *adj syn see* FALSE 1
rel apparent, seeming; colorable, plausible; beguiling; illogical, spurious; empty, hollow, idle, nugatory, vain
ant valid
speciousness *n syn see* FALLACY 2
rel speciosity
ant validity
speck *n* 1 *syn see* POINT 11
rel pinpoint; tick
2 *syn see* PARTICLE
speck *vb syn see* SPECKLE 1
speckle *vb* 1 to produce on or mark with small spots, speckles, or blemishes <a *speckled* egg>
syn bespeckle, dot, freckle, pepper, speck, sprinkle, stipple; *compare* SPOT 1
rel dapple, flake, fleck
2 *syn see* SPOT 2
spectacle *n syn see* EXHIBITION 1
spectacled *adj syn see* BESPECTACLED
spectacular *adj syn see* MARVELOUS 1
rel eye-popping, sensational, striking, thrilling; dramatic, histrionic, stagy, theatrical
ant unspectacular
spectator *n* one who sees or looks upon something <sports *spectators*>
syn beholder, by-sitter, bystander, eyewitness, looker-on, observer, onlooker, stander-by, viewer, watcher, witness
rel gazer; perceiver; seer
specter *n syn see* APPARITION
spectral *adj syn see* GHASTLY 2
rel phantom, phantomlike, shadowlike; disembodied, unearthly; spooky
spectrum *n syn see* APPARITION
speculate *vb syn see* THINK 5
rel excogitate, review, study, weigh
idiom ‖beat one's brains, turn over in one's mind, ‖use the gray matter
speculation *n* 1 *syn see* THOUGHT 1
rel excogitation, review, studying, weighing
2 *syn see* THEORY 2
speculative *adj syn see* THEORETICAL 1
2 *syn see* THOUGHTFUL 1
rel musing, ruminating; curious, inquiring, questioning

ant unspeculative
speech *n* 1 communication, expression, or interchange of thoughts in spoken words <considered *speech* as a means of reproducing for one's listeners the images in one's mind>
syn discourse, speaking, talk, utterance, verbalization; *compare* VOCALIZATION
rel articulation, uttering, vocalization, vocalizing, voice, voicing; expressing, expression; language
idiom oral communication, vocal expression
2 a usually formal discourse delivered to an audience <a televised *speech* to the nation>
syn address, allocution, lecture, talk
rel debate, parlance, parley; declamation, harangue, oration, speechification
3 *syn see* LANGUAGE 1
speechcraft *n syn see* ORATORY
speechless *adj* 1 *syn see* DUMB 1
rel aphonic
2 *syn see* SILENT 2
3 *syn see* SILENT 3
speed *n* 1 *syn see* HASTE 1
rel alacrity, legerity; headway
con dilatoriness, tardiness
2 rate of movement, performance, or occurrence <ran through the exercise at a high *speed*>
syn ‖bat, celerity, gait, pace, quickness, rapidity, rapidness, swiftness, velocity; *compare* TEMPO
rel fastness, fleetness; clip, hickory
speed *vb* 1 *syn see* HURRY 2
idiom make haste
ant slow (up *or* down)
2 *syn see* COURSE
3 to cause to move fast or faster <*sped* our craft forward>
syn accelerate, hasten, hurry, quicken, shake up, step up, swiften
rel advance, aid, ease, encourage, expedite, facilitate, forward, further, help (along), smooth; cheer (on), drive (on), goad (on), spur (on); burn (up)
idiom ‖get the lead out
con hamper, restrain, retard; check, stay; delay, postpone, put off
ant slow (up *or* down)
speedily *adv syn see* FAST 2
idiom against the clock, hell-bent for leather, like a bat out of hell, like all forty, ‖like all get-out, on the double, to beat the band
con deliberately, languidly, leisurely; lazily, lethargically, sluggishly; crawlingly, creepingly
ant slow, slowly
speediness *n syn see* HASTE 1
ant slowness
speedy *adj syn see* FAST 3
rel agile, brisk, nimble; prompt, ready
idiom fast as greased lightning, speedy as an arrow
ant dilatory; slow
speerings *n pl syn see* NEWS
‖**spelder** *vb syn see* SPRAWL 1
spell *n* a spoken word or set of words believed to have magic power <cause death by muttering *spells* over her>
syn charm, conjuration, ‖devil-devil, incantation, rune

rel bewitching, enchanting, hexing

spell *vb syn* see BEWITCH 1

spell *vb syn* see MEAN 2

spell *vb* 1 *syn* see RELIEVE 3
2 *syn* see REST 3

spell *n* 1 a limited period or amount of activity <each *spell* of work was followed by a brief rest >
syn bout, go, shift, stint, time, tour, trick, turn
rel streak; ||patch, period; stretch; relay
2 *syn* see WHILE 1
3 *syn* see ATTACK 3

spellbind *vb syn* see ENTHRALL 2

spell out *vb syn* see EXPLAIN 1

spend *vb* 1 to distribute or consume in payment or expenditure <*spent* fifty dollars for that dress >
syn disburse, expend, fork (out), give, lay out, outlay, pay, shell out
rel blow, drop, hand out; contribute; consume, dissipate, lavish, squander, throw away, waste
ant save
2 *syn* see GO 4
3 to cause or permit to elapse <*spent* the summer at the beach >
syn pass, while (away)

spender *n syn* see SPENDTHRIFT
ant saver

spending money *n syn* see POCKET MONEY

spendthrift *n* one who dissipates his resources foolishly and wastefully <a *spendthrift* who lost his estate through gambling >
syn high roller, prodigal, profligate, scattergood, spender, squanderer, unthrift, waster, wastethrift, wastrel
con hoarder, miser, saver

spent *adj syn* see EFFETE 2

spew *vb* 1 *syn* see VOMIT
2 *syn* see ERUPT 1
rel flood, gush

sphere *n* 1 *syn* see BALL
2 *syn* see FIELD
rel circle, jurisdiction, realm

sphere *vb syn* see BALL

spice *n* 1 *syn* see HINT 2
2 *syn* see FRAGRANCE

spick-and-span *adj* 1 *syn* see BRAND-NEW
2 *syn* see NEAT 2

spicy *adj* 1 *syn* see SWEET 2
2 *syn* see PUNGENT
rel fiery, gingery, high-spirited, spirited, zestful
3 *syn* see RISQUÉ
rel sophisticated; piquant

spider *n syn* see FRYING PAN

spiel *n* voluble, glib, or extravagant talk often intended to impress, persuade, or deceive <gave her a long sales *spiel* >
syn ||line, pitch, song and dance
rel demagoguery; dramatics, pyrotechnics, sensationalism

||spieler *n syn* see SWINDLER

spiff *vb syn* see DRESS UP 1

---

syn synonym(s)   *rel* related word(s)
ant antonym(s)   *con* contrasted word(s)
idiom idiomatic equivalent(s)
|| use limited; if in doubt, see a dictionary

spiffy *adj syn* see DAPPER

||spifflicated *adj syn* see INTOXICATED 1

spigot *n syn* see FAUCET

spike *vb syn* see IMPALE

spill *vb* 1 to cause or allow (something) to fall, flow, or run out and be lost or wasted <accidentally dropped the cup and *spilled* his tea >
syn slop, squab
rel dribble, drip, drop; spatter, splash, spray
2 *syn* see OVERFLOW 2
3 *syn* see REVEAL 1

spilth *n syn* see REFUSE

spin *vb* 1 to turn or cause to turn rapidly <pinwheels *spinning* in the wind >
syn gyrate, gyre, ||pirl, pirouette, ||purl, twirl, whirl, whirligig; *compare* TURN 1
rel revolve, rotate, wheel; swirl; oscillate, pendulate, vibrate
idiom spin like a top
2 to feel as if revolving <her head was *spinning* with figures >
syn reel, swim, turn, whirl
rel dizzy, giddy; fluster, mix up, muddle
idiom be in a whirl

spin (out) *vb syn* see EXTEND 3

spin *n syn* see DRIVE 1

spinal column *n syn* see SPINE

spindling *adj syn* see GANGLING

spindly *adj syn* see GANGLING

spine *n* the articulated column of bones that is the central and axial structure of a vertebrate skeleton <fractured his *spine* >
syn back, backbone, rachis, spinal column, vertebrae, vertebral column
rel spinal cord

spineless *adj syn* see WEAK 4
rel weak-kneed, weak-willed
idiom as spineless as an amoeba
con self-willed, strong-willed

spin-off *n syn* see OUTGROWTH 2

spinster *n* a woman who is past the common age for marrying or who seems unlikely ever to marry <a gentle *spinster*, happy in her solitary life >
syn maiden lady, old maid, spinstress, ||tabby

spinstress *n syn* see SPINSTER

spiny *adj syn* see THORNY

spiral *vb syn* see WIND 2

spiring *adj syn* see LOFTY 6

spirit *n* 1 *syn* see SOUL 1
2 *syn* see APPARITION
3 *syn* see SOUL 2
4 *syn* see TEMPER 1
5 a lively or brisk quality in a person or his actions <a man of great *spirit* and courage >
syn animation, brio, dash, élan, esprit, gimp, life, oomph, verve, vim, zing; *compare* VIGOR 2
rel ardor, briskness, enthusiasm, liveliness; drive, get-up-and-go, ginger, go, pep, snap, starch, vigor, vitality, zip; character, force, substance
6 *syn* see COURAGE
rel ardor, fervor, passion, zeal; energy, force, might, power, strength
7 often **spirits** *pl syn* see LIQUOR

spirit (away) *vb syn* see KIDNAP

spirit (up) *vb syn* see ELATE

spirited *adj* 1 *syn* see LIVELY 1

rel sharp; fiery, gingery, peppery
idiom full of life (*or* go)
ant spiritless
2 having or manifesting a high degree of vitality, spirit, and daring <the lawyer gave a *spirited* defense of his client>
syn beany, fiery, gingery, high-hearted, high-spirited, mettlesome, peppery, spunky
rel game, gritty, resolute; audacious, bold, brave, courageous, dauntless, fearless, intrepid, nervy, plucky, valiant; avid, eager, hot, keen; ardent, enthusiastic, fervent, hot, passionate, peppy, zealous
con unenthusiastic; flabby, languid, limp; boneless, spineless
ant spiritless

spiritless *adj* **1** *syn* see DEAD 1
2 *syn* see DOWNCAST
idiom down in the dumps
3 *syn* see LANGUID
rel tame; broken, subdued, submissive
ant spirited

spiritual *adj* **1** *syn* see IMMATERIAL 1
rel supernatural, supramundane
ant physical
2 *syn* see SACRED 2
3 *syn* see ECCLESIASTICAL
4 appealing to, coming from, or related to the higher emotions or to the aesthetic senses <man's *spiritual* and intellectual life as opposed to his animal instincts>
syn numinous
rel cerebral, intellectual, mental; elevated, high, high-minded, lofty; saintly
con low, lower; base
ant animal

spirituous *adj* containing a considerable amount of alcohol <*spirituous* liquors>
syn alcoholic, ardent, hard, strong
rel spiked; inebriating, intoxicating, intoxicative; heady
con nonalcoholic, nonintoxicating, soft
‖**spirity** *adj syn* see LIVELY 1

spit *vb syn* see IMPALE

spit *n* **1** *syn* see SALIVA
2 *syn* see IMAGE 1
rel counterpart; look-alike; twin

spit *vb* **1** *syn* see SPUTTER 1
2 *syn* see SPUTTER 2

spite *n syn* see MALICE
rel rancor; revenge, revengefulness, vengeance, vengefulness, vindictiveness
con sympathy; affection, love, tenderness

spiteful *adj syn* see MALICIOUS
rel antagonistic, hostile; revengeful, vengeful, vindictive
con charitable; sympathetic; affectionate, loving
ant spiteless

spitefulness *n syn* see MALICE
spitish *adj syn* see MALICIOUS
spitting image *n syn* see IMAGE 1
rel mirror image
spittle *n syn* see SALIVA
spit up *vb syn* see VOMIT
‖**spiv** *n* **1** *syn* see PARASITE
2 *syn* see SLACKER

splash *vb* to dash a liquid or semiliquid substance upon or against <*splashed* water onto her face>
syn douse, plash, slop, slosh, spatter, splatter, splosh, splurge, spurtle, swash
rel dash, throw; spray; sprinkle; ‖sprent; squirt; drench, drown, soak, sop, wet

splashy *adj syn* see SHOWY
splathering *adj syn* see CLUMSY 1
splatter *vb syn* see SPLASH
splay *adj syn* see CLUMSY 1
spleen *n syn* see MALICE
rel revenge, revengefulness, vindictiveness; wrath

splendid *adj* **1** *syn* see GRAND 2
rel baroque, flamboyant
2 extraordinarily or transcendently impressive <a *splendid* new city>
syn glorious, gorgeous, magnificent, proud, resplendent, splendiferous, splendorous, sublime, superb
rel eminent, illustrious; grand, impressive, lavish, luxurious, royal, sumptuous; divine, exquisite, lovely; incomparable, matchless, peerless, superlative, supreme, unparalleled, unsurpassed; surpassing, transcendent
con common, ordinary, run-of-the-mill
ant unimpressive

splendiferous *adj syn* see SPLENDID 2
rel dazzling, marvelous, smashing, walloping; rattling, ripping, screaming, terrific
splendorous *adj syn* see SPLENDID 2
splice *vb syn* see MARRY 2
splinter *vb syn* see SHATTER 1
splinterize *vb syn* see SHATTER 1
split *vb* **1** *syn* see CUT 5
rel crack, rive
2 *syn* see TEAR 1
‖**3** *syn* see BETRAY 2
split (up) *vb syn* see SEPARATE 1
split *n* **1** *syn* see CRACK 3
2 *syn* see SCHISM 3
3 *syn* see BREACH 3
rel alienating, estranging
split second *n syn* see INSTANT 1
splitter *vb syn* see SHATTER 1
split-up *n syn* see SEPARATION 1
‖**splodge** *vb syn* see SPLOTCH
splosh *vb syn* see SPLASH
splotch *vb* to mark or spot with irregular patches especially of contrasting color <a pallid face *splotched* with red>
syn blotch, mottle, ‖splodge
rel blot, stain; dapple, fleck, marble, motley, variegate; bespot, spot; harlequin
‖**splunge** *vb syn* see PLUNGE 2
splurge *n syn* see SPREE 1
rel extravagance; splash
splurge *vb syn* see SPLASH
splurt *vb syn* see SQUIRT
splutter *vb* **1** *syn* see SPUTTER 2
2 *syn* see SPUTTER 1
spoil *n* something taken from another by force or craft <gold, jewels, and paintings are often *spoils* of war>
syn boodle, booty, loot, plunder, plunderage, prize, ‖spreaghery, ‖spulzie, swag
rel acquisition, grab, haul, take; pickings, stealings; pillage, spoliation
spoil *vb* **1** *syn* see RAVAGE
2 *syn* see INJURE 1
rel ‖snafu; ruin, wreck; demolish, destroy
3 *syn* see RAPE
4 *syn* see BABY
rel accommodate, favor, oblige
idiom spoil (one) rotten, spoil to death
5 *syn* see DECAY
spoiled *adj* **1** *syn* see DAMAGED
ant unspoiled

2 *syn* see BAD 5
rel off, tainted; putrefying, rotting
ant unspoiled
spoiler *n syn* see MARAUDER
spoken *adj* 1 *syn* see ORAL 2
ant written
2 *syn* see VOCAL 1
ant unspoken
spokesman *n* one who speaks as a representative of another <selected as *spokesman* for the party's views>
syn mouth, mouthpiece, speaker, spokesperson, spokeswoman
rel delegate, deputy, representative; champion, protagonist; prophet
spokesperson *n syn* see SPOKESMAN
spokeswoman *n syn* see SPOKESMAN
spoliate *vb syn* see RAVAGE
rel raid; maraud; gut, ravish, sweep
spoliator *n syn* see MARAUDER
sponge *n* 1 *syn* see DRUNKARD
2 *syn* see PARASITE
sponger *n syn* see PARASITE
spongy *adj syn* see SOFT 6
idiom as soft as a sponge
sponsor *n* one that accepts responsibility for another person or thing <the major *sponsor* of this project is the government>
syn angel, backer, backer-up, guarantor, patron, surety
rel advocate, champion, mainstay, supporter, upholder; preferrer, promoter; benefactor, Maecenas
sponsorship *n syn* see BACKING
spontaneity *n syn* see UNCONSTRAINT
rel extemporaneousness, offhandedness, unpremeditatedness
spontaneous *adj* acting or activated without apparent thought or volition <a *spontaneous* burst of applause>
syn automatic, impulsive, instinctive, involuntary, unmeditated, unpremeditated, unprompted, will-less
rel unconstrained, unforced; unreasoned, unstudied; extemporaneous, extempore, impromptu, improvised, offhand; natural, simple, unsophisticated
con deliberate, intended, intentional, planned, predetermined, preplanned, studied, thought-out, voluntary, willed, willful; forced, prompted; conventional, formal, stylized
ant premeditated
spontoon *n syn* see CUDGEL
spoof *vb syn* see DUPE
spoof *n syn* see IMPOSTURE
spook *n* ‖1 *syn* see APPARITION
‖2 *syn* see ECCENTRIC
3 *syn* see SPY
‖**spook** *vb* 1 *syn* see FRIGHTEN
2 *syn* see GHOSTWRITE
spooky *adj* 1 *syn* see WEIRD 1
rel spookish; ominous
2 *syn* see NERVOUS
‖**spoon** *n syn* see DUNCE
spoony *adj syn* see SIMPLE 3
spoony (over *or* on) *adj syn* see ENAMORED 1

spoor *n syn* see FOOTPRINT
sporadic *adj* 1 *syn* see FITFUL
ant regular
2 *syn* see INFREQUENT
rel separate, single
ant frequent
sporadically *adv syn* see OCCASIONALLY
ant regularly
sport *vb syn* see PLAY 1
sport *n* 1 *syn* see PLAY 1
2 **sports** *pl syn* see ATHLETICS
3 *syn* see FUN 1
rel jollification; antics, high jinks, horseplay
4 *syn* see LAUGHINGSTOCK
5 *syn* see CHANGE 2
sporting girl *n syn* see PROSTITUTE
sporting house *n syn* see BROTHEL
sportive *adj syn* see PLAYFUL 1
sportiveness *n syn* see MISCHIEVOUSNESS
sportsmanlike *adj syn* see FAIR 5
ant unsporting, unsportsmanlike
sportsmanly *adj syn* see FAIR 5
ant unsporting, unsportsmanlike
sporty *adj syn* see WILD 7
spot *n* 1 *syn* see STIGMA
2 *syn* see DRAM
3 *syn* see PARTICLE
4 *syn* see PLACE 1
rel scene; section, sector
5 *syn* see JOB 2
idiom job slot
6 *syn* see PREDICAMENT
spot *vb* 1 to mark or stain (something) with spots <a white dress *spotted* with red mud>
syn bespatter, bespot, spatter; *compare* SPECKLE 1
rel blot, blotch, mottle; fleck, marble, streak, stripe; dot, pepper, speck, speckle, sprinkle, stipple; splash; dirty, soil, stain
2 to form or appear as spots on <a bleak landscape *spotted* with cottages>
syn dot, pimple, speckle, sprinkle, stud
rel intersperse
3 *syn* see IDENTIFY
rel ascertain; see
4 *syn* see FIND 1
spot *adj syn* see RANDOM
spotless *adj* 1 *syn* see CLEAN 1
rel hygienic, sanitary
2 *syn* see CHASTE
ant spotted
spotty *adj* 1 lacking uniformity <*spotty* illumination>
syn irregular, patchy, uneven
rel unequal; flickering, fluctuating
con equal, even, regular, uniform
2 *syn* see FITFUL
spousal *n syn* see WEDDING
spousal *adj syn* see MATRIMONIAL
spouse *n* a marriage partner <consulted with her *spouse* before buying the dress>
syn consort, mate
spouseless *adj syn* see SINGLE 1
con espoused
‖**spout** *vb syn* see PAWN
spout *n syn* see WATERFALL
spraddle *vb syn* see SPRAWL 1
sprain *vb* to injure (a joint) by a sudden twisting motion that stretches and lacerates the ligaments <*sprained* her ankle>
syn ‖rick, turn, twist, wrench

---

syn synonym(s)   *rel* related word(s)
ant antonym(s)   *con* contrasted word(s)
idiom idiomatic equivalent(s)
‖ use limited; if in doubt, see a dictionary

rel pull, strain, stretch; tear; dislocate, throw; break, fracture

sprangle *vb syn* see SPRAWL 2

sprat *n syn* see TWERP

||**sprauchle** *vb syn* see SCRAMBLE 1

sprawl *vb* 1 to lie or sit with arms and legs stretched out carelessly and awkwardly < the dog lay *sprawled* out on the sofa >
syn drape, ||scamble, ||spelder, spraddle, spread-eagle
rel loll, lounge; slouch, slump

2 to grow, develop, or spread irregularly and without apparent design or plan < the city *sprawls* down the whole coast >
syn ramble, scramble, sprangle, spread-eagle, straddle, straggle
rel extend, stretch; spread

spread *vb* 1 to extend or cause to extend over a considerable area or space < they *spread* the news far and wide > < clouds *spread* over the sky >
syn circulate, diffuse, disperse, disseminate, distribute, propagate, radiate, strew; *compare* STREW 1
rel deal, dispense; broadcast, communicate, pass (on), transmit; dissipate, scatter, sow; peddle, push, retail
idiom spread abroad (*or* far and wide)
con hold (in); contain; compress

2 *syn* see OPEN 4

con fold; close

3 *syn* see SET 5

spread *n* 1 *syn* see EXPANSION 2
rel diffusion; profusion; stretch, sweep

2 *syn* see EXPANSE

3 *syn* see DINNER

4 *syn* see BEDSPREAD

spread-eagle *vb* 1 *syn* see SPRAWL 1

2 *syn* see SPRAWL 2

||**spreaghery** *n syn* see SPOIL

spree *n* 1 an unrestrained indulgence in or outburst of an activity < a shopping *spree* >
syn binge, fling, orgy, rampage, splurge

2 *syn* see BINGE

spree *vb syn* see REVEL 1

sprightful *adj syn* see LIVELY 1

sprightly *adj* 1 *syn* see LIVELY 1
rel perky; breezy

2 *syn* see ANTIC 2
rel sportive; coltish, frisky

3 *syn* see AGILE

4 *syn* see CLEVER 5
rel pungent, sharp; keen-witted, quick-witted

spring *vb* 1 to have something as a source < the primitive cultures from which civilization *springs* >
syn arise, birth, come (from), derive (from), emanate, flow, head, issue, originate, proceed, rise, stem, upspring; *compare* BEGIN 2
rel appear, emerge, come out, loom; arrive, come; begin, commence, hatch, start

2 *syn* see SKIP 1

3 *syn* see JUMP 1

4 *syn* see START 1

||5 *syn* see FREE

spring *n* 1 *usu* **springs** *pl syn* see SPA 1

2 *syn* see SOURCE

3 *syn* see YOUTH 1
ant autumn

4 *syn* see MOTIVE 1

rel excitant, impetus, incitement, stimulant, stimulus

5 the season between winter and summer < planting flowers in the *spring* >
syn budtime, springtide, springtime
rel ||blackberry winter
idiom prime of the year
con autumn, fall

spring *adj syn* see VERNAL

springe *n syn* see PITFALL

springlike *adj syn* see VERNAL

springtide *n* 1 *syn* see SPRING 5

2 *syn* see YOUTH 1
ant autumn

springtime *n* 1 *syn* see SPRING 5

2 *syn* see YOUTH 1
ant autumn

springy *adj syn* see ELASTIC 1
rel rebounding, recoiling
ant rigid; springless

sprinkle *vb* 1 to scatter (something) in small drops or particles < *sprinkle* chocolate shot on whipped cream >
syn besprinkle, dust, powder, ||strinkle; *compare* STREW 1
rel shake; scatter; pepper; sparge

2 *syn* see SPECKLE 1

3 *syn* see SPOT 2

4 *syn* see BAPTIZE

5 to rain lightly < it's only *sprinkling*, so we can still take our walk >
syn drizzle, ||mizzle
rel mist; shower; spit
con pour, stream

sprinkling *n* 1 *syn* see HINT 2

2 *syn* see DUSTING

3 *syn* see FEW

sprint *vb syn* see RUN 1

sprit *vb syn* see SQUIRT

sprite *n syn* see FAIRY

||**spritz** *vb syn* see SQUIRT

spruce *adj syn* see DAPPER
ant slouchy

spruce (up) *vb syn* see DRESS UP 1

sprucy *adj syn* see DAPPER

spry *adj syn* see AGILE
rel prompt, quick, ready; energetic, vigorous; healthy, robust, sound
ant doddering

spuddy *adj syn* see ROTUND 2

||**spulzie** *n syn* see SPOIL

spume *n syn* see FOAM

spunk *n* 1 *syn* see FORTITUDE
rel bulldoggedness, doggedness
idiom clear (*or* true) grit
ant funk

2 *syn* see COURAGE

spunkless *adj syn* see COWARDLY
ant spunky

spunky *adj* 1 *syn* see BRAVE 1
idiom full of spunk
ant spunkless; funky

2 *syn* see SPIRITED 2
ant funky

spur *n syn* see STIMULUS
rel excitant; activation, actuation
ant checkrein; curb

spur *vb syn* see URGE
rel rowel; arouse, awaken, rally, rouse, stir; instigate; countenance, favor
ant curb

spurious *adj* 1 *syn* see ILLEGITIMATE 1

2 *syn* see ARTIFICIAL 2

3 of doubtful authenticity <claimed they had bought a *spurious* painting>
syn apocryphal, bastard, unauthentic, ungenuine; *compare* ARTIFICIAL 2, COUNTERFEIT
rel bogus, counterfeit, fake, phony, pseudo, sham; false, unreal
idiom not what (*or* all) it's cracked up to be
con actual, real, true; bona fide, genuine, veritable
ant authentic
4 *syn* see ARTIFICIAL 3
rel make-believe, pretend, pretended, pseudo
5 *syn* see COUNTERFEIT

spuriousness *n syn* see FALLACY 2

spurn *vb syn* see DECLINE 4
rel conspue, contemn, despise, disdain, scorn, scout; flout, scoff, sneer
con crave, desire, want
ant embrace

spur-of-the-moment *adj syn* see EXTEMPORANEOUS

spurt *vb syn* see SQUIRT

spurtle *vb syn* see SPLASH

sputter *vb* **1** to utter (words or ejaculations) hastily, explosively, and sometimes indistinctly <pompously *sputtering* his objections>
syn rip (out), spit, splutter
rel ejaculate, eject, throw (out); gibber, jabber, bluster, heckle, hector, rage, rant, rave, storm
2 to make a series of sudden short crackling or popping sounds <bacon *sputtering* in the pan>
syn spatter, spit, splutter
rel crackle, pop; hiss

spy (on *or* upon) *vb* to make furtive, stealthy, or secret observations of <had private detectives *spying* on his wife>
syn ‖stag
rel stake out; watch

spy *n* one who keeps secret watch to obtain information <was convicted on evidence produced by a *spy*>
syn agent, spook, undercover man; *compare* INFORMER
rel detective, investigator, sleuth; scout; beagle
idiom inside man, secret agent

spying *n syn* see ESPIONAGE

squab *adj syn* see STOCKY

‖squab *vb syn* see PRESS 1

squab *vb syn* see SPILL 1

squabble *n syn* see QUARREL

squabble *vb* **1** *syn* see QUARREL
rel clash, encounter
idiom have a squabble over
2 *syn* see ARGUE 2
idiom get into (*or* have) a hassle, have a verbal wrestling match

squalid *adj* **1** *syn* see DIRTY 1
rel disheveled, slipshod, sloppy, slovenly, unkempt; frowzy, slatternly; dingy, shoddy, sleazy
2 *syn* see SHABBY 1

3 *syn* see BASE 3

squall *vb* **1** to make a raucous noise <angry street urchins fighting and *squalling* at each other>
syn caw, ‖quawk, squark, squawk, yawp (*or* yaup)
rel bellow, howl, roar, shout, yell; bark, yap, yip; croak
2 *syn* see BAWL 2
rel squeal; screech, shriek; yelp

squall *n syn* see QUARREL

squander *vb syn* see WASTE 2
idiom make ducks and drakes of, play ducks and drakes with

squander *n syn* see EXTRAVAGANCE 2

squanderer *n syn* see SPENDTHRIFT

square *n* **1** *syn* see COMMON 2
2 *syn* see FOGY

square *adj* **1** having four equal sides and four right angles <a large *square* Georgian mansion>
syn foursquare, quadrate, quadratic, quadratical
rel boxlike, boxy, squarish
2 *syn* see EVEN 5
3 *syn* see FAIR 4
4 *syn* see CONVENTIONAL 1

square *vb* **1** *syn* see ADAPT
2 *syn* see CLEAR 5
3 *syn* see BRIBE
4 *syn* see AGREE 4
rel balance; coincide

square *adv syn* see JUST 1

squarehead *n syn* see DUNCE

squarely *adv* **1** *syn* see EVENLY 1
2 *syn* see JUST 1

squark *vb syn* see SQUALL 1

squash *vb* **1** *syn* see PRESS 1
2 *syn* see CRUSH 2
3 *syn* see CRUSH 5
4 *syn* see PRESS 7

squash *n* **1** *syn* see SQUELCH
2 *syn* see CROWD 1

squashing *n syn* see REPRESSION 1

squashy *adj syn* see SOFT 6
ant firm

squat *vb* to sit on one's haunches <they were *squatting* around the fire>
syn hunker (down), ‖quat, ‖swat; *compare* CROUCH
rel crouch; hunch; stoop

squat *adj syn* see STOCKY
rel squattish, squatty
con long, tall; twiggy
ant lanky

‖squaw *n syn* see WIFE

squawk *vb* **1** *syn* see SQUALL 1
2 *syn* see GRIPE
rel yap, yip

squawker *n syn* see INFORMER

squawky *adj syn* see HARSH 3
con liquid, mellow, smooth

squdgy *adj syn* see STOCKY

squeak *vb* **1** to utter or make a short shrill cry or noise <mice *squeaking* in the barn>
syn ‖queak; *compare* SQUEAL 2
rel creak, grate, screak, screech, squeal; pipe; scream
2 *syn* see TALK 6
3 *syn* see INFORM 3

squeak *n syn* see OPPORTUNITY

‖squeaker *n syn* see INFORMER

squeal *vb* 1 *syn* see SCREAM 1
  idiom squeal like a stuck pig
  2 to make a harsh piercing sometimes rasping noise <tires *squealing* on wet pavement>
  syn screak, scream, screech, shriek; *compare* SQUEAK 1
  rel creak, grate, rasp
  3 *syn* see INFORM 3
  4 *syn* see TALK 6
  5 *syn* see YELL 2
  rel bitch, bleat, complain, gripe, squawk
  idiom raise a howl, scream bloody murder

squealer *n* *syn* see INFORMER

squeam *n* *syn* see QUALM

squeamish *adj* 1 inclined to become nauseated <felt *squeamish* after the heavy meal on the ship>
  syn ‖pensy, qualmish, qualmy, queasy, queer, ‖wambly; *compare* NAUSEATED
  rel unsettled, upset; dizzy, shaky, vertiginous
  2 *syn* see NAUSEATED
  idiom sick at (or to) one's stomach
  3 *syn* see NICE 1

squeamishness *n* *syn* see NAUSEA

squeamy *adj* *syn* see NICE 1

squeeze *vb* 1 *syn* see PRESS 1
  rel contract, ‖scruze
  2 *syn* see EMBRACE 1
  3 *syn* see EXTORT 1
  4 *syn* see EKE OUT 2
  5 *syn* see PRESS 8
  6 *syn* see PRESS 7

squeezy *adj* *syn* see CRAMPED

squelch *n* a sound of or as if of semiliquid matter under suction <the *squelch* of his feet in the mud>
  syn squash, squidge, squish

squelch *vb* *syn* see SUPPRESS 2

squelching *n* *syn* see REPRESSION 1

squelchy *adj* *syn* see SOFT 6

‖squench *vb* 1 *syn* see EXTINGUISH 1
  2 *syn* see QUENCH 4

squidge *n* *syn* see SQUELCH

squiffed *adj* *syn* see INTOXICATED 1

squiggle *vb* 1 *syn* see WRIGGLE
  2 *syn* see SCRIBBLE

squinch *vb* 1 *syn* see RECOIL
  2 *syn* see SQUINT

squinny *vb* *syn* see SQUINT

squinny *adj* *syn* see THIN 1

squint *vb* to look or peer with the eyes partly closed <*squinted* in the bright sunlight>
  syn ‖sken, squinch, squinny
  idiom look asquint, screw up one's eyes
  ant goggle

squirm *vb* 1 *syn* see WRIGGLE
  2 *syn* see WRITHE 1

squirrel *vb* *syn* see HOARD

squirt *vb* to come forth in a sudden rapid usually narrow stream <water *squirting* from the hose>
  syn jet, splurt, sprit, ‖spritz, spúrt, ‖squitter
  rel pour, stream, surge; spatter; spray
  con dribble, drip, trickle

squirt *n* ‖1 squirts *pl* *syn* see DIARRHEA
  2 *syn* see TWERP

squish *n* 1 *syn* see PRESS 1
  2 *syn* see SQUELCH

squishy *adj* *syn* see SOFT 6

‖squit *n* *syn* see TWERP

‖squitter *vb* *syn* see SQUIRT

squush *vb* *syn* see PRESS 1

squushy *adj* *syn* see SOFT 6

stab *n* 1 *syn* see PRICK 1
  2 *syn* see POKE 1
  3 *syn* see FLING 1

stab *vb* *syn* see THRUST 2
  rel dagger, dirk, poniard, prong

stabbing *adj* *syn* see SHARP 8

stabile *adj* *syn* see STEADY 2

stabilify *vb* *syn* see STABILIZE

stabilitate *vb* *syn* see STABILIZE

stability *n* the ability to withstand force or stress without alteration of position and without material change <the structural *stability* of the bridge>
  syn firmness, security, soundness, stableness, steadiness, strength
  rel dependability, durability, reliability; solidity, solidness, sturdiness; cohesion, toughness
  con insecurity, undependability, unreliability, unsoundness, unsteadiness; weakness
  ant instability, unstability

stabilize *vb* to make or keep stable, steadfast, or firm <a policy that *stabilized* the economy>
  syn ballast, poise, stabilify, stabilitate, steady
  rel balance, counterbalance, counterpoise, equalize, equipoise; prop, support, sustain; fix, secure, set, settle
  ant unstabilize

stable *adj* 1 *syn* see SURE 1
  rel balanced, poised; fixed, set, solid, sound, steadfast
  con wobbling, wobbly
  ant instable, unstable
  2 *syn* see STEADY 2
  3 *syn* see LASTING
  rel constant, steady; safe, secure, sound; staunch, steadfast, resolute
  4 marked by solidity, firmness, and stability especially in design or construction <a *stable* foundation for the building>
  syn firm, secure, solid, sound; *compare* FAST 4, SURE 1
  rel strong, sturdy; unassailable, unshakable
  idiom as firm as (the rock of) Gibraltar, solid as a rock
  con insecure, shaky, unsound, weak, wobbling, wobbly
  ant instable, unstable

stableness *n* *syn* see STABILITY
  ant unstableness

stack *n* *syn* see PILE 1

stack *vb* *syn* see HEAP 1

‖stacked *adj* *syn* see CURVACEOUS

stade *n* *syn* see STADIUM

stadium *n* a large usually unroofed structure with tiered seats enclosing a field used especially for sports <a football *stadium*>
  syn bowl, coliseum, stade
  rel arena, garden, gymnasium

‖stag *vb* *syn* see SPY (on or upon)

stage *n* 1 *used with the* *syn* see DRAMA
  2 *syn* see DEGREE 1
  rel level; phase; period

stage *vb* to present on the stage < *staged* a play >
  syn mount, produce, put on, show
  rel bring out, open; give, present; do, execute, perform, play
stage set *n syn see* SCENE 1
stage setting *n syn see* SCENE 1
stagger *vb* 1 *syn see* REEL 2
  2 *syn see* LURCH 2
  idiom pitch and plunge
  3 *syn see* TEETER
  rel ||stiver, ||stoit, ||stoiter, ||stot
  4 *syn see* HESITATE
  5 to affect with great wonder or bewilderment < a plot so bizarre as to *stagger* the imagination >
  syn boggle, dumbfound, nonplus
  rel perplex, puzzle, stump; amaze, astonish, astound, flabbergast; bowl (over), floor, knock over; devastate, overpower, overwhelm, shatter; paralyze
  idiom take (one) aback
stagger (on *or* along) *vb syn see* SHIFT 5
||**stagger** *n syn see* FLING 1
staggering *adj syn see* MARVELOUS 1
stagnant *adj syn see* STATIC
stagnate *vb* 1 *syn see* VEGETATE
  2 *syn see* STULTIFY
stagnation *n syn see* DEPRESSION 3
staid *adj syn see* SERIOUS 1
  rel decorous, formal; collected, composed, cool; priggish, smug; starchy, stuffy
  con breezy, devil-may-care, easy, frivolous; debonair, jaunty; playful, sportive; hoydenish, rakish; fresh, irreverent; uncontrolled, unrestrained
  ant unstaid
stain *vb* 1 to soil often permanently with foreign matter < a shirt *stained* with grease >
  syn bestain, blot, discolor, smut; *compare* SOIL 2
  rel tinge; bedaub, daub, smear; besmirch, smirch, smudge, smutch
  2 *syn see* TAINT 1
  3 *syn see* DEBASE 1
stain *n* 1 *syn see* STIGMA
  rel blemish, defect, flaw
  idiom blot on the escutcheon
  2 *syn see* COLOR 6
stainless *adj syn see* CHASTE
  con tainted, tarnished
  ant stained
stake *n* 1 *syn see* BET
  2 *syn see* INTEREST 1
stake *vb* 1 *syn see* GAMBLE 1
  rel stake down
  2 *syn see* CAPITALIZE
stale *adj* 1 *syn see* MALODOROUS 1
  2 *syn see* TRITE
  rel dusty, fusty; dead
  ant fresh
||**stale** *n syn see* LURE 2
stalemate *n syn see* DRAW 4
stalk *vb* 1 to pursue (game) stealthily or under cover < *stalk* deer >
  syn still-hunt
  rel follow, track; drive, chase, pursue; walk up; flush (out); ambush

---

  2 *syn see* STRIDE 1
stalky *adj syn see* THIN 1
stall *vb* ||1 *syn see* SATIATE
  2 *syn see* ARREST 1
  rel brake, slow (down); hold off, put off, stand off, suspend; shut down
  idiom pull the checkstring
  con spur
stalwart *adj* 1 *syn see* STRONG 2
  rel athletic, brawny, husky, muscular, sinewy
  2 *syn see* BRAVE 1
stamina *n syn see* TOLERANCE 1
stammer *vb* 1 to make involuntary stops and repetitions in uttering syllables and words < the frightened child *stammered* and fell silent >
  syn ||hammer, ||stut, stutter
  rel falter, hesitate; stumble; splutter, sputter; gibber, jabber
  ||2 *syn see* TEETER
stamp *vb* 1 *syn see* TRAMPLE 2
  rel clomp, clump, stump
  2 *syn see* IMPRESS 3
  rel etch, imprint, infix, inscribe, print
  idiom impress on the mind
stamp *n* 1 *syn see* IMPRESSION 1
  2 *syn see* TYPE
  3 *syn see* SEAL
stampede *vb* 1 *syn see* ROUT 1
  2 to take to sudden headlong flight in panic < cattle *stampeding* across the plain >
  syn pell-mell; *compare* RUSH 1
  rel bolt, charge, chase, crash, dash, fling, hurry, rush, shoot, tear
  idiom run like a pack of scalded dogs
stamping ground *n syn see* HABITAT
  2 *syn see* RESORT 2
stance *n* 1 *syn see* POSTURE 1
  2 *syn see* POSITION 1
stanch *vb syn see* STEM
stand *vb* 1 *syn see* BEAR 10
  idiom ||hack it, take lying down
  2 *syn see* TREAT 3
stand (on *or* upon) *vb syn see* DEPEND (on *or* upon) 1
  idiom be contingent on
stand *n syn see* POSITION 1
standard *n* 1 *syn see* FLAG
  2 *syn see* MODEL 2
  3 a means of determining what a thing should be < each generation has its own *standards* of morality >
  syn benchmark, criterion, gauge, measure, touchstone, yardstick
  rel average, mean, median, norm, par; axiom, belief, fundamental, principle; law, rule; exemplar, model, pattern
  idiom rule of thumb
  4 a fixed, customary, or official measure (as of quantity, quality, or price) < governmental *standards* of weights and measures >
  syn assize
  rel ||dick
stander-by *n syn see* SPECTATOR
stand-in *n syn see* SUBSTITUTE
  rel second; assistant
standing *n* 1 *syn see* TERM 5
  2 *syn see* STATUS 1
  3 *syn see* STATUS 2
standoff *adj syn see* UNSOCIABLE

standoff *n syn* see DRAW 4

standoffish *adj* 1 *syn* see UNSOCIABLE
2 *syn* see ANTISOCIAL

stand out *vb* 1 *syn* see BULGE
2 *syn* see LOOM 3

standout *adj syn* see SUPERB 3

stand over *vb syn* see DEFER

standpat *n syn* see DIEHARD 1

standpatter *n syn* see DIEHARD 1

standpoint *n syn* see VIEWPOINT 2

standstill *n* cessation of movement < the
car came to a *standstill* in the mud>
syn stay, stillstand, stop
rel arrest, check; pause; cessation, halt
con start; movement
ant start-up

stand up *vb syn* see RISE 1

stand–up *adj syn* see ERECT
con lowered; flat, horizontal

‖stang *vb syn* see SMART

staple *n syn* see LOOP 2

staple *n syn* see BODY 3

star *n syn* see CHIEF 1

starch *n syn* see VIGOR 2

star–crossed *adj syn* see UNLUCKY

stare *vb* 1 *syn* see LOOK 7
idiom ‖take a gander at
2 *syn* see GAZE 1
idiom fix (or rivet) one's eyes on

stare down *vb* to overcome (someone) by
or as if by staring < the teacher could not
stare the boy *down*>
syn look down, outstare
rel glare; master, quell, subdue, suppress;
overcome, overwhelm

stark *adj* 1 *syn* see UTTER
2 *syn* see NUDE 2
3 *syn* see EMPTY 1

stark–naked *adj syn* see NUDE 2
idiom bare (or naked) as a newborn babe,
‖naked as a jaybird, naked as the day one
was born

‖starny *adj syn* see STELLAR 1

starry *adj syn* see STELLAR 1

start *vb* 1 to move suddenly and violently
from a state of stillness or rest < *started*
from his bed at the sound of shots>
syn bolt, jump, spring, startle
rel dart; bounce; bound, leap; draw
(back), flinch, recoil
idiom jump out of one's skin, start aside
ant stay
2 *syn* see RECOIL
3 *syn* see BEGIN 2
rel proceed, spring
ant end
4 *syn* see FOUND 2
5 *syn* see BEGIN 1
ant stop

start *n* 1 *syn* see BEGINNING
ant finish
2 *syn* see ADVANTAGE 3

startle *vb* 1 *syn* see START 1
2 *syn* see SHOCK 2
3 *syn* see FRIGHTEN
rel astonish, surprise
idiom make one jump out of one's skin,
‖scare the pants off

startlish *adj syn* see EXCITABLE

starved *adj syn* see HUNGRY
rel underfed, undernourished; weakened;
half-famished, half-starved
con fed, nourished; overfed

ant well-fed

starving *adj syn* see HUNGRY
rel craving, famishing, hungering; dying,
perishing
idiom crazy for food

stash *vb* 1 *syn* see HOARD
2 *syn* see HIDE
rel hoard, squirrel

stasis *n syn* see BALANCE 1

state *n* 1 the way in which one manifests
existence or the circumstances under
which one exists or by which one is given
distinctive character < remained in a
weakened *state* for weeks>
syn condition, mode, posture, situation,
status
rel circumstances; attitude, position,
stand
idiom state of being
2 *syn* see STATUS 1
3 *syn* see STATUS 2

state *vb* 1 *syn* see RELATE 1
rel elucidate, explain, expound, interpret;
set forth
2 *syn* see ENUNCIATE 1
3 *syn* see SAY 1
4 *syn* see EXPRESS 2
ant imply

stated *adj syn* see FIRM 4

stately *adj* 1 *syn* see CEREMONIAL
rel dignified, grand, noble; imperial,
kingly, princely, regal, royal
2 *syn* see COURTLY
3 *syn* see GRAND 1
con lowly, poor; shabby; cheap

statement *n* 1 *syn* see EXPRESSION 1
rel outgiving, articulation, presentation,
presentment, verbalization, vocalization
2 *syn* see WORD 1
rel description, narrative, recital
3 *syn* see BILL 1

static *adj* characterized by relatively little
or no movement, progression, or change
(as in conditions) < a *static* economy>
syn immobile, stagnant, stationary, unmoving; *compare* STEADY 2
rel constant, stabile, stable, unchanging,
unfluctuating; fixed, immovable, rigid,
sticky; inactive, inert; stalled, stopped,
stuck
idiom at a standstill, standing still
con active, changing, mobile, moving,
progressing; erratic, fluctuating, inconstant, unstable
ant dynamic

station *n* 1 *syn* see PLACE 1
2 *syn* see RAILROAD STATION
3 *syn* see STATUS 1

station *vb* to appoint or assign to an office
or duty < *stationed* guards around the
camp>
syn post, set
rel appoint, assign; place, position

stationary *adj syn* see STATIC
rel motionless, stock-still
ant moving

station house *n syn* see RAILROAD STA-
TION

statuesque *adj syn* see SHAPELY

stature *n* 1 *syn* see QUALITY 2
rel prestige, standing, status; ability, capacity; competence, qualification
2 *syn* see STATUS 2

status *n* **1** rating or positioning in relation to others (as in a social order, community, class, or profession) <his *status* as a slave>
　syn capacity, character, footing, place, position, quality, rank, situation, standing, state, station
　rel rating
2 social or professional importance or distinction <a lawyer of international *status*>
　syn cachet, consequence, dignity, position, prestige, rank, standing, state, stature
　rel caliber, merit, worth; distinction, renown; eminence, prominence
　con inconsequence, insignificance, unimportance
3 *syn* see STATE 1
　rel status quo
　idiom state of affairs

statute *n syn* see LAW 1
　rel act, enactment

staunch *adj* **1** *syn* see SURE 1
2 *syn* see FAITHFUL 1
　rel firm, strong
　idiom as staunch as an oak, tried and true
　con mercurial; shaky, unsteady

stave *vb syn* see HURRY 2

stave off *vb* **1** *syn* see FEND (off)
　rel beat off, drive (off), fight (off); block, parry
2 *syn* see PREVENT 2

staving *adv syn* see VERY 1
　ant barely

stay *vb* **1** *syn* see ARREST 1
　rel postpone, prorogue, put off
2 to continue to be in one place for a noticeable time <*stayed* late at the office>
　syn abide, bide, linger, remain, stick around, tarry, wait
　rel dally, delay, dillydally, lag, procrastinate; hang around, loiter; outstay, stay out
　ant go
3 *syn* see VISIT 3
　rel bide, dwell, live
4 *syn* see DEFER

stay *n syn* see STANDSTILL

stay *n syn* see SUPPORT 3

stay *vb syn* see BASE

stead *vb syn* see HELP 1

steadfast *adj* **1** *syn* see IMMOVABLE 1
2 *syn* see INFLEXIBLE 2
　ant unsteadfast, vacillating
3 *syn* see SURE 2
　ant capricious
4 *syn* see FAITHFUL 1
　rel unfaltering, unflinching, unquestioning, unwavering

steadfastly *adv syn* see HARD 7
　rel staunchly, strongly

steadiness *n syn* see STABILITY
　ant unsteadiness

steady *adj* **1** *syn* see SURE 2
　rel unswerving; eternal, never-ending

---

2 being neither markedly varying nor variable in course or extent <a *steady* rain> < *steady* prices>
　syn constant, equable, even, stabile, stable, unchanging, unfluctuating, uniform, unvarying; *compare* STATIC
　rel steady-going; certain, changeless, fixed, set, sure, unchangeable; unflickering, unwavering; durable, reliable
　con inconstant, uneven, unstable; changeable; changing, fluctuating, uncertain, undependable, undulating, unsure, varying, wavering
　ant unsteady
3 *syn* see FAITHFUL 1

steady *vb syn* see STABILIZE

steady *n* **1** *syn* see BOYFRIEND 2
2 *syn* see GIRL FRIEND 2

steal *vb* **1** to take another's possession illegally and without his knowledge <*stole* a car>
　syn abstract, annex, appropriate, cabbage, ‖clout, ‖cly, collar, ‖coon, ‖cop, ‖crook, filch, ‖heist, hook, lift, nab, ‖nail, ‖nick, nim, nip, pilfer, pillage, pinch, pocket, ‖prig, purloin, smouch, ‖snaffle, ‖snake, snitch, swipe, thieve, vulture
　rel mooch; fleece, frisk; grab, grasp, seize, snatch, take; hijack, shanghai; poach, rustle; burglarize, rob; loot, plunder, rifle
　idiom make off (*or* away) with, run away (*or* off) with
2 *syn* see SNEAK
3 to move or go quietly so as not to disturb <*stole* out of the sickroom on tiptoe>
　syn creep, glide, mouse, slide, slip; *compare* SNEAK
　rel tiptoe
　con clump, stamp, stomp, stump

steal *n* **1** *syn* see THEFT
2 *syn* see BARGAIN 1

stealage *n syn* see THEFT

stealer *n syn* see THIEF

stealing *n syn* see THEFT

stealthily *adv syn* see SECRETLY
　ant openly

stealthy *adj* **1** *syn* see SECRET 1
　rel crafty, cunning, sly, wily; skulking, slinking, sneaking; catlike
　con direct, straight, straightforward
　ant open
2 being so quiet, slow, and deliberate in movement as to escape observation <the *stealthy* movements of the cat burglar>
　syn catlike, catty, feline, furtive; *compare* SECRET 1
　rel noiseless, pantherine, pantherish, quiet, silent; shifty, skulking, sly, sneak, sneaking, sneaky

steam *n syn* see POWER 4

steamroller *vb syn* see WHIP 2

steam up *vb syn* see ANGER 1

steel *vb* **1** *syn* see GIRD 3
　rel rally; nerve; buck up; reinforce
　idiom grit one's teeth, set one's jaw, take the bit in one's teeth
　ant unsteel
2 *syn* see ENCOURAGE 1

steep *adj* **1** having an incline approaching the perpendicular <a *steep* trail up the mountain>

---

syn synonym(s)　　*rel* related word(s)
ant antonym(s)　　*con* contrasted word(s)
idiom idiomatic equivalent(s)
‖ use limited; if in doubt, see a dictionary

syn abrupt, arduous, precipitate, precipitous, sheer, sideling, steepdown, steep-to, steep-up, ‖stickle

rel elevated, lifted, raised; steepish; high, lofty; prerupt; perpendicular, straight-up; breakneck

con easy, gentle, gradual, moderate; shelvy, shelving, shelvy

2 *syn* see EXCESSIVE 1

steep *vb* 1 *syn* see SOAK 1

2 *syn* see INFUSE 1

steepdown *adj syn* see STEEP 1

steep-to *adj syn* see STEEP 1

steep-up *adj syn* see STEEP 1

steer *vb syn* see GUIDE

idiom steer one's course

steer *n syn* see TIP

stellar *adj* 1 of, relating to, or suggestive of a star or group of stars < *stellar* light >

syn astral, sidereal, ‖starny, starry, stellular

rel gleaming, luminous, lustrous, shining, starlike, twinkling; star-spangled

con starless

2 *syn* see CHIEF 2

stellify *vb syn* see EXALT 1

stellular *adj syn* STELLAR 1, astral, sidereal, ‖starny, starry

stem *vb syn* see SPRING 1

stem *vb* to hinder or prevent by or as if by damming < *stem* the flow of blood >

syn stanch, stop

rel arrest, check, control

stemma *n syn* see GENEALOGY

stench *vb syn* see SMELL 3

stenchful *adj syn* see MALODOROUS 1

stenchy *adj syn* see MALODOROUS 1

stentorian *adj syn* see LOUD 1

rel orotund; clamorous, vociferous; gravelly, rough; clarion-voiced, loudmouthed, loud-voiced, trumpet-tongued

stentorious *adj syn* see LOUD 1

rel orotund; clamorous, vociferous; gravelly, rough; clarion-voiced, loudmouthed, loud-voiced, trumpet-tongued

stentorophonic *adj syn* see LOUD 1

step *n* 1 *syn* see FOOTPRINT

2 *syn* see DEGREE 1

3 *syn* see MEASURE 7

rel act, action; motion

step *vb* 1 *syn* see WALK 1

2 *syn* see DANCE 1

step-by-step *adj syn* see GRADUAL

step in *vb* 1 *syn* see VISIT 2

2 *syn* see INTERPOSE 2

step up *vb syn* see SPEED 3

ant step down

stereotyped *adj syn* see TRITE

idiom worn thin

stereotypical *adj syn* see TRITE

ant original

sterile *adj* 1 lacking the power to bear offspring or produce fruit < a hybrid that is completely *sterile* >

syn barren, effete, impotent, infecund, infertile, unfruitful

rel sterilized; fallow, fruitless, unproductive; unprolific; arid, bare, dry; dead, desolate

con potent, productive, rich; bearing, fruiting, fruitive, producing, turning out, yielding; fecund, fruitful, prolific, teeming

ant fertile

2 *syn* see UNORIGINAL

rel flat, insipid, jejune, vapid; stale; effete, worn-out; impotent

con fertile, fruitful, potent, producing, productive, prolific

ant fecund

sterilize *vb* to make incapable of producing offspring < *sterilizing* animals in medical experiments >

syn alter, castrate, change, desexualize, fix, geld, mutilate, neuter, unsex

rel emasculate; caponize, poulardize; spay

sterling *adj syn* see HONORABLE 1

rel pure, true

stern *adj syn* see SEVERE 1

rel grim, implacable, unrelenting; inexorable, inflexible

ant lenient, soft

‖**stern** *n syn* see BUTTOCKS

stew *n* 1 *syn* see BROTHEL

2 *usu* stews *pl syn* see RED-LIGHT DISTRICT

3 *syn* see SLUM

4 *syn* see MISCELLANY 1

5 *syn* see SNIT

rel boil

6 *syn* see COMMOTION 2

stew *vb* 1 *syn* see BOIL 2

2 *syn* see WORRY 3

idiom be in a stew

stewardly *adj syn* see SPARING

‖**stewed** *adj syn* see INTOXICATED 1

stick *n* 1 *syn* see BAR 1

2 *syn* see DECOY 1

3 sticks *pl,* used with the *syn* see FRONTIER 2

idiom the middle of nowhere

stick *adv syn* see ALL 1

stick *vb* 1 *syn* see THRUST 2

2 to become or cause to become closely and firmly attached < papers all *stuck* together >

syn adhere, cleave, cling, cohere

rel affix, attach, fasten, fix; glue; cement; fuse, weld; braze, solder

idiom stick close, stick like a wet shirt, stick like the paper on the wall, stick like wax, stick to like a barnacle (*or* leech)

con loosen; detach, disengage

ant unstick

3 *syn* see SET 1

4 *syn* see NONPLUS 1

5 *syn* see FLEECE 1

6 *syn* see OVERCHARGE 1

‖7 *syn* see BEAR 10

8 *syn* see DEMUR

stickage *n syn* see ADHERENCE 1

stick around *vb syn* see STAY 2

stick-at-nothing *adj syn* see UNSCRUPULOUS

sticker *n syn* see SEAL

sticking *n syn* see ADHERENCE 1

stick-in-the-mud *n syn* see FOGY

‖**stickle** *adj syn* see STEEP 1

stickle *vb syn* see DEMUR

rel hold out, stall; contend, kick, object, protest

stick out *vb* 1 *syn* see BULGE

rel outstretch, outthrust, protend, push

2 *syn* see STRIKE 1

3 *syn* see BEAR 10

stick up *vb syn* see ROB 1

sticky *adj* 1 having the quality of sticking by or as if by adhesion < *sticky* syrup >

syn adhesive, ‖claggy, ‖clarty, cloggy, gluey, gooey, gummy, stodgy
rel tacky; viscid, viscous
2 *syn* see HUMID
3 *syn* see HARD 6
4 *syn* see SENTIMENTAL

‖**stickybeak** *n syn* see BUSYBODY

sticky–fingered *adj syn* see LARCENOUS

stiff *adj* **1** incapable of or highly resistant to bending or flexing <a *stiff* cardboard packing box>
syn immalleable, impliable, incompliant, inelastic, inflexible, rigid, unbending, unflexible, unyielding; *compare* INFLEXIBLE 2
rel stiffish; hard, resistant; hardened, petrified; stark
idiom stiff as a board (*or* poker)
con soft, softened; yielding; bendable, pliable, pliant; limber, supple, willowy
ant flexible, flexile
2 *syn* see INTOXICATED 1
3 *syn* see OBSTINATE
4 characterized by a lack of ease, grace, or spontaneity especially in style <a play whose dialogue and characters were *stiff* and perfunctory>
syn buckram, cardboard, muscle-bound, stilted, wooden
rel rigid, set, studied; machine-made, mechanical, stereotyped, stock; arid, dry, dull
con expressive, graphic, vivid; easy, fluent, graceful, smooth
5 *syn* see EXCESSIVE 1

stiff *n* **1** *syn* see CORPSE
2 *syn* see DRUNKARD
3 *syn* see MISER

stiff–necked *adj syn* see OBSTINATE

stifle *vb* **1** *syn* see SUFFOCATE
2 *syn* see MUFFLE 2
3 *syn* see SUPPRESS 3
4 *syn* see STULTIFY

stifling *adj* **1** producing or seeming to produce suffocation <a *stifling* heat>
syn smothering, smothery, ‖smudgy, suffocating, suffocative; *compare* HUMID, STUFFY 1
rel oppressive, overpowering; unbearable, unendurable
2 *syn* see STUFFY 1

stifling *n syn* see REPRESSION 1

stigma *n* a mark of shame or discredit <the *stigma* of personal cowardice>
syn bar sinister, black eye, blot, blur, brand, odium, onus, slur, spot, stain
rel besmirchment, disfigurement, smudge, smutch, taint, tainting; disgrace, dishonor, shame
con credit, distinction, glory, honor; bay(s), crown, laurel(s)

still *adj* **1** *syn* see MOTIONLESS
2 *syn* see CALM 1
rel peaceful, unperturbed
con roiled, roily, turbid
3 devoid of or making no stir, sound, or noise <the streets were *still* at 3:00 A.M.>

---

syn hush, hushful, noiseless, quiet, silent, soundless, stilly, whist
rel calm, hushed, peaceful, placid, serene, tranquil; deathlike, deathly
idiom deathly still, still as death
ant noisy

still *vb* **1** *syn* see CALM
ant agitate
2 *syn* see SILENCE

still *adv* **1** *syn* see HOWEVER
2 *syn* see YET 1
idiom still (*or* even) more
3 *syn* see ALSO 2

still *n syn* see SILENCE 1

still and all *adv syn* see HOWEVER

still–hunt *vb syn* see STALK 1

stillness *n syn* see SILENCE 1

stillstand *n syn* see STANDSTILL

stilly *adj* **1** *syn* see STILL 3
con agitated, disturbed, noisy
ant noiseful
2 *syn* see CALM 1

stilted *adj* **1** *syn* see RHETORICAL
2 *syn* see STIFF 4
3 *syn* see GENTEEL 3
rel conventional, formal; decorous; prim

stimulant *n syn* see STIMULUS

stimulate *vb* **1** *syn* see PROVOKE 4
rel enliven, vivify; activate, dynamize, energize, vitalize
idiom build a fire under, get one started (*or* moving)
con unnerve; deaden
2 *syn* see ELATE

stimulating *adj* **1** *syn* see EXCITING
rel enlivening, lively; provocative, seminal, suggestive; incitory, stimulative, stimulatory
2 *syn* see INVIGORATING

stimulative *adj syn* see INVIGORATING

stimulus *n* something that rouses the mind or spirits or incites to activity <the war proved a *stimulus* to the economy> <sought a *stimulus* to take her mind off her own troubles>
syn catalyst, goad, impetus, impulse, incentive, incitation, incitement, instigation, motivation, propellant, provocative, push, spur, stimulant; *compare* MOTIVE 1
rel boost, encouragement, inducement, invitation, urging; cause, motive; excitement, piquing, provocation, stimulation

sting *vb syn* see SMART

stingy *adj* being unwilling or showing unwillingness to share with others <too *stingy* to tip the waiter>
syn cheeseparing, ‖chinchy, close, close-fisted, costive, hardfisted, hardhanded, ironfisted, mean, mingy, miserly, ‖narrow, narrow-fisted, narrowhearted, niggard, niggardly, parsimonious, penny-pinching, penny-wise, penurious, pinching, pinch-penny, save-all, ‖scant, scrimpy, scrimy, tight, tightfisted, ungenerous, ungiving; *compare* SPARING
rel economical, frugal, Scotch, sparing, thrifty; scaly, screwy
idiom as close as a vise, as close (*or* tight) as paper on a wall, as tightfisted as a kulak, near (*or* close *or* tight) as the bark on a tree
con bountiful, giving, liberal, munificent, open-handed, philanthropic, unsparing, unstinting; prodigal

ant generous
stink vb syn see SMELL 3
stinkard n syn see SNOT 1
stinkaroo n syn see SNOT 1
stinker n syn see SNOT 1
stinking adj syn see MALODOROUS 1
  idiom stinking to high heaven
  ||2 syn see INTOXICATED 1
||**stinko** adj syn see INTOXICATED 1
stinky adj syn see MALODOROUS 1
stint vb 1 syn see SCRIMP
  2 syn see SPARE 3
stint n 1 syn see RESTRICTION 1
  2 syn see TASK 1
  rel amount, quantity; allotment, apportionment; participation, share
  3 syn see SPELL 1
stipend n syn see WAGE
  rel award, consideration, payment
stipple vb syn see SPECKLE
stipulate vb syn see SPECIFY 3
  rel designate; state; provide
stipulated adj syn see FIRM 3
  rel designated, pinned down
  con implied, unstated, unwritten
stipulation n syn see CONDITION 1
  rel specification; circumscription, limit
stir vb 1 to cause to shift from quiescence or torpor into activity <a teacher who *stirred* the minds of his most sluggish students>
  syn arouse, awaken, bestir, challenge, kindle, rally, rouse, wake, waken, whet; compare PROVOKE 4
  rel excite, galvanize, inspire, provoke, quicken, stimulate; agitate, foment, incite, instigate; activate, energize, vitalize; actuate, drive, move, impel; ||roust, rout
  idiom make (or have) an impact on, set astir, set on fire
  2 syn see WAKE 1
  3 syn see SEETHE 4
stir (up) vb syn see INCITE
  idiom add fuel to the flame, apply the torch, feed the fire, pour oil on the fire, stir the embers
stir n 1 signs of excited activity, hurry, or commotion <noticed a *stir* within the crowd>
  syn ado, bustle, flurry, furore, fuss, pother, whirl, whirlpool, whirlwind; compare COMMOTION 4
  rel agitation, disquiet, stir-up; commotion, disturbance; din, hubbub, pandemonium, stirabout, tumult
  con calm, peace, placidity; inaction, inactivity
  ant tranquillity
  2 syn see MOTION 1
||**stir** n syn see JAIL
||**stirra** n syn see MAN 3
stirring n syn see MOTION 1
stirring adj syn see EXCITING
  rel heart-stirring, soul-stirring
stitch n syn see PAIN 1
stivy adj syn see STUFFY 1
stock n 1 syn see FAMILY 1
  2 syn see ESTIMATION 1
  3 syn see TRUST 1
  4 syn see SUPPLY
  5 syn see RESERVE
stock vb to equip, furnish, supply, or have material requisites (as for sale) <a bar that *stocks* all the best brands of liquor>

syn carry, keep
  rel have; furnish, supply
  idiom have (or keep) in stock, keep on hand
stockade n syn see JAIL
stockpile n 1 syn see PILE 1
  2 syn see RESERVE
stockpile vb syn see ACCUMULATE
stock-still adj syn see MOTIONLESS
stocky adj being compact and broad in build and often short in stature <a *stocky* but quick and hard-hitting catcher>
  syn ||chuffy, ||chumpy, chunky, dumpy, heavyset, squab, squat, squdgy, stubby, ||stuggy, stumpy, thick, thick-bodied, thickset
  rel plump, stout; bunty, low-set, short; lumpish, lumpy, pudgy; corpulent, fat
  con lean, skinny, thin, wiry
stodge vb 1 syn see SATIATE
  2 syn see PLOD 1
stodgy adj 1 syn see STICKY 1
  2 syn see DULL 9
  rel unexciting; pedantic; heavy, ponderous, weighty
  3 syn see TACKY 2
stoic adj syn see IMPASSIVE 1
  rel aloof, detached, indifferent, unconcerned; self-controlled, Spartan; indomitable, unassailable; long-suffering, patient, resigned
stoicism n syn see APATHY 1
  rel backbone, fortitude, grit, guts, pluck, sand
||**stolt** vb syn see LURCH 2
||**stoiter** vb syn see LURCH 2
stolid adj syn see IMPASSIVE 1
  rel blunt, dull, obtuse; dense, dull, dumb, slow, stupid; inactive, inert, passive, supine
  ant sensitive
stolidity n syn see APATHY 1
  rel dullness, dumbness, slowness, stupidity; inactiveness, inactivity, inertia, passivity
  con aptness, quickness, readiness; animation, enlivening, quickening; ardor, enthusiasm, fervor, passion, zeal; fire
  ant sensitivity
stomach n 1 syn see ABDOMEN
  2 syn see APPETITE 1
stomach vb syn see BEAR 10
stomachache n abdominal pain <she has a terrible *stomachache*>
  syn bellyache, colic, collywobbles, gripe(s)
  rel distress, misery
||**stomachy** adj syn see IRASCIBLE
stomp vb syn see TRAMPLE 2
stone-blind adj syn see BLIND 1
stone-broke adj syn see POOR 1
stoned adj 1 syn see INTOXICATED 1
  2 syn see DRUGGED
stone-still adj syn see MOTIONLESS
stony adj 1 syn see UNFEELING 2
  ant soft
  2 syn see POOR 1
stonyhearted adj syn see UNFEELING 2
  rel flinty, hard, stonelike
  idiom as cold as marble
  ant softhearted
stooge n 1 one who plays a subordinate or compliant role to a principal <an executive who was only a *stooge* with no real power>

syn Charlie McCarthy, dummy, yes-man
2 syn see TOOL 2

stool n syn see INFORMER

||**stool** vb syn see INFORM 3

stoolie n syn see INFORMER

stool pigeon n syn see INFORMER

stoop vb 1 to descend from one's level (as of rank or dignity) usually to do something <a king who would not *stoop* to consider the common people>
syn condescend, deign
rel relax, thaw, unbend; accord, concede; accommodate, favor, oblige
idiom be so good as to, come (or get) down from one's high horse, lower oneself
2 to drop in status or dignity by indulgence in pettiness or unworthy behavior <a man who would not *stoop* to tell a lie>
syn descend, sink
idiom act beneath oneself, debase (or demean) oneself, lower oneself
3 syn see DUCK 2

stop vb 1 syn see STEM
2 syn see FILL 1
rel disrupt, hinder, interrupt; cut off, shut off, turn off
ant unstop
3 to suspend or cause to suspend activity <the conversation *stopped*>
syn cease, desist, ||deval, discontinue, give over, halt, knock off, leave off, quit, surcease; compare ARREST 1
rel ||can, refrain (from); arrest, check, cut off, interrupt; stay, suspend; ||cheese, lay off; break off, break up, end, terminate
con continue, go on, keep (on), keep up, persist
ant start
4 to come to a standstill <the car *stopped* at the intersection>
syn bring up, draw up, fetch up, halt, haul up, pull up
con start; move; pull out
ant go

stop (in or by) vb syn see VISIT 2

stop (over) vb syn see VISIT 3
idiom make a stopover

stop n 1 syn see END 2
ant start
2 syn see BAR 2
3 syn see STANDSTILL

stopcock n syn see FAUCET

stopgap adj syn see MAKESHIFT

stopgap n syn see RESOURCE 3

stopover n syn see SOJOURN

stopper vb syn see FILL 1
ant unstopper

store vb syn see STOW

store (up) vb syn see ACCUMULATE
rel deposit; cache

store n 1 syn see RESERVE
2 syn see SUPPLY
3 syn see DEPOT 2
4 a business establishment where goods are shown for sale <a food *store*>
syn market, outlet, shop, showroom
rel discounter, discount house, discount store, emporium

---

syn synonym(s)   rel related word(s)
ant antonym(s)   con contrasted word(s)
idiom idiomatic equivalent(s)
|| use limited; if in doubt, see a dictionary

store adj syn see READY-MADE

store–bought adj syn see READY-MADE

||**store–boughten** adj syn see READY=MADE

storehouse n syn see DEPOT 2

storm n 1 syn see COMMOTION 4
2 syn see BARRAGE

storm vb syn see ATTACK 1

storm and stress n syn see UNREST

stormful adj syn see WILD 6
rel threatening; dusty, murky; foul; howling, riproaring, roaring
ant calm

stormily adv syn see HARD 2

stormy adj syn see WILD 6
rel threatening; dusty, murky; foul; howling, riproaring, roaring
ant calm

story n 1 syn see ACCOUNT 7
2 a recital of real or imaginary happenings that is less elaborate than a novel <told the *story* of his escape> <a simple *story* of heartwarming devotion>
syn anecdote, narration, narrative, tale, yarn; compare ACCOUNT 7
rel conte; description; fable; folktale, legend, märchen; Canterbury tale, cock-and-bull story, fabrication, fairy tale, fiction
3 syn see LIE

storyteller n syn see LIAR

||**stot** vb syn see LURCH 2

stout adj 1 syn see BRAVE 1
idiom bold as a lion
con irresolute; fainthearted
2 syn see STRONG 2
rel resolute, steadfast; hard; indomitable, invincible
idiom as strong (or stalwart) as an English oak
3 syn see FAT 2
rel thick-bodied; ||plenitudinous
ant spare

stouthearted adj syn see BRAVE 1

stow vb to put (articles) into a storage space <*stowed* his gear belowdecks>
syn bestow, pack, store, warehouse
ant unstow

straddle vb 1 syn see BESTRIDE 2
2 syn see SPRAWL 2

straggle vb 1 syn see WANDER 1
2 syn see SPRAWL 2

straggler n syn see LAGGARD

straight adv 1 syn see AWAY 3
2 syn see DIRECTLY 1

straight adj 1 syn see DIRECT 2
idiom as straight as an arrow
ant circuitous
2 syn see STRAIGHTFORWARD 2
3 free from admixture or extraneous matter <a shot of *straight* liquor>
syn neat, plain, pure, unadulterated, undiluted, unmixed
rel unmodified; concentrated; strong
con adulterated, blended, mixed; watered=down; weak
4 syn see CONVENTIONAL 1

straight n syn see RIGHT 1

straightaway adv syn see AWAY 3

straightforward adj 1 syn see DIRECT 2
2 free from all that is dishonest or secretive <a *straightforward* answer>
syn aboveboard, forthright, plain dealing, straight; compare FRANK

rel pretenseless; honest, honorable, just, upright, upstanding; candid, frank, open, plain, unequivocal; direct, outspoken
con equivocal, evasive, shuffling; indirect; prevaricative; dishonest, untruthful
ant devious
3 *syn* see FRANK
rel barefaced, straight-from-the-shoulder
4 *syn* see CLEAR 5
straightly *adv syn* see DIRECTLY 1
straight off *adv syn* see AWAY 3
straight-out *adj syn* see UTTER
straight-up *adj* 1 *syn* see ERECT
2 *syn* see VERTICAL
straightway *adv syn* see AWAY 3
strain *n* 1 *syn* see HINT 2
2 *syn* see MELODY
3 *syn* see MOOD 1
strain *vb* 1 *syn* see TRY 2
rel stretch
idiom put a strain on
2 to injure (as a body part) by overuse or misuse < *strained* a muscle while lifting weights>
syn pull
3 *syn* see LABOR 1
4 *syn* see EXUDE
5 *syn* see DEMUR
strain *n syn* see STRESS 1
strained *adj syn* see FORCED
rel taut, tense, tight
con unforced, unlabored; unconstrained
ant unstrained
strait *n syn* see JUNCTURE 2
rel bind, squeeze; difficulty, hardship, rigor, vicissitude; bewilderment, mystification, perplexity
straitlaced *adj syn* see PRIM 1
rel hidebound, intolerant, narrow, narrow-minded; rigorous, strict
idiom prim and proper
con easygoing, relaxed; broadminded, liberal, liberal-minded; libertine
strake *vb syn* see STREAK
‖**stramash** *n syn* see CRASH 3
strand *n syn* see SHORE
strand *vb syn* see SHIPWRECK 1
stranded *adj syn* see AGROUND
idiom high and dry, run aground
strange *adj* 1 *syn* see EXOTIC 2
2 *syn* see UNFAMILIAR 1
rel unknown; alien
3 *syn* see MARVELOUS 1
4 deviating from what is ordinary, usual, or to be expected < a *strange* unpredictable man>
syn bizarre, curious, eccentric, erratic, idiosyncratic, odd, oddball, outlandish, peculiar, quaint, queer, ‖rum, rummy, singular, uncouth, unusual, weird; *compare* EXCEPTIONAL 1, MYSTERIOUS
rel aberrant, abnormal, atypical, off, off-the-wall; fishy, funny; far-out, freaky, ‖kinky, kooky, offbeat, outré, ‖scatty; crazy, nutty; fantastic, grotesque
idiom as strange as they come
con common, ordinary, unexceptional, usual; expected, predictable
ant familiar
stranger *n* a nonresident or an unknown person in a community < he felt he had become a *stranger* in a foreign land>
syn alien, auslander, foreigner, inconnu, outcomer, outlander, outsider

rel out-of-stater, outstater; transient; visitor; immigrant; wanderer
idiom stranger within the gates
con inhabitant, resident; aboriginal, aborigine, autochthon, indigene, native
strangle *vb* 1 *syn* see CHOKE 1
2 *syn* see SUPPRESS 2
strangling *n syn* see REPRESSION 1
strapped *adj syn* see POOR 1
stratagem *n syn* see TRICK 1
rel conspiracy, intrigue, machination, plot
strategy *n syn* see PLAN 1
stratospheric *adj syn* see EXCESSIVE 1
straw *adj syn* see BLOND 1
rel strawish, strawy
straw *vb syn* see STREW 1
stray *vb* 1 *syn* see WANDER 1
2 *syn* see ERR
idiom stray from the straight and narrow
3 *syn* see DIGRESS 1
idiom get off the track, get sidetracked
stray *adj syn* see ERRATIC 1
rel random, sporadic
streak *n syn* see HINT 2
streak *vb* to make irregular lines or stripes of contrasting colors on or in < hair *streaked* with gray>
syn strake, striate, stripe
rel dapple, fleck, spot; marble, variegate, vein
stream *n* 1 *syn* see CREEK 2
2 *syn* see FLOW
stream *vb syn* see POUR 2
streamer *n syn* see FLAG
streamline *vb syn* see SIMPLIFY
‖**streel** *n syn* see SLATTERN 1
street *n syn* see WAY 1
rel ruelle, streetlet; drive
street arab *n syn* see VAGABOND
street girl *n syn* see PROSTITUTE
streetwalker *n syn* see PROSTITUTE
streetwalking *n syn* see PROSTITUTION
strength *n* 1 *syn* see POWER 4
rel brawn; sturdiness, toughness; healthiness, soundness
con feebleness
ant weakness
2 *syn* see STABILITY
3 *syn* see SUBSTANCE 2
strengthen *vb* 1 *syn* see ENCOURAGE 1
2 to make strong or stronger < exercise is needed to *strengthen* the body>
syn energize, fortify, invigorate, reinforce
rel brace, support, undergird; anneal, ruggedize, sinew, tone (up), toughen; cheer, embolden, encourage, enhearten, ensteel, hearten, inspirit, nerve, steel
con cripple, debilitate, disable, enfeeble, tear down, undermine; deject, discourage, dishearten, dispirit; emasculate, enervate, unman, unnerve
ant weaken
3 *syn* see GIRD 3
idiom gather one's resources, recruit one's strength
‖**strengthy** *adj syn* see STRONG 1
strenuous *adj* 1 *syn* see VIGOROUS
2 *syn* see HARD 6
rel breathless, energy-consuming; mean, wicked; Herculean
idiom a long hard pull, an uphill climb, tough going
con comfortable, cushy, light, unburdensome

ant effortless

stress *n* the action or effect of force exerted within or upon a thing < the *stress* and buckled under the weight of the deck >
　syn pressure, strain, tension
　rel pinch; burden, weight
　2 *syn* see EMPHASIS
　rel import, importance

stress *vb* 1 *syn* see TRY 2
　2 *syn* see EMPHASIZE

stretch *vb* 1 *syn* see RUN 8
　rel range, roll
　2 *syn* see EXTEND 3
　con abbreviate, shorten; condense, curtail, cut, trim
　3 *syn* see EMBROIDER

stretch (out) *vb* *syn* see REST 1

stretch *n* 1 *syn* see RANGE 2
　2 *syn* see DISTANCE 1
　3 *syn* see EXPANSE
　rel area, region, tract
　4 *syn* see WHILE 1

stretch *adj syn* see ELASTIC 1

stretchy *adj syn* see ELASTIC 1

strew *vb* 1 to spread (something) loosely or at intervals usually over a substantial area < *strew* seed for birds >
　syn bestrew, broadcast, disject, disseminate, scatter, sow, straw; *compare* SPREAD 1, SPRINKLE 1
　rel dust, pepper; dissipate; cover
　2 *syn* see SPREAD 1

striate *vb syn* see STREAK

strict *adj* 1 *syn* see RIGID 3
　rel exacting, oppressive, unsparing; dour, forbidding, grim, hard-boiled, harsh, tough
　idiom not to be trifled (*or* messed) with
　con easy, easygoing; lax, loose; permissive
　ant lenient
　2 *syn* see TRUE 3

stricture *n* 1 *syn* see RESTRICTION 1
　2 *syn* see ANIMADVERSION

‖striddle *vb* 1 *syn* see BESTRIDE 2
　2 *syn* see STRIDE 1

stride *vb* 1 to move or walk with long often purposeful steps < *strode* to the door and slammed it >
　syn march, sling, stalk, ‖striddle
　rel clump, stamp, stomp, tramp, tromp
　2 *syn* see BESTRIDE

strident *adj syn* see HARSH 3
　rel loud, stentorian, stertorous
　2 *syn* see VOCIFEROUS

stridulent *adj syn* see HARSH 3

stridulous *adj syn* see HARSH 3

strife *n* 1 *syn* see DISCORD
　rel argument, controversy, dispute; altercation, quarrel, squabble, wrangle; brawl, broil, fracas; affray, combat, fight, fray
　ant accord
　2 *syn* see CONTEST 1

strike *vb* 1 to engage in a temporary work stoppage to effect compliance with demands made on an employer < they *struck* for higher wages >
　syn stick out, walk out

---

syn synonym(s)　　*rel* related word(s)
ant antonym(s)　　*con* contrasted word(s)
idiom idiomatic equivalent(s)
‖ use limited; if in doubt, see a dictionary

idiom go (*or* be) on strike
　2 to deliver (a blow) in a strong, vigorous manner < angrily *struck* the boy >
　syn ‖biff, catch, clout, ‖devel, ding, hit, ‖nail, pop, slog, ‖slosh, smite, sock, swat, whack; *compare* SLAM 1, SLAP 1
　rel beat, pummel, ‖slat, ‖swap, ‖wap, whop; cudgel, hammer, mace; ‖plug, poke, ‖puck, punch; bang, bash, crash, ‖pandy, slam; ‖stoush, thrash
　idiom hang one on, let one fly
　3 *syn* see GIVE 10
　4 *syn* see AFFLICT
　5 *syn* see SEIZE 1
　6 *syn* see ATTACK 1
　7 *syn* see OCCUR 2
　8 *syn* see AFFECT
　9 *syn* see DON 2

strike *n syn* see DISCOVERY

strike out *vb syn* see HEAD 3

striker *n syn* see HELPER

striking *adj syn* see NOTICEABLE
　rel showy; forceful, powerful; cogent, compelling, telling

strikingly *adv syn* see VERY 1

string *n* 1 *syn* see LINE 5
　2 *syn* see RESOURCE 3
　3 *syn* see SUCCESSION 2
　4 **strings** *pl syn* see POWER 1

string (up) *vb syn* see HANG 2

string along *vb syn* see TRIFLE 1
　idiom keep (someone) dangling

stringent *adj* 1 *syn* see RIGID 3
　rel binding, confining, drawing
　2 *syn* see GRIM 1

strings *n pl syn* see CONDITION 1

stringy *adj syn* see MUSCULAR 1

‖strinkle *vb syn* see SPRINKLE 1

strip *vb* 1 to remove the clothing of < guards *stripped* and searched the prisoners >
　syn denude, disrobe, unclothe, undress
　rel doff, peel, take off; bare, denudate, expose, uncover; disfrock, unfrock
　idiom strip to the buff
　con clothe, dress, robe; cover
　2 to take something (as honors, privileges, functions, or trappings) away from < an exiled king now *stripped* of his power >
　syn bankrupt, bare, denudate, denude, deprive, dismantle, disrobe, divest; *compare* DEPRIVE 2
　rel bereave, deplenish, disfurnish, ‖displenish, dispossess; despoil, rob
　con clothe, endow, furnish, grant, vest; install
　ant invest
　3 *syn* see RAVAGE
　4 *syn* see SKIN 2

strip *n syn* see STRIPTEASE

strip *n* 1 a relatively long and narrow piece or section < tear old linen into *strips* for bandages >
　syn band, bandeau, banding, fillet, ribbon, stripe
　rel piece; section; segment; shred
　2 *syn* see BAR 1

stripe *vb syn* see WHIP 1

stripe *n* 1 *syn* see STRIP 1
　2 *syn* see TYPE

stripe *vb syn* see STREAK

stripling *n syn* see BOY 1

stripped *adj* 1 *syn* see NUDE 2

con attired; covered
ant clothed, dressed
2 *syn* see OPEN 2
con covered, unexposed; protected
stripper *n syn* see STRIPTEASER
stripping *n syn* see STRIPTEASE
striptease *n* entertainment in which a female performer removes her clothing piece by piece in view of an audience <a nightclub featuring *striptease*>
syn strip, stripping
idiom exotic dancing
stripteaser *n* one who performs a striptease <worked part-time as a model and *stripteaser*>
syn ecdysiast, peeler, stripper, stripteuse, teaser
idiom exotic dancer, ‖pantie peeler, ‖strip-and-shake artist, strip artist
stripteuse *n syn* see STRIPTEASER
strive *vb* 1 *syn* see LABOR 1
2 *syn* see TRY 5
rel labor, toil, travail, work; drive, strain
striving *n* 1 *syn* see CONTEST 1
rel contending; combat, fight
2 *syn* see ATTEMPT
rel labor, toil, travail, work
stroll *vb syn* see SAUNTER
stroll *n syn* see WALK 1
strong *adj* 1 having great physical strength <had the *strong* hands and arms of a wrestler>
syn mighty, powerful, ‖strengthy, wieldy; compare MUSCULAR 2
rel firm, robust, stark, strapping, sturdy, two-handed; able-bodied, tough; brawny, muscular, sinewy, lusty, vigorous
idiom strong as a bull (*or* ox)
con feeble, frail; puny, weak-bodied; forceless, impotent, powerless, strengthless
ant weak
2 having or manifesting great force or power (as in acting or resisting) <a *strong* constitution>
syn stalwart, stout, sturdy, tenacious, tough
rel hardy, robust, rugged, strapping; firm, solid, staunch; durable, enduring; forceful, potent, powerful; lusty, vigorous
con frail; forceless, impotent, powerless, strengthless; depleted, failing
ant weak
3 being rich in a characteristic ingredient <*strong* coffee>
syn concentrated, full-bodied, lusty, potent, robust
rel strong-flavored, strong-tasting; straight, undiluted, unmixed; rich; heroic, large, powerful
con diluted, mixed, watered-down
ant weak
4 *syn* see SPIRITUOUS
5 *syn* see SURE 1
rel solid, substantial, unmoving, unyielding
6 *syn* see MALODOROUS 1
strong arm *n* 1 *syn* see POWER 4
2 *syn* see THUG 1
strong-arm *vb syn* see INTIMIDATE
stronghold *n syn* see FORT
strongly *adv syn* see HARD 1
ant weakly
strong man *n syn* see TYRANT

strong suit *n syn* see FORTE
structure *n* 1 *syn* see BUILDING
rel construction, erection, pile
2 *syn* see EDIFICE
3 something made up of more or less interdependent elements and having a definite organizational pattern <the complex bureaucratic *structure* of modern government>
syn framework
rel anatomy, skeleton; build, construction, frame; arrangement, composition, form, format, makeup, morphology; complex, network, system
struggle *vb syn* see TRY 5
rel compete, vie
idiom make a valiant attempt (*or* try)
ant give up
struggle *n syn* see ATTEMPT
strum *vb syn* see HUM
strumpet *n syn* see WANTON
‖**strunt** *vb syn* see STRUT 2
‖**strunt** *n syn* see LIQUOR 2
strut *vb* 1 *syn* see SASHAY
2 to walk with an air of pomposity or affected dignity <a pompous general *strutting* off the parade ground>
syn ‖strunt, swagger
rel flaunt, parade
con cower, cringe; slink
stubborn *adj* 1 *syn* see OBSTINATE
rel contumacious, insubordinate, rebellious; cantankerous, ornery; ‖stunkard, ‖stunt
idiom set in one's ways, stubborn as a mule
con adaptable, pliable, pliant; amenable, tractable
ant docile
2 *syn* see INFLEXIBLE 2
stubbornness *n syn* see DEFIANCE 2
rel cantankerousness, orneriness
stubby *adj syn* see STOCKY
stube *n syn* see ALEHOUSE
stuck-up *adj syn* see VAIN 3
idiom too big for one's breeches, wise in one's own conceit
stud *vb syn* see SPOT 2
studied *adj syn* see DELIBERATE 1
rel thoughtful; intentional, voluntary, willful, willing
con natural, offhand
ant unstudied
studio *n* the working place of an artist (as a painter) <moved to a larger *studio*>
syn atelier, bottega
rel shop, workroom, workshop
studious *adj syn* see DELIBERATE 1
ant impromptu
study *n* 1 *syn* see REVERIE
2 *syn* see ATTENTION 1
rel contemplation, weighing; abstraction, meditation, musing, pondering, rumination
3 *syn* see EXERCISE 4
study *vb* 1 *syn* see CONSIDER 1
idiom give careful study to
2 *syn* see SCRUTINIZE 1
stuff *n* 1 *syn* see PERSONAL EFFECTS
2 *syn* see MONEY
3 *syn* see THING 4
4 *syn* see ESSENCE 2
stuff *vb syn* see CRAM 1
rel overfill, overstuff

idiom fill to overflowing, fill to the brim

stuffed *adj syn* see FULL 1

stuffed shirt *n* a smug usually pompous person with an inflexibly conservative or reactionary outlook < a *stuffed shirt* with a starched smile >
syn Blimp, Colonel Blimp, fuddy-duddy
rel diehard; prig, prude, smug
con freethinker, latitudinarian, liberal, libertarian, libertine; avant garde

stuffing *n syn* see ENTRAILS
rel ||tar

stuffy *adj* 1 marked by a heavy oppressive quality of air < a *stuffy* room that needed airing >
syn airless, breathless, close, stifling, stivy, suffocating, sultry; *compare* HUMID, STIFLING 1
rel heavy, oppressive, thick; stagnant; shut-up, unventilated
con airy, breezy; open, ventilated; bracing, invigorating, refreshing, stimulating
2 *syn* see PRIM 1
rel dull, humdrum, stodgy; hidebound, illiberal, narrow, narrow-minded
3 *syn* see POMPOUS 1

||stuggy *adj syn* see STOCKY

stultify *vb* to deprive of vitality and render futile especially by enfeebling or repressive influences < artistic creativity *stultified* by the intrusion of propaganda >
syn constipate, stagnate, stifle, trammel
rel discourage, inhibit, restrain; check, stunt; enfeeble, impair, weaken; deaden, dull; repress, smother, suffocate, suppress; invalidate, nullify
con encourage, foster, nourish; pique, provoke, stimulate

stultiloquence *n syn* see CHATTER

stumble *vb* 1 *syn* see WALLOW 2
rel falter, waver; trip; fall
2 *syn* see DEMUR
3 to move so clumsily and awkwardly as to lose one's balance or trip and fall < *stumbled* across the darkened room and fell >
syn blunder, bumble, lurch, ||snapper; *compare* WALLOW 2
rel reel, stagger, totter; trip; pitch, topple
4 *syn* see LUMBER
5 *syn* see TEETER
rel careen, swing
6 to act, proceed, or execute in a hesitant and clumsily faltering manner < *stumbled* through his Latin translation >
syn limp, muddle, shuffle
rel falter, hesitate, wobble; blunder, bumble; botch, bungle, ||muck
ant breeze
7 *syn* see HAPPEN 2
idiom come (*or* run) up against, fall upon, stub one's toe upon (*or* on)
8 *syn* see PUZZLE

stumblebum *n* a clumsy inept or blundering person < a staff consisting of third-raters and *stumblebums* >
syn blunderbuss, blunderer, bungler
rel incompetent

---

syn synonym(s)   *rel* related word(s)
ant antonym(s)   *con* contrasted word(s)
idiom idiomatic equivalent(s)
|| use limited; if in doubt, see a dictionary

con crackerjack, ||dab, ||darb, expert, top-notcher, whiz; natural; professional

stumbling block *n syn* see OBSTACLE

stump *vb* 1 *syn* see NONPLUS 1
2 *syn* see LUMBER

stump *n syn* see DEFIANCE 1

stumpy *adj syn* see STOCKY

||stumpy *n syn* see MONEY

stun *vb syn* see DAZE 2
rel nonplus; amaze, astound, flabbergast; knock out
idiom strike dumb (*or* dead)

stunner *n* 1 *syn* see WONDER 1
2 *syn* see BEAUTY

stunning *adj* 1 *syn* see EXCELLENT
2 *syn* see BEAUTIFUL

||stunpoll *n syn* see DUNCE

stunt *adj syn* see STUNTED

stunt *vb* to hinder the normal growth and development of < the inhospitable climate had *stunted* all vegetation >
syn dwarf, suppress
rel check, curb, hold back; impair

stunt *n syn* see TRICK 3

stunted *adj* having had one's growth and development hindered or arrested < the children were *stunted* from malnutrition >
syn runted, runtish, runty, ||scrunty, ||stunt
rel undersized; dwarf
con able-bodied, robust well-set, well-set-up; giant, oversize; healthy, strong, sturdy, vigorous

||stupe *n syn* see DUNCE

stupefy *vb* 1 *syn* see DULL 5
2 *syn* see DAZE 2
rel addle, faze, rattle; nonplus

stupendous *adj* 1 *syn* see MARVELOUS 1
2 *syn* see MONSTROUS 1

stupid *adj* 1 lacking in or exhibiting a lack of power to absorb ideas or impressions < a willing boy but too *stupid* to succeed in school >
syn beefheaded, beef-witted, beetleheaded, blear-eyed, blear-witted, blockheaded, blockish, chuckleheaded, dense, doltish, dull, dumb, dunnical, fatheaded, goosey, hammerheaded, numskulled, pinhead, pinheaded, thick, thickheaded, thick-witted; *compare* RETARDED, SIMPLE 3
rel asinine, fatuous, foolish, silly, simple; brute, brutish, dummel, lumbering, oafish, slow, slow-witted, sluggish; ||half-assed; crass; backward, half-witted, retarded; idiotic, imbecilic
idiom ||dead above (*or* between) the ears, ||dead from the neck up, having a block for a head, having cotton between the ears, ||muscle-bound between the ears
con acute, alert, bright, clever, keen, knowing, quick, quick-witted, sharp, smart; sage, wise; brilliant; able, competent
ant intelligent
2 *syn* see LETHARGIC

stupid *n syn* see DUNCE

stupor *n syn* see LETHARGY 1
rel sopor; anesthesia, insensibility

sturdy *adj syn* see STRONG 2
rel sound, substantial
ant decrepit

Sturm und Drang *n syn* see UNREST

||stut *vb syn* see STAMMER 1

stutter *vb syn* see STAMMER 1

sty *n* 1 an extremely unkempt or filthy place < the basement was a rat-infested *sty* >
syn dump, pigpen, pigsty
2 *syn* see SINK 1

stygian *adj syn* see INFERNAL 2

style *n* 1 *syn* see VEIN 1
2 *syn* see NAME 1
3 *syn* see FASHION 3
4 an individual's characteristic attitudes and taste as expressed or indicated in his way of life < she liked the man's sophisticated *style* >
syn manner, way
rel behavior; bearing; carriage; characteristic; trait; idiosyncrasy, peculiarity

style *vb syn* see NAME 1

stylish *adj* being in accordance with or conforming to current fashion < she was a *stylish* dresser >
syn a la mode, chic, ‖classy, dashing, exclusive, fashionable, in, modish, posh, sharp, smart, snappy, swank, swish, tonish, tony, ‖trendy, trig, ultrafashionable, with-it; *compare* DAPPER
rel new, new-day, newfangled, new-fashioned; modern, modernistic, up-to-date; chichi, doggish, doggy, natty, rakish, sassy, swagger; ostentatious, pretentious, ritzy, showy, swell; sleek, slick
idiom in fashion, in the mode
con styleless; old-fashioned, outmoded, out-of-date; drab, tasteless
ant dowdy, unstylish

suasible *adj syn* see RECEPTIVE 1

suave *adj* being conspicuously and ingratiatingly tactful and well-mannered < a man of *suave*, well-bred equanimity >
syn bland, civilized, smooth, urbane; *compare* TACTFUL
rel affable, cordial, genial, gracious, sociable; courteous, courtly, polite; diplomatic, politic; cultivated, cultured, distingué, polished, refined, well-bred; sophisticated, worldly; ingratiating, soft, soft-spoken; fulsome, slick, unctuous
con clumsy, unpolished, unskilled; tactless, undiplomatic, untactful
ant bluff

sub *adj syn* see SUBORDINATE

sub *n syn* see SUBSTITUTE

subaltern *n syn* see INFERIOR

subaquatic *adj syn* see SUBMARINE

subaqueous *adj syn* see SUBMARINE

subaverage *adj syn* see LOW 9

subconscious *n* mental activities that occur just below the threshold of consciousness < a motive probably rooted in his *subconscious* >
syn underconsciousness, undersense
rel subconsciousness; subliminal self
idiom subconscious (*or* submerged) mind
con consciousness; awareness

subdolous *adj syn* see SLY 2

subdue *vb syn* see CONQUER 1
rel extinguish, put down, quash, quell, quench, squelch, suppress

subdued *adj* 1 *syn* see QUIET 4
2 reduced or lacking in force, intensity, or vividness < *subdued* colors > < she answered his questions in a timid *subdued* voice >

syn low-key, low-keyed, sober, soft, softened, toned down
rel moderated, tempered; controlled, restrained; mellow; neutral; quiet
con enlivened, intensified; bright, intense, strong; brilliant, vivid; saturated; blaring, glaring, harsh, screaming
3 *syn* see TAME
ant unsubdued

subduer *n syn* see VICTOR 1

subfusc *adj syn* see DULL 8

subitaneous *adj syn* see PRECIPITATE 1

subjacent *adj syn* see INFERIOR 1
ant superjacent

subject *n* 1 *syn* see CITIZEN 2
2 the basic idea or the principal object of attention in a discourse or artistic composition < the Puritans as soldiers of Christ was the *subject* of her paper >
syn argument, head, matter, motif, motive, point, subject matter, text, theme, topic
rel material, substance; problem, question; leitmotiv; core, meat
con elaboration, enlargement, enlarging, expatiation; development, explication

subject *adj* 1 *syn* see SUBORDINATE
rel servile, slavish, subservient
ant dominant, sovereign
2 *syn* see LIABLE 2
rel apt, likely

subject *vb syn* see EXPOSE 1

subjective *adj* peculiar to a particular individual as modified by individual bias and limitations < *subjective* judgments >
syn unobjective
rel biased, prejudiced; abstract, nonobjective, nonrepresentational, nonrepresentative
ant objective

subject matter *n syn* see SUBJECT 2

subjoin *vb syn* see ADD 1
rel combine, conjoin, unite
con part, separate, sever

subjugate *vb* 1 *syn* see CONQUER 1
rel compel, coerce, force
2 *syn* see ENSLAVE
ant liberate

subjugator *n syn* see VICTOR 1

sublease *vb syn* see SUBLET

sublet *vb* to turn over to another one's right of occupancy of (rented or leased housing) < *sublet* her apartment to a friend >
syn sublease, underlease, underlet

sublime *vb syn* see EXALT 1

sublime *adj* 1 *syn* see GRAND 3
2 *syn* see SPLENDID 2
rel abstract, ideal, transcendent, transcendental; divine, holy, sacred, spiritual; august, majestic, noble, stately

sublimity *n syn* see APEX 2

sublunary *adj syn* see EARTHLY 1

submarine *adj* being, acting, growing, or used under water < a *submarine* camera >
syn subaquatic, subaqueous, underwater

submerge *vb* 1 *syn* see DIP 1
rel drench, impregnate, saturate, soak
2 *syn* see DELUGE 1
3 *syn* see SINK 1

submerse *vb* 1 *syn* see DIP 1
2 *syn* see SINK 1

submission *n syn* see SURRENDER

rel bowing, submitting; acquiescence, compliance, resignation; cringing, servility; prostration

ant resistance

submissive *adj* 1 *syn* see TAME

rel complying, conformable, obeying; bowing down, unerect; menial, servile, slavish, subservient

ant rebellious

2 *syn* see PASSIVE 2

submit *vb* 1 *syn* see YIELD 2

ant resist, withstand

2 to offer or commit (something) for consideration, study, or decision < *submitted* his report directly to the general >

syn hand in, refer

rel bring, deliver, present; offer, proffer, tender; send in; provide

3 *syn* see SUGGEST 4

4 *syn* see FALL 3

ant hold out, resist

subnormal *adj syn* see LOW 9

rel subpar

subordinate *adj* placed in or occupying a lower class, rank, or status < making the executive *subordinate* to the legislative branch >

syn collateral, dependent, secondary, sub, subject, tributary, under

rel adjuvant, auxiliary, contributory, subsidiary; satellite; inferior, subaltern, subalternate; accessory, parergal, supplementary

con chief, first, leading, main; dominant, master, superior

subordinate *n syn* see INFERIOR

sub rosa *adv syn* see SECRETLY

ant aboveboard

sub-rosa *adj syn* see SECRET 1

ant aboveboard

subscribe *vb* 1 *syn* see SIGN 1

2 *syn* see CONTRIBUTE 1

3 *syn* see ASSENT

rel approve, endorse, favor, sanction

subsequent *adj* 1 being, occurring, or carried out at a time after something else < *subsequent* events disproved his predictions >

syn after, ensuing, later, posterior, postliminary, subsequential

rel following, next, succeeding; consequential, resultant, resulting

con exordial, introductory, prefatory, preliminary, preludial; anterior, precedent, preceding, prior

ant antecedent

2 *syn* see CONSECUTIVE

ant antecedent

subsequential *adj* 1 *syn* see SUBSEQUENT 1

2 *syn* see CONSECUTIVE

ant antecedent

subsequently *adv syn* see AFTER

ant antecedently, priorly

subsequent to *prep syn* see AFTER 2

subservient *adj* 1 *syn* see AUXILIARY

2 showing extreme compliance or abject obedience < a *subservient* minor bureaucrat >

---

syn synonym(s)   *rel* related word(s)
ant antonym(s)   *con* contrasted word(s)
idiom idiomatic equivalent(s)
‖ use limited; if in doubt, see a dictionary

syn menial, obeisant, obsequious, servile, slavish

rel acquiescent, compliant, resigned, submissive; cowering, cringing, fawning, truckling; abject, ignoble, mean

idiom as obedient as a dog

con aggressive; arrogant, haughty; rebellious; independent, irrepressible, uncontainable

ant domineering, overbearing

subside *vb syn* see ABATE 4

idiom dwindle down

subsidiary *adj syn* see AUXILIARY

rel back-up; minor, tributary

subsidize *vb syn* see ENDOW 2

rel back; promote; help

subsidy *n syn* see APPROPRIATION

rel subsidization; gift, reward

subsist *vb syn* see BE

subsistence *n syn* see LIVING

substance *n* 1 *syn* see TENOR 1

rel import, meaning

idiom the general drift

2 the inner significance or central meaning of something written or said < just give me the *substance* of his speech >

syn amount, body, burden, core, crux, gist, kernel, matter, meat, nub, nubbin, pith, purport, sense, short, strength, sum and substance, sum total, thrust, upshot; *compare* BODY 3, ESSENCE 2, MEANING 1, TENOR 1

rel center, focus, heart, nucleus; point; import, meaningfulness

3 *syn* see BODY 3

rel drift, tenor

4 *syn* see ESSENCE 2

5 *syn* see THING 4

6 *syn* see WEALTH 2

substantial *adj* 1 *syn* see MATERIAL 1

con airy, ethereal

ant unsubstantial

2 *syn* see IMPORTANT 1

rel key, principal; strong; serious

3 *syn* see PROSPEROUS 3

rel solid, solvent

substantiate *vb* 1 *syn* see EMBODY 1

rel substantialize, substantify

2 *syn* see CONFIRM 2

rel demonstrate, prove, test, try

substitutable *adj syn* see INTERCHANGEABLE

substitute *n* 1 a person who takes the place of or acts instead of another < found a *substitute* for the sick teacher >

syn alternate, fill-in, locum tenens, pinch hitter, replacement, stand-in, sub, succedaneum, surrogate

rel relay, relief; deputy, procurator, proxy; supply; double, understudy

2 *syn* see RESOURCE 3

substitute *vb syn* see EXCHANGE 2

substitute *adj* 1 serving or fitted for use as a substitute < a *substitute* driver was needed for the long trip >

syn alternate, alternative, surrogate

rel additional, another; other, second; back-up, reserve; supplemental, supplementary, suppletory

2 *syn* see ARTIFICIAL 2

substract *vb syn* see DEDUCT 1

substratal *adj syn* see ELEMENTAL 1

substratum *n* **1** *syn* see BASIS 1
  rel core, meat, stuff, substance
  2 *syn* see BASE 1
substruction *n* *syn* see BASE 1
substructure *n* *syn* see BASE 1
  ant superstructure
subsume *vb* *syn* see INCLUDE
subterfuge *n* *syn* see DECEPTION 1
subterrane *n* *syn* see CAVE
subterranean *adj* being, lying, functioning, or operating under the surface of the earth < *subterranean* hot springs that emerge as geysers >
  syn subterrestrial, underearth, underfoot, underground
  con aboveground, surface, surficial
subterranean *n* *syn* see CAVE
subterrestrial *adj* *syn* see SUBTERRANEAN
subtile *adj* *syn* see THIN 2
subtle *adj* **1** *syn* see THIN 2
  2 *syn* see FINE 1
  ant unsubtle
  3 *syn* see LOGICAL 2
  rel dexterous, skillful
  con blunt; dense
  4 *syn* see SLY 2
  ant unsubtle
subtract *vb* *syn* see DEDUCT 1
  ant add
subtraction *n* *syn* see DEDUCTION 1
  ant addition
suburbs *n pl* *syn* see ENVIRONS 2
  rel fringes; suburbia
subvention *n* *syn* see APPROPRIATION
subversion *n* *syn* see SABOTAGE
  rel demolishing, destroying, destruction
subvert *vb* *syn* see SABOTAGE
  rel overthrow, overturn, upset; demolish, destroy, ruin; corrupt, debase, deprave, pervert
  con sustain, uphold
succedaneum *n* *syn* see SUBSTITUTE
succedent *adj* *syn* see CONSECUTIVE
succeed *vb* **1** *syn* see FOLLOW 1
  ant precede
  2 to result favorably according to plans and desires < that advertising campaign really *succeeded* >
  syn click, come off, go, go over, pan out, prove out
  rel catch on; prevail
  idiom go over big, go over with a bang, hit the mark, make a hit, turn out well
  ant fail, flop
  3 to attain or be attaining a desired end < how to *succeed* in big business >
  syn arrive, flourish, go, make out, prosper, score, thrive
  rel ‖dow; get ahead; boom; achieve, attain, gain, reach; accomplish, effect, fulfill; conquer, prevail, triumph, win (out)
  idiom do all right by oneself, do well, gain one's end, get places, get somewhere, get to the top of the ladder, make a success, make it (big), make one's mark, ‖make the big time, make the grade
  con dwindle, languish; fall down, flounder, founder; lose (out); bust
  ant fail
succeeding *adj* *syn* see CONSECUTIVE
succès fou *n* *syn* see SMASH 6
success *n* a succeeding fully or in accordance with one's desires < attributed his

business *success* to hard work and attention to detail >
  syn arrival, ‖do, flying colors, go, prosperity, successfulness
  rel accomplishment, achievement, attainment; triumph, victory
  ant failure; nonsuccess, unsuccessfulness
successful *adj* resulting in or having gained success < a *successful* business venture >
  syn prosperous, thriving; *compare* FLOURISHING
  rel extraordinary, notable, noteworthy, outstanding, smash, smashing
  idiom crowned (*or* blessed *or* flushed) with success, ‖out front
  con failing, thriveless, unprosperous; defeated, disappointed, failed, frustrated; bankrupt, broken, destroyed, ruined
  ant successless, unsuccessful
successfully *adv* *syn* see WELL 5
  ant unsuccessfully
successfulness *n* *syn* see SUCCESS
  ant nonsuccess, unsuccessfulness
succession *n* **1** *syn* see ORDER 5
  2 a number of things that follow each other in some order < another *succession* of price hikes >
  syn alternation, chain, consecution, course, order, progression, row, sequel, sequence, series, string, suite, train; *compare* CYCLE 1
  rel successiveness; round, round robin
successional *adj* *syn* see CONSECUTIVE
successive *adj* *syn* see CONSECUTIVE
  rel alternating, rotating
successively *adv* *syn* see TOGETHER 2
succinct *adj* *syn* see CONCISE
  rel blunt, brusque
  idiom right to the point
  ant discursive
succinctly *adv* *syn* see BRIEFLY
  ant discursively
succor *n* *syn* see HELP 1
  rel ministration, ministry; maintenance, nourishment, sustenance
succubus *n* *syn* see DEVIL 2
succulent *adj* full of juice < a *succulent* roast >
  syn juicy, ‖sappy
succumb *vb* **1** *syn* see YIELD 2
  rel abandon, relinquish, resign
  2 *syn* see FALL 3
  idiom hand over one's sword, meet one's Waterloo, show (*or* wave) the white flag, strike (*or* haul down) one's colors
  3 *syn* see COLLAPSE 2
  idiom bite the dust, ‖take the count
  4 *syn* see DIE 1
  idiom yield one's breath
such *adj* **1** being previously characterized or specified < authorized to seize illegally parked cars and impound *such* vehicles >
  syn aforementioned, aforesaid, said
  2 being of so extreme a degree or quality < *such* nonsense as I had never heard before >
  syn that
  3 *syn* see LIKE
such *pron* **1** *syn* see SUCH A ONE
  2 *syn* see SUCHLIKE
  idiom the like
such a one *pron* someone or something that has been, is being, or will be stated,

implied, or exemplified < the area is full of caverns; *such a one* may be found here>
  syn such

suchlike *adj syn* see LIKE

suchlike *pron* a person or thing of the same or similar kind < airplanes, missiles, rockets, and *suchlike* >
  syn such

‖**suck** *n syn* see SYCOPHANT

sucker *n* 1 *syn* see PARASITE
  2 *syn* see FOOL 3
  idiom easy pickings

sucker *vb syn* see CHEAT

suck in *vb syn* see DECEIVE

‖**suck-in** *n syn* see DECEPTION 1

suckle *vb syn* see NURSE 1

sudden *adj syn* see PRECIPITATE 1
  rel accelerated, quickened, speeded; expeditious, fast, fleet, rapid, swift

sudden *adv* 1 *syn* see UNAWARES
  2 *syn* see SHORT 1

suddenly *adv* 1 *syn* see SHORT 1
  2 *syn* see UNAWARES
  idiom of (*or* on) a sudden, on the sudden

suds *n pl but sing or pl in constr* 1 *syn* see SADNESS
  2 *syn* see FOAM

sue *vb syn* see ADDRESS 8
  idiom make (*or* pay) suit to, press one's suit

sue (for *or* to) *vb syn* see PETITION

suffer *vb* 1 *syn* see BEAR 10
  rel accept, admit, receive
  idiom grin and abide
  2 *syn* see EXPERIENCE 1
  3 *syn* see LET 2
  rel countenance; accept, admit, receive; acquiesce, bow, submit, yield
  ‖4 *syn* see HURT 4

sufferable *adj syn* see BEARABLE
  ant insufferable

sufferance *n syn* see PERMISSION

suffering *n syn* see DISTRESS
  rel adversity, misfortune

suffice *vb syn* see SERVE 3

sufficiency *n syn* see ENOUGH
  ant insufficiency

sufficient *adj* 1 being what is requisite or needed especially without superfluity < there is *sufficient* bread left for breakfast>
  syn adequate, comfortable, competent, decent, enough, satisfactory, sufficing; *compare* DECENT 4
  rel ample, plenteous, plentiful, plenty; commensurable, commensurate, due, proportionate; acceptable, agreeable, pleasing
  con inadequate, unsufficing; deficient; failing, lacking, missing, wanting
  ant insufficient
  2 *syn* see DECENT 4
  idiom fair to middling

sufficient *n syn* see ENOUGH

sufficiently *adv syn* see ENOUGH 1
  ant insufficiently

sufficing *adj syn* see SUFFICIENT 1

---

syn synonym(s)   *rel* related word(s)
ant antonym(s)   *con* contrasted word(s)
idiom idiomatic equivalent(s)
‖ use limited; if in doubt, see a dictionary

suffocate *vb* to stop the respiration of (as by asphyxiation) < the child was *suffocated* in an old refrigerator>
  syn asphyxiate, choke, ‖quackle, smother, stifle; *compare* CHOKE 1
  rel stive; strangle

suffocating *adj* 1 *syn* see STIFLING 1
  2 *syn* see STUFFY 1

suffocative *adj syn* see STIFLING 1

suffrage *n* the right, privilege, or power of expressing one's choice or wish (as in an election or in the determination of policy) < universal *suffrage* >
  syn ballot, franchise, vote
  rel voice

suffuse *vb syn* see INFUSE 1
  rel interject, interpose, introduce

‖**sugar** *n syn* see MONEY

sugar (over) *vb syn* see SUGARCOAT 1

sugarcoat *vb* 1 to make (something difficult or unpleasant) superficially easy or attractive < *sugarcoated* the reproach with a smile>
  syn candy, honey, sugar (over), sweeten
  rel edulcorate
  2 *syn* see PALLIATE

sugarplum *n syn* see SOP 2

suggest *vb* 1 to convey an idea indirectly < designing attractive books with jackets that truly *suggest* their contents >
  syn connote, hint, imply, insinuate, intimate; *compare* POINT 2
  rel advert, allude, refer; denote
  idiom bring to mind
  con demonstrate, display, exhibit, manifest, set out, show
  ant express
  2 *syn* see POINT 2
  rel promise
  idiom be the sign of, point in the direction of
  3 *syn* see PROPOSE 1
  4 to offer (as an idea or theory) for consideration < this, I *suggest*, is what really happened >
  syn submit, theorize
  rel conjecture; imagine
  5 to represent another thing indirectly, figuratively, and sometimes obscurely by evoking a thought, image, or conception of it < the meaning of a poem is often *suggested* in its title>
  syn adumbrate, shadow (forth); *compare* ADUMBRATE 1
  rel outline, sketch; betoken, symbolize; typify
  con display, flaunt, parade
  ant manifest

suggestion *n* 1 *syn* see PROPOSAL
  2 *syn* see HINT 1
  rel implication, innuendo
  3 *syn* see ASSOCIATION 4
  rel allusion; reminder
  con demonstration, display, exhibition, manifestation, show
  ant expression
  4 *syn* see HINT 2

suggestive *adj* 1 *syn* see EVOCATIVE
  rel significative
  2 *syn* see RISQUÉ
  rel erotic, sexy

suicide *n* the act or an instance of taking one's own life voluntarily and intention-

ally <committed *suicide* by shooting herself>
syn felo-de-se, hara-kiri, self-destruction, self-murder, self-slaughter, self-violence

suit *n* 1 a legal proceeding instituted for the sake of demanding justice or enforcing a right <filed a *suit* to recover her property>
syn action, case, cause, lawsuit
2 *syn* see PRAYER
rel asking, request, requesting, solicitation, soliciting

suit *vb* 1 *syn* see AGREE 4
idiom be in accord with, check out to the letter
2 *syn* see SERVE 3
3 *syn* see ADAPT
4 to be suitable for or to <the right word is the one that *suits* the occasion>
syn agree (with), become, befit, fit, go (together or with); compare SUIT 6
rel harmonize (with); benefit; please, satisfy
idiom answer a need (or the purpose), hit the spot
con clash, conflict, disaccord, disagree
5 *syn* see FLATTER
6 to meet the needs or desires of <this arrangement *suits* me fine>
syn please, satisfy; compare SUIT 4
con discontent, displease, dissatisfy; disappoint, fail, let down

suitability *n* *syn* see ORDER 11
ant unsuitability

suitable *adj* 1 *syn* see GOOD 2
ant unsuitable
2 *syn* see JUST 3
rel reasonable; advisable, expedient, politic
ant unsuitable
3. *syn* see FIT 1
rel nice, presentable, seemly
ant unbecoming, unsuitable
4 *syn* see ELIGIBLE
ant unsuitable

suitableness *n* *syn* see ORDER 11
ant unsuitableness

suitably *adv* *syn* see WELL 4
ant unsuitably

suite *n* 1 *syn* see ENTOURAGE
2 *syn* see GROUP 3
3 *syn* see APARTMENT 1
4 *syn* see SUCCESSION 2

suited *adj* *syn* see ASSORTED 2
ant unsuited

suitor *n* 1 *syn* see SUPPLIANT
2 one who courts a woman or seeks to marry her <a *suitor* for the king's daughter>
syn spark, sparker, swain, wooer
rel beau, boyfriend; cavalier, gallant; lover, man, paramour

sulk *vb* to be sullen or morose in mood usually because of a grievance <*sulked* all day when he didn't call>
syn ‖dort, grump, ‖mump, pet, pout, ‖sull
rel frown, glower, lower, scowl; brood, gloom, mope, take on
idiom be in a sulk, have the sulks, ‖take the dods

sulk *n.* often sulks *pl* the state, condition, or mood of one sulking <sat in a *sulk* all day after being reprimanded>

syn ‖dods, ‖dorts, grumps, mulligrubs, mumps, pouts, sullens
rel sourness, sulkiness, surliness; glumness, grouchiness
idiom a case of the sulks

sulky *adj* *syn* see SULLEN
rel cranky, testy, touchy; cantankerous, irritable, querulous
idiom having the sulks

‖**sull** *vb* *syn* see SULK

sullen *adj* showing a forbidding or disagreeable mood <stalked out in *sullen* silence>
syn ‖chuff, ‖chuffy, crabbed, crabby, ‖dorty, dour, gloomy, glum, morose, mumpish, saturnine, sulky, surly, ugly
rel moody; tenebrific, tenebrose, tenebrous; frowning, glowering, lowering, scowling; cross, fretful, grumpy, ill-humored, peevish, petulant, pouting, pouty, sour, sourpussed; black, hostile, malevolent, malicious, malign, ‖runty; cynical, pessimistic
con easy, gay, high-spirited, insouciant, lighthearted, smiling

sullens *n pl* *syn* see SULK

sully *vb* *syn* see TAINT 1
rel disgrace, shame

sulphurous *adj* *syn* see INFERNAL 1

sultry *adj* 1 *syn* see HUMID
rel smothering, smothery, ‖smudgy, stifling, suffocating
2 *syn* see STUFFY 1
3 *syn* see HOT 1
idiom hot as Hades, ‖hot as old Billy Hell
4 *syn* see SENSATIONAL 2

sum *n* 1 *syn* see WHOLE 1
2 *syn* see WHOLE 2
rel body, bulk, mass; structure
3 *syn* see SUMMARY

sum *vb* 1 *syn* see ADD 2
2 *syn* see EPITOMIZE 1

sum (to or into) *vb* *syn* see AMOUNT 1

sum and substance *n* 1 *syn* see SUBSTANCE 2
2 *syn* see MEANING 1

summarize *vb* *syn* see EPITOMIZE 1
rel recapitulate, résumé, retrograde

summary *adj* 1 *syn* see CONCISE
rel compact, compacted
ant circumstantial
2 done or executed on the spot and without formality <a *summary* trial and speedy execution>
syn drumhead

summary *n* a short restatement of the main points <a *summary* of the news>
syn epitome, recapitulation, résumé, sum, summation, summing-up, sum-up
rel outline; run-through; roundup; inventory
con amplification, elaboration, enlargement, expansion

summate *vb* 1 *syn* see ADD 2
2 *syn* see EPITOMIZE 1

summation *n* *syn* see SUMMARY

summative *adj* *syn* see CUMULATIVE

summer *n* the season between spring and autumn <liked to swim during the *summer*>
syn summertide, summertime
rel midsummer

summerhouse *n* a covered structure in a garden or park designed to provide a shady resting place <watched the sea from the *summerhouse* >
syn alcove, belvedere, garden house, gazebo, pagoda

summertide *n syn* see SUMMER

summertime *n syn* see SUMMER

summing-up *n syn* see SUMMARY

summit *n* 1 *syn* see TOP 1
2 *syn* see APEX 2

summon *vb* 1 *syn* see CONVOKE
2 to demand or request the presence or service of <were *summoned* to the principal's office>
syn call, call in, convene, summons; *compare* CONVOKE
rel bid, command, enjoin, order; cite, subpoena
idiom bid come

summons *vb syn* see SUMMON 2

‖**sump** *n syn* see SWAMP

sumptuous *adj* 1 *syn* see LUXURIOUS 3
rel gorgeous, resplendent, splendid, superb; lavish, rich
2 *syn* see GRAND 2
rel awe-inspiring, grandiose, imposing

sum total *n* 1 *syn* see WHOLE 1
2 *syn* see SUBSTANCE 2

sum up *vb syn* see EPITOMIZE 1

sum-up *n syn* see SUMMARY

sun *n* 1 the heavenly body about which the earth rotates <up in time to see the *sun* rise>
syn daystar, phoebus, Sol
rel celestial body, luminary, orb, star
idiom old Sol
2 the radiation of the sun <enjoying the warm spring *sun* >
syn sunlight, sunshine
rel daylight; radiance, radiation

sun *vb* to expose to sunshine <*sunned* himself too long and got badly burned>
syn bask, insolate
rel sunbathe; sunburn, sun-cure, sun-dry, tan

sunbeamy *adj syn* see CHEERFUL 1

Sunday best *n syn* see FINERY
idiom Sunday-go-to-meeting clothes

sunder *vb* 1 *syn* see SEPARATE 1
rel cleave, rend, rive
2 *syn* see CUT 5

‖**sundowner** *n syn* see VAGABOND

sundries *n pl* miscellaneous small articles, details, or items <supplied such *sundries* as needles, pins, and thread>
syn etceteras, oddments, odds and ends, this and that(s)
rel notions

sundry *adj syn* MANY, legion, multifarious, multitudinal, multitudinous, numerous, populous, ‖several, various, voluminous
idiom all and sundry
2 *syn* see SEVERAL 3
idiom all sorts of

sundry *pron, pl in constr* an indeterminate number of more than one or two <*sundry* were interviewed; a few were selected>

---

syn synonym(s)   *rel* related word(s)
ant antonym(s)   *con* contrasted word(s)
idiom idiomatic equivalent(s)
‖ use limited; if in doubt, see a dictionary

---

syn divers, many, ‖several, various
idiom all and sundry, quite a few

sunk *adj syn* see DOWNCAST

sunlight *n syn* see SUN 2

sunny *adj* 1 *syn* see FAIR 2
rel bright, brilliant
idiom bright and sunny
2 *syn* see CHEERFUL 1

sunrise *n syn* see DAWN 1

sunset *n syn* see EVENING 2

sunshine *n syn* see SUN 2

sunshine *adj syn* see FAIR 2

sunshining *adj syn* see FAIR 2

sunshiny *adj syn* see FAIR 2

sunup *n syn* see DAWN 1

sup (off *or* up) *vb syn* see DRINK 1

super *adj syn* see MARVELOUS 2
idiom out of this world

super *adv* 1 *syn* see VERY 1
2 *syn* see EVER 6

superabundant *adj* abounding to a great, abnormal, or excessive degree <*superabundant* harvests had brought down prices>
syn overabounding, overabundant, overflowing
rel abounding, abundant, cornucopian, plenteous, plentiful; excess, excessive, overmuch, surplus; crawling, teeming; overspilling; epidemic, rampant

superadd *vb syn* see ADD 1

superannuate *vb* 1 *syn* see OUTDATE
2 *syn* see RETIRE 2

superb *adj* 1 *syn* see GRAND 3
rel noble; majestic
2 *syn* see SPLENDID 2
rel imposing, stately; opulent
3 consummately impressive and supremely excellent of its kind <the writer's style is brilliant and his command of words and imagery, *superb*>
syn magnificent, outstanding, standout, superexcellent, superlative; *compare* SUPREME
rel gorgeous, glorious, marvelous, resplendent; crashing, rousing, sensational, slambang, super, superfine, wonderful; best, optimal, optimum, prime; sublime
idiom very best
con inferior, mediocre, poor, substandard; atrocious, awful, dreadful, shocking; deplorable, dismal, lamentable, pitiful, woeful; abominable, execrable, outrageous, shameful
ant wretched

superbity *n syn* see PRIDE 3

supercilious *adj syn* see PROUD 1
rel sniffish, sniffy, snifty, snippy, snuffy; sneering

superciliousness *n syn* see PRIDE 3

supererogant *adj* *syn* see SUPEREROGATORY

supererogative *adj* *syn* see SUPEREROGATORY

supererogatory *adj* given or done without compulsion, need, or warrant <people who offer *supererogatory* advice>
syn gratuitous, supererogant, supererogative, unasked, uncalled-for, wanton
rel nonessential, superfluous, supernumerary, unnecessary, unneeded
con essential, indispensable, vital; compulsory, obligatory; called-for, needful, required, requisite, sought, wanted

superexcellent *adj syn* see SUPERB 3
rel incomparable, matchless, unparalleled, unsurpassed

superficial *adj* 1 *syn* see SHALLOW 1
2 lacking in depth, solidity, and comprehensiveness <wrote only a *superficial* report on the situation>
syn cursory, depthless, shallow, sketchy, uncritical
rel bird's-eye, general; one-dimensional, skin-deep; smattery
con comprehensive, full, inclusive; deep, detailed, in-depth, thorough; critical
ant exhaustive

superficies *n syn* see TOP 2

superfluent *adj syn* see SUPERFLUOUS

superfluity *n* 1 *syn* see EXCESS 1
rel overflowing, swarming, teeming
2 *syn* see LUXURY

superfluous *adj* exceeding what is needed or indispensable <omitted all *superfluous* information>
syn de trop, excess, extra, recrementitious, spare, superfluent, supernumerary, surplus
rel unnecessary, unneeded, unwanted; needless, useless; dispensable, nonessential; gratuitous, supererogatory, unasked, uncalled-for
con critical, crucial, imperative; essential, fundamental, vital; consequential, important, momentous, notable, noteworthy; defective, inadequate
ant deficient

superhuman *adj* 1 *syn* see SUPERNATURAL 1
2 *syn* see SUPERNATURAL 2

superhuman *n syn* see SUPERMAN

superincumbent *adj* 1 *syn* see SUPERIOR 1
2 *syn* see ONEROUS

superintend *vb syn* see SUPERVISE

superintendence *n syn* see OVERSIGHT 1
rel direction, presidence

superintendency *n syn* see OVERSIGHT 1
rel direction, presidence

superior *adj* 1 being or regarded as being above the level of another <the new assistant received a *superior* rating for his work>
syn greater, higher, over, overlying, superincumbent, superjacent
rel major, primary, senior
con lesser, lower, nether, under
ant inferior
2 *syn* see SUPERNATURAL 1
3 *syn* see BETTER 2
ant inferior
4 being of higher quality, accomplishment, or merit <a class of *superior* students>
syn exceptional, premium; *compare* MARVELOUS 2
rel noteworthy, remarkable, unusual
con commonplace, ordinary, unexceptional, unremarkable
ant average
5 *syn* see CHOICE
6 *syn* see EXCELLENT
ant inferior
7 *syn* see PROUD 1

superior *n* one standing above another in a hierarchy of rank <was always respectful to his *superiors* in the department>

syn better, brass hat, elder, higher-up, senior
rel heavyweight
ant inferior

superiority *n syn* see BETTER 2
rel ascendancy, dominance, supremacy
ant inferiority

superjacent *adj syn* see SUPERIOR 1
ant subjacent

superlative *adj syn* see SUPERB 3
rel accomplished, consummate, finished

superman *n* a person of extraordinary power or achievement <a space program run by scientific *supermen*>
syn demigod, superhuman
idiom Triton among the minnows
con also-ran, loser, underdog
ant subhuman

supermundane *adj syn* see SUPERNATURAL 1

supernatural *adj* 1 of, relating to, or proceeding from an order of existence beyond the visible observable universe <many then believed in a *supernatural* force that directs history>
syn metaphysical, miraculous, numinous, preternatural, superhuman, superior, supermundane, suprahuman, supramundane, supranatural, unearthly
rel paranormal, rare, unusual; spiritual; celestial, heavenly; divine
2 being much more than is natural or normal <had a *supernatural* ability to win money>
syn superhuman, supernormal, superordinary, supranormal, uncanny, unnatural
rel extraordinary, outstanding, phenomenal, remarkable; paranormal
3 *syn* see EXCESSIVE 1

supernormal *adj syn* see SUPERNATURAL 2
ant subnormal

supernumerary *adj syn* see SUPERFLUOUS

superordinary *adj syn* see SUPERNATURAL 2
ant ordinary

superpatriot *n syn* see PATRIOTEER

superscribe *vb syn* see ADDRESS 6

supersede *vb syn* see REPLACE 3
rel reject, repudiate; abandon, desert, forsake; discard

superseded *adj syn* see OBSOLETE

supersensible *adj syn* see PSYCHIC 1

supersensory *adj syn* see PSYCHIC 1

supertemporal *adj syn* see INFINITE 1

supervene *vb syn* see FOLLOW 1

supervenient *adj syn* see ADVENTITIOUS

supervise *vb* to have or exercise the charge, direction, and oversight of <*supervised* the construction of the new stadium>
syn boss, chaperon, overlook, oversee, quarterback, superintend, survey
rel guide, steer; administer, conduct, direct; manage, run; control; monitor, proctor

supervision *n syn* see OVERSIGHT 1

supper club *n syn* see NIGHTCLUB

supplant *vb* 1 to supersede (another) by or as if by force, trickery, or treachery <a wife who found herself *supplanted* by another woman>

syn cut out, displace, usurp

rel crowd (out), force (out); bounce, cast (out), eject, expel, oust

idiom give the bum's rush, give the old heave-ho, step into the shoes of

2 *syn* see REPLACE 3

supple *adj* 1 *syn* see ELASTIC 1

ant stiff

2 *syn* see PLASTIC

3 showing freedom and ease of bodily movement (as in bending or twisting) <the light *supple* spring of a cat>

syn limber, lissome, lithe, lithesome

rel agile, graceful, willowy, wiry, withy

con awkward, clumsy, gawky, maladroit, unhandy; ungraceful; arthritic, creaky, decrepit

ant stiff

supplement *n* 1 *syn* see COMPLEMENT 1

2 *syn* see APPENDIX 1

suppliant *n* one who asks (as for a favor or gift) humbly <a room full of *suppliants* waiting to see the king>

syn asker, beggar, petitioner, prayer, suitor, supplicant, supplicator

rel solicitant, solicitor

supplicant *n* *syn* see SUPPLIANT

supplicate *vb* *syn* see BEG

idiom ask on bended knee, ‖come down on one's marrowbones

supplication *n* *syn* see PRAYER

supplicator *n* *syn* see SUPPLIANT

supply *vb* *syn* see GIVE 3

rel fulfill, outfit, provision

supply *n* an accumulation of something that is a source from which things may be drawn <an unending *supply* of new talent>

syn armamentarium, fund, inventory, stock, store

rel accumulation; reserve, reservoir, stockpile, surplus; hoard

supply *adj* *syn* see TEMPORARY

support *vb* 1 *syn* see BEAR 10

2 to favor actively in the face of opposition <*support* an unpopular economic policy>

syn advocate, back, backstop, champion, side (with), uphold

rel applaud, approve, endorse, favor, plunk (for), pull (for); root; adopt, embrace, espouse; defend, maintain, sustain

idiom align oneself with, be on (someone's) side, take (someone's) side

con battle, combat, counter, fight, oppose; withstand

ant buck

3 to supply what is needed for sustenance <*support* his family>

syn maintain, provide (for)

idiom boil the pot, bring home the bacon, make a living for, take care of

4 to hold up in position by serving as a foundation or base for <pillars *supporting* an arch>

syn bear up, bolster, brace, buttress, carry, prop, shore (up), sustain, upbear, uphold

rel stand

5 to keep from yielding, sinking, or losing courage or stability <her friends *supported* her during the crisis>

syn bolster, buoy (up), prop, sustain, underprop, uphold; compare ENCOURAGE 1

rel encourage; fortify, stiffen, strengthen

support *n* 1 *syn* see HELP 1

2 *syn* see HELP 2

3 a supporting means, agency, medium, or device <girders as structural *supports*> <strong economic *support* for the government>

syn brace, buttress, column, prop, shore, stay, underpinner, underpinning, underpropping

rel base, foundation; sustentation

4 *syn* see LIVING

supportable *adj* *syn* see BEARABLE

ant insupportable, unsupportable

supporter *n* 1 *syn* see FOLLOWER

2 *syn* see EXPONENT

ant antagonist

supposable *adj* *syn* see THINKABLE 2

ant insupposable

supposal *n* *syn* see THEORY 1

suppose *vb* 1 *syn* see UNDERSTAND 3

rel presuppose

2 *syn* see CONJECTURE

suppose *n* *syn* see THEORY 2

supposed *adj* 1 accepted or advanced as true or real on the basis of less than conclusive evidence <the *supposed* efficiency of the new machine>

syn conjectural, hypothetical, putative, reputed, suppositional, suppositious, supposititious, suppositive, suppository; compare ALLEGED

rel assumed, postulated, postulatory, presumed, presupposed; provisional, tentative; academic, speculative, theoretical; alleged

con sure; known, proved, proven; ascertained, demonstrated, observed, recognized

ant certain

2 *syn* see ALLEGED

ant proved, proven

supposition *n* 1 *syn* see ASSUMPTION 2

2 *syn* see THEORY 2

suppositional *adj* *syn* see SUPPOSED 1

suppositious *adj* 1 *syn* see FICTITIOUS 1

2 *syn* see SUPPOSED 1

rel doubtful, dubious, questionable; pretended, simulated

supposititious *adj* 1 *syn* see ILLEGITIMATE 1

2 *syn* see FICTITIOUS 1

3 *syn* see SUPPOSED 1

supposititiousness *n* *syn* see ILLEGITIMACY 1

suppositive *adj* *syn* see SUPPOSED 1

suppository *adj* *syn* see SUPPOSED 1

suppress *vb* 1 *syn* see CRUSH 5

idiom ride roughshod over

2 to hold back more or less forcefully someone or something that seeks an outlet <management tried to *suppress* the workers' discontent> <there was no way to *suppress* her short of murder>

syn muffle, ‖quelch, repress, shush, squelch, strangle; compare CRUSH 5

---

syn synonym(s)   *rel* related word(s)
ant antonym(s)   *con* contrasted word(s)
idiom idiomatic equivalent(s)
‖ use limited; if in doubt, see a dictionary

rel curb, restrain; arrest, check, interrupt; put down, slap down; quash, quell, squash; cut off, spike; abolish, annihilate, extinguish
idiom bring to naught, crack (*or* clamp) down on, put the kibosh on
3 to keep from public knowledge < *suppress* all news from the front >
syn burke, hush (up), stifle
rel repress; censor; silence
idiom put the lid on
con disclose, divulge, leak, ||let out, reveal; broadcast, circulate, diffuse, publish, spread
4 *syn* see COMPOSE 4
rel drown; swallow
5 *syn* see STUNT

suppression *n* **1** *syn* see REPRESSION 1
2 *syn* see REPRESSION 2

supra *adv syn* see ABOVE 2
ant infra

suprahuman *adj syn* see SUPERNATURAL

supramundane *adj syn* see SUPERNATURAL 1

supranatural *adj syn* see SUPERNATURAL 1

supranormal *adj syn* see SUPERNATURAL 2

supremacy *n* the position of being first (as in rank, power, or influence) < Britain once enjoyed *supremacy* on the seas >
syn ascendancy, ascendant, dominance, domination, dominion, masterdom, preeminence, preponderance, preponderancy, preponderation, prepotence, prepotency, sovereignty
rel authority, control, driver's seat, power, sway; mastership, mastery, principality, superiority; transcendence

supreme *adj* developed to the utmost and not exceeded by any other in degree, quality, or intensity < dying for one's principles is an example of *supreme* sacrifice >
syn incomparable, preeminent, surpassing, towering, transcendent, ultimate, unequalable, unmatchable, unsurpassable; *compare* ALONE 3, EXCELLENT, MARVELOUS 2, MAXIMUM, SUPERB 3
rel crowning, master, sovereign; unequaled, unmatched, unparalleled, unrivaled, unsurpassed; final, last; absolute, perfect

surcease *vb syn* see STOP 3

sure *adj* **1** firmly settled or established < trying to find a *sure* footing on the rugged slope >
syn fast, firm, secure, stable, staunch, strong; *compare* FAST 4, STABLE 4
2 free from doubt, hesitation, or fear < upheld a *sure* faith >
syn abiding, enduring, firm, fixed, never-failing, steadfast, steady, unfaltering, unqualified, unquestioning, unshakable, unshaken, unwavering, wholehearted
rel assured, changeless, constant, unchangeable, unchanging, uncompromising, unfailing, unvarying; certain, fixed, set
con insecure, uncertain, unreliable, feeble, infirm, shaky, unsound; doubtful, dubious, hesitant
ant unsure
3 *syn* see INFALLIBLE 1

4 *syn* see INFALLIBLE 2
5 marked by unwavering assurance especially as to the rightness of one's views or actions < was *sure* he knew the answer >
syn certain, cocksure, confident, positive
rel assured, self-assured, self-possessed, self-satisfied; arrogant, cocky, pert; decided, decisive
con doubtful, hesitant, uncertain
ant unsure
6 *syn* see POSITIVE 3
rel convincing, telling; absolute, definite; genuine, real, valid

sure-enough *adj* **1** *syn* see ACTUAL 2
2 *syn* see AUTHENTIC 2

surefire *adj syn* see INFALLIBLE 2

sureness *n syn* see CERTAINTY
ant unsureness

sure thing *n* one that is bound to be successful < was deemed a *sure thing* in the race >
syn shoo-in
rel certainty; winner

surety *n* **1** *syn* see CERTAINTY
2 *syn* see GUARANTEE 1
3 *syn* see SPONSOR

surface *n syn* see TOP 2
rel exterior, outside; cover, covering
con body, mass; inside, interior; lining

surface *vb* to come to the surface (as of water) < a submarine *surfaced* outside the harbor >
syn rise
rel come up
con go down, go under; submerge; dive

surfeit *n syn* see EXCESS 1

surfeit *vb syn* see SATIATE
rel overfill, overindulge
idiom have all one can take (*or* stand)
ant whet

surfeited *adj syn* see SATIATED
ant unsatisfied

surge *vb syn* see POUR 2

surly *adj syn* see SULLEN
rel discourteous, ill-mannered, rude, ungracious; bearish, boorish, churlish; fractious, irritable, snappish, waspish
idiom as surly as a bear
con affable, cordial, genial, gracious
ant amiable

surmise *vb syn* see CONJECTURE
rel consider, regard; hypothesize, theorize
idiom risk assuming, venture a guess

surmount *vb* **1** *syn* see OVERCOME 1
rel best, better, outdo, outstrip, outtop, outtower, surpass
idiom rise superior to
2 *syn* see CLEAR 8
3 to stand or lie at the top of < a cross *surmounts* the cupola >
syn cap, crest, crown, top
rel finish; terminate
4 *syn* see TOP

surpass *vb* **1** to be or become greater than or superior to < *surpassed* all his fellows in scholarship >
syn ||bang, beat, best, better, cap, cob, ding, exceed, excel, outdo, outgo, outmatch, outshine, outstrip, pass, top, transcend, trump
rel distance, outdistance, outpace, outperform, outpoint, outrange, outrival, outrun, outvie; eclipse, outrank, outtop, outtower, outweigh, overshadow, overtop, rank

idiom have it all over, put to shame
2 *syn* see EXCEED 1

surpassing *adj syn* see SUPREME

surpassingly *adv syn* see VERY 1

surplus *n* 1 *syn* see EXCESS 1
ant deficiency
2 *syn* see EXCESS 2
ant shortage

surplus *adj syn* see SUPERFLUOUS

surplusage *n* 1 *syn* see EXCESS 2
ant shortage, underage
2 *syn* see EXCESS 1
ant shortage

surprise *vb* 1 to attack unawares < hijackers *surprised* the truck driver and took his cargo >
syn ambush, lay (for), waylay
rel bushwhack, dry-gulch; capture, catch; grab, grasp, seize, take
2 to impress forcibly through unexpectedness, startlingness, or unusualness < was *surprised* by his violent jealousy >
syn amaze, astonish, astound, dumbfound, flabbergast
rel startle; bewilder, confound, discomfit, disconcert, dismay, nonplus, ‖swan; faze, rattle, rock; bowl (over), floor, stagger; stun, stupefy
idiom leave open-mouthed (*or* aghast), take aback (*or* by surprise)

surprising *adj syn* see MARVELOUS 1
rel unexpected, unforeseen, unlooked-for; eye-opening, eye-popping

surrender *vb* 1 *syn* see RELINQUISH
rel commit, consign, entrust
2 *syn* see FALL 3
rel give in, give up
idiom haul down one's colors, strike the (*or* one's) flag

surrender *n* the yielding of one's person, forces, or possessions to another < the victors demanded unconditional *surrender* >
syn capitulation, dedition, submission
rel appeasement, Munich; relenting, succumbing, yielding; white flag

surreptitious *adj syn* see SECRET 1
rel skulking, slinking, slinky, sneaking, sneaky
con obvious, open, overt
ant brazen

surreptitiously *adv syn* see SECRETLY
con openly, overtly, plainly
ant brazenly

surrogate *n* 1 *syn* see SUBSTITUTE
2 *syn* see RESOURCE 3

surrogate *adj syn* see SUBSTITUTE 1

surround *vb* 1 to close in or as if in a ring about something < a crowd *surrounded* the accident victim >
syn begird, beset, circle, compass, encircle, encompass, environ, gird, girdle, hem, loop, ring, round
rel embosom, enclave, enclose, envelop; circumscribe, circumvent, confine, limit
2 *syn* see BORDER 1

surroundings *n pl syn* see ENVIRONMENT

surveillance *n* 1 *syn* see EYE 3

---

syn synonym(s)   *rel* related word(s)
ant antonym(s)   *con* contrasted word(s)
idiom idiomatic equivalent(s)
‖ use limited; if in doubt, see a dictionary

---

idiom peeled eye
2 *syn* see LOOKOUT 3
rel surveyance
idiom watchful (*or* weather) eye

survey *vb* 1 *syn* see ESTIMATE 1
rel measure, size, size up
2 *syn* see SUPERVISE
3 to view from or as if from a high place or position < *surveyed* the view from his penthouse window >
syn overlook, oversee
4 *syn* see SCRUTINIZE 1

survey *n* 1 *syn* see EXAMINATION
2 *syn* see COMPENDIUM 1

‖**survigrous** *adj syn* see VIGOROUS

survive *vb* 1 *syn* see OUTLIVE
2 to continue to exist or function in spite of a usually adverse condition or development < a company that managed to *survive* the recession >
syn come through, pull through, ride (out)
rel carry on, carry through, continue, endure, last, persist; live down, outlast, outlive; recover, revive
idiom come out of it, live to fight again, make it through, ride out (*or* weather) the storm
con collapse, crash, fold, fold up, go down, go under; founder, sink; close (down), close up; bankrupt, bust
ant perish

susceptible *adj* 1 *syn* see LIABLE 2
rel disposed, inclined, predisposed
ant immune, unsusceptible
2 *syn* see EASY 3
rel nonresistant, soft; movable, persuadable
ant unsusceptible
3 *syn* see SENTIENT 3
rel affected, impressed, influenced, swayed, touched; aroused, roused, stirred
ant unsusceptible

susceptive *adj syn* see SENTIENT 3

suscitate *vb syn* see PROVOKE 4

suspect *adj syn* see DOUBTFUL 1
idiom ‖a bit thin (*or* thick), open to suspicion

suspect *vb* 1 *syn* see DISTRUST
idiom have doubts about
2 *syn* see UNDERSTAND 3
idiom be inclined to think

suspend *vb* 1 *syn* see EXCLUDE
2 *syn* see DEFER
rel arrest, check, interrupt; cease, discontinue, stop
idiom lay on the table, put on the shelf
3 *syn* see HANG 1

suspended *adj* hung or seeming as if hung from a support < bunches of grapes *suspended* from the vines >
syn hanging, pendent, pendulant, pendulous, pensile
rel dangling, swinging

suspenders *n pl* a pair of supporting bands worn across the shoulders to support trousers, skirt, or belt < *suspenders* are out of style>
syn braces, ‖gallows, ‖galluses

suspense *n syn* see SUSPENSION 2

suspension *n* 1 *syn* see ABEYANCE
2 a temporary withholding of action or cessation of activity < asked for *suspension*

of judgment until all the evidence was in >
   syn moratorium, suspense
   rel cessation, concluding, conclusion, end, ending, finish, period, termination
   con resumption; continuance

suspicion *n* 1 *syn* see UNCERTAINTY
   rel apprehension, foreboding, misgiving, presentiment; distrust
   2 *syn* see HINT 2

‖**suspicion** *vb syn* see DISTRUST

suspicious *adj* 1 *syn* see DOUBTFUL 1
   rel questionable; queer
   2 given or prone to suspicion < was *suspicious* of everyone's motives >
   syn distrustful, jealous, mistrustful
   rel careful, cautious; leery, wary, watchful; skeptical, unbelieving
   con trustful, trusting, unsuspecting; naive; dupable, easy, exploitable, gullible
   ant unsuspicious

suspiciously *adv syn* see ASKANCE 2
   rel distrustingly, mistrustingly
   ant unsuspiciously

suspire *vb* 1 *syn* see SIGH 1
   idiom draw a long breath
   2 *syn* see LONG

sustain *vb* 1 *syn* see MAINTAIN 1
   rel nourish, support; prolong
   2 *syn* see SUPPORT 4
   rel lug, pack, tote
   3 *syn* see SUPPORT 5
   rel befriend, favor
   idiom stand by
   con abandon, forsake; ignore
   4 *syn* see BEAR 10
   5 *syn* see EXPERIENCE 1
   rel bear, endure

sustainable *adj syn* see BEARABLE
   ant unsustainable

sustenance *n* 1 *syn* see FOOD 2
   idiom bodily sustenance
   2 *syn* see LIVING

sustentation *n syn* see PRESERVATION 1

susurration *n syn* see MURMUR 1

‖**swack** *n syn* see CUFF

‖**swacked** *adj syn* see INTOXICATED 1

swad *n syn* see SOLDIER

swaddle *vb syn* see SWATHE
   rel ‖sweel
   ant unswaddle

‖**swaddy** *n syn* see SOLDIER

swag *vb* 1 *syn* see SEESAW
   2 *syn* see DROOP 3

swag *n* 1 *syn* see SPOIL
   2 *syn* see MONEY

swagger *vb* 1 *syn* see LORD
   rel swash, swashbuckle
   2 *syn* see STRUT 2
   rel bluster, brandish, flourish
   con blench, quail; shrink, wince; truckle

‖**swagger** *n syn* see VAGABOND

‖**swagman** *n syn* see VAGABOND

swain *n* 1 *syn* see BOYFRIEND 1
   2 *syn* see SUITOR 2

swainish *adj syn* see BOORISH

swallow *vb* 1 to receive through the esophagus into the stomach < *swallowed* the pills easily with a sip of water >
   syn down, take
   rel drop, gulp, ‖quilt, toss; ingest, ingurgitate
   2 *syn* see DRINK 1

3 *syn* see BELIEVE 1
   idiom swallow (something) hook, line, and sinker
   4 *syn* see BEAR 10
   5 *syn* see ACCEPT 2
   6 *syn* see MUMBLE

swamp *n* wet spongy land saturated and sometimes partially covered with water < hunted alligators in the Florida *swamps* >
   syn baygall, bog, ‖fen, marsh, marshland, mire, morass, ‖moss, muskeg, ‖purgatory, ‖puxy, quag, quagmire, slough, ‖sump, swampland, ‖swang, ‖vlei
   rel bottoms, ‖holm; ‖glade; ‖heel; quake ooze; shaking prairie, trembling prairie

swamp *vb* 1 *syn* see DELUGE 1
   2 *syn* see DELUGE 3

swampland *n syn* see SWAMP

‖**swang** *n syn* see SWAMP

swank *vb syn* see LORD

swank *adj* 1 *syn* see SHOWY
   2 *syn* see STYLISH

swap *vb* 1 *syn* see EXCHANGE 2
   2 *syn* see TRADE 1
   idiom ‖swap horses, swap out of

‖**swap** *n syn* see BLOW 1

‖**swapping** *adj syn* see HUGE

‖**swart** *vb syn* see FAINT

swarm *vb syn* see TEEM
   idiom gather (or swarm) like bees

swarming *adj syn* see ALIVE 5

swart *adj syn* see DARK 3

swarth *adj syn* see DARK 3

swarthy *adj syn* see DARK 3

swash *vb* 1 *syn* see SLOSH 1
   2 *syn* see SPLASH

swashy *adj syn* see INSIPID 3

swat *vb* ‖1 *syn* see SQUAT
   2 *syn* see STRIKE 2
   rel blip, box, buffet, cuff, smack; belt, clobber, slug, smash, wallop

swat *n syn* see HIT 1

swathe *vb* to cover or bind completely with clothing or material < legs *swathed* in bandages > < the baby was *swathed* in a warm shawl >
   syn drape, enswathe, envelop, enwrap, roll, swaddle, wrap (up); compare ENFOLD 1
   rel enfold; encase; cover
   con bare, denude, expose, strip, uncover, unswaddle, unwrap
   ant unswathe

sway *vb* 1 *syn* see SWING 2
   2 *syn* see LURCH 2
   3 *syn* see GOVERN 1
   4 *syn* see AFFECT
   rel bias, dispose, incline, predispose; conduct, control, direct, manage; govern, rule

sway *n syn* see POWER 1
   rel range, reach, scope, sweep; amplitude, expanse, spread, stretch

swayable *adj syn* see RECEPTIVE 1

swear *vb* 1 *syn* see VOW
   idiom swear on a stack of Bibles, swear to God, swear up and down
   2 *syn* see TESTIFY 2
   3 to use profane, blasphemous, or obscene language < *swore* when the horse threw him >
   syn bedamn, curse, cuss, damn, execrate, imprecate

rel blaspheme; rail, rant; abuse, revile, vilify, vituperate

idiom ||chew the dirty rag, curse and swear, fall a-cursing, ||let out religion, make the air blue, пp (*or* rap) out an oath, swear like a sailor (*or* trooper), use language

swear *n syn* see SWEARWORD

swearing *n syn* see BLASPHEMY 1

swearword *n* a profane, blasphemous, or obscene word <let loose with a string of *swearwords*>

syn curse, cuss, cussword, expletive, oath, swear

rel four-letter word, obscenity, scurrility

idiom blue word, one-horse oath, raw one, ripe (*or* juicy) word, sailor's blessing, six-cornered oath, strong word

sweat *vb* 1 *syn* see EXUDE

2 *syn* see FLEECE 1

sweat *n* 1 *syn* see WORK 2

2 *syn* see SNIT

||3 *syn* see SOLDIER

sweatful *adj syn* see SWEATY

sweating *adj syn* see SWEATY

sweat out *vb syn* see BEAR 10

sweaty *adj* producing, accompanied by, or characterized by sweat <he still held the racket tight in *sweaty* hands>

syn asweat, perspiring, perspiry, ||puggy, sweatful, sweating

rel clammy; sticky; wet

idiom bathed in sweat, covered with sweat, drenched with (*or* in) sweat, in a muck of a sweat, wet with sweat (*or* perspiration)

sweep *vb syn* see FLY 4

sweep *n syn* see RANGE 2

sweeping *n* sweepings *pl syn* see REFUSE

sweeping *adj* 1 *syn* see ALL-AROUND 2

rel all-embracing, all-encompassing

2 *syn* see INDISCRIMINATE 1

rel all-out, out-and-out, whole-hog; across-the-board, blanket

sweet *adj* 1 distinctly pleasing or charming <a *sweet* smile>

syn dulcet, engaging, winning, winsome

rel agreeable, pleasant, pleasing; beautiful, fair, lovely; delectable, delicious, delightful, luscious; angelic, heavenly

con disagreeable, unpleasant; displeasing, obnoxious, repulsive

ant bitter

2 having a pleasant smell <the *sweet* odor of flowers and incense>

syn ambrosial, aromal, aromatic, balmy, fragrant, perfumed, perfumy, redolent, savory, scented, spicy; *compare* ODOROUS

rel clean, fresh; sweetish

con funky, fusty, musty, noisome, putrid, rancid, rotten, stale, stinking, strong, whiffy; fetid, foul, olid, rank, smelly

ant malodorous

3 *syn* see MELODIOUS 1

sweet *n syn* see SWEETHEART 1

sweeten *vb* 1 *syn* see PACIFY

2 *syn* see SUGARCOAT 1

sweetheart *n* 1 one who is dearly beloved — often used as a term of endearment

<was her childhood *sweetheart*> < *sweetheart*, you know I'll wait>

syn beloved, darling, dear, flame, heartthrob, honey, honeybunch, love, loveling, sweet, sweetling, turtledove

rel ||cutie pie, deary, pigsney; pet, puggy

2 *syn* see GIRL FRIEND 2

rel doll baby, lovey-dovey, ||tootsie

3 *syn* see BOYFRIEND 2

rel paramour; ||dreamboat

sweetheart *vb syn* see ADDRESS 8

sweetie *n syn* see GIRL FRIEND 2

rel sweetie pie

sweetling *n syn* see SWEETHEART 1

sweetness and light *n syn* see AMENITY 1

sweet-talk *vb syn* see COAX

swell *vb* 1 *syn* see EXPAND 3

rel balloon, belly, bloat, blow up, bosom; pouch, pout; overblow

con compress, condense, constrict, contract

ant shrink

2 *syn* see LORD

rel puff

idiom act the grand seigneur, swell it

swell *n syn* see EXPERT

swell *adj syn* see MARVELOUS 2

swelled head *n syn* see CONCEIT 2

swellheadedness *n syn* see CONCEIT 2

swelling *adj syn* see RHETORICAL

||**swelt** *vb* 1 *syn* see DIE 1

2 *syn* see FAINT

swelter *vb syn* see BURN 3

sweltering *adj syn* see HOT 1

idiom ||hot as the hinges of hell

ant frigid

sweltry *adj syn* see HOT 1

swerve *vb* 1 to turn or be turned away abruptly from a straight line or course < *swerved* the car to avoid collision>

syn dip, sheer, skew, slue, train off, veer

2 to be deflected from a fixed or right course of action or conduct <never *swerved* from the concept of duty, honor, country>

syn depart, deviate, digress, diverge

rel shift; waver; err, stray, wander

idiom deviate from the straight and narrow, get off the proper course (*or* path)

swift *adj syn* see FAST 3

rel headlong, precipitate, sudden; double-quick; supersonic

ant sluggish

swift *adv syn* see FAST 2

ant sluggishly

swiften *vb syn* see SPEED 3

swiftly *adv syn* see FAST 2

con slowly

ant sluggishly

swiftness *n* 1 *syn* see SPEED 2

ant sluggishness

2 *syn* see HASTE 1

ant slowness

swig *n syn* see DRINK 3

swig *vb syn* see DRINK 3

swill *vb* 1 *syn* see DRINK 3

2 *syn* see CONSUME 5

swill *n* 1 *syn* see REFUSE

2 *syn* see DRINK 3

swillbowl *n syn* see DRUNKARD

swiller *n syn* see DRUNKARD

swim *vb syn* see SPIN 2

---

syn synonym(s)	*rel* related word(s)	
ant antonym(s)	*con* contrasted word(s)	
idiom idiomatic equivalent(s)		
|| use limited; if in doubt, see a dictionary		

idiom have one's head swim

swimming *adj syn* see DIZZY 2
   rel fluctuating, swaying, wavering
swimmingly *adv syn* see WELL 5
swimmy *adj syn* see DIZZY 2
swindle *vb syn* see CHEAT
   rel rogue; victimize
   idiom sell one a bill of goods, take for a ride, take for a sucker
swindle *n syn* see IMPOSTURE
swindler *n* one who defrauds usually of money and especially by imposture or by gaining the victim's confidence <lost their savings to *swindlers* in a get-rich-quick scheme>
   syn bunco steerer, cheat, cheater, chiaus, come-on, confidence man, con man, defrauder, diddler, double-dealer, flimflammer, ‖grifter, gyp, gypper, ‖mace, mountebank, Peter Funk, rogue, sharper, sharpie, skin, slicker, ‖spieler, trickster
   rel bilk, bilker, blackleg, charlatan, chiseler, crook, deceiver, dodger, fraud, gouger, harpy, highbinder, hoaxer, operator, rook, shark, sharp, sharpster, tricker; scoundrel
swing *vb* 1 *syn* see HANDLE 2
   2 to move rhythmically to and fro, up and down, or back and forth <the clock's pendulum *swung* slowly>
   syn oscillate, pendulate, sway
   rel undulate, wave; rock, roll; revolve, rotate, switch, wheel; jiggle, wag, waggle, wiggle, wigwag
   3 *syn* see TURN 6
   4 *syn* see LURCH 2
swing *n* 1 *syn* see RHYTHM
   2 *syn* see HANG
‖**swingeing** *adj syn* see EXCELLENT
swinish *adj syn* see BRUTISH
swipe *n syn* see HIT 1
swipe *vb syn* see STEAL 1
swirl *vb* to move swiftly in circles, eddies, or undulations <water *swirled* into the storm drains>
   syn eddy, gurge, purl, swoosh, whirl, whirlpool, whorl
   rel boil, roil; gush, surge
swish *vb syn* see HISS
swish *adj syn* see STYLISH
switch *vb* 1 *syn* see WAG
   2 *syn* see EXCHANGE 2
   3 *syn* see SHUNT 1
‖**swither** *vb syn* see RUSH 1
swivet *n syn* see SNIT
swizzle *vb syn* see DRINK 3
swollen *adj syn* see RHETORICAL
swoon *vb syn* see FAINT
   rel die away, drown
swoon *n syn* see FAINT
swoosh *vb syn* see SWIRL
sworn *adj syn* see INVETERATE 1
sybarite *n syn* see HEDONIST
sybaritic *adj* marked by or given to luxury or voluptuous living <the *sybaritic* grandeur of a sultan's harem> <a man of *sybaritic* and self-indulgent habits>
   syn hedonistic, onanistic, self-indulgent, sybaritical, sybaritish; *compare* SENSUOUS
   rel apolaustic, pleasure-loving; epicurean, luxurious; carnal, sensual, voluptuous
sybaritical *adj syn* see SYBARITIC
sybaritish *adj syn* see SYBARITIC

sycophancy *n syn* see DETRACTION
sycophant *n* a base or servilely attentive flatterer and self-seeker <*sycophants* who slavishly curried favor with the king>
   syn apple-polisher, bootlick, bootlicker, ‖brownnose, ‖brownnoser, ‖clawback, creature, ‖easy rider, footlicker, groveler, lickspit, lickspittle, minion, reptile, spaniel, ‖suck, toad, toadeater, toadier, toady, truckler, yes-man; *compare* PARASITE
   rel flunky, gopher, lackey, slave, stooge; flatterer, self-seeker; snob, tuft-hunter
sycophant *adj syn* see FAWNING
sycophantic *adj syn* see FAWNING
sycophantical *adj syn* see FAWNING
sycophantish *adj syn* see FAWNING
syllable *n syn* see PARTICLE
syllabus *n syn* see COMPENDIUM 1
sylloge *n syn* see COMPENDIUM 1
symbol *n* 1 something that stands for something else by reason of relationship, association, convention, or accidental resemblance <the lion is often used as a *symbol* of courage>
   syn attribute, emblem; *compare* INDICATION 3
   rel indication, token, type; badge, mark, note, sign, stamp; character, design, device, figure, motif, pattern; representation
   2 *syn* see CHARACTER 1
symbolism *n syn* see ALLEGORY 1
symbolization *n syn* see ALLEGORY 1
symbolize *vb syn* see REPRESENT 2
symmetrical *adj syn* see PROPORTIONAL
symmetry *n* beauty of form or arrangement arising from balanced proportions <the superb *symmetry* of the design>
   syn balance, harmony, proportion
   rel arrangement, order; agreement, conformity; equality, evenness, regularity; rhythm; finish
   con asymmetry, dissymmetry; disproportion, imbalance, irregularity, unbalance
sympathetic *adj* 1 *syn* see CONSONANT 1
   ant unsympathetic
   2 favorably inclined <found his hearers *sympathetic* to his proposal>
   syn friendly, receptive, ‖sib, well-disposed
   rel agreeable, congenial, favorable; amenable, open, open-minded, receptive, responsive
   con ill-disposed, unfriendly, unreceptive; cool, indifferent, lukewarm; neutral
   ant unsympathetic
   3 *syn* see TENDER
   rel benign, benignant, kind, kindly; appreciating, comprehending, understanding
   ant unsympathetic
sympathize (with) *vb syn* see COMPASSIONATE
   rel appreciate, comprehend, understand
sympathy *n* 1 *syn* see ATTRACTION 2
   ant antipathy
   2 a feeling for or a capacity for sharing in the interests of another <he was in *sympathy* with her desire to succeed>
   syn compassion, empathy, fellow feeling
   rel responsiveness, sensitivity; feelings, heart; tenderness, warmheartedness, warmth; benignancy, benignness, kindliness, kindness
   con disinterest, unconcern
   3 *syn* see PITY

symphonic *adj syn* see HARMONIOUS 1

symphonious *adj syn* see HARMONIOUS 1

symphonize *vb syn* see HARMONIZE 4

symphony *n syn* see ORCHESTRA
rel concert band, symphony band; symphony orchestra

symptom *n syn* see INDICATION 3

synchronal *adj syn* see CONTEMPORARY 1

synchronic *adj syn* see CONTEMPORARY 1

synchronous *adj syn* see CONTEMPORARY 1

syncope *n syn* see FAINT

syndicate *n* a combination of interlocked companies or enterprises <a large newspaper *syndicate*>
syn cartel, chain, combine, conglomerate, group, pool, trust
rel association, organization; partnership, union

syndrome *n syn* see DISEASE 1

synergetic *adj syn* see COOPERATIVE
ant counteractive

synergic *adj syn* see COOPERATIVE
ant counteractive

synopsis *n syn* see ABRIDGMENT

synopsize *vb syn* see EPITOMIZE 1
idiom hit the high spots, put it in a nutshell

synthesize *vb syn* see HARMONIZE 4

synthetic *adj* formed or developed by human art, skill, or effort and not by natural processes <*synthetic* plastics>
syn artificial, factitious, man-made; *compare* ARTIFICIAL 2
rel manufactured; constructed, fabricated, made
con natural

syrupy *adj syn* see SENTIMENTAL

system *n* 1 an organized integrated whole made up of diverse but interrelated and interdependent parts <the capitalist *system*>
syn complex; *compare* WHOLE 2
rel aggregation, array; mesh, network; arrangement, disposition, scheme, setup; order, pattern
con disorganization; chaos
2 *syn* see WHOLE 2
3 *syn* see ORDER 8
rel proceeding, procedure, process
4 *syn* see METHOD 1

systematic *adj syn* see ORDERLY 1
rel arranged, ordered, organized, systematized; analytical, logical
con disorganized; chaotic
ant unsystematic

systematize *vb syn* see ORDER 1
rel contrive, frame
con confuse, disorder, jumble

T

tab *n* 1 *syn* see EYE 3
2 *syn* see BILL 1
3 *syn* see CHECK 2
4 *syn* see PRICE 1

tabby *n* 1 *syn* see GOSSIP 1
‖2 *syn* see SPINSTER

tabernacle *n syn* see HOUSE OF WORSHIP

table *n* 1 a piece of furniture on which food is customarily served <a feast on the *table*>
syn board, dining table, dinner table, mahogany, ‖table-board
rel bar, buffet, counter, sideboard
2 a condensed ordered enumeration of items usually arranged in columns <a *table* of weights and measures>
syn chart, tabulation
rel list; diagram
3 *syn* see PLATEAU

‖**table-board** *n syn* see TABLE 1

tableland *n syn* see PLATEAU

tabloid *adj syn* see SENSATIONAL 2

taboo *n* a restraint imposed by social usage or as a protective measure <a society rife with antiquated moral *taboos*>
syn ban, forbiddance, interdiction, prohibition, proscription
rel inhibition, limitation, reservation, restraint, restriction; regulation, sanction; don't
con acceptance, toleration; approval, authorization, permission, permit, permittance

taboo *vb syn* see FORBID

tabulation *n syn* see TABLE 2

tacit *adj* 1 expressed or conveyed without words, speech, or forthright reference <they made a *tacit* agreement to work together>
syn implicit, implied, inarticulate, inferred, undeclared, understood, unexpressed, unsaid, unspoken, unuttered, wordless
rel alluded (to), hinted (at), intimated, suggested; assumed
con expressed, spoken, verbal; categorical, explicit, express, unequivocal
2 *syn* see UNSPOKEN 1

taciturn *adj syn* see SILENT 3
rel laconic, unexpressive; brooding, dour
con chatty, communicative, loquacious, talkative; convivial, uninhibited, unreserved, unrestrained
ant garrulous

tack *n syn* see TURN 2
rel alteration; digression, tangent; swerve, zigzag

tackle *n syn* see EQUIPMENT

tackle *vb syn* see ATTACK 2
rel take on, undertake; plunge into, set about
idiom get on the job, put one's shoulder to the wheel, start the ball rolling

---

syn synonym(s)   *rel* related word(s)
ant antonym(s)   *con* contrasted word(s)
idiom idiomatic equivalent(s)
‖ use limited; if in doubt, see a dictionary

con avoid, delay, hesitate, put off

tackling *n syn see* EQUIPMENT

tacky *adj* 1 *syn see* SHABBY 1
rel dowdy, outmoded, unstylish; messy, sloppy, slovenly, unkempt, untidy; blowsy, frowzy, frumpish
idiom gone to seed
2 marked by a lack of style or good taste <an old *tacky* scarf spoiled her outfit>
syn dowdy, frumpish, frumpy, outmoded, out-of-date, stodgy, unstylish
rel unbecoming; crude, inelegant, tasteless; incorrect, unsuitable; cheap, gaudy
con ‖mod, modern, modish, smart, stylish, tasteful; elegant

tact *n* skill and grace in dealing with others <handled the embarrassing situation with great *tact*>
syn address, delicatesse, diplomacy, poise, savoir faire, tactfulness; *compare* ADDRESS 1
rel control, head, presence, repose; amenity, courtesy, gallantry; policy, politicness, smoothness, suavity, urbanity; adroitness, deftness, skill; acumen, finesse, perception, sensitivity
con abruptness, bluntness, coarseness, discourtesy, rudeness
ant tactlessness

tactful *adj* marked by or exhibiting tact <his *tactful* skill in handling negotiations>
syn delicate, diplomatic, politic, tactical; *compare* SUAVE
rel polished, suave, urbane; adroit, deft, skilled, skillful; perceptive, sensitive
con clumsy, unpolished, unskilled; discourteous, impolite, rude; undiplomatic
ant blunt, tactless, untactful

tactfulness *n syn see* TACT
rel civility, civilness, politeness; polish
ant tactlessness

tactic *adj syn see* TACTILE 2

tactical *adj* 1 made or carried out with only a limited or immediate end in view <had time only for *tactical* decisions and not strategic planning>
syn short-range
con long-range
ant strategic
2 *syn see* EXPEDIENT
3 *syn see* TACTFUL

tactile *adj* 1 *syn see* TANGIBLE 1
2 of or relating to the sense of touch <*tactile* responses>
syn tactic, tactual

tactility *n syn see* TOUCH 3

taction *n syn see* TOUCH 3

tactless *adj* marked by a lack of tact <his *tactless* remark hurt her>
syn brash, impolitic, maladroit, undiplomatic, unpolitic, untactful
rel impolite, inconsiderate, indelicate, rude; bungling, inept
con diplomatic, polite, tactical
ant tactful

tactual *adj syn see* TACTILE 2

tad *n syn see* BOY 1

tag *n* 1 *syn see* COMMONPLACE
2 *syn see* TICKET 2

tag *vb syn see* TAIL

tag and rag *n syn see* RABBLE 2

tag end *n syn see* TAIL END 2

tagrag *adj syn see* SHABBY 1

tagrag and bobtail *n syn see* RABBLE 2

tail *n syn see* BUTTOCKS

tail *vb* to follow (someone) for purposes of surveillance <detectives *tailing* the suspects>
syn bedog, dog, shadow, tag, trail; *compare* EYE 2, FOLLOW 2
rel hound, pursue

tail end *n* 1 *syn see* BUTTOCKS
2 the hindmost end of something <watched the *tail end* of the parade march off>
syn tag end

tailor *vb syn see* ADAPT
rel style; dovetail; shape up

tailor-made *adj syn see* CUSTOM-MADE

tailor-make *vb syn see* ADAPT

taint *vb* 1 to touch or affect with something bad or undesirable <his good reputation was *tainted* by the scandal>
syn besmear, besmirch, blur, cloud, defile, dirty, discolor, smear, smudge, smut, smutch, soil, stain, sully, tar, tarnish; *compare* CONTAMINATE 1
rel discredit; brand, stigmatize; blacken; damage, harm, hurt
idiom cast a slur upon; give a bad name to, give a black mark to
con brighten, cleanse, clear
2 *syn see* DECAY
rel befoul, contaminate, foul
3 *syn see* CONTAMINATE 1

taintless *adj syn see* CLEAN 1
ant tainted

take *vb* 1 *syn see* CATCH 1
2 *syn see* SEIZE 2
idiom make off with
con drop, dump, give up, relinquish, surrender
3 *syn see* APPROPRIATE 1
con relinquish, yield
4 to lay hold of (as with the hands or an instrument) <*took* the ax by the handle>
syn clasp, grasp, grip
rel hold; handle
idiom take hold of
con drop, release
5 *syn see* SEIZE 3
rel contract, get; harrow, reach, torment
6 *syn see* CATCH 7
7 *syn see* ATTRACT 1
8 *syn see* SWALLOW 1
9 *syn see* EAT 1
10 to bring into and accept in a particular capacity or relationship <*took* his son as a member of the firm>
syn admit, receive, take in
rel bring; accept; have, include
11 *syn see* BUY 1
12 *syn see* CHOOSE 1
13 *syn see* DEMAND 2
14 to obtain from another source by means of derivation <*takes* his name from his father's>
syn derive, draw
rel get, obtain; borrow
15 *syn see* BEAR 10
rel withstand; undergo; ‖hack
idiom take it lying down, take it on the chin
16 *syn see* CONTRACT 1
idiom take sick with

17 *syn* see APPREHEND 1
18 *syn* see UNDERSTAND 3
19 *syn* see DEDUCT 1
20 *syn* see TREAT 2
21 *syn* see CHEAT
  rel bamboozle, hoodwink
  idiom take for a ride
22 *syn* see ACT 5
take (from) *vb syn* see DECRY 2
take (to) *vb syn* see HABITUATE 2
  rel enjoy, fancy, favor, like
  idiom get used to
take away *vb* 1 *syn* see REMOVE 2
  rel separate
2 *syn* see DEDUCT 1
3 *syn* see DECRY 2
take back *vb* 1 *syn* see RETURN 4
2 *syn* see REPOSSESS 3
3 *syn* see ABJURE
take down *vb syn* see DISMOUNT
take in *vb* 1 *syn* see TAKE 10
2 *syn* see INCLUDE
3 *syn* see APPREHEND 1
  rel perceive; ‖savvy; absorb, assimilate,
  digest
4 *syn* see DECEIVE
  rel flimflam, take; trick
take off *vb* 1 *syn* see REMOVE 2
2 *syn* see REMOVE 3
3 *syn* see DEDUCT 1
4 *syn* see KILL 1
5 *syn* see MIMIC
  idiom do a takeoff on
6 *syn* see GET OUT 1
7 *syn* see HEAD 3
  idiom hit the road (*or* trail)
8 *syn* see GO 2
takeoff *n syn* see CARICATURE 2
take on *vb* 1 *syn* see DON 2
2 *syn* see ADD 1
3 to proceed to deal with < *took on* a new
  job with more responsibilities>
  syn take up, undertake
  rel begin, commence, enter (upon); attempt, endeavor, try; launch, venture
  idiom set about, take upon oneself
  con abandon, drop, forsake
  ant give up
4 *syn* see ENGAGE 5
5 *syn* see EMPLOY 2
6 *syn* see ADOPT
  ant give up
take out *vb* 1 *syn* see REMOVE 2
2 *syn* see REMOVE 4
3 *syn* see DEDUCT 1
4 *syn* see DATE
take out (on) *vb* to find release for (as
  emotions) < *took out* his anger on the
  dog>
  syn loose, release, unleash, vent
  idiom give vent to, let loose (*or* fly)
  con control, govern, restrain; bottle (up),
  check, keep down, quell, smother; repress,
  suppress
take over *vb syn* see RELIEVE 3
take up *vb* 1 *syn* see LIFT 1
2 *syn* see BEGIN 1
3 *syn* see TAKE ON 3

---

syn synonym(s)   *rel* related word(s)
ant antonym(s)   *con* contrasted word(s)
idiom idiomatic equivalent(s)
‖ use limited; if in doubt, see a dictionary

---

  rel assume; tackle
  idiom address oneself to
4 *syn* see ADOPT
  rel support; affiliate
5 *syn* see RESUME 2
taking *adj syn* see INFECTIOUS 3
tale *n* 1 *syn* see STORY 2
  rel myth, saga
2 *syn* see DETRACTION
3 *syn* see LIE
  rel fiction; yarn
4 *syn* see WHOLE 1
tale *vb syn* see COUNT 1
talebearer *n* 1 *syn* see INFORMER
2 *syn* see GOSSIP 1
talent *n syn* see GIFT 2
  rel art, craft, skill; endowment; expertise,
  forte
talisman *n syn* see CHARM 2
  idiom good-luck piece, lucky piece (*or*
  charm)
talk *vb* 1 *syn* see SPEAK 3
2 *syn* see SPEAK 1
3 *syn* see CONVERSE
4 *syn* see CHAT 1
  rel palaver, spout off
  idiom talk one's arm (*or* ear *or* leg) off,
  flap (*or* wag) the (*or* one's) tongue
5 *syn* see GOSSIP
6 to reveal secret or confidential information usually concerning illegal acts < at
  last the suspect *talked* to the police>
  syn sing, squeak, squeal; *compare* IN-
  FORM 3
  rel inform (on); divulge; reveal; confess
  idiom spill one's guts, spill the beans, tell
  all
7 to give a talk < he *talks* to community
  groups on ecology>
  syn address, lecture, prelect, speak
  rel declaim, harangue, hold forth, perorate, speechify, spout
talk (into) *vb syn* see INDUCE 1
talk *n* 1 *syn* see SPEECH 1
2 *syn* see CONVERSATION 2
3 *syn* see CHAT 2
4 a formal or prearranged discussion,
  exchange, or negotiation usually of a political nature < summit *talks* on nuclear
  arms>
  syn conference, meeting, parley, powwow
  rel dialogue, discussion, exchange; negotiation; deliberation
5 *syn* see REPORT 1
6 *syn* see SPEECH 2
  rel spiel; conference, discussion
talkative *adj* given to talk or talking < a
  talkative, sociable man>
  syn babblative, chatty, gabby, garrulous,
  loose-lipped, loose-tongued, loquacious,
  mouthy, multiloquent, multiloquious,
  talky, tonguey; *compare* GLIB
  rel articulate, eloquent, fluent; vocal,
  voluble; buzzy, gossipy
  con closemouthed, laconic, reserved, reticent, uncommunicative; speechless
  ant silent
talkee-talkee *n syn* see CHATTER
talky *adj syn* see TALKATIVE
tall *adj syn* see HIGH 1
  rel high-reaching, sky-high, skyscraping
  idiom higher than a cat's back
  con abbreviated, truncated; low

ant short

tally *n syn* see SCORE 5

tally *vb* 1 *syn* see INVENTORY
2 *syn* see COUNT 1
3 *syn* see AGREE 4
rel equal, match; balance, complement
con conflict (with), differ (from), disagree (with)

tame *adj* docilely tractable < a *tame* lion >
syn domestic, domesticated, domitae naturae, subdued, submissive
rel broken (in), ||busted, housebroken, trained; amenable, biddable, docile, obedient, tractable; pliable, pliant; meek, mild
idiom gentle as a lamb
con fierce, savage, tameless; undomesticated, untrained; unbridled, unbroken
ant untamed, wild

tame *vb syn* see DOMESTICATE

tamp *vb syn* see CRAM 1
rel fill up (*or* in), plug up; concentrate

tamper (with) *vb* 1 *syn* see BRIBE
2 *syn* see MEDDLE
rel interpose, intervene; doctor, manipulate

tang *n syn* see TASTE 3
rel bite, nip, piquancy, twang; aroma, pungency; spiciness, tanginess

tangible *adj* 1 capable of being perceived especially by the sense of touch < primitives who find *tangible* expression of divinity in idols >
syn palpable, tactile, touchable; *compare* PERCEPTIBLE
rel corporeal, physical; embodied, material, real, substantial
con ethereal, spiritual, unreal
ant intangible
2 *syn* see MATERIAL 1
3 *syn* see PERCEPTIBLE
rel distinct, evident, manifest, obvious, patent, plain
con clouded, cloudy, imperceptible, indistinct, unclear
ant intangible

tangle *vb* 1 *syn* see INVOLVE 1
idiom make a party to
ant untangle
2 *syn* see CATCH 3
ant untangle
3 *syn* see ENTANGLE 1
rel foul up, mix up
4 *syn* see COMPLICATE
ant untangle

tangle *n syn* see MAZE 1

tanked *adj syn* see INTOXICATED 1

tank town *n syn* see BURG

tank up *vb syn* see DRINK 3

tantalize *vb syn* see WORRY 1
rel badger, bait; frustrate

tantamount *adj syn* see SAME 2
rel alike, like, uniform; selfsame, very
idiom as much as to say

tap *n* 1 *syn* see FAUCET
2 *syn* see BAR 5

tap *vb syn* see DRAIN 1

tap *vb* 1 to strike or hit audibly and usually lightly < *tapped* her pencil on the desk >
syn bob, knock, rap, tunk
rel bang, beat, hammer, hit, pound, smite, strike, thud, thump
2 *syn* see DESIGNATE 2

tapa *n syn* see SNACK

taper *vb syn* see DECREASE

taper off *vb syn* see DECREASE

taproom *n syn* see BAR 5

tapster *n syn* see BARTENDER

tar *n syn* see MARINER

tar *vb syn* see TAINT 1

taradiddle *n syn* see LIE

tardy *adj* not arriving, occurring, or done at the set, due, or expected time < be *tardy* for school >
syn behindhand, belated, late, lated, overdue, unpunctual
rel delayed, detained; dilatory, laggard, slow; delinquent
con beforehand, early; convenient, opportune, seasonable, timely; precise, punctilious
ant prompt, punctual

target *n* 1 an object of ridicule, attack, or abuse < made him the chief *target* of political satire >
syn butt, mark, sitting duck
rel victim; fall guy, scapegoat, whipping boy
2 *syn* see AMBITION 2
3 *syn* see USE 4

tariff *n* 1 *syn* see TAX 1
2 *syn* see PRICE 1

||**tarnation** *adj syn* see UTTER

tarnish *vb syn* see DULL 1
2 *syn* see SOIL 2
rel contaminate, defile, pollute, stain, taint
con clean, cleanse; shine (up)
ant polish
3 *syn* see INJURE 1
4 *syn* see TAINT 1
rel defame, disgrace, embarrass; slander

tarpaulin *n syn* see MARINER

tarriance *n syn* see SOJOURN

tarry *vb* 1 *syn* see DELAY 2
rel falter, flag
2 *syn* see STAY 2
rel dawdle; sojourn
3 *syn* see VISIT 3

tart *adj syn* see SOUR 1
rel piquant, pungent
ant flat

tart *n syn* see DOXY 1

Tartarean *adj syn* see INFERNAL 1

Tartuffe *n syn* see HYPOCRITE

Tartuffery *n syn* see HYPOCRISY

Tartuffism *n syn* see HYPOCRISY

task *n* 1 a piece of work assigned or to be done < laboratory *tasks* assigned to chemistry students >
syn assignment, chare, chore, devoir, duty, job, stint
rel enterprise, project, undertaking; errand, labor, toil, work; charge, function, mission, office, province; business, calling, employment, occupation, vocation
2 a necessary undertaking that is usually difficult, dull, disagreeable, or problematic < deciphering his handwriting is a real *task* >
syn chore, effort, job, taskwork
rel burden, onus, strain, tax; bother, headache, nuisance, pain, trouble
idiom a hard (*or* long) row to hoe
con child's play, cinch, duck soup, picnic, ||pipe, sinecure, snap

3 syn see LOAD 3

task vb syn see BURDEN

taskmaster n syn see SLAVE DRIVER

taskwork n syn see TASK 2

taste vb syn see FEEL 2
idiom be exposed to, run up against

taste n 1 syn see HINT 2
rel bit, sample, sampling
2 syn see APPETITE 1
3 the property of a substance which makes it perceptible to the gustatory sense <children often dislike the *taste* of olives>
syn flavor, relish, sapidity, sapor, smack, tang
4 a liking for or enjoyment of something because of the pleasure it gives <had a *taste* for fast cars>
syn gusto, heart, palate, relish, zest
rel appreciation, comprehension, understanding; partiality, predilection, prepossession; disposition, inclination, predisposition
con dislike, disrelish; allergy, aversion, repugnance, repulsion
ant antipathy; distaste
5 syn see APPETITE 3
ant distaste
6 the power or practice of discerning and enjoying whatever constitutes excellence (as in the fine arts) <a room whose decoration reflected her exquisite *taste*>
syn tastefulness
rel correctness; finesse, polish, refinement; elegance, grace
con gracelessness, inelegance, unrefinement; incorrectness, vulgarity
ant tastelessness

tasteful adj 1 syn see PALATABLE
rel rich
ant savorless, tasteless
2 syn see QUIET 4
ant tasteless

tastefulness n syn see TASTE 6
ant tastelessness

tasteless adj 1 syn see UNPALATABLE 1
rel bland, dull, stale, vapid; unflavored; uninteresting
con flavorful, pleasing
ant tasteful, tasty
2 syn see BARBARIC 1
rel inelegant, unpolished, unrefined
idiom in bad taste
ant tasteful, tasty

tasty adj 1 syn see PALATABLE
idiom fit for a king
con unsavory; bland, flavorless, unpalatable
ant savorless, tasteless
2 syn see QUIET 4
ant tasteless

||**tats** n pl syn see DICE

||**tatter** vb syn see HURRY 2

tatterdemalion n syn see RAGAMUFFIN

tattered adj syn see RAGGED
2 syn see SHABBY 1

tatters n pl syn see RAGS 1

tattle vb syn see GOSSIP

idiom tell tales out of school

tattle n syn see REPORT 1

tattler n syn see INFORMER

tattletale n syn see INFORMER

tatty adj syn see CHEAP 2

taunt vb syn see RIDICULE
rel banter, chaff; provoke; upbraid; disdain, scorn; affront, insult, offend, outrage

taut adj syn see TIGHT 3
rel firm, trim; stretched
con flabby; relaxed
ant slack

tautology n syn see VERBIAGE 1
rel reiteration, repetition, repetitiousness; padding

tavern n 1 syn see BAR 5
2 syn see HOTEL

tavern car n syn see PARLOR CAR

taverner n syn see SALOONKEEPER

tawdry adj syn see GAUDY
rel common, sleazy; flaring, screaming

tax vb 1 syn see BURDEN
rel overtax
idiom press hard upon, tax the strength of, weigh heavy on (or upon)
2 syn see ACCUSE

tax n 1 a charge usually of money imposed by authority upon persons or property for public purposes <federal, state, and local *taxes* bear heavily on the thrifty>
syn assessment, ||cess, duty, impost, levy, tariff
rel tithe, tribute; boodle, boondoggle, giveaway, pork barrel
2 syn see LOAD 3
rel difficulty, strain; demand, imposition

taxi n syn see TAXICAB

taxicab n an automobile that carries passengers for a fare <took a *taxicab* from the airport to his hotel>
syn cab, hack, taxi
rel ||crawler, nighthawk

taxing adj syn see ONEROUS
rel wearing; tedious, troublesome

TB n syn see TUBERCULOSIS

||**tea** n syn see MARIJUANA

teach vb to cause to acquire knowledge or skill <*teach* a child to read>
syn discipline, educate, instruct, school, train
rel communicate, impart; implant, inculcate, instill; edify, enlighten, indoctrinate; fit, ground, prepare, rear; drill, exercise, practice; coach, tutor; lesson
idiom give instruction

teaching n syn see EDUCATION 1

teachy adj syn see DIDACTIC

tear vb 1 to separate (one part of a substance or object from another) forcibly <*tore* a chunk from the loaf on the table>
syn cleave, rend, rip, rive, split
rel cut, gash, incise, slash, slit; devil, pull (apart), rift, sever, sunder; ribbon, shred; break, crack, rupture; damage, impair, injure
2 syn see EXTRACT 1
3 syn see RUSH 1
4 syn see COURSE

tear n syn see BINGE 1

tear down vb 1 syn see DESTROY 1
ant build up
2 syn see MALIGN

---

syn synonym(s)   rel related word(s)
ant antonym(s)   con contrasted word(s)
idiom idiomatic equivalent(s)
|| use limited; if in doubt, see a dictionary

ant build up

teardrops *n pl syn* see TEARS

tearful *adj* flowing with or accompanied by tears < *tearful* entreaties >
syn lachrymose, teary, weeping, weepy
rel lamenting, mournful; sniveling; bawling, blubbering, crying, sobbing
con dry-eyed
ant tearless

tearing *adj syn* see EXCRUCIATING

tear-jerking *adj syn* see SENTIMENTAL

tears *n pl* a profuse secretion of saline fluid that overflows the eyelids and dampens the face < a blow that brought *tears* to his eyes >
syn teardrops, water

teary *adj syn* see TEARFUL
ant tearless

tease *vb syn* see WORRY 1
rel disturb, importune
idiom give a bad time

teaser *n syn* see STRIPTEASER

tease up *vb syn* see TOUCH UP

‖**tec** *n syn* see DETECTIVE

teched *adj syn* see INSANE 1

technique *n syn* see METHOD 1

tedious *adj* 1 *syn* see IRKSOME
2 *syn* see ARID 2
rel dragging, mortal, slow, tiresome

tedium *n* a state of dissatisfaction and weariness < incessant routine without variety breeds *tedium* >
syn boredom, doldrums, ennui, yawn
rel irksomeness, tediousness, tiresomeness, wearisomeness; dullness, monotony
con enlivenment, interest, invigoration, refreshment

teem *vb* to be abundantly stocked or provided < rivers *teeming* with fish >
syn abound, crawl, flow, pullulate, ‖sny, swarm
rel bristle, bustle; cram, crowd, jam, pack; overbrim, overflow, overrun
con lack, want

teem *vb syn* see POUR 3

teeming *adj syn* see ALIVE 5
rel multitudinous, populous, pregnant; bristling
con rare, sparse, uncommon; empty, lacking, void, wanting

teensy *adj syn* see TINY

teensy-weensy *adj syn* see TINY

teenty *adj syn* see TINY

teeny *adj syn* see TINY

teeny-weeny *adj syn* see TINY

tee off *vb syn* see BEGIN 1

teeter *vb* to progress (as by walking) unsteadily < *teetered* along on 4-inch heels >
syn falter, lurch, stagger, ‖stammer, stumble, topple, totter, wobble; *compare* LURCH 2, SEESAW
rel sway, weave

teethy *adj syn* see TOOTHY 1

teetotal *adj syn* see DRY 3

tehee *vb syn* see LAUGH

telephone *vb* to communicate with (a person) by telephone < *telephoned* him yesterday >
syn ‖buzz, call, phone, ‖ring (up)
idiom ‖get (one) on the horn, give (one) a buzz (*or* ring)

telestic *adj syn* see MYSTICAL 1

tell *vb* 1 *syn* see COUNT 1

2 *syn* see SAY 1
rel communicate, convey, impart
3 *syn* see REVEAL 1
rel recite, recount, rehearse, relate; acquaint, apprise, inform
4 *syn* see INFORM 2
5 *syn* see COMMAND
6 *syn* see WEIGH 3

telling *adj syn* see VALID
rel power-packed; influential, weighty, significant, striking

tell off *vb syn* see SCOLD 1
rel call down; denounce
idiom give (one) a piece of one's mind, tell (one) a thing or two, tell (one) where to get off

telltale *n* 1 *syn* see GOSSIP 1
2 *syn* see HINT 1

tellurian *adj syn* see EARTHLY 1

telluric *adj syn* see EARTHLY 1

temblor (*or* **trembler**) *n syn* see EARTHQUAKE

temerarious *adj syn* see ADVENTUROUS
rel heedless, imprudent, incautious, injudicious

temerity *n* conspicuous or flagrant boldness (as in speech, behavior, or action) < had the *temerity* to order an attack when hopelessly outnumbered >
syn assurance, audacity, brashness, hardihood, hardiness, nerve
rel daring, foolhardiness, heedlessness, rashness, recklessness, venturesomeness; impetuosity, precipitateness; impertinence, intrusiveness
con deliberation, judgment, judiciousness, prudence; heed, heedfulness
ant caution

temper *vb syn* see MODERATE 1
rel dilute, season; ease, pacify, soften; adjust, modify; curb, tune down
idiom take the edge off

temper *n* 1 a general or prevailing quality or characteristic (as of moral or social attitudes and behavior) < riots reflected the *temper* of the times >
syn mood, spirit, timbre, tone
rel atmosphere, aura, climate; orientation, outlook; disposition, drift, leaning, tendency, trend; character, nature, peculiarity
2 *syn* see DISPOSITION 3
rel condition, posture, state; attribute, property, quality; style, type, way
idiom turn of mind
3 *syn* see MOOD 1
idiom frame (*or* state) of mind
4 an outbreak or display of anger < a childish fit of *temper* >
syn passion
rel anger, fury, ire, rage; conniption, fit, outburst, tantrum

temperament *n syn* see DISPOSITION 3
rel mentality, mind; kind, type, way
idiom inner nature

temperamental *adj* 1 *syn* see MOODY
2 *syn* see INCONSTANT 1
ant steady

temperance *n* 1 an avoidance of extremes (as in action, thought, or feeling) < a man who knew no *temperance* in his opinions >
syn measure, moderateness, moderation
rel reasonableness; constraint, restraint

idiom happy medium

con extremeness, radicalism; excess, excessiveness; immoderateness, immoderation, unconstraint, unreasonableness, unrestraint

ant intemperance, intemperateness

2 strict habitual and usually complete self-denial in the gratification of appetites or passions <an ascetic who practiced complete *temperance* >

syn abstinence, continence, sobriety

rel abnegation, eschewal, forbearance, forgoing, refrainment, sacrifice, self-denial, self-deprivation; control, restraint, self-control, self-discipline; asceticism, austerity, mortification

con intemperance, intemperancy, intemperateness, prodigality

ant excess

temperate *adj* **1** *syn* see MODERATE 2

rel constant, equable, even, steady; checked, curbed, regulated, restrained

ant intemperate

2 *syn* see ABSTEMIOUS

rel indulgent; self-indulgent

con intemperate; dissipated, prodigal, profligate

ant excessive

3 *syn* see CONSERVATIVE 2

4 *syn* see SOBER 3

temperish *adj syn* see IRASCIBLE

tempersome *adj syn* see ILL-TEMPERED

tempestuous *adj syn* see WILD 6

rel tumultuous, unbridled, unrestrained, violent

ant calm, quiet

temple *n syn* see HOUSE OF WORSHIP

tempo *n* rate of performance or delivery <increased sales and production *tempo* >

syn pace, time; *compare* SPEED 2

rel speed; momentum

temporal *adj* **1** *syn* see MATERIALISTIC

ant nontemporal

2 *syn* see PROFANE 1

rel material, physical; nonsacred, nonspiritual, unhallowed, unsanctified, unspiritual

con celestial, heavenly

ant spiritual

temporary *adj* lasting, continuing, or serving for a limited time <was *temporary* president of the company for nine months>

syn acting, ad interim, interim, pro tem, pro tempore, supply; *compare* TRANSIENT

rel alternate, substitute; interimistic, provisional, provisory; jackleg, make-do, makeshift, stopgap

ant permanent

tempt *vb syn* see LURE

rel provoke, rouse; court, invite, solicit, vamp, woo

idiom whet the appetite

con discourage; dissuade; repel, repulse, revolt

temptation *n syn* see LURE 2

tempting *adj syn* see ENTICING

rel appetizing, mouth-watering; provoking, rousing, tantalizing

con repellent, repulsive

ant untempting

temptress *n syn* see SIREN

ten *n syn* see BREAK 4

tenable *adj* **1** capable of being defended against attack <the platoon's position was no longer *tenable* >

syn defendable, defensible

rel impregnable, secure

con insecure, vulnerable; defenseless, helpless, unprotected; dangerous, precarious, risky

ant untenable

2 *syn* see JUSTIFIABLE

rel believable, credible, maintainable, plausible

con indefensible, inexcusable, unbelievable, unjustifiable

ant untenable

tenacious *adj* **1** *syn* see STRONG 2

rel bulldogged, bulldoggish, bulldoggy, dogged, obstinate, pertinacious, stubborn; resolute, steadfast, true; persevering, persisting

2 *syn* see VISCOUS

rel cohesive; tacky; sticky

3 *syn* see FAST 4

con lax, slack

tenant *vb syn* see INHABIT

tenantable *adj syn* see LIVABLE 1

idiom fit to live in

con uninhabitable

tend *vb* **1** *syn* see TILL

2 to supervise or take charge of <employed a girl to *tend* the children each day>

syn attend, care (for), mind, watch

rel cherish, cultivate, foster, minister, nurse, nurture, serve; defend, guard, protect, safeguard, shield; supervise

idiom look after, see after, see to, take care of, take under one's wing

con disregard, ignore, neglect

tend *vb* **1** to have or exhibit an inclination or tendency <he *tends* to praise people too highly>

syn incline, lean, look; *compare* INCLINE 3

idiom be disposed

2 *syn* see CONTRIBUTE 2

tendency *n* **1** a movement or course having a particular direction and character <a growing *tendency* to underestimate the potential strength of that nation >

syn current, drift, run, tenor, trend

rel curve, inclination, leaning, propensity; turn; shift; custom, habit, usage, way

2 *syn* see LEANING 2

tendentious *adj syn* see BIASED 2

tender *adj* showing or expressing affectionate interest in another <his mother was very *tender* with her wayward son>

syn compassionate, kindhearted, responsive, softhearted, sympathetic, warm, warmhearted

rel gentle, lenient, mild, soft, yielding; considerate, solicitous, thoughtful; affectionate, fond, loving; benevolent, charitable, humane, mild; commiserative; forgiving, merciful, tolerant

con callous, hard, harsh; inhumane, uncharitable, unfeeling

ant rough, severe

---

syn synonym(s)   *rel* related word(s)
ant antonym(s)   *con* contrasted word(s)
idiom idiomatic equivalent(s)
‖ use limited; if in doubt, see a dictionary

tender *vb syn* see OFFER 1
rel propose, purpose, submit, suggest

tenderfoot *n syn* see NOVICE

tenderloin *n syn* see RED-LIGHT DISTRICT

tenebrific *adj syn* see GLOOMY 3

tenebrous *adj* 1 *syn* see DARK 1
2 *syn* see OBSCURE 3

tenement *n syn* see APARTMENT 1

tenet *n syn* see DOCTRINE
rel belief, conviction, persuasion, view

tenor *n* 1 the course of thought that is retained through something spoken or written < the *tenor* of the book is first expressed in the introduction >
syn drift, purport, substance; *compare* BODY 3, MEANING 1, SUBSTANCE 2
rel intent; inclination, trend; mood, tone; core, gist, meat, stuff
2 *syn* see TENDENCY 1

tense *adj* 1 *syn* see TIGHT 3
rel strained, stretched
ant relaxed
2 feeling or showing nervous tension < the soldiers were *tense* as they waited for the order to advance >
syn edgy, nervy, restive, uneasy, uptight
rel queasy; jittery, rusty, unquiet; anxious, concerned, overanxious
con easy; calm, cool, ‖loose, placid, unconcerned; firm, nerveless, unshaken
ant relaxed

tension *n* 1 *syn* see STRESS 1
rel tautness, tenseness, tightness
idiom stress and strain
ant relaxation
2 emotional strain < was suffering from nervous *tension* >
syn unease, uptightness
rel strain, stress; anxiety, nerves, nervousness, uneasiness; agitation, discomfort, disquiet, misease

ten–strike *n syn* see SMASH 6

tent *vb syn* see CAMP

tentative *adj* 1 *syn* see CONDITIONAL 1
rel acting, ad interim, makeshift, temporary; probationary; experimental, test, trial
con conclusive, decisive, definitive
ant final
2 *syn* see VACILLATING 2
rel disinclined, reluctant

tenue *n syn* see BEHAVIOR

tenuous *adj* 1 *syn* see THIN 2
2 *syn* see THIN 1
rel aerial, airy, ethereal, fine
con abundant
ant dense
3 having little substance or strength and usually not firmly based < only a *tenuous* link in the chain of evidence >
syn feeble, insubstantial, unsubstantial; *compare* IMPLAUSIBLE
rel flimsy, weak; insignificant
con significant, sound, strong
ant substantial

tenure *n syn* see HOLD

tepid *adj* 1 moderately warm < a *tepid* bath >
syn lukewarm, milk-warm, warmish
rel mild, temperate, warm
con cold, cool, freezing, frozen; heated, hot, steaming
2 lacking in animation, force, passion, conviction, or commitment < gave only a *tepid* endorsement to the candidate >
syn halfhearted, lukewarm, unenthusiastic; *compare* ARID 2
rel indifferent; colorless, dull, lifeless, unlively; feeble, marrowless, pithless, sapless, spiritless; dim, faint, forceless, weak
con animated, forceful; fiery, impassioned, passionate, spirited

tergiversate *vb* 1 *syn* see DEFECT
idiom fall away from
2 *syn* see EQUIVOCATE 2
idiom beg the question

tergiversation *n* 1 *syn* see DEFECTION
rel about-face, reversal, reverse; denial, disavowal, forswearing, renunciation, repudiation
2 *syn* see AMBIGUITY

tergiversator *n syn* see RENEGADE

tergiverse *vb* 1 *syn* see DEFECT
2 *syn* see EQUIVOCATE 2

term *n* 1 *syn* see LIMIT 1
rel terminus
2 a limited, definite, or measurable extent of time during which something exists, lasts, or is in progress < the office has a *term* of four years >
syn duration, span, time
rel phase; go, period, spell, stretch; hitch, tour, turn; standing
3 *syn* see WORD 2
4 terms *pl syn* see CONDITION 1
rel detail, item, particular, point; limit
5 terms *pl* mutual social relationship or relative position < fight on equal *terms* > < the two were on *terms* of great intimacy >
syn footing, standing
rel coequality, equipollence, status; equality, equivalence, par, parity; balance

term *vb syn* see NAME 1

termagant *n syn* see VIRAGO

termagant *adj syn* see TURBULENT 1

terminable *adj* liable to be terminated or subject to termination < marriage is a *terminable* institution >
syn determinable, endable
rel finite, limited; limitable

terminal *adj syn* see LAST
con beginning, starting
ant initial

terminate *vb* 1 *syn* see CLOSE 3
rel abolish, extinguish; discontinue, wind down
idiom put the lid on
ant initiate
2 *syn* see ADJOURN 2
3 *syn* see DISMISS 3
4 *syn* see QUIT 6

terminated *adj syn* see COMPLETE 4

terminating *adj syn* see LAST
ant initial

termination *n syn* see END 2
rel issue, outcome, ‖pay-off, result
con source; beginning, start
ant initiation

terminology *n* the specialized or technical terms and expressions peculiar to a field, subject, or trade < the *terminology* of the plastics industry >
syn cant, dictionary, jargon, language, lexicon, palaver, vocabulary; *compare* DIALECT 2

rel shoptalk; gibberish, gobbledygook

terminus *n syn* see END 2

terra firma *n syn* see EARTH 2

terrain *n* 1 the physical configuration and features of a tract of land <made an analysis of the *terrain* via aerial photos>
syn topography
rel contour, form, profile, shape
2 an area devoted to a specified activity <the whole county had become breeding and racing *terrain*>
syn territory, turf
3 *syn* see FIELD

terrene *adj* 1 *syn* see EARTHLY 1
2 *syn* see EARTHY 1

terrestrial *adj* 1 *syn* see EARTHLY 1
rel earthbound, prosaic; profane, secular, unspiritual
ant empyreal
2 *syn* see EARTHY 1

terrible *adj* 1 *syn* see FEARFUL 3
2 *syn* see HARD 6
3 *syn* see INTENSE 1
4 *syn* see GHASTLY 1

terribly *adv syn* see VERY 1

terrific *adj* 1 *syn* see FEARFUL 3
rel terrorizing; agitating, disquieting, upsetting
2 *syn* see MARVELOUS 2
rel magnificent, superb; rattling, screaming

terrified *adj syn* see AFRAID 1
rel horrified, shocked; terrorized; frozen, paralyzed
con unfearful, unfearing, unfrightened
ant unafraid

terrify *vb syn* see FRIGHTEN
rel freeze, paralyze, petrify, stun, stupefy
idiom put the fear of God into, strike fear into the heart of

terrifying *adj syn* see GHASTLY 1
ant unterrifying

territory *n* 1 *syn* see AREA 1
2 *syn* see FIELD
3 *syn* see TERRAIN 2

terror *n syn* see FEAR 1
rel awe, fearfulness

terroristic *adj* characterized by or practicing terror as a means of coercion <used torture and other *terroristic* tactics to extract confessions>
syn gestapo
rel coercive, strong-arm; brutal, cruel, merciless; immoral, improper, unsanctioned

terrorize *vb* 1 *syn* see FRIGHTEN
idiom scare to death
2 *syn* see INTIMIDATE
idiom use gestapo tactics on

terse *adj syn* see CONCISE
rel close, compact; lean, precise; clear-cut, crisp, incisive; taut
con circuitous; pleonastic, redundant, repetitious

tersely *adv syn* see BRIEFLY
rel closely, compactly; crisply, incisively, precisely; abruptly, curtly
idiom in as few words as possible

ant prolixly

test *n syn* see EXPERIMENT
rel inspection, scrutiny; confirmation, corroboration, substantiation, verification

test *vb* 1 *syn* see TRY 1
rel assay, essay; confirm, substantiate, verify
idiom bring to test
2 *syn* see PROVE 1

test (out) *vb syn* see EXPERIMENT

test *adj syn* see EXPERIMENTAL 2
rel proving, testing, trying; probationary, speculative

testament *n syn* see TESTIMONY

testify *vb* 1 to serve as evidence of <present conditions *testify* to the accuracy of his predictions>
syn attest, point (to)
rel affirm; demonstrate, show; prove
con discredit, disprove, invalidate; confute, refute
2 to make a solemn declaration under oath for the purpose of establishing a fact (as in court) <*testified* against the defendant>
syn depone, depose, ||mount, swear
idiom give testimony
3 *syn* see INDICATE 2

testimonial *n* 1 *syn* see TESTIMONY
rel indication, manifestation, show, sign, symbol, token
2 *syn* see CREDENTIALS
3 an expression of great approval and high esteem <a dinner was planned as a *testimonial* in his honor>
syn appreciation, salvo, tribute
rel salute; triumph; jubilee; commemoration, memorialization, remembrance
4 *syn* see MONUMENT 2

testimony *n* something that serves as tangible verification <the results are remarkable *testimony* to the accuracy of his predictions>
syn attestation, confirmation, evidence, proof, testament, testimonial, witness; *compare* INDICATION 3
rel demonstration, illustration; affirmation, corroboration, documentation, substantiation, verification

testy *adj syn* see IRASCIBLE
rel annoyed, exasperated, grouchy, irritable

tetchy *adj syn* see IRASCIBLE
rel ill-humored; cantankerous

tête-à-tête *n* a private conversation between two people <had a *tête-à-tête* with her in a quiet corner>
syn vis-à-vis
rel causerie, chat, coze; conversation, talk; argument, discussion

tetrad *n syn* see QUARTET

||**tew** *vb syn* see WORRY 3

text *n syn* see SUBJECT 2
rel consideration, issue; fundamentals; idea

texture *n* 1 *syn* see ESSENCE 1
2 a basic often highly complex underlying scheme, structure, or pattern <war destroys the very *texture* of a society>
syn fabric, fiber, web
rel framework, structure; composition, constitution, makeup; pattern, scheme

thalassic *adj syn* see MARINE 1

---

syn synonym(s)   *rel* related word(s)
ant antonym(s)   *con* contrasted word(s)
idiom idiomatic equivalent(s)
|| use limited; if in doubt, see a dictionary

thankful *adj syn* see GRATEFUL 1
con unappreciative, ungrateful
ant thankless, unthankful

thankless *adj* 1 not inclined to give thanks
< a *thankless* guest >
syn unappreciative, ungrateful, unthankful
rel self-centered; careless, heedless,
thoughtless; unappreciative, ungrateful,
unmindful
con appreciative, grateful, mindful; careful, heedful, thoughtful
ant thankful
2 not likely to obtain thanks < a *thankless*
job >
syn unappreciated, ungrateful, unthankful
rel disagreeable, distasteful, unpleasant;
miserable, wretched
con thankworthy

thanks *n pl syn* see GRACE 1
thanksgiving *n syn* see GRACE 1
thankworthy *adj syn* see WORTHY 1
thank-you-ma'am *n syn* see BUMP 3
that *adj* 1 being the other < we argued it
this way and we argued it *that* way >
syn another
ant this
2 *syn* see SUCH 2

thaumaturgic *adj syn* see MAGIC 1
thaumaturgy *n syn* see MAGIC 1
thaw *vb syn* see LIQUEFY
theater *n syn* see DRAMA
theatral *adj syn* see DRAMATIC 1
theatric *adj syn* see DRAMATIC 1
theatrical *adj* 1 *syn* see DRAMATIC 1
2 having qualities resembling a stage play
or an actor's performance < he slowly
made an exaggerated *theatrical* bow >
syn dramatic
rel histrionic, melodramatic, staged; affected, artificial, exaggerated, mannered,
unnatural

theft *n* the unlawful taking and carrying
away of property without the consent of
its owner < was found guilty of auto
theft >
syn larceny, lift, pinch, purloining, steal,
stealage, stealing, thievery, thieving,
‖touch
rel filching, pilferage, pilfering, swiping;
robbery, robbing, ‖stouth, ‖stouthrief;
‖score

theme *n* 1 *syn* see SUBJECT 2
2 *syn* see ESSAY 2
then *adv* 1 at another time < science as it
was taught *then* >
syn again, anon, when; *compare* BEFORE
2
rel before, formerly
2 *syn* see AGAIN 4
3 *syn* see THEREFORE
thence *adv* 1 *syn* see AWAY 1
2 *syn* see THEREFROM
thenceforth *adv* from that time forward
< the island which was *thenceforth* to be
their home >
syn thenceforward, thereafter; *compare*
HENCEFORTH
idiom from then on
thenceforward *adv syn* see THENCE-
FORTH
theorem *n syn* see PRINCIPLE 1
theoretical *adj* 1 concerned principally
with abstractions and theories < *theoretical* versus applied physics >

syn academic, closet, speculative
rel conjectural, hypothetical, notional,
suppositional, unproved; analytical, prob-
lematical
con practical; factual; proved
ant applied
2 *syn* see ABSTRACT 1
rel idealized, ivory-tower
ant concrete

theorize *vb syn* see SUGGEST 4

theory *n* 1 a belief, policy, or procedure
proposed or followed as the basis of action < an educational system that was
based on the *theory* that men learn best
by experience >
syn hypothesis, supposal; *compare* AS-
SUMPTION 2
rel base, basis, grounds, position, premise, understanding
ant practice
2 something taken for granted especially
on trivial or inadequate grounds < her
theory that the house was haunted >
syn conjecture, perhaps, speculation,
suppose, supposition
rel guess, guesswork, surmise; feeling,
hunch, impression, presentiment, suspicion
con assurance, certainty, knowledge

there *adv* to or into that place < they seldom go *there* anymore >
syn thither, thitherward, yon
rel yonder
ant here

thereafter *adv syn* see THENCEFORTH
thereby *adv* in consequence of that < lied
to the jury, *thereby* negating his testimony >
syn therethrough; *compare* THEREFROM
therefore *adv* for this or that reason < I
think, *therefore* I am >
syn accordingly, consequently, ergo,
hence, so, then, thereupon, thus
rel thence, therefrom
therefrom *adv* from that thing, fact, or
circumstance < public opinion and a policy deriving *therefrom* >
syn thence, thereof; *compare* THEREBY
thereof *adv syn* see THEREFROM
thereon *adv* on or upon that < knew both
the text and commentary *thereon* >
syn thereupon
rel therein, thereof, thereto
therethrough *adv syn* see THEREBY
theretofore *adv* up to that time < *theretofore* obscure communities >
syn thereuntil
rel ‖afore, before, previously
idiom before then
thereuntil *adv syn* see THERETOFORE
idiom until then
thereupon *adv* 1 *syn* see THEREON
2 *syn* see THEREFORE
thesis *n* 1 a position assumed or a point
made especially in controversy < his *thesis*
about the assassination was arguable >
syn contention, contestation
rel point, position; argument; belief, opinion, sentiment(s), view(s)
2 *syn* see ASSUMPTION 2
3 *syn* see DISCOURSE 2
rel exposition; argument, argumentation
thespian *adj syn* see DRAMATIC 1
thespian *n syn* see ACTOR 1

thew *n syn* see MUSCLE 1
thick *adj* **1** *syn* see STOCKY
rel broad, wide; bulky, burly, husky; blubber, blubbery, massive, obese
con slender, slight, slim; lanky, spare; skeletal
2 *syn* see CLOSE 4
rel concentrated, crammed; localized
con dispersed, scattered
ant diffuse
3 *syn* see STUPID 1
4 *syn* see FAMILIAR 1
idiom hand in glove, thick as thieves
5 *syn* see IMPLAUSIBLE
idiom a little too thick
thick-bodied *adj syn* see STOCKY
thickhead *n syn* see DUNCE
rel ||clot
thickheaded *adj syn* see STUPID 1
thickset *adj syn* see STOCKY
rel fleshy, portly
thickskull *n syn* see DUNCE
rel lout
thick-witted *adj syn* see STUPID 1
thief *n* one who steals <a *thief* took her money>
syn filcher, larcener, larcenist, nimmer, pilferer, prig, purloiner, stealer; *compare* ROBBER
rel burglar, cat burglar, cat man, housebreaker; hijacker, robber; ||booster, ||dip, lifter, shoplifter; nip, pickpocket
thieve *vb syn* see STEAL 1
thievery *n syn* see THEFT
thieving *adj syn* see LARCENOUS
thieving *n syn* see THEFT
thievish *adj syn* see LARCENOUS
thin *adj* **1** not thick, heavy, or broad (as in configuration or physique) <a *thin* body>
syn attenuate, reedy, slender, slight, slim, squinny, stalky, tenuous, twiggy; *compare* LEAN
rel lank, lanky, lathy, lean, macilent, spare; cadaverous, gaunt, pinched, skeletal, wasted; meager, puny, small, twiglike
con broad, wide; compact, dense, solid; heavy, massive; corpulent, fat, obese
ant thick
2 characterized by wide separation of component particles <*thin* air at high altitudes>
syn attenuate, attenuated, rare, rarefied, subtile, subtle, tenuous
rel diffuse, diluted, dispersed; fine, refined
con heavy, thick
ant dense
3 *syn* see DILUTE
4 *syn* see ACUTE 4
rel high-pitched
con low, low-pitched; guttural; deep
5 *syn* see IMPLAUSIBLE
rel vapid; transparent; questionable; untenable
idiom a bit thin
con believable, convincing, sound, substantial
thin *vb* **1** to make thin or thinner <a once powerful frame *thinned* by privation>

syn attenuate, extenuate, wiredraw
rel diminish, reduce; weaken
con broaden, enlarge; strengthen
ant thicken
2 to make or become less dense <the air *thinned* at high altitudes>
syn attenuate, rarefy
ant densify
3 *syn* see DILUTE
thing *n* **1** *syn* see AFFAIR 1
2 *syn* see OCCURRENCE
3 *syn* see ACTION 1
rel exploit, feat, stunt
4 whatever is apprehended as having actual, distinct, and demonstrable existence <there is a place for each *thing* in the lab>
syn article, object
rel entity, item
5 that which can be known as having existence in space or time <virtue is not a *thing*, but an attribute of a *thing*>
syn being, entity, individual, material, matter, object, stuff, substance
rel item, particular
con attribute, characteristic, property, quality
6 *syn* see ENTITY 1
ant nonentity, nonexistence
7 things *pl syn* see POSSESSION 2
8 things *pl syn* see PERSONAL EFFECTS
9 things *pl syn* see CLOTHES
10 *syn* see POINT 1
11 *syn* see FASHION 3
12 *syn* see FETISH 2
thingum *n syn* see DOODAD
thingumajig *n syn* see DOODAD
thingumbob *n syn* see DOODAD
thingummy *n syn* see DOODAD
think *vb* **1** to form an idea of something in the mind <try to *think* exactly how the accident happened>
syn conceive, envisage, envision, fancy, feature, image, imagine, project, realize, see, vision, visualize
rel consider, contemplate, study, weigh; appreciate, comprehend, understand; cerebrate, ideate; conjecture, guess, surmise
2 *syn* see UNDERSTAND 3
3 *syn* see CONJECTURE
4 *syn* see FEEL 3
rel estimate; regard
5 to use one's powers of conception, judgment, or inference <the power to *think* sets humans apart from other animals>
syn cerebrate, cogitate, deliberate, reason, reflect, speculate
rel consider, contemplate; brood, meditate, mull, muse, ponder, ruminate; intellectualize, logicalize, logicize, rationalize; conclude, deduce, infer, judge
idiom put on one's thinking cap, set one's brain to work, use one's head, use the old bean
think (out *or* over) *vb syn* see CONSIDER 1
think (over) *vb syn* see RECONSIDER
thinkable *adj* **1** capable of being thought about <concepts that are easy enough to be *thinkable*>
syn cogitable
rel imaginable, presumable, supposable; comprehendible, comprehensible
con unimaginable; incomprehensible, uncomprehensible

ant unthinkable

2 capable of being made actual <nationalism at this time would be scarcely *thinkable* >
syn conceivable, imaginable, supposable
rel likely, possible; convincing, plausible; feasible, practicable, practical
con inconceivable, unimaginable; impossible, unlikely; implausible; impractical, unfeasible
ant unthinkable

thinking *adj syn* see THOUGHTFUL 1
ant unthinking

third degree *n syn* see CROSS-EXAMINATION

third estate *n syn* see COMMONALTY

thirst *vb syn* see LONG
rel covet; desire, wish

thirsting *adj syn* see THIRSTY 1

thirsty *adj* 1 experiencing a desire for drink <the long hot walk had made him *thirsty* >
syn athirst, dry, thirsting
rel juiceless, parched, sapless
2 *syn* see DRY 1
3 *syn* see EAGER
idiom hungry for, itching for, wild for
ant sated, satiated

this and that *n, often* this and thats *pl*
syn see SUNDRIES

thither *adv syn* see THERE
ant hither

thitherward *adv syn* see THERE
ant hitherward

thorny *adj* bristling with perplexities, points of controversy, or other conflicting elements <the *thorny* question of states' rights>
syn nettlesome, prickly, spiny
rel troublesome, vexatious; difficult; tricky

thorough *adj* 1 *syn* see EXHAUSTIVE
rel absolute
2 *syn* see CIRCUMSTANTIAL

thoroughbred *adj syn* see PUREBRED
con mixed, mongrel

thoroughfare *n syn* see WAY 1

thoroughgoing *adj* 1 *syn* see EXHAUSTIVE
2 *syn* see UTTER

thoroughly *adv* 1 *syn* see WELL 3
2 in a detailed and complete manner < *thoroughly* investigated the accusations>
syn completely, detailedly, exhaustively, in and out, inside out, up and down
idiom item by item, to the last detail
con casually, offhandedly, sketchily, superficially
ant cursorily
3 *syn* see VERY 1
4 *syn* see HARD 3

though *adv syn* see HOWEVER

though *conj* in spite of the fact that < *though* they know the war is lost, they continue to fight>
syn albeit, although, howbeit, much as, when, whereas, while

thought *n* 1 the act or process of thinking <sat immersed in deep *thought* >
syn brainwork, cerebration, cogitation, deliberation, reflection, speculation
rel contemplation; meditation, musing, pondering, rumination

2 *syn* see IDEA

thoughtful *adj* 1 characterized by or exhibiting the power to think <the doctor had a shrewd rather than a *thoughtful* face>
syn cogitative, contemplative, meditative, pensive, ||pensy, pondering, reflecting, reflective, ruminative, speculative, thinking
rel analytical, calculating, logical, rational; earnest, grave, melancholy, serious, sober, studious; brainy, intellectual; deep, inseeing, introspective
con irrational; dull, slow, stupid, unthinking; empty-headed, shallow, vacuous
ant thoughtless
2 *syn* see MINDFUL 2
3 mindful of others <the thank-you note was a *thoughtful* gesture>
syn attentive, considerate
rel anxious, careful, concerned, heedful, mindful, solicitous; chivalrous, civil, courteous, gallant, gracious, polite, well-bred
con careless, heedless, inattentive, negligent, remiss, unconcerned, unmindful, unthinking; inconsiderate; discourteous, impolite
ant thoughtless, unthoughtful

thoughtfully *adv syn* see WELL 2
rel courteously, politely, solicitously
con discourteously, impolitely; inconsiderately, heedlessly, unkindly
ant thoughtlessly, unthoughtfully

thoughtless *adj* 1 *syn* see RASH 1
2 *syn* see CARELESS 1
con mindful
ant thoughtful
3 *syn* see SHORT 5
rel discourteous, impolite, rude; selfish
ant thoughtful

thought-out *adj syn* see DELIBERATE 1
rel investigated; analyzed
idiom thought over (*or* through)

thousand *n syn* see SCAD

thrall *n syn* see BONDAGE

thralldom *n syn* see BONDAGE

thrash *vb* 1 *syn* see BEAT 1
2 *syn* see WHIP 2
3 *syn* see WHIP 1
rel strike; paddywhack, ||pail

thrashing *n syn* see DEFEAT 1

thrash out *vb syn* see DISCUSS 1

threadbare *adj* 1 *syn* see SHABBY 1
rel damaged, impaired, injured; frayed, ragged; shopworn, timeworn, worn
idiom the worse for wear, worn to rags (*or* threads)
2 *syn* see TRITE
rel common, familiar; imitative, uncreative; set, stock; banal, corny
con fresh; new; different, novel, original, unconventional, unusual; memorable

threaten *vb* to announce or forecast impending danger or evil <bullies *threatening* the child with a beating>
syn menace
rel browbeat, bulldoze, cow, intimidate; augur, forebode, portend, presage; caution, forewarn, warn
idiom make (*or* utter) threats against

threatening *adj* 1 *syn* see IMMINENT 2
rel impending; forthcoming, upcoming; close, near
2 *syn* see OMINOUS

threesome *n syn* see TRIAD

threshold *n syn* see VERGE 2

thrift *n syn* see ECONOMY
　rel austerity, economizing; saving; parsimony
　ant waste

thriftiness *n syn* see ECONOMY
　ant thriftlessness

thriftless *adj syn* see IMPROVIDENT
　ant thrifty

thrifty *adj* 1 *syn* see FLOURISHING
　rel blooming, burgeoning; growing
　2 *syn* see SPARING
　rel foresighted, prudent; conserving, preserving
　con extravagant, improvident
　ant wasteful

thrill *vb* to fill with emotions that stir or excite or to be so excited <an audience *thrilled* by the brilliant spectacle>
　syn electrify, enthuse, send
　rel animate, excite, galvanize, move, quicken, stimulate; arouse, inspire, rally, rouse, stir
　idiom thrill to pieces (*or* to bits)
　con bore, ennui, weary

thrill *n* sudden emotional stimulation, excitement, or enjoyment <they both got a *thrill* out of small-boat racing>
　syn bang, boot, kick, wallop
　rel excitement, lift, stimulation, titillation

thriller *n* a work of fiction or drama designed to hold the interest by use of a high degree of intrigue, adventure, or suspense <wrote cheap detective *thrillers*>
　syn chiller, shocker, thriller-diller
　rel gothic, mystery; dime novel, penny dreadful, shilling shocker

thriller-diller *n syn* see THRILLER

thrive *vb* 1 *syn* see BOOM
　rel come on, develop, grow; increase; prosper
　con stagnate; fail; bust
　2 *syn* see SUCCEED 3
　rel advance, progress
　idiom make a go, turn out well

thriving *adj* 1 *syn* see FLOURISHING
　rel blooming, growing; advancing, progressing
　idiom going strong
　con shriveling; dying
　2 *syn* see SUCCESSFUL

thriving *n syn* see PROSPERITY 2

throb *vb syn* see PULSATE
　rel thump; resonate

throe *n* 1 *syn* see ATTACK 3
　rel convulsion
　2 *syn* see PAIN 1
　rel stab

throne *n syn* see TOILET

throng *n syn* see CROWD 1
　rel assemblage, assembly, collection, congregation, gathering; bunch, flock, group, pack

thronged *adj syn* see ALIVE 5
　rel crawling

throttle *vb syn* see CHOKE 1

---

　rel garrote

throttling *n syn* see REPRESSION 1

through *prep* 1 *syn* see VIA 1
　2 *syn* see VIA 2
　3 *syn* see OVER 6
　4 *syn* see ABOUT 4
　idiom clear through

through *adv* 1 from beginning to end <the region has a mild climate the whole year *through*>
　syn around, over, round, throughout
　2 *syn* see OVER 5

through *adj* 1 *syn* see DIRECT 2
　con obstructed; interrupted
　2 *syn* see COMPLETE 4
　3 having no further value, strength, or resources <when he lost his voice, his singing career was *through*>
　syn done for, finished, washed-up
　rel ended; over
　4 being at the very end of a course, concern, or relationship <was *through* with his wife>
　syn done, washed-up
　rel finished

through-and-through *adv syn* see DOWN 2

throughout *adv* 1 *syn* see EVERYWHERE 1
　2 *syn* see THROUGH 1

throughout *prep* 1 *syn* see ABOUT 4
　2 *syn* see DURING

throw *vb* 1 to cause to move swiftly through space by a propulsive movement or a propelling force <*throw* a ball to first base>
　syn ‖bung, cast, fire, fling, heave, hurl, launch, pitch, sling, toss
　rel ding, drive, impel, precipitate, shoot; project, propel, push, shove, thrust; flick, flip; ‖chuck, shy, tumble; lift, lob
　2 to dislodge from one's seat especially in horseback riding <was *thrown* while taking a hurdle>
　syn buck (off), pitch, unhorse, unseat
　rel ding (off), fling (off)
　3 *syn* see OVERCOME 1
　4 *syn* see DON 1
　5 *syn* see EXERT
　6 *syn* see ADDRESS 3

throw away *vb* 1 *syn* see DISCARD
　ant salvage
　2 *syn* see WASTE 2
　con lay away, lay by, lay up

throw back *vb syn* see REVERT 2

throwback *n syn* see REVERSION 1

throw down *vb syn* see FELL 1
　rel cast down

throw in *vb syn* see INTRODUCE 6
　rel contribute

throwing away *n syn* see DISPOSAL 2
　ant salvaging

throw off *vb* 1 *syn* see RID
　2 *syn* see SHAKE 5
　3 *syn* see EMIT 2
　rel disgorge, eject, exhaust, expel
　4 *syn* see CONFUSE 2

throw out *vb* 1 *syn* see EJECT 1
　2 *syn* see DISCARD
　3 *syn* see SAY 1
　4 *syn* see CONFUSE 2

throw over *vb syn* see ABANDON 1

throw up *vb* 1 to construct or erect hastily and often carelessly <makeshift buildings *thrown up* almost overnight>

---

syn jerry-build, run up
rel roughcast, roughhew
idiom slap together, throw together
2 *syn* see VOMIT

thrum *vb syn* see HUM
rel birr, purr

thrust *vb* 1 *syn* see PUSH 1
rel crowd, jam; bump, elbow, jostle,
nudge, prod, shoulder
2 to cause (as a pointed instrument) to
penetrate forcibly < *thrust* the dagger
through her heart>
syn dig, drive, plunge, ram, run, sink,
stab, stick
rel jab, shove; impale; pierce; embed; put

thrust *n syn* see SUBSTANCE 2

thud *vb* to make a dull sound by or as if
by striking a surface with something thick
and heavy < heard footsteps *thudding*
down the hall>
syn clonk, clunk, thump
rel tunk; hit, smite, strike; beat, pound

thug *n* 1 a person inclined or hired to treat
another roughly, brutally, or murderously
< was beaten and robbed by *thugs*>
syn ‖gorilla, ‖hood, hoodlum, hooligan,
ruffian, strong arm; *compare* TOUGH
rel bully, ‖larrikan, plug-ugly, roughneck,
rowdy, tough; punk; cutthroat, gangster,
gunman, mobster; goon, hatchet man
2 *syn* see TOUGH

thumb *vb syn* see HITCHHIKE
idiom thumb a ride

thumb (through) *vb syn* see BROWSE

thump *vb syn* see THUD
rel hammer, knock

thunder *n* the sound that follows a flash of
lightning and is caused by sudden expansion of the air in the path of the electrical
discharge < he was more afraid of *thunder*
than of lightning>
syn thunderclap, thundercrack, thundering
rel fulmination

thunderbolt *n* a single discharge of lightning with the accompanying thunder < he
was startled by the *thunderbolt*>
syn bolt, thunderstroke

thunderclap *n syn* see THUNDER

thundercrack *n syn* see THUNDER

thundering *n syn* see THUNDER

thunderstroke *n syn* see THUNDERBOLT

thunderstruck *adj syn* see AGHAST 2
rel bewildered, staggered; breathless,
stunned
idiom struck dumb

thus *adv* 1 in this or that manner < summoned his counselors and spoke *thus* to
them>
syn so, thus and so, thus and thus, thusly
2 *syn* see THEREFORE

thus and so *adv syn* see THUS 1

thus and thus *adv syn* see THUS 1

thus far *adv syn* see HITHERTO 1

thusly *adv syn* see THUS 1

thwack *n syn* see BLOW 1

thwart *adj syn* see TRANSVERSE

thwart *vb syn* see FRUSTRATE 1
rel curb, restrain, scotch; cross; foul up,
gum up, queer; stymie
con aid, assist, help, support; abet, encourage

‖**tick** *n syn* see INSTANT 1

ticket *n* 1 a slip giving information (as of
ownership, identity, or price) < the price
of the iron is on the *ticket*>
syn label, tag
rel card; slip; sticker
2 a card of admission < theater *tickets*>
syn carte d'entrée
rel pass
3 a list of candidates for appointment,
nomination, or election < vote the party
ticket>
syn slate
rel choice; lineup; list
4 *syn* see BALLOT 1
5 *syn* see PASSPORT

ticklish *adj* 1 *syn* see UNSTABLE 2
2 *syn* see DELICATE 7
rel critical
3 *syn* see INCONSTANT 1

tick off *vb* 1 *syn* see ENUMERATE 2
2 *syn* see REPROVE

tidbit (*or* titbit) *n syn* see DELICACY

‖**tiddly** *adj syn* see INTOXICATED 1

tide *n syn* see FLOW

tidings *n pl syn* see NEWS

tidy *adj syn* see NEAT 2
rel sleek, spruce
ant untidy

tie *n* 1 *syn* see BOND 3
rel fastener, fastening; attachment
2 *syn* see DRAW 4

tie *vb* 1 to make fast and secure < *tie* a
bundle with strong cord>
syn bind, tie up
rel attach, fasten; connect, join, link;
anchor, moor, rivet, secure; lash, truss
(up); band, cinch, gird, rope
con loose, loosen; disconnect
ant untie
2 *syn* see MARRY 2
3 *syn* see HAMPER
idiom tie hand and foot, tie one's hands
ant untie
4 *syn* see EQUAL 3

tier *n* 1 *syn* see LINE 5
rel layer
2 *syn* see CLASS 1

tie up *vb* 1 *syn* see TIE 1
2 *syn* see HAMPER

tie-up *n syn* see ASSOCIATION 1
rel linkup

tiff *n syn* see QUARREL

tiff *vb syn* see QUARREL

tiffany *adj syn* see FILMY

tight *adj* 1 *syn* see FAST 4
rel clasped; solid, steadfast
con lax, limp; shaky
ant loose
2 *syn* see CLOSE 4
ant loose
3 fitting, drawn, or stretched so that there
is no slackness or looseness < a *tight*
drumhead>
syn close, taut, tense
rel skintight; constricted, contracted,
drawn, tightened; inflexible, rigid, stiff
con loosened, slack, unconstricted
ant loose
4 difficult to cope with, get through, or
circumvent < a very *tight* diplomatic situa-
tion>
syn arduous, rough, tricksy, trying
rel difficult; exacting; tense; critical; punishing; distressing, disturbing, upsetting

5 *syn* see STINGY

6 *syn* see INTOXICATED 1

idiom tight as a tick

tight *adv syn* see HARD 7

tightfisted *adj syn* see STINGY

rel grudging, mean, shabby

tight-laced *adj syn* see PRIM 1

tight-lipped *adj syn* see SILENT 3

idiom with one's lips sealed

tightly *adv syn* see HARD 7

tight-mouthed *adj syn* see SILENT 3

tightwad *n syn* see MISER

till *prep syn* see UNTIL

till *conj* up to the time when < be sure to wait *till* I come >

syn until

till *vb* to prepare (soil) for the raising of crops < *till* the soil >

syn cultivate, dress, ‖labor, tend, work

rel harrow, hoe, mulch, plow, turn; plant, sow

tillable *adj syn* see ARABLE

ant untillable

tilt *vb* 1 *syn* see SLANT 1

2 *syn* see SEESAW

tilt *n syn* see SLOPE

tilted *adj syn* see INCLINED 3

tilter *vb syn* see SEESAW

tilting *adj syn* see INCLINED 3

timber *n* 1 *syn* see FOREST

2 a large squared or dressed piece of wood < roof *timbers* >

syn balk, beam

rel girder, rafter

timberland *n syn* see FOREST

timbre *n syn* see TEMPER 1

time *n* 1 *syn* see WHILE 1

rel season

2 *syn* see OCCASION 5

3 *syn* see OPPORTUNITY

idiom the proper moment

4 *syn* see PERIOD 2

5 *syn* see TERM 2

6 *syn* see SEASON

7 *syn* see TEMPO

8 *syn* see SPELL 1

‖**9** *syn* see BINGE 1

time *vb* 1 to arrange or set the time of < *timed* his visits to coincide with her vacations >

syn book, schedule

rel plan, program, set up

2 to ascertain or record the time, duration, or rate of < *timed* the car at 100 mph >

syn clock

idiom hold the clock on

time and again *adv syn* see OFTEN

timeless *adj* 1 *syn* see CONTINUAL

2 *syn* see ETERNAL 4

timely *adv syn* see EARLY 1

timely *adj* 1 done or occurring at a suitable time < await a more *timely* moment >

syn auspicious, favorable, opportune, propitious, prosperous, seasonable, timeous, well-timed

rel appropriate, fit, fitting, meet, proper, suitable; likely, promising

con improper, inappropriate, unfitting; inauspicious, inopportune, unfavorable, unpropitious, unsuitable; ill-timed

ant untimely

2 *syn* see PUNCTUAL 2

timeous *adj syn* see TIMELY 1

timetable *n syn* see PROGRAM 1

rel table; plan

timeworn *adj* 1 *syn* see ANCIENT 1

2 *syn* see TRITE

timid *adj* 1 *syn* see SHY 1

rel humble; shrinking

ant bold

2 marked by or exhibiting a lack of boldness, courage, or determination < was too *timid* to ski >

syn timorous, ‖timorsome, undaring

rel gentle, mild, milk-toast, milky; cautious, chary, wary; jumpy, nervous, skittish; afraid, apprehensive, fainthearted, fearful; chicken, chickenhearted, henhearted, mouselike, mousy, pigeonhearted; cowardly, yellow; funky, panicky

con audacious, brave, courageous, daring, doughty, fearless, intrepid, lionhearted, unafraid, valiant, valorous

ant bold

3 *syn* see VACILLATING 2

timorous *adj syn* see TIMID 2

rel quailing, recoiling, shrinking; quivering, shivering, shuddering, trembling

ant assured

‖**timorsome** *adj syn* see TIMID 2

tincture *n* 1 *syn* see COLOR 6

2 *syn* see HINT 2

rel smattering

tincture *vb syn* see TINT

rel pigment; stain

ting *vb syn* see TINKLE 1

tinge *vb syn* see TINT

rel streak

tinge *n* 1 *syn* see COLOR 1

rel coloration, coloring, tincture; stain

2 *syn* see HINT 2

tingle *vb* 1 *syn* see TINKLE 1

rel chime

2 *syn* see JINGLE

tinker *vb syn* see FIDDLE 2

idiom play around

tinkle *vb* 1 to make a repeated light high-pitched ringing sound < wind-bells *tinkling* in the breeze >

syn plink, ting, tingle

rel clink, jangle, jingle

2 *syn* see JINGLE

3 *syn* see CHAT 1

tinsel *adj syn* see GAUDY

tint *n syn* see COLOR 1

rel tincture, touch; coloration; pigmentation; dye, stain, wash

tint *vb* to color with a slight shade or stain < white blossoms *tinted* with pale pink >

syn complexion, tincture, tinge

rel color, dye; shade, touch (up); stain, wash

tintamarre *n syn* see DIN

tiny *adj* exceptionally or remarkably small < the first *tiny* buds of spring flowers >

syn ‖bitsy, diminutive, dwarf, dwarfish, itsy-bitsy, itty-bitty, lilliputian, midget, miniature, minikin, minute, peewee, pint-size, pocket, pocket-size, pygmy, teensy, teensy-weensy, teenty, teeny, teeny-weeny, wee, weensy, weeny; *compare* SMALL 1

---

syn synonym(s)   *rel* related word(s)

ant antonym(s)   *con* contrasted word(s)

idiom idiomatic equivalent(s)

‖ use limited; if in doubt, see a dictionary

rel minuscular, minuscule; infinitesimal, microscopic, minim
con colossal, enormous, gigantic, immense, mammoth, vast
ant huge

tip *n syn see* POINT 9
tip *vb syn see* SLANT 1
tip *vb syn see* TIPTOE
  rel creep, mince, pussyfoot, steal
tip (over) *vb syn see* OVERTURN 1
  idiom turn upside down
tip *n syn see* GRATUITY
tip *n* a piece of advice or confidential information given by one thought to have access to special or inside sources < gave him a *tip* on which horse would win >
  syn point, pointer, steer, tip-off
  rel advice; information; clue, cue, hint; forecast, prediction
  idiom a bit of inside advice, a bug in the ear, a word to the wise
tip-off *n syn see* TIP
tipped *adj syn see* INCLINED 3
tipple *vb syn see* DRINK 3
  idiom drown one's cares (*or* sorrows)
tipple *n syn see* LIQUOR 2
tippler *n syn see* DRUNKARD
tipster *n syn see* INFORMER
tipsy *adj syn see* INTOXICATED 1
  rel dazed, unsteady
tiptoe *vb* to walk or proceed quietly on or as if on the ends of the toes < *tiptoed* through the dark house >
  syn tip, toe
  rel creep, gumshoe, pussyfoot, steal
  con clomp, clump, stamp, stomp, stump
tirade *n* a violent, often protracted, and usually denunciatory speech or writing < lashed out with a vicious *tirade* of angry protest >
  syn diatribe, harangue, jeremiad, philippic
  rel rant, rodomontade, screed; abuse, invective, revilement, vituperation; censure, condemnation, denunciation; berating, tongue-lashing; lecture, sermon
tire *vb* 1 to deplete the strength and energy of < the plane trip *tired* him >
  syn drain, fatigue, jade, wear, wear down, weary; *compare* EXHAUST 4
  rel debilitate, enervate, enfeeble, sap, weaken; exhaust, wear out
  con brace (up), invigorate, strengthen; animate, energize, enliven, pep (up), quicken, stimulate, vitalize
  2 *syn see* BORE
  rel jade, wear; irk; disgust, nauseate, sicken
  idiom make one tired, put one to sleep
tired *adj* 1 being depleted of strength and energy < was too *tired* to go on >
  syn fatigued, jaded, wearied, weary, worn, worn down
  rel overtaxed, overworked; drained, rundown; ||beat, ||bushed, dog-tired, exhausted, fagged, frazzled, overworn, ||pooped, ||tucked up, tuckered, worn-out; collapsing, consumed, knocked out, prostrate, spent
  idiom worn to a frazzle
  con active, energetic, lively, strong, tireless
  ant rested; fresh, untired
  2 *syn see* SHABBY 1

3 *syn see* FED UP
  rel annoyed, bothered, displeased, irked
  idiom having a bellyful of, having about enough of
  4 *syn see* TRITE
tiredness *n syn see* FATIGUE
  rel collapse, prostration
tireless *adj syn see* INDEFATIGABLE
  rel active, enthusiastic
  con inactive, listless, tired, unenergetic, unenthusiastic, weak
tiresome *adj syn see* IRKSOME
  rel dull; jading; burdensome, onerous, oppressive; difficult, hard
tiring *adj syn see* IRKSOME
Titan *adj syn see* HUGE
titanic *adj syn see* HUGE
title *n* 1 *syn see* CLAIM 1
  rel argument, ground, justification, proof, reason; desert, due, merit
  2 *syn see* NAME 1
title *vb syn see* NAME 1
titter *vb syn see* LAUGH
  rel twitter
  idiom laugh behind (*or* in) one's hand, laugh in one's beard
tittle *n syn see* PARTICLE
  rel fleck, flyspeck, speck; crumb, grain, scrap, snippet
tittle-tattle *n* 1 *syn see* CHATTER
  2 *syn see* REPORT 1
titubate *vb syn see* REEL 2
titular *adj syn see* NOMINAL
tizzy *n syn see* SNIT
to *prep* 1 in the direction of and as far as < was driving *to* the city >
  syn into
  rel toward
  ant from
  2 *syn see* AGAINST 2
  rel on, over, upon
  3 *syn see* BEFORE 1
  4 *syn see* UNTIL
  5 for the particular purpose of < a market study tailored *to* your needs >
  syn for
  idiom in contemplation (*or* consideration) of, with an eye to, with a view to
  6 in complement to < played Romeo *to* her Juliet >
  syn opposite
toad *n syn see* SNOT 1
toad *n syn see* SYCOPHANT
toadeater *n syn see* SYCOPHANT
toadier *n syn see* SYCOPHANT
toady *n syn see* SYCOPHANT
toady *vb syn see* FAWN
  rel follow, tag, tail, trail
toadying *adj syn see* FAWNING
toadyish *adj syn see* FAWNING
to-and-fro *n* 1 *syn see* HESITATION
  2 *syn see* QUARREL
toast *n syn see* DRINK 2
to-be *n syn see* FUTURE
tocsin *n syn see* ALARM 1
  rel sign, signal
today *adv* at the present time < youth *today* do not know what poverty is >
  syn now, nowadays, presently
  idiom in this day and age, these days
  con then, yesteryear
today *n syn see* PRESENT
todayish *adj syn see* PRESENT

to-do *n* 1 *syn* see COMMOTION 4

  2 *syn* see COMMOTION 3

toe *vb syn* see TIPTOE

tog (out *or* up) *vb syn* see DRESS UP 1

together *adv* 1 at one and the same time <events that occurred *together*>
  syn at once, coincidentally, coincidently, coinstantaneously, concurrently, simultaneously
  idiom all at once, all together
  ant separately

  2 in succession usually without intermission <was moody for days *together*>
  syn consecutively, continually, continuously, hand running, night and day, running, successively, unintermittedly, uninterruptedly
  idiom on end

  3 in or by combined action or effort <students and faculty protested *together*>
  syn conjointly, jointly, mutually
  rel collectively, concertedly, unanimously
  idiom in one breath, in the same breath, with one accord, with one voice
  ant separately

togetherness *n* 1 *syn* see ASSOCIATION 1

  2 *syn* see SOLIDARITY

‖**toggle** *vb syn* see DRESS UP 1

togs *n pl syn* see CLOTHES

toil *n syn* see WORK 2
  idiom sweat of one's brow, toil and trouble

toil *vb* 1 *syn* see LABOR 1

  2 *syn* see DRUDGE

  3 *syn* see PLOD 1

toil *n, usu* toils *pl syn* see WEB 2

toiler *n syn* see SLAVE 2

toilet *n* a fixture for defecation and urination
  syn ‖can, convenience, ‖donicker, head, john, johnny, latrine, lavatory, ‖loo, ‖pot, ‖potty, privy, ‖throne, water closet
  rel hopper

toilful *adj syn* see HARD 6

toilsome *adj syn* see HARD 6

toilsomely *adv syn* see HARD 8

token *n* 1 *syn* see INDICATION 3
  rel harbinger, omen, portent; characteristic, earmark; indicator, smack

  2 *syn* see REMEMBRANCE 3

  3 *syn* see EXPRESSION 3

  4 *syn* see PLEDGE 1

‖**tokus** *n syn* see BUTTOCKS

tolerable *adj* 1 *syn* see BEARABLE
  ant intolerable

  2 *syn* see RESPECTABLE 5

  3 *syn* see DECENT 4
  rel fair, goodish, OK, tidy
  idiom better than nothing, good enough
  ant intolerable

tolerably *adv syn* see ENOUGH 2

tolerance *n* 1 the capacity to bear something unpleasant, painful, or difficult <had always had a high *tolerance* to pain>
  syn endurance, stamina, toleration

  rel fortitude, grit, guts; strength, vigor; long-suffering, patience, sufferance; steadfastness, steadiness; opposition, resistance
  ant intolerance

  2 *syn* see FORBEARANCE 2
  rel liberality, liberalness, open-mindedness, permissiveness
  con narrow-mindedness; prejudice; dogmatism; bigotry
  ant intolerance

tolerant *adj* 1 *syn* see LIBERAL 3
  rel open-minded; permissive
  con narrow, narrow-minded; prejudiced; dogmatic; bigoted
  ant intolerant

  2 *syn* see FORBEARING
  rel benevolent, humane; condoning, excusing, forgiving, sympathetic, understanding
  con severe, stern; uncompromising, unforgiving, unsympathetic
  ant intolerant

tolerate *vb* 1 *syn* see ACCEPT 2
  rel condone, countenance; allow, consent (to), permit; have, bear (to)

  2 *syn* see BEAR 10
  rel sustain

toleration *n* 1 *syn* see FORBEARANCE 2

  2 *syn* see TOLERANCE 1

toll *n syn* see EXPENSE 2

toll *vb syn* see LURE

toll *vb syn* see RING

‖**tomato** *n syn* see PROSTITUTE

tomb *n syn* see GRAVE
  rel box, coffin, ‖trough

tomb *vb* 1 *syn* see BURY 1
  ant untomb

  2 *syn* see ENTOMB 1
  ant disentomb, untomb

tomboy *n* a girl exhibiting boyish behavior <a *tomboy* who still rode, fished, and fought with her brothers>
  syn gamine, hoyden
  rel romp

tombstone *n* an inscribed memorial stone set at a place of interment <read the epitaph on the *tombstone* of her ancestor>
  syn footstone, grave marker, gravestone, headstone, ledger, monument
  rel memorial; cenotaph

tome *n syn* see BOOK 1

tomfool *n syn* see FOOL 1

tomfool *adj syn* see FOOLISH 2

tomfoolery *n* 1 *syn* see NONSENSE 2

  2 *syn* see PRANK

tommyrot *n syn* see NONSENSE 2

Tom o' Bedlam *n syn* see LUNATIC 1

Tom Thumb *n syn* see DWARF

ton *n* 1 *syn* see FASHION 3

  2 *syn* see SMART SET

tone *n* 1 *syn* see INFLECTION

  2 *syn* see VEIN 1

  3 *syn* see COLOR 1
  rel blend

  4 the state of a living body or any of its organs or parts in which the functions are healthy and performed with due vigor <diet and exercise contributed to his good muscle *tone*>
  syn tonicity, tonus
  rel health, healthiness; elasticity, resiliency; strength, vigor

---

syn synonym(s)   *rel* related word(s)
ant antonym(s)   *con* contrasted word(s)
idiom idiomatic equivalent(s)
‖ use limited; if in doubt, see a dictionary

5 *syn* see TEMPER 1
rel current, movement
idiom (the) state of things
6 *syn* see MOOD 1
toned down *adj syn* see SUBDUED 2
tongue *n syn* see LANGUAGE 1
tongue *vb syn* see SCOLD 1
tongue–lash *vb syn* see SCOLD 1
idiom give one the rough side of one's
tongue
tongue–tied *adj syn* see INARTICULATE 3
con loose-lipped, loose-tongued
‖**tongue–walk** *vb syn* see SCOLD 1
idiom give one the rough side of one's
tongue
tonguey *adj syn* see TALKATIVE
tonic *adj* 1 increasing or restoring physical
or mental tone <the *tonic* effect of a
syn astringent, restorative, roborant
rel invigorating, refreshing, renewing,
strengthening; bracing, sharp
con debilitating, enfeebling, weakening;
enervating; exhausting, grueling, sapping
2 *syn* see INVIGORATING
tonicity *n syn* see TONE 4
tonish *adj syn* see STYLISH
tonus *n syn* see TONE 4
tony *adj syn* see STYLISH
too *adv* 1 *syn* see ALSO 1
2 *syn* see EVER 6
rel exorbitantly, immoderately, unconscio-
nably, unmeasurably
3 *syn* see VERY 1
‖**toodle–oo** *interj syn* see GOOD-BYE
tool *n syn* see IMPLEMENT
rel machine, mechanism
2 one used or manipulated by another to
accomplish his purposes <had no intention of being used as a *tool* by either fac-
tion>
syn cat's-paw, pawn, puppet, stooge
rel agent, hireling, vehicle; chump, sucker
tool *vb syn* see DRIVE 5
toot *vb syn* see DECLARE 1
toot *n syn* see BINGE 1
toothful *n syn* see DRAM
toothsome *adj syn* see PALATABLE
rel agreeable, pleasant, pleasing
toothy *adj* 1 having or showing prominent
teeth <a wide *toothy* grin>
syn teethy
2 *syn* see PALATABLE
too–too *adj syn* see GENTEEL 3
rel chichi
‖**tootsie** *n syn* see DOXY 1
top *n* 1 the highest point <hiked to the *top*
of the mountain>
syn apex, crest, crown, fastigium, peak,
roof, summit, vertex
rel acme, climax, culmination, height,
pinnacle; cusp, head, point, tip
con base, foot, sole; nadir
ant bottom
2 the outer or upper part <the *top* of the
table>
syn face, superficies, surface
3 *syn* see BEST
ant bottom
top *vb* 1 to remove or cut back the top of
<*top* a tree>
syn crop, detruncate, pollard, truncate
rel clip, dock, prune, trim; curtail,
shorten

2 *syn* see SURPASS 1
3 *syn* see SURMOUNT 3
top *adj* 1 of, relating to, or being at the top
<the *top* floor of the house>
syn apical, highest, loftiest, topmost,
uppermost
con bottommost, lowest
ant bottom
2 *syn* see EXCELLENT
3 *syn* see MAXIMUM
top–drawer *adj syn* see EXALTED 1
tope *vb syn* see DRINK 3
toper *n syn* see DRUNKARD
Tophet *n syn* see HELL
topic *n syn* see SUBJECT 2
rel proposition; issue
topless *adj syn* see LOFTY 6
toploftical *adj syn* see PROUD 1
toplofty *adj syn* see PROUD 1
rel inflated, puffed; egotistic
con crestfallen
topmost *adj* 1 *syn* see TOP 1
ant bottommost
2 *syn* see MAXIMUM
top–notch *adj syn* see EXCELLENT
top off *vb syn* see CLIMAX
topography *n syn* see TERRAIN 1
topple *vb* 1 *syn* see FALL 2
2 *syn* see TEETER
3 *syn* see OVERTURN 1
4 *syn* see OVERTHROW 2
top–ranking *adj syn* see EXALTED 1
topsy–turviness *n syn* see CONFUSION 3
topsy–turvy *adj* 1 *syn* see UPSIDE-DOWN
1
2 *syn* see UPSIDE-DOWN 2
rel cockeyed, disarranged, disjointed,
disordered, unhinged
torch *n syn* see INCENDIARY
toreador *n syn* see BULLFIGHTER
torero *n syn* see BULLFIGHTER
torment *vb* 1 *syn* see AFFLICT
rel distress, trouble; hurt, pain, punish
2 *syn* see MOLEST
tormented *adj syn* see DISTRAUGHT
tormenting *adj syn* see EXCRUCIATING
torn *adj syn* see LACERATED
tornado *n* a violent destructive whirling
wind accompanied by a funnel-shaped
cloud extending downward from a cumu-
lonimbus cloud <the *tornado* caused
extensive destruction>
syn cyclone, twister; *compare* HURRI-
CANE, WHIRLWIND 1
torpedo *n syn* see ASSASSIN
torpid *adj syn* see LETHARGIC
rel dull, leaden, sodden; motionless,
static; numb
con lively; frisky, sprightly, vigorous; fast
ant active
torpidity *n syn* see LETHARGY 1
rel listlessness, passivity, stagnation
torpidness *n syn* see LETHARGY 1
ant activeness
torpor *n syn* see LETHARGY 1
rel stolidity; passivity
ant activity; animation
torrent *n syn* see FLOOD 2
rel flux, rush
torrid *adj* 1 *syn* see HOT 1
idiom burning hot, hot enough to roast
an ox
ant arctic

2 *syn* see IMPASSIONED

rel sultry

ant frigid

tort *n syn* see EVIL 3

tortuous *adj syn* see WINDING

rel involute, vermiculate; cranky; involved

torture *vb* 1 *syn* see AFFLICT

rel oppress, persecute, wrong; hurt, wound; maim, mangle, mutilate

idiom put on the rack, put to torture

2 *syn* see DEFORM

torturing *adj syn* see EXCRUCIATING

torturous *adj syn* see EXCRUCIATING

tory *n syn* see DIEHARD 1

rel loyalist, traditionalist

tory *adj syn* see CONSERVATIVE 1

tosh *n syn* see NONSENSE 2

toss *vb* 1 *syn* see THROW 1

2 to rise and fall often rhythmically or with alternate motions <a small boat *tossing* in heavy seas>

syn heave, pitch, rock, roll; *compare* SEE-SAW

rel bob; sway

3 *syn* see DRINK 1

4 *syn* see WRITHE 1

idiom toss and turn

toss (around) *vb syn* see DISCUSS 1

rel bandy (about)

tosspot *n syn* see DRUNKARD

tot *n syn* see DRAM

tot *vb syn* see ADD 2

total *adj* 1 *syn* see WHOLE 4

rel overall; comprehensive, full, inclusive, plenary; teetotal

ant partial

2 *syn* see UTTER

3 *syn* see TOTALITARIAN 1

rel authoritative; absolute, arbitrary, despotic; omnipotent

4 *syn* see TOTALITARIAN 2

rel monopolistic

5 concentrating and employing all resources on a single objective <a *total* offensive>

syn all-out, full-blown, full-out, full-scale, totalitarian, unlimited

rel out-and-out, unreserved, unrestricted

con hampered, impeded, trammeled; restrained, restricted; stinted

ant limited

total *n* 1 *syn* see WHOLE 1

2 *syn* see BODY 5

total *vb* 1 *syn* see ADD 2

2 *syn* see AMOUNT 1

rel comprise, consist (of); stack up; equal, result (in), yield

idiom mount up to, pile up to

3 to make a total wreck of < *totaled* his car when he hit the wall>

syn demolish, wreck; *compare* DESTROY 1

rel crack up, smash

totalistic *adj syn* see TOTALITARIAN 1

con democratic; individualistic

totalitarian *adj* 1 of or relating to centralized control by one autocratic leader or party considered to be infallible <Nazi Germany was a *totalitarian* state>

syn authoritarian, total, totalistic; *compare* ABSOLUTE 4, DICTATORIAL

con democratic, popular; constitutional

2 having or exercising dictatorial powers often tending toward monopoly <antitrust legislation reversing the trend toward the *totalitarian* collectivism of big business>

syn total

3 *syn* see TOTAL 5

totalitarianism *n syn* see TYRANNY

totality *n* 1 *syn* see WHOLE 1

2 *syn* see ENTIRETY 1

3 *syn* see WHOLE 2

rel configuration, form

totalize *vb syn* see ADD 2

totally *adv syn* see ALL 1

tote *vb syn* see CARRY 1

rel cart, haul; shoulder

tote *n syn* see WHOLE 1

tote *vb syn* see ADD 2

totter *vb* 1 *syn* see TEETER

rel shimmy

2 *syn* see REEL 2

rel blunder, stumble, trip; dodder, ||dotter; flounder

touch *vb* 1 to probe with a sensitive part of the body (as a finger) so as to get or produce a sensation often in the course of examining or exploring < *touch* an iron to test its temperature>

syn feel, finger, handle, palpate, paw

rel brush, graze; caress, fondle, rub, stroke, toy (with); palm, thumb; examine, inspect, probe, scrutinize; investigate

2 *syn* see ADJOIN

3 *syn* see EQUAL 3

4 *syn* see AFFECT

rel arouse, stir; excite, quicken, stimulate

idiom touch a chord

5 *syn* see AMOUNT 2

rel come (to), verge (on)

touch *n* 1 *syn* see CONTACT 1

rel junction; communication

2 an act of touching or feeling <woke her with a light *touch* on her hand>

syn palpation, taction

rel brush, pat, stroke; contact

3 tactile sensitivity <a blanket soft to the *touch*>

syn feel, tactility

rel feeling

4 a specified sensation conveyed through the tactile receptors <the velvety *touch* of a fabric>

syn feel, feeling

5 *syn* see HINT 1

6 distinctive manner or method <this house needs a woman's *touch*>

syn hand

rel manner, style, way

||7 *syn* see THEFT

touchable *adj syn* see TANGIBLE 1

ant untouchable

touch down *vb syn* see ALIGHT

touching *prep* 1 *syn* see AGAINST 2

idiom up against

2 *syn* see APROPOS

touching *adj* 1 *syn* see ADJACENT 3

rel meeting; impinging; overlapping

2 *syn* see MOVING 2

rel compassionate, responsive, sympathetic, tender; piteous, pitiable, pitiful, tear-jerking

---

syn synonym(s)   *rel* related word(s)

ant antonym(s)   *con* contrasted word(s)

idiom idiomatic equivalent(s)

|| use limited; if in doubt, see a dictionary

touch-me-not-ish *adj syn* see UNSOCIABLE

touchstone *n syn* see STANDARD 3
rel check, test, trial; barometer, scale; demonstration, proof

touch up *vb* to improve or perfect by small additional strokes or alterations < *touch up* a picture >
syn brush up, retouch, tease up
rel improve, perfect, polish; do (up), fix (up)
idiom put finishing touches on

touchy *adj* 1 *syn* see IRASCIBLE
rel hypersensitive, oversensitive, sensitive, thin-skinned; temperamental, volatile; miffy
ant imperturbable
2 *syn* see DELICATE 7
rel dicey, risky, unpredictable; harmful, hazardous, unsafe

tough *adj* 1 *syn* see STRONG 2
rel flinty, hard, unyielding; resistant, unbreakable, withstanding
idiom tough as leather (*or* nails)
con breakable; brittle; yielding
ant fragile
2 *syn* see VISCOUS
3 advocating a persistently firm course of action < a *tough* foreign policy >
syn hard-line, inflexible, uncompromising, unyielding
rel stiff, taut; fixed, confirmed, hard-shell, narrow, rigid; arbitrary, immutable, unalterable; hard-boiled, hardened, obdurate; harsh, procrustean, rigorous, severe, strict; drastic
con liberal, relaxed; compromising, flexible, laissez-faire, yielding
ant soft
4 having or exhibiting great physical endurance (as to strain, hardship, or labor) < the rigorous climate created a *tough* people >
syn hardy, rugged
rel conditioned, hard-bitten, hardened, seasoned, steeled; fit, healthy, lusty, robust, vigorous; stalwart, strong, sturdy
con delicate, fragile, frail, tender; half-hardy, puny; weakened
ant weak
5 *syn* see OBSTINATE
rel hardfisted, hardhanded, hardheaded, tough-minded
6 *syn* see HARD 6
ant soft
7 *syn* see ONEROUS
ant soft
8 frequented by rowdy or criminal elements < lived in a *tough* neighborhood >
syn bad, rough
rel disorderly, rowdy; dangerous, unsafe; ghetto, inner-city, underprivileged
con orderly, quiet, safe

tough (out) *vb syn* see ACCEPT 2

tough *n* a rough or unruly person often taking part in bullying or violent behavior < attacked by a gang of *toughs* >
syn ‖b'hoy, bullyboy, mucker, mug, plug-ugly, punk, rough, roughneck, rowdy, ruffian, thug, toughie, yahoo; *compare* BULLY 1, THUG 1
rel goon, hood, hoodlum, hooligan

toughen *vb syn* see HARDEN 2

rel develop, strengthen
ant weaken

toughie *n syn* see TOUGH
rel ‖heavy

tour *n* 1 *syn* see SPELL
2 a journey in which one eventually returns to the starting point < made a quick *tour* of all the bars >
syn circuit, round, roundabout, round trip; *compare* TRIP 1
rel turn; circle tour

tour de force *n* 1 *syn* see FEAT 2
2 *syn* see MASTERPIECE 1

tourist *n* one who makes a tour for pleasure or culture < *tourists* going through the castle >
syn rubberneck, sightseer, ‖tripper
rel day-tripper, excursionist; traveler; visitor

tout *n syn* see LOOKOUT 3

tout *vb* to overly publicize < was *touted* as the world's most modern shopping center >
syn ballyhoo, herald, trumpet
rel proclaim, publicize; plug, promote; acclaim, laud, praise
idiom praise to the skies

tow *vb syn* see PULL 2
rel propel; push
idiom take in tow

toward *adj syn* see GOOD
ant untoward

toward *prep* 1 *syn* see APROPOS
2 *syn* see AGAINST 1

tower (above *or* over) *vb syn* see OVERLOOK 2

towering *adj* 1 *syn* see LOFTY 6
rel altitudinous, high, tall; stratospheric
2 *syn* see SUPREME
3 *syn* see MONSTROUS 1
4 reaching a high point of greatness, intensity, or violence < a *towering* rage >
syn monumental, overwhelming
rel ‖crashing; overpowering, mind-blowing
con minor, petty, piddling, puny, trivial
5 *syn* see EXCESSIVE 1

towery *adj syn* see LOFTY 6

to wit *adv syn* see NAMELY

towner *n syn* see TOWNSMAN

townish *adj* of, relating to, or characteristic of a town or of urban life < enjoyed a fast-paced, competitive, *townish* life-style >
syn towny
rel city, metropolitan, urban
con bucolic, rural; isolated, lonely, solitary

townman *n syn* see TOWNSMAN

townsman *n* a town dweller < population composed mostly of *townsmen* and a few countrymen >
syn burgher, cit, citizen, towner, townman, towny

towny *n syn* see TOWNSMAN

towny *adj syn* see TOWNISH

tow-row *n syn* see COMMOTION 4

toxic *adj syn* see POISONOUS
ant nontoxic

toxicant *adj syn* see POISONOUS

toy *n* 1 *syn* see KNICKKNACK
2 something for a child to play with < games, dolls, and other *toys* >
syn ‖die, ‖play-pretty, plaything, ‖pretty

toy *vb 1 syn* see TRIFLE 1
rel disport, frolic, play, sport; fiddle (with), tease; caress, cosset, cuddle, dandle, pet
idiom fool (*or* mess) around with

trace *n 1 syn* see TRACK 1
rel evidence, proof
2 *syn* see VESTIGE 1
rel mark, token
3 *syn* see HINT 2

trace *vb syn* see TRACK 1

track *n 1* detectable evidence that something has passed < the *track* of a sleigh in the snow>
syn trace, tread
rel impress, imprint, mark, print; sign, vestige
2 *syn* see TRAIL
rel footpath, footway, walk
idiom beaten path
3 *syn* see WAY 1
rel roadway, trackway
4 *syn* see FOOTPRINT
rel scent, slot

track *vb 1* to follow the tracks or traces of < *track* a wounded deer>
syn trace, trail
rel follow; dog, shadow, tail; chase, pursue; find, hunt (down), smell (out)
idiom be hot on the trail of
2 *syn* see TRAVEL 2

tract *n 1 syn* see AREA 1
rel amplitude, spread, stretch; part, portion, section, sector
2 *syn* see LOT 3
3 *syn* see FOOTPRINT

tractable *adj syn* see OBEDIENT
rel flexible, pliable, pliant; manageable; subdued
con headstrong, unmanageable, willful; obstinate, refractory, stubborn
ant intractable, unruly

tractate *n syn* see DISCOURSE 2

trade *n 1* a pursuit followed as an occupation or means of livelihood and requiring technical knowledge and skill < the *trade* of a carpenter>
syn art, calling, craft, handicraft, métier, profession, vocation
rel employment, occupation, pursuit, work
con avocation, hobby
2 *syn* see BUSINESS 4
rel market
3 *syn* see PATRONAGE 2

trade *vb 1* to give one thing in return for another with an expectation of gain < *traded* furs for tobacco and rum>
syn bargain, barter, exchange, swap, traffic, truck; *compare* EXCHANGE 2
rel market, merchandise, sell; deal; argue, chaffer, dicker, haggle, wrangle
idiom make (*or* strike) a bargain, make a deal
2 *syn* see EXCHANGE 2

trademark *n syn* see MARK 7
trader *n syn* see MERCHANT
tradesman *n syn* see MERCHANT

tradition *n 1* an inherited or established way of thinking, feeling, or doing < America's Puritan *tradition* is still very much alive>
syn heritage
rel culture; convention, custom, ethic, form; birthright, inheritance, legacy
2 *syn* see LORE 2

traditional *adj 1* of or relating to tradition < a *traditional* interpretation of the Bible>
syn conventional, tralatitious; *compare* CONVENTIONAL 1
rel ancestral, immemorial, old; customary, habitual, usual; acknowledged, established, establishmentarian, fixed; common, popular
con new; unconventional, unusual; individualistic, original, personal
2 *syn* see ORAL 2

traditionalist *n syn* see PURIST

traditionalistic *adj syn* see CONSERVATIVE 1

traduce *vb syn* see MALIGN
rel mock; disgrace; betray; violate

traducing *adj syn* see LIBELOUS

traffic *n 1 syn* see BUSINESS 4
2 *syn* see COMMERCE 2
rel relations, relationship; closeness, connection, familiarity, intimacy
3 *syn* see PATRONAGE 2
4 the number or volume of vehicles or pedestrians moving along a route < freeway *traffic* is heavy during the rush hour>
syn travel

traffic *vb 1 syn* see TRADE 1
2 to engage in illegal or disreputable business or activity < *trafficked* in drugs>
syn truck
rel deal (in), push, shove; black-market; bootleg, moonshine; fence
idiom handle (*or* deal in) under the counter

trafficable *adj syn* see MARKETABLE

trafficker *n syn* see MERCHANT

tragedy *n 1 syn* see DISASTER
rel blow, shock
2 *syn* see MISFORTUNE
rel unluckiness; curse, lot; woe(s)
con prosperity, success
ant triumph

trail *vb 1 syn* see DRAG 3
2 *syn* see DELAY 2
rel plod, trudge; falter, flag; halt
3 *syn* see TRACK 1
rel nose (out), sniff (out)
idiom follow a scent
4 *syn* see TAIL
5 *syn* see FOLLOW 2

trail *n* a rough course or way formed by or as if by repeated chance footsteps < an old Indian *trail*>
syn path, pathway, track, ||trod
rel footpath, footwalk, footway

trail *vb syn* see LURE

train *n 1 syn* see ENTOURAGE
2 *syn* see SUCCESSION 2
rel course, run; line, thread; gradation, scale, tier

train *vb 1 syn* see TEACH
rel cultivate, develop, shape; accustom, habituate; harden, season

---

syn synonym(s)   *rel* related word(s)
ant antonym(s)   *con* contrasted word(s)
idiom idiomatic equivalent(s)
|| use limited; if in doubt, see a dictionary

2 *syn* see DIRECT 2
training *n syn* see EDUCATION 1
train off *vb syn* see SWERVE 1
traipse *vb 1 syn* see WANDER 1
  2 *syn* see WALK 1
  3 *syn* see DRAG 3
traipse *n syn* see SLATTERN 1
trait *n 1 syn* see QUALITY 1
  2 *syn* see CHARACTERISTIC 1
  rel denominator; attribute, quality
traitorous *adj syn* see FAITHLESS
  rel apostate, renegade; mutinous, rebellious, seditious; alienated, disaffected, estranged; unpatriotic
  con faithful; patriotic
traject *vb syn* see CONDUCT 4
tralatitious *adj syn* see TRADITIONAL 1
  idiom handed down from time immemorial
traluceat *adj syn* see TRANSLUCENT 3
trammel *vb 1 syn* see ENTANGLE 3
  2 *syn* see HAMPER
  rel circumscribe, confine, limit; bind, enchain, handcuff, manacle
  3 *syn* see STULTIFY
tramp *vb 1* to walk, tread, or step especially heavily <heard hobnailed boots *tramping* across the square>
  syn trample, tromp; *compare* PLOD 1
  rel march; thud; footslog, stodge, trudge; stamp, stomp
  2 *syn* see HIKE 2
  3 *syn* see TRAMPLE 2
tramp *n 1 syn* see VAGABOND
  2 *syn* see WANTON
  3 a journey on foot or a walking trip <took a long *tramp* through the woods>
  syn hike, walkabout
  rel ramble, saunter, stroll, walk; traipse
tramper *n syn* see VAGABOND
trample *vb 1 syn* see TRAMP 1
  2 to tread on forcibly and repeatedly so as to crush or injure <was *trampled* to death by his horse>
  syn stamp, stomp, tramp, tromp
  rel ||stoach, ||stramp, ||stunt; pound; tread (on); override
trance *vb syn* see TRANSPORT 2
trance *n syn* see REVERIE
tranquil *adj syn* see CALM 2
  rel irenic, pacific, peaceful; quiet, still; stable, steady
  con stirred up, troubled
  ant agitated
tranquilize *vb syn* see CALM
  rel hush; sedate; subdue
  idiom pour oil on troubled waters
  ant agitate
transaction *n syn* see CONTRACT 2
transcend *vb syn* see SURPASS 1
  idiom go beyond, rise above
transcendent *adj 1 syn* see SUPREME
  rel accomplished, consummate, finished; entire, intact, perfect, whole
  2 *syn* see ABSTRACT 1
  rel absolute, ultimate; boundless, eternal, infinite
transcendental *adj 1 syn* see OTHERWORLDLY 1
  2 *syn* see ABSTRACT 1
  rel supernatural, supranatural, ultimate
transfer *vb 1 syn* see MOVE 4
  rel carry, convey; relocate

2 *syn* see GIVE 3
  rel convey, transmit
  3 *syn* see TRANSFORM
  4 to shift the title of (property) from one owner to another <to preserve the farm intact he *transfers* it to a single heir>
  syn abalienate, alien, alienate, assign, cede, convey, deed, make over, remise, sign (over)
transfigure *vb syn* see TRANSFORM
transfix *vb syn* see IMPALE
transform *vb* to make over to a radically different form, composition, state, or disposition <the interaction of social forces *transforms* custom and produces a new tradition>
  syn change, commute, convert, metamorphize, metamorphose, mutate, transfer, transfigure, translate, transmogrify, transmute, transpose, transubstantiate; *compare* CHANGE 1
  rel alter; denature
transformation *n syn* see CONVERSION 2
transfuse *vb syn* see PERMEATE
transgress *vb 1 syn* see VIOLATE 1
  2 *syn* see TRESPASS 1
transgression *n syn* see BREACH 1
  rel erring, error, lapse, slip; overstepping; misbehavior, misstepping
transient *adj* lasting or staying only a short time <features of a *transient* culture now extinct>
  syn ephemeral, evanescent, fleeting, fugacious, fugitive, impermanent, momentaneous, momentary, passing, short-lived, transitory, volatile; *compare* TEMPORARY
  rel deciduous, flitting, unstable; temporal, temporary; insubstantial
  idiom as transient as the clouds, here today and gone tomorrow
  con lasting, perdurable, permanent, substantial; durable, stable
  ant perpetual
transit *n 1 syn* see PASSAGE 1
  2 *syn* see TRANSITION
  3 *syn* see TRANSPORTATION 1
  4 public conveyance of passengers or goods as a commercial enterprise <mass *transit*>
  syn transport, transportation
transition *n* passage from one state or condition to another <the *transition* from boyhood to manhood>
  syn alteration, passage, shift, transit
  rel change, conversion, metamorphosis, transformation; development, evolution; growth, progress
transitional *adj* involving or characterized by passage from one stage, condition, or state to another <a *transitional* phase of social development>
  syn transitive, transitory
  rel developing, evolving; altering, changing, shifting
  idiom being in a state of flux
transitive *adj syn* see TRANSITIONAL
transitory *adj 1 syn* see TRANSIENT
  rel changeable; nonpermanent, unenduring; brief, short-term
  2 *syn* see TRANSITIONAL
translate *vb 1* to make a version of in another language <*translated* many secret documents from French to English>

syn put, render, transpose, turn
rel transliterate; transcribe; interpret; metaphrase, paraphrase
2 *syn* see TRANSFORM
translate (into) *vb syn* see PARAPHRASE
translation *n syn* see VERSION 1
translucent *adj* 1 *syn* see TRANSPARENT 1
2 *syn* see CLEAR 4
rel apparent, obvious, unmistakable
3 admitting and diffusing light so that objects beyond cannot be clearly distinguished < *translucent* amber >
syn clear, tralucent, translucid, transparent; *compare* TRANSPARENT 1
rel lucent, lucid
translucid *adj syn* see TRANSLUCENT 3
transmarine *adj syn* see OVERSEAS
transmigrate *vb syn* see MIGRATE
transmigratory *adj syn* see MIGRATORY
transmit *vb* 1 *syn* see SEND 1
rel convey, transport
2 *syn* see COMMUNICATE 1
3 *syn* see HAND DOWN
rel instill; transfuse, translate
4 *syn* see CONDUCT 4
transmogrify *vb syn* see TRANSFORM
transmundane *adj syn* see OTHER-WORLDLY 1
transmute *vb syn* see TRANSFORM
transparent *adj* 1 admitting light without appreciable diffusion or distortion so that objects beyond are entirely visible < a sheet of *transparent* plastic >
syn clear, limpid, pellucid, see-through, translucent; *compare* TRANSLUCENT 3
rel crystal, crystalline, glassy; diaphanous
idiom clear as glass (*or* crystal)
con dark, smoky; cloudy, foggy hazy, misty, nubilous
ant opaque
2 *syn* see FILMY
3 *syn* see TRANSLUCENT 3
4 *syn* see CLEAR 4
rel distinguishable, recognizable; articulate, distinct, plain; unambiguous, unequivocal
con muddy, turbid
transpicuous *adj syn* see CLEAR 4
transpierce *vb syn* see IMPALE
transpire *vb* 1 *syn* see GET OUT 2
2 *syn* see HAPPEN 1
rel eventuate, result
transplace *vb syn* see REVERSE 1
rel remove; rearrange
transport *vb* 1 *syn* see CARRY 1
2 to carry away by strong and usually pleasant emotion < *transported* with ecstasy >
syn enrapture, enravish, entrance, ravish, trance
rel excite, move, provoke, quicken, stimulate; agitate, inflame, stir (up); elevate, uplift; carry away, delight, imparadise, ‖send, slay, thrill, ‖wow
3 *syn* see BANISH
transport *n* 1 *syn* see TRANSPORTATION 1

2 *syn* see ECSTASY
rel ardor, enthusiasm, fervor, passion; happiness
3 *syn* see VEHICLE 3
4 *syn* see TRANSIT 4
transportable *adj syn* see PORTABLE
transportation *n* 1 an act, process, or instance of transporting or being transported < arranged for the *transportation* of his luggage >
syn carriage, carrying, conveyance, transit, transport, transporting
rel hauling, moving
2 *syn* see VEHICLE 3
3 *syn* see TRANSIT 4
transporting *n syn* see TRANSPORTATION 1
transpose *vb* 1 *syn* see TRANSFORM
2 *syn* see TRANSLATE 1
3 *syn* see REVERSE 1
transubstantiate *vb syn* see TRANSFORM
transude *vb syn* see EXUDE
transversal *adj syn* see TRANSVERSE
rel bent; intersecting
transverse *vb syn* see TRAVERSE 4
transverse *adj* extended or lying in a direction across something else < the *transverse* arches of the cathedral ceiling >
syn crossing, crosswise, thwart, transversal, traverse
rel diagonal, oblique; across, crossed
con perpendicular
ant longitudinal
transversely *adv syn* see OVER 1
transversely *adv syn* see OVER 1
trap *n* 1 *syn* see LURE 2
rel artifice, feint, gambit, maneuver, ploy, ruse, stratagem, wile; birdlime, net; ambuscade, ambush; conspiracy, intrigue, machination, plot
‖2 *syn* see POLICEMAN
‖3 *syn* see MOUTH 1
trap *vb syn* see CATCH 3
rel mousetrap, snag
trapfall *n syn* see PITFALL
traps *n pl syn* see PERSONAL EFFECTS
trash *n* 1 *syn* see REFUSE
rel leavings
2 *syn* see NONSENSE 2
3 *syn* see RABBLE 2
‖**trash** *vb syn* see VANDALIZE
trash *vb syn* see PLOD 1
trashy *adj syn* see CHEAP 2
rel third-rate
trauma *n* intense mental, emotional, or physical disturbance resulting from stress < a broken home may produce persistent *trauma* in children >
syn shock, traumatism
rel blow, stress; traumatization; derangement, disturbance, upset; collapse
traumatism *n syn* see TRAUMA
travail *n* 1 *syn* see WORK 2
rel task; struggle
idiom toil and trouble
con relaxation, rest
2 *syn* see LABOR 2
rel contractions, pains
idiom birth throe
travel *vb* 1 *syn* see GO 1
rel move (on); voyage; roam, trek; explore

---

syn synonym(s)   *rel* related word(s)
ant antonym(s)   *con* contrasted word(s)
idiom idiomatic equivalent(s)
‖ use limited; if in doubt, see a dictionary

2 to journey over (as by conveyance) <certain roads can be *traveled* only on horseback >
syn cover, do, pass (over), track, traverse
rel cross

travel *n* 1 *syn* see PASSAGE 1
2 *often* **travels** *pl syn* see JOURNEY
3 *syn* see TRAFFIC 4

travelable *adj syn* see PASSABLE

‖**traveler** *n syn* see VAGABOND

traverse *n syn* see OBSTACLE

traverse *vb* 1 *syn* see RESIST
2 *syn* see DENY 4
rel oppose; dismiss; squash, squelch
3 *syn* see TRAVEL 2
4 to extend or lie across (something) <a highway *traversing* the entire state>
syn cross, transverse
rel crisscross, intersect, quarter
idiom cut across
5 to pass over, along, or to and fro especially on foot <deep in thought he *traversed* the terrace again and again>
syn perambulate, walk
rel peregrinate; track, tread; pace

traverse *adj syn* see TRANSVERSE

travesty *n* 1 *syn* see CARICATURE 2
rel mimicry; distortion, exaggeration; ridicule
2 *syn* see MOCKERY 2

travesty *vb syn* see MIMIC

treacherous *adj* 1 *syn* see FAITHLESS
rel undependable, unreliable, untrustworthy; betraying, deceptive, double-crossing, falsehearted, misleading, Punic
ant dependable; trustworthy
2 *syn* see DANGEROUS 1
rel deceptive, ticklish, tricky; precarious

treacherousness *n syn* see TREACHERY
ant dependability; trustworthiness

treachery *n* betrayal of a trust or confidence <corruption in public office is little short of *treachery* >
syn disloyalty, faithlessness, perfidiousness, perfidy, treacherousness, treason; *compare* INFIDELITY
rel falseheartedness, falseness; double-cross, double-dealing; sellout
idiom dirty pool, dirty work at the crossroads
con incorruptibility, reliability, probity, rectitude, uprightness; constancy, fidelity, loyalty, staunchness
ant dependability; trustworthiness

tread *vb* 1 *syn* see DANCE 1
2 *syn* see WALK 1
rel march, stride; tromp

tread *n syn* see TRACK 1

treadmill *n syn* see ROUTINE

treason *n* 1 *syn* see TREACHERY
rel deceit, deceitfulness; duplicity; Machiavellianism
idiom breach of trust (*or* faith)
con allegiance, loyalty
ant staunchness
2 *syn* see SEDITION
rel disloyalty, treacherousness, treachery; high treason; misprision
ant allegiance

treasure *n syn* see FIND 1
rel catch, plum, prize; pearl

treasure *vb syn* see APPRECIATE 1
rel conserve, guard, preserve, save; idolize, revere, reverence, venerate, worship
idiom hold dear

treasure-house *n* 1 *syn* see TREASURY 1
2 *syn* see BONANZA

treasure trove *n* 1 *syn* see FIND 1
2 *syn* see BONANZA

treasury *n* 1 a place (as a room or building) where valuables are kept <priceless gold candlesticks kept in the *treasury* of the cathedral>
syn treasure-house
rel archive(s), gallery, museum; depository, repository, storehouse
idiom treasure room
2 the place of deposit, retention, and disbursement of collected funds <the union *treasury* held emergency strike funds>
syn chest, coffer, exchequer, war chest
rel depositary, depository
3 *syn* see BONANZA

treat *vb* 1 *syn* see CONFER 2
rel consider, study, weigh; deliberate, reason, think
2 to have to do with or behave toward (a person or thing) in a specified manner <*treat* all employees fairly and impartially>
syn deal (with), handle, play, serve, take, use
rel conduct, do with, manage, ‖wield; regard, respect; account, consider, hold; appraise, estimate, evaluate, rate, value
idiom act with regard to, conduct oneself toward, do by
3 to pay for another's entertainment <*treated* her to a few drinks>
syn blow, set up, ‖shout, stand
rel stake
idiom go treat, pick up the tab for, stand treat
4 to give medical treatment to <was *treated* by an eye specialist>
syn doctor
rel attend, care (for), minister (to), nurse

treat *n syn* see DELICACY

treatise *n syn* see DISCOURSE 2
rel writing; book; argument, discussion, exposition

treaty *n* a formal, usually written, arrangement made by negotiation between two or more political authorities <the two nations finally signed an arms-limitation *treaty*>
syn agreement, concord, convention, pact; *compare* CONTRACT
rel arrangement, entente, understanding; bargain, contract; charter, compact, concordat, covenant; alliance, cartel, league; accord, reconciliation, settlement

treble *adj syn* see ACUTE 4
ant bass

tree *vb syn* see CORNER

trek *n syn* see JOURNEY

tremble *vb* 1 *syn* see SHAKE 1
rel shrink, wince
idiom tremble like a leaf
2 *syn* see SHAKE 2

trembling *adj syn* see TREMULOUS
ant steady

tremendous *adj* 1 *syn* see FEARFUL 3
2 *syn* see MONSTROUS 1
3 *syn* see HUGE
rel amazing, astounding, flabbergasting; terrific

idiom great big
ant minute

tremendousness *n syn* see ENORMITY 2
  rel bigness, largeness
tremor *n syn* see EARTHQUAKE
tremor *vb* 1 *syn* see SHAKE 1
  2 *syn* see SHAKE 2
tremorous *adj syn* see TREMULOUS
tremulant *adj syn* see TREMULOUS
tremulous *adj* characterized by or affected
  with trembling or tremors <her *tremulous*
  hands could scarcely hold the book>
  syn aquake, aquiver, ashake, ashiver,
  quaking, quaky, quivering, quivery, shaking, shaky, shivering, shivery, trembling,
  tremorous, tremulant
  rel aguish; aspen; palpitating; vibrating
  idiom having the shakes
  con firm, settled, stable, steady, unmoving
trench *n* a long narrow furrow in the
  ground <dig a *trench* for a sewer pipe>
  syn cut, ditch
  rel gully; drill, furrow; fosse; trough;
  drain, sink
trench *vb syn* see BORDER 3
trenchant *adj* 1 *syn* see INCISIVE
  rel piercing, probing, razor-sharp; sarcastic, sardonic, satiric; acrid; piquant, poignant, pungent
  2 *syn* see CAUSTIC 1
  rel scalding, scorching
trend *n* 1 *syn* see TENDENCY 1
  rel movement; flow; direction, orientation; swing, wind; progression
  2 *syn* see FASHION 3
||**trendy** *adj syn* see STYLISH
  rel ultramodern
  con dated, outmoded
trepidation *n syn* see FEAR 1
  ant unapprehensiveness
trepidity *n syn* see FEAR 1
  ant intrepidity, intrepidness
trespass *n syn* see BREACH 1
  rel encroachment, entrenchment, invasion;
  intrusion, obtrusion
trespass *vb* 1 to commit an offense <ex-
  hibited scrupulous fairness even to those
  who *trespassed* against him>
  syn offend, sin, transgress
  rel deviate, err, lapse
  idiom do wrong by
  2 to make inroads on the property, territory, or rights of another <warned the
  hunters not to *trespass* on his land>
  syn encroach, entrench, infringe, invade
  rel enter, penetrate, pierce, probe; interlope, intermeddle, intrude; transgress
  idiom crash the gate
trestle *n syn* see SAWHORSE
triad *n* a union or group of three often
  closely related individuals or things <a
  triad of deities>
  syn threesome, trine, trinity, trio, triple,
  triumvirate, triune, troika; *compare* TRI-
  UMVIRATE 1
trial *n* 1 the state or fact of being tested
  (as by suffering) <the Vietnam war period was a time of great national *trial*>

syn affliction, calvary, cross, crucible,
  ordeal, tribulation, visitation
  rel agony, distress, misery, suffering;
  anguish, grief, heartbreak, sorrow, woe;
  adversity, misfortune; difficulty, hardship,
  rigor, vicissitude
  idiom crown of thorns, fiery ordeal, trial
  and tribulation
  2 a source of vexation or annoyance <liv-
  ing in a crowded hotel is a real *trial*>
  syn care, trouble, worry
  rel complication, difficulty; annoyance,
  distress, misfortune; ordeal
  3 *syn* see EXPERIMENT
  4 *syn* see ATTEMPT
trial *adj syn* see EXPERIMENTAL 2
trial and error *n syn* see EXPERIMENT
trial balloon *n syn* see FEELER
  rel trial
trial run *n syn* see EXPERIMENT
tribe *n syn* see FAMILY 1
tribulation *n syn* see TRIAL 1
  rel oppression, persecution, wronging
tribunal *n syn* see COURT 2
tributary *adj syn* see SUBORDINATE
  rel conquered, subdued, subjugated, vanquished; accessory, minor; satellite
tribute *n* 1 *syn* see TESTIMONIAL 3
  rel recognition; monument
  2 *syn* see ENCOMIUM
trice *n syn* see INSTANT 1
trick *n* 1 an indirect, ingenious, and often
  cunning means to gain an end <used
  every *trick* in the bag to cover up the
  scandal>
  syn artifice, chouse, device, feint, gambit,
  gimmick, jig, maneuver, play, ploy, ||prat,
  ruse, shenanigan, sleight, stratagem, whizzer, wile; *compare* PRANK
  rel contrivance, craft, expediency; blind,
  bluff, diversion, dodge, dodgery, red herring; curve, deception, sham, stall; fraud,
  ||rort, scheme, shift, skin game
  2 *syn* see PRANK
  rel boutade; escapade; practical joke
  3 an ingenious or dexterous act or procedure designed to puzzle or amuse <a
  juggler's *trick*>
  syn feat, stunt
  rel accomplishment
  4 **tricks** *pl syn* see PERSONAL EFFECTS
  5 *syn* see HANG
  6 *syn* see HABIT 1
  7 *syn* see SPELL
trick *adj* somewhat defective and inclined
  to function abnormally on occasion <a
  trick lock that doesn't always catch>
  syn tricky, undependable
  rel catchy, touchy; unreliable, untrustworthy; insecure, shaky, unstable; defective, dysfunctioning, malfunctioning
trick *vb syn* see DUPE
  rel outtrick, outtrump, outwit; have
  idiom take (someone) for a ride
trick (off, out, *or* up) *vb syn* see DRESS UP
  1
trickery *n syn* see DECEPTION 1
  rel double-cross; underhandedness
  idiom underhand dealing
trickle *vb syn* see DRIP
  ant gush
trickster *n* 1 *syn* see SWINDLER
  idiom gyp artist

2 *syn* see MAGICIAN 2

tricksy *adj syn* see TIGHT 4

tricky *adj* **1** *syn* see SLY 2
rel deceptive, delusive; delusory, misleading; deceitful, dishonest
2 *syn* see UNSTABLE 2
rel catchy, difficult, trappy; quirky
3 *syn* see DELICATE 7
4 *syn* see TRICK

tried *adj syn* see RELIABLE 1
rel constant, faithful, staunch, steadfast; demonstrated, proved, tested; approved, certified
ant untried

tried and true *adj syn* see RELIABLE 1

trifle *n* **1** *syn* see KNICKKNACK
rel rope yarn
2 *syn* see HINT 2

trifle *vb* **1** to behave amorously without serious intent <was interested only in *trifling* with her, not marrying her>
syn coquet, dally, flirt, fool, lead on, string along, toy, wanton
rel play (with); mess around, ‖muck, mucker; philander; mash
2 *syn* see FIDDLE 1

trifle (away) *vb syn* see WASTE 2
rel misuse; burn (up), use up
con retain, save

trifling *n syn* see SMALL TALK

trifling *adj syn* see PETTY 2
rel banal, inane, insipid, jejune, vapid; empty, frivolous, hollow, idle, nugatory, otiose, vain; insignificant, unimportant

trig *adj* **1** *syn* see NEAT 2
2 *syn* see STYLISH
‖**3** *syn* see FULL 1

triggerman *n syn* see ASSASSIN

trill *vb syn* see DRIP

trillion *n syn* see SCAD

trim *vb* **1** *syn* see ADORN
2 *syn* see WHIP 2
rel ‖skin
3 *syn* see CUT 6

trim *adj* **1** *syn* see NEAT 2
rel clean, clean-cut, fit, spruce; shapely, streamlined, symmetrical
con disordered, shapeless, straggly
ant frowsy
2 *syn* see SHAPELY

trim *n syn* see ORDER 10
rel commission; whack

trine *n syn* see TRIAD

trinity *n syn* see TRIAD

trinket *n syn* see KNICKKNACK
rel plaything, frippery, showpiece, tinsel; trinketry, trinkums

trio *n syn* see TRIAD

trip *vb syn* see SKIP 1

trip *n* **1** a single passage of a vehicle between two points or to a point and return <a regular bus *trip* to and from the city>
syn run; compare DRIVE 1, JOURNEY, TOUR 2
rel drive; progress
2 *syn* see JOURNEY
rel run
3 *syn* see ERROR 2

tripes *n pl syn* see ENTRAILS

triple *n syn* see TRIAD

tripped out *adj syn* see DRUGGED

‖**tripper** *n syn* see TOURIST

triste *adj syn* see SAD 2

trite *adj* used or occurring so often as to have lost interest, freshness, or force <unrequited love has become a *trite* theme>
syn bathetic, chain, cliché, clichéd, commonplace, corny, hack, hackneyed, musty, old hat, shopworn, stale, stereotyped, stereotypical, threadbare, timeworn, tired, twice-told, warmed-over, well-worn, worn-out
rel common, ordinary; banal, dull, flat, jejune, mildewed, vapid; bedridden, drained, exhausted, used-up; bromidic, platitudinous, prosaic, ready-made, set, stock
con first, new, seminal; novel, unique; creative, imaginative; uncopied; memorable; distinctive
ant fresh, original

triturate *vb syn* see PULVERIZE 1

triumph *n* **1** *syn* see VICTORY 1
rel ascendancy, gain; surmounting, vanquishing, vanquishment
ant defeat
2 *syn* see EXULTATION
rel joy; festivity, merriment, reveling

triumph *vb* **1** *syn* see EXULT
rel gloat
2 *syn* see WIN 1
rel prosper, succeed; conquer, surmount
idiom get the best (*or* better) of
con lose
ant fail
3 *syn* see CONQUER 2

triumphal *adj syn* see EXULTANT

triumphant *adj syn* see EXULTANT
rel rejoicing, triumphing

triumvirate *n* **1** an administrative or ruling body of three <a monarchy replaced by a *triumvirate* of generals>
syn troika; compare TRIAD
rel junta
2 *syn* see TRIAD

triune *n syn* see TRIAD

trivia *n pl but sometimes sing in constr* unimportant matters <they became bored with the *trivia* of everyday life>
syn minutia(e), small beer, small change, small potato(es), triviality

trivial *adj* **1** *syn* see LITTLE 3
rel slight; negligible
idiom no great shakes
con considerable
ant momentous, weighty
2 *syn* see PETTY 2
rel captious, fribbling, frivolous; shallow, superficial

triviality *n syn* see TRIVIA
rel shallowness, superficiality, unimportance
con basic(s), essential(s), fundamental(s)

‖**trod** *n syn* see TRAIL

troika *n* **1** *syn* see TRIUMVIRATE 1
2 *syn* see TRIAD

trollop *n syn* see WANTON
idiom (a) fast number

trollop *vb syn* see SLOUCH

tromp *vb* **1** *syn* see TRAMP 1
2 *syn* see HIKE 2
rel slog, trudge
3 *syn* see TRAMPLE 2
4 *syn* see BEAT 1

troop n 1 syn see COMPANY 4
  rel assemblage, assembly, collection, gathering; army, host, legion, multitude
  2 **troops** pl members of a nation's military units < Marines, GI's, and Seabees were among the *troops* sent to war >
  syn armed forces, forces, military, servicemen
  rel combatants; soldiers, troopers
  idiom fighting men

troop vb syn see WALK 1

trophy n syn see REMEMBRANCE 3

tropic adj syn see TROPICAL
  rel baking, broiling, scorching, sweltering
  con arctic

tropical adj of, relating to, or occurring in the tropics < *tropical* fruits >
  syn tropic
  rel equatorial, semitropical, subtropical; warm; hot, sultry, torrid
  con temperate

tropical cyclone n syn see HURRICANE

tropical storm n syn see HURRICANE

trot n 1 syn see HAG 2
  2 syn see PONY

troth n syn see ENGAGEMENT 2

trot out vb syn see SHOW 4

troubadour n syn see BARD 1
  rel balladist; rhymer, rhymester

trouble vb 1 to cause to be uneasy or upset < *sorrows* that *trouble* the strongest of men >
  syn ail, cark, distress, upset, worry
  rel agitate, concern, discompose, disquiet, disturb, perturb, rowel, ‖worrit; annoy, bother, fret, irk, vex; ‖destroy, haunt
  2 syn see TRY 2
  rel upset, worry; disconcert, disturb; harry, irritate; afflict, torment
  3 syn see INCONVENIENCE
  rel annoy, pester, plague, worry; impose (on or upon), intrude

trouble n 1 syn see TRIAL 2
  2 syn see EFFORT 1
  rel ado, bustle, flurry, fuss, pother; bother, inconvenience; difficulty, hardship, rigor; strain, stress
  3 a condition of annoyance, disturbance, or distress < got him into *trouble* by repeating gossip >
  syn Dutch, hot water
  rel bind, difficulty, predicament

troubled adj syn see DISTRAUGHT

troublemaker n a person who consciously or unconsciously causes trouble < a *troublemaker* who set father against daughter >
  syn bad actor, mischief-maker
  rel agitator, inciter, inflamer, instigator

troublesome adj giving trouble or anxiety < a *troublesome* infection >
  syn mean, pesky, troublous, ugly, vexatious, wicked
  rel annoying, bothersome, vexing; alarming, disquieting, disturbing, upsetting; infestive; painful
  con untroublesome
  ant innocuous

troublesomeness n syn see INCONVENIENCE
  rel difficulty; irritation, vexation

troublous adj syn see TROUBLESOME
  rel troubling

trounce vb syn see WHIP 2
  idiom walk all over

trouncing n syn see DEFEAT 1

troupe n syn see COMPANY 4

trouper n syn see ACTOR 1
  rel entertainer; artiste

trove n syn see ACCUMULATION

truce n a suspension of or an agreement for suspending hostilities < the high command ordered a *truce* for the holidays >
  syn armistice, cease-fire
  rel break, ‖breather, letup, lull, pause, respite; de-escalation, ‖wind-down; accord, reconciliation; peace

truck vb 1 syn see TRADE 1
  rel handle; peddle, retail
  2 syn see TRAFFIC 2
  idiom have truck with

truck n syn see COMMERCE 2

truckle vb syn see FAWN
  rel knuckle down, knuckle under, succumb; follow, tag, tail, trail
  idiom kiss (or lick) one's boots, lick the feet of, make a doormat of oneself

truckler n syn see SYCOPHANT

truckling adj syn see FAWNING

truculent adj 1 syn see FIERCE 1
  rel browbeating, bullying, cowing, intimidating; frightening, terrifying, terrorizing
  2 syn see ABUSIVE
  rel caustic, mordacious, mordant, scathing, sharp, trenchant; harsh, rough, severe; vitriolic
  3 syn see BELLIGERENT

trudge vb syn see PLOD 1

true adj 1 syn see FAITHFUL 1
  rel sincere, unfeigned, whole-hearted, whole-souled
  ant false, fickle
  2 syn see UPRIGHT 2
  rel creditable, estimable, worthy; high-principled, right-minded, truehearted
  3 conformable to fact or to a standard, rule, or model < gave a *true* account of the accident >
  syn faithful, just, right, strict, undistorted, veracious, veridical
  rel careful, conscientious, meticulous, punctilious, scrupulous; finicky, fussy, overnice; accurate, precise; absolute, mathematical
  idiom true to the letter
  con imprecise, inaccurate, incorrect, inexact; erroneous, false
  ant untrue
  4 syn see GENUINE 3
  con deceitful
  5 syn see AUTHENTIC 2
  rel genuine, kosher; sincere, unfaked, unfeigned
  con artificial, fake, faked, feigned; insincere
  ant false
  6 syn see REAL 3
  rel natural, normal, regular, typical
  ant false
  7 being such as it should be < meanings presented in their *true* relationship >

syn appropriate, desired, fitting, proper
rel acceptable; applicable, befitting, likely, suitable
con inappropriate, unfitting

8 being such by right < the *true* heir >
syn legitimate, rightful
rel lawful, legal, proper
con illegitimate, spurious, supposititious
ant false

9 that can be relied on < polls can provide a *true* projection of public sentiment >
syn authoritative, dependable, trustable, trustworthy
rel meaningful, significant; expressive, indicative, suggestive
con independable, undependable, untrustworthy; doubtful, questionable

trueloye *n* 1 *syn* see GIRL FRIEND 2
2 *syn* see BOYFRIEND 2
idiom one and only

true-tongued *adj syn* see TRUTHFUL

truism *n* 1 *syn* see VERACITY 2
2 *syn* see MAXIM
3 *syn* see COMMONPLACE

trull *n syn* see WANTON

truly *adv* 1 *syn* see VERY 2
rel absolutely, positively
2 *syn* see EVEN 3
rel confidently, really
3 *syn* see WELL 7
rel probably; surely

trump *n syn* see TRUMP CARD

trump *vb syn* see SURPASS 1

trump card *n* something decisive or telling often held in reserve < kept a political *trump card* up his sleeve till election eve >
syn clincher, trump
rel ace; coup, coup de grace, coup de main
idiom ace in the hole

trumpery *n syn* see NONSENSE 2
trumpery *adj syn* see CHEAP 2
trumpet *vb syn* see TOUT

truncate *vb syn* see TOP 1
rel abbreviate, abridge; cut off, lop; shear

truncheon *n syn* see CUDGEL

trust *n* 1 complete assurance and certitude regarding the character, ability, strength, or truth of someone or something < they continue to have *trust* in his judgment >
syn confidence, dependence, faith, hope, reliance, stock
rel assurance, certainty, certitude, conviction; belief, credence, credit; positiveness, sureness; entrustment; overconfidence, oversureness
con doubt, dubiety, dubiosity, skepticism, suspicion, uncertainty
ant mistrust
2 *syn* see SYNDICATE
3 *syn* see CUSTODY

trust *vb syn* see ENTRUST
rel commit, consign, hand over

trust (in *or* to) *vb syn* see RELY (on *or* upon)
rel assume, imagine, presume
idiom have no reservations

trustable *adj syn* see TRUE 9
ant trustless

trustless *adj syn* see UNRELIABLE 1
rel unworthy; unfaithful; suspect, suspicious; dishonest; deceitful; treacherous

ant trustable, trustworthy

trustworthy *adj* 1 *syn* see RELIABLE 1
rel veracious, truthful; honest, scrupulous, upright
con deceitful; dishonest
ant untrustworthy
2 *syn* see TRUE 9
rel accurate, exact; valid; realistic
con inaccurate, inexact; invalid; unrealistic; suspect
ant untrustworthy
3 *syn* see AUTHENTIC 1

trusty *adj* 1 *syn* see RELIABLE 1
rel predictable, stable; firm, sound; responsible, ||straight
con capricious
ant untrusty
2 *syn* see AUTHENTIC 1
ant untrusty

truth *n* 1 *syn* see VERACITY 1
rel precision, rightness, trueness; authenticity, genuineness, veritableness; candor
idiom unvarnished truth (*or* truthfulness)
con equivocation, evasion, hedging; deception, deceptiveness, falseness
ant falsity, untruth
2 *syn* see VERACITY 2
rel reality
idiom (the) gospel truth, (the) truth of the matter
ant lie, untruth

truthful *adj* observant of or telling the truth < a *truthful* witness >
syn true-tongued, truth-speaking, truth-telling, veracious, veridical
rel candid, frank, honest, sincere; accurate, factual; real, realistic
con false, insincere; truthless, uncandid; inaccurate; unrealistic
ant untruthful

truthfulness *n syn* see VERACITY 1
ant untruthfulness

truthlessness *n syn* see MENDACITY
truth-speaking *adj syn* see TRUTHFUL
truth-telling *adj syn* see TRUTHFUL

try *vb* 1 to subject to testing < *try* the door to be sure it's locked >
syn check, examine, prove, test
rel inspect, scrutinize; appraise, judge, weigh
idiom make trial of, put to proof, put to the test
2 to subject to stress < the fine print *tried* her eyes >
syn distress, harass, irk, pain, strain, stress, trouble
rel annoy, bother, vex
3 *syn* see AFFLICT
4 *syn* see PROVE 1
5 to make an effort to do or accomplish something < the baby is *trying* to walk >
syn assay, attempt, endeavor, essay, offer, seek, strive, struggle, undertake
rel aim, aspire, hope, strike
idiom do one's best (*or* utmost) to, have a go at

try (out) *vb syn* see EXPERIMENT
rel examine, inspect, scrutinize; demonstrate, prove
idiom cut and try, put to trial, try for size

try *n* 1 *syn* see ATTEMPT
2 *syn* see FLING 1

rel dab, jab

trying *adj* 1 *syn* see TIGHT 4
rel annoying, bothersome, irksome, irritating, troublesome, vexing; strenuous; sticky, tricky
2 *syn* see ONEROUS

try on *vb syn* see EXPERIMENT

tryst *n syn* see ENGAGEMENT 3

‖**tub** *n syn* see FATTY

tub *vb syn* see BATHE 1

tubby *adj syn* see ROTUND 2
idiom plump as a dumpling (*or* partridge)

tuberculosis *n* a communicable bacterial disease typically marked by wasting, fever, and formation of cheesy tubercles often in the lungs < Victorian heroines fading away with *tuberculosis* >
syn consumption, phthisis, TB, white plague

tuck (in) *vb syn* see BED
rel snug (down *or* up), snuggle

‖**tuck** *n syn* see FOOD 1

tuck *n syn* see ENERGY 2

‖**tucked up** *adj syn* see CRAMPED

tucker *vb syn* see EXHAUST 3
rel gruel; wilt; drop
idiom take the tuck out of

tug *vb* 1 *syn* see CONTEND 1
2 *syn* see LABOR 1
3 *syn* see PULL 2

tug–of–war *n syn* see CONTEST 1

tuition *n syn* see EDUCATION 1

tumble *vb* 1 *syn* see FALL 2
rel trip; come (down), descend
2 *syn* see PLUMMET
rel depreciate; sag, slump
idiom take a downward spiral, take a nosedive
3 *syn* see HAPPEN 1
4 *syn* see DISCOVER 3
5 *syn* see OVERTHROW 2
6 *syn* see FELL 1
7 *syn* see CONFUSE 5
8 *syn* see DISORDER 1

tumble (to) *vb syn* see APPREHEND 1

tumble *n syn* see CLUTTER 2

tumescent *adj* 1 *syn* see INFLATED
rel bloated; bulging
2 *syn* see RHETORICAL

tumid *adj* 1 *syn* see INFLATED
rel dilated, distended, expanded, swollen
2 *syn* see RHETORICAL

tummy *n syn* see ABDOMEN

tumulary *adj syn* see SEPULCHRAL 1

tumult *n* 1 *syn* see COMMOTION 1
rel disturbance, turmoil, uproar
2 *syn* see COMMOTION 4
rel babel, din, hullabaloo, pandemonium, racket
con calm, hush, lull, quietude
3 *syn* see COMMOTION 2
rel seething; disorder, unsettlement; ferment, maelstrom, paroxysm
4 *syn* see DIN
rel noise; ‖corroboree
idiom ‖all hell broken loose

tumultuous *adj syn* see TURBULENT 1

tumultuously *adv syn* see HARD 2

---

syn synonym(s)   *rel* related word(s)
ant antonym(s)   *con* contrasted word(s)
idiom idiomatic equivalent(s)
‖ use limited; if in doubt, see a dictionary

---

tun *n syn* see CASK
rel vat

tune *n* 1 *syn* see MELODY
rel carol; composition, number, piece
2 *syn* see HARMONY 1
3 *syn* see HARMONY 2
4 *syn* see ORDER 4

tune *vb* 1 *syn* see SING 1
2 *syn* see HARMONIZE 3
rel fix, regulate
3 to adjust with respect to resonance < *tune* a TV set to a local station >
syn dial

tune (up) *vb syn* see ADJUST 2

tuned *adj syn* see MELODIOUS 2

tuneful *adj* 1 *syn* see MELODIOUS 2
2 *syn* see MELODIOUS 1
ant tuneless

tunk *vb syn* see TAP 1

turbid *adj* clouded with or as if with roiled sediment < a *turbid* stream >
syn muddy, riley, roily
rel dark, dense, obscure; mucky, thick; clouded, cloudy, murky, opaque, smoky; dull
con translucent; lucid, pellucid, transparent; crystal, crystalline; clean, pure, undefiled
ant clear, limpid

turbulence *n syn* see COMMOTION 2
rel babel, din, pandemonium, uproar; unruliness; fracas, fight
con calmness, composure, placidity, quiet

turbulent *adj* 1 given to insubordination and disorder < a *turbulent* and irresponsible group >
syn boisterous, disorderly, rambunctious, raucous, rowdy, rowdydowdy, rowdyish, rumbustious, termagant, tumultuous, unruly; *compare* UNRULY 1
rel mutinous; fast, roisterous, uncontrollable, uninhibited, wild; clamorous, loudmouthed; brawling, quarrelsome, rough, roughhouse; hell-for-leather, rip-roaring, tempestuous
con calm, placid, quiet, tranquil; controlled, orderly, peaceful, restrained
2 *syn* see WILD 6
rel agitated, convulsed, moiling, stirred up; boiling, roily, ruffled, swirling; howling, riotous, roaring; tempest-tossed

turbulently *adv syn* see HARD 2
rel blusteringly

turf *n syn* see TERRAIN 2
rel area, region, sphere

turgid *adj* 1 *syn* see INFLATED
rel swelling, turgescent
2 *syn* see RHETORICAL

turmoil *n* 1 *syn* see COMMOTION 2
rel jitteriness, nervousness, restlessness, unease, uneasiness; disorder, disruption; moil; riot, strife, uproar
2 *syn* see UNREST
rel distress; anxiety, anxiousness
ant tranquillity
3 *syn* see COMMOTION 4

turn *vb* 1 to move or cause to move in a curved or circular path on or as if on an axis < *turned* the wheel sharply to avoid a collision >
syn circle, circumduct, gyrate, gyre, revolve, roll, rotate; *compare* SPIN 1

rel orbit; pirouette, spin, twirl, whirl; twist, weave, wind; circulate, eddy, swirl; oscillate, sway, swing, vibrate
2 *syn* see SPRAIN
3 *syn* see REVERSE 1
4 *syn* see PLOW
5 *syn* see UPSET 5
rel discompose, undo; unbalance
6 to change or cause to change course or direction < *turned* his car down a side road>
syn avert, deflect, divert, pivot, sheer, swing, veer, volte-face, wheel, whip, whirl; *compare* SHUNT 1
rel depart, detract, deviate, digress, diverge; move, shift; switch, swivel, twist, zigzag; call off, double (back), reverse; shunt, sidetrack; bend, curve, sway; detour, rechannel, turn away
7 *syn* see DIRECT 2
con call off, detract (from), distract, divert (from), draw (away)
8 *syn* see ADDRESS 3
rel employ, use; plunge (into), undertake
idiom turn one's hand (*or* energies) to
con avoid, escape, shy (away)
9 *syn* see CURDLE
10 *syn* see DECAY
11 *syn* see CHANGE 1
12 *syn* see TRANSLATE 1
13 *syn* see DULL 3
14 *syn* see SPIN 2
15 *syn* see DEFECT
16 *syn* see RESORT 2
17 *syn* see BECOME 1
rel change (into), pass (into)

turn (on *or* upon) *vb syn* see DEPEND (on *or* upon) 1

turn *n* **1** *syn* see REVOLUTION 1
2 an often sudden change in course or trend <his health took a *turn* for the better>
syn bend, deflection, deviation, double, shift, tack, yaw
rel course, drift, trend
3 *syn* see REVERSAL 1
4 a point at which a change of course takes place <hidden by a *turn* in the road>
syn angle, bend, bow, flection, flexure, turning
rel curve, twist; corner
5 *syn* see WALK 1
6 *syn* see DRIVE 1
7 *syn* see SPELL 1
8 *syn* see CHANGE 1
9 *syn* see GIFT 2
rel bias, disposition, predisposition
10 an unusual, unexpected, or special interpretation or construction <gave a new *turn* to the old joke>
syn twist
rel construction, interpretation; device, gimmick, trick
11 *syn* see ATTACK 1

turnabout *n* **1** *syn* see REVERSAL 1
2 *syn* see RENEGADE
rel backslider, coward, quitter, turnback

turn back *vb syn* see RETURN 1

turncoat *n syn* see RENEGADE
rel deserter, straggler, betrayer, quisler, quisling, traitor; spy

turn down *vb syn* see DECLINE 4

turned on *adj syn* see DRUGGED

turn in *vb syn* see RETIRE 4
ant turn out

turning *n* **1** *syn* see TURN 4
2 *syn* see DEVIATION 1
rel detour
3 *syn* see REVERSAL 1

turning point *n syn* see JUNCTURE 2
rel climax, culmination, peak
idiom moment of truth

turnip *n syn* see DUNCE

turn off *vb* **1** *syn* see DISMISS 3
2 *syn* see HANG 2

turn out *vb* **1** *syn* see FURNISH 1
rel deck, dress (out)
2 *syn* see BEAR 9
3 *syn* see ROLL OUT

turnout *n* **1** *syn* see COSTUME
2 *syn* see OUTPUT

turn over *vb* **1** *syn* see OVERTURN 1
2 *syn* see PLOW
3 *syn* see PONDER 2
idiom turn over in one's mind
4 *syn* see GIVE 3
rel assign, confer, consign, convey, delegate, relegate; give up, relinquish, ‖turn up
idiom come across with, put into the hands of
con get back, reclaim, recover, regain, retrieve, take back
5 *syn* see COMMIT 1

turnover *n syn* see SHAKE-UP

turn up *vb* **1** *syn* see FIND 1
rel see; uncover, unearth; track (down)
idiom come across
‖**2** *syn* see RELINQUISH
3 to arrive when or where expected < *turned up* for dinner promptly at seven o'clock>
syn show, show up
rel appear, arrive, come, materialize; blow in, pop (in), punch in, roll (in), weigh in
idiom make one's appearance, put in an appearance
4 *syn* see COME 1

turtledove *n syn* see SWEETHEART 1

tussle *vb syn* see WRESTLE
rel scrap, skirmish, spar; hassle
idiom get into a tussle

tutelage *n syn* see EDUCATION 1

twaddle *n syn* see NONSENSE 2
rel gabble; wish-wash

twaddle *vb* **1** *syn* see BABBLE 2
2 *syn* see CHAT 1

twang *n syn* see HINT 2

‖**twat** *n syn* see BUTTOCKS

tweedle *vb syn* see CHIRP

tween *prep syn* see BETWEEN 2

tweet *vb syn* see CHIRP

twerp *n* a usually young or insignificant upstart who meddles beyond his competence or concern <ignored the protests of that insolent *twerp*>
syn pup, puppy, sprat, squirt, ‖squit
rel upstart; ‖squib; fool, jerk, ‖twit; brat
idiom small-time big shot

twice-told *adj syn* see TRITE

twiddle *vb syn* see FIDDLE 1
rel finger, manipulate, palpate; monkey (with), toy (with)
idiom twiddle around with

twiddle *vb syn* see CHAT 1

twig *vb* **1** *syn* see SEE 1

2 *syn* see APPREHEND 1

||**twig** *n syn* see FASHION 3

twiggy *adj syn* see THIN 1

twilight *n* 1 *syn* see EVENING 1
rel afterglow, afterlight
2 *syn* see EVENING 2
rel decline; end

twin *adj* made up of two very closely
matched or identical aspects, elements,
individuals, or parts <the *twin* threats of
inflation and recession>
syn double, dual, paired
rel bifold, binary, twofold; identical,
matched, matching; like, similar
con independent, separate; dissimilar,
unlike

twin *n syn* see MATE 5

twine *vb syn* see WIND 2
rel interweave; undulate; enmesh, entangle, tangle

twinge *n syn* see PAIN 1

twinkle *vb* 1 *syn* see BLINK 2
rel illuminate, light, light up; shine
2 *syn* see FLASH 1
3 *syn* see WINK

twinkle *n* 1 *syn* see INSTANT 1
2 *syn* see FLASH 1

twinkling *n syn* see INSTANT 1
idiom the twinkling of an eye

twirl *vb syn* see SPIN 1

twist *vb* 1 *syn* see SPRAIN
2 *syn* see MISREPRESENT
3 *syn* see WIND 2
ant untwist

twist *n syn* see TURN 10

twister *n syn* see TORNADO

twisting *adj syn* see CROOKED 1

twit *vb syn* see RIDICULE
rel jive, josh, tease; chide, reproach, reprove; blame, censure, reprehend

twitch *vb syn* see JERK
rel clutch, grasp, pluck, snatch; nip,
pinch

twitter *vb* 1 *syn* see CHIRP
2 *syn* see CHAT 1
3 *syn* see SHAKE 1

twittery *adj syn* see NERVOUS
rel flustered; twittering
idiom all atwitter, all fluttery, all of a
twitter

twitty *adj syn* see IRRITABLE

twixt *prep syn* see BETWEEN 2

twofold *adj* 1 having two parts, elements,
or aspects <the problem is *twofold*: to
find gasoline and to be able to pay for
it>
syn bifold, binary, double, double-barreled, dual, dualistic, duple, duplex
rel dyadic; paired, twin
con distinct, separate
2 being twice as large, as great, or as
many <a *twofold* increase in enrollment>
syn double, double-barreled
idiom twice over

two-handed *adj* 1 designed for or requiring the use of both hands <a *two-handed*
sword>
syn bimanual

2 having or being efficient with two hands
< *two-handed* tennis players are rare>
syn ambidextrous, bimanual

twosome *n syn* see COUPLE

two-time *vb syn* see DECEIVE

two-wheeler *n syn* see BICYCLE

tycoon *n syn* see MAGNATE

tyke *n syn* see DOG 1

type *n* a number of individuals thought of
as a group because of a common quality
or qualities <political radicals of whatever *type*>
syn breed, cast, character, class, cut,
description, feather, ilk, kidney, kind, lot,
mold, nature, order, persuasion, sort,
species, stamp, stripe, variety, way
rel blazon, brand, form; sample, specimen; category, group, rubric

typhoon *n syn* see HURRICANE

typic *adj syn* see GENERAL 1
rel average, ordinary

typical *adj* 1 constituting or having the
nature of a type <a *typical* instance of
guilt by association>
syn archetypal, classic, classical, exemplary, ideal, model, paradigmatic, prototypal, prototypical, quintessential, representative
rel characteristic; emblematic, symbolic;
absolute, consummate, perfect
con uncharacteristic; unusual
ant atypical, untypical
2 *syn* see GENERAL 1
rel old hat, unexceptional; collective,
quintessential, representative; characteristic, specific
idiom being the rule and not the exception
con distinctive; exceptional, extraordinary,
unusual; abnormal
ant atypical, untypical

typification *n syn* see ALLEGORY 1

typify *vb* 1 *syn* see REPRESENT 2
2 *syn* see EPITOMIZE 2
rel model

tyrannical *adj syn* see ABSOLUTE 4
rel brutal, harsh, oppressive; roughshod

tyrannize *vb* to exercise arbitrary power
over often with unjust and oppressive
severity <a country *tyrannized* by a dictator and his secret police>
syn despotize
rel dictate, dominate, domineer, overlord;
crush, oppress, trample; shackle; terrorize

tyrannous *adj syn* see ABSOLUTE 4
rel lordly; fascistic, totalitarian

tyranny *n* absolute government in which
unlimited power is vested in a single usually severe and oppressive ruler <the
tyranny of Hitler>
syn autocracy, despotism, dictatorship,
totalitarianism
rel monocracy; absolutism, authoritarianism, fascism; domination, oppression,
totality; terrorism
idiom iron heel (*or* boot)
con democracy; freedom; anarchy

tyrant *n* a ruler who exercises absolute
power oppressively and brutally <Hitler
and Stalin as twentieth-century *tyrants*>
syn despot, dictator, duce, oppressor,
strong man
rel autocrat, totalitarian

---

syn synonym(s)   *rel* related word(s)
ant antonym(s)   *con* contrasted word(s)
idiom idiomatic equivalent(s)
|| use limited; if in doubt, see a dictionary

idiom man on horseback
tyro *n* 1 *syn* see AMATEUR 2

2 *syn* see NOVICE

U

aberrima fides *n syn* see GOOD FAITH

ubiquitous *adj syn* see OMNIPRESENT

ugly *adj* 1 *syn* see GRAVE 3
2 unpleasing to the sight <an *ugly* decaying neighborhood>
syn hideous, ill-favored, ill-looking, unbeautiful, uncomely, unsightly
rel homely, plain; bizarre, grotesque; repelling, repugnant, repulsive; unattractive, uninviting, unpleasing, unprepossessing
idiom homely as a mud (*or* hedge) fence, not much to look at, short on looks
con comely, fair, good-looking, handsome, lovely, pretty; attractive, prepossessing
ant beautiful
3 *syn* see BASE 3
4 *syn* see TROUBLESOME
5 *syn* see SULLEN

ukase *n syn* see EDICT 1

ulterior *adj* lying behind what is manifest or avowed <an *ulterior* motive>
syn buried, concealed, covert, guarded, hidden, obscured, privy, shrouded
rel ambiguous, cryptic, dark, enigmatic, equivocal, obscure
idiom hidden under the rug, kept behind a screen, under cover, under wraps
con clear, open, overt, plain, straightforward; explicit, expressed

ultimate *adj* 1 *syn* see LAST
2 *syn* see SUPREME
3 being so fundamental as to stand at the extreme limit of the actually or conceivably knowable <*ultimate* realities>
syn absolute, categorical
rel empyreal, empyrean, sublime, transcendental; exalted, grand, lofty

ultimate *n syn* see APOTHEOSIS 1

ultimate *vb syn* see CLOSE 3

ultimately *adv syn* see YET 2

ultra *adj* 1 *syn* see EXTREME 3
2 *syn* see OUTLANDISH 3

ultraconservative *n syn* see REACTIONARY

ultrafashionable *adj syn* see STYLISH

ultraist *n syn* see RADICAL

ultraist *adj syn* see EXTREME 3

ultramarine *adj syn* see OVERSEAS

ululate *vb syn* see HOWL 1
rel bewail, lament

umbra *n* 1 *syn* see APPARITION
2 *syn* see SHADE 1

umbrage *n* 1 *syn* see SHADE 1
2 *syn* see FOLIAGE
3 *syn* see OFFENSE 2
rel annoyance, irking, vexation; exasperation, irritation, nettling, provoking; fury, ire, rage, wrath

umbrage *vb* 1 *syn* see SHADE
2 *syn* see ANGER 1

umbrageous *adj syn* see SHADY 1

umbrous *adj syn* see SHADY 1

umpire *n syn* see JUDGE 1

umpire *vb syn* see JUDGE 1

unabashed *adj syn* see SHAMELESS
ant abashed

unabbreviated *adj syn* see UNABRIDGED
ant abbreviated

unabridged *adj* not shortened by omission of parts (as words) <published an *unabridged* edition of Shakespeare's plays>
syn complete, unabbreviated, uncondensed, uncut, whole-length
rel entire, intact, whole
con condensed, cropped, curtailed, cut, incompleted, shortened, trimmed
ant abridged

unacceptable *adj syn* see OBJECTIONABLE
ant acceptable

unaccompanied *adj syn* see ALONE 1
ant accompanied, companioned

unaccomplished *adj syn* see AMATEURISH
ant accomplished, skilled

unaccountable *adj* 1 *syn* see INEXPLICABLE
ant accountable
2 *syn* see MYSTERIOUS

unaccustomed *adj syn* see UNFAMILIAR 1
ant accustomed, familiar

unacquaintance *n syn* see IGNORANCE 2
ant acquaintance

unacquainted *adj syn* see IGNORANT 2
ant acquainted

unacquaintedness *n syn* see IGNORANCE 2
ant acquaintance

unacquired *adj syn* see INNATE 1
ant acquired

unadorned *adj syn* see PLAIN 1
ant adorned

unadulterated *adj* 1 *syn* see PURE 2
2 *syn* see STRAIGHT 3
ant adulterated

unadvisable *adj syn* see INADVISABLE
ant advisable

unadvised *adj syn* see RASH 1
ant advised, thought-out

unaffable *adj syn* see UNDEMONSTRATIVE
ant affable

unaffected *adj syn* see NATURAL 5
ant affected, artificial

unafraid *adj syn* see BRAVE 1
rel composed, cool, imperturbable; assured, confident, sure
con apprehensive, fearful
ant afraid

unaimed *adj syn* see RANDOM

unalert *adj syn* see INCAUTIOUS 1
ant alert

unalike *adj syn* see DIFFERENT 1
ant alike
unalloyed *adj syn* see PURE 2
unalluring *adj syn* see PLAIN 5
ant alluring, attractive
unalterable *adj syn* see INFLEXIBLE 3
ant alterable
unambiguous *adj* 1 *syn* see CLEAR 4
ant ambiguous, obscure
2 *syn* see EXPLICIT
ant ambiguous
3 *syn* see CLEAR 5
unanimated *adj syn* see DEAD 1
unanimous *adj* being of one mind <they were *unanimous* in their determination to win>
syn consentaneous, consentient, solid
rel agreed, agreeing, concordant, concurrent, harmonious
idiom of one accord, of one (*or* the same) mind, with one voice
con differing, disagreed, disagreeing, discordant, inharmonious
unanticipatedly *adv syn* see UNAWARES
unapparent *adj syn* see IMPERCEPTIBLE
ant apparent, detectable
unappeasable *adj* 1 *syn* see INSATIABLE
ant appeasable
2 *syn* see GRIM 3
ant appeasable, placable
unappetizing *adj syn* see UNPALATABLE 1
ant appetizing
unappreciable *adj syn* see IMPERCEPTIBLE
ant appreciable
unappreciated *adj syn* see THANKLESS 2
ant appreciated
unappreciative *adj syn* see THANKLESS 2
ant appreciative
unapproachable *adj* 1 *syn* see INACCESSIBLE
ant approachable, attainable
2 *syn* see UNSOCIABLE
ant accessible, approachable
unapt *adj* 1 *syn* see IMPROPER 1
2 *syn* see UNSKILLFUL 1
ant apt
unarm *vb syn* see DISARM 2
unartful *adj syn* see NATURAL 5
ant artful
unarticulate *adj syn* see DUMB 1
ant articulate
unartificial *adj syn* see NATURAL 5
ant affected, artificial
unasked *adj* 1 not asked or invited <annoyed by his *unasked* advice>
syn unbidden, uninvited, unrequested, unsought
rel arrogant, impudent, overbearing, presumptuous; spontaneous, voluntary; unacceptable, unwanted, unwelcome
con desired, invited, sought, wanted; acceptable, welcome
ant asked
2 *syn* see SUPEREROGATORY
unassailable *adj syn* see INVINCIBLE 1
rel stalwart, stout, strong, sturdy, tenacious, tough

---

syn synonym(s)   *rel* related word(s)
ant antonym(s)   *con* contrasted word(s)
idiom idiomatic equivalent(s)
‖ use limited; if in doubt, see a dictionary

ant assailable
unassertive *adj syn* see SHY 1
ant aggressive, assertive
unassorted *adj syn* see MISCELLANEOUS
unassuming *adj syn* see HUMBLE 1
ant assuming, presumptuous
unassured *adj* 1 *syn* see UNSAFE
2 *syn* see SHY 1
ant assured
3 *syn* see INSECURE 1
unattainable *adj* 1 *syn* see INACCESSIBLE
ant attainable
2 *syn* see IMPOSSIBLE 1
unattractive *adj syn* see PLAIN 5
ant alluring, attractive
unauthentic *adj syn* see SPURIOUS 3
ant authentic, genuine
unavailable *adj syn* see FUTILE
unavailing *adj syn* see FUTILE
unavoidable *adj syn* see INEVITABLE
ant avoidable
unavoidably *adv syn* see WILLY-NILLY
unaware *adv syn* see UNAWARES
unaware *adj syn* see IGNORANT 2
ant aware, conscious
unawaredly *adv syn* see UNAWARES
unawareness *n syn* see IGNORANCE 2
ant awareness, consciousness
unawares *adv* without warning <caught *unawares* by company>
syn aback, short, sudden, suddenly, unanticipatedly, unaware, unawaredly, unexpectedly
rel unprepared, unready
idiom like a bolt from the blue, off base, out of a clear sky, out of the blue
unbalance *vb syn* see MADDEN 1
unbalance *n syn* see INSANITY 1
rel disorientation, instability
unbalanced *adj* 1 *syn* see LOPSIDED
ant balanced
2 *syn* see INSANE 1
unbearable *adj syn* see INSUFFERABLE
ant bearable, supportable
unbearing *adj syn* see BARREN 2
unbeatable *adj syn* see INVINCIBLE 1
ant beatable, defeatable
unbeauteous *adj syn* see PLAIN 5
ant beauteous
unbeautified *adj syn* see PLAIN 1
ant beautified, embellished
unbeautiful *adj* 1 *syn* see PLAIN 5
ant beautiful
2 *syn* see UGLY 2
ant beautiful
unbecoming *adj* 1 *syn* see INDECOROUS
rel awkward, clumsy, gauche, inept, maladroit
ant becoming, seemly
2 *syn* see IMPROPER 1
unbecomingness *n syn* see IMPROPRIETY 1
ant becomingness, seemliness
unbefitting *adj syn* see IMPROPER 1
ant apropos, befitting
unbegotten *adj syn* see SELF-EXISTENT
unbelief *n* the attitude or state of mind of one who does not believe <after so much deception, so many lies, she could offer nothing but *unbelief* to his words>
syn disbelief, incredulity, unbelievingness, unfaith

rel doubt, dubiety, dubiosity, skepticism, uncertainty; distrust, mistrust, suspicion; apprehension, misgiving, qualm
con assurance, certitude, security, trust; dependence, reliance, stock, store
ant belief

unbelievable *adj* 1 *syn* see INCREDIBLE 1
ant believable, credible
2 *syn* see IMPLAUSIBLE
ant believable, credible

unbelieve *vb* *syn* see DISBELIEVE
ant believe, credit

unbeliever *n* *syn* see SKEPTIC
ant believer

unbelieving *adj* *syn* see INCREDULOUS
ant believing

unbelievingness *n* *syn* see UNBELIEF

unbend *vb* 1 *syn* see RELAX 1
2 *syn* see REST 2

unbendable *adj* *syn* see INFLEXIBLE 2
ant bendable

unbending *adj* 1 *syn* see STIFF 1
ant bendable
2 *syn* see INFLEXIBLE 2
3 *syn* see UNSOCIABLE

unbiased *adj* *syn* see FAIR 4
rel aloof, uninterested
ant biased

unbidden *adj* *syn* see UNASKED

unbind *vb* 1 *syn* see LOOSE 3
ant bind
2 *syn* see FREE
ant bind

unblamable *adj* *syn* see GOOD 11
ant blamable, blameworthy

unblemished *adj* 1 *syn* see WHOLE 1
ant blemished, flawed
2 *syn* see CHASTE

unblenched *adj* *syn* see BRAVE 1

unblenching *adj* *syn* see BRAVE 1

unblock *vb* *syn* see OPEN 1
ant block

unblunted *adj* *syn* see SHARP 1
ant blunt, blunted

unblurred *adj* *syn* see CLEAR 4
ant blurred

unblushing *adj* *syn* see SHAMELESS

unbodied *adj* *syn* see IMMATERIAL 1
ant bodied, incarnate

unbookish *adj* *syn* see UNSCHOLARLY
ant bookish

unbosom *vb* *syn* see REVEAL 1

unbounded *adj* *syn* see LIMITLESS
ant bounded, limited

unbrace *vb* *syn* see WEAKEN 1
ant brace, reinforce

unbroken *adj* *syn* see WHOLE 1
ant broken

unbrookable *adj* *syn* see INSUFFERABLE

unbuild *vb* *syn* see DESTROY 1
ant build

unburden *vb* *syn* see RID
rel discharge, disencumber, unload
con encumber, lade, load, saddle, tax, weight
ant burden

unbury *vb* *syn* see EXHUME
ant bury

uncalled-for *adj* 1 *syn* see UNNECESSARY
ant required
2 *syn* see SUPEREROGATORY
3 *syn* see BASELESS

rel absurd, foolish, preposterous, silly; impertinent, intrusive, officious
ant well-founded
4 *syn* see RUDE 6

uncandid *adj* *syn* see DISINGENUOUS
ant candid

uncanny *adj* 1 *syn* see WEIRD 1
2 *syn* see SUPERNATURAL 2

uncared-for *adj* *syn* see NEGLECTED
ant cared-for

uncareful *adj* *syn* see IRRESPONSIBLE
ant careful

uncaring *adj* *syn* see CARELESS 1
ant careful

uncaused *adj* *syn* see SELF-EXISTENT

unceasing *adj* *syn* see CONTINUAL

uncelebrated *adj* *syn* see OBSCURE 5
ant celebrated, noted

uncelestial *adj* *syn* see EARTHLY 1
ant celestial

unceremonious *adj* 1 *syn* see INFORMAL 1
ant ceremonious
2 *syn* see SHORT 5

uncertain *adj* 1 not stable, consistent, or predictable < was in very *uncertain* health >
syn capricious, chancy, erratic, fluctuant, iffy, incalculable, unpredictable, whimsical; *compare* INCONSTANT 1
rel questionable, undependable, unsettled; fickle, inconstant, insecure, unstable, unsure; changeable, mutable, protean, variable; unexpectable, unforeseeable
idiom in a state of uncertainty, in suspense
2 *syn* see INCONSTANT 1
3 *syn* see MUTABLE 2
4 *syn* see DOUBTFUL 1
ant certain
5 *syn* see MOOT
ant certain
6 *syn* see OBSCURE 3
7 *syn* see VACILLATING 2
idiom at a loss
ant certain, set

uncertainty *n* a feeling of unsureness about someone or something < troubled by a growing *uncertainty* about the future >
syn concern, doubt, doubtfulness, dubiety, dubiosity, dubitancy, incertitude, mistrust, query, skepticism, suspicion, uncertitude, wonder
rel anxiety, bother, disquiet, trouble, worry; agitation, distress, perturbation, uneasiness; disfaith, distrust; hesitation, reserve, salt
con assurance, certitude, confidence, conviction; complacency, content, satisfaction
ant certainty

uncertitude *n* *syn* see UNCERTAINTY
ant certitude

unchain *vb* *syn* see FREE
ant chain

unchangeable *adj* *syn* see INFLEXIBLE 3
ant changeable

unchanging *adj* 1 *syn* see STEADY 2
2 *syn* see SAME 3
ant changeable, changing

uncharnel *vb* *syn* see EXHUME

unchaste *adj* 1 *syn* see IMPURE 1
ant chaste

2 *syn* see FAST 7
  ant chaste
unchristian *adj syn* see OUTRAGEOUS 1
  ant ‖Christian
uncivil *adj* 1 *syn* see BARBARIAN 1
  2 *syn* see RUDE 6
  rel coarse, crass, crude
  con polished, smooth, urbane
  ant civil
uncivilized *adj* 1 *syn* see BARBARIAN 1
  ant civilized
  2 *syn* see BOORISH
  ant civilized
  3 *syn* see OUTRAGEOUS 1
unclad *adj syn* see NUDE 2
unclean *adj* 1 *syn* see IMPURE 1
  ant clean, pure
  2 *syn* see DIRTY 1
  ant clean, cleanly
  3 *syn* see IMPURE 3
  ant clean; purified
uncleanly *adj* 1 *syn* see IMPURE 1
  ant cleanly
  2 *syn* see DIRTY 1
  ant clean, cleanly
unclear *adj* 1 *syn* see OBSCURE 3
  ant clear
  2 *syn* see FAINT 2
  ant clear, distinct
  3 *syn* see DOUBTFUL 1
  ant clear
uncloak *vb syn* see EXPOSE 4
  ant cloak
unclose *vb* 1 *syn* see OPEN 1
  ant close
  2 *syn* see REVEAL 1
unclosed *adj syn* see OPEN 1
  ant closed
unclothe *vb* 1 *syn* see STRIP 1
  ant clothe, dress
  2 *syn* see OPEN 2
unclothed *adj syn* see NUDE 2
  ant clothed, dressed
unclouded *adj syn* see FAIR 2
  ant clouded, cloudy
uncluttered *adj syn* see NEAT 2
  ant cluttered
uncolored *adj syn* see FAIR 4
  ant colored, partial
uncombed *adj syn* see SLOVENLY 1
uncombine *vb syn* see SEPARATE 1
  ant combine
un—come-at-able *adj syn* see INACCESSI-
BLE
  ant come-at-able
uncomely *adj* 1 *syn* see IMPROPER 1
  2 *syn* see PLAIN 5
  ant comely
  3 *syn* see UGLY 2
  ant comely
uncomfortable *adj* causing or likely to
cause discomfort <kept an *uncomfortable*
chair for uninvited callers>
  syn comfortless, discomforting, harsh,
uncomforting, uncomfy
  rel distressing, easeless, uneasy
  con comforting, easy, soothing
  ant comfortable

---

syn synonym(s)   *rel* related word(s)
ant antonym(s)   *con* contrasted word(s)
idiom idiomatic equivalent(s)
‖ use limited; if in doubt, see a dictionary

uncomforting *adj syn* see UNCOMFORT-
ABLE
  ant comforting
uncomfy *adj syn* see UNCOMFORTABLE
  ant comfy
uncommon *adj* 1 *syn* see INFREQUENT
  con commonplace, everyday, ordinary
  ant common
  2 *syn* see EXCEPTIONAL 1
  ant common, commonplace
‖**uncommon** *adv syn* see EXTRA
uncommonly *adv* 1 *syn* see OCCASION-
ALLY
  ant commonly
  2 *syn* see EXTRA
uncommunicative *adj* 1 *syn* see SILENT 3
  ant communicative
  2 *syn* see UNSOCIABLE
uncompanionable *adj syn* see UNSOCIA-
BLE
  ant companionable
uncompassionate *adj syn* see UNFEEL-
ING 2
  ant compassionate
uncompensated *adj syn* see UNPAID 1
  ant compensated
uncomplainingness *n syn* see PATIENCE
  ant complainingness, discontent
uncomplete *adj syn* see DEFICIENT 1
  ant complete
uncompliant *adj syn* see INFLEXIBLE 2
  ant compliant
uncomplimentary *adj syn* see DEROGA-
TORY
  ant complimentary
uncomprehensible *adj syn* see INCOM-
PREHENSIBLE 1
  ant comprehensible, graspable
uncompromising *adj* 1 *syn* see INFLEXI-
BLE 2
  2 *syn* see TOUGH 3
unconcealed *adj syn* see FRANK
unconceivable *adj syn* see IMPLAUSIBLE
  ant conceivable
unconcern *n syn* see APATHY 1
  ant concern
unconcerned *adj syn* see INDIFFERENT 2
  rel collected, composed, cool, nonchalant
  con anxious, careful, solicitous, worried
  ant concerned
uncondensed *adj syn* see UNABRIDGED
  ant condensed
unconfident *adj syn* see INSECURE 1
  ant confident
unconfined *adj syn* see FREE 2
  ant confined
uncongenial *adj* 1 *syn* see ANTIPATHETIC
2
  rel displeasing, unattractive, unlikable,
unpleasing
  ant congenial
  2 *syn* see INHARMONIOUS 2
unconnected *adj syn* see INCOHERENT 2
  ant connected, ordered
unconquerable *adj* 1 *syn* see INVINCIBLE
1
  rel insuperable, unsurmountable; proof,
resistant, secure, tight
  idiom more than a match for
  con beatable, vincible; expugnable, preg-
nable, vulnerable; insecure, open, unprotected
  ant conquerable

2 *syn* see INSUPERABLE
ant conquerable

unconscionable *adj* 1 *syn* see UNSCRUPULOUS
ant conscientious, conscionable
2 *syn* see EXCESSIVE 1
3 *syn* see UNREASONABLE 2
4 *syn* see OUTRAGEOUS 1

unconscious *adj syn* see INSENSIBLE 2
ant conscious

unconsequential *adj syn* see PETTY 2
ant consequential

unconsidered *adj* 1 *syn* see PETTY 2
2 *syn* see RANDOM
ant considered, planned
3 *syn* see RASH 1
ant considered

unconsolable *adj syn* see INCONSOLABLE
ant consolable

unconspicuous *adj syn* see INCONSPICUOUS
ant conspicuous

unconstrained *adj* 1 *syn* see EASYGOING 3
2 *syn* see DEMONSTRATIVE
ant constrained

unconstraint *n* freedom from constraint or pressure <had always been used to the *unconstraint* of a happy affectionate family>
syn abandon, ease, naturalness, spontaneity, unrestraint; compare ABANDON 2
rel impulsiveness, instinctiveness; ingenuousness, naiveté, simplicity, unsophistication
con pressure, strain, stress, tension; formality, rigidity; sophistication
ant constraint

uncontainable *adj syn* see IRREPRESSIBLE

uncontent *adj syn* see DISCONTENTED
ant content, contented

uncontented *adj syn* see DISCONTENTED
ant content, contented

uncontestable *adj syn* see POSITIVE 3
ant contestable

uncontinuous *adj syn* see INCOHERENT 2

uncontrite *adj syn* see REMORSELESS
ant contrite

uncontrollable *adj* 1 *syn* see UNRULY 1
ant controllable
2 *syn* see IRREPRESSIBLE
ant controllable

uncontrovertible *adj syn* see POSITIVE 3
ant controvertible, disputable

unconversant *adj syn* see INEXPERIENCED
ant conversant, versed

unconvincing *adj syn* see IMPLAUSIBLE
ant convincing

uncooked *adj syn* see RAW 1
ant cooked

‖**uncorporal** *adj syn* see IMMATERIAL 1

uncorrectable *adj syn* see HOPELESS 2
ant correctable

uncostly *adj syn* see CHEAP 1
ant costly

uncountable *adj* 1 *syn* see INNUMERABLE
ant countable
2 *syn* see INCALCULABLE 1

uncounted *adj syn* see INNUMERABLE

uncouple *vb syn* see DETACH

ant couple

uncourteous *adj syn* see RUDE 6
ant courteous

uncouth *adj* 1 *syn* see STRANGE 4
2 *syn* see DERELICT 1
3 *syn* see COARSE 3
ant couth
4 *syn* see RUDE 6

uncover *vb* 1 *syn* see REVEAL 1
2 *syn* see EXPOSE 1
3 *syn* see OPEN 2
ant cover

uncovered *adj syn* see OPEN 2

uncreate *vb syn* see ANNIHILATE 2

uncreated *adj syn* see SELF-EXISTENT
ant created

uncreative *adj syn* see UNORIGINAL
ant creative

uncritical *adj syn* see SUPERFICIAL 2
rel imprecise, inaccurate, inexact; careless, casual, offhand, perfunctory, slipshod
con accurate, exact, precise; careful; discerning, discriminating, penetrating
ant critical

uncrown *vb syn* see DEPOSE 1
ant coronate, crown

unction *n syn* see OINTMENT

unctious *adj syn* see FULSOME

unctuous *adj* 1 *syn* see FATTY 2
2 *syn* see FULSOME

uncultivated *adj* 1 *syn* see COARSE 3
ant cultivated
2 *syn* see BARBARIAN 1
ant cultivated
3 *syn* see WILD 1
ant cultivated

uncultured *adj* 1 *syn* see BOORISH
ant cultured
2 *syn* see COARSE 3

uncurable *adj syn* see HOPELESS 2
ant curable

uncurbed *adj syn* see AUDACIOUS 4
ant curbed

uncurious *adj syn* see INDIFFERENT 2
ant curious

uncurtain *vb syn* see REVEAL 1

uncustomary *adj syn* see EXCEPTIONAL 1
ant customary

uncut *adj syn* see UNABRIDGED
ant cut

undamaged *adj syn* see WHOLE 1
ant damaged

undaring *adj syn* see TIMID 2
ant daring

undarkened *adj syn* see FAIR 2

undauntable *adj syn* see BRAVE 1

undaunted *adj syn* see BRAVE 1
ant daunted

undear *adj syn* see CHEAP 1
ant dear

undeceive *vb syn* see DISABUSE
ant deceive

undecided *adj* 1 *syn* see PENDING
ant decided
2 *syn* see DOUBTFUL 1

undecipherable *adj syn* see ILLEGIBLE
ant decipherable

undecisive *adj syn* see VACILLATING 2
ant decisive

undeclared *adj syn* see TACIT 1

undecorated *adj syn* see PLAIN 1
ant decorated

undecorous *adj syn* see INDECOROUS

ant decorous

undefeatable *adj syn see* INVINCIBLE 1
  ant defeatable
undefiled *adj syn see* CHASTE
undefined *adj syn see* FAINT 2
  ant defined
undeflowered *adj syn see* VIRGIN 1
  ant deflowered
undelude *vb syn see* DISABUSE
  ant delude
undemonstrated *adj syn see* UNTRIED 1
  ant demonstrated
undemonstrative *adj* not socially outgoing < a shy *undemonstrative* person yet capable of deep feeling >
  syn aseptic, restrained, retiring, shrinking, unaffable, unexpansive, withdrawn; *compare* UNSOCIABLE
  rel chill, cold, frigid, glacial, icy; emotionless, indifferent, unemotional, uninterested; aloof, distant, reserved, standoffish
  con free and easy, hail-fellow-well-met, outgiving, outgoing, palsy-walsy; sociable
  ant demonstrative
undeniable *adj* 1 *syn see* POSITIVE 3
  ant deniable
  2 *syn see* REAL 3
undenominational *adj syn see* NONSECTARIAN
  ant denominational
undependable *adj* 1 *syn see* UNRELIABLE 1
  ant dependable
  2 *syn see* UNSAFE
  ant dependable
  3 *syn see* TRICK
  ant dependable
under *adv syn see* BELOW 1
  ant above, over
under *prep syn see* BELOW 1
  ant over
under *adj* 1 *syn see* INFERIOR 1
  2 *syn see* SUBORDINATE
underage *n syn see* FAILURE 3
  ant overage
underconsciousness *n syn see* SUBCONSCIOUS
undercover *adj syn see* SECRET 1
undercover man *n syn see* SPY
undercroft *n syn see* CRYPT
underdeveloped *adj syn see* BACKWARD 6
underdog *n syn see* VICTIM 2
  ant overdog, top dog
underearth *adj syn see* SUBTERRANEAN
underfoot *adj* 1 *syn see* SUBTERRANEAN
  2 *syn see* DOWNTRODDEN
undergo *vb syn see* EXPERIENCE 1
  rel abide, bear, endure, tolerate; bow, defer, submit, yield
underground *adj syn see* SUBTERRANEAN
underhand *adj* characterized by sly unobtrusive craft or deceit < ready to use the most *underhand* methods to gain his ends >
  syn devious, duplicitous, guileful, indirect, shifty, sneaking, sneaky, underhanded; *compare* SECRET 1, SLY 2

rel deceitful, dishonest; crooked, oblique; crafty, cunning, insidious, sly, tricky, wily; furtive, hangdog
con candid, frank, open, plain; forthright, straight-forward
ant aboveboard
underhanded *adj* 1 *syn see* UNDERHAND
  ant aboveboard
  2 *syn see* SHORTHANDED
underivative *adj syn see* PRIMARY 5
  ant derivative
underived *adj syn see* PRIMARY 5
  ant derived
underlease *vb syn see* SUBLET
underlet *vb syn see* SUBLET
underline *vb syn see* EMPHASIZE
underline *n syn see* CAPTION
underling *n syn see* INFERIOR
underly *adj syn see* UNWELL
underlying *adj* 1 *syn see* FUNDAMENTAL 1
  rel cardinal, essential, vital; critical, crucial; indispensable, necessary, needful
  2 *syn see* ELEMENTAL 1
undermanned *adj syn see* SHORT-HANDED
  ant overmanned
undermine *vb* 1 *syn see* WEAKEN 1
  rel ruin, wreck; foil, frustrate, thwart
  idiom bore from within
  ant reinforce
  2 *syn see* SABOTAGE
undermining *n syn see* SABOTAGE
undermost *adj syn see* BOTTOMMOST
  ant uppermost
underneath *prep syn see* BELOW 1
underneath *adv syn see* BELOW 1
‖**underneath** *adj syn see* SECRET 1
underneath *n syn see* BOTTOM 1
underpinner *n syn see* SUPPORT 3
underpinning *n* 1 *syn see* BASIS 1
  2 *syn see* BASE 1
  3 *syn see* SUPPORT 3
underprivileged *adj* deficient in basic economic and social resources < the role of the school in bettering the lot of *underprivileged* children >
  syn depressed, deprived, disadvantaged
  rel handicapped; hapless, ill-fated, ill-starred, unfortunate, unlucky; impoverished, needy, poor
  idiom badly off, in adverse circumstances, out of luck
  con advantaged, fortunate, privileged; coddled, indulged, spoiled
underprize *vb syn see* DEPRECIATE 1
  ant overprize
underprop *vb syn see* SUPPORT 5
underpropping *n syn see* SUPPORT 3
underrate *vb syn see* DEPRECIATE 1
  ant overrate
underscore *vb syn see* EMPHASIZE
undersense *n syn see* SUBCONSCIOUS
undersexed *adj syn see* FRIGID 3
  ant oversexed
underside *n syn see* BOTTOM 1
understaffed *adj syn see* SHORTHANDED
  ant overstaffed
understand *vb* 1 *syn see* APPREHEND 1
  idiom get the drift
  ant misunderstand
  2 *syn see* KNOW 1
  idiom get the hang of

---

syn synonym(s)   *rel* related word(s)
ant antonym(s)   *con* contrasted word(s)
idiom idiomatic equivalent(s)
‖ use limited; if in doubt, see a dictionary

3 to view as plausible or likely < I *understand* he is expected home soon >
syn assume, believe, ‖conceit, conceive, expect, gather, surmise; suspect, take, think, ‖wit; *compare* CONJECTURE
rel conclude, deduce, infer; conjecture, guess, presume, surmise; fancy; consider
con know; challenge, doubt, question

understandable *adj* of a kind to be readily understood < her style was smooth and easy, her language *understandable* >
syn apprehensible, comprehendible, comprehensible, fathomable, graspable, intelligible, knowable, lucid, luminous; *compare* CLEAR 4, 5
rel clear-cut, unambiguous, unblurred; plain, simple, straightforward; exoteric, lay, popular
con mysterious, obscure, strange, vague; cryptic, esoteric, hidden

understanding *n* 1 *syn* see REASON 5
rel discernment, discrimination, insight, penetration; awareness, intuition; apprehension, comprehension, grasp
2 *syn* see AGREEMENT 2
3 *syn* see MEANING 1

understood *adj syn* see TACIT 1

understrapper *n syn* see INFERIOR

understructure *n syn* see BASE 1
ant superstructure

undersurface *n syn* see BOTTOM 1

undertake *vb* 1 *syn* see TRY 5
rel begin, commence, start
idiom put (*or* set) one's hand to
2 *syn* see TAKE ON 3
3 *syn* see PROMISE 1
rel certify, warrant
idiom stand back of (*or* behind)

undertaker *n* 1 *syn* see ENTREPRENEUR 1
2 *syn* see MORTICIAN

undertaking *n* 1 *syn* see ATTEMPT
2 *syn* see PROJECT 2

under-the-table *adj syn* see SECRET 1
ant aboveboard

undertone *n* 1 *syn* see MURMUR 1
2 *syn* see ASSOCIATION 4

undervalue *vb syn* see DEPRECIATE 1
ant overvalue

underwater *adj syn* see SUBMARINE

underwit *n syn* see FOOL 4

underworld *n syn* see HELL

undescribable *adj syn* see UNUTTERABLE
ant describable

undesignated *adj syn* see ANONYMOUS

undesigned *adj syn* see UNINTENTIONAL
ant designed

undesigning *adj syn* see GENUINE 3
ant designing

undesirable *adj syn* see OBJECTIONABLE
ant desirable

undesired *adj syn* see UNWELCOME 1
ant desired

undestroyable *adj syn* see INDESTRUCTIBLE
ant destroyable, destructible

undeterminable *adj syn* see INDEFINITE 1
ant determinable

undetermined *adj* 1 *syn* see PENDING
ant determined

2 *syn* see FAINT 2

undeveloped *adj* 1 *syn* see BACKWARD 6
ant developed
2 *syn* see PRIMITIVE 3
ant advanced

undeviatingly *adv syn* see DIRECTLY 1

undevised *adj syn* see UNINTENTIONAL
ant devised

undexterous *adj syn* see UNSKILLFUL 1
ant dexterous

undifferenced *adj syn* see LIKE

undifferentiated *adj syn* see LIKE
ant differentiated

undiluted *adj* 1 *syn* see STRAIGHT 3
ant diluted
2 *syn* see PURE 2

undiplomatic *adj syn* see TACTLESS
ant diplomatic

undiscernible *adj syn* see IMPERCEPTIBLE
ant discernible

undisciplinable *adj syn* see UNRULY 1

undisciplined *adj syn* see UNRULY 1
ant disciplined

undiscriminated *adj syn* see INDISCRIMINATE 1
ant discriminate, discriminated

undiscriminating *adj syn* see INDISCRIMINATE 1

undisguised *adj syn* see FRANK

undisputable *adj syn* see POSITIVE 3
ant controvertible, disputable

undissembled *adj* 1 *syn* see GENUINE 3
ant dissembled, feigned
2 *syn* see FRANK

undissembling *adj syn* see FRANK
ant dissembling

undistinct *adj syn* see FAINT 2
ant clear, distinct

undistinctive *adj syn* see FAIR 4

undistinguishing *adj syn* see INDISCRIMINATE 1

undistorted *adj syn* see TRUE 3
ant distorted

undistracted *adj syn* see WHOLE 5

undivided *adj syn* see WHOLE 5
ant divided

undo *vb* 1 *syn* see LOOSE 3
2 *syn* see OPEN 1
rel loose, untie
3 *syn* see ABOLISH 1
4 *syn* see DESTROY 1
5 *syn* see OUTWIT
idiom bring down (*or* low), bring to naught
6 *syn* see SEDUCE 2

undocked *adj syn* see UNABRIDGED
ant docked

undoing *n syn* see DOWNFALL 2

undomesticated *adj syn* see WILD 1
ant domesticated

undoubtable *adj syn* see POSITIVE 3
ant doubtable, questionable

undoubted *adj syn* see AUTHENTIC 2
ant doubtful, questionable

undoubtedly *adv syn* see WELL 7

undoubtful *adj syn* see CONFIDENT 1
ant doubtful

undress *vb* 1 *syn* see STRIP 1
ant dress
2 *syn* see EXPOSE 4
ant dress up

undressed *adj* 1 *syn* see NUDE 2

ant dressed
2 *syn* see RUDE 1
ant dressed, finished
undubitable *adj syn* see AUTHENTIC 2
ant dubitable
undue *adj* 1 *syn* see IMPROPER 1
2 *syn* see EXCESSIVE 1
3 *syn* see UNREASONABLE 2
undulate *vb syn* see SLITHER 2
unduly *adv syn* see EVER 6
ant duly
unduteous *adj syn* see IMPIOUS 2
ant duteous
undutiful *adj syn* see IMPIOUS 2
ant dutiful
undying *adj syn* see IMMORTAL 1
rel continuing, persistent; interminable, unceasing; inextinguishable, unquenchable
ant mortal
uneager *adj syn* see DISINCLINED
ant eager
unearth *vb syn* see DISCOVER 3
rel exhibit, expose, show; disclose, reveal; delve, dig
unearthing *n syn* see DISCOVERY
unearthly *adj* 1 *syn* see SUPERNATURAL 1
2 *syn* see WEIRD 1
3 *syn* see FOOLISH 2
unease *n* 1 *syn* see CARE 2
2 *syn* see TENSION 2
3 *syn* see EMBARRASSMENT
ant ease, easiness
uneasiness *n* 1 *syn* see CARE 2
2 *syn* see EMBARRASSMENT
ant ease, easiness
uneasy *adj* 1 *syn* see TENSE 2
rel anxious, careful, concerned, solicitous, worried; agitated, disquieted, disturbed, perturbed
idiom on pins and needles
ant easy
2 *syn* see RESTLESS
3 *syn* see DOUBTFUL 1
uneatable *adj syn* see INEDIBLE
ant eatable
uneducated *adj syn* see IGNORANT 1
ant educated, lettered
unelaborate *adj syn* see PLAIN 1
ant elaborate
unembellished *adj syn* see PLAIN 1
ant embellished
unembodied *adj syn* see IMMATERIAL 1
unembroidered *adj syn* see PLAIN 1
unemotional *adj* 1 *syn* see COLD 2
rel dispassionate; unfeeling; impassive
con affective, feeling; affectionate, demonstrative
ant emotional
2 *syn* see UNFEELING 2
unemphatic *adj syn* see INCONSPICUOUS
unemployed *adj* lacking a gainful occupation <the problems of *unemployed* workers>
syn jobless, workless
rel free, unengaged, unoccupied; underemployed; fired, laid off
idiom at liberty, let go, on layoff, out of work

ant employed
unending *adj* 1 *syn* see EVERLASTING 1
2 *syn* see CONTINUAL
unendurable *adj syn* see INSUFFERABLE
ant endurable
unenlarged *adj syn* see ILLIBERAL
unenlightened *adj syn* see BACKWARD 5
ant enlightened
unennobled *adj syn* see IGNOBLE 1
ant ennobled, noble
unentangle *vb syn* see EXTRICATE 2
ant entangle
unenthusiastic *adj syn* see TEPID 2
ant enthusiastic
unequal *adj* 1 *syn* see DIFFERENT 1
2 *syn* see LOPSIDED
unequalable *adj syn* see SUPREME
unequaled *adj syn* see ALONE 3
ant equaled
unequipped *adj syn* see UNFIT 2
unequitable *adj syn* see INEQUITABLE
ant equitable
unequivocal *adj* 1 *syn* see CLEAR 5
ant equivocal
2 *syn* see POSITIVE 1
ant equivocal
3 *syn* see POSITIVE 3
unequivocally *adv syn* see EASILY 2
uneradicable *adj syn* see INDELIBLE
ant eradicable
unerasable *adj syn* see INDELIBLE
ant erasable
unerring *adj syn* see INFALLIBLE 1
unescapable *adj syn* see INEVITABLE
ant escapable
unessential *adj* 1 *syn* see UNNECESSARY
ant essential
2 *syn* see DISPENSABLE
ant essential
unethical *adj syn* see CORRUPT 2
ant ethical
unevadable *adj syn* see INEVITABLE
ant evadable
uneven *adj* 1 *syn* see ROUGH 1
ant even
2 *syn* see LOPSIDED
ant even
3 *syn* see SPOTTY 1
rel differing, disparate, unequal; discrepant, inconsistent
con consistent, equal, regular
unevenness *n* 1 *syn* see DISPARITY
2 *syn* see INEQUALITY 1
uneventful *adj syn* see COMMON 6
ant eventful
unevolved *adj syn* see PRIMITIVE 3
ant advanced, evolved
unexaminable *adj syn* see MYSTERIOUS
unexampled *adj syn* see ONLY 2
unexceptionable *adj syn* see DECENT 4
ant exceptionable
unexceptional *adj* 1 *syn* see DECENT 4
2 *syn* see COMMON 6
ant exceptional
unexcessive *adj syn* see CONSERVATIVE 2
ant excessive
unexpansive *adj syn* see UNDEMONSTRATIVE
ant expansive
unexpectedly *adv syn* see UNAWARES
unexpedient *adj syn* see INADVISABLE
ant expedient
unexperienced *adj syn* see INEXPERIENCED

---

syn synonym(s)   *rel* related word(s)
ant antonym(s)   *con* contrasted word(s)
idiom idiomatic equivalent(s)

‖ use limited; if in doubt, see a dictionary

ant experienced

unexpert *adj syn see* INEFFICIENT 2
ant expert

unexplainable *adj syn see* INEXPLICABLE
ant explainable, explicable

unexplicit *adj syn see* OBSCURE 3
ant explicit

unexpressed *adj* 1 *syn see* UNSPOKEN 1
ant expressed
2 *syn see* TACIT 1
ant expressed

unexpressible *adj syn see* UNUTTERABLE
ant expressible

unexpressive *adj syn see* EXPRESSION-
LESS
ant expressive

unextreme *adj syn see* CONSERVATIVE 2

unfabled *adj syn see* REAL 3
ant fabled

unfacile *adj syn see* UNSKILLFUL 1

unfailing *adj* 1 *syn see* SAME 3
2 *syn see* INFALLIBLE 2
ant fallible

unfair *adj syn see* INEQUITABLE
ant fair

unfairness *n syn see* INJUSTICE 1
ant fairness

unfaith *n syn see* UNBELIEF
ant faith

unfaithful *adj syn see* FAITHLESS
ant faithful

unfaithfulness *n syn see* INFIDELITY
ant faithfulness

unfaltering *adj syn see* SURE 2

unfamed *adj syn see* OBSCURE 5
ant famed

unfamiliar *adj* 1 not well known <trying
to find her way about the *unfamiliar*
room in the dark>
syn new, strange, unaccustomed
rel exotic, foreign; curious, peculiar, remarkable; unknown
con accustomed, commonplace, customary, ordinary, usual, wonted
ant familiar
2 *syn see* IGNORANT 2
ant familiar

unfamiliarity *n syn see* IGNORANCE 2

unfantastic *adj syn see* REALISTIC
ant fantastic

unfashioned *adj syn see* RUDE 1

unfasten *vb syn see* LOOSE 3
ant fasten

unfastidious *adj syn see* SLOVENLY 1
ant fastidious

unfathered *adj syn see* ILLEGITIMATE 1

unfathomable *adj* 1 *syn see* BOTTOMLESS
2
ant fathomable
2 *syn see* INCOMPREHENSIBLE 1
ant fathomable

unfathomed *adj syn see* HUGE

unfavorable *adj* 1 *syn see* ADVERSE 2
ant favorable
2 *syn see* EVIL 5

unfavorably *adv syn see* AMISS 2

unfearful *adj syn see* BRAVE 1
ant fearful

unfearing *adj syn see* BRAVE 1
ant fearing

unfeasible *adj syn see* IMPOSSIBLE 1
ant feasible, practicable

unfeeling *adj* 1 *syn see* INSENSATE 1

ant feeling
2 lacking in normal human sympathy
<an *unfeeling* response to a plea for
help>
syn callous, cold-blooded, coldhearted,
compassionless, hard-boiled, hardened,
hardhearted, heartless, ironhearted, marblehearted, obdurate, stony, stonyhearted,
uncompassionate, unemotional, unsympathetic; *compare* PITILESS
rel brutal, cruel, indurated, merciless,
roughhearted, ruthless, tough; exacting,
severe; unamiable, uncordial, unkind;
cantankerous, churlish, crotchety, curmud-
geonly, surly
idiom hard of heart
con considerate, gentle, thoughtful; kind,
merciful; compassionate, sympathetic,
warmhearted
ant feeling
3 *syn see* NUMB 1

unfeigned *adj* 1 *syn see* SINCERE 1
ant feigned
2 *syn see* GENUINE 3
ant dissembled, feigned

unfertile *adj syn see* BARREN 2
ant fertile

unfinished *adj* 1 *syn see* RUDE 1
ant dressed, finished
2 *syn see* AMATEURISH
ant finished

unfit *adj* 1 not adapted or appropriate to a
particular end <land *unfit* for farming>
syn ill-adapted, ill-suited, inappropriate,
inapt, unfitted, unmeet, unsuitable, unsuited
rel discordant, inharmonious; improper,
infelicitous, unbecoming; incompatible,
incongruous, uncongenial
idiom out of drawing, out of one's element, out of place
con adapted, appropriate, apt, suitable,
suited; congruous, harmonious
ant fit
2 lacking essential qualifications <politi-
cians *unfit* to govern>
syn disqualified, incapable, incompetent,
ineligible, unequipped, unfitted, unqualified
rel awkward, blundering, bungling; butterfingered, heavyhanded, maladjusted,
maladroit, unhandy; inefficient, inexpert,
unproficient, unskillful
con capable, competent, qualified; adroit,
dexterous, handy; expert, skilled
ant fit

unfitted *adj* 1 *syn see* UNFIT 1
2 *syn see* UNFIT 2
ant fitted

unfitting *adj syn see* IMPROPER 1
ant fitting

unfix *vb* 1 *syn see* LOOSE 3
ant fix
2 *syn see* DETACH

unfixedness *n syn see* INSTABILITY

unflagging *adj syn see* INDEFATIGABLE
rel constant, steady
ant flagging

unflappable *adj syn see* COOL 2
rel easy, relaxed

unflawed *adj syn see* PERFECT 2
ant flawed

unfledged *adj syn see* YOUNG 1
ant fledged

unfleshed *adj syn* see INEXPERIENCED

unfleshly *adj syn* see IMMATERIAL 1
   ant fleshly

unflexible *adj syn* see STIFF 1
   ant flexible

unflinching *adj syn* see GRIM 3

unfluctuating *adj syn* see STEADY 2
   ant fluctuant, fluctuating

unfold *vb* 1 *syn* see OPEN 4
   ant fold
   2 *syn* see SOLVE 2
   3 to disclose by degrees to the sight or understanding <shyly she *unfolded* her hopes for the future>
   syn develop, elaborate, evolve
   rel demonstrate, evidence, evince, manifest, show; disclose, display, exhibit, expose, reveal

unfolding *n syn* see DEVELOPMENT

unforbearing *adj syn* see INTOLERANT 1
   ant forbearing

unforced *adj syn* see VOLUNTARY
   ant forced

unforgivable *adj syn* see INEXCUSABLE
   ant forgivable

unformed *adj* 1 *syn* see FORMLESS
   rel unfinished
   ant formed
   2 *syn* see RUDE 1

unfortunate *adj* 1 *syn* see UNLUCKY
   rel infelicitous; deplorable, miserable, sad, wretched; malefic
   con auspicious, favorable, propitious
   ant fortunate
   2 *syn* see INFELICITOUS
   3 *syn* see DEPLORABLE

unfounded *adj syn* see BASELESS
   rel deceptive, misleading; dishonest, mendacious, untruthful
   ant well-founded

unframe *vb syn* see DESTROY 1

unfrank *adj syn* see DISINGENUOUS
   ant frank

unfrequent *adj syn* see INFREQUENT
   ant frequent

unfrequently *adv syn* see SELDOM
   ant frequently

unfriendly *adj syn* see HOSTILE 1
   ant friendly

unfruitful *adj syn* see STERILE 1
   con fecund, fertile
   ant fruitful, prolific

unfunctional *adj syn* see IMPRACTICABLE 2
   ant functional

unfussy *adj syn* see EASYGOING 3
   ant fussy

ungainly *adj syn* see CLUMSY 1
   rel blundering, lubberly, maladroit
   con graceful, supple, willowy; gainly

ungarnished *adj syn* see PLAIN 1
   ant garnished

ungenerous *adj* 1 *syn* see PETTY 2
   ant generous
   2 *syn* see STINGY
   ant generous

ungenial *adj syn* see ANTIPATHETIC 2
   ant genial

ungenuine *adj syn* see SPURIOUS 3
   ant genuine

ungetatable *adj syn* see INACCESSIBLE
   ant getatable

ungifted *adj syn* see AMATEURISH
   ant gifted

ungiving *adj syn* see STINGY

ungodly *adj* 1 *syn* see IMPIOUS 1
   ant godly
   2 *syn* see INDECOROUS
   3 *syn* see OUTRAGEOUS 1

ungovernable *adj syn* see UNRULY 1
   ant governable

ungoverned *adj syn* see AUDACIOUS 4

ungracious *adj* 1 *syn* see RUDE 6
   ant gracious
   2 *syn* see SHORT 5
   ant gracious

ungraded *adj syn* see UNREFINED 3

ungraspable *adj syn* see INCOMPREHENSIBLE 1
   ant comprehensible, graspable

ungrateful *adj* 1 *syn* see THANKLESS 1
   ant grateful
   2 *syn* see THANKLESS 2
   3 *syn* see OFFENSIVE

ungratified *adj syn* see DISCONTENTED
   ant gratified

ungrounded *adj syn* see BASELESS

unguarded *adj syn* see INCAUTIOUS 1
   ant guarded

unguent *n syn* see OINTMENT

unguessed *adj syn* see MYSTERIOUS

unguilty *adj syn* see INNOCENT 2
   ant guilty

unhallowed *adj* 1 *syn* see IMPIOUS 1
   2 *syn* see FIENDISH

unhampered *adj syn* see AUDACIOUS 4
   ant hampered

unhandsome *adj* 1 *syn* see PLAIN 5
   ant handsome
   2 *syn* see RUDE 6

unhandy *adj* 1 *syn* see UNWIELDY
   2 *syn* see UNSKILLFUL 1
   ant handy
   3 *syn* see AWKWARD 2
   ant handy

unhappiness *n* 1 *syn* see MISERY 1
   ant happiness
   2 *syn* see SADNESS
   ant happiness

unhappy *adj* 1 *syn* see UNLUCKY
   ant happy
   2 *syn* see INFELICITOUS
   ant happy
   3 *syn* see AWKWARD 2
   ant happy
   4 *syn* see SAD 1
   ant happy
   5 *syn* see BAD 8
   6 *syn* see GLOOMY 3

unharmed *adj syn* see SAFE 1

unharmonious *adj* 1 *syn* see DISSONANT 1
   ant harmonious
   2 *syn* see INHARMONIOUS 2
   ant harmonious

unhasty *adj syn* see SLOW 2
   ant hasty

unhealth *n syn* see SICKNESS 1
   ant health

unhealthful *adj syn* see UNWHOLESOME 1
   ant healthful

unhealthiness *n syn* see INFIRMITY 1

---

syn synonym(s)   *rel* related word(s)
ant antonym(s)   *con* contrasted word(s)
idiom idiomatic equivalent(s)
‖ use limited; if in doubt, see a dictionary

ant healthiness

unhealthy *adj* 1 *syn* see UNWHOLESOME 1
ant healthy
2 *syn* see DANGEROUS 1
3 *syn* see VICIOUS 2

unheard–of *adj* *syn* see OBSCURE 5

unheavy *adj* *syn* see LIGHT 1
ant heavy

unheeding *adj* 1 *syn* see INATTENTIVE
ant heedful, heeding
2 *syn* see CARELESS 1
ant heedful, heeding

unhewn *adj* *syn* see RUDE 1

unhinge *vb* 1 *syn* see UPSET 5
2 *syn* see MADDEN 1
3 *syn* see DISCOMPOSE 1

unholy *adj* 1 *syn* see IMPIOUS 1
ant holy
2 *syn* see BLAMEWORTHY
3 *syn* see OUTRAGEOUS 1

unhonest *adj* *syn* see DISHONEST
ant honest

unhorse *vb* 1 *syn* see THROW 2
2 *syn* see OVERTHROW 2

unhurried *adj* *syn* see SLOW 2
ant hurried

unhurt *adj* *syn* see WHOLE 1

unicity *n* *syn* see UNIQUENESS

unidealistic *adj* *syn* see REALISTIC
ant idealistic

unification *n* a bringing together or being brought together into an integrated whole < *unification* of mass transit facilities is increasingly needed >
syn coadunation, coalition, combination, consolidation, melding, mergence, merger, merging, union; *compare* ALLIANCE 2
rel affiliation, connection, interlocking, joining, linkage; coupling, hookup
con dissociation, disunion, division, parting, partition, separation
ant disunification

uniform *adj* 1 *syn* see LIKE
ant various
2 *syn* see STEADY 2
rel compatible, consistent, consonant, ordered, orderly, regular
ant multiform

uniformly *adv* *syn* see EVENLY 3
ant variably

unify *vb* 1 to gather or combine parts or elements into a close mass or a coherent whole < minorities that are *unified* by persecution >
syn compact, concentrate, consolidate, integrate; *compare* UNITE 2
rel articulate, concatenate; order, organize, systematize; bind, tie
idiom make one
con divide, part, scatter; disorder, disorganize; disunite, divide, separate
ant break up, disunify
2 *syn* see HARMONIZE 4
ant disunify

unifying *adj* *syn* see INTEGRATIVE
ant disunifying

unilluminated *adj* *syn* see DARK 1
ant illuminated

unimaginable *adj* 1 *syn* see INCONCEIVABLE 1
ant imaginable
2 *syn* see EXCEPTIONAL 1

3 *syn* see INCREDIBLE 1

unimpaired *adj* *syn* see WHOLE 1
ant impaired

unimpassioned *adj* 1 *syn* see MATTER-OF-FACT 3
ant impassioned
2 *syn* see SOBER 3
rel impassive, phlegmatic, stoic, stolid; calm, placid, tranquil
con ardent, fervent, fervid, heated, keen
ant impassioned, passionate

unimpeachable *adj* *syn* see DECENT 4

unimportant *adj* *syn* see LITTLE 3
ant important

unimpressible *adj* *syn* see INSUSCEPTIBLE
ant impressible

unimpressionable *adj* *syn* see INSUSCEPTIBLE
ant impressionable

unindifferent *adj* *syn* see BIASED 2
ant indifferent

unindulgent *adj* *syn* see INTOLERANT 1
ant indulgent

uninflammable *adj* *syn* see NONCOMBUSTIBLE
ant flammable, inflammable

uninformed *adj* *syn* see IGNORANT 2
ant informed

uninhibited *adj* *syn* see AUDACIOUS 4
ant inhibited

uninhibitedness *n* *syn* see ABANDON 2

uninitiate *n* *syn* see AMATEUR 2

uninjured *adj* *syn* see WHOLE 1
ant injured

uninjurious *adj* *syn* see SAFE 3

uninspired *adj* 1 *syn* see UNORIGINAL
ant inspired
2 *syn* see PONDEROUS 2
ant inspired

uninstructed *adj* 1 *syn* see IGNORANT 2
2 *syn* see IGNORANT 1

unintelligent *adj* *syn* see SIMPLE 3
ant intelligent

unintelligible *adj* 1 *syn* see INCOMPREHENSIBLE 1
ant intelligible
2 *syn* see OBSCURE 3
ant intelligible

unintended *adj* *syn* see UNINTENTIONAL
ant intended

unintentional *adj* not the result of intent or design < her slight of the newcomer was quite *unintentional* >
syn inadvertent, undesigned, undevised, unintended, unplanned, unpremeditated, unpurposed, unthought; *compare* ACCIDENTAL, EXTEMPORANEOUS
rel causeless, chance, haphazard, purposeless, random; unanticipated, unexpected, unforeseen, unlooked-for; unthinking, unwitting
con deliberate, designed, devised, intended, planned, premeditated, purposed
ant intentional

uninterested *adj* *syn* see INDIFFERENT 2
ant interested

uninteresting *adj* *syn* see ARID 2
ant interesting

unintermitted *adj* *syn* see CONTINUAL
ant intermitted, intermittent

unintermittedly *adv* *syn* see TOGETHER 2

unintermittent *adj* *syn* see CONTINUAL
ant intermitted, intermittent

uninterrupted *adj* **1** *syn* see CONTINUAL
ant interrupted
2 *syn* see DIRECT 2
uninterruptedly *adv* . *syn* see TOGETHER 2
ant interruptedly
uninventive *adj* *syn* see UNORIGINAL
ant inventive
uninvited *adj* *syn* see UNASKED
ant invited
union *n* **1** *syn* see UNIFICATION
ant disunion
2 *syn* see ASSOCIATION 2
3 *syn* see JOINT 1
4 *syn* see ALLIANCE 2
unique *adj* **1** *syn* see ONLY 2
2 *syn* see SINGLE 2
3 *syn* see ALONE 3
4 *syn* see EXCEPTIONAL 1
uniqueness *n* the quality or state of standing alone and without a peer < the time she rode in an old-time sleigh — never would she forget the *uniqueness* of that experience >
syn oneness, singleness, unicity, uniquity
rel curiousness, oddity, peculiarity, quaintness, singularity, strangeness; import, mark, moment, note, significance; memorability, notability, remarkableness, unusualness
con commonness, commonplaceness, ordinariness, routineness; monotony, sameness, tediousness
uniquity *n* *syn* see UNIQUENESS
unite *vb* **1** *syn* see JOIN 1
rel amalgamate, blend, merge, mix
ant alienate; disunite, divide
2 to join forces especially in order to act more effectively < citizen groups *uniting* to further the fight against crime >
syn band, coadjute, combine, concur, conjoin, cooperate, league; *compare* UNIFY 1
rel affiliate, ally, associate, confederate; coalesce, commingle, fuse, mingle, weld
idiom draw together, hook up with, join forces (with), make common cause (with), throw in with
con break up, disband, separate, split (up)
ant disunite, part
unity *n* **1** the condition of being or consisting of one < *unity* — the idea conveyed by whatever we visualize as one thing >
syn individuality, oneness, singleness, singularity, singularness
rel identity, selfsameness, soleness, uniqueness, uniquity
ant multiplicity
2 *syn* see HARMONY 3
rel agreement, identity, oneness, union; solidarity; conformance, congruity
ant disunity
universal *adj* **1** *syn* see OMNIPRESENT
2 present or significant throughout the world < *universal* aspirations for a better world >
syn catholic, cosmic, cosmopolitan, ecumenical, global, planetary, worldwide

rel all-embracing, all-inclusive; broad, extensive, sweeping; all, entire, total, whole
con narrow, petty, provincial
ant parochial
3 *syn* see GENERAL 2
ant particular
universe *n* the totality of physical entities < theories of the expanding *universe* >
syn cosmos (*or* kosmos), creation, macrocosm, macrocosmos, megacosm, nature, world
univocal *adj* *syn* see CLEAR 5
ant ambiguous
unjust *adj* *syn* see INEQUITABLE
ant just
unjustifiable *adj* **1** *syn* see UNREASONABLE 2
ant justifiable
2 *syn* see INEXCUSABLE
ant justifiable
unjustness *n* *syn* see INJUSTICE 1
ant justice, justness
unkempt *adj* *syn* see SLOVENLY 1
ant kempt
unknow *vb* *syn* see FORGET 1
unknowable *adj* **1** *syn* see INCOMPREHENSIBLE 1
ant knowable
2 *syn* see INCONCEIVABLE 1
ant knowable
3 *syn* see MYSTERIOUS
unknowing *adj* *syn* see IGNORANT 2
ant knowing
unknowingness *n* *syn* see IGNORANCE 2
ant knowingness
unknown *adj* *syn* see OBSCURE 5
ant well-known
unlade *vb* *syn* see UNLOAD
ant lade, load
unlawful *adj* contrary to or prohibited by law < the spread of *unlawful* wiretapping >
syn criminal, illegal, illegitimate, illicit, lawless, wrongful
rel flagitious, iniquitous, nefarious; black-market, bootleg, under-the-counter; exceptionable, improper, intolerable, objectionable
idiom against the law
con condign, due, rightful; allowable, justifiable, permissible
ant lawful
unlawfulness *n* *syn* see ILLEGALITY
ant lawfulness
unlax *vb* **1** *syn* see RELAX 2
2 *syn* see REST 2
unlearned *adj* *syn* see UNSCHOLARLY
ant erudite, learned
unleash *vb* *syn* see TAKE OUT (on)
unless *conj* *syn* see EXCEPT 1
unlettered *adj* *syn* see IGNORANT 1
ant educated, lettered
unlevel *adj* *syn* see ROUGH 1
ant level
unlike *adj* *syn* see DIFFERENT 1
ant like
unlikely *adj* *syn* see IMPROBABLE 1
ant likely
unlikeness *n* *syn* see DISSIMILARITY
rel incompatibility, incongruousness, inconsistence
ant likeness

---

syn synonym(s)   *rel* related word(s)
ant antonym(s)   *con* contrasted word(s)
idiom idiomatic equivalent(s)
‖ use limited; if in doubt, see a dictionary

unlimited *adj* 1 *syn* see LIMITLESS
ant limited, measured
2 *syn* see TOTAL 5
ant limited

unload *vb* to remove cargo or the cargo of < *unload* cattle from a truck >
syn disburden, discharge, off-load, unlade, unship, unstow
rel disencumber, dump, jettison, lighten; stevedore; debark, disembark, land
idiom break bulk
ant lade, load

unloose *vb syn* see LOOSE 3
unloosen *vb syn* see LOOSE 3
unloyal *adj syn* see FAITHLESS
ant loyal

‖**unluck** *n syn* see MISFORTUNE
ant luck

unlucky *adj* 1 *syn* see OMINOUS
2 involving or suffering misfortune that results from chance <in spite of careful planning the expedition was *unlucky* from the start >
syn hapless, ill-fated, ill-starred, luckless, misfortunate, star-crossed, unfortunate, unhappy, untoward
rel calamitous, cataclysmic, catastrophic, dire, disastrous, tragical
idiom down on one's luck, out of luck
con fortunate, happy, providential; prosperous, successful; coming, made
ant lucky

unmake *vb* 1 *syn* see DESTROY 1
2 *syn* see DEPOSE 1
ant make

unman *vb syn* see UNNERVE
rel deplete, drain, exhaust, impoverish; abase, degrade; disqualify, paralyze, prostrate, unfit
idiom knock the bottom (*or* stuffing) out of
con brace, fortify
ant man

unmanageable *adj syn* see UNRULY 1
ant manageable

unmanly *adj* 1 *syn* see COWARDLY
ant manly
2 *syn* see EFFEMINATE
ant manly

unmannered *adj* 1 *syn* see RUDE 6
2 *syn* see FRANK

unmannerly *adj syn* see RUDE 6
ant mannerly

unmarred *adj syn* see WHOLE 1
ant marred

unmarried *adj syn* see SINGLE 1
ant married, wed

unmarry *vb syn* see DIVORCE 2
unmask *vb syn* see EXPOSE 4
unmatchable *adj syn* see SUPREME
unmatched *adj* 1 *syn* see ALONE 3
2 *syn* see ODD 1
ant matched

unmaterial *adj syn* see IMMATERIAL 1
ant material

unmeaning *adj syn* see SENSELESS 5
ant meaningful

unmeasurable *adj* 1 *syn* see INCALCULABLE 1
ant measurable
2 *syn* see EXCESSIVE 1

unmeasured *adj* 1 *syn* see INCALCULABLE 1

ant measurable
2 *syn* see LIMITLESS
ant limited, measured

unmeditated *adj syn* see SPONTANEOUS
ant meditated

unmeet *adj syn* see UNFIT 1
ant meet

unmeetness *n syn* see IMPROPRIETY 1
unmellowed *adj syn* see YOUNG 1
con developed, matured, ripened
ant mellow, mellowed

unmerciful *adj syn* see PITILESS
ant merciful

unmindful *adj syn* see FORGETFUL
con anxious, careful, concerned
ant mindful; solicitous

unmindfulness *n syn* see APATHY 2
ant mindfulness

unmistakable *adj syn* see CLEAR 5
ant mistakable

unmitigated *adj* 1 *syn* see PURE 2
2 *syn* see UTTER

unmixable *adj syn* see INCONSONANT 1
unmixed *adj* 1 *syn* see STRAIGHT 3
ant blended, mixed
2 *syn* see PURE 2

unmodern *adj syn* see OLD-FASHIONED
ant modern

unmodifiable *adj syn* see INFLEXIBLE 3
ant modifiable

unmovable *adj* 1 *syn* see IMMOVABLE 1
ant mobile, movable
2 *syn* see INFLEXIBLE 3

unmoving *adj syn* see STATIC
ant mobile

unmusical *adj syn* see DISSONANT 1
ant musical

unnamed *adj syn* see ANONYMOUS
unnatural *adj* 1 *syn* see IRREGULAR 1
2 *syn* see SUPERNATURAL 2
ant natural

unneat *adj syn* see SLOVENLY 1
ant neat

unnecessary *adj* not needed or unavoidable < *unnecessary* loss of life >
syn inessential, needless, uncalled-for, unessential, unneeded, unneedful, unrequired
rel excess, redundant, superfluous, surplus; lavish, prodigal, profuse; gratuitous, supererogatory
con essential, needed, required, vital; inevitable, unescapable
ant necessary; unavoidable

unneeded *adj syn* see UNNECESSARY
ant needed; unavoidable

unneedful *adj syn* see UNNECESSARY
ant needful; unavoidable

unnerve *vb* to deprive of strength, spirit, and vigor <a man so *unnerved* as to be bereft of sense and judgment >
syn castrate, emasculate, enervate, unman, unstring
rel enfeeble, sap, undermine, weaken; bewilder, confound, distract; agitate, perturb, upset
con brace (up), inspirit, invigorate, reinforce, strengthen; encourage, hearten, steel
ant nerve

unneutral *adj syn* see BIASED 2
ant neutral

unnoted *adj syn* see OBSCURE 5
rel unconsidered, unobserved, unremarked

ant noted

unnoteworthy *adj syn* see COMMON 6
ant noteworthy

unnoticeable *adj syn* see INCONSPICUOUS
ant noticeable

unnoticing *adj syn* see INATTENTIVE
ant noticing

unnumberable *adj syn* see INNUMERA-
BLE

unnumbered *adj syn* see INNUMERABLE
ant numbered

unobjectionable *adj syn* see DECENT 4
ant objectionable

unobjective *adj syn* see SUBJECTIVE
ant objective

unobservable *adj syn* see IMPERCEPTIBLE

unobservant *adj syn* see INATTENTIVE
ant observant, observing

unobserving *adj syn* see INATTENTIVE
ant observant, observing

unobstructed *adj syn* see OPEN 1
con clogged, plugged
ant obstructed

unobtainable *adj syn* see INACCESSIBLE

unobtrusive *adj syn* see QUIET 4
ant obtrusive

unoffending *adj syn* see HARMLESS
ant offending

unoffensive *adj syn* see HARMLESS
ant offensive

unofficial *adj syn* see INFORMAL 1

unoften *adv syn* see SELDOM
ant often

unordinary *adj syn* see EXCEPTIONAL 1
ant ordinary

unorganized *adj syn* see INCOHERENT 2
ant organized

unoriginal *adj* lacking or manifesting a
lack of capacity for originality <a good
man but with a mind stolid and *unoriginal* >
syn noncreative, sterile, uncreative, uninspired, uninventive, unoriginative; *compare*
ARID 2
rel arid, barren, dry; dull, prosaic, staid,
stodgy, stuffy, unfired
con creative, inspired, inventive, originative; alert, aware, keen; constructive, productive
ant original

unoriginated *adj syn* see SELF-EXISTENT

unoriginative *adj syn* see UNORIGINAL
ant originative

unornamented *adj syn* see PLAIN 1

unorthodox *adj syn* see HERETICAL
ant orthodox

unorthodoxy *n syn* see HERESY
ant orthodoxy

unostentatious *adj syn* see PLAIN 1
ant ostentatious

unpaid *adj* 1 serving without pay <a charity manned by *unpaid* assistants >
syn uncompensated, unrecompensed,
unremunerated
rel freewill, gratuitous, voluntary, volun-
teer
con compensated, recompensed, remunerated

ant paid

2 not cleared by payment <an *unpaid*
bill >
syn due, mature, outstanding, overdue,
owing, payable, unsettled
idiom in arrears
con cleared, discharged, liquidated, settled
ant paid

unpaired *adj syn* see ODD 1
ant paired

unpalatable *adj* 1 lacking appeal to the
sense of taste <threw together a greasy
unpalatable meal >
syn distasteful, flat, flavorless, ill-flavored,
insipid, savorless, tasteless, unappetizing,
unsavory
rel loathsome, nauseous, sickening; thin,
washy, watery, weak
con appetizing, delectable, delicious, flavorsome, sapid, savory, tasty
ant palatable

2 *syn* see BITTER 2

unparagoned *adj syn* see ALONE 3
ant paragoned

unparalleled *adj syn* see ALONE 3
ant paralleled

unpardonable *adj syn* see INEXCUSABLE
ant pardonable

unparented *adj syn* see ORPHAN

unpassioned *adj syn* see NEUTRAL
ant impassioned, passionate

unpatient *adj syn* see IMPATIENT 1
ant patient

unpeace *n syn* see DISCORD
ant peace

unpeaceful *adj syn* see RESTLESS
ant peaceful

unpedantic *adj syn* see LIVELY 1
ant pedantic

unperceivable *adj syn* see IMPERCEPTI-
BLE

unperceiving *adj* 1 *syn* see IMPERCEP-
TIVE
ant perceiving, perceptive, percipient

2 *syn* see INATTENTIVE

unperceptive *adj syn* see IMPERCEPTIVE
ant perceiving, perceptive, percipient

unperishable *adj syn* see INDESTRUCTI-
BLE
ant perishable

unpermissive *adj syn* see RIGID 3
ant permissive

unphysical *adj syn* see IMMATERIAL 1
ant physical

unpierceable *adj syn* see IMPASSABLE 1
ant pierceable

unpitying *adj syn* see PITILESS
ant pitying

unplanned *adj* 1 *syn* see RANDOM
ant planned

2 *syn* see UNINTENTIONAL
ant planned

unpleasant *adj syn* see BAD 8

unpliable *adj syn* see OBSTINATE
ant pliable, pliant

unpliant *adj syn* see OBSTINATE
ant pliable, pliant

unpolished *adj* 1 *syn* see RUDE 1
idiom in the rough
ant polished

2 *syn* see RUDE 6

3 *syn* see BOORISH

---

syn synonym(s)   *rel* related word(s)
ant antonym(s)   *con* contrasted word(s)
idiom idiomatic equivalent(s)

‖ use limited; if in doubt, see a dictionary

unpolished
unpolitic *adj syn* see TACTLESS
ant politic
unpractical *adj syn* see IMPRACTICAL 1
ant practical
unpracticed *adj* 1 *syn* see UNTRIED 1
2 *syn* see INEXPERIENCED
ant practiced
unpredictable *adj syn* see UNCERTAIN 1
ant predictable
unprejudiced *adj syn* see FAIR 4
ant prejudiced
unpremeditated *adj* 1 *syn* see SPONTANE-
OUS
2 *syn* see UNINTENTIONAL
ant premeditated
unprepossessed *adj syn* see FAIR 4
ant prepossessed
unprescribed *adj syn* see VOLUNTARY
ant prescribed
unpretentious *adj syn* see PLAIN 1
ant pretentious
unpretty *adj syn* see PLAIN 5
ant pretty
unprevailing *adj syn* see FUTILE
unprincipled *adj* 1 *syn* see UNSCRUPU-
LOUS
ant principled
2 *syn* see ABANDONED 2
rel corrupt, crooked, unscrupulous; dishonest, unconscientious, unethical
3 *syn* see CORRUPT 2
ant principled
unproductive *adj* 1 *syn* see BARREN 2
rel impotent, infecund, unprolific
ant productive
2 *syn* see FUTILE
ant productive
unprofane *adj syn* see HOLY 1
ant profane
unproficient *adj syn* see UNSKILLFUL 1
ant proficient, skilled
unprogressive *adj* 1 *syn* see BACKWARD
6
ant progressive
2 *syn* see BACKWARD 5
ant progressive
unprompted *adj syn* see SPONTANEOUS
unpropitious *adj syn* see OMINOUS
rel adverse, antagonistic, counter
con cheering, encouraging, reassuring
ant propitious
unproportionate *adj syn* see LOPSIDED
ant proportionate
unprosperous *adj syn* see POOR 1
ant prosperous
unprosperousness *n syn* see POVERTY 1
ant prosperousness
unprotected *adj syn* see HELPLESS 1
rel undefended, unguarded, unsheltered,
unshielded; insecure, unsafe
ant protected
unproved *adj syn* see UNTRIED 1
ant proved
unpunctual *adj syn* see TARDY
ant punctual
unpurposed *adj* 1 *syn* see UNINTEN-
TIONAL
2 *syn* see FECKLESS 1
unqualified *adj* 1 *syn* see UNFIT 2
rel unskilled; unsuitable
ant qualified
2 *syn* see SURE 2

rel unconditional, unlimited, unreserved;
clear, explicit, express; entire, perfect,
utter
ant qualified
3 *syn* see UTTER
4 *syn* see PURE 2
unquenchable *adj syn* see INSATIABLE
ant quenchable
unquestionable *adj* 1 *syn* see AUTHENTIC
2
ant doubtable, questionable
2 *syn* see POSITIVE 3
rel dependable, reliable; established, well-
founded, well-grounded
ant doubtable, questionable
3 *syn* see DOWNRIGHT 2
unquestionably *adv syn* see EASILY 2
ant questionably
unquestioning *adj syn* see SURE 2
ant questioning
unquiet *adj syn* see RESTLESS
ant quiet
unravel *vb syn* see SOLVE 2
rel disentangle, extricate, untangle
unreachable *adj syn* see INACCESSIBLE
ant reachable
unreadable *adj syn* see ILLEGIBLE
ant legible, readable
unreal *adj syn* see FICTITIOUS 1
ant real
unrealistic *adj syn* see IMPRACTICAL 1
ant realistic
unrealizable *adj syn* see IMPOSSIBLE 1
ant realizable
unreasonable *adj* 1 *syn* see ILLOGICAL
rel incongruous, loose, self-contradictory
ant reasonable
2 exceeding the bounds of reason or right
< the constitutional guarantees against
unreasonable searches and seizures >
syn unconscionable, undue, unjustifiable,
unwarrantable, unwarranted
rel arbitrary, peremptory; excessive, immoderate, inordinate, overmuch; improper,
unlawful, unrightful, wrongful
con lawful, licit; proper, right, tolerable
ant reasonable
unreasoned *adj syn* see ILLOGICAL
ant reasoned
unrecking *adj syn* see CARELESS 1
unreckonable *adj syn* see INCALCULA-
BLE 1
unrecompensed *adj syn* see UNPAID 1
ant recompensed
unrecoverable *adj syn* see HOPELESS 2
unrefined *adj* 1 *syn* see BOORISH
ant refined
2 *syn* see COARSE 3
ant refined
3 not freed from unwanted material
< shipped the *unrefined* ore >
syn crude, impure, native, raw, run-of-
mine, ungraded, unsorted
rel rough, roughcast, roughhewn; coarse,
natural, undressed, unprocessed
idiom in the rough
con dressed, processed
ant refined
unreflective *adj syn* see CARELESS 1
unregretful *adj syn* see REMORSELESS
ant regretful
unregular *adj syn* see IRREGULAR 1
ant regular

unrehearsed *adj syn see* EXTEMPORANE-OUS
ant rehearsed
unrelenting *adj syn see* GRIM 3
ant relenting
unreliable *adj* 1 not to be counted on < it is certain that much of the testimony was *unreliable* >
syn dubious, fly-by-night, questionable, trustless, undependable, unsure, untrustworthy, untrusty
rel fickle, inconstant, unstable, vacillating; faithless, false, untrue; falsehearted, perfidious; shifty, slick, slippery, tricky; inaccurate, inexact, unfaithful
idiom not to be depended (*or* relied) on
con dependable, trustworthy, trusty; constant; faithful, true
ant reliable
2 *syn see* UNSAFE
ant reliable
unreligious *adj syn see* IRRELIGIOUS
ant religious
unremarkable *adj syn see* ORDINARY 1
unremitting *adj syn see* CONTINUAL
unremittingly *adv syn see* HARD 3
unremorseful *adj syn see* REMORSELESS
ant remorseful
unremunerated *adj syn see* UNPAID 1
ant remunerated
unrenowned *adj syn see* OBSCURE 5
ant renowned
unrepealable *adj syn see* IRREVOCABLE
ant repealable
unrepeatable *adj syn see* ONLY 2
unrepentant *adj syn see* REMORSELESS
ant repentant
unrepresentative *adj syn see* ABNORMAL 1
unrequested *adj syn see* UNASKED
unrequired *adj* 1 *syn see* UNNECESSARY
ant required
2 *syn see* DISPENSABLE
ant required
unreserved *adj* 1 *syn see* FRANK 1
ant reserved
2 *syn see* DEMONSTRATIVE
ant reserved
3 *syn see* EASYGOING 3
unresistant *adj syn see* PASSIVE 2
ant resistant, resisting
unresisting *adj syn see* PASSIVE 2
ant resistant, resisting
unresolved *adj syn see* VACILLATING 2
ant resolved
unrespectable *adj syn see* DISREPUTABLE 1
ant respectable
unresponsive *adj* 1 *syn see* INSUSCEPTIBLE
ant responsive
2 *syn see* FRIGID 3
unresponsiveness *n syn see* APATHY 1
ant responsiveness
unrest *n* a disturbed uneasy state < that popular *unrest* that, unchecked, can lead to insurrection and anarchy >
syn ailment, disquiet, disquietude, ferment, inquietude, restiveness, restlessness,

storm and stress, Sturm und Drang, turmoil
rel agitation, commotion, confusion, convulsion, tumult, turbulence, upheaval; anarchy, chaos, disorder
con calm, easiness, peace, quiet
unrestful *adj* 1 *syn see* RESTLESS
ant restful
2 *syn see* NERVOUS
unrestrainable *adj syn see* IRREPRESSIBLE
ant restrainable
unrestrained *adj* 1 *syn see* EXCESSIVE 2
2 *syn see* FREE 2
ant restrained
3 *syn see* AUDACIOUS 4
rel candid, frank, open; forthright, plainspoken, straightforward; bluff, blunt, brusque
ant restrained
4 *syn see* DEMONSTRATIVE
ant restrained
unrestraint *n* 1 *syn see* UNCONSTRAINT
ant restraint
2 *syn see* ABANDON 2
unrestricted *adj syn see* OPEN 4
unriddle *vb syn see* SOLVE 2
unrighteous *adj syn see* INEQUITABLE
ant righteous
unripe *adj syn see* YOUNG 1
unrivaled *adj syn see* ALONE 3
unromantic *adj syn see* REALISTIC
ant romantic
unruffled *adj syn see* COOL 2
ant discomposed, ruffled
unruly *adj* 1 resistant to discipline or control < a stubborn *unruly* boy >
syn fractious, indocile, indomitable, intractable, recalcitrant, uncontrollable, undisciplinable, undisciplined, ungovernable, unmanageable, untoward, wild; *compare* OBSTINATE, TURBULENT 1
rel contumacious, incorrigible, insubordinate, rebellious; contrary, froward, perverse, wayward; boisterous, obstreperous, rampageous; disorderly, raffish, rambunctious, rowdy, turbulent
idiom out of hand
con controlled, easy, mild, restrained; disciplined, governable, manageable; amenable, biddable, obedient; correct, proper
ant docile, tractable
2 *syn see* TURBULENT 1
rel hard, ruffianly, tough
3 *syn see* DISOBEDIENT
unsacred *adj syn see* PROFANE 1
ant sacred
unsafe *adj* not to be depended on or trusted < an *unsafe* investment >
syn unassured, undependable, unreliable, untrustworthy
rel insecure, shaky, tottery, unsound, unstable; chancy, hazardous, risky; dangerous, jeopardous, perilous; erratic, uncertain
con dependable, trustworthy; secure, sound, stable, substantial
ant safe
unsaid *adj syn see* TACIT 1
unsalutary *adj syn see* UNWHOLESOME 1
ant salutary
unsandaled *adj syn see* BAREFOOT 1
ant sandaled

unsane *adj syn* see INSANE 1
ant sane
unsatiate *adj syn* see INSATIABLE
ant satiate, satiated
unsatisfactory *adj syn* see BAD 1
ant satisfactory
unsatisfiable *adj syn* see INSATIABLE
ant satisfiable
unsavory *adj syn* see UNPALATABLE 1
ant savory
unsay *vb syn* see ABJURE
unscathed *adj syn* see SAFE 1
unscholarly *adj* not devoted to scholarly
pursuits < *unscholarly* concerns >
syn inerudite, unbookish, unlearned, unstudious
rel unenlightened, uninformed, uniniti-
ated; callow, green, unripe; inexperienced,
naive
con bookish, erudite, learned; enlightened,
informed; experienced
ant scholarly
unschooled *adj* 1 *syn* see IGNORANT 1
2 *syn* see NATURAL 5
unscramble *vb syn* see EXTRICATE 2
unscrupulous *adj* 1 lacking in moral scruples < *unscrupulous* conduct of political
leaders >
syn conscienceless, stick-at-nothing, unconscionable, unprincipled
rel crafty, deceitful, scheming; improper,
unseemly, wrongful; corrupt, crooked,
dishonest; questionable, shady, sinister,
underhand
con conscientious, dutiful, proper, upright; dependable, reliable, responsible
ant scrupulous
2 *syn* see CORRUPT 2
con meticulous, particular, punctilious,
strict
ant scrupulous
unseasonable *adj* 1 involving or occurring
at an inappropriate or unexpected time
< his wife's sudden return proved most
unseasonable >
syn ill-seasoned, ill-timed, inopportune,
malapropos, mistimed, untimely
rel deplorable, inappropriate, inconvenient, unsuitable; inauspicious, infelicitous,
undesirable, unfavorable, unfortunate
con apropos, opportune, timely, well-
timed
ant seasonable
2 *syn* see IMPROPER 1
unseasoned *adj syn* see INEXPERIENCED
ant seasoned
unseat *vb syn* see THROW 2
unsectarian *adj syn* see NONSECTARIAN
ant sectarian
unseemliness *n syn* see IMPROPRIETY 1
ant propriety, seemliness
unseemly *adj* 1 *syn* see INDECOROUS
rel coarse, crude, inelegant, unrefined;
raffish, rowdy, ruffianly
con prim, restrained, starchy, stiff, stilted;
elegant, gracious, polished, refined
ant seemly
2 *syn* see IMPROPER 1
ant seemly
unselfish *adj syn* see SELFLESS
ant selfish
unsentimental *adj syn* see REALISTIC
ant sentimental

unserviceable *adj syn* see IMPRACTICA-
BLE 2
ant serviceable
unsettle *vb* 1 *syn* see DISORDER 1
rel agitate, disquiet, perturb; discommode, incommode, trouble
con calm, ease, quiet, stabilize, steady
ant settle
2 *syn* see UPSET 5
ant settle
3 *syn* see DISCOMPOSE 1
unsettled *adj* 1 *syn* see RESTLESS
2 *syn* see CHANGEABLE 1
ant settled
3 *syn* see DOUBTFUL 1
4 *syn* see PENDING
ant settled
5 *syn* see BACK 1
6 *syn* see UNPAID 2
ant settled
unsettledness *n syn* see INSTABILITY
unsex *vb syn* see STERILIZE
unshackle *vb syn* see FREE
ant shackle
unshakable *adj syn* see SURE 2
ant shakable
unshaken *adj syn* see SURE 2
ant shaken
unshaped *adj syn* see FORMLESS
ant shaped
unshared *adj syn* see SOLE 4
ant shared
unship *vb syn* see UNLOAD
unshod *adj syn* see BAREFOOT 1
ant shod
unshroud *vb syn* see EXPOSE 4
ant shroud
unshut *vb syn* see OPEN 1
ant shut
unsightly *adj syn* see UGLY 2
rel ill-shaped, unshapely; unesthetic; drab,
dull, lackluster
ant sightly
unsimilar *adj syn* see DIFFERENT 1
ant similar
unskilled *adj* 1 *syn* see AMATEURISH
ant skilled
2 *syn* see INEFFICIENT 2
ant skilled
unskillful *adj* 1 lacking in skill or proficiency < an ardent but *unskillful* home
mechanic >
syn inadept, inapt, inept, inexpert, unapt,
undexterous, unfacile, unhandy, unproficient
rel incapable, incompetent; unfitted, unqualified, unready
con adept, apt, dexterous, expert, handy,
proficient
ant skillful
2 *syn* see INEFFICIENT 2
unsleeping *adj syn* see WATCHFUL
ant sleeping
unsmooth *adj syn* see ROUGH 1
ant smooth
unsober *adj syn* see INTOXICATED 1
ant sober
unsociable *adj* disinclined to active social
intercourse < tried to hide his basically
shy *unsociable* nature under a professional
heartiness of manner >
syn aloof, cool, distant, insociable, offish,
reserved, shut-in, solitary, standoff, standoffish, touch-me-not-ish, unapproachable,

unbending, uncommunicative, uncompanionable, withdrawn; *compare* INDIFFERENT 2, UNDEMONSTRATIVE
  rel self-contained, self-sufficient; exclusive, inaccessible, remote; prickly, sensitive; brooding, secretive; diffident, shy, timid
  con cordial, genial, hearty, outgoing; companionable, friendly, gregarious
  ant sociable, social

unsoiled *adj syn see* CLEAN 1
  ant soiled, sullied

unsoluble *adj syn see* INSOLUBLE
  ant soluble, solvable

unsolvable *adj syn see* INSOLUBLE
  ant soluble, solvable

unsophisticated *adj syn see* NATURAL 5
  rel authentic, bona fide, genuine; callow, crude, green, uncouth
  con finished, polished, smooth, suave
  ant sophisticated

unsorry *adj syn see* REMORSELESS
  ant sorry

unsorted *adj* 1 *syn see* MISCELLANEOUS
  2 *syn see* UNREFINED 3
  ant sorted

unsought *adj* 1 *syn see* UNASKED
  2 *syn see* UNWELCOME 1

unsound *adj* 1 *syn see* INSANE 1
  ant sound
  2 *syn see* WEAK 1
  rel damaged, faulty, flawed, imperfect
  con solid, strong, substantial
  ant sound
  3 *syn see* FALSE 1
  ant sound
  4 *syn see* DANGEROUS 1

unsparing *adj syn see* LIBERAL 1
  ant close, sparing

unspeakable *adj syn see* UNUTTERABLE
  rel loathsome, offensive, repulsive, revolting; abominable, detestable, hateful, odious; distasteful, obnoxious, repellent, repugnant; atrocious, disgusting, outrageous

unspoiled *adj syn see* VIRGIN 2

unspoken *adj* 1 not put into words <met regularly by a sort of *unspoken* agreement>
  syn silent, tacit, unexpressed, unuttered, unvoiced, wordless
  rel implicit, implied, understood; hinted, intimated, suggested; mute, unsaid, unstated
  con mentioned, said, stated, told, voiced
  ant spoken
  2 *syn see* TACIT 1
  ant spoken

unstability *n syn see* INSTABILITY
  ant stability

unstable *adj* 1 *syn see* MOVABLE
  ant stable
  2 difficult to manage because of lack of physical steadiness <the canoe is an inherently *unstable* craft>
  syn rocky, ticklish, tricky
  rel insecure, uncertain, unsteady
  con secure, steady
  ant stable
  3 *syn see* WEAK 2

---

syn synonym(s)   *rel* related word(s)
ant antonym(s)   *con* contrasted word(s)
idiom idiomatic equivalent(s)
|| use limited; if in doubt, see a dictionary

---

  ant stable
  4 *syn see* INCONSTANT 1
  rel buoyant, effervescent, elastic, resilient; freakish
  ant stable
  5 *syn see* CHANGEABLE 1
  ant stable
  6 *syn see* MUTABLE 2
  ant stable
  7 *syn see* DOUBTFUL 1

unstableness *n syn see* INSTABILITY
  ant stability, stableness

unsteadfast *adj syn see* MOVABLE
  ant steadfast

unsteadfastness *n syn see* INSTABILITY
  ant steadfastness

unsteadiness *n syn see* INSTABILITY
  ant steadiness

unsteady *adj* 1 *syn see* MOVABLE
  2 *syn see* CHANGEABLE 1
  ant steady
  3 *syn see* MUTABLE 2
  ant steady

unsteel *vb syn see* DISARM 2

unstop *vb syn see* OPEN 1
  ant stop

unstow *vb syn see* UNLOAD

unstrengthen *vb syn see* WEAKEN 1
  ant strengthen

unstring *vb syn see* UNNERVE

unstudied *adj* 1 *syn see* NATURAL 5
  ant studied
  2 *syn see* EXTEMPORANEOUS

unstudious *adj syn see* UNSCHOLARLY
  ant studious

unstylish *adj syn see* TACKY 2
  ant stylish

unsubstantial *adj* 1 *syn see* TENUOUS 3
  ant substantial
  2 *syn see* IMPLAUSIBLE
  3 *syn see* IMMATERIAL 1
  ant substantial
  4 *syn see* WEAK 1
  rel insecure, shaky, undependable
  ant substantial

unsuccess *n syn see* FAILURE 2
  ant success, successfulness

unsuccessfulness *n syn see* FAILURE 2
  ant success, successfulness

unsufferable *adj syn see* INSUFFERABLE
  ant sufferable

unsufficient *adj syn see* SHORT 3
  ant sufficient

unsuitable *adj* 1 *syn see* UNFIT 1
  rel undesirable, unhappy
  ant suitable
  2 *syn see* IMPROPER 1
  ant suitable

unsuited *adj syn see* UNFIT 1
  rel inadmissible, objectionable, unacceptable; disappointing, inadequate
  ant suited

unsullied *adj* 1 *syn see* CHASTE
  ant sullied
  2 *syn see* CLEAN 1
  ant soiled, sullied

unsupportable *adj syn see* INSUFFERABLE
  ant bearable, supportable

unsure *adj* 1 *syn see* INSECURE 1
  ant sure
  2 *syn see* WEAK 2
  3 *syn see* DOUBTFUL 1

ant sure

4 *syn* see UNRELIABLE 1

unsurmountable *adj syn* see INSUPER-ABLE

ant surmountable

unsurpassable *adj syn* see SUPREME

ant surpassable

unsusceptible *adj syn* see INSUSCEPTIBLE

ant susceptible

unsuspecting *adj syn* see CREDULOUS

ant suspecting, suspicious

unsuspicious *adj syn* see CREDULOUS

ant suspecting, suspicious

unswayable *adj syn* see INFLEXIBLE 2

ant suasible

unswerving *adj syn* see WHOLE 5

rel constant, steadfast, steady, unremitting; firm, unfaltering, unwavering

unsymmetrical *adj syn* see LOPSIDED

ant symmetrical

unsympathetic *adj* 1 *syn* see ANTIPATHETIC 2

rel dislikable, unlikable; displeasing, unpleasing

con appealing, congenial, likable; pleasant, pleasing

ant sympathetic

2 *syn* see UNFEELING 2

rel cold, cool, frigid; disinterested, half-hearted, indifferent, lukewarm

ant sympathetic

untactful *adj syn* see TACTLESS

ant tactful

untangle *vb syn* see EXTRICATE 2

ant entangle, tangle

untapped *adj syn* see VIRGIN 2

untaught *adj syn* see IGNORANT 1

untellable *adj syn* see UNUTTERABLE

ant expressible

untempered *adj syn* see EXCESSIVE 2

ant temperate, tempered

untenable *adj syn* see INEXCUSABLE

untended *adj syn* see NEGLECTED

untested *adj syn* see UNTRIED 1

ant tested, tried

unthankful *adj* 1 *syn* see THANKLESS 2

2 *syn* see THANKLESS 1

ant thankful

unthinkable *adj* 1 *syn* see EXCEPTIONAL 1

2 *syn* see INCREDIBLE 1

ant thinkable

unthinking *adj syn* see CARELESS 1

unthorough *adj syn* see SLIPSHOD 3

ant thorough

unthought *adj syn* see UNINTENTIONAL

ant aforethought

unthrift *n* 1 *syn* see EXTRAVAGANCE 2

ant thrift

2 *syn* see SPENDTHRIFT

unthrift *adj syn* see IMPROVIDENT

unthrifty *adj syn* see IMPROVIDENT

ant thrifty

untidy *adj* 1 *syn* see SLOVENLY 1

ant tidy

2 *syn* see SLIPSHOD 3

untie *vb syn* see EXTRICATE 2

untighten *vb syn* see LOOSE 5

ant tighten

until *prep* up to a stipulated time <we never met him *until* last night>

syn before, in advance of, prior to, till, to, up till, up to; *compare* BEFORE 1

until *conj syn* see TILL

untimely *adj* 1 *syn* see EARLY 2

ant timely

2 *syn* see UNSEASONABLE 1

con opportune, pat, seasonable, well-timed

ant timely

3 *syn* see IMPROPER 1

ant timely

untiring *adj syn* see INDEFATIGABLE

con casual, disinterested, intermittent

untold *adj* 1 *syn* see HUGE

2 *syn* see INNUMERABLE

untouchable *n syn* see OUTCAST

rel déclassé, outcaste, outsider

untouched *adj* 1 *syn* see WHOLE 1

2 *syn* see VIRGIN 2

untoward *adj* 1 *syn* see UNRULY 1

2 *syn* see UNLUCKY

3 *syn* see INDECOROUS

untowardness *n syn* see IMPROPRIETY

untrammeled *adj syn* see AUDACIOUS 4

untranquil *adj syn* see RESTLESS

untried *adj* 1 not subjected to test or proof (as by experience or use) <the fledgling's *untried* wings>

syn undemonstrated, unpracticed, unproved, untested

rel inexperienced, unseasoned; callow, green, immature; fresh, half-baked, unripe

con practiced, proven, tested; accomplished, finished, skilled; initiated

ant tested, tried

2 *syn* see INEXPERIENCED

untroubled *adj syn* see CALM 1

ant troubled

untroublesome *adj syn* see EASY 1

untrue *adj* 1 *syn* see FAITHLESS

ant true

2 *syn* see FALSE 1

rel imprecise, inexact, unprecise; forsworn, perjured

con exact, precise

ant true

untruism *n syn* see LIE

ant truism

untrustworthy *adj* 1 *syn* see UNRELIABLE 1

ant trustworthy

2 *syn* see UNSAFE

ant trustworthy

untrusty *adj syn* see UNRELIABLE 1

ant trusty

untruth *n* 1 *syn* see FALLACY 1

ant truth

2 *syn* see LIE

ant truth

untruthful *adj syn* see DISHONEST

rel deceptive, delusive, delusory, misleading; false, wrong; inaccurate, incorrect

ant truthful

untruthfulness *n syn* see MENDACITY

ant truthfulness

untune *vb syn* see DISCOMPOSE 1

untutored *adj* 1 *syn* see IGNORANT 1

2 *syn* see NATURAL 5

untwine *vb syn* see EXTRICATE 2

untypical *adj syn* see ABNORMAL 1

ant typical

ununderstandable *adj syn* see INCONCEIVABLE 1

ant understandable

unusable *adj syn* see IMPRACTICABLE 2

ant usable

unused *adj syn* see VACANT 4

unusual *adj* 1 *syn* see EXCEPTIONAL 1
idiom the exception rather than the rule
ant usual
2 *syn* see STRANGE 4
ant usual

unusually *adv syn* see EXTRA

unutterable *adj* being beyond human power to tell or describe < *unutterable* spiritual bliss>
syn incommunicable, indefinable, indescribable, ineffable, inenarrable, inexpressible, undescribable, unexpressible, unspeakable, untellable
rel inconceivable, incredible, unbelievable, unimaginable; awesome, awful, marvelous, prodigious, wonderful, wondrous
idiom beyond expression
con commonplace, humdrum, ordinary; monotonous, samely, unvarying

unuttered *adj* 1 *syn* see UNSPOKEN 1
ant uttered
2 *syn* see TACIT 1
ant uttered

unvarnished *adj syn* see FRANK

unvarying *adj* 1 *syn* see STEADY 2
ant varying
2 *syn* see SAME 3
ant variable, varying

unveil *vb* 1 *syn* see OPEN 2
ant veil
2 *syn* see REVEAL 1
ant veil

unveracity *n syn* see MENDACITY
ant veracity

unversed *adj syn* see INEXPERIENCED
ant versed

unvigilant *adj syn* see INCAUTIOUS 1
ant vigilant

unvital *adj syn* see PETTY 2
ant vital

unvocal *adj syn* see INARTICULATE 3
ant vocal

unvoiced *adj syn* see UNSPOKEN 1
ant voiced

unwanted *adj* 1 *syn* see UNWELCOME 1
ant wanted
2 *syn* see OBJECTIONABLE

unwarrantable *adj syn* see UNREASONABLE 2
ant warrantable

unwarranted *adj* 1 *syn* see BASELESS
2 *syn* see UNREASONABLE 2

unwary *adj* 1 *syn* see INCAUTIOUS 1
ant wary
2 *syn* see CREDULOUS
3 *syn* see RASH 1
ant wary

unwashed *adj syn* see IGNOBLE 1

unwashed *n syn* see RABBLE 2

unwasteful *adj syn* see SPARING
ant wasteful

unwatchful *adj* 1 *syn* see INATTENTIVE
ant watchful
2 *syn* see INCAUTIOUS 1
ant watchful

unwatered *adj syn* see DRY 1

ant watered

unwavering *adj syn* see SURE 2
ant wavering

unweariable *adj syn* see INDEFATIGABLE
ant weariable

unwearying *adj syn* see INDEFATIGABLE
rel constant, steady; interminable, unceasing

unwed *adj syn* see SINGLE 1
ant married, wed

unwelcome *adj* 1 not of a kind to be welcome <an *unwelcome* interruption that scattered his train of thought>
syn undesired, unsought, unwanted, unwished
rel distasteful, obnoxious, repellent; unasked; undesirable, unpleasant, unpleasing
con desired, sought, wanted; agreeable, desirable, pleasant, pleasing
ant welcome
2 *syn* see OBJECTIONABLE
ant welcome

unwell *adj* somewhat disordered in health <had felt *unwell* from the moment she got up>
syn ailing, ‖donsie, indisposed, low, mean, off-color, offish, poorly, sickly, underly; *compare* SICK 1
rel rocky, shaky, wobbly; feeble, frail, infirm, weakly; ill, sick; qualmish, queasy, squeamish
idiom out of sorts, under the weather
ant well

unwholesome *adj* 1 likely to be detrimental to physical, mental, or moral health <an *unwholesome* crime-ridden neighborhood>
syn insalubrious, insalutary, noisome, noxious, sickly, unhealthful, unhealthy, unsalutary
rel baneful, deleterious, detrimental, pernicious; harmful, hurtful, injurious, mischievous
con healthful, hygienic, salubrious, salutary
ant wholesome
2 *syn* see OFFENSIVE
ant wholesome

unwieldy *adj* clumsy and difficult to handle usually because of excessive weight and awkward form <a massive *unwieldy* sledgehammer>
syn cumbersome, cumbrous, ponderous, unhandy; *compare* HEAVY 1
rel awkward, inconvenient; uncontrollable, unmanageable; bulky, clumsy, lumbering, massive; burdensome, encumbering, onerous
con compact, neat, trig, trim; adaptable, convenient, handy; easy, facile, light
ant wieldy

unwilling *adj syn* see DISINCLINED
ant willing

unwind *vb syn* see RELAX 2

unwise *adj* not marked by or according with good sense or sound judgment <his decision to quit school was most *unwise*>
syn ill-advised, ill-judged, impolitic, imprudent, indiscreet, injudicious
rel senseless, thoughtless, witless; impractical, unsound; fatuous, inane, inept; inappropriate, undesirable, unfortunate; fool-

---

syn synonym(s)   *rel* related word(s)
ant antonym(s)   *con* contrasted word(s)
idiom idiomatic equivalent(s)
‖ use limited; if in doubt, see a dictionary

ish, misguided, unintelligent; childish, immature, naive
idiom penny-wise and pound-foolish
con discreet, judicious, prudent; sane, sensible, sound; appropriate, apt, desirable
ant wise

unwished *adj syn* see UNWELCOME 1
unwishful *adj syn* see DISINCLINED
ant wishful
unwitting *adj* 1 *syn* see FORGETFUL
ant witting
2 *syn* see IGNORANT 2
ant witting
unwitty *adj syn* see SIMPLE 3
ant ||witty
unwonted *adj syn* see EXCEPTIONAL 1
ant wonted
unworkable *adj* 1 *syn* see IMPOSSIBLE 1
2 *syn* see IMPRACTICABLE 2
ant workable
unworked *adj syn* see RUDE 1
ant worked, wrought
unworkmanlike *adj syn* see INEFFICIENT 2
ant workmanlike, workmanly
unworldly *adj* 1 *syn* see DREAMY 1
2 *syn* see NATURAL 5
ant worldly
unworthy *adj syn* see WORTHLESS 1
ant worthy
unwritten *adj syn* see ORAL 2
ant written
unwrought *adj syn* see RUDE 1
ant worked, wrought
unyielding *adj* 1 *syn* see STIFF 1
ant yielding
2 *syn* see OBSTINATE
rel firm, fixed, rigid
ant yielding
3 *syn* see GRIM 3
4 *syn* see TOUGH 3
ant yielding
5 *syn* see INFLEXIBLE 2
up *adj* 1 *syn* see BAD 1
2 *syn* see FAMILIAR 3
3 *syn* see UP-TO-DATE
up *vb* 1 *syn* see RISE 4
2 *syn* see RAISE 9
up-and-coming *adj syn* see ENTERPRISING 2
rel alert, eager, keen, ready
idiom in prospect, on the horizon
up and down *adv syn* see THOROUGHLY 2
up-and-down *adj syn* see DOWNRIGHT 2
upbear *vb syn* see SUPPORT 4
upbeat *adj syn* see OPTIMISTIC
upbraid *vb syn* see SCOLD 1
upchuck *vb syn* see VOMIT
upclimb *vb syn* see ASCEND 1
upcoming *adj syn* see FORTHCOMING
rel foreseen, prospective
idiom in prospect, on the horizon
up-country *n syn* see FRONTIER 2
update *vb syn* see RENEW 1
upend *vb syn* see WHIP 2
upgo *vb syn* see ASCEND 1
upgrade *vb syn* see ADVANCE 2
ant downgrade
upgrade *n syn* see RISE 3
upgrading *n syn* see ADVANCEMENT 1
ant downgrading
upgrowth *n syn* see DEVELOPMENT
upheaval *n syn* see COMMOTION 1

rel cataclysm, catastrophe, disaster; alteration, change; churning, heaving, stirring
upheaved *adj syn* see ELEVATED 1
ant downthrown
uphill *adj syn* see HARD 6
uphold *vb* 1 *syn* see SUPPORT 5
rel defend, justify, maintain, vindicate; aid, assist, help
ant contravene; subvert
2 *syn* see SUPPORT 2
3 *syn* see SUPPORT 4
4 *syn* see LIFT 1
upholstered *adj* 1 *syn* see LUXURIOUS 3
2 *syn* see FAT 2
upland *n syn* see PLATEAU
uplay *vb syn* see ACCUMULATE
uplift *vb* 1 *syn* see LIFT 1
2 *syn* see ILLUMINATE 2
ant degrade
uplifted *adj syn* see ELEVATED 1
upon *prep* 1 *syn* see OVER 3
2 *syn* see OVER 4
upper class *n syn* see ARISTOCRACY
upper crust *n syn* see ARISTOCRACY
rel (the) Four Hundred
upper hand *n syn* see BETTER 2
uppermost *adj syn* see TOP 1
ant lowermost
||**upper story** *n syn* see MIND 1
||**upperworks** *n pl syn* see MIND 1
uppish *adj syn* see PRESUMPTUOUS
uppity *adj syn* see PRESUMPTUOUS
upraise *vb* 1 *syn* see LIFT 1
2 *syn* see COMFORT
ant depress
upraised *adj syn* see ELEVATED 1
uprear *vb* 1 *syn* see LIFT 1
2 *syn* see BUILD 1
3 *syn* see EXALT 1
con bust, demote, downgrade
ant degrade
4 *syn* see RISE 4
upright *adj* 1 *syn* see ERECT
2 having or manifesting a strict regard for what is morally right <an *upright* man ready to give even the devil his due>
syn conscientious, honest, honorable, just, right, scrupulous, true
rel ethical, moral, principled, righteous, virtuous; equitable, fair, impartial; elevated, high-minded, noble; blameless, exemplary, good, pure
con crooked, devious, oblique; depraved; base, low, vile; ignoble, mean
ant corrupt
uprightness *n syn* see GOODNESS
rel nobility, reputability, worthiness; honesty, integrity
ant corruption
uprise *vb* 1 *syn* see RISE 1
2 *syn* see ROLL OUT
uprisen *adj syn* see ELEVATED 1
uproar *n* 1 *syn* see DIN
rel chaos, confusion, disorder; brawl, broil, fracas, melee; commotion, confusion, turbulence, turmoil
con calm, peace, quiet
2 *syn* see COMMOTION 4
3 *syn* see COMMOTION 3
uproarious *adj syn* see NOISY
uproot *vb* 1 *syn* see ANNIHILATE 2
rel demolish, destroy; overthrow, overturn, subvert; displace, replace, supersede, supplant; move, shift, transplant

ant establish; inseminate

upset *vb* 1 *syn* see OVERTURN 1
rel invert, reverse; bend, curve, turn
2 *syn* see DISCOMPOSE 1
rel bewilder, confound, distract; unman, unnerve
idiom rock the boat
3 *syn* see TROUBLE 1
4 *syn* see DISORDER 1
5 to disturb the normal functioning especially of body or mind < her stomach was badly *upset* by too many sweets >
syn derange, disorder, sicken, turn, unhinge, unsettle
rel afflict, indispose, lay up; ail, suffer; debilitate, incapacitate, invalid

upshot *n* 1 *syn* see EFFECT 1
rel ending, termination; climax, culmination; completion, conclusion, finish
2 *syn* see SUBSTANCE 2

upside-down *adj* 1 having the upper and lower parts reversed in position < *upside-down* letters >
syn inverted, topsy-turvy
rel reversed
2 confused utterly even to the point of inversion of the normal or reasonable < *upside-down* logic that confused cause with effect >
syn arsy-varsy, downside-up, topsy-turvy
rel inverted, reversed; chaotic, confused, helter-skelter, jumbled, mixed-up; fouled-up, haywire, ||snafu
con orderly, well-ordered; logical, reasonable, sensible, sound; legitimate, plausible

upspring *vb* 1 *syn* see SPRING 1
2 *syn* see RISE 1

upstanding *adj* *syn* see ERECT

upstart *n* a usually crude and pushing person who has recently reached a position of prominence, power, or wealth < declared the new executive an *upstart* lacking all breeding and culture >
syn arriviste, nouveau riche, parvenu, roturier
rel bounder, cad, outsider; guttersnipe, mucker, slob, vulgarian; boor, lout, roughneck, rowdy; comer; social climber

upsurge *vb* *syn* see INCREASE 2

uptight *adj* *syn* see TENSE 2

uptightness *n* *syn* see TENSION 2

up till *prep* *syn* see UNTIL

up to *prep* *syn* see UNTIL

up-to-date *adj* completely modern (as in style or outlook) < using *up-to-date* methods of study >
syn abreast, au courant, contemporary, down-to-date, red-hot, up, up-to-the-minute
rel convenient, opportune, timely; expedient, fitting, suitable; advanced, modern, stylish; a la mode, dashing, modish
idiom abreast of the times
con dusty, rusty, stale, timeworn; antiquated, outmoded, superannuated
ant out-of-date; archaic

up-to-the-minute *adj* *syn* see UP-TO-DATE

---

syn synonym(s)   *rel* related word(s)
ant antonym(s)   *con* contrasted word(s)
idiom idiomatic equivalent(s)
‖ use limited; if in doubt, see a dictionary

upturn *n* *syn* see COMMOTION 1

uranian *adj* *syn* see HOMOSEXUAL

uranian *n* *syn* see HOMOSEXUAL

uranist *n* *syn* see HOMOSEXUAL

urban *adj* of, relating to, or characteristic of a city < *urban* disorders >
syn burghal, city, municipal
rel inner city; metropolitan; civic, popular, public; oppidan, town, village
ant rural

urbane *adj* 1 *syn* see COSMOPOLITAN 1
2 *syn* see SUAVE
rel balanced, poised
ant bucolic, clownish
3 *syn* see GENTEEL 1
rel affable, civil, courteous, gracious, obliging
ant rude

urchin *n* a pert or roguish youngster < *urchins* pilfering apples on their way from school >
syn gamin, imp, monkey
rel brat, bratling, cub, dickens, pup, whelp, whippersnapper; guttersnipe, mudlark, ragamuffin, street arab; hobbledehoy

urge *vb* to press or impel to action, effort, or speed < his conscience *urged* him to tell the truth >
syn egg (on), exhort, goad, prick, prod, prompt, propel, sic, spur
rel hurry, hustle, push, rush, shove; blandish, cajole, coax, encourage, incite, needle, solicit, wheedle; constrain, drive, high-pressure, press, pressure; provoke, set (on), tar (on)
idiom bring pressure to bear on, twist one's arm
con brake, check, constrain, curb, hold back, inhibit, restrain

urge *n* *syn* see DESIRE 1
rel goad, incentive, motive, spring, spur

urgent *adj* *syn* see PRESSING
rel driving, impelling; demanding

usable *adj* *syn* see OPEN 5
ant unusable

usage *n* 1 *syn* see HABIT 1
rel choice, preference; procedure, proceeding, process; guidance, guiding, lead
2 *syn* see FORM 3
rel ceremony, formality

usance *n* *syn* see USE 1

use *n* 1 the act or practice of using something or the state of being used < all tools must be kept ready for instant *use* >
syn appliance, application, employment, operation, play, usance; *compare* EXERCISE 1
con desuetude, disuse
ant nonuse
2 *syn* see EXERCISE 1
3 the quality of being appropriate or valuable to some end < even the scraps had some *use* >
syn account, advantage, applicability, appropriateness, avail, fitness, relevance, service, serviceability, usefulness, utility
rel adaptability, availability, benefit, efficacy; profit, value, worth
con inadequacy, inapplicability, inappropriateness, insufficiency, unfitness, unserviceability, uselessness, worthlessness
4 a particular service or end < industrial *uses* of atomic energy >

syn duty, function, goal, mark, object, objective, purpose, target

5 *syn* see HABIT 1

rel ceremony, formality

6 *syn* see NEED 3

use *vb* 1 *syn* see ACCUSTOM

2 to put into action or service <it is necessary to *use* resources wisely>

syn apply, bestow, employ, exercise, exploit, handle, utilize

rel manipulate, operate, ply, wield; control, govern, manage, regulate

idiom avail oneself of, bring into play, fall back (on *or* upon), make use of, press into service, put into action, put to use

con dissipate, exhaust, use up; waste

3 *syn* see OPERATE 3

4 *syn* see SPEAK 3

5 *syn* see EXPLOIT 2

idiom make the most of, make use of

6 *syn* see TREAT 2

used up *adj syn* see EFFETE 2

useful *adj* 1 *syn* see PRACTICAL 2

2 *syn* see GOOD 1

ant useless

3 *syn* see GOOD 2

ant useless

usefulness *n syn* see USE 3

ant uselessness

useless *adj* 1 *syn* see FUTILE

ant useful

2 *syn* see IMPRACTICABLE 2

ant useful

3 *syn* see FECKLESS 1

use up *vb* 1 *syn* see CONSUME 1

2 *syn* see GO 4

3 *syn* see DEPLETE

usher *vb syn* see PRECEDE 3

usher in *vb syn* see INTRODUCE 3

usual *adj* 1 familiar through frequent or regular repetition <the sort that would perform her *usual* chores while waiting for the end of the world>

syn accepted, accustomed, chronic, customary, habitual, routine, wonted

rel natural, normal, regular, typical; common, familiar, ordinary; current, prevailing, prevalent, rife

idiom that make up one's daily round

con exceptional, rare, unaccustomed; remarkable, strange, unexpected

ant unusual

2 *syn* see GENERAL 1

3 *syn* see ORDINARY 1

usually *adv* 1 by or in accord with habit or custom <establishments of a kind *usually* restricted to back streets>

syn as usual, consistently, customarily, habitually, wontedly

2 more often than not <he is *usually* late for work>

syn as a rule, by ordinary, commonly, frequently, generally, ordinarily

rel now and again (*or* now and then), occasionally, once and again, sometimes

idiom for the most part, in the main

con infrequently, seldom, uncommonly

ant rarely

usurer *n syn* see LOAN SHARK

usurp *vb* 1 *syn* see ARROGATE 1

ant abdicate

2 *syn* see SUPPLANT 1

utensil *n syn* see IMPLEMENT

utile *adj syn* see PRACTICAL 2

ant inutile

utilitarian *adj syn* see REALISTIC

utility *n syn* see USE 3

ant inutility

utilize *vb syn* see USE 2

rel advance, forward, further, promote

utmost *adj* 1 *syn* see EXTREME 5

2 *syn* see MAXIMUM

3 *syn* see EXTREME 1

utopia *n* an often imaginary place or situation of perfection and delight <able to make an enduring *utopia* of the humblest house>

syn arcadia, Cockaigne, fairyland, heaven, lubberland, paradise, promised land, Shangri-la, wonderland, Zion

rel dreamland, dreamworld, never-never

utopian *adj* 1 *syn* see IDEALISTIC

rel abstract, ideal, transcendental

2 *syn* see AMBITIOUS 2

rel impossible, impracticable, unfeasible; arcadian, edenic, millennial, otherworldly

utopian *n syn* see DREAMER

utter *adj* being such without qualification — used especially to intensify the noun modified <acted like an *utter* idiot>

syn absolute, all-fired, arrant, black, blamed, blank, blankety-blank, blasted, bleeding, blessed, blighted, blinding, ‖blinking, blithering, ‖blooming, blue, complete, confounded, ‖consarned, consummate, crashing, dad-blamed, dad=blasted, dad-burned, damned, dang, darn (*or* durn), dashed, deuced, doggone, double-distilled, double-dyed, downright, flat-out, goldarn, gross, hell-fired, infernal, out-and-out, outright, perfect, positive, ‖proper, pure, ‖puredee (*or* pure-D), rank, regular, sheer, stark, straight-out, ‖tarnation, thoroughgoing, total, unmitigated, unqualified; *compare* PURE 2

utter *vb* 1 *syn* see SPEAK 1

idiom give utterance to

2 *syn* see SAY 1

utterance *n* 1 *syn* see WORD 1

2 *syn* see VOCALIZATION

3 *syn* see EXPRESSION 1

4 *syn* see SPEECH 1

uttering *n syn* see VOCALIZATION

utterly *adv* 1 *syn* see WELL 3

2 *syn* see ALL 1

uttermost *adj* 1 *syn* see EXTREME 5

2 *syn* see EXTREME 1

V

vacancy *n syn* see VACUITY 2
  rel desertedness
  ant occupancy

vacant *adj* 1 *syn* see EMPTY 1
  rel tenantless, unfilled, unoccupied, untaken
  con inhabited, tenanted
  ant occupied
  2 *syn* see VACUOUS 2
  3 *syn* see EXPRESSIONLESS
  rel empty-headed, inane, thoughtless, witless
  4 not being put to normal or appropriate use < *vacant* land >
  syn idle, unused
  rel bare, empty; unfilled, unoccupied
  con filled; used
  ant occupied

vacate *vb* 1 *syn* see ANNUL 4
  rel repeal, rescind, retract, reverse, revoke
  idiom declare null and void
  2 to make something (as an office, post, or dwelling) vacant or empty < *vacate* a house >
  syn clear, empty, void
  rel abandon, give up, part (with *or* from), relinquish; leave, quit

vacation *n* a period spent away from one's usual activity or work often in travel or recreation < took a two-week *vacation* to Florida >
  syn holiday, leave
  rel break, breathing space (*or* breathing spell), intermission, recess; time off; respite, rest; furlough

vacillant *adj syn* see VACILLATING 2

vacillate *vb syn* see HESITATE
  rel swag, sway, ‖swither; alternate, seesaw, teeter, teeter-totter, wag, waggle, wigwag, wobble; dally, dawdle, fiddle-faddle
  idiom blow hot and cold, hem and haw, swing from one thing to another
  con decide, resolve, settle

vacillating *adj* 1 *syn* see WEAK 2
  rel unfixed; unsettled, unsteady; changeable, fickle, inconstant; eccentric, erratic, mercurial, volatile
  con constant, steady, unchanging; strong
  2 given to or manifesting hesitation or vacillation < a *vacillating* witness >
  syn double-minded, faltering, halting, hesitant, hesitating, indecisive, irresolute, pendulous, shilly-shally, shilly-shallying, tentative, timid, uncertain, undecisive, unresolved, vacillant, vacillatory, wavering, weak-kneed, whiffling, wiggle-waggle, wobbly

vacillation *n syn* see HESITATION
  rel dallying, demurral, dillydallying, stalling

vacillatory *adj syn* see VACILLATING 2
  rel alternating, seesawing, varying; indecisive, irresolute, uncertain

vacuity *n* 1 *syn* see HOLE 3
  2 the condition, fact, or quality of being vacuous < the utter *vacuity* of his expression >
  syn blankness, emptiness, vacancy, vacuousness, voidness
  rel bareness, barrenness, bleakness, desolateness, hollowness; dullness, inaneness, inanity, stupidity
  3 *syn* see NOTHINGNESS

vacuous *adj* 1 *syn* see EMPTY 1
  2 characterized by a lack of substance, thought, or intellectual content < a *vacuous* mind >
  syn empty-headed, vacant; *compare* STUPID 1
  rel shallow, superficial; blank, empty; dull, foolish, inane, silly

vacuousness *n syn* see VACUITY 2

vade mecum *n syn* see HANDBOOK

vag *n syn* see VAGABOND

vagabond *adj syn* see ITINERANT
  rel vagabondish

vagabond *n* a person who wanders at will or as a habit < a park full of *vagabonds* sleeping on benches >
  syn arab, ‖bindle stiff, bum, canter, clochard, derelict, drifter, floater, ‖gangrel, hobo, piker, roadster, runagate, ‖shack, street arab, ‖sundowner, ‖swagger, ‖swagman, tramp, tramper, ‖traveler, vag, vagrant, Weary Willie
  rel roamer, rover, wanderer; boomer, migrant, runabout, straggler, stray, transient; bohemian, gypsy, picaro, picaroon; ‖casual; stiff; beggar, rogue
  idiom knight of the road

vagabond *vb syn* see WANDER 1

vagabondage *n syn* see VAGRANCY

vagabondia *n syn* see VAGRANCY

vagabondism *n syn* see VAGRANCY

vagabondize *vb syn* see WANDER 1

vagarious *adj syn* see ARBITRARY 1
  rel unreasonable; kinky

vagary *n syn* see CAPRICE
  rel daydream, dream, fantasy; kink, quirk
  idiom passing fancy

vagrancy *n* the act or state of wandering from place to place usually with no means of support < dropped out of society and lived a life of *vagrancy* >
  syn hoboism, vagabondage, vagabondia, vagabondism

---

syn synonym(s)   *rel* related word(s)
ant antonym(s)   *con* contrasted word(s)
idiom idiomatic equivalent(s)

‖ use limited: if in doubt, see a dictionary

rel itineracy, itinerancy, nomadism; rambling, roaming, roving, wandering

vagrant *n syn* see VAGABOND

vagrant *adj syn* see ITINERANT
rel aimless, errant, erratic; straying; sauntering, strolling

vague *adj* 1 *syn* see OBSCURE 3
rel indeterminate, indistinct, unplain; cloudy, dim, hazy, nebulous; muddy
con clear, distinct
ant express
2 *syn* see FAINT 2
rel nebulous, unsubstantial; indefinite, unplain; uncertain, unrecognizable; dreamlike, dreamy
3 *syn* see HAZY
rel bleared, bleary, blurry

vain *adj* 1 devoid of worth or significance <the *vain* pursuits of a luxurious life>
syn empty, hollow, idle, nugatory, otiose
rel profitless, unprofitable, useless, valueless, void, worthless; ineffective, ineffectual, inefficacious; bootless, fruitless; abortive, futile
con useful, valuable, worthy; effective, effectual, efficacious
2 *syn* see FUTILE
rel paltry, petty, puny, trifling, trivial; delusive, delusory, misleading
3 having or exhibiting undue or excessive pride especially in one's appearance or achievements <was *vain* about his clothes>
syn conceited, ||conceity, narcissistic, self-conceited, stuck-up, vainglorious; *compare* PROUD 1
rel arrogant, egocentric, egoistic, haughty, ||pensy, proud, self-important, swollen-headed; boastful, self-exalting; coxcombical, dandyish, foppish
idiom stuck on oneself
con humble, meek, modest; bashful, diffident, retiring, shy

vainglorious *adj syn* see VAIN 3
rel boastful, bragging, vaunting; disdainful, insolent, supercilious

vainglory *n syn* see CONCEIT 2
rel arrogance, haughtiness; boastfulness, bombast; exhibition, flaunting, parading
con lowliness, meekness; bashfulness, diffidence, self-effacement, shyness; modesty
ant humility

vainness *n syn* see CONCEIT 2

vale *n syn* see VALLEY

valedictory *adj syn* see PARTING

valiance *n syn* see HEROISM
con feebleness, ineffectiveness; fear

valiancy *n syn* see HEROISM
con feebleness, ineffectiveness; fear

valiant *adj syn* see BRAVE 1
ant pusillanimous

valid *adj* having the power to impress others as right and well-founded <a *valid* conclusion>
syn cogent, convincing, satisfactory, satisfying, solid, sound, telling
rel persuasive, potent, strong; attested, confirmed, corroborated, demonstrated, determined, established, substantiated, validated, verified; lawful, legal, licit; effective, effectual; conclusive, decisive, definitive, determinative; acceptable

con groundless, shaky, unconvincing, unfounded, unsound; fallacious, false, misleading, sophistical; counterfeit, fictitious
ant invalid

validate *vb syn* see CONFIRM 2
rel approve, endorse, legalize, ratify, rubber-stamp, sanction
con abolish, abrogate, annul, cancel, repeal; void
ant invalidate

validity *n syn* see POINT 3
rel efficacy, gravity, soundness; persuasiveness, potency
con inconsistency; unsoundness; fallacy, falsity
ant invalidity, invalidness

validness *n syn* see POINT 3
ant invalidity, invalidness

valley *n* an elongate depression of the earth's surface commonly situated between ranges of hills or mountains <small farms dotted the floor of the *valley*>
syn ||combe, dale, glen, vale
rel dell, dingle, hollow; ||rincon; canyon

valor *n syn* see HEROISM
rel mettle, resolution, spirit, tenacity; indomitableness, invincibility, unconquerableness; backbone, fortitude, guts, sand
con cowardliness, fear
ant pusillanimity, pusillanimousness

valorous *adj syn* see BRAVE 1
ant pusillanimous

valorousness *n syn* see HEROISM
rel chivalrousness, chivalry; manliness
con cowardliness
ant pusillanimity, pusillanimousness

valuable *adj syn* see PRECIOUS 1
rel dear, expensive; appreciated, prized, treasured, valued; admired, esteemed, respected
idiom of great value
con cheap, inexpensive, trashy; unmarketable, unsalable; unworthy
ant valueless, worthless

valuate *vb syn* see ESTIMATE 1

valuation *n* 1 *syn* see ESTIMATE 1
rel judgment, opinion, rating
2 *syn* see WORTH 1
rel charge, cost, price

value *n* 1 *syn* see WORTH 1
rel appraisal, assessment; charge, cost, expense, price
2 *syn* see QUALITY 2

value *vb* 1 *syn* see ESTIMATE 1
rel compute, figure, gauge, reckon
idiom place a value (or price) on
2 *syn* see APPRECIATE 1
rel care (for); revere, reverence, venerate
idiom set much by

valueless *adj syn* see WORTHLESS 1
ant valuable

valve *n syn* see FAUCET
rel shutoff

||**vamoose** *vb syn* see GET OUT 1

vamp *vb syn* see MEND 2
rel brush up, fix up, touch up; furbish, refurbish

vamp (up) *vb syn* see CONTRIVE 2

vamp *n syn* see FLIRT
rel charmer, enchantress, enticer, femme fatale, gold digger, inveigler, seductress, siren, temptress

vandal *n* one who willfully destroys or mars something valuable < *vandals* had knocked off the head of the statue >
  syn defacer, despoiler, destroyer, ruinator, ruiner, wrecker
  rel hoodlum, hooligan, lout, ruffian; devastator, ravager, spoiler, spoliator; looter, pillager, plunderer, iconoclast

vandalize *vb* to destroy or deface (as public or private property) willfully or maliciously < youths *vandalized* the shop >
  syn ‖trash, wreck
  rel ‖rip off; destroy, tear up

vanish *vb* to pass from view or out of existence < the moon *vanished* behind a cloud >
  syn clear, disappear, evanesce, evanish, evaporate, fade
  rel dematerialize, dissolve, melt (away); die
  idiom do the vanishing act, vanish from sight, vanish into thin air, vanish like a dream
  con arise, break out (*or* through), come (forth *or* out), emerge, issue, loom (up), materialize, show (up)
  ant appear

vanished *adj syn* see EXTINCT 2
  rel expired, passed away; annihilated, no more, perished

vanity *n syn* see CONCEIT 2
  rel autotheism, self-worship

vanquish *vb syn* see CONQUER 1
  rel surmount; overturn, subvert; humble, trample

vanquisher *n syn* see VICTOR 1
  rel champ, champion
  con loser

vanquishment *n syn* see DEFEAT 1
  rel mastery, subdual, subjugation

vantage *n syn* see ADVANTAGE 3
  ant disadvantage

vapid *adj syn* see INSIPID 3
  rel flavorless, milk-toast, tasteless, weak; dull, unimaginative, uninteresting
  idiom neither hot nor cold, neither one thing nor the other
  con brisk, lively, tangy, zesty; crisp, forceful, incisive, trenchant; expressive, meaningful, pregnant, significant, telling

vaporous *adj* 1 *syn* see HAZY
  2 *syn* see AIRY 3
  rel unsubstantial, wispy; illusory, unreal

vapory *adj* 1 *syn* see HAZY
  2 *syn* see AIRY 3
  rel gaseous

variable *adj syn* see CHANGEABLE 1
  rel fitful, spasmodic; irregular, unequable, unequal, ununiform
  con unchanging, unvarying; immobile, stable, unmoving; equable, equal, uniform
  ant constant, invariable
  2 *syn* see MUTABLE 2
  3 *syn* see INCONSTANT 1

variance *n* 1 the quality, state, or fact of being variable < a daily *variance* of 1°F. >
  syn difference, variation
  rel change, deviation, fluctuation

  ant invariance
  2 *syn* see DISCORD
  rel division, separation, severing, sundering

variation *n* 1 *syn* see CHANGE 1
  rel difference, dissimilarity; deflection, discrepancy
  con stability, unchangeableness
  2 *syn* see VARIANCE 1
  rel shift; divergence; discrepancy, disparity
  con uniformity

varicolored *adj syn* see VARIEGATED
  ant solid

varied *adj syn* see MISCELLANEOUS

variegated *adj* having a pattern involving different colors or shades of color < *variegated* leaves >
  syn dappled, discolor, motley, multicolor, multicolored, multihued, parti-color, particolored, polychromatic, polychrome, varicolored, versicolor, versicolored
  rel checked, checkered; piebald, pied, skewbald; freaked, streaked; flecked; stippled; marbled; mottle, mottled, spattered, speckled, spotted; calico; pinto
  ant solid

variety *n* 1 the quality or state of being composed of different parts, elements, or individuals < the *variety* of the city's cultural life >
  syn diverseness, diversity, multeity, multifariousness, multiformity, multiplicity, variousness
  rel diversification, heterogeneity, variation
  2 a collection of different things, forms, or qualities especially of a particular class < had a great *variety* of jobs in his lifetime >
  syn assortment
  rel conglomeration, medley, miscellany
  3 *syn* see TYPE
  rel classification; grade, rank

various *adj* 1 *syn* see MANY
  rel assorted, heterogeneous, miscellaneous, omnifarious, omnigenous
  2 *syn* see DIFFERENT 1
  rel changing, variant, varied, varying; distinct, separate; distinctive, individual, peculiar
  ant uniform
  3 *syn* see SEVERAL 3
  ant many, numerous
  4 *syn* see DISTINCT 1
  5 *syn* see CERTAIN 2

various *pron, pl in constr syn* see SUNDRY

variously *adv syn* see OTHERWISE 1

variousness *n syn* see VARIETY 1

varnish *vb syn* see PALLIATE

vary *vb* 1 *syn* see CHANGE 1
  rel modulate, qualify
  2 *syn* see DIFFER 1
  3 *syn* see DIFFER 2
  rel depart, deviate, digress, diverge; divide, part, separate
  ant agree
  4 *syn* see RANGE 3

vast *adj syn* see HUGE
  rel big, large; ample, capacious, spacious; broad, expansive, far-flung, wide, widespread; astronomical, cosmic
  con confined, limited, narrow, restricted

vastness *n syn* see ENORMITY 2

---

syn synonym(s)   *rel* related word(s)
ant antonym(s)   *con* contrasted word(s)
idiom idiomatic equivalent(s)
‖ use limited; if in doubt, see a dictionary

vatic *adj syn see* PROPHETIC

vaticinal *adj syn see* PROPHETIC

vaticinate *vb syn see* FORETELL

vault *n syn see* CRYPT

vault *vb* 1 *syn see* JUMP 1
rel upleap, upspring; overjump, overleap; clear; rise, soar; ascend, mount; surmount
2 *syn see* CLEAR 8

vaulting *adj syn see* AMBITIOUS 1
rel enthusiastic; opportunistic

vaunt *vb syn see* BOAST
rel brandish, display, exhibit, expose, flaunt, parade, show off
idiom puff oneself

vaunter *n syn see* BRAGGART

vaunting *adj syn see* BOASTFUL

vector *n* an agent capable of transmitting a pathogen from one organism to another < fleas are *vectors* of bubonic plague >
syn carrier, vehicle

veer *vb* 1 *syn see* TURN 6
2 *syn see* SWERVE 1
rel depart, deviate, digress, diverge; angle off, bear off; twist; pivot, turn, wheel

vegetate *vb* to lead a passive existence without exertion of body or mind < he never really lived his life—he merely *vegetated* >
syn stagnate
rel idle; languish; hibernate
idiom idle life away, live the life of a clam, pass the time

vehement *adj syn see* INTENSE 1
rel emphatic, pronounced; energetic, hearty, lively, zealous; forceful, potent, powerful; ardent, fervent, fervid, heated, impassioned, passionate, perfervid; delirious, frantic, furious, rabid, wild

vehicle *n* 1 *syn see* VECTOR
rel agent
2 *syn see* MEAN 2
rel implement, tool
3 a means of transporting goods or passengers < his *vehicle* was an old battered coupe >
syn conveyance, transport, transportation

veil *n syn see* MASK 2

veil *vb syn see* ENFOLD 1
rel mantle, overspread, spread (over); blanket, curtain; camouflage, cloak, cover (up), disguise, mask; conceal, hide, screen, secrete
con exhibit, lay (open), open up, reveal, uncover, unmask; bare, expose, show
ant unveil

vein *n* 1 a distinctive method of expression < wrote his speech in the proper *vein* for a very sophisticated audience >
syn fashion, manner, mode, style, tone
rel way; line; mood, tenor
2 *syn see* HINT 1
3 *syn see* MOOD 1
rel complexion, disposition, fettle, temperament; character, nature, spirit

velitation *n syn see* ENCOUNTER

velleity *n syn see* WILL 1
rel volition; wish

vellicate *vb syn see* JERK
rel nip, pinch; fidget, jig, jiggle

velocipede *n syn see* BICYCLE

velocity *n syn see* SPEED 2
rel headway, impetus, momentum; dispatch, expedition, haste, hurry

velutinous *adj syn see* VELVETY

velvetlike *adj syn see* VELVETY
idiom soft as velvet

velvety *adj* 1 having the extreme softness associated with the surface or appearance of velvet < wore a *velvety* red flower in her hair >
syn velutinous, velvetlike
rel plush, plushy, smooth, soft; glossy, sleek, slick; satiny, silken, silky
2 *syn see* SOFT 3

venal *adj* 1 open to corrupt influence and especially bribery < a *venal* legislator >
syn bribable, buyable, corruptible, purchasable; *compare* CORRUPT 2, CROOKED 2
rel corrupt, flagitious, infamous, iniquitous, nefarious, vicious; hack, hireling, mercenary, paid; ignoble, sordid; unethical, unprincipled, unscrupulous
2 *syn see* CORRUPT 2

vend *vb* 1 *syn see* SELL 2
2 *syn see* PEDDLE 2
3 *syn see* DECLARE 1

vendee *n syn see* PURCHASER

vendetta *n* a prolonged mutual enmity marked by bitter hostility and conflict < a long-standing *vendetta* between two rival gangs >
syn feud
rel dispute, quarrel; rhubarb, row, wrangle; conflict, fight, set-to; blood feud, blood vengeance

vendible *adj syn see* MARKETABLE
ant unvendible

vendible *n, usu* **vendibles** *pl syn see* MERCHANDISE

vendor *n syn see* PEDDLER

veneer *n syn see* MASK 2

veneer *vb syn see* PALLIATE

venerable *adj* 1 deserving to be venerated usually by reason of prolonged testing (as of character) < a *venerable* judge with an impressive knowledge of the law >
syn patriarchal, revered, reverend, reverential; *compare* HONORABLE 1
rel dignified, imposing, stately; admirable, estimable; honored, reverenced; worshipful; sacred
ant unvenerable
2 *syn see* ANCIENT 1
rel elderly; patriarchal, reverenced, reverend, venerated
con contemporary, current; fresh, inexperienced, new, untried, unused

venerate *vb syn see* REVERE
rel honor; idolize
idiom put on a pedestal

venery *n syn see* HUNTING

venge *vb syn see* AVENGE
idiom even (up) the score, repay in kind, settle accounts (or an account)

vengeance *n syn see* RETALIATION
rel return; repayment; revengefulness, vengefulness

vengeful *adj syn see* VINDICTIVE
rel antagonistic, hostile, inimical, rancorous
con charitable, forgiving, kind; benevolent, benign, inoffensive

venial *adj* of a kind that can be remitted and that does not warrant punishment or penalty < the *venial* indiscretions of youth >

syn excusable, forgivable, pardonable, remittable

rel allowable, unobjectionable; insignificant, minor, trifling, trivial; harmless, tolerable

con criminal, damning, deadly, mortal; grievous, outrageous, serious; inexcusable, unforgivable, unpardonable, unremittable

ant heinous

venom *n syn* see POISON

rel ill will, malignity, rancor, venomousness, virulence, vitriol

con antidote, remedy

venomous *adj syn* see POISONOUS

rel malevolent, malign, malignant; baleful, malefic, maleficent; viperish, viperlike, viperous

vent *vb* 1 *syn* see EMIT 2

rel cast out, discharge, exhaust

2 *syn* see EXPRESS 2

rel utter, voice; assert, declare

idiom come out with, give vent to

con check, curb, inhibit, restrain; repress, suppress

3 *syn* see TAKE OUT (on)

vent *n* 1 *syn* see APERTURE

2 *syn* see EXPRESSION 1

rel articulation, verbalization, vocalization

venter *n syn* see ABDOMEN

ventilate *vb* 1 *syn* see BROACH

2 *syn* see EXPRESS 2

rel go into, take up; debate, deliberate, discourse (about), discuss, ||rap (about), talk over (*or of or* about); thresh out; advertise, broadcast, publish

idiom chew the fat (*or* the rag)

ventilation *n syn* see CONFERENCE 1

venture *vb* 1 to expose to risk or loss < *ventured* their capital in foreign trade >

syn adventure, chance, hazard, risk, wager; *compare* GAMBLE 2

rel endanger, imperil, jeopard, jeopardize, jeopardy, peril; expose, lay (open)

idiom take chances (*or* risks) on (*or* with)

2 *syn* see GAMBLE 2

rel bet, operate, play (for), speculate, stake; jeopard, jeopardize, jeopardy

idiom luck it

3 *syn* see FACE 3

venture *n syn* see ADVENTURE

rel attempt, undertaking; crack, fling; dare, gamble, risk, speculation

idiom leap in the dark

venturesome *adj syn* see ADVENTUROUS

rel stalwart, stout, sturdy; brave; overbold

con timid, timorous; afraid, apprehensive, fearful

venturous *adj syn* see ADVENTUROUS

rel aggressive, enterprising, hustling

veracious *adj* 1 *syn* see TRUTHFUL

rel direct; undeceitful, undeceptive

con equivocal; deceitful, dishonest, insincere; false, untruthful

ant unveracious

2 *syn* see TRUE 3

rel unquestionable, valid

con illusory, invalid, wrong

---

syn synonym(s)   *rel* related word(s)
ant antonym(s)   *con* contrasted word(s)
idiom idiomatic equivalent(s)
|| use limited; if in doubt, see a dictionary

ant unveracious

veraciousness *n syn* see VERACITY 1

rel artlessness, openness; trustworthiness

con falseness, insincerity

veracity *n* 1 the quality or state of keeping close to fact and avoiding distortion or misrepresentation < questions the *veracity* of that witness >

syn truth, truthfulness, veraciousness, veridicality, verity

rel accuracy, correctness, exactness, factualness; frankness, honesty

con inaccuracy, incorrectness; deception, dishonesty, untruth, untruthfulness

ant unveracity

2 something that is true < can make lies sound like *veracities* >

syn gospel, truism, truth, verity

rel verisimilitude; actuality; fact

con lie, untruth

ant unveracity

verbal *adj* 1 *syn* see ORAL 2

2 *syn* see VERBATIM

verbalism *n* 1 *syn* see WORDING

rel styling

2 *syn* see VERBOSITY

verbality *n syn* see VERBIAGE 1

rel verbalism, verboseness, verbosity, wordiness

verbalization *n syn* see SPEECH 1

verbalize *vb syn* see SPEAK 1

rel air, express, give, say, state, vent, ventilate, word

idiom couch in terms, find words to express

verbatim *adv* in the same words < repeated their earlier conversation *verbatim* >

syn direct, directly, literally, literatim, word for word

rel accurately, exactly, precisely

idiom to the letter

con basically, essentially, in essence; carelessly, imprecisely, inaccurately, inexactly

verbatim *adj* using the same words < court stenographers took down the *verbatim* testimony >

syn literal, verbal, word-for-word

rel close, faithful, strict; exact, precise

idiom following the letter, true to the letter

con careless, imprecise, inaccurate, inexact

verbiage *n* 1 a stylistic fault involving excessive wordiness that obscures or unduly complicates expression < the *florid verbiage* of the dissertation >

syn circumambages, circumbendibus, circumlocution, periphrase, periphrasis, pleonasm, redundancy, roundabout, tautology, verbality; *compare* VERBOSITY

rel nimiety; repetition; expansiveness, floridity, floridness; longiloquence, long-windedness

idiom purple prose

con breviloquence, brevity, briefness, terseness

ant concision

2 *syn* see WORDING

verbose *adj syn* see WORDY

rel flowery, grandiloquent, magniloquent; circumlocutory, periphrastic, pleonastic, tautologous

con precise; close, compact, lean, tight

ant concise; laconic

verboseness *n syn see* VERBOSITY

ant conciseness

verbosity *n* the quality or state or an instance of being wordy <his two-hour lecture was the epitome of *verbosity* > <flowery *verbosities* weakened his speech>

syn prolixity, prolixness, verbalism, verboseness, windiness, wordiness; *compare* VERBIAGE 1

rel bombast, grandiloquence; long-windedness; redundancy

con conciseness, preciseness, succinctness, terseness; leanness, tightness

verboten *adj syn see* FORBIDDEN

rel disallowed, disapproved; unauthorized, unlicensed, unsanctioned; outlawed, taboo

con allowed, permitted; authorized, licensed; approved, endorsed, sanctioned

verdure *n syn see* FOLIAGE

verge *n* 1 *syn see* BORDER 1

2 a time interval or set of circumstances marking the imminent beginning of a new state, condition, or action <on the *verge* of war>

syn brink, edge, point, threshold

rel border line

verge *vb* 1 *syn see* BORDER 1

rel approach; incline, lean, tend (to *or* toward); touch (on *or* upon)

2 *syn see* ADJOIN

3 *syn see* BORDER 3

veridical *adj* 1 *syn see* TRUTHFUL

2 *syn see* REAL 3

3 *syn see* TRUE 3

rel uncolored, undistorted, unvarnished; actual, real

con invalid; illusory, unreal

veridicality *n syn see* VERACITY 1

rel genuineness

verificatory *adj syn see* CORROBORATIVE

verify *vb syn see* CONFIRM 2

rel demonstrate, prove, test, try; document, establish, settle

verily *adv syn see* EVEN 3

verisimilitude *n* the quality of a representation that causes it to appear true <his characters are too stilted for *verisimilitude*>

syn color, plausibility, verisimility

rel authenticity, genuineness, veritableness; likeness, resemblance, similarity

verisimility *n syn see* VERISIMILITUDE

veritable *adj syn see* AUTHENTIC 2

rel undenied, unrefuted; actual, factual

con doubtful, questionable; imaginary, unreal, untrue; artificial, factitious; counterfeit, false, spurious

veritably *adv syn see* VERY 2

verity *n* 1 *syn see* VERACITY 2

ant falsity

2 *syn see* VERACITY 1

vernacular *adj* of or relating to everyday speech <*vernacular* Welsh differs greatly from literary Welsh>

syn colloquial, vulgar, vulgate

vernacular *n* 1 *syn see* LANGUAGE 1

rel mother tongue

idiom native tongue

2 *syn see* DIALECT 2

3 a commonly spoken as opposed to a prestige variety of a language <literary Chinese and the various *vernaculars* >

syn colloquial, patois, vulgate; *compare* DIALECT 2

rel dialect, lingo, slang

vernacularism *n syn see* BARBARISM

vernacularity *n syn see* BARBARISM

vernal *adj* of, relating to, or resembling the spring of the year <*vernal* sunshine>

syn spring, springlike

versant *adj syn see* FAMILIAR 3

ant unversed

versatile *adj* having a wide range of skills, aptitudes, or interests <a *versatile* artist, who is at home in any medium>

syn adaptable, all-around, ambidextrous, many-sided, mobile, myriad-minded

rel elastic, flexible, plastic, pliable; adroit, dexterous, facile; able, skilled, skillful; accomplished, conversant; gifted, talented; well-rounded

con inadequate, limited

verse *n* 1 *syn see* POETRY 1

2 *syn see* POEM

rel jingle; ballad, lay; sonnet; lyric; ode; epic

versed *adj* 1 *syn see* EXPERIENCED

rel competent

con incompetent

ant unversed

2 *syn see* FAMILIAR 3

ant unversed

verseman *n syn see* POETASTER

versemonger *n syn see* POETASTER

verser *n syn see* POETASTER

versesmith *n syn see* POETASTER

versicolor *adj syn see* VARIEGATED

versicolored *adj syn see* VARIEGATED

versificator *n syn see* POETASTER

versifier *n syn see* POETASTER

version *n* 1 a restating often in simpler language of something previously stated or written <a simple *version* of Beowulf for the use of children>

syn paraphrase, rendering, restatement, translation

rel rendition; clarification, interpretation; condensation, simplification; rewording; restipulation

2 *syn see* ACCOUNT 7

rel tale

3 *syn see* INTERPRETATION 2

versus *prep* 1 in conflict with <the case of John Doe *versus* Richard Roe>

syn against

rel con, contra

idiom at cross-purposes with (*or* to), at odds with, at outs with, at variance with, on the outs with

2 in contrast with <the age-old argument about free trade *versus* protection>

syn over against, vis-à-vis

idiom as opposed to

vertebrae *n syn see* SPINE

vertebral column *n syn see* SPINE

vertex *n syn see* TOP 1

rel cap; tip-top; apogee, zenith

idiom upper extremity

vertical *adj* situated at right angles to the plane of the horizon or extending from that plane at such an angle <*vertical* walls>

syn perpendicular, plumb, straight-up

rel erect, upright; steep, up-and-down

con flat, plane

ant horizontal

verticalism *n syn* see VERTICALITY

verticality *n* the quality or state of being vertical < the soaring *verticality* of the spires >
syn perpendicularity, plumbness, verticalism, verticalness
rel erectness, uprightness
con flatness, lowness
ant horizontality

verticalness *n syn* see VERTICALITY

vertiginous *adj syn* see DIZZY 2

verve *n syn* see SPIRIT 5
rel liveliness, vivacity; bounce, buoyancy, elasticity, resiliency, spring; fire, gusto, zest

very *adj* 1 *syn* see AUTHENTIC 2
rel hundred-percent, perfect; correct, exact, right
con fake, fraudulent, mock, sham
2 *syn* see PRECISE 4
rel especial, express, special
3 *syn* see PERFECT 3
4 being as stated without addition or superfluity < the *very* thought of it makes me ill >
syn bare, mere
5 *syn* see SAME 1
idiom (the) very same

very *adv* 1 to a high or exceptional degree < a *very* successful meeting >
syn ‖awful, awfully, ‖big, ‖crazy, damned, ‖dreadful, dreadfully, eminently, exceedingly, exceptionally, extremely, greatly, highly, hugely, insatiably, ‖larruping, ‖main, mightily, mighty, ‖monstrous, ‖mortacious, mortally, most, much, notably, parlous, pesky, ‖pure, rattling, remarkably, right, ‖right smart, snapping, so, spanking, staving, strikingly, super, surpassingly, terribly, thoroughly, too, vitally, whacking, whopping
rel passing, quite, somewhat; perfectly, seriously, significantly, tellingly
idiom nothing if not
con inconsiderably, little, scarcely, slightly
2 in actual fact < told the *very* same story >
syn actually, de facto, genuinely, really, truly, veritably
rel exactly, precisely; almost, nearly, practically, well-nigh
idiom in point of fact, in truth
con apparently, ostensibly, outwardly, seemingly

vest *vb* 1 *syn* see INVEST 2
2 *syn* see BELONG 2

vestibule *n* an entrance chamber between the outer door and the interior of a building < the *vestibule* of a theater >
syn foyer, lobby
rel entrance hall, entry, entryway; portal, portico; antechamber, anteroom; narthex

vestige *n* 1 something (as a mark or visible sign) left by a material thing formerly present but now lost or unknown < digging for the *vestiges* of past civilizations >
syn memento, relic, shadow, trace
rel remainder, remains; rag, remnant, scrap, tag
2 *syn* see FOOTPRINT
rel path; trail

vet *vb syn* see SCRUTINIZE 1
idiom go over with a fine-tooth comb

vet *adj syn* see EXPERIENCED

vet *n syn* see VETERAN

veteran *n* one having knowledge or ability gained through long experience < was a political campaign *veteran* of long standing >
syn longtimer, old hand, old-timer, vet
rel expert, master, past master
con amateur, freshman, youngster
ant novice

veteran *adj syn* see EXPERIENCED
rel wise; sophisticated, worldly
idiom dry behind the ears, not born yesterday, wise in the ways of the world
con inexperienced, unpracticed, unversed; unqualified, unskilled, untrained

veto *vb* to refuse to admit or approve < the President *vetoed* the bill >
syn kill, negative, ‖nix, non-placet
rel decline, deny, disallow, forbid, prohibit, refuse, reject; defeat
idiom put one's veto on
con admit, approve, assent (to); pass

vex *vb syn* see ANNOY 1
rel ‖chaw, embarrass; plague; anger, infuriate
con appease, mollify, pacify, propitiate, smooth (over); please, regale
ant soothe

vexation *n syn* see ANNOYANCE 1
rel aggravation, irritation

vexatious *adj syn* see TROUBLESOME

vexing *n syn* see ANNOYANCE 1

via *prep* 1 over a route that passes through < shipped to New York *via* the Panama Canal >
syn by, by way of, through
rel along; over
2 using as a means of approach or action < reached the voters *via* mass-media advertising >
syn by, by dint of, by means of, by virtue of, by way of, per, through, with
idiom through the medium of

viable *adj syn* see POSSIBLE 1

viands *n pl syn* see FOOD 1
rel fare

vibrant *adj syn* see RESONANT

vibrate *vb syn* see SHAKE 2

vice *n* 1 degrading or immoral habits and practices < an exposé of *vice* and crime in the city >
syn corruption, depravity, immorality, wickedness
rel decay, rot, squalor; evil, ill, sin, wrong; indecency, unchastity; debasement, debauchery, licentiousness, perversion
con morality; respectability; uprightness
ant virtue
2 *syn* see FAULT 2
rel shortcoming
idiom weak point
3 *syn* see BLEMISH

vice versa *adv syn* see AGAIN 5

vicinage *n syn* see LOCALITY 1

vicinity *n* 1 *syn* see LOCALITY 1

2 *syn* see ORDER 4

vicious *adj* 1 *syn* see WRONG 1

2 highly offensive or reprehensible in character, nature, or conduct < *vicious* parents who were a bad influence on their children>

syn corrupt, degenerate, depraved, flagitious, infamous, miscreant, nefarious, perverse, putrid, rotten, unhealthy, villainous

rel bad, faulty, poor, unsound; opprobrious, reprehensible; contaminated, obnoxious, septic

con good, moral, righteous, right-minded

ant virtuous

3 *syn* see SAVAGE 1

rel brutish; bloodthirsty

4 *syn* see MALICIOUS

5 *syn* see INTENSE 1

rel severe

vicissitude *n* 1 *syn* see CHANGE 2

rel alternation; reversal; transposition; progression; diversity, variety

2 *syn* see DIFFICULTY 1

rel chop and change, ups and downs; adversity, mischance, misfortune; affliction, trial, tribulation

victim *n* 1 a living being sacrificed (as in a religious rite) < offered up human *victims* to appease their bloodthirsty gods>

syn offering, sacrifice

2 one subjected to oppression, loss, or suffering < *victims* of social injustice>

syn bottom dog, casualty, prey, underdog

rel quarry

3 *syn* see FOOL 3

idiom easy mark, easy pickings

victimize *vb* 1 *syn* see SACRIFICE 1

2 *syn* see DUPE

victor *n* 1 one that defeats an enemy < the Allies were the *victors* of World War II >

syn conqueror, defeater, master, subduer, subjugator, vanquisher

rel winner

con conquered, defeated, subjugated; loser

ant vanquished

2 a successful contender < emerged as *victor* in the swimming meet >

syn winner

rel champ, champion; first, top

idiom conquering hero

ant loser

Victorian *adj* *syn* see PRIM 1

rel old-fashioned, old-maidish; hidebound; starchy

con easy going; trendy, with-it

victory *n* 1 the overcoming of an opponent < won a knockout *victory* in the first round >

syn conquest, triumph, win

rel command, control, dominion, mastery, subjugation; superiority, supremacy; walkaway, walkover

idiom a feather in one's cap

con loss; bust, failure, fizzle, flop, ‖flopperoo, washout; comedown, cropper

ant defeat

2 *syn* see BETTER 2

victuals *n pl syn* see FOOD 1

videlicet *adv syn* see NAMELY

vie *vb* 1 *syn* see COMPETE 1

rel challenge; match; outvie

2 *syn* see OPPOSE 1

view *n* 1 *syn* see LOOK 1

rel examination, inspection, scan, scrutiny

2 *syn* see EXAMINATION

3 *syn* see EYE 4

4 what is revealed to the vision or can be seen < the *view* from the window>

syn outlook, scene, sight

rel panorama, picture, prospect, vista

5 extent or range of vision < there were still no ships in *view* >

syn sight

rel look; apprehension, scan

6 something (as an aim, end, or motive) to or by which the mind is directed < kept this *view* in mind while negotiating>

syn object

rel intent, intention, purpose; aim, ambition, goal, objective; design, plan, project; consideration, notion; expectation

7 *syn* see OPINION

rel concept, conception; deduction, inference

view *vb* 1 *syn* see SCRUTINIZE 1

2 *syn* see EYE 1

rel observe

3 *syn* see SEE 1

4 *syn* see CONSIDER 3

viewable *adj syn* see VISUAL 1

viewer *n syn* see SPECTATOR

viewpoint *n* 1 *syn* see EYE 4

2 the position or attitude that determines how something is seen, presented, or evaluated < from this *viewpoint* the picture looks askew> < consider totalitarianism from the German *viewpoint* >

syn angle, direction, outlook, side, slant, standpoint; *compare* EYE 4

rel estimation; attitude, position, posture, stand; long view, perspective

idiom frame of reference, point of view, vantage point

viewy *adj syn* see IMPRACTICAL 1

vigil *n syn* see LOOKOUT 3

vigilance *n syn* see LOOKOUT 3

vigilant *adj syn* see WATCHFUL

rel agog, anxious, avid, eager, keen; acute, sharp, sharp-eyed; attentive

idiom on one's guard, with a weather eye open

con lax, neglectful, negligent, remiss, slack; forgetful, oblivious, unmindful

vigor *n* 1 *syn* see POWER 4

2 a quality of physical or mental force or forcefulness < the *vigor* of youth>

syn bang, drive, getup, get-up-and-go, go, pep, punch, push, snap, starch, vitality; *compare* ENERGY 2, ENTERPRISE 4, SPIRIT 5

rel bounce, energy, force, might, muscularity, power, strength; healthiness, soundness; lustiness, manliness, virility

con slowness, sluggishness

ant weakness

3 *syn* see ENERGY 2

rel dash, drive, dynamism, fire, punch, starch, steam, vim, zing, zip; ability, capability, capacity

con ineffectiveness; impotence; incompetence, uselessness, worthlessness

vigorous *adj* having or manifesting great vitality and force < seemed as *vigorous* as a youth half his age>

syn dynamic, energetic, lusty, red=
blooded, strenuous, ||survigrous, vital
rel brisk, dashing, lively, slashing; exuberant, mettlesome, proud, spirited; driving,
hard-driving, hard-hitting, robust, rough-
and-ready, zealous; bouncing, hardy,
healthy, hearty, masterful, potent, powerful, strong, tough; rude, stout, sturdy;
athletic, husky, muscular, sinewy
con languorous, unenergetic; decrepit,
feeble, infirm, weak; impotent
ant lethargic

vigorously *adv syn* see HARD 1
rel alertly, eagerly; boldly, firmly, purposefully, resolutely, unfalteringly, zealously; lustily, robustly
con aimlessly, languorously; falteringly,
indecisively; impotently

vile *adj* 1 *syn* see BASE 3
rel corrupted, debased, debauched, depraved, perverted; coarse, gross, obscene,
vulgar; disgusting, foul, nasty; abhorrent,
contemptible, loathsome, offensive, repulsive, revolting
2 *syn* see OFFENSIVE

vilify *vb syn* see MALIGN
rel abuse, mistreat, misuse, outrage; assail, attack, berate; denounce
con commend, compliment; acclaim, exalt; celebrate, glorify, honor; adore, worship
ant eulogize

vilifying *adj syn* see LIBELOUS

villa *n syn* see MANSION

villain *n* 1 a low, mean, reprehensible person utterly lacking in principle < was an
insufferable bully, a tyrant, and a *villain*
in general >
syn blackguard, heel, knave, lowlife, miscreant, rascal, reprobate, rogue, roperipe,
scoundrel, ||slubberdegullion; *compare*
SNOT 1, DEVIL 2
rel meanie; evildoer, offender, sinner;
criminal, malefactor
2 *syn* see SCAMP

villainize *vb syn* see MALIGN
ant eulogize

villainous *adj syn* see VICIOUS 2
rel contrary, detestable, objectionable,
offensive; debased, perverted; atrocious,
heinous, outrageous; abandoned, dissolute,
profligate

villenage *n syn* see BONDAGE

vim *n syn* see SPIRIT 5
rel pepper; kick, push

vinculum *n syn* see BOND 3

vindicable *adj syn* see JUSTIFIABLE
con indefensible, unjustifiable; inexcusable, unforgivable; heinous, mortal

vindicate *vb* 1 *syn* see AVENGE
2 *syn* see MAINTAIN 2
rel advocate, plead (for), second, support,
uphold; rationalize; bear out, prove
3 *syn* see EXCULPATE
rel confute, disprove, refute; defend,
guard, protect, shield
con accuse, attack, calumniate

ant convict

vindictive *adj* showing or motivated by a
desire for vengeance < *vindictive* hatred
for his brother >
syn revengeful, vengeful, wreakful
rel grim, implacable, merciless, relentless,
unrelenting; malicious, malign, malignant,
spiteful
con charitable, forgiving, merciful, relenting
ant unvindictive

vinegarish *adj syn* see CANTANKEROUS

vinegary *adj syn* see CANTANKEROUS

vintage *adj* 1 being of old, recognized, and
enduring interest, importance, or quality
< a *vintage* comedy from the silent movie
era >
syn classic, classical
2 *syn* see OLD-FASHIONED

violate *vb* 1 to fail to keep < people who
thoughtlessly *violate* the law >
syn breach, break, contravene, infract,
infringe, offend, transgress
rel disregard, trample (on *or* upon); err,
sin; overpass, trespass
con abide by, carry out, fulfill, submit
(to); heed, keep, mind
ant observe; obey
2 *syn* see RAPE

violation *n* 1 *syn* see BREACH 1
rel break; encroachment; illegality, misdemeanor, offense, wrong
ant observance
2 *syn* see PROFANATION
rel defacement, defacing

violence *n syn* see FORCE 4
rel frenzy, fury, savagery; assault, attack,
clash, foul play, onslaught, rampage,
struggle, tumult, uproar
con passiveness, passivity; peace, peacefulness
ant nonviolence

violent *adj syn* see INTENSE 1
rel forceful, forcible, mighty, potent, powerful, strong; extreme, immoderate, inordinate; acute, cutting, piercing, splitting
con calm, moderate, peaceful
ant nonviolent

violently *adv syn* see HARD 2
rel combatively; destructively, ruinously
idiom like fury, with a vengeance

VIP *n syn* see NOTABLE 1

virago *n* a woman of extremely pugnacious
temperament < an overbearing *virago* who
screamed at her children and squabbled
with her neighbors >
syn amazon, fishwife, harpy, ogress,
scold, shrew, termagant, vixen, Xanthippe
rel cat; dragon; fury

virgin *adj* 1 never having had sexual relations < *virgin* girls were sacrificed >
syn intact, maiden, undeflowered, virginal
rel innocent, untouched; single, spouseless, unmarried, unwed; abstinent, celibate
2 not marred or altered from a natural or
original state < a *virgin* forest >
syn unspoiled, untapped, untouched,
virginal
rel primeval, pristine; fresh, new; unmarried, unsullied

virginal *adj* 1 *syn* see VIRGIN 1
2 *syn* see VIRGIN 2

virginity *n* the quality or state of being a
virgin < lost her *virginity* >

syn ||cherry, maidenhead, maidenhood
rel chasteness, chastity, purity

virile *adj* 1 *syn* see POTENT 3
2 characterized by the energy and drive considered typical of a man or of men < developed a strong *virile* prose style >
syn male, manlike, manly, masculine
rel manful, mannish; decisive, driving, forceful; energetic, potent, robust; ultramasculine
con effeminate, womanish; emasculated, weak, weakened; impotent

virtual *adj* 1 *syn* see IMPLICIT 2
rel basic, essential, fundamental
ant actual

virtuality *n* *syn* see ESSENCE 2

virtually *adv* not absolutely or actually, yet so nearly so that the difference is negligible < that request is *virtually* an order >
syn in essence, morally, practically; *compare* ALMOST 2
rel basically, essentially, fundamentally; absolutely, actually
idiom for all practical purposes, in effect, in substance, to all intents and purposes

virtue *n* 1 *syn* see GOODNESS
rel fealty, fidelity, loyalty, piety; virtuousness
con dishonesty; disloyalty, infidelity; evil; immorality; depravity
ant vice
2 *syn* see EXCELLENCE
rel attribute, characteristic, feature, property; effectiveness, effectualness, efficacy; force, might, power, strength
3 *syn* see QUALITY 1
4 *syn* see QUALITY 2
5 *syn* see POWER 4

virtuosic *adj* *syn* see CONSUMMATE 1

virtuoso *n* 1 *syn* see EXPERT
2 *syn* see MUSICIAN

virtuous *adj* 1 *syn* see EFFECTIVE
ant virtueless
2 *syn* see MORAL 1
rel spotless, unsullied, untainted, untarnished; worthy
con dishonest; unjust; unworthy; impure, tainted; immodest, immoral, indecent; vicious, wicked
ant unvirtuous, virtueless
3 *syn* see GOOD 11
rel faultless, sinless
idiom innocent as a lamb, in the clear, without reproach
con bad, impure, unrighteous
ant unvirtuous, virtueless; vicious

virulent *adj* 1 *syn* see POISONOUS
rel malign, malignant
2 *syn* see BITTER 3
rel biting, cutting, scathing, sharp, stabbing; hateful, spiteful, unfriendly

virus *n* *syn* see POISON
rel corruption, taint

visage *n* 1 *syn* see FACE 1
2 *syn* see LOOK 2

vis-à-vis *n* 1 *syn* see OPPOSITE NUMBER
2 *syn* see TÊTE-À-TÊTE

vis-à-vis *prep* 1 *syn* see AGAINST 1
rel opposite
2 *syn* see VERSUS 2

viscera *n pl* *syn* see ENTRAILS

visceral *adj* 1 *syn* see INNER 2

2 *syn* see INSTINCTIVE 1

viscerous *adj* *syn* see INNER 2

viscid *adj* *syn* see VISCOUS
rel jellylike, slabby

viscose *adj* *syn* see VISCOUS
rel smeary

viscous *adj* having a glutinous adhesive consistency or quality < a *viscous* scum covered the surface of the platter >
syn tenacious, tough, viscid, viscose
rel ||slab, slimy, thick; glutinous, gummy, ropy, sticky; semifluid; stiff

visibility *n* the quality or state of being visible < very poor *visibility* due to fog >
syn visuality

visible *adj* *syn* see VISUAL 2
rel seen

vision *n* 1 *syn* see REVELATION
rel apparition, phenomenon, presence
2 *syn* see FANCY 4
rel muse
idiom phantom of the mind
3 *syn* see EYE 2

vision *vb* *syn* see THINK 1

visional *adj* *syn* see VISUAL 1

visionary *adj* 1 *syn* see DREAMY 1
rel abstracted, introspective, musing; impractical
idiom out of this world, up in the clouds
2 *syn* see IDEALISTIC
rel exalted, grandiose, lofty, noble, pretentious
ant pragmatic, pragmatical
3 *syn* see AMBITIOUS 2
rel radical

visionary *n* *syn* see DREAMER
ant pragmatist

visionless *adj* *syn* see BLIND 1

visit *vb* 1 *syn* see INFLICT 2
rel afflict, bother, pain, trouble; avenge, punish
idiom bring down upon
2 to make a social call upon < *visited* friends briefly in the evening >
syn call, come by, come over, drop (in *or* by), look in, look up, pop (in), run in, see, step in, stop (in *or* by)
3 to reside with temporarily as a guest < *visited* with friends in the country for a few weeks >
syn sojourn, stay, stop (over), tarry
rel frequent; reside
4 *syn* see CONVERSE

visit *n* 1 a coming to stay with another temporarily and usually briefly < pay a *visit* to friends >
syn call, visitation
2 *syn* see SOJOURN

visitant *n* *syn* see VISITOR 1

visitation *n* 1 *syn* see VISIT 1
2 *syn* see TRIAL 1
rel mischance; calamity, catastrophe, disaster

visitor *n* 1 one who visits another < there are *visitors* in the living room >
syn caller, guest, visitant; *compare* COMPANY 2
rel invitee
2 visitors *pl syn* see COMPANY 2

visor *n* 1 a projecting front brim on a cap or hat for shading the eyes < the *visor* kept out the sun >
syn bill, peak

rel eyeshade

2 *syn* see MASK 1

vista *n* an extensive or distant view <a long flat tree-lined *vista*>
syn lookout, outlook, perspective, prospect, scape
rel panorama, scene, sight, view; range, scope, survey
idiom long view

visual *adj* 1 of or relating to or used in vision <the *visual* sense>
syn ocular, optic, optical, visional

2 capable of being seen <*visual* objects>
syn ocular, seeable, viewable, visible
rel discernible, perceivable, perceptible

visuality *n syn* see VISIBILITY

visualize *vb* 1 *syn* see THINK 1
rel picture, view; objectify; call up, conjure (up)
idiom bring (or call) to mind, conjure up a mental image (or picture) of, see in the mind's eye

2 *syn* see FORESEE

vital *adj* 1 *syn* see LIVING 1
rel breathing

2 *syn* see VIGOROUS

3 *syn* see ESSENTIAL 2
rel indispensable, needed, needful, required, requisite; integral, prerequisite

vital force *n syn* see SOUL 1

vitality *n syn* see VIGOR 2
rel animation, life, liveliness, pulse; endurance, energy, spirit, vim

vitalize *vb* to arouse to activity, animation, or life <atomic energy is a force that can *vitalize* or destroy human civilization>
syn actify, activate, activize, energize
rel animate, enliven, invigorate, quicken, vivify; dynamize, excite, galvanize, provoke, stimulate; pep up, strengthen
idiom put life into
con eviscerate, weaken
ant atrophy; devitalize

vitalizing *adj syn* see INVIGORATING
ant devitalizing

vitally *adv syn* see VERY 1

vitiate *adj syn* see DEBASED
ant purified

vitiate *vb* 1 *syn* see INJURE 1
rel twist, warp

2 *syn* see DEBASE 1
rel defile, soil, sully, taint; prostitute; contaminate
idiom drive to the dogs
ant purify

3 *syn* see ABOLISH 1

vitiated *adj syn* see DEBASED
rel contaminated, defiled, polluted, tainted; impaired, injured, spoiled
ant purified

vitriolic *adj syn* see BITTER 3

vituperate *vb syn* see SCOLD 1
rel condemn, lambaste; asperse, calumniate, malign, traduce; bark (at), growl (at), yell (at); abuse, curse
idiom rip into
con applaud, commend, compliment; eulogize, extol, praise

vituperation *n syn* see ABUSE
rel blame, censure, revilement, scolding, tongue-lashing
con eulogy, extolment
ant acclaim, praise

vituperative *adj syn* see ABUSIVE
rel censorious, critical; severe; railing, scolding

vituperatory *adj syn* see ABUSIVE
rel censorious, critical; severe; railing, scolding

vituperous *adj syn* see ABUSIVE
rel censorious, critical; severe; railing, scolding

vivacious *adj* 1 *syn* see LIVELY 1
rel breezy, vibrant, zesty; frolicsome, playful, sportive
idiom gay as a lark
ant languid

2 *syn* see EXUBERANT 1

viva voce *adj syn* see VOCAL 1

vivid *adj* 1 *syn* see COLORFUL

2 *syn* see GRAPHIC 1
rel acute, intense, keen, sharp; dramatic, dramaturgic, theatrical; eloquent, expressive, meaningful, rich; animated, lively, spirited, vigorous

vivificate *vb syn* see QUICKEN 1
rel revive

vivify *vb syn* see QUICKEN 1
rel refresh, renew, restore; excite, galvanize
idiom give life to, imbue with life, put new life into

vivres *n pl syn* see FOOD 1

vixen *n syn* see VIRAGO

vizard *n syn* see MASK 1

‖**vlei** *n syn* see SWAMP

vocable *n syn* see WORD 2
rel verbalism

vocabulary *n* 1 the sum or set of words employed by a language, group, individual, or work or in relation to a subject <Latin contributes heavily to the *vocabulary* of English>
syn lexicon, word-hoard, word-stock
idiom stock of words

2 *syn* see TERMINOLOGY
rel phraseology

vocal *adj* 1 uttered by the voice or having to do with such utterance <the infant's primitive *vocal* sounds from which language develops>
syn articulate, oral, sonant, spoken, viva voce, voiced
rel intonated; expressed, uttered
con unexpressed, unuttered, unvoiced
ant nonvocal

2 *syn* see VOCALIC
ant consonantal

3 being able to express oneself clearly or easily <he was hardly *vocal*: he could scarcely express the simplest concepts>
syn articulate, eloquent, fluent, smooth-spoken
rel expressing, voicing; expressive; outspoken, stentorian, venting
con faltering, halting, hesitant, stumbling

4 *syn* see OUTSPOKEN

vocalic *adj* marked by, consisting of, or functioning as a vowel or vowels <*vocalic* and consonantal sounds>

---

syn vocal, vowel, vowely
rel vowellike

vocalism *n syn* see VOCALIZATION

vocalization *n* the exercise of the vocal organs in song or speech < his *vocalization* of a previously unstated thought >
syn articulation, utterance, uttering, vocalism; *compare* SPEECH 1
rel mouth, mouthing; sounding, voice, voicing; diction, enunciation, verbalization; speaking, speech

vocalize *vb* 1 *syn* see SPEAK 1
rel emit, let out; express; enunciate, pronounce; communicate, convey, impart
idiom execute vocally
2 *syn* see SING 1

vocation *n* 1 *syn* see TRADE 1
2 *syn* see MISSION

vocative *adj syn* see GLIB
rel chatty, garrulous, loquacious, talkative, windy; slick, smooth

vociferant *adj syn* see VOCIFEROUS

vociferate *vb syn* see CALL 1

vociferous *adj* so loud, noisy, and insistent as to compel attention < the crowd made *vociferous* protests against the speaker's statement >
syn blatant, boisterous, clamorous, ‖dinsome, loudmouthed, multivocal, obstreperous, openmouthed, strident, vociferant
rel distracting; loud, noisy, shrill
con close-lipped, reserved, silent, uncommunicative; noiseless, quiet, still

vogue *n syn* see FASHION 2
rel bon ton, fashionableness, stylishness

voice *n* 1 *syn* see EXPRESSION 1
rel speech
2 the right to express a wish, choice, or opinion or to influence a situation < even the youngest had a *voice* in planning the party >
syn say, say-so

voice *vb syn* see SPEAK 1
rel sound; articulate, enunciate, pronounce; formulate, phrase, present, put; recount, tell

voiced *adj syn* see VOCAL 1

voiceless *adj syn* see DUMB 1

void *adj* 1 *syn* see EMPTY 1
ant full
2 *syn* see DEVOID
rel scant, short, shy; bare, bereft, denuded, deprived
3 *syn* see NULL
rel negated

void *n syn* see HOLE 3

void *vb* 1 *syn* see VACATE 2
rel evacuate; deplete, drain, eliminate; eject, remove, throw out
2 *syn* see DISCHARGE 5

void *vb syn* see ANNUL 4
idiom declare (*or* make) null and void

voidness *n syn* see VACUITY 2
ant fullness

volage *adj syn* see GIDDY 1

volant *adj syn* see AGILE

volatile *adj* 1 *syn* see ELASTIC 2
rel capricious, fickle, inconstant, mercurial, unstable; flighty, flippant, frivolous, light-minded; changeable, protean, variable
2 *syn* see EXCITABLE
rel explosive

3 *syn* see INCONSTANT 1
4 *syn* see TRANSIENT

volatility *n syn* see LIGHTNESS
rel animation, sprightliness; inconstancy, instability, mercurialness; changeability, variability

volition *n syn* see WILL 2
rel choice, election, option, selection; desire, preference
con coercion, compulsion, duress, force

volley *n syn* see BARRAGE

volte-face *n syn* see REVERSAL 1

volte-face *vb syn* see TURN 6
rel about-face, face (about), right-about-face

voluble *adj syn* see GLIB

volume *n* 1 *syn* see BOOK 1
2 *syn* see BULK 1
rel amount, content, quantity
3 *syn* see BODY 4

voluminous *adj syn* see MANY

voluntary *adj* consisting of or proceeding from an exercise of free will < the law requires that a confession be *voluntary* >
syn deliberate, intentional, unforced, unprescribed, willful, willing, witting
rel chosen, elected, opted, volitional; autonomous, free, independent
con coerced, compelled, forced; unintentional, unplanned, unwilling, unwitting
ant involuntary

voluptuous *adj syn* see SENSUOUS
rel indulgent, self-gratifying; abandoned, dissipated, dissolute, excessive, wanton
con self-contained, self-denying
ant ascetic

vomit *vb* to discharge the contents of the stomach through the mouth < the churning seas made several passengers *vomit* >
syn barf, bring up, ‖cack, ‖cascade, ‖cast, ‖cat, disgorge, ‖heave, shoot, sick (up), spew, spit up, throw up, upchuck
rel gag, regurgitate, retch; keck; eject, expel
idiom ‖blow one's lunch, holler New York, lose one's cookies

voodoo *n* 1 *syn* see MAGICIAN 1
2 *syn* see JINX

voodoo *vb syn* see BEWITCH 1

voodooist *n syn* see MAGICIAN 1

voracious *adj* excessively greedy (as in appetite, reactions, or behavior) < the wolverine is an extremely *voracious* eater >
syn edacious, gluttonous, rapacious, ravening, ravenous
rel acquisitive, covetous, grasping, greedy; devouring, gorging, satiating, sating, surfeiting; avid, insatiable

vortex *n syn* see EDDY
rel spiral, spout

votary *n* 1 *syn* see ADDICT
rel disciple; freak
2 *syn* see AMATEUR 1
rel hound

vote *n* 1 *syn* see BALLOT 1
2 *syn* see SUFFRAGE

vote (in) *vb syn* see ELECT 2
rel choose, decide
idiom cast one's vote for

vouch *vb syn* see CERTIFY 1
rel support, uphold; confirm, corroborate, prove, substantiate, verify; assure, guarantee

vouchsafe *vb syn* see GRANT 1
  rel condescend, deign, stoop; accommodate, favor, oblige

vow *vb* to promise solemnly < *vowed* never to leave each other >
  syn covenant, pledge, plight, swear; *compare* PROMISE 1
  rel assert, declare, ‖swan; promise
  idiom give (*or* make) a solemn promise, give one's word of honor

vowel *adj syn* see VOCALIC

vowely *adj syn* see VOCALIC

voyage *n* a journey by water < took the new ship on a long *voyage* >
  syn cruise
  rel journey, tour, trip

voyeur *n syn* see PEEPING TOM

vulgar *adj* 1 *syn* see VERNACULAR
  rel conversational, spoken; idiomatic
  2 *syn* see PUBLIC 4
  3 *syn* see COARSE 3
  4 *syn* see OBSCENE 2
  rel base, low, vile; loathsome, offensive,

repulsive, revolting; indecorous, indelicate, uncouth
  con decent, delicate, refined; high-minded, lofty, noble
  5 *syn* see BARBARIC 1
  rel inelegant, ungraceful; improper, incorrect, unseemly; uncouth, unpolished, unrefined
  idiom in very poor taste
  con elegant, graceful; correct, proper, seemly

vulgarism *n syn* see BARBARISM

vulgate *adj syn* see VERNACULAR

vulgate *n syn* see VERNACULAR 3

vulnerability *n syn* see EXPOSURE
  rel vincibility

vulnerableness *n syn* see EXPOSURE
  rel weakness

vulnerary *adj syn* see CURATIVE

vulpine *adj syn* see SLY 2

vulture *vb syn* see STEAL 1

vulturine *adj syn* see RAPACIOUS 1

vulturish *adj syn* see RAPACIOUS 1

vulturous *adj syn* see RAPACIOUS 1

W

‖**wack** *n syn* see ECCENTRIC

wacky *adj* 1 *syn* see FOOLISH 2
  2 *syn* see INSANE 1

wad *n* 1 *syn* see LUMP 1
  2 *often* wads *pl syn* see SCAD
  3 *syn* see FORTUNE 4

wade (in *or* into) *vb syn* see PITCH IN 1

‖**waffle** *vb syn* see BABBLE 2

wag *vb* to move to and fro < the dog *wagged* his tail briskly >
  syn beat, lash, switch, waggle, wave, woggle
  rel shake, twitch, wiggle; oscillate; wigwag

wag *n* 1 a person full of sportive humor < a gay young *wag*, always full of fun >
  syn card, comedian, humorist, joker, zany
  rel clown, cutup, madcap, prankster, show-off; jester, kidder, quipster, wisecracker, wit
  idiom life of the party
  2 *syn* see ZANY 2
  3 *syn* see HUMORIST 1

wage *n, often* wages *pl* the price paid a person for his labor or services < high *wages* are often seen as a factor in inflation >
  syn emolument, fee, hire, pay, pay envelope, salary, stipend
  rel compensation, recompense, remuneration, reward; earnings, income, receipts, return(s), take

wager *n syn* see BET

wager *vb* 1 *syn* see VENTURE 1
  2 *syn* see GAMBLE 1

  idiom lay a wager

waggery *n* 1 *syn* see MISCHIEVOUSNESS
  2 *syn* see JOKE 1

waggish *adj syn* see PLAYFUL 1
  rel facetious, humorous, jocose, jocular, witty; comic, comical, droll, funny, laughable, ludicrous; arch, pert, saucy
  con earnest, grave, sedate, serious, sober, staid

waggishness *n syn* see MISCHIEVOUSNESS

waggle *vb syn* see WAG
  rel sway, waddle, wobble

wail *vb* 1 *syn* see CRY 2
  idiom make an outcry
  2 *syn* see HOWL 1
  3 *syn* see BAWL 2
  4 *syn* see COMPLAIN

wailful *adj syn* see MELANCHOLY 2

waistband *n syn* see BELT 1

wait *vb syn* see STAY 2
  rel anticipate, foresee; await, expect
  idiom bide one's time, cool one's heels, look forward to, mark time
  con depart, go, leave

wait (on) *vb syn* see MINISTER (to)

waive *vb* 1 *syn* see RELINQUISH
  rel allow, concede, grant
  con claim, demand, exact, require; assert, defend, maintain
  2 *syn* see DEFER

wake *vb* 1 to stop sleeping < she usually *woke* before dawn >
  syn awake, awaken, rouse, stir, waken
  rel arise, get up, roll out
  con catnap, doze, drowse, nap, nod, snooze; sleep, slumber
  2 *syn* see STIR 1
  rel freshen, renew
  con calm, ease, mollify, relax

waken *vb* 1 *syn* see STIR 1
  rel freshen, renew

---

syn synonym(s)   *rel* related word(s)
ant antonym(s)   *con* contrasted word(s)
idiom idiomatic equivalent(s)
‖ use limited; if in doubt, see a dictionary

con calm, ease, mollify, relax
2 *syn* see WAKE 1

wale *n syn* see WHEAL

walk *vb* 1 to advance on foot step by step
< often *walked* to work on pleasant
mornings >
syn ambulate, foot (it), hoof, pace, step,
traipse, tread, troop
rel circumambulate, perambulate, promenade, ramble, stroll; hike, tramp; lumber,
plod, slog, stride, stump, trudge; leg, race,
run
idiom beat one's feet, heel and toe it, ride
shanks' mare
con drive, ride
2 *syn* see TRAVERSE 5

walk *n* 1 a usually brief journey on foot
for pleasure or exercise < always took a
walk before breakfast >
syn constitutional, ramble, saunter, stroll,
turn
rel hike, march, tramp; deambulation,
parade, promenade; airing, stretch
2 *syn* see FIELD

walkabout *n syn* see TRAMP 3

walkaway *n syn* see RUNAWAY

walk out *vb syn* see STRIKE 1

walkover *n syn* see RUNAWAY

wall *n syn* see BAR 2

wall *vb syn* see ENCLOSE 1

wallop *n* 1 *syn* see BLOW 1
2 *syn* see IMPACT
3 *syn* see THRILL

wallop *vb* 1 *syn* see BEAT 1
2 *syn* see WHIP 2
3 *syn* see SLAM 1

walloping *adj syn* see HUGE

wallow *vb* 1 to roll or move in an indolent
and ungainly yet comfortable fashion
< hogs *wallowing* in a cool mudhole >
syn welter
rel flounder, roll, tumble; cuddle, nestle,
snuggle
2 to move or progress unsteadily and
clumsily as if beset by obstacles < *wal-
lowed* through the mire for miles trying to
get help >
syn blunder, flounder, lurch, stumble;
compare STUMBLE 3
rel reel, stagger, sway, totter, wamble,
welter
idiom make heavy weather (of)
3 to become deeply or excessively involved
in or with something subjectively felt as
pleasant < *wallowing* in luxury >
syn bask, indulge, luxuriate, revel, roll,
rollick, welter
rel baby, humor, pamper, spoil; appreciate, delight (in), enjoy, relish
con abstain, refrain; avoid, eschew, shun

waltz *vb syn* see BREEZE

‖**wambly** *adj syn* see SQUEAMISH 1

‖**wampum** *n syn* see MONEY

wan *adj* 1 *syn* see PALE 1
rel cadaverous, haggard, worn; blanched,
bleached, washed-out; anemic, bloodless
2 *syn* see WEAK 4

wander *vb* 1 to move about from place to
place more or less aimlessly and without
obvious plan < *wandering* through the
forest >
syn bat, circumambulate, drift, gad, gallivant, maunder, meander, mooch, ‖project,
ramble, range, roam, roll, rove, straggle,

stray, traipse, vagabond, vagabondize;
compare SAUNTER
rel amble, saunter, stroll; divagate, diverge; trail; boom, bum, tramp
2 *syn* see DIGRESS 2
3 *syn* see ERR

wanderer *n syn* see ROVER

wandering *adj* 1 *syn* see ITINERANT
2 *syn* see ERRATIC 1
3 *syn* see DELIRIOUS 1

wane *vb* 1 *syn* see ABATE 4
ant wax
2 *syn* see FAIL 3
ant wax

wangle *vb syn* see ENGINEER
rel outflank, outgeneral, outmaneuver,
overreach

waning *n syn* see FAILURE 4
ant waxing

wanky *adj syn* see WEAK 1

want *vb* 1 *syn* see LACK
idiom be found wanting, fall short, feel
the want of
2 *syn* see DESIRE 1
rel choose, prefer
idiom could do with, have a mind (*or* an
eye) to
3 to have as a duty or responsibility
< you *want* to behave yourself >
syn must, ought, should
rel become, befit, behoove; need (to)
idiom be wise to, had better (*or* best)

want *n* 1 *syn* see ABSENCE
rel exigency, necessity, need
con sufficiency
2 *syn* see POVERTY 1
rel exiguousness, meagerness, scantiness,
skimpiness; inadequacy, insufficiency
con riches
3 *syn* see REQUIREMENT 1

wanting *adj syn* see ABSENT 1
2 *syn* see SHORT 3
3 *syn* see DEFICIENT 1

wanting *prep syn* see WITHOUT 2

wanton *adj* 1 *syn* see FAST 7
rel lax, slack, wayward
idiom of easy virtue, of loose morals
con austere, puritanical, restrained, self=
restrained
ant chaste
2 *syn* see SUPEREROGATORY
rel malevolent, malicious, spiteful; contrary, perverse, wayward

wanton *n* a woman who engages in lewd
unseemly conduct < giddy *wantons* flaunting themselves in bars >
syn baggage, ‖bim, ‖bimbo, cyprian,
hussy, jade, jezebel, ‖pig, slattern, slut,
strumpet, tramp, trollop, trull, wench;
compare DOXY, HARLOT 1, PROSTITUTE
idiom loose woman

wanton *vb syn* see TRIFLE 1

wantwit *n syn* see DUNCE

war *vb syn* see CONTEND 1
rel attempt, endeavor, essay, strive, struggle; challenge, engage, take on
idiom draw the sword against, lift one's
hand against, take up the cudgels

warble *n syn* see MELODY

war chest *n syn* see TREASURY 2

war club *n syn* see CUDGEL

war cry *n syn* see BATTLE CRY

ward *n* 1 *syn* see GUARD 2

2 *syn* see DEFENSE 1

3 *syn* see CUSTODY

ward *vb* 1 to cause to miss an objective by or as if by turning aside < *warded* the stroke of his enemy's sword with his shield >
syn deflect, fend, parry
rel block, check, halt, stay, stymie; avert, divert, turn
idiom keep at arm's length, turn aside

2 *syn* see PREVENT 2
rel balk, foil, frustrate, thwart; check, interrupt
ant conduce (to)

ward (off) *vb syn* see FEND (off)
ant bring on

warden *n syn* see CUSTODIAN

ware *adj syn* see AWARE

warehouse *vb syn* see STOW
rel accommodate; guard, protect, shelter

wares *n pl syn* see MERCHANDISE

warfare *n syn* see CONTEST 1

warhorse *n syn* see COURSER

warlike *adj* 1 *syn* see BELLIGERENT
ant peaceable

2 *syn* see MARTIAL
rel battling, contending, fighting, warring
ant unwarlike

warlock *n syn* see MAGICIAN 1

warm *adj* 1 *syn* see ENTHUSIASTIC

2 *syn* see TENDER
rel ardent, fervent, passionate; affable, cordial, gracious; heartfelt, hearty, sincere, wholehearted
ant cool; austere

warmed–over *adj syn* see TRITE

warmhearted *adj syn* see TENDER
rel benign, benignant, kind, kindly, outgoing
con austere, cold, cool, frigid, frosty, severe, stern
ant coldhearted

warning *n syn* see DEFEAT 1

warmish *adj syn* see TEPID 1

warn *vb* 1 to let one know of approaching danger or risk < police and the weather service join to *warn* travelers of hazardous road conditions >
syn caution, forewarn
rel advise, alert, apprise, inform, notify, tip; counsel, direct, guide
idiom address a warning to, give warning, put a flea in one's ear, put one on guard

2 *syn* see INFORM 2

3 *syn* see COMMAND

warning *n* something and especially a statement that warns or is intended to warn < gave them *warning* that disobedience would lead to punishment >
syn admonition, caution, caveat, commonition, forewarning, monition
rel advice, counsel, guidance, recommendation; hint, suggestion, tip
idiom flea (or word) in the ear, word to the wise

warning *adj syn* see MONITORY

warp *vb* 1 *syn* see DEBASE 1
rel contort, crook, distort, twist

con disentangle, rectify, straighten, unkink

2 *syn* see DEFORM
rel bend, crook, kink, twist

3 *syn* see MISREPRESENT

war paint *n* 1 *syn* see FINERY

2 *syn* see MAKEUP 3

warped *adj syn* see BIASED 2
ant unwarped

warrant *n* 1 *syn* see PLEDGE 1

2 *syn* see BASIS 3

3 *syn* see WORD 8

warrant *vb* 1 *syn* see MAINTAIN 2
rel state; assure, ensure, insure

2 to give assurance of the worth of something especially in respect to quality, quantity, or condition < *warranted* the merchandise to be exactly as described in the catalog >
syn certify, guarantee, guaranty
rel assure, insure, secure; back, sponsor, stipulate; affirm, claim, state
idiom stand behind

3 *syn* see JUSTIFY 4
rel endorse; call (for), need, require

warrantable *adj syn* see JUSTIFIABLE
ant unwarrantable

warranty *n syn* see GUARANTEE 1

warrior *n syn* see SOLDIER

wary *adj* 1 *syn* see CAUTIOUS
rel distrustful, doubting, leery, suspicious; vigilant, watchful
idiom on one's guard
con careless, heedless, thoughtless; devil=may-care, reckless, venturesome
ant foolhardy; unwary

2 *syn* see SPARING

wash *vb* 1 *syn* see BATHE 1

2 *syn* see BATHE 2

3 *syn* see DRIFT 1

4 *syn* see SLOSH 1

washed–out *adj syn* see EFFETE 2

washed–up *adj* 1 *syn* see THROUGH 3

2 *syn* see THROUGH 4

wash out *vb* 1 *syn* see FAIL 4

2 *syn* see DISCARD

wash up *vb syn* see GO 4

washy *adj syn* see DILUTE

waspish *adj* 1 *syn* see IRRITABLE
rel contrary, impatient, perverse; malicious, sharp, spiteful; crabbed, cross=grained

2 *syn* see CANTANKEROUS

waspy *adj* 1 *syn* see IRRITABLE
rel contrary, impatient, perverse; malicious, sharp, spiteful; crabbed, cross=grained

2 *syn* see CANTANKEROUS

wassail *n* 1 *syn* see BINGE 1

2 *syn* see REVELRY 2

wassail *vb syn* see REVEL 1

waste *n* 1 an area of the earth unsuitable for cultivation or general habitation < the scattered dwellers of southern Africa's dry *wastes* >
syn badland, barren, desert, wasteland, wild, wilderness, wild land, wildness
rel brush, brushland, bush; jungle

2 *syn* see EXTRAVAGANCE 2

3 *syn* see REFUSE
rel rubble, rummage

waste *vb* 1 *syn* see RAVAGE
idiom reduce to a shambles

---

syn synonym(s)   *rel* related word(s)
ant antonym(s)   *con* contrasted word(s)
idiom idiomatic equivalent(s)

‖ use limited; if in doubt, see a dictionary

ant conserve

2 to spend or expend freely and usually foolishly or futilely < *wasted* his inheritance on women and gambling > < *waste* one's time on trifles >

syn blow, blunder (away), cast away, consume, dissipate, dribble (away), drivel, fool (away), fritter, frivol away, muddle (away), ||piss away, potter (away), prodigalize, riot (away), squander, throw away, trifle (away)

rel disburse, expend, spend; dispense, distribute; deplete, drain, exhaust, impoverish; dispel, disperse, scatter; misspend

idiom let slip through one's fingers, pour down the drain, throw good money after bad

ant save; conserve

waste (away) *vb syn* see FAIL 3

wasted *adj syn* see EMACIATED

rel meager; shriveled, withered, wizened

con healthy, robust; stalwart, stout, strong, sturdy

wastefulness *n syn* see EXTRAVAGANCE 2

ant frugality

wasteland *n syn* see WASTE 1

waster *n* 1 *syn* see SPENDTHRIFT

rel dissipater, fritterer; idler, loafer, lounger

2 *syn* see WASTREL 1

wastethrift *n syn* see SPENDTHRIFT

wastrel *n* 1 a worthless, self-indulgent, and reprehensible person < loafers and other *wastrels* lounging on the corner >

syn ||bad lot, good-for-nothing, ne'er-do-well, no-good, profligate, rounder, scapegrace, waster

rel lecher, libertine, rake, rip, roué; blackguard, black sheep, knave, rascal, rogue, scoundrel; rapscallion, scalawag, scamp

idiom sad case

2 *syn* see SPENDTHRIFT

rel dissipater, fritterer; idler, loafer, lounger

watch *vb* 1 *syn* see SEE 2

rel examine, follow, inspect, scan, scrutinize

idiom keep an eye on, keep tabs on

2 *syn* see EYE 2

3 *syn* see TEND 2

idiom keep watch over

4 *syn* see LOOK 1

watch *n* 1 *syn* see LOOKOUT 3

2 *syn* see GUARD 2

3 *syn* see EYE 3

watch and ward *n syn* see LOOKOUT 3

watchdog *n syn* see CUSTODIAN

watcher *n syn* see SPECTATOR

watchfire *n syn* see BEACON 1

watchful *adj* paying close attention usually with a view to anticipating approaching danger or opportunity < adopted a policy of *watchful* waiting >

syn alert, open-eyed, unsleeping, vigilant, wakeful, wide-awake

rel cautious, chary, circumspect, wary; prompt, quick, ready

idiom keeping one's eyes peeled (*or* open), on the watch (*or* lookout)

con careless, heedless, thoughtless; inadvertent; absentminded, abstracted, faraway

ant unwatchful

watchman *n syn* see GUARD 2

watch out *vb syn* see BEWARE

watchword *n* 1 *syn* see PASSWORD 1

2 *syn* see PASSWORD 3

3 *syn* see CATCHWORD

water *n* 1 *syn* see TEARS

2 *syn* see SALIVA

water *vb syn* see DROOL 1

water closet *n syn* see TOILET

watercourse *n syn* see CHANNEL 1

watered-down *adj syn* see DILUTE

waterfall *n* a precipitous descent of water or the site of this < heard the roar of the *waterfall* >

syn cascade, cataract, chute, fall(s), ||force, sault, spout

rel rapid(s), riffle, shoot; eddy, surge, vortex, whirlpool

watering hole *n* 1 *syn* see RESORT 2

2 *syn* see BAR 5

3 *syn* see NIGHTCLUB

watering place *n* 1 *syn* see SPA 1

2 *syn* see RESORT 3

3 *syn* see BAR 5

4 *syn* see NIGHTCLUB

waterish *adj* 1 *syn* see DILUTE

2 *syn* see PALE 2

3 *syn* see INSIPID 3

waterless *adj syn* see DRY 1

ant watered

waterlog *vb syn* see SOAK 1

watery *adj* 1 *syn* see DILUTE

2 *syn* see PALE 2

3 *syn* see INSIPID 3

wave *vb syn* see WAG

waver *vb syn* see HESITATE

rel palter, shift, trim; seesaw, teeter

idiom back and fill, hem and haw

wavering *n syn* see HESITATION

wavering *adj* 1 *syn* see VACILLATING 2

ant unwavering

2 *syn* see WEAK 2

wax *vb* 1 *syn* see INCREASE 2

ant wane

2 *syn* see BECOME 1

wax *n syn* see RISE 3

ant wane

waxen *adj syn* see PALE 1

waxy *adj syn* see ANGRY

way *n* 1 a public and unobstructed passage leading from one place to another < tracing the remains of an old lumberman's *way* >

syn artery, avenue, boulevard, ||drag, highway, path, road, street, thoroughfare, track

rel course, line, passage, route; alley, byway, lane, ride, row

2 that along which one passes in going from one place to another < his *way* led through wooded hills >

syn course, line, passage, path, road, route

3 *syn* see DOOR 2

4 *syn* see METHOD 1

rel custom, habit, habitude, practice, usage, use, wont

5 *syn* see STYLE 4

6 *syn* see HABIT 1

7 *syn* see DISTANCE 2

8 *syn* see TYPE

||**wayback** *n syn* see RUSTIC

wayfaring *adj syn* see ITINERANT

waylay *vb syn* see SURPRISE 1
  rel lurk, prowl, skulk, slink
  idiom lay wait for, lie in wait for
ways *n pl but sing in constr syn* see DIS-
  TANCE 2
wayward *adj* 1 *syn* see CONTRARY 3
  rel capricious, fickle, inconstant, unstable,
    variable
  con complaisant, good-natured
  2 *syn* see ARBITRARY 2
weak *adj* 1 lacking physical, mental, or
  moral strength <a *weak* spirit in a *weak*
  body>
  syn decrepit, feeble, flimsy, fragile, frail,
    infirm, insubstantial, puny, unsound, un-
    substantial, ||wanky, weakly
  rel debilitated, enfeebled, sickly, spindly,
    weakened; forceless, impotent, impuissant,
    powerless
  con stalwart, stout, sturdy, tenacious,
    tough; dynamic, energetic, forceful, vigor-
    ous
  ant strong
  2 deficient in stability <a love too *weak*
  to bear the trials of daily life>
  syn dickey, fluctuant, insecure, rootless,
    shaky, unstable, unsure, vacillating, wa-
    vering, wobbly; *compare* RICKETY
  rel hesitant, irresolute, trimming, uncer-
    tain; insubstantial, undependable, unreli-
    able
  con certain, secure, solid, stable, sure;
    dependable, reliable, substantial
  ant strong
  3 *syn* see IMPLAUSIBLE
  4 not equal to the requirements and demands of a situation <a *weak* executive>
  syn boneless, emasculate, forceless, impo-
    tent, inadequate, ineffective, ineffectual,
    invertebrate, slack-spined, spineless, wan
  rel unfit, unqualified, unsuitable; bun-
    gling, incompetent, inept
  con able, competent, effective, efficient;
    adequate, fit, qualified, satisfactory, suffi-
    cient, suitable; manly, masculine, virile
  ant strong
  5 *syn* see DILUTE
  ant strong
weaken *vb* 1 to lose or cause to lose
  strength, vigor, or energy <his hesitation
  weakened the force of his argument>
  syn attenuate, blunt, cripple, debilitate,
    disable, enfeeble, sap, unbrace, undermine,
    unstrengthen; *compare* PARALYZE 1
  rel emasculate, enervate, incapacitate,
    unman, unnerve; damage, impair, injure;
    lessen, minimize, reduce; dilute, thin
  con better, improve; activate, energize,
    invigorate, vitalize
  ant strengthen
  2 *syn* see FAIL 1
  3 *syn* see FAIL 3
  4 *syn* see DILUTE
weak-headed *adj syn* see SIMPLE 3
weak-kneed *adj syn* see VACILLATING 2
weakling *n* a person lacking in stamina
  and character <his speech deplored the
  characterless *weaklings* in critical posi-
  tions>

  syn baby, doormat, invertebrate, jellyfish,
    milksop, Milquetoast, ||molly, mollycod-
    dle, namby-pamby, pantywaist, sissy,
    sissy-pants (*or* sissy-britches), sop
  rel butt, mark, pushover, sucker; drip,
    mama's boy, misfit, mother's boy, sad
    sack, weak sister
  idiom shrinking violet
weakly *adv syn* see SOTTO VOCE
  ant strongly
weakly *adj syn* see WEAK 1
weak-minded *adj syn* see SIMPLE 3
weakness *n syn* see APPETITE 3
weal *n syn* see WHEAL
weald *n syn* see FOREST
wealth *n* 1 *syn* see MEAN 3
  2 one's worldly possessions <at that
  point his *wealth* consisted of the clothes
  he stood in and a solitary quarter>
  syn fortune, property, resources, riches,
    substance, worth
  rel assets, estate, goods, holdings, posses-
    sions
wealthy *adj syn* see RICH 1
  con impoverished, penniless, poor
  ant indigent
wean *vb syn* see ESTRANGE
  ant addict
wear *vb* 1 *syn* see ABRADE 1
  2 *syn* see TIRE 1
wear (away) *vb syn* see EAT 3
wear down *vb syn* see TIRE 1
wearied *adj syn* see TIRED 1
  ant refreshed; unwearied, unweary
weariful *adj syn* see ARID 2
weariless *adj syn* see INDEFATIGABLE
weariness *n syn* see FATIGUE
  2 *syn* see ARID 2
wear out *vb* 1 *syn* see EXHAUST 4
  ||2 *syn* see WHIP 1
weary *vb* 1 *syn* see TIRE 1
  rel debilitate, enfeeble, weaken; depress,
    oppress, weigh
  con animate, energize, vitalize; enliven,
    quicken, vivify
  ant refresh
  2 *syn* see BORE
weary *adj* 1 *syn* see TIRED 1
  ant refreshed, unwearied, unweary
  2 *syn* see FED UP
Weary Willie *n syn* see VAGABOND
weasel *n syn* see SNEAK
weasel *vb syn* see EQUIVOCATE 2
weathery *adj syn* see CHANGEABLE 1
weave *vb syn* see LURCH 2
web *n* 1 *syn* see TEXTURE 1
  2 something by which one is ensnared,
  held fast, or inextricably involved <di-
  plomacy caught in its own *web* of double-
  dealing>
  syn cobweb, entanglement, mesh(es),
    toil(s); *compare* ENTANGLEMENT 1
  rel complexity, complication; labyrinth,
    maze, morass, skein, snarl, tangle; em-
    broilment, enmeshment, ensnarement,
    entrapment, involvement
  idiom a tangled web
  3 *syn* see MAZE 1
wed *vb* 1 *syn* see MARRY 1
  2 *syn* see MARRY 2
  3 *syn* see JOIN 1
wedded *adj syn* see MATRIMONIAL
  con unwed, unwedded

---

syn synonym(s)   *rel* related word(s)
ant antonym(s)   *con* contrasted word(s)
idiom idiomatic equivalent(s)
|| use limited; if in doubt, see a dictionary

wedding n the marriage ceremony usually with its accompanying festivities <one of the most elaborate *weddings* of the social season>
syn bridal, espousal(s), marriage, nuptial(s), spousal

wedlock n *syn* see MARRIAGE 1

wee adj *syn* see TINY

weed n *syn* see MARIJUANA

weensy adj *syn* see TINY

weeny adj *syn* see TINY

weep vb 1 *syn* see DEPLORE 1
2 *syn* see EXUDE
3 *syn* see CRY 2
4 *syn* see DRIP

weeping adj *syn* see TEARFUL

weepy adj *syn* see TEARFUL

weigh vb 1 *syn* see CONSIDER 1
rel appraise, evaluate, rate
2 *syn* see BURDEN
3 to carry intellectual weight <this evidence *weighed* heavily against him>
syn count, militate, tell
rel import, matter, register, signify
idiom amount to some shucks, be something, carry weight, cut (some) ice
4 *syn* see MATTER

weigh down vb *syn* see DEPRESS 2
ant raise (one's spirits)

weight n 1 *syn* see LOAD 2
2 *syn* see IMPORTANCE
3 *syn* see INFLUENCE 1
rel effectiveness, efficacy; forcefulness, forcibleness, potency, powerfulness
4 *syn* see LOAD 3

weight vb 1 *syn* see ADULTERATE
rel burden, cumber, encumber; contaminate, corrupt, foul up, spoil
2 *syn* see BURDEN

weightiness n *syn* see IMPORTANCE

weightless adj *syn* see LIGHT 1
ant weighty

weighty adj 1 *syn* see IMPORTANT 1
2 *syn* see SERIOUS 1
3 *syn* see SERIOUS 2
4 *syn* see HEAVY 1
ant weightless
5 *syn* see FAT 2
6 *syn* see ONEROUS

weird n 1 *syn* see FATE
2 *syn* see PREDICTION

weird adj 1 fearfully and mysteriously strange or fantastic <shuddered at the *weird* unearthly glow that swept across the sky>
syn eerie, spooky, uncanny, unearthly
rel creepy, haunting, unnatural; preternatural, supernatural; supernal; curious, odd, peculiar, queer, strange; inscrutable, mysterious; awe-inspiring, awful, dreadful, fearful, horrific
con common, commonplace, everyday, quotidian; natural, normal, ordinary
2 *syn* see STRANGE 4

welcome adj *syn* see PLEASANT 1
rel congenial, cordial, genial, sympathetic; contenting, satisfying
ant unwelcome

welfare n a state of thriving and progress <parents who seek their children's *welfare*>
syn advantage, benefit, good, interest, prosperity, well-being

rel fortune, luck, success; contentment, felicity, happiness, satisfaction
ant illfare

welkin n *syn* see SKY

well n 1 wells pl *syn* see SPA 1
2 *syn* see SOURCE

well adv 1 in a good, proper, or acceptable manner <the children behaved very *well* at the party>
syn aright, befittingly, correctly, decently, decorously, fitly, fittingly, justly, nicely, properly, rightly
rel bearably, passably, tolerably, unobjectionably; considerately, pleasantly, thoughtfully, white; appropriately
con badly, improperly, objectionably, obnoxiously, outrageously
ant ill
2 in a pleasant, cooperative, or thoughtful manner <he speaks *well* of your new proposal>
syn considerately, generously, heedfully, kindly, thoughtfully
rel concernedly, interestedly; approvingly
con contemptuously, disdainfully, scornfully
3 to a full extent or degree <you are *well* aware of the problems we face>
syn à fond, altogether, clear, ‖cleverly, completely, entirely, fully, perfectly, ‖plumb, quite, right, roundly, ‖slam, ‖slap, thoroughly, utterly, wholly
rel certainly, obviously, surely, undoubtedly, unquestionably; sublimely
idiom all the way
con barely, hardly, scarcely
4 in an adequate or appropriate manner <any large box will answer our need very *well*>
syn acceptably, adequately, amply, appropriately, becomingly, fittingly, properly, right, satisfactorily, suitably
5 in a desirable or pleasing manner <everything went *well* on the trip>
syn favorably, fortunately, happily, prosperously, satisfyingly, successfully, swimmingly
rel comfortably, easily, smoothly
con amiss, wrong
ant badly
6 *syn* see EASILY 1
7 in all likelihood <the fighting may *well* continue for years>
syn doubtlessly, easily, indeed, really, truly, undoubtedly
rel conceivably, perhaps, possibly; likely, probably
8 to a considerable extent or degree <they landed *well* beyond the wharf>
syn considerably, far, quite, rather, significantly, somewhat
idiom by a long way, by a wide margin

well adj 1 *syn* see PROSPEROUS 3
2 *syn* see HEALTHY 1
ant ill, unwell
3 *syn* see LUCKY

well—behaved adj *syn* see GOOD 13

well—being n 1 *syn* see PROSPERITY 2
ant ill-being
2 *syn* see WELFARE
ant ill-being

well—bred adj *syn* see GENTEEL 1
ant ill-bred

well-conditioned *adj syn* see HEALTHY 1
well-developed *adj syn* see CURVACEOUS
well-disposed *adj syn* see SYMPATHETIC 2
   ant ill-disposed
well-favored *adj syn* see BEAUTIFUL
   ant ill-favored
well-fixed *adj syn* see PROSPEROUS 3
   ant badly off
well-founded *adj* having a firm foundation in fact or logic <offered *well-founded* arguments to support his position>
   syn cogent, good, just, justified, well-grounded
   rel sound, substantial, telling, valid; rational, reasonable, reasoned; fundamental, meaty, pithy
   con unjustified; insubstantial, invalid, unsound; irrational, unreasonable
well-groomed *adj* 1 *syn* see NEAT 2
   2 *syn* see DAPPER
well-grounded *adj syn* see WELL-FOUNDED
wellhead *n syn* see SOURCE
well-heeled *adj syn* see PROSPEROUS 3
   ant badly off
well-hung *adj syn* see GLIB
well-known *adj* much talked about <a *well-known* hospital>
   syn famous, leading, noted, notorious, popular, prominent; *compare* FAMOUS 2
   rel conspicuous, important, outstanding
   idiom on everyone's tongue
   con inconspicuous, obscure, unheard-of, unimportant, unnoted, unpopular
   ant unknown
well-liked *adj syn* see FAVORITE 2
well-liking *adj syn* see HEALTHY 1
well-mannered *adj syn* see CIVIL 2
   ant ill-mannered
well-nigh *adv* 1 *syn* see NEARLY
   2 *syn* see ALMOST 2
well-off *adj syn* see PROSPEROUS 3
   ant badly off
well over *vb syn* see OVERFLOW 2
well-paying *adj syn* see ADVANTAGEOUS 1
well-proportioned *adj syn* see SHAPELY
wellspring *n syn* see SOURCE
well-thought-of *adj syn* see RESPECTABLE 1
well-timed *adj syn* see TIMELY 1
   con premature, untimely; behindhand, late, tardy
   ant ill-timed
well-to-do *adj syn* see PROSPEROUS 3
   ant badly off
well-turned *adj syn* see SHAPELY
well-worn *adj syn* see TRITE
welsh *vb syn* see BACK DOWN
welt *n* 1 *syn* see WHEAL
   ‖2 *syn* see BLOW 1
weltanschauung *n syn* see IDEOLOGY
welter *vb* 1 *syn* see WALLOW 1
   rel strive, struggle; toss, tumble; writhe; grovel
   2 *syn* see WALLOW 3
welter *n syn* see WITHER

---

syn synonym(s)   *rel* related word(s)
ant antonym(s)   *con* contrasted word(s)
idiom idiomatic equivalent(s)
‖ use limited; if in doubt, see a dictionary

---

wench *n* 1 *syn* see GIRL 1
   2 *syn* see WANTON
wend *vb syn* see GO 1
western *n* a motion picture or radio or television play with its scene laid in the western U.S. and having cowboys as its main characters <young boys delighting in Saturday morning *westerns*>
   syn horse opera, oater
   rel shoot-'em-up
wet *vb* to make wet by or as if by saturating with water <they were *wet* thoroughly by the pouring rain>
   syn deluge, douse, drench, drown, soak, sop, souse; *compare* SOAK 1
   rel damp, dampen, moisten; humidify, humify; fill, impregnate, saturate; irrigate; lave, rinse, wash
   ant desiccate, dry
wet *adj* 1 containing or impregnated with liquid <change *wet* clothing for dry>
   syn drenched, dripping, madid, saturate, saturated, soaked, soaking, sodden, sopping, soppy, soused, wringing-wet
   rel soggy, water-logged; damp, dank, moist, wettish
   idiom dripping (*or* soaking *or* sopping) wet
   con bone-dry, dehydrated, desiccated, parched, sere, waterless
   ant dry
   2 *syn* see INTOXICATED 1
‖**wet** *n syn* see DRAM
wettish *adj syn* see DAMP
whack *vb syn* see STRIKE 2
whack *n* 1 *syn* see BLOW 1
   2 *syn* see FLING 1
whacking *adj syn* see HUGE
whacking *adv syn* see VERY 1
whale *n syn* see GIANT
whale *vb syn* see WHIP 1
whaling *adj syn* see HUGE
wham *n syn* see BANG 2
whammy *n syn* see JINX
whangdoodle *n syn* see NONSENSE 2
wharf *n* a structure used by boats and ships for taking on or landing cargo and passengers <brought the boat alongside the *wharf* and moored her>
   syn berth, dock, jetty, levee, pier, quay, slip
what-do-you-call-it *n* a thing or person that the speaker cannot (as from not knowing or from forgetting) name <hand me one of those little *what-do-you-call-its*> <went to *what-do-you-call-her's* house last week>
   syn what-is-it, whatsis, what's its name, what-you-call-it, whatyoumayjigger; *compare* DOODAD, GADGET 1
what-is-it *n syn* see WHAT-DO-YOU-CALL-IT
whatnot *n syn* see KNICKKNACK
whatsis *n syn* see WHAT-DO-YOU-CALL-IT
what's its name *n syn* see WHAT-DO-YOU-CALL-IT
what-you-call-it *n syn* see WHAT-DO-YOU-CALL-IT
what-you-may-call-it *n syn* see WHAT-DO-YOU-CALL-IT
whatyoumayjigger *n syn* see WHAT-DO-YOU-CALL-IT

wheal *n* a ridge raised on the skin by or as if by a stroke of a lash <the convict's back was covered with *wheals* and old scars>
  syn wale, weal, welt, whelk, ‖whelp
  rel strake, streak, stripe

wheedle *vb syn* see COAX

wheel *n* 1 *syn* see CYCLE 1
  2 *syn* see REVOLUTION 1
  3 *syn* see LEAGUE 4

wheel *vb* 1 *syn* see REEL 2
  2 *syn* see DRIVE 5
  3 *syn* see TURN 6

wheeze *vb syn* see HISS

wheeze *n syn* see PRANK

whelk *n syn* see WHEAL

whelm *vb* 1 *syn* see DELUGE 1
  2 *syn* see DELUGE 3
  3 *syn* see OVERWHELM 4

‖whelp *n syn* see WHEAL

when *adv syn* see THEN 1

when *conj syn* see THOUGH

whence *n syn* see SOURCE

where *adv* 1 *syn* see WHEREVER
  2 *syn* see WHITHER 1

where *n syn* see PLACE 1

whereabouts *adv syn* see WHITHER 1
  con hereabouts, thereabouts

whereas *conj* 1 *syn* see BECAUSE
  2 *syn* see THOUGH

‖whereaway *adv syn* see WHITHER 1

wherefore *n syn* see REASON 3

whereto *adv syn* see WHITHER 2

whereunto *adv syn* see WHITHER 2

wherever *adv* at, in, or to any or every place in or to which <he goes *wherever* he is needed>
  syn everywhere, where
  con here, there

‖wherret *vb syn* see SLAP 1

‖wherret *vb syn* see WORRY 1

whet *vb* 1 *syn* see SHARPEN
  2 *syn* see STIR 1

whet *n* ‖1 *syn* see WHILE 1
  2 *syn* see APPETIZER

whether or no *adv syn* see WILLY-NILLY

whetted *adj syn* see SHARP 1

whicker *vb syn* see NEIGH

whiff *n syn* see HINT 2

whiffet *n syn* see NONENTITY

whiffle *vb syn* see HESITATE

whiffling *adj syn* see VACILLATING 2

whiffy *adj syn* see MALODOROUS 1

whigmaleerie *n* 1 *syn* see CAPRICE
  2 *syn* see KNICKKNACK

while *n* a somewhat indefinite period of time <sat down to rest for a *while*>
  syn bit, space, spell, stretch, time, ‖whet
  2 *syn* see OCCASION 5
  3 *syn* see EFFORT 1

while *conj syn* see THOUGH

while *vb* to pass time and especially leisure time without boredom or in pleasant ways <*whiled* odd hours away in dreaming>
  syn beguile, fleet, wile
  rel amuse, divert, entertain; brighten, enliven, lighten

while (away) *vb syn* see SPEND 3

whilom *adj syn* see FORMER 2

whim *n syn* see CAPRICE
  rel idea; disposition, inclination, thought; dream, fantasy, vision

whimper *vb* to cry feebly and often plaintively or peevishly <a baby *whimpering* in its sleep>
  syn pule, whine; *compare* CRY 2

whimsical *adj* 1 *syn* see ARBITRARY 1
  2 *syn* see UNCERTAIN 1

whimsied *adj syn* see ARBITRARY 1

whimsy *n syn* see CAPRICE
  rel idea; disposition, inclination, thought; dream, fantasy, vision

whim-whams *n pl syn* see JITTERS

whine *vb* 1 *syn* see WHIMPER
  2 *syn* see COMPLAIN

‖whinner *vb syn* see NEIGH

whinny *vb syn* see NEIGH

whiny *adj syn* see IRRITABLE

whip *vb* 1 to strike repeatedly with or as if with a lash or rod <*whip* a dog for stealing from the table>
  syn flagellate, flog, hide, ‖larrup, lash, lather, scourge, stripe, thrash, ‖wear out, whale, ‖yerk
  rel beat, belabor, drub, wallop; bastinado, birch, bludgeon, cane, cudgel, quirt, switch
  2 to defeat utterly <*whipped* their traditional rival by a score of 40 to 7>
  syn beat, blast, ‖bowl (down *or* out), ‖clean up (on), ‖clobber, ‖cream, curry, drub, dust, lambaste, ‖larrup, lick, mop (up), overrun, overwhelm, rout, shellac, skunk, smear, smother, steamroller, thrash, trim, trounce, upend, wallop, whomp; *compare* CONQUER 1, DEFEAT 2
  rel conquer, defeat, overcome, subdue, vanquish
  idiom cook one's goose, deal a crushing defeat, settle one's hash, snow one under
  3 to agitate with an instrument so as to stiffen and increase the bulk of by incorporation of air <*whip* cream for a shortcake>
  syn beat, whisk
  4 *syn* see TURN 5

whip (up) *vb syn* see INCITE
  ant calm (down)

whip hand *n syn* see BETTER 2

whippersnapper *n syn* see NONENTITY

whipping boy *n syn* see SCAPEGOAT

whippy *adj syn* see ELASTIC 1

whipster *n syn* see NONENTITY

whirl *vb* 1 *syn* see SPIN 1
  2 *syn* see SWIRL
  3 *syn* see TURN 6
  4 *syn* see HURRY 2
  5 *syn* see SPIN 2

whirl *n* 1 *syn* see REVOLUTION 1
  2 *syn* see EDDY
  3 *syn* see COMMOTION 4
  4 *syn* see STIR 1
  5 *syn* see FLING 1

whirlblast *n syn* see WHIRLWIND 1

whirligig *vb syn* see SPIN 1

whirlpool *n* 1 *syn* see EDDY
  2 *syn* see STIR 1

whirlpool *vb syn* see SWIRL

‖whirlpuff *n syn* see WHIRLWIND 1

whirlwind *n* 1 a rotating windstorm of limited extent that is often accompanied by a column of dust or vapor <*whirlwinds* moved across the plowed land>
  syn whirlblast, ‖whirlpuff, whirly; *compare* HURRICANE, TORNADO

rel dust devil, rainspout, sand column, sand spout, waterspout
2 *syn* see STIR 1

whirly *n syn* see WHIRLWIND 1

whish *vb* 1 *syn* see HISS
2 *syn* see HURRY 2

whisk *vb* 1 *syn* see HURRY 2
2 *syn* see WHIP 3

whisker *n syn* see HAIR

whiskered *adj* 1 *syn* see BEARDED
2 *syn* see HAIRY 1

whiskers *n pl syn* see BEARD

whisper *vb* 1 *syn* see HISS
2 *syn* see CONFIDE 1

whisper *n* 1 *syn* see MURMUR 1
2 *syn* see HINT 1

whispering *n syn* see REPORT 1

whist *adj syn* see STILL 3

whistle–stop *n syn* see BURG

whit *n syn* see PARTICLE

white *adj syn* see FAVORABLE 5
ant black

white *n syn* see REACTIONARY
ant red

white *vb* 1 *syn* see WHITEN 1
2 *syn* see PALLIATE

whited sepulcher *n syn* see HYPOCRITE

white–haired *adj syn* see FAVORITE 1

white–headed *adj syn* see FAVORITE 1

white–hot *adj* 1 *syn* see HOT 1
2 *syn* see IMPASSIONED

white lightning *n syn* see MOONSHINE 2

white–livered *adj syn* see COWARDLY

whiten *vb* 1 to free from color and make white or whiter < *whiten* linen in the sun >
syn blanch, bleach, blench, decolor, decolorize, white
rel dim, dull, fade, lighten, pale; etiolate; frost, grizzle, silver
con color, darken
ant blacken
2 *syn* see PALLIATE

white plague *n syn* see TUBERCULOSIS

whitewash *vb syn* see PALLIATE

whither *adv* 1 to what place < *whither* did they go? >
syn where, whereabouts, ‖whereaway
2 to what point, conclusion, or end < *whither* is our nation drifting? >
syn whereto, whereunto

whiz *vb* 1 *syn* see HISS
2 *syn* see HURRY 2

whiz *n syn* see EXPERT
ant dub, dud, duffer

whiz–bang *adj syn* see EXCELLENT

whizzer *n syn* see TRICK 1

whole *adj* 1 free from damage, defect, or flaw < feared the eggs were broken but found them *whole* >
syn entire, flawless, good, intact, perfect, sound, unblemished, unbroken, undamaged, unhurt, unimpaired, uninjured, unmarred, untouched
rel complete, plenary; healthy, well
con broken, damaged, defective, impaired, injured, marred
2 *syn* see HEALTHY 1

---

3 lacking nothing that properly belongs to it < the effect of the *whole* mural >
syn choate, complete, entire, full, integral, perfect
rel orbicular, rounded, well-rounded
ant partial

4 including every constituent element or individual < the *whole* community rose to his defense >
syn all, complete, entire, gross, outright, total
ant partial

5 not scattered or dispersed < gave the matter his *whole* attention >
syn concentrated, exclusive, fixed, undistracted, undivided, unswerving

whole *n* 1 the total supply or amount < the *whole* of our creative literature >
syn aggregate, all, be-all and end-all, entirety, gross, sum, sum total, tale, total, totality, ‖tote
rel amount, supply; result, resultant, summation; bulk, mass, quantity, quantum
con detail, division, fraction, fragment, portion, section, segment, share
ant part

2 an organized array of parts or elements forming or functioning as a unit < stars, planets, galaxies — all but parts of one stupendous *whole*, the universe >
syn entity, integral, integrate, sum, system, totality; *compare* SYSTEM 1
rel being, organism, organization; coherence, cohesion, linkage; unity
con accumulation, aggregation, heap, pile, mass; section, segment; selection
ant part; agglomeration

wholehearted *adj* 1 *syn* see SURE 2
2 *syn* see SINCERE 1
rel ardent, fervent, impassioned, passionate; earnest, serious; authentic, bona fide, genuine

whole–hog *adj syn* see EXHAUSTIVE

whole–length *adj syn* see UNABRIDGED

wholeness *n* 1 *syn* see HEALTH
rel integrity; heartiness, robustness, vigor
2 *syn* see ENTIRETY 1
3 *syn* see INTEGRITY 2

whole number *n syn* see NUMBER

wholesale *adj syn* see INDISCRIMINATE 1

wholesome *adj* 1 *syn* see HEALTHFUL
ant noxious; unwholesome
2 *syn* see CURATIVE
3 *syn* see HEALTHY 1
4 *syn* see SAFE 3
ant noxious

whole–souled *adj syn* see SINCERE 1
rel ardent, fervent, impassioned; earnest, intense, serious

wholly *adv* 1 *syn* see WELL 3
2 *syn* see ALL 1

whomp *vb syn* see WHIP 2

whoop *vb syn* see SHOUT 1

whoop *n syn* see PARTICLE

whoop–de–do *n syn* see REVELRY 2

whoopee *n* 1 *syn* see REVELRY 2
2 *syn* see MERRYMAKING

whoopla *n* 1 *syn* see COMMOTION 4
2 *syn* see REVELRY 2

whoop–up *n syn* see REVELRY 2

whoosh *vb syn* see HISS

whop *vb syn* see BEAT 1

---

syn synonym(s)   *rel* related word(s)
ant antonym(s)   *con* contrasted word(s)
idiom idiomatic equivalent(s)
‖ use limited; if in doubt, see a dictionary

whop n syn see BLOW 1

whopping adj syn see HUGE

whopping adv syn see VERY 1

whore n 1 syn see HARLOT 1

2 syn see PROSTITUTE

whoredom n syn see PROSTITUTION

whorehouse n syn see BROTHEL

whoreson n syn see BASTARD 1

whorish adj syn see FAST 7

whorl vb syn see SWIRL

who's who n syn see ARISTOCRACY

why n 1 syn see REASON 3

2 syn see MYSTERY

whyfor n syn see REASON 3

wicked adj 1 syn see WRONG 1

ant upright

2 syn see PLAYFUL 1

3 syn see RISQUÉ

4 syn see MALICIOUS

5 syn see DANGEROUS 1

6 syn see TROUBLESOME

7 syn see OUTRAGEOUS 1

8 syn see SKILLFUL 1

9 syn see ABLE

wickedness n 1 syn see EVIL 2

2 syn see VICE 1

wide adj 1 syn see SPACIOUS

2 syn see EXTENSIVE 1

3 syn see LIBERAL 3

wide-awake adj syn see WATCHFUL

rel alive, awake, aware, conscious, sensible

widen vb syn see BROADEN

wideness n syn see BREADTH 2

widespread adj syn see PREVAILING

widget n syn see GADGET 1

width n syn see RANGE 2

wield vb 1 syn see HANDLE 2

rel conduct, control

2 syn see EXERT

wieldy adj syn see STRONG 1

wiener n syn see FRANKFURTER

wienerwurst n syn see FRANKFURTER

‖**wienie** n syn see FRANKFURTER

wife n the female partner in a marriage < wives unwilling to share responsibility >

syn ‖ball and chain, lady, ‖little woman, ‖missus, Mrs., ‖old lady, ‖old woman, ‖rib, ‖squaw, woman

rel consort, helpmate, helpmeet, mate, other half, spouse; bride, dowager, matron; concubine

idiom better half

con maid, maiden; widow

wig n syn see REBUKE

wig n syn see SCOLD 1

wiggle vb syn see WRIGGLE

wiggle-waggle adj syn see VACILLATING 2

wiggle-waggle vb syn see HESITATE

wiggy adj syn see POMPOUS 1

wight n syn see HUMAN

wild adj 1 living and growing in a state of nature and without human intervention < lived on wild plants and game animals >

syn agrarian, agrestal, native, natural, uncultivated, undomesticated; compare SAVAGE 1

rel escaped, feral; unsubdued, untamed

ant cultivated, domesticated

2 syn see SAVAGE 1

ant tame, tamed

3 syn see IRRESPONSIBLE

rel adventurous, audacious, daring, dashing; brash, cocksure, rash

4 syn see FURIOUS 2

rel bewildered, distracted, perplexed; agitated, perturbed, upset; addled, confused, muddled; crazy, demented, deranged, mad

con easy, relaxed

5 syn see UNRULY 1

6 marked by turmoil and fury especially of natural elements < a wild night of howling winds and driving snow >

syn blustering, blustery, ‖coarse, dirty, furious, raging, rough, stormful, stormy, tempestuous, turbulent

rel blatant, boisterous, clamorous, ungovernable, unruly; brutal, harsh, severe

con calm, peaceful, placid, quiet, stormless; halcyon, irenic, serene

7 given to unrestrained self-indulgence and pursuit of pleasure < her son got in with a wild bunch and took to drink >

syn devil-may-care, fast, gay, raffish, rakehell, rakish, sporty

rel boisterous, roisterous, rollicking, swaggering; careless, heedless, irresponsible, thoughtless; lewd, loose, unchaste, wanton

con moderate, restrained, sober, sparing, temperate; bridled, controlled, curbed; self-controlled

8 syn see EXTRAVAGANT 1

9 syn see BARBARIAN 1

ant cultivated, cultured

10 syn see BARBARIC 1

wild n syn see WASTE 1

wilderness n syn see WASTE 1

rel backcountry, backland(s), hinterland

idiom back of beyond

wild land n syn see WASTE 1

wildly adv syn see HARD 2

wildness n syn see WASTE 1

wile n syn see TRICK 1

rel chicane, chicanery, trickery; cunning, deceit, dissimulation, guile

con candor, frankness, openness, plain dealing, straightforwardness, unconstraint; artlessness, naturalness, sincerity

wile vb 1 syn see ATTRACT 1

2 syn see WHILE

wiliness n syn see CUNNING 2

will vb to be inclined < you may decide whichever way you will >

syn choose, elect, like, please, wish

rel crave, desire, want

idiom have a mind to, see (or think) fit

will n 1 a desire to act in a particular way or have a particular thing < I've no will to be sociable tonight >

syn fancy, inclination, liking, mind, pleasure, velleity

rel appetite, desire, passion, urge; hankering, longing, pining, yearning

idiom heart's desire

con aversion, dislike, distaste, repugnance, repulsion, revulsion

2 the aspect of mind involved in choosing or deciding < problems arise when one's will and judgment come in conflict >

syn volition

rel design, intent, purpose, wishes; character, disposition, temper

3 power of controlling one's actions, impulses, or emotions <a self-indulgent man of feeble character and little *will* >
syn discipline, self-command, self-control, self-discipline, self-government, self-mastery, self-restraint, willpower
rel aplomb, assurance, confidence, poise, self-possession; control, discretion, restraint
con gratification, indulgence, self-indulgence

will *vb* to give to another by will < *will* family treasures to a relative >
syn bequeath, devise, leave, legate

willful *adj* 1 *syn* see OBSTINATE
rel contumacious, factious
idiom having the bit in one's teeth, not yielding an inch
con amenable, docile, obedient, tractable
ant biddable

2 *syn* see VOLUNTARY
rel intentional, purposive; decided, determined, resolved; dogged, obstinate, pertinacious, stubborn
con accidental, chance, involuntary, unintentional, unplanned

willies *n pl syn* see JITTERS

willing *adj* 1 prepared in mind or by disposition < *willing* to help >
syn disposed, fair, inclined, minded, predisposed, prone, ready
rel agreeable, compliant, favorable; forward, game, prompt
idiom in the mood
con averse, disinclined, indisposed, loath, reluctant, unminded
ant unwilling

2 *syn* see VOLUNTARY
rel disposed, inclined, predisposed; open, prone

will—less *adj syn* see SPONTANEOUS

willpower *n syn* see WILL 3

willy—nilly *adv* surely and without regard to plans or inclination <it seems that we must drift *willy-nilly* toward disaster >
syn helplessly, inescapably, inevitably, perforce, unavoidably, whether or no
idiom as a matter of course, come what may, of necessity, without let or choice

‖**willy—nilly** *n syn* see HURRICANE

wilt *vb* 1 *syn* see WITHER
2 *syn* see COLLAPSE 2
3 *syn* see DROOP 3

wily *adj syn* see SLY 2
rel sagacious, shrewd; clever, knowing
con aboveboard, forthright, straightforward; guileless, open, trusting

win *vb* 1 to gain the victory <the home team *won* by a wide margin >
syn beat, overcome, prevail, triumph; *compare* CONQUER 1
idiom bear off the palm (*or* prize), bring home the bacon, carry the day, come out first (*or* ahead), finish in front
ant lose

2 *syn* see GAIN 1
3 *syn* see EARN 1
rel produce, yield

---

syn synonym(s)   **rel** related word(s)
ant antonym(s)   **con** contrasted word(s)
idiom idiomatic equivalent(s)
‖ use limited; if in doubt, see a dictionary

---

4 *syn* see GET 1
ant lose

win (over) *vb* 1 *syn* see DISARM 2
2 *syn* see INDUCE 1

win *n syn* see VICTORY 1

wince *vb syn* see RECOIL
rel dodge, duck, jib, sheer, swerve, turn; cower, cringe

wind *n* 1 *syn* see NOTHING 1
2 *syn* see HINT 1

wind *vb syn* see BLOW 1

wind *vb* 1 *syn* see DEFORM
2 to follow a circular, spiral, or writhing course <the vine *wound* its way up the pillar >
syn coil, corkscrew, curl, entwine, spiral, twine, twist, wreathe; *compare* CURVE
rel bend, curve, meander, weave; circle, encircle, enlace, gird, girdle, surround; enclose, envelop

windbaggery *n syn* see NONSENSE 2

windiness *n syn* see VERBOSITY

winding *adj* curving repeatedly first one way then another <a *winding* country road >
syn anfractuous, convoluted, flexuous, meandering, meandrous, serpentine, sinuous, snaky, tortuous; *compare* CROOKED 1
rel bending, curving, twisting; crooked, devious; circuitous, indirect, roundabout
con direct, straight

window dressing *n syn* see MASK 2

windrow *n syn* see PILE 1

wind up *vb* 1 *syn* see CLOSE 3
2 *syn* see SETTLE 7

windup *n syn* see FINALE

windy *adj* 1 marked by more wind than usual <a *windy* March day >
syn airy, blowy, breezy, gusty
rel brisk, fresh; drafty
con breathless, motionless, still
ant windless

2 *syn* see INFLATED
3 *syn* see WORDY

wing *n syn* see ANNEX
rel expansion, prolongation; bulge, projection, protrusion, protuberance

wing *vb syn* see FLY 4

wink *vb* to close and open the eyelids quickly < *winking* involuntarily as the light struck his eyes >
syn bat, blink, nictate, nictitate, twinkle
rel squinch, squinny, squint; flutter

wink (at) *vb syn* see CONNIVE 1

wink *n* 1 *syn* see INSTANT 1
2 *syn* see HINT 1

winker *n syn* see EYE 1

winner *n syn* see VICTOR 2
ant loser

winning *adj syn* see SWEET 1

winnow *vb* 1 *syn* see BLOW 1
2 *syn* see SORT 2

winsome *adj syn* see SWEET 1
rel adorable, lovable, lovesome

wipe (out) *vb* 1 *syn* see ERASE
2 *syn* see ANNIHILATE 1
3 *syn* see SLAUGHTER 3

wipe *n* 1 *syn* see HIT 1
‖2 *syn* see HANDKERCHIEF

‖**wiped out** *adj syn* see DRUGGED

‖**wiper** *n syn* see HANDKERCHIEF

‖**wire** *n syn* see PICKPOCKET

wiredraw *vb syn* see THIN 1

wiry *adj syn* see MUSCULAR 1

wisdom *n* 1 *syn* see KNOWLEDGE 2

2 *syn* see SAGACITY

3 *syn* see SENSE 6

rel judiciousness, sageness, saneness, sapience; perspicacity, sagacity, shrewdness

ant folly

wise *n syn* see METHOD 1

wise *adj* 1 having or exhibiting a capacity for discernment and the intelligent application of knowledge <to be *wise* is to use knowledge well>

syn discerning, gnostic, insighted, insightful, knowing, knowledgeable, perceptive, sagacious, sage, sophic, wisehearted

rel aware, grasping, intuitive, sensing; acute, keen, perspicacious; cogitative, contemplative, reflective, thoughtful; astute, sharp, shrewd

con dull, obtuse, slow, slow-witted; insensitive, unaware, unknowing

ant unwise

2 exercising or involving sound judgment < *wise* management of scarce resources>

syn judgmatic, judicious, prudent, sage, sane, sapient, sensible; *compare* SHREWD

rel canny, discreet, foresighted, provident; astute, perspicacious, sagacious, shrewd; alert, bright, intelligent, keen, smart

con careless, heedless, injudicious; improvident, imprudent, indiscreet, shortsighted

ant foolish, unwise

3 *syn* see EXPEDIENT

4 shrewdly aware and subtly resourceful <a *wise* operator with his eye always on the main chance>

syn canny, hep, knowing, nimble-witted, quick, quick-witted, sharp, sharp-witted, slick, smart; *compare* INTELLIGENT 2, SHREWD

rel cagey, foresighted, shrewd; artful, crafty, cunning, slippery, smooth, tricky, wily; steel-trap

idiom in the groove, not born yesterday, on the beam

con narrow, prim, puritanical, straitlaced; conservative, plodding, ‖square

5 presumptuously confident and self-assured <a bunch of. *wise* kids tearing up the neighborhood>

syn ‖biggety, bold, bold-faced, cheeky, forward, fresh, impudent, nervy, pert, procacious, sassy, smart, smart-alecky

rel arrogant, brash, cocky, insolent; flip, flippant, impertinent, lippy, saucy

con demure, mannerly, modest, proper; dull, priggish, stuffy

wise (up) *vb syn* see INFORM 2

wiseacre *n syn* see SMART ALECK

wisecrack *n syn* see JOKE 1

wisecracker *n syn* see SMART ALECK

wise guy *n syn* see SMART ALECK

wisehead *n syn* see SMART ALECK

wisehearted *adj syn* see WISE 1

wise man *n syn* see SAGE

wisenheimer *n syn* see SMART ALECK

wish *vb* 1 *syn* see DESIRE 1

rel expect, hope; fancy

2 *syn* see WILL

3 *syn* see IMPOSE 4

wishy-washy *adj* 1 *syn* see INSIPID 3

rel enervated, languid, listless, spiritless; flavorless, savorless

idiom neither flesh, fowl, nor good red herring, neither one thing nor the other

2 *syn* see CHARACTERLESS

wistful *adj syn* see PENSIVE 2

‖**wit** *vb syn* see UNDERSTAND 3

wit *n* 1 *syn* see MIND 1

rel perspicacity, sagacity; apprehension, awareness, comprehension

2 *often* wits *pl* mental soundness and health <frightened nearly out of her *wits*>

syn lucidity, ‖marbles, mind, reason, saneness, sanity, sense(s), soundness

rel balance, rationality

con aberration; craziness, derangement, insanity, lunacy, madness, mania

ant witlessness

3 acuteness of perception or judgment <had the *wit* to know that he was out of his depth in such a discussion>

syn acumen, astucity, astuteness, clearsightedness, discernment, discrimination, keenness, penetration, percipience, perspicacity, shrewdness; *compare* PRUDENCE 1

rel awareness, comprehension, grasp, insight, perception, understanding; prudence, sagaciousness, sagacity, sageness, sapience, wisdom; clairvoyance, divination, ESP, sensing

con aridity, dullness, prosaicness, unimaginativeness, fatuity, foolishness, inanity, silliness, stupidity

4 *syn* see INTELLIGENCE 1

5 a talent for banter or persiflage <a jolly man, noted for his kindly *wit*>

syn esprit, humor

rel alertness, keenness, quick-wittedness; brilliance, cleverness, intelligence, smartness

6 *syn* see HUMOR 5

7 *syn* see HUMORIST 2

witch *n* 1 a woman who practices the black arts <ancient laws against *witches*>

syn bruja, enchantress, hag, hex, lamia, sorceress, witchwoman; *compare* MAGICIAN 1

2 *syn* see HAG 2

witch *vb syn* see BEWITCH 1

witchcraft *n* 1 *syn* see MAGIC 1

2 *syn* see CHARM 3

witchery *n* 1 *syn* see MAGIC 1

2 *syn* see CHARM 3

witching *n syn* see MAGIC 1

witchwoman *n syn* see WITCH 1

witchy *adj syn* see MAGIC

with *prep* 1 *syn* see OVER 3

2 *syn* see FOR 2

3 *syn* see VIA 2

withal *adv* 1 *syn* see ALSO 2

2 *syn* see HOWEVER

withdraw *vb* 1 *syn* see REMOVE 2

ant deposit

2 *syn* see ABJURE

3 *syn* see GO 2

rel quail, recoil, retreat, shrink; recede

idiom give ground, give way

con advance, progress; arrive, come

4 *syn* see RETREAT 2

ant advance

withdrawal *n syn* see DEPARTURE 1

ant approach

withdrawn *adj* 1 *syn* see UNDEMONSTRA-
TIVE
ant outgiving
2 *syn* see INDIFFERENT 2
3 *syn* see UNSOCIABLE
ant outgoing

wither *vb* to lose substance and freshness
by or as if by loss of natural moisture
< projects that *wither* and die from lack
of popular interest >
syn dry up, mummify, mummy, shrivel,
welter, wilt, wizen
rel cave in, collapse, deflate, fold; constrict, contract, shrink; decline, wane
con freshen, revive, revivify; develop,
grow, increase, wax
ant flourish

withhold *vb* 1 *syn* see RESTRAIN 1
2 *syn* see KEEP 5
con award, concede, grant, vouchsafe
ant accord
3 *syn* see DENY 2
4 *syn* see REFRAIN 1

within *adv* *syn* see INDOORS
ant without

within *n* *syn* see INTERIOR
ant without

withindoors *adv* *syn* see INDOORS
ant withoutdoors

withinside *adv* *syn* see INDOORS
ant withoutside

with–it *adj* *syn* see STYLISH

without *prep* 1 *syn* see BEYOND 1
2 not having < living *without* decent housing or adequate food >
syn awanting, lacking, minus, sans, wanting

without *adv* *syn* see OUTDOORS
ant within

without *n* *syn* see OUTDOORS

‖**without** *conj* *syn* see EXCEPT 1

withoutdoors *adv* *syn* see OUTDOORS
ant indoors, withindoors

with respect to *prep* *syn* see APROPOS

withstand *vb* *syn* see RESIST
rel bear, endure, stand, suffer, tolerate
con capitulate, submit, yield

witless *adj* 1 *syn* see SIMPLE 3
2 *syn* see INSANE 1

witlessness *n* *syn* see FOOLISHNESS

witness *n* 1 *syn* see TESTIMONY
2 *syn* see SPECTATOR

witness *vb* 1 *syn* see CERTIFY 1
rel affirm; endorse, subscribe
2 *syn* see INDICATE 2

witticism *n* *syn* see JOKE 1

wittiness *n* *syn* see HUMOR 4

witting *adj* 1 *syn* see AWARE
ant unwitting
2 *syn* see VOLUNTARY
ant unwitting

witty *adj* provoking or intended to provoke
mirth < a whimsical *witty* discussion on
the foreignness of honesty to politics >
syn facetious, humorous, jocose, jocular
rel amusing, diverting, entertaining; scintillating, sparkling; penetrating, piercing,
probing; funny, ridiculous, risible

con foolish, senseless, silly; brash, cheeky,
fresh; earnest, serious, sober, solemn
ant unwitty

wiz *n* *syn* see EXPERT
ant dub, dud, duffer

wizard *n* 1 *syn* see MAGICIAN 1
2 *syn* see EXPERT
ant dub, dud, duffer

wizardly *adj* *syn* see MAGIC

wizardry *n* *syn* see MAGIC 1

wizen *vb* *syn* see WITHER
rel decrease, diminish, dwindle, reduce

wobble *vb* 1 *syn* see LURCH 2
2 *syn* see TEETER
3 *syn* see SHAKE

wobbly *adj* 1 *syn* see RICKETY
2 *syn* see WEAK 2
3 *syn* see VACILLATING 2

woe *n* 1 *syn* see SORROW
rel bemoaning, bewailing, deploring, lamentation
con bliss, felicity, happiness
2 *syn* see MISERY 1
3 *usu* woes *pl* *syn* see DISASTER

woebegone *adj* 1 *syn* see DOWNCAST
rel lugubrious, melancholy
con alert, concerned, interested, spirited;
lively, vigorous; avid, eager, keen
2 *syn* see GLOOMY 3
rel dilapidated, outworn, shabby, worn
con bright, crisp, fresh, gay

woeful *adj* 1 full of or expressive of woe
< a *woeful* countenance >
syn afflicted, doleful, dolent, dolorous,
miserable, rueful, ruthful, sorrowful,
wretched
rel harrowed, racked, tortured, wrung;
crushed, overcome, stricken; disconsolate,
heartsick, inconsolable; dejected, depressed, dispirited, downcast, downhearted, low-spirited
idiom cut to the heart, cut up, in the
dumps (*or* depths *or* doldrums), on the
rack
con content, satisfied; easy, peaceful,
quiet; cheerful, gay, lighthearted
ant joyful
2 *syn* see MELANCHOLY 2
3 *syn* see DEPLORABLE
rel dismal, grave, sad; unprecedented

woggle *vb* *syn* see WAG

wolf *n* a man forward, direct, and zealous
in amorous pursuit of women < known
far and wide as a lecherous old *wolf* >
syn Casanova, chaser, Don Juan, ladies'
man, lady-killer, masher, philander, philanderer, womanizer
rel amorist; lecher, libertine, Lothario,
profligate, rip, roué, rounder
idiom man on the make, skirt chaser

wolf *vb* 1 *syn* see GULP
2 *syn* see PHILANDER

wolfish *adj* *syn* see FIERCE 1

woman *n* 1 *syn* see WIFE
2 *syn* see MISTRESS

womanize *vb* *syn* see PHILANDER

womanizer *n* *syn* see WOLF

wonder *n* 1 something that causes fascinated astonishment or admiration < the
seven *wonders* of the ancient world >
syn marvel, miracle, phenomenon, portent, prodigy, sensation, stunner
rel curiosity, cynosure, gazingstock, spectacle

---

syn synonym(s)   *rel* related word(s)
ant antonym(s)   *con* contrasted word(s)
idiom idiomatic equivalent(s)
‖ use limited; if in doubt, see a dictionary

idiom one for the book(s), something to shout (*or* write home) about

2 the complex emotion aroused by the strange and incomprehensible and especially the awe-inspiring < stood gazing in wide-eyed *wonder* at the scene unveiled before her >

syn admiration, amaze, amazement, marveling, wonderment

rel awe, fear, reverence; bewilderment, perplexity, puzzlement; astonishment, marvel, shock

con disinterest, incuriosity, indifference, unconcern; dispassion, impassivity; casualness, offhandedness; boredom, ennui

3 *syn* see UNCERTAINTY

rel assailability, vulnerability

con unconcern

wonderful *adj* 1 *syn* see MARVELOUS 1

2 *syn* see MARVELOUS 2

ant lousy

wonderland *n syn* see UTOPIA

wonderment *n syn* see WONDER 2

wondrous *adj syn* see MARVELOUS 1

wont *n syn* see HABIT 1

wont *vb syn* see ACCUSTOM

wonted *adj syn* see USUAL 1

ant unwonted

wontedly *adv syn* see USUALLY 1

ant unwontedly

woo *vb syn* see ADDRESS 8

idiom bill and coo, pitch woo

wood *n, often* woods *pl but sing or pl in constr syn* see FOREST

wooden *adj* 1 *syn* see STIFF 4

rel awkward, clumsy; heavy, ponderous, weighty

con limber, supple; plastic, pliable, pliant

2 *syn* see AWKWARD 2

woodenhead *n syn* see DUNCE

woodland *n syn* see FOREST

woods colt *n syn* see BASTARD 1

woodsy *n syn* see RUSTIC

wooer *n syn* see SUITOR 2

woolly *adj syn* see HAIRY 1

word *vb* to convey (as an impression, a thought, or a need) in words < seemed scarcely to know how to *word* her appeal >

syn couch, express, formulate, phrase, put; *compare* EXPRESS 2

rel convey, offer, submit; say, state, tell

word *n* 1 something that is said < didn't tell a *word* about his plans >

syn statement, utterance

rel announcement, declaration, pronouncement

2 a pronounceable sound or combination of sounds that expresses and symbolizes an idea < be sure you learn the meaning of each *word* >

syn term, vocable

rel expression, idiom, locution, phrase

3 *syn* see COMMAND 1

4 *syn* see NEWS

5 *syn* see REPORT 1

6 *syn* see MESSAGE 1

7 *syn* see SAYING

8 a statement whose weight or worth depends on the truthfulness or authority of its maker < had the doctor's *word* that no operation would be needed >

syn assurance, guarantee, pledge, warrant; *compare* PROMISE

rel commitment, engagement, undertaking; oath, vow; promise

9 *syn* see PROMISE

10 *usu* words *pl syn* see QUARREL

11 *syn* see PASSWORD 3

12 *syn* see PASSWORD 1

wordage *n syn* see WORDING

word for word *adv syn* see VERBATIM

word-for-word *adj syn* see VERBATIM

word-hoard *n syn* see VOCABULARY 1

wordiness *n syn* see VERBOSITY

con crispness, pithiness, trenchancy

ant laconicism, laconism

wording *n* manner or style of verbal expression < take care with the *wording* of a formal invitation >

syn diction, parlance, phrase, phraseology, phrasing, verbalism, verbiage, wordage

rel language, mode, style

wordless *adj* 1 *syn* see TACIT 1

2 *syn* see SILENT 2

3 *syn* see SILENT 3

4 *syn* see UNSPOKEN 1

ant wordy

word-of-mouth *adj syn* see ORAL 2

word-stock *n syn* see VOCABULARY 1

wordy *adj* using or marked by the use of more words than are needed to express an idea < tired of dull *wordy* editorials >

syn diffuse, long-winded, palaverous, prolix, redundant, verbose, windy

rel flatulent, inflated, tumid, turgid; garrulous, glib, loquacious, talkative, voluble; bombastic, highfalutin, rhetorical

con compendious, concise, pithy, succinct, summary, terse; lean, taut

ant laconic

work *n* 1 the activity that affords one his livelihood < laborers hurrying to *work* at dawn >

syn business, calling, employment, job, line, occupation, pursuit, ||racket; *compare* JOB 2

rel art, craft, handicraft, métier, profession, trade, vocation, walk

2 strenuous activity that involves difficulty and effort and usually affords no pleasure < had done much hard *work* during his life >

syn bullwork, donkeywork, drudge, drudgery, grind, labor, moil, plugging, slavery, slogging, sweat, toil, travail

rel effort, exertion, pains, trouble; chore, duty, job; elucubration; striving; spadework

ant play

3 works *pl syn* see FACTORY

work *vb* 1 *syn* see OPERATE 3

2 *syn* see TILL

3 *syn* see SOLVE 1

4 *syn* see LABOR 1

5 *syn* see FUNCTION 3

6 *syn* see ACT 5

work (for) *vb syn* see BENEFIT

workable *adj syn* see POSSIBLE 1

rel applicable, exploitable, usable

ant unworkable

workaday *adj* 1 *syn* see PROSAIC 3

2 *syn* see ORDINARY 1

workday *adj syn* see PROSAIC 3

worker *n* one who earns a living by labor and especially by manual labor < weary *workers* straggling home each night >

syn hand, laborer, ‖mozo, operative, roustabout, workhand, workingman, workman
rel artisan, craftsman, handicraftsman, mechanic; employee
ant idler

workhand *n syn* see WORKER

workhorse *n* 1 *syn* see SLAVE 2
2 *syn* see SAWHORSE

work in *vb syn* see INSINUATE 3

working *adj* 1 *syn* see ACTIVE 1
2 *syn* see BUSY 1

workingman *n syn* see WORKER

workless *adj syn* see UNEMPLOYED

workman *n syn* see WORKER

workmanlike *adj syn* see SKILLFUL 2
ant unworkmanlike

workmanly *adj syn* see SKILLFUL 2

work off *vb syn* see FOIST 3

work out *vb syn* see SOLVE 1

work over *vb syn* see REVISE

work-shy *adj syn* see LAZY

work up *vb syn* see GENERATE 3

world *n* 1 *syn* see EARTH 1
2 *syn* see UNIVERSE

worldly *adj* 1 *syn* see EARTHLY 1
ant otherworldly
2 *syn* see MATERIALISTIC
ant otherworldly, unworldly
3 *syn* see SOPHISTICATED 2
ant unworldly

worldly-wise *adj syn* see SOPHISTICATED 2
rel callous, hard-boiled, hardened
con naive, unsophisticated, unworldly

worldwide *adj syn* see UNIVERSAL 2
con parochial

world-wise *adj syn* see SOPHISTICATED 2

world-without-end *adj syn* see EVERLASTING 1

world-without-end *n syn* see ETERNITY 2

worm *n syn* see WRETCH 1

worm *vb* 1 *syn* see INSINUATE 3
2 *syn* see WRIGGLE

wormling *n syn* see WRETCH 1

worn *adj* 1 *syn* see TIRED 1
2 *syn* see HAGGARD

worn down *adj syn* see TIRED 1

worn-out *adj* 1 *syn* see EFFETE 2
2 *syn* see TRITE

worried *adj syn* see DISTRAUGHT
ant unworried

worry *vb* 1 to disturb one or destroy one's peace of mind by repeated or persistent tormenting attacks <vain regrets that *worry* his spirit>
syn annoy, bedevil, beleaguer, dun, gnaw, hagride, harass, harry, needle, pester, plague, tantalize, tease, ‖wherret
rel beset, bother, fret, pelt, trouble, vex; goad, test, try; afflict, torment, torture; aggrieve, oppress, persecute, wrong
idiom give one gyp
con comfort, console, solace; alleviate, assuage, ease, relieve
2 *syn* see TROUBLE 2

3 to experience concern, disquietude, or anxiety <*worrying* over her children's health>
syn cark, fret, fuss, pother, stew, ‖tew
rel carry on, take on; despair, give up; bother, concern (oneself); agitate, disquiet, disturb, trouble
idiom be upset, bite one's nails
con accept, submit; abide, bear, endure, stand, support; disregard, ignore, overlook, pass over

worry *n* 1 *syn* see CARE 2
rel presentiment; doubt, mistrust, uncertainty; anguish, heartache, woe
con composure, equanimity, sangfroid; assurance, certainty, certitude, confidence, security
2 *syn* see TRIAL 2

worrywart *n syn* see PESSIMIST

worsen *vb syn* see DETERIORATE 1
rel blast, blight, debase, degrade, humble, lower; corrupt, foul, taint
idiom get worse, grow worse
ant better

worship *n syn* see ADORATION

worship *vb* 1 *syn* see REVERE
con contemn, despise, disdain, flout, scorn; curse, execrate, vilify
2 *syn* see ADORE 3
ant abominate; scorn
3 *syn* see LOVE 2

worst *vb syn* see DEFEAT 2

worth *n* 1 equivalence in good qualities (as utility, importance, or desirability) express or implied <impossible to estimate the *worth* of such a man to the community>
syn account, valuation, value
rel class, excellence, merit, perfection, quality, virtue; rate; use, usefulness, utility; consequence, importance, mark, moment, note, significance, weight
con baseness, meanness, paltriness, poorness
ant worthlessness
2 *syn* see QUALITY 2
3 *syn* see WEALTH 2

worthless *adj* lacking all excellence or value <gave me a *worthless* check>
syn draffy, drossy, good-for-nothing, inutile, ‖no-account, no-good, nothing, unworthy, valueless
rel inferior, mediocre, poor, second-rate; defective, flawed, imperfect; bootless, ineffectual, unavailing, useless; contemptible, dusty, mean, sad, sorry
idiom dear at any price, of no earthly value (or worth)
con esteemed, precious; useful, valuable, worthwhile; invaluable, priceless
ant worthful
2 *syn* see FECKLESS 1
rel incapable, incompetent, unqualified

worthwhile *adj syn* see ADVANTAGEOUS 1

worthy *adj* 1 having worth or merit <a *worthy* custom handed down from our ancestors>
syn admirable, commendable, deserving, estimable, laudable, meritable, meritorious, praisable, praiseworthy, thankworthy
rel invaluable, precious, priceless; desirable, pleasing, satisfying; divine
con good-for-nothing, ‖no-account, no-good, valueless; contemptible, sad, sorry

---

syn synonym(s)   *rel* related word(s)
ant antonym(s)   *con* contrasted word(s)
idiom idiomatic equivalent(s)
‖ use limited; if in doubt, see a dictionary

ant worthless
2 *syn* see HONORABLE 1
ant unworthy
wound *vb syn* see INJURE 3
wow *n syn* see SMASH 6
‖**wowser** *n syn* see PRUDE
wrack *vb syn* see DESTROY 1
wrackful *adj syn* see DESTRUCTIVE
wraith *n syn* see APPARITION
wrangle *vb* 1 *syn* see QUARREL
2 *syn* see ARGUE 2
wrangle *n syn* see QUARREL
wrap *vb syn* see ENFOLD 1
rel camouflage, cloak, mask
ant unwrap
wrap (up) *vb* 1 *syn* see BUNDLE UP
2 *syn* see SWATHE
wrapped *adj syn* see INTENT
wrapped up *adj syn* see INTENT
wrap up *vb syn* see CLOSE 3
wrath *n syn* see ANGER
rel acerbity, acrimony, asperity; offense,
resentment
wrathful *adj syn* see ANGRY
wrathy *adj syn* see ANGRY
‖**wraxle** *vb syn* see WRESTLE
wreak *vb syn* see INFLICT 2
wreakful *adj syn* see VINDICTIVE
wreath *n* a circlet of intertwined leaves or
flowers worn upon the head as an ornament or as a mark of honor or esteem
< received the laurel *wreath* of victory
from the emperor's own hand >
syn anadem, chaplet, coronal, coronet,
crown, garland
rel bay(s), laurel
wreathe *vb syn* see WIND 2
wreck *n* 1 *syn* see CRASH 3
2 *syn* see COLLAPSE 2
3 *syn* see JALOPY
wreck *vb* 1 *syn* see VANDALIZE
2 *syn* see DESTROY 1
rel despoil, loot, plunder, ravage; cripple,
disable
3 *syn* see TOTAL 3
4 *syn* see SABOTAGE
5 *syn* see SHIPWRECK 1
6 *syn* see RUIN 3
7 *syn* see INFLICT 2
wreckage *n* 1 *syn* see SABOTAGE
2 *syn* see DRIFTWOOD
wrecker *n syn* see VANDAL
wreckful *adj syn* see DESTRUCTIVE
wrecking *n syn* see SABOTAGE
wrench *vb* 1 to shift the position of or
move by or as if by vigorous twisting
< suddenly *wrenched* her around to face
him >
syn wrest, wring, wry
rel bend, twist; coerce, compel, constrain,
force; drag, rend, tear; contort, distort
2 *syn* see SPRAIN
3 *syn* see MISREPRESENT
4 *syn* see EXTORT 1
wrest *vb* 1 *syn* see WRENCH 1
rel arrogate, confiscate, usurp; elicit,
extort, extract
2 *syn* see EXTORT 1
3 *syn* see MISREPRESENT
wrestle *vb* to struggle with an opponent at
close quarters < determined to solve the
problem if he had to *wrestle* with it all
night >

syn grapple, scuffle, tussle, ‖wraxle
rel contend, fight, struggle; endeavor,
essay; labor, moil, toil, travail, work; exert, strain, stretch, strive
wretch *n* 1 a worthless and often vicious
or contemptible person < a treacherous
drink-sodden *wretch* >
syn ‖blighter, lowlife, mucker, no-good,
worm, wormling
rel good-for-naught, good-for-nothing,
ne'er-do-well; blackguard, caitiff, devil,
knave, rapscallion, rascal, rogue, rotter,
scalawag, scoundrel, villain
idiom sad case
2 *syn* see SNOT 1
wretched *adj* 1 *syn* see WOEFUL 1
rel melancholy; abject, mean, sordid;
piteous, pitiable, pitiful; despairing, despondent, forlorn, hopeless
con animated, gay, lively; content, contented, satisfied; gratified, pleased
2 *syn* see BASE
wretchedness *n syn* see MISERY 1
wriggle *vb* to move or advance with worm-
like motions < the attackers *wriggled*
stealthily through the underbrush >
syn squiggle, squirm, wiggle, worm,
writhe
rel flow, glide, ooze, slide, slip
wring *vb* 1 *syn* see EXTORT 1
2 *syn* see WRENCH 1
rel press, squeeze
3 *syn* see AFFLICT
wringing–wet *adj syn* see WET 1
wrinkle *n* a small linear prominence or
depression on a surface < a benign old
face netted with *wrinkles* >
syn corrugation, crease, crinkle, fold,
furrow, plica, ridge, rimple, rivel, ruck
rel crow's foot; pleat, pucker
wrinkle *vb syn* see CRUMPLE 1
write *vb* to form characters or words on a
surface (as of paper) usually with pen or
pencil < learned to *write* at an early age >
syn engross, indite, inscribe, scribe
rel dot (down), jot, note; chalk, pen,
pencil; scratch, scrawl, scribble; draft,
draw, make out; write down, write up
idiom push one's pen, put in writing, take
down
write down *vb syn* see DEPRECIATE 1
ant write up
write off *vb* 1 *syn* see DEPRECIATE 1
2 *syn* see DECRY 2
write–up *n syn* see PUFF 3
writhe *vb* 1 to twist and turn in physical
or mental distress < *writhing* in anguish
with a throbbing tooth- ache >
syn agonize, squirm, toss
rel blench, flinch, recoil, shrink, wince;
contort, distort; bend, twist; thrash, tumble
2 *syn* see WRIGGLE
writing *n syn* see PRINT 2
writing desk *n syn* see DESK
wrong *n* 1 *syn* see INJUSTICE 2
2 *syn* see EVIL 2
3 *syn* see EVIL 3
4 *syn* see INJUSTICE 1
wrong *adj* 1 rejecting or deviating from the
dictates of moral or divine law < had a
wrong outlook on life > < *wrong* principles
of conduct >

syn bad, evil, immoral, iniquitous, reprobate, sinful, vicious, wicked
  rel blamable, blameworthy, censurable,
reprehensible; corrupt, debauched, depraved; abandoned, dissolute, infamous,
villainous; blasphemous, unholy, unrighteous; accursed, unblessed
  con ethical, high-principled, moral, righteous, upright; chaste, innocent, pure,
virtuous
  ant right
2 syn see FALSE 1
  idiom at fault, barking up the wrong tree,
in error, on the wrong track
  con exact, precise
  ant right
3 syn see BAD 1
  rel improper, inappropriate, inapt, infelicitous, unfit, unfitting, unhappy, unsuitable
  con appropriate, fit, fitting, proper, suitable
4 syn see MISTAKEN
  ant right
5 syn see INSANE 1
wrong *adv syn* see AMISS 2

  ant right
wrong *vb* to inflict injury on another without justification < these men who have
wronged the public trust deserve no consideration >
  syn aggrieve, oppress, outrage, persecute
  rel abuse, ill-treat, maltreat, mistreat;
harm, hurt, injure; offend
  idiom do wrong to (or by)
  con guard, protect, safeguard; care (for),
cherish; honor, love, respect
wrongdoing *n* **1 syn see EVIL 3**
2 syn see MISCONDUCT
wrongful *adj syn see UNLAWFUL*
  ant rightful
wrongheaded *adj* **1 syn see OBSTINATE**
2 syn see CONTRARY 3
wrongly *adv syn see AMISS 1*
  ant rightly
wroth *adj syn see ANGRY*
wrothful *adj syn see ANGRY*
wrothy *adj syn see ANGRY*
wry *vb syn see WRENCH 1*
wry *adj syn see SARDONIC*

X

X *n syn see ERROR 1*
X (out) *vb syn see ERASE*

Xanthippe *n syn see VIRAGO*
Xmas *n syn see CHRISTMAS*

Y

yaboo *n syn see TOUGH*
yak *n syn see CHATTER*
yak *vb syn see CHAT 1*
‖**yak** *n syn see JOKE 1*
yakety-yak *n syn see CHATTER*
yakety-yak *vb syn see CHAT 1*
yak-yak *n syn see CHATTER*
yak-yak *vb syn see CHAT 1*
yammer *vb* **1 syn see GRIPE**
2 syn see CHAT 1
yank *vb* **1 syn see JERK**
  rel tug; clutch, grab, snatch
2 syn see EXTRACT 1
yap *n* **1 syn see RUSTIC**
‖**2 syn see MOUTH 1**
yard *n syn see COURT 1*
yardstick *n syn see STANDARD 3*
yare *adj syn see AGILE*
yarn *n* **1 syn see STORY 2**
2 syn see CHAT 2
yarn *vb syn see CONVERSE*
yatter *n syn see CHATTER*
yatter *vb syn see CHAT 1*

yaw *n syn see TURN 2*
yaw *vb syn see SEESAW*
yaw *vb syn see YAWN*
yawn *vb* to breathe deeply with jaws widespread usually in reaction to fatigue or
boredom < *yawned* again and again in the
stuffy room >
  syn gape, yaw
  rel doze, drowse, nap, snooze
yawn *n syn see TEDIUM*
yawning *adj syn see CAVERNOUS 1*
yawp (or yaup) *vb* **1 syn see SQUALL 1**
2 syn see GRIPE
yea *adv* **1 syn see ALSO 2**
2 syn see YES 1
3 syn see EVEN 3
yearbook *n* a book issued yearly to chronicle a particular part of the preceding
year's activities < sports editor of his
school *yearbook* >
  syn annual, annuary
yearn *vb syn see LONG*
  rel covet, desire, wish; pant
  ant dread
years *n pl syn see OLD AGE*
yeast *n syn see FOAM*
yeasty *adj syn see GIDDY 1*
yegg *n syn see ROBBER*
yell *vb* **1 syn see SHOUT 1**

---

syn synonym(s)   *rel* related word(s)
ant antonym(s)   *con* contrasted word(s)
idiom idiomatic equivalent(s)
‖ use limited; if in doubt, see a dictionary

2 to complain vigorously or vociferously < let the opposition *yell;* we got the vote >
syn howl, scream, squeal, yip, yowl
rel cry, lament, squall, wail, weep; bemoan, bewail, deplore
idiom beat one's breast, make an outcry, tear one's hair, yell to high heaven
con acclaim, applaud, cheer, hail
3 *syn* see CALL 1

yellow *adj syn* see COWARDLY
yellowback *n syn* see DIME NOVEL
yellowbelly *n syn* see COWARD
rel fink, rat, stinker
yellow dog *n syn* see CAD
yen *vb syn* see LONG
∥**yep** *adv syn* see YES 1
ant ∥nope
∥**yerk** *vb syn* see WHIP 1
yes *adv* **1** —used as a function word to express assent, agreement, understanding, or acceptance < *yes,* I can do that >
syn agreed, all right, aye, OK (*or* okay), ∥okeydoke, yea, ∥yep
rel assuredly, certainly, gladly, willingly; undoubtedly, unquestionably
idiom beyond a doubt, beyond any shade (*or* shadow) of doubt, with all my heart, without the least doubt
2 *syn* see EXACTLY 3
yes *vb syn* see ASSENT
yes-man *n* **1** *syn* see STOOGE 1
2 *syn* see SYCOPHANT
yesterday *n syn* see PAST
ant tomorrow
yesteryear *n syn* see PAST
yet *adv* **1** beyond this — used as an intensive to stress the comparative degree < in spite of her protest he went *yet* faster >
syn even, still
2 at some future time < just wait, we'll get there *yet* >
syn eventually, finally, someday, sometime, somewhen, sooner or later, ultimately
idiom after a while, in due course, in the course of time
3 *syn* see ALSO 2
4 *syn* see HITHERTO 1
5 *syn* see HOWEVER
yet *conj syn* see ONLY
yield *vb* **1** *syn* see RELINQUISH
con appropriate, arrogate, confiscate
2 to give way before a force that one cannot longer resist < *yielded* to temptation >
syn bow, buckle (under), capitulate, cave, defer, knuckle, knuckle under, submit, succumb
rel accord, award, concede, grant; cede, surrender, waive; break, fail
idiom give ground, give place, give way
con bear up, hold out, resist
ant withstand
3 *syn* see BEAR 9

4 *syn* see GIVE 7
rel discharge, eject, emit, vent
5 to produce as return or revenue < an investment that *yields* 10 percent >
syn bring in, pay, return
rel afford, furnish, provide, supply; hold out, offer, proffer, tender
idiom afford (*or* give *or* provide) a return of, put at one's disposal
6 *syn* see GIVE 12
yield *n syn* see OUTPUT
yielding *adj* **1** *syn* see SOFT 6
ant unyielding
2 *syn* see PASSIVE 2
yip *vb syn* see YELL 2
∥**yob** *n syn* see RUSTIC
yoke *n* **1** *syn* see BONDAGE
2 *syn* see BOND 3
yoke *vb* **1** *syn* see HITCH 2
2 *syn* see JOIN 1
yokel *n syn* see RUSTIC
yon *adv* **1** *syn* see BEYOND 1
2 *syn* see THERE
yonder *adv syn* see BEYOND 1
yore *n syn* see PAST
young *adj* **1** being in an early stage of life, growth, or development < *young* shoots of new grass >
syn callow, green, immature, infant, juvenile, unfledged, unripe, youthful
rel fresh, new; crude, raw, unfinished, unformed
con full-grown, grown-up, mature, ripe; aged, elderly, superannuated
ant old; adult
2 *syn* see INEXPERIENCED
youngling *n syn* see CHILD 1
young man *n syn* see BOYFRIEND 1
young one *n syn* see CHILD 1
youngster *n syn* see CHILD 1
youth *n* **1** the period of life in which one passes from childhood to maturity < the thought of regaining one's *youth* >
syn adolescence, greenness, juvenility, prime, puberty, pubescence, spring, springtide, springtime, youthfulness, youthhood
rel callowness, immaturity, inexperience, unripeness; dewiness
idiom awkward age, flower (*or* springtime *or* May) of life, salad days
ant age
2 *syn* see CHILD 1
youthful *adj syn* see YOUNG 1
rel beardless, boyish, puerile; maiden, virgin, virginal
con adult, matured
ant aged, elderly
youthfulness *n syn* see YOUTH 1
youthhood *n syn* see YOUTH
yowl *vb* **1** *syn* see YELL 2
2 *syn* see BAWL 2
yule *n syn* see CHRISTMAS
yuletide *n syn* see CHRISTMAS
yummy *adj syn* see DELIGHTFUL

Z

zakuska *n syn* see APPETIZER

zany *n* 1 *syn* see CLOWN 3
  rel comic, farceur, funnyman
  2 one who makes an exhibition of himself for the amusement of others <tired of having her parties spoiled by drunken *zanies*>
  syn clown, cutup, farceur, joker, jokester, wag
  rel practical joker, pranker, prankster, trickster; exhibitionist, show-off
  3 *syn* see WAG 1
  4 *syn* see FOOL 4

zeal *n syn* see PASSION 6
  rel energy, gusto, spirit, zest; fierceness, intensity, vehemence; avidity, keenness, readiness, urgency; earnestness, seriousness, sincerity
  con coolness, halfheartedness, indifference, lukewarmness; carelessness, heedlessness, insouciance, negligence, unmindfulness; disinterest, lackadaisy, unconcern
  ant apathy

zealot *n syn* see ENTHUSIAST
  rel adherent, disciple, follower, partisan, sectary

zealous *adj syn* see ENTHUSIASTIC
  rel afire, ardent, fervent, fervid, fired; avid, eager; dedicated, fanatic, frenetic, rabid, wild-eyed; infatuated, obsessed, possessed
  con cool, halfhearted, indifferent, lukewarm; careless, heedless, insouciant, negligent, unmindful; disinterested, lackadaisical, uninterested
  ant apathetic

zemi *n syn* see CHARM 2

zenith *n syn* see APEX 2
  ant nadir

zero *n* 1 a numerical symbol 0 denoting the absence of all magnitude or quantity <wrote a row of *zeros* after the decimal point>
  syn aught (*or* ought), cipher, goose egg, naught (*or* nought), nothing, zilch
  rel blank, nil, void
  2 *syn* see NONENTITY

zero (in) *vb syn* see DIRECT 2

zero hour *n syn* see JUNCTURE 2

zest *n syn* see TASTE 4
  rel ardor, eagerness, enthusiasm, fervor, passion, zeal; delectation, delight, enjoyment, pleasure, satisfaction; bliss, ecstasy, elation

zesty *adj syn* see PUNGENT

zetetic *n syn* see SKEPTIC

zilch *n* 1 *syn* see ZERO 1
  2 *syn* see NONENTITY

zing *n* 1 *syn* see EAGERNESS
  2 *syn* see SPIRIT 5

Zion *n* 1 *syn* see HEAVEN 2
  2 *syn* see UTOPIA

zip *vb* 1 *syn* see BREEZE
  2 *syn* see HURRY 2

zippy *adj syn* see AGILE
  rel alert, keen, ready; dynamic, forceful, intense

zoetic *adj syn* see LIVING 1

Zoilus *n syn* see CRITIC

zombie *n* 1 *syn* see DUNCE
  2 *syn* see ECCENTRIC

zone *n syn* see AREA 1
  rel section, sector, segment

zonked *adj* 1 *syn* see INTOXICATED 1
  2 *syn* see DRUGGED
